Second Edition

CONSTITUTIONAL LAW

GOVERNMENTAL POWERS AND INDIVIDUAL FREEDOMS

Daniel E. Hall, J.D., Ed.D.
Miami University, Hamilton

John P. Feldmeier, J.D., Ph.D.
Wright State University

D0127051

PEARSON

Boston   Columbus   Indianapolis   New York   San Francisco   Upper Saddle River   Amsterdam
Cape Town   Dubai   London   Madrid   Milan   Munich   Paris   Montreal   Toronto   Delhi
Mexico City   São Paulo   Sydney   Hong Kong   Seoul   Singapore   Taipei   Tokyo

Editorial Director: Vernon Anthony
Acquisitions Editor: Gary Bauer
Editorial Project Manager: Linda Cupp
Director of Marketing: David Gesell
Senior Marketing Manager: Stacey Martinez
Marketing Assistant: Les Roberts
Production Manager: Susan Hannahs
Senior Art Director: Jayne Conte
Cover Designer: Suzanne Behnke
Cover Art: Shutterstock
Chapter Opening Image: © JustASC/Shutterstock
Full-Service Project Management: Niraj Bhatt, Aptara®, Inc.
Composition: Aptara®, Inc.
Text Printer/Bindery: Edwards Brothers Malloy
Cover Printer: Lehigh-Phoenix Color
Text Font: 10.5/12.5 Times

Credits and acknowledgments borrowed from other sources and reproduced, with permission, in this textbook appear on the appropriate page within the text.

Library of Congress Cataloging-in-Publication Data
Hall, Daniel (Daniel E.)
  Constitutional law : governmental powers and individual freedoms / Daniel E. Hall, John P. Feldmeier.—2nd ed.
    p. cm.
  Rev. ed. of: Constitutional values / Daniel E. Hall, John P. Feldmeier. c2009.
  Includes bibliographical references and index.
  ISBN-13: 978-0-13-510950-2
  ISBN-10: 0-13-510950-7
 1. Constitutional law—United States.   2. Constitutional history—United States.   3. Civil rights—
    United States.   4. Separation of poweres—United States.   5. United States—Politics and
    government.   I. Feldmeier, John P. (John Phillip)   II. Hall, Daniel (Daniel E.) Constitutional
    values.   III. Title.
  KF4550.H344 2013
  342.73—dc23

                                                                              2011033211

www.pearsonhighered.com

10 9 8 7 6 5 4

PEARSON

ISBN 10:   0-13-510950-7
ISBN 13: 978-0-13-510950-2

Dedication

To Grace and Eva from Daddy, who, in spite of repeated attempts by the Father, don't yet appreciate that it's the Constitution that protects their toys from the Burgermeister. D.E.H.

To Melissa, who has inspired and supported me throughout my professional life. To Emma and Jack, who offered me many welcome breaks during the preparation of this book. J.P.F.

CONTENTS

PREFACE

Having taught constitutional law courses to undergraduate students for a number of years, we have received many questions from students about matters that the U.S. Supreme Court has not yet addressed: Does the message on my t-shirt constitute fighting words? Can we begin our student government meetings with a prayer? Is our university's affirmative action policy constitutional? In most cases, we have found that students want definitive answers to these questions. Much like the results received from computer searches or the numbers produced from mathematical formulas, students often expect certainty when it comes to addressing their constitutional questions. And in their view, such certainty is warranted, especially in a constitutional context, where much of "the law" (the Constitution) has remained textually unchanged.

The problem, of course, is that the Constitution is not written like an owner's manual for a car, where you can turn to the troubleshooting section to find the answers to many questions. Comparatively speaking, the Constitution is a relatively short, ill-defined, and vaguely written document that, at times, offers few clearly explained and universally accepted resolutions to constitutional dilemmas. As a result, the answers to constitutional questions often depend not so much on *which* question is asked, but rather on to *whom* the question is directed. Just survey legal scholars and practitioners as to whether the Constitution allows a local government to erect a nativity scene during the holidays, protects a woman's right to have an abortion, or gives the president the ability to order domestic wiretaps without a warrant, and you will likely get varied and conflicting responses. Even members of the Supreme Court—jurists who have received some of the finest and most substantial educations regarding the Constitution—often cannot agree on the Constitution's meaning.

In reality, we have found that constitutional law involves the application of human values. Whether turning to historical documents to determine the original intent of a constitutional provision or considering modern-day realities as informative of constitutional terms, those who interpret the Constitution make value judgments about how to determine the meaning of constitutional language. Just as some political scientists have come to define *politics* as "the authoritative allocation of values," we have found that constitutional law involves much the same enterprise. Judges and others with legal authority assign or allocate values to constitutional provisions in order to give them meaning and effect. As a result, we endeavor to help students appreciate that constitutional law is not divorced from the political process, but rather is a continuation of this process. To this end, we have attempted to provide a text that enables students to understand the values that have been used to shape our current state of constitutional law and to assist them in developing their own constitutional values.

TEXT FEATURES

We have written this book for use in undergraduate classes. It is **flexible in its design,** allowing use in split (governmental powers vs. civil liberties) and combined courses. The **writing style** and language are intended to challenge, but not overwhelm, the undergraduate student. When legalese is used, it is defined. A running **glossary** of terms reinforces learning of legal terms.

Excerpts of significant cases are embedded in the text. Although each case has been well edited, we have been careful to retain the material needed to accomplish our pedagogical objectives. These include reinforceing the black-letter law presented in our narrative, developing analytical skills, and giving students exposure to judicial writing. These excerpted opinions also provide briefing opportunities for those students who want to engage in this traditional practice used for legal research and writing projects. To remain true to our flexibility objective, we have designed the text so that the cases may be omitted without losing any black-letter learning. For those who want access to full-length opinions, the book provides links to many opinions on its companion website; additional references in the book are provided in a feature entitled *Cyber Constitution*, which offers web-based links to supplemental materials.

Illustrations, charts, and photos appear throughout the text. They are used to assist students in conceptualizing challenging subjects, to summarize complex topics, and to break up dense sections.

Your Constitutional Values is a special feature designed to make students aware that constitutional law occurs at all levels, branches, and areas of government— it is not just something that happens at the U.S. Supreme Court. Consistent with the adage that "all politics is local," we have included excerpts of constitutional law cases that did not make it "all the way to the Supreme Court," but that nonetheless contain interesting issues and facts relevant to constitutional jurisprudence. These sections within each chapter allow students to consider and apply key constitutional principles and terms to constitutional disputes using their own constitutional values.

Modern Challenges is a feature appearing within each chapter that provides predictive observations regarding constitutional questions that courts might face in the next few years. These forward-thinking assessments seek to stimulate creative and analytical thinking among students and provide further opportunities for readers to appreciate the dynamic nature of constitutional law.

Each chapter also contains a **Summary** section that reviews the main points outlines terms and concepts used by today's practicioner's in constitutional law. The terms are placerines found within text of the chapter. This section allows students to assess whether they have captured the primary points and principles after reading the full-length materials. There are also **Review Questions** that appear at the end of every chapter that require a short answer or brief analytical response.

Constitutional Law in Action is a feature at the end of each chapter that provides students with real-life exercises and assignments that reflect the work of legal professionals in facing issues of constitutional law. This feature provides students with work assignments and tasks often faced by legal professionals in real cases involving constitutional questions. These might include outlining an argument for an appellate brief, preparing a legal memorandum, identifying the courtroom rules for a given jurisdiction, or preparing a binder for an appellate argument. Students are then asked to complete the assignments within the parameters of the instructions given by a hypothetical supervisor within an office setting. These assignments require students to apply key constitutional principles to tangible situations, using the knowledge gained from the chapter.

There are three types of assignments provided in this feature. The first is called **The Constitution in Your Community,** which contains assignments asking students to locate and apply the standards of constitutional law and civil liberties within their own state or local jurisdiction. This section allows students to tailor their general understanding of constitutional law and civil liberties to own legal environment and courts. The second type assignment is called **Going Federal,** which provides assignments based on more national issues and controversies facing the nation as a whole. It is designed to allow students to appreciate constitutional law on a much larger scale. These assignments might involve locating and reviewing an appellate brief, researching governmental policies on issues of federal funding, religion, affirmative action, and other constitutional issues. The last assignment is called **Moot Court,** which invites students to organize and prepare a five-minute oral argument on a constitutional issue that might be presented to the Supreme Court.

CHAPTER TOPICS AND ORGANIZATION

This book is divided into two parts. Part One focuses on the organization and authorities of the U.S. government and the government of the states. Part Two focuses on civil liberties and, consequently, limitations on the authorities of governments.

The first chapter provides the student with a brief historical framework from which to understand our Constitution. The Articles of Confederation, the Philadelphia Convention, and the ratification debates are featured in this chapter. The chapter also addresses the essence and process of "doing" constitutional law, which is grounded in the doctrines of judicial review and constitutional interpretation. The chapter then provides a historical overview of some of the trends and developments of constitutional interpretation over the years.

In Chapter 2, the text moves to a discussion of basic governmental structures. Federalism, separation of powers, and checks and balances are introduced. Essentially, this chapter explains that there are two basic divisions of power under the U.S. Constitution—the division between the federal and state governments (federalism) and the division between and among the branches of government (separation of powers and checks and balances). These three primary constitutional dynamics—federalism, separation of powers, and checks and balances—are the primary structural backdrops for most of constitutional law.

Chapters 3, 4, and 5 are devoted to detailed discussions of the three branches of government. In Chapter 3, the book addresses the structure and power of federal courts, their role in our nation, and the power of judicial review. This chapter also covers the jurisdiction of federal courts. Included in these chapters are discussions of how these principles apply to real cases with which the student may have contact. The chapter provides students with an overview of the different methods courts use to interpret and apply constitutional language.

In Chapter 4, the powers of Congress are addressed, featuring the core constitutional authorities under the Commerce Clause, Necessary and Proper Clause, and Tax and Spending Clause. This chapter also discusses some of the constitutional conflicts between Congress and other bodies of power, such as the president, the judiciary, and the states.

Chapter 5 discusses the explicit and implicit powers of the president under Article II. Included in this chapter are treatments of the commander in chief, appointment, and chief executive powers. The chapter also addresses the president's veto power under Article I and explores many of the constitutional debates surrounding modern presidential action in the so-called war on terror.

Chapter 6 covers the importance of administrative agencies in the United States—the so-called fourth branch of government. Here, students will examine the creation of agencies, delegation of powers to agencies, and presidential and congressional control of agencies, as well as other contemporary topics.

Finally, building on the discussion in Chapter 2, Chapter 7 examines federalism in greater detail through issues such as intergovernmental immunity and preemption. In addition, a complete discussion of the revival in state constitutional law is included.

Part Two of the book addresses individual liberties as protected by the First and Fourteenth Amendments to the Constitution. Chapter 8 discusses the nature of individual liberties, their possible sources, and the construction of the Bill of Rights. This chapter also explains how most liberties within the Bill of Rights are applied to state and local governments through the incorporation doctrine.

In Chapter 9, the book analyzes the freedom of speech as protected by the First Amendment. As a part of this discussion, the text distinguishes speech from conduct, identifies the various forms of expression—political, symbolic, commercial, sexual, and so on—and provides students with a framework for addressing future free speech controversies.

Chapter 10 reviews the religion clauses of the First Amendment by providing students with excerpts of the seminal cases in Establishment Clause and Free Exercise Clause jurisprudence and by identifying the various tests used by the Supreme Court to resolve religion-based constitutional disputes.

In Chapter 11, the book discusses constitutional protections for the right of privacy and other bodily freedoms. As a part of this discussion, the text reviews the constitutional origins for the right of privacy and rights of due process that protect various forms of individual activity not specifically listed in the Constitution. Among other topics, this chapter covers the constitutional controversies over abortion, the right to die, and governmental restrictions on sexual activity.

Chapter 12 examines the notions of equality and due process as protected by the Fifth and Fourteenth Amendments. This chapter addresses cases involving school desegregation, affirmative action, sex-based discrimination, and same-sex marriage. It also reviews governmental intrusions upon fundamental rights and economic liberties.

Chapter 13 addresses civil liberties in the criminal context. Specifically, the chapter discusses the right against unreasonable searches and seizure, the right against self-incrimination, the exclusionary rule, the right to counsel, the right against double jeopardy, the right to a fair trial, and the right against cruel and unusual punishment.

Appendices include the Constitution of the United States, the history of U.S. Supreme Court justices by seat, a special feature on how to brief a case, and selected Executive Orders and other memoranda.

CHANGES IN THIS EDITION

- In order to excite the readers' interests in the subject and to expose them to the uniqueness of the U.S. form of constitutionalism, the judicial review material that was placed in Chapter 3 in the first edition has been moved into Chapter 1, following the discussion of rule of law.
- For context, the political background of the *Marbury* decision has been more fully developed. A new subsection on the impact of U.S. constitutionalism on nations around the world has been added.
- The discussion of the judiciary, which previously was spread over two chapters, has been edited and merged into one chapter.
- New material has been added through the book, including a new subsection on executive signing statements, the role of the solicitor general, additional background on FDR's internment and relocation orders, unitary executive theory, executive and congressional power in national emergencies, short biographies of current justices, and more on constitutional amendments.
- The text also includes materials addressing the relationship between President Lincoln and Chief Justice Taney, the role of the solicitor general, recent developments on the Second Amendment right to bear arms, and state and federal courts decisions regarding same-sex marriage and free speech for corporations.
- The appendix on how to brief cases was expanded and an example brief has been added.
- A new appendix containing examples of presidential executive orders and memoranda has been added.

- The law has been updated through early 2011 throughout, with a new case excerpt added.
- New photos also have been added throughout the book.
- New exhibits, diagrams, and case summaries have been added to illustrate particularly dense and difficult subjects, including a chart of current justices, who appointed them, and their basic political affiliation, a summary of the Court's various eras as identified by its federalism perspective, and a diagram of Dormant Commerce Clause analysis.
- Several new end-of-chapter features have been added, including Modern Challenges and Constitution Law in Action. These features provide students with several opportunities to research, review, and analyze contemporary constitutional cases and issues in real-world settings.
- A *Cyber Constitution* feature has also been added to provide web-based links to updated supplements to important constitutional principles and cases.

STUDENT RESOURCES

Within each chapter, the ***Cyber Constitution*** notes in the margin refer the reader to website sources containing full-length cases, court documents, legal resources, and other materials that highlight the realities of working on cases involving constitutional questions. In addition, the companion website at www.pearsonhighered.com/Hall helps to illustrate and explore the core practice of constitutional law and civil liberties in today's world. Practice Tests are included to allow students to check their knowledge. The companion website also contains links to **May It Please the Court,** a series of video and audio recordings of appellate oral arguments. These videos illustrate many of the modern-day constitutional debates facing courts today and demonstrate the practical realities of practicing constitutional law. Overall, the companion website provides students with many supplemental materials that allow the text to grow with the ever-changing dynamics of constitutional law.

INSTRUCTOR RESOURCES

For the convenience of instructors, the following ancillary materials are provided:

Instructor's Manual—The instructor's manual includes chapter outlines, answers to questions in the text, and a test bank with answers.

PowerPoint Lecture Presentation—The PowerPoint Lecture Presentation package provides screens outlining key concepts discussed in each chapter.

Pearson MyTest Electronic Testing Program—Pearson MyTest is a powerful assessment generation program that helps instructors easily create and print quizzes and exams. Questions and tests can be authored online, allowing instructors ultimate flexibility and the ability to efficiently manage assessments anytime, anywhere. Educator access to MyTest is already included in Pearson's Instructor Resource Center (IRC) Educator suite. Simply go to www.pearsonmytest.com and log in with your existing IRC login name and password.

The Instructor's Manual, Pearson MyTest program, and PPT Package can be downloaded from our Instructor's Resource Center. To access supplementary materials online, instructors need to request an instructor access code. Go to **www.pearsonhighered.com/irc**, where you can register for an instructor access code. Within 48 hours of registering you will receive a confirming e-mail including an instructor access code. Once you have received your code, locate your text in the online catalog and click on the **Instructor Resources** button on the left side of the catalog product page. Select a supplement and a log-in page will appear. Once you have logged in, you can access instructor material for all Pearson textbooks.

ACKNOWLEDGMENTS

The Authors thank the following reviewers for their suggestions on revising the text for the new edition.

Alvin L. McDonald, *New Mexico State University at Alamogordo*

Ann Lucas, *San Jose State University*

Sonia M. Gipson Rankin, *JD, University of New Mexico*

Brian J. McCully, *Fresno City College*

Charlotte A. Weybright, *Brown Mackie College, Fort Wayne*

Woodrow W. Colbert, *Vatterott College*

ABOUT THE AUTHORS

Daniel E. Hall, a native of Indiana, earned his bachelor's degree at Indiana University, Juris Doctor at Washburn University, and Doctor of Education in higher education curriculum and instruction at the University of Central Florida. He worked as an intern in the U.S. House of Representatives and at the Brookings Institution before attending law school, as law clerk to both the Honorable Gene E. Brooks, Chief Judge, U.S. District Court for the Southern District of Indiana and the Supreme Court of the Federated States of Micronesia immediately following law school. He has practiced law in both the United States and the Federated State of Micronesia, where he served as assistant attorney general following his judicial clerkship with the Supreme Court of Micronesia. In this capacity he litigated some of the young nation's first cases addressing important constitutional and traditional law issues. He has been a member of the faculties of the University of Central Florida, the University of Toledo, and Miami University, where he is currently professor of political science/criminal justice and former dean of the Hamilton Campus. From 2010 to 2013 he is also visiting professor of law at Sun Yat-sen University in Goungzhou, China. He is the author or coauthor of eighteen textbooks, including revisions, and a dozen journal articles on public law subjects. He is father of Grace Kathryn Hall and Eva Joan Hall. You can learn more about Daniel at Danielhall.org. He welcomes your comments and suggestions for this book, which may be sent to hallslaw@yahoo.com.

John P. Feldmeier earned his bachelor's degree in political science from Ohio Dominican College, Juris Doctor from Capital University Law School, and M.A. and Ph.D. in political science from Miami University. Before joining the academy, Dr. Feldmeier practiced law in Ohio, handling numerous cases involving important constitutional issues, including one that reached the U.S. Supreme Court. Dr. Feldmeier has published several articles on constitutional subjects in law reviews and political science journals. He is currently an associate professor of political science at Wright State University and is serving of counsel with the law firm of Sirkin Kinsley. John resides in Cincinnati, Ohio, with his wife, Melissa, and his two children, Emma and Jack.

1

Constitutionalism and Rule of Law

An assembly of demi-gods.

THOMAS JEFFERSON, COMMENTING ON THE DELEGATES TO
THE CONSTITUTIONAL CONVENTION

As the British Constitution is the most subtle organism which has proceeded from the womb and long gestation of progressive history, so the American Constitution is, so far as I can see, the most wonderful work ever struck off at a given time by the brain and purpose of man.

WILLIAM E. GLADSTONE (BRITISH PRIME MINISTER)

LEARNING OBJECTIVES
At the end of this chapter you should be able to:

- Identify and discuss the important historical events and political philosophies that led to, and shaped, the U.S. Constitution.
- Explain rule of law, including its elements and how it relates to constitutionalism.
- Define constitutional law as an academic field of study.
- Define judicial review, discuss its political and legal history, explain how it is an important element of the U.S. rule of law, and contrast it with at least two other models from around the world.
- Identify the major eras of the Supreme Court in the context of its approach to federalism.
- Identify the basic architecture and style of judicial opinions.
- Identify the elements of a brief.

1.1 CONSTITUTIONS AND RULE OF LAW

This book examines U.S. constitutional law. A complete understanding of constitutional law requires an understanding of the text of the Constitution, the Constitution's history, the institutions that interpret and enforce the Constitution, the Constitution's relationship to other forms of law, the current state of the law, and the most pressing constitutional issues of the day. But before these subjects are explored, one must understand what a constitution is and why it is important, particularly in the U.S. context. *Ballentine's Legal Dictionary* defines *constitution* as "[t]he system of fundamental principles by which a nation . . . is governed. A nation's constitution may be written or unwritten." In terms of a hierarchy, a constitution sits at the apex, and all forms of law below it (statutes, ordinances, regulations, executive orders) must conform to it. In the United States, the Constitution provides the basic architecture of government, protects individual rights, and is the foundation upon which all other laws are created.

1

The influence of the U.S. Constitution is much broader than commonly realized. For example, the daily actions of police officers are guided by many constitutional provisions, such as the Fourth Amendment (which prohibits unreasonable searches and seizures) and the Fifth Amendment (which protects against coerced confessions). Attorneys, process servers, and legal assistants must contend with constitutional law in nearly every case. As examples, the due process guarantees of the Fifth and Fourteenth Amendments regulate service of process (especially on out-of-state defendants), the Full Faith and Credit Clause provides the law for enforcing foreign judgments, and many clients present cases that arise directly under the U.S. Constitution. Even more, the freedom to speak, to write, to worship (or not), to meet with others, to disagree with the government, and a host of other protections found in the Constitution and its amendments play out in the daily lives of all people in the United States.

A constitution may be written or unwritten. The United States has a written constitution, whereas England has an unwritten one. In England, the rights of citizens are secured through the common law, customs, and several acts of Parliament. There is no single constitutional document. Some commentators argue that England does not have a constitution because Parliament is free to abolish all the rights enjoyed by the people. Others contend that these rights are so much a part of English society that they are secure against parliamentary intrusion.

Today, most nations have written constitutions. The Constitution of the United States is the oldest written constitution in the world and has been the model for many other nations as they debated and drafted their own documents.

This book examines the law of the U.S. Constitution. Important historical and social influences are discussed, as are institutions (e.g., the U.S. Supreme Court), constitutional methodology, and case law. American constitutional law is commonly divided into two fields of study: one focusing on governmental authorities and structures and another examining civil liberties. This text addresses both, as well as the values that underpin the Constitution.

In terms of development, legal systems and nations are often characterized by the degree to which they adhere to rule of law. The phrase "rule of law" has been used for hundreds of years. The English legal scholar A. V. Dicey brought attention to the concept in his discussions of the English law, and the phrase has been defined differently by scholars. In 2010, the World Justice Project issued its first report on rule of law around the world.[1] For purposes of its research, the World Justice Project defined the elements of rule of law as the level of legal accountability of government officials; whether laws are enacted and administered in a fair and efficient manner; the degree to which laws are clear and stable and protect fundamental rights; and whether access to justice is administered by fair and independent judicial officers.[2]

For purposes of this text, rule of law is achieved in a legal system if the following elements are present:

1. There is fundamental law
2. that limits the authority of government and
3. is enforceable by citizens.[3]

The first element, fundamentalism, refers to two characteristics of law. First, it must be primary, reflecting the most important liberty, social control, and governmental organization principles of a nation. Second, it must be superior law; all other forms of law must yield to it.

The second element is that it must limit the authority of the lawmakers and law enforcers. In some jurisdictions, it is not courts but special constitutional councils that exercise the authority to review legislation for constitutionality. In some of these cases, it is only legislation that may be invalidated, not the actions of the executive branch.

The last requirement is that it must be enforceable by citizens. In the United States this is accomplished through judicial review. You will learn more about judicial review later in this chapter. For now, understand that judicial review in the United States empowers courts, based upon their interpretation of the Constitution, to strike down legislation and executive actions that are unconstitutional. Historically, judicial review has provided a mechanism for all individuals to protect their rights and has served as a vehicle through which minority rights are protected from the prejudices and disadvantages of the majority. It has also served, with limitations, as a check on the balance of authority between the states and federal government and between the three branches of government.

In most jurisdictions that have rule of law, their fundamental law is expressed through a written constitution. Having a written constitution that recognizes individual rights does not mean that rule of law exists. For example, consider the following language that appears in the Constitution of the People's Republic of China:

Article 33. All persons holding the nationality of the People's Republic of China are citizens of the People's Republic of China. All citizens of the People's Republic of China are equal before the law. Every citizen enjoys the rights and at the same time must perform the duties prescribed by the Constitution and the law.

Article 34. All citizens of the People's Republic of China who have reached the age of 18 have the right to vote and stand for election, regardless of nationality, race, sex, occupation, family background, religious belief, education, property status, or length of residence, except persons deprived of political rights according to law.

Article 35. Citizens of the People's Republic of China enjoy freedom of speech, of the press, of assembly, of association, of procession, and of demonstration.

Article 36. Citizens of the People's Republic of China enjoy freedom of religious belief. No state organ, public organization, or individual may compel citizens to believe in, or not to believe in, any religion, nor may they discriminate against citizens who believe in, or do not believe in, any religion. The state protects normal religious activities. No one may make use of religion to engage in activities that disrupt public order, impair the health of citizens, or interfere with the educational system of the state. Religious bodies and religious affairs are not subject to any foreign domination.

Article 37. The freedom of person of citizens of the People's Republic of China is inviolable. No citizen may be arrested except with the approval or by decision of a people's procuratorate or by decision of a people's court, and arrests must be made by a public security organ. Unlawful deprivation or restriction of citizens' freedom of person by detention or other means is prohibited, and unlawful search of the person of citizens is prohibited.

Article 38. The personal dignity of citizens of the People's Republic of China is inviolable. Insult, libel, false charge, or frame-up directed against citizens by any means is prohibited.

Article 39. The home of citizens of the People's Republic of China is inviolable. Unlawful search of, or intrusion into, a citizen's home is prohibited.

Article 40. The freedom and privacy of correspondence of citizens of the People's Republic of China are protected by law. No organization or individual may, on any ground, infringe upon the freedom and privacy of citizens' correspondence except in cases where, to meet the needs of state security or of investigation into criminal offences, public security or procuratorial organs are permitted to censor correspondence in accordance with procedures prescribed by law.

Article 41. Citizens of the People's Republic of China have the right to criticize and make suggestions to any state organ or functionary. Citizens have the right to make to relevant state organs complaints and charges against, or exposures of, violation of the law or dereliction of duty by any state organ or functionary, but fabrication or distortion of facts with the intention of libel or frame-up is prohibited. In case of complaints, charges, or exposures made by citizens, the state organ concerned must deal with them in a responsible manner after ascertaining the facts. No one may suppress such complaints, charges, and exposures, or retaliate against the citizens making them. Citizens who have suffered losses through infringement of their civil rights by any state organ or functionary have the right to compensation in accordance with the law.

Article 42. Citizens of the People's Republic of China have the right as well as the duty to work. . . .

Article 43. Working people in the People's Republic of China have the right to rest. . . .

Article 44. The state prescribes by law the system of retirement for workers and staff in enterprises and undertakings and for functionaries of organs of state. The livelihood of retired personnel is ensured by the state and society.

Article 45. Citizens of the People's Republic of China have the right to material assistance from the state and society when they are old, ill, or disabled. . . .

Article 46. Citizens of the People's Republic of China have the duty as well as the right to receive education. The state promotes the all-round moral, intellectual, and physical development of children and young people.

Article 47. Citizens of the People's Republic of China have the freedom to engage in scientific research, literary and artistic creation, and other cultural pursuits. The state encourages and assists creative endeavors conducive to the interests of the people made by citizens engaged in education, science, technology, literature, art, and other cultural work.

Article 48. Women in the People's Republic of China enjoy equal rights with men in all spheres of life: political, economic, cultural and social, and family life. The state protects the rights and interests of women, applies the principle of equal pay for equal work for men and women alike, and trains and selects cadres from among women.

Article 49. Marriage, the family, and mother and child are protected by the state. Both husband and wife have the duty to practise family planning. Parents have the duty to rear and educate their minor children, and children who have come of age have the duty to support and assist their parents. Violation of the freedom of marriage is prohibited. Maltreatment of old people, women, and children is prohibited.

Article 50. The People's Republic of China protects the legitimate rights and interests of Chinese nationals residing abroad and protects the lawful rights and interests of returned overseas Chinese and of the family members of Chinese nationals residing abroad.

Many of these provisions are likely familiar to you, as they are also found in the U.S. Constitution. Interestingly, the Chinese Constitution also recognizes many rights that are not protected by the U.S. Constitution. The rights to work and retirement are examples. Even though the Chinese Constitution's recognition of individual rights is broader than that of the U.S. Constitution, the rights are balanced by the needs of the many, as seen in the following provisions:

Article 51. The exercise by citizens of the People's Republic of China of their freedoms and rights may not infringe upon the interests of the state, of society, and of the collective, or upon the lawful freedoms and rights of other citizens.

Article 52. It is the duty of citizens of the People's Republic of China to safeguard the unity of the country and the unity of all its nationalities.

YOUR CONSTITUTIONAL VALUES

In each of the following chapters, you will find a special feature entitled *Your Constitutional Values*. In this feature you will find examples of constitutional conflicts that did not make it to the Supreme Court of the United States for resolution. These case studies illustrate that constitutional law occurs at all levels and in all branches of government. Consistent with the adage "all politics is local," these case studies illustrate that constitutional conflicts occur with relative frequency in communities all around the nation.

As your read *Your Constitutional Values*, consider the following:

(1) What values are in conflict?
(2) What is the state of the law? Does precedent adequately consider all the values at stake? If not, how can you distinguish this case from the existing precedent?
(3) Has this or a similar case occurred in your community or state?

Article 53. Citizens of the People's Republic of China must abide by the constitution and the law, keep state secrets, protect public property, and observe labor discipline and public order and respect social ethics.

Article 54. It is the duty of citizens of the People's Republic of China to safeguard the security, honor, and interests of the motherland; they must not commit acts detrimental to the security, honor, and interests of the motherland.

An equally significant limitation on constitutionalism is the absence of constitutional accountability by the government. The Chinese Constitution is not enforceable by citizens in courts, nor does China have a constitutional council with the authority to invalidate legislation. As Paul Gewirtz penned of the Chinese Constitution's status, "The most basic question is whether the PRC Constitution is 'law' at all. Many perceive it to be more of an ideological document, a political document, or an aspirational document, than a legal one. Certainly it does not function in Chinese society the way constitutions function in other societies where the constitution is viewed as law. It has not been used by the courts in the course of deciding cases [citation omitted]. Indeed, it is not regularly interpreted by any government body. It does not function day-to-day as a superior law."[4] Indeed, the final authority to interpret all national law, including the Constitution rests with the National People's Congress through its standing committee.[5] Moreover, it the Communist Party that truly answers all important political and legal questions and the party is not accountable to the people. So, while the nation's fundamental legal principles are announced through a written constitution, China lacks rule of lack because of the absence of enforceability.

To understand why the framers chose the particular governmental architecture they did, and why they protected a certain set of liberties, a brief historical context must be drawn.

Cyber Constitution
The World Justice Project has an index on rule of law around the world. See www.worldjusticeproject. org/ Similarly, the World Bank has a governance indicator that includes rule of law. See http:// info.worldbank.org/ governance/wgi/index.asp

1.2 ARTICLES OF CONFEDERATION

After the colonists arrived in what is now known as the United States, they established colonies. The original thirteen states were established from the geographical boundaries of these colonies. Although the colonies were largely autonomous and self-governing, they remained, ultimately, governed by England. Each colony's governmental structure and relationship with England varied, but all shared common grievances with their mother country that led to the war for independence. Their Declaration of Independence was issued in 1776. Independence was won in 1781.

Even before independence was declared, the colonies had established a body to meet and address issues of national concern: the Continental Congress. The Continental

Congress first met in Philadelphia on September 5, 1774. It operated from this date until 1781. This organization, though national in representation, did not have the authority to make binding laws. Its authority was primarily limited to raising an army and conducting diplomacy.

By the time the Declaration of Independence was adopted, there had been discussions in the Continental Congress concerning the adoption of a constitution to formally recognize a confederacy of the thirteen colonies. On June 7, 1776, Richard Henry Lee, a delegate to the Congress from Virginia, introduced a resolution that declared the "United Colonies" to be "free and independent states, that they are absolved from all allegiance to the British Crown, and that all political connection between them and the State of Great Britain is, and ought to be, totally dissolved." Additionally, the resolution called for the development of a plan of confederation to be submitted to the states.[6] The resolution was adopted on July 2, 1776, and was incorporated into the Declaration of Independence, which was largely drafted by Thomas Jefferson on July 4, 1776.

It was not until 1781 that the colonies adopted the Articles of Confederation and Perpetual Union, the first constitution of the United States. Under the Articles, the Continental Congress was disbanded and replaced by the Confederation Congress. Although the new Congress had more authority than its predecessor, the states continued to be the most powerful political entities. It was proclaimed in the Articles that "[e]ach state retains its sovereignty, freedom and independence, and every power, jurisdiction and right, which is not expressly delegated to the United States, in Congress assembled." Politically, the United States was a loose union of independent and sovereign states, and members of the Congress were little more than ambassadors representing their respective states. As expressly stated in the Articles, the states entered into a "firm league of friendship."[7]

Not many years passed before this league proved unworkable. The states were distant from one another. In an age without modern travel and technological means to disseminate information, this was problematic. Compounding the problem, the states were distant in more ways than miles; they differed in history, culture, and politics. The result was parochialism, localism, and an interest in empowering the states rather than the national government. In the end, the states proved to be too independent and powerful, and the national government too dependent and powerless.

Under the Articles of Confederation, the national government was responsible for negotiating treaties with foreign governments. That authority, however, was thwarted by the authority of the states to tax imports and exports, regardless of any treaties negotiated by the national government. Although the national government had the authority to declare war, it had no authority to establish a standing army. If it declared war, it could enlist volunteers, but lacked the power of conscription. It could request the assistance of state militias, but the states could refuse. Even more, funding for war efforts came from the states.[8]

Also, each state could prohibit the export and import of goods. The consequence was inconsistent and often competing commercial laws between the states. For the same reasons, foreign governments and merchants were discouraged from trading with the United States.

Jealousies between the states led to factionalism. Nine of the thirteen states had their own navies. Territorial disputes, as well as disputes over the authority to control the nation's waterways, plagued the nation.[9] Many of the states were engaged in economic war with one another, and there were concerns that civil war would destroy the union.

The national government was clearly financially subservient to the states. Specifically, it did not have the authority to raise revenues directly from its citizens. The Articles provided that the states were to make contributions to the national treasury. However, the contributions were to be raised by the action of each state, and the national government lacked the authority to compel a state to contribute. As a result, the national government suffered financial difficulties because many of the states were regularly in arrears in their payments. As a result, the national government itself could not pay debts it owed to foreigners and citizens.

Governmental structure under the Articles was also confused. There was no independent executive. The president of the Congress served as the nation's highest executive officer, but the role of the president was not clearly understood, which resulted in confusion between legislative and executive authority. Many executive responsibilities were performed by legislative committees rather than by the president—a practice that proved to be ineffective.

There was no national judiciary, except that the Congress selected four judges to hear cases in the territory northwest of the Ohio River and a Court of Capture heard appeals from the state courts in admiralty cases.[10] Otherwise, there was no national court to bring the national perspective to litigation or to develop a uniform national jurisprudence. Accordingly, cases involving national law were heard and decided by state courts, sometimes with differing interpretations of national law.

The private sector was also affected. Inflation was high and the laws governing commerce differed from state to state. Inconsistent and often competing laws regulating interstate commerce impeded economic development. Again, the national government was virtually powerless to remedy the nation's ills. Lack of confidence in the future of the nation resulted in little investment and a significant decrease in the value of land.

In 1786, the nation's economic problems provoked a group of radical farmers in Massachusetts, led by Daniel Shays, to rebel against the local government. The rebels—angered by the poor state of the economy, the imprisonment of small farmers who could not pay their debts, and court-ordered land forfeitures—took control of a number of courts and prevented them from operating. There was no national authority to defeat the rebellion, and initially many local authorities were reluctant to become involved. Eventually, **Shays' Rebellion** was quelled by a privately financed (merchants and creditors), state-legislature-authorized militia, but it was further proof that the nation's problems needed to be addressed.

The inadequacies of the Articles became critical. James Madison stated that the "insufficiency of present confederation [threatened the] preservation of the union." He continued, "we may indeed with propriety be said to have reached almost the last stage of national humiliation. There is scarcely anything that can wound the pride or degrade the character of an independent nation which we do not experience."[11] Madison was speaking for many. The mood of the nation was one for change in order to save the union. The proponents of change recognized the problem to be the weakness of the national government. However, the colonists had also learned a lesson about unchecked centralized power while under British rule: it can be unfair and arbitrary.

These two experiences—the excesses of British power and the inadequacies of the Confederation—resulted in a reserved and cautious attitude in favor of strengthening the national government. Some people, notably George Washington, Alexander Hamilton, James Madison, John Marshall, and John Hancock, favored a strong national government and thus are known as **Federalists.** There were also people who opposed the creation of a strong national government. This group, known as the **anti-Federalists,** had among its ranks Thomas Jefferson, Luther Martin, George Mason, and Patrick Henry.

1.3 PHILADELPHIA CONVENTION

The prevailing attitude was that a stronger national government could provide economic and political stability for the young nation. For several years the Congress had called for an increase in national authority to cure the nation's ills. James Madison zealously fought for a constitutional convention. The highly respected George Washington bitterly complained of the impotence of the national government. But the states were reluctant to give up any power, and this caused delay. Finally, there came a chance to mend the nation's problems.

Shays' Rebellion
Daniel Shays, a veteran of the American Revolutionary War, and a group of fellow farmers rebelled in protest of economic conditions. This incident was cited by many as justification for abandoning the Articles of Confederation, the theory being that a stronger national government could provide better economic conditions and that a national military would be most effective in defeating rebellions.

Federalist
(1) A person who supports a strong, centralized government.
(2) A political party that advocates a strong, centralized government.

anti-Federalist
(1) A person who opposes establishment of a strong, centralized government in favor of local control.
(2) A party that opposes establishment of a strong, centralized government in favor of local control.

1.3(a) The Delegates and Their Mandate

In 1786, a group of prominent Americans met in Annapolis, Maryland, to discuss interstate commerce issues. The meeting had been urged by the Virginia state legislature and was supported by many politicians from other states. However, little occurred, as only five states were represented. One important product did result from this meeting, however. Alexander Hamilton submitted, and the body approved, a recommendation to the Continental Congress that a convention be held to examine the problems of the nation and its constitution. The Continental Congress approved such a meeting.

The congressional resolution approving of the convention read, in part, "Resolved that . . . on the second Monday in May next a Convention of delegates who shall have been appointed by the several states be held at Philadelphia for the sole and express purpose of revising the Articles of Confederation." There was no mandate to the delegates to create a new constitution. Even more, they were representatives of the states and, arguably, not the people. In spite of this, they chose to act as representatives of the people. Consequently, they chose to begin the new constitution with "We the People," rather than the suggested "We the States."

Philadelphia was an appropriate location for such an auspicious gathering. It was the city where the first Continental Congress met, where George Washington was appointed Commander of the Continental Army by the Second Continental Congress, and where two important documents—the Declaration of Independence and the Articles of Confederation—had been signed. Philadelphia would add the new constitution to its impressive list.

In total, seventy-four delegates were selected to attend the convention (see Figure 1-1), although only fifty-five actually attended. The reasons for not attending

---

Connecticut
Oliver Ellsworth
Roger Sherman
William Samuel Johnson

Delaware
Richard Bassett
Jacob Broom
Johnson Dikinson
George Read
Gunning Bedford Jr.

Georgia
Abraham Baldwin
William Houston
William Pierce
William Few

Maryland
Daniel Carroll
Daniel of St. Thomas Jenifer
James McHenry
Luther Martin
John Francis Mercer

Massachusetts
Elbridge Gerry

Nathaniel Gorham
Rufus King
Caleb Strong

New Hampshire
John Langdon
Nicholas Gilman

New Jersey
David Brearley
Jonathan Dayton
William Churchill Houston
William Livingston
William Paterson

New York
Alexander Hamilton
John Lansing Jr.
Robert Yates

North Carolina
William Blount
William Richardson Davie
Alexander Martin
Richard Dobbs Spaight
Hugh Williamson

Pennsylvania
Benjamin Franklin
George Clymer
Thomas Fitzsimons
Jared Ingersoll
Thomas Mifflin
Gouverneur Morris
Robert Morris
James Wilson

Rhode Island
None

South Carolina
Charles Pinckney
Charles Cotesworth Pinckney
Pierce Butler
John Rutledge

Virginia
George Washington
James Madison
George Mason
Edmund Randolph
John Blair
James McClurg
George Wythe

FIGURE 1-1

The states' delegates to the Constitutional Convention of 1787

varied—some personal, others political. Patrick Henry rejected his appointment because he "smelt a rat."[12] He correctly foresaw what the convention would produce: not a revision of the Articles, but a whole new constitution, creating a whole new government. Later, during the ratification debates in the states, he would prove to be a vocal and vehement opponent of the new constitution.

The delegates who attended were the who's-who of colonial life. They were among the most respected men of politics, law, and business. It is said that Thomas Jefferson, who was in Paris during the convention, remarked that it was "an assembly of demi-gods" when he learned who the delegates were.

Of the attending delegates, one-half were college graduates, most were attorneys, and all were part of America's political or economic aristocracy.[13] Eight were foreign-born and eighteen had worked or studied abroad. Some were obviously influenced by what they had learned from the political experiences of other peoples in other nations. A few delegates were clergymen, but this did not affect the secular atmosphere of the convention.[14]

The convention was scheduled to open on May 14, 1787. Because of the absence of a quorum, though, the proceedings did not begin until May 25. They continued until September 17 with only two breaks, two days to celebrate Independence Day and another work-related, ten-day recess.

Of the thirteen states, all but one were represented at the convention. Rhode Island refused to send delegates. Two matters were immediately considered and agreed upon. First, with little discussion, George Washington was selected to chair the convention. Second, the delegates decided that what was to transpire was to remain secret until the final document was completed. Although there were small leaks during the convention, the rule was generally complied with by the members.

The absence of information from the delegates led to speculation and rumor about what was transpiring inside the hall. So wild was one rumor, to the effect that the delegates were considering a monarchy, that they issued a statement on August 15 to the contrary. Interestingly, there were a few delegates who supported the establishment of some form of monarchy. Alexander Hamilton, for example, proposed an "elective monarchy." Under this system, the president would have been elected for life, as would the Senate. Hamilton advocated for an English-like government, equating the House of Representatives to England's House of Commons, the Senate to the House of Lords, and the president to the Crown. Edmund Randolph admitted to preferring the English system, but he also recognized that the people of the United States would never accept such a government.[15] Hamilton's and Randolph's feelings did not represent those of most of the delegates. As a whole, they were faithful to republican (representative democratic, if you will) principles and were mindful not to place too much authority in any one person's or group's hands.

1.3(b) The Debates

Details of what transpired at the convention are not known. An official journal was kept and provides some insights. More thorough than the convention journal are the notes of James Madison, who was so diligent in his record keeping that he never

Independence Hall, Philadelphia, Pennsylvania
Photos.com/Thinkstock

left the convention for more than an hour. In total, his notes occupy three volumes. These items, as well as the personal notes and correspondence of all the delegates, give us an idea of what the delegates discussed and debated during that hot summer of 1787.

On the second day of the convention, Edmund Randolph, governor of Virginia, presented the Virginia Plan, which was in large measure the work of James Madison. Although the Virginia Plan was not the only proposal presented to the convention,[16] it was to be the most influential. The Virginia Plan, or Virginia Resolves, set the tone for the convention and controlled the issues that would be considered. Many of the plan's initial concepts were made a part of the Constitution, in whole or in part. Although the Virginia Plan claimed to be a revision of the Articles of Confederation, it was clear to the delegates that it was more than that: It was a proposal to replace the existing confederation with a strong, centralized, and supreme national government. The convention took up the plan resolve by resolve. Some of the issues debated at the convention are discussed here.

The nature of the national legislature, Congress, was of particular importance to the delegates. What would be each state's representation in the new Congress? How would its members be selected? What powers would it possess? These are all issues that were considered, debated, and resolved by the delegates.

General Charles Pinckney objected to the discussions and reminded the delegates that they were authorized only to revise the Articles of Confederation, not to replace them. Later, Edmund Randolph commented, "when the salvation of the Republic is at stake . . . it would be treason to our trust not to propose what we find necessary."

The Virginia Plan called for a separation of powers: legislative, executive, and judicial. Madison, Hamilton, and other delegates were influenced by the theories of

Cyber Constitution
The National
Constitution Center http://
constitutioncenter.org/

European Renaissance and Enlightenment philosophers, such as John Locke and Charles de Montesquieu, who had written extensively about the importance of dividing the functions and powers of government to preserve liberty. As stated by Madison, "The accumulation of all powers, legislative, executive, and judiciary, in the same hands may justly be pronounced the very definition of tyranny."[17] There was little discussion about the concept, as it was generally accepted. Additionally, all agreed, as evidenced by the final product, that few decisions should be made by one branch alone. The branches should check one another to maintain a balance of power.

As for a national legislature, the Virginia Plan provided for a bicameral Congress. There appears to have been little disagreement with this idea. However, the remaining questions were not so easily answered. Concerning each state's representation, the plan called for state representation to be based upon each state's number of free people or, in the alternative, based upon each state's contribution to the national treasury. The small states opposed the proposal, as they were accustomed to being treated as equals under the Articles of Confederation. These states were convinced that the larger states would always have their will, unless all were equals in Congress. They particularly feared the West, which represented potentially large and wealthy states in the future. Roger Sherman commented, "The smaller states will never agree to the plan on any other principle than an equality of suffrage in this branch." The larger states objected to equal representation, contending that this would devalue the franchise of their citizens.

Ultimately, an agreement known as the "Great Compromise" was reached. Representation in the lower house, the House of Representatives, would be based on population (the number of free persons, excluding Indians that were not taxed, and three-fifths of others); representation in the upper house, the Senate, was to be equal. Initially, the delegates agreed that each state would be entitled to one representative to the Senate, but later this was changed, with no debate, to two. Included in this compromise was the resolution of another troubling issue: whether slaves were to be part of the equation for deciding representation. Because the delegates had decided, after debate, that the national government's taxes were to be based upon the same equation, the issue was doubly important.

This issue divided the delegates. Philosophically, the division was geographic, North versus South, over whether slavery should be permitted. But the delegates did not seriously debate this issue. However, the division over whether to count slaves for the purpose of representation and taxation transcended the North/South divide. The South would pay more in taxes if slaves were counted. At the same time, the added numbers could increase its representation. Some of the southern delegates contended that southern white citizens would never accept being placed on a one-to-one basis with slaves.

Northern delegates were also split. Some contended that because slaves were property, they should not be included. Others insisted that all people should be included in the census. The two sides compromised and allowed three-fifths of slaves to be counted in determining both taxation and representation. The drafters of the Constitution were careful not to use the term *slave,* referring to "other persons" instead.

The number of representatives was thus set, but how were they to be selected? This proved to be another hotly debated issue. Delegates such as Elbridge Gerry and Roger Sherman believed that the people could not be trusted to choose their own representatives. To them, the people were an uninformed mass, subject to being "duped" by unscrupulous, charismatic politicians. They proposed that the state legislatures be empowered to appoint the representatives.

George Mason wanted the power to rest with the states, not because he distrusted the people, but because he was a states' rights advocate. "Whatever power may be necessary for the national government, a certain portion must necessarily be left in the states . . . . The state legislatures also sought to have some means of defending themselves against encroachments of the national government . . . . And what better means can we provide than to make them a constituent part of the national establishment."

John Dickinson felt similarly. He contended that direct election would result in the total annihilation of the states as political entities.

Others believed that the people should directly elect their representatives. This issue was central to the convention. Were they creating a government of the states, or of the people? George Mason and James Madison were proponents of the direct election of at least one chamber of Congress. Mason pointed out that under the Articles of Confederation, the national government represented the states, which then represented the people. He contended that the states should not stand between the people and the national government, as the interests of the states are sometimes at odds with the people's. Oliver Ellsworth warned that the "people will not readily subscribe to the national constitution if it should subject them to be disfranchised." The decision went to the heart of how to define this new democratic republic.

Again, the ideas of John Locke, Charles de Montesquieu, and Thomas Hobbes. Natural law theory was a part of the delegates' collective political ideology. If the authority to create a constitution emanates from the people, some delegates wondered how the people could be disenfranchised. Again, a compromise was reached. The members of the House of Representatives would be elected directly; senators were to be selected by the state legislatures. This method for selecting senators remained until the adoption of the Seventeenth Amendment in 1913, which provided for direct election.

The delegates also tackled the issue of qualifications to vote. There was discussion of limiting the right to vote to landowners. There were concerns that the less wealthy would sell their votes. This idea was defeated, and the franchise was extended to all free men.

There was little debate over the powers that should be possessed by Congress. These were spelled out in the first article of the Constitution. The framers intended for the national government to be a limited government. Said another way, the national government possesses no authority that is not specifically granted through the Constitution. However, in the enumeration of its powers, Congress was granted the authority to regulate interstate commerce and to make all laws "necessary and proper" for enforcing its other enumerated powers. These clauses, matched with social, political, and technological changes, have proven instrumental to the growth of the national government and are concomitantly responsible for decreasing the authority of the states.

Another thorny issue for the delegates was the Virginia Plan's resolve that provided the national Congress with veto power over state laws. The original proposal allowed the legislative veto of state laws that were in conflict with the national constitution. Later in the convention, this was extended to all laws that Congress found improper. Madison supported the idea, as did Pinckney. They contended that it was an effective and necessary means of keeping the states from encroaching upon the national sphere. There were strong objections. Elbridge Gerry argued that through such power, the national government could "enslave the states." It was suggested that the new constitution could enumerate the instances when Congress could exercise the power, but that idea was rejected, as was the entire proposal. The legislative veto was dead. Madison was not happy, but was consoled by the fact that the judiciary would apparently have the authority to protect the national government from the excesses of the states.

What were the framers' thoughts on the executive branch? Under the Virginia Plan, the executive power would have rested in one person, who was to be limited to one term and selected by Congress. George Mason thought there should be three coequal executives. It was decided, with little debate, that executive authority should reside with one person. Nevertheless, the framers feared a monarchy and were careful not to create one. The title *President* was chosen over other more regal titles, such as *His Highness,* to avoid the appearance of monarchy.

One of the hardest decisions for the delegates to reach was the method of selecting the president. For the same reasons discussed earlier in regard to selecting members of Congress, direct election was not seriously considered. It was proposed that Congress make the selection. However, there was general agreement that this would place too much authority with the legislature and create too much executive dependence on the legislature. Others wanted greater state involvement in the process. Perhaps the state legislatures should select the highest executive? Most agreed that this process would be too political and too regional, likely resulting in each state supporting one of its own. There was intense debate over the issue. The result was the electoral college. Under the electoral college system, each state has a number of electors equal to the total number of national Congress members (members of the House and Senate) it possesses. These persons constitute the electoral college. The president is selected by this electoral college. Alexander Hamilton said of this system:

> It was desirable that the sense of the people should operate in the choice of the person to whom so important a trust was to be confided. This end will be answered by committing the right of making it, not to any preestablished body, but to men chosen by the people for the special purpose, and at the particular conjuncture.
>
> It was equally desirable that the immediate election should be made by men most capable of analyzing the qualities adapted to the station and acting under circumstances favorable to deliberation, and to a judicious combination of all the reasons and inducements which were proper to govern their choice. A small number of persons, selected by their fellow citizens from the general mass, will be most likely to possess the information and discernment requisite to so complicated an investigation.[18]

The delegates agreed that, in the event of a tie in the electoral college, the House of Representatives would choose between the candidates. The Senate was originally considered, but the delegates felt that they had already significantly empowered the Senate and that, in the interest of balance, this responsibility should be placed with the House of Representatives.

In regard to presidential responsibilities, the delegates agreed that the president should be the commander-in-chief of the military, negotiate and make treaties, and nominate the cabinet members, members of the national judiciary, and other government officials, with the advice and consent of the Senate. They also decided to give the president the power to veto legislation, but checked that power by providing that Congress could override the veto with a two-thirds vote. Edmund Randolph believed that the total grant of authority to the president was excessive and characterized it as the "fetus of monarchy."

The final issue to be discussed concerning the executive also concerns the judiciary. It was proposed that a council be established comprising the president and several justices of the Supreme Court to review acts of Congress for constitutionality. Under the proposal, acts contrary to the Constitution could be declared void or revised by the council. Gerry opposed the measure because he believed it to be superfluous, as the judiciary has the power to nullify laws contrary to the Constitution. James Madison agreed, "A law violating a constitution established by the people themselves . . . would be considered by judges as null and void." Rufus King also opposed the council. He contended that because it was the responsibility of the courts to review laws before them, and nullify those repugnant to the Constitution, it would be an improper mixing of functions to have judges participate in revising or voiding laws with the executive. Still another voice was heard in this vein. Luther Martin stated, "[A]s to the Constitutionality of laws, that point will come before the judges in their proper official character. In this character they have a negative on the laws." The measure was defeated, but the president was given the veto power, subject to override.

Interestingly, the delegates did not specifically mention, in the Constitution, the power of the judiciary to declare the acts of its coordinate branches or the states unconstitutional. However, the Supreme Court has determined that such a power is implicit in the judicial function. (This issue is discussed again in Chapter 3.)

Another issue the delegates debated was the role the national judiciary should play in the new United States. Some contended that they should create a system of national courts through the new constitution. Others feared, however, that if they created national courts, state courts would be displaced and divested of their authority. The compromise agreement was that the Supreme Court of the United States would be created by the new constitution along with "inferior Courts as the Congress may from time to time ordain and establish." Without a system of lower national courts, many delegates feared that national laws would go unenforced. To remedy this problem, the delegates included a provision in the new constitution requiring state courts to enforce national laws. This is embodied in Article VI, and reads, in relevant part:

> This Constitution, and the Laws of the United States which shall be made in Pursuance thereof: and all Treaties made, or which shall be made, under the Authority of the United States, shall be the supreme Law of the Land; and the Judges in every State shall be bound thereby, any Thing in the Constitution of any State to the Contrary notwithstanding.

This compromise satisfied the delegates who wanted to control the size of the national government and also assured that national laws would be enforced. Congress exercised its power to create inferior national courts when it enacted the Judiciary Act of 1798, which established thirteen district and three circuit courts.

There was little debate concerning the jurisdiction of the national judiciary by the delegates. This issue is examined more closely in Chapters 3 and 4.

1.3(c) Individual Rights and Slavery

To many people, there were two glaring problems with the Constitution. First, it did not explicitly set out individual rights. Second, it did not address slavery.

First, it must be pointed out that the delegates did not totally ignore issues of individual liberty. The Constitution does contain a number of provisions intended to protect civil rights. For example, Article I, section 9, provides for writs of **habeas corpus.** Section 10 prohibits Congress from passing any **bills of attainder** or **ex post facto laws.** Article III, Section 3, provides that no person shall be convicted of treason except upon the testimony of two witnesses to the same act or upon a confession in open court.

In spite of this, the first ten amendments, commonly known as the Bill of Rights, were added to assure that the government would not encroach upon civil liberties. At the Constitutional Convention, George Mason argued for the inclusion of a bill of rights, and Elbridge Gerry moved for such a bill to be included in the Constitution. Alexander Hamilton saw no need to include a bill of rights, because the government lacked the authority to encroach upon an individual's liberty: "Why declare that things shall not be done, which there is no power to do."

Hamilton did not foresee the significant change that would come to the United States. Industrialization, a huge growth in population, and a specialization of functions have led to increased interdependence among people. Today, few persons live so remotely that their activities do not affect others, and few supply their own food, clothes, and other necessities. Contemporary life in the United States involves continuous and frequent contact with other people. As human contact increases, so do conflicts and, accordingly, rules to regulate conduct. We look to government to establish and enforce most of these rules. To protect ourselves from an overzealous government, which we have entrusted with an ever-increasing amount of authority, we need a bill of rights.

Hamilton's view prevailed. The delegates decided not to include a bill of rights in the original document because they simply did not believe the government had the authority to legislate in the areas a bill of rights would cover. After the convention voted ten to zero to exclude it, Gerry moved that the freedom of the press should at least be included. For the same reason—that the delegates did not believe the government had the authority to regulate the press—this motion was also defeated. There was no bill of rights in the original Constitution.

Nevertheless, the absence of a bill of rights was troubling to the nation. A few states, such as New York and Virginia, attached to their resolutions of approval of the

habeas corpus
Latin term for "you have the body." A writ whose purpose is to obtain immediate relief from illegal imprisonment by having the "body" (that is, the prisoner) delivered from custody and brought before that court. A writ of habeas corpus is a means for attacking the constitutionality of the statute under which, or the proceedings in which, the original conviction was obtained. There are numerous writs of habeas corpus, each applicable in different procedural circumstances. The full name of the ordinary writ of habeas corpus is *habeas corpus ad subjiciendum.*

bill of attainder
A legislative act that inflicts capital punishment upon named persons without a judicial trial. Congress and the state legislatures are prohibited from issuing bills of attainder by the Constitution.

ex post facto law
A law making a person criminally liable for an act that was not criminal at the time it was committed. The Constitution prohibits both Congress and the states from enacting such laws.

Constitution proposals to amend the new constitution to add a bill of rights. In total, over 200 amendments to the constitution were discussed in the state ratifying conventions.[19] It was a popular idea, and only three years after the Constitution was ratified, the Bill of Rights was ratified.

Slavery was a divisive issue. The issue arose in the context discussed previously: taxation and representation. It was at that juncture that many delegates voiced their objections to slavery. Luther Martin asserted that the slave trade was "inconsistent with the principles of the revolution and dishonorable to the American character to have such a feature in the Constitution."

The issue of slavery also arose in the context of the importation of slaves. Under the new constitution, this was an area under national jurisdiction, but many delegates representing the southern states did not want the national government to interfere with the importation of slaves. Again, some delegates who were opposed to slavery believed that the document should include a provision prohibiting the importation of slaves into the United States. George Mason, himself a slave owner, opposed slavery and wanted to include such a provision in the new constitution.

There were also delegates who opposed slave traffic but believed that the constitution should not prohibit it. Roger Sherman was in this group. He thought the states were moving toward abolition and that this movement should be permitted to run its course. Charles Pinckney warned that South Carolina would not accept any constitution that forbade the importation of slaves. He voiced what all the delegates feared: factionalism. They did not want to include a provision so repugnant to any particular region that ratification would be jeopardized. Benjamin Franklin, president of the Pennsylvania Society for the Abolition of Slavery, refused to present a petition from the group to the convention, fearing that it would drive an irreparable wedge between the states.

A compromise was reached. First, as discussed earlier, three-fifths of slaves were included in the initial determination of representation and taxation. As to the importation of slaves, the delegates agreed that Congress could not prohibit the importation of slaves until 1808 and capped the tax on each slave at $10. On January 1, 1808, Congress prohibited the importation of slaves. This did not, however, end slavery. It took a civil war to accomplish that goal.

Subsequent to the civil war, the Thirteenth, Fourteenth, and Fifteenth Amendments, and federal legislation, were enacted to extend legal protections and equality to all persons, regardless of color, race, or ethnicity. You will learn more about this subject later in this text.

1.3(d) Women and the Franchise

Women were not extended the right to vote by the new constitution. In fact, it appears that there was no discussion of the issue at the Constitutional Convention. Women were not excluded entirely from political processes during this period, however. For example, the New Jersey Constitution of 1776 extended the right to vote to women who owned property (African Americans were also allowed to vote). This was changed, however, in 1807, when the New Jersey Constitution was amended to restrict suffrage to "men."[20]

The women's suffrage movement can be traced back to Abigail Adams, wife of President John Adams. Later, feminists such as Elizabeth Cady Stanton and Susan B. Anthony led the women's suffrage movement that resulted in the Nineteenth Amendment (1920), which extended the right to vote to women. You will learn later that the Fourteenth Amendment's Equal Protection and Due Process clauses, as well as federal legislation, have since been interpreted to ensure equal protection under the law in many instances beyond voting.

1.4 RATIFICATION

James Madison, Alexander Hamilton, Gouverneur Morris, and Rufus King were responsible for the actual drafting of the Constitution. Although it was Madison who brought many of the ideas to the convention that were eventually adopted, it was Gouverneur Morris who wrote most of the text, including the entire preamble. A local clerk was hired to actually pen the document. It took him forty hours to write the 4,400 words on a four-page parchment made of either calf or lamb skin. He was paid $30 for this task.

The signing occurred on September 17, 1787. Thirty-nine delegates signed. Three delegates, George Mason, Edmund Randolph, and Elbridge Gerry, refused to sign. Edmund Randolph was the delegate who introduced the Virginia Plan, from which the Constitution was constructed. He, like Mason and Gerry, was concerned that too much power had been vested in the national government. Later, however, during the Virginia Ratification Convention, Randolph supported the Constitution to avoid dividing the nation.[21] Mason and Gerry, in contrast, later opposed the Constitution in their state conventions. Mason commented that he would rather cut off his hand than see the Constitution ratified.

S I D E B A R

RATIFICATION OF THE CONSTITUTION

Article VII of the Constitution of the United States reads, in part, "The Ratification of the Conventions of nine States, shall be sufficient for the Establishment of this Constitution between the States so ratifying the Same." The delegates had decided that ratification would occur through conventions to be conducted in each state. Further, it took nine states' approval before the Constitution could be ratified, and then it would apply only among the ratifying states. It took two and a half years, but eventually all thirteen states accepted the Constitution. The order of state approval was as follows:

December 7, 1787	Delaware
December 12, 1787	Pennsylvania
December 18, 1787	New Jersey
January 2, 1788	Georgia
January 9, 1788	Connecticut
February 6, 1788	Massachusetts
April 28, 1788	Maryland
May 23, 1788	South Carolina
June 21, 1788	New Hampshire
June 25, 1788	Virginia
July 26, 1788	New York
November 21, 1789	North Carolina
May 29, 1790	Rhode Island

Rhode Island remained obstinate. Congress voted to sever the new nation's commercial relations with Rhode Island, which helped push that state to approval. Finally, on May 29, 1790, Rhode Island gave its approval. The nation was united under the Constitution.

The delegates transmitted a copy to the Congress, where it was received on September 20, 1787. Richard Henry Lee opposed sending the Constitution on to the states for ratification, and there was discussion of sending it on with objections. The Congress decided to do neither. Instead, it was transmitted to the states without any comment whatsoever.

The delegates had debated the method of ratification. Special conventions won out over state legislatures. Further, the delegates decided that it should take only nine states to ratify the document, rather than the total of thirteen, and that ratification would be effective only among the ratifying states. All thirteen states would have at least one ratification convention. The state conventions were limited to ratifying or rejecting the document; no revisions or conditional ratifications were allowed. However, concerns were voiced during the ratification process, and at least one, the absence of a bill of rights, was so serious that the framers promised to immediately add the protections after ratification in order to secure the support needed to ratify the document. The conventions began in November 1787 and ended in May 1790.

During this period, numerous articles were published in magazines and newspapers, pamphlets were distributed, and speeches were made, arguing the pros and cons of the new constitution. The most influential writings were those of James Madison, Alexander Hamilton, and John Jay, who published a series of eighty-five articles under the pseudonym *Publius.* Today, we know these as the *Federalist Papers.* Through these articles, these men made forceful arguments in support of the Constitution. The anti-Federalists had their outlet as well. Another series of articles, entitled the *Federal Farmer,* was published in opposition to ratification.

Cyber Constitution
Federalist Papers
www.foundingfathers.
info/federalistpapers/

During the debates in the state conventions, three common objections were made to the Constitution. First, it was missing a bill of rights. Second, it emasculated the sovereignty of the states. Third, the delegates had exceeded their authority in replacing the Articles of Confederation. Delegates Luther Martin, Elbridge Gerry, and George Mason passionately opposed ratification.

Delaware was the first state to approve the Constitution, doing so on December 7, 1787. New Hampshire approved on June 21, 1788. It was the critical ninth state to approve, so the Constitution was then ratified and the Articles of Confederation superseded, and a new government could be formed. During the formation of the new government, the state conventions continued. By the time North Carolina ratified on July 26, 1788, every state but Rhode Island had joined the Union and the nation's first electoral college had selected George Washington the first president under the Constitution. In April of that year, Congress had its first meeting. John Jay was selected as the nation's first chief justice during 1789.

1.5 AMENDMENTS

The framers of the Constitution lived in an era when changes to government came either by edicts of kings or by revolution. They desired to have a more fair and civil method. At the same time, they did not want to empower Congress to amend the Constitution. After all, the Constitution is fundamental law, intended to restrict the power of government in many instances.

The framers devised two methods to amend the Constitution. They are found in Article V. The first method is initiated by Congress. With a two-thirds vote in both houses, Congress may propose an amendment to the states. In the alternative, two-thirds of the state legislatures may call for a convention to make proposals. Congressional initiation is the only method of proposal that has been used to date.

A proposal is then ratified either by the legislatures of three-fourths of the states or by conventions in three-fourths of the states. Congress designates the ratification method. Thomas Jefferson believed that this process realized the dream of providing for bloodless change by the people. He said,

[h]appily for us, that when we find our constitutions defective and insufficient to secure the happiness of our people, we can assemble with all the coolness of philosophers, and set them to rights, while every other nation on earth must have recourse to arms to amend or to restore their constitutions.[22]

Although the states were given only two alternatives in regard to the Constitution (adoption or rejection), many states attached lists of proposed amendments to their adoption resolutions anyway. A few states, such as Virginia and New York, called for a bill of rights. Eight states called for an amendment protecting the sovereignty of the states. To satisfy these concerns, it was agreed that a bill would be added immediately after the original Constitution was ratified. James Madison initially suggested a single general statement affirming that the source of all governmental power is derived from the people. This was rejected and he eventually composed a bill of seventeen amendments. After House of Representatives and Senate revisions, twelve rights remained. Ten of the twelve were ratified on November 3, 1791. They have become known as the Bill of Rights. The Bill of Rights includes protections of individual rights and liberties and a provision intended to preserve the integrity of state sovereignty. The two provisions that were not ratified concerned the number of representatives in the lower house and compensation for members of Congress. See Chapter 9 for a more thorough discussion of this topic.

Today, there are a total of twenty-seven amendments. Ratification of the Twenty-Seventh Amendment, which provides that changes in the compensation of members of Congress shall not be implemented until there has been an intervening election of the House of Representatives, traveled an interesting road. It was one of the two amendments proposed by Madison that was not ratified as part of the original Bill of Rights. Ratification restarted in 1978. Ultimately, it was ratified in 1992, two hundred and one years after it was proposed.[23] The ratifying state, Michigan, did not exist at the time the amendment was proposed. The final proposal that was part of the original twelve concerns how seats in the House of Representatives are to be apportioned among the states. Like the amendment ratified in 1992, it does not have a sunset provision, so it is still active. However, only eleven states have ratified it. There are three other amendments pending before the states: an 1810 proposal that forbids U.S. citizens from holding titles of nobility from other nations, an 1861 proposal to forbid the federal Constitution from authorizing Congress to interfere with slavery and other matters in the states, and a 1926 proposal to delegate the authority to regulate child labor to Congress. Two other proposals, the Equal Rights Amendment and the District of Columbia Voting Rights Amendment, failed to be ratified in the states and are no longer active.

One amendment was enacted to repeal another. The Twenty-First Amendment repealed the Eighteenth Amendment's prohibition of alcohol. Several amendments were enacted to reverse Supreme Court interpretations of the Constitution, or at least had that effect. The Eleventh Amendment removed lawsuits from citizens of one state against another state from federal court jurisdiction, reversing *Chisolm v. Georgia,* 2 U.S. (2 Dall.) 419 (1793). This amendment was introduced, passed, and ratified by the states in a little more than a year.

The Thirteenth and Fourteenth Amendments, which forbid slavery and extended citizenship to African Americans, respectively, reverse the Supreme Court's infamous *Dred Scott v. Sanford,* 60 U.S. 393 (1857) decision that slaves of African descent were not citizens and, accordingly, not fully protected by the Constitution. The Sixteenth Amendment's delegation of taxing authority to Congress reversed *Pollock v. Farmers' Loan and Trust Co.,* 157 U.S. 429 (1895). The Twenty-Sixth Amendment, which set the voting age at 18, reversed *Oregon v. Mitchell,* 400 U.S. 112 (1970), which permitted the states to set their own voting ages for state elections; the Nineteenth Amendment's guarantee of the vote to women reversed *Minor v. Happersett,* 21 Wall. (88 U.S.) 162 (1875).

Although the number of amendments that have been passed by the House of Representatives and sent to the states is relatively small, the number of proposals to amend the Constitution that have been proposed in Congress is staggering. By 2004, the number of proposals introduced in Congress exceeded 11,000.[24] The proposed amendments span the spectrum in subject matter. You will learn more about the amendments, with an emphasis on the rights protected by them, in the second part of this book.

1.6 VALUES, POLITICS, AND CONSTITUTIONAL LAW

The remainder of this book examines how the Constitution has been applied and interpreted. Examining the decisions of the courts of the United States, particularly of the U.S. Supreme Court, is the most common method of learning this subject. Be aware, however, that the judiciary does not exist in a vacuum. Its coequal branches (president and Congress) interpret the Constitution, apply its principles, and, in certain ways, influence the judiciary's interaction with and interpretation of the Constitution.

For example, administrative agencies are largely responsible for the administration of government in this nation. They are the front line of government. To function, administrative agencies must interpret the law, often before any court has had an opportunity to address objections to that law. In some cases, a party may obtain pre-enforcement judicial review of a law, and in such instances the agency's role is diminished. When pre-enforcement review is not sought or is unavailable, the agency's role becomes more significant. In instances when a law is valid as written, but the agency's method of enforcement is questionable, the agency's role is again emphasized.

The perceived constitutionality of a bill may also affect legislative decision making. A bill that is seen as unconstitutional may not make it out of committee. Individual legislators may oppose proposed legislation that seems unconstitutional. This is not always the case, however. For political reasons, legislators may support a bill known to be unconstitutional. For example, the Supreme Court invalidated a Texas statute that protected the U.S. flag from desecration by a political protester in the 1989 case of *Texas v. Johnson.*[25] The Court reasoned that the protester's right to political expression under the First Amendment outweighed Texas's interest in protecting the integrity of the flag. One year later, the Congress enacted similar legislation, even though it clearly contradicted the Supreme Court's ruling in *Texas v. Johnson.* For that reason, the new law was quickly invalidated as well.

Also, Congress possesses considerable authority over the jurisdiction of the federal courts. Political concerns could, therefore, cause legislators to limit the jurisdiction of the judiciary over certain issues.

Many of the petitions filed with the Supreme Court are filed by the United States through the solicitor general of the United States. Such filings are examined with special care by the Court when it determines whether to hear the appeals. The executive branch therefore influences the Court by its partial control over the issues presented to the Court. Outside of the Supreme Court, the Justice Department and the many U.S. Attorneys file and defend cases that involve constitutional issues in the lower federal courts.

Although the Supreme Court is generally insulated from politics, it is likely that politics and public opinion play at least a minor role in influencing the Court's decision making. Because the Court has no method of enforcing its orders, it relies on the executive branch. This unenforceability, some contend, keeps the Court's decisions within the bounds of reason—that is, within a range the public will tolerate and the executive will enforce.

Politics also plays a role in the selection of Article III judges. Supreme Court justices and judges of federal district and appellate courts are selected by the political branches of government—the president nominates and the Senate must confirm. In recent years, the process has been criticized as being too political, focusing on the political and ideological beliefs of nominees rather than on other qualifications, such as education, employment experience, prior judicial experience, intellectual ability, and the like. The confirmation hearings of Robert Bork (nominated by President Reagan and rejected by the Senate) and Clarence Thomas (nominated by President Bush and confirmed by the Senate) are used to illustrate this point. Because lower courts are bound by precedent of higher courts, but the Supreme Court is the final word on the Constitution's meaning, Supreme Court justices are more likely to resolve policy and value-laden questions, with a national, binding consequence. For this reason, senators are more likely to investigate the values and philosophy of a Supreme Court justice nominee than those of a nominee to a lower court. Once appointed, an Article III judge maintains his or her position until one of three occurrences: retirement, death, or impeachment. The power to impeach a judge rests with Congress. Congress may impeach for high crimes and misdemeanors. This is, therefore, another limitation upon the judiciary by an external force. Congress has been true to the purpose of impeachment and has not used the power to achieve political objectives.

When possible, the authors recognize and refer to political or social influences, as well as to other actors, that influence constitutional law. However, it is the judiciary that is charged with interpreting the law, and since 1803 the Supreme Court of the United States has the final word on what the Constitution means. Judicial review, as it is known, goes to the heart of the U.S. version of rule of law; it is fundamental to U.S. constitutionalism.

1.7 JUDICIAL REVIEW

What is a court to do when faced with applying a statute (or other law or action) that is contrary to the Constitution? What is a court to do when it is hearing a criminal case and the government has used unfair techniques to obtain evidence or to prove its case? Must courts defer to the other branch's (or state's) determinations of the constitutionality of their actions? The Constitution is silent on these matters but the questions were answered by the adoption of judicial review by the Supreme Court.

The doctrine of judicial review provides that the judiciary may invalidate the actions of other governmental actors that are violative of the Constitution. The Constitution does not expressly grant this authority to the judiciary. The power extends from the judiciary's authority to interpret and declare the meaning of law. (See Figure 1-2 for a summary.)

1.7(a) Historical Basis

Recall that one of the functions performed by courts in the United States is protection of individual liberties. Through judicial review, the courts act to control the government and thus protect individual rights.

In the early years of the British monarchy, the Crown was sovereign and virtually unchecked. However, theories of **natural law** and **natural rights** eventually led the Crown to acknowledge that certain laws and rights were fundamental and superior

natural law
A term referring to the concept that there exists, independent of manmade law, a law laid down (depending upon one's beliefs) by God or by nature, which human society must observe in order to be happy and at peace.

natural right
A right existing under natural law, independent of manmade law.

JUDICAL REVIEW—A SUMMARY

Defined: The authority of the judiciary to review the acts of its coequal branches (and possibly its co-sovereign) for constitutionality. An unconstitutional act is declared void.

Structure: Diffused. With the exception of a few local courts, all courts in the United States, both federal and state, possess the power of judicial review.

Source (federally): Not expressly provided for in the Constitution. Implicit in the general grant of judicial power in Article III. *Marbury v. Madison* is the landmark case on judicial review.

Impact: Less than 1 percent of all federal statutes are invalidated by the Supreme Court.

FIGURE 1-2
Summary of judicial review

to the monarch's imperative. See Chapter 9 for further discussion of natural law. This occurred in 1215, when the feudal nobles of England coerced King John into signing the Magna Carta, a document that recognized particular natural rights. Though a landmark in law, the Magna Carta did not declare rights for all Englishmen and was hardly what contemporary Western cultures would consider a comprehensive declaration of human rights. Further, the Magna Carta fell into disuse, and the abuses it was intended to curb resurfaced.

However, natural law theories were later used by philosophers, such as John Locke and Charles Montesquieu, to advance theories of representative government, separation of powers, and use of the judiciary to protect individuals from governmental abuse. These philosophers advanced the theory that sovereignty rests not with the monarch but with the people. Natural law theories were the foundation of both the French Declaration of Rights and the French Revolution and their U.S. counterparts.

England, from which the United States as a nation derived its common law, does not have a written constitution, at least not in the sense that the United States has one. Nor is there an independent judiciary. Parliament is the highest body (except for the symbolic role the Crown continues to play) in the nation.

Generally, parliamentary law is supreme. Many British insist, however, that they have a constitution, that is, a body of fundamental law. What could be supreme to parliamentary law in a system in which Parliament is supreme?

English fundamental law is not found in one written document. Instead, there are a number of laws that, taken together, make up the British "constitution." First, certain common law principles and customs are so sacred that they are considered part of England's fundamental law. Second, several acts of Parliament are considered fundamental. For example, the Bill of Rights of 1689 established that the monarch must be Protestant, that the Crown could not raise an army without parliamentary approval, that Parliament was the supreme lawmaker, and that Protestant subjects possessed a right to petition the Crown and bear arms. It also prohibited excessive fines and cruel and unusual punishment. The Act of Settlement of 1701 is also considered part of England's fundamental law. Through this act, the proposition that the Crown ruled through Parliament was furthered. For example, it provides, in part, that the Crown must have the consent of Parliament to remove judges.

In spite of apparent parliamentary supremacy, the idea that Parliament is limited by a higher form of law (natural law) can be found as early as 1610. In *Dr. Bonham's Case*, Lord Coke wrote, "[w]hen an Act of Parliament is against common right and reason, or repugnant, or impossible to be performed, the common law will controul [sic] it, and adjudge such Act to be void."[26] Regardless of this famous statement by Lord Coke, which was made during a period when natural law theory was popular, judicial review did not take hold in England. In fact, Parliament immediately reenacted the law the Coke court challenged and Coke was removed from the bench, in part because of the *Bonham* decision.[27]

That judicial review has not developed in England can be attributed, in part, to Parliament's self-restraint. It has not attempted, in recent times, to abrogate any fundamental freedoms, such as the freedom of the press. If it did, the issue of parliamentary supremacy might be reconsidered. The framers of the U.S. Constitution were heavily influenced by natural law and natural rights theories. Natural law was the foundation of the Declaration of Independence and the American Revolution. The framers believed that certain matters were beyond the control of government and that certain rights were inalienable. Further, they believed in the role of the courts as guardians of freedom. It is not surprising, considering this history, that eight of the thirteen states had expressly adopted judicial review even before the Constitution was written. A number of statements by delegates during the Constitutional Convention indicate that they intended for the judiciary to possess the power. For example, the delegates considered establishing a council comprised of the president and a number of justices of the Supreme Court to review legislation for constitutionality. The proposal was opposed and rejected as unnecessary because it was thought that the judiciary possessed the power to nullify unconstitutional laws. Again, natural law was the foundation of this belief. James Madison stated at the convention, "a law violating a constitution established by the people . . . would be considered by judges as null and void." The proposal was thus rejected.

The same argument was made by delegates who opposed giving Congress the authority to veto laws that are contrary to the national constitution. It was argued that the interests of the national government would be adequately guarded by the national judiciary, which possesses the power to negate state laws that contravene the national constitution. Alexander Hamilton later wrote in the *Federalist Papers*, "where the will of the legislature declared in its statutes, stands in opposition to that of the people, declared in the constitution, the judges ought to be governed by the latter, rather than the former. They ought to regulate their decisions by the fundamental laws." Further, he stated that the power to declare unconstitutional legislative acts void belonged to the judiciary.[28] John Marshall stated, "[i]f they [Congress] were to make a law not warranted by any of the powers enumerated, it would be considered by the judges as an infringement of the Constitution which they are to guard. They would not consider such a law as coming under their jurisdiction. They would declare it void." Luther Martin, James Wilson, and others made similar statements.[29]

There is also evidence that judicial review was practiced in state courts before 1789. In *The American Doctrine of Judicial Supremacy,*[30] Haines traces the history of the doctrine back to state and colony courts. The idea that legislative enactments were to be limited by natural law, natural rights, or a written constitution is found in the state efforts to create constitutional tribunals. These groups were known as *councils of censors* and *councils of revision* and existed in Pennsylvania, New York, and Vermont. The Pennsylvania Constitution of 1776 provided that the Constitution was not to be violated and established a council, composed of persons chosen from each city and county, charged with overseeing the constitutionality of executive and legislative branch actions. In addition, this body was delegated the authority to pass public censures, to order impeachments, to recommend that unconstitutional laws be repealed, and to call constitutional conventions.

Vermont's council of censors was nearly identical in structure to Pennsylvania's. New York, in contrast, did not elect laymen to sit on its council. Rather, the governor, chancellor, and justices of the state Supreme Court sat together on a council of revision, which reviewed bills for constitutionality before they became law. The group possessed veto power, but its vetoes could be overridden by a two-thirds majority vote in the state legislature.

All three councils were eventually abolished. They are important to constitutional history, however, because they illustrate that the framers did not embrace the English concept of legislative supremacy.

There is additional, more direct, evidence of support for judicial review. In several cases that predate the Constitution, judicial review was either exercised or recognized. For example, *Holmes v. Walton,*[31] a 1780 decision from New Jersey, involved a statute that provided for a six-man jury. The defendant objected, claiming that a twelve-man jury was required by the state constitution. The court agreed and invalidated the statute. There are other examples.[32]

In summary, the concept of judicial review was not new when the Supreme Court first invoked it to nullify a law in 1803. However, there is also evidence that the framers did not intend for the judiciary to possess the power. After all, if the framers had intended it, why was it not explicitly provided for in the Constitution? Possibly, they did not specifically mention judicial review because they believed it to be inherent in the judicial power, which they granted wholly to the judiciary in Article III. In the end, the evidence is inconclusive about whether the framers intended for the courts to possess the authority of judicial review.

1.7(b) Congressional Action

The power of judicial review can be traced to decisions of the Supreme Court as far back as 1796.[33] However, the landmark case of *Marbury v. Madison* was where the Court first used judicial review to invalidate federal action.

An understanding of the political context, the facts that gave rise to the dispute, and the major players will enrich your understanding of *Marbury v. Madison*. Two political philosophies, each represented by a political party, are central to the story. The Federalists, founded by Alexander Hamilton and others, advanced the notion of a strong national government, the creation of a national bank, and good relations with England, among other policies. The Federalists were fiercely opposed by the Republicans (also known as Democrat-Republicans), led by Thomas Jefferson. James Madison was another prominent founder to fall into these ranks. The Republicans opposed having a strong federal government and deepening the nation's ties with England. Interestingly, both Hamilton and Jefferson served in important capacities in George Washington's administration, the former as Secretary of the Treasury and the latter as Secretary of State.

An independent with Federalist leanings, President George Washington attempted to keep the peace between Jefferson and Hamilton, but the growing divide between the men, and their political parties, reached a fevered pitch during the election of 1796.

The controlling constitutional provision of the time provided that the candidate with the largest number of electoral college votes for president assumed the presidency and the candidate with the second highest number of votes assumed the vice presidency.

COURT DECISIONS AND OPINIONS

Many of the decisions made by judges are written. Many of these are published. The higher the court is, the more likely it is that its decisions will be published.

The decisions of the Supreme Court are published in the United States Reports (abbreviated as U.S.), a federal government publication. In addition, West Publishing Company reports the Supreme Court's decisions in the Supreme Court Reporter (S. Ct.). Lawyers Cooperative Publishing Company also publishes these decisions in the Lawyers Edition, which is now in its second series (L. Ed. or L. Ed. 2d). These last two sources are parallel to the official U.S. reporter. Generally, cite only the official reporter when available. All cites indicate the court, volume, page, and year the decision was rendered. The volume precedes the court, and the page on which the case begins follows the court designation:

Roe v. Wade, 410 U.S. 113, 93 S. Ct. 705, 35 L. Ed. 2d 147 (1973)

This citation shows that the case *Roe v. Wade* can be located in volume 410 of the United States Reports at page 113. The decision was issued in 1973. This citation style is used for all reported court decisions.

United States Courts of Appeals decisions are reported in the Federal Reporter, now in the third series (F., F.2d, F.3d). Not only are the reporter volume and page part of the cite, but so is the specific court that issued the decision:

FSK Drug Corp. v. Perales, 960 F.2d 6 (2d Cir. 1992)

The parenthetical information indicates that the decision was rendered by the U.S. Court of Appeals for the Second Circuit.

District court decisions are published in the Federal Supplement (F. Supp.) and are cited as such: Wimberg v. University of Evansville, 761 F. Supp. 587 (S.D. Ind. 1989)

This decision was issued by the U.S. District Court for the Southern District of Indiana.

State court decisions are reported in a system of regional reporters. Some states have their own official reporters as well.

BRIEFING CASES

Appendix B provides a discussion of reading and briefing cases.

Alien and Sedition Acts
Four federal laws were enacted in 1798: Naturalization Act, Alien Friends Act, Alien Enemies Act, and Sedition Act. Enacted in anticipation of war with France, the laws required alien registration, empowered the president to deport all aliens from nations that were at war with the United States, empowered the president to deport any alien deemed dangerous, and made it a crime for any person to speak or write falsely, maliciously, or scandalously about the federal government or its high officers. Enacted during the Adams administration and supported by Federalists, including Alexander Hamilton, the acts were controversial and bitterly opposed by Republicans, including Thomas Jefferson and James Madison. The Naturalization Act was repealed and the other acts sunset early in the 1800s. Jefferson pardoned everyone convicted under the laws, most of whom were newspaper editors with Republican political views.

In a very close and acrimonious race in 1796, John Adams, who had served two terms as vice president under George Washington, closely defeated Thomas Jefferson for President. This left Jefferson, as the runner-up, vice president to Adams. This was a difficult situation that is difficult to imagine today. The **Alien and Sedition Acts** provide an excellent example. The Adams administration and the Federalist-controlled Congress enacted four laws in 1798 that are collectively known as the Alien and Sedition Acts. The laws were enacted in response to increased anxiety about a possible war with France. They required registration, and permitted increased tracking of aliens, empowered the president to deport aliens deemed dangerous, and most controversially, enabled the prosecution of any person who spoke or wrote maliciously, scandalously, or falsely about the federal government. The laws were used to persecute Republicans who opposed Federalists and Federalist policies. Jefferson, Adam's vice president, was so opposed to the laws that he, along with Madison, worked with the legislatures of Kentucky and Virginia to enact state laws invalidating the federal acts, under the theory that each state had the authority to invalidate unconstitutional federal legislation. Later, as president, Jefferson pardoned everyone who had been convicted under the Sedition Act. Having opponents serve together in these capacities proved to be so unworkable that in 1804 the Twelfth Amendment was adopted; it provides for separate votes for president and vice president, enabling electors to vote for a "ticket" with a president and vice president of the same party.

The John Adams presidency, which was accompanied by a Federalists-controlled Congress, was successful in enacting Federalist legislation, thereby establishing the foundation for a strong federal government. Ironically, even though Adams was successful in advancing many of Hamilton's ideas, Hamilton was a vocal opponent of Adams. Faced with opposition from Hamilton and other Federalists as well as from Republicans, he lost his 1800 re-election bid to Thomas Jefferson and Aaron Burr (they actually tied in the electoral college, and it took 36 votes in the House of Representatives before Jefferson prevailed). In addition to losing the presidency, the Federalists also lost their majority in Congress.

To extend the influence of the Federalist Party beyond Adams's administration, Congress and President Adams attempted to fill as many judicial appointments, which survive changes in administrations, with Federalists. Sixteen new circuit judge positions were created by Congress (previously, justices of the Supreme Court and district judges sat as circuit judges). The size of the Supreme Court was decreased by one, to prevent the new administration and Congress from replacing retiring Associate Justice William Cushing. Chief Justice Oliver Ellsworth retired early so that Adams could nominate his replacement. President Adams nominated his Secretary of State, John Marshall, to become the new (third) chief justice. The Senate quickly confirmed Marshall's nomination. Congress also created forty-two new justices of the peace for the District of Columbia.

The final days of the Adams administration were hurried and hectic. Adams's nominations for the justice of the peace positions were confirmed only one day before the new president was to be inaugurated. President Adams signed the commissions late into the night of his last day in office (the judges have become known as the midnight judges) and gave them to John Marshall, who was then still Secretary of State, for delivery. Marshall, however, was unable to deliver four of the justice of the peace commissions before the Jefferson administration assumed power. President Jefferson ordered his Acting Secretary of State, Levi Lincoln, and eventually, Secretary of State, James Madison, not to deliver the commissions. William Marbury was one of the four men who did not receive their commissions. Marbury filed suit against James Madison in the Supreme Court seeking in order (a writ of mandamus) compelling delivery of the commissions.

The suit was filed in 1801, but no decision was rendered until 1803 because the new administration effectively canceled the 1802 term. This was accomplished by first changing the two terms of the Court, beginning in 1802, from February and August to June and December. Then in April 1802, before the Court held its first session, Congress again changed the Court's term to every February. Therefore, the Court did not meet from December 1801 to February 1803. In addition, the new Republican Congress repealed the circuit judgeships created by the lame duck Federalist Congress.

Although highly controversial, both politically and constitutionally, these actions were never judicially reviewed. By the time the case was heard by the Supreme Court, John Marshall had assumed the position of chief justice. In fact, he authored the Court's opinion.

Cyber Constitution
To read the full text of *Marbury v. Madison*, go to http://caselaw.lp. findlaw.com/scripts/ getcase.pl? court=US& vol=5&invol=137

Marbury v. Madison
5 U.S. (1 Cranch) 137 (1803)

Chief Justice Marshall delivered the Court's decision. [Vote: 4–0–2. Cushing and Moore did not participate.]

In the order in which the court has viewed the subject, the following questions have been considered and decided.

1st. Has the applicant a right to the commission he demands?

2ndly. If he has a right, and that right has been violated, do the laws of his country afford him a remedy?

3rdly. If they do afford him a remedy, is it a mandamus issuing from this court?

The first object of inquiry is, 1st. Has the applicant a right to the commission he demands?

His right originates in an act of congress passed in February 1801, concerning the district of Columbia . . . [which provides] "that there shall be appointed . . . such number of discreet persons to be justices of the peace as the president of the United States shall, from time to time think expedient, to continue in office for five years."

It is therefore, decidedly the opinion of the court, that when a commission has been signed by the president [after confirmation by the Senate], the appointment is made, and that the commission is complete, when the seal of the United States has been affixed to it by the secretary of state. . . .

Mr. Marbury, then, since his commission was signed by the President and sealed by the secretary of state, was appointed: and as the law creating the office gave the officer a right to hold for five years independent of the executive, the appointment was not revocable, but vested in the officer legal rights, which are protected by the laws of this country.

To withhold his commission therefore, is an act deemed by the court not warranted by law, but violative of a vested legal right.

This brings us to the second inquiry; which 2ndly if he has a right, and that right has been violated, do the laws of his country afford him a remedy?

The very essence of civil liberty certainly consists in the right of every individual to claim the protection of the laws whenever he receives an injury. One of the first duties of government is to afford that protection.

[The Court found that the President and his immediate subordinates are entitled to immunity from the judicial process when performing certain discretionary functions, but not necessarily when performing ministerial functions.] . . . But where a specific duty is assigned by law and individual rights depend upon the performance of that duty, it seems, equally clear that the individual who considers himself injured has a right to resort to the laws of his country for a remedy.

It is then the opinion of the court. [t]hat, having this legal title to the office, he has a consequent right to the commission; a refusal to deliver which, is a plain violation of that right, for which the laws of his country afford him a remedy.

It remains to be inquired whether 3rdly. He is entitled to the remedy for which he applies. This depends on, 1st. The nature of the writ applied for, and, 2ndly. The power of this court.

1st. The nature of the writ. [The Court explained that at common law writs of mandamus could be used to compel government officers to take actions required by law.]

This, then, is a plain case for a mandamus, either to deliver the commission, or a copy of it from the record; and it only remains to be inquired.

Whether it [the writ of mandamus] can issue from this court.

The act to establish the judicial courts of the United States authorizes the supreme court "to issue writs of mandamus, in cases warranted by the principles and usages of law, to any courts appointed, or persons holding office, under the authority of the United States."

The secretary of state, being a person holding an office under the authority of the United States, is precisely within the letter of the description; and if this court is not authorized to issue writ of mandamus to such an officer, it must be because the law is unconstitutional, and therefore absolutely incapable of conferring the authority, and assigning the duties which its words purport to confer and assign.

The constitution vests the whole judicial power of the United States in one supreme court, and such inferior courts as congress shall, from time to time, ordain and establish. This power is expressly extended to all cases arising under the laws of the United States; and consequently, in some form, may be exercised over the present case; because the right claimed is given by a law of the United States.

In the distribution of this power it is declared that "the supreme court shall have original jurisdiction in all cases affecting ambassadors, other public ministers and consuls, and those in which a state shall be a party. In all other cases, the supreme, court shall have appellate jurisdiction."

It has been insisted, at the bar, that as the original grant of jurisdiction, to the supreme and inferior courts, is general, and the clause, assigning original jurisdiction to the supreme court, contains no negative or restrictive words; the power remains to the legislature, to assign original jurisdiction to that court in other cases than those specified in the article which has been recited; provided those cases belong to the judicial power of the United States.

If it had been intended to leave it in the discretion of the legislature to apportion the judicial power between the supreme and inferior courts according to the will of that body, it would certainly have been useless to have proceeded further than to have defined the judicial power, and the tribunals in which it should be vested. The subsequent part of the section is mere surplusage, is entirely without meaning, if such is to be the construction. If congress remains at liberty to give this court appellate jurisdiction, where the constitution has declared their jurisdiction shall be original; and original jurisdiction where the constitution has declared it shall be appellate, the distribution of jurisdiction, made in the constitution, is form without substance.

Affirmative words are often, in their operation, negative of other objects than those affirmed; and in this case, a negative or exclusive sense must be given to them or they have no operation at all.

It cannot be presumed that any clause in the constitution is intended to be without effect, and therefore such a construction is inadmissible, unless words require it.

When an instrument organizing fundamentally a judicial system, divides it into one supreme, and so many inferior courts as the legislature may ordain and establish; then enumerate its powers, and proceeds so far to distribute them, as to define the jurisdiction of the supreme court by declaring the cases in which it shall take the original jurisdiction, and that in others it shall take appellate jurisdiction; the plain import of the words seems to be, that in one class of cases its jurisdiction is original, and not appellate, in the other it is appellate, and not original. If any other construction would render the clause inoperative, that is an additional reason for rejecting such other construction, and for adhering to their obvious meaning.

To enable this court then to issue a mandamus, it must be shown to be an exercise of appellate jurisdiction, or to be necessary to enable the court to exercise appellate jurisdiction. . . .

It is an essential criterion of appellate jurisdiction, that it revises and corrects the proceedings in a cause already instituted, and does not create that cause. Although, therefore, a mandamus may be directed to courts, yet to issue such a writ to an officer for the delivery of a paper, is in effect the same as to sustain an original action for that paper, and therefore seems not to belong to appellate, but to original jurisdiction neither is it necessary in such a case as this, to enable the court to exercise its appellate jurisdiction.

The authority, therefore, given to the supreme court, by the act establishing the judicial courts of the United States, to issue writs of mandamus to public officers, appears not to be warranted by the constitution; and it becomes necessary to inquire whether a jurisdiction, so conferred, can be exercised.

The question, whether an act, repugnant to the constitution, can become the law of the land, is a question deeply interesting to the United States, but, happily, not of an intricacy proportioned to its interest. It seems only necessary to recognize certain principles, supposed to have been long and well established, to decide it.

That the people have an original right to establish, for their future government, such principles as, in their operation, shall most conduce to their own happiness, is the basis, on which the whole American fabric has been erected. The exercise of this original right is a very great exertion, nor can it, nor ought it to be frequently repeated. The principles, therefore, so established, are deemed fundamental. And as the authority, from which they proceed, is supreme, and can seldom act, they are designed to be permanent.

This original and supreme will organizes the government, and assigns, to different departments, their respective powers. It may either stop here, or establish certain limits not to be transcended by those departments.

The government of the United States is of the latter description. The powers of the legislature are defined, and limited, and that those limits may not be mistaken, or forgotten, the constitution is written. To what purpose are powers limited, and to what purpose is that limitation committed to writing, if these limits may, at any time, be passed by those intended to be restrained? The distinction, between a government with limited and unlimited powers, is abolished, if those limits do not confine the persons on whom they are imposed, and if acts prohibited and acts allowed, are of equal obligation. It is a proposition too plain to be contested, that the constitution controls any legislative act repugnant to it; or, that the legislature may alter the constitution by an ordinary act.

Between these alternatives there is no middle ground. The constitution is either a superior, paramount law, unchangeable by ordinary means, or it is on a level with ordinary legislative acts, and like other acts, is alterable when the legislature shall please to alter it.

If the former part of the alternative be true, then a legislative act contrary to the constitution is not law; if the latter part be true, then written constitutions are absurd attempts, on the part of the people, to limit a power, in its own nature illimitable.

Certainly all those who have framed written constitutions contemplate them as forming the fundamental and paramount law of the nation, and consequently the theory of every such government must be, that an act of the legislature, repugnant to the constitution, is void.

This theory is essentially attached to a written constitution, and is consequently to be considered, by this court, as one of the fundamental principles of our society. It is not therefore to be lost sight of in the further consideration of this subject.

If an act of the legislature, repugnant to the constitution, is void, does it, notwithstanding its invalidity, bind the courts, and oblige them to give it effect? Or, in other words, though it be not law, does it constitute a rule as operative as if it was a law? This would be to overthrow in fact what was established in theory; and would seem, at first view, an absurdity too gross to be insisted on. It shall, however, receive more attentive consideration.

It is emphatically the province and duty of the judicial department to say what the law is. Those who apply the rule to particular cases, must of necessity expound and interpret that rule. If two laws conflict with each other, the courts must decide on the operation of each.

So if a law be in opposition to the constitution; if both the law and the constitution apply to a particular case, so that the court must either decide that case conformably to the law, disregarding the constitution; or conformably to the constitution, disregarding the law; the court must determine which of these conflicting rules governs the case. This is of the very essence of judicial duty.

If then the courts are to regard the constitution; and the constitution is superior to any ordinary act of the legislature, the constitution, and not such ordinary act, must govern the case to which they both apply.

Those then who controvert the principle that the constitution is to be considered, in court, as a paramount law, are reduced to the necessity of maintaining that courts must lose their eyes on the constitution, and see only the law.

This doctrine would subvert the very foundation of all written constitutions. It would declare that an act, which, according to the principles and theory of our government, is entirely void; is yet, in practice, completely obligatory. It would declare, that if the legislature shall do what is expressly forbidden, such act, notwithstanding the express prohibition, is in reality effectual. It would be giving to the legislature a practical and real omnipotence, with the same breath which professes to restrict their powers within narrow limits. It is prescribing limits, and declaring that those limits may be passed at pleasure.

That it thus reduces to nothing what we have deemed the greatest improvement on political institutions—a written constitution—would itself be sufficient, in America, where written constitutions have been viewed with so much reverence, for rejecting the construction. But the peculiar expressions of the constitution of the United States furnish additional arguments in favour of its rejection.

The judicial power of the United States is extended to all cases arising under the constitution.

Could it be the intention of those who gave this power, to say that, in using it, the constitution should not be looked into? That a case arising under the constitution should be decided without examining the instrument under which it arises?

This is too extravagant to be maintained.

In some cases then, the constitution must be looked into by the judges. And when they open it at all, what part of it are they forbidden to read, or to obey?

There are many other parts of the constitution which serve to illustrate this subject.

It is declared [in the constitution] that "no tax or duty shall be laid on articles exported from any state." Suppose a duty on the export of cotton, of tobacco, or of flour; and suit instituted to recover it. Ought judgment to be rendered in such a case? Ought the judges to close their eyes on the constitution, and only see the law?

The constitution declares that "no bill of attainder or ex post facto law shall be passed."

If, however, such a bill should be passed and a person should be prosecuted under it; must the court condemn to death those victims whom the constitution endeavors to preserve?

"No person," says the constitution, "shall be convicted of treason unless on the testimony of two witnesses to the same overt act, or on confession in open court."

Here the language of the constitution is addressed especially to the courts. It prescribes, directly for them, a rule of evidence not to be departed from. If the legislature should change that rule, and declare one witness, or a confession out of court, sufficient for conviction, must the constitutional principle yield to the legislative act?

From these, and many other selections which might be made, it is apparent, that the framers of the constitution contemplated that instrument, as a rule for the government of the *courts,* as well as of the legislature.

Why otherwise does it direct judges to take an oath to support it? This oath certainly applies, in an especial manner, to their conduct in their official character. How immoral to impose it on them, if they were to be used as the instruments, and the knowing instruments, for violating what they swear to support!

The oath of office, too, imposed by the legislature, is completely demonstrative of the legislative opinion on this subject. It is in these words, "I do solemnly swear that I will administer justice without respect to persons, and do equally right to the poor and to the rich; and that I will faithfully and impartially discharge all the duties incumbent on me as, according to the best of my abilities and understanding, agreeably to *the constitution*, and laws of the United States."

Why does a judge swear to discharge his duties agreeable to the constitution of the United States, if that constitution forms no rule for his government? If it is closed upon him, and cannot be inspected by him?

If such be the real state of things, this is worse than solemn mockery. To prescribe, or to take this oath, becomes equally a crime.

It is also not entirely unworthy of observation, that in declaring what shall be the *supreme* law of the United States generally, the *constitution* itself is first mentioned; and not the laws of the United States generally, but those only which shall be made in *pursuance* of the constitution, have that rank.

Thus, the particular phraseology of the constitution of the United States confirms and strengthens the principles, supposed to be essential to all written constitutions, that a law repugnant to the constitution is void; and that *courts,* as well as other departments, are bound by that instrument.

The rule must be discharged.

Cyber Constitution
Marbury v. Madison The full case can be read at http://supreme.justia.com/us/5/137/case.html

The facts of *Marbury v. Madison* have all the intrigue and politics of a suspense novel. Some of the country's most prominent citizens were involved, some in ways that would not be permitted today. For example, using contemporary ethics standards, Chief Justice Marshall would have been expected to recuse himself from deciding the case because of his involvement in the dispute. In fact, he had already been appointed to the Supreme Court but was still acting as Secretary of State when he began delivering the midnight judges commissions.

Chief Justice Marshall carefully constructed this opinion. He did not want a confrontation with President Jefferson, for fear that the judiciary as an institution would be harmed. At the same time, Marshall wanted both to establish the Court's authority and to announce that President Jefferson's actions were unlawful. He accomplished this by ruling against Marbury, due to a lack of jurisdiction, and thereby avoiding a direct confrontation with the executive. But he simultaneously declared that the judiciary can check the actions of the other branches for constitutionality and that President Jefferson had acted improperly. How exactly did he reach these conclusions?

First, he found that Marbury had been properly appointed and that President Jefferson (through his Secretary of State James Madison) had wrongly withheld his commission. To avoid a potentially harmful confrontation with the executive, however, the Court did not order Jefferson to deliver the commission. Rather, the Court concluded that it could not issue the writ of mandamus because it lacked jurisdiction over the case. Congress had included a provision in the Judiciary Act of 1789 that provided the Supreme Court with original jurisdiction to issue writs of mandamus against public officials. Marshall found that the Constitution's statement of original jurisdiction was exclusive, could not be extended by Congress, and did not provide for original jurisdiction in mandamus cases. Therefore, that provision of the Judiciary Act was unconstitutional.

Marshall then had to address the issue of whether the Court had the authority to invalidate (by not enforcing) a coequal branch's actions. For a number of reasons, he concluded that the judiciary possesses such authority. Marshall posed the problem: what is the judiciary to do when faced with applying a statute that is repugnant to the Constitution? Because the Constitution is the higher form of law, it must be followed and not the statute. This does not address the central issue, however—that is, why is the Supreme Court the final word on the meaning of the Constitution? Why should it not defer to the legislature's interpretation? Marshall concluded that it is the responsibility of the judiciary to declare the meaning of the law. In his words, "[i]t is emphatically the province and duty of the judicial department to say what the law is." If two laws conflict, it is a court that must decide which governs a case. "This is of the very essence of judicial duty," said Marshall. Because the Constitution is the highest form of law in the land, a court must choose to apply it over any other law.

In support of his conclusions, Marshall pointed to several provisions of the Constitution. Recall that there is no express delegation of judicial review in the Constitution. First, Article III, Section 2, provides that the "judicial Power shall extend to all Cases . . . arising under this Constitution." Implicit in this assertion is the belief that the judicial power includes being the final arbiter of the meaning of the Constitution. After all, could not the judicial power extend to all cases arising under the Constitution even though the judiciary defers to the legislature's interpretations of the Constitution?

Second, Marshall pointed to particular provisions in the Constitution to establish that the framers intended for the courts to independently determine the meaning of the Constitution, regardless of legislation. For example, the treason provision requires the testimony of two witnesses to the same overt act, or a confession, before a person may be convicted of treason. Marshall reasoned that the framers would not want a court to enforce a law that allowed conviction for treason upon the testimony of one person. Therefore, Marshall concluded that the framers intended the Constitution to bind the judiciary, as well as the other branches. This being so, courts must independently interpret, comply with, and enforce the Constitution.

One other constitutional provision was relied upon by Marshall. The Supremacy Clause of the Constitution declares that the laws of the national government are the supreme laws of the United States. Marshall noted that, in declaring what laws are supreme, the framers mentioned the Constitution first. He deduced from this that the Constitution is paramount to statutes and other law.

Finally, Marshall noted that judges are required to take an oath of office. Through that oath, judges swear to uphold the laws of the nation, including the Constitution. In order to uphold the Constitution, he asserted, it must be interpreted and treated as paramount law.

For these reasons, Marshall concluded that Congress had improperly conferred original jurisdiction upon the Court and that the Court therefore lacked the authority to issue the mandamus. For the first time, judicial review was used to nullify federal action—particularly, an act of Congress. In addition to concluding that the judiciary can review congressional actions, Marshall also stated that executive actions can be reviewed. This statement was **dictum,** however, because the Court had determined that it lacked jurisdiction to issue the mandamus. Regardless, the power has since extended over the executive branch as well.

1.7(c) Executive Action

The Burger Court reiterated in the *Nixon* tapes case what the Marshall Court stated in *Marbury v. Madison* 171 years earlier: it is the duty of the judiciary to say what the law is. This does not mean that the executive and legislative branches should not make their own interpretations; it simply means that the judiciary is the final word on the subject. Consider the sensitivity of issuing an order to a coequal branch. Consider further the enforcement aspect of such an order. The Court has no method of enforcing its orders— it is the duty of the executive to enforce court orders. As such, it is uncomfortable to courts to order the executive branch to do something the executive opposes.

dictum (obiter dictum) Expressions or comments in a court opinion that are not necessary to support the decision made by the court; they are not binding authority and have no value as precedent. If nothing else can be found on point, an advocate may wish to attempt to persuade by citing cases that contain dicta.

Cyber Constitution **Marbury v. Madison** **video** www.youtube.com/ watch?v=uLRO5iCWpps

---

United States v. Nixon
418 U.S. 683 (1974)

[On June 17, 1972, members of President Richard Nixon's committee for re-election were caught burglarizing the Democratic National Headquarters in the Watergate Hotel in Washington, DC.

Archibald Cox, the special prosecutor appointed to investigate the Watergate affair, asked President Nixon to produce documents and audiotapes recorded by Nixon of conversations in the Oval Office. President Nixon refused to provide the documents and recordings to the special prosecutor. Cox then sought and obtained court orders compelling Nixon to produce the requested documents and tapes.

Enraged, President Nixon ordered the Attorney General to fire the special prosecutor. The Attorney General resigned rather than comply. President Nixon then ordered the second highest official in the Department of Justice to discharge the special prosecutor. That official also resigned. Finally, Solicitor General Robert Bork acquiesced and fired the special prosecutor, in what became known as the "Saturday Night Massacre." A new special prosecutor,

Leon Jaworski, was appointed. He continued the Watergate investigation, eventually obtaining indictments against several White House officials. President Nixon was not indicted, but was named as a co-conspirator in the indictments. At this point, impeachment was being considered by Congress.

Both Congress and Jaworski insisted that President Nixon produce the previously requested tapes and documents. Special Prosecutor Jaworski sought and obtained a subpoena compelling complete production by President Nixon. President Nixon responded by producing the documents and edited versions of the audiotapes, one of which included an eighteen-minute period that appeared to have been erased. Additionally, on May 1, 1974, President Nixon moved to quash the subpoena, claiming executive privilege. The district court denied the motion. Because of the significance and sensitivity of the case, the Supreme Court granted certiorari before the court of appeals heard the appeal.]

Chief Justice Burger delivered the opinion of the Court. [Vote: 8–0–1. Justice Rehnquist did not participate.]

[W]e turn to the claim that the subpoena should be quashed because it demands "confidential conversations between a President and his close advisors that it would be inconsistent with the public interest to produce." The first contention is a broad claim that the separation of powers doctrine precludes judicial review of a President's claim of privilege. The second contention is that if he does not prevail on the claim of absolute privilege, the court should hold as a matter of constitutional law that the privilege prevails over the subpoena *duces tecum*.

In the performance of assigned constitutional duties each branch of the Government must initially interpret the Constitution, and the interpretation of its powers by any branch is due great respect from the others. The President's counsel, as we have noted, reads the Constitution as providing an absolute privilege of confidentiality for all Presidential communications. Many decisions of this Court, however, have unequivocally reaffirmed the holding of *Marbury v. Madison* (1803) that "it is emphatically the province and duty of the judicial department to say what the law is."

No holding of the Court had defined the scope of judicial power specifically relating to the enforcement of a subpoena for confidential Presidential communications for use in a criminal prosecution, but other exercises of power by the Executive Branch and the Legislative Branch have been found invalid as in conflict with the Constitution.

Notwithstanding the deference each branch must accord the others, the "judicial power of the United States" vested in the federal courts by Art. III, Sec. 1, of the Constitution can no more be shared with the Executive Branch than the Chief Executive, for example, can share with the judiciary the power to override a Presidential veto. Any other conclusion would be contrary to the basic concept of separation of powers and the checks and balances that flow from the scheme of a tripartite government. We therefore reaffirm that it is the province and duty of this Court "to say what the law is" with respect to the claim of privilege presented in this case.

In support of his claim of absolute privilege, the President's counsel urges two grounds, one of which is common to all governments and one of which is peculiar to our system of separation of powers. The first ground is the valid need for protection of communications between high Government officials and those who advise and assist them in the performance of their manifold duties; the importance of this confidentiality is too plain to require further discussion. Human experience teaches that those who expect public dissemination of their remarks may well temper candor with a concern for appearances and for their own interests to the detriment of the decisionmaking process. Whatever the nature of the privilege of confidentiality of Presidential communications in the exercise of Art. II powers, the privilege can be said to derive from the supremacy of each branch within its own assigned area of constitutional duties. Certain powers and privileges flow from the nature of enumerated powers; the protection of the confidentiality of Presidential communications has similar constitutional underpinnings.

The second ground asserted by the President's counsel in support of the claim of absolute privilege rests on the doctrine of separation of powers. Here it is argued that the independence of the Executive Branch within its own sphere insulates the President from a judicial subpoena in an ongoing criminal prosecution, and thereby protects confidential Presidential communications.

However, neither the doctrine of separation of powers, nor the need for confidentiality of high-level communication, without more, can sustain an absolute, unqualified Presidential privilege of immunity from judicial process under all circumstances. The President's need for complete candor and objectivity from advisers calls for great deference from the courts. However, when the privilege depends solely on the broad, undifferentiated claim of public interest in the confidentiality of such conversations, a confrontation with other values arise. Absent a claim of need to protect military, diplomatic, or sensitive national security secrets, we find it difficult to accept the argument that even the very important interest in confidentiality of Presidential communications is significantly diminished by production of such material for *in camera* inspection with all the protection that a district court will be obliged to provide.

The impediment that an absolute, unqualified privilege would place in the way of the primary constitutional duty of the Judicial Branch to do justice in criminal prosecutions would plainly conflict with the function of the courts under Art. II. In designing the structure of our Government and dividing and allocating the sovereign power among three co-equal branches, the Framers of the

Constitution sought to provide a comprehensive system, but the separate powers were not intended to operate with absolute independence.

. . . To read the Art. II powers of the President as providing an absolute privilege as against a subpoena essential to enforcement of criminal statutes on no more than a generalized claim of the public interest in confidentiality of nonmilitary and nondiplomatic discussions would upset the constitutional balance of "a workable government" and gravely impair the role of the courts under Art. III.

Since we conclude that the legitimate needs of the judicial process may outweigh Presidential privilege, it is necessary to resolve those competing interests in a manner that preserves the essential functions of each branch. The right and indeed the duty to resolve that question does not free the judiciary from according high respect to the representations made on behalf of the President.

The expectation of a President to the confidentiality of his conversations and correspondence, like the claim of confidentiality of judicial deliberations, for example, has all the values to which we accord deference for the privacy of all citizens and, added to those values, is the necessity for protection of the public interest in candid, objective, and even blunt or harsh opinions in Presidential decision making. A President and those who assist him must be free to explore alternatives in the process of shaping policies and making decisions and to do so in a way many would be unwilling to express except privately. These are the considerations justifying a presumptive privilege for Presidential communications. The privilege is fundamental to the operation of Government and inextricably rooted in the separation of powers. . . .

But this presumptive privilege must be considered in light of our historic commitment to the rule of law. This is nowhere more profoundly manifest than in our view that "the twofold aim [of criminal justice] is that guilt shall not escape or innocence suffer." We have elected to employ an adversary system of criminal justice in which the parties contest all issues before a court of law. The need to develop all relevant facts in the adversary system is both fundamental and comprehensive. The ends of criminal justice would be defeated if judgments were to be founded on a partial or speculative presentation of the facts. The very integrity of the judicial system and public confidence in the system depend on full disclosure of the facts, within the framework of the rule of evidence. To ensure that justice is done, it is imperative to the function of courts that compulsory process be available for the production of evidence needed either by the prosecution or by the defense.

In this case the President challenges a subpoena served on him as a third party requiring the production of materials for use in a criminal prosecution; he does so on the claim that he has a privilege against disclosure of confidential communications. He does not place his claim of privilege on the ground they are military or diplomatic secrets. As to these areas of Art. II duties the courts have traditionally shown the utmost deference to Presidential responsibilities. . . .

No case of the Court, however, has extended this high degree of deference to a President's generalized interest in confidentiality. Nowhere in the Constitution, as we have noted earlier is there any explicit reference to a privilege of confidentiality, yet to the extent this interest relates to the effective discharge of a President's powers, it is constitutionally based.

The right to the production of all evidence at a criminal trial similarly has constitutional dimensions. The Sixth Amendment explicitly confers upon every defendant in a criminal trial the right "to be confronted with the witnesses against him" and "to have compulsory process for obtaining witnesses in his favor." Moreover, the Fifth Amendment also guarantees that no person shall be deprived of liberty without due process of law. It is the manifest duty of the courts to vindicate those guarantees, and to accomplish that it is essential that all relevant and admissible evidence be produced.

In this case we must weigh the importance of the general privilege of confidentiality of Presidential communications in performance of the President's responsibilities against the inroads of such a privilege on the fair administration of criminal justice. The interest in preserving confidentiality is weighty indeed and entitled to great respect. However, we cannot conclude that advisers will be moved to temper the candor of their remarks by the infrequent occasions of disclosure because of the possibility that such conversations will be called for in the context of a criminal prosecution.

On the other hand, the allowance of the privilege to withhold evidence that is demonstrably relevant in a criminal trial would cut deeply into the guarantee of due process of law and gravely impair the basic function of the courts. . . .

We conclude that when the ground for asserting privilege as to subpoenaed materials sought for use in a criminal trial is based only on the generalized interest in confidentiality, if cannot prevail over the fundamental demands of due process of law in the fair administration of criminal justice. The generalized assertion of privilege must yield to the demonstrated, specific need for evidence in a pending criminal trial.

We have no doubt that the District Judge will at all times accord to Presidential records that high degree of deference suggested in *United States v. Burr,* and will discharge his responsibility to see to it that until released to the Special Prosecutor no in camera material is revealed to anyone. This burden applies with even greater force to excised material; once the decision is made to excise, the material is restored to its privileged status and should be returned under seal to its lawful custodian. Since this matter came before the Court during the pendency of a criminal prosecution, and on representations that time is of the essence, the mandate shall issue forthwith.

Cyber Constitution
Listen to the Nixon tapes
at http://nixontapes.org/

President Nixon complied with the order, thereby averting a constitutional crisis. Even though he supplied all the tapes, the eighteen-minute erasure remains a mystery. Impeachment looming, President Nixon resigned on August 9, 1974, thus becoming the only president ever to resign. Additional litigation later resulted from the Watergate affair. Some of the other prominent cases are discussed further in Chapter 6, which discusses the role, authority, and responsibilities of the president.

Although judicial review is established law, most recent presidents have asserted their authority to interpret the Constitution, independent of the judiciary. Under a theory known as Departmental Review or Coordinate Review, all three branches have the authority to be the final interpreter of the Constitution. Under this theory, conflicts in interpretation between the branches would be resolved through established political processes, such as elections, impeachment, and amendment of the Constitution. Although this theory is as old as the Constitution, nearly all presidents in the past twenty-five years, Republican and Democrat, have asserted the theory, often cast as the theory of Unitary Executive Power, in varying degrees. It has manifested itself in different forms, in different contexts. For example, presidents have questioned judicial decisions that limited executive authority, and in other cases, presidents have questioned the legitimacy of congressionally created "independent administrative agencies" where presidential authority to oversee their operations is limited.

1.7(d) State Action

As previously discussed, the federal judiciary exercises constitutional review over the actions of its two coequal branches. Does it possess the same power over the states?

The Supreme Court answered this question for the first time in 1810, when it declared a Georgia statute unconstitutional.[34] Six years later, the Supreme Court issued *Martin v. Hunter's Lessee,* wherein it asserted the power of judicial review over the decisions of the states' high courts.

Martin v. Hunter's Lessee
14 U.S. (1 Wheat.) 304 (1816)

Justice Story delivered the opinion of the Court. [Vote 6–0–1. Chief Justice Marshall did not participate.]

[Denny Martin, a citizen and resident of England, inherited a 300,000-acre tract of Virginia land in 1781 from his uncle, Lord Fairfax, who had been living in the United States. However, a Virginia statute forbade "enemies" of the United States from inheriting property. Therefore, Virginia took possession of the property and began selling it. The state sold some of the land to Hunter. Simultaneously, Martin began selling the property. One tract of the land was sold to Chief Justice John Marshall and his brother. For this reason, Marshall did not participate in this case.

Martin contested the state's assertion that he had no interest in the land. Martin prevailed at the trial level; however, that decision was reversed by the Court of Appeals of Virginia, the court of last resort in Virginia. The decision of the Virginia appellate court was appealed to, and reversed by, the Supreme Court of the United States. The Supreme court held that the Virginia statute was unconstitutional because it conflicted with the Treaty of Paris. The Virginia Court of Appeals was ordered to enforce the decision by recognizing Martin's interests.]

The Virginia Court of Appeals refused to comply with the order. Further, it concluded that the provision of the Judiciary Act of 1789 that endowed the Supreme Court with appellate jurisdiction in the case was unconstitutional and, hence, void. The Virginia Court of Appeals was asserting, in essence, that it was not subordinate to the Supreme Court and that it had the authority to independently interpret the Constitution of the United States. Martin again appealed to the Supreme Court for relief.]

The questions involved in the judgment are of great importance and delicacy. Perhaps it is not too much to affirm, that, upon their right decision, rest some of the most solid principles which have hitherto been supposed to sustain and protect the constitution itself. The great respectability, too, of the court whose decisions we are called upon to review, and the entire deference which we entertain for the learning and ability of that court, add much to the difficulty of the task which has so unwelcomely fallen upon us. It is, however, a source of consolation, that we have had the assistance of the most able and learned arguments to aid our inquires; and that the opinion which is now to be pronounced has been weighed with every solicitude to come to a correct result, and matured after solemn deliberation.

Before proceeding to the principal questions, it may not be unfit to dispose of some preliminary considerations which have grown out of the arguments at the bar.

The constitution of the United States was ordained and established, not by the states in their sovereign capacities, but emphatically, as the preamble of the constitution declares, by "the people of the United States." There can be no doubt that it was competent to the people to invest the general government with all the powers which they might deem proper and necessary; to extend or restrain the powers according to their own good pleasure, and to give them a paramount and supreme authority. As little doubt can there be, that the people had a right to prohibit to the states the exercise of any powers which were, in their judgment, incompatible with the objects of the general compact; to make the powers of state governments, in given cases, subordinate to those of the nation, or to reserve to themselves those sovereign authorities which they might not choose to delegate to either. The constitution was not, therefore necessarily carved out of existing state institutions, for the powers of the states depend upon their own constitutions; and the people of every state had the right to modify and restrain them, according to their own views of policy or principle. On the other hand, it is perfectly clear that the sovereign powers vested in the state governments, by the respective constitutions, remained unaltered and unimpaired, except so far as they were granted to the government of the United States.

These deductions do not rest upon general reasoning, plain and obvious as they seem to be. They have been positively recognized by one of the articles in amendment of the constitution, which declares, that "the powers not delegated to the United States by the constitution, nor prohibited by it to the states, are reserved to the *states* · respectively, or *to the people*."

The government, then, of the United States, can claim no powers which are not granted to it by the constitution, and the powers actually granted, must be such as are expressly given, or given by necessary implication. On the other hand, this instrument, like every other grant, is to have reasonable construction, according to the import of its terms; and where a power is expressly given in general terms, it is not to be restrained to particular cases, unless that construction grow out of the context expressly, or by necessary implication. The words are to be taken in their natural and obvious sense, and not in a sense unreasonably restricted or enlarged.

The constitution unavoidably deals in general language. It did not suit the purposes of the people, in framing this great charter of our liberties, to provide for minute specifications of its powers, or to declare the means by which those powers should be carried into execution. It was foreseen that this would be a perilous and difficult, if not an impracticable, task. The instrument was not intended to provide merely for the exigencies of a few years, but was to endure through a long lapse of ages, the events of which were locked up in the inscrutable purposes of Providence. It could not be foreseen what new changes and modifications of power might be indispensable to effectuate the general objects of the charter; and restrictions and specifications, which at the present, might seem salutary, might, in the end, prove the overthrow of the system itself. Hence its powers are expressed in general terms, leaving to the legislature, from time to time, to adopt its own means to effectuate legitimate objects, and to mould and model the exercise of its powers, as its own wisdom, and the public interests, should require.

With these principles in view, principles in respect to which no difference of opinion ought to be indulged, let us now proceed to . . . consideration of the great question as to the nature and extent of the appellate jurisdiction of the United States. . . .

If the constitution meant to limit the appellate jurisdiction to cases pending in the courts of the United States, it would necessarily follow that the jurisdiction of these courts would, in all the cases enumerated in the constitution, be exclusive of state tribunals. How otherwise could the jurisdiction extend to *all* cases arising under the constitution, laws, and treaties of the United States, or to *all* cases of admiralty and maritime jurisdiction? If some of these cases might be entertained by state tribunals, and no appellate jurisdiction as to them should exist, then the appellate power would not extend to *all*, but to *some*, cases. If state tribunals might exercise concurrent jurisdiction over all or some of the other classes of cases in the constitution without control, then the appellate jurisdiction of the United States might, as to such cases, have no real existence, contrary to the manifest intent of the constitution. Under such circumstances, to give effect to the judicial power, it must be construed to be exclusive; and this not only when the *casus faederis* [federal cause of action] should arise directly, but when it should arise, incidentally, in cases pending in state courts. This construction would abridge the jurisdiction of such court far more than has been ever contemplated in any act of Congress.

On the other hand, if, as has been contended, a discretion be vested in congress to establish, or not to establish, inferior courts at their own pleasure, and congress should not establish such courts, the appellate jurisdiction of the supreme court would have nothing to act upon, unless it could act upon cases pending in state courts. . . .

It must, therefore, be conceded that the constitution not only contemplated, but meant to provide for cases within the scope of the judicial power of the United States, which might yet depend before state tribunals. It was foreseen that in the exercise of their ordinary jurisdiction, state courts would incidentally take cognizance of cases arising under the constitution, the laws, and treaties of the United States. Yet to all these cases the judicial power, by the very terms of the constitution, is to extend. . . .

It has been argued that such an appellate jurisdiction over state courts is inconsistent with the genius of our governments, and the spirit of the constitution. That the latter was never designed to act upon state sovereignties, but only upon the people, and that if the power exists, it will materially impair the sovereignty of the states, and the independence of their courts. We cannot yield to the force of this reasoning, it assumes principles which we cannot admit, and draws conclusions to which we do not yield our assent.

It is a mistake [to assert] that the constitution was not designed to operate upon states, in their corporate capacities. It is crowded with provisions which restrain or annul the sovereignty of the states in some of the highest branches of their prerogatives. The tenth section of the first articles contains a long list of disabilities and prohibitions imposed upon the states. Surely, when such essential portions of state sovereignty are taken away, or prohibited to be exercised, it cannot be correctly asserted that the constitution does not act upon the states. The language of the constitution is also imperative upon the states as to the [performance of many duties. It is imperative upon the state legislatures to make laws prescribing the time, places, and manner of holding elections for senators and representatives, and for electors of president and vice-president. And in these, as well as some other cases, congress have a right to revise, amend, or supersede the laws which may be passed by state legislatures. . . .

The courts of the United States can, without question, revise the proceedings of the executive and legislative authorities of the states, and if they are found to be contrary to the constitution, may declare them to be of no legal validity. Surely the exercise of the same right over judicial tribunals is not a higher or more dangerous act of sovereign power.

Nor can such a right be deemed to impair the independence of state judges . . . . In respect to the powers granted to the United States, they are not independent, they are expressly bound to obedience by the letter of the constitution; and if they should unintentionally transcend their authority, or misconstrue the constitution, there is no more reason for giving their judgments an absolute and irresistible force, than for giving it to the acts of the other co-ordinate departments of state sovereignty.

It is further argued, that no great public mischief can result from a construction which shall limit the appellate power of the United States to cases in their own courts; first, because state judges are bound by an oath to support the constitution of the United States, and must be presumed to be men of learning and integrity; and, secondly, because congress must have an unquestionable right to remove all cases within the scope of the judicial power from the state courts to the courts of the United States, at any time before final judgment, though not after final judgment. As to the first reason—admitting that the judges of the state courts are, and always will be, of as much learning, integrity, and wisdom, as those of the courts of the United States, (which we very cheerfully admit,) it does not aid the argument. It is manifest that the constitution has proceeded upon a theory of its own . . . . The constitution has presumed (whether rightly or wrongly we do not require) that state attachments, state prejudices, state jealousies, and state interests, might sometimes obstruct, or control, or be supposed to obstruct or control, the regular administration of justice. Hence, in controversies between states; between citizens of different states . . . it enables the parties, under the authority of congress, to have the controversies heard, tried, and determined before the national tribunals . . . In respect to other enumerated cases—the cases arising under the constitution, laws, and treaties of the United States . . . reasons of higher and more extensive nature, touching the safety, peace and sovereignty of the nation, might well justify a grant of exclusive jurisdiction.

This is not all. A motive of another kind, perfectly compatible with the most sincere respect for state tribunals, might induce the grant of appellate power over their decisions. That motive is the importance and even necessity of *uniformity* of decisions throughout the whole United States, upon all subjects within the purview of the constitution.

Judges of equal learning and integrity, in different states, might differently interpret a statute, or a treaty of the United States, or even the constitution itself: If there were no revising authority to control these jarring and discordant judgments, and harmonize them into uniformity, the laws the treaties, and the constitution of the United States would be different in different states, and might, perhaps, never have precisely the same construction, obligation, or efficacy, in any two states.

On the whole, the court are of the opinion, that the appellate power of the United States does extend to cases pending in state courts.

It is the opinion of the whole court, that the judgment of the court of appeals of Virginia, rendered on the mandate in this cause, be reversed, and the judgment of the district court, held at Winchester, be, and the same is hereby affirmed.

Today, the power of the federal courts to review state actions is well established. All federal courts, whether district, appellate, or the Supreme Court, possess the constitutional power of judicial review. Federal courts may review the actions of any governmental entity (local, state, or national) for compliance with the Constitution, provided the Court has jurisdiction and there is not some other limiting doctrine.

State courts also exercise judicial review as to both state and federal laws. Under the Supremacy Clause of Article VI, state courts must apply federal law, even if contrary to their own state's laws. This includes nullifying state laws that are violative of the U.S. Constitution. A state's attempt to limit the jurisdiction of its courts to hear federal cases violates the Supremacy Clause unless the rule is neutral and established as part of a larger administrative scheme. A state may not decide that a certain class of cases that are recognized by federal law cannot be heard by state courts. For example, frustrated by the large number of frivolous lawsuits filed by inmates, New York divested its trial courts of jurisdiction over the cases in favor of having all the cases heard by a court of claims. The change also eliminated attorney's fees awards, punitive damages, and injunctive relief. The new law applied to all inmate claims, state and federal. The Supreme Court found the law to be contrary to the Supremacy Clause in *Haywood v. Drown,* 129 S. Ct. 2108 (2009).

Because state judges must hear federal cases, they also have a responsibility of reviewing federal laws for constitutionality. Of course, the decision will have precedential effect only within each particular court's geographical jurisdiction. Through its appellate jurisdiction, the Supreme Court eventually will have an opportunity to review state court decisions interpreting the Constitution. In some instances, review by a lower federal court, or removal of cases involving federal law, is possible as well.

1.7(e) Shield or Sword?

Although the power of judicial review is well established today, the debate over whether the framers intended for the judiciary to have the exclusive power, or whether it ought to have that power, continues. Is judicial review a shield with which the judiciary protects the individual, minorities, and the integrity of our system, or is it a sword used by judges to maintain a judicial supremacy over the coordinate branches and the states?

The frequency of invocation of the judicial review power by the Supreme Court is informative. Since 1790, the Supreme Court has declared approximately 1,500 acts of local, state, and federal government unconstitutional.[35] This may appear significant, but it represents only a small fraction of a percentage of the total laws enacted. Congress enacted over 60,000 laws from 1790 to 1990, and the Supreme Court declared less than 1 percent unconstitutional.[36]

Former federal Judge Robert Bork, whose nomination to the Supreme Court by President Reagan was not confirmed, asserted that the Court is continually deferring less to the decisions of the states and its coordinate branches. For example, he points out that during the ninety-three-year period from 1803 to 1896, the Court declared 19 acts of Congress and 167 state laws unconstitutional. In the twenty-seven years from 1897 to 1924, the Court declared 28 acts of Congress and 212 state laws unconstitutional. Between 1940 and 1970, the Court held about the same number of acts of Congress unconstitutional, but the number of state laws invalidated increased to 278. According to Judge Bork,

> With each successive case, the Court shrinks the sphere of legislative decision making and expands the role of the judiciary: We observe . . . the increasing importance of the one counter-majoritarian institution in the American democracy. . . . What is worrisome is that so many of the Court's increased number of declarations of unconstitutionality are not even plausibly related to the actual Constitution. This means that we are increasingly governed not by law or elected representatives but by an unelected, unrepresentative, unaccountable committee of lawyers applying no will but their own.[37]

Later, Bork summarized his concerns by referring to contemporary judicial activism as "politics masquerading as law."[38] It is generally agreed by constitutional scholars that the Court is playing a larger role than it had in the past. But Judge Bork's other assertions—that the Court is doing this at the expense of legislative power, and therefore is undermining democracy and freedom, and that many of the Court's decisions are not well grounded in the Constitution—are the subject of considerable and ongoing debate.

The theory that there is a negative correlation between the authority of the Court and its coordinate branches and the states assumes that the power of government as a whole has not changed since 1789: that governmental power is a zero-sum game. However, it is possible that the authority of the Court has increased concomitantly with the increase in power of government. Today, government regulates the personal and commercial life of its citizens to a much greater degree than it did just 100 years ago. Therefore, possibly, the enlargement of the role of the Court has not meant a decrease in the power of legislatures. Judge Bork's assertion that the Court's decisions are not "plausibly related" to the Constitution is also easier understood when one knows his constitutional ideology: He is an originalist.

In any event, the total number of laws invalidated by the Court remains small. In instances in which the Court has nullified a law, it has generally been successful in protecting the individual from arbitrary and unreasonable governmental actions and in helping its coordinate branches, the states, and the federal government maintain the delicate balance of power conceived by the framers.

In addition, the Court has created a number of rules and doctrines governing its decision making that are intended to respect the integrity and independence of the other branches, as well as of the states. Some of these have been discussed, such as the presumption that legislation is constitutional and the rule requiring the Court to construe a statute as constitutional, if reasonable. Also, through the political question doctrine, the Court refuses to adjudicate cases that are inherently political in nature or involve disputes that are best resolved by the executive or legislative branches. Therefore, it appears that the Court can serve the "guardian and protector" function while not excessively interfering with the functions of its coordinate branches or of the states.

The judiciary plays its role in the system through its administration of justice. That is, federal courts do not make rules on their own initiative; rather, they make decisions of law within the context of adjudication of cases. Importantly, the authority of the federal courts to hear cases, which is referred to as *jurisdiction,* is limited. The jurisdiction of the federal courts is examined in Chapter 4.

1.7(f) A Diffused Model

Recall that all courts, state and federal, are called upon to interpret the Constitution. Through Article VI of the Constitution, state courts have an obligation to apply federal law even if contrary to their own state's laws. Section 2 of Article VI reads:

> This Constitution, and the Laws of the United States, which shall be made in Pursuance thereof; and all Treaties made, or which shall be made, under the Authority of the United States, shall be the supreme Law of the Land; and the Judges in every State shall be bound thereby, any Thing in the Constitution or Laws of any State to the Contrary notwithstanding.

Hence, the power of judicial review is diffused to all state and federal courts (except that certain limited jurisdiction courts, such as traffic courts, may not possess this authority). Every day, every judge stands as a barrier between potentially oppressive government conduct and the citizen.

Although a few nations have followed the model used in the United States,[39] this model of judicial review remains one of the most extreme in the world. Consider, for example, that there is no judicial review whatsoever in some nations; nations with a socialist legal system usually fall into this category. In others, judicial review is concentrated in one tribunal or court. For example, the Constitutional Council in France is the only body in that nation that may declare a law unconstitutional, and that body falls outside the judiciary. Germany also employs a concentrated model of judicial review. Unlike France, however, the power is held by a judicial entity, the *Bundesverfassungsgericht.*[40] The scope of review authority differs between nations as well. In some, constitutional tribunals are limited to reviewing proposed legislation. This is true of France's Constitutional Council. In others, standing is much more limited

---

JUDICIAL REVIEW—COMPARATIVE MODELS

Structure	*Nation/legal family*
Diffused review	• United States—power held by nearly all courts • Mexico—power held by federal courts
Concentrated review	• France—power held by Constitutional Council (nonjudicial tribunal composed of political leaders) • Germany—Bundesverfassungsgericht, a judicial tribunal
No review	• Socialist nations • Most Islamic nations

FIGURE 1-3
Comparison of judicial review models

than in the United States. Again, looking to France, standing to challenge legislation is limited to certain political leaders. The composition and term of appointment of constitutional judges also vary around the world. In many nations with constitutional tribunals, the judges are political appointees or retired political leaders. In many cases, the individuals serve fixed terms, very different than the lifetime appointment of U.S. federal judges.

A comparison of judicial review around the world evinces that the United States (and the nations with similar models) has the most diffused system in many ways. Not only may legislation be challenged, but so may executive and judicial action. Standing is also diffused. Any person who is affected by a law or government action may invoke the authority of judicial review. Even our structure—for example, lifetime tenure and review authority by all courts—has the effect of reinforcing judicial review. These points illustrate the significance of judicial independence and review in the United States (see Figure 1-3). Simply stated, judicial review is an important part of American legal culture.

Of course, a court's authority of judicial review is limited by stare decisis. If a higher court has already interpreted the Constitution in a particular manner, a lower court may not render a conflicting reinterpretation. Recall, however, that a court may distinguish a case under review from a prior binding case. To do so, the court must determine that the facts of the prior case are so dissimilar as to make it useless as precedent. Also, in certain rare instances, a lower court will interpret a case in a manner that is inconsistent with a precedential case. Finding that a precedential case is so old that its law is no longer viable is an example. Such decisions may, of course, be reviewed by higher courts.

As a practical matter, judges in lower courts are less likely to declare laws unconstitutional than are judges of higher courts. Similarly, state judges are less likely to declare acts of Congress or the president unconstitutional than are federal courts. Although federal trial courts and state courts both hear cases involving federal issues, various procedural and substantive laws increase the likelihood that a case of national significance will first be resolved by a federal court or, in rare circumstances, by the Supreme Court.

1.7(g) An International Model

Although nearly singular in its breadth and depth, the U.S. model of judicial review has been a model for the world, particularly in the past seventy years. According to William E. Nelson, several Latin American nations adopted some form of judicial review before 1920, and Austria, Germany, and Czechoslovakia were the first European nations to do so, each around 1920.[41]

But it was in the post–World War II years that judicial saw its greatest expansion. Japan, Germany, and Italy adopted it, in part because of the U.S. influence on the redevelopment of the political and legal systems of the Axis nations. Similarly, many of the Pacific Islands that had been freed from Japan following the war were united in the Trust Territory of the Pacific Islands. With the United States acting as trustee with the obligation of assisting the islands in working toward political, legal, and economic independence, it is no surprise that judicial review found its way into the legal fabric of those islands, often along with a recognition of their customary law. The Federated States of Micronesia (FSM) and the Commonwealth of the Northern Marianas Islands are examples. Judicial review has taken hold in islands outside of the FSM as well.

India adopted judicial review in 1947 following its independence from Great Britain. As you have already learned, constitutional councils have been instituted in many nations, particularly in Europe. Although functionally different and not as powerful as the diffused U.S. model, they nonetheless represent the idea of legislative inferiority to larger legal, and sometimes political, principles. Also, the European Union's tribunals exercise review of member states in some circumstances.[42] Other nations, including Ireland, Scotland, and Hong Kong, also empower their courts, in varying degrees, to review the acts of government officials for constitutionality. According to the United Nations Development Programme, judicial review is spreading in Arab nations, through both constitutional councils and courts. This includes Algeria, Egypt, Kuwait, Lebanon, Morocco, Sudan, Syria, Tunisia, United Arab Emirates, and Yemen.[43] Indeed, constitutionalism has been one of the United States's greatest exports. Nearly all nations of the world have adopted a written constitution, many using the U.S. Constitution as the model from which they constructed their own. As you have read, the idea of rule of law, as actualized through judicial or other forms of constitutional review, has taken hold around the world as well.

1.8 JUDICIAL ERAS

Just as judicial review is the hallmark of U.S. constitutionalism, the Supreme Court is constitutionalism's icon. At the top of the judicial hierarchy sits the Supreme Court of the United States. Accordingly, it is a major player in U.S. constitutionalism. Scholars have discovered that the Court's decisions often follow the ideologies of the justices. There have been several significant "eras" in the history of the Supreme Court. These eras are marked by particular ideologies that were dominant on the Court. These often, but not always, coincide with chief justice terms. The respective powers of the national and state governments are the primary point of reference for the periods discussed below. You will learn more the relationship of state and federal authorities, about lower courts, and the jurisdiction of all courts, later in this book.

1.8(a) Early Court: The Least Dangerous Branch

Even though the Constitution was intended to centralize governmental authority more than existed under the Articles of Confederation, state authority, especially judicial authority, was much greater in 1789 than it is now. As a result, the status of the Supreme Court was uncertain for many years. The early years of the Court were characterized by resignations for other positions that today would be less desirable. John Jay, one of the three authors of the *Federalist Papers* and the nation's first chief justice, assumed office in 1789 and resigned in 1795 to run for governor of New York. John Rutledge was also nominated by President Washington and confirmed in 1789, but he never appeared for duty. He resigned in 1791 and was later nominated to replace John Jay as chief justice. He began serving immediately but ultimately was not confirmed by the Senate. Oliver Ellsworth (1796–1800) followed John Rutledge as chief justice. There were few significant decisions rendered in the early years of the Court. One exception is *Chisholm v. Georgia*, 2 U.S. 419 (1793), which held that states may be liable in federal court. The decision was so unpopular that it led to the adoption of the Eleventh Amendment in 1795. The Court began to establish itself as an important legal institution during the tenure of Chief Justice John Marshall.

1.8(b) Marshall Court: Expanding Federal Authority

John Marshall was chief justice of the United States from 1801 to 1836. Nominated by President John Adams, he was a strong nationalist (Federalist). As you learned earlier, Marshall had been President Adams's secretary of state. Adams lost his re-election bid to an anti-Federalist, Thomas Jefferson. In an effort to continue to influence government, Adams, with the support of a lame-duck Federalist Congress, made a number of appointments of Federalists to vacant judicial positions. Marshall was one of these appointees.

The Marshall Court is known for establishing the supremacy of the national government over the state governments. A number of important decisions were handed down by the Marshall Court, including *Marbury v. Madison*, 5 U.S. (1 Cranch) 137 (1803); *McCulloch v. Maryland*, 17 U.S. (4 Wheat) 316 (1819); and *Martin v. Hunter's Lessee*, 14 U.S. (1 Wheat) 304 (1816). (These decisions are discussed in Chapter 3.) In *McCulloch*, Marshall addressed the power of Congress; this decision is discussed further in Chapter 4. *Hunter's Lessee* concerned the division of authority between the national government and state governments and is the subject of more thorough examination in Chapter 7. The theme of *Marbury v. Madison* was different. In that case, the power of **judicial review** was established. Judicial review is the authority of the judiciary, as the final interpreter of the law, to declare the acts of the other coordinate branches unconstitutional. *Marbury v. Madison* and judicial review are discussed fully in Chapter 3.

judicial review
The power of the judiciary, as the final interpreter of the law, to declare an act of a coordinate governmental branch of state unconstitutional. The power is not expressly stated in the Constitution, but the Supreme Court announced that the judiciary possesses this power in *Marbury v. Madison*, 5 U.S. (1 Cranch) 137 (1803).

1.8(c) Taney Court: States Rights

Roger Taney replaced John Marshall as chief justice of the United States in 1836. Between 1836 and 1843, four other justices were appointed: Philip Barbour, John Catron, John McKinley, and Peter Daniel. McKinley and Daniel filled two new seats, expanding the number of justices on the Court to nine. Eight other justices would join the Court during Taney's tenure as chief justice, which did not end until 1865.

During this era, the Court's philosophy changed from strongly nationalist to one favoring states' rights. The Taney Court was not activist; that is, it was not aggressive in reversing the decisions of the Marshall Court. The Court did favor states' rights, however, when new issues were raised concerning the balance of power between the national and state governments.

The Taney Court is best known for *Dred Scott v. Sandford*, 60 U.S. (19 How.) 393 (1856). In that decision, the Supreme Court held that slaves were property and possessed no rights or privileges under the Constitution. Further, for the second time in history, the first being *Marbury v. Madison*, the Court relied upon judicial review to invalidate a statute. In *Dred Scott*, the Court held a federal statute that conferred rights upon slaves unconstitutional. In short, the Court concluded that slavery was an issue of local, not national, concern.

1.8(d) Reconstruction Era: Federal Authority Expands

Salmon P. Chase became chief justice in 1865 and remained in that position until 1874. The Civil War had ended and the nation was rebuilding. The South had been defeated and slavery abolished. Most significant, the war proved that the states were not independent members of a league, but parts of a larger, more powerful nation. The nation's political identity changed as a result of the war. People began to identify more closely with their national citizenship and less with their state affiliations. The consequence was a strengthening of the national government and a concomitant weakening of the state governments.

During this period, the so-called reconstruction amendments were adopted. The Thirteenth Amendment, ratified in 1865, forbids slavery. The Fourteenth Amendment, ratified in 1868, has four sections, but the first is the most significant, as it provides that every state shall extend to all persons due process and equal protection of the law. The Fourteenth Amendment extends to Congress the power to enact legislation to enforce its mandates. Congress did that through the Civil Rights Acts, found at 42 U.S.C. §1981, 1982, and 1983. The Fifteenth Amendment, ratified in 1870, assures the franchise to persons of all color and race.

The Thirteenth and Fourteenth Amendments were not ratified under the most favorable of circumstances. The southern states were coerced into ratification. In fact, most of the southern states initially rejected the Fourteenth Amendment and acquiesced only after Congress enacted a reconstruction act that denied each state representation in Congress until it ratified the amendment. Such coercion would not be acceptable today, but the methods used by the national government in coercing the states into ratifying the reconstruction amendments have to be considered in light of the circumstances of the day.

It would be decades before the full force of these amendments would be realized. However, the reconstruction period marks an important point in constitutional history. Today, the reconstruction amendments and statutes are applied often and with significant effect on state actions. For example, the Fourteenth Amendment and federal discrimination statutes forbid state governments from discriminating against individuals on the account of race, religion, or gender when hiring employees or providing benefits to citizens.

1.8(e) Pre–New Deal Era: Protecting Commercial Interests

Salmon Chase was followed by Morrison Waite (1874–1888), Melville Fuller (1888–1910), Edward White (1910–1921), and William Taft (1921–1930) as chief justices. Again, the Court's philosophy changed during the tenure of these men, at least regarding federalism issues. During this period, the Fourteenth Amendment was used to limit the power of the states to regulate intrastate commerce. For example, in *Lochner v. New York,* 198 U.S. 45 (1905), the Court invalidated a state statute that set maximum working hours for bakers. The Court found the statute to be an unwarranted burden upon the right to contract, a liberty interest protected by the Fourteenth Amendment.

The authority of the federal government to regulate interstate commerce was also limited during this period, often for Tenth Amendment reasons (the federal government was encroaching upon the domain of the states).

Ironically, while the Court was using the Fourteenth Amendment to protect economic interests, it did not concomitantly protect the rights of black citizens, the primary goal of the amendment. The case that established the "separate but equal" doctrine, *Plessy v. Ferguson,* 163 U.S. 537 (1896), was rendered during this period. Not until 1954, when *Brown v. Board of Education,* 381 U.S. 479 (1954) was decided, was the separate but equal doctrine overturned as violative of the Fourteenth Amendment.

1.8(f) New Deal Era: Expanding Federal Authority

The next significant judicial era occurred during the Great Depression. President Franklin D. Roosevelt was elected with a popular mandate to correct the nation's serious economic crisis. Roosevelt's New Deal plan included significant federal government involvement in economic matters. A number of programs were created with the intention of stimulating the economy. Additionally, national governmental regulation of commercial activities increased during the New Deal.

Early in Roosevelt's administration, the Court rendered a number of unpopular decisions invalidating some of the New Deal legislation. In 1935, the Court held the National Industrial Recovery Act unconstitutional in *Panama Refining Co. v. Ryan,* 293 U.S. 388 (1935), as it found that Congress had made an unlawful delegation of legislative authority to the president (violating separation of powers principles). There were other decisions unfavorable to President Roosevelt: *Schechter Poultry Corp. v. United States,* 295 U.S. 495 (1935); *Railroad Retirement Board v. Alton Railroad,* 295 U.S. 330 (1935); and *United States v. Butler,* 297 U.S. 1 (1936). (This line of cases is more fully discussed in Chapters 5 and 7.) In short, they stood for the principle of a limited national government, one whose authority to regulate interstate commerce is limited by the right of individual contract and by federalism principles. These cases asserted the importance of separation of powers, substantive due process, and limitations on the authority that may be delegated by Congress to administrative agencies.

These decisions angered President Roosevelt, who reacted with the famous "court-packing" plan. In an effort to "pack" the Court with justices sympathetic to his objectives, President Roosevelt proposed that for every justice over seventy years of age, an additional justice be appointed. At the time the suggestion was made, there were six justices over age seventy on the Court. He contended that the additional justices were needed to meet the Court's heavy burden. Congress saw the proposal for what it was—an attempt to control the Court by President Roosevelt—and ultimately it was defeated. Also contributing to the defeat were two decisions issued by the Court upholding the New Deal legislation. The decisions represented a change in direction from the court. Justice Roberts, the swing vote on the divided Court, is credited with saving the nine-member court by changing his vote, favoring federal authority in commerce cases. This has become commonly known as the *switch in time that saved nine.* Roosevelt's court-packing scheme presented one of the most serious threats to the integrity and independence of the Court in its history.

As it turned out, Roosevelt did not need the court-packing scheme to gain the ideological sympathy of the Court. Recall that six justices were over the age of seventy when he made his proposal. As might be expected, a number left the Court during the New Deal era. By 1941, Roosevelt had nominated seven new justices, all of whom were confirmed.

The new membership on the Court transformed its attitude and approach to substantive due process and federalism. Beginning in 1938, and continuing thereafter, the Court consistently upheld the New Deal legislation.

1.8(g) Warren Court: Expanding Individual Rights

In 1953, Earl Warren, a nominee of President Eisenhower, became the new chief justice. Warren presided over a Court that is best known for its decisions protecting individual rights (civil liberties). Three other justices were prominent during this time for their "liberal" philosophies: William Douglas, William Brennan, and Hugo Black. In 1967, two years before the end of Warren's tenure, another liberal justice, Thurgood Marshall, was added to the Court.

Much constitutional law was established during the Warren Court era. Included in this Court's decisions are the following: the invalidation of the separate but equal doctrine of *Plessy,* in *Brown v. Board of Education;* the finding that privacy is protected by the Constitution, in *Griswold v. Connecticut,* 381 U.S. 479 (1965); the establishment of much of the First Amendment free speech law used today; and enhanced protection of the rights of persons accused of crimes, including *Katz v. United States,* 389 U.S. 347 (1967) (Fourth Amendment protects reasonable expectations of privacy), *United States v. Wade,* 338 U.S. 218 (1967) (right to counsel at pretrial [postarrest or charge] identifications), and *Miranda v. Arizona,* 384 U.S. 436 (1966) (right to counsel during interrogations), to name only a few.

1.8(h) Burger Court: A Moderate Approach

Warren Burger was nominated by President Richard M. Nixon to follow Earl Warren as chief justice in 1969. President Nixon appointed three other justices, Harry Blackmun,

Lewis Powell, and William Rehnquist, who were either conservative or moderate, to replace three more liberal members of the Warren Court: Earl Warren, Abe Fortas, and Hugo Black.

Although the Burger Court was more conservative than the Warren Court, it was not activist in its approach. Few decisions of the Warren Court were reversed; in fact, the early years of the Burger Court continued in the Warren Court tradition, emphasizing the preservation of civil liberties. However, just as the Burger Court did not proactively pursue a conservative agenda, it did not continue the liberal activism of the Warren Court. Rather, on the whole, the Court maintained the status quo, neither disturbing precedent nor engaging in social engineering.

This is not to say that the Burger Court did not issue important decisions. Important precedents concerning the freedom of speech, the rights of racial minorities, and the rights of women were established during the Burger era. For example, the Burger Court decided *Roe v. Wade,* 410 U.S. 113 (1973), wherein the Court determined that the right to privacy protects a woman's right to elect abortion in some situations. The Burger Court was also responsible for ordering President Nixon to hand over tape recordings of Oval Office conversations that related to the Watergate affair, in *Nixon v. United States,* 418 U.S. 683 (1974), *reh'g denied,* 433 U.S. 916 (1977). It was during the Burger era that the first woman joined the Court. Justice Sandra Day O'Connor was nominated by President Reagan and confirmed by the Senate in 1981.

1.8(i) Rehnquist Court: Protecting States' Rights

William Rehnquist was appointed associate justice of the Supreme Court in 1972, and he succeeded Warren Burger as chief justice in 1986. Between 1988 and 1991, Associate Justices Lewis Powell Jr., William Brennan Jr., and Thurgood Marshall retired. Their replacements, Justices Anthony Kennedy, David Souter, and Clarence Thomas, were all more conservative than the justices they replaced. Accordingly, the Court had a more conservative leaning during the Rehnquist tenure than during the Warren and Burger eras. This was particularly true for issues concerning economic and states' rights.

Some of the important federalism cases decided during Rehnquist's term are *United States v. Lopez,* 115 S. Ct. 1624 (1995) and *Morrison v. United States,* 529 U.S. 598 (2000), both limiting Congress's power over interstate commerce. In *United States Term Limits v. Thornton,* 115 S. Ct. 1842 (1996), the Court invalidated state-imposed term limits on U.S. Congress members, and *Bush v. Gore,* 531 U.S. 98 (2000) brought closure to the closest presidential election in history. Another important decision was *Casey v. Planned Parenthood,* 112 S. Ct. 2791 (1992), wherein the Court reaffirmed the basic holding of the Burger Court decision in *Roe v. Wade,* namely, that women have a privacy right to elect abortions in some situations. However, the Rehnquist Court invalidated the trimester analysis established in *Roe* in favor of another test. Justice Rehnquist died in office in 2005.

1.8(j) Roberts Court: An Unfolding Story

John G. Roberts was confirmed as Chief Justice Rehnquist's successor in 2005, making him the Court's seventeenth chief justice. It is difficult to make generalizations about the "Roberts" Court because there were three retirements and three appointments in the first five years of the Roberts's era. By 2010, following the appointment of the third new justice, Elana Kagan, the Court was evenly split between conservative and liberal justices with one moderately conservative "swing" justice. Whether the Roberts Court will continue to embolden state rights, as the Rehnquist Court did, remains to be seen. In its early years, the Roberts Court appears to be shifting its federalism focus from whether the federal government possesses specific authorities and state sovereignty (which precludes federal involvement) to federal preemption, and if its early decisions (e.g., *Reigel v. Medtronic,* 552 U.S. 312 (2008) and *Waters v. Wachovia,* 550

U.S. 1 (2007)) foreshadow what is coming, the Court is not likely to expand on the New Federalism of the Rehnquist Court.

See Appendix E for a chronological chart of all of the members of the Supreme Court since its inception.

1.9 THE COURT TODAY

In the 2010/2011 term, the Supreme Court had five justices appointed by Republican presidents—three women and two ethnic minorities (African American and Puerto Rican)—and the once Protestant-dominated Court had six Catholic and three Jewish members. There was some economic diversity on the Court with Justices Thomas and Sotomayor both hailing from less financially fortunate childhoods. There was little diversity in their higher education. All attended prestigious colleges for their under-graduate education, and six earned their law degrees at Harvard University; the other three at Yale University. The Court was philosophically split, with Roberts, Scalia, Thomas, and Alito comprising a conservative block and Ginsburg, Breyer, Sotomayor, and Kagan comprising a liberal block. Justice Kenney has proved to be a moderate with conservative leanings. As Justice O'Connor was for many years, Kennedy is the fifth, crucial swing vote in many cases because of his status in the philosophical center. See the exhibit in this chapter for a summary of the current members of the court, the presidents who nominated them, and their general philosophical leaning.

Chief Justice John Roberts was born on January 27, 1955, in New York and spent his young years in Indiana. He was reared, and remains, Catholic. He attended Harvard College and Harvard Law School; clerked for both a federal appellate judge and subsequently for Chief Justice Rehnquist; practiced law for many years, including extensive experience before the Supreme Court; and served in both the Attorney General's and White House Counsel's offices under President Reagan.

He was nominated by President George H. W. Bush to serve on the U.S. Court of Appeals for the D.C. Circuit in 1992. The Senate judiciary committee failed to act on his nomination and it lapsed. He then went into private practice and served as a part-time faculty member at the Georgetown University School of Law.

In 2001, the second President Bush nominated Roberts to the U.S. Court of Appeals for the D.C. Circuit. A repeat of the earlier nomination, his nomination was not taken to vote. When the balance in the Senate changed from Democrat to Republican, President Bush again nominated him to the appellate court and he was confirmed in 2003. Two years later President Bush nominated him to fill the seat vacated by Justice Sandra O'Connor. Before his confirmation, however, Chief Justice Rehnquist died. President Bush then changed his nomination of Roberts to chief justice. He was confirmed as chief justice with the largest number of votes in history (78) and was sworn in on September 28, 2005. He is also distinguished as the youngest chief justice since John Marshall, two hundred years earlier. With conservative leanings, he is considered more centrist than justices Thomas and Scalia.

Antonin Scalia, born on March 11, 1936, is a second-generation Italian-American who was born in New Jersey but spent much of his youth in New York. Like the chief justice, he is a life-long Catholic. He attended Georgetown University as an undergraduate and Harvard Law School. After law school he practiced law for a short time followed by a stint as professor of law at the University of Virginia. Subsequently, he worked in several roles in President Nixon's administration, as a resident scholar at the American Enterprise Institute, a conservative think-tank, and he held faculty positions at the law schools of Georgetown University and the University of Chicago. He was appointed judge to the U.S. Court of Appeals for Washington, DC, in 1982. He was nominated to the Supreme Court by President Reagan to fill the vacancy created by William H. Rehnquist's elevation from associate justice to chief justice. He was confirmed in 1986, becoming the most senior associate justice.

Cyber Constitution
For profiles on current and past justice of the Supreme Court, go to www.oyez.org/courts

Strongly conservative, Justice Scalia believes in judicial restraint and free market. While he opposes expansive interpretation of rights, he has surprised many scholars with some of his decisions supporting free speech, such as his vote in favor of the First Amendment right to burn the U.S. flag in *Texas v. Johnson*.

The second most senior associate justice is Anthony Kennedy. He was born on July 23, 1936, in Sacramento, California. He is a Catholic. Kennedy earned his undergraduate degree at Stanford University and law degree at Harvard. After law school he practiced law in California. He worked for Ronald Reagan, who was Governor of California at the time, in various capacities during this period. He also taught constitutional law part-time at the University of the Pacific's McGeorge School of Law. Ronald Reagan suggested his appointment to the U.S. Court of Appeals for the Ninth Circuit to President Ford, who agreed, and when confirmed by the Senate in 1975, Kennedy was the youngest federal appellate judge in the nation at 39.

In 1987, Justice Lewis Powell retired and President Reagan nominated Robert Bork to fill his seat. However, Bork faced considerable opposition in the Senate and his nomination failed. President Reagan then nominated Douglas Ginsburg, a federal appellate judge, who withdrew his candidacy after a scandal ensued concerning his admitted past marijuana use. Kennedy, Reagan's third nominee, faced little opposition in the Senate and was confirmed and took his oath in February 1988. Although he falls to the conservative side on many issues, Justice Kennedy is regarded as the bridge between the conservative and liberal blocks on the Court, often rendering the "pivot" vote in close cases.

Clarence Thomas, born on June 23, 1948, brings both racial and economic diversity to the Court as an African American who grew up poor in a racially segregated Georgia. A Catholic, his original career objective was to join the priesthood. Uncomfortable with the racism he experienced, he quit. He earned his bachelor's degree at the College of the Holy Cross and law degree at Yale University. Thomas's first position after law school was in the Missouri Attorney General's Office. Subsequently he worked as a corporate attorney and for Senator John Danforth of Missouri. He was appointed assistant secretary of civil rights in the U.S. Department of Education and eventually director of the U.S. Equal Employment Opportunity Commission (EEOC) in the Reagan administration. Much of his work at the EEOC was met with opposition by civil rights groups who believed he was not adhering to the commission's mission of advancing civic rights in the workplace.

President George H. W. Bush nominated Thomas, and he was confirmed, to the U.S. Court of Appeals for the District of Columbia in 1990. Only one year later he was nominated by President Bush to take the seat previously held by Associate Justice Thurgood Marshall. He weathered opposition from civil rights groups and allegations of sexual harassment by Anita Hill, an employee of Thomas at both the U.S. Department of Education and EEOC to be confirmed on October 15, 1991.

Justice Thomas, as expected, is a member of the Court's conservative block. Civil rights groups continue to find him to be a foe of their interests. He is equally conservative on other issues (e.g., criminal justice) and in his judicial philosophy. In addition to his political ideology, Justice Thomas is well known for his silence on the bench. As of 2011, Justice Thomas had not spoken the first word during oral arguments (like all justices, he occasionally reads the decisions of the Court from the bench) in over five years. Although his colleagues vary considerably in the number of questions and comments they make, none had let a single year pass without speaking during oral arguments. Justice Thomas has suggested various reasons for his silence, including being self-conscious about his southern dialect and out of respect for the attorneys who appear before the Court.[44]

The first non-Catholic justice of the present Court to be profiled is Ruth Bader Ginsburg. Born on March 15, 1933, in New York City, New York, Justice Ginsburg, who is Jewish and from a lower-middle economic background, was nominated by

President William J. Clinton and confirmed by the Senate in 1993. She attended Cornell University as an undergraduate student and began her legal education at Harvard Law School. But after her family moved to New York to access cancer treatment for her husband, she attended and graduated from Columbia University School of Law. She remained at Columbia Law School as a research associate following her graduation until 1963, when she joined the law faculty at Rutgers University. She returned to Columbia in 1972, the first woman with tenure on the law faculty. During this period she appeared before the U.S. Supreme Court on several occasions. An advocate of women's rights, she was an active member of the American Civil Liberties Union before assuming her duties on the Supreme Court. She was nominated to the U.S. Court of Appeals for the District of Columbia by President Jimmy Carter, a post he held from 1981 until her appointment to the Supreme Court in 1993, replacing Justice Byron White. Justice Ginsburg has strong leanings to the right, although like most justices, she is not monolithic and occasionally votes with the conservative members of the Court.

Stephen Breyer is the second Jewish member of the Court and the second democratic appointee profiled so far. Hailing from a middle-class family in California, he married into a family of considerable wealth. He attended Stanford University as an undergraduate, studied economics at the University of Oxford (England), and earned his law degree at Harvard. He clerked for Justice Arthur Goldberg in the 1964/1965 term and subsequently worked in the U.S. Department of Justice's antitrust division.

A TENTH JUSTICE?

SIDEBAR

One of the most important executive positions in the United States is the Solicitor General. This position was established in 1870 by Congress as part of the newly created Department of Justice (DOJ). Originally, the Solicitor General was the second highest office in the DOJ, following the Attorney General. Today, it falls a bit lower in hierarchy but is nonetheless regarded as one of the most powerful positions in the government. The Solicitor General is the chief litigator for the United States before the Supreme Court, and as desired, lower courts. Although the Solicitor General is nominated by the president, confirmed by Congress, and reports to the Attorney General, past Solicitors have exercised considerable independence in their decision making. Federal officials and agencies who want to appeal to the Supreme Court must do so through the Solicitor General, and historically, the Solicitor has demonstrated considerable restraint in what cases the office is willing to seek certiorari. Once appealed, however, the likelihood of the Supreme Court hearing a Solicitor General's request is much higher than for all other attorneys. Today, about two-thirds of all cases decided on the merits by the Court have the United States involved in some manner.

The Solicitor General enjoys a special relationship with the Supreme Court. First, the Solicitor General maintains offices in both the DOJ and the Supreme Court. Second, in addition to hearing a high percentage of cases brought to it by the Solicitor General, the Supreme Court bestows several privileges upon the Solicitor General. For example, the Solicitor General's opinion is often sought in cases where the United States is not a party. In such cases, the Solicitor General files amicus curiae (friend of the court) briefs. In such cases, it is rare for amicus parties to be given oral argument time before the Court. But the Solicitor General's requests are frequently granted.

One way Solicitor Generals maintain their credibility with the Court is through the practice of confessing error. This practice involves cases where the United States won in a lower court where the Solicitor General was not involved but the Solicitor General believes the United States' position (likely argued by a U.S. Attorney) was wrong or that the United States should have lost in the lower court. The Solicitor General may appeal such a case and confess error, indicating to the Court that it should find contrary to the United States.

The close relationship between the Court and the Solicitor General has resulted in the common referral to the Solicitor General as the tenth justice of the Court. Indeed, several Solicitor Generals joined the judiciary after leaving the DOJ. This includes William Howard Taft, Stanley Reed, Thurgood Marshall, and Elena Kagan. Other Solicitor Generals went on to accomplished legal and political careers outside the judiciary.

Source: U.S. DOJ website, www.justice.gov/osg/

He left the Department of Justice for an appointment to the Harvard law faculty. In 1974 he accepted the position as legal counsel to the Senate's judiciary committee. He was nominated to the U.S. Court of Appeals for the First District by President Reagan, was confirmed in 1980, and retained that position until his appointment to the Supreme Court in 1994, having been nominated by President Clinton. While on the appellate court, Breyer also served on the influential Federal Sentencing Commission, which established the federal criminal sentencing guidelines. Justice Breyer has proven to be an ideological moderate member of the Court.

President George W. Bush's only appointee to the Court is Justice Samuel Alito Jr. Alito was confirmed only after President Bush's first nominee, Harriet Miers, withdrew her name amid questions about her qualifications. Alito's confirmation did not come without a fight, with Democratic members of the Senate opposing him because of his conservative views on abortion rights, civil rights, criminal justice issues, state and federal authorities, and executive power. A graduate of Princeton University and Yale University School of Law, he came to the Supreme Court after fifteen years on the U.S. Court of Appeals for the Third Circuit. He took the oath of office on January 30, 2006.

One of two appointees of President Barack Obama is Justice Sonia Sotomayor. Replacing Justice David Souter, she is the first Hispanic and third woman to serve on the Court. Justice Sotomayor, born on June 25, 1955, in New York is Catholic and of Puerto Rican descent. A product of a lower economic background, her academic success won her a seat at Princeton University and Yale University School of Law. Following law school she worked as a prosecutor and private attorney. In 1992, President H. W. Bush nominated Sotomayor to a federal trial court judgeship. Five years later she was elevated to the U.S. Court of Appeals for the Second Circuit by President Clinton. Justice Sotomayor took the oath of office on August 8, 2009.

The least senior and youngest member of the Court is Justice Elana Kagan. Justice Kagan was born on April 28, 1960, in New York City, New York. She is Jewish and from an upper middle class family. She is the Court's fourth female justice, with three serving together at the time of the writing of this text. Like so many of her colleagues, she attended Princeton University, University of Oxford, and Harvard University School of Law. She clerked for both a federal appellate court and Justice Thurgood Marshall of the Supreme Court, served President Clinton as Associate White House Counsel and as a policy advisor, and held a faculty position at University of Chicago School of Law. She served as dean of the Harvard Law School after her nomination to the U.S. Court of Appeals for the D.C. Circuit lapsed without action by the Senate. President Obama nominated and she was confirmed Solicitor General of the United States in January 2009. In May 2010, President Obama nominated her

Justice	Nominated by	General Philosophy
John Roberts, Chief	George W. Bush (R)	Conservative
Antonin Scalia	Ronald Reagan (R)	Conservative
Anthony Kennedy	Ronald Reagan (R)	Moderately conservative
Clarence Thomas	George H. W. Bush (R)	Conservative
Ruth Bader Ginsburg	William H. Clinton (D)	Liberal
Stephen Breyer	William H. Clinton (D)	Liberal
Samuel Alito Jr.	George W. Bush (R)	Conservative
Sonia Sotomayor	Barack Obama (D)	Liberal
Elana Kagan	Barack Obama (D)	Liberal

Exhibit: Supreme Court Justices in 2011

to the Supreme Court to fill the line previously held by Justice John P. Stevens. Her confirmation hearings were uneventful and she was easily confirmed. She was sworn on August 7, 2010.

1.10 MODERN CHALLENGES

As you learned earlier, there have been thousands of attempts to amend the U.S. Constitution. Only twenty-seven were successful. Early proposals include a prohibition of interracial marriages, protection of the authority of states to decide whether to permit or prohibit slavery, and a prohibition of citizens of the United States from holding titles of nobility in other countries. Hot topics in the past few decades have been capital punishment, flag desecration, war powers, equal rights, school prayer, same-sex marriage, and abortion.

What will be the hot button issues that will lead to proposals to amend the Constitution in the years to come? It is likely that the dramatic changes that President Obama's administration ushered in will result in amendment proposals. Specifically, controlling the size of the federal government may be a theme. The massive changes in health-care administration and in the regulation of the finance and other industries, often to the exclusion of the states, will likely lead to proposals not only to control the size of the federal government but also to strengthen state authority in the federal scheme. The recent **tea party movement** and the successes of the Republican and tea party candidates in the midterm election of 2010 indicate that there is concern about these issues. Many of the victorious candidates ran on a platform of smaller government, lower taxes, reducing the federal debt, state rights, commercial libertarianism, and "stricter constitutionalism." This combination of values, matched with congressional victories, lend them to the probability that amendment proposals are on the way. What are your predictions?

Tea Party Movement
A political movement that begun in response to the policies advanced by President Obama to revitalize the economy, such as the bailouts of the banking and other industries and the health-care reform program. Named for the Boston Tea Party, adherents advocate for smaller government, less taxes, lowering the national debt, states rights, commercial liberty, and "strict constitutionalism."

1.11 SUMMARY

Under the Articles of Confederation, the nation was fragmented and the national government was too weak to effectively deal with the challenges facing our young nation. The framers gathered in Philadelphia to revise the Articles of Confederation. Understanding that their task was greater than this, the delegates chose to abolish the Articles of Confederation and to write a new constitution. They knew that presenting a new constitution would be controversial. To preserve the integrity of the process, they agreed to keep their proceedings secret until the final document was completed.

They created a new governmental structure in the new constitution. The national government would be stronger, but it was limited to the authorities directly given it by the people through the Constitution. Although they intended to strengthen the federal government, they were careful to preserve local governmental authority. The concern about excessive federal authority was so great that the principle of dual sovereignty, or concurrent federal and state authority, was reinforced through the Tenth Amendment only two years after the Constitution was enacted. Thus, powers that appeared inherently national were delegated to the national government, such as foreign relations and war. In addition, control over interstate, foreign, and Indian commerce was assigned to Congress. Everyday matters, such as intrastate commerce, crime, and social concerns, were left to the states.

The first state to accept the new constitution was Delaware. The delegates decided that ratification would occur when the ninth state ratified. This happened in New Hampshire on June 21, 1788. The last of the thirteen states to ratify was Rhode Island, which did so on May 29, 1790. The Bill of Rights was added to the Constitution one year later.

The framers were successful in establishing a stronger national government and are credited with saving the Union from economic disaster and civil war. For reasons that will be more fully discussed later in this book, the federal government has continually grown in size and authority under this Constitution. Whether the federal government has become too large and powerful is the subject of continual discussion. Federalism, or the division of governmental powers among the federal and state governments, is the subject of Chapters 2 and 8. The division of authority between the three branches is a work in progress as well. But what could have proved to be a very weak and ineffective branch, the judiciary, was given a power shot by John Marshall's Supreme Court, particularly through *Marbury's* unabashed assertion of courts as final interpreters and arbiters of the Constitution. The power of the judiciary to review the acts of its coordinate branches and the states for constitutionality is significant. Although not specifically provided for in the Constitution, Chief Justice John Marshall stated in *Marbury v. Madison* that the power is inherent in the general grant of judicial power found in Article III. Accordingly, all Article III judges possess the power of judicial review. This diffusion of authority establishes significant judicial power in the American political and legal systems. Judicial review is used every day in courts across the land when judges review statutes, other written law, and the actions of government officials (such as law-enforcement officers) for constitutionality. Although the power is frequently invoked, data indicate that courts do not use it often to invalidate legislation. Of course, this is a subjective determination, and many jurists argue that it is used too frequently and that it is used in important policy cases that would be more properly decided by elected representatives.

The framers' legacy extends well beyond having established the oldest written constitution in continuous existence. Their ripple turned into a constitutional wave that has swept the world.

REVIEW QUESTIONS

1. What were the names of the national legislative bodies before and during the period of the Articles of Confederation and Perpetual Union?

2. Distinguish Federalists from anti-Federalists. State the basic philosophical differences between the two.

3. Identify two of the weaknesses of the Articles of Confederation that contributed to the need for a new constitution.

4. What was the mandate of the delegates to the Philadelphia convention?

5. Name the only one of the original thirteen colonies that was not represented at the Philadelphia convention.

6. Edmund Randolph introduced a plan, largely written by James Madison, that became the working document at the Philadelphia convention. What is the common name of this plan?

7. The delegates considered empowering the Congress with the authority to invalidate state laws. The idea was rejected. Madison, a proponent of the idea, was disappointed, but was consoled by what fact?

8. The delegates agreed to strengthen the national (federal) government but maintain considerable state powers. Describe the relationship between the federal government and state governments as envisioned by the framers.

9. What were the terms of the Great Compromise?

10. Why did Alexander Hamilton oppose including a bill of rights in the original Constitution?

11. What is judicial review and in what Supreme Court case did Chief Justice Marshall announce the power on behalf of the federal judiciary?

12. The United States employs a diffused model of judicial review. What does this mean?

13. Compare and contrast the U.S. model of judicial review from the constitutional council model of review.

14. Why did the framers of the Constitution make it so difficult to amend the Constitution?

15. Do you believe judicial review is essential to ensuring freedom and the protection of civil liberties? Explain your answer.

ASSIGNMENTS: CONSTITUTIONAL LAW IN ACTION

The Constitution in Your Community

Judicial review is a well-accepted, frequently exercised authority by local, state, and federal courts. The most frequent use is in reviewing the arrests, searches, and other activities of government in criminal justice. It is frequently used in noncriminal cases too. While many constitutional challenges to laws and executive actions rely on the U.S. Constitution, many state constitutional challenges to state actions exist as well.

Assume that you are working for a local prosecutor's office. One of the assistant prosecutors in the office is involved with a case where the defense attorney is challenging the constitutionality of the state criminal code being used to prosecute the defendant. The defense attorney has filed a motion asking the trial court to exercise its power of judicial review and declare the criminal statute unconstitutional under the state's constitution. Without getting into the particulars of the code or its possible defects, the assistant prosecutor would like for you to research the power of judicial review held by courts within your state.

Going Federal

Assume that you are working for a law firm that has been retained to challenge the constitutionality of the recently enacted federal health-care law. See "Is Health Care Law Constitutional?" www.washingtonpost.com/wp-dyn/content/article/2010/03/19/AR2010031901470.html. A senior partner has asked you to help her prepare for a meeting with the client. Prepare a short (1–3 pages) analysis of the federal constitutional questions raised by the law.

Moot Court

On October 12, 2010, U.S. District Court Judge Virginia Phillips ordered the United States to stop enforcing its "don't ask, don't tell" policy in the armed forces, which she had previously found to be violative of the First and Fourteenth Amendments in *Log Cabin Republicans v. United States of America* (Case No. CV-0408425-VAP, Cen. Dist. CA, October 12, 2010). The "don't ask, don't tell" policy prohibits asking members of the military about their sexual preferences but also provides for the discharge of admitted gay and lesbian members. Judge Phillips's order applied throughout the United States, to all of the armed forces. The Obama administration challenged the authority of Phillips, who is judge of a federal trial court with jurisdiction in central California, to issue a nation-wide order. The United States requested a stay of the order pending appeal. Judge Phillips refused to stay her order, but the Ninth Circuit Court of Appeals granted the United States' request. (See *Log Cabin Republicans v. United States of America* (Case No. 10-56634, 9th Cir., October 20, 2010).)

Set aside any statutory issues concerning Judge Phillips's authority to issue such an order. Instead, focus on whether a federal trial court should have the authority to exercise judicial review and issue nation-wide orders. Consider the possibility of conflicting judgments between districts or circuits (federal appellate courts). Remember the Supreme Court exercises discretionary jurisdiction in nearly all cases. That is, it does not have to hear most cases that are appealed to it. On the other hand, consider the limitation on rule of law that would exist if only the Supreme Court had such authority. Working in teams of two, the first team should prepare a five-minute oral argument favoring judicial review at all levels of the judiciary. The second team should prepare a five-minute oral argument opposing this authority at all levels. The second team should present and defend an alternative model.

NOTES

1. World Justice Project Rule of Law Index 2010 at www.worldjusticeproject.org/.
2. The study looked at 49 quantitative factors in determining the extent to which the studied nations adhere to rule of law. The World Justice Project selected the factors that have meaning to ordinary persons, such as individual access to government and courts and levels of fear of governmental abuse. The 2010 report included 35 nations, which the World Justice Project intends to increase to 100 by 2012. Report, p. 7.
3. Documents preceding the Constitution, such as the Declaration of Independence, have no legal authority.
4. Paul Gewirtz, "Approaches to Constitutional Interpretation: Comparative Constitutionalism and Chinese Characteristics," 31 *Hong Kong Law Journal* 200–223 (No. 208 2002).
5. Ibid., 211.
6. A. McLaughlin, *A Constitutional History of the United States* 99–100 (D. Appleton-Century 1935).
7. Articles of Confederation and Perpetual Union, Article III.
8. Thomas and Thomas, *The War-Making Powers of the President* 3–4 (SMU Press 1982).
9. Catherine Bowen, *Miracle at Philadelphia* 9 (Little, Brown, & Co. 1966).
10. *Judges of the United States,* 2d ed. (Bicentennial Committee of the Judicial Conference of the United States 1983).
11. The Federalist No. 15.
12. George Anastaplo, *The Constitution of 1787* (Johns Hopkins University Press 1989).
13. For a comprehensive discussion of the delegates' respective wealth and how their personal economic interests may have been a factor in their decision making at the convention, see Charles Beard's *Economic Interpretation of the Constitution* (1913) and Forrest McDonald's *We the People: The Economic Origins of the Constitution* (Transaction Publishers 1992).
14. William Peters, *A More Perfect Union* 25 (Crown Publishers 1982).
15. Neil MacNeil, "The First Congress, a Republic If You Can Keep It," 1 *Constitution* 5–6 (No. 3 1989).
16. The other significant proposal was introduced by William Paterson. His plan became known as the New Jersey Plan and was in most respects the antithesis of the Virginia Plan. It called for continuing the Articles of Confederation with revision. Notable differences between the two plans are as follows: the Virginia Plan saw the Constitution's authority emanating from the people, whereas the New Jersey Plan continued to view the national government as representing the states; the Virginia Plan provided for a bicameral Congress, the New Jersey Plan for a unicameral Congress; the Virginia Plan gave the national government wide-sweeping jurisdiction, whereas the New Jersey Plan severely limited the jurisdiction of the national government.
17. The Federalist No. 47.
18. The Federalist No. 68.
19. "The Fourth Amendment," *The Bill of Rights and Beyond.* Bicentennial Calendar (Commission on the Bicentennial of the Constitution 1991).
20. Sara M. Shumer, "Ratifying the Constitution." In *New Jersey,* Gillespie et al., eds. (1989), 76–77.
21. *The Creation of the Constitution* 58. Opposing Viewpoints Series (Greenhaven Press 1995).
22. Letter to C.W.F. Dumas, September 1787, cited in Richard Bernstein, *Amending America* 222 (Random House 1993).
23. It was originally the Second Amendment. The other unenacted amendment provided for an increase in the membership of the House of Representatives as the nation's population increased. It has never been enacted.

24. See U.S. Senate document www.senate.gov/reference/resources/pdf/proposedamend.pdf#search='number%20of%20amendments%20constitution%20introduced%20congress and Richard B. Bernstein, *Amending America: If We Love the Constitution So Much, Why Do We Keep on Trying to Change It?* xii (Random House 1993).

25. 491 U.S. 397 (1989).

26. 8 Co. Rep. 107(a) (1610).

27. M. Graber and M. Perhac, eds, *Marbury v. Madison: Documents and Commentary* (CQ Press, Washington, DC 2002, p. 2).

28. The Federalist No. 78.

29. Haines, *The American Doctrine of Judicial Supremacy,* 2d ed., 136 (1959).

30. *Id.*

31. Austin Scott, *Holmes v. Walton: The New Jersey Precedent,* Rutgers College Publication No. 5, 4 *American Historical Review* (No. 456 April 1899).

32. *Id.*, chapters V and VI.

33. See *Hylton v. United States,* 3 Dall. 171 (1796), wherein the Court implicitly exercised the power by reviewing and upholding a federal taxing statute.

34. *Fletcher v. Peck,* 10 U.S. (6 Cranch) 87 (1810).

35. L. Baum, *The Supreme Court,* 4th ed. (Congressional Quarterly Press 1992).

36. *Id.*; C. Herman Pritchett, *Constitutional Law of the Federal System* (Prentice-Hall 1984), citing in part Sen. Doc. No. 134, 93d Cong., S127–S135 (1974), provides the following numbers: between 1865 and 1979, the Court held 120 acts of Congress unconstitutional; between 1953 and 1969 (Warren Court), 25 acts of Congress were held unconstitutional; between 1969 and 1979 (Burger Court), 21 acts of Congress were held unconstitutional; and between 1789 and 1974, 848 acts of state and local governments were held unconstitutional. See also Henry J. Abraham, *The Judicial Process,* 4th ed. 271 (Oxford University Press 1980); *Constitution of the United States: Analysis and Interpretation,* S. Doc. No. 16, 99th Cong. (1982).

37. Robert H. Bork, *The Dangers of Political Law: The Tempting of America: The Political Seduction of Law* 130 n. 1 (Free Press 1989).

38. Robert H. Bork, *Coercing Virtue: The Worldwide Rule of Judges* (American Enterprise Institute Press 2003).

39. Examples include Canada, Ireland, and Japan.

40. Philip B. Reichel, *Comparative Criminal Justice Systems* 163 (Prentice-Hall 1994).

41. William E. Nelson, *Marbury v. Madison: The Origins and Legacy of Judicial Review* (University of Kansas Press 2000), 104–105.

42. See James D. Dinnage and John F. Murphy, *The Constitutional Law of the European Union* (Anderson Publishing 1996), chapter 8, for more.

43. United Nations Development Programme, Program on Governance in the Arab Region, www.undp-pogar.org/publications/judiciary/nbrown/tprovisions.html (2010).

44. "No Argument: Thomas Keeps 5-Year Silence," *The New York Times,* February 12, 2011, www.nytimes.com/2011/02/13/us/13thomas.html.

2

Dividing Governmental Power

The accumulation of all power, legislative, executive and judiciary in the same hands, whether hereditary, self-appointed, or elective, may justzly be pronounced the very definition of tyranny.

JAMES MADISON[1]

LEARNING OBJECTIVES
At the end of this chapter you should be able to:

- Define federalism and separation of powers, identify the major sources of state and federal authorities explicit in the Constitution, and explain why the division of powers architecture was important to the framers.

- Distinguish dual, hierarchical, and cooperative federalism, and from the last chapter, identify the various times the Supreme Court has favored dual or hierarchical federalism.

- List ten or more examples of checks and balances among the three federal branches that are explicit in the Constitution.

- Identify the most significant forms of federal and state laws.

- Demonstrate comfort and familiarity with the style and format of judicial opinions.

- Brief a judicial opinion with little outside assistance. You should be successful in identifying the relevant facts. You should be successful in identifying the legal issue and analyzing the court's rationale in at least 33 percent of your briefs.

2.1 FEDERALISM

The men who met in Philadelphia during the hot summer of 1787 firmly believed that a new government would have to be formed to solve the nation's many problems. Under the Articles of Confederation, the nation's first constitution, the nation floundered. Economic and political instability were generally attributed to the weakness of the national government. Therefore, a new, stronger national government was established.

The framers were concerned, however, with the centralization of power. Too much power residing in any one person or group could lead to tyranny. The belief that absolute power corrupts absolutely predominated the political philosophy of the framers, as can be seen in James Madison's opening quote to this chapter.

Also, the framers were protective of state sovereignty. They wanted a stronger national government, but not to the point of obliterating the states. So the Constitution they created reflects a balancing of these interests. Three important concepts were included in the Constitution to prevent both the centralization of power and the death of state sovereignty: federalism, separation of powers, and checks and balances. This chapter introduces those concepts. Chapters 3 through 6 expand the discussion to include particular cases in which the concepts have been raised and applied.

The Constitution recognizes two forms of government: the national (which shall be referred to as the federal government in the remainder of this book) government and the government of the states. The division of governmental power between the federal and state governments is called **federalism.** Federalism represents a vertical division of power.

The Constitution specifically enumerates the powers of the federal government. Articles I, II, and III set forth the powers of the national Congress, president, and judiciary. The powers of the states are not specifically enumerated, for the most part. The absence of an enumeration of state powers concerned state rights advocates. The Tenth Amendment was included in the Bill of Rights to appease these concerns. That amendment reads, "The powers not delegated to the United States by the Constitution, nor prohibited by it to the States, are reserved to the States respectively, or to the people."

James Madison said, of the balance of powers between the national government and the states:

> The powers delegated by the proposed Constitution to the federal government are few and defined. Those which are to remain in the State governments are numerous and indefinite. The former will be exercised principally on external objects, such as war, peace, negotiation, and foreign commerce; with which last the power of taxation will, for the most part, be connected. The powers reserved to the several States will extend to all the objects which, in the ordinary course of affairs, concern the lives, liberties, and properties of people, and the internal order, improvement, and prosperity of the State.[2,3]

Several other clauses of the Constitution are critical to understanding federalism in the United States. First, Articles I, II, and III enumerate the powers of the national government by defining its three branches. Article I, Section 8, for instance, lists the various powers of Congress. There are many, including, for example, the power to coin and borrow money, establish a post office, establish and maintain military forces, promote the arts and sciences, and create immigration laws. Article I, Section 8, clause 18, is known as the **Necessary and Proper Clause.** This clause provides that Congress shall have the power to "make all Laws which shall be necessary and proper for carrying into execution the foregoing Powers, and all other Powers vested by this Constitution in the Government of the United States, or in any Department or Officer thereof." The "foregoing Powers" referred to in the clause are the enumerated powers of Congress, the president, and the judiciary. This clause, as discussed in Chapter 5, has been used to increase federal jurisdiction.

The **Commerce Clause,** also found in Article I, Section 8, clause 3, states that Congress has the power to regulate foreign and interstate commerce. Like the Necessary and Proper Clause, the Commerce Clause has been used to expand the realm of the federal government.

Article VI contains another important provision, the **Supremacy Clause.** The relevant part of Article VI provides that "This Constitution, and the Laws of the United States which shall be made in Pursuance thereof; and all Treaties made, or which shall be made, under the Authority of the United States, shall be the supreme Law of the Land; and the Judges in every State shall be bound thereby, any Thing in the Constitution or Laws of any State to the Contrary notwithstanding." In other words, any state or local law that conflicts with the Constitution or a treaty of the United States is invalid. Also, any state or local law that conflicts with any national law, when the policy area is exclusively national, is invalid.

Finally, the Civil War Amendments—Amendments 13, 14, and 15—contributed to an increase in federal power. The Fourteenth Amendment, for example, adopted in 1868, increased the authority of the federal government as against the states in regard to civil liberties. A post–Civil War amendment, it protects due process and equal protection rights of all persons in the United States. The amendment further provides that Congress "shall have power to enforce, by appropriate legislation, the provisions of this article." Legislation enacted to enforce this and the other Civil War Amendments limits the authority of the states.

Cyber Constitution
For quick interesting facts about the Constitution, including quizzes and games, visit www.constitutionfacts.com/

Federalism
(1) Pertaining to a system of government that is federal in nature. (2) The system by which the states of the United States relate to one another and to the federal government.

Necessary and Proper Clause
Article I of the Constitution grants to Congress the power to make all laws "necessary and proper" for carrying out its constitutional responsibilities. The Supreme Court has long interpreted this provision to mean that Congress has the right to enact not only those laws that are absolutely indispensable, but any laws that are reasonably related to effectuating the powers expressly granted to it by the Constitution.

Commerce Clause
The clause in Article I, Section 8, of the Constitution that gives Congress the power to regulate commerce between the states and between the United States and foreign countries. Federal statutes that regulate business and labor are based upon this power.

Supremacy Clause
The provision in Article VI of the Constitution that "this Constitution and the laws of the United States . . . shall be the supreme law of the land, and the judges in every state shall be bound thereby."

2.1(a) Dual, Hierarchical, and Cooperative Federalism

The balancing of federal and state powers has not been an easy task, and conflicts continue to arise. How exactly is the Tenth Amendment to be construed—as a limitation upon the national authority, or as a truism? How far does Congress's power over interstate commerce extend? What is necessary and proper?

Different theories have been developed concerning the nature of the federal–state relationship. One theory is that the federal government and state governments are co-equal sovereigns. This is known as **dual federalism.** Under this approach, the Tenth Amendment is read broadly and the Supremacy, Necessary and Proper, and Commerce Clauses are read narrowly. Only if the national government clearly has jurisdiction are its laws supreme over the states. Further, the Tenth Amendment is construed as establishing a particular sphere of state power; that is, it is considered an independent source of states' rights. As a result, there is a large group of exclusive state powers, a smaller group of exclusive federal powers, and few, if any, concurrently held powers. This approach predominated until the early twentieth century.

Another theory, **hierarchical federalism,** asserts that the federal government is supreme in the scheme. Using this approach, the Supremacy, Necessary and Proper, and Commerce Clauses are read expansively, whereas the Tenth Amendment is interpreted as not creating any specific state powers. Dual federalists, alternatively, view the Tenth Amendment as an independent source of states' rights. It is seen as establishing a state domain upon which the federal government may not encroach. Under the hierarchical federalism approach, the Tenth Amendment is viewed as a truism, a negative statement of state power. No domain is staked out; rather, the states are left with whatever the federal government cannot lawfully regulate. In addition, there is a large area over which the federal and state governments exercise concurrent jurisdiction, albeit with federal law reigning supreme. Intrastate commercial ventures that affect interstate commerce are examples.

A third model, which is less authority focused and more relationally focused, is cooperative federalism. A characteristic of cooperative federalism is increased interaction between the states and national government (and local forms of government) in an effort to effectively regulate and administer law and programs. The War on Drugs

dual federalism
The theory that the national government and the state governments are coequal sovereigns. The national government is supreme only when its jurisdiction is explicitly granted by the Constitution.

hierarchical federalism
The theory that the national government is supreme to the state governments. The powers of the national government are read broadly, and the Tenth Amendment is read as not granting any specific powers to the states.

SIDEBAR

THE FIRST PRESIDENT OF THE UNITED STATES AND THE FIRST CONSTITUTION OF THE UNITED STATES

Who was the first president of the United States? George Washington would be a common response. However, this is a matter of perspective.

The first national government maintained by the colonists was that under the Continental Congress. On September 5, 1774, Peyton Randolph was the first man elected president of that body; thus, he could be considered the first president of the United States. However, he possessed no executive authority and had less authority over the Continental Congress than the Speaker of the House of Representatives has over the House today.

John Hanson is another possible first president. He was the first president elected under the Articles of Confederation, although he also had little authority in this position.

Finally, the third possible first president is George Washington, the first person elected president under the current Constitution of the United States.

The current Constitution is not this nation's first. The Articles of Confederation and Perpetual Union, commonly known as the Articles, were adopted in 1781. In most people's eyes, this was the nation's first constitution. However, the colonists operated under British rule prior to winning independence. Although the British do not have a single document expounding their fundamental law, they do have a body of law that, when taken together, constitutes the British "Constitution." During this period, the colonists were subject to and received the benefits of the British Constitution. Arguably, then, the nation's first fundamental law was that of England.

Finally, it has been suggested that the fundamental laws of the several Native American nations represent the true first constitutions of this land.

waged during the Reagan and George H. W. Bush administrations and the War on Terror waged during the George W. Bush administration are examples of cooperative federalism, as federal law-enforcement agencies worked more closely with their counterpart state agencies, including sharing and coordinating resources, all toward policy objectives that were identical or substantially similar.

This aspect of cooperative federalism is a product of the political branches, the executive and legislative. The judiciary has little to do with the cooperative aspect because it does not engage in creation or development of programs and therefore does not interact with state authorities in the administration of those programs. The judiciary usually becomes involved when there is a dispute over jurisdiction; accordingly, it is normally concerned with defining the relative powers of the national and state governments.

The judiciary has had to deal with federalism issues in three contexts, and through its decisions in these contexts, it has advanced the supremacy of national power. First, under the **preemption doctrine,** state laws are invalidated if they interfere or conflict with national legislation. For example, the federal government has preempted state regulation of aviation. Thus, a state cannot enact airline safety regulations, because the federal government has completely regulated the area.

preemption doctrine
Doctrine that state laws that interfere with federal laws are invalid pursuant to the Supremacy Clause.

Illegal immigration.
Private individuals who refer to themselves as minutemen voluntarily patrol the border for illegal crossings. State officials have supported their actions while some federal border officials have been critical of their actions. Immigration will continue to be a hot federalism topic for years to come.
© Fred Greaves/Corbis

dormant Commerce Clause doctrine
The idea that state laws that unduly burden interstate commerce, even if the subject is unregulated by the national government, are invalid under federalism principles, because the regulation of interstate and foreign commerce belongs exclusively to the federal government.

intergovernmental immunity doctrine
The doctrine that both the states and the national government possess some immunity from the regulation of the other under federalism principles. Generally, the federal government enjoys greater immunity than do the states.

Second, state laws that interfere with interstate commerce, even if largely unregulated by the federal government, are invalidated. This is known as the **dormant Commerce Clause doctrine.** Pursuant to this doctrine, laws that discriminate against out-of-state market participants have been invalidated. Hence, a state law that prohibited the sale of milk produced outside New York at a lower price than milk produced within the state was held unconstitutional.[4]

Third, through the **intergovernmental immunity doctrine,** the national government possesses greater immunity from state regulation than the states do from federal regulation. That is, the federal government has greater authority to impose obligations upon the states than vice versa. Accordingly, federal overtime and wage laws apply against the states, but similar state laws do not protect federal employees. These three doctrines are discussed more fully in Chapter 7.

Which theory has been applied in the United States? Both the dual and hierarchical models have been applied by the Court cyclically. As discussed in Chapter 1, the Marshall Court was strongly nationalist. It operated under a hierarchical federalism approach. The same was true of the post–Civil War and late New Deal Courts. It was also true of the Burger Court in its late years.

The Taney Court, Pre–New Deal Court, and the early Burger Court followed the dual federalism approach. Notice that the Burger Court is split between the two theories. This is because the Court issued two opinions, only seven years apart, reaching opposite conclusions concerning the allocation of power between the national and state governments.[5] (See Figure 2-1.)

In many respects, it is easy to understand why the federal government would today possess broader authority than during the framers' time. At the time the Constitution was created, most commercial activities occurred locally. Industries were small and affected their local areas only. Travel and mobility were much more limited than today. National communication was minimal. People's social lives did not stretch far beyond their local communities.

Today, industries are large and have the ability to significantly affect not only other states, but also the nation and even the world. Through cyberspace and other forms of high-tech communication, nearly all persons are connected. Travel is no longer a local matter. Long-distance air, land, and sea carriers have become commonplace, as have immigration and emigration. Cross-national, international, and terrorism crime are more common and a larger threat than ever before. These changes have caused an

Era	Approach
Marshall	Hierarchical
	Ex: *McCulloch v. Maryland*
Taney to New Deal	Dual
	Ex: *New York v. Miln*
New Deal to Burger	Hierarchical
Burger	Dual (e.g., *National League*) shifting to hierarchical (e.g., *Garcia*)
Rehnquist	Dual
	Ex: *New York v. U.S.* (1992)
Roberts	Not yet clear, although focus appears to be shifting from state sovereignty to preemption.
	Ex: *Cuomo v. Clearing House, 557 U.S. ___ (2009)*

FIGURE 2-1
Supreme Court federalism eras

ILLEGAL IMMIGRATION: FEDERAL, STATE, OR LOCAL AUTHORITY?

Article I, Section 8, of the U.S. Constitution delegates the authority to "establish a uniform rule of naturalization" to the Congress of the United States. This provision, in combination with many other provisions delegating foreign affairs powers to the United States, makes it clear that immigration and naturalization are largely federal policy issues. And indeed, the United States has regulated immigration since the early days of the Constitution, beginning with the Alien Act of 1798. Today, the most significant legislation regulating the field is the Immigration and Naturalization Act of 1952, with several subsequent amendments. This law generally regulates who may enter the United States, for how long, and under what conditions. Many other federal laws exist, such as the Alien Registration Act of 1940, the Immigration Reform and Control Act of 1986, the Immigration Act of 1990, Patriot Act, and Enhanced Border Security and Visa Entry Reform Act, which, when taken in aggregate, amount to near-federal preemption of immigration.

Although immigration is nearly preempted, many state and local governments are confronting challenges that are a consequence of immigration. Immigrants impact state and local resources, as well as political and social life. Accordingly, there is an ongoing tug of war between federal and state control of immigration-related issues that have a local dimension. For example, may a state make aliens ineligible for welfare, education, or other benefits? May a state or local government impose registration requirements or impose conditions upon their residence? Generally, if the federal government has regulated the area, local law is invalid, even if not directly contradictory. For example, a state law that imposed registration and fingerprinting requirements beyond what federal law required was stricken down in *Hines v. Davidowitz,* 312 U.S. 52 (1941). On the other hand, the inherent authority (police power) of local authorities to arrest aliens for criminal violations is not seriously questioned. Whether a local authority may retain custody for purposes of trial against the wishes of the United States, which may want to begin deportation proceedings, is a more difficult constitutional question. While it is generally understood that state and local officers may make arrests while enforcing federal criminal laws, whether local officials may make arrests to enforce federal administrative and civil laws is not as clear.

In recent years, the immigration of illegal Mexicans into the United States has been controversial. By the early years of the 2000s, at least ten million illegal immigrants, most of whom were Mexican, resided in the United States. For many years, the impact these individuals had was most acutely felt by border states. By the late 1990s, many midwestern communities, who were home to large numbers of Mexican immigrants, were impacted as well.

Many people were of the opinion that the federal government should do more to control the influx of illegal Mexicans and that it could do more to locate and deport them after entry. As the impact of these individuals on localities grew, so did local reaction. An example is what transpired in Butler County, Ohio, in the first decade of the new century. Like many regions in the Midwest, Butler County had experienced a large influx of illegal immigrants. According to the sheriff of Butler County, Richard Jones, the county spent over $1 million in one year housing over 900 illegal aliens who were accused of criminal violations.

Concerned that the federal government was not adequately responding to illegal immigration, Sheriff Jones sent President Bush a letter imploring him to act. He also sent the U.S. Bureau of Immigration and Customs Enforcement (ICE) a bill for the costs associated with housing the illegal immigrants. The bill was not paid. Sheriff Jones also advocates the use of local police to identify and seize suspected illegal immigrants. Sheriff Jones found an ally in a local state representative, who proposed that legislation be enacted allowing illegal immigrants, who have been lawfully stopped by police for an unrelated traffic or other violation, to be charged with trespassing. Whether the state has the authority to make and enforce such a law is an interesting unanswered constitutional question. It is unlikely that this particular case will find itself before the Supreme Court because the sheriff averted the constitutional showdown by partnering with the United States in a good example of cooperative federalism. The United States authorized a handful of the sheriff's deputies to enforce federal immigration laws against individuals who are incarcerated in the Butler County jail for non-alien status crimes. ICE stationed agents in the sheriff's office for a short time to train deputies and facilitate cooperation. In essence, the sheriff's office will help process the deportation of individuals incarcerated in the jail even though the sheriff's office was not given carte blanche immigration enforcement authority.[6] Concerning the relative authorities of the state/local authorities as opposed to federal authorities, what constitutional values are implicated? Precedent aside, how would you weigh these conflicting interests?

Cyber Constitution
Cooperative Federalism
Many examples of cooperative federalism can be found on the Internet. Here are but a few: Antitrust Federalism, www.justice.gov/atr/public/speeches/250635.htm; Securities Federalism, www.sec.gov/info/smallbus/sbcoop.shtml; Consumer protection Federalism, www.fda.gov/downloads/ICECI/Inspections/IOM/UCM123506.pdf; Highways and Roads Federalism, http://cfr.vlex.com/vid/3-cooperation-authority-highway-departments-19725469; Environmental Federalism, www.epa.gov/compliance/resources/publications/monitoring/fifra/manuals/fifra/fiframanch_04.pdf

increase in the federal government's sphere. In some instances, the need for uniformity of law has caused the federal government to become involved. In others, the impetus has been the lack of resources of the states. In still others, social, technological, or political change has converted what was once a traditional state issue into a national one.

Finally, note that examples of cooperative federalism can be found during periods where dual and hierarchical federalism are dominant. Need, finances, and whether dual or hierarchical federalism is dominant all influence the extent to which states of the federal government cooperate.

2.1(b)   State and National Powers Compared

Some powers are held exclusively by the national government, others are held exclusively by the states, and some are held concurrently (see Figure 2-2). Then there are some actions that neither may take, because of rights retained by the people.

The powers of the national government are set out in the Constitution. Many of these are found in Article I, which enumerates the powers of Congress. Examples of

Exclusive National Powers	Concurrently Held Powers
Coining money	Taxing citizens
Foreign diplomacy	Chartering banks
Making treaties	Constructing roads
Regulating interstate and foreign commerce	Borrowing money
Establishing a post office	Eminent domain
Taxing imports and exports	Punishing crime
Regulating naturalization of citizenship	
Regulating immigration and emigration	**Powers Denied to Both**
Establishing bankruptcy law	Ex post facto laws
	Bills of attainder
Exclusive State Powers	Other encroachments upon civil rights
Providing for the health and welfare of state citizens	protected by the Constitution
General police and fire protection	
Licensing most professions	
Providing education, Regulate domestic relations	

FIGURE 2-2
Comparing state and federal powers

exclusive national powers are coining money, declaring war, conducting foreign diplomacy, making treaties, regulating interstate and international commerce, establishing a post office, taxing imports and exports, regulating naturalization of citizenship, and establishing bankruptcy law.

Article II, which establishes the national executive, grants to the president of the United States the responsibility of conducting foreign diplomacy and negotiating treaties. Treaties must be ratified by the Senate, however. The states are forbidden from engaging in diplomacy and entering into agreements with other nations.

Although the sovereignty of the states has diminished since the Constitution was created, certain areas remain within the exclusive domain of the states. Regulating for the health and welfare of citizens and regulating domestic affairs are within the state sphere.[7] Providing police and fire protection is another matter within a state's control. These functions make up what is generally referred to as the **police power.** The licensing of professions, such as physicians, plumbers, electricians, and attorneys, is regulated by the states. Education has also been a traditional state function. Just as the national government has the exclusive authority to regulate interstate and foreign commerce, the states possess the exclusive authority to regulate intrastate commerce.

police power
The power of government to make and enforce laws and regulations necessary to maintain and enhance the public welfare and to prevent individuals from violating the rights of others.

Finally, some powers are held concurrently. The power to tax citizens, charter banks and corporations, and build roads are examples.

If the authority over a policy area has been delegated to the federal or state governments, the delegatee is generally permitted to engage in regulation of any type—civil, administrative, or criminal. Frequently, the result is an overlapping of administrative functions, as well as civil and criminal laws. For example, the U.S. Department of Transportation has overlapping jurisdiction with state agencies charged with highway administration. Also, robbery of a federally insured or chartered bank is a violation of both state and federal criminal law. The state in which the robbery occurred has jurisdiction pursuant to its general police powers, and the federal government has jurisdiction by virtue of its charter or insurance coverage.

Finally, civil rights, or rights of the people, are a limitation upon the authority of both the states and the national government. Some of these rights are found in the original Constitution. For example, Article I forbids Congress from enacting ex post facto laws and bills of attainder. The Bill of Rights also protects a number of civil rights, such as freedom from self-incrimination, freedom of the press, freedom of assembly, and freedom from cruel and unusual punishment. The rights specifically mentioned in the Constitution are not intended to be exclusive. The Tenth Amendment, often referred to as the *state rights amendment,* also reserves powers to the people. Further, the Ninth Amendment reserves rights not mentioned in the Constitution exclusively to the people. It states, "The enumeration in the Constitution, of certain rights, shall not be construed to deny or disparage others retained by the people." To date, the Supreme Court has not read this amendment as solely reserving any particular right. Although it has cited it as supporting rights founded largely upon another right, for example, due process.

Be aware, however, that the Supreme Court has determined that the Bill of Rights was intended to be a limitation upon the national government, not the states. Support for this decision can be found in the reaction to James Madison's proposed Bill of Rights. He proposed seventeen rights that were eventually consolidated and winnowed to twelve, from which the ten we know today were ratified. One that was rejected provided that states may not "violate the equal right of conscience, freedom of the press, or trial by jury in criminal cases."

This changed, however, as a result of the post–Civil War Amendments (Amendments 13–15). Specifically, the Court has determined that the Fourteenth Amendment's Due Process Clause "incorporates" most of the amendments. Any amendment incorporated applies against the states. Nearly every amendment has been incorporated, and

incorporation
The Bill of Rights
was intended to be
applied only against the
national government.
However, the Supreme
Court determined that
most of the rights
contained therein were
"incorporated" by the
Due Process Clause of the
Fourteenth Amendment.
A right is *incorporated*
if it is fundamental
and necessary to an
ordered liberty. Once
incorporated, the right
applies against the states.

therefore, the Bill of Rights limits the authority of the states as well as of the national government.[8] See Chapters 5 and 9 for more thorough discussions of **incorporation.**

The debate over the balancing of federal and state authorities continues today. Proponents of "states' rights" claim that the national government, through all three of its branches, has emasculated state sovereignty. The national government has extended its authority in two primary ways. First, the sphere of the national government's jurisdiction has widened considerably, through a liberal reading of the Constitution's delegation of authority to the national government (i.e., Commerce and Necessary and Proper Clauses) and a narrow interpretation of the Tenth Amendment. This has already been mentioned and is the subject of further discussion later in the chapters on Congress and contemporary federalism.

Second, if the federal government wants to effectuate a policy objective that falls within the exclusive (or concurrent) jurisdiction of the states, it may impose its will on the states through economic coercion. It does this by attaching conditions to subsidies, grants, and appropriations made to the states. For example, to further the national government's policy of racial integration at public events, one condition placed on money awarded to states is that it may not be used to fund segregated functions. The fifty-five-mile-per-hour speed limit is another example. The regulation of state and local highways is outside the direct regulation of the national government. When the federal government wanted to impose a nationwide fifty-five-mile-per-hour speed limit, it accomplished that aim by threatening to withhold funding from states that did not adopt the fifty-five-mile-per-hour limit. The federal government similarly coerced the states to come into compliance with federal clean air laws by threatening to withhold federal highway funds.[9]

Various presidents have attempted to address states' rights concerns, such as Presidents Nixon and Ford, who advocated a "new federalism," whereby the federal government would place fewer conditions on the use of federal subsidies. President Carter implemented rules requiring federal administrative officers to work directly with state officials to accomplish policy objectives. President Carter's approach, as you have learned, is a form of *shared and cooperative federalism.* President Reagan advocated states' rights, claiming that authority should be returned to the states; however, little authority was actually transferred during his administration.

As we have seen, the political branches of government are not alone in struggling with the complexity of federalism. The Supreme Court has wavered between dual and hierarchical federalism, with its approach being dependent upon the ideology of its members.

Undoubtedly, the debate over the allocation of authorities between the states and national government will continue as an inherent feature of a federalist system like that of the United States. The vacillation between dual and hierarchical federalism will also continue, as a result of political, social, and economic factors. At times when national or international concerns consume the nation's attention and conscience, such as war and economic crisis, hierarchical federalism will predominate. During periods when there are fewer pressing national problems, dual federalism is more likely to predominate.

2.2 SEPARATION OF POWERS

Under the Articles of Confederation, there was no national judiciary. Also, there was no independent executive, as the president was a member of, and selected by, the Congress. The framers were heavily influenced by the theories of philosophers James Harrington, John Locke, and Charles de Montesquieu.[10] These men advanced the theory that, to avoid tyranny, a separation or division of governmental authority must exist. To the framers, the need for a separation of powers was more than a theory. They had had

SEPARATION OF POWERS			
		Executive	Legislative	Judicial

FEDERALISM	United States	President ■ Executive officers ■ Inferior officers and most federal agencies	Congress ■ Senate ■ House	Federal courts ■ Article III ■ Supreme Court ■ Appeals courts ■ Trial courts
	States	Governor ■ Executive officers and most state agencies	State legislatures ■ Typically bicameral	State courts ■ Highest court ■ Intermediate appeal ■ Trial

FIGURE 2-3
Dividing governmental power

experience with a centralized authority, the English Crown, and had found it arbitrary and unjust. Concerning the centralization of powers, James Madison stated, "[t]he accumulation of all power legislative, executive and judiciary in the same hands, whether hereditary, self-appointed, or elective, may justly be pronounced the very definition of tyranny."[11]

Although the phrase "separation of powers" does not appear in the Constitution, the framers employed its architecture in their design of the new government. Hence, there is a horizontal division of governmental authority, just as there is a vertical division (federalism) (see Figure 2-3).

Horizontally, the national government's authorities are divided among three branches: the legislative, executive, and judicial. This division is found in the first three articles of the Constitution. Article I establishes Congress and sets forth its authorities. Congress is comprised of two chambers: the House of Representatives and the Senate. Article II establishes the presidency and also sets forth the authorities of the executive. Article III establishes the Supreme Court and such inferior courts as Congress may establish and sets forth the authorities of the judiciary. Indeed, Congress has exercised the authority to create lower judicial tribunals on several occasions. Today, there are three levels of federal courts. The trial-level courts are called *district courts*. Appeals are taken to the courts of appeals, which are divided into thirteen circuits. Finally, the Supreme Court sits at the apex of the judiciary. In addition, there are a few specialty courts in the federal system. See Figure 2-4, which diagrams the federal court structure.

The authority and responsibilities of the three branches are not equally well defined by the Constitution. Congress's authority is the best defined, with the president's and the judiciary's falling second and third, respectively.

Congress is responsible for making the nation's laws; the president is responsible for administering and enforcing the nation's laws, conducting foreign affairs, and negotiating treaties, and is the commander-in-chief of the military; the judiciary is responsible for administering justice, resolving disputes, and interpreting the law. Today, the judiciary also plays a role in preserving the balance of powers and protecting civil liberties.

As a general proposition, one branch may not exercise the functions of any other coordinate branches. However, no one function is vested entirely in one branch. The framers went one step further in preventing abuse—they incorporated a system of checks and balances.

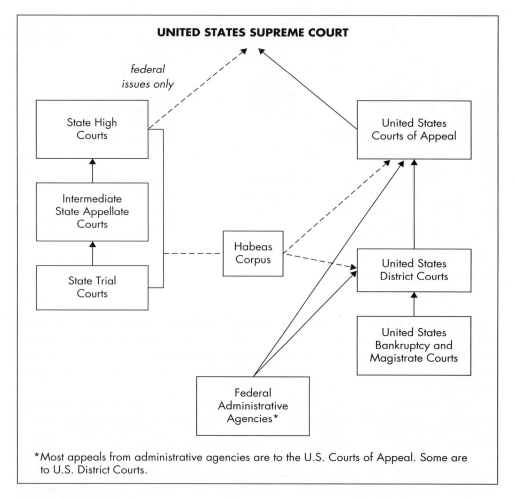

FIGURE 2-4
Courts and appellate procedure

2.3 CHECKS AND BALANCES

Although the framers intended to separate the three governmental branches, they did not intend for the branches to be "wholly unconnected with each other."[12] The branches do come into contact with one another on occasion. For example, executive officials and judges may testify at congressional hearings concerning their functions and needs. The president, justices of the Supreme Court, and the entire Congress assemble for the president's State of the Union address. The branches also come into contact (albeit often indirect contact) as a result of the many checks and balances found in the Constitution.

Through checks and balances, the framers prevented one branch from possessing absolute authority over any particular function. Rather, the functions delegated to one branch are "checked" by, or shared with, another branch. This provides balance to the system by keeping each branch accountable to its coordinate branches, and ultimately, the people. Several checks can be found in the Constitution (see Figure 2-5). Some scholars argue that the system of checks and balances is so robust that there is no genuine "separation of powers."

Congress is responsible for making the law. It is checked in this function by the president, who may veto legislation. The president is then checked by Congress, which can override a veto with a two-thirds majority. Also, Congress enacts laws, but it depends on the president to enforce them. The judiciary also checks Congress. Legislation that conflicts with the Constitution may be declared void by the courts.

The president conducts foreign affairs and negotiates treaties. Congress, the Senate in particular, must ratify treaties. The president is the commander-in-chief of the

Authority	Checked By
President negotiates treaties	Senate ratification
President nominates judges and officers	Senate confirmation
President oversees federal bureaucracy	Congress creates, funds, and establishes responsibilities and authorities of agencies, and sets qualifications for officers
Congress enacts laws	Presidential approval and judicial review
Presidential veto of bills passed by Congress	Congressional override
President is commander-in-chief of the military	Congress declares war, creates rules regulating the military, and establishes military budgets
Courts exercise judicial review	Impeachment by Congress and constitutional amendment process
Performance of Elected Officials	People, through the vote

FIGURE 2-5
Examples of checks and balances

military, but Congress possesses significant authority over the military as well. It is charged with making rules regulating the military and is responsible for declaring war. The president has been delegated the authority to nominate federal judges and other governmental officers, but the appointments are final only after confirmation by the Senate. As a check on both the president and the judiciary, Congress holds the authority of impeachment. Finally, through judicial review, the judiciary checks the president's actions for constitutionality.

The judiciary is also checked. Article III judges are nominated by the president, and the Senate must approve the nominations. Congress has the authority to remove cases from the appellate jurisdiction of the Supreme Court and, presumably, could limit the jurisdiction of lower courts. Also, because the courts inferior to the Supreme Court were created by Congress, they may be abolished by Congress. As previously mentioned, judges may be removed through impeachment by Congress. The states and Congress (the people) check the constitutional pronouncements of the Court through the amendment process.

Therefore, no branch is completely independent in the performance of its functions. Because of these checks, interbranch cooperation, especially between Congress and the president, is increased and the potential for unlawful, unethical, and unreasonable governmental behavior is decreased.

Another method of checking government is through the varying methods of selecting governmental officials. This authority is diffused—that is, no one entity is responsible for choosing the representatives of the people. Even within Congress, for example, two methods of selection were incorporated by the original framers: members of the House of Representatives were elected directly by the people, and senators were chosen by state legislatures. The method of selecting senators by the states did not change until the Seventeenth Amendment was adopted in 1913. Today, members of both houses are selected by direct election.

The president is elected by the electoral college, a small group of people chosen at the state level nationwide. Federal judges are nominated by the president and must be confirmed by the Senate. Other federal officials, such as diplomats and cabinet officials, must undergo the same process.

Federalism, separation of powers, and checks and balances are all intended to prevent tyranny and the usurpation of state sovereignty. In the following five chapters, these issues are examined more closely. In Chapters 3, 4, and 5, the authorities of the national legislative, executive, and judicial branches are discussed. Chapter 6 discusses a particular separation of powers problem, that of delegations to administrative agencies.

The authorities of the states as opposed to the national government are explored in greater detail in Chapter 7. The remainder of the text is devoted to the rights of the people.

2.4 FORMS OF STATE AND FEDERAL LAW

The division of governmental authority into state and federal levels and between branches at each level creates a complex system within which there are many forms of law, from many sources, at many levels.

Of course, the fundamental law of the nation, and the subject of this text, is the U.S. Constitution. Each state also has a constitution. The U.S. Constitution is the highest form of law. The U.S. Constitution recognizes, inherently through its structural provisions and explicitly in the Ninth and Tenth Amendments, that certain authorities belong to the states. Accordingly, state constitutions are the highest form of law for state law subjects. Similarly, the highest court of each state is the final arbiter of state law, not the Supreme Court of the United States. When in conflict, state law falls to federal law under the Supremacy Clause of Article VI, and the Supreme Court of the United States is the final interpreter of federal law.

As you will learn in a later chapter, the Constitution assigns the authority to make federal law to the U.S. Congress. The laws enacted by this body are known as public laws or statutes. These laws are organized by subject matter into the U.S. Code. Each state also has a legislature that makes law. Many lawmaking bodies also exist at the local level, such as city councils, county councils, and school boards. Local laws are generally known as ordinances.

Although largely an enforcement officer, the president, as well as his gubernatorial counterparts, has limited lawmaking authority. The common vehicle for presidential lawmaking is the executive order. If legitimate, an executive order has the authority of a statute. The president has the authority to make law in those subject areas that are inherently executive or where Congress has appropriately delegated the authority to the president. Orders managing the operations of government are examples of the former because as the chief executive, the president is responsible for managing the daily operations of government. Many examples of congressional delegations of authority enabling presidents to issue executive orders can be found and will be discussed later in this text. Other executive tools exist through which "law" is sometimes made, such as military orders and presidential proclamations. Statute requires that all executive orders be published in the *Federal Register,* a U.S. government publication of new regulations, executive orders and proclamations, notices by government agencies of impending action, and other documents required to be published by government agencies.

Administrative rulemaking is another form of law. Congress often empowers administrative agencies to create rules, also known as regulations, to enforce their mandates. When properly created, administrative rules have the authority of legislation. In most cases, the authority to make rules must be delegated from the legislative authority. Administrative regulations are always subordinate to legislation. Today, there are more administrative rules than statutes. By the 1990s, the Code of Federal Regulations, where all federal rules can be found, exceeded 135,000 pages. State agencies have, in varying degrees, similar authority to make regulations.

At the state level and, to a lesser extent, the federal level, the common law continues to be an important source of law. The common law, which is of English heritage, has a judicial origin. Before Parliament existed in England, judges developed legal principles to guide their decision making. These legal principles generally followed the customs and practices of the time. For political and prudential reasons, the doctrine of *stare decisis et non quieta movera* (Latin for "stand by precedents and do not disturb settled points") was developed in early English courts. This doctrine requires that all lower courts adhere to the law announced by a superior court when the facts of the present case are identical or nearly identical to the facts of the earlier case. The application of this

Cyber Constitution
Federal Administrative Law and Records To see the Federal Register, Code of Federal Regulations, and other administrative documents, go to www.gpo.gov/fdsys/

Cyber Constitution
Common Law For more information on Common Law, go to www.britannica.com/EBchecked/topic/128386/common-law

doctrine over time had the effect of homogenizing the law. Said another way, the law began to be common to all. The colonists who founded the United States brought the English common law with them. Today, Congress and the state legislatures, and administrative agencies as described earlier, are the primary source of new laws. The common law continues to fill in the gaps where legislatures have not spoken, and it continues to be important in understanding and defining existing law. Of course, any common law principle that is contrary to the Constitution of the United States, or a state common law principle if inconsistent with a state constitution, is invalid. For example, ancient courts would often declare an act to be criminal, and therefore create a precedent of the act's criminality, on a case-by-case basis. So, there had to be a first case where a court declared murder to be a crime. Now that we have legislatures, some courts have found that the creation of common law crimes violates the Due Process Clause's guarantee of notice of which acts are criminal. This idea is expressed in the Latin phrase *nulla poena sine lege,* meaning "there shall be no crime if there is no statute."

Finally, judicial decisions interpreting the Constitution and statutes are another form of law. A perennial debate exists over whether this is lawmaking or simply interpretation. For some people, departures from precedent by the Supreme Court amount to lawmaking. For others, interpretation is a natural process, and the limits on this authority, such as the ability to amend a constitution or statute that is being interpreted, keep it from being pure lawmaking.

2.5 MODERN CHALLENGES

Dividing governmental power and constructing checks on the allocations of powers are essential to free society to democracy. Recent events have challenged these notions. The new and very different "war" against terror; the worldwide economic depression, including the economic destabilization of several nations; the rise and threat of technology to nation-states, as evinced by the 2009 Wikileaks event; and the breakdown of several trusted institutions in the United States and elsewhere have resulted in an increase in federal, particularly executive, authorities. This rise in executive power has not been without its critics. Concerns about maintaining a balance of authority and for losses of civil liberties are genuine and will be part of the nation's discussion as it transforms in the upcoming years.

2.6 SUMMARY

Even though the framers wanted to increase the national government's authority from its weak position under the Articles of Confederation, they did not want to centralize all governmental authority into one hand or into a small number of hands. Instead, they controlled authority through structure. First, they created a federation. Second, they further divided federal authority into three departments or branches. These authority divisions are not absolute, however. The federal and state governments often share jurisdiction, and the three branches of the federal government check each other. These additional features of the U.S. government are intended to protect the people against tyranny.

The precise relationship between the federal and state governments is continually being redefined. The social, economic, and political circumstances of each case determine the legal outcome of any jurisdictional conflicts. The Supreme Court has vacillated between the dual and hierarchical federalism perspectives since the Constitution was enacted. There is no question, however, that the federal government has experienced enormous growth and increases in authority during the past two hundred years. Some of this can be attributed to population growth and the globalization of economic, travel, political, and social aspects of the world. Other factors, such as internal politics, have also contributed to the current federal scheme. As you will learn later, there was a shift on the Supreme Court during the Rehnquist years favoring limited federal authority and reinforcing state authority. The Roberts Court appears to be shifting its focus from the traditional state versus federal power questions that interested the Rehnquist Court to more complex federal preemption, legislative and administrative, of state laws.

REVIEW QUESTIONS

1. Define federalism and separation of powers.
2. Why did the framers separate governmental authority?
3. List two authorities held exclusively by the federal government, two held exclusively by the state governments, and two held concurrently.
4. Identify two checks and balances provided for in the Constitution.
5. Briefly describe the functions of each of the three branches of government.

ASSIGNMENTS: CONSTITUTIONAL LAW IN ACTION

The Constitution in Your Community

Assume that you are working for a law firm that has just been retained by Steve Smith, a local home owner who is upset with his local government's enforcement of a zoning code prohibiting him from building a fence in his front yard. Mr. Smith is thinking about challenging the legitimacy of the zoning code. But before examining the zoning code, your supervising attorney would like to get some background research on the makeup and structure of the local government. From where does the zoning board get its authority (e.g., state constitution, state statute, local ordinance), and is this delegation of authority consistent with the state constitution? If legitimate, does the zoning board have the authority to make the fencing decision? Is there a provision for appeal? Prepare a short brief answering these questions.

Going Federal

Assume the following facts:

With presidential approval, Congress enacts the following statute:

Green Construction and Conservation Act

Section One Purpose and Constitutional Source The existing decentralized system of building and construction codes is inefficient, wasteful, and disparate. Uniform standards that challenge the nation to increase energy efficiency and enable businesses to easily conduct business across state lines without confronting different standards will lessen the nation's dependence on oil and improve the economy. Therefore, pursuant to its authority under the Commerce Clause of Article I of the Constitution of the United States, Congress enacts this law.

Section Two Establishment and Mission of DBCC There is established a Department of Building Construction and Conservation (DBCC), an executive department of the United States. The mission of the DBCC is to maximize the energy efficiency of all building, renovation, and construction of homes and businesses in the United States. The Director of DBCC shall be appointed by the president with the advice and consent of the Senate. The Director shall report to the Secretary of Commerce. The Director shall appoint the necessary inspectors and other officials to execute the responsibilities delegated herein.

Section Three Standards The Director shall establish through formal rulemaking procedures a set of standards for all construction, building, and renovation.

These standards shall be designed to maximize energy efficiency and safety. The standards shall provide minimum standards of energy efficiency and shall provide incentives for builders to exceed the minimum standards. The Director shall also establish through formal rulemaking the procedures and processes for the issuance of building, construction, and renovation permits, including inspection, approval, fines and other punitive action, and appeals of decisions.

Section Four Preemption These provisions shall preempt all state and local laws that regulate construction and building.

The DBCC was formed, the Director and other employees were appointed, and the standards were promulgated. John Rodriguez, a local builder, has received notice from the DBCC that he has been charged with noncompliance with the minimum energy standards in the construction of an office building. His hearing on the matter before an administrative law judge is scheduled for six weeks from the date he received the notice. Although he applied and received a permit for the project, he objects to the federal government's regulation of the industry as exceeding its constitutional authority. He noted his objection on his permit application. It is true that he did not comply with the energy standards, which he believes are so expensive to implement that they are onerous. Mr. Rodriguez lost his case before the administrative law judge and he was fined $10,000. He has appealed the decision to a federal trial court. He has raised only one issue on appeal, whether Congress has the authority to regulate the construction industry. You work for the U.S. district judge hearing the case. Prepare a memorandum for him analyzing the preemption question raised by Mr. Rodriguez. Include a final recommendation to the judge about how to rule.

Moot Court

The U.S. separation of powers between the branches, particularly between the president and Congress and within Congress itself, was on the international stage in 2011 during the debt ceiling debates. Federal law establishes a limit to how much debt the United States may carry. Changes to the debt ceiling must undergo standard lawmaking procedure, (e.g., approval by both houses of Congress and presentation to the president). The debt ceiling, as it is commonly known, has been raised on many occasions by both Republic and Democratic presidents and by congresses dominated by both parties. If the nation were to reach its debt ceiling and no legislation were enacted to increase it, all of the federal government, with the exception of certain national security and other agencies, would have to close.

As the United States neared the debt ceiling in 2011, negotiations between the Obama administration and the leadership of both houses of Congress began. The discussions went on for months and were punctuated by disagreements, inflammatory rhetoric, and walk-outs. The 2011 debt ceiling discussions were more difficult than in the past because of the election of a number of "tea party" members and other fiscal conservatives in Congress whose political and economic philosophies (and campaign platforms) included smaller government and less federal debt. Most of these individuals desired to see cuts in entitlement programs, such as social security and Medicare/Medicaid. These individuals, newly elected in 2010 with a sense of a strong mandate from the people to lower the debt, were unwavering in their demands for a plan to lower the national debt, sometimes putting them at odds with their own party's leadership in Congress. President Obama, on the other hand, strongly opposed reductions in some entitlement programs. Of course, these discussions happened in larger geo-economic climate that was characterized by a worldwide recession, austerity measures, and even violence. A deal was reached two days before the debt ceiling was reached, avoiding the closing of many federal agencies and the suspension of many services. The compromise called for increasing the preexisting $14 trillion debt ceiling by an additional $2.4 trillion with subsequent decreases of $2.4 trillion over ten years. Many viewed the difficulties in the discussions, as well as the eleventh-hour compromise, as evidence of a broken political system. Others, such as conservative commentator George Will, suggested that what transpired is entirely what the framers intended. Applying what you have learned about the framers' philosophies, objectives, and the structure of government they created, debate, in groups of two, whether the debt ceiling discussions of 2011 are an example of the success of the U.S. separation of powers or whether they represent a defect in the system. Each team of two should prepare a five-minute argument.

Sources   http://topics.nytimes.com/topics/reference/timestopics/subjects/n/national_debt_us/index.html, www.charlierose.com/view/interview/11834

NOTES

1. The Federalist No. 47.
2. The Federalist No. 45.
3. Essay published in the *New York Journal* on October 18, 1787, taken from *The Creation of the Constitution* 109–111. Opposing Viewpoints Series (Greenhaven Press 1995).
4. *Baldwin v. G.A.F. Seelig, Inc.*, 294 U.S. 511 (1935).
5. The two cases are *National League of Cities v. Usery*, 426 U.S. 833 (1976), and *San Antonio Independent School District v. Rodriguez*, 411 U.S. 1 (1973).
6. Butler County Sheriff Reveals Federal Partnership, www.wlwt.com/news/15015422/detail.html.
7. See *Elk Grove Unified School District v. Newdow*, 542 U.S. 1 (2004) in Chapter 4.
8. The amendments that have not been incorporated are the right to a jury trial in civil cases (Seventh Amendment), the right to grand jury indictment (Fifth Amendment), and the right to have a twelve-person jury (Sixth Amendment and case law).
9. For a discussion of this topic, see William Klein, "Pressure or Compulsion? Federal Highway Fund Sanctions of the Clean Air Act Amendments of 1990," 26 *Rutgers L.J.* 855 (1995).
10. See James Harrington, *Oceana* (1656); John Locke, *Civil Government* (1690); and Charles de Montesquieu, *Spirit of the Laws* (1748).
11. The Federalist No. 47.
12. The Federalist No. 48.

3

The Judiciary: Its Role and Jurisdiction

We are under a Constitution, but the Constitution is what the judges say it is, and the judiciary is the safeguard of our liberty and of our property under the Constitution.

CHIEF JUSTICE CHARLES EVANS HUGHES[1]

Interpretation is inescapably a kind of legislation.

JEROME FRANK[2]

LEARNING OBJECTIVES
At the end of this chapter you should be able to:

- Outline the structure of the federal court system, as defined by the Constitution and statute.

- Explain the appointment and removal processes for federal judges, both Article III and other; discuss the formal and informal constraints on judges and courts; and explain the role and responsibilities of courts in the United States.

- Explain the jurisdictions of federal and state courts, including the application of federal and state laws by both.

- Explain the jurisdiction of federal courts in detail, including the various limitations on federal judicial jurisdiction.

- Identify, compare, and contrast the four primary methods of interpreting the Constitution.

- Identify and explain three canons of construction.

- Define and explain stare decisis and its application by the Supreme Court and lower courts.

- Identify and discuss a contemporary issue concerning federal court jurisdiction.

- Demonstrate comfort with reading judicial opinions.

- Brief a judicial opinion with little outside assistance. You should be successful in identifying the relevant facts. You should be successful in identifying the legal issue and analyzing the court's rationale in at least 33 percent of your briefs.

- Apply, with assistance, what you have learned to a new set of facts that are given to you.

3.1 THE FEDERAL COURT SYSTEM

Chapters 3 through 5 cover the three branches of the federal government in detail. Because of the special role the judiciary plays in constitutional law, that branch is examined first, followed by the legislative and executive branches.

You already learned about a very important judicial authority, judicial review, in Chapter 1. Indeed, judicial review is a hallmark of United States constitutionalism and rule of law. In what follows, learn more about U.S. courts, beginning with the structure of the federal court system.

Article III, Section 1, of the federal Constitution provides that the "judicial power of the United States, shall be vested in one Supreme Court, and such inferior Courts as the Congress may from time to time ordain and establish." There is no mention of the number of judges that shall sit on the Supreme Court or of how or what lower courts may be established. Further, the jurisdictional statement (which is discussed later in this chapter) is vague. It is true, as shown in Chapters 4 and 5, that the framers gave considerably more attention to defining the legislative and executive branches. This probably reflects their fears that the executive and legislative branches posed a greater threat to freedom and state sovereignty than did the judiciary. Alexander Hamilton said that although the executive "holds the sword of the community" and the legislature holds the purse strings and the power to make the laws, the judiciary,

> on the contrary, has no influence over either the sword or the purse; no direction either of the strength or of the wealth of the society, and can take no active resolution whatever. It may truly be said to have neither FORCE nor WILL but merely judgment; and must ultimately depend upon the aid of the executive arm even for the efficacy of its judgments. . . . It proves incontestably that the judiciary is beyond comparison the weakest of the three departments of power.[3]

The framers expressly created the Supreme Court. They left it to Congress (through legislation involving the president) to determine the number of justices that would sit on the Court. Initially, the number was set at six—one chief justice and five associate justices—by the Judiciary Act of 1789. The number changed to five between 1801 and 1807. In 1807 it rose to nine justices. In 1837, the Court had its greatest number of justices, ten. In 1866, the number returned to seven, and in 1869 the number again became nine, where it has remained ever since.

Franklin D. Roosevelt, displeased with decisions of the Court that invalidated some of his New Deal reforms, proposed increasing the size of the Court. Convinced that younger justices, or possibly justices he nominated, would be more receptive to his attempts to pull the nation out of the Depression, he proposed that one additional justice be appointed for every justice over the age of seventy. Had his proposal become law, he would have been able to appoint six new justices, increasing the size of the Court to fifteen. The proposal was controversial, and ultimately unsuccessful, and represents the boldest attempt yet by a president to control the decision-making of the Court.

appellate jurisdiction
The authority of one court to review the proceedings of another court or of an administrative agency.

original jurisdiction
The jurisdiction of a trial court, as distinguished from the jurisdiction of an appellate court.

The Supreme Court sits at the apex of the judiciary of the United States and for the most part exercises **appellate jurisdiction.** Appeals from the U.S. courts of appeals and from the highest courts of the states (on federal issues) are taken to the Supreme Court. In rare instances, the Supreme Court acts as a court of **original jurisdiction,** which means that a case does not come to the Court by appeal, but rather is initiated in the Supreme Court. See Figure 2-4 for a chart of the federal court system. The original and appellate jurisdiction of the Supreme Court is discussed at greater length later in this chapter.

Congress immediately created inferior federal courts through the Judiciary Act of 1789. Through that statute, three circuit courts of appeals and thirteen district courts were created. Initially, there were no circuit judges. Circuit court panels were comprised of one district judge and two Supreme Court justices.

The organization of the system changed on several occasions, most notably in 1891, when ninety new judgeships were created.

Today, there are eleven geographical circuits with a court of appeals in each. There are two additional courts of appeals, one in the District of Columbia and another for the federal circuit. Hence, there are thirteen courts of appeals in the federal system.

The courts of appeals are the intermediate-level appellate courts of the federal system. (See Figure 3-1, which diagrams the judicial circuits of the United States.) These courts hear appeals from district courts, specialty courts, and, in some instances, administrative tribunals. Each court of appeals has many associate judges (e.g., eleven)

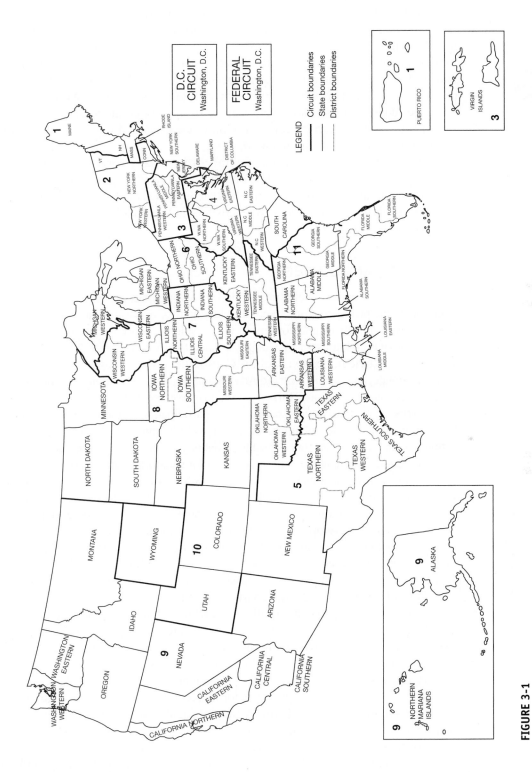

FIGURE 3-1

U.S. courts of appeals and U.S. district courts

en banc
French term for "on the bench." A court, particularly an appellate court, with all the judges sitting together (sitting en banc) in a case.

Cyber Constitution
Federal Courts
The official website of the federal courts is www. uscourts.gov

and one chief judge. Cases are usually heard by three judges, although a court may sit **en banc** so that all the members of the court hear a single case.

In addition, there are ninety-four district courts in the United States. These are the federal trial courts. Each state has at least one district court, and larger states have as many as four. Districts may be further geographically divided into divisions.

The number of judges in each district varies according to need. District judges usually sit individually. However, Congress has provided for three-judge district courts in particular cases. Even when a three-judge court is statutorily mandated, one judge may be designated as the chief of the panel and be delegated the authority to make some decisions alone, such as whether preliminary injunctions or stays should be ordered. All three judges must sit, however, at trial. In most three-judge district court trials, appeal is taken directly to the Supreme Court. See Chapter 4 for a discussion of when three-judge district courts are required.

Finally, Congress has created a number of specialty courts. The Claims Court, the Court of International Trade, the Foreign Intelligence Surveillance Act (FISA), the Tax Court, and the Court of Customs and Patent Appeals are examples. In addition, a system of bankruptcy courts and U.S. magistrate-judges handles a considerable amount of the federal caseload.

3.2 FEDERAL JUDGES

The framers considered several proposals for the appointment of federal judges: first, selection by the president alone; second, selection by Congress alone; third, selection by Congress with the advice and consent of the president; fourth, selection by the president with the advice and consent of Congress, specifically, the Senate.[4] Their decision is embodied in Article II, Section 2, of the Constitution, which provides that the president "shall nominate, and by and with the Advice and Consent of the Senate, shall appoint . . . Judges of the supreme Court." First, a nominee is selected by the president. The language of the clause appears to anticipate senatorial participation in the form of "advice." The final nomination decision is, however, exclusively the president's. A president's nomination is sent to the Senate for "consent"—that is, the Senate may either deny or confirm the nomination. A simple majority is required for senatorial confirmation.

The Constitution does not specify criteria for either nomination or confirmation. There is no requirement, for example, that a nominee be trained in, or have experience in, law. The qualifications criteria are left to the president and Senate to define. Over time, a process has developed for nominations. Presidents consult their closest political advisors about potential nominees to the Supreme Court, and the U.S. Department of Justice screens such candidates. For years, the American Bar Association also screened the candidates. President George W. Bush ended this practice in 2001.

For judges of federal district courts, a practice has evolved of inviting the senator of the state where the judgeship shall reside, who is of the same party as the president, to make a recommendation of one or more candidates to the president. For each circuit court, all of which encompass more than one state, a procedure, such as assignment of specific seats to states, has been established.

Presidents commonly accept the recommendations of home state senators. A president who does not accept a senatorial recommendation faces a possible veto through *senatorial courtesy*. Through this informal practice, which dates to a 1789 decision not to confirm a nomination to a nonjudicial position by President Washington that was opposed by a home state senator, senators agree not to confirm a nominee who does not have the support of a senator from the state where the judge will reside. Attorney General Robert Kennedy described the process as senatorial nomination with senatorial confirmation. Over the years, several presidents and a few senators have attempted to abolish or modify the senatorial courtesy practice. Presidents Carter and Reagan were both somewhat successful in watering down the system, and in 2002,

Senator Orrin Hatch, a Republican and chair of the Senate Judiciary Committee, instituted a policy of allowing hearings on nominees who were not supported by home state senators. This led to the use of the filibuster by Democratic senators to block several nominees to lower courts. The future of senatorial courtesy is unknown.

On occasion, presidents have made appointments when the Senate is in recess, as provided for in Article II, Section 2, clause 3. *Recess appointments* expire at the close of the next session of the Senate. Accordingly, such appointees must be nominated and undergo Senate confirmation to receive a life appointment.

There is little disagreement that presidential nomination discretion is nearly unlimited. Historically, presidents have attempted to influence U.S. policy by nominating justices and judges who possess a desired political or legal philosophy. Research confirms that presidents usually nominate individuals of similar political ideology to the Supreme Court.[5]

There is a long-standing debate, however, about the Senate's confirmation role. One school of thought holds that the Senate should limit its review to basic qualifications and that it should confirm nominees unless they are scoundrels or clearly incompetent. Several presidents, including John Adams, have held this view. Another school of thought holds that the president and Senate are coequals in the process and that the Senate has an obligation to thoroughly examine nominees. If this is true, another question arises: Should the Senate focus exclusively on nonpolitical qualifications, or may it consider a nominee's political and legal values and philosophy?

In recent years, some commentators have suggested that the confirmation process is becoming increasingly political, focusing too much on candidate ideology and not enough on objective abilities and qualifications. The failure to confirm federal appellate judge Robert Bork as associate justice of the Supreme Court is often cited as an example. Constitutional scholars Lee Epstein and Jeffrey A. Segal disagree. They assert that ideology and politics have long been factors in both nomination and confirmation processes. Since the earliest nominations, according to Epstein and Segal, presidents and senators have been partisan in their appointments to the bench. In 1800, after President John Adams, a Federalist, lost his re-election bid to Thomas Jefferson, a Republican, he and the Federalist-controlled Senate quickly filled several judicial vacancies and created and filled several new judgeships with individuals who shared their political affiliation. This resulted in one of the most important judicial decisions in the U.S. history, *Marbury v. Madison,* which was discussed in greater detail in Chapter 1. Consider further that 60 percent of all nominees personally knew the president who nominated them.[6]

Even the creation of judgeships has been, at times, political. Consider, for example, the 1891 creation of ninety new judgeships mentioned earlier. The law establishing the new positions passed the day before the membership in the House of Representatives was to change. Previously, Republicans held the House, Senate, and presidency. After the election of 1890, Republicans continued to hold the majority in the Senate and the presidency but not the House. Republicans quickly passed the new legislation, while they controlled the House and then left it to the Republican Senate and president to fill the positions, undoubtedly with an eye toward appointing judges with right-leaning values.

Nomination and confirmation data suggest that senators have historically respected presidential nominations, but not to the point of acting as a rubber stamp. As of 2006, the Senate failed to confirm, through negative votes, withdrawals, and failures to vote, 30 of the 144 nominees (79 percent) to the Supreme Court. Many nominees to lower courts have also not been confirmed.[7]

While some have criticized the selection process as too political, others have criticized the lifetime tenure rule (discussed later in this section) as creating a judiciary that is not sufficiently political. In particular, they criticize the federal courts as being **countermajoritarian institutions.** A countermajoritarian institution is one whose members are not elected by, or directly accountable to, the people. In fact, federal judges are only marginally accountable even to the people's elected representatives.

countermajoritarian institution
Because its members are not elected by the people, are not accountable to the people, and are not required to consider public opinion in their decision making, the Supreme Court is considered by most to be a countermajoritarian institution. This does not mean, however, that the Court has historically been countermajoritarian in its decision making.

Clearly, the Court is countermajoritarian in structure. But is it countermajoritarian in practice? Research indicates that the Court is largely a majoritarian institution, issuing decisions that are consistent with public opinion:

> Empirically, the results of our analysis are easily summarized. For most of the period since 1956, a reciprocal relationship appears to have existed between the ideology of the public mood in the United States and the broad ideological tenor of Supreme Court decisions. . . . [T]he evidence suggests that public opinion exercises important influence on the decisions of the Court even in the absence of changes in the composition of the Court or in the partisan and ideological makeup of Congress and the presidency. That the effects of public opinion take five years, on average, to register on the Court's decisions probably reflects both the time it takes for a change in public opinion to be reflected in presidential elections and the time required before a newly elected president has a Court vacancy to fill. . . . [T]he results appear to reassure those committed to democratic principles and concerned about the countermajoritarian potential of the Court. Our analyses indicate that for most of the period since 1956, the Court has been highly responsive to majority opinion. Its decisions not only have conformed closely to the aggregate policy opinions of the American public but have thereby reinforced and helped legitimate emergent majoritarian concerns.[8]

The findings correlating public opinion and the Court's decisions include only fundamental changes in public opinion, not ordinary fluctuations or mood swings. Interestingly, the strong correlation between public opinion and the Court's decision began to diminish in 1981, when the Court's decisions became increasingly more conservative and the public mood became increasingly more liberal. The result was that the Court was more countermajoritarian under Presidents Reagan and Bush than under the previous administrations.[9]

Why did the framers establish an institution with a countermajoritarian potential? The framers believed strongly in the independence of the judiciary. Although they created a republican form of government, they believed that the will of the majority should be checked in some circumstances. This is because, upon occasion, such as during times of national emergency, the popular will may be at odds with republican, democratic principles. It is the duty of the judiciary to keep a cool, deliberative, rational head and not ride the waves of populism. The judiciary, as an institution, acts as the nation's democratic conscience. If the judiciary were dependent upon the people directly, or upon one of the other two political branches, this role would be compromised.

Once confirmed, federal judges receive lifetime tenure. Also, the Constitution prohibits Congress from decreasing the salaries of federal judges during their tenure. These provisions were intended to shield the judiciary from overreaching by the other two branches. By assuring judges lifetime tenure and income, Congress cannot financially coerce judges; thereby, the independence of the judiciary is protected. Remember that the framers believed that an independent judiciary was necessary to protect civil liberties. Alexander Hamilton stated, in the *Federalist Papers*, the following about the selection process and lifetime appointment:

> If, then, the courts of justice are to be considered as the bulwarks of a limited Constitution against legislative encroachments, this consideration will afford a strong argument for the permanent tenure of judicial offices, since nothing will contribute so much as this to that independent spirit in the judges which must be essential to the faithful performance of so arduous a duty.
>
> This independence of the judges is equally requisite to guard the Constitution and the rights of individuals from the effects of those ill humors which the arts of designing men, or the influence of particular conjunctures, sometimes disseminate among the people themselves, and which, though they speedily give place to better information, and more deliberate reflection, have a tendency, in the meantime, to occasion dangerous innovations in the government, and serious oppressions of the minor party in the community. . . .
>
> That inflexible and uniform adherence to the rights of the Constitution, and of individuals, which we perceive to be indispensable in the courts of justice, can certainly not be expected from judges who hold their offices by a temporary commission. Periodical appointments, however regulated, or by whomsoever made, would in some way or other, be fatal to their necessary independence. If the power of making them was committed either to the executive or legislature there would be danger of an improper complaisance to the branch which

possessed it; if to both, there would be an unwillingness to hazard the displeasure of either; if to the people, or to persons chosen by them for the special purpose, there would be too great a disposition to consult popularity to justify a reliance that nothing would be consulted but the Constitution and the laws.

There is yet a further weighty reason for the permanency of the judicial offices . . . [A] temporary duration in office which would naturally discourage such characters from quitting a lucrative line of practice to accept a seat on the bench would have a tendency to throw the administration of justice into the hands less able and less well qualified to conduct it with utility and dignity.[10]

John Marshall declared the same principle during the Virginia Constitutional Convention. "I have always thought, from my earliest youth until now, that the greatest scourge an angry Heaven ever inflicted upon an ungrateful and sinning people was an ignorant, a corrupt, or a dependent judiciary."[11]

TRADITIONS OF THE SUPREME COURT OF THE UNITED STATES

SIDEBAR

The Supreme Court met for the first time on February 2, 1790, in New York City, the nation's first capital. John Jay was the Court's first chief justice. The Court has many long-standing practices, some dating back to the Court's first sessions.

By statute, the Court's term begins the first Monday of October, every year. The Court operates under a continuous single term designated by the month and year (for example, the October 1998 Term). Public sessions begin at 10:00 A.M. and close at 3 P.M. There are no public sessions on Thursdays or Fridays. Wednesdays are split between oral arguments in the morning and a conference of the justices in the afternoon. Thursdays are reserved for conducting research, preparing opinions, and the like. The justices meet on Fridays to discuss and decide pending cases and petitions for certiorari. Approximately twelve cases are argued during the Monday, Tuesday, and Wednesday sessions. Public sessions in May and June are used to announce the Court's decisions. When all the decisions have been announced, the Court recesses for the summer, although in recess, the Court continues to manage petitions for certiorari during the summer.

At the justices' conferences, the chief justice begins the discussion by explaining his position and what he expects his final vote to be. The most senior associate justice then does the same, and the process continues until the least senior associate justice has made a statement. After a vote is finalized, the chief justice assigns a justice to write the Court's opinion, if the chief justice is in the majority. If not, the most senior associate justice in the majority makes the assignment. The opinion is circulated among the justices in the majority for comment. An opinion may be amended at this stage if the justices unanimously agree. A justice who is in the majority but does not want to join in the majority's opinion may write a concurring opinion. This means that the justice agrees with the outcome, but not necessarily with the Court's rationale. Justices in the minority may draft dissenting opinions for publication.

Chief Justice Fuller initiated a practice during the late nineteenth century that continues today, the "conference handshake." Before each session and prior to their conferences, the justices shake hands. Through this, they symbolize their cooperation and harmony, in spite of any differences of opinion they have.

A visitor to the Courtroom may notice that the justices' chairs are different. The practice of each justice selecting his or her own chair is another tradition of the Court.

Six justices constitute a quorum; although rare, there have been cases in which a quorum could not be reached due to recusals and absences. The chief justice is seated in the center chair. The senior associate justice is seated to the chief justice's immediate right, the justice next in seniority is seated to the chief justice's immediate left, and so on, alternating from right to left.

Since at least 1800, the justices have worn black robes. Chief Justice Jay and other justices initially wore robes with a red facing, emulating English judges, but this practice was discontinued. However, Chief Justice Rehnquist wore a black robe with stripes on the sleeves, a departure from recent practice. Similarly, a wig was worn by at least one justice initially, but this practice did not continue.

Quill pens are also a tradition of the Court. A white quill pen is placed at each counsel table before each session.

In the Court's early years, attorneys appeared wearing formal attire, including tails. Today, this practice is followed by attorneys appearing on behalf of the government. It is optional for others. Most attorneys today appear in dark suits.

Lifetime appointment is not absolute. Judges may be removed by Congress. Article III provides that judges shall remain in office during "good behavior." Article II, Section 4, allows removal of any civil officer of the national government, including a judge, for treason, bribery, or other high crimes and misdemeanors.

Article I vests the power of impeachment in the House of Representatives. However, impeachment is not removal; it is an accusation. The Senate tries impeachment cases and decides whether to remove the accused official. There are two other methods of ending the appointment of a federal judge: death and resignation for disability, retirement, or other reasons.

Today, there are ninety-four district courts, some with multiple judges, and thirteen appellate courts. In addition, Congress has created a number of courts and judgeships that are considered *legislative courts* rather than *constitutional courts.* Whether a court is legislative or constitutional largely depends on the status of the judges who sit on the court. If the judges are empowered under Article III of the Constitution—and therefore must undergo the nomination and confirmation process, are assured lifetime tenure, and cannot have their pay reduced—the court is constitutional. District, appellate, and Supreme Court judges are all constitutional judges.

In contrast, if the judges do not have these characteristics, they are empowered by Congress and not the Constitution. The U.S. Claims Court, the U.S. Court of International Trade, the U.S. Tax Court, and administrative law tribunals are examples of non–Article III courts. The judges of these courts are federal judicial officers, but they are not empowered by the Constitution; rather, their positions are created by Congress and are not formally part of the judicial branch. For this reason, they are commonly referred to as *Article I judges.*

In addition to the judges who sit on the foregoing non–Article III courts, Congress has created a system of bankruptcy courts, presided over by bankruptcy judges. Also, through the Federal Magistrate Act, a system of magistrate-judges was created to relieve some of the burden on district judges without the commitment of lifetime tenure.

Neither bankruptcy judges nor magistrate-judges undergo the nomination and confirmation process. Instead, Congress has delegated the appointment power to Article III judges. Also, such judges do not benefit from lifetime appointment. Bankruptcy judges are appointed for fourteen years and magistrate-judges for seven years. Both may be reappointed. Through appointment by Article III judges and other measures, Congress has created a degree of independence (from Congress and the executive) for these non–Article III judges. Nevertheless, there are some limitations upon

---

S I D E B A R

FEDERAL AND STATE JUDGES

THEN AND NOW

Through the Judiciary Act of 1789, six Supreme Court justiceships were created (one chief justice and five associate justices). Additionally, Congress provided for thirteen district judgeships. In total, nineteen federal judicial positions were created. At the same time, there were approximately one hundred state judges.

Compare those numbers to contemporary figures. In 2011, there were 678 district judges, 179 appellate judges, 352 bankruptcy judges, 551 magistrate-judges, and 9 Supreme Court justices in the federal system, totaling 1,769 federal judges. In 2008, there were 356 high, 984 intermediate appellate, and 29,929 trial court judges in the United States. Approximately 95% of all cases are heard by state courts.

Source of contemporary state statistics: State Court Caseload Statistics, Conference on State Court Administrators, Bureau of Justice Statistics, and National Conference on State Courts (2010), www.ncsconline.org/D_Research/csp/2008_files/StateCourtCaseloadStatisticsFINAL.pdf

Source of contemporary federal statistics: Federal Judicial Center, Washington, DC, www.fjc.gov/federal/courts.nsf

what functions they may perform, as they are not constitutionally empowered. For example, magistrate-judges may not preside over the critical stages of a felony criminal trial without the consent of the parties.[12] Also, at present, it appears that bankruptcy judges may not preside over jury trials.[13] Regardless, both these types of judicial officers are valuable members of the federal judiciary.

3.3 FORMAL AND INFORMAL CONTROLS ON THE FEDERAL JUDICIARY

As will be discussed later in this chapter, through judicial review, a court may declare executive, congressional, or state action void as unconstitutional. This is an awesome and controversial authority. Regardless, it is a well-established authority.

Now consider the federal judiciary. As you have learned, federal judges are appointed for life. They are assured no reduction in their salaries. They are, for the most part, independent. Does this mean that the United States is governed by an imperial and unconstrained judiciary? No, there are a number of formal and informal constraints on the judiciary (see Figure 3-2). Our discussion begins with formal constraints.

3.3(a) Formal Constraints

First, the political branches are responsible for the selection of judges. The president nominates a candidate. The Senate must confirm the nomination before it can become final. Through this process, the political branches control the membership of the Court. As one would expect, presidents have tended to nominate individuals who hold ideologies similar to their own. However, ideology has increased in importance lately, and contemporary presidents and Senates have increasingly probed deeper into the backgrounds, philosophies, and records of candidates.

In spite of efforts to nominate persons with a particular judicial philosophy, presidents occasionally end up dissatisfied with their selections. President Eisenhower appointed Earl Warren as chief justice. Later he said of this choice that it was "[t]he greatest damn-fool mistake I ever made!" President Truman remarked, "whenever you put a man on the Supreme Court, he ceases to be your friend."[14]

The effect a president can have on the philosophy of the nation's judiciary can be profound. This is especially true of two-term presidents and periods during which successive presidents are of the same ideological fabric. For example, Presidents Reagan and Bush appointed over 600 federal judges, out of a total of only 828 federal judges.[15] Even if a small percentage prove to be philosophically disappointing to the nominator, these two presidents have had a significant and long-lasting effect on the judiciary.

Formal

1. Presidential nomination and Senate confirmation of Article III judges
2. Removal through impeachment
3. Congressional control of jurisdiction
4. Congressional control of number of justices and lower federal courts
5. Justiciability requirements
6. Constitution and statutory amendments intended to reverse judicial decisions
7. Congressional control of increases in salaries and provision of other resources

Informal

1. Judicial reliance on executive branch for the enforcement of orders
2. Public opinion
3. Interest in preserving the integrity of the judiciary

FIGURE 3-2

Controls on federal judicial power—summary

jurisdiction
A term used in several senses: (1) In a general sense, the right of a court to adjudicate lawsuits of a certain kind. (2) In a specific sense, the right of a court to determine a particular case; in other words, the power of the court over the subject matter of, or the property involved in, the case at bar. (3) In a geographical sense, the power of a court to hear cases only within a specific territorial area.

Removal of judges by Congress is the second formal control on the judiciary. The House of Representatives has the power to impeach a justice. An article of impeachment is the equivalent of bringing charges. However, the Constitution limits impeachment to removal from office. Once a judge is impeached, the Senate tries the matter. A two-thirds vote is required to remove a justice. Either house, or both, may assign their respective responsibilities to a committee that will hear the evidence and report its findings and recommendations.

Only one Supreme Court justice, Samuel Chase, has ever been impeached, and he was not convicted by the Senate. Twelve appellate and district judges have been impeached, and seven of those were convicted. Many others have resigned because of controversy or impending impeachment.[16]

Third, as you will see later in this chapter, Congress possesses significant authority to control the types of cases that may be heard by the judiciary. It can do this because the Constitution grants to Congress the authority to control the **jurisdiction** of the Court in some circumstances. *Jurisdiction* refers to the authority of a court to hear a case. If a court has the authority to hear a case, then it has jurisdiction.

Fourth, Congress determines the number of justices to sit on the Supreme Court. However, if Congress were to try to use this power to influence the Court's decision making, by packing the Court with members of a particular ideological view, it would need to have a president who shared its philosophy, because the nominations must be made by the executive. As previously discussed, Franklin D. Roosevelt proposed a court-packing plan that was defeated in Congress. The size of the Supreme Court has not been changed since 1870, when it was finally set at nine.

Fifth, so-called *justiciability requirements* also are controlling factors. A number of doctrines limit the power of the Court to render decisions. Mootness, ripeness, standing, political question, and case-or-controversy requirements all limit the authority of the judiciary (discussed in Chapter 4).

Sixth, the Court's decisions can be changed through political processes. An unfavorable interpretation of a statute can be changed by congressional amendment of the law. Although more difficult than amending a statute, constitutional decisions can be changed through the Article IV amendment process. See §1.5 for a description of the process of amending the Constitution. The Constitution has been amended four times to reverse Supreme Court decisions:

1. The Eleventh Amendment, which provides for state immunity in federal court. Enacted in response to *Chisholm v. Georgia,* 2 U.S. (2 Dall.) 419 (1793).
2. The Fourteenth Amendment, which provides for due process and equal protection in the states. Enacted, partly, in response to *Dred Scott v. Sandford,* 60 U.S. (19 How.) 393 (1856).
3. The Sixteenth Amendment, which provides for the federal income tax. Enacted in response to *Pollock v. Farmer's Loan & Trust Co.,* 157 U.S. 429 (1895), in which the Court ruled a federal income tax unconstitutional.
4. The Twenty-Sixth Amendment, which provides that all individuals age eighteen and older possess the right to vote in state and national elections. Enacted in response to *Oregon v. Mitchell,* 400 U.S. 112 (1970).

Seventh, although the pay of Article III judges may not be decreased, Congress does control increases and the provision of other resources to the courts.

3.3(b) Informal Constraints

The Court is also constrained by informal forces. The most significant informal force is the Court's inability to enforce its own commands. The Court does not have a battery of officers, an army, or the administrative network necessary to enforce its orders. The framers vested the executive with the responsibility of enforcing the law. This includes enforcement of court orders.

Some legal scholars believe that some justices fear that the integrity of the Court would be put in jeopardy if the Court were to issue an order knowing that the president would refuse to enforce its mandate. President Andrew Jackson once responded to a decision of the Supreme Court by stating, "John Marshall has made his decision, now let him enforce it."[17] This fear constrains the justices to making decisions that they believe the president will enforce. To issue a decision that will not be enforced would result in disrespect for the Court and could potentially set a devastating precedent that the executive may be selective in the orders it wishes to enforce.

Similarly, judicial decision making may be limited by public opinion. Directly, the Court has been insulated from such concerns through lifetime tenure and assured salaries. Justices do not, however, live in a special dormitory separated from society. They are exposed to the media, family, friends, and acquaintances. They may not consider public opinion directly, but surely they have some awareness of contemporary issues, norms, and beliefs that then influences their conceptions of what is just, fair, and expected by the people. Justice Rehnquist stated, concerning the influence of public opinion on judicial decision making:

> Judges, so long as they are relatively normal human beings, can no more escape being influenced by public opinion in the long run than can people working at other jobs. And, if a judge on coming to the bench were to decide to hermetically seal himself off from all manifestations of public opinion, he would accomplish very little; he would not be influenced by the state of public opinion at the time he came to the bench.[18]

There have been a few cases in the Supreme Court's history about which it is speculated that public opinion and political pressures unduly influenced the Court's decision making. For example, in the early 1930s the Court invalidated several statutes (or portions thereof) that were critical parts of President Roosevelt's New Deal plan. These decisions were met with considerable resistance from Roosevelt, Congress, and the public. President Roosevelt attempted his famous court-packing scheme as a result, and Congress considered limiting the appellate jurisdiction of the Court. By 1937, the Court had changed its approach and thereafter upheld statutes that it previously might have invalidated.[19]

In *Korematsu v. United States,*[20] the internment of Japanese residents—many of them citizens of the United States—during World War II was challenged. The Court upheld the government's actions, and many jurists believe it did so because of political and public pressures. Of course, the fact that the nation was embroiled in a war with Japan was a significant factor. As you will learn in Chapter 6, the authority of the president is greater during times of war than during times of peace.

In most cases the effect of public opinion on the judiciary is fairly subtle. Nevertheless, it is a factor that must be considered when analyzing judicial decision making.

Returning to the appointment and removal of justices, there is evidence that political actors, particularly presidents, can influence the tenure of federal judges and justices. For example, it is alleged that President Lyndon B. Johnson coerced Justice Arthur Goldberg into retiring so President Johnson could appoint a friend and colleague to the bench. President Johnson accomplished this by threatening to disclose alleged improper fundraising by Justice Goldberg and by offering him the position of ambassador to the United Nations. Justice Goldberg accepted, was subsequently appointed to the post, and President Johnson nominated his friend Abe Fortas to the bench. Similarly, lower federal court judges, whose nomination is recommended by the senator of the state, have been known to retire at the request of party officials to permit the appointment of a successor before his or her party loses the White House or a senatorial seat.[21]

3.4 THE ROLE OF THE FEDERAL JUDICIARY

What role does the judiciary play in a republican form of government? This is the first question that must be addressed. Once answered, a second question must be asked: What roles do the state and federal courts play in our federal republic?

Historically, courts have served two primary functions: dispute resolution and the administration of criminal justice. The former refers to the process of adjudicating civil claims made by individuals, business entities, or governmental entities against others. The latter refers to the adjudication of criminal cases.

In colonial America, both of these functions were performed by state and local courts. Prior to the Constitution, there were no national courts. This was one of the weaknesses of the Articles of Confederation.

The Constitution did create a national judiciary: It specifically established the Supreme Court. Further, it provided that Congress could create inferior federal courts. What role were these courts to play in the new system? Clearly, the framers did not intend for federal courts to displace state courts. The traditional jurisdiction of state courts was to continue. To the framers, there was no question that most disputes and criminal cases belonged in state courts. At the Constitutional Convention, anti-Federalists opposed creating a national judiciary, fearing that it would usurp the authority of state courts. Similarly, the Federalists strongly favored creating a national judiciary to protect the United States from the states. They compromised by creating only the Supreme Court, leaving the inferior courts to Congress, and by delegating most judicial authority to the states.

The framers had personally observed the economic and political turmoil caused by a lack of national unity, interstate conflicts, and conflicts between the national and state governments under the Articles of Confederation. Therefore, certain disputes were delegated to the federal judiciary so that a national perspective would be part of judicial decision making. Cases in which the United States is a party are the most obvious example.

diversity jurisdiction
The jurisdiction of a federal court arising from diversity of citizenship, when the jurisdictional amount has been met.

Diversity jurisdiction is another form of federal jurisdiction. Cases involving disputes between a citizen of one state and another state, between two states, between citizens of different states, or between a foreign nation or one of its citizens and a state or one of the state's citizens are examples of diverse cases. Federal jurisdiction also extends to cases involving ambassadors, public ministers, and consuls.

federal jurisdiction
The jurisdiction of the federal courts. Such jurisdiction is based upon the judicial powers granted by Article III of the Constitution and by federal statutes.

Finally, there is federal jurisdiction any time national law is at issue, whether constitutional, statutory, treaty, administrative, or other. This is known as **federal jurisdiction** or *federal question jurisdiction*. These forms of jurisdiction are recognized in the Constitution. Generally, they are considered permissive grants of jurisdiction. That is, they do not automatically create federal jurisdiction; rather, they permit federal jurisdiction to be assumed. Congress has enforced the provisions primarily through two statutes, one providing for diversity of citizenship jurisdiction[22] and the other for federal question jurisdiction.[23]

Since the adoption of the Constitution, the federal judiciary has grown significantly, both in size and in jurisdiction. The increase in jurisdiction is mostly attributable to federal question jurisdiction. As the national government has extended its sphere through the Necessary and Proper and Commerce Clauses, the jurisdiction of the federal judiciary has grown concomitantly. The Reconstruction Amendments (Thirteen through Fifteen) and civil rights legislation enacted to enforce them have also contributed to the expansion of the jurisdiction of federal courts, probably far beyond what the framers imagined. Although federal courts hear a large variety of cases today, including many the framers did not anticipate, they have not usurped the role of state courts. In fact, over 95 percent of all civil and criminal cases are heard by state courts.

Another role the judiciary plays is that of guardian and protector. This role has two related features. First, the judiciary acts as the guardian of liberty, justice, and civil liberties. Second, the judiciary acts as a governmental referee, overseeing the state and federal governments to be sure that separation of powers and federalism principles are adhered to.

It is the obligation of the courts to stand between the government and the individual, checking the government's behavior and shielding the individual from any wrongs by the government. Alexander Hamilton wrote, "[t]he courts were designed to be an intermediate body between the people and the legislature, in order, among other things, to keep the latter within the limits assigned to their authority."

This role extends beyond protection of the individual to protection of minorities. The United States is a *republic,* an impure form of democracy. Majority rule is the benchmark of governmental decision making in a democracy. However, the framers also recognized the dangers attendant to majoritarianism. A small group, a minority, can be disadvantaged for the benefit of the majority. The judiciary, with its counter-majoritarian attributes, is responsible for protecting minorities from the abuses of the community. Alexander Hamilton commented on this role of the judiciary:

> The independence of judges is equally requisite to guard the Constitution and the rights of individuals from the effects of those ill humors which the arts of designing men, or the influence of particular conjunctures, sometimes disseminate among the people themselves, and which, though they speedily give place to better information, and more deliberate reflection, have a tendency, in the meantime, to occasion dangerous innovations in the government, and serious oppressions of the minor party in the community. . . . [I]t is not to be inferred from this principle that the representatives of the people, whenever a momentary inclination happens to lay hold of a majority of their constituents incompatible with the provisions in the existing Constitution, would, on that account, be justifiable in a violation of those provisions; or that the courts would be under a greater obligation to connive at infractions in this shape than when they had proceeded wholly from the cabals of the representative body. Until the people have, by some solemn and authoritative act, annulled or changed the established form, it is binding upon themselves collectively, as well as individually; and no presumption, or even knowledge, of their sentiment can warrant their representatives in a departure from it prior to such an act. But it is easy to see that it would require an uncommon portion of fortitude in the judges to do their duty as faithful guardians of the Constitution, where legislative invasions of it had been instigated by the major voice of the community.[24]

Today this function is more critical than ever, and it is likely to continue to increase in significance. At the time the Constitution was adopted, the United States was largely homogeneous. Today, the United States is a pluralistic and heterogeneous nation. There simply are more minorities that require attention today than there were two hundred years ago.

Slavery and the later segregation of blacks from the white community are examples of the oppression feared by Hamilton. Slavery was not ended by the judiciary. That occurred through the political branches and a civil war. It was, however, the judiciary that ended the separate-but-equal doctrine. Bear in mind that the term *minorities,* as used by Hamilton, refers to any minority, not just racial or ethnic groups. Political, religious, and social minorities are included.

3.5 FEDERAL JUDICIAL JURISDICTION

Article III, Section 1, of the Constitution provides that the "judicial power of the United States shall be vested in one Supreme Court, and such inferior Courts as the Congress may from time to time ordain and establish." Only the existence of the Supreme Court is assured by the Constitution. However, the framers empowered Congress to create additional federal courts. This was done by the first Congress through the Judiciary Act of 1789, and even more federal courts (and restructuring of existing federal courts) were added by later congressional action.

As you learned earlier, the Supreme Court was established by the Constitution, it is commonly known as a *constitutional court* or an *Article III* court. Some lower federal courts are Article III courts also. Others derive their jurisdiction entirely from Congress and, as a result, are known as *legislative courts* or *Article I* courts. There has even been an executive court (Article II court) in U.S. history. These courts are discussed more fully later in this chapter. The distinction between Article III courts and other courts is important. Jurisdiction, appointment procedures, length of appointment, and authority differ among Article III and other courts (see Figure 3-3).

FEDERAL COURTS—CONSTITUTIONAL SOURCES		
	Nature	*Examples*
ARTICLE I	Creation by president pursuant to treaty or military powers. Ad hoc in nature.	Tiede Court
ARTICLE II	Creation by Congress. May be ad hoc or permanently established.	U.S. magistrate-judges, bankruptcy judges, administrative law judges
	Judges are not "constitutionally established," so no lifetime tenure or salary guarantee.	
ARTICLE III	Supreme Court created by Constitution; district and circuit judges provided for by Constitution but established by Congress. Lifetime tenure and salary guarantees.	Chief justice, associate justices, district judges, court of appeals judges

FIGURE 3-3
Federal courts—constitutional sources

3.5(a) Case-or-Controversy Requirement

Article III provides that the judicial power of federal courts extends to cases and controversies. An actual case or dispute must exist before an Article III court has jurisdiction. Because of this and other limitations, federal courts are considered **courts of limited jurisdiction,** as opposed to **courts of general jurisdiction.**

Therefore, federal courts do not have jurisdiction over hypothetical cases, nor can they issue **advisory opinions.** For example, Congress may not petition the Supreme Court to decide whether a proposed law, if enacted, would be constitutional. In such a case there is no dispute, no injury. However, if the law is enacted and enforced against a person who believes it to be unconstitutional, then there is jurisdiction, because there is a genuine dispute between the government and the individual resisting enforcement of the law. The Supreme Court was forced to resolve this issue early in the nation's history.[25] Thomas Jefferson, while secretary of state to President George Washington, requested an advisory ruling on treaty matters. Chief Justice John Jay refused to issue an opinion because there was no case or controversy.

Similarly, private parties cannot consent to, or create, jurisdiction in Article III courts when there is no genuine dispute. Nor can Congress declare a party to have interest when it does not. That was the issue in the 1911 case of *Muskrat v. United States.*[26] *Muskrat* involved a set of statutes that changed the ownership of Cherokee tribal property to individual ownership and also concerned rights of alienation of that property. One statute provided that certain individuals could sue to test the constitutionality of the laws in the Court of Claims, with appeal to the Supreme Court. A group of plaintiffs brought an action, as provided for in the statute, before they were engaged in a real dispute over ownership. As provided for by the law, the United States was made a party to the case. The Supreme Court held that Congress had improperly granted jurisdiction to the federal courts because the law did not require an actual controversy in its jurisdictional provision. The Court concluded that Congress had created a mechanism for individuals to circumvent the case-or-controversy requirement. Adding the United States as a party was specious, because the United States was not claiming ownership of any of the properties in dispute, nor did it have any other genuine interest in the outcome of the case. If there had been an ownership dispute between two citizens over a piece of land, or if the government had voided a sale or lease because the contract violated the alienation provisions of the law, then the case-or-controversy requirement would have been satisfied.

In most instances, prevailing parties can not appeal their victories to the Supreme Court because they don't possess the concrete injury expected by the case or contro-

court of limited jurisdiction
A court whose jurisdiction is limited to civil cases of a certain type or that involve a limited amount of money, or whose jurisdiction in criminal cases is confined to petty offenses and preliminary hearings. A court of limited jurisdiction is sometimes called a *court of special jurisdiction*

court of general jurisdiction
Generally, another term for trial court, that is, a court having jurisdiction to try all classes of civil and criminal cases except those that can be heard only by a court of limited jurisdiction.

advisory opinion
A judicial interpretation of a legal question requested by the legislative or executive branch of government. Typically, courts prefer not to give advisory opinions and federal courts are generally prohibited from rendering advisory opinions.

versy requirement. However, there are exceptions. For example, the Supreme Court held in the 2011 case Camreta v. Greene, that it has jurisdiction to hear appeals from government officials who were sued under federal civil rights laws, won because they were immune, but where the lower courts decided new law that will bind them in the future. Camreta involved a lawsuit by a child protective services employee and a deputy sheriff. The two interviewed a nine-year-old child without a warrant or the consent of her parents during an investigation of her father for sexually abusing her. Eventually the father was charged, the jury hung, and the charges were dismissed. The mother sued the child protective services worker and deputy for interviewing the daughter without a warrant or parental consent under the Fourth Amendment, which requires all searches be reasonable. Civil rights law provides immunity to officials unless they violate clearly established rights and there is no clearly established right of children to have parents or a warrant in such circumstances. So, the lower court found for the officials but also held that in all future cases, all officers should either have a warrant or parental consent before conducting such an interview. Even though they were held not liable because they were immune, the lower court's decision of law will remove their immunity in the future and could subject them to liability. This, the Court concluded, created the personal stake in the decision to establish a case or controversy.[27]

The case-or-controversy requirement was intended by the framers to limit the authority of the judiciary. If the rule were otherwise, the judiciary could act as a super-legislature and superexecutive, issuing opinions and orders and voiding the laws and actions of the other branches as it pleased. Hence, the case-or-controversy provision preserves the integrity of the doctrine of separation of powers.

The case-or-controversy requirement affects only Article III courts. Article I and Article II courts, therefore, may issue advisory opinions. Hence, Congress may establish a court whose responsibility it is to render advisory opinions to both Congress and the executive. Of course, the decisions rendered by such a body could be only advisory and would not directly influence Article III judicial decision making.

In some instances, however, a plaintiff may request that a court review a case and declare the respective rights and obligations of the parties before there has been an injury. That is, in fact, the purpose of declaratory relief. Even though no injury has occurred, the Supreme Court has held that Article III courts have jurisdiction, so long as there is a genuine controversy between two or more parties.[28]

Supreme Court Justices (front row from left) Clarence Thomas, Antonin Scalia, John G. Roberts, Anthony Kennedy, Ruth Bader Ginsburg; (back row from left) Sonia Sotomayor, Stephen Breyer, Samuel Alito, and Elena Kagan
ROGER L. WOLLENBERG/UPI/Newscom

prayer
Portion of a bill in equity
or a petition that asks
for equitable relief and
specifies the relief sought.

In the *Wallace* case, an appeal from the Supreme Court of Tennessee, the Supreme Court addressed the issue of whether declaratory relief is permitted under the case-or-controversy requirement. According to this case, the issue is not what form of remedy is **prayed** for; rather, it is the nature of the case itself. Actual injuries and damages do not have to be present to establish Article III jurisdiction, but there must be real parties—adversaries—who have a genuine dispute.

Nashville, Cincinnati, and St. Louis Railway v. Wallace
288 U.S. 249 (1933)

Mr. Justice Stone delivered the opinion of the Court.

Appellant brought suit in the Chancery Court of Davidson County, Tenn., under the Uniform Declaratory Judgments Act of that state, Chapter 29, Tennessee Public Acts 1923, to secure a judicial declaration that a state excise tax levied on the storage of gasoline . . . as applied to appellant, [was] invalid under the commerce clause and the Fourteenth Amendment of the Federal Constitution. A decree for appellees was affirmed by the Supreme Court of the State, and the case comes here from appeal under section 237(a) of the Judicial Code (28 USCA § 344[a]).

After the jurisdictional statement required by Rule 12 (28 USCA § 354) was submitted, this Court, in ordering the cause set down for argument, invited the attention of counsel to the question "whether a case or controversy is presented, in view of the nature of the proceedings in the state courts." This preliminary question, which has been elaborately briefed and argued, must first be considered, for the judicial power with which this Court is invested by article 3, § 1, of the Constitution, extends by article 3, § 2, only to "case" and "controversies"; if no "case" or "controversy" is presented for decision, we are without power to review the decree of the court below.

In determining whether this litigation presents a case within the appellate jurisdiction of this Court, we are concerned, not with form, but with substance. Hence, we look not to the label which the Legislature has attached to the procedure followed in the state courts, or to the description of the judgment which is brought here for review in popular parlance, as "declaratory," but to the nature of the proceeding which the statute authorizes, and the effect of the judgment rendered upon the rights which the appellant asserts.

Section 1 of the Tennessee Declaratory judgments Act confers jurisdiction on courts of record "to declare rights . . . whether or not further relief is or could be claimed" and provides that "no action or proceeding shall be open to objection on the ground that a declaratory judgment or decree is prayed for. The declaration may be either affirmative or negative in form and effect; and such declaration shall have the force and effect of a final judgment or decree." By section 2 it is provided that "any person . . . whose rights, status or other legal relations are affected by a statute . . . may have determined any question or construction or validity arising under the . . . statute . . . and obtain a declaration of rights . . . thereunder."

Under section 6, the court may refuse to render a declaratory judgment where, if rendered, it "would not terminate the uncertainty or controversy giving rise to the proceeding."

The statute has been often considered by the highest court of Tennessee, which has consistently held that its provisions may only be invoked when the complainant asserts rights which are challenged by the defendant, and presents for decision an actual controversy to which he is a party, capable of final adjudication by the judgment or decree to be rendered. . . .

Proceeding in accordance with this statute, appellant filed its bill of complaint in the state chancery court, joining as defendants the appellees, the Attorney General and the state officials charged with the duty of collecting the gasoline privilege tax imposed by the Tennessee statute. The complaint alleged that appellant is engaged in purchasing gasoline outside the state, which it stores within the state pending its use within and without the state in the conduct of appellant's business as an interstate rail carrier; that appellees assert that the statute taxes the privilege of storing gasoline within the state and is applicable to appellant; that they have demanded payment of the tax in a specified amount and have determined to enforce their demand; and that, under the circumstances alleged, the statute as applied to appellant is invalid under the Commerce Clause and the Fourteenth Amendment. [The chancery court found the tax to be lawful and dismissed the complaint.]

. . . Obviously the appellant, whose duty to pay the tax will be determined by the decision of this case, is not attempting to secure an abstract determination by the Court of the validity of a statute . . . or a decision advising what the law would be on an uncertain or hypothetical state of facts . . . Thus the narrow question presented for determination is whether the controversy before us, which would be justiciable in this Court if presented in a suit for injunction, is any the less so because through a modified procedure appellant has been permitted to present it in the state courts, without praying for an injunction.

While the ordinary course of judicial procedure results in a judgment requiring an award of process or execution to carry it into effect, such relief is not an indispensable adjunct to the exercise of the judicial function.

The issues raised here are the same as those which under old forms of procedure could be raised only in a suit for an injunction or one to recover the tax after its payment.

But the Constitution does not require that the case or controversy requirement should be presented by traditional forms of procedure, invoking only traditional remedies. The judiciary clause of the Constitution defined and limited judicial power not the particular method by which that power might be invoked. . . . The states are left free to regulate their own judicial procedure. Hence changes merely in the form or method of procedure by which federal rights are brought to final adjudication in the state courts are not enough to preclude review of the adjudication of this Court so long as the case retains the essentials of an adversary proceeding, involving a real, not hypothetical, controversy, which is finally determined by judgment below. . . . Accordingly, we must consider the constitutional questions raised by the appeal. [The Supreme Court then concluded that the tax was constitutional.]

The case-or-controversy requirement is also at issue when considering **declaratory relief.** Generally, parties seek money damages (legal relief) or an order from a court requiring or prohibiting some action (equitable relief). For example, in a breach-of-contract case, the plaintiff may seek compensation for losses resulting from the breach. He may also request an order requiring the defendant to complete the contract (specific performance). These are the standard legal and equitable remedies sought by plaintiffs. They create no case-or-controversy problem.

> **declaratory judgment (declaratory relief)**
> A judgment that specifies the rights of the parties but orders no relief. Nonetheless, it is a binding judgment and the appropriate remedy for the determination of an actionable dispute when the plaintiff is in doubt as to his or her legal rights.

3.5(b) Federal Question and Diversity Jurisdiction

Federal judicial jurisdiction is further limited by Article III, Section 2, to cases that involve federal legal issues or where diversity of citizenship exists. Congress has enacted statutes controlling the precise contours of judicial jurisdiction. This is because the Constitution delegated to Congress the authority to define jurisdiction. In doing so, Congress may not increase the jurisdiction of the judicial branch beyond the limits set by the Constitution. Do not be surprised when you learn that Congress has declared diversity jurisdiction to be narrower than allowed by the Constitution. A more thorough discussion of congressional control of federal judicial jurisdiction follows in this chapter.

Federal Question Jurisdiction As to the first form of jurisdiction, Article III, Section 2, states that the judicial power "shall extend to all Cases, in Law and Equity, arising under the Constitution, the Laws of the United States, and Treaties made, or which shall be made, under their Authority." The section continues by specifying jurisdiction in particular cases, including those that involve federal public officials such as ambassadors and cabinet officers. This provision is enforced by a federal statute, 28 U.S.C. § 1331. Accordingly, cases founded upon federal law may be heard by federal courts. This is known as federal question jurisdiction. Recall, however, that federal claims may also be heard by state courts, unless Congress declares otherwise. The opposite is not true. Federal courts do not freely hear state claims.

Federal question jurisdiction extends beyond constitutional claims. The previously mentioned provision refers to all laws and treaties of the United States. This includes statutes, administrative regulations, executive orders, and similar proclamations. Accordingly, all of the following are examples of cases in which federal question jurisdiction is found:

1. A plaintiff sues a police officer and a police department for violating a federally secured constitutional right, such as the right to be free from unreasonable searches and seizures (Fourth Amendment).
2. A plaintiff sues a private employer to recover unpaid overtime income under the Fair Labor Standards Act.
3. The administrators of a nuclear power plant sue to enjoin the enforcement of an administrative regulation, promulgated by the Nuclear Regulatory Commission, that they contend was created in an improper manner.
4. A plaintiff sues the United States for breach of contract after the president orders that the employment of the plaintiff and other striking employees of the federal government be terminated.

There are thousands of "laws" of the United States. As you can see from these examples, such laws govern more than the relationship between the government and its citizens. Relationships between individuals are also subject to federal regulation, as can be seen in the following case.

Grable & Sons v. Darue Engineering
545 U.S. 308 (2005)

Justice Souter Delivered the Opinion of the Court

The question is whether want of a federal cause of action to try claims of title to land obtained at a federal tax sale precludes removal to federal court of a state action with non-diverse parties raising a disputed issue of federal title law. We answer no, and hold that the national interest in providing a federal forum for federal tax litigation is sufficiently substantial to support the exercise of federal question jurisdiction over the disputed issue on removal, which would not distort any division of labor between the state and federal courts, provided or assumed by Congress.

I

In 1994, the Internal Revenue Service seized Michigan real property belonging to petitioner Grable & Sons Metal Products, Inc., to satisfy Grable's federal tax delinquency. Title 26 U.S.C §6335 required the IRS to give notice of the seizure, and there is no dispute that Grable received actual notice by certified mail before the IRS sold the property to respondent Darue Engineering & Manufacturing. Although Grable also received notice of the sale itself, it did not exercise its statutory right to redeem the property within 180 days of the sale, §6337(b)(1), and after that period had passed, the Government gave Darue a quitclaim deed. §6339.

Five years later, Grable brought a quiet title action in state court, claiming that Darue's record title was invalid because the IRS had failed to notify Grable of its seizure of the property in the exact manner required by §6335(a), which provides that written notice must be "given by the Secretary to the owner of the property [or] left at his usual place of abode or business." Grable said that the statute required personal service, not service by certified mail.

Darue removed the case to Federal District Court as presenting a federal question, because the claim of title depended on the interpretation of the notice statute in the federal tax law. The District Court declined to remand the case at Grable's behest after finding that the "claim does pose a significant question of federal law," Tr. 17 (Apr. 2, 2001), and ruling that Grable's lack of a federal right of action to enforce its claim against Darue did not bar the exercise of federal jurisdiction. On the merits, the court granted summary judgment to Darue, holding that although §6335 by its terms required personal service, substantial compliance with the statute was enough. 207 F. Supp. 2d 694 (WD Mich. 2002).

The Court of Appeals for the Sixth Circuit affirmed. 377 F.3d 592 (2004) . . .

Darue was entitled to remove the quiet title action if Grable could have brought it in federal district court originally, 28 U.S.C. § 1441(a), as a civil action "arising under the Constitution, laws, or treaties of the United States," §1331. This provision for federal-question jurisdiction is invoked by and large by plaintiffs pleading a cause of action created by federal law (*e.g.*, claims under 42 U.S.C. § 1983). There is, however, another longstanding, if less frequently encountered, variety of federal "arising under" jurisdiction, this Court having recognized for nearly 100 years that in certain cases federal question jurisdiction will lie over state-law claims that implicate significant federal issues. *E.g.*, *Hopkins v. Walker,* 244 U.S. 486, 490–491 (1917). The doctrine captures the commonsense notion that a federal court ought to be able to hear claims recognized under state law that nonetheless turn on substantial questions of federal law, and thus justify resort to the experience, solicitude, and hope of uniformity that a federal forum offers on federal issues, see ALI, Study of the Division of Jurisdiction Between State and Federal Courts 164–166 (1968).

The classic example is *Smith v. Kansas City Title & Trust Co.,* 255 U.S. 180 (1921), a suit by a shareholder claiming that the defendant corporation could not lawfully buy certain bonds of the National Government because their issuance was unconstitutional. Although Missouri law provided the cause of action, the Court recognized federal-question jurisdiction because the principal issue in the case was the federal constitutionality of the bond issue. *Smith* thus held, in a somewhat generous statement of the scope of the doctrine, that a state-law claim could give rise to federal-question jurisdiction so long as it "appears from the [complaint] that the right to relief depends upon the construction or application of [federal law]." *Id.,* at 199.

The *Smith* statement has been subject to some trimming to fit earlier and later cases recognizing the vitality of the basic doctrine, but shying away from the expansive view that mere need to apply federal law in a state-law claim will suffice to open the "arising under" door. As early as 1912, this Court had confined federal-question jurisdiction over state-law claims to those that "really and substantially involv[e] a dispute or controversy respecting the validity, construction or effect of [federal] law." *Shulthis v. McDougal,* 225 U.S. 561, 569 (1912). This limitation was the ancestor of Justice

Cardozo's later explanation that a request to exercise federal-question jurisdiction over a state action calls for a "common-sense accommodation of judgment to [the] kaleidoscopic situations" that present a federal issue, in "a selective process which picks the substantial causes out of the web and lays the other ones aside." *Gully v. First Nat. Bank in Meridian*, 299 U.S. 109, 117–118 (1936). It has in fact become a constant refrain in such cases that federal jurisdiction demands not only a contested federal issue, but a substantial one, indicating a serious federal interest in claiming the advantages thought to be inherent in a federal forum . . .

But even when the state action discloses a contested and substantial federal question, the exercise of federal jurisdiction is subject to a possible veto. For the federal issue will ultimately qualify for a federal forum only if federal jurisdiction is consistent with congressional judgment about the sound division of labor between state and federal courts governing the application of §1331. Thus, *Franchise Tax Bd.* explained that the appropriateness of a federal forum to hear an embedded issue could be evaluated only after considering the "welter of issues regarding the interrelation of federal and state authority and the proper management of the federal judicial system." *Id.*, at 8. Because arising-under jurisdiction to hear a state-law claim always raises the possibility of upsetting the state-federal line drawn (or at least assumed) by Congress, the presence of a disputed federal issue and the ostensible importance of a federal forum are never necessarily dispositive; there must always be an assessment of any disruptive portent in exercising federal jurisdiction. See also *Merrell Dow, supra,* at 810.

These considerations have kept us from stating a "single, precise, all-embracing" test for jurisdiction over federal issues embedded in state-law claims between non-diverse parties. . . .

This case warrants federal jurisdiction. Grable's state complaint must specify "the facts establishing the superiority of [its] claim," Mich. Ct. Rule 3.411(B)(2)(c) (West 2005), and Grable has premised its superior title claim on a failure by the IRS to give it adequate notice, as defined by federal law. Whether Grable was given notice within the meaning of the federal statute is thus an essential element of its quiet title claim, and the meaning of the federal statute is actually in dispute; it appears to be the only legal or factual issue contested in the case. The meaning of the federal tax provision is an important issue of federal law that sensibly belongs in a federal court. The Government has a strong interest in the "prompt and certain collection of delinquent taxes," *United States v. Rodgers,*, 461 U.S. 677, 709 (1983), and the ability of the IRS to satisfy its claims from the property of delinquents requires clear terms of notice to allow buyers like Darue to satisfy themselves that the Service has touched the bases necessary for good title. The Government thus has a direct interest in the availability of a federal forum to vindicate its own administrative action, and buyers (as well as tax delinquents) may find it valuable to come before judges used to federal tax matters. Finally, because it will be the rare state title case that raises a contested matter of federal law, federal jurisdiction to resolve genuine disagreement over federal tax title provisions will portend only a microscopic effect on the federal-state division of labor. . . .

The judgment of the Court of Appeals, upholding federal jurisdiction over Grable's quiet title action, is affirmed.

It is so ordered.

Diversity of Citizenship Jurisdiction   There is a second form of federal judicial jurisdiction: **diversity of citizenship** jurisdiction. Again the jurisdictional statement is found in Article III, Section 2, which provides that federal judicial jurisdiction includes controversies between two or more states, between citizens of different states, and between a citizen or state of the United States and a foreign nation or one of its citizens. This form of jurisdiction is commonly known as diversity jurisdiction. Diversity jurisdiction arises most frequently in cases in which a citizen of one state sues a citizen of another state. For example, diversity jurisdiction might exist if a citizen of New York were to injure a citizen of Florida in an automobile accident while vacationing in Florida. The injured Floridian is not required to file his personal injury action in New York; rather, using diversity jurisdiction, he may be able to establish jurisdiction in a federal district court located in Florida.

Congress enacted a statute, 28 U.S.C. § 1332, that brings diversity jurisdiction to life. The Supreme Court has interpreted that statute as conferring narrower jurisdiction than the Constitution allows. In particular, the Supreme Court held that *complete diversity* of citizenship is required before a federal court may exercise jurisdiction in cases of multiple defendants and plaintiffs.[29] That is, every plaintiff must be diverse from, or from a different location than, every defendant. If any plaintiff is from the same forum as any of the defendants in the case, then jurisdiction is destroyed.

Consider this example. John and Samantha, husband and wife, live in New York. They are sitting in their automobile, which was manufactured in Michigan by

diversity of citizenship
A ground for invoking the original jurisdiction of a federal district court, the basis of jurisdiction being the existence of a controversy between citizens of different states.

a company incorporated in Michigan and purchased in New York at a dealership incorporated in New York, in the driveway to their home. Unexpectedly, as a result of negligent design, the car slips out of park into drive and runs into their garage door. They suffer both property damage and personal injury. If the couple decides to sue both the manufacturer and the distributor in Michigan, they must file their negligence action in a Michigan court, because complete diversity does not exist to establish federal court jurisdiction.

Recall that the preceding Florida motorist example stated that diversity jurisdiction *may* exist. This is because more than diversity of citizenship must be shown. Pursuant to 28 U.S.C. § 1332, not the Constitution, an additional requirement must be met to establish diversity jurisdiction: a minimum amount in controversy. A plaintiff must have a minimum amount of damages before he or she can invoke federal jurisdiction. Otherwise, the case belongs in state court. The amount is set by Congress and is currently $75,000, though it is likely that this amount will increase in the next few years.[30]

Accordingly, there are two requirements to establish diversity jurisdiction. First, there must be complete diversity of the parties; second, there must be a minimum amount in controversy. (By the way, no specific amount in controversy is required to establish federal question jurisdiction.)

It is easy to understand why the framers would want federal question cases to be heard by federal courts. But why diversity cases? The purpose of diversity jurisdiction is to avoid local bias. The nation was different in 1789. People were less mobile, were more closely affiliated with their communities and states, and the states competed against one another to a greater extent than today. Consequently, the framers believed that the possibility of local prejudice in state courts was great. Accordingly, they created diversity jurisdiction to bring traditional state cases out of state court into a federal forum, where it was assumed that the foreign person would receive fair treatment. Why would a noncitizen receive fairer treatment in a federal court in Virginia than in a state court in Virginia? It was thought that because federal judges are appointed by, paid by, and owe their allegiance to the federal government, they will not bring as much local bias to the courtroom. In addition, unlike most state judges, they have lifetime appointments, which allow them to make unpopular decisions without fearing for their jobs. Whether diversity jurisdiction makes sense today is heavily debated. There have been proposals to abolish diversity jurisdiction, but to date, Congress has opted merely to reduce the number of cases subject to diversity jurisdiction (by increasing the amount-in-controversy requirement) rather than to eliminate it altogether.

3.5(c) Pendent Jurisdiction, Removal, and Other Practice Issues

The relationship and coordination between the federal and state court systems can be complex. Plaintiffs must sometimes choose between filing in federal or state court (due to concurrent jurisdiction), and the defendant may disagree with the plaintiff's choice of forum. As the preceding discussion shows, a forum decision involves more than strategic considerations—there are constitutional concerns as well.

pendent jurisdiction
The rule that even though there is no diversity of citizenship, a federal court has the right to exercise jurisdiction over a state matter if it arises out of the same transaction as a matter already before the federal court.

Pendent Jurisdiction The framers of the Constitution intended for state trial courts to have general jurisdiction over both state and federal claims. It remains true today that federal claims may be filed in state courts, unless otherwise provided by statute. Federal courts, in contrast, possess limited jurisdiction. As a result, federal courts are generally prohibited from hearing state claims. There are exceptions. For example, through **pendent jurisdiction,** a federal court may hear a state claim if the state claim is related to a legitimate federal claim. Claims are related if they stem from a "common nucleus of operative facts." The federal claim provides the basis of the federal court's jurisdiction, and the state claim is heard in the interests of efficiency. As an example, assume that Defendant Don, a local police officer, is sued by Perry Plaintiff under a federal civil rights statute. Perry claims that Don used excessive force while arresting Perry. Perry files his action in federal court, using the federal civil rights statute to establish jurisdiction. Through pendency, Perry may also attach his state claims for deprivation of civil rights, assault and battery, and intentional infliction of emotional distress. If the rule were otherwise, a plaintiff who desires to have a federal claim heard in federal court would have to file any state claims separately in state court. This is judicially inefficient and more costly in time and expenses for the litigants.

Removal   If a plaintiff files an action in federal court when no federal jurisdiction exists, the case should be dismissed under Federal Rule of Civil Procedure 12. In cases of concurrent jurisdiction, is the plaintiff's choice of forum final? No. The Supreme Court has held that defendants have a right to have their cases heard in federal court when such jurisdiction exists, even if the plaintiff originally filed in state court.* Defendants enforce this constitutional principle through removal procedures.

   Removal is the term used to describe the process of transferring a case from state court to federal court. For removal to be proper, there must be concurrent jurisdiction at the time the action is originally filed. Removal in the United States occurs automatically after a defendant has complied with all the procedural requirements (e.g., filing a petition for removal with the federal court, serving the petition on the parties, and serving a notice on the state court). Congress has provided that, in certain circumstances, a criminal case may be removed from state court to federal court. In the criminal context, the purpose of removal is to preserve the sovereignty of the federal government and to assure a fair trial to particular criminal defendants. Otherwise, the states could interfere with the functioning of the federal government by harassing federal officials through criminal proceedings.

   Whether the action is civil or criminal, a federal official sued in state court may remove the case to the federal district court in which the action is pending, if the suit concerns the performance of her official duties.[31] Similarly, 28 U.S.C. § 1442(a) provides for **removal of cases,** whether civil or criminal, filed against members of the U.S. armed forces for actions taken in the course of their duties. In addition, 28 U.S.C. § 1443 provides for removal of certain civil rights cases.

> **removal of case**
> The transfer of a case from a state court to a federal court.

   Removal of criminal cases is the same as for civil: The defendant must file a notice of, and petition for, removal.[32] Improperly removed actions are remanded to the state court from which they came.[33] Cases that are improperly removed (no federal jurisdiction) are returned to the state court through **remand** procedures. At both removal and remand stages, constitutional and statutory jurisdiction issues must be resolved.

   The case-or-controversy requirement of Article III, as well as the dual kinds of jurisdiction (federal question and diversity), forms the foundation of federal jurisdiction (see Figure 3-4). With an understanding of those subjects, you are now prepared to examine the jurisdictions of the Supreme Court and lower federal courts more specifically.

> **remand**
> The return of a case by an appellate court to the trial court for further proceedings, for a new trial, or for entry of judgment in accordance with an order of the appellate court.

---

*Federal statutes clearly give the U.S. Supreme Court the jurisdiction to review state court decisions for compliance with the U.S. Constitution. The jurisdiction of U.S. district courts to hear appeals of constitutional issues from state courts is complex, especially when concurrent cases exist and the state court issues its decision first. See *Exxon Mobile Corp. v. Saudi Basic Industries Corp.,* 544 U.S. 280 (2005), *District of Columbia Court of Appeals v. Feldman,* 460 U.S. 462 (1983), and *Rooker v. Fidelity Trust Co.,* 263 U.S. 413 (1923).

FEDERAL JUDICIARY—JURISDICTION

Two forms of federal judicial jurisdiction are authorized by Article III of the Constitution. Both have been implemented by Congress via statute.

Federal Question	*Diversity of Citizenship*
Law: 28 U.S.C. § 1331	Law: 28 U.S.C. § 1332
Jurisdiction: Cases arising under the federal Constitution or other federal law	Jurisdiction: Cases in which all plaintiffs are from different states from all defendants (complete diversity) and there is a minimum amount in controversy ($75,000)

Removal: Cases originally filed in state court, but for which federal jurisdiction exists, may be removed to federal court by the defendant, 28 U.S.C. § 1441.

Remand: Improperly removed cases (no federal jurisdiction) may be returned to the state courts from which they were removed, 28 U.S.C. § 1447.

FIGURE 3-4
Federal judiciary—jurisdiction

YOUR CONSTITUTIONAL VALUES

DOES A PRISONER HAVE A CONSTITUTIONAL RIGHT TO A CENTER SLICE OF BREAD?

For most of U.S. history, state laws exclusively governed the conditions under which state prisoners were held. This began to change in the 1960s, when the Supreme Court "incorporated" the Eighth Amendment's prohibition of cruel and unusual punishments. One of the first cases to incorporate the Eighth Amendment's prohibition of cruel and unusual punishments was *Robinson v. California*, 370 U.S. 660 (1962), wherein the Court held that it was cruel and unusual for the State of California to make it a crime to be addicted to drugs. A person may be punished for the use of drugs, but the Court found that a person's status cannot be the basis of criminal liability.

By incorporating the Cruel and Unusual Punishments Clause, the Supreme Court determined that the right was so fundamental and necessary to an ordered liberty that it should limit state, as well as federal, authority. Since its incorporation, a large body of federal case law defining the rights of state prisoners has developed and many local jails and state prisons have been sued in federal court. The conditions at many of these institutions were found to be inadequate, and such institutions have, for varying periods of time, been under court order and supervision to monitor improvements. The case law now defines what punishments may be imposed for crimes (proportionality), the responsibilities of corrections officials to care for inmates, and the minimum conditions to which inmates are entitled.

As to minimally constitutional conditions, courts have held *inter alia* that inmates are entitled to access a legal library, to adequate medical and dental care, to a nutritious diet, to adequate heat and ventilation, to reasonable space, and to periodic exercise.

But how far do inmate rights extend? Inmates have asserted some interesting rights. In *Helling v. McKinley*, 509 U.S. 25 (1993), the Supreme Court held that prisoners may be entitled to a tobacco-smoke-free environment. In 2006, several inmates in Wisconsin prisons sued the state, alleging that state legislation prohibiting the use of state monies to fund sex-change procedures, the Sex Change Prevention Act, was cruel and unusual. A settlement was reached where the State of Wisconsin agreed to allow the plaintiff to wear women's undergarments and the plaintiff agreed to withdraw her surgery claim. In late 2010, the inmate-plaintiff reversed course, claiming that the settlement had been coerced. The case made its way to the U.S. Seventh Circuit Court of Appeals where the Wisconsin Sex Change Prevention Act was found to be violative of the Eighth Amendment's Cruel and Unusual Punishments Clause in 2011. The Court likened denying hormone and other treatments to denying cancer treatment.[34] In the early 1990s, inmates in an Indiana jail claimed that their conditions were cruel and unusual. Specifically, they alleged that the jail was poorly maintained and poorly lighted and had inadequate ventilation. Additionally, they alleged that the food was not sufficiently nutritious. Their complaint included an allegation that they should receive more meals from McDonald's and that they consistently received only the heels of bread. The district court, which found for the inmates on some of their claims, said of the last allegation, that any way you slice it, the allegation that the inmates are entitled to a center slice of the loaf does not rise to the level of an Eighth Amendment violation.

Source for Wisconsin story: Ryan J. Foley, *Wis. Inmate Rejects Women's Underwear, Insists on Sex Change* (Associated Press, November 10, 2010), found at www.startribune.com/lifestyle/health/107059208.html

3.5(d) Supreme Court Jurisdiction

Article III, Section 2, clause 2, states:

> In all Cases affecting Ambassadors, other public Ministers and Consuls, and those in which a State shall be a Party, the supreme Court shall have original Jurisdiction. In all the other Cases before mentioned, the supreme Court shall have appellate Jurisdiction, both as to Law and Fact, with such Exceptions, and under such Regulations as the Congress shall make.

Original Jurisdiction   Article III, Section 2, delegates to the Supreme Court original jurisdiction in all "[c]ases affecting Ambassadors, other public Ministers and Consuls, and those in which a State shall be a Party." Congress has implemented this provision through statutes. *Marbury* taught us that Congress may not extend the Supreme Court's original jurisdiction beyond this constitutional limit. Nevertheless, Congress may decide whether the Supreme Court's original jurisdiction is exclusive or is held concurrently with other courts.[35]

By statute, 28 U.S.C. § 1251, the Supreme Court is required to hear cases between two or more states. Section 1251 jurisdiction is exclusive; therefore, no other court may originally hear these cases. The Supreme Court has ruled, however, that the statute does not confer exclusive jurisdiction over cases involving political subdivisions of states, such as counties and municipalities.[36] Few of these cases come to the Supreme Court, but when one does, the Court usually refers it to a **special master** to conduct the trial and make findings of fact. Otherwise, the Court actually sits as a trial court, receiving evidence in addition to hearing the arguments of counsel.

special master
A person appointed by the court to assist with certain judicial functions in a specific case.

As to cases involving ambassadors, public ministers, and other public officials of foreign nations, or disputes between the United States and a state, or disputes between a state and citizens of another state or aliens, the Supreme Court has concurrent original jurisdiction with the federal district courts. In such cases, the Supreme Court is unlikely to accept jurisdiction; accordingly, the true court of original jurisdiction is the district court. The Supreme Court stated in one case: "[i]t has long been this Court's philosophy that our original jurisdiction should be invoked sparingly."[37] The seriousness of the claims and the availability of an alternate forum are important factors in the decision of whether to deny original jurisdiction. The Court has stated that its policy is justified because it needs to reserve time for its appellate duties.

Although 28 U.S.C. § 1251 was enacted to implement the Court's original jurisdiction, the Court has stated that such legislation is unnecessary, because the constitutional delegation of original jurisdiction is self-executing.[38] Said another way, the Constitution itself is the basis of the Supreme Court's original jurisdiction and Congress is not needed to make this so. Further, Congress may not eliminate this jurisdiction. Although self-execution of constitutional provisions is the norm, in some circumstances, it is not. If a constitutional provision is not self-executing, some additional action, commonly a statute, is necessary to make it enforceable.

Cyber Constitution
Supreme Court
The Supreme Court's official website is www.supremecourt.gov/

rule of four
An internal rule of the Supreme Court, which provides that a case will be reviewed by the Court if four justices wish it to be reviewed.

Appellate Jurisdiction   Article III, Section 2, clause 2, provides that in all cases in which the Supreme Court does not have original jurisdiction, but there is federal judicial power, the Supreme Court has appellate jurisdiction. The clause continues by stating that this appellate jurisdiction is subject to "regulations" and "exceptions" by Congress. Before delving into congressional control of the Court's appellate jurisdiction, let us examine the forms of appellate jurisdiction, certiorari, and appeal by right.

The Supreme Court receives far more appeals than it can hear. In recent years the Court has entertained only a small percentage of the cases brought to it. In fact, less than 2 percent of cases are granted certiorari. See Figure 3-5 for a breakdown of cases filed with the court over a three-year period.

Most of the cases heard by the Court arrive through certiorari procedure. *Certiorari* is a common law writ ordering a lower court to transmit a file to a higher court for review. The Supreme Court (as well as state appellate courts) uses certiorari to control its caseload. Individuals desiring Supreme Court review petition the Court to grant the writ. Under the **rule of four,** if any four justices vote in favor of granting certiorari, the case is placed on the docket. Granting the writ does not indicate which party will prevail, only that the Court feels the case is of sufficient importance to be heard. Certiorari is purely discretionary. The Court decides, upon its best judgment, what cases it will hear. It is prone to entertain cases that pose novel issues of federal law (also known as *cases of first impression*), especially constitutional law; cases in which there is a conflict in interpretation of federal law between state high courts or U.S. courts of appeals; and cases wherein a state high court or U.S. court of appeals has failed to follow the Supreme Court's precedents.[39] In addition, 28 U.S.C. § 1254 provides that any party to a civil or criminal action in a U.S. court of appeals may petition for certiorari. Also, a court of appeal may certify a question to the Supreme Court when it needs guidance or instructions. Under 28 U.S.C. § 1257, any party to

The Supreme Court receives thousands of petitions for certiorari each year. Most come in the form of a petition to proceed *in forma pauperis*(IFP). An IFP is a request to proceed without paying the required fees. Statistically, IFPs are less likely to be granted than paid petitions. The Court also receives a small number of original case petitions yearly. The data in this figure reflect the total cases on the Court's docket each term, whether newly filed or carried over from the previous term.

	October Term 2003	October Term 2004	October Term 2005
Total Cases	7,814	7,496	8,521
IFP Cases (*in forma pauperis*)	6,092	5,755	6,846
Paid	1,722	1,741	1,671
Argued	91	87	87
Opinions	73	74	69

Note: The percentage of filings granted review in any year is typically between 1.5% and 3%.

FIGURE 3-5
Supreme Court filings and cases

a case before a state high court may petition for certiorari when one of the following occurs:

1. The validity of a treaty is questioned.
2. The validity of a federal statute is questioned.
3. A state statute is challenged as violative of federal law, whether constitutional, statutory, or other.
4. A party asserts a title, right, privilege, or commission secured by federal law.

If, after granting a writ of certiorari, a majority of the Court determines that the case should not be heard, it is removed from the Court's docket and the decision of the lower court stands. A denial of a petition for a writ of certiorari also leaves the lower court's decision intact. A denial of certiorari has no precedential value, because no decision concerning the merits of the case is rendered.

A second avenue to the Supreme Court is through appeal by right. Unlike certiorari, the Supreme Court must hear cases of this nature. Appeals have always been outnumbered by certiorari, but since amendments to 28 U.S.C. § 1254 and § 1257 in 1988, the number of appeals has fallen, because cases that previously came to the Court through appeal were shifted to certiorari procedure. Today, the only cases that come to the Court by appeal are those in which three-judge district courts were empaneled. Few cases today require a three-judge district court, so these cases constitute only a small percentage of the high court's business. Pursuant to 28 U.S.C. § 1253, appeals from orders granting or denying injunctive relief from three-judge district courts may be made directly to the Supreme Court. Under 28 U.S.C. § 2284, three-judge district courts are required whenever specified by Congress through special legislation and in political apportionment cases. That is, if a congressional district or state legislative district is challenged as being improperly apportioned, a three-judge district court, as opposed to the usual one-judge court, must hear the case.

There are several instances, which occur infrequently, in which a three-judge district court is required with direct appeal to the Supreme Court—for example, enforcement of the Twenty-Sixth Amendment (voting rights) by the United States against the states,[40] civil rights actions filed by the Attorney General of the United States in employment cases[41] and cases concerning access to public accommodations,[42] actions by the United States against a state to enjoin a poll tax,[43] and actions filed by members of Congress concerning the constitutionality and enforcement of certain spending statutes.[44] In recent years, Congress has decreased the number of cases in which mandatory appeals were possible. Less than 1 percent of the Court's total caseload has come through mandatory appeals in recent years.

In some cases, appeal to the Supreme Court from a district court follows neither appeal nor certiorari procedure. Rather, a hybrid procedure is followed by which direct appeal to the Court is permitted but the appeal is discretionary. For example, a party in antitrust litigation may bring an appeal directly to the Supreme Court from the district court. However, the Supreme Court may dispose of the appeal "in the same manner as any other direct appeal . . . or in its discretion, deny the direct appeal and remand the case to the court of appeals."[45]

Also, as a matter of procedure, there must be a quorum of justices (five) before the Court may hear an appeal (certiorari or mandatory). A quorum may not be present because of vacancies on the Court or recusal of justices (e.g., when a justice has an interest in the case). By statute, the chief justice may remand a case to a U.S. court of appeals for hearing if a quorum cannot be reached. The decision of the court of appeals is final in such a case. In cases brought through certiorari, the judgment of the court from which the appeal is brought (i.e., court of appeals or state high court) is treated as affirmed if the qualified justices determine that a quorum does not exist and will not exist during the Court's next term.[46]

Recall that Article III, Section 2, clause 2, provides that Congress may establish "exceptions" to the appellate jurisdiction of the Supreme Court. The structure of the

Cyber Constitution
Supreme Court
Beyond the Supreme Court's official website, you can learn about the Court at www.oyez. org, www.law.cornell. edu/supct/, and www. supremecourthistory. org/, among other sites. Federal court opinions, at all levels; other federal law and state laws; and judicial opinions can be found at http://lp.findlaw. com/, www.oyez.com, and www.law.cornell.edu

clause makes it clear that the exceptions provision applies only to the Court's appellate jurisdiction and not its original jurisdiction. To what extent may Congress regulate the Court's appellate jurisdiction? Like many other clauses, the exceptions provision is vague. May Congress eliminate the Court's appellate jurisdiction entirely? This appears to be more than an "exception." What types of exceptions may Congress announce? May the jurisdiction of the Court be revoked as to a single case or during the pendency of a case? What role does the doctrine of separation of powers play in the exceptions analysis? These are difficult questions. The leading case in this area is *Ex Parte McCardle.*

LAW CLERKS

SIDEBAR

Nearly all federal judges employ at least one attorney, usually a recent law graduate, as a judicial law clerk. Although federal clerkships at all levels are prestigious, the most highly coveted are those for Supreme Court justices. Each justice of the Supreme Court has at least three clerks. Justice Horace Gray was the first to employ (at his own expense) a recent law school graduate to serve as secretary or law clerk.

Most clerks serve for only one or two years, although some clerks have served for longer periods. Clerks are appointed by, and exclusively serve, individual justices. Excepting the attorneys of the parties during oral arguments and the other members of the Court, law clerks are the only attorneys with whom a justice may confer. As a result, the law clerk becomes an important sounding board and source of ideas for many justices.

Selection criteria for law clerks vary, but it is common for justices to hire clerks from particular law schools (perhaps where the justice studied), from particular geographic areas of the country, who have prior clerking experience, and are personally compatible. For example, Oliver Wendell Holmes Jr., Louis Brandeis, and William Brennan favored Harvard Law School graduates. Justices William O. Douglas and Earl Warren favored individuals from the western United States. A former clerk stated that the best clerk for Justice Hugo Black was an Alabama boy who went to an Alabama law school.

The duties of a clerk are defined by his or her justice and vary significantly. Dean Acheson, who clerked for Justice Brandeis, commented that he wrote the footnotes of opinions. Clerks to Justices Butler and Murphy, in contrast, wrote nearly all the opinions of those justices. Justice Warren would have his clerks prepare a draft opinion from which he would cast his final opinion. Most justices have their law clerks conduct legal research, prepare memoranda examining legal issues and parties' briefs, and screen petitions for certiorari. Justice Frankfurter used his law clerks to lobby the clerks of other justices, and sometimes the justices themselves, in an effort to "line up" votes.

The degree to which law clerks influence the development of the law is unknown, but it is unquestionable that as the caseload of all federal courts has increased, so has the role played by clerks.

Source: David O'Brien, *Storm Center: The Supreme Court in American Politics,* 3d ed. (W.W. Norton 1993).

Ex Parte McCardle
74 U.S. (7 Wall.) 506 (1869)

[McCardle, a civilian, was arrested and detained by military authorities. He was charged with printing "incendiary and libelous" articles in a newspaper in violation of the Reconstruction Acts. Alleging unlawful detention, McCardle sought habeas corpus (judicial review of the constitutionality of detention) in the United States Court of Appeals. When this was denied, he appealed to the U.S. Supreme Court under a statute allowing such an appeal. The Supreme Court received the case and heard arguments but, before it issued a decision, Congress repealed the statute under which McCardle had appealed. President Andrew Johnson (who was involved in his own impeachment at the time) vetoed the bill, but it was overridden by two-thirds votes in both houses of Congress.]

Chief Justice Chase delivered the opinion of the Court.

The first question necessarily is that of jurisdiction; for, if the act of March, 1868, takes away the jurisdiction defined by the act of February, 1867, it is useless, if not improper, to enter into any discussion of other questions.

It is quite true, as was argued by the counsel for the petitioner, that the appellate jurisdiction of this court is not derived from acts of Congress. It is, strictly speaking, conferred by the Constitution. But it is conferred "with such exceptions and under such regulations as Congress shall make."

It is unnecessary to consider whether, if Congress had made no exceptions and no regulations, this court might not have exercised general appellate jurisdiction under rules prescribed by itself. For among the earliest acts of the first Congress, at its first session, was the act of September 24th, 1789, to establish the judicial courts of the United States. That act provided for the organization of this court, and prescribed regulations for the exercise of its jurisdiction.

The source of that jurisdiction, and the limitations of it by the Constitution and by statute, have been on several occasions subjects of consideration here. In the case of *Durousseau v. United States* (6 Cranch 312, 3 L. Ed. 232 [1810]) particularly, the whole matter was carefully examined, and the court held, that while "the appellate powers of this court are not given by the judicial act, but are given by the Constitution," they are, nevertheless, "limited and regulated by that act, and by such other acts as have been passed on the subject." The court said, further, that the judicial act was an exercise of the power given by the Constitution to Congress "of making exceptions to the appellate jurisdiction of the Supreme Court." "They have described affirmatively," said the court, "its jurisdiction, and this affirmative description has been understood to imply a negation of the exercise of such appellate power as is not comprehended within it."

The principle that the affirmation of appellate jurisdiction implies the negative of all such jurisdiction not affirmed having been established, it was an almost necessary consequence that acts of Congress, providing for the exercise of jurisdiction, should come to be spoken of as acts granting jurisdiction, and not as acts making exceptions to the constitutional grant of it.

The exception to appellate jurisdiction in the case before us, however, is not an inference from the affirmation of other appellate jurisdiction. It is made in terms. The provision of the act of 1867, affirming the appellate jurisdiction of this court in cases of *habeas corpus* is expressly repealed. It is hardly possible to imagine a plainer instance of positive exception.

We are not at liberty to inquire into the motives of the legislature. We can only examine into its power under the Constitution; and the power to make exceptions to the appellate jurisdiction of this court is given by express words.

What, then, is the effect of the repealing act upon the case before us? We cannot doubt as to this. Without jurisdiction the court cannot proceed at all in any cause. Jurisdiction is the power to declare the law, and when it ceases to exist, the only function remaining to the court is that of announcing that fact and dismissing the cause.

And this is not less clear upon authority than upon principle. . . .

[T]he general rule, supported by the best elementary writers, is, that "when an act of the legislature is repealed, it must be considered, except as to transactions past and closed, as if it never existed." . . .

It is quite clear, therefore, that this court can not proceed to pronounce judgment in this case, for it has no longer jurisdiction of the appeal; and judicial duty is not less fitly performed by declining ungranted jurisdiction than in exercising firmly that which the Constitution and laws confer. . . .

The appeal of the petitioner in this case must be dismissed for want of jurisdiction.

McCardle stands for the proposition that Congress possesses broad authority over the Supreme Court's appellate jurisdiction. Some jurists interpret the exceptions clause (and the *McCardle* decision) as granting Congress nearly absolute control over the Supreme Court's appellate jurisdiction. Justice Frankfurter interpreted the exceptions clause in this literal manner. He said, "Congress cannot give this Court any appellate power; it may withdraw appellate jurisdiction once conferred and it may do so even while a case is *sub judice*."[47]

Whether the Supreme Court would interpret the exceptions clause this broadly today is questionable. Justice Douglas stated in a 1962 opinion, "[t]here is a serious question whether the *McCardle* case could command a majority view today."[48] There are several reasons to believe that congressional authority over the Court's appellate jurisdiction might be interpreted more narrowly than advanced by Justice Frankfurter. First, *McCardle* was issued at a time when the federal courts played less of a role in government than today. Increasingly, the public has looked to the Court to maintain the balance of government and to secure civil liberties. Accordingly, separation of powers principles could be used to block the wholesale elimination of the Court's appellate jurisdiction. Indeed, distinguished jurist Henry Hart stated that the exceptions clause cannot be used to "destroy the essential role of the Supreme Court in the constitutional plan."[49] Today, the Court's essential role may be its status as a referee of the relationships between the federal government's branches, between the states and the federal government, between states, and between governments and citizens. If this is accepted, Congress would be prohibited from using the exceptions clause to prevent review of its actions that are alleged to violate civil liberties or separation of powers. To date, the Supreme Court has not announced such a limitation upon Congress's authority under the exceptions clause.

The second limitation upon the exceptions clause has a separation of powers foundation. Congress may not use the exceptions clause to exercise a judicial power. That is, Congress may not use the exceptions clause to decide an individual case. Any withdrawal of jurisdiction must be neutral. To be neutral, such a law would have to apply generally, as opposed to applying to an individual or a specific group of individuals. Congress may not use the exceptions clause to direct the outcome of a specific case. The issue of selective withdrawal of jurisdiction came before the Court in *United States v. Klein.*

The Court concluded in *Klein* that Congress was not eliminating appeals in a class of cases. Rather, it was using jurisdiction to decide specific cases—a judicial function. In addition to attempting to usurp judicial power, the Court also held that Congress was usurping executive power. This is in direct conflict with the doctrine of separation of powers, so the statute was held void. Even in *McCardle,* the Court referred to state cases in which state courts had invalidated state laws dealing with judicial jurisdiction as interfering with the judicial power. This principle appears to be a well-entrenched limitation upon the exceptions clause.

Third, the exceptions clause may be limited by other constitutional provisions. In cases where a congressional decision to limit jurisdiction conflicts with another constitutional provision, the Court would be forced to decide which provision prevails. For example, there is considerable First Amendment jurisprudence concerning whether governments may allow displays or exhibits of a religious nature (a Christian manger scene, for example) on public property. The plaintiffs in these cases are often individuals of nonmajority religious faiths. It would be unconstitutional (violative of equal protection, as guaranteed by the Fifth and Fourteenth Amendments) for Congress to withdraw the Supreme Court's appellate jurisdiction in cases in which Muslims, Jews, Hindus, or people of other faiths were plaintiffs, while preserving the right of Christians to seek relief.

United States v. Klein
80 U.S. 128 (1871)

[Klein sued to recover property that had been seized by the United States during the Civil War. Pursuant to the authorizing statute, to be eligible to recover his property, a claimant had to prove that he did not aid the Confederacy. Klein received a presidential pardon (pursuant to a general pardon offered by the President to all citizens who aided the Confederacy) for his war activities. In his petition to recover his property, Klein relied on a Supreme Court decision that declared pardons to be conclusive proof that an individual did not aid in the rebellion. Klein won his case at the trial level, in the U.S. Court of Claims, but while his appeal to the Supreme Court was pending, Congress enacted a statute reversing the Supreme Court's earlier decision. That statute declared that this specific pardon was irrebuttable proof that the pardoned citizen had aided the Confederacy. The statute further required cases in the Court of Claims to be dismissed, thereby denying the return of property, if the claimant had accepted the pardon without a disclaimer ("I accept the pardon even though I did not support the enemy"). Finally, the Supreme Court's jurisdiction over appeals from the Court of Claims in these cases was withdrawn.]

Mr. Chief justice Chase delivered the opinion of the court.

The Court of Claims is thus constituted one of those inferior courts which Congress authorizes, and has jurisdiction of contracts between the Government and the citizen, from which appeal regularly lies to this Court.

Undoubtably, the Legislature has complete control over the organization and existence of that court and may confer or withhold the right of appeal from its decisions. And if this Act did nothing more, it would be our duty to give it effect. If it is simply denied the right of appeal in a particular class of cases, there could be no doubt that it must be regarded as an exercise of the power of Congress to make "such exceptions from the appellate jurisdiction" as should seem to it expedient.

But the language of the proviso shows plainly that it does not intend to withhold appellate jurisdiction except as a means to an end. Its great and controlling purpose is to deny to pardons granted by the President the effect which this court had adjudged them to have. . . .

It seems to us that this is not an exercise of the acknowledged power of Congress to make exceptions and prescribe regulations of the appellate power.

The court is required to ascertain the existence of certain facts and thereupon to declare that its jurisdiction on appeal has ceased, by dismissing the bill. What is this but to prescribe a rule for the decision of a cause in a particular way? . . .

We must think that Congress has inadvertently passed the limit which separates the legislative from the judicial power.

It is of vital importance that these powers be kept distinct. The Constitution provides that the judicial power of the United States shall be vested in one Supreme Court and such inferior courts as Congress shall from time to time ordain and establish. The same instrument, in the last clause of the same article, provides that in all cases other than those of original jurisdiction "the Supreme Court shall have appellate jurisdiction both as to law and fact, with such exceptions and under such regulations as the Congress shall make."

The Congress has already provided that the Supreme Court shall have jurisdiction of the judgments of the Court of Claims on appeal. Can it prescribe a rule in conformity with which the court must deny to itself the jurisdiction thus conferred, because and only because its decision, in accordance with settled law, must be adverse to the Government and favorable to the suitor? This question seems to us to answer itself.

The rule prescribed is also liable to just exception as impairing the effect of a pardon, and thus infringing the constitutional power of the Executive.

It is the intention of the Constitution that each of the great coordinate departments of the Government—the Legislative, the Executive and the Judicial—shall be, in its sphere, independent of the others. To the Executive alone is intrusted the power of pardon; and it is granted without limit. It blots out the offense pardoned and removes all its penal consequences. . . .

Now, it is clear that the Legislature cannot change the effect of such a pardon any more than the Executive can change a law. Yet this is attempted by the provision under consideration. [The motion to dismiss was denied and the judgment of the Court of Claims was affirmed.]

The issue appears to be one, at least in part, of legislative motive. In such a case, Congress's motive would be to direct the outcome of a specific class of cases. The line between a neutral law and an improperly motivated law is thin. Even more, motive-based tests are tricky. They create evidence problems: How does a plaintiff prove that all the members of Congress who voted in favor of a bill shared a motive? Legislative history may be used, but often it does not reflect the true intentions of legislators. In any event, it is likely that a jurisdictional statute that encroaches upon equal protection or due process will be invalidated. Through dicta, the Court has stated as much.[50]

The final issue is that of complete withdrawal. The Supreme Court handed down *Ex Parte Yerger*[51] during the same year it decided *McCardle*. The Court held that it had jurisdiction to hear an appeal in *Yerger*, even though the case was similar to *McCardle*. Jurisdiction was present in *Yerger*, however, because the appeal was brought through certiorari procedure and not through the repealed statute that was at issue in *McCardle*. The Court held that Congress had withdrawn only one method of reaching the Court and that the Court's discretion to grant certiorari had not been withdrawn. Some commentators have suggested that the outcome in *McCardle* would have been different if the holding in *Yerger* had not been possible. That is, repeal of a remedy is valid so long as other remedies are available to an aggrieved party.

The *McCardle* Court recognized that the repeal of appellate jurisdiction at issue was limited. "Counsel seems to have supposed, if effect be given to the repealing act in question, that the whole appellate power of the court, in cases of habeas corpus, is denied. But this is an error. The act of 1868 does not except from the jurisdiction any cases but appeals from Circuit Court under the act of 1867."[52] It may be that if Congress had eliminated all classes of appeals in habeas corpus cases, or if it had eliminated habeas corpus in all federal courts, the decision might have been different. The issue is what is an exception? The use of the term *exception* itself indicates that the Supreme Court will retain the bulk of its appellate jurisdiction outlined in the Constitution. Many interpretations are possible. Can an exception be horizontal (that is, withdrawing jurisdiction that affects many classes of cases, such as excepting all cases that arise out of the Fourteenth Amendment), or vertical (withdrawing jurisdiction in one type of case only, such as school prayer), or both? Can Congress except all cases arising during a specified period of time (e.g., the Supreme Court shall not hear any appeals from cases arising between January 1, 1997, and January 1, 1998)? Can Congress except cases arising in certain regions of the nation (e.g., the Supreme Court shall not hear any appeals from cases arising out of the Seventh Circuit Court of Appeals)? Although no such cases have been litigated, the former is likely violative of separation of powers and the latter violative of equal protection. Exception to jurisdiction in particular cases, as discussed earlier, is the clearest case for overreaching by Congress.

Finally, Congress could use the exceptions clause to control the Court's review of cases by subject matter (e.g., the Supreme Court shall not hear any appeals from cases involving abortion rights). That issue has not reached the Court, and it is unknown whether such a law would be constitutional. The following factors would be considered for this determination:

1. What is being excepted from review? Does the withdrawal conflict with another constitutional provision, such as due process or equal protection?
2. Is the withdrawal of jurisdiction neutral?
3. Does the withdrawal of jurisdiction comport with separation of powers principles?
4. Does the withdrawal interfere with the Court's performance of its essential role?
5. Does the withdrawal of jurisdiction leave the states to decide federal constitutional law?

This is not a precise formulation, and this area of law is uncertain.[53] It does, however, provide a good guide as to whether a congressional withdrawal of jurisdiction would be valid.

There are arguments favoring a broad interpretation of the exceptions clause. Proponents of the countermajoritarian theory contend that congressional control over the Court's jurisdiction is not only proper, but also necessary, to check the Court. Otherwise, the Court is likely to become a body of philosopher-kings. Of course, individuals who subscribe to the literal school of interpretation contend that the clause is unambiguous—Congress has been delegated the authority to decide the what and when of the Supreme Court's appellate jurisdiction. Remember, withdrawal of Supreme Court jurisdiction does not mean that no court will hear the case. Rather, a state or federal appellate court will become the court of final resort.

On the other side, a more narrow interpretation of the clause insulates the Supreme Court from riding the wave of public opinion. Recall that the nation was founded upon the ideal of limited government and individual freedom. Although other courts, state and federal, may enforce the law in a fair and neutral manner, the Supreme Court's place at the top of the judicial hierarchy gives law uniformity. If the Court's appellate jurisdiction is eliminated in an area, lower-court decisions (those of state high courts, U.S. courts of appeals, etc.) would become final. As a result of conflicting interpretations, citizens in different geographic areas of the country could be treated differently under the Constitution. For example, affirmative action could be lawful in some areas but violative of equal protection in others.

Also, a narrow reading of the clause preserves the integrity of the Court in the tripartite system. To give Congress plenary authority over the Court's jurisdiction is like allowing the fox to guard the henhouse, as one of the roles of the Court (at least since *Marbury*) is to review the actions of its coordinate branches (see Figure 3-6).

SUPREME COURT JURISDICTION

Original: Cases involving ambassadors, other public ministers, and consuls, and those in which a state is a party

Congressional control: Congress may not extend the Court's original jurisdiction. It may, however, provide that the Court's original jurisdiction is held concurrently with other federal courts or that it is exclusive.

Appellate: All cases where federal judicial power exists and the Court does not have original jurisdiction.

Congressional control: Congress may establish "regulations" and "exceptions." The extent of congressional control is undefined.

FIGURE 3-6
The U.S. Supreme Court—jurisdiction

3.5(e) Lower Courts' Jurisdictions

Article III Courts   Although Article III expressly creates only the Supreme Court, it provides that Congress may create "inferior Courts." Courts created under this provision, like the Supreme Court, are commonly known as *constitutional courts* or *Article III courts.* Although these courts are established by Congress, the Constitution is the source of their existence. As Article III entities, these courts are limited in jurisdiction to "cases and controversies." Congress may not extend their jurisdiction beyond the Constitution's limits. Judges of Article III courts are assured lifetime tenure and no reduction in pay. Certain classes of cases, as well as certain parts of cases, must be heard by Article III judges.

The first Congress established Article III lower courts in the Judiciary Act of 1789. Through that statute, three circuit courts of appeals and thirteen district courts were created. Initially, there were no circuit judges. Circuit court panels were comprised of one district judge and two Supreme Court justices.

The organization of the system has since changed. Today, there are eleven geographical circuits with a court of appeals in each. There are two additional courts of appeals, one in the District of Columbia and another for the Federal Circuit. Hence, there are thirteen courts of appeals in the federal system.

These courts represent the intermediate-level appellate courts of the federal system. (See Figure 2-4 for a diagram of the federal appellate circuits.) They hear appeals from district courts, specialty courts, and, in some instances, administrative tribunals.

It is generally agreed that because Congress possesses the power to create these courts, it has control over their jurisdiction. Recall, however, that as Article III courts, their jurisdiction cannot be extended by Congress beyond the Constitution's case-and-controversy, diversity, and federal question limitations. But it appears that, within those limitations, Congress has nearly total control over the cases that may be entertained by these courts.

> It would seem to follow, also, that, having a right to prescribe, Congress may withhold from any court of its creation jurisdiction of any of the enumerated controversies. Courts created by statute can have no jurisdiction but such as the statute confers.[54]

Similarly, the Court stated:

> As regards the inferior courts to be established, Congress may give them such jurisdiction, both original and appellate, within the limits of the Constitution, as it may see fit to confer. . . . The whole subject is remitted to the unfettered discretion of Congress.[55]

Of course, some jurists argue that Congress may have control over the jurisdiction of lower courts, but its authority is not **plenary.** Rather, jurisdictional declarations

plenary
Full; complete.

must be consonant with other constitutional mandates, as was previously discussed in regard to Supreme Court appellate jurisdiction. In the extreme, it has been argued that, because of the importance of federal courts in assuring due process and equal protection of citizens, Congress could not totally eliminate all lower federal courts. For example, it is generally accepted that Congress may withdraw cases from being heard in state courts. Also, Congress may withhold the original jurisdiction of lower federal courts and the appellate jurisdiction of the Supreme Court. In such cases, no court would possess jurisdiction to resolve the federal constitutional claim. Although the jurisdictional mandates may be valid individually, as a whole they are constitutionally unsound. Whether the line is drawn at this extreme point, or earlier, is unknown.

This analysis applies only to constitutionally secured rights. If a right is established by Congress, it may eliminate that right or withhold the jurisdiction of all courts to enforce the right while leaving it intact. Recall, however, that state judges have an obligation to follow federal law, even if contrary to their own state's law. Thus, a citizen may assert the federal Constitution as a defense to state action. Congress cannot withdraw this remedy from the state courts. However, this example refers to cases involving the federal government. For example, suppose Congress enacts a new environmental statute that prohibits the owners of wetlands from building on or otherwise developing their property. These types of laws are often challenged as constituting a taking of property under the Fifth Amendment. In a taking, the federal government is required to compensate the property owner. It is hard to imagine that it would be constitutionally sound to withdraw jurisdiction from every state and federal court in such a case. In fact, it appears that the framers intended for all federal claims to be heard by a federal court. At the inception of the Constitution, this role could be handled by the Supreme Court. Today, however, the Court cannot hear all these cases. Therefore, lower courts are now not a luxury—they are a constitutional necessity.

Through diversity and federal question jurisdiction, federal courts hear nearly all the cases allowed by the Constitution. Congress could expand the jurisdiction of the federal courts if it wished. For example, the statute providing for diversity jurisdiction has been interpreted as limiting that jurisdiction to cases of complete diversity (all defendants diverse from all plaintiffs), although the Court has held that the Constitution permits incomplete diversity.[56] Also, several statutes limit original and appellate jurisdiction directly, such as a statute that generally forbids federal courts from enjoining state court proceedings.[57]

Article I and Article II Courts Congress may establish nonconstitutional courts. The judges of these courts are not entitled to lifetime tenure, their pay may be reduced while they are in office, and they need not be selected through the constitutional nomination and confirmation process. These courts are commonly referred to as *Article I courts*. The Constitution's jurisdictional limitations do not apply to these courts. Accordingly, Congress may delegate to these tribunals hypothetical questions and other nondisputes.

There are many Article I judges and courts in the federal system. The U.S. bankruptcy courts, U.S. magistrate-judges, military courts, territorial courts, the Claims Court, the Tax Court, and some District of Columbia courts are examples. Although their nonconstitutional nature enables Article I judges to perform some functions prohibited to Article III judges, it also limits their authority in particular instances. Article I judges may not be delegated the authority to perform essential judicial functions. For example, in some instances a litigant may possess a right to appear before a constitutionally empowered judge. In such a case, an Article I judge may not render the final decision in the case, nor may he or she preside over some critical stage of the proceeding.

This is true of U.S. magistrate-judges. These official positions are the creation of Congress, although they reside within the judicial branch. The system of magistrates was created in an effort to reduce the burden on district judges without establishing new Article III judgeships. Congress was careful to keep magistrates accountable to Article III judges and therefore less susceptible to constitutional challenge. Magistrates are appointed by, and may be removed by, Article III judges. The decisions of magistrates are reviewed, **de novo,** by Article III judges. Party consent is required before a magistrate may conduct a trial.

de novo
Anew; over again; a second time.

Under the Federal Magistrates Act,[58] certain responsibilities are delegated to magistrates (though their actions are reviewable by district judges) and district judges are empowered to delegate further responsibilities. However, in *Gomez v. United States*[59] and *Peretz v. United States,*[60] the Court ruled that a magistrate may not preside over the critical stages of a criminal trial over the objection of one of the parties. Because Congress carefully drafted the Magistrates Act, however, magistrates may preside over nearly all other pretrial and trial proceedings, subject to review by a district judge. If Congress were to amend the Magistrates Act to make the decision of a magistrate final, it would likely be invalid.

An interesting question, which remains open today, is whether federal bankruptcy judges may conduct jury trials. The Seventh Amendment preserves the right to a jury in federal common law cases when the amount in controversy exceeds $20. There is no right to a jury trial in equity cases. Although most of the legal issues presented to bankruptcy judges are equitable in nature, some are not.

In 1989, the Supreme Court issued *Granfinanciera, S.A. v. Nordberg,*[61] in which it ruled that litigants in bankruptcy actions involving a common law issue possess a right to have those disputes heard by a jury. The Supreme Court did not answer the next logical question: Whether Article I bankruptcy judges may preside over bankruptcy-related jury trials. This question has not been answered by the Court, and there is a split of authority among the lower federal courts.[62] The powers and limitations of non–Article III tribunals are discussed in greater depth in Chapter 7.

In total, the federal courts dispose of a significant amount of litigation annually. In 1993, the district courts handled 275,850 cases; courts of appeals, 50,000 cases; and bankruptcy courts, 896,000 cases. The Supreme Court had 5,832 cases on its docket during that year. What is amazing is that this accounts for less than 5 percent of all litigation in the United States (the remainder falls into the state courts).

Congress has created a number of specialty courts. The Court of Claims, the Court of International Trade, the Tax Court, and the Court of Customs and Patents Appeals are examples. The Court of Claims was created by statute in 1855. It has jurisdiction over most claims against the United States.[63]

Another form of non–Article III federal courts are those created under both Articles I and IV, courts in the territories of the United States. They are created by Congress, hence the Article I reference. The source of their creation is also Article IV, Section 3, which provides that "The Congress shall have Power to dispose of and make all needful Rules and Regulations respecting the Territory or other property belonging to the United States. . . ." The courts of American Samoa, Commonwealth of the Marianas Islands, Guam, and the U.S. Virgin Islands are examples. Interestingly, Puerto Rico does not fall into this category because Congress established full Article III courts there. This is also true of the courts in the District of Columbia. Finally, there are the anomalous courts established by the executive under Article II of the Constitution. These are rare, but known to the law. For example, the State Department established a court in Berlin, West Germany, in 1978 to try airline hijackers. The hijackers were not terrorists, but East Germans who had commandeered a plane and forced it to land in West Germany, in an attempt to escape the repression of the Eastern Bloc. The United States, West Germany, and East Germany were signatories to an international agreement criminalizing hijacking, and the United States continued to have authority over its section of West Germany as a residual power from World War II. East Germany insisted on prosecution, and West Germany convinced the United States to try the individuals under U.S. authority. Hence, a court was created under the authority of the president.

The defendants were tried by a jury and convicted. An Article III judge, Herbert Stern, was selected to try the matter, and he caused the State Department some consternation by applying U.S. constitutional law. The State Department insisted that the Constitution has no force outside the United States and that the defendants were not entitled to the rights and protections found therein, such as the right to a jury trial. Judge Stern disagreed and ruled that the defendants were protected by the Constitution; accordingly, they were entitled to due process and a jury trial. As to the claim that the court was an Article II tribunal subject to orders from the secretary of state, Judge Stern stated, "[d]ue process requires that if the United States convenes this Court, it must come before the Court as a litigant and not as a commander." The judge was careful to distinguish the case from military courts-martial, espionage cases, and military trials during times of war, in which the outcomes would be different.[64]

Interesting issues are raised by such a case. Can courts be established under Article II to try criminal cases? Unquestionably, such a court could not be used within the United States. But what about international circumstances such as those presented in the Berlin case? What about international war crimes trials, such as the Nuremberg trials? If permitted, to what extent must the judge be independent? Also, to what extent does the Constitution apply in such a case? These questions have not been answered and are as much political as they are legal.[65]

Cyber Constitution
Administrative Law Judges
For the qualifications to serve as a federal administrative law judge, visit www.opm.gov/qualifications/alj/alj.asp

Administrative Tribunals   As discussed in greater detail in Chapter 7, administrative agencies perform "quasi-judicial" functions. Also, as discussed earlier, these agencies are not Article III tribunals. Accordingly, they are limited by the Constitution to a greater extent than are Article III judges in some ways; in others, they may possess broader jurisdiction than Article III judges. For example, an agency can be delegated the authority to render advisory opinions. However, because such an agency is not constitutionally empowered, its interpretations of law would not be binding on Article III courts. Similarly, the case-or-controversy requirement that limits the jurisdiction of federal courts has no constitutional effect on administrative agencies.

The jurisdictional authority of administrative agencies is established by Congress. Administrative tribunals are characterized as informal, when compared to courts, and operate under a different set of procedural and evidentiary rules than do court proceedings. There are over 1,000 administrative law judges (ALJs) in the federal administrative system. ALJs hear more cases each year than do all the federal courts combined. One agency alone, the Social Security Administration, hears more cases than the entire civil docket of the federal courts.[66] Greater detail about the powers, limits, and role of administrative tribunals is provided in Chapter 7.

3.6 LIMITATIONS ON FEDERAL JUDICIAL POWER

As previously discussed, Article III limits the jurisdiction of federal courts to actual cases and controversies. Article III courts may not hear hypothetical cases, no matter how important to the nation. Article III is also the source of other limitations.

Additionally, other constitutional provisions, such as the Eleventh Amendment, restrict the power of federal courts. A case that may be heard by a federal court is said to be *justiciable,* and the following rules are known, in combination, as the **justiciability doctrine.** What follows is a discussion of the most significant limitations on federal judicial power.

justiciability doctrine
Rules that limit the authority of federal courts to hear cases, such as ripeness, mootness, political question, and standing.

3.6(a) Ripeness and Mootness

As previously pointed out, Article III limits the jurisdiction of federal courts to genuine disputes. This rule affects the timing of lawsuits.

Ripeness   If a suit is filed before a harm has occurred or before the threat of harm is imminent, there is no genuine dispute and hence no jurisdiction. The case is said to be *unripe.*

The most significant decision in this area is the 1947 Supreme Court decision in *United Mine Workers v. Mitchell.*[67] This case centered around the Hatch Act, a federal statute that prohibited executive branch employees from participating in political campaigns. One employee had violated the statute, but several employees challenged it. The Court heard the case and concluded that only the employee who was subject to punishment for actually violating the statute had presented a justiciable claim. The other employees had presented their claim prematurely. The Court stated, "[a] hypothetical threat is not enough. We can only speculate as to the kinds of political activity the appellants desire to engage in or as to the contents of their proposed public statements. . . . Should the courts [hear such cases,] they would become the organ of political theories."[68]

Similarly, if a law is not enforced and there is no reason to believe that it will be enforced, an action seeking to have the law declared unconstitutional is not ripe. This occurred in *Poe v. Ullman,*[69] in which a law criminalizing the use of contraceptives was challenged. The Court found that because the law was not enforced, there was no justiciable issue.

Mootness   Just as a case may be filed prematurely, it may also be heard by a court too late to be justiciable. A case for which the disputed issues have been resolved or dissipated during litigation is moot. Consider a hypothetical example. Latoya is the president of SITUS (State Income Tax Is Unlawful Society). At each monthly SITUS meeting, Latoya burns the state flag in protest of the state income tax. In January, the state legislature enacts a statute criminalizing desecration of the state flag. Latoya receives a letter the following week from the local prosecutor indicating that if she continues her practice, she will be prosecuted under the new law. Latoya responds by filing a petition asking the federal district court to declare the law unconstitutional under the First Amendment. During the pendency of the suit, the prosecutor comes to believe that the law is unconstitutional and issues a public statement that no person will be prosecuted under the new law. This action renders the case moot.

An example of mootness that reached the Supreme Court is *DeFunis v. Odegaard.*[70] DeFunis was denied admission to the University of Washington Law School in 1971. He filed an action in state court seeking an order declaring the admissions process violative of equal protection. DeFunis claimed that minority applicants were unlawfully favored for admission. He prevailed at the trial level, and an order was issued to the university to admit him. During his legal studies, the Supreme Court of Washington reversed the trial court's decision. The Supreme Court issued a stay of that court's decision and set the matter for hearing. By the time the case reached the Supreme Court, DeFunis was in his third year of law school, and the university indicated that he would be allowed to complete his graduate degree regardless of the outcome of the appeal. Due to these facts, the Supreme Court held that the case was moot.

Important to the mootness inquiry is whether an action is filed by an individual or on the behalf of a class. Individual actions become moot more easily than do **class actions.** For example, had DeFunis filed his action on behalf of all Caucasian applicants, past and future, who were or might be discriminated against as a result of the university's affirmative action policy, the entire action might not have been dismissed as moot.[71]

Exceptions to Mootness   There are exceptions to the mootness doctrine. The first concerns behavior that is **capable of repetition yet evading review.** Three elements must be proved to satisfy this test. First, there must have been a legal or factual issue when the case was filed that became moot during the pendency of the proceedings. Second, the harm at issue must be capable of recurring. Third, the nature of the issue must be such that it evades review. Typically, a case evades review because its facts change before review can be had. That was true in the well-known case of *Roe v. Wade,*[72] wherein the Supreme Court held that women possess the right to elect to abort pregnancies, in some circumstances.

Roe, a plaintiff using a **pseudonym,** challenged a Texas statute that prohibited her from obtaining an abortion. By the time the case reached the Court, there was no

class action
An action brought by one or several plaintiffs on behalf of a class of persons. A class action may be appropriate when there has been injury to so many people that their voluntarily and unanimously joining in a lawsuit is improbable and impracticable. In such a situation, injured parties who wish to do so may, with the court's permission, sue on behalf of all. A class action is sometimes referred to as a *representative action.*

capable of repetition yet evading review
An exception to the mootness doctrine, providing that if an alleged harm may be repeated, but by its nature cannot be judicially determined in the normal legal process, that harm may become the basis of jurisdiction.

pseudonym
A fictitious name. A plaintiff may sometimes be permitted to file a case using a fictitious name, if the plaintiff has a legitimate interest in protecting his or her privacy, such as when the facts of the case are embarrassing or the plaintiff's life may be threatened.

Cyber Constitution
Roe v. Wade
To read *Roe v. Wade*, go to http://caselaw.lp.findlaw. com/cgi-bin/getcase. pl?court=us&vol=410& invol=113

voluntary cessation of illegal acts
An exception to the mootness doctrine, providing that if an alleged harm has been ceased in order to avoid review, and there is a reasonable likelihood that the harm will reoccur or be recommenced, then the case may be heard.

collateral consequences
An exception to the mootness doctrine providing for jurisdiction in cases in which the primary issue is moot, but secondary—*collateral*— issues remain.

standing
The legal capacity to bring and to maintain a lawsuit. A person is without standing to sue unless some interest of his or hers has been adversely affected or unless he or she has been injured by the defendant. The term "standing to sue" is often shortened simply to "standing."

chance that Roe was still pregnant (at least not the pregnancy that was the basis of her complaint), as two years had passed. Regardless, the Supreme Court heard the case. The Court stated:

the normal 266-day human gestation period is so short that the pregnancy will come to term before the usual appellate process is complete. If that termination makes a case moot, pregnancy litigation seldom will survive much beyond the trial stage, and appellate review would be effectively denied. Pregnancy provides a classic justification for a conclusion of non-mootness. It truly could be capable of repetition yet evading review.[73]

A second exception to mootness applies in cases when the defendant appears to have stopped the alleged violation in order to avoid judicial review. This is commonly referred to as the **voluntary cessation of illegal acts** doctrine. This is similar to the "capable of repetition yet evading review" rule, except that the defendant is responsible for the case becoming moot. If it appears that such an action is intended only to avoid review and that the behavior may resume, jurisdiction to hear the case exists.

A third exception applies when the actual subject of litigation becomes moot but **collateral consequences** continue to linger. For example, assume that a state punishes thefts of items valued at less than $100 with a fine and no more than three months' imprisonment. It is not possible for a case to be reviewed by an appellate court before the sentence is served. Even though the sentence may have been completed, there are collateral consequences: An offender may be placed on probation, sentences in future convictions may be enhanced due to the conviction, and the offender may be stigmatized in the community. For these reasons, the issue is justiciable even though the actual sentence has been fully served. So long as a party has some interest, tangible or intangible, in the litigation, the case is not moot.

Parties may not create fictional disputes in order to get a legal question answered. For example, in *United States v. Johnson*,[74] the plaintiff sued his landlord, alleging that the rent he paid was in excess of what federal regulations permitted. The United States intervened (which explains why it is in the case title) in defense of the law. The trial court ruled that the law was unconstitutional. The United States then sought reconsideration because it claimed that the original parties had acted in collusion to create jurisdiction. In support of this, the United States pointed out that the plaintiff had brought the suit (using a fictitious name) at the defendant's request, the plaintiff's counsel had never met the plaintiff, and, most important, the defendant had paid the plaintiff's attorney fees. Based upon these facts, the Supreme Court found that the parties were attempting to have a legal question answered, not to have a dispute resolved.

3.6(b) Standing

Standing is concerned with *who* may file a claim or assert a defense—in other words, who may be a plaintiff or defendant. An individual must have standing to be a party to litigation. To have standing, a party must have a genuine interest in the outcome of the litigation. A party must possess "such a personal stake in the outcome of a controversy as to assure that concrete adverseness which sharpens the presentation of issues upon which the Court so largely depends for illumination of difficult constitutional questions."[75]

In some cases, standing may be evident from a statute. Congress may have created a right and expressly provided that certain classes of individuals have standing to enforce the created right. In other cases, such as when Congress creates a right but does not express who should have standing, and in cases in which a constitutional right is asserted, standing is more problematic.

Generally, standing exists if three requirements are met. This test was announced by the Supreme Court in *Baker v. Carr.*[76]

1. The plaintiff must have suffered an injury in fact, and
2. The injury must have been caused by the challenged action, and
3. A favorable decision will redress the injuries suffered.

Injury in Fact What is an *injury in fact?* Clearly, tangible injuries, such as personal and financial, satisfy this requirement. As examples, a physician who performs abortions has standing to challenge a statute proscribing that procedure;[77] owners of bookstores have standing to challenge a law that restricts the display of sexually explicit materials, because the law may reduce sales.[78]

Sierra Club v. Morton
405 U.S. 727 (1972)

The Mineral King Valley is an area of great natural beauty nestled in the Sierra Nevada Mountains in Tulare Country, California, adjacent to Sequoia National Park. It has been part of the Sequoia National Forest since 1926, and is designated as a national game refuge by special Act of Congress. Though once the site of extensive mining activity, Mineral King is now used almost exclusively for recreational purposes. Its relative inaccessibility and lack of development have limited the number of visitors each year, and at the same time have preserved the valley's quality as a quasi-wilderness area largely uncluttered by the products of civilization.

The United States Forest Service, which is entrusted with the maintenance and administration of national forests, began in the late 1940s to give consideration to Mineral King as a potential site for recreational development. Prodded by a rapidly increasing demand for skiing facilities, the Forest Service published a prospectus in 1965, inviting bids from private developers for the construction and operation of a ski resort that would serve as a recreation area. The proposal of Walt Disney Enterprises, Inc., was chosen from those of six bidders, and Disney received a three-year permit to conduct surveys and explorations in the valley in connection with its preparation of a complete master plan for the resort.

The final Disney plan, approved by the Forest Service in January 1969, outlines a $35 million complex of motels, restaurants, swimming pools, parking lots, and other structures designed to accommodate 14,000 visitors daily.

Representatives of the Sierra Club, who favor maintaining Mineral King largely in its present state, followed the progress of recreational planning for the valley with close attention and increasing dismay. They unsuccessfully sought a public hearing on the proposed development in 1965, and in subsequent correspondence with officials of the Forest Service and the Department of the Interior, they expressed the Club's objections to Disney's plan as a whole and to particular features included in it. In June 1969 the Club filed the present suit in the United States District Court for the Northern District of California, seeking a declaratory judgment that various aspects of the proposed development contravene federal laws and regulations governing the preservation of national parks, forests, and game refuges, and also seeking preliminary and permanent injunction restraining federal officials involved from granting their approval or issuing permits . . .

The first question presented is whether the Sierra Club has alleged facts that entitle it to obtain judicial review of the challenged action. Whether a party has sufficient stake in an otherwise justiciable controversy to obtain judicial resolution of that controversy is what has traditionally been referred to as the question of standing to sue. Where the party does not rely on any specific statute authorizing invocation of the judicial process, the question of standing depends upon whether the party has alleged such a "personal stake in the outcome of the controversy," . . . as to ensure that "the dispute sought to be adjudicated will be presented in an adversary context and in a form historically viewed as capable of judicial resolution."

The injury alleged by the Sierra Club will be incurred entirely by reason of the change in the uses to which Mineral King will be put, and the attendant change in the aesthetics and ecology of the area. Thus, in referring to the road to be built through Sequoia National Park, the complaint alleged that the development "would destroy or otherwise adversely affect the scenery, natural and historic objects and wildlife of the park and would impair the enjoyment of the park for future generations."

The trend of cases arising [under federal law] authorizing judicial review of federal agency action has been toward recognizing that injures other than economic harm are sufficient to bring a person within the meaning of the statutory language, and toward discarding the notion that an injury that is widely shared is *ipso facto* not an injury sufficient to provide the basis for judicial review. We noted this development in [a prior case], in saying that the interest alleged to have been injured "may reflect 'aesthetic, conservational and recreational' as well as economic values." But broadening the categories of injury that may be alleged in support of standing is a different matter from abandoning the requirement that the party seeking review must himself have suffered an injury.

Some courts have indicated a willingness to take this latter step by conferring standing upon organizations that have demonstrated "an organizational interest in the problem" of environmental or consumer protection. . . . But a mere "interest in a problem," no matter how qualified the organization is in evaluating the problem, is not sufficient in itself [to establish standing].

[The Court found that there was no standing because the Sierra Club had failed to allege that it or its members used the Mineral King site.]

Although a mere metaphysical or intellectual interest is not adequate to establish standing, in recent years the Court has expanded the injury-in-fact category to include aesthetic, conservational, and recreational injuries. In the *Morton* case, the Court held that a personal interest in the environment is adequate to establish standing.[79]

Although the Court held that an aesthetic, conservational, or recreational interest is adequate to establish standing, it also held that such an interest must be held by the party asserting the harm. Hence, had Sierra Club held its meetings at Mineral King, for example, standing could have been found.

Another way a special interest group can establish standing is by representing individuals who have suffered an injury in fact. The lesson of *Sierra Club* was not learned by the plaintiffs in *Lujan v. Defenders of Wildlife.*[80] *Lujan* centered around the Endangered Species Act (ESA), a statute intended to protect animal species from extinction. The ESA provided that agencies were not to commit acts that were likely to jeopardize the continued existence of an endangered species.

Pursuant to the ESA, the Fish and Wildlife Service and National Marine Fisheries Service jointly promulgated regulations stating that the ESA applied to agency actions in foreign nations. The agencies later changed their position and promulgated a regulation stating that the ESA had force only in the United States and on the high seas. This action was challenged by the plaintiffs, who sought an order compelling the Secretary of the Interior to issue a regulation restoring the ESA's international scope.

The Supreme Court held that the plaintiffs did not have standing. The plaintiff wildlife preservation organizations relied upon the affidavits of two members to establish standing. In those affidavits, the members asserted that they had been abroad and intended at some unknown date to return, and that they had an interest in observing endangered species while abroad. The Court found this interest inadequate to confer standing. The Court reiterated the principles set out in *Sierra Club v. Morton*; that is, an organization can maintain an action so long as at least one member of that organization can individually establish standing, the organization can adequately represent the member's interest, and the subject of the lawsuit is one in which the organization has a special interest and expertise. An intent to return to a foreign land at some unplanned and unknown date is too conjectural and hypothetical to confer standing.

It would have been easy to satisfy the standing requirements in *Lujan*. Had a member been a scientist who studied endangered species abroad, there would have been standing. Also, Justice Kennedy, in a concurring opinion, asserted that if the members had obtained airline tickets and made plans to visit one of the areas in dispute, there would have been standing.

Causation   In addition to proving an injury in fact, a plaintiff must also show a nexus between the injury and the alleged act. In terms of governmental conduct, a plaintiff must prove that the injury was caused by the government's conduct.

Allen v. Wright teaches that there must be a connection between the injury in fact and the conduct alleged to be unlawful. The injury must be "fairly traceable" to the conduct to satisfy this prong of the standing test. It is not always easy to determine when an injury is fairly traceable. In *Duke Power Co. v. Carolina Environmental Study Group,*[81] a federal statute that limited the liability of the owners of nuclear power plants for nuclear accidents was at issue. The plaintiff lived near the site where a plant was to be constructed and would suffer environmental injury in the event of an accident. The plaintiff challenged the law, claiming that it increased the likelihood that the plant would be built; accordingly, his potential injuries would be fairly traceable to the statute. The Court agreed. The line between *Allen v. Wright* and *Duke Power* is thin.

Allen v. Wright
468 U.S. 737 (1984)

[This case was filed by several parents of black school-children. They sued the Internal Revenue Service (IRS) for declaratory and injunctive relief, claiming that the IRS had an obligation to deny tax-exempt status to schools that discriminated against children on the basis of race. The parents claimed that this behavior of the IRS undermined desegregation. The parents prevailed at the lower levels.]

Justice O'Connor delivered the opinion of the Court.

Article III of the Constitution "confines the federal courts to adjudicating actualy 'cases' and 'controversies.'" As the Court explained in *Valley Forge Christian College v. Americans United for Separation of Church and State, Inc,* 454, U.S. 464, 471–476 (1982), the "case or controversy" requirement defines with respect to the Judicial Branch the idea of separation of powers on which the Federal Government is founded. The several doctrines that have grown up to elaborate that requirement are "founded in concern about the proper—and properly limited—role of the courts in a democratic society." . . . The case-or-controversy doctrines state fundamental limits of federal judicial power in our system of government.

The Art. III doctrine that requires a litigant to have "standing" to invoke the power of a federal court is perhaps the most important of these doctrines. "In essence the question of standing is whether the litigant is entitled to have the court decide the merits of the dispute or of particular issue." Standing doctrine embraces several judicially self-imposed limits on the exercise of federal jurisdiction, such as the general prohibition on a litigant's raising another person's legal right, the rule barring adjudication of generalized grievances more appropriately addressed in the representative branches, and the requirement that a plaintiff's complaint fall within the zone of interests protected by the law invoked. [The] requirement of standing, however, has a core component derived directly from the Constitution. A plaintiff must allege personal injury fairly traceable to the defendant's allegedly unlawful conduct and likely to redressed by the requested relief . . .

Like the prudential component, the constitutional component of standing doctrine incorporates concepts concededly not susceptible of precise definition. The injury alleged must be for example, "distinct and palpable," . . . not "abstract" or "conjectural" or "hypothetical." [The] injury must be "fairly" traceable to the challenged action, and relief from the injury must be "likely" to follow from a favorable decision. [These principles] cannot be defined so as to make application of the constitutional standing requirement a mechanical exercise. . . .

Respondents [parents] allege two injuries in their complaint to support their standing to bring this lawsuit. First, they say that they are harmed directly by the mere fact of Government financial aid to discriminatory private school. Second, they say that the federal tax exemptions to racially discriminatory private school in their communities impair their ability to have their public school desegregated.

[Respondents'] first claim of injury [might be] a claim simply to have Government avoid the violation of law alleged in respondents' complaint. Alternatively, it might be a claim of stigmatic injury, or denigration, suffered by all members of a racial group when the Government discriminates on the basis of race. Under neither interpretation is this claim of injury judicially cognizable.

This Court has repeatedly held that an asserted right to have the Government act in accordance with law is not sufficient standing, alone to confer jurisdiction on a federal court. . . .

Neither do they have standing to litigate their claims based on the stigmatizing injury often caused by racial discrimination. There can be no doubt that this sort of noneconomic injury is one of the most serious consequences of discriminatory government action and is sufficient in some circumstances to support standing.

[This Court's] case makes clear, however, that such injury accords a basis for standing only to "those persons who are personally denied equal treatment" by the challenged conduct . . . [If] the abstract stigmatic injury were cognizable, standing would extend nationwide to all members of the particular racial groups against which the Government was alleged to be discriminating by its grants of tax exemption to a racially discriminatory school, regardless of the location of that school . . . Recognition of standing in such circumstances would transform the federal courts into "no more than a vehicle for the vindication of the value interests of concerned bystanders." It is in their complaint's second claim of injury that respondents allege harm to a concrete, personal interest that can support standing in some circumstances. The injury they Identify—their children's diminished ability to receive an education in a racially integrated school—is, beyond any doubt, not only judicially cognizable but, as shown in *Brown v. Board of Education* . . . one of the most serious injuries recognized in our legal system. Despite the constitutional importance of curing the injury alleged by respondents, however, the federal judiciary may not redress it unless standing requirements are met. In this case, respondents' second claim of injury cannot support standing because the injury alleged is not fairly traceable to the Government conduct respondents challenge as unlawful.

The illegal conduct challenged by respondents is the IRS's grant of tax exemptions to some racially discriminatory school. The line of causation between that conduct and desegregation of respondents' schools is attenuated at best. From the perspective of the IRS, the injury to respondents is highly indirect and "results form the independent action of some third party not before the court."

The diminished ability of respondents' children to receive a desegregated education would be fairly traceable to unlawful IRS grants of tax exemptions only if there were enough racially discriminatory private school receiving tax exemptions in respondents' communities for withdrawal of those exemptions to make an appreciable difference in public-school integration. Respondents have made no such allegation. It is, first uncertain how many racially discriminatory private schools are in fact receiving tax exemptions. Moreover, it is entirely speculative [that] withdrawal of a tax exemption from any particular school would lead the school to change its policies. [It is also] speculative whether any given parents of a child attending such a private school would decide to transfer the child to public school as a result of any changes in educational or financial policy made by the private school once it was threatened with loss of tax-exempt status. It is also pure speculation whether, in a particular community, a large enough number of the numerous relevant school official and parents would reach decisions that collectively would have a significant impact on the racial composition of the public school.

The links in the chain of causation between the challenged Government conduct and the asserted injury are far too weak for the chain as a whole to sustain respondents's standing.

The idea of separations of powers that underlies standing doctrine explains why our cases preclude the conclusion that respondents's alleged injury "fairly can be traced to the challenged actions of the IRS." That conclusion would pave the way generally for suits challenging, not specifically identifiable Government violations of law, but the particular programs agencies establish to carry out their legal obligations.

The Constitution, after all, assigns to the Executive Branch, and not to the Judicial Branch, the duty to "take Care that the Laws be faithfully executed."

"The necessity that the plaintiff who seeks to invoke the judicial power stand to profit in some personal, interest remains an Act. III requirement." . . . Respondents have not met this fundamental requirement. The judgment of the Court of Appeals [which had ruled in the respondents favor] is accordingly reversed, and the injunction issued by that court is vacated.

Administrative Law Standing In most administrative law cases, standing issues revolve around an enabling statute. Even though Congress may not expand federal court jurisdiction beyond what is permitted in Article III, Congress may create a right and grant standing to enforce that right to a class of individuals. The enabling statute may thus provide standing even when traditional standing law does not. However, in most instances, standing in administrative cases parallels traditional standing law.

If a plaintiff is suing under a statute, he must prove that his injury is within the zone of interests intended to be protected by that law to have standing. If he does so, then he has standing to challenge an agency's conduct. *Association of Data Processing Service Organizations v. Camp*[82] is such a case. The plaintiffs in *Camp* challenged a ruling by the Comptroller of the Currency declaring that banks could make data-processing services available to each other and to bank customers. The plaintiffs were in the business of selling these services and did not want the additional competition. The Court found that, as competitors, the plaintiffs would suffer some financial injury; accordingly, they met the injury-in-fact prong of the standing test. Then the Court determined that to meet the second prong of the test, they would have to prove that they were in the zone intended to be protected by law. The plaintiffs claimed that the Comptroller's ruling was contrary to statutes regulating banks. The Court ruled that as a competitor who might suffer economic loss, the association had standing. See Chapter 7 for further discussion of standing and administrative law.

Citizen and Taxpayer Standing As *Allen v. Wright* taught, having a generalized interest in the affairs of government does not give one standing to challenge governmental actions. Status as a citizen does not provide a sufficient interest to give one standing to challenge governmental conduct. Similarly, being a taxpayer does not give a person standing to challenge the expenditure of public funds in most circumstances. *Flast v. Cohen*[83] represents an exception to this general rule. *Flast* involved a challenge to a statute that provided financing for reading, arithmetic, and other nonreligious courses in religious schools. The plaintiff, a taxpayer, filed an action alleging that the expenditure violated the Establishment Clause of the First Amendment.

The Court held that taxpayers may have standing if a nexus between the taxpayers' status and the expenditure can be shown and it can be further shown that the statute exceeds a constitutional limitation. The plaintiff in *Flast* satisfied these requirements because the Court found that the expenditure was significant, that the plaintiff was in the group of taxpayers whose funds were being spent, and that the First Amendment was clearly implicated. Note that the First Amendment was "implicated." No actual violation need be found to confer standing. On the contrary, standing is a preliminary matter. At this stage, a court must only decide that the Constitution is implicated (somehow involved). If so, then the party has standing and the case proceeds further. When standing is found to exist, a person is allowed to participate in the proceedings, but no final decision has been rendered on the merits.

Although *Flast* continues to be the law, the Court seriously limited its scope in four decisions, the 1982 decision *Valley Forge Christian College v. Americans for Separation of Church & State, Inc.*,[84] the 2006 decision *DaimerChrysler Corp. v. Cuno.*, the 2007 decision *Hein v. Freedom from Religion Foundation,* and the 2001 decision *Arizona Christian School Tuition Organization v. Winn.* In *Valley Forge*, a delegation of authority from Congress to the Secretary of Health, Education, and Welfare (now Secretary of Education) that allowed the Secretary to transfer surplus property at discounted rates to schools for educational use was at issue. The plaintiffs complained that the Secretary's transfer of property to a Christian school at a 100 percent discount violated the Constitution. The Court disagreed and upheld the transfer because the delegation from Congress to the Secretary was not made under Congress's taxing and spending power, but under the property clause of Article IV of the Constitution. Furthermore, the Court stated that because the decision to award the grant was made by an administrative agency, not Congress, the taxpayer lacked standing. Said another way, a taxpayer only has standing to challenge the actual body responsible for levying a tax or authorizing an expenditure of tax revenues.

In *DaimerChrysler*, residents of Toledo, Ohio, challenged both Toledo and Ohio tax reductions to DaimerChrysler as violative of the Commerce Clause. Relying on *Flast*, they asserted standing as both municipal and state taxpayers. The Court rejected their standing, finding that individual taxpayer contributions to state (or federal) budgets are minute, fluctuating, and too uncertain. The Court also reasoned that federalism principles advise against federal court jurisdiction over state and local budgetary matters. Finally, the Court found that the plaintiffs' Commerce Clause claim was not as compelling as the plaintiff's First Amendment Establishment Clause (no establishment of religion) claim in *Flast*.

As a general rule, one person does not have standing to assert the rights of another. There are exceptions to this rule. First, a close personal relationship may pave the way to third-party standing. Parents may stand in for their children and guardians for their wards, for example. A professional relationship may also suffice to establish third-party standing. In *Singleton v. Wulff*,[85] it was held that a doctor has standing to assert a patient's privacy interest in securing an abortion against a statute prohibiting that medical procedure. In support of this decision, the Court pointed out that the physician–patient relationship is intimate and that the patient could be deterred from asserting her claim by potential public embarrassment.

The impact of *Flast* was further limited in the 2007 *Hein* decision.

Hein v. Freedom from Religion Foundation, Inc.
551 U.S. 587 (2007)

Justice Alito announced the judgment of the Court and delivered an opinion in which the Chief Justice and Justice Kennedy join.

In 2001, the President issued an executive order creating the White House Office of Faith-Based and Community Initiatives within the Executive Office of the President. Exec. Order No. 13199, 3 CFR 752 (2001 Comp.). The purpose of this new office was to ensure that "private and charitable community groups, including religious ones . . . have the fullest opportunity permitted by law to compete on a level playing field, so long as they achieve valid public purposes" and adhere to "the bedrock principles of pluralism, nondiscrimination, evenhandedness, and neutrality." *Ibid.* The office was specifically charged with the task of eliminating unnecessary bureaucratic, legislative, and regulatory barriers that could impede such organizations' effectiveness and ability to complete equally for federal assistance.

By separate executive orders, the President also created Executive Department Centers for Faith-Based and Community Initiatives within several federal agencies and departments. These centers were given the job of ensuring that faith-based community groups would be eligible to compete for federal financial support without impairing their independence or autonomy, as long as they did "not use direct Federal financial assistance to support any inherently religious activities, such as worship, religious instruction, or proselytization." Exec. Order No. 13279, 3 CFR §2(f), p. 260 (2002 Comp.). To this end, the President directed that "[n]o organization should be discriminated against on the basis of religion or religious belief in the administration or distribution of Federal financial assistance under social service programs," and that "[a]ll organizations that receive Federal financial assistance under social services programs should be prohibited from discriminating against beneficiaries or potential beneficiaries of the social services programs on the basis of religion or religious belief." Petitioners, who have been sued in their official capacities, are the directors of the White House Office and various Executive Department Centers.

No congressional legislation specifically authorized the creation of the White House Office or the Executive Department Centers. Rather, they were "created entirely within the executive branch . . . by Presidential executive order." Nor has Congress enacted any law specifically appropriating money for these entities' activities. Instead, their activities are funded through general Executive Branch appropriations. For example, the department of Education's Center is funded from money appropriated for the Office of the Secretary of Education, while the Department of Housing and Urban Development's Center is funded through that Department's salaries and expenses account.

The respondents are Freedom from Religion Foundation, Inc., a nonstock corporation "opposed to government endorsement of religion," and three of its members. Respondents brought suit in the United States District Count for the Western District of Wisconsin, alleging that petitioners violated the Establishment Clause by organizing conferences at which faith-based organizations allegedly "are singled out as being particularly worthy of federal funding . . . and the belief in God is extolled as distinguishing the claimed effectiveness of faith-based social services." Respondents further alleged that the content of these conferences sent a message to religious believers "that they are insiders and favored members of

the political community" and that the conferences sent the message to nonbelievers "that they are outsiders" and "not full members of the political community." In short, respondents alleged that the conferences were designed to promote, and had the effect of promoting, religious community groups over secular ones.

The only asserted basis for standing was that the individual respondents are federal taxpayers who are "opposed to the use of Congressional taxpayer appropriations to advance and promote religion." In their capacity as federal taxpayers, respondents sought to challenge Executive Branch expenditures for these conferences, which, they contended, violated the Establishment Clause. . . .

Article III of the Constitution limits the judicial power of the United States to the resolution of "Cases" and "Controversies," and 'Article III standing . . . enforces the Constitutions's case-or-controversy requirement." . . . "No principle is more fundamental to the judiciary' proper role in our system of government than the constitutional limitation of federal-court jurisdiction to actual cases or controversies."

"[O]ne of the controlling elements in the definition of a case or controversy under Article III" is standing. The requisite elements of Article III standing are well established: "A plaintiff must allege personal injury fairly traceable to the defendant's allegedly unlawful conduct and likely to be redressed by the requested relief."

The constitutionally mandated standing inquiry is especially important in a case like this one, in which taxpayers seek "to challenge laws of general application where their own injury is not distinct from that suffered in general by other taxpayers or citizens." This is because "[t]he judicial power of the United States defined by Art. III is not an unconditioned authority to determine the constitutionality of legislative or executive acts." *Valley Forge Christian College v. Americans United for Separation of Church and State, Inc.*, 454 U. S. 464, 471 (1982). The federal courts are not empowered to seek out and strike down any governmental act that they deem to be repugnant to the Constitution. Rather, federal courts sit "solely, to decide on the rights of individuals," *Marbury v. Madison*, 1 Cranch 137, 170 (1803), and must "refrai[n] from passing upon the constitutionality of an act . . . unless obliged to do so in the proper performance of our judicial function, when the question is raised by a party whose interests entitle him to raise it." *Valley Forge, supra*, at 474 (quoting *Blair v. United States*, 250 U. S. 273, 279 (1919)). . . .

As a general matter, the interest of a federal taxpayer in seeing that Treasury funds are spent in accordance with the Constitution does not give rise to the kind of redressable "personal injury" required for Article III standing. Of course, a taxpayer has standing to challenge the *collection* of a specific tax assessment as unconstitutional; being forced to pay such a tax causes a real and immediate economic injury to the individual taxpayer. That is not the interest on which respondents assert standing here. Rather, their claim is that, having paid lawfully collected taxes into Federal Treasury at some point, they have a continuing, legally cognizable interest in ensuring that those funds are not *used* by the Government in a way that violates the Constitution.

We have consistently held that this type of interest is too generalized and attenuated to support Article III standing. In *Frothingham*, a federal taxpayer sought to challenge federal appropriations for mother's and children's health, arguing that federal involvement in this area intruded on the rights reserved to the states under the Tenth Amendment and would "increase the burden of future taxation and thereby take [the plaintiff's] property without due process of law." 262 U. S., at 486. We concluded that the plaintiff lacked the kind of particularized injury required for Article III standing:

> [I]interest in the moneys of the Treasury . . . is shared with millions of others; is comparatively minute and indeterminable; and the effect upon future taxation, of any payment out of the funds, so remote, fluctuating and uncertain, that no basis is afforded for an appeal to the preventive powers of a court of equity.

"The administration of any statute, likely to produce additional taxation to be imposed upon a vast number of taxpayers, the extent of whose several liability is indefinite and constantly changing, is essentially a matter of public and not of individual concern." Because the interests of the taxpayer are, in essence, the interests of the interests of the public-at-large, deciding a constitutional claim based solely on taxpayer standing "would be[,] not to decide a judicial controversy, but to assume a position of authority over the governmental acts of another and co-equal department, an authority which plainly we do not possess."

In *Flast* [*v. Cohen*, 392 *v.* U.S. 83 (1968)], the Court carved out a narrow exception to the general constitutional prohibition against taxpayer standing. The taxpayer-plaintiff in that case challenged the distribution of federal funds to religious schools under the Elementary and Secondary Education Act of 1965, alleging that such aid violated the Establishment Clauses. The Court set out a two-part test for determining whether a federal taxpayer has standing to challenge an allegedly unconstitutional expenditure:

> First, the taxpayer must establish a logical link between that status and the type of legislative enactment attacked. Thus, a taxpayer will be a proper party to allege the unconstitutionality only of exercises of congressional power under the taxing and spending clause of Art. I, §8, of the Constitution. It will not be sufficient to allege an incidental expenditure of tax funds in the administration of an essentially regulatory statute. . . . Secondly, the taxpayer must establish a nexus between that status and the precise nature of the constitutional infringement alleged. Under this requirement, the taxpayer must show that the challenged enactment exceeds

specific constitutional limitations imposed upon the exercise of the congressional taxing and spending power and not simply that the enactment is generally beyond the powers delegated to Congress by Art. I, §8. *Flast*, 392 U. S., at 102–103.

The Court held that the taxpayer-plaintiff in *Flast* had satisfied both prongs of this test: the plaintiff's "constitutional challenge [was] made to an exercise by Congress of its power under Art. I, §8, to spend for the general welfare," and she alleged a violation of the Establishment Clause, which "operates as a specific constitutional limitation upon the exercise by Congress of the taxing and spending power conferred by Art. I, §8."

Respondents argue that this case falls within the *Flast* exception, which they read to cover any "expenditure of government funds in violation of the Establishment Clause." But this broad reading fails to observe "the rigor with which the *Flast* exception to the *Frothingham* principle ought to be applied." *Valley Forge*, 454 U. S., at 481.

The expenditures at issue in *Flast* were made pursuant to an express congressional mandate and a specific congressional appropriation. The plaintiff in that case challenged disbursements made under the Elementary and Secondary Education Act of 1965. That Act expressly appropriated the sum of $100 million for fiscal year 1966 and authorized the disbursement of those funds to local educational agencies for the education of low-income students, see *Flast, supra*, at 86. The Act mandated that local educational agencies receiving such funds "ma[k]e provision for including special educational services and arrangements (such as dual enrollment, educational radio and television, and mobile educational services and equipment)" in which students enrolled in private elementary and secondary schools could participate. In addition, recipient agencies were required to ensure that "library resources, textbooks, and other instructional materials" funded through the grants "be provided on an equitable basis for the use of children and teachers in private elementary and secondary schools,"

The expenditures challenged in *Flast*, then, were funded by a specific congressional appropriation and were disbursed to private schools (including religiously affiliated schools) pursuant to a direct and unambiguous congressional mandate. Indeed, the *Flast* taxpayer-plaintiff's constitutional claim was premised on the contention that if the Government's actions were "within the authority and intent of the Act, the Act is to that extent unconstitutional and void." *Flast*, 392 U. S., at 90. And the judgment reviewed by this Court in *Flast* solely concerned the question whether "if [the challenged] expenditures are authorized by the Act the statute constitutes a 'law respecting an establishment of religion' and law 'prohibiting the free exercise thereof'" under the First Amendment.

Given that the alleged Establishment Clause violation in *Flast* was funded by a specific congressional appropriation and was undertaken pursuant to an express congressional mandate, the Court concluded that the taxpayer-plaintiffs had established the requisite "logical link between [their taxpayer] status and the type of legislative enactment attacked." In the Court's words, "[t]hier constitutional challenge [was] made to an exercise by Congress of its power under Art. I, §8, to spend for the general welfare." But as this Court later noted, *Flast* "limited taxpayer standing to challenges directed 'only [at] exercises of congressional power'" under the Taxing and Spending Clause. *Valley Forge*, 454 U. S., at 479.

The link between congressional action and constitutional violation that supported taxpayer standing in *Flast* is missing here. Respondents do not challenge any specific congressional action appropriation; nor do they ask the Court to invalidate any congressional enactment or legislatively created program as unconstitutional. That is because the expenditures at issue here were not made pursuant to any Act of Congress. Rather, Congress provided general appropriations to the Executive Branch to fund its day-to-day activities. These appropriations did not expressly authorize, direct, or even mention the expenditures of which respondents complain. Those expenditures resulted from executive discretion, not congressional action. . . .

Respondents argue that it is "arbitrary" to distinguish between money spent pursuant to congressional mandate and expenditures made in the course of executive discretion, because "the injury to taxpayers in both situations is the very injury targeted by the Establishment Clause and *Flast*—the expenditure for the support of religion of funds exacted from taxpayers." The panel majority below agreed, based on its observation that "there is so much that executive officials could do to promote religion in ways forbidden by the Establishment Clause."

But *Flast* focused on congressional action, and we must decline this invitation to extend its holding to encompass discretionary Executive Branch expenditures. *Flast* itself distinguished the "incidental expenditure of tax funds in the administration of an essentially regulatory statute," *Flast, supra*, at 102, and we have subsequently rejected the view that taxpayer standing "extends to 'the Government as a whole, regardless of which branch is at work in a particular instance,'" *Valley Forge, supra.* Moreover, we have repeatedly emphasized that the *Flast* exception has a "narrow application in our precedent," and that must be applied with "rigor," *Valley Forge, supra*, . . .

While respondents argue that Executive Branch expenditures in support of religion are no different from legislative extractions, *Flast* itself rejected this equivalence: "It will not be sufficient to allege an incidental expenditure of tax funds in the administration of an essentially regulatory statute."

Because almost all Executive Branch activity is ultimately funded by some congressional appropriation, extending the *Flast* exception to purely executive expenditures would effectively subject every federal action—be it a conference, proclamation or speech—to Establishment Clause challenge by any taxpayer in federal court. To see the wide swathe of activity that respondents' proposed rule would cover, one need look no further than the amended complaint in this action, which focuses largely on speeches and presentations made by Executive Branch officials. . . .

Over the years, *Flast* has been defended by some and criticized by others. But the present case does not require us to reconsider that precedent. The Court of Appeals did not apply *Flast*; it extended *Flast*. It is a necessary concomitant of the doctrine of *stare decisis* that a precedent is not always expanded to the limit of its logic. That was the approach that then-Justice Rehnquist took in his opinion for the Court in *Valley Forge,* and it is the approach we take here. We do not extent *Flast*, but we also do not overrule it. We leave *Flast* as we found it.

Justice Scalia says that we must either overrule *Flast* or extend it to the limits of its logic. His position is not "[in]sane," inconsistent with the "rule of law," or "utterly meaningless." But it is wrong. Justice Scalia does not seriously dispute either (1) that *Flast* itself spoke in terms of "legislative enactment[s]" and "exercises of congressional power," or (2) that in the four decades since *Flast* was decided, we have never extended its narrow exception to a purely discretionary Executive Branch expenditure. We need go no further to decided this case. Relying on the provision of the Constitution that limits our role to resolving the "Cases" and "Controversies" before us, we decide only the case at hand.

For these reasons, the judgment of the Court of Appeals for the Seventh Circuit is reversed.

It is so ordered.

Justice Kennedy, concurring.

The separation-of-powers design in the Constitution is implemented, among other means, by Article III's case-or-controversy limitation and the resulting requirement of standing. See, *e.g., Lujan v. Defenders of Wildlife*, 504 U.S. 555, 559–560 (1992). The Court's decision in *Flast v. Cohen*, 392 U. S. 83 (1968), and in later cases applying it, must be interpreted as respecting separation-of-powers principles but acknowledging as well that these principles, in some cases, must accommodate the First Amendment's Establishment Clause. The clause expresses the Constitution's special concern that freedom of conscience not be compromised by government taxing and spending in support of religion. In my view the result reached in *Flast* is correct and should not be called into question. For the reasons set forth by Justice Alito, however, *Flast* should not be extended to permit taxpayer standing in the instant matter. And I join his opinion in full.

. . .

It must be remembered that, even where parties haves no standing to sue, members of the Legislative and Executive Branches are not excused from making constitutional determinations in the regular course of their duties. Government officials must make a conscious decision to obey the Constitution whether or not their acts can be challenged in a court of law and then must conform their actions to these principled determinations.

Justice Scalia, with whom Justice Thomas joins, concurring in the judgment.

Today's opinion is, in one significant respect, entirely consistent with our previous cases addressing taxpayer standing to raise Establishment Clause challenges to government expenditures. Unfortunately, the consistency lies in the creation of utterly meaningless distinctions which separate the case at hand from the precedents that have come out differently, but which cannot possibly be (in any sane world) the reason it comes out differently. If this Court is to decide cases by rule of law rather than show of hands, we must surrender to logic and choose sides: Either *Flast v. Cohen*, 392 U. S. 83 (1968), should be applied to (at a minimum) *all* challenged to the governmental expenditure of general tax revenues in a manner alleged to violate a constitutional provision specifically limiting the taxing and spending power, or *Flast* should be repudiated. For me, the choice is easy. *Flast* is wholly irreconcilable with the Article III restrictions on federal-court jurisdiction that this Court has repeatedly confirmed are embodied in the doctrine of standing.

. . .

Justice Souter, with whom Justice Stevens, Ginsburg, and Justice Breyer join, dissenting.

Flast v. Cohen, U. S. 83, 102 (1968), held that plaintiffs with an Establishment Clause claim could "demonstrate the necessary stakes as taxpayers in the outcome of the litigation to satisfy Article III requirement." Here, the controlling, plurality opinion declares that *Flast* does not apply, but a search of that opinion for a suggestion that these taxpayers have any less stake in the outcome than the taxpayers in *Flast* will come up empty: the plurality makes no such finding, nor could it. Instead, the controlling opinion closes the door on these taxpayers because the Executive Branch, and not the Legislative Branch,

caused their injury. I see no basis for this distinction in either logic or precedent, and respectfully dissent. . . .

The plurality points to the separation of powers to explain its distinction between legislative and executive spending decisions, but there is no difference on that point of view between a Judicial Branch review of an executive decision and a judicial evaluation of a congressional one. We owe respect to each of the other branches, no more to the former than to the latter, and no one has suggested that the Establishment Clause lacks applicability to executive uses of money. It would surely violate the Establishment Clause for the Department of Health and Human Services to draw on a general appropriation to build a chapel for weekly church services (no less than if a statute required it), and for good reason: if the Executive could accomplish through the exercise of discretion exactly what Congress cannot do through legislation, Establishment Clause protection would melt away. . . .

Flast speaks for this Court's recognition (shared by a majority of the Court today) that when the Government spends money for religious purposes a taxpayer's injury is serious and concrete enough to be "judicially cognizable," *Allen, supra*, at 752. The judgment of sufficient injury takes account of the Madisonian relationship of tax money and conscience, but it equally reflects the Founders' pragmatic "conviction that individual religious liberty could be achieved best under a government which was stripped of all power to tax, to support, or otherwise to assist any or all religions," *Eversion v. Board of Ed. of Ewing*, 330 U. S. 1, 11 (1947), and the realization continuing to the modern day that favoritism for religion "'sends the . . . message to . . . nonadherents' that they are outsiders, not full members of the political community," *McCreary Country v. American Civil Liberties Union of Ky.*, 545 U. S. 844, 860 (2005) (quoting *Santa Fe Independent School Dist v. Doe*, 530 U. S. 290, 306–310 (2000), in turn quoting *Lynch v. Donnelly*, 465 U. S. 668, 688 (1984) (O'Connor, J., concurring); [omissions in original].

The Court further limited the impact of *Flast* in its 2011 decision *Arizona Christian School Tuition Organization v. Winn* (131 S.Ct. 1436 [Apr. 4, 2011]) where the Court held that taxpayers lacked standing to challenge an Arizona law that provided tax credits to taxpayers who made contributions to school tuition organizations that used the funds to provide scholarships to private schools, secular and religious. While two justices would have overruled *Flast*, three justices were careful to distinguish the decision from *Flast*, finding that empowering individuals to choose what schools to support is different than direct government support for religious schools, which would violate the First Amendment's prohibition of governmental establishment of religion.

The bottom line is that the *Flast* exception has been considerably narrowed, particularly as Justice Kagan argued in her dissent in *Arizona Christian School*, it has been devastated in establishment cases.

Association Standing   *Sierra Club v. Morton* establishes that a special interest organization may represent its members in federal courts. Organizational representation is permitted so long as at least one of the organization's members has standing; the organization will adequately represent the members' interest, and participation by the individual member is unnecessary; the issues of the case fall within the purview of the organization's expertise and mission.[86] Organizational representation is most common in environmental, labor (unions representing workers), and consumer protection cases.

Government Standing and Parens Patriae   The government does not have to meet the association test to represent its citizens. A state, or the federal government, may file actions or intervene in actions when a public interest exists. The government's interest in the health and welfare of its citizens is adequate to confer standing. The state stands in **parens patriae** to its citizens. It may obtain injunctive relief on behalf of the public. For example, a state agency may obtain an injunction prohibiting unlawful business practices. In addition, the government may seek to have individuals compensated when a governmental interest is involved. Thus, the state may seek compensation for those individuals harmed by a company's unlawful business practices. In actions against other states or the federal government, a state may seek declaratory and injunctive relief, but it has no standing to present the claims of individuals who are seeking damages.[87]

parens patriae
Latin for "the parent of the country."

Congressperson Standing   Members of Congress have filed civil cases challenging both presidential and congressional action on many occasions. The issue is whether a person's status as a member of Congress establishes standing to challenge governmental actions. The courts have held that in some cases it may.

For the case-or-controversy requirement to be satisfied, a congressperson must establish

1. That she suffered a distinct and palpable injury,
2. That the injury was fairly traceable to the act that is the subject of the complaint, and
3. That a remedy is available that will redress the injury.[88]

An act that diminishes the member's influence or nullifies his legislative vote is "distinct and palpable." For example, in *Goldwater v. Carter,*[89] it was decided that a congressman had standing to challenge President Carter's decision to terminate a treaty with the Republic of China without first obtaining Senate approval. Because the integrity of a senator's vote was in question, standing existed. Note, however, that the Court found in favor of Carter on the larger issue: It held that President Carter could unilaterally terminate the treaty.

Another case illustrates the point. In *Kennedy v. Sampson,*[90] it was decided that a member of Congress has standing to seek an order requiring executive branch officials to recognize the existence of a law. A bill had been passed and presented to the president. The presentment indicated that the bill could be returned to the Secretary of the Senate if the Senate was in recess. The Senate went into its Christmas recess, but the president never returned the bill. In spite of the rule that bills not returned in ten days become law, the executive branch refused to recognize the law. Because this action had the effect of nullifying Senator Kennedy's vote, he had standing to challenge it. Furthermore, he prevailed in the larger issue: The court found that the bill had become law. The Supreme Court did not review this decision.

Members of Congress generally lack standing to challenge acts of Congress, because they have available to them the best remedy: using their position to advocate and vote to amend or repeal the law. Similarly, a member does not have standing to protect the executive or judicial branch from legislative encroachments.[91] (Members of those branches do, of course, have standing in such circumstances.) Also, like all citizens, a member's generalized objection to the manner in which the executive branch enforces a law, or does not enforce a law, is not adequate to confer standing.[92]

Third-Party Standing   As a general proposition, one party may not assert another's constitutional rights. The theory is that constitutional rights are personal. In *Elk Grove Unified School District v. Newdow*, 542 U.S. 1 (2004), the issue of standing was raised in the context of a parent–child relationship.

Elk Grove Unified School District v. Newdow
542 U.S. 1 (2004)

Each day elementary school teachers in the Elk Grove Unified School District (School District) lead their classes in a group recitation of the Pledge of Allegiance. Respondent, Michael A. Newdow, is an atheist whose daughter participates in that daily exercise. Because the Pledge contains the words "under God," he views the School District's policy as a religious indoctrination of his child that violates the First Amendment. A divided panel of the Court of Appeals for the Ninth Circuit agreed with Newdow. In light of the obvious importance of that decision, we granted certiorari to review the First Amendment issue and, preliminarily, the question whether Newdow has standing to invoke the jurisdiction of the federal courts. We conclude that Newdow lacks standing and therefore reverse the Court of Appeals' decision.

"The very purpose of a national flag is to serve as a symbol of our country," *Texas v. Johnson,* 491 U.S. 397, 405 (1989), and of its proud traditions "of freedom, of equal opportunity, of religious tolerance, and of good will for other peoples who share our aspirations," *id.,* at 437 (Stevens, J., dissenting). As its history illustrates, the Pledge of Allegiance evolved as a common public acknowledgement of the ideals that our flag symbolizes. Its recitation is a patriotic exercise designed to foster national unity and pride in those principles . . .

Under California law, "every public elementary school" must begin each day with "appropriate patriotic exercises." Cal. Educ. Code Ann. §52720 (West 1989). The statute provides that "[t]he giving of the Pledge of Allegiance to the Flag of the United States of America shall satisfy" this requirement. *Ibid.* The Elk Grove Unified School District has implemented the state law by requiring that "[e]ach elementary school class recite the pledge of allegiance to the flag once each day." Consistent with our case law, the School District permits students who object on religious grounds to abstain from the recitation.

In March 2000, Newdow filed suit in the United States District Court for the Eastern District of California against the United States Congress, the President of the United States, the State of California, and the Elk Grove Unified School District and its superintendent. At the time of filing, Newdow's daughter was enrolled in kindergarten in the Elk Grove Unified School District and participated in the daily recitation of the Pledge. Styled as a mandamus action, the complaint explains that Newdow is an atheist who was ordained more than 20 years ago in a ministry that "espouses the religious philosophy that the

true and eternal bonds of righteousness and virtue stem from reason rather than mythology." The complaint seeks a declaration that the 1954 Act's addition of the words "under God" violated the Establishment and Free Exercise Clauses of the United States Constitution, as well as an injunction against the School District's policy requiring daily recitation of the Pledge. It alleges that Newdow has standing to sue on his own behalf and on behalf of his daughter as "next friend."

[The district court dismissed the action holding that the Establishment Clause was not violated by the policy. The appellate court reversed.]

After the Court of Appeals' initial opinion was announced, Sandra Banning, the mother of Newdow's daughter, filed a motion for leave to intervene, or alternatively to dismiss the complaint. She declared that although she and Newdow shared "physical custody" of their daughter, a state-court order granted her "exclusive legal custody" of the child, "including the sole right to represent [the daughter's] legal interests and make all decision[s] about her education" and welfare. Banning further stated that her daughter is a Christian who believes in God and has no objection either to reciting or hearing others recite the Pledge of Allegiance, or to its reference to God. Banning expressed the belief that her daughter would be harmed if the litigation were permitted to proceed, because others might incorrectly perceive the child as sharing her father's atheist views. Banning accordingly concluded, as her daughter's sole legal custodian, that it was not in the child's interest to be a party to Newdow's lawsuit . . .

In a second published opinion, the Court of Appeals reconsidered Newdow's standing in light of Banning's motion. The court noted that Newdow no longer claimed to represent his daughter, but unanimously concluded that "the grant of sole legal custody to Banning" did not deprive Newdow, "as a noncustodial parent, of Article III standing to object to unconstitutional government action affecting his child." The court held that under California law Newdow retains the right to expose his child to his particular religious views even if those views contradict the mother's, and that Banning's objections as sole legal custodian do not defeat Newdow's right to seek redress for an alleged injury to his own parental interests . . .

[O]ur standing jurisprudence contains two strands: Article III standing, which enforces the Constitution's case or controversy requirement, see *Lujan v. Defenders of Wildlife* . . .; and prudential standing, which embodies "judicially self-imposed limits on the exercise of federal jurisdiction," *Allen*, 468 U.S., at 751. The Article III limitations are familiar: The plaintiff must show that the conduct of which he complains has caused him to suffer an "injury in fact" that a favorable judgment will redress. See *Lujan*. . . . Although we have not exhaustively defined the prudential dimensions of the standing doctrine, we have explained that prudential standing encompasses "the general prohibition on a litigant's raising another person's legal rights, the rule barring adjudication of generalized grievances more appropriately addressed in the representative branches, and the requirement that a plaintiff's complaint fall within the zone of interests protected by the law invoked." . . .

One of the principal areas in which this Court has customarily declined to intervene is the realm of domestic relations. Long ago we observed that "[t]he whole subject of the domestic relations of husband and wife, parent and child, belongs to the laws of the States and not to the laws of the United States." . . .

Nothing that either Banning or the School Board has done, however, impairs Newdow's right to instruct his daughter in his religious views . . .

When hard questions of domestic relations are sure to affect the outcome, the prudent course is for the federal court to stay its hand rather than reach out to resolve a weighty question of federal constitutional law. There is a vast difference between Newdow's right to communicate with his child—which both California law and the First Amendment recognize—and his claimed right to shield his daughter from influences to which she is exposed in school despite the terms of the custody order. We conclude that, having been deprived under California law of the right to sue as next friend, Newdow lacks prudential standing to bring this suit in federal court.

The judgment of the Court of Appeals is reversed.

Standing principles are also important in the criminal law context. A criminal defendant may not assert another person's constitutional rights in an effort to have evidence excluded at trial. For example, Sam is at Norma's home. He forgets to take his briefcase with him when he leaves her home. He has cocaine in the briefcase. Later that day the police conduct a search of Norma's home, looking for evidence of an unrelated crime. They discover the briefcase and its contents, but the search is later determined to be unlawful by a court. Accordingly, any evidence seized may not be used to prosecute Norma. However, the contents of the briefcase may be used to prosecute Sam (Norma implicated him) because he does not have standing to assert Norma's Fourth Amendment right to be free from unlawful searches and seizures.

This doctrine applies to the assertion of all constitutional rights and in all contexts, whether civil, criminal, or administrative. Recall from the preceding discussion of standing that organizations may establish standing to represent their members if they can prove that at least one member satisfies the traditional standing test and that the subject of the litigation is related to the purposes of the organization.

3.6(c) Political Questions

political question
A nonjudicial issue. The political question doctrine states that, under the Constitution, certain questions belong to the nonjudicial branches of the federal government to resolve.

Another limitation upon judicial power is the so-called **political question** doctrine. The Supreme Court has long held that certain cases are nonjusticiable due to their political nature. The theory holds that the political branches—the executive and legislative—are better equipped to deal with these political issues than is a court of law.

The political question doctrine is based somewhat upon Article III, but primarily upon separation principles. It is a self-imposed restraint of judicial power. The doctrine applies in cases where it otherwise appears that judicial jurisdiction exists. Because of this, courts are careful not to extend their jurisdiction too far. Chief Justice John Marshall said in *Cohens v. Virginia*:[93]

It is most true that this court will not take jurisdiction if it should not; but it is equally true, that it must take jurisdiction when it should. The judiciary cannot, as the legislature may, avoid a measure because it approaches the constitution. . . . [W]e have no more right to decline the exercise of jurisdiction which is given, than to usurp that which is not given. The one or the other would be treason to the constitution.

However, this same chief justice stated in *Marbury v. Madison* that political questions "can never be made in this court."[94]

The Court has not been entirely consistent in its application of the doctrine, and the phrase "political question" is really a misnomer. Nearly all cases before courts, especially the Supreme Court, have political aspects. That does not mean they are not heard. The political question doctrine is more concerned with keeping the judiciary out of the business of the executive and legislative branches than with avoiding questions of politics.

One of the first Supreme Court cases that dealt with the political question doctrine was *Luther v. Borden*.[95] In 1841, Rhode Island's government was operating as it did under its royal charter of 1663. By this date, other states had adopted constitutions that established republican forms of government. Rhode Island's colonial charter did not provide for amendment, limited the vote to "freeholders" of land, and had other provisions that led many people in the state, after failing to persuade government officials to make changes, to meet and elect delegates to draft a new constitution. A constitution was drafted and approved by a majority of voters. The charter legislature denied the legitimacy of the constitution, and when the new government made plans to take control by force, the charter legislature declared martial law. Ultimately, the charter government's militia was successful in defeating the insurgent forces. Subsequently, Martin Luther, one of the insurgents, had his home searched. Luther sued for trespass, alleging that the defendants violated the guarantee of a republican form of government clause in Article IV, Section 4. The clause reads, "The United States shall guarantee to every States in this Union a Republican Form of Government, and shall protect each of them against Invasion; and on Application of the Legislature, or of the Executive (when the Legislature cannot be convened) against domestic Violence." Upon review of his claim by the Supreme Court, it held that it could not interfere both because of the intense political nature of the dispute and because the Constitution vested federal authority over the subject to Congress and the president.

Subsequently, the Court, using *Luther* as precedent, has refused to extend judicial authority over several types of political controversy. One type of case the Court shied away from for years were those alleging political **gerrymandering,** that is, the realignment of political districts by a party in power to favor its candidates in future elections. In 1946, the Court said that its involvement in a reapportionment case would be "hostile to a democratic system."[96] This changed in *Baker v. Carr,* where the Court held that gerrymandering cases may be heard.[97] In *Baker v. Carr*, the Court announced the factors or issues that implicate the political question doctrine. Justice William Brennan, writing for the Court, stated that the presence of any of the following suggests a political question:

gerrymandering
Manipulating the boundary lines of a political district to give an unfair advantage to one political party or to dilute the political strength of voters of a particular race, color, or national origin.

1. The case involves a power that is delegated by the Constitution to the legislative or executive branch of government and not to the courts.
2. There are no judicially discoverable and manageable standards for resolving the issue of the case.
3. It is impossible to decide the case without an initial policy determination of a kind clearly for nonjudiciable discretion.
4. It is impossible for the court to undertake independent resolution without expressing lack of respect due to the coordinate branches of government.
5. There is an unusual need for unquestioning adherence to a political decision already made.
6. There is the potential of embarrassment from multifarious pronouncements by various departments on one question.

These standards reflect separational, functional, and political concerns. The Court decided, in *Baker v. Carr,* that the issue of whether legislative apportionment satisfies equal protection is not a political question, because the issue does not pose a separation of power issue and there are judicial standards to be applied in such Fourteenth Amendment cases.

Coleman v. Miller,[98] a 1939 Supreme Court decision, illustrates a case that was nonjudiciable because its core question was delegated by the Constitution to one of the Court's coordinate branches. Several issues were raised in *Coleman* concerning the constitutional amendment process, including whether a state that rejects an amendment can later ratify it and whether an amendment has been ratified within an appropriate period of time. The Supreme Court found these two issues to be within the purview of Congress and not fit for judicial review.

The plaintiff in *Powell v. McCormack,*[99] Adam Clayton Powell Jr., had been elected to the House of Representatives, but, because of allegations of misuse of public funds and unbecoming conduct, the House refused to seat him. The issues centered around two provisions of the Constitution. Article I, Section 5, clause 1, states, "[e]ach House shall be the Judge of the Elections, Returns, and Qualifications of its own members." Clause 2 of the same section provides that "[e]ach House may determine the Rules of its Proceedings, punish its Members for disorderly Behavior, and, with the Concurrence of two thirds, expel a Member."

The Court stated, in dicta, that a congressional decision to expel a member would be nonjusticiable as a political question because the Constitution clearly delegates such decisions to Congress. However, the Court concluded that Powell had not been expelled because he was never permitted to take his place in the House. Accordingly, the Court treated the case as arising under the former clause.

The Court held that congressional authority to exclude members under this clause is narrower than its authority to expel sitting members. The Court reasoned that the Constitution provides that a house may exclude a member because of lack of qualification, such as not satisfying the age or citizenship requirements, but that it does not permit a house to exclude elected representatives for other reasons. Accordingly, a court could not review a decision to exclude a member that is based upon the qualifications clause. For example, if Congress were to exclude an elected representative because it determined that the representative did not satisfy the age requirement, there could be no judicial review under the political question doctrine. It would not violate separation principles, however, for a court to review exclusions for other reasons, as such power has not been delegated to Congress. Because there was no question that Powell satisfied the Constitution's qualification requirements, the Court ordered that he be seated in the House.

In 1984, Frank McCloskey and Richard McIntyre were opposing candidates in the closest congressional election in history. The initial vote count showed McCloskey a winner by 72 votes. However, after a recount, the Indiana Secretary of State declared McIntyre the victor by 34 votes. The House of Representatives intervened and conducted its own investigation and recount. The House's recount showed McCloskey to be the winner, by only four votes. The final count was 116,645 to 116,641.

McIntyre challenged the decision in state court. McCloskey removed the case to the U.S. District Court for the Southern District of Indiana. That court held the issue to be nonjusticiable. This decision of the trial court was affirmed on appeal. The appellate court stated that questions concerning vote counting in congressional elections are left to the appropriate house of Congress, not to the judiciary.[100]

Impeachment cases are also nonjusticiable. The House of Representatives impeaches officials and the Senate tries impeachment cases. Other than providing that the chief justice shall preside at the Senate trial, the Constitution does not establish a role for the judiciary in such actions. Accordingly, the decisions to impeach and convict are political, and they are finally decided in the appropriate house of Congress.

Foreign Affairs, National Security, and Military   It is also generally accepted that foreign affairs, national security, and military questions are not judiciable. The Court stated of this policy:

The President, both as Commander-in-Chief and as the Nation's organ for foreign affairs, has available intelligence services whose reports are not and ought not to be published to the world.

It would be intolerable that courts, without the relevant information, should review and perhaps nullify actions of the Executive taken on information properly held secret. Nor can courts sit in camera in order to be taken into executive confidences. But even if courts could require full disclosure, the very nature of executive decisions are wholly confided by our constitution to the political departments of government.[101]

The decision to declare war is left to Congress. The decision to negotiate a treaty and, in most cases, whether a treaty is in effect, and whether a treaty has been violated by a foreign power, is left to the president. Whether to recognize a foreign government is also a political question. The Supreme Court has refused to decide whether the United States was dealing with the proper representative of a foreign nation while negotiating a treaty. This is an executive decision.[102] The decision of whether a state of war exists between nations was also held to be a political question best left to the executive.[103] In *United States v. Alvarez-Machain*,[104] the Court was faced with an unlawful abduction of a criminal defendant by U.S. authorities. The defendant was kidnapped in Mexico and returned to the United States for trial. The Court concluded that it had jurisdiction to determine whether the United States/Mexico extradition treaty had been violated, but, since it had not, the decision on whether to return the man to Mexico belonged to the president. This is logical, as a treaty provides a court with standards from which it can render a decision. Beyond that, the decision rests upon political considerations that are beyond the competence of the judiciary. In 2005, the Supreme Court affirmed a Civil War decision that prohibits U.S. spies from suing the United States in *Tenet v. Doe*.

Tenet v. Doe
544 U.S. 1 (2005)

Chief Justice Rehnquist Delivered the Opinion of the Court.

In *Totten v. United States,* 92 U.D. 105 (1876), we held that public policy forbade a self-styled Civil War spy from suing the United States to enforce its obligations under their secret espionage agreement. Respondents here, alleged former Cold War spies, filed suit against the United States and the Director of the Central Intelligence Agency (CIA), asserting estoppel and due process claims for the CIA's alleged failure to provide respondents with the assistance it had promised in return for their espionage services. Finding that *Totten* did not bar respondents' suit, the District Court and the Court of Appeals for the Ninth Circuit held that the case could proceed. We reverse because this holding contravenes the longstanding rule, announced more than a century ago in *Totten*, prohibiting suits against the Government based on covert espionage agreements.

Respondents, a husband and wife who use the fictitious names John and Jane Doe, brought suit in the United States District Court for the Western District of Washington. According to respondents, they were formerly citizens of a foreign country that at the time was considered to be an enemy of the United States, and John Doe was a high-ranking diplomat for the country. After respondents expressed interest in defecting to the United States, CIA agents persuaded them to remain at their posts and conduct espionage for the United States for a specified period of time, promising in return that the Government "would arrange for travel to the United States and ensure financial and personal security for life." App. to Pet. for Cert. 122a. After "carrying out their end of the bargain" by completing years of purportedly high-risk, valuable espionage services, *Id.*, at 123a, respondents defected (under new names and false backgrounds) and became United States citizens, with the Government's help. The CIA designated respondents with "PL—110" status and began providing financial assistance and personal security.

With the CIA's help, respondent John Doe obtained employment in the State of Washington. As his salary increased, the CIA decreased his living stipend until, at some point, he agreed to a discontinuation of benefits while he was working. Years later, in 1997, John Doe was laid off after a corporate merger. Because John Doe was unable to find new employment as a result of CIA restrictions on the type of jobs he could hold, respondents contacted the CIA for financial assistance. Denied such assistance by the CIA, they claim they are unable to properly provide for themselves. Thus, they are faced with the prospect of either returning to their home country (where they say they face extreme sanctions), or remaining in the United States in their present circumstances.

Respondents assert, among other things, that the CIA violated their procedural and substantive due process rights by denying them support and by failing to provide them with a fair internal process for reviewing their claims. They seek injunctive relief ordering the CIA to resume monthly financial support pending further agency review. They also request a declaratory judgment stating that the CIA failed to provide a constitutionally adequate review process, and detailing the minimal process the agency must provide. Finally, respondents seek a mandamus order requiring the CIA to adopt agency procedures, to give them fair review, and to provide them with security and financial assistance. . . .

[The United States's motion to dismiss the claim was denied by both the district court and the appellate court.]

In *Totten*, the administrator of William A. Lloyd's estate brought suit against the United States to recover compensation for services that Lloyd allegedly rendered as a spy during the Civil War. 92 U.S. 105. Lloyd purportedly entered into a contract with President Lincoln in July 1861 to spy behind Confederate lines on troop placement and fort plans, for which he was to be paid $200 a month. *Id.*, at 105–106. The lower court had found that Lloyd performed on the contract but did not receive full compensation. *Id.*, at 106. After concluding with "no difficulty," *Ibid.*, that the President had the authority to bind the United States to contracts with secret agents, we observed that the very essence of the alleged contract between Lloyd and the Government was that it was secret, and had to remain so:

> The service stipulated by the contract was a secret service; the information sought was to be obtained clandestinely, and was to be communicated privately; the employment and the service were to be equally concealed. Both employer and agent must have understood that the lips of the other were to be for ever sealed respecting the relation of either to the matter. This condition of the engagement was implied from the nature of the employment, and is implied in all secret employments of the government in time of war, or upon matters affecting our foreign relations, where a disclosure of the service might compromise or embarrass our government in its public duties, or endanger the person or injure the character of the agent.

Ibid.

Thus, we thought it entirely incompatible with the nature of such a contract that a former spy could bring suit to enforce it. *Id.*, at 106–107.

We think the Court of Appeals was quite wrong in holding that *Totten* does not require dismissal of respondents' claims. That court, and respondents here, reasoned first that *Totten* developed merely a contract rule, prohibiting breach-of-contract claims seeking to enforce the terms of espionage agreements but not barring claims based on due process or estoppel theories. In fact, *Totten* was not so limited: "[P]ublic policy forbids the maintenance of *any* suit in a court of justice, the trial of which would inevitably lead to the disclosure of matters which the law itself regards as confidential." *Id.*, at 107 [emphasis added]; see also *ibid.* ("The secrecy which such contracts impose precludes *any action* for their enforcement" [emphasis added]). No matter the clothing in which alleged spies dress their claims, *Totten* precludes judicial review in cases such as respondents' where success depends upon the existence of their secret espionage relationship with the Government. . . .

We adhere to *Totten*. . . . The possibility that a suit may proceed and an espionage relationship may be revealed, if the state secrets privilege is found not to apply, is unacceptable: "Even a small chance that some court will order disclosure of a source's identity could well impair intelligence gathering and cause sources to 'close up like a clam.'" *CIA v. Sims*, 471 U.S. 159, 175 (1985). Forcing the Government to litigate these claims would also make it vulnerable to "graymail," *i.e.*, individual lawsuits brought to induce the CIA to settle a case (or prevent its filing) out of fear that any effort to litigate the action would reveal classified information that may undermine ongoing covert operations. And requiring the Government to invoke the privilege on a case-by-case basis risks the perception that it is either confirming or denying relationships with individual plaintiffs.

The judgment of the Court of Appeals is reversed.

It is so ordered.

Exceptions   Although these issues represent the clearest cases of political questions, there may be exceptions. The Court stated in *Baker v. Carr,* "it is error to suppose that every case or controversy which touches foreign relations lies beyond judicial cognizance." Where is the limit? Consider the following hypothetical case. The Constitution expressly delegates to Congress the authority to declare war. In spite of this, presidents often initiate wars. The power of the executive in this area is now recognized, primarily due to historical precedent. What if the president were to commit troops or order other military action after Congress had considered and rejected the idea of declaring war? What if the president refused to engage in war after Congress declared it? Whether this would be nonjusticiable is unknown, but may represent an extreme political case in which the Court might intervene.

Nixon v. United States
506 U.S. 224 (1993)

Chief Justice Rehnquist delivered the opinion of the Court.

Petitioner Walter L. Nixon, Jr., asks this court to decide whether Senate Rule XI, which allows a committee of Senators to hear evidence against an individual who has been impeached and to report that evidence to the full Senate, violates the Impeachment Trial Clause, Art. I, Section 3, cl. 6. That Clause provides that the "Senate shall have the sole Power to try all impeachments." But before we reach the merits of such a claim, we must decide whether it is "justiciable," that is, whether it is a claim that may be resolved by the courts. We conclude that it is not.

Nixon, a former Chief Judge of the United States District Court for the Southern District of Mississippi, was convicted by a jury of two counts of making false statements before a federal grand jury and sentenced to prison. . . . The grand jury investigation stemmed from reports that Nixon had accepted a gratuity from a Mississippi businessman in exchange for asking a local district attorney to half the prosecution of the businessman's son. Because Nixon refused to resign from his office as a United States District Judge, he continued to collect his judicial salary while serving out his prison sentence. . . .

On May 10, 1989, the House of Representatives adopted three articles of impeachment for high crimes and misdemeanors. . . . After the House presented the articles to the Senate, the Senate voted to invoke its own impeachment Rule XI, under which the presiding officer appoints a committee of Senators to "receive evidence and take testimony." . . . The Senate committee held four days of hearings. . . . [The Senate then convicted Nixon.]

Nixon thereafter commenced the present suit, arguing that Senate Rule XI violates the constitutional grant of authority to the Senate to "try" all impeachments because it prohibits the whole Senate from taking part in the evidentiary hearing. . . . [Nixon lost at both the trial and appellate levels.]

A controversy is nonjusticiable—i.e. involves a political question—where there is "a textually demonstrable constitutional commitment of the issue to a coordinate political department; or a lack of judicially discoverable and manageable standards for resolving it. . . ."

In this case we must examine Art. I, Section, 3, cl. 6, to determine the scope of the authority conferred upon the Senate by the Frames regarding impeachment. It provides:

> The Senate shall have the sole Power to try all impeachments. When sitting for that Purpose, they shall be on Oath or Affirmation. When the President of the United States is tried, the Chief Justice shall preside. And no person shall be convicted without the Concurrence of two thirds of the Members present.

The language and structure of the Clause are revealing. The first sentence is a grant of authority to the Senate, and the word "Sole" indicates that this authority is reposed in the Senate and nowhere else. The next two sentences specify requirements to which the Senate proceedings shall conform: the Senate shall be on oath or affirmation, a two-third vote is required to convict, and when the President is tried the Chief Justice shall preside.

Petitioner argues that the world "try" in the first sentences imposes by implication an additional requirement on the Senate in that the proceeding must be in the nature of a judicial trial. From there the petitioner goes on to argue that this limitation precludes the Senate from delegating to a select committee the task of hearing the testimony of witnesses, as we done pursuant to Senate Rule XI. "'Try' means more than simply 'vote on' 'review' or 'judge' in 1787 and today, trying a case means hearing the evidence, not scanning a cold record." Brief for Petitioner 25. Petitioner concludes from this that courts may review whether or not the Senate "tried" him before convicting him.

There are several difficulties with the position which lead us ultimately to reject it. The word "try," both in 1787 and later, has considerably broader meanings than those to which petitioner would limit it. Older dictionaries define *try* as "to examine" or "to examine as a judge." See 2 S. Johnson, *A Dictionary of the English Language* (1785). In more modern usage the term has various meanings. For example, *try* can mean "to examine or investigate judicially," "to conduct the trial of," or "to put to the test by experiment, investigation, or trial" *Webster's Third New International Dictionary*. . . .

Petitioner submits that "try," as contained in T. Sheridan, *Dictionary of the English Language* (1796), means "to examine as a judge; to bring before a judicial tribunal." Based on the variety of definitions, however, we cannot say that the Framers used the work "try" as an implied limitation on the method by which the Senate might proceed in trying impeachments. . . .

The conclusion that the use of the word "try" in the first sentence of the Impeachment Trial Clause lacks sufficient precision to afford any judicially manageable standard of review of the Senate's action is fortified by the existence of the three very specific requirements that the Constitution does impose on the Senate when trying impeachments: the members must be under oath, a two-thirds vote is required to convict, and the Chief Justice presides when the President is tried. These limitations are quite precise, and their nature suggests that the Framers did not intend to impose additional limitations on the form of the Senate proceedings by the use of the word "try" in the first sentence.

. . . We think that the word "sole" is of considerable significance. Indeed, the word "sole" appears only one other time in the Constitution—with respect to the House of Representatives' sole Power of Impeachments. . . . The common sense meaning of the world "sole" is that the Senate alone shall have authority to determine [whether] an individual should be acquitted or convicted. The dictionary definition beats this out. "sole" is defined as "having no companion," "solitary," "being the only one," and "functioning . . . independently and without assistance or interference." . . . If the courts may review the actions of the Senate in order to determine whether that body "tried" an impeached official, if is difficult to see how the Senate would be "functioning . . . independently and without assistance or interference."

Nixon asserts that the word "sole" has no substantive meaning. To support his contention, he argues that the word is nothing more than a mere "cosmetic edit" added by the Committee of Style after the delegates had approved the substance of the Impeachment Trial Clause. . . . [W]e must presume that the Committee's reorganization or rephrasing accurately captured what the Framers meant in their unadorned language. . . . Second, carrying Nixon's argument to its logical conclusion would constrain us to say that the second to last draft would govern in every instance where the Committee of Style added an arguably substantive word. Such a result is at odds with the fact that the Convention passed the Committee's version, and with the well established rule that the plain language of the enacted text is the best indicator of intent. . . .

The history and contemporary understanding of the impeachment provisions support our reading of the constitutional language. The parties do not offer evidence of a single word in the history of the Constitutional Convention or in contemporary commentary that even alludes to the possibility of judicial review in the context of impeachment powers. . . .

There are two additional reasons why the judiciary, and the Supreme Court in particular, were not chosen to have any role in impeachments. First, the Framers recognized that most likely there would be two sets of proceedings for individuals who commit impeachable offenses—the impeachments trial and a separate criminal trial, In fact, the Constitution explicitly provides for two separate proceedings. See Art. I, Sec. 3, Cl. 7. The Frames deliberately separated the two forums to avoid raising the specter of bias. . . .

Second, judicial review would be inconsistent with the Framers' insistence that our system be one of checks and balances. In our constitutional system impeachment was designed to be the only check on the Judicial Branch by the Legislature. . . . For the foregoing reasons, the judgment of the Court of Appeals is Affirmed.

Finally, in the political question arena, there is *United States v. Nixon*.[105] This case resulted from the Watergate affair, a political scandal during the Nixon presidency that involved break-ins of the Democratic National Committee Headquarters in the Watergate Building in Washington, DC. President Nixon and many of his closest advisors were implicated in the scandal, and a special prosecutor sought to enforce a subpoena for documents and tapes against Nixon. See Chapter 6 for a more thorough discussion of the Watergate affair. Before the high court, President Nixon claimed executive privilege as to the information and also claimed that his actions were nonjusticiable as political questions. The Court rejected the nonjusticiability claim and ordered that the prosecutor be permitted an *in camera* inspection of the documents. The Court reasoned that the issues of the case were traditionally vested in the judiciary—specifically, whether evidence that is relevant to an ongoing criminal investigation should be produced. Accordingly, the courts were to determine the extent of President Nixon's immunity under the executive privilege doctrine. See Chapter 6 for a discussion of executive privilege.

3.6(d) Abstention

In spite of Chief Justice John Marshall's statement in *Cohens v. Virginia*[106] that the Court has no right to relinquish jurisdiction, it does in abstention cases.[107] There are three forms of abstention. The first occurs when there is an unsettled state law issue, the second arises when a federal court is faced with an issue that has traditionally been left to state courts to decide, and the third occurs when comity principles demand it. The first two forms of abstention occur most often in diversity of citizenship cases.

Unsettled State Law   As to the first situation, a federal court will abstain from hearing a case, but will retain jurisdiction, whenever a case rests upon an unsettled issue of state law. Even though jurisdiction exists, the federal court will stay the case until a state court has had an opportunity to resolve the state legal issue. This occurs most often when diversity of citizenship is used to establish federal judicial jurisdiction, but the underlying state legal issue is controversial and unresolved. The more sensitive the state legal issue, the more likely it is that abstention will be invoked. Also, if it is possible that a state court's interpretation of its laws or orders will avoid a federal constitutional issue, the likelihood of abstention is increased. For example, suppose that there are two possible interpretations of a state statute, one that raises federal constitutional issues and one that does not. A federal court may abstain from resolving the issue in hopes that a state court will interpret the statute in the manner that avoids the federal constitutional issue.

To facilitate the process and policy underlying abstention, many states have enacted certification procedures through which a federal court can certify questions of state law to be presented to the state high courts for resolution. This can occur during the pendency of the federal proceeding. If no certification procedure is available, the plaintiff must initiate a new state court action to have the state issues answered. This does not preclude federal judicial review; rather, it postpones such review until the state court has rendered its decision. Whatever procedure is used, abstention usually delays resolution of a case.

Traditional State Law Issues Abstention may be declared in a second class of cases. Questions that have traditionally been resolved by state courts, or otherwise strike at the heart of traditional state powers, are left to state courts to answer. For example, domestic issues, such as divorce and child custody, have belonged to the states. The Supreme Court announced this as early as 1859.[108] Accordingly, federal courts abstain from hearing domestic cases even if diversity jurisdiction can be established. Consider the marriage of Herman and Mariza, for example. Recall that to establish diversity jurisdiction, there must be a diversity of citizenship between the plaintiff and the defendant, and the amount in controversy must exceed $50,000. Herman and Mariza were married in Oregon and remained there until they separated in 1998. Herman moved to Florida and Mariza moved to Maryland at that time. The total value of their marital property is $200,000. Using these facts, federal court diversity jurisdiction exists. However, because this area of law is left to the states, no federal court will entertain the case. Similarly, federal courts abstain from estate and probate cases.

Younger Doctrine Federal courts also generally abstain from interfering with pending state court cases, even if a federal constitutional issue is raised. If a criminal defendant in state court, for example, alleges that his federal constitutional rights are being violated, he may not obtain federal court intervention in most instances. Rather, the federal issues must be resolved through the appellate and habeas corpus processes. This is generally known as the **Younger doctrine,** after the 1971 Supreme Court case that announced the principle.[109] Pursuant to the Younger doctrine, federal courts are to abstain from interfering with state court criminal cases unless a federal constitutional right is asserted, the defendant will suffer irreparable harm without intervention, the harm will be both great and immediate, and the state authorities are acting in bad faith. This is a rigorous standard for a state criminal defendant to meet; as a result, *Younger* demands abstention in nearly all cases.

Younger has been extended to civil cases as well. For *Younger* to apply in a civil proceeding, the "[s]tate's interests in the proceeding [must be] so important that exercise of the federal jurisdiction power would disregard the comity between the states and National Government."[110] Enforcement of judgments and contempt proceedings are examples of important state interests. *Younger* may also apply to administrative proceedings.[111]

An individual has standing to seek federal intervention if a prosecution has been initiated or there is a legitimate and serious threat of impending prosecution. If a federal court decides that intervention is appropriate, it will issue an injunction staying the

Younger doctrine
The doctrine, drawn from *Younger v. Harris*, that federal courts will abstain in most cases from interfering with state court proceedings, even if federal constitutional issues are present. Except in extreme cases, federal review of federal constitutional issues must wait until appeal or habeas corpus review.

state court proceeding so that it may hear the federal issue. In some instances, the case may be brought to final judgment in the federal court; in others the federal issue will be resolved and the case remanded to the state court for final adjudication.

The Supreme Court has stated that there are three policy reasons for the *Younger* abstention doctrine. First, as a general rule, equity does not operate except when a party has no adequate remedy at law. Because a party seeking federal review is in a state court of law, equity is generally unavailable. This hurdle can be overcome by showing that the state courts will not hear the constitutional claim. However, failure to raise the issue in the state court is not adequate. Second, *comity*—that is, respect for federalism principles—also justifies the doctrine. Third, federal courts avoid constitutional issues whenever possible. It is possible that the state court, if allowed to proceed, will deal with the case in a manner that does not implicate the federal constitution.

3.6(e) Sovereign Immunity and the Eleventh Amendment

sovereign immunity
The principle that the government—specifically, the United States or any state of the United States—is immune from suit except when it consents to be sued.

In old England, the Crown could not be held accountable for its actions. This is the historical source of **sovereign immunity.** This doctrine was accepted and adopted by the states and national government early in U.S. history, albeit not without criticism. However, in the United States, the people are regarded as sovereign, not the state. One court said, "[i]n preserving the sovereign immunity theory, courts have overlooked the fact that the Revolutionary War was fought to abolish that 'divine right of the kings' on which the theory was based."[112]

Regardless of any controversy, sovereign immunity continues to be the law for both states and the federal government. Local forms of government are not protected by this immunity, however.

In 1793, the Supreme Court handed down *Chisholm v. Georgia,*[113] wherein it decided that the citizen of one state could sue another state in federal court. Believing that it was shielded from suits by the doctrine of sovereign immunity, Georgia refused to defend itself and a default judgment was entered against it. The public response was sure and swift. The Eleventh Amendment was initiated and ratified in five years. That Amendment reads:

> The Judicial power of the United States shall not be construed to extend to any suit in law or equity, commenced or prosecuted against one of the United States by Citizens of another State, or by Citizens or Subjects of any Foreign State.

The intention of the Eleventh Amendment is clear. States shall be immune from suit in federal court from cases filed by citizens of other states or nations. It was, in the opinion of its drafters, a ratification of the doctrine of sovereign immunity. Because a case may not be prosecuted in federal court does not necessarily mean that a party is without a remedy, though. If a state has waived immunity in its own courts, the plaintiff may pursue her action there.

In spite of its plain language to the contrary, the Supreme Court interpreted the Eleventh Amendment as barring suits by citizens against their own states in *Hans v. Louisiana.*[114] This decision was based upon original intention analysis.

There are several exceptions to the Eleventh Amendment. First, states are not immune from actions brought by other states or the United States. This includes actions filed by the United States on behalf of citizens, even if the citizens could not have filed the actions themselves. For example, the U.S. Department of Labor was permitted to prosecute a case against a state alleging that the state was violating the federal labor rights of certain employees. The employees themselves would have been barred from bringing such an action.[115]

Second, a state may waive its immunity. This is normally accomplished through state statute. A waiver must be clearly expressed in a statute or must be implied strongly.[116] A court may not read a waiver into a law.

A third exception to the Eleventh Amendment applies to political subdivisions of states. Counties, municipalities, districts, and other governmental subdivisions are not shielded by the Eleventh Amendment. State agencies do, however, fall under the immunity of the amendment.

To address special interstate issues, two or more states will sometimes join with the federal government in the creation of an agency. In such cases, the Eleventh Amendment may shield the agency with immunity. This was the issue in *Hess v. Port Authority,*[117] a 1994 Supreme Court case. Two states (New York and New Jersey) and the federal government created a port authority. Employees of the port who were injured while on the job sued the authority for their damages under the Federal Employers Liability Act. The authority claimed that it was immune from being sued in federal court.

The Supreme Court held that in determining whether such bilateral agencies are immune, a court should consider whether the states and federal government intended for the agency to be immune and the degree to which the agency is independent and self-sustaining. If an agency's losses directly affect the state treasury, then the agency is most likely immune. In *Hess,* the Court stated that because the agency paid its own debts and generated its own revenues, it was sufficiently independent of the states to fall outside the protection of the Eleventh Amendment.

Fourth, state officials may be sued in federal court for unconstitutional actions pursuant to the Ex Parte Young doctrine.[118] The theory underlying this exception is that unconstitutional acts are by their nature not state action. Such a suit must be directed against the official and not the state. Thus, suits seeking declaratory and injunctive relief against public officials are permitted. So are suits alleging that a state official violated a person's constitutional rights. However, if the suit seeks money from the state treasury, then it is barred, regardless of whether it is filed against an individual in her personal or official capacity. In such a case, the real party is the state, not the public official. The trial court may use its contempt powers to prod state officials into compliance. Oddly, the Supreme Court has held that both the official and the state may be fined for refusals to comply.[119] The fact that a state will expend state funds while complying with an injunction does not mean that it is a real party in Eleventh Amendment terms. For example, an order to desegregate will involve costs to a state, but these expenditures are ancillary.

The Ex Parte Young doctrine was extended in the 2011 case Virginia Office for Protection and Advocacy v. Stewart[120] to permit agencies of the same state to sue one another. In the case, the State of Virginia chose to participate in a program financially supported by the federal government. To be eligible for federal funding to provide assistance to the mentally ill and those with developmental disabilities, Virginia was required to have an agency, either private or state, that had the authority to sue and advocate for the intended populations, independent of state executive control. Virginia delegated the authority to its independent agency, the Office of Protection and Advocacy (OPA). While investigating patient deaths and injuries at state mental hospitals the OPA requested records from the responsible state agency. The agency refused to produce the documents, the OPA sued the agency in federal court claiming it was in violation of federal law, and the agency sought dismissal, asserting Eleventh

---

PERSONAL AND OFFICIAL CAPACITIES

Lawsuits against government officials may be filed in "official capacity" or "personal capacity." Generally, a claim filed in official capacity makes the government itself a party. Claims against individuals are personal and usually do not make the employer-government a real party in interest. The title of the claim is not dispositive; the issue is who will bear the burden of any resulting judgment.

S I D E B A R

Amendment immunity. The Supreme Court applied Ex Parte Young and permitted the OPA to seek prospective relief from the applicable agency officials. The Court found no reason to distinguish between suits brought by persons from those brought by state agencies. Indeed, Virginia agreed that if it had delegated the authority to advocate and sue under the law to a private agency, which was permitted under federal law, then the suit would be permitted under Ex Parte Young. While the Court acknowledged that there must be a limit to the extent to which a court can affect a state' internal operations, herein by enabling a state to be divided against itself, it didn't believe this narrow case exceeded the limit.

Fifth, Congress may authorize suits against states in federal courts in some instances. This congressional power stems from Amendments 13 through 15 (Civil War Amendments prohibiting slavery, assuring due process, etc.), 19 (women's right to vote), 23 (no poll taxes), and 26 (franchise of eighteen-year-olds). These amendments specifically provide that Congress may enact legislation to enforce their mandates. Because these amendments postdate the Eleventh Amendment, they are interpreted as limitations upon both state sovereignty (Tenth Amendment) and state immunity (Eleventh Amendment). For example, a state can be sued in federal court for refusing to permit eighteen-year-old citizens to vote, and individuals can sue their states to collect the costs of cleaning up environmental toxins that are the responsibility of the state.[121]

Congress has enacted many civil rights statutes prohibiting discrimination in various sectors of life, including employment and access to public facilities. These laws are generally designed to apply to private parties. Congress may, but usually does not, extend the remedies under these laws to state action. Congressional intent to abrogate state immunity will not be inferred lightly; rather, there must be an "unequivocal expression of congressional intent." This issue was addressed by the Supreme Court in *Atascadero State Hospital v. Scanlon,* a 1985 case.

Atascadero State Hospital v. Scanlon
473 U.S. 678 (1985)

Justice Powell delivered the opinion of the Court.

This case presents the question whether States and state agencies are subject to suit in federal court by litigants seeking retroactive monetary relief under § 504 of the Rehabilitation Act of 1973 . . . or whether such suits are proscribed by the Eleventh Amendment.

Respondent, Douglas James Scanlon, suffers from diabetes mellitus and has no sight in one eye. In November 1979, he filed this action against petitioners, Atascadero State Hospital and the California Department of Mental Health, in the United States District Court for the Central District of California, alleging that in 1978 the hospital denied him employment. . . . solely because of his physical handicaps. Respondent charged that the hospital's discriminatory refusal to hire him violated § 504 of the Rehabilitation Act of 1973. . . .

Petitioners moved for dismissal of the complaint on the ground that the Eleventh Amendment barred the federal court from entertaining respondent's claims. . . . In January 1980, the District Court granted petitioner's motion to dismiss the complaint on the ground that respondent's claims were barred by the Eleventh Amendment. On

appeal, the United States Court of Appeals for the Ninth Circuit affirmed [on different judgment]. . . . We granted certiorari . . . vacated the judgment . . . and remanded the case for further consideration. . . . On remand, the Court of Appeals reversed the judgment of the District Court. It held that "the Eleventh Amendment does not bar [respondent's] action because the State, If it has participated in and received funds from programs under the Rehabilitation Act, has implicitly consented to be sued."

The [court of appeals] decision in this case is in conflict with those of the Court of Appeals for the First and Eight Circuits. . . . We granted certiorari to resolve this conflict.

The Eleventh Amendment provides. "The Judicial power of the United States shall not be construed to extend to any suit in law or equity, commenced or prosecuted against one of the United States by Citizens of another States, or by Citizens or Subjects or any Foreign State." As we have recognized, the significance of this Amendment "lies in its affirmation that the fundamental principle of sovereign immunity limits the grants of judicial authority in Act. III" of the Constitution. . . .

There are, however, certain well-established exceptions to the reach of the Eleventh Amendment. For example, if a State Waives its immunity and consents to suit in federal court, the Eleventh Amendment does not bar the action. . . .

Moreover, the Eleventh Amendment is "necessarily limited by the enforcement provisions of § 5 of the Fourteenth Amendment," that is by Congress' power to enforce by appropriate legislation, the substantive provisions of the Fourteenth Amendment.

But because the Eleventh Amendment implicates the fundamental constitutional balance between the Federal Government and the States, this Court consistently has held that these exceptions apply only when certain specific conditions are met. Thus, we have held that a State will be deemed to have waived its immunity "only where stated by the most express language or by such overwhelming implication from the text as [will] leave no room for any other reasonable construction. . . . Likewise, in determining whether Congress in exercising its Fourteenth Amendment powers has abrogated the State's Eleventh Amendment immunity, we have required "an unequivocal expression of congressional intent to overturn the constitutionally guaranteed immunity of the several states."

In this case, we are asked to decide whether the State of California is subject to suit in federal court for alleged violations of [the Rehabilitation Act]. . . .

Respondent argues that the State of California has waived its immunity to suit in federal court . . . The test for determining whether a State has waived its immunity from federal court jurisdiction is a stringent one. Although a State's general waiver of sovereign immunity may subject it to suit in state court, it is not enough to waive the immunity guaranteed by the Eleventh Amendment. . . . As we explained just last Term, "a State's constitutional interest in immunity encompasses not merely whether it may be sued, but where it may be sued." . . . In view of these principles, we do not believe that Art. III, § 5, of the California Constitution constitutes a waiver of the State's constitutional immunity. This provision does not specifically indicate the State's willingness to be sued in federal court. Indeed, this provision appears simply to authorize the legislature to waive the State's sovereign immunity. In the absence of an unequivocal waiver . . . we decline to find the California has waived its constitutional immunity.

Respondent also contends that is enacting the Rehabilitation Act, Congress abrogated the State's constitutional immunity. . . .

Only recently the Court reiterated that "the States occupy a special and specific position in our constitutional system. . . ." By guaranteeing the sovereign immunity of the States against suit in federal court, the Eleventh Amendment serves to maintain this balance. "Our reluctance to infer that a State's immunity from suit in the federal courts has been negated stems from recognition of the vital role of the doctrine of sovereign immunity in our federal system."

For these reasons, we hold . . . that Congress must express its intention to abrogate the Eleventh Amendment in unmistakable language in the statute itself.

In light of these principles, we must decide whether Congress, in adopting the Rehabilitation Act, has chosen to override the Eleventh Amendment. Section 504 of the Rehabilitation Act provides in pertinent part:

No otherwise qualified handicapped individual in the United States . . . shall, solely by reason of his handicap, be excluded from the participation in, be denied the benefits of, or be subjected to discrimination under any program or activity receiving Federal financial assistance or under any program or activity conducted by an Executive agency or by the United States Postal Service.

Section 505, which was added to the Act in 1978, describes . . . the available remedies under the Act, including provisions pertinent to this case:

(a) (2) The remedies, procedures, and rights set forth in title VI of the Civil Rights Act of 1964 . . . shall be available to any person aggrieved by any act or failure to act by any recipient of Federal assistance or Federal provider of such assistance . . .

(b) In any action or proceeding to enforce or charge a violation of a provision of this subchapter, the court, in its discretion, may allow the prevailing party, other than the United States, a reasonable attorneys fee as part of the costs.

The statute thus provides remedies for violations of § 504 by "any recipient of Federal assistance." There is no claim here that the State of California is not a recipient of federal aid under the statute. But given their constitutional role, the States are not like any other class of recipients of federal aid. A general authorization for suit in federal court is not the kind of unequivocal statutory a language sufficient to abrogate the Eleventh Amendment. . . . Accordingly, we hold that the Rehabilitation Act does not abrogate the Eleventh Amendment bar to suits against the States.

[The Court concluded by holding that, in itself, state receipt of federal funds also does not abrogate a state's immunity.]

Federal sovereign immunity continues to be recognized by the courts. This is not as serious a barrier as it was a hundred years ago, as Congress has waived immunity in most cases. For example, through the Federal Tort Claims Act,[122] the United States permits individuals to prosecute cases against it for certain torts. There are other similar laws.[123] In cases in which the United States has not waived immunity, the court is to dismiss the case.

FEDERAL JUDICIAL JURISDICTION LIMITING DOCTRINES	
Doctrine	*Source*
1. Ripeness	1. Art. III
2. Mootness	2. Art. III
3. Standing	3. Art. III
4. Political question	4. Art. III and separation of powers principles
5. Abstention	5. Tenth Amendment
6. Cases against states	6. Eleventh Amendment
7. Canons of construction	7. Judicial restraint

FIGURE 3-7
Federal judicial jurisdiction limiting doctrines

3.6(f) Other Limitations

The federal courts have developed several rules intended to restrain their own power (see Figure 3-7 for a complete list). As a matter of policy, federal courts avoid constitutional issues whenever possible. One canon of statutory construction holds that if multiple interpretations of a statute are possible, some holding the law constitutional and others not, a construction that supports the law's constitutionality is to be selected. Similarly, a court will decide a case without addressing a constitutional issue, if possible (alternative grounds). "It is [the Court's] settled policy to avoid an interpretation of a federal statute that engenders a constitutional issue if a reasonable alternative interpretation poses no constitutional question."[124]

Another canon of construction provides that a statute is presumed constitutional and the burden of proving otherwise lies with the challenger. If part of a statute is held unconstitutional, the remaining parts are to remain viable as long as it is logical to do so. The unconstitutional clauses are to be severed, and the courts should enforce the remaining parts of the law.

Finally, federal judicial review of state court decisions is prevented when the lower court decision is based upon **adequate and independent state grounds,** even if federal claims were presented to that court. Of course, the state-law basis for the decision must be consistent with the U.S. Constitution for this rule to apply.

This rule is the product of federalism, comity, and economy principles. State courts are the final arbiters of state law. A state high court, usually entitled State Supreme Court, is the court of last resort for state-law principles. The Supreme Court is a lower court in these terms and is bound by state court interpretations of state laws. Accordingly, if a state court can resolve a case by applying state law without violating federal law, then no federal judicial review of any federal constitutional issues is necessary.

State law is adequate in these cases if it logically resolves the issue without the support of federal constitutional law. The more troubling issue concerns the second prong: independence. Often, the issue is whether a state court decided a case upon state or federal constitutional principles. It is common for a state court to cite both state and federal constitutional provisions in support of a decision. In such cases, the question of whether the state court relied upon federal or state case law, state or federal constitutional history, and the like must be considered. Generally, it must be plain that a decision is made upon state grounds to avoid review of federal legal issues.

adequate and independent state grounds doctrine
Federal judicial review of a state decision in a case that included both state and federal claims will not occur if the lower court's decision rested upon adequate and independent state law.

3.7 STATE COURT JURISDICTION

State courts possess general jurisdiction. They may hear all state-law cases, whether arising under ordinance, statute, regulation, state constitution, or common law. Also, since the merger of equity and common law courts in most jurisdictions, state courts entertain claims for equitable relief as well. State courts are, as previously noted, the final interpreters of state law.

In addition, state courts are presumed to have jurisdiction over federal claims and Congress may compel state courts to entertain federal claims.[125] Congress may withdraw state court jurisdiction over federal claims in certain cases,[126] such as when a right and its remedy were created by Congress. However, Congress may not withdraw the authority and obligation of state judges to enforce the U.S. Constitution. Recall that the Supremacy Clause, Article VI, commands state judges to treat federal law as supreme, even over their own state's laws. State courts must follow federal precedents when applying federal law.

In a case in which federal jurisdiction exists concurrently with state jurisdiction, and the case was filed in state court, removal to federal court is possible. Removal is optional, so if no party files a petition to remove, the case remains in the state court. As a result of the anti-injunction act and comity doctrines (such as the *Younger* doctrine), federal courts rarely interfere with exclusive state-law cases. However, in extreme cases, if a party will be immediately, greatly, and irreparably harmed and bad faith can be shown to exist at the state level, a federal court may stay its proceedings and review any federal constitutional issues.

State courts are not bound by Article III's case-or-controversy requirement, even when interpreting federal law. Accordingly, a litigant who cannot establish standing in a federal court may be able to have her federal claim heard in state court. This creates a situation where state court interpretations of federal law cannot be reviewed by federal courts.

This paradoxical situation was tempered by the 1989 decision in *Asarco Inc. v. Kadish.*[127] *Asarco* involved a challenge to an Arizona statute that permitted leasing of state-owned mineral rights. A group of taxpayers and public school teachers challenged the statute as violative of federal law. The Arizona Supreme Court ruled in favor of the plaintiffs and invalidated the law. The lessees of the mineral rights appealed to the Supreme Court, which held that the plaintiffs in the state court action (taxpayers and teachers with a generalized interest) were without standing. Regardless, the Supreme Court agreed to review the case because the defendant lessees had suffered a "distinct and palpable" injury from the Arizona Supreme Court decision. (The decision would have been different had the defendant prevailed in the state court and the plaintiffs appealed.)

Thus, it is now possible for the Supreme Court to entertain a case in which standing was lacking at the trial level. In essence, the Court concluded that an adverse decision, even when no standing exists, may itself create an injury that gives rise to standing.[128]

America's state courts continue to be the largest dispensers of justice. Over 95 percent of all cases, civil and criminal, are filed in and resolved by state courts.

When adjudicating cases, courts interpret statutes, ordinances, court decisions, administrative regulations, and other law. This is called *interpretation.* The most important document interpreted is the Constitution. The most influential interpretation of that document comes from the Supreme Court.

3.8 CONSTITUTIONAL INTERPRETATION

The Constitution does not state how it is to be interpreted. In many ways, the issue of what method of interpreting the Constitution should be used parallels the question, what role should the judiciary play in the United States? We have delegated

CONSTITUTION INTERPRETATION METHODS

Method	Description	Evidence
Originalism	Constitution is interpreted and applied in a manner consistent with the framers' intentions	• Convention records • Writings of the framers and their Contemporaries (e.g., *Federalist Papers*) • Ratification debate records • Laws of the era and preexisting constitution
Modernism/ Instrumentalism	Constitution is interpreted and applied in contemporary terms	• Objective indicators of public values • Social scientific evidence
Literalism— historical	Constitution is interpreted and applied by focusing on its terms, syntax, and other linguistic features that were in use at the time of adoption/ratification	• Text of the Constitution • Evidence of language use at time of adoption/ratification
Literalism— contemporary	Constitution is interpreted and applied by focusing on its terms, syntax, and other linguistic features that are currently in use	• Text of the Constitution • Evidence of contemporary language use
Democratic/normative reinforcement	Constitution is interpreted and applied in a manner that reinforces the document's underlying democratic themes	• Evidence of framers' intentions • Structure/organization internet in Constitution • Objective evidence of reinforcement of norms

FIGURE 3-8

Methods of interpreting the Constitution

the authority to make policy to the legislative and, to a lesser degree, the executive branches, which are accountable to the people through the voting booth. However, federal judges are not elected, and once installed, they leave office only through death, retirement, or impeachment. Therefore, the issue is whether the Constitution should be interpreted in a manner that permits justices to consider policy matters. Should they be guided by their own ideologies? The nation's?

The most common methods of interpreting the Constitution are originalism, modernism, historical literalism, contemporary literalism, and democratic reinforcement (see Figure 3-8).

3.8(a) Originalism

Originalists follow the so-called doctrine of **original intent.** It is not truly a constitutional doctrine; rather, it is an approach to interpreting the Constitution. Originalists hold that the Constitution should be interpreted to mean what the framers originally intended it to mean.

They contend that by examining the records from the Constitutional Convention, letters written by the framers, the *Federalist Papers* and related publications, the records from the state ratification debates, and other documents, it is possible to determine the framers' intent. Originalists assert that by using this approach, the Court's decision will be less normative. Said another way, decisions will not be the result of the personal opinions (beliefs, mores, biases, etc.) of justices; they will be "objectively" arrived at. This being so, the Court's decisions will be more predictable and stable and will be perceived as objective, not as a product of the Court's ideological bent. Thereby, the institution itself will command greater respect. Originalists argue that once the original intent has been declared, change can come only through the amendment process.

Opponents of the original intent approach argue that the very premise of originalism is unfounded. They ask how one intention can be attributed to the entire group of

original intent
A term applied to the view of some scholars and jurists that judicial interpretation of the Constitution should be based on the words of the Constitution itself and the framers' "original intent," not on a contemporary understanding of the Constitution in the context of current realities. Adherents of this doctrine are sometimes referred to as *strict constructionists.* An approach to interpreting the Constitution that uses historical analysis to assess what the authors of the Constitution meant or intended by a particular term or provision, including the term "liberty" within the Due Process Clauses.

framers; individual delegates may have had different reasons for supporting a particular provision of the Constitution.

Also, because the document was ratified by the states, should the intent of all the participants at the state conventions be considered? Maybe the intent of the framers is not even relevant—after all, the Constitution is a document of the people. Should an attempt to understand the people's general beliefs and attitudes be made? Furthermore, there is evidence that some provisions were intentionally drafted vaguely (such as the Due Process Clause of the Fifth Amendment), so that the precise meaning could be developed at a later date. What of these provisions? There is also some evidence that the framers did not intend for their subjective intentions to live in perpetuity. For example, James Madison believed that a document must speak for itself and that any meaning derived from its reading should not be displaced by a contrary finding of original intent. He also stated, "[a]s a guide in expounding and applying the provisions of the Constitution, the debates and incidental decisions of the Convention can have no authoritative character." He believed that the "public meaning" of the Constitution should prevail over the individual intentions of the framers. Public meaning could be shown, according to Madison, through precedent and consensus. That is, if there is consensus in the government and with the people as to what the Constitution means, and they have acted accordingly for some time, then the meaning is established, regardless of any original intent.[129]

It is also argued that original intention cannot be discerned in most instances, because the framers did not consider every possibility. This is especially true when one considers the significant changes the nation has seen since the Constitution was ratified. The Industrial Revolution, technological revolution, rapid modernization, population explosion (there were fewer than four million people in the United States at the time the Constitution was ratified), and changes in social, political, and economic attitudes brought with them problems that could not have been foreseen by the framers.

Opponents also disagree with the conclusion that predictability and stability will be assured. Courts can differ in their interpretation of intent and even in the method of determining original intention; therefore, decisions could be changed because of differences in opinion concerning the framers' original intentions.

3.8(b) Modernism

Many of those who criticize originalism are modernists, also known as *instrumentalists.* Associate Justice William Brennan Jr. was of this ideological group. He contended that the Constitution should be interpreted as if it were to be ratified today—a "contemporary ratification," "living constitution," or **modernism** approach. Originalists discover the meaning of the Constitution by examining the intent of the framers. Modernists find meaning by reading the language of the Constitution in light of contemporary life. Through this approach, the judiciary contributes to the social and moral evolution of the nation. Some oppose this method as countermajoritarian. That is, they contend that it is not the function of nine unelected individuals to make policy decisions for the nation. Proponents hold that, as an institution, the Court must engage in this form of decision making to perform its function of shielding the individual from governmental excesses and to assure that its decisions will be respected.

> **Modernism**
> An approach to interpreting the Constitution that allows courts to consider changes in social, economic, and political forces.

In addition to the philosophies previously mentioned, the adherents of this school oppose the doctrine of original intention because it causes the Constitution to become dated and out of touch with contemporary problems. They contend that the Constitution's strength comes from its dynamic, flexible nature. Although it affirmatively establishes certain principles, it does so in language that permits it to change as America changes—not revolutionary changes, but measured evolutionary changes. Change outside of the perimeters of reason must occur by amendment. Justice Brennan said:

> We current justices read the Constitution in the only way that we can: as Twentieth Century Americans. We look to the history of the time of framing and to the intervening history of

interpretation. But the ultimate question must be, what do the words of the text mean in our time. For the genius of the Constitution rests not in any static meaning it might have had in a world that is dead and gone, but in the adaptability of its great principles to cope with current problems and current needs . . . As augmented by the Bill of Rights and the Civil War Amendments, this text is a sparkling vision of the supremacy of the human dignity of every individual. This vision is reflected in the very choice of democratic self-governance: the supreme value of a democracy is the presumed worth of each individual. And this vision manifests itself most dramatically in the specific prohibitions of the Bill of Rights . . . It is a vision that has guided us as a people throughout our history, although the precise rules by which we have protected fundamental human dignity have been transformed over time in response to both transformations of social condition and evolution of our concepts of human dignity.[130]

YOUR CONSTITUTIONAL VALUES

IS THERE A CONSTITUTIONAL RIGHT TO PLAY GOLF?

Not all constitutional cases evolve from complex intergovernmental disputes or result from governmental intrusions into homes and businesses. Many cases concern the government's treatment of individuals when providing or regulating services. Generally, both state and federal governments must comply with constitutional limitations in all their activities, regulatory and social welfare. Accordingly, the Fourteenth Amendment's due process and equal protection mandates limit governmental conduct not only when administering criminal cases, but also when governments provide education and social services. Sometimes the reach of these clauses can be quite far. The case of *Crane v. Indiana High School Athletic Association*, 975 F.2d 1315 (7th Cir. 1992), reh. den. 1992 U.S. App. Lexis 33956 (19902) is an example of an everyday dispute that became a federal constitutional case.

In the late 1980s, the Indiana High School Athletic Association (IHSAA), which regulated high school interscholastic athletics, had a rule that made high school students who transferred schools ineligible to participate in interscholastic athletics during the remainder of the school year. Apparently the rule was intended to prevent students from transferring for athletic reasons, such as to play for a superior team or coach or to avoid disciplinary action. Applying this rule, the IHSAA declared Ryan Crane ineligible to play golf.

Ryan's parents divorced in 1978. After the divorce, Ryan lived with his father until he was five, when he began living with his mother in Ft. Wayne, Indiana. He lived with his mother until the close of his freshman year in high school. In 1989, Ryan's mother, citing "disciplinary problems" and falling grades in school, asked Mr. Crane to take custody of Ryan. At that time, Ryan's parents decided that it would not be a good idea for Ryan to change schools in the middle of the school year. So, Ryan stayed with his mother and finished his freshman year at Snider. After completion of the school year, however, Ryan's parents decided that it was in Ryan's best interests to live with his father. Accordingly, in June 1990, Ryan moved to his father's home in Washington, Indiana, where he enrolled in Washington High School. Citing the transfer rule, the IHSAA declared him ineligible to play varsity golf for one year. Mr. Crane, on behalf of his son, filed suit in state court. The IHSAA then removed the case to federal court on the grounds that the plaintiff raised federal constitutional claims.

The plaintiff sought to have the eligibility rule stricken and asked the court to issue an injunction prohibiting the application of the rule, thereby making him eligible to play golf. The district court granted the requested injunctive relief, holding that the rule unfairly burdened children of divorced parents in violation of the due process, and presumably, Equal Protection Clauses. The IHSAA appealed the case to the Seventh Circuit Court of Appeals. During the pendency of the appeal, Ryan played the entire season. The Court of Appeals agreed to hear the appeal, even though the season had ended, because IHSAA rules allowed for retroactive penalties against teams and athletes who have been allowed to play pursuant to a court order that is subsequently reversed or vacated. The Seventh Circuit Court of Appeals ultimately affirmed the district court's decision, although on state law, not federal constitutional, grounds. Judge Posner of that court dissented for several reasons, including that "the decision today may signal a willingness on the part of some members of this court to consider the court an arbiter of purely local disputes related, however remotely, to family status. I do not relish such a role. I think it carries us well beyond our constitutional mandate." After all of this, Ryan's performance on the greens proved to be modest.

This case is a good example of how process can manifest itself as substance. The court did not find that golf is constitutionally protected, but it did find that the student's right to a fair process resulted in a constitutionally protected right to play golf. Do you believe his claim warranted a federal case? Do you believe the framers intended to extend due process legal protection this far? Does what the framers intended matter?

Justice Brennan is in good company. Associate Justice Benjamin Cardozo commented, "the great generalities of the Constitution have a content and a significance that vary from age to age."[131] Chief Justice Fred Vinson responded to originalists by stating, "To those who would paralyze our government in the face of impending threat by encasing it in a semantic straitjacket, we must reply that all concepts are relative."[132]

Modernists do not discard original intention or stare decisis; they recognize them as factors in judicial decision making. But the needs of society are also taken into account, as is the nature of the dispute that gave rise to the case before the Court. To the modernist, the framers could not anticipate every issue that would be presented to the Court, nor did they try. It is the duty of the Court to read the Constitution and apply its terms in a manner that gives due deference to the nation's history and customs, as well as contemporary conditions and norms.

The results of scientific research may also play a role in judicial decision making. Judges following the modernist tradition are more likely to be receptive to the use of scientific data than if they were following another method. For example, in *Brown v. Board of Education*,[133] the evidence produced by social scientists indicating that segregation has detrimental effects on black people was relied upon in striking down the separate but equal doctrine. Critics charge that, by its nature, much scientific data, particularly the results of social science research, are unreliable and are used by the Court only to justify policy objectives (social engineering), a task better left to Congress and the states.

Reference to contemporary values may also be part of modern analysis. For example, the Eighth Amendment prohibits cruel and unusual punishments. The Court applies both original and modern approaches in Eighth Amendment cases. First, all punishments believed by the framers to be cruel and unusual are forever forbidden. Second, the Court has held that the Eighth Amendment is not "bound by the sparing humanitarian concessions of our forebears" and that punishments must be in accord with "evolving standards of decency that mark the progress of a maturing society."[134] The Court has said that when necessary to determine contemporary values, it will look to "objective factors," such as how other states punish the crime in question, how the jurisdiction in question punishes other crimes, and (in death penalty cases) how often sentencing juries choose the punishment.

3.8(c) Historical and Contemporary Literalism

literalism
An approach to interpreting the Constitution that focuses on the literal meanings of its words, rather than on other factors, such as the original intent of the framers. There are two forms of literalism, historical and contemporary. *Historical literalism* defines terms in the context of when the particular provision being considered was ratified. *Contemporary literalism* uses contemporary definitions.

plain-meaning rule
The rule that in interpreting a statute whose meaning is unclear, the courts will look to the "plain meaning" of its language to determine legislative intent. The plain-meaning rule is in opposition to the majority view of statutory interpretation, which takes legislative history into account.

Another approach to interpreting the Constitution is **literalism,** also known as *textualism.* This method focuses on the actual text of the Constitution. Literalists believe that the words of the document must be examined first. Words have objective meaning that may differ from the drafters' intentions. Language is paramount, not the intentions of the framers. The framers were particular in their choice of language, and accordingly, those words should be respected. The first tenet of literalism is the **plain-meaning rule,** which states that if the meaning of a term is immediately apparent, then that meaning must be accepted and applied, regardless of any other factors.

However, the meanings of words change. The phrase "modern means of production" is historically contextual. It had a different meaning in 1999 than it did in 1799. The same can be said of the language of the Constitution. Does the phrase "cruel and unusual punishment" mean the same today as it did in 1791?

Those in the historical literalism camp believe that the meaning of the words at the time the provision was ratified must be used. This approach is similar to originalism. However, do not confuse the two approaches. An originalist may transcend the language of the document in order to find the original intent; a literalist would not.

There is a second group of literalists that advocate contemporary literalism, that is, the view that contemporary definitions should be applied. They are similar to modernists, but focus on language more than a modernist does.

Historical literalists assert, as do originalists, that their method de-emphasizes the effect the ideologies of judges have on decisions and, further, that it makes the law more predictable and stable. Contemporary literalists concede that because the meanings of terms evolve, this method may result in slightly less stability. Nevertheless, they believe that they strike the proper balance between keeping the Constitution current and preventing justices from engaging in policymaking.

3.8(d) Democratic Reinforcement

Another approach to interpreting the Constitution has been termed *democratic* or *representation reinforcement.* Proponents of this theory suggest that the framers did not intend to establish a set of specific substantive principles. Rather, they created a document that defines the processes, structures, and relationships that constitute the foundation of the American democracy. The first three articles of the Constitution, for example, establish the structure of the national government, define the powers of the national government and its actors, and establish the procedures that must be followed in deciding who will occupy high government positions. Even rights usually thought of as purely substantive have procedural or structural aspects. For example, the First Amendment's religion clauses are recognized as protecting the individual's substantive right to choose and exercise religious beliefs, but they also establish a structure separating governmental and religious institutions. Although structural components of the Constitution are generally easy to define, substantive portions are not. This is because the language of the Constitution is vague or broad when it comes to substance. "Due process," "equal protection," and "cruel and unusual punishments" are examples.

From these facts, some analysts glean that the framers did not intend to establish a precise set of substantive laws. Rather, they intended to define the who, what, where, and when of substantive rulemaking. Following this theory, judicial interpretation should be guided by the general republican principles underlying the Constitution. However, the analysis is contemporary. The basic republican themes established by the framers are used as a base, but those themes are interpreted within the context of contemporary society. By allowing change in this way, constitutional law actually reflects the will of people. Accordingly, the Supreme Court is not viewed as a countermajoritarian institution, but one that reinforces democracy and republicanism.[135]

3.8(e) The Interpretation Process

Few judges subscribe exclusively to any one approach. The same judge may favor originalism for one issue and modernism for another. This does not necessarily mean that the judge is inconsistent; rather, each judge develops his or her own approach to interpretation. For example, all judges must begin with the language of the Constitution. Nearly all judges believe they have an obligation to enforce language that is plain and clear on its face. In this sense, they are literalists subscribing to the plain-meaning doctrine. However, exceptions to this rule can be found. For example, in *Hans v. Louisiana,* 134 U.S. 1 (1890), the Court determined that the Eleventh Amendment shields states from suits by their citizens in federal courts, regardless of the plain language of the amendment, which provides for state immunity in federal courts from suits filed only by citizens of other states or other nations. The Eleventh Amendment reads:

> The Judicial power of the United States shall not be construed to extend to any suit in law or equity, commenced or prosecuted against one of the United States by Citizens of another State, or by Citizens or Subjects of any Foreign State.

Many originalists and modernists subscribe to the plain-meaning doctrine. However, when the meaning of a term is not plain, they diverge into their respective approaches. They may again find themselves on similar tracks if the originalist cannot determine what the intent of the framers was or if it is determined that the framers intended to create an evolutionary concept. In such cases, the originalist finds herself on another track, possibly the same track as the modernist.

In some cases, interpretation is guided by customs, practices, and the common law. If a practice is long-standing, it is more likely to be found consistent with the Constitution than if it were new.

Common law decisions predating the Constitution may also be considered. For example, processes that were approved at common law have traditionally been approved under the Fifth and Fourteenth Amendments' Due Process Clauses. In fact, many constitutional provisions are codifications of common law doctrines, and thus the common law is depended upon to shed light on the meaning of the Constitution. For example, the Court said of the Fourth Amendment's probable cause and warrants requirements that the "provision was not intended to establish a new principle but to affirm and preserve a cherished rule of the common law designed to prevent the issue of groundless warrants."[136] This is only one example of many instances in which reference to the common law is part of interpretation of the Constitution.

The effect that a particular decision will have on the nation, the nation's institutions (including the Court itself), and the parties to the case before the Court is also a factor in judicial decision making.[137] For example, in *Bibb v. Navajo Freight Lines,*[138] the issue was whether a state could require trucks engaged in interstate commerce to comply with its safety requirements. In support of its decision holding that states may not regulate interstate trucking in this manner, the Court pointed out the consequence of an opposite decision: Disruption of interstate commerce would result from differing safety requirements. The Court reasoned that truck drivers would be forced to stop at the border of every state and reconfigure their trucks to be in compliance with the next state's safety regulations. In short, the effect of a Court ruling permitting such state regulation would be disruption of the interstate trucking industry.

A judge may also consider the interpretations of other actors, such as Congress, the president, or administrative agencies. Even though it is not required of the Supreme Court, in some cases it has exhibited deference to the interpretations of its coordinate branches when there is no dispute between them.

Although there are proponents and opponents of every approach discussed here, there is no one correct method. Justices differ in their approaches, and legal scholars differ sharply on the subject as well. Be aware of the different methods and look for their application in the cases in this text. Understanding them will increase your understanding of constitutional law and will also enhance your ability to predict the outcome of future cases.

3.8(f) Stare Decisis, Canons, and Practices Affecting Interpretation

stare decisis
Latin term for "standing by the decision." Stare decisis is the doctrine that judicial decisions stand as precedents for cases arising in the future. It is a fundamental policy of our law that, except in unusual circumstances, a court's determination on a point of law will be followed by courts of the same or lower rank in later cases presenting the same legal issue, even though different parties are involved and many years have elapsed.

A number of rules and practices also affect constitutional judicial decision making. **Stare decisis** is an important rule. This common law doctrine (the name of which translates from Latin as "let the decision stand") actually comes from the Latin phrase *stare decisis et non quieta movere* or "stand by matters that have been decided and do not disturb what is tranquil." Stare decisis is a legal principle that requires courts to respect precedent. It dates back to medieval England and was so well established by the eighteenth century that Blackstone included it in his famous *Commentaries.* The doctrine of stare decisis holds that if a court has established a legal principle that applies to a certain set of facts, it should adhere to that principle in future cases with identical or substantially similar facts. If the new case is different from the prior case in issues of law or fact, the doctrine is not applicable.

As a matter of policy, the courts adopted the practice of respecting precedent in order to make the law predictable, stable, and secure. Three additional benefits are derived from the doctrine: uniformity, efficiency, and constraint. If state courts and lower federal courts were not bound by the decisions of the Supreme Court, the Constitution and other federal laws would not have one meaning and application, but several. The Supreme Court said of the importance of following precedent, "[u]nless we wish anarchy to prevail within the federal judicial system, a precedent of this Court must be followed by the lower federal courts no matter how misguided the judges of those courts may think it to be."[139]

As for efficiency, Justice Cardozo commented, "[t]he labor of judges would be increased almost to the breaking point if every past decision could be reopened in every case, and one could not lay one's own course of bricks on the secure foundation of the courses laid by others who had gone before him."[140] In addition, adherence to precedent is "a basic self-governing principle within the Judicial Branch, which is entrusted with the sensitive and difficult task of fashioning and preserving a jurisprudential system that is not based upon an arbitrary discretion."[141]

Having a legal question answered has its own value, even if it is answered wrongly. "The Court has noted in the past that stare decisis is a principle of policy, . . . and it is usually the wise policy, because in most matters it is more important that the applicable rule of law be settled than it be settled right."[142]

Courts are bound only by their own decisions and the decisions of courts superior to them. For example, the Supreme Court is superior to all other courts, state and federal, in interpreting national law, and therefore its decisions are binding upon them all. In regard to issues of state law, the high court of each state is the final arbiter and even the Supreme Court is bound by that court's declarations. Indeed, federal courts often hear cases that have both federal and state law issues. In some cases, federal courts will send the state law issue, if novel, back to a state court for decision while the case is pending in the federal court.

Unlike the decisions of the Supreme Court, which have national precedential authority, the decisions of the U.S. courts of appeals are binding only upon the courts within their geographical circuits. For example, the Eleventh Circuit includes Alabama, Georgia, and Florida, so the decisions of the court of appeals for that circuit are precedent for the state and federal courts in those states. A decision of a district court is precedent within its district only. These limitations concern the precedential value of interpretive decisions, not the power of these courts to issue process or orders.

Courts must defer to precedent set by a superior court. As a matter of policy, courts should also respect their own prior decisions. However, a court may overturn a prior decision. The Supreme Court has done this on many occasions, for example,

Brown v. Board of Education,[143] wherein it set aside the separate but equal doctrine that it established in *Plessy v. Ferguson.*[144] The Court also did this in *Payne v. Tennessee,*[145] which overruled its decision in *Booth v. Maryland.*[146] In *Booth* the Supreme Court had held that the Eighth Amendment's prohibition of cruel and unusual punishments forbade the use of victim impact evidence at an offender's sentencing. This holding was reversed in *Payne,* only four years after *Booth* was issued. It also did this in *Lawrence v. Texas,* 539 U.S. 558 (2003), holding that private, consensual, same-sex sodomy is outside the reach of government regulate, reversing its decision in *Bowlers v. Hardwick,* 478 U.S. 186 (1986).

The extent to which a Supreme Court justice will respect stare decisis depends on many factors: the nature of the prior decision, including the nature of the decision-making process; how squarely the precedent fits the case before the Court; the age of the decision; whether citizens or legislators have acted in reliance on a previous decision; whether settled rights or obligations will be dislodged by a change; the ideologies of the justices that issued the prior decision; the number of justices that joined in the prior majority opinion; whether the decision accomplished its objectives; what the results of reversing or reaffirming the prior decision will be; how the parties before the Court will be affected by the decision; any subsequent social, political, or economic changes the nation has undergone; and the justices' conclusions concerning the propriety of the prior decision. Of course, a particular justice's approach to constitutional interpretation will determine which of these factors, if any, will be considered, and the weight to be given to each. For example, an originalist would not be interested in subsequent social, political, or economic changes. The originalist would be interested, however, in the decision-making process. Particularly, she would want to know whether the Court used an originalist approach. Presumably, a justice is more likely to vote to set aside precedent if it is based on an approach contrary to her own than she would if a decision with which she disagrees was reached using her favored approach.

It is generally accepted that because the high Court's constitutional decisions can be altered only through the amendment process, they should have less precedential effect than interpretations of statutes, which can be freely amended by Congress. The Court has stated that respect for precedent is strongest "in the area of statutory construction, where Congress is free to change this Court's interpretation of its legislation."[147]

There may be a qualification of the general rule that constitutional precedents are more freely reversed than statutory precedents: Precedents that have been relied upon that secure fundamental individual liberties should not be changed without significant justification.

> To overturn a constitutional decision is a rare and grave undertaking. To overturn a constitutional decision that secured a fundamental personal liberty to millions of persons would be unprecedented in our 200 years of constitutional history. Although the doctrine of stare decisis applies with somewhat diminished force in constitutional cases generally . . . even in ordinary constitutional cases "any departure from . . . stare decisis demands special justification" . . . This requirement of justification applies with unique force where, as here, the Court's abrogation of precedent would destroy people's firm belief, based on past decisions of this Court, that they possess an unabridgeable right to undertake certain conduct.[148]

Two principles are reflected here. The first concerns reliance interests. As public reliance on a precedent increases, so does the need to leave it undisturbed. Otherwise, the public's ability to rely on and predict the law will be hindered. Also, precedents securing fundamental rights should not be set aside as freely as other constitutional precedents. A judge who does not regularly adhere to stare decisis is commonly referred to as *activist.* More broadly, **judicial activism** describes two phenomena: a pattern by a judge of disrupting precedent in favor of his own conceptions and beliefs, and a pattern of using judicial decisions to engage in social engineering or policymaking. In recent years, activism has been associated with political and legal liberalism. For example, the Warren Court is noted (and often criticized by conservatives) for its

judicial activism
(1) Use of judicial decisions to engage in social engineering. (2) A judicial philosophy that gives little deference to precedent, and therefore commonly results in the abrogation of prior decisions.

judicial activism in the social engineering and policymaking context. However, activism transcends ideology. The "conservative" Rehnquist Court proved to be as activist as the "liberal" Warren Court. A justice faces a dilemma when confronting precedent with which she disagrees. On the one hand, stare decisis serves laudable objectives. On the other hand, the individual justice has sworn to uphold and defend the Constitution. The two are at odds when a justice believes that precedent runs afoul of the Constitution. This difficulty is not new. In 1851, Justice Roger Taney said that if a "former decision was founded in error, and that the error, if not corrected, must produce serious public as well as private inconvenience and loss, it becomes our duty not to perpetuate it."[149] In another opinion, the Supreme Court stated, "[s]tare decisis is not an inexorable command; rather, it is a principle of policy and not a mechanical formula of adherence to the latest decision."[150] It is generally agreed that stare decisis plays a larger role in nonconstitutional cases than in constitutional ones. Associate Justice William O. Douglas commented:

> The place of stare decisis in constitutional law is even more tenuous. A judge looking at a constitutional decision may have compulsions to revere past history and accept what was once written. But he remembers above all else that it is the Constitution which he swore to support and defend, not the gloss which his predecessors may have put upon it. So he comes to formulate his own views, rejecting some earlier ones as false and embracing others.[151]

Associate Justices William Brennan Jr. and Thurgood Marshall were notorious for their approach to death penalty cases. Even though the Court held that capital punishment is not inherently cruel and unusual in *Gregg v. Georgia*[152] in 1976, and many times thereafter both men refused to adhere to this ruling and dissented in every denial of certiorari in death penalty appeals, on the theory that the punishment was in fact violative of the Eighth Amendment's cruel and unusual punishments prohibition. Justice Brennan, while acknowledging that judges have a general obligation to follow precedent, said of his practice in death penalty cases:

> I must add a word about a special kind of dissent: the repeated dissent in which a justice refuses to yield to the views of the majority although persistently rebuffed by them. . . . For me . . . the fatal constitutional infirmity of capital punishment is that it treats members of the human race as nonhumans, as objects to be toyed with and discarded . . . This is an interpretation to which a majority of my fellow justices—not to mention, it would seem, a majority of my fellow countrymen—do not subscribe. Perhaps you find my adherence to it, and my recurrent publication of it, simply contrary, tiresome, or quixotic. Or perhaps you see in it a refusal to abide by the judicial principle of stare decisis, obedience to precedent. . . . Yet, in my judgment, when a justice perceives an interpretation of the text to have departed so far from its essential meaning, that justice is bound, by a larger constitutional duty to the community, to expose the departure and point toward a different path. . . . [T]his type of dissent constitutes a statement by the judge as an individual; "Here I draw the line."[153]

Although it does so only with gravest caution, the Supreme Court has discarded precedent on many occasions. For example, from 1971 to 1991, the Supreme Court overruled thirty-three of its prior constitutional decisions.[154] In total, the Court has reversed itself on over two hundred occasions, and three-quarters of those were constitutional decisions.[155] Regardless, stare decisis continues to be the rule, so a party seeking to overturn precedent has the burden of convincing the Court that it should disregard its previous decisions.

A judge can avoid the issue of stare decisis by determining that a prior case is not precedent for the case at bar. This can occur in two ways. First, if it is determined that the case **sub judice** is different in fact from a previous case, then the previous case has no, or limited, precedential influence. This is known as **distinguishing on the facts.** Of course, the facts must differ to such a degree that it is illogical to apply the earlier case to the one sub judice.

Second, a judge can avoid a prior decision by framing the issues differently than the court did in the prior case. For example, suppose a State Supreme Court determined

sub judice
Before the court for consideration and determination.

distinguishing on the facts
Choosing not to apply a rule from a previous case because its facts differ from the case sub judice.

that the state's constitutional due process requirement does not confer greater rights on a criminal defendant than does the Due Process Clause of the Constitution of the United States in regard to a confession made to the police. In a later case, the State Supreme Court could avoid this decision by recharacterizing the issue as one of the right to be free from self-incrimination under the state constitution, rather than due process. In so doing, the court could reach a different result from the prior case even though the facts are identical, and it can do so without reversing itself.

Judicial decision making is also affected by the **canons of construction and interpretation.** The canons are a set of rules governing the interpretation of written law, such as statutes and constitutions. The canons have been developed by the courts through the common law.

canons of construction and interpretation
A set of judicially created rules that govern the interpretation of written law, such as statutes, regulations, and constitutions.

A number of canons have been recognized by the Supreme Court. For example, the strict necessity rule limits the exercise of judicial review to cases in which it is strictly necessary. Under this canon, constitutional issues are not to be adjudicated if a case can be adequately adjudicated on nonconstitutional grounds.

Another rule under which the Court operates is the presumption that statutes are constitutional. Accordingly, the burden of persuasion falls upon the party challenging a statute to prove that it is violative of the Constitution.

Similarly, another canon holds that if two or more reasonable constructions of a statute are possible, a court is to select a construction that is consistent with the Constitution, and thereby uphold the statute, if possible. Associate Justice Louis Brandeis stated, "[w]hen the validity of an act of the Congress is drawn in question, and even if a serious doubt of constitutionality is raised, it is a cardinal principle that this Court will first ascertain whether a construction of the statute is fairly possible by which the question may be avoided."[156] Of course, if every reasonable interpretation leads to the conclusion that the law is unconstitutional, it must be so declared.

Another interpretation rule provides that, if possible, an unconstitutional provision of a statute (or other law) is to be severed from the statute to allow the remainder to continue to be enforceable. For the **severability rule** to apply, the court must determine that removal of the unconstitutional portion does not disrupt the nature or thwart the objectives of the law.[157] Occasionally, Congress avoids this possibility by prohibiting severance. In such cases, the entire statute is valid or not.

severability rule
A rule of interpretation that allows a court to remove unconstitutional portions from a law and leave the remainder intact.

Certain practices also affect constitutional adjudication. The Supreme Court has long engaged in the **avoidance** of constitutional issues. That is, the Court will address constitutional issues only if necessary. In most cases, the Court will decide a case upon nonconstitutional grounds rather than delving unnecessarily into constitutional issues.

avoidance
The Supreme Court's practice of avoiding constitutional issues by deciding cases upon nonconstitutional grounds.

The Court also avoids constitutional issues in another way. If a case has reached the Supreme Court via appeal from a state high court, the Supreme Court may remand the case to the state for further consideration if it appears that the case can be disposed of through state law.[158] However, the certiorari process weeds most of these cases out before the appeal is heard by the Court.

To avoid policymaking, the Court usually limits its decisions to the facts of the specific cases or cases before it. By tailoring its opinions and orders to fit a specific case, it is less likely to create wide-sweeping constitutional mandates.

There are problems with relying on canons and practices, however. First, the canons may themselves be in conflict. For example, cases can be found to support the principle that if a provision has a plain meaning, that obvious meaning must be enforced regardless of outcome or policy. Other decisions require courts to set aside interpretations that lead to absurd results. Even further, at least one Supreme Court case permits an examination into legislative intent at any time, regardless of a statute's plain meaning. In *United States v. American Trucking Ass'n,* the Court said, "when aid to construction of the meaning of words, as used in the statute, is available, there certainly can be no 'rule of law' which forbids its use, however clear the words may appear on 'superficial examination.'"[159] Although *American Trucking* involved the interpretation of a statute, by analogy the reasoning could be extended to constitutional interpretation.

The second problem with rules of interpretation is that the Supreme Court is not consistent in their application. The rules have been developed by the courts and can be disregarded by them as well. Third, it is not always easy to determine whether a rule is truly a canon or simply a principle intended to apply in an individual case.

In the following chapters you will learn a number of other ways in which constitutional adjudication is avoided by the Supreme Court. For example, the Constitution limits the Court's jurisdiction to "cases or controversies." Therefore, abstract or hypothetical disputes may not be heard. An *abstract case* is one through which an individual challenges a law on constitutional grounds, even though he or she has not been harmed by it. Also prohibited to federal courts is hypothetical jurisdiction. *Hypothetical jurisdiction* refers to the issuance of advisory opinions, a practice not permitted because no genuine case exists. For example, the president may not request advice from the Supreme Court concerning possible prospective action, such as whether it would be constitutional to commit troops in some nation. A number of other limiting doctrines stem from the Article III case-or-controversy requirement. If an issue is political, the Court may refuse to hear it under the self-imposed political question doctrine. Further, the Court defers to the decision making of its coordinate branches in some circumstances. In such cases, the Court's decision-making role is diminished.

As is apparent, understanding constitutional adjudication is not an easy task. All the factors discussed here, and many to be discussed in the remainder of this text, affect constitutional adjudication. If you read the cases closely, paying attention to context, patterns, and trends, you will find that your understanding of constitutional law is greatly enhanced.

3.8(g) Political Values and Judicial Decisions

As discussed earlier, politics unquestionably plays a role in both the nomination and the confirmation process. But does it influence judicial decision making? This is not an easy question to answer. Lifetime tenure and the guarantee of no reduction in pay greatly reduce the direct influence political actors have over judges. Said another way, judges probably do not allow politics or transient waves of public opinion to influence their decisions in most instances. Several presidents have commented, in fact, that they have regretted their nominations to the Supreme Court. Recall President Eisenhower's comment that Earl Warren was the "biggest damn fool mistake" he made as president. There may be a few exceptions where politics has directly influenced the decisions of Supreme Court justices, such as the famous *switch in time that saved nine*. Regardless, judges are creatures of the period in which they live and of the prevailing culture. Although justices of the Supreme Court are not bound by lower-court decisions or by the Supreme Court's own precedents, undoubtedly these are also influencing factors.

Most significant, however, is the indirect, sometimes unconscious, impact of personal philosophy and values. Everyone has a worldview that shapes his or her understanding and interpretation of events, policy, and law. Indeed, researchers have found that there is a positive correlation between the decisions of the justices and each justice's individual political ideology.[160] Conservative justices, such as Thomas and Scalia, voted conservatively in most cases, and liberal justices, such as Marshall and Douglas, cast liberal votes in most cases.

3.9 MODERN CHALLENGES

There are three related challenges to the nation that are becoming increasingly pressing. The first is the rise of globalization. Global issues, such as hunger, civil rights, the environment, biological safety, and the threat by nonstate actors have created a

Cyber Constitution
Civic Responsibility and Education
There are many organizations committed to improving civic life and participatory democracy through education. See, for example, National Conference on Citizenship, www.ncoc.net/; National Collaborative for the Study of University Engagement, http://ncsue.msu.edu/; Clearninghouse and National Review Board for Scholarship of Engagement, http://schoe.coe.uga.edu/index.html; Campus Compact, www.compact.org/; American Association of State Colleges and Universities American Democracy Project, www.aascu.org/programs/adp/about.htm; Talliores Project, www.tufts.edu/talloiresnetwork/; Association of American Colleges and Universities, www.aacu.org/resources/civicengagement/index.cfm

demand for unprecedented international cooperation and collaboration. Because of an increasing global workplace, people are more likely to work with, or do business with, people from other nations. A second challenge is the increasing diversity in the United States. The nation is becoming more diverse in its ethnic, religious, and social makeup. Because of an increasing globalization of the world's markets, employees are more likely to work or do business with people from other nations.

Another challenge falls to the people. With the exception of the 2008 presidential election, voter participation in the United States is on the decline. Participation in government, beyond voting and at all levels, is even lower. For a democracy to be successful, an educated, participating population is necessary. This may be especially important to check potentially dangerous expansion in the power of any one branch or agency (e.g., federal executive authority). Yet most Americans report that they are too busy for, and lack an interest in, civic involvement, evidence that nation has failed in inculcating deliberative democracy values. In the years to come, educators (K–Ph.D.), education policy makers, community activists, leaders in government, and others must unite to prepare a new generation of citizens that will need to be prepared for a diverse, interconnected world. Our next generation of citizens will need to value participation in government, appreciate diverse people and ideas, understand how to contribute civilly, and contribute both locally and globally. And our courts will need to adapt to these changes. It may need to reconceptualize its existing understandings of how the U.S. form of democracy operates and how the nation interacts with other nations.

3.10 SUMMARY

Although the framers intended for most cases to remain in the state courts, they also determined that a national judiciary was necessary to protect the newly formed national government from the states and, to a lesser degree, to protect individuals from the excesses of governments. The latter function has increased in importance as a result of the expansion of federal jurisdiction, particularly in the area of civil rights. Today, federal courts play an important role in checking states and state officials and generally in preserving individual liberties.

The power of the federal courts is not, however, unbounded. Several formal institutional and informal limits exist to control the power of federal courts. In addition, even though federal jurisdiction has grown significantly in the past one hundred years, most judicial authority continues to reside in the states.

Article III mandates the existence of only one federal court: the Supreme Court. But Article III grants Congress the power to establish other courts. The first Congress did this, and the federal judiciary has grown continuously since that time. Today, the Supreme Court of eight associate justices and one chief justice sits at the judicial apex, with the courts of appeals directly below it. Below the appellate courts are the nation's district courts. They are the federal trial courts. All district, appellate, and Supreme Court judges and justices are empowered under Article III. This means that they must undergo the presidential confirmation and senatorial confirmation process. Once sworn, an Article III judge receives the benefit of lifetime tenure and no reduction in salary.

District courts have original jurisdiction over two classes of cases: diversity and federal question. Having only limited jurisdiction, these courts may not freely entertain state-law claims. A few exceptions exist, such as pendent claims. In some circumstances, district courts act in an appellate capacity, such as when they hear appeals from non–Article III courts. The courts of appeals hear appeals from district courts and some administrative agencies and possess general appellate powers. The Supreme Court, pursuant to Article III, possesses both original and appellate jurisdiction. The high court's original jurisdiction is limited to a narrow class of cases, such as those involving states. The Supreme Court most often acts as appellate court, hearing cases through appeal or certiorari. Appeals must be heard, whereas certiorari is discretionary. Only a few cases (i.e., where three-judge district courts are empanelled) come to the Court by appeal. Otherwise, the Supreme Court receives a majority of its cases through certiorari procedure, and it grants certiorari in only 2 to 5 percent of the cases filed.

Although the power of the federal judiciary is significant, especially in regard to constitutional interpretation, it is limited in many respects. Most cases continue to be litigated in state courts, and the federal courts themselves have created a number of limitations (e.g., abstention) on their power. Congress exercises considerable power over federal courts through its powers to create lower federal courts and to define judicial jurisdiction. Congress may not enlarge the judicial power beyond that provided for in Article III; thus, only genuine controversies may be heard. This prohibits federal courts from entertaining hypothetical disputes and issuing advisory opinions. So long as a genuine dispute exists, however, federal courts may render declaratory judgments, as well as issue injunctions and award damages. Today, federal practice is a specialty within law because federal jurisdiction and procedure are so complex.

Interpretation of the Constitution, legislation, and agency rules is a function all judges perform. There are as many methods of interpretation as there are judges. Regardless, most constructions can be classified as primarily originalist, modernist, literalist, or normative. The Constitution is silent as to whether the framers' intentions are to be followed, and there is no other concrete evidence in the matter. In reality, most judges treat the Constitution as a living document, while adhering to the plain-meaning rule or original intent when the outcome is clear and obvious.

The judiciary has become an important institution in American legal culture. The public expects courts to be available to redress their injuries and to protect them from governmental abuse.

REVIEW QUESTIONS

1. What is meant by the assertion that the Supreme Court is a countermajoritarian institution?
2. Briefly describe the roles the Supreme Court plays in the U.S. governmental system.
3. Chart the structure of the current federal court system, noting the names of the courts at each level. Which courts were established under the Constitution? Which by Congress?
4. Briefly distinguish between originalism, modernism, and historical and contemporary literalism as methods of interpreting the Constitution.
5. Define *stare decisis*. When does it apply and what does *distinguishing on the facts* mean?
6. What is the rule of severability?
7. Define *certiorari*.
8. State two informal and two formal constraints on federal judicial power.
9. What article of the Constitution establishes the Supreme Court and defines its jurisdiction?
10. What is the significance of *Marbury v. Madison* to U.S. constitutional law?
11. Name the two forms of federal judicial jurisdiction.
12. Define the political question doctrine.
13. Define the *Younger* doctrine and state its elements in criminal cases.
14. Define standing and explain its three primary elements.
15. Define sovereign immunity and explain the importance of the Eleventh Amendment to this concept.

16. Identify the three categories of cases in which a federal court may abstain from exercising jurisdiction.

17. State courts are courts of general jurisdiction and federal courts possess limited jurisdiction. Explain these principles.

ASSIGNMENTS: CONSTITUTIONAL LAW IN ACTION

The Constitution in Your Community

Assume that your law firm has been retained by Ima T. Partier, a local activist who is upset with the decisions and behavior of some state and local officials. Specifically, Mr. Partier believes that your state's governor and your city's mayor (or other chief executive) should be removed from office due to malfeasance and other shortcomings in office. Mr. Partier has retained your firm to research the legal process for taking removal action against these officials. Prepare a short memorandum (1–3 pages) describing the process, as defined by your state's constitution and applicable statutes and local ordinances.

Going Federal

Assume you are working for a local attorney. You have a client who is scheduled to appear before a federal judge, and she would like to know as much about the judge as possible. Identify one of the U.S. District Court judges in the federal district where you live or work. Determine what president nominated the judge and who in your state recommended his appointment to the president. Has the judge issued any controversial decisions? Can you easily label those decisions as liberal, moderate, or conservative? Is this in alignment with the nominating president's political leanings?

Moot Court

As you learned in this chapter, state courts are the final arbiters of state law. But federal courts often hear cases that have both federal and state issues. In some cases, the federal court hearing such a case will send the state question back to the Supreme Court of the state for decision. This happened in 2011 when the U.S. Court of Appeals for the Ninth Circuit was hearing a challenge to California's same-sex marriage prohibition, known as Proposition 8. After losing on appeal, the state refused to continue to defend Proposition 8 on appeal. However, a private group that opposes same-sex marriages wanted to continue to defend the proposition when the state itself has chosen to not defend the law. The Ninth Circuit was not sure if California allowed nonstate defendants to defend state laws, and it asked the California Supreme Court to answer the question. Break into groups of two and argue the question.

NOTES

1. Addresses and Papers of Charles Evans Hughes (New York 1908).
2. Jerome Frank, "Words and Music," 47 *Colum. L. Rev.* 1259, 1269 (1947).
3. The Federalist No. 78.
4. Strauss and Sunstein, "The Senate, the Constitution and the Confirmation Process," 101 *Yale L.J.* 1491 (1992).
5. Epstein and Segal, infra., ch. 5.
6. Lee Epstein and Jeffrey A. Segal, *Advice and Consent: The Politics of Judicial Appointments* 2–4, 27 (Oxford University Press 2005).
7. Outline of U.S. Legal System, http://usinfo.state.gov/products/pubs/legalotln/judges.htm (2006).

8. See William Mishler and Reginald S. Sheehan, "The Supreme Court as a Countermajoritarian Institution? The Impact of Public Opinion on Supreme Court Decisions," 87 *Am. Pol. Sci. Rev.* 87, 96–97 (March 1993).

9. *Id.* at 97–98.

10. The Federalist No. 78.

11. Robert Katzman, ed., *Judges and Legislators* 32 (Brookings 1988).

12. *Gomez v. United States,* 490 U.S. 858 (1989).

13. *Granfinanciera S.A. v. Nordberg*, 492 U.S. 33 (1989).

14. *New York Times,* April 7, 1994, at A13.

15. See Peter Schuck, "Public Law Litigation and Social Reform [book review]," 102 *Yale L.J.* 1763, 1786 (1993).

16. Emily Field van Tassel, "Resignations and Removals: A History of Federal Judicial Service—and Disservice—1789–1992," 142 *U. Pa. L. Rev.* 333, 335 (1993).

17. Richard M. Frank, "The Scorpions' Dance: Judicially Mandated Attorney's Fees—the Legislative Response and Separation-of-Powers Implications," 1 *Emerging Issues St. Const. Law* 73 (1988), citing H. Hockett, *Political and Social Growth of the United States* 502 (1937).

18. Mishler and Sheehan, supra n. 5, at 89.

19. See Daniel E. Hall, *Administrative Law: Bureaucracy in a Democracy*, 3rd ed., ch. 5 (Pearson Prentice Hall 2006).

20. 323 U.S. 214 (1944).

21. Epstein and Segal, p. 29, and author Hall's interview with a retired district judge.

22. 28 U.S.C. § 1332.

23. 28 U.S.C. § 1331.

24. The Federalist No. 78.

25. This case and many before it came before the Court through private correspondence. Prior to this instance, individual members of the Court had informally, through letters, rendered advice to the president and other government officials.

26. 219 U.S. 346 (1911).

27. Camreta v. Greene, 563 U.S. __ (2011).

28. *Aetna Life Insurance Co. v. Haworth,* 300 U.S. 227 (1937).

29. *Strawbridge v. Curtiss,* 3 Cranch 267 (1806).

30. The amount-in-controversy requirement has increased through the years. It was increased from $50,000 to $75,000 in 2007 following a recommendation from a federal courts study committee that it be increased to $100,000.

31. 28 U.S.C. § 1442.

32. 28 U.S.C. § 1446.

33. 28 U.S.C. § 1447.

34. *Fields v. Smith* (7th Cir. August 5, *2011*).

35. *Ames v. Kansas,* 111 U.S. 449 (1884).

36. *Illinois v. Milwaukee,* 406 U.S. 91 (1972).

37. *Id.* at 93.

38. *California v. Arizona,* 440 U.S. 59, 64 (1979).

39. See Supreme Court Rule 10.

40. 42 U.S.C. § 1973bb. Other voting rights cases for which direct appeal to the Supreme Court is provided can be found at 42 U.S.C. §§ 1971, 1973b, 1973aa-2, and 1973c.

41. 42 U.S.C. § 2000e-6.

42. 42 U.S.C. § 2000a-5.

43. 42 U.S.C. § 1973h.

44. 2 U.S.C. § 922.

45. 15 U.S.C. § 29.

46. 28 U.S.C. § 2109.

47. *National Mutual Insurance Co. v. Tidewater Transfer Co.,* 337 U.S. 582, 655 (1949).

48. *Glidden Co. v. Zdanok,* 370 U.S. 530 (1962).

49. Henry Hart, "The Power of Congress to Limit the Jurisdiction of Federal Courts: An Exercise in Dialectic," 66 *Harv. L. Rev.* 1362, 1365 (1953).

50. *United States v. Bitty,* 208 U.S. 393, 399–400 (1908).

51. 75 U.S. (8 Wall.) 85 (1869).

52. 74 U.S. (7 Wall.) 506, 515 (1871).

53. For a more thorough discussion of congressional authority over the Supreme Court's jurisdiction, *see* Henry Hart, "The Power of Congress to Limit the Jurisdiction of Federal Courts: An Exercise in Dialectic," 66 *Harv. L. Rev.* 1362 (1953); William Dodge, "Congressional Control

of Supreme Court Appellate Jurisdiction: Why the Original Jurisdiction Clause Suggests an Essential Role," 100 *Yale L.J.* 1013 (1991); Ratner, "Majoritarian Constraints on Judicial Review: Congressional Control of Supreme Court Jurisdiction," 27 *Vill. L. Rev.* 929 (1982).

54. *Sheldon v. Sill,* 8 U.S. (How.) 441, 448 (1850).

55. *Home Life Insurance Co. v. Dunn,* 86 U.S. 214, 226 (1873). See also *The Francis Wright,* 105 U.S. 381 (1881).

56. *State Farm Fire & Casualty Co. v. Tashire,* 386 U.S. 523 (1967).

57. 28 U.S.C. § 2283.

58. 28 U.S.C. § 636.

59. 490 U.S. 858 (1989).

60. 501 U.S. 923 (1991).

61. 492 U.S. 33 (1989).

62. *See* William Kelleher, III, "The Continuing Saga of Jury Trials in Bankruptcy Court—Is There an Answer? An Argument for Jury Trials in Bankruptcy Court," 2 *Am. Bankr. Inst. L. Rev.* 477 (1994); Conrad Cyr, "The Right to Trial by Jury in Bankruptcy: Which Judge Is to Preside?" 63 *Am. Bankr. L.J.* 53 (1989).

63. *See* 28 U.S.C. § 1491 *et seq.*

64. *United States v. Tiede,* 86 F.R.D. 227 (Berlin Ct. 1979).

65. *See* Farber, Eskridge, and Frickey, *Constitutional Law* 1005–06 (West Publishing 1993), which cites Herbert Stern, *Judgment in Berlin* (1984), for a full discussion of this case. Herbert Stern was the judge in the case.

66. Resnik, "Regarding 'The Federal Court': Revising the Domain of Federal Court Jurisprudence at the End of the Twentieth Century," 47 *Vand. L.R.* 1021, 1026 (1994).

67. 330 U.S. 75 (1947).

68. *Id.* at 90–91.

69. 367 U.S. 497 (1961).

70. 416 U.S. 312 (1974).

71. *See Sosna v. Iowa,* 419 U.S. 393 (1975), for a discussion of how class action procedure can be used to save an otherwise moot case.

72. 410 U.S. 113 (1973).

73. *Id.* at 124.

74. 319 U.S. 302 (1943).

75. *Baker v. Carr,* 369 U.S. 186 (1962).

76. 369 U.S. 186 (1962).

77. *Singleton v. Wulff,* 428 U.S. 106 (1976).

78. *Virginia v. American Booksellers Ass'n.,* 484 U.S. 383 (1988).

79. For a more thorough discussion of environmental law, *see* Harold Hickok, *Introduction to Environmental Law* (Delmar/Lawyers Cooperative 1996).

80. 524 U.S. 555 (1992).

81. 438 U.S. 59 (1978).

82. 397 U.S. 150 (1970).

83. 392 U.S. 83 (1968).

84. 454 U.S. 464 (1982).

85. 428 U.S. 106 (1976).

86. *Hunt v. Washington State Apple Advertising Commission,* 432 U.S. 333 (1977).

87. *North Dakota v. Minnesota,* 263 U.S. 365 (1923).

88. *Boehner v. Anderson,* 30 F.3d 156 (D.C. Cir. 1994).

89. 617 F.2d 697 (D.C. Cir. 1979).

90. 511 F.2d 430 (D.C. Cir. 1974).

91. *Dornan v. Secretary of Defense,* 851 F.2d 450 (D.C. Cir. 1988).

92. *Daughtery v. Carter,* 584 F.2d 1050 (D.C. Cir. 1974).

93. 19 U.S. 264 (1821).

94. 5 U.S. at 170.

95. *48 U.S. 1 (1849).*

96. 328 U.S. 459 (1946).

97. *Baker v. Carr, 369* U.S. 186 (1962). See also *Davis v. Bandemer,* 478 U.S. 109 (1986).

98. 307 U.S. 433 (1939).

99. 395 U.S. 486 (1969).

100. *McIntyre v. Fallahay,* 766 F.2d 1078 (7th Cir. 1985), citing *Roudenbush v. Hartke,* 405 U.S. 15 (1972).

101. *Chicago & Southern Air Lines v. Waterman Steamship Corp.,* 333 U.S. 103 (1948).

102. *Doe v. Braden,* 57 U.S. (16 How.) 635 (1853).

103. *The Divina Pastora: The Spanish Consul,* 17 U.S. 52 (1819).

104. 504 U.S. 655 (1992).

105. 418 U.S. 683 (1974).

106. 19 U.S. (6 Wheat.) 264, 404 (1821).

107. See *Railroad Commission v. Pullman Co.,* 312 U.S. 496 (1941), and *Colorado River Water Conservation District v. United States,* 424 U.S. 800 (1976), for discussions of abstention.

108. See *Barber v. Barber,* 62 U.S. (21 How.) 582 (1859); *Popovici v. Agler,* 280 U.S. 379 (1930).

109. *Younger v. Harris,* 401 U.S. 37 (1971).

110. *Pennzoil v. Texaco,* 481 U.S. 1, 10 (1987).

111. *Aiona v. Hawaii,* 17 F.3d 1244 (9th Cir. 1993).

112. *Molitor v. Kaneland Community Unit District No. 302,* 18 Ill. 2d 11, 163 N.E.2d 89, 94 (1959).

113. 2 U.S. (2 Dall.) 419 (1793).

114. 134 U.S. 1 (1890).

115. *Employees of Department of Public Health & Welfare v. Missouri Department of Public Welfare,* 411 U.S. 279 (1973).

116. *Port Authority Trans-Hudson Corp. v. Feeny,* 495 U.S. 299 (1990).

117. 115 S. Ct. 394 (1994).

118. Ex Parte Young, 209 U.S. 123 (1908).

119. *Hutto v. Finney,* 437 U.S. 678 (1978).

120. 563 U.S. __ (2011).

121. *Pennsylvania v. Union Gas,* 491 U.S. 1 (1989).

122. 28 U.S.C. §§ 1291, 1346, 1402, 1504, 2110, 2401–2402, 2411–2412, 2671–2678, 2680.

123. See Daniel Hall, *Administrative Law: Bureaucracy in Democracy,* 3rd ed., ch. 10 (Pearson Prentice Hall Publishing 2005) for a more thorough discussion of the Federal Tort Claims Act and other statutes through which the United States has waived immunity from liability.

124. *Gomez v. United States,* 490 U.S. 858, 863 (1991).

125. *Testa v. Katt,* 330 U.S. 389 (1947).

126. *The Moses Taylor,* 4 Wall 411 (1867).

127. 490 U.S. 605 (1989).

128. For a discussion of this topic and a proposal to apply Article III to state courts hearing federal claims, see William Fletcher, "The 'Case or Controversy' Requirement in State Court Adjudication of Federal Questions," 78 *Cal. L. Rev.* 263 (1990).

129. See H. Jefferson Powell, "The Original Understanding of Original Intent," 98 *Harv. L. Rev.* 885 (1985).

130. William J. Brennan Jr., "The Constitution of the United States: Contemporary Ratification," 27 *S. Tex. L. Rev.* 433 (1986).

131. Benjamin Cardozo, *The Nature of the Judicial Process* 17 (1921).

132. *Dennis v. United States,* 341 U.S. 494 (1951). For further discussion of the Eighth Amendment's cruel and unusual punishments clause, see Daniel Hall, "When Caning Meets the Eighth Amendment: Whipping Offenders in the United States," 4 *Widener J. Pub. L.* 903 (1995).

133. 347 U.S. 483 (1954).

134. *Ford v. Wainwright,* 477 U.S. 399, 406 (1986) (further citations omitted); *Trop v. Dulles,* 356 U.S. 86, 101 (1958).

135. See John H. Ely, *Democracy and Distrust: A Theory of Judicial Review* (Harvard University Press 1980).

136. *McGrain v. Daugherty,* 273 U.S. 135, 156 (1927).

137. See Johnson and Canon, *Judicial Policies: Implementation and Impact* (Congressional Quarterly Press 1984) for further discussion of this topic.

138. 359 U.S. 520 (1959).

139. *Rummel v. Estelle,* 445 U.S. 263, 375 (1980).

140. Cardozo, *The Nature of the Judicial Process 149* (1921).

141. *Patterson v. McLean Credit Union,* 491 U.S. 164, 172 (1989); Alexander Hamilton, The Federalist No. 78.

142. *Holder v. Hall,* 114 S. Ct. 2581, 2618 (1994) (concurring opinion).

143. 347 U.S. 483 (1954).

144. 163 U.S. 537 (1896).

145. 501 U.S. 808 (1991).

146. 482 U.S. 496 (1987).

147. *Illinois Brick Co. v. Illinois,* 431 U.S. 720, 736 (1977).

148. *Webster v. Reproductive Health Services, Inc.,* 492 U.S. 490, 558 (1989). (concurring/dissenting opinion), citing *Arizona v. Rumsey,* 467 U.S. 203, 212 (1984).

149. *Genesee Chief v. Fitzhugh*, 12 How. 443 (1852).

150. *Helvering v. Hallock,* 309 U.S. 106, 119 (1940), cited in *Payne v. Tennessee,* 111 S. Ct. 2597, 2609 (1991).

151. William O. Douglas, "*Stare Decisis*," 49 *Colum. L. Rev.* 735, 736 (1949).

152. 428 U.S. 153 (1976).

153. William J. Brennan Jr., "In Defense of Dissents," 37 *Hastings L.J.* 427, 437–38 (1986).

154. *Payne v. Tennessee,* 111 S. Ct. 2597, 2610 (1991).

155. See Paul Linton, "*Planned Parenthood v. Casey:* The Flight from Reason in the Supreme Court," 13 *St. Louis U. Pub. L. Rev.* 15 n. 273 (1993), citing an unpublished work by A. Blaustein and C. Willner entitled *Stare Decisis.*

156. *Ashwander v. TVA,* 297 U.S. 288, 346 (1936).

157. See *Alaska Airlines v. Brock*, 480 U.S. 678 (1987); *Immigration & Naturalization Service v. Chadha*, 462 U.S. 919 (1983).

158. *Government & Civic Employees Organizing Committee v. Windsor,* 353 U.S. 364 (1957).

159. *United States v. American Trucking Ass'n*, 310 U.S. 534 (1940). See also *Cass v. United States*, 417 U.S. 72 (1974).

160. Epstein and Segal, infra., ch. 5.

4

Congress

Laws are like sausage. It's better not to see them being made.

OTTO VON BISMARCK[1]

LEARNING OBJECTIVES
At the end of this chapter you should be able to:

- Outline the structure of Congress, including terms of office, how representation in Congress is determined, and how members are disciplined. Detail the required qualifications to be a member of the House of Representatives or Senate.

- List and explain the authorities of Congress that are enumerated in the Constitution.

- Explain the evolution of federal authority from 1789 to present day, and identify and discuss in detail the enumerated authorities upon which Congress has relied in expanding its authority. You should also be able to identify and explain the Supreme Court cases that have been important in this evolution.

- Identify and explain three canons of construction. Define and explain stare decisis and its application by the Supreme Court and lower courts.

- Identify a contemporary issue concerning legislative authority, and discuss the most likely future scenarios, referencing both historical analogs and case law.

- Brief a judicial opinion with little outside assistance. You should be successful in identifying the relevant facts. You should be successful in identifying the legal issue and analyzing the court's rationale in at least 33 percent of your briefs.

- Apply what you have learned to a new set of facts that are given to you with little assistance.

4.1 LEGISLATURES GENERALLY

Courts are responsible for resolving disputes. As part of that function, they interpret and apply law. Where does the law come from? Of course, the Constitution is a source of law. In a common law system, some law is created by the courts. But today, the primary source of lawmaking is legislative bodies.[2] In the United States, these bodies are groups of elected representatives.

Whereas courts are largely reactive (become involved only after a dispute has arisen), legislatures are largely proactive. When a court hears a case, it is concerned with individual facts; legislatures consider large systemic issues. Individual cases are used only as anecdotal evidence. Legislation is concerned with policy issues and large groups of people, whereas courts are usually concerned with dispensing justice among a small number of people. Courts look to the past in resolving disputes; legislatures are concerned with the future.

Legislatures are responsible for making law. In making the law, legislators must consider competing policies and interests. Legislatures are free to enact any law, so long as that law is consonant with the Constitution. Legislatures are free to alter, amend, and abolish the common law of their jurisdictions if they wish, except for the common law that is now embodied in the Constitution.

In a republic such as the United States, any person may petition his representative to propose a law, but only members of legislatures are authorized to propose new laws to the legislature. In some jurisdictions, citizen-initiated amendments to state and local fundamental law are possible. These are outside the scope of this text. A proposed law is referred to as a **bill.** Procedures vary among legislatures, but generally new bills are sent to committees. These committees review the bill, hold hearings and **mark-up** sessions, and eventually vote on whether the bill should proceed further. If so, the bill may be sent to another committee, to a subcommittee, or to the entire body for vote. In **bicameral** legislatures, additional (conference) committee work may be necessary to resolve any problems that the bill has between the two houses. If the bill receives congressional approval and is signed by the president (or a presidential veto is overridden by Congress), it becomes a public law or **statute,** which is the written law of the body. Statutes are then compiled and arranged according to subject matter in the process of **codification.** These combined statutes are known as **codes,** such as the Code of Civil Procedure or the Administrative Code.

Congress also adopts resolutions. These are formal statements by Congress but are not intended to be statutes. For example, Congress may by resolution express its opinion to the president concerning a matter that is exclusively executive. Resolutions may be issued by a single house, known as a simply resolutions, or both houses, in which case they are referred to as *concurrent.* A **joint resolution** is one passed by both houses and approved by the president. Such a resolution has the force of a statute. The point of reference for the names is to what bodies pass the resolution, not what body initiates. All resolutions and bills must be initiated in one house and then move to the other. So, "joint" in joint resolution refers to the need for both the House and Senate to review and pass the measure not to the resolution being introduced jointly.

bill
A proposed law, presented to the legislature for enactment, that is, a legislative bill.

mark-up
The detailed revision of a bill by a legislative committee.

bicameral
Two-chambered, referring to the customary division of a legislature into two houses (a Senate and a House of Representatives).

statute
A law enacted by a legislature; an act.

codification
(1) The process of arranging laws in a systematic form covering the entire law of a jurisdiction or a particular area of the law; the process of creating a code. (2) The process of turning a common law rule into a statute.

code
(1) The published statutes of a jurisdiction, arranged in systematic form. (2) A portion of the statutes of a jurisdiction, especially the statutes relating to a particular subject.

joint resolution
A resolution passed by both houses of a bicameral legislature and eligible to become a law if signed by the chief executive or passed over the chief executive's veto.

POSITIVE LAW AND WHEN A CODE IS NOT A LAW `SIDEBAR`

When a bill is enacted, it becomes a *public law* or *session law*—a statute. The statutes are published by year of enactment, but these compilations can be confusing to the researcher. That is because the text of a public law does not necessarily refer to existing related law. For convenience, public laws are arranged into codes. A *code* is a group of laws organized by subject matter, such as a code of criminal procedure. As laws are enacted, they are made a part of the existing code. Generally, only permanent substantive laws are included in the code. Appropriations bill is an example of public laws that are not included in a code. Hence, the organization of codes reflects the current state of the law, not a chronological ordering of enactments.

The first codification of federal statutes occurred in 1874. This was revised in 1878. Between 1878 and 1924, the federal codes fell into disarray. Congress, as well as the public, suffered from legislative confusion. For example, Congress amended laws that had previously been repealed. To remedy the problem, Congress arranged for a new codification of federal statutes in 1924. The new code was completed one year later.

Decisions concerning the state of the law had to be made during the codification process. For example, editorial decisions concerning whether statutes had been "amended" or "repealed" by subsequent statutes were made, technical errors were corrected, and obsolete provisions were removed. The result was a written product that could vary from what Congress enacted. Consequently, unless a code section is formally enacted into *positive law* by Congress, it is not law. Congress has enacted many of the code sections found in the U.S. Code (U.S.C.), but not all. Generally, the unenacted sections of the U.S. Code are unquestioned. But when they are challenged as inaccurate, a court must resort to the Statutes at Large (Stat.) to determine the state of the law.

For more information see http://uscode.house.gov/codification/legislation.shtml. For more information on codification, see http://uscode.house.gov/codification/Positive%20 Law%20Codification.pdf

There is little legal difference between bills and resolution and indeed, the terms are sometimes used interchangeably. In practice, the distinction is often drawn between laws of general applicability, which are intended to be added to the United States Code, and more specialized laws that appropriate smaller amounts of funds, to propose a constitutional amendment, or regulate Congress itself with the former starting as bills and the latter as resolutions. Like bills, most resolutions require approval of both houses and presentment to the president. However, resolutions to regulate one house of Congress need only be passed by the applicable house, resolutions to regulate both houses need both House and Senate approval, and proposals to amendment the Constitution are not presented to the president. Instead, proposed amendments are sent to the states following approval by both houses of Congress.

4.2 THE STRUCTURE AND ORGANIZATION OF CONGRESS

Article I, Section 1, of the Constitution reads:

> All legislative Powers herein granted shall be vested in a Congress of the United States, which shall consist of a Senate and House of Representatives.

This provision makes clear that the authority make federal law is delegated entirely to Congress, subject to the checks and balances found elsewhere in the Constitution. The U.S. Congress is bicameral, having both a Senate and a House of Representatives. The second and third sections of Article I describe the requirements for being a senator or representative, as well as the processes of selection. We will return to this topic shortly.

According to Section 4, clause 2, Congress is to assemble at least once yearly beginning on the first Monday in December, unless it selects another day. A public journal of the proceedings is to be maintained, except when the body votes for secrecy. The *Congressional Record* is the official record of Congress and can be found in most public libraries. Records of how members vote are to be kept, so long as one-fifth of the members present at a session desire it.[3] Each house is permitted to make its own rules to govern its proceedings.[4] A house may order that its members be present and can punish absences.[5] The House elects its leaders, including the highest officer of the body, the Speaker of the House. Similarly, the Senate is empowered to elect its leaders, including the President Pro Tempore (commonly known as the Pro Tem).[6] However, the presiding officer of the Senate is the vice-president, who is selected by the Electoral College following the national election. The President Pro Tempore presides in the absence of the vice-president.

Bills may be introduced by any member. If a bill is approved by both houses, it is presented to the president. The president may sign the bill, making it law, or may veto the bill. Vetoes may be overcome by two-thirds votes in both houses. If the president does not return a bill within ten days, it becomes law, unless Congress is adjourned. If adjourned, the bill dies. This is known as a **pocket veto.**

With one exception, a bill may originate in either house. Article I, Section 7, clause 1, establishes the exception, as it reads, "[a]ll Bills for raising Revenues shall originate in the House of Representatives." A law that does not have revenue raising as its primary purpose, but raises revenues incidentally, may originate in either house. As an example, a statute that requires federal criminal offenders to pay a special assessment into a crime victims fund is not revenue raising for the purposes of the **origination clause.** The Court has also held that origination claims are justiciable.[7]

Note that neither house of Congress may adjourn longer than three days without the consent of the other house. Also, both houses are required to conduct their work in the same location.[8]

4.3 MEMBERSHIP IN CONGRESS

The Constitution has provisions concerning the qualifications a person must possess to be a member of Congress, removal of congresspersons, and related matters.

Cyber Constitution
You can learn more about the House of Representatives at www.house.gov and the Senate at www.senate.gov. including biographies of senators and representatives, pending legislation, committees, leadership, and history.

pocket veto
The veto of a congressional bill by the president by retaining it until Congress is no longer in session, neither signing nor vetoing it. The effect of such inaction is to nullify the legislation without affirmatively vetoing it. The pocket veto is also available to governors under some state constitutions.

origination clause
Article I, Section 7, clause 1, of the U.S. Constitution, which requires all revenue-raising bills to originate in the House of Representatives.

4.3 (a) Qualifications

To be a member of the House of Representatives, a person must be at least twenty-five years old, a citizen of the United States for at least seven years, and an inhabitant of the state where he will run for election. Members of the House, commonly referred to as representatives, congressmen and congresswomen, congresspersons, or members, serve two-year terms. The number of representatives that serve from each state varies according to population. Representatives serve districts and, accordingly, are elected by the voters of each district, not by the voters of the state generally. Each congressperson possesses one vote in the House. There are also a few nonvoting members of the House. For example, the representatives from the District of Columbia, Puerto Rico, and American Samoa may not vote.

To be a senator, a person must be at least thirty years old, a citizen of the United States for at least nine years, and an inhabitant of the state where she will be a candidate for election. Senators serve six-year terms. The terms of the senators are staggered so that the terms of one-third of all senators expire every other year. Every state, regardless of population, has two senators, each with one vote.

YOUR CONSTITUTIONAL VALUES

MAY A PUBLIC UNIVERSITY STUDENT GOVERNMENT OPEN A MEETING WITH A PRAYER?

Congress shall make no law respecting an establishment of religion, or prohibiting the free exercise thereof; or abridging the freedom of speech, or of the press; or the right of the people peaceably to assemble, and to petition the government for a redress of grievances.—U.S. Constitution, Amendment I

In the second part of this book, you will learn more about the Constitution's protection of civil liberties. This discussion will include the First Amendment, which contains several important protections. These include, inter alia, freedom of speech, of religion, and from government establishment of religion. The latter two are commonly known as the Free Exercise and Establishment Clauses. The two religion clauses have been the subject of considerable litigation and Supreme Court case law. This is because there is a highly contentious zone where the two meet and are at odds with each other: when individuals seek to practice their religion in public areas. May the federal government refer to God on our currency? May Congress, a state legislature, or a local legislative body open its meeting with a prayer? May a government employee hang a religious object on the wall in his or her office? May a local government have a Christmas tree or menorah on government property in a community square? Is a government-paid Santa Claus constitutional? May the federal government extend tax relief to religious organizations? May federal property that is rented to citizens be rented to a religious organization to hold a mass or revival? The questions seem to be endless. Several have arisen in the context of public schools and colleges. For example, may a university student government open its meetings with a prayer?

The Supreme Court decided in *Lee v. Weisman*, 505 U.S. 577 (1992), that public-school-sponsored prayers are violative of the Establishment Clause. Later, in *Santa Fe School District v. Doe*, 530 U.S. 290 (2000), the Court held that a system that permitted students, by vote, to determine whether invocations and benedictions would be delivered at commencement and athletic events violated the Establishment Clause as well. However, the Court noted that it was possible for student prayers that were less endorsed or regulated by school policies to be considered private speech and the private exercise of religion.

There has been less Supreme Court case law arising out of the public college and universities context than out of the primary and secondary school context. The assumption of many scholars is that age matters. That is, the balance between the Establishment Clause and the Free Exercise Clause shifts with maturity, with greater protection from an establishment of religion in the younger years. The assumption underlying this rationale is that adults are less impressionable and less likely to feel coerced. For example, even though sponsored invocations at voluntary athletic events are not permitted at public high schools, two U.S. courts of appeals, in *Chaudhuri v. Tennessee,* 130 F.3d 232, 237 (6th Cir. 1997), and *Tanford v. Brand,* 104. F.3d 982 (7th Cir. 1997), have permitted them at public university athletic events. The age, maturity, and education level of college students were significant factors in both cases. However, another U.S. court of appeals invalidated a prayer at a public university in *Mellen v. Bunting.* But the facts of this case, which involved mandatory prayer before meals at the Virginia Military Institute, are more extreme and easily distinguishable from *Chaudhuri* and *Tanford.* So what about a decision of a public university student government to open its meetings with a prayer? The answer is unclear. As the "official" student government, the decision to employ an invocation is more questionable than if made by a voluntary student organization that has been formally recognized by a university. Weighing the other direction is *Chaudhuri* and *Tanford's* focus on the maturity of those involved and the voluntary nature of attendance and participation; do you believe the practice is consonant with the First Amendment?

Initially, according to Article I, Section 3, senators were selected by the state legislatures. This reflected the attitude of the framers concerning the role of the Senate. Unlike the House, which was intended to be a true body of the people, the Senate was a body representing the interests of the states. Many of the framers were troubled by the proportional representation in the House. They feared that the smaller states would be taken advantage of by the larger states. Therefore, the Senate, with its equal representation, was devised. However, populism led to the direct election of senators by the people, now enshrined in the Seventeenth Amendment.

No person may simultaneously serve in Congress and in a "civil Office under the Authority of the United States."[9] This requirement avoids obvious conflicts of interest. It is common practice to allow government officials to keep their positions until the time of election, or in some cases, until they are sworn in as a senator or representative.

The Constitution does not limit the number of terms a person may serve in either house. Concerns that the Congress is filled with professional politicians who have lost touch with the people and have incurred detrimental obligations to special interests prompted some states to enact term limits legislation in the early 1990s. The Republican-controlled Congress of 1994 also promised term limits as part of its "Contract with America." In 1995, however, the Supreme Court invalidated an Arkansas constitutional amendment limiting House members to three terms and senators to two terms. In *United States Term Limits, Inc. v. Thornton,*[10] the Court held that the Constitution establishes qualifications and that it would take a constitutional amendment to change them. In support of its decision, the Court found the following:

1. State-imposed qualification restrictions are contrary to the fundamental principle of our representative democracy, and the people should be empowered to choose whom they please to govern.
2. State-imposed qualifications are inconsistent with the framers' vision of a uniform national legislature.
3. Historical evidence leads to the conclusion that the qualifications appearing in the Constitution are exclusive and neither Congress nor the states may add to them.

The decision whether a person possesses the qualifications to be a member of Congress is left to the applicable house. Article I, Section 5, clause 1, provides that "[e]ach House shall be the Judge of the Elections, Returns, and Qualifications of its own Members." This has been interpreted to mean that each house has the authority to decide whether a member meets the age, citizenship, and domicile requirements. Also, the decision as to who prevailed in an election belongs to the house in which the candidate would be seated. In other words, if there is a dispute as to what votes should be counted, the final decision rests with Congress, not the state where the election was held or any court.[11]

If the Senate or House were to exclude a member for one of these reasons, its decision would be unreviewable by a court pursuant to the political question doctrine. However, a decision to exclude persons for other reasons is reviewable, as the clause limits the exclusion power to qualifications. This was the issue in *Powell v. McCormack*:[12] Adam Clayton Powell Jr. had been elected to the House of Representatives, but, due to allegations of misuse of public funds and unbecoming conduct, the House refused to seat him. The Supreme Court held that the issue was justiciable and ordered that he be seated.

Each chamber has its own leadership. The Constitution expressly provides that the vice-president shall act as the president of the Senate. The vice-president does not get a vote except in the case of a tie. This authority has been weakened in recent years by an increasing number of issues for which the Senate requires, through its own procedures, a two-thirds vote. The Senate otherwise selects its leaders, such as its

Speaker Boehner takes oath in 2011. Later he and other members would read the constitution on the floor, a new practice

Ron Sachs-CNP-PHOTOlink.net/Newscom

Charles Rangel during a news conference calling for an ethics investigation of his own conduct

Scott J. Ferrell/Congressional Quarterly/Newscom

President Pro Tempore who acts as chair in the absence of the vice-president and the chairs of its various committees. The House of Representatives is led by the Speaker of the House, who is elected by the members. Although the Constitution does not explicitly require it, all speakers have been members of the House. Compared to the vice-president's weak role in the Senate, the Speaker wields considerable authority over appointments and process in the House and is second in line behind the vice-president for the presidency. All other leaders are selected by the House pursuant to its rules.

4.3(b) Discipline and Punishment

Another provision of the Constitution was also at issue in the *Powell* case. The second clause of Article I, Section 5, provides that "[e]ach House may determine the Rules of its Proceedings, punish its Members for disorderly Behavior, and, with the Concurrence of two thirds, expel a member."

Expulsion   The Court concluded that Powell had not been expelled because he had never been seated. The Court also stated, in dictum, that a House's power to expel is much broader than its power to exclude. Still, the language of the clause leads to the conclusion that the power is not plenary. Could Powell have been expelled for behavior that occurred before his election? One reasonable construction of the expulsion clause is that it applies to postelection and not preelection conduct.

Censorship and Other Discipline   In addition to expulsion, the Constitution allows each house to punish its members in other ways, including reprimand and, the most serious, censorship. In 1881 the Supreme Court went so far as to state:

> punishment may in a proper case be imprisonment, and that it may be for refusal to obey some rule on that subject made by the House for the preservation of order. So, also, the penalty which each House is authorized to inflict in order to compel the attendance of absent members may be imprisonment, and this may be for a violation of some order or standing rule on that subject.[13]

Again, the decision concerning what conduct warrants punishment, including expulsion, is political. An act need not be criminal to be subject to punishment. In December 2010 the House censured its twenty-third member, Charles Rangel of New York, for failing to pay federal taxes, failing to report income, and soliciting corporate donations to Charles B. Rangel Center for Public Service at the City College of New York in violation of House rules.[14] The Senate has expelled fifteen members in its history, fourteen for supporting the Confederacy, and censured nine of its members.[15]

4.3(c) Immunity

Both senators and representatives are entitled to a limited immunity from civil arrest while serving. Article I, Section 6, clause 1, expresses that all members of Congress

> shall in all Cases, except Treason, Felony and Breach of the Peace, be privileged from Arrest during their Attendance at the Session of their respective Houses, and in going to and returning from the same; and for any Speech and Debate in either House, they shall not be questioned in any other Place.

The first half of this provision, the freedom from arrest clause, has been interpreted very narrowly. First, because the phrase "treason, felony, and breach of the peace" historically included all ordinary crimes, it has been held that the clause shields congresspersons from civil, but not criminal, arrest. Accordingly, a congressperson may be arrested, detained, or imprisoned, if convicted during a session of Congress, for any crime, felony, or misdemeanor. The immunity applies only to civil arrests, which were more common at the time the Constitution was ratified than they are today.

Second, members of Congress are immune from civil arrest, but not civil process. Members may be served with complaints and other process during a session. A congressperson may not, however, be arrested in order to secure his or her testimony at a civil trial. These immunities apply when a congressperson is in transit to and returning from a session of Congress.

The second half of this provision contains the speech and debate clause. No congressperson may be sued or otherwise made to answer for any statements made during congressional proceedings. Unlike the freedom from arrest clause, the speech and debate clause is interpreted broadly. It was the intent of the framers to encourage open and candid debates and discussions in Congress. Fear of civil liability, such as an action for defamation of character, could chill full and frank debate. This provision applies to both civil and criminal cases. Therefore, the government could not use the statements of a congressperson made on the floor of the house in his prosecution for defrauding the government and violating a conflicts of interest law.[16]

The clause has force in any congressional proceeding, whether it be a meeting of the entire house or a committee. Statements made to reporters or during news conferences are not privileged. Although committee reports are privileged, individual dissemination of the same information by members of Congress to the public is not.[17] Such dissemination of information is not considered an essential part of the legislative process.

In addition to statements made in congressional meetings, the clause has been interpreted to grant immunity to members for "things generally done in a session of the House by one of its members in relation to the business before it."[18] This extends the immunity beyond speech to include actions. Actions are protected so long as they are an integral part of the deliberative and communicative processes of committee and house proceedings.

Gravel v. United States
408 U.S. 606 (1972)

Opinion of the Court by Mr. Justice White.

These cases arise out of the investigation by a federal grand jury into possible criminal conduct with respect to the release and publication of a classified Defense Department study entitled History of the United States Decision-Making Process on Viet Nam Policy. This document, popularly known as the Pentagon Papers, bore a Defense security classification of Top Secret Sensitive. The crime being investigated included the retention of public property or records with intent to covert (18 U.S.C. §641), the gathering and transmitting of national defense information (18 U.S.C. § 793), the concealment or removal of public records or documents (18 U.S.C. § 2071), and conspiracy to commit such offenses and to defraud the United States (18 U.S.C. § 371).

Among the witnesses subpoenaed were Leonard S. Rodberg, an assistant to Senator Mike Gravel of Alaska and a resident fellow at the institute of Policy Studies, and Howard Webber, Director of M.I.T. Press. Senator Gravel, as intervenor of filed motion to quash the subpoenas and to require the Government to specify the particular question to be addressed to Rodberg. He asserted that requiring these witnesses to appear and testify would violate his privilege under the speech or debate clause of the United States Constitution, Art 1, § 6, cl 1.

It appeared that on the night on June 29, 1971 Senator Gravel, as Chairman of the Subcommittee on Buildings and Grounds of the Senate Public Works Committee, convened a meeting of the subcommittee and there read extensively from a copy of the Pentagon Papers. He then placed the entire 47 volumes of the study in the public record. Rodberg had been added to the Senator's staff earlier in the day and assisted Gravel in preparing for and conducting the hearing. Some weeks later there were press reports that Gravel had arranged for the papers to be published by Beacon Press and that members of Gravel's staff had talked with Webber as editor of M.I.T. Press.

The District Court overruled the motions to quash and to specify questions but entered an order proscribing certain categories of questions.

The Court of Appeals affirmed the denial of the motions to quash but modified the protective order to reflect its own views of the scope to the congressional privilege. . . .

Because the claim is that a Member's aide shares the Member's constitutional privilege, we consider first whether and to what extent Senator Graval himself is exempt from process or inquiry by a grand jury investigating the commission of a crime. Our frame of reference is Art. 1, § 6, cl. 1, of the Constitution:

> The Senators and Representatives shall receive a Compensation for their Services, to be ascertained by Law, and paid out of the Treasury of the United States. They shall in all Cases, except Treason, Felony and Breach of the Peace be privileged from Arrest during their Attendance at the Session of their respective Houses, and in going to and returning from the same; and for any Speech or Debate in either House, they shall not be questioned in any other Place.

[Gravel] points out that the last portion of § 6 affords Members of Congress another vital privilege—they may not be questioned in any other place for any speech or debate in either House.

[Gravel insists] that the speech and debate clause protects him from criminal or civil liability and from questioning elsewhere than in the Senate, with respect to the events occurring at the sub-committee hearings at which the Pentagon Papers were introduced into the public record. To us this claim is incontrovertible. The speech or debate clause was designed to assure to co-equal branch of the government wide freedom of speech, debate, and deliberation without intimidation or threats from the Executive Branch. . . .

Even so, the United States strongly urges that because the speech or debate clause confers a privilege only upon "Senators and Representatives," Rodberg himself has no valid claim to constitutional immunity from grand jury inquiry. . . . We agree with the Court of Appeals that for the purpose of construing the privilege a Member and his aide are to be "treated as one." . . . It is literally impossible, in view of the complexities of the modern legislative process, with Congress almost constantly in session and matters of legislative concern constantly proliferating, for Members of Congress to perform their legislative tasks without the help of aides and assistants; that the day-to-day work of such aides is so critical to the Members' performance that they must be treated as the latter's alter ego. . . .

The United States fears the abuses that history reveals have occurred when legislators are invested with the power to relieve others from the operation of otherwise valid civil and criminal laws. But these abuses, it seems to us, are for the most part obviated if the privilege applicable to the aide is viewed, as it must be as the privilege of the Senator, and invocable only by the Senator or by the aide on the Senator's behalf, and if in all events the privilege available to the aide is confined to those services that would be immune legislative conduct if performed by the Senator himself. The view places beyond the speech or debate clause a variety of services characteristically performed by aides for Members of Congress, even though within the scope of employment. It likewise provides no protection for criminal conduct threatening the security of the person or property of others, whether performed at the direction of the Senator [or not]. Neither does it immunize Senator or aide from testifying at trial or grand jury proceedings involving third-party crimes where the questions do not require testimony about or impugn a legislative act. Senator and aide . . . does not mean that Rodberg is for all purposes exempt from grand jury questioning.

We are convinced also that the Court of Appeals correctly determined that Senator Gravel's alleged arrangement with Beacon Press to publish the Pentagon Papers was not protected speech or debate within the meaning of Art 1, § 6, cl. 1. of the Constitution.

Historically, the English legislative privilege was not viewed as protecting republication of an otherwise immune libel on the floor of the House. . . . [An English case] recognized that [f]or speeches made in Parliament by a member to the prejudice of any other person or hazardous to the public peace, that member enjoys complete impunity." But it was clearly stated that "If the calumnious or inflammatory speeches should be reported and published, the law will attach responsibility on the publisher." . . .

Thus, voting by Members and Committee reports are protected; and we recognize today—as the Court has recognized before . . . that a Member's conduct at legislative committee hearings, although subject to judicial review in various circumstances, as is legislation itself, may not be made the basis for a civil or criminal judgment against a Member because that conduct is within the "sphere of legitimate legislative activity." . . .

But the Clause had not extended beyond the legislative sphere. That Senators generally perform certain acts in their official capacity as Senators does not necessarily make all such acts legislative in nature. . . .

Legislative acts are not all-encompassing. The heart of the Clause is speech or debate in either House. Insofar as the Clause is construed to reach other matters, they must be an integral part of the deliberative and communicative processes by which Members participate in committee and House Proceedings with respect to the consideration and passage or rejection of proposed legislation or with respect to other matters which the Constitution places within the jurisdiction of either House. . . .

Here private publication by Senator Gravel through the cooperation of Beacon Press was in no way essential to the deliberations of the Senate; nor does questioning as to private publication threaten the integrity or independence of the Senate by impermissibly exposing its deliberations to executive influence. The Senator has conducted his hearings; the record and any report that was forthcoming were available both to this committee and the Senate. Insofar as we are advised, neither Congress nor the full committee ordered or authorized the publication. We cannot but conclude that the Senator's arrangements with Beacon Press were not part and parcel of the legislative process.

There are additional considerations Article 1, § 6. cl. 1, as we have emphasized, does not purport to confer a general exemption upon Members of Congress from liability or process in criminal cases. Quite the contrary is true. While the speech or debate clause recognizes speech, voting, and other legislative acts as exempt from liability that might otherwise attach, it does not privilege either Senator or aide to violate an otherwise valid criminal law in preparing for or implementing legislative acts. If republication to these classified papers would be a crime under an Act of Congress, it would not be entitled to immunity under the speech or debate clause. It also appears that the grand jury was pursuing this very subject in the normal course of a valid investigation. The speech or debate clause does not in our view extend immunity to Rodberg, as a Senator's aide, from testifying before the grand jury about the arrangement between Senator Gravel and Beacon Press or about his own participation, if any, in the alleged transaction, so long as legislative acts of the Senator are not impugned.

We must finally consider, in the light of the foregoing, whether the protective order entered by the Court of Appeals is an appropriate regulation of the pending grand jury proceedings.

Focusing first on paragraph two of the order, we think the injunction against interrogating Rodberg with respect to any act, "in the broadest sense," performed by him within the scope of his employment, overly restricts the scope of grand jury inquiry. Rodberg's immunity, testimonial or otherwise extends only to legislative acts as to which the Senator himself would be immune. The grand jury, therefore, if relevant to its investigation into the possible violations of the criminal law, and absent. Fifth Amendment objections, may require from Rodberg answers to questions relating to his or the Senator's arrangements, if any, with respect to republication or with respect to third-party conduct under valid investigation by the grand jury, as long as the questions do not implicate legislative action of the Senator. Neither do we perceive any constitutional or other privilege that shields Rodberg, any more than any other witness, from grand jury questions relevant to tracing the source of obviously highly classified documents that came into the Senator's possession and are the basic subject matter of injury in this case, so long as no legislative act is implicated by the questions.

Because the speech or debate clause privilege applies both to Senator and aide, it appears to us that paragraph one of the order alone, would afford ample protection for the privilege if it forbade questioning any witness, including Rodberg: (1) concerning the Senator's conduct or the conduct of his aides, at the June 29, 1971, meeting of the subcommittee; (2) concerning the motives and purposes behind the Senator's conduct, or that of his aides, at that meeting; (3) concerning communications between the Senator and his aides during the term of their employment and related to said meeting or any other legislative act of the Senator (4) except as it proves relevant to investigating possible third-day crime, concerning any act, in itself not criminal performed by the Senator, or by his aides in the course of their employment.

The judgment of the Court of Appeals is vacated and the cases are remanded to the court for further proceedings consistent with this opinion.

The boundaries of the speech and debate clause immunity were examined in *Gravel v. United States.* The Court held in *Gravel* that a congressman's aide is shielded with immunity to the same extent that the congressman is himself. Further, the Court held that the aide could not be compelled to testify at a grand jury hearing concerning the actions committed by himself and his employer-senator in preparation for the committee hearing. Nor could the aide be compelled to answer questions concerning the senator's motives. These matters go to the heart of the legislative process.

The aide could, however, be required to testify concerning matters that did not directly implicate the deliberative and communicative aspects of the legislative process, such as any knowledge he possessed concerning the private publication of the papers. The private publication of information, even if contained in a public record, is not part of the legislative process and is not shielded by the speech and debate clause.

In 1995, it was held that the speech and debate clause did not foreclose the prosecution of Congressman Daniel Rostenkowski of Illinois for fraud, embezzlement, and misappropriation of congressional funds.[19] Rostenkowski was accused in that case, among other things, of having congressional staff perform personal services, purchasing items from the House store at a reduced rate for personal use, and purchasing automobiles with congressional funds for personal use. The Court found that these acts were not part of the legislative process and, as such, were not protected.

The speech and debate clause provides, when applicable, *absolute immunity.* This means that a member of Congress is immune not only from liability, but also from suit or from having to defend herself. Therefore, members are entitled to an immediate appeal from trial court decisions finding no immunity, under the collateral order doctrine.[20] This is contrary to the general appellate rule that requires appeals to be filed after final judgment is rendered in a case.

In May 20, 2006, special agents of the Federal Bureau of Investigation (FBI), armed with a judicially issued search warrant, conducted a search of U.S. Congressman William Jefferson's congressional office in the Rayburn Office Building. It was the first search of an office at Capitol in U.S. history. At the time of the search, Representative Jefferson had been under investigation for bribery for over a year and the evidence of his guilt was building. One individual had already pled guilty to bribing Mr. Jefferson with more than $400,000, one of Mr. Jefferson's aides was convicted and sentenced to eight years in prison for brokering deals for Mr. Jefferson, and Mr. Jefferson had been videotaped accepting a $100,000 bribe money from a government informant. That money was later found in Mr. Jefferson's freezer during a search of his home. No one in the House of Representatives or Senate objected to the search of his home or to the surveillance that resulted in the videotape. In fact, the House of Representatives had initiated its own investigation. But the search of Mr. Jefferson's office ruffled some feathers. The Speaker of the House of Representatives, Dennis Hastert, as well as other members, objected to the search as violative of the Constitution's separation of powers and the speech and debate clause. The FBI seized, for example, Mr. Jefferson's computer. As such, the FBI had access to Mr. Jefferson's legitimate and confidential congressional data. Given the coequal status of the branches and the executive oversight role of the Congress, the search raised serious concerns.

U.S.A v. Rayburn House Office Building, Room 2113, Washington, D.C. 20515
497 F.3d 654 (C.A.D.C. 2007), cert. den. 128 S.Ct. 1738 (2008)

This is an appeal from the denial of a motion, filed pursuant to *Rule 41(g) of the Federal Rules of Criminal Procedure*, seeking the return of all materials seized by the Executive upon executing a Search warrant for non-legislative materials in the congressional office of a sitting Member of Congress. The question on appeal is whether the procedures under which the search was conducted were sufficiently protective of the legislative privilege created by the speech or debate clause *Article 1, section 6, clause 1 of the United States Constitution.* Our precedent establishes that the testimonial privilege under the Clause extends to non-disclosure of written legislative materials. Given the Department of Justice's voluntary freeze of its review of the seized materials and the procedures mandated on remand by this court in granting the Congressman's motion for emergency relief pending appeal, the imaging and keyword Search of the Congressman's computer hard drives and electronic media exposed no legislative material to the Executive and therefore did not violate the speech or debate clause, but the review of the Congressman's paper files when the Search was executed exposed legislative material to the Executive and accordingly violated the Clause. Whether the violation requires, as the Congressman suggests, the return of all seized items, privileged as well as non-privileged, depends upon a determination of which documents are privileged and then, as to the non-privileged documents, a balancing of the separation of powers underlying the speech or debate clause and the Executive's Article II, section 3 law enforcement interest in the seized materials. The question of whether the seized evidence must be suppressed under the Fourth Amendment is not before us.

We hold that the compelled disclosure of privileged material to the Executive during execution of the search warrant for Rayburn House Office Building Room 2113 violated the speech or debate clause and that the Congressman is entitled to the return of documents that the court determines to the privileged under the Clause. We do not, however, hold, in the absence of a claim by the Congressman that the operations of his office have been disrupted as a result of not having the original versions of the non-privileged documents, that remedying the violation also requires the return of the non-privileged documents. The Congressmen has suggested no other reason why return of such documents is required pursuant to *Rule 41(g)* and, in any event, it is doubtful that the court has jurisdiction to entertain such arguments following the return of the indictment against him while this appeal was pending.

I.

On May 18, 2006, the Department of Justice filled an application for a search warrant for Room 2113 of the Rayburn House Office Building, the congressional office of Congressman William J. Jefferson. The attached affidavit of Special Agent Timothy R. Thibault of the Federal Bureau of Investigation ("FBI") described how the apparent victim of a fraud and bribery scheme who had come forward as a cooperating witness led to an investigation into bribery of a public official, wire fraud, bribery of a Foreign official, and conspiracy to commit these crimes. The investigation included speaking with the Congressman's staff, one of whom had advised that records relevant to the investigation remained in the congressional office. Based on the investigation, the affiant concluded there was probable cause to believe that Congressman Jefferson, acting with other targets of the investigation, had sought and in some cases already accepted financial backing and or concealed payments of cash or equity interests in business ventures located in the United States, Nigeria, and Ghana in exchange for his undertaking official acts as a Congressman while promoting the business interests of himself and the targets.

Attachments A and B, respectively, described Room 2113 and the non-legislative evidence to be seized. The affiant asserted that the Executive had exhausted all other reasonable methods to obtain these records in a timely manner.

The warrant affidavit also described "special procedures" adopted by the Justice Department prosecutors overseeing the investigation. According to the affidavit,

these procedures were designed: (1) "to minimize the likelihood that any potentially politically sensitive, non-responsive items in the Office will be seized and provided to the [p]rosecution [t]eam," and (2) "to identify information that may fall within the purview of the speech or debate clause privilege, *U.S. Const., art. I § 6 cl. 1* or any other pertinent privilege." Essentially the procedures called for the FBI agents conducting the Search to "have no substantive role in the investigation" and upon reviewing and removing materials from Room 2113, not to reveal politically sensitive or non-responsive items "inadvertently seen . . . during the course of the Search." The FBI agents were to review and seize paper documents responsive to the warrant, copy all electronic files on the hard drives or other electronic media in the Congressman's office, and then turn over the file for review by a filter team consisting of two justice Department attorneys and an FBI agent. The Filter team would determine: (1) whether any of the seized documents were not responsive to the Search warrant, and return any such documents to the Congressmen; and (2) whether any of the seized documents were subject to the Speech of Debate Clause privilege or other privilege. Materials determined to be privileged or not responsive would be returned without dissemination to the prosecution team. Materials determined by the filter team not to be privileged would be turned over to the prosecution team, with copies to the Congressman's attorney within ten business days of the Search. Materials determined by the filter team to be potentially privileged would absent the Congressman's consent to Executive use of a potentially privileged document, be submitted to the district court for review, with a log and copy of such documents provided to the Congressmen's attorney within 20 business days of the Search. The filter team would make similar determinations with respect to the data on the copied computer hard drives, following an initial electronic screening by the FBI's Computer Analysis and Response Team.

The district court found probable cause for issuance of Search warrant and signed it on May 18, 2006, directing the search to occur on or before May 21 and the U.S. Capitol Police to "provide immediate access" to Room 2113. Beginning on Saturday night, May 20, more than a dozen FBI agents spent about 18 hours in Room 2113. The FBI agents reviewed every paper record and copied the hard drives on all of the computers and electronic data stored on other media in Room 2113. The FBI agents seized and carried away two boxes of documents and copies of the hard drives and electronic data. According to the brief for the Executive, the Office of the Deputy Attorney General directed an immediate freeze on any review of the seized materials.

On May 24, 2006, Congressman Jefferson challenged the constitutionality of the Search of his congressional office and moved for return of the seized property pursuant to *FED R. CRIM P. 41(g)*. He argued *inter alia* that the issuance and execution of the search warrant violated the Speech of Debate Clause and sought an order enjoining FBI and Justice Department review or inspection of the seized material. The following day, the President of the United States directed the Attorney General, acting through the Solicitor General, to preserve and seal the records and to make sure no use was made of the materials and that no one had access to them; this directive would expire on July 9, 2006.

On July 10, 2006, the direct court denied the Congressman's motion for return of the seized materials. Concluding that execution of the warrant "did not impermissibly interfere with Congressman Jefferson's legislative activities," *In re Search of the Rayburn House Office Bldg. Room No. 2113 Washington, D.C 20515*, 432 F. Supp. 2d 100, 113 (D.D.C. 2006), the district court noted that the warrant sought only materials that were outside of the "legitimate legislative sphere." The district court rejected the Congressman's claim that he had a right to remove documents he deemed privileged before execution of the warrant, reasoning that although "some privileged material was incidentally captured by the search" and was subject to "incidental review," "the preconditions for a properly administered warrant that seeks only unprivileged material that falls outside the sphere of legitimate legislative activity are sufficient to protect against" undue Executive intrusion. The Justice Departments, therefore, could regain custody of the seized materials and resume review as of July 10, 2006. On July 11, 2006, Congressman Jefferson filed a notice of appeal and a motion for a stay pending appeal. According to the brief for the Executive, the Attorney General ordered the FBI to regain custody of the seized materials and imposed an immediate freeze on any review until the district court and this court considered the Congressman's request for a stay pending appeal. The district court denied a stay . . .

This court, upon consideration of the Congressman's emergency motion for a stay pending appeal filed on July 20, 2006, enjoined the United States, acting through the Executive, from resuming its review of the seized materials. Three days later, the court remanded the record to the district court to make findings regarding "which, if any, documents (physical or electronic) removed . . . from [the] Congressman['s] . . . office pursuant to a Search warrant executed on May 20, 2006, are records of legislative acts." The court instructed the district court to: (1) copy and provide the copies of all the seized documents to the Congressman; (2) "using the copies of computer files made by [the Executive], search for the terms listed in the warrant, and provide a list of responsive records to Congressman Jefferson"; (3) provide the Congressman an opportunity to review the records and, within two days, to submit, *ex parte*, any claims that specific documents are legislative in nature; and (4) "review *in camera* any specific documents or records identified as legislative and make findings regarding whether the specific documents or records are legislative in nature." In the meantime, the court enjoined the Executive from reviewing any of the seized documents pending further order of this court. Subsequently, the court allowed the Executive to review seized

materials that the Congressman "has conceded on remand are not privileged under the speech or debate clause." Order of Nov. 14, 2006. The court ordered expedition of this appeal and oral argument was heard on May 15, 2007.

On June 4, 2007, the grand jury returned a sixteen-count Indictment against Congressman Jefferson in the Eastern District of Virginia. *United States v. Jefferson*, No. 07-0209 (E.D. Va.indictment filed June 4, 2007). The indictment included charges of racketeering, solicitation of (and conspiracy to solicit) bribes, money laundering, wire fraud, and obstruction of justice. Trial is scheduled to begin with jury selection in January 2008. . . .

The speech or debate clause provides that "for any Speech or Debate in either House, [Members of Congress] shall not be questioned in any other Place." U.S. CONST. art. I, § 6, cl. 1. The version of the Clause adopted by the Founders closely resembles the language adopted in the English Bill of Rights of 1689, which came out of the long struggle for governmental supremacy between the English monarchs and the Parliaments, during which the criminal and civil law used to intimidate legislators. By the time of the Constitutional Convention, the privilege embodied in the speech or debate clause was "recognized as an important protection of the independence and integrity of the legislature," *United States v. Johnson*, 383 U.S. 169, 178, 86 S.Ct. 749, 15 L.Ed.2d 681 (1966), and was to serve as a protection against possible "prosecution by an unfriendly executive and conviction by a hostile judiciary," *id*. At 179.

In defining the protections afforded by the Clause, the Supreme Court has limited the scope to conduct that is an integral part of "the due functioning of the legislative process." *United States v. Brewster*, 408 U.S. 501, 513, 92 S.Ct. 2531, 33 L.ED.2d 507 (1972). The Congressman does not dispute that congressional offices are subject to the operation of the Fourth Amendment and thus subject to a search pursuant to a search warrant issued by the federal district court. The Executive acknowledges, in connection with the execution of a search warrant, that there is a role for a Member of Congress to play in exercising the Member's rights under the speech or debate clause. The parties disagree on precisely when that should occur and what effect any violation of the Member's Speech or Debate right should have. The Congressman contends that the exercise of his privilege under the Clause must precede the disclosure of the contents of his congressional office to agents of the Executive and that any violation of the privilege requires return of all of the seized materials. The Executive offers that the special procedures described in the warrant affidavit "are more than sufficient to protect Rep[resentative] Jefferson's rights . . . under the Clause," and that any violation of the privilege does not deprive the Executive of the right to retain all nonprivileged materials within the scope of the search warrant.

The Supreme Court has not spoken to the precise issue at hand. May 20–21, 2006 was the first time a sitting Member's congressional office has been searched by the Executive. The Court has made clear, however, in the context of a grand jury investigation, that "[t]he speech or debate clause was designed to assure a co-equal branch of the government wide freedom of speech, debate, deliberation without intimidation or threats from the Executive Branch." *Gravel v. United States*, 408 U.S. 606, 616, 92 S.Ct. 2614, 33 L.Ed.2d 583 (1972). Although in *Gravel* the Court held that the Clause embraces a testimonial privilege, to date the Court has not spoken on whether the privilege conferred by the Clause includes a non-disclosure privilege. However, this court has.

Beginning with the observation that the prohibition in the speech or debate clause is "deceptively simple," this court held in *Brown & Williamson*, that the Clause includes a non-disclosure privilege. Noting that the purpose of the speech or debate clause is "'to insure that the legislative function the Constitution allocates to Congress may be performed independently,' without regard to the distractions of private civil litigation or the periods of criminal prosecution," . . . the court rejected the view that the testimonial immunity of the speech or debate clause applies only when Members or their aides are personally questioned.

Documentary evidence can certainly be as revealing as oral communications—even if only indirectly when, as here, the documents in question . . . do not detail specific congressional actions. But indications as to what Congress is looking at provide clues as to what Congress is doing, or might be about to do—and this is true whether or not the documents are sought for the purpose of inquiring into (or frustrating) legislative conduct or to advance some other goals. . . . We do not share the Third Circuit's conviction that democracy's "limited toleration for secrecy" is inconsistent with an interpretation of the speech or debate clause that would permit Congress to insist on the confidentiality of investigative files.

As "[d]iscovery procedures can prove just as intrusive" as naming Members or their staffs as parties to a suit, the court held that "[a] party is no more entitled to compel congressional testimony—or production of documents—than it is to sue congressmen," . . . Further, the court noted that when the privilege applies it is absolute. As such, "if the toughstone is interference with legislative activities," then "the nature of the use to which documents will be put—testimonial or evidentiary—is immaterial." *Id.* at 421. In the same vein, the court indicated that the degree of disruption caused by probing into legislative acts is immaterial.

Thus, our opinion in *Brown & Williamson* makes clear that a key purpose of the privilege is to prevent intrusions in the legislative process and that the legislative process is disrupted by the disclosure of legislative material, regardless of the use to which the disclosed materials are put. . . .

The search of Congressman Jefferson's office must have resulted in the disclosure of legislative materials to agents of the Executive. Indeed, the application accompanying the warrant contemplated it. In order to determine whether the documents were responsive to the search

warrant, FBI agents had to review all of the papers in the Congressman's office, of which some surely related to legislative acts. This compelled disclosure clearly tends to disrupt the legislative process: exchanges between a Member of Congress and the Member's staff or among Members of Congress on legislative matters may legitimately involve frank or embarrassing statement; the possibility of compelled disclosure may therefore chill the exchange of views with respect to legislative activity. The chill runs counter to the Clause's purpose of protecting against disruption of the legislative process. . . .

The special procedures outlined in the warrant affidavit would not have avoided the violation of the speech or debate clause because they denied the Congressman any opportunity to identify and assert the privilege with respect to legislative materials before their compelled disclosure to Executive agents. Indeed, the Congressman, his attorney and counsel for the House of Representatives were denied entry into Room 2113 once the FBI arrived. The special procedures described in the warrant affidavit called for review by FBI agents and the several members of the Justice Department filter team before the Congressman would be afforded an opportunity to identify potentially privileged materials. This procedure is significantly different even from those the Executive has on occasion afforded to other privileges not protected in the Constitution; for example, in *United States v. Search of Law Office,* 341 F.3d 404, 407 (5th Cir. 2003), the privilege holder was allowed an opportunity to identify documents protected under the attorney-client privilege at the point the search was completed. Although the Supreme Court in *Weatherford v. Bursey*, 429 U.S. 545, 558, 97 S.Ct. 837, 51 L.Ed 2d 30 (1977), distinguished between the receipt of privileged information by an agent of the Executive and by the prosecution team in the context of a civil rights claim based on a Sixth Amendment violation, the nature of the considerations presented by a violation of the speech or debate clause is different. If the testimonial privilege under the Clause is absolute and there is no distinction between oral and written materials within the legislative sphere, then the non-disclosure privilege for written materials described in *Brown & Williamson*, 62 F.3d at 421, is also absolute, and thus admits of no balancing. The compelled disclosure of legislative materials to FBI agents executing the search warrant was not unintentional but deliberate—a means to uncover responsive non-privileged materials.

There would appear to be no reason why the Congressman's privilege under the speech or debate clause cannot be asserted at the outset of a search in a manner that also protects the interest of the Executive in law enforcement. To the extent the Executive expresses concern about the burdens placed upon the district court and attendant delay during judicial review of seized materials, the Remand Order illustrates streamlined approach by narrowing the number of materials the district court may be required to review. The historical record utterly devoid of Executive searchers of congressional offices suggests the imposition of such a burden will be, at most, infrequent. Regardless of whether the accommodation is by initially sealing the office to be Searched before the Member is afforded an opportunity to identify potentially privileged legislative materials prior to any review by Executive agents to by some other means, seriatim initial reviews by agents of the Executive of a sitting Member's congressional office are inconsistent with the privilege under the Clause. How that accommodation is to be achieved is best determined by the legislative and executive branches in the first instance. Although the court has acknowledged, where it is not a Member who is subject to criminal proceedings, that the privilege might be less stringently applied when inconsistent with a sovereign interest this observation has no bearing her and is relevant if at all, to the question to remedy for a violation, not the determination of whether a violation has occurred.

Accordingly, we hold that a Search that allows agents of the Executive to review privileged materials without the Member's consent violates the Clause. The Executive's search of the Congressman's paper files therefore violated the Clause, but its copying of computer hard drives and other electronic media is constitutionally permissible because the Remand Order affords the Congressman an opportunity to assess the privilege prior to disclosure of privileged materials to the Executive; the Executive advises, that no FBI agent or other Executive agent has seen any electronic document that, upon adjudication of the Congressman's claim of privilege may be determined by the district court to be privileged legislative material.

III.

The question remains what the appropriate remedy under Rule 41(g) for a violation of the speech or debate clause. . . . Our task is to determine how to reconcile the scope of the protection that is afforded to a Member of Congress under the speech or debate clause with the Executive's Article II responsibilities for law enforcement.

Clearly a remedy in this case must show particular respect to the fact that the speech or debate clause "reinforces the separation of powers and protects legislative independence." . . .

Although the search of Congressmen Jefferson's paper files violated the speech or debate clause, his argument does not support granting the relief that he seeks, namely the return of all seized documents, including copies, whether privileged or not. Taking his assertion in reverse order, such relief is unnecessary to deter future unconstitutional acts by the Executive. There is no indication that the Executive did not act based on a good faith interpretation of the law, as reflected in the district court's prior approval and later defense of the special procedures set forth in the warrant affidavit. . . . Additionally, with respect to concern about future actions by the Executive, this is the only time in this Nation's history that the Executive has Searched the office of a sitting Member of Congress. Our holding regarding the compelled disclosure of privileged documents to agents of the Executive during the search makes clear that the special procedures described in the warrant affidavit are insufficient to protect the privilege under the speech or debate clause. This too should ameliorate concerns about deterrence.

At the same time, the remedy must give effect not only to the separation of powers underlying the speech or debate clause but also to the sovereign's interest under Article II, section 3 in law enforcement. The following principles govern our conclusion. The speech or debate clause protects against the compelled disclosure of privileged documents to agents of the Executive, but not the disclosure of non-privileged materials. . . . This particular search needlessly disrupted the functioning of the Congressman's office by allowing agents of the Executive to view legislative materials without the Congressman's consent, even though a search of a congressional office is not prohibited *per se*. Still, the Congressman makes no claim in his brief, much less any showing, that the functioning of his office has been disrupted as a result of not having possession of the original versions of the non-privileged seized materials. Most important, to construe the speech or debate clause as providing an absolute privilege against a seizure of non-privileged materials essential to the Executive's enforcement of criminal statutes pursuant to Article II, section 3 on no more than a generalized claim that the separation of powers demands no less would, as the Supreme Court has observed, albeit as to a qualified privilege, "upset the constitutional balance of a 'workable government.'" The Supreme Court has instructed that the Clause is to be applied "in such a way as to insure the independence of the legislature without altering the historic balance of the three co-equal branches of Government." Applying these principles, we conclude that the Congress is entitled, as the district court may in the first instance determine pursuant to the Remand Order, to the return of all materials (including copies) that are privileged legislative materials under the speech or debate clause. Where the Clause applies its protection is absolute. For the reasons stated, absent any claim of disruption of the congressional office by reason of lack of original versions, it is unnecessary to order the return of non-privileged materials as a further remedy for the violation of the Clause. . . .

Accordingly, we hold that the Congressman is entitled to the return of all legislative materials (original and copies) that are protected by the speech or debate clause seized from Rayburn House Office Building Room 2113 on May 20–21, 2006. Further, as contemplated by the warrant affidavit, the FBI agents who executed the search warrant shall continue to be barred from disclosing the contents of any privileged or "politically sensitive and non-responsive items, and they shall not be involved in the pending prosecution or other charges arising from the investigation described in the warrant affidavit other than as regards responsiveness."

Mr. Jefferson was indicted on bribery, corruption, obstruction of justice, and other charges in 2007, and he was convicted of conspiring to commit bribery, money laundering, using his congressional office as a criminal enterprise, and other charges, and was sentenced to thirteen years in prison in 2009.[21] As previously discussed, Congress may punish its members. So even if a member is immune from other processes, her house may sanction her conduct, including inappropriate statements made on the floor of the house. The protections of the speech and debate clause are not extended to state legislators who are sued or prosecuted in federal court.[22]

4.3(d) Vacancies

If a representative or senatorial position becomes vacant in between elections (e.g., by a member's death), the Constitution provides that the governor of the state may call an election to fill the seat (Article I, § 2 [representative]; Amendment 17 [senator]). Amendment 17 further provides that the legislature of the state may empower the governor to make a temporary senatorial appointment pending replacement by election.

4.4 CONGRESSIONAL AUTHORITY GENERALLY

Over what matters and peoples may Congress legislate? Recall from earlier discussions that the framers intended to create a limited national government. Through the Tenth Amendment, they affirmatively provided that all powers not "delegated to the United States by the Constitution, nor prohibited by it to the States, are reserved to the States respectively, or to the people." It is clear that the framers intended to carve out a well-defined sphere of authority for the national government that could not be enlarged without amendment. In theory, there are no inherent federal authorities. There *is* inherent state authority. In fact, all authority not belonging to the people or the national government fall into the jurisdiction of the states. Hence, there is a triad of authority: the federal government, the states, and the people. The power of the people is further buttressed by the Ninth Amendment, which provides that "[t]he enumeration in the Constitution, of certain rights, shall not be construed to deny or disparage others retained by the people." To understand this triad of power, consider the following analysis. First, determine whether the act in question may be regulated by any government. That is, is this a right of the people? If so, then no further analysis is required. If not, then determine if the federal government may regulate the area. If so, then ask if the states may concurrently regulate the area. (Later in this text, it will be shown that other issues, such as preemption, must be considered at this point.) Finally, if the subject is not delegated to the national government and is not prohibited to any government, then it belongs to the states (see Figure 4-1).

To analyze a problem in these terms, constitutional governmental powers and constitutional civil rights must both be understood. We begin with the authorities of Congress. Congress's authority is limited to the delegations found in the Constitution. Most of those are found in Article I. What follows is a discussion of the express and implied delegations of authority to Congress. As is discussed in the following sections, the concept of a limited national government has fallen away; through several provisions of the Constitution, the national government has increased in both size and jurisdiction. The discussion begins with the Commerce Clause.

4.5 COMMERCE POWER

Article I, section 8, clause 3, states that Congress shall have the power to "regulate Commerce with foreign Nations, and among the several states, and with the Indian Tribes." This is the **Commerce Clause.**

Commerce Clause
The clause in Article I, Section 8, of the Constitution that gives Congress the power to regulate commerce between the states and between the United States and foreign countries. Federal statutes that regulate business and labor are based upon this power.

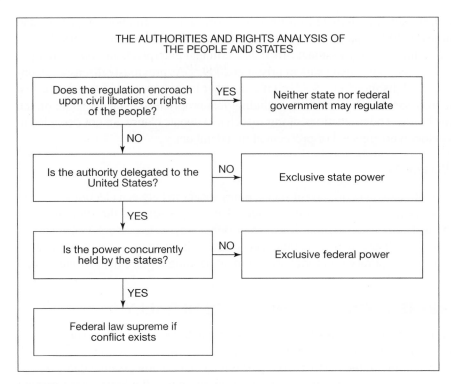

THE AUTHORITIES AND RIGHTS ANALYSIS OF
THE PEOPLE AND STATES

Does the regulation encroach upon civil liberties or rights of the people? — YES → Neither state nor federal government may regulate

NO ↓

Is the authority delegated to the United States? — NO → Exclusive state power

YES ↓

Is the power concurrently held by the states? — NO → Exclusive federal power

YES ↓

Federal law supreme if conflict exists

FIGURE 4-1

Respective authorities of the states, the federal government, and rights of the people

State rivalries and conflicts over foreign and interstate commerce were problems under the Articles of Confederation. The national government was virtually powerless to regulate the area, and there was little uniformity of law. The Commerce Clause was among several constitutional provisions intended to remedy these problems.

Gibbons v. Ogden
22 U.S. (9 Wheat.) 1 (1824)

[New York granted Robert Livingston and Robert Fulton an exclusive license to operate steamships on all New York waterways. Ogden obtained a right to operate a ferry on a New York waterway from Livingston and Fulton. Gibbons under license from the federal government authorized by federal statute operated a ship in Ogden's zone. Ogden obtained an injunction in state court prohibiting Gibbons from operating his ship in New York waters.]

Chief Justice Marshall delivered the opinion of the Court. . . .

The words are, "Congress shall have the power to regulate commerce with foreign nations, and among the several States, and with the Indian tribes."

The subject to be regulated is commerce; and our constitution being, as was aptly said at the bar, one of enumeration, and not of definition, to ascertain the extent of the power, it becomes necessary to settle the meaning of the word. The counsel for the appellee would limit it to traffic, to buying and selling, or the interchange of commodities, and do not admit that it comprehends navigation. This would restrict a general term, applicable to many objects, to one of its significations. Commerce, undoubtably, is traffic, but it is something more; it is intercourse. It describes the commercial intercourse between nations, and parts of nations, in all its branches, and is regulated by prescribing rules for carrying on that intercourse. The mind can scarcely conceive a system for regulating commerce between nations, which shall exclude all laws concerning navigation, which shall be silent on the admission of vessels of the one nation into the ports of the other, and be confined to prescribing rules for the conduct of individuals, in the actual employment of buying and selling, or of barter.

If commerce does not include navigation, the government of the Union has no direct power over the subject, and can make no law prescribing what shall constitute American vessels, or requiring that they shall be navigated by American seamen. Yet this power has been exercised from the commencement of the government, has been exercised with the consent of all, and has been understood by all to be commercial regulation. All

America understands, and has uniformly understood, and word "commerce" to comprehend navigation.

If the opinion that "commerce" as the word is used in the constitution, comprehends navigation also, requires any additional confirmation, that additional confirmation is, we think, furnished by the words of the instrument itself. . . . The 9th section of the 1st article declares, that "no preference shall be given, by any regulation of commerce or revenue, to the ports of one state over those of another." This clause cannot be understood as applicable to those laws only which are passed for the purposes of revenue, because it expressly applied to commercial regulations; and the most obvious preference which can be given to one port over another, in regulating commerce, relates to navigation. But the subsequent part of the sentence is still more explicit. It is, "nor shall vessels bound to or from one state, be obliged to enter, clear, or pay duties, in another." These words have a direct reference to navigation.

The universally acknowledged power of the government to impose embargoes must also be considered as showing that all America is united in that construction which comprehends navigation in the word commerce. . . .

Commerce among the states cannot stop at the external line of each state, but may be introduced into the interior. It is not intended to say that these words comprehend that commerce, which is completely internal which is carried on between man and man in a State, or between different parts of the same State, and which does not extend to or affect other states [is to be regulated]. . . .

Comprehensive as the word "among" is, it may very properly be restricted to that commerce which concerns more States than one. The phrase is not one which would probably have been selected to indicate the completely interior traffic of a State. . . . The completely internal commerce of a state, then, may be considered as reserved for the state itself.

But, in regarding commerce with foreign nations, the power of Congress does not stop at the jurisdictional lines of the several states. It would be a very useless power, if it could not pass those lines. . . . The deep streams which penetrate our country in every direction, pass through the interior of almost every state. . . . If it exists within the States, if a foreign voyage may commence or terminate at a port within a State, then the power or Congress may be exercised within a State.

We are now arrived at the inquiry—What is this power?

It is the power to regulate; that is, to proscribe the rule by which commerce is governed. This power, like all others vested in Congress, is complete in itself, may be exercised to its utmost extent, and acknowledges no limitations, other than those prescribed in the constitution. . . .

The power of Congress, then, comprehends navigation, within the limits of every state in the Union; so far as that navigation may be, in any manner, connected with "commerce with foreign nations, or among the several States, or with the Indian tribes." It may, of consequence, pass the jurisdictional line of New York, and act upon the very waters to which the prohibition now under consideration applies.

4.5(a) Early Commerce Clause Cases

The clause delegates the authority to regulate interstate, international, and Indian commerce to the United States. Because the federal government is, in theory, a limited one, it does not have the authority to regulate intrastate commerce. This power is left to the states.

Several troubling issues have surfaced in the commerce area. One concerns a fundamental question. When is commerce interstate in character? The examination of the clause begins with that inquiry.

Chief Justice Marshall defined *interstate commerce* as "commerce that concerns more states than one." According to Chief Justice Marshall, only commerce that is entirely internal is not subject to federal regulation. Further, Congress may regulate activities within states if those activities affect interstate commerce. For example, in 1922 the Court ruled that the Chicago stockyards could be federally regulated because they were a point through which interstate commerce flowed. The Court held that intrastate activities could be regulated if they were part of the "stream or current of commerce."[23] Chief Justice Marshall's broad interpretation of the authority of the federal government to regulate commerce remained the prevailing view until the 1930s.

4.5(b) The New Deal and the Commerce Clause

For a brief period, during the New Deal administration of President Franklin D. Roosevelt, the Court changed its approach to the Commerce Clause. The Court adopted a more territorial approach to commerce, carving out an area that belonged to the states. In several cases, the Court invalidated New Deal legislation that was intended to remedy the economic depression. In *Railroad Retirement Board v. Alton Rail Co.*,[24] a 1935 decision of the Supreme Court, the Railroad Retirement Act was held to exceed Congress's authority over commerce. The Act governed pensions for railroad employees. In short, the Court found no connection between interstate commerce and the financial security of railroad employees.

Schechter Poultry Corp. v. United States,[25] another 1935 case, represented another defeat for the New Deal's recovery efforts. This case challenged the authority of the president to approve "codes of fair competition" for the poultry industry. The defendant corporation was convicted of violating the code, which had been established by an agency at the direction of the president, over its objections that the delegation to the president was unlawful and that Congress had exceeded its authority under the Commerce Clause. The Court ruled for the defendant on both counts. The first issue, unlawful delegation of authority to the president, is discussed in Chapter 7. As to the second issue, the majority held that the intrastate activities of a poultry business did not have sufficient connection to interstate commerce to allow federal regulation.

There were other cases in which the Court read the Commerce Clause as conferring less federal authority than had previously been allowed.[26] Also, several New Deal statutes were invalidated under excessive delegation and substantive due process theories. These cases are discussed in Chapter 6. (Recall also that these decisions led to President Franklin D. Roosevelt's court-packing plan and the *switch in time that saved nine*, previously discussed in Chapter 3.)

4.5(c) The Commerce Clause Today

The Court's change in direction occurred in 1937, when the Court upheld the National Labor Relations Act (NLRA), a federal labor statute that governs collective bargaining and unfair labor practices. The Court held that the law's jurisdictional provision, which confined the NLRA's reach to transactions affecting or obstructing commerce, was valid.[27] Under this new approach, the fact that a business may have an economic impact on the nation—regardless of whether it otherwise appears to be intrastate in nature—creates federal jurisdiction. Furthermore, the Tenth Amendment, which had previously been used by the Court to create a state commerce domain, was rejected as a limitation upon federal authority.

Since this time, congressional authority has grown significantly, virtually unchecked by the judiciary. Federal jurisdiction has been found in some cases where common sense leads to the opposite conclusion. In many respects, the power of Congress to regulate has extended into what were once thought to be exclusively state issues. Most notably, Congress now regulates for the general welfare of the people. The power to regulate health, welfare, and security is known as the **police power.** The framers rejected a national police power at the Philadelphia Convention in favor of leaving such subjects to the states. Chief Justice Marshall acknowledged that the police powers rested with the states in *McCulloch v. Maryland*,[28] wherein he announced the **pretext principle.** Marshall, writing for the Court, stated that Congress could enact no law under one of its enumerated powers when its true intent was to regulate a subject that belonged to the states.

Today, the pretext principle has been rendered a dead letter because the Court generally refuses to examine the motives of Congress. That body is now free, so long as a connection to interstate commerce can be established, to regulate for welfare purposes;[29] Congress is no longer limited to strictly commercial concerns. The test is whether the statute bears a rational relationship to its objective. If so, it is constitutional. This is not a hard test to satisfy. As a consequence, a host of labor laws have been approved, including child labor and occupational safety regulations. President Roosevelt's social security program is another example. It was upheld against Tenth Amendment and other challenges in two cases, *Stewart Machine Co. v. Davis*, 301 U.S. 548 (1937) and *Helvering v. Davis*, 301 U.S. 619 (1937).

police power
The power of government to make and enforce laws and regulations necessary to maintain and enhance the public welfare and to prevent individuals from violating the rights of others.

pretext principle
A law that is enacted by Congress supposedly under one of its enumerated powers, when the law's true purpose is to regulate a subject belonging to the states, is invalid. Today, the affectation doctrine has made the pretext principle of little significance.

Affectation and Cumulative Affects To what extent must an intrastate regulation relate to commerce to be subject to federal control? In a few early cases, the Court restricted Congress to regulating activities that directly affected interstate commerce. However, since the late 1930s, the power of Congress to regulate activities that indirectly affect interstate commerce has increased. It is through this **affectation doctrine** that Congress often regulates for the general welfare. When considering whether an activity indirectly affects interstate commerce, Congress may consider the cumulative effects of seemingly local activity. That is, even though an individual's act may not affect interstate commerce, the cumulative effect of all people who engage in the activity may affect interstate commerce. If so, Congress may regulate the activity. This is the legal issue discussed in *Wickard v. Filburn*.

affectation doctrine
Rule that provides Congress with authority to regulate intrastate activities that affect interstate commerce. Even though individual activity may not affect interstate commerce, the total effect of all individuals who engage in the activity may affect interstate commerce and provide Congress with the jurisdiction to regulate the activity.

Wickard v. Filburn
317 U.S. 111 (1942)

[The defendant farmer was penalized $117 for violating the Agricultural Adjustment Act, which set a quota on wheat production. Farmers were prohibited from producing more wheat than allotted. The defendant (Fiburn) was a dairy farmer and raised wheat primarily to feed his family and livestock. The defendant sought an injunction prohibiting the Secretary of Agriculture (Wickard) from enforcing the penalty.]

Mr. Justice Jackson delivered the opinion of the Court. . . .

It is urged that under the Commerce Clause [Congress] does not possess the power it has in this instance sought to exercise. The question would merit little consideration but for that this Act extends federal regulation to production not intended in any part to form commerce but wholly for consumption on the farm. [The quotas at issue] not only embrace all that may be sold without penalty but also what may be consumed on the premises. . . .

Appellee says that this is a regulation of production and consumption of wheat. Such activities are, he urges, beyond the reach of Congressional power under the Commerce Clause, since they are local in nature, and their effects upon interstate commerce are at most "indirect." In answer the Government argues that the statute regulates neither production nor consumption, but only marketing; and, in the alternative, that if the Act does go beyond the regulation of marketing it is sustainable as a "necessary and proper" implementation of the power of Congress over interstate commerce. . . . [The Court reviewed the precedents in the area, including cases requiring activities to directly affect interstate commerce if they are to come under federal authority.]

The Court's recognition of the relevance of the economic effects in the application of the Commerce Clause exemplified by the statement has made the mechanical application of legal formulas no longer feasible. Once an economic measure of the reach of the power granted to Congress in the Commerce Clause is accepted, questions of federal power cannot be decided simply by finding the activity in question to be "production," nor can consideration of its economic effects be foreclosed by calling them "indirect." . . . Whether the subject of the regulation in question was "production," "consumption," or "marketing" is, therefore, not material for purposes of deciding the question of federal power before us. That an activity is of local character may help in a doubtful case to determine whether Congress intended to reach it. . . . But even if appellee's activity be local and though it may not be regarded as commerce, it may still, whatever its nature, be reached by Congress if it exerts a substantial economic effect on interstate commerce and this irrespective of whether such effect is what might at some earlier time have been defined as "direct" or "indirect."

The parties have stipulated a summary of the economics of the wheat industry. Commerce among the states in wheat is large and important. Although wheat is raised in every state but one, production in most states is not equal to consumption. . . .

The wheat industry has been a problem industry for some years. Largely as a result of increased foreign production and import restrictions, annual exports of wheat and flour from the United States during the ten-year period ending in 1940 averaged less than 10 per cent of total production, while during the 1920's they averaged more than 25 per cent. The decline in the export trade has left a large surplus in production which in connection with an abnormally large supply of other grains in recent years caused congestion in a number of markets; tied up railroad cars; and caused elevators in some instance to turn away grains, and railroads to institute embargoes to prevent further congestion. . . .

The effect of consumption of homegrown wheat on interstate commerce is due to the fact that it constitutes the most variable factor in the disappearance of the wheat crop. Consumption on the farm where grown appears to vary in the amount greater than 20 per cent of average production. The total amount of wheat consumed as food varies but relatively little, and use as seed is relatively constant.

The maintenance by government regulation of a price for wheat undoubtedly can be accomplished as effectively by sustaining or increasing the demand as by limiting the supply. The effect of the statute before us is to restrict the amount which may be produced for market and the extent as well to which one may forestall resort to the market by producing to meet his own needs. That appellee's own contribution to the demand for wheat may be trivial by itself is not enough to remove him from the scope of federal regulation where, as here, his contribution, taken together with that of many others similarly situated, is far from trivia. . . .

Home grown wheat in this sense competes with wheat in commerce. The stimulation of commerce is a use of the regulatory function quite as definitely as prohibitions or restrictions thereon. This record leaves us in no doubt that Congress may properly have considered that wheat consumed on the farm where grown is wholly outside the scheme of regulation would have a substantial effect in defeating and obstructing [congress's] purpose to stimulate trade therein at increased prices.

The following are other examples of congressional regulations approved by the Supreme Court:

1. Congress may regulate surface mining because coal travels in interstate commerce and the environmental effects of the activity may stretch beyond one state.[30]
2. Congress may prohibit discriminatory practices by hotels because such practices affect the interstate travel of black people. The claim that the law was intended to regulate morals, not commercial activities, was rejected. The motive of Congress in enacting a regulation under the Commerce Clause is not material. The issue is whether the activity regulated is interstate in character. If so, the regulation is valid.[31]
3. A locally owned and operated restaurant that served only intrastate customers was subject to federal civil rights laws requiring that it serve black persons because some of the food it served had traveled in interstate commerce.[32]

Cyber Constitution
The U.S. Code can be found in several locations, including http://www.gpoaccess.gov/uscode/ and http://www.law.cornell.edu/uscode/

The Outer Limit For over sixty years the Supreme Court did not invalidate one act of Congress as exceeding federal authority under the Commerce Clause. It appeared as though there was no limit to what Congress could regulate, especially in a nation where virtually every enterprise, no matter how small, has contact with people or goods that travel in interstate commerce. And Congress has used its commerce power extensively. Through the Commerce Clause, Congress regulates the environment, poverty, cyberspace, and criminal matters.

In the criminal law arena, Congress now regulates crimes that once were thought to be local. The Mann Act criminalizes the interstate movement of women for immoral purposes.[33] Movement between states in order to commit domestic violence, including violating protective orders, is a federal crime.[34] The Uniform Flight to Avoid Prosecution Act makes flight from one state to another to avoid prosecution of a state crime a federal offense.[35] It is unlawful for certain persons to transport firearms in interstate commerce.[36] The transportation of children in interstate commerce for immoral purposes and the interstate transportation of child pornography are both federal crimes.[37] The Consumer Credit Protection Act, which applies to local extortionate credit transactions (loan-sharking), was upheld on the theory that the cumulative effect of all loan-sharking affects interstate commerce.[38] Congress criminalized carjacking in 1992 in a law codified as 18 U.S.C. § 2119. That statute provides that "whoever, with the intent to cause death or serious bodily harm takes a motor vehicle that has been transported, shipped, or received in interstate or foreign commerce from . . . another by force or violence or by intimidation" has committed a federal crime. The law has been upheld as a valid exercise of the commerce power by at least one appellate court.[39]

Unquestionably, these laws are motivated by health and welfare, not commercial, concerns. Again, the Court made it clear in *Heart of Atlanta Motel* and other cases that Congress may exercise police powers. In addition, it also appeared that there was no genuine requirement of affectation; that is, no true connection between interstate commerce and the regulation appeared to be required. This changed with the 1995 decision in *United States v. Lopez.*

Lopez was the first case since the 1940s in which a statute was invalidated as extending federal power under the Commerce Clause too far. It teaches that there must be a genuine connection between commerce and a regulation before Congress may act. The Court's decision was that the possession of a gun near a school is not a commercial activity subject to the congressional regulation under the Commerce Clause. Thus, Congress had no authority to regulate it. Remember, this decision does not forbid the *states* from creating gun-free school zones. States have the authority to enact such laws under their general police powers. The *Lopez* Court identified the things over which Congress may exercise jurisdiction under the Commerce Clause:

United States v. Lopez
514 U.S. 549 (1995)

Chief Justice Rehnquist delivered the opinion of the Court.

In the Gun-Free School Zone Act of 1990, Congress made it a federal offense "for any individual knowingly to possess a firearm at [a] place that the individual knows, or has reasonable cause to believe, is a school zone." . . . The Act neither regulates a commercial activity nor contains a requirement that the possession be connected in any way to interstate commerce. We hold that the Act exceeds the authority of Congress "[t]o regulate Commerce . . . among the several states. . . ." U.S. Const., Art. I. § 8, cl. 3.

On March 10, 1992, respondent, who was then a 12th-grade student, arrived at. Edison High School in San Antonio, Texas, carrying a concealed 38 caliber handgun and live bullets. Acting upon an anonymous tip, school authorities confronted respondent, who admitted that he was carrying the weapon. He was arrested and charged under Texas law with firearm possession on school premises. . . . The next day, the state charges were dismissed after federal agents charged respondent by complaint with violating the Gun-Free School Zone Act of 1990. . . . [The defendant was indicted and moved to dismiss the indictment on the ground that the statute was beyond congressional powers. The district court denied the motion and the appellate court reversed the trial court conviction.]

We start with first principles. The Constitution creates a Federal Government of enumerated powers. . . . As James Madison wrote, "[t]he powers delegated by the proposed Constitution to the federal government are few and defined. Those which are to remain in the State governments are numerous and indefinite. *The Federalist* No. 45. . . . This constitutionally mandated division of authority "was adopted by the Framers to ensure protection of our fundamental liberties." . . . [The Court then summarized the history of its Commerce Clause decisions.]

Consistent with this structure, we have identified three broad categories of activity that Congress may regulate under its commerce power. . . . First, Congress may regulate the use of the channels of interstate commerce . . . . Second, Congress is empowered to regulate and protect the instrumentalities of interstate commerce, or persons or things in interstate commerce, even though the threat may only from intrastate activities. . . . Finally, commerce authority includes the power to regulate those activities having a substantial relation to interstate commerce, . . . i.e., those activities that substantially affect interstate commerce. . . .

Within the final category, admittedly, our case law has not been clear whether an activity must "affect" or "substantially affect" interstate commerce in order to be within Congress' power to regulate it under the Commerce Clause. . . . We conclude, consistent with the great weight of our case law, that the proper test requires an analysis of whether the regulated activity "substantially affects" interstate commerce.

We now turn to consider the power of Congress, in the light of this framework, to [en]act [the Gun-Free School Zone Law]. The first two categories of authority may be quickly disposed of [the statute] is not a regulation of the use of the channels of interstate commerce, nor is it an attempt to prohibit the interstate transportation of [a] commodity through the channels of commerce; nor can [the statute] be justified as a regulation by which Congress has sought to protect an instrumentality of interstate commerce or a thing in interstate commerce. Thus, if [the statute] is to be sustained, it must be under the third category as a regulation of an activity that substantially affects interstate commerce.

First, we have upheld a wide variety of congressional Acts regulating intrastate economic activity where we have concluded that the activity substantially affected interstate commerce. Examples include the regulation of intrastate coal mining . . . intrastate extortionate credit transactions . . . restaurants utilizing substantial interstate supplies . . . and production and consumption of home-grown wheat. These examples are by no means exhaustive, but the pattern is clear. Where economic activity substantially affects interstate commerce, legislation regulating that activity will be sustained.

Even *Wickard*, which is perhaps the most far reaching example of Commerce Clause authority over intrastate activity, involved economic activity in a way that the possession of a gun in a school zone does not. . . .

[The Gun-Free Zone Law] is criminal statute that by its terms has nothing to do with "commerce" or any sort of economic enterprise, however broadly one might define those terms. [The statute] is not an essential part of a larger regulation of economic activity, in which the regulatory scheme could be undercut unless the intrastate activity were regulated. It cannot, therefore, be sustained under our cases upholding regulations of activities that arise out of or are connected with a commercial transaction, which viewed in the aggregate, substantially affects interstate commerce. . . .

Second, [the statute] contains no jurisdictional elements which would ensure, through case-by-case inquiry, that the firearm possession in question affects interstate commerce. For example, . . . 18 U.S.C. § 1202(a), which made it a crime for a felon to "receive[e], posses[s], or transpor[t] in commerce or affecting commerce . . . any firearm." . . . The Court interpreted the possession component of § 1202(a) to require an additional nexus to interstate commerce both because the statute was ambiguous and because "unless Congress conveys its purpose clearly, it will not be deemed to have significantly changed the federal-state balance." . . . The [Court in a case arising under § 1202(a)] set aside the conviction because although the Government had demonstrated that [the defendant] had possessed a firearm, it had failed "to show the interpreted statute to reserve the constitutional question whether Congress could regulate, without more, the 'mere possession' of firearms." . . . Unlike the statute in [this prior case], [the gun-free school zone statute] has no express jurisdictional element which might limit its reach to a discrete set of firearm possessions that additionally have an explicit connection with or effect on interstate commerce. . . .

The Government argues that possession of a firearm in a school zone may result in violent crime and that violent crime can be expected to affect the functioning of the national economy in two ways. First, the costs of violent crime are substantial, and, through the mechanism of insurance, those costs are spread throughout the population. . . . Second, violent crime reduces the willingness of individuals to travel to areas within the country that are perceived to be unsafe. . . . The Government also argues that the presence of guns in schools poses a substantial threat to the educational process by threatening the learning environment. A handicapped educational process, in turn will result in a less productive citizenry. That, in turn, would have an adverse effect on the Nation's economic well-being. . . .

We pause to consider the implications of the Government's arguments. The Government admits, under its "costs of crime" reasoning, that Congress could regulate not only all violent crime, but all activities that might lead to violent crime, regardless of how tenuously they relate to interstate commerce. . . . Similarly, under the Government's "national productivity" reasoning, Congress could regulate any activity that it found was related to the economic productivity of individual citizens: family law . . . for example. Under the theories that the Government presents in support of [the

statute], it is difficult to perceive any limitation on federal power, even in areas such as criminal law enforcement or education where States historically have been sovereign. Thus, if we were to accept the Government's arguments, we are hard-pressed to posit any activity by a individual that Congress is without power to regulate. . . .

For instance, if Congress can, pursuant to its Commerce Clause power, regulate activities that adversely affect the learning environment, then, a fortiori, it also can regulate the educational process directly. Congress could determine that a school's curriculum has a "significant" effect on the extent of classroom learning. As a result, Congress could mandate a federal curriculum for local elementary and secondary schools because what is taught in local schools has a significant "effect on classroom learning". . . and that, in turn, has a substantial effect on interstate commerce. . . .

We do not doubt that Congress has authority under the Commerce Clause to regulate numerous commercial activities that substantially affect interstate commerce and also affect the educational process. That authority, though broad, does not include the authority to regulate each and every aspect of local schools.

Admittedly, a determination whether an intrastate activity is commercial or noncommercial may in some cases result in legal uncertainty. But, so long as Congress' authority is limited to those powers enumerated in the Constitution, and so long as those enumerated powers are interpreted as having judicially enforceable outer limits, congressional legislation under the Commerce Clause will always engender "legal uncertainty." . . .

These are not precise formulations, and in the nature of things they cannot be. But we think they point the way to a correct decision of this case. The possession of a gun in a local school zone is in no sense an economic activity that might, through repetition elsewhere, substantially affect any sort of interstate commerce. Respondent was a local student at a local school; there is no indication that he had recently moved in interstate commerce, and there is no requirement that his possession of the firearm have any concrete tie to interstate commerce.

To uphold the Government's contentions here, we would have to pile inference upon inference in a manner that would bid fair to convert congressional authority under the Commerce Clause to a general police power of the sort retained to the States. Admittedly, some of our prior cases have taken long steps down that road, giving great deference to congressional action. . . . The broad language in these opinions has suggested the possibility of additional expansion, but we decline here to proceed any further. . . .

For the foregoing reasons the judgment of the Court of Appeals is Affirmed.

1. The channels of interstate commerce.
2. The instrumentalities of interstate commerce, or persons or things in interstate commerce, even though the threat may come only from intrastate activities.
3. Those activities having a substantial relation to interstate commerce, that is, those activities that substantially affect interstate commerce.

Commerce Power **171**

Lopez was concerned with the third category, and the Court made it clear that an activity cannot be regulated unless it *substantially* affects interstate commerce. The cumulative effect an intrastate activity has on interstate activity can continue to be the basis of federal power, however.

Generally, Congress uses two models to assert its interstate commerce power. First, Congress can make a finding of interstate character for an entire class of cases. For example, in committee reports and a piece of legislation itself, Congress can indicate that it has determined that an activity "substantially affects" interstate commerce. Second, Congress can require that the commerce requirement be satisfied on a case-by-case basis. That is, the elements of a crime or civil action may include an interstate connection, such as requiring proof that drugs have traveled in interstate commerce before allowing federal prosecution for their transportation or sale.

Two years following *Lopez, Printz v. United States*[40] was handed down. The federal Brady Handgun Violence Protection Act was invalidated using the same rationale found in *Lopez*. The Brady law required the federal government to construct a background checking system for gun buyers. The law required local police officials to conduct the checks until the federal system was operational. The Court found this to be an excessive encroachment of state authority. Although the states have fared well post-*Lopez*, some extensions of federal authority over interstate commerce have been upheld. For example, the federal carjacking statute, which criminalizes the forcible taking of an automobile that has been transported, shipped, or received in interstate commerce, was upheld.[41]

The issue surfaced again in the following 2000 case.

United States v. Morrison
529 U.S. 598 (2000)

Chief Justice Rehnquist delivered the opinion of the Court.

In these cases we consider the constitutionality of 42 U.S.C. § 13981 which provides a federal civil remedy for the victims of gender-motivated violence. The United States Court of Appeals for the Fourth Circuit, sitting en banc, struck down §13981 because it concluded that Congress lacked constitutional authority to enact the section's civil remedy. Believing that these cases are controlled by our decisions in *United States v. Lopez,* 514 U.S. 549 (1995), *United States v. Harris,* 106 U.S. 629 (1883), and the *Civil Rights Cases,* 109 U.S. 3 (1883), we affirm.

Facts

Petitioner Christy Brzonkala enrolled at Virginia Polytechnic Institute (Virginia Tech) in the fall of 1994. In September of that year, Brzonkala met respondents Antonio Morrison and James Crawford, who were both students at Virginia Tech and members of its varsity football team. Brzonkala alleges that, within 30 minutes of meeting Morrison and Crawford, they assaulted and repeatedly raped her. After the attack, Morrison allegedly told Brzonkala, "You better not have any . . . diseases." In the months following the rape, Morrison also allegedly announced in the dormitory's dining room that he "like[d] to get girls drunk and. . . ." The omitted portions, quoted verbatim in the briefs on file with this Court, consist of boasting, debased remarks about what

Morrison would do to women, vulgar remarks that cannot fail to shock and offend.

Brzonkala alleges that this attack caused her to become severely emotionally disturbed and depressed. She sought assistance from a university psychiatrist, who prescribed antidepressant medication. Shortly after the rape Brzonkala stopped attending classes and withdrew from the university.

In early 1995, Brzonkala filed a complaint against respondents under Virginia Tech's Sexual Assault Policy. . . . [and she later sued the men and the University in federal court. The defendants moved to dismiss the complaint as unconstitutional and for other reasons. The federal trial court granted the motion, having concluded that Congress lacked the authority to enact the Violence Against Women Act.]

Section 13981 was part of the Violence Against Women Act of 1994, §40302, 108 Stat. 1941–1942. It states that "[a]ll persons within the United States shall have the right to be free from crimes of violence motivated by gender." 42 U.S.C. § 13981(b). To enforce that right, subsection (c) declares [that individuals who commit crimes of violence motivated by gender may be sued for damages in federal court.]

End Facts

Every law enacted by Congress must be based on one or more of its powers enumerated in the Constitution. "The powers of the legislature are defined and limited; and that those limits may not be mistaken or forgotten, the constitution is written." *Marbury v. Madison*, 1 Cranch 137, 176 (1803) (Marshall, C. J.). Congress explicitly identified the sources of federal authority on which it relied in enacting §13981. It said that a "federal civil rights cause of action" is established "[p]ursuant to the affirmative power of Congress . . . under section 5 of the Fourteenth Amendment to the Constitution, as well as under section 8 of Article I of the Constitution." 42 U.S.C. § 13981(a). We address Congress' authority to enact this remedy under each of these constitutional provisions in turn. . . .

Lopez emphasized, however, that even under our modern, expansive interpretation of the Commerce Clause, Congress' regulatory authority is not without effective bounds.

"[E]ven [our] modern-era precedents which have expanded congressional power under the Commerce Clause confirm that this power is subject to outer limits. In *Jones & Laughlin Steel*, the Court warned that the scope of the interstate commerce power 'must be considered in the light of our dual system of government and may not be extended so as to embrace effects upon interstate commerce so indirect and remote that to embrace them, in view of our complex society, would effectually obliterate the distinction between what is national and what is local and create a completely centralized government.'"

As we observed in *Lopez*, modern Commerce Clause jurisprudence has "identified three broad categories of activity that Congress may regulate under its commerce power." . . . "First, Congress may regulate the use of the channels of interstate commerce . . . "Second, Congress is empowered to regulate and protect the instrumentalities of interstate commerce, or persons or things in interstate commerce, even though the threat may come only from intrastate activities." . . . "Finally, Congress' commerce authority includes the power to regulate those activities having a substantial relation to interstate commerce, . . . *i.e.*, those activities that substantially affect interstate commerce."

Petitioners do not contend that these cases fall within either of the first two of these categories of Commerce Clause regulation. They seek to sustain §13981 as a regulation of activity that substantially affects interstate commerce. Given §13981's focus on gender-motivated violence wherever it occurs (rather than violence directed at the instrumentalities of interstate commerce, interstate markets, or things or persons in interstate commerce), we agree that this is the proper inquiry.

Since *Lopez* most recently canvassed and clarified our case law governing this third category of Commerce Clause regulation, it provides the proper framework for conducting the required analysis of §13981. In *Lopez*, we held that the Gun-Free School Zones Act of 1990, 18 U.S.C. § 922(q)(1)(A), which made it a federal crime to knowingly possess a firearm in a school zone, exceeded Congress' authority under the Commerce Clause. See 514 U.S., at 551. Several significant considerations contributed to our decision. . . .

First, we observed that [the law reviewed in *Lopez*] was "a criminal statute that by its terms has nothing to do with 'commerce' or any sort of economic enterprise, however broadly one might define those terms." . . .

The second consideration that we found important in analyzing §922(q) was that the statute contained "no express jurisdictional element which might limit its reach to a discrete set of firearm possessions that additionally have an explicit connection with or effect on interstate commerce." Such a jurisdictional element may establish that the enactment is in pursuance of Congress' regulation of interstate commerce.

Third, we noted that neither §922(q) "nor its legislative history contain[s] express congressional findings regarding the effects upon interstate commerce of gun possession in a school zone." . . .

Finally, our decision in *Lopez* rested in part on the fact that the link between gun possession and a substantial effect on interstate commerce was attenuated. The United States argued that the possession of guns may lead to violent crime, and that violent crime "can be expected to affect the functioning of the national economy in two ways. First, the costs of violent crime are substantial, and, through the mechanism of insurance, those costs are spread throughout the population. Second, violent crime reduces the willingness of individuals to travel to areas within the country that are perceived to be unsafe." (citation omitted). The Government also argued that the presence of guns at schools poses a threat to the educational process, which in turn threatens to produce a less efficient and productive workforce, which will negatively affect national productivity and thus interstate commerce.

We rejected these "costs of crime" and "national productivity" arguments because they would permit Congress to "regulate not only all violent crime, but all activities that might lead to violent crime, regardless of how tenuously they relate to interstate commerce." . . .

With these principles underlying our Commerce Clause jurisprudence as reference points, the proper resolution of the present cases is clear. Gender-motivated crimes of violence are not, in any sense of the phrase, economic activity. While we need not adopt a categorical rule against aggregating the effects of any noneconomic activity in order to decide these cases, thus far in our Nation's history our cases have upheld Commerce Clause regulation of intrastate activity only where that activity is economic in nature.

Like the Gun-Free School Zones Act at issue in *Lopez*, §13981 contains no jurisdictional element establishing that the federal cause of action is in pursuance of Congress' power to regulate interstate commerce. Although *Lopez* makes clear that such a jurisdictional element would lend support to the argument that §13981 is sufficiently tied to interstate commerce, Congress elected to cast §13981's remedy over a wider, and more purely intrastate, body of violent crime. . . .

Given these findings and petitioners' arguments, the concern that we expressed in *Lopez* that Congress might use the Commerce Clause to completely obliterate the Constitution's distinction between national and local authority seems well founded. See *Lopez, supra*, at 564. The reasoning that petitioners advance seeks to follow the but-for causal chain from the initial occurrence of violent crime (the suppression of which has always been the prime object of the States' police power) to every attenuated effect upon interstate commerce. If accepted, petitioners' reasoning would allow Congress to regulate any crime as long as the nationwide, aggregated impact of that crime has substantial effects on employment, production, transit, or consumption. Indeed, if Congress may regulate gender-motivated violence, it would be able to regulate murder or any other type of violence since gender-motivated violence, as a subset of all violent crime, is certain to have lesser economic impacts than the larger class of which it is a part.

Petitioners' reasoning, moreover, will not limit Congress to regulating violence but may, as we suggested in *Lopez*, be applied equally as well to family law and other areas of traditional state regulation since the aggregate effect of marriage, divorce, and childrearing on the national economy is undoubtedly significant. Congress may

have recognized this specter when it expressly precluded §13981 from being used in the family law context. See 42 U.S.C. § 13981(e)(4). Under our written Constitution, however, the limitation of congressional authority is not solely a matter of legislative grace. See *Lopez, supra*, at 575–579 (Kennedy, J., concurring); *Marbury*, 1 Cranch, at 176–178.

We accordingly reject the argument that Congress may regulate noneconomic, violent criminal conduct based solely on that conduct's aggregate effect on interstate commerce. The Constitution requires a distinction between what is truly national and what is truly local. *Lopez*, 514 U.S., at 568 (citing *Jones & Laughlin Steel*, 301 U.S., at 30). In recognizing this fact we preserve one of the few principles that has been consistent since the Clause was adopted. The regulation and punishment of intrastate violence that is not directed at the instrumentalities, channels, or goods involved in interstate commerce has always been the province of the States. . . . [the Court then discussed and rejected the plaintiff's claim that Congress had the authority under the Fourteenth Amendment to enact the Violence Against Women Act.]

Gonzales v. Raich
545 U.S. (2005)

California is one of at least nine States that authorize the use of marijuana for medicinal purposes. The question presented in this case is whether the power vested in Congress by Article I, §8, of the Constitution "[t]o make all Laws which shall be necessary and proper for carrying into Execution" its authority to "regulate Commerce with foreign Nations, and among the several States" includes the power to prohibit the local cultivation and use of marijuana in compliance with California law.

California has been a pioneer in the regulation of marijuana. In 1913, California was one of the first States to prohibit the sale and possession of marijuana, and at the end of the century, California became the first State to authorize limited use of the drug for medicinal purposes. In 1996, California voters passed Proposition 215, now codified as the Compassionate Use Act of 1996. The proposition was designed to ensure that "seriously ill" residents of the State have access to marijuana for medical purposes, and to encourage Federal and State Governments to take steps towards ensuring the safe and affordable distribution of the drug to patients in need. The Act creates an exemption from criminal prosecution for physicians, as well as for patients and primary caregivers who possess or cultivate marijuana for medicinal purposes with the recommendation or approval of a physician. A "primary caregiver" is a person who has consistently assumed responsibility for the housing, health, or safety of the patient.

Respondents Angel Raich and Diane Monson are California residents who suffer from a variety of serious

medical conditions and have sought to avail themselves of medical marijuana pursuant to the terms of the Compassionate Use Act. They are being treated by licensed, board-certified family practitioners, who have concluded, after prescribing a host of conventional medicines to treat respondents' conditions and to alleviate their associated symptoms, that marijuana is the only drug available that provides effective treatment. Both women have been using marijuana as a medication for several years pursuant to their doctors' recommendation, and both rely heavily on cannabis to function on a daily basis. Indeed, Raich's physician believes that forgoing cannabis treatments would certainly cause Raich excruciating pain and could very well prove fatal.

Respondent Monson cultivates her own marijuana, and ingests the drug in a variety of ways including smoking and using a vaporizer. Respondent Raich, by contrast, is unable to cultivate her own, and thus relies on two caregivers, litigating as "John Does," to provide her with locally grown marijuana at no charge. These caregivers also process the cannabis into hashish or keif, and Raich herself processes some of the marijuana into oils, balms, and foods for consumption.

On August 15, 2002, county deputy sheriffs and agents from the federal Drug Enforcement Administration (DEA) came to Monson's home. After a thorough investigation, the county officials concluded that her use of marijuana was entirely lawful as a matter of California law. Nevertheless, after a 3-hour standoff, the federal agents seized and destroyed all six of her cannabis plants.

Respondents thereafter brought this action against the Attorney General of the United States and the head of the DEA seeking injunctive and declaratory relief prohibiting the enforcement of the federal Controlled Substances Act (CSA). . . .

[Relying on *Lopez* and *Morrison*, the lower courts found for the defendants, having found the federal law to be invalid as applied.] . . .

Respondents in this case do not dispute that passage of the CSA, as part of the Comprehensive Drug Abuse Prevention and Control Act, was well within Congress' commerce power. Brief for Respondents 22, 38. Nor do they contend that any provision or section of the CSA amounts to an unconstitutional exercise of congressional authority. Rather, respondents' challenge is actually quite limited; they argue that the CSA's categorical prohibition of the manufacture and possession of marijuana as applied to the intrastate manufacture and possession of marijuana for medical purposes pursuant to California law exceeds Congress' authority under the Commerce Clause.

Our case law firmly establishes Congress' power to regulate purely local activities that are part of an economic "class of activities" that have a substantial effect on interstate commerce. See, *e.g., Perez*, 402 U.S., at 151; *Wickard v. Filburn*, 317 U.S. 111, 128–129 (1942). As we stated in *Wickard*, "even if appellee's activity be local and though it may not be regarded as commerce, it may still, whatever its nature, be reached by Congress if it exerts a substantial economic effect on interstate commerce." *Id.*, at 125. We have never required Congress to legislate with scientific exactitude. When Congress decides that the "total incidence" of a practice poses a threat to a national market, it may regulate the entire class. See *Perez*, 402 U.S., at 154–155 (quoting *Westfall v. United States*, 274 U.S. 256, 259 (1927) ("[W]hen it is necessary in order to prevent an evil to make the law embrace more than the precise thing to be prevented it may do so.") In this vein, we have reiterated that when "a general regulatory statute bears a substantial relation to commerce, the *de minimis* character of individual instances arising under that statute is of no consequence." *E.g., Lopez*, 514 U.S., at 558 (emphasis deleted) (quoting *Maryland v. Wirtz*, 392 U.S. 183, 196, n. 27 (1968)).

Our decision in *Wickard,* 317 U.S. 111, is of particular relevance. . . .

Wickard thus establishes that Congress can regulate purely intrastate activity that is not itself "commercial," in that it is not produced for sale, if it concludes that failure to regulate that class of activity would undercut the regulation of the interstate market in that commodity.

The similarities between this case and *Wickard* are striking. Like the farmer in *Wickard*, respondents are cultivating, for home consumption, a fungible commodity for which there is an established, albeit illegal, interstate market. Just as the Agricultural Adjustment Act was designed "to control the volume [of wheat] moving in interstate and foreign commerce in order to avoid surpluses . . ." and consequently control the market price, *id.*, at 115, a primary purpose of the CSA is to control the supply and demand of controlled substances in both lawful and unlawful drug markets. See nn. 20–21, *supra*. In *Wickard*, we had no difficulty concluding that Congress had a rational basis for believing that, when viewed in the aggregate, leaving home-consumed wheat outside the regulatory scheme would have a substantial influence on price and market conditions. Here too, Congress had a rational basis for concluding that leaving home-consumed marijuana outside federal control would similarly affect price and market conditions.

More concretely, one concern prompting inclusion of wheat grown for home consumption in the 1938 Act was that rising market prices could draw such wheat into the interstate market, resulting in lower market prices. *Wickard*, 317 U.S., at 128. The parallel concern making it appropriate to include marijuana grown for home consumption in the CSA is the likelihood that the high demand in the interstate market will draw such marijuana into that market. While the diversion of homegrown wheat tended to frustrate the federal interest in stabilizing prices by regulating the volume of commercial transactions in the interstate market, the diversion of homegrown marijuana tends to frustrate the federal interest in eliminating commercial transactions in the interstate market in their entirety. In both cases, the regulation is squarely within Congress' commerce power because production of the commodity meant for home consumption, be it wheat or marijuana, has a substantial effect on supply and demand in the national market for that commodity.

In assessing the scope of Congress' authority under the Commerce Clause, we stress that the task before us is a modest one. We need not determine whether respondents' activities, taken in the aggregate, substantially affect interstate commerce in fact, but only whether a "rational basis" exists for so concluding. Given the enforcement difficulties that attend distinguishing between marijuana cultivated locally and marijuana grown elsewhere, 21 U.S.C. §801(5), and concerns about diversion into illicit channels, we have no difficulty concluding that Congress had a rational basis for believing that failure to regulate the intrastate manufacture and possession of marijuana would leave a gaping hole in the CSA. Thus, as in *Wickard*, when it enacted comprehensive legislation to regulate the interstate market in a fungible commodity, Congress was acting well within its authority to "make all Laws which shall be necessary and proper" to "regulate Commerce . . . among the several States." U.S. Const., Art. I, §8. That the regulation ensnares some purely intrastate activity is of no moment. As we have done many times before, we refuse to excise individual components of that larger scheme.

Respondents also raise a substantive due process claim and seek to avail themselves of the medical necessity defense. These theories of relief were set forth in their complaint but were not reached by the Court of Appeals.

We therefore do not address the question whether judicial relief is available to respondents on these alternative bases. We do note, however, the presence of another avenue of relief. As the Solicitor General confirmed during oral argument, the statute authorizes procedures for the reclassification of Schedule I drugs. But perhaps even more important than these legal avenues is the democratic process, in which the voices of voters allied with these respondents may one day be heard in the halls of Congress. Under the present state of the law, however, the judgment of the Court of Appeals must be vacated. The case is remanded for further proceedings consistent with this opinion.

In 2005, the Court chose not to extend *Lopez* to a California state law that permitted the medical use of marijuana, in contravention of federal law. In *Gonzales v. Raich* (2005) (excerpt above), the Court ruled that, under the Commerce Clause, federal authorities could still prosecute individuals for federal marijuana crimes, even though California had legalized the medicinal use of the substance.

Congressional power under the Commerce Clause is broad. As the nation and world grow more closely connected, more activities will become subject to federal regulation, but congressional authority over commerce is not unlimited. Unquestionably the *Lopez, Printz,* and *Morrison* decisions, for example, require that a true nexus between commerce and a regulated activity must exist. If an activity is not commercial and is entirely intrastate in character, its regulation belongs entirely to the states.

On March 23, 2010, President Barack Obama signed the Patient Protection and Affordable Care Act (PPACA) into law. It was followed seven days later by a second health-care reform bill, the Health Care and Education Reconciliation Act (HCERA). The PPACA and HCERA represent the largest social service reform in the United States since the creation of the social security system in the 1930s. The arena is large with health care representing 15 percent and 20 percent of the U.S. gross national product.

The legislation is huge, both literally and figuratively. The bill, for example, was over 2,400 pages in length. President Obama asserted that the law will expand coverage to tens of millions of people who were previously uninsured, and the Congressional Budget Office estimates that the national deficit will be reduced by over $100 billion in the first ten years and $1.2 trillion in years eleven to twenty.

The laws include expanding Medicaid eligibility, incentives for employers to provide insurance to employees, the creation of health exchanges where the uninsured can secure coverage with subsidies for low-income individuals and families, creation of additional exchanges for small businesses, providing insurance regardless of preexisting conditions, mandatory insurance coverage for the individual, longer periods pharmaceutical companies can market drugs before generics may be marketed, support for medical research, and various taxes and fees on high-income individuals, tanning parlors, and medical and pharmaceutical companies. There are hundreds of other provisions of the law regulating all dimensions of health care.

Implementation of this massive, diverse, and complex policy area is no small task. Although estimates vary, most agree that when done, more than 100 new agencies, boards, commissions, offices, and other entities will be created to implement the bill. Although the precise number is unknown now, there is little doubt that tens of thousands of new federal employees will be required.

Although many agencies will be involved (e.g., Internal Revenue Service, Department of Labor), the U.S. Department of Health and Human Services (HHS) is primarily responsible for implementation and oversight of the PPACA. HHS has announced the creation of several new agencies, boards, and offices to fulfill its mandate, including an Office of Consumer Information and Insurance Oversight, Office of Insurance Programs, Office of Oversight, Office of Health Insurance Exchanges, Office of Consumer Support, Independent Payment Advisory Board, Innovation Center, and Patient-Centered Outcomes Research Institute. New agencies with congressional mandates and new delegations to existing agencies will also mean new regulations. Indeed, the Internal Revenue Service, Department of Labor, and HHS have already promulgated their first set of regulations.

Of course, no policy initiative this large can go unchallenged. The first legal challenges came from a majority of the states. Virginia, for example, is opposed to the law on federalism grounds. It has a statute that explicitly permits its residents to not be insured, in contrast with the PPACA, which mandates coverage. In March 23, 2010, the same day President Obama signed the PPACA into law, Virginia Attorney General Ken Cuccinelli filed suit in federal district court challenging the law's constitutionality. Virginia asserts two constitutional flaws in the PPACA. First, the federal government lacks the authority under the Commerce Clause to require individuals to purchase coverage, the so-called individual mandate. It recognizes in its complaint that the federal government has created social security and Medicaid, but these programs were funded by tax dollars, and Virginia contends that the United States "lacks the political will" to fund health care so it is resorting to mandating coverage and payment to the individual. Second, the United States lacks the authority to mandate coverage when the State of Virginia has contrary law. In essence, Virginia is asserting a Tenth Amendment, or at least the absence of federal authority, argument. Fifteen additional states, led by Florida, filed a separate lawsuit asserting Virginia's first argument but because they do not have contrary legislation, not its second. Another issue concerns taxes and fines, which are provided for in the PPACA. It is clear that Congress possesses both of these authorities under Articles I and XVI of the Constitution, but some people question if they may be used as outlined in the PPACA.

Even though many legal scholars believe the Commerce Clause and federalism arguments will fail, citing *Helvering v. Davis* and *Stewart Machine Co. v. Davis,* the federal trial judge hearing the Virginia case issued an opinion on December 13, 2010, holding the law unconstitutional in regard to individual mandate. The Virginia federal trial court acknowledged that precedent empowered Congress to regulate economic activity that, when aggregated, impacted the market and that precedent permitted federal regulation of non-economic activity that is closely related to the targeted market. But there is no precedent to permit Congress to regulate inactivity, nor is there precedent that empowers Congress to force individuals to engage in economic activity (e.g., to purchase health insurance). While the Court found for Virginia, it denied Virginia's request to stop implementation of the law.[42] The United States appealed the decision that Congress exceeded its authority under the Commerce Clause, and Virginia appealed the court's refusal to stay implementation of the law. Both appeals were pending at the time of the writing of this book.

In a similar challenge by 26 states and a couple of private parties, the Eleventh Circuit Court of Appeals also ruled that the imposition of the individual mandate exceeded Congress's authority under the Commerce Clause in August 2011. The Court upheld other provisions of the Act, and unlike the trial court, which declared the entire law unconstitutional because it found the individual mandate provision to be inseverable from the remainder of the law, the court of appeals ruled that the individual mandate provision could be severed. In its analysis, the appellate court found that both health care and insurance have traditionally been treated as a police power, and accordingly, within the regulatory authority of the states. In its conclusion, the judges penned:

> [T]he individual mandate exceeds Congress's enumerated commerce power and is unconstitutional. This economic mandate represents a wholly novel and potentially unbounded assertion of congressional authority: the ability to compel Americans to purchase an expensive health insurance product they have elected not to buy, and to make them re-purchase that insurance product every month for their entire lives. We have not found any generally applicable, judicially enforceable limiting principle that would permit us to uphold the mandate without obliterating the boundaries inherent in the system of enumerated congressional powers. "Uniqueness" is not a constitutional principle in any antecedent Supreme Court decision. The individual mandate also finds no refuge in the aggregation doctrine, for decisions to *abstain* from the purchase of a product or service, whatever their cumulative effect, lack a sufficient nexus to commerce.[43]

The Eleventh Circuit Court also rejected the suggestion that Congress could enact the individual mandate, and the accompanying fine on individuals for failing to secure insurance, under its taxing authorities in Article I and the Sixteenth Amendment,

---

FEDERAL COMMERCE POWER—SUMMARY

Article I, Section 8, clause 3 provides that Congress shall have the power to "regulate Commerce with foreign Nations, and among the several States, and with the Indian Tribes."
This power may be exercised over

1. The channels of interstate commerce

2. The instrumentalities of interstate commerce

3. Persons or things in interstate commerce, even though from intrastate commerce

4. Activities having substantial relation to interstate commerce, including activities that substantially affect interstate commerce

---

FIGURE 4-2
Federal commerce power—summary

finding the individual mandate to be a regulatory penalty, not a tax. The significance of the law, the legal questions it raises, and the opposition from the states are all factors that will likely propel one or more cases before the Supreme Court for final resolution.

See Figure 4-2 for a summary of the elements of the congressional commerce power.

4.6 TAXING, SPENDING, AND BORROWING POWERS

For most of the nation's early history, revenues were generated through customs laws (tariffs). Congress imposed the first income tax to finance the Civil War. Various taxes were imposed until the Supreme Court held the federal income tax unconstitutional in *Pollock v. Farmers Loan & Trust Co.*[44] Several proposals to amend the Constitution to allow a federal tax were proposed. One finally passed Congress and was ratified in 1913, as the Sixteenth Amendment. Today, the federal income tax is firmly established. Other important constitutional provisions provide that Congress has the authority to collect taxes and import duties and that all import duties must be uniform throughout the United States.[45] The Constitution also provides that there shall be no federal tax on articles exported from any state.[46]

One issue that the Court has had to deal with in the taxing area is whether Congress may use the federal taxing power to regulate for the general welfare of the people. The Court has generally approved of the use of the taxing power to achieve police power objectives. Again, the Tenth Amendment does not delegate this type of regulation to the states exclusively. Other constitutional provisions act to limit the taxing power. For example, if a taxing requirement creates a "real and appreciable" possibility of incrimination by the taxpayer, then it is violative of the Fifth Amendment's protection against self-incrimination. Thus, a taxing statute that requires a taxpayer to disclose and pay taxes on money earned from illegal activity (e.g., sale of drugs), but does not protect the information from disclosure to law enforcement officials, is unconstitutional.

The authority of Congress to spend is also found in the Constitution. Article I, Section 8, clause 1, states that Congress shall have the power to "pay the Debts and provide for the common Defense and general Welfare of the United States." What is the limit of federal spending power? Unquestionably, Congress may spend in furtherance of any of its enumerated powers, such as its power over commerce. May it spend for the general welfare? Again, Congress has broad authority and appropriations will not be invalidated because they concern the general welfare.

Even more, the federal government has used its spending power to coerce the states into complying with federal policies, including those with police power objectives. It does this by attaching conditions to grants to states. If a state does not comply with the conditions, it loses the money. The national fifty-five-mile-per-hour speed limit was achieved in this manner.

This use of the spending power has been approved by the Supreme Court. In *South Dakota v. Dole,*[47] a federal law that withheld highway funds from states that did not prohibit the purchase and consumption of alcohol by individuals under twenty-one years of age was validated. The state objected, claiming that the repeal of prohibition (Twenty-First Amendment) left the states with exclusive control over the issue. The Court rejected the claim, holding that even though Congress could not regulate the subject directly, it could do so indirectly through its taxing and spending powers. State claims that these conditional grants are violative of the Tenth Amendment have been consistently rejected. There is a limit, however, as seen in the 2011 Eleventh Circuit Court of Appeal's decision striking down the individual mandate provision of the PPACA discussed in the last section, where it was held that Congress may not disguise a regulation as a tax in an attempt to regulate a subject over which it has no other form of jurisdiction (e.g., commerce).

The Constitution delegates other fiscal powers to Congress. The power to coin money belongs to the national government, as does the power to punish counterfeiters.[48] The power to coin money includes the power to establish national banks.[49] Congress may borrow money on behalf of the nation,[50] and is authorized to establish national bankruptcy laws.[51]

4.7 INTERNATIONAL, WAR, AND MILITARY POWERS

Congress and the president share authority over foreign, international, and military affairs. The Constitution does not specifically define what is presidential and what is congressional power. The relationship is an "arena of conflict."

The Constitution is clear in creating a civilian led military. It provides that the president is the commander-in-chief of the military and is responsible for all forms of diplomacy, including the negotiation of treaties. These powers are balanced by the following powers that are expressly delegated to Congress in Article I, Section 8:

1. Establishing duties and imports (clause 1).
2. Regulating commerce with foreign nations (clause 3).
3. Establishing uniform rules of naturalization (clause 4).
4. Punishing crimes on the high seas and offenses against the law of nations (clause 10).
5. Declaring war, granting letters of marque and reprisal, and making rules concerning captures on land and water (clause 11).
6. Establishing rules and regulations to govern the U.S. armed forces (clause 14).
7. Creating and regulating the national militia (clauses 15 and 16).

Article I, Section 9, clause 1, further provides that Congress shall regulate immigration.

These provisions are clear in delegating to Congress the authority to regulate commerce with foreign nations. Also, Congress alone possesses the power to declare war, although, in reality, presidents have initiated most military encounters without a congressional declaration of war. Congress regulates the military by creating the rules under which it operates, including disciplinary laws, but the president is the commander-in-chief. The relationship between the president and the Congress concerning warmaking is discussed in Chapter 6.

The power to declare war is much broader than simply making declarations. Congress is empowered to prepare the nation for war and to promote war efforts generally. Accordingly, Congress may demand conscription, seize industries and private property necessary to war efforts, close nonessential businesses, establish price controls and rent controls,[52] and ration foods and supplies. The internment of "enemy aliens" residing in the United States has also been approved by the Court.[53]

The war power extends to postwar recovery efforts as well. For example, laws encouraging the reemployment of returning service personnel would be permissible.

4.8 EMERGENCY POWERS

In addition to the national military, the Constitution grants Congress the authority to provide for the use of state militias (National Guard units) to suppress insurrections and defend the nation. In addition, Congress may regulate the organization, arming, and disciplining of state militias.[54] This includes delegating to the president the power to call militias into active duty outside the United States without the consent of state executive officials. Federal power is supreme in terms of military affairs.[55]

In times of unrest, Congress may declare martial law in the affected areas of the nation. Congress alone possesses the authority to suspend habeas corpus. Article I, Section 9, clause 2, states: "[t]he privilege of the Writ of Habeas Corpus shall not be suspended, unless when in Cases of Rebellion or Invasion the Public Safety may require it."

The greater the emergency, the more governmental action may encroach upon civil liberties. For example, in *Korematsu v. United States,* the Supreme Court upheld the actions taken against Japanese Americans during World War II.[56] Military officials, under the authority of statute and executive order, excluded people of Japanese ancestry, even U.S. citizens, from certain West Coast areas, established curfews, and interned many in camps. The action was justified, the Court said, by the fear of espionage, sabotage, West Coast invasion by the Japanese Empire, and the disloyalty by some persons of Japanese ancestry on the West Coast.

4.9 INVESTIGATORY POWERS

To acquire information about the subjects it regulates, Congress conducts investigations. Hearings are a part of the investigatory function. At congressional hearings, witnesses testify and other evidence is received. Hearings educate both members of Congress and the public. The data received are often incorporated into the official record (committee reports, etc.) and are sometimes considered by courts when deciding legislative intent.

Although not expressly stated in the Constitution, a power to conduct hearings is implied in the legislative power. Further, the power to subpoena witnesses, documents, and other evidence is held by both houses of Congress. This power may be delegated to committees and subcommittees.

The power to subpoena carries enforcement powers with it. Recalcitrant witnesses can be held in contempt and jailed by Congress. Congress may conduct the contempt trial and punish witnesses without referring the matter to a court. Regardless, Congress has enacted a statute providing that its contempt cases are to be referred to a federal court for disposition. Once referred, a defendant is entitled to all the rights and privileges afforded to any criminal defendant in federal court, even if the right would not have been extended to the defendant if tried by Congress. Today, Congress may punish a contemnor under either its inherent power or this statute.

In addition to punishing witnesses who refuse to testify, Congress may punish other misbehaviors as well. Disruption of congressional proceedings and perjury are examples.

There are limitations upon the congressional investigatory power and, accordingly, its contempt power. First, Congress may not extend an investigation into a matter over which it has no authority to regulate. Therefore, attempts to expose the private affairs of individuals when there is no possibility of producing legislation is unlawful. However, Congress does have the authority to investigate corruption and incompetence in the other branches.[57]

Second, a committee can punish a witness for refusing to testify only if the appropriate house of Congress has authorized the committee to investigate the subject at issue. Subcommittees must be empowered by the full committee, which is empowered by the appropriate house of Congress.

Third, certain constitutional rights limit the congressional investigatory power. The privilege against self-incrimination, found in the Fifth Amendment, limits the authority of Congress to extract information from witnesses. The committee may inquire into why a defendant believes that his testimony is potentially incriminating in order to determine whether a claim is legitimate. A committee may not, however, demand that a question be answered in order to determine its legitimacy. Also, a Fifth Amendment claim may be overcome by providing **use immunity** to a witness.

use immunity
A guaranty given to a person that if he or she testifies against others, his or her testimony will not be used against him or her if he or she is prosecuted for involvement in the crime.

The First Amendment also restricts the power of Congress to investigate. Generally, Congress may not punish a witness for refusing to answer questions concerning speech, religion, political beliefs, or association. However, if the public interest in obtaining the information outweighs the individual's interest in nondisclosure, a witness can be compelled to testify. In one case, for example, a witness was legitimately required to answer inquiries about his Communist Party affiliations.[58]

The Fourth Amendment's protection against unreasonable searches and seizures applies to congressional investigations. Therefore, a subpoena that is not supported by probable cause, is overly broad, or is otherwise unreasonable is invalid.

Of course, the due process clause of the Fifth Amendment requires that all actions by investigatory committees be fair. Questions must be clear, what is required of a potential contemnor-witness must be articulated, and the witness should be advised that a refusal to answer may lead to a contempt citation.

Finally, the power of Congress to investigate is limited by structural and institutional forces. Separation of powers principles prevent congressional investigations that delve into matters belonging exclusively to the executive or judicial branch. For example, Congress may not investigate individual court cases. Congress may investigate such cases when considering larger issues, such as whether tort reform is necessary.

4.10 CONFIRMATION AND IMPEACHMENT POWERS

4.10(a) Appointment and Confirmation

The president, vice-president, and members of Congress are elected officials. Lower executive officials, such as cabinet members and ambassadors, are appointed. Federal judges are also appointed. The appointment process includes presidential nomination and Senate confirmation. Or, in the words of the Constitution, the president shall "nominate . . . by and with the Advice and Consent of the Senate."[59]

Current Supreme Court justice Elena Kagan at her confirmation hearing
Kristoffer Tripplaar/ Sipa Press/Newscom

The Senate's role in the appointment process is hotly debated. Some commentators would limit the Senate's role to objective evaluation of the nominee's qualifications and character. According to this view, if a nominee is of good character and is qualified, she should be confirmed regardless of her political beliefs. Other people believe that the Senate should play a more active role and that it may appropriately consider a nominee's political beliefs. In the context of judicial nominations, the issue is whether a judge possesses the favored legal philosophy. The history of the appointments clause sheds little light on the subject, and the issue is not likely to be resolved soon.

In recent years, the process has been politicized. The confirmation hearings of Robert Bork (not confirmed to the Supreme Court because he was perceived as too legally conservative), Douglas Ginsburg (nomination to Supreme Court withdrawn after he admitted to marijuana use), Clarence Thomas (confirmed as associate justice after controversial hearings wherein he was accused of sexual harassment), and Dr. Henry Foster (confirmed as surgeon general after a controversy centering around abortion) are examples.

4.10(b) Impeachment

Once confirmed, most executive employees may be removed by the president. In addition, they may be removed by **impeachment.** Other than death and retirement, impeachment is the only method of removing a federal judge. (Figure 4-3 illustrates the impeachment process.)

impeachment
The constitutional process by which high elected officers of the United States, including the president, may be removed from office. The accusation (articles of impeachment) is made by the House of Representatives and tried by the Senate, which sits as an impeachment court. Under the Constitution, the grounds for impeachment are "treason, bribery, or other high crimes and misdemeanors."

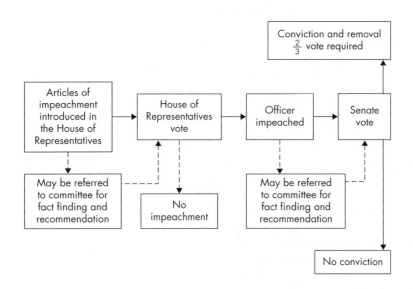

IMPEACHMENT PROCESS

Article II, Section 4, provides that the president, vice-president, and all civil officers of the United States shall be removed from office on impeachment for, and conviction of, treason, bribery, or other high crimes and misdemeanors.

Article III, Section 1, states that federal judges shall hold their offices during times of good behavior.

Article I, Section 2, vests the power of impeachment in the House of Representatives.

Article I, Section 3, vests the power to try impeachment cases in the Senate. Article III, Section 2, makes it clear that there is *no* right to jury in impeachment cases.

This procedure may occur prior to, after, or simultaneous with any related criminal trial of the officer.

FIGURE 4-3
The impeachment process

Article I, Section 2, clause 5, vests the power of impeachment in the House of Representatives, and Article I, Section 3, clause 6, gives the Senate the responsibility of trying impeachment cases. *Impeachment* is a charge against a public official. Conviction in impeachment cases results in removal from public office. Technically, an official is impeached once charged by the House of Representatives. In common usage, though, the term is used to describe the removal of public officials who have been convicted in the Senate.

The House and Senate may delegate the responsibility of conducting impeachment investigations and hearing evidence to committees. The Constitution requires that a vote of the full house be taken, and a two-thirds majority is required for conviction in the Senate. Impeachment decisions are political questions and are not reviewable by courts. See *Nixon v. United States*, a case involving an impeached and convicted federal judge, in Chapter 4 for a discussion of the political question doctrine in this context. Also, see Figure 4-4a for the actual articles of impeachment against President Nixon, as recommended by the House Judiciary Committee in July 1974.

Article II, Section 4, provides that the "President, Vice-President and all civil Officers of the United States shall be removed from Office on Impeachment for, and Conviction of Treason, Bribery, or other high Crimes and Misdemeanors." In addition to the president and vice-president, any federal officer who undergoes the nomination and confirmation process may be impeached. This includes ambassadors, cabinet officers, and judges. Members of Congress may not be impeached, as they are not "civil officers." They are subject to exclusion and expulsion, however, by their house.

What qualifies as a high crime or misdemeanor is not well defined. It is generally believed that this phrase includes more than violations of criminal law. Said another way, Congress decides what a high crime or misdemeanor is without any necessary reference to the criminal laws. Article II, Section 2, clause 1, exempts impeachments from the pardon power of the president.

Article I, Section 3, clause 7, limits the power of impeachment to removal from office. It further provides that "the Party convicted shall nevertheless be liable and subject to Indictment, Trial, Judgment, and Punishment, according to Law." Alcee Hastings, a federal judge, was acquitted of crimes before he was impeached. He appealed his conviction, claiming that the Constitution requires removal before criminal trial. His claim was rejected by the appellate court.[60] It appears, therefore, that the two events may occur in any order and at any time. There is, however, contrary original intent evidence. Alexander Hamilton, for example, penned in *The Federalist No. 69,* "The President of the United States would be liable to be impeached, tried, and, upon conviction of treason, bribery, or other high crimes or misdemeanors, removed from office; and would *afterwards be liable to prosecution and punishment* in the ordinary course of law" [emphasis added].

Between the adoption of the Constitution and 1994, there were seventeen impeachments, including one president, one senator, a Supreme Court justice, and twelve lower-court judges.[61] Not all the impeached officials were convicted. President Andrew Johnson, for example, was impeached but not convicted. The same is true of the only justice impeached, Samuel Chase. President Richard Nixon resigned after articles of impeachment were introduced in the House but before they were acted upon. (See Figure 4-3.) Of the thirteen federal judges impeached, only seven were convicted.

Conviction of an official prior to removal creates interesting legal and political problems. District judge Harry Claiborne was convicted of tax fraud and sentenced to two years in prison. He refused to resign and was imprisoned for five months before Congress removed him from office. He was the first sitting federal judge to be imprisoned. The possible legal problems presented by having a federal judge incarcerated in a federal prison are obvious. On the political side, federal judges who are not removed, but are convicted of crimes and sentenced to prison, continue to receive their pay and benefits. Although constitutionally required, such circumstances engender public disrespect for the judiciary and government generally.

**ARTICLES OF IMPEACHMENT AGAINST PRESIDENT RICHARD M. NIXON
RECOMMENDED BY THE HOUSE JUDICIARY COMMITTEE**

Resolved, That Richard M. Nixon, President of the United States, is impeached for high crimes and misdemeanors, and that the following articles of impeachment be exhibited to the Senate:

Articles of impeachment exhibited by the House of Representatives of the United States of America in the name of itself and of all of the people of the United States of America, against Richard M. Nixon, President of the United States of America, in maintenance and support of its impeachment against him for high crimes and misdemeanors.

Article I

In his conduct of the office of President of the United States, Richard M. Nixon, in violation of his constitutional oath faithfully to execute the office of President of the United States and, to the best of his ability, preserve, protect, and defend the Constitution of the United States, and in violation of his constitutional duty to take care that the laws be faithfully executed, has prevented, obstructed, and impeded the administration of justice, in that:

On June 17, 1972, and prior thereto, agents of the Committee for the Re-election of the President committed unlawful entry of the headquarters of the Democratic National Committee in Washington, District of Columbia, for the purpose of securing political intelligence. Subsequent thereto, Richard M. Nixon, using the powers of his high office, engaged, personally and through his subordinates and agents, in a course of conduct or plan designed to delay, impede, and obstruct the investigation of such unlawful entry; to cover up, conceal and protect those responsible; and to conceal the existence and scope of other unlawful covert activities.

The means used to implement this course of conduct or plan included one or more of the following:

1. Making or causing to be made false or misleading statements to lawfully authorized investigative officers and employees of the United States;

2. Withholding relevant and material evidence of information from lawfully authorized investigative officers and employees of the United States;

3. Approving, condoning, acquiescing in, and counseling witnesses with respect to the giving of false or misleading statements to lawfully authorized investigative officers and employees of the United States and false or misleading testimony in duly instituted judicial and congressional proceedings;

4. Interfering or endeavoring to interfere with the conduct of investigations by the Department of Justice of the United States, the Federal Bureau of Investigation, the Office of Watergate Special Prosecution Force, and Congressional committees;

5. Approving, condoning, and acquiescing in, the surreptitious payment of substantial sums of money for the purpose of obtaining the silence or influencing the testimony of witness, potential witnesses or individuals who participated in such illegal entry and other illegal activities;

6. Endeavoring to misuse the Central Intelligence Agency, an agency of the United States;

7. Disseminating information received from officers of the Department of Justice of the United States to subjects of investigations conducted by lawfully authorized investigative officers and employees of the United States, for the purpose of aiding and assisting such subjects in their attempts to avoid criminal liability;

8. Making false or misleading public statements for the purpose of deceiving the people of the United States into believing that a thorough and complete investigation had been conducted with respect to allegations of misconduct on the part of personnel of the executive branch of the United States and personnel of the Committee for the Re-election of the President, and that there was no involvement of such personnel in such misconduct; or

9. Endeavoring to cause prospective defendants, and individuals duly tried and convicted, to expect favored treatment and consideration in return for their silence or false testimony, or rewarding individuals for their silence or false testimony.

In all of this, Richard M. Nixon has acted in a manner contrary to his trust as President and subversive of constitutional government, to the great prejudice of the cause of law and justice and to the manifest injury of the people of the United States.

Wherefore Richard M. Nixon, by such conduct, warrants impeachment and trial, and removal from office.

Article II

Using the powers of the office of president of the United States, Richard M. Nixon, in violation of his constitutional oath faithfully to execute the office of president of the United States and, to the best of his ability, preserve, protect and defend the Constitution of the United States, and in disregard of his constitutional duty to take care that the laws be faithfully executed, has repeatedly engaged in conduct violating the constitutional rights of citizens, impairing the due and proper administration of justice and the conduct of lawful inquires, or contravening the laws governing agencies of the executive branch and the purposes of these agencies.

FIGURE 4-4
Articles of impeachment against President Richard M. Nixon

This conduct has included one or more of the following:

1. He has, acting personally and through his subordinated and agents, endeavored to obtain from the Internal Revenue Service, in violation of the constitutional rights of citizens, confidential information contained in income tax returns for purposes not authorized by law and to cause, in violation of the constitutional rights of citizens, income tax audits or other income tax investigations to be initiated or conducted in a discriminatory manner.

2. He misused the Federal Bureau of Investigation, the Secret Service and other executive personnel in violation or disregard of the constitutional rights of citizens by directing or authorizing such agencies or personnel to conduct or continue electronic surveillance or other investigations for purposes unrelated to national security, the enforcement of laws or any other lawful function of his office; and he did direct the concealment of certain records made by the Federal Bureau of Investigation of electronic surveillance.

3. He has, acting personally and through his subordinates and agents, in violation or disregard of the constitutional rights of citizens authorized and permitted to be maintained a secret investigative unit within the office of the president, financed in part with money derived from campaign contributions to him, which unlawfully utilized the resources of the Central Intelligence Agency, engaged in covert and unlawful activities and attempted to prejudice the constitutional right of an accused to a fair trial.

4. He has failed to take care that the laws were faithfully executed by failing to act when he knew or had reason to know that his close subordinates endeavored to impede and frustrate lawful inquiries by duly constituted executive, judicial and legislative entities concerning the unlawful entry into the headquarters of the Democratic National Committee and the cover-up thereof, and concerning other unlawful activities including those relating to the confirmation of Richard Kleindienst as attorney general of the United States, the electronic surveillance of private citizens, the break-in into the office of Dr. Lewis Fielding and the campaign financing practices of the Committee to Re-elect the President.

5. In disregard of the rule of law, he knowingly misused the executive power by interfering with agencies of the executive branch, including the Federal Bureau of Investigation, the Criminal Division and of Office of Watergate Special Prosecution Force, of the Department of Justice and the Central Intelligence Agency, in violation of his duty to take care that the laws be faithfully executed.

In all of this, Richard M. Nixon has acted in a manner contrary to his trust as president and subversive of constitutional government, to the great prejudice of the cause of law and justice and to the manifest injury of the people of the United States.

Wherefore Richard M. Nixon, by such conduct, warrants impeachment and trial and removal from office.

Article III

In his conduct of the office of president of the United States, Richard M. Nixon, contrary to his oath faithfully to execute the office of president of the United States and, to the best of his ability, preserve, protect and defend the Constitution of the United States, and in violation of his constitutional duty to take care that the laws be faithfully executed, has failed without lawful cause or excuse to produce papers and things as directed by duly authorized subpoenas issued by the Committee on the Judiciary of the House of Representatives on April 11, 1974; May 15, 1974; May 30, 1974, and June 24, 1974, and willfully disobeyed such subpoenas.

The subpoenaed papers and things were deemed necessary by the committee in order to resolve by direct evidence fundamental, factual questions relating to presidential direction, knowledge or approval of actions demonstrated by other evidence to be substantial grounds for impeachment of the president.

In refusing to produce these papers and things Richard M. Nixon, substituting his judgment as to what materials were necessary for the inquiry, interposed the powers of the presidency against the lawful subpoenas of the House of Representatives, thereby assuming to himself functions and judgments necessary to the exercise of the sole power of impeachment vested by the Constitution in the House of Representatives.

In all of this, Richard M. Nixon has acted in a manner contrary to his trust as president and subversive of constitutional government, to the great prejudice of the cause of law and justice and the manifest injury of the people of the United States.

Wherefore, Richard M. Nixon by such conduct, warrants impeachment and trial and removal from office.

* * *

FIGURE 4-4
Continued

FAMOUS IMPEACHMENTS

Three of the most famous impeachments in the United States were those of Justice Samuel Chase, President Andrew Johnson, and President William J. Clinton.

Samuel Chase was impeached by the House of Representatives in 1805. Samuel Chase, a Federalist, had a history of service to the nation. In addition to serving as a Supreme Court justice, he was a signer of the Declaration of Independence. Justice Chase, while acting as a district judge, made statements from the bench attacking anti-Federalist (Republican) policies. Eight charges were brought against Justice Chase arising from these statements. His Senate trial lasted one month. He was acquitted by one vote. Interestingly, Aaron Burr, the vice-president of the United States, presided over Chase's trial. At the time of the trial, Aaron Burr was under indictment in two states (New York and New Jersey) for the death of Alexander Hamilton, whom he killed in a duel. Aaron Burr was later tried and acquitted. Both he and Chase were represented by the same lawyer, Luther Martin.

President Andrew Johnson was impeached by the House of Representatives in 1868. Johnson had been President Lincoln's vice-president and assumed the presidency upon Lincoln's assassination. Johnson's reconstruction program was bitterly opposed by Republican members of Congress. Two bills that had the effect of limiting presidential power were vetoed by Johnson. Both vetoes were overridden by two-thirds majorities in both houses. One was the Tenure of Office Act, which restricted the president's power to remove federal officials. When Johnson attempted to remove the secretary of war, Edwin Stanton, who was a Republican sympathizer, the House of Representatives impeached Johnson. Eleven articles of impeachment were filed, most involving the removal of Stanton. On the first charge, Johnson prevailed by one vote. The Senate adjourned for ten days, and when it reconvened, votes on the second and third articles were taken. Johnson was again acquitted. The impeachment was abandoned and votes were never held on the remaining articles.

Impeachment of President Andrew Johnson
Antonio Abrignani/Shutterstock

President William J. Clinton was impeached by the House of Representatives in 1998 for obstruction of justice and perjury, arising out of his testimony in a civil suit filed against him by Paula Jones. Ms. Jones alleged sexual discrimination against President Clinton when he was governor of Arkansas. He was alleged to have committed perjury about an alleged affair he had with a White House intern, Monica Lewinsky. With fifty-five votes to convict on the perjury charge and fifty votes to convict on the obstruction of justice charge, the Senate failed to convict by the required two-thirds. Later, the federal district judge hearing the Jones case found President Clinton in contempt of court for failing to comply with her orders. Subsequently, President Clinton settled the Jones lawsuit for $850,000, agreed to relinquish his right to practice law in Arkansas for five years, and resigned his admission to practice before the U.S. Supreme Court after having his admission suspended by that Court.

These three impeachment trials stand as evidence that impeachment is intended, as the Constitution states, for high crimes and misdemeanors. Scholars generally agree that the impeachments of both Chase and Johnson were politically motivated. Many believe that is true of the Clinton impeachment as well. Today, it is accepted, in part because of the failures in these cases, that public officials may not be impeached for political reasons. Rather, the political remedy lies in the ballot box.

Sources: William Rehnquist, *Grand Inquests* (William Morrow 1992); Gene Smith, *High Crimes and Misdemeanors* (William Morrow 1977).

4.11 INITIATION OF CONSTITUTIONAL AMENDMENTS

Article 5 of the Constitution states, in part:

> The Congress, whenever two thirds of both Houses shall deem it necessary, shall propose Amendments to this Constitution, or, on the Application of the Legislatures of two thirds of the several States, shall call a Convention for proposing Amendments, which, in either Case, shall be valid to all Intents and Purposes, as part of this Constitution, when ratified by the Legislatures of three fourths of the several States, or by Conventions in three fourths thereof, as the one or the other Mode of Ratification may be proposed by the Congress. . . .

Accordingly, there are two methods of initiating a constitutional amendment. Congressional resolution is the first. Two-thirds majorities in both houses of Congress are required. The president does not play a role in this process. Second, with two-thirds of the state legislatures or more, a convention can be convened to propose amendments. To date, initiation by Congress is the only method that has been successfully used to initiate amendments.

Regardless of which method of proposal is employed, Congress is empowered to decide the method of ratification. There are two methods: by concurrence of three-fourths of the state legislatures or by conventions in three-fourths of the states.

Congress holds considerable authority in the amendment process. It may establish a time limit for ratification of a proposal, regardless of the method of proposal, and it is empowered to decide whether an amendment has been ratified.

There are twenty-seven amendments to the Constitution. The twenty-seventh, ratified in 1992, provides that Congress may increase its pay in future congressional terms, but not in the present term. This amendment was part of the original twelve amendments of 1789. This and one other were not ratified, but the remaining ten were and are known as the Bill of Rights. No time limit was placed on ratification, and the Twenty-Seventh Amendment now holds the record for longest ratification waiting period, having been ratified 203 years after its proposal.

The preceding amendment, the twenty-sixth, holds the opposite record; that is, its ratification was the fastest ever. The Twenty-Sixth Amendment lowered the voting age in federal and state elections to eighteen. The amendment was, in part, a response to World War II, the Korean Conflict, and a Supreme Court decision. Many Americans, including President Eisenhower and Senator Randolph (who had urged a change in law since World War II), believed that if the nation could require eighteen-year-old men to risk their lives at war, they should be empowered to vote for their political leaders. In 1970, Congress enacted legislation lowering the voting age to eighteen for both federal and state elections. The Supreme Court held, in *Oregon v. Mitchell*,[62] that Congress could lower the voting age for federal elections, but not state and local elections. Within three months of the Court's decision in *Oregon v. Mitchell*, an amendment was introduced in Congress to change the law established in that case. Three months after the proposal was sent to the states, the needed three-fourths of the states ratified the proposal. So, on June 30, 1971, the franchise was extended to eighteen-year-old citizens.[63]

By the mid-1990s, over 10,000 proposals to amend the Constitution had been introduced in Congress. Individual states have called for constitutional conventions over four hundred times.[64] Proposals have spanned the spectrum, including over fifty proposals to prohibit polygamy; hundreds to prohibit abortion or to declare that life begins at conception; to prohibit duels; to mandate a balanced budget; to prohibit child labor; to allow school prayer; to change the name of the United States of America to the United States of the World;[65] and to establish a Court of the Union, comprised of State Supreme Court justices, that would have the authority to review and reverse Supreme Court decisions.[66]

Four amendments have been adopted to reverse constitutional decisions of the Supreme Court:

1. The Eleventh Amendment, which provides for state immunity in federal court. Enacted in response to *Chisholm v. Georgia*.[67]
2. The Fourteenth Amendment, which provides for due process and equal protection in the states. Enacted, partly, in response to *Dred Scott v. Sandford*.[68]
3. The Sixteenth Amendment, which provides for the federal income tax. Enacted in response to *Pollock v. Farmer's Loan & Trust Co.*,[69] in which the Court ruled the federal income tax unconstitutional.
4. The Twenty-Sixth Amendment, which provides that all individuals eighteen years of age and older possess the right to vote in state and national elections. Enacted in response to *Oregon v. Mitchell*.[70]

One amendment has been ratified to repeal another. The Eighteenth Amendment's prohibition of alcohol (1919) was repealed by the Twenty-First Amendment (1933). Amendments may concern any subject, with one exception. The final clause of Article V states, "no State, without its consent, shall be deprived of its equal Suffrage in the Senate." This provision creates an interesting paradox: May the Constitution be amended to allow inequal suffrage amendments without individual state consent? On the one hand, a literal reading leads to the conclusion that under no circumstances can a state's suffrage be changed without its consent. On the other hand, it is possible to circumvent this amendment by amending it, permitting state suffrage to be changed pursuant to normal amendment procedures. If this is accepted, the state suffrage provision is rendered meaningless. There is no case law directly examining the meaning of this provision at this time.

4.12 POWER OVER FEDERAL COURTS

Article III grants Congress considerable authority over the federal judiciary. Section 1, for example, establishes the Supreme Court, but leaves the creation of all other courts to Congress. This power is first mentioned in Article I, Section 8, clause 9. If Congress had wished, the Supreme Court would be the only federal court.

Section 2, clause 2, then grants Congress the authority to make exceptions to the appellate jurisdiction of the Supreme Court. The precise contours of this provision have not been defined. Recall from *Marbury v. Madison* that Congress may not extend or restrict the jurisdiction of a federal court beyond the limits of the Constitution. For example, Congress may not give the Supreme Court original jurisdiction where it has none under the Constitution. See Chapter 3 for a complete discussion of Congress's power over the judicial branch.

4.13 FEDERAL PROPERTY, TERRITORIES, AND NATIVE AMERICANS

Congress may control, by appropriate legislation, the purchase and sale of property. It may also provide for the use of eminent domain; however, whenever the federal government takes property from a person, the Fifth Amendment demands just compensation.

Congress may regulate federal properties, including establishing criminal laws that apply on these properties. Some properties are held by the federal government exclusively; others are concurrently held with the states. In many instances, the federal government enters into agreements with states and localities that provide for the application of local laws, as well as for local law enforcement. Accordingly, local and state police agencies are responsible for enforcing federal, state, and local laws in many federal lands.

Article IV, Section 3, clause 2, delegates to Congress the power to "dispose of and make all needful Rules and Regulations respecting the Territory or other Property belonging to the United States." This includes the power to acquire, dispose of, establish governments in, and tax territories.

There are many forms of affiliation with the United States. A *territory* is an area that has a political affiliation with the United States, but it is not a state. A people, or geographical area, may be a territory, commonwealth, or free association state.

Territories may be *unorganized;* that is, no specific statute establishes a territorial government. In such cases, the president of the United States possesses the authority to establish laws and institutions in the territory. American Samoa is an example of an unorganized territory.

A territory may also be *organized.* To be organized, Congress must establish and provide for territorial government by statute, known as the organic act. Typically, organic act provides for a tripartite government resembling that of the United States, and it also recognizes individual rights similar to those found in the Bill of Rights. Once this occurs, the president loses the authority to regulate such matters. Rather, congressional action is required. Because it is more difficult to obtain the necessary majority in Congress to enact laws than it is for the president to act unilaterally, organized territories are thought to enjoy greater independence than unorganized territories. Puerto Rico, Guam, and the Commonwealth of the Northern Marianas Islands are examples of organized territories.

The extent to which the Constitution of the United States applies to territories varies, and the determination of the Constitution's reach into any particular territory is complex and not well defined. The Supreme Court has held that the extent to which the U.S. Constitution applies in a territory is Congress's decision. If a territory is *incorporated*, then the Constitution is fully applicable. If unincorporated, the Court has held that the Constitution is applicable, lest Congress would be without its authority to regulate the area, but only "fundamental rights" are applied. A territory is incorporated if Congress has made clear its intention of extending statehood to the territory at some future date.[71]

Today, all U.S. territories are unincorporated. The last two incorporated territories were Alaska and Hawaii. As to what rights are fundamental, the Court has rejected the fundamental rights definition used elsewhere (e.g., due process) in constitutional analysis. Sensitive that the application of some rights could be excessively disruptive to an indigenous culture, the Court has held that a right may not be extended to a territory if it is *impractical and anomalous*. Using this test, the Supreme Court refused to extend jury trials to one territory and to strike down indigenous customs concerning the ownership and use of land that would not survive equal protection scrutiny in an incorporated territory or elsewhere in the United States. A lower court said in the latter case, "Bill of Rights was not intended to interfere with our international obligations. Nor was it intended to operate as a genocide pact for diverse native cultures . . . Its bold purpose was to protect minority rights, not to enforce homogeneity."

The term *commonwealth*, which should not be confused with its use for certain U.S. states, is sometimes used to describe territories. From a constitutional perspective, this descriptor is not very useful. In most instances, such as Puerto Rico and Commonwealth of Northern Marianas Islands, it refers to a form of organized territory where the people of the territory have been more involved in the creation of the territory than in others. The significant legal classifications are organized/unorganized and incorporated/unincorporated.

The most detached relationship is one of *free association.* The Federated States of Micronesia, the Republic of the Marshall Islands, and the Republic of Palau are examples of freely associated states. Freely associated states are sovereign and self-governing, that is, free to develop and enforce their own domestic laws and policies. The U.S. Constitution is not applicable in freely associated states. The United States provides monies and technical support to enhance the states' political and economic development. In addition, the United States provides military protection. In exchange, the free association state agrees to extend military rights to the United States, such as the right to establish and maintain bases and to exclude the military of other nations from the area. In most cases, the freely associated state is permitted to conduct its own foreign affairs, but it does so in consultation with the United States. Citizens of freely associated states normally also possess greater rights than other foreigners to travel to or live and work in the United States. Concurrently, the same is true of U.S. citizens who want to travel to the associated state. Either the United States or the freely associated state may terminate the agreement with notice (e.g., six months). The president may not terminate the agreement without the concurrence of Congress. A plebiscite is required for most freely associated states to terminate their affiliation with the United States.

Congress also has the authority to regulate the lands belonging to Native American tribes. Also, the Commerce Clause provides that Congress may regulate commerce with "Indian tribes."

4.14 ENFORCEMENT OF CIVIL RIGHTS

Congressional jurisdiction over civil rights matters stems from several sources. The Commerce Clause, for example, has been relied upon by Congress when regulating the availability of public accommodations (such as hotels) to all people regardless of race or color.

The Thirteenth, Fourteenth, and Fifteenth Amendments all contain the following language: "Congress shall have the power to enforce this article by appropriate legislation." The three amendments are commonly referred to as the Civil War, Reconstruction, and Civil Rights Amendments. The Thirteenth (1865) abolishes slavery, the Fourteenth (1868) provides for due process and equal protection of laws, and the Fifteenth (1870) assures that all citizens may enjoy the franchise, regardless of race or color.

Katzenbach v. Morgan
384 U.S. 641 (1966)

[The Voting Rights Act of 1965 (§ 4) provided that Puerto Ricans who had completed at least the sixth grade shall be entitled to vote, regardless of English language skills. The statute was intended to preempt a New York state law that required voters to be English-literate. There were thousands of Puerto Ricans living in New York at the time. The Court had previously upheld the New York law, but now was addressing the issue of Congress's statute, which was intended to set aside New York's law.]

Mr. Justice Brennan delivered the opinion of the Court . . . .

[We] hold that, in the application challenged in these cases, § 4(e) [of the Voting Rights Act] is a proper exercise of the powers granted to congress by § of the Fourteenth Amendment [allowing Congress to enforce that amendment with appropriate legislation] and that by force of the Supremacy Clause, Article VI, the New York English literacy requirement cannot be enforced to the extent that it is inconsistent with § 4(e).

Under the distribution of powers effected by the Constitution, the States establish qualification for voting. [O]f course, the States have no power to grant or withhold franchise on conditions that are forbidden by the Fourteenth Amendment, or any other provision of the Constitution. Such exercises of state power are no more immune to the limitations of the Fourteenth Amendment than any other state action. The Equal Protection Clause itself has been held to forbid some state laws that restrict the right to vote.

The Attorney General of the State of New York argues that an exercise of congressional power under § 5 of the Fourteenth Amendment that prohibits the enforcement of state law can only be sustained if the judicial branch determines that the state law is prohibited by the provisions of the Amendment that Congress sought to enforce. More specifically, he urges that § 4(e) cannot be sustained as appropriate legislation to enforce the Equal protection Clause unless the judiciary decided—even with the guidance of a congressional judgment—that the application of the English literacy requirement prohibited by § 4(e) is forbidden by the Equal Protection Clause itself. We disagree. Neither the language nor history of § 5 support such a construction. As was said in regard to § 5 in *Ex Parte Virginia* 100 U.S. 339, 345 "It is the power of Congress which has been enlarged Congress is authorized to *enforce* the prohibitions by appropriate legislation. Some legislation is contemplated to make the amendments fully effective." . . .

Thus our task in this case is not to determine whether the New York English literacy requirement as applied to deny the right to vote to a person who successfully completed the sixth grade in a Puerto Rican school violates the Equal Protection Clause. . . . [Rather, the issue is] whether Congress [may] prohibit the enforcement of the state law by legislation under § 5 of the Fourteenth Amendment? In answering this question, our task is limited to determining whether such legislation is, as required by § 5 of appropriate legislation to enforce the Equal Protection Clause.

By including § 5 the draftsmen sought to grand to Congress, by a specific provision application to the Fourteenth Amendment, the same broad powers expressed in the Necessary and Proper Clause. . . .

There can be no doubt that § 4(e) may be regarded as an enactment to enforce the Equal Protection Clause. Congress explicitly declared that it enacted § 4(e) "to secure the right under the fourteenth amendment of persons educated in American-flag school in which the predominant classroom language was other than English." [Section] 4(e) may be viewed as a measure to secure for the Puerto Rican community residing in New York nondiscriminatory treatment by government—both in the imposition of voting qualifications and the provision or administration of governmental services, such as public school, public housing and law enforcement.

Section 4(e) may be readily seen as "plainly adapted" to furthering these aims of the Equal protection Clause. The practical effect of § 4(e) is to prohibit New York from denying the right to vote to large segments of its Puerto Rican community. . . . It is well within congressional authority to say this need of the Puerto Rican minority for the vote warranted federal intrusion upon any state interests served by the English literacy requirement. It was for Congress, as the branch that made this judgment, to assess and weigh that various conflicting consideration—the risk or pervasiveness of the discrimination in governmental services, the effectiveness of eliminating the state restriction on the right to vote as a means of dealing with the evil, the adequacy or availability of alternative remedies, and the nature and significance of the state interests that would be affected by the nullification of the English literacy requirement as applied to residents who have successfully completed the sixth grade in a Puerto Rican school. It is not for us to review the congressional resolution of these factors. . . .

We therefore conclude that § 4(e), in the application challenged in this case, is appropriate legislation to enforce the Equal Protection Clause and that the judgment of the District Court must be and hereby is reversed.

The courts have construed these provisions broadly, so that Congress has considerable authority and flexibility in remedying America's civil rights ills. Congress may regulate both private and civil associations. For example, Congress has prohibited racial discrimination in employment, regardless of whether it occurs in the private or public sector.

Several statutes have been enacted providing for equal treatment in housing, contract relationships, and employment. The "appropriate legislation" provision includes the power to create both civil and criminal remedies for violations. Because there is a specific constitutional grant of authority in this area, congressional regulation may extend to areas that have traditionally been regulated by the states and may apply against the states as well.

In addition, the Court has held that Congress's power under these amendments extends beyond fashioning remedies for strict constitutional violations. It may go further and create rights and remedies under these amendments. This is illustrated in *Katzenbach v. Morgan.*

As *Katzenbach* demonstrates, Congress may preempt state laws in this area. However, congressional authority to regulate civil rights is limited. You read an excerpt from *United States v. Morrison* earlier in this chapter, where the Court determined that Congress did not have the authority under the Commerce Clause to regulate violent criminal behavior that had no connection to interstate commerce. In the following excerpt from the same case, the Court addressed whether the Fourteenth Amendment provided Congress with the authority to regulate violent conduct that has traditionally been within the sphere of state authority. Also, it may extend rights under the Civil War Amendments further than they would otherwise reach. The purpose here is not to explain the state of civil rights law; rather, it is to demonstrate the authority Congress has in this area.

United States v. Morrison
529 U.S. 598 (2000)

In these cases we consider the constitutionality of 42 U.S.C. §13981, which provides a federal civil remedy for the victims of gender-motivated violence. The United States Court of Appeals for the Fourth Circuit, sitting en banc, struck down §13981 because it concluded that Congress lacked constitutional authority to enact the section's civil remedy. Believing that these cases are controlled by our decisions in [*Lopez and others*], we affirm.

In December 1995, Brzonkala sued Morrison, Crawford, and Virginia Tech in the United States District Court for the Western District of Virginia. Her complaint alleged that Morrison's and Crawford's attack violated §13981 and that Virginia Tech's handling of her complaint violated Title IX of the Education Amendments of 1972. . . . Morrison and Crawford moved to dismiss the complaint on the grounds that it failed to state a claim and that §13981's civil remedy is unconstitutional. The United States intervened to defend the [constitutionality of the law].

Section 13981 was part of the violence Against Women Act of 1994. . . . It states that [a]ll persons within the United States shall have the right to be free from crimes of violence motivated by gender. . . . To enforce that right, subsection (c) declares:

> A person (including a person who acts under color of any statute, ordinance, regulation, custom, or usage of any State) who commits a crime of violence motivated by gender and thus deprives another of the right declared in subsection (b) of this section shall be liable to the party injured, in an action for the recovery of compensatory and punitive damages, injunctive and declaratory relief, and such other relief as a court may deem appropriate.

Every law enacted by Congress must be based on one or more of its powers enumerated in the Constitution. "The powers of the legislature are defined and limited; and that those limits may not be mistaken or forgotten, the constitution is written." *Marbury v. Madison* . . . Congress explicitly identified the sources of federal authority on which it relied in enacting §13981. It said that a "federal civil rights cause of action" is established "[p]ursuant to the affirmative power of Congress . . . under section 5 of the Fourteenth Amendment to the Constitution, as well as under section 8 of Article I of the Constitution." We address Congress' authority to enact this remedy under each of these constitutional provisions in turn.

[The Court discussed *Lopez* and its other cases concerning the economic or commercial aspect of the Commerce Clause.] With these principles underlying our Commerce Clause jurisprudence as reference points, the proper resolution of the present cases is clear. Gender-motivated crimes of violence are not, in any sense of the phrase, economic activity. While we need not adopt a categorical rule against aggregating the effects of any noneconomic activity in order to decide these cases, thus far in our Nation's history our cases have upheld Commerce Clause regulation of intrastate activity only where that activity is economic in nature.

We accordingly reject the argument that Congress may regulate noneconomic, violent criminal conduct based solely on that conduct's aggregate effect on interstate commerce. The Constitution requires a distinction between what is truly national and what is truly local. In recognizing this fact we preserve one of the few principles that has been consistent since the Clause was adopted. The regulation and punishment of intrastate violence that is not directed at the instrumentalities, channels, or goods involved in interstate commerce has always been the province of the States. . . .

Because we conclude that the Commerce Clause does not provide Congress with authority to enact §13981, we address petitioner's alternative argument that the section's civil remedy should be upheld as an exercise of Congress' remedial power under §5 of the Fourteenth Amendment. As noted above, Congress expressly invoked the Fourteenth Amendment as a source of authority to enact §13981. [The Court concluded by also rejecting Brzonkala's Fourteenth Amendment claim. Accordingly, the provisions of the statute establishing a federal civil cause of action were stricken.]

4.15 OTHER POWERS

Congress possesses many other powers. It exercises control over aliens and immigration. The power to establish a post office and postal roads is expressly delegated to Congress. Control of patents and copyrights also falls into Congress's domain. Bankruptcy law is exclusively federal, and Congress has enacted an entire scheme of bankruptcy law and has created a system of bankruptcy courts to enforce those laws. Because of the importance of admiralty issues to the federal government, the framers delegated them to Congress. Congress may regulate national elections. The admission of new states to the union is a congressional responsibility, as is assuring each state a Republican form of government.

In terms of the structure of the federal government, Congress controls where the Constitution does not. For example, Congress is responsible for creating and abolishing agencies and determining the organizational structure of America's bureaucracy. In addition, Congress creates governmental and quasi-governmental corporations to accomplish governmental objectives. The first corporation chartered by Congress was the Bank of the United States in 1791. Since that time, Congress has created many corporations, such as the Federal Deposit Insurance Corporation (FDIC), which insures bank deposits, and the National Railroad Passenger Corporation (Amtrak), which was created to save passenger train travel from extinction. Congress normally provides for government selection of corporate officers, but may otherwise make these corporations independent. Even though a corporation may be declared independent, if it is created by Congress and serves a governmental purpose, and a majority of its board members and officers are appointed by governmental officials, its actions are considered governmental for purposes of constitutional analysis. Thus, Amtrak's decision not to allow political messages on its billboards was subject to First Amendment free speech limitations.[72]

4.16 NECESSARY AND PROPER POWERS

One of the most important enumerations of authority in Article I is the Necessary and Proper Clause of Section 8, clause 18. Congress shall have the power to "make all Laws which shall be necessary and proper for carrying into Execution the foregoing Powers, and all other Powers vested by this Constitution in the Government of the United States, or in any Department or Officer thereof." This clause represents an exception to the concept of a limited federal government. It is an expression that there is implied, unenumerated federal authority that extends from enumerated authorities.

This last point is important. The Necessary and Proper Clause is not an independent source of authority. Instead, it empowers Congress to undertake whatever actions are necessary to fully enforce delegated authorities. For example, Article I, Section 8, authorizes Congress to "establish Post Office and post Roads." To do this, it must create an agency to oversee the operation (the Department of the Treasury), provide for employees appropriate funds, and make other laws, such as to protect the mails from interference and misuse. None of these authorities are enumerated in the Constitution but are necessary in order to create a sound postal system. The risk of abuse by Congress was not lost on the framers and others during the time of the Constitution's adoption. There were fears that the Necessary and Proper Clause would be used by Congress to enlarge its realm beyond the powers enumerated. Note that the clause applies to more than congressional power. Congress may enact legislation to expand any power delegated to the federal government or officer or department thereof. Therefore, Congress may enact laws that support presidential (or other executive officials') authority. For example, the president is responsible for diplomacy. Congress may therefore enact laws establishing the State Department, providing for the foreign service, or authorizing the expenditure of funds.

The Necessary and Proper Clause was relied upon by Justice Marshall in *McCulloch v. Maryland,* wherein the Court upheld the power of the federal government to create a national bank. There is no express provision allowing the establishment of a national bank, but the Court reasoned that a national bank was a proper extension of Congress's fiscal powers to collect taxes and borrow money, which are expressly authorized by the Constitution. The Court stated, in *McCulloch v. Maryland,* that a law is valid under the Necessary and Proper Clause if it supports a legitimate objective and is "plainly adapted to that end."

In 2010 the Supreme Court upheld a federal civil detention statute as a necessary and proper power in *United States v. Comstock.*

United States v. Comstock,
130 S. Ct. 1949 (2010)

Justice Breyer delivered the opinion of the Court.

A federal civil-commitment statute authorizes the Department of Justice to detain a mentally ill, sexually dangerous federal prisoner beyond the date the prisoner would otherwise be released. 18 U. S. C. §4248. We have previously examined similar statutes enacted under state law to determine whether they violate the Due Process Clause. See *Kansas v. Hendricks*, 521 U. S. 346, 356–358 (1997); *Kansas v. Crane*, 534 U. S. 407 (2002). But this case presents a different question. Here we ask whether the Federal Government has the authority under Article I of the Constitution to enact this federal civil-commitment program or whether its doing so falls beyond the reach of a government "of enumerated powers." *McCulloch v. Maryland*, 4 Wheat. 316, 405 (1819). We conclude that the Constitution grants Congress the authority to enact §4248 as "necessary and proper for carrying into Execution" the powers "vested by" the "Constitution in the Government of the United States."

Art. I, §8, cl. 18.

The federal statute before us allows a district court to order the civil commitment of an individual who is currently "in the custody of the [Federal] Bureau of Prisons," §4248, if that individual (1) has previously "engaged or attempted to engage in sexually violent conduct or child molestation," (2) currently "suffers from a serious mental illness, abnormality, or disorder," and (3) "as a result of" that mental illness, abnormality, or disorder is "sexually dangerous to others," in that "he would have serious difficulty in refraining from sexually violent conduct or child molestation if released." . . .

If the Government proves its claims by "clear and convincing evidence," the court will order the prisoner's continued commitment in "the custody of the Attorney General," who must "make all reasonable efforts to cause" the State where that person was tried, or the State where he is domiciled, to "assume responsibility for his custody, care, and treatment." §4248(d). If either State is willing to assume that responsibility, the Attorney General "shall release" the individual "to the appropriate official" of that State. §4248(d). But if, "notwithstanding such efforts, neither such State will assume such responsibility," then "the Attorney General shall place the person for treatment in a suitable [federal] facility." . . .

The question presented is whether the Necessary and Proper Clause, Art. I, §8, cl. 18, grants Congress authority sufficient to enact the statute before us. . . .

First, the Necessary and Proper Clause grants Congress broad authority to enact federal legislation. Nearly 200 years ago, this Court stated that the Federal "[G]overnment is acknowledged by all to be one of enumerated powers," *McCulloch*, 4 Wheat., at 405, which means that "[e]very law enacted by Congress must be based on one or more of" those powers, *United States v. Morrison*, 529 U. S. 598, 607 (2000). But, at the same time, "a government, entrusted with such" powers "must also be entrusted with ample means for their execution." . . . We have since made clear that, in determining whether the Necessary and Proper Clause grants Congress the legislative authority to enact a particular federal statute, we look to see whether the statute constitutes a means that is rationally related to the implementation of a constitutionally enumerated power. . . .

Thus, the Constitution, which nowhere speaks explicitly about the creation of federal crimes beyond those related to "counterfeiting," "treason," or "Piracies and Felonies committed on the high Seas" or "against the Law of Nations," Art. I, §8, cls. 6, 10; Art. III, §3, nonetheless grants Congress broad authority to create such crimes. See *McCulloch*, 4 Wheat., at 416 ("All admit that the government may, legitimately, punish any violation of its laws; and yet, this is not among the enumerated powers of Congress"); see also *United States v. Fox*, 95 U. S. 670, 672 (1878). And Congress routinely exercises its authority to enact criminal laws in furtherance of, for example, its enumerated powers to regulate interstate and foreign commerce, to enforce civil rights, to spend funds for the general welfare, to establish federal courts, to establish post offices, to regulate bankruptcy, to regulate naturalization, and so forth. . . .

Similarly, Congress, in order to help ensure the enforcement of federal criminal laws enacted in furtherance of its enumerated powers, "can cause a prison to be erected at any place within the jurisdiction of the United States, and direct that all persons sentenced to imprisonment under the laws of the United States shall be confined there." *Ex parte Karstendick*, 93 U. S. 396, 400 (1876). Moreover, Congress, having established a prison system, can enact laws that seek to ensure that system's safe and responsible administration by, for example, requiring prisoners to receive medical care and educational training, see, *e.g.*, 18 U. S. C. §§4005–4006; §4042(a)(3), and can also ensure the safety of the prisoners, prison workers and visitors, and those in surrounding communities by, for example, creating further criminal laws governing entry, exit, and smuggling, and by employing prison guards to ensure discipline and security. See, *e.g.,* §1791 (prohibiting smuggling contraband); §751 *et seq.* (prohibiting escape and abetting thereof); 28 CFR §541.10 *et seq.* (2009) (inmate discipline).

Neither Congress' power to criminalize conduct, nor its power to imprison individuals who engage in that conduct, nor its power to enact laws governing prisons and prisoners, is explicitly mentioned in the Constitution. But Congress nonetheless possesses broad authority to do each of those things in the course of "carrying into Execution" the enumerated powers "vested by" the "Constitution in the Government of the United States," Art. I, §8, cl. 18— authority granted by the Necessary and Proper Clause.

Second, the civil-commitment statute before us constitutes a modest addition to a set of federal prison-related mental-health statutes that have existed for many decades. . . . Here, Congress has long been involved in the delivery of mental health care to federal prisoners, and has long provided for their civil commitment. . . . [The Court then detailed how Congress enlarged the civil commitment power to extend beyond the terms of imprisonment for the underlying crimes of prisoners, first in the late 1940s and on several occasions leading the law under review, which included sexual predators for the first time.]

Third, Congress reasonably extended its longstanding civil-commitment system to cover mentally ill and sexually dangerous persons who are already in federal custody, even if doing so detains them beyond the termination of their criminal sentence. For one thing, the Federal Government is the custodian of its prisoners. As federal custodian, it has the constitutional power to act in order to protect nearby (and other) communities from the danger federal prisoners may pose. . . .

Fourth, the statute properly accounts for state interests. Respondents and the dissent contend that §4248 violates the Tenth Amendment because it "invades the province of state sovereignty" in an area typically left to state control. . . . But the Tenth Amendment 's text is clear: "The powers *not delegated to the United States* by the Constitution, nor prohibited by it to the States, are reserved to the States respectively, or to the people." (Emphasis added.) The powers "delegated to the United States by the Constitution" include those specifically enumerated powers listed in Article I along with the implementation

authority granted by the Necessary and Proper Clause. Virtually by definition, these powers are not powers that the Constitution "reserved to the States." . . . [The Court further discussed the statute's deference to state sovereignty by requiring the Attorney General to give a state the first option to take custody of any civil detainee under the law.]

Fifth, the links between §4248 and an enumerated Article I power are not too attenuated. Neither is the statutory provision too sweeping in its scope. . . . Our necessary and proper jurisprudence contains multiple examples of similar reasoning. For example, in *Sabri* we observed that "Congress has authority under the Spending Clause to appropriate federal moneys" and that it therefore "has corresponding authority under the Necessary and Proper Clause to see to it that taxpayer dollars" are not "siphoned off" by "corrupt public officers." We then further held that, in aid of that implied power to criminalize graft of "taxpayer dollars," Congress has the *additional* prophylactic power to criminalize bribes or kickbacks even when the stolen funds have not been "traceably skimmed from specific federal payments." *Ibid.* Similarly, in *United States v. Hall* we held that the Necessary and Proper Clause grants Congress the power, in furtherance of Art. I, §8, cls. 11–13, to award "pensions to the wounded and disabled" soldiers of the armed forces and their dependents. . . .

To be sure, as we have previously acknowledged,

> The Federal Government undertakes activities today that would have been unimaginable to the Framers in two senses; first, because the Framers would not have conceived that *any* government would conduct such activities; and second, because the Framers would not have believed that the *Federal* Government, rather than the States, would assume such responsibilities. Yet the powers conferred upon the Federal Government by the Constitution were phrased in language broad enough to allow for the expansion of the Federal Government's role.
>
> *New York, 505 U. S., at 157.*

> The Framers demonstrated considerable foresight in drafting a Constitution capable of such resilience through time. As Chief Justice Marshall observed nearly 200 years ago, the Necessary and Proper Clause is part of "a constitution intended to endure for ages to come, and, consequently, to be adapted to the various crises of human affairs."
>
> *McCulloch* . . . .

We take these five considerations together. They include: (1) the breadth of the Necessary and Proper Clause, (2) the long history of federal involvement in this arena, (3) the sound reasons for the statute's enactment in light of the Government's custodial interest in safeguarding the public from dangers posed by those in federal custody, (4) the statute's accommodation of state interests, and (5) the statute's narrow scope. Taken together, these considerations lead us to conclude that the statute is a "necessary and proper" means of exercising the federal authority that permits Congress to create federal criminal laws, to punish their violation, to imprison violators, to provide appropriately for those imprisoned, and to maintain the security of those who are not imprisoned but who may be affected by the federal imprisonment of others. The Constitution consequently authorizes Congress to enact the statute.

We do not reach or decide any claim that the statute or its application denies equal protection of the laws, procedural or substantive due process, or any other rights guaranteed by the Constitution. Respondents are free to pursue those claims on remand, and any others they have preserved.

[Justice Thomas, joined by Justice Scalia, point out in their dissent, *inter alia*, that the Necessary and Proper Clause does not empower Congress to make laws to further other laws. Instead, the necessary and proper law must further a specific enumerated power. Accordingly, they dismissed the majority's discussion of the history of the history of statutes allowing federal civil commitment of offenders. They also disagreed with the majority's contention that the civil commitment law is analogous to laws that authorize prison officials to care for prisoners because (1) there is no connection between the underlying crime and civil commitment. The federal statute permits commitment of any prisoner, the counterfeiter, bank robber, or assassin beyond the date of his sentence if sexually dangerous. (2) Civil commitment occurs after the offender has served his prison time. (3) The commitment may occur for a future state crime, not federal, since most sexual crimes fall within the jurisdiction of the states. (4) the right of first refusal for the states is not adequate to protect the sovereignty of the states under the Tenth Amendment.]

When combined, the Necessary and Proper Clause, the Commerce Clause, the Civil Rights Amendments, and the general expansion of the other enumerated powers provide the foundation for a very powerful federal government in the early years of the twenty-first century.

4.17 MODERN CHALLENGES

While resources have always been important to politics, money did not play as great of a role in electoral politics in 1789 as it has in recent decades. In the earliest elections, there were no political parties as we think of them today, and of course, there was no television or Internet campaigning. While the Constitution of 1789 provided for direct election of the members of the House of Representatives, the president of the United States was, and continues to be, selected by the Electoral College, and Senators were chosen by their respective state legislatures. Because of these procedures, a man's personal status and influence among his elite peers played a large role. That is not to say that money was not a factor. According to one source, Abraham Lincoln was bankrupted by the expenses of his 1858 senatorial campaign and Andrew Jackson's bid for reelection as president was resisted by the Second Bank of the United States, with which he had been embattled during his first term. The bank spent $40,000 in its attempt to defeat him.[73]

Cyber Constitution
The Dirksen Congressional Center is a nonprofit organization devoted to improving an understanding of Congress through education and research. http://www.dirksencenter.org/

Even though money was a factor in early elections, the rising costs of political campaigns in recent years is well documented. According to an independent, nonpartisan, and nonprofit campaign finance research organization, the costs of federal elections rose from $1.6 billion in 1998 to an astonishing $5.3 billion in 2008.[74] If the 1998 figure had increased at the rate of inflation only, the elections would have cost only $2.1 billion.[75]

Many people fear that money has become too great a factor in electoral politics. Additionally, there are concerns that voter education does not increase with the dollars spent; quite the opposite, voters are misled and turned off by most campaign advertising. Congress has responded to these concerns by requiring greater disclosure of financial support for candidates and by limiting contributions. The first significant statute to regulate campaign finances was the Federal Election Campaign Act (FECA) of 1972. FECA required contribution disclosure by candidates and limited individual contributions to $1,000 and political action committee contributions to $5,000. Congress followed with the creation of the Federal Election Commission to oversee enforcement of the FECA in 1975.

FECA proved only marginally successful because it only regulated "hard money," or direct contributions to candidates. In 2002 the Bipartisan Campaign Reform Act (aka McCain-Feingold) regulated "soft money," or gifts to political parties and "issue" campaigning. The latter refers to advertising and other support for issues, not specific candidates. Often, however, such campaigning has the effect of supporting specific candidates. In 2010 the Supreme Court handed down *Citizens United v. Federal Election Commission,* which struck a damaging blow to campaign reform. Citizens United was a politically conservative organization that had produced a documentary that was critical of Hillary Clinton. The case arose because of Citizens United plans to run television advertisements about the film during the 2010 presidential election wherein Ms. Clinton was a presidential candidate. The advertisements violated McCain-Feingold's restrictions on the use of a corporation's or union's general funds to oppose or support candidates independent of candidate campaigns. The Supreme Court, reversing its 1990 decision *Austin v. Michigan Chamber of Commerce*, struck down the law as violating the First Amendment free speech rights of the corporations. The impact of the decision on the 2010 mid-year elections was huge. Advertising by corporations including so-called attack ads for candidates and issues was ubiquitous. Supported by free speech advocates and conservatives, the Court's decision has been heavily criticized by campaign finance reformers, legal scholars, and the general public. President Obama opined, "[w]ith its ruling today, the Supreme Court has given a green light to a new stampede of special interest money in our politics . . . It is a major victory for big oil, Wall Street banks, health insurance companies and the other powerful interests that marshal their power every day in Washington to drown out the voices of everyday Americans."[76]

There is little doubt that the situation will worsen, money will continue to play a larger role, and the nation will return to the drawing board to try to identify ways to lessen the impact of money on elections.

4.18 SUMMARY

The framers intended for two groups to be represented in Congress: the people (House of Representatives) and the states (Senate). Equal representation in the Senate assured that the larger states would not take advantage of the smaller states. Although originally selected by the states, today senators are popularly elected, as are members of the House of Representatives.

In recent decades, federal power has grown considerably. The growth appears to be the natural consequence of a nation (and world) that is becoming rapidly interconnected and interdependent. The Commerce Clause, the Necessary and Proper Clause, the Civil Rights Amendments (13 to 15), and the Supremacy Clause have facilitated this increased power.

The Supreme Court has been largely permissive of federal expansion and in contemporary times has read the Tenth Amendment as not establishing a distinct sphere of state power. Congress has attempted on occasion to check itself. For example, when the Republicans regained a majority in the House of Representatives in 2011, the newly elected Speaker John Boehner implemented a rule requiring every bill to include a statement of Congress's constitutional source of authority to enact the law.[77]

Attempts to stem the tide are not likely to have a major impact on the growth of federal power. Moving into the twenty-first century, it is reasonable to anticipate that federal power will continue to increase. In addition, the emerging globalization of the world's economies, cultures, and laws will present new constitutional issues to the judiciary of the twenty-first century.

REVIEW QUESTIONS

1. Define the affectation doctrine.
2. What is the cumulative effects doctrine?
3. May the president declare war? May Congress?
4. Describe the process for removing the president, vice-president, an Article III judge, and other public officials from office.
5. Does the Fifth Amendment freedom from self-incrimination apply in congressional hearings?
6. Is a member of Congress immune from criminal arrest during session? From a civil summons and complaint?
7. Describe the procedures to amend the Constitution.
8. What is the Necessary and Proper Clause? Explain its significance.
9. Do the states or federal government have jurisdiction over post offices? Patents and copyrights? Murder? Education?

ASSIGNMENTS: CONSTITUTIONAL LAW IN ACTION

The Constitution in Your Community

You are employed by a law firm that has been retained by Mae Shen, a prominent and wealthy business leader in your community. Dissatisfied with your city's support for businesses, she is considering running for city council to bring a business voice to the council. You have been asked by the senior partner of the firm to answer the following questions for her:

1. What is the term of office and how does she go about getting her name on the ballot?
2. How much of her money may she invest in her campaign? How much may she receive from individual and corporate donors to support her campaign?
3. What are the rules for posting yard and street signs?

Prepare a brief, not to exceed two pages, answering these questions with references to the applicable law.

Going Federal

After a term on the city council, Mae Shen decided that to really make a difference for businesses, she needed to be involved in federal lawmaking. She has again retained your firm, and you have been assigned the responsibility of answering the following questions:

1. What is the term of office and how does she go about getting her name on the ballot?
2. How much of her money may she invest in her campaign? How much may she receive from individual and corporate donors to support her campaign?

Moot Court

Congress's authority to regulate has expanded considerably since 1789. The cumulative effects doctrine has been one theory that has paved the way for greater congressional authority, including over health care. While the federal government has considerably increased its involvement in some aspects of medicine, it has not yet regulated the actual practice of medicine. This authority currently belongs to the states. In teams of two, prepare to debate whether Congress should have the jurisdiction to regulate medical licensing, for example, eligibility and qualifications to practice medicine.

NOTES

1. Robert Byrne, comp. *1,911 Best Things Anybody Ever Said* (Fawcett Columbine 1988).
2. While legislatures are the primary lawmakers, administrative agencies are the creators of the greatest number of laws. Agencies, however, acquire their authorities from legislatures and their regulations may not conflict with statutory law or the intentions of the legislatures that have created and empowered them.
3. Art. I, § 5, clause 3.
4. Art. I, § 5, clause 2.
5. Art. I, § 5, clause 1.
6. Art. I, §§ 2 and 3.
7. *United States v. Munoz-Flores*, 495 U.S. 385 (1990).
8. Art. I, § 5.
9. Art. I, § 6, clause 2.
10. *United States Term Limits v. Thornton,* 514 U.S. 779, 115 S. Ct. 1842 (1995).
11. *McIntyre v. Fallahay,* 766 F.2d 1098 (7th Cir. 1985).
12. 395 U.S. 486 (1969).
13. *Kilbourn v. Thompson,* 103 U.S. 168, 189 (1881).
14. Rangel's Censure, Online *Wall Street Journal*, December 3, 2010.
15. U.S. Senate website, www.senate.gov/artandhistory/history/common/briefing/Expulsion_Censure.htm.
16. *United States v. Johnson*, 383 U.S. 169 (1966).
17. *Hutchinson v. Proxmire,* 443 U.S. 111 (1979).
18. *Kilbourn,* 103 U.S. at 204.
19. *United States v. Rostenkowski,* 59 F.3d 1291 (D.C. Cir. 1995).
20. *Id.*
21. David Stout, "Ex-Louisiana Congressman Sentenced to 13 Years," *New York Times*, November 13, 2009, available at www.nytimes.com/2009/11/14/us/politics/14jefferson.html.
22. *United States v. Gillock*, 445 U.S. 360 (1980).
23. *Stafford v. Wallace,* 258 U.S. 495 (1922).
24. 295 U.S. 330 (1935).
25. 295 U.S. 495 (1935).
26. See *Carter v. Carter Coal Co.*, 298 U.S. 238 (1936).
27. *NLRB v. Jones & Laughlin Steel Corp.*, 301 U.S. 1 (1937).
28. 17 U.S. 316 (1819).
29. *Heart of Atlanta Motel Inc. v. United States*, 379 U.S. 241, 257 (1964).
30. *Hodel v. Virginia Surface Mining & Reclamation Ass'n*, 452 U.S. 264 (1981).
31. *Heart of Atlanta Motel Inc. v. United States*, 379 U.S. 241 (1964).
32. *Katzenbach v. McClung,* 379 U.S. 294 (1964).
33. 18 U.S.C. § 2421.
34. 18 U.S.C. § 2261 *et seq.*
35. 28 U.S.C. § 1073.
36. 28 U.S.C. § 921 *et seq.*
37. 28 U.S.C. § 2251 *et. seq.*
38. *Perez v. United States,* 402 U.S. 146 (1971).
39. The law was invalidated by a U.S. district court in *United States v. Cortner,* 834 F. Supp. 242 (M.D. Tenn. 1993), but the Sixth Circuit Court of Appeals has found to the contrary. See *United States v. Johnson,* 22 F.3d 106 (6th Cir. 1994); *United States v. Osteen,* 30 F.3d 135 (6th Cir. 1994).
40. 521 U.S 98.
41. *United States v. Oliver,* 60 F.3d 547 (9th Cir. 1995); *United States v. Carolina,* 61 F.3d 917 (10th Cir. 1995).
42. *Commonwealth of Virginia v. Sebelius,* Memorandum Opinion, U.S. Dist., E.D. Va., Civil Action No. 3:10CV188-HEH, December 13, 2010.

43. *Florida v. HHS*, 11th Cir.Ct. App., case no. Nos. 11-11021 and 11-1106, August 12, 2011.
44. 157 U.S. 429 (1895).
45. Art. I, § 2, clause 3.
46. Art. I, § 9, clause 5.
47. 483 U.S. 203 (1987).
48. Art. I, § 8, clauses 5 and 6.
49. *McCulloch v. Maryland*, 17 U.S. (4 Wheat.) 316 (1819).
50. Art. I, § 8, clause 2.
51. Art. I, § 8, clause 4.
52. *Woods v. Cloyd W. Miller Co.*, 333 U.S. 138 (1948).
53. *Korematsu v. United States*, 323 U.S. 214 (1944).
54. Art. I, § 8, clauses 15 and 16.
55. *Perpich v. Department of Defense*, 496 U.S. 334 (1990).
56. 323 U.S. 214 (1944).
57. *Watkins v. United States,* 354 U.S. 178, 200 (1957).
58. *Barenblatt v. United States*, 360 U.S. 109 (1959).
59. Art. II, § 2, clause 2.
60. *Hastings v. United States,* 681 F.2d 706 (11th Cir. 1982). See also *United States v. Claiborne,* 727 F.2d 842 (9th Cir. 1984).
61. Michael Broyde, "Expediting Impeachment: Removing Article III Federal Judges after Criminal Conviction," 17 *Harv. J. L. & Pub. Pol'y* 157 (1994).
62. 400 U.S. 112 (1970).
63. Jerome Angel, *Amending America* 138–39 (Random House 1993). This book is recommended to those who are interested in the history of constitutional amendments.
64. Maggie McComas, "Amending the Constitution," *Constitution* 26 (Spring–Summer 1992).
65. This information was taken from *Amending America, supra* n. 56.
66. John Vile, "Proposals to Amend the Bill of Rights: Are Fundamental Rights in Jeopardy?" 75 *Judicature* 62 (Aug./Sept. 1991).
67. 2 U.S. (2 Dall.) 419 (1793).
68. 60 U.S. (19 How.) 393 (1856).
69. 157 U.S. 429 (1895).
70. 400 U.S. 112 (1970).
71. For more on this topic, see Daniel E. Hall, "Curfews, Custom, and Culture in American Samoa," 2 *Asian-Pacific Law and Policy Journal* 69 (2001) available at http://www.hawaii.edu/aplpj/articles/APLPJ_02.1_hall.pdf
72. *Lebron v. National Railroad Passenger Corp.*, 513 U.S. 374, 115 S. Ct. 961 (1995).
73. Wikipedia, Campaign Finance Reform (2010).
74. Opensecrets.org (click on historical elections).
75. The inflation calculator at USinflationcalculator.com was used to arrive at this figure.
76. See Jeff Zeleny, *New York Times* blog http://thecaucus.blogs.nytimes.com/2010/01/21/political-fallout-from-the-supreme-court-ruling/.
77. Jennifer Steinhauer, Congress to Return With G.O.P. Vowing to Alter Rules, *New York Times*, January 4, 2011.

5

The Presidency

Tho we cannot, affirmatively, tell you what we are doing; we can negatively, tell you what we are not doing—we never once thought of a King.[1]

STATEMENT FROM PHILADELPHIA CONVENTION[2]

LEARNING OBJECTIVES
At the end of this chapter you should be able to:

- Outline the presidency, including term of office, method of election, required qualifications, and temporary removal for disability and permanent removal through impeachment.

- List and explain the authorities of the president that are enumerated in the Constitution.

- Explain the theory of the unitary president as well as differing conceptions of presidential authority.

- Explain the evolution of presidential authority from 1789 to present day, including a full description of the circumstances under which presidential authority is at its highest and lowest. You should also be able to identify and discuss the most significant Supreme Court decisions that contributed to the shaping of presidential authority.

- Define the relationship between the president and Congress in foreign affairs, in war, and during times of insurrection and rebellion. Cite the most significant historical events and the Supreme Court decisions in this area.

- Explain presidential privilege and immunity, citing and discussing the most significant Supreme Court decisions in the area.

- Identify a contemporary issue concerning presidential authority and discuss the most likely future scenarios, referencing both historical analogs and caselaw.

- Brief a judicial opinion with little outside assistance. You should be successful in identifying the relevant facts. You should be successful in identifying the legal issue and analyzing the court's rationale in at least 50 percent of your briefs.

- Apply what you have learned to a new set of facts that are given to you with no assistance.

5.1 MODELS OF PRESIDENTIAL AUTHORITY

One of the defects of the Articles of Confederation was the absence of a strong executive with unified powers. The president of the Continental Congress served as the nation's highest executive, but held little authority. Even more, many functions that are today considered "executive" were performed by legislative committees. This proved to be inefficient, and many people believed the nation needed a strong, central figure.

Many proposals were considered at the Philadelphia Convention, including installing a monarch and having multiple presidents. The framers finally agreed on what is now found in Article II, Section 1, clause 1, which states:

> The executive Power shall be vested in a President of the United States of America. He shall hold his Office during the Term of Four Years, and, together with the Vice President, chosen for the same Term, be elected. . . .

Specific authorities of the president follow in Sections 2 and 3. These include, *inter alia*, acting as commander and chief of the military, the authority to grant pardons and reprieves, the authority to make treaties with the advice and consent of the Senate, the authority to make certain nominations and appointments, to receive ambassadors and foreign ministers, and to faithfully execute the laws of the nation. In spite of these specific authorities, the general delegation of executive authority to the president is quite broad and, some would say, vague. Consequently, there is disagreement over the scope of presidential authority. Two models of presidential authority, representing two ends of the authority spectrum, have developed. Each model had the support of a prominent framer.

Alexander Hamilton advocated for a strong executive, or as he described it, a "vigorous executive." In *Federalist No. 70,* he wrote:

> Energy in the Executive is a leading character in the definition of good government. It is essential to the protection of the community against foreign attacks; it is not less essential to the steady administration of the laws; to the protection of property against those irregular and high-handed combinations which sometimes interrupt the ordinary course of justice; to the security of liberty against the enterprises and assaults of ambition, of faction, and of anarchy. . . . A feeble Executive implies a feeble execution of the government.

He continued by describing the elements needed to have an effective executive, while remaining faithful to the democratic principles undergirding the Constitution.

> The ingredients which constitute energy in the Executive are, first, unity; secondly, duration; thirdly, an adequate provision for its support; fourthly, competent powers.
>
> The ingredients which constitute safety in the republican sense are, first, a due dependence on the people, secondly, a due responsibility.

At the extreme, proponents of this model advance the notion of a **unitary executive.** Under this theory, Article II creates a unified, hierarchical executive branch by vesting all executive authority in the president. Proponents of a "strong" unitary executive believe that the president possesses the authority to make all executive decisions and that all executive officers must be accountable to the president either directly or through the executive chain-of-command. In a strong unitary executive system, Congress has little influence over executive decision making, or over administrative agencies, and is without the authority to delegate executive authorities independent of the president's oversight. Independent agencies, which are headed by individuals free from direct presidential control and removal, are inconsistent with unitary executive theory. For the related theory of coordinate (aka departmental) review of constitutional interpretation, see the discussion of judicial review of executive action in Chapter 3.

unitary executive
A theory that the Constitution vests all executive authority in the president of the United States. In a strong unitary executive system, Congress is without the authority to delegate executive authority, independent of the president, to any officer or agency or to limit presidential authority to remove or direct executive subordinates.

Many of the other framers, for various reasons, advocated for a less powerful president. States' rights advocates, for example, sought to limit the authority of the entire federal government. Still others who favored a stronger federal government also opposed Hamilton's vision. James Madison, for example, was a tireless promoter of balance. It was Madison, in *Federalist No. 47*, who penned, "The accumulation of all powers, legislative, executive, and judiciary, in the same hands, whether of one, a few, or many, and whether hereditary, self-appointed, or elective, may justly be pronounced the very definition of tyranny." For Madison and others, the advent of independent agencies, congressional oversight of executive functions, and spirited debate about presidential nominations would not only be acceptable, but would also evidence that our system of checks and balances is working.

These are not two distinct models of presidential authority. Rather, they are two points on a continuum. Because the Constitution is somewhat vague, the authorities of the respective branches, particularly between the president and Congress, will continue to shift, influenced by the personal philosophies of future presidents and congresspersons, public opinion, foreign affairs and security concerns, economic circumstances, and other factors. As you progress through this text, you will learn that the Supreme Court has interpreted the Constitution as constructing a moderate unitary executive system. The Court has permitted Congress to create independent agencies and to engage in oversight of federal officers, subject, however, to some Article II limitations.

YOUR CONSTITUTIONAL VALUES

THE YOLK'S ON OSAMA BIN LADEN

Following the attacks on the United States on September 11, 2001, Patricia Thomas, a public high school teacher at Dixie M. Hollins High School in St. Petersburg, Florida, found herself immersed in an interesting First Amendment dispute. Ms. Thomas had a project in her physics class that required students to construct devices intended to protect eggs from breaking in a thirty-foot fall. Each year, at her expense, Ms. Thomas rented a "cherry picker" and had a large plastic-coated poster embossed with a photo constructed. The students' eggs were dropped from the cherry picker onto the poster, with the photo acting as the target. The objective was for her students to construct devices that protected the eggs from breaking.

Ms. Thomas allowed her students to select the photo each year, and prior to 2001, they had selected cartoon characters and other uncontroversial targets. In response to the attacks on September 11, 2001, her students chose Osama bin Laden as the target in 2001. But school administrators, who were initially supportive, balked at permitting the use of bin Laden's photo. One administrator said he had reviewed the project with "a couple of people and I thought perhaps, especially with our emphasis on multicultural issues . . . that it would not be a good thing to do. . . ." He suggested a poster with the word "terrorism" embossed on it would be better.

The First Amendment free speech rights of students have been addressed by the Supreme Court on several occasions. In *Tinker v. Des Moines Independent Community School District,* 393 U.S. 503 (1969), the right of a public school student to wear a black armband in protest of the Vietnam War was upheld. The Court held, however, that student speech that could reasonably be expected to lead to a material or substantial disruption of education or order may be regulated. Another line of cases focuses on the pedagogical dimensions of the speech and its regulation. For example, the Supreme Court upheld a school decision to redact two articles in a student newspaper in *Hazelwood School District v. Kuhlmeier,* 484 U.S. 260 (1988), because the newspaper was school sponsored, as opposed to public, and because the school had legitimate pedagogical reasons for redacting the articles. There have been no Supreme Court decisions directly addressing the in-class free speech rights of students. Lower courts have analyzed in-class speech cases differently, some applying *Tinker's* public concern analysis to student in-class speech and others applying *Hazelwood's* school sponsorship test. As students turn to state-provided Internet for both communication and personal reflection, such as through e-mails, blogs, and facebook, conflicts between free speech rights and the opposing forces of slander, security, and safety and the need to maintain harmonious school environments are going to increase. In the case involving the egg drop, the situation is made more complex because there was more than student speech rights at stake. The teacher's free speech rights are also a factor.

Although the First Amendment free speech rights of public school teachers have received less attention by the Supreme Court than those of students, a few cases have been issued that inform the area. In *Pickering v. Board of Education,* 391 U.S. 563 (1968), a teacher was fired for writing a letter to a newspaper criticizing his school board's misuse of funds. The Supreme Court held that public employees possess First Amendment free speech rights when expressing matters of "public concern." The Court also held that such rights are limited by the need for public employers to maintain an efficient, harmonious working environment. For the Court, *Pickering's* concerns about the use of public tax dollars did rise to the level of a public concern. In *Connick v. Myers*, 461 U.S. 138 (1983), the Court upheld the termination of a prosecuting attorney who distributed a survey questioning office practices to her coworkers, even though one of the questions raised a matter of public concern, because in balance, the public concern was outweighed by the need for office efficiency. In a case with similar facts, *Garcetti v. Ceballos,* the Court reaffirmed *Connick* in 2006. Ceballos, a deputy prosecuting attorney, filed a free speech claim against his supervisors, alleging that he was disciplined for work-related memoranda he drafted. The Court held that two questions have to be asked in such cases: (1) Did the employee speak as a citizen on a matter of public concern? (2) If so, did the government employer have adequate justification for treating the employee differently than other members of the public? If the answer to question one is no, then no free speech rights under the First Amendment exist. The Court drew a clear line: When public employees make "statements pursuant to their official duties, the employees are not speaking as citizens for First Amendment purposes, and the Constitution does not insulate their communications from employer discipline." The Court reasoned that both federalism and separation of powers principles advise against courts scrutinizing governmental operations to the extent that would be required if work-related speech were constitutionally protected. For Ceballos, his memoranda were clearly work product. Therefore, he did not prevail. The Court specifically did not decide the extent to which the *Ceballos* decision applies to academic settings. Justice Souter, who dissented, commented that the decision could have significant ramifications on academic freedom. Justice Kennedy, writing for the majority, penned, "expression related to academic scholarship or classroom instruction implicates additional constitutional interests that are not fully accounted for by the Court's customary employee-speech jurisprudence. We need not [decide that today]." Note the Court's careful limitation of possible protection to academic scholarship and teaching, not other work-related speech.

Again, there are lower-court decisions concerning the in-class statements of teachers. Clearly, teachers can be disciplined for speaking about matters outside their assigned subjects, even if a public concern, because schools have a legitimate pedagogical interest in restricting teachers to their subjects. Similarly, teachers can be disciplined for insulting students, for making offensive statements, and for violating a school's harassment policy. Age and maturity are factors. Accordingly, the same case could have different outcomes at the primary, secondary, and postsecondary levels.

So where does this leave the physics class at Dixie Hollins? If banned by the school board, a reviewing court would have to engage in two sets of analyses, one for the students' free speech rights and another for Ms. Thomas's free speech rights. In regard to the students, *Tinker* stands for the proposition that political speech, unrelated to a specific academic objective of the school, may be protected, so long as it is not materially disruptive. Apparently, the school board did not assert that the use of the photo would lead to a material disruption. Accordingly, the court would then weigh the students' rights against the school board's interest in advancing its cultural sensitivity agenda. In this analysis, courts give schools considerable latitude. That is, they defer to schools as curricula and pedagogical experts. In the case of the egg drop, the school board would have to establish that the use of Osama bin Laden's photo would undermine its efforts to teach tolerance of people of different faiths and cultures. This would be difficult to do. As Ms. Thomas said, the target "was not meant to take aim at Muslims but at a specific person . . . There's nobody here who would be offended except other terrorists. . . . " In regard to Ms. Thomas's free speech rights, a reviewing court would have to determine whether an academic freedom exception to the *Ceballos* decision exists, and if so, whether the school board's interest outweighs the benefits of the particular speech under review. Because the content of the speech at question was far outside the boundaries of physics, her claim appears to have less merit than her students' claim.

After a public outcry of support for the students and Ms. Thomas, the school board permitted the photo to be used, averting a constitutional controversy. The drop occurred; there was no disruption, and no reported loss of respect for Muslims. In the end, the yolk was solely on Osama bin Laden.

5.2 SELECTION, TENURE, AND SUCCESSION

Article II, Section 1, provides for one president and one vice-president, each to serve four years. Not every American qualifies to be president. The Constitution requires that a person be a natural-born citizen, thirty-five years of age, and at least fourteen years a resident of the United States.[1] *Natural-born citizen* has not been defined, but it appears to exclude naturalized citizens. Citizens born abroad on U.S. soil qualify.

The president is not elected by direct, popular vote. Rather, a system of electors, known as the **electoral college,** selects the president. Each state has a group of electors equal to the number of representatives it has in the House and Senate. The Twenty-Third Amendment gives the District of Columbia the number of electors it would have if were a state. However, that number may not exceed that of the smallest states, currently 3 and the District's population entitles it to that number. This places 538 electors in the College, 270 required to elect the president and vice-president. Accordingly, the United States does not have one presidential election, but fifty-one elections that are combined through the electoral college system.

Each state legislature is empowered to decide how electors are chosen. In the early years of the nation, state legislatures typically selected electors directly. Today, electors are popularly elected in each of the fifty states and the District of Columbia. Initial selection of electors varies between the states. In all jurisdictions, the political parties are central to the process. The nominees are then elected at the general presidential election. The electoral candidates appear on the ballot with the presidential and vice-presidential candidates in some states and not in others.

In all but two states, the candidates who receive the largest popular vote receive all the electoral votes. In Maine and Nebraska, some of the electors follow the statewide popular vote and the remaining electors vote consistent with the popular vote of a particular congressional district. The practice is for all electors to vote as a block in favor of the candidate who receives the greatest number of popular votes in the state. However, electors in many states have the authority, although rarely exercised, to vote in any manner. In recent years, a few isolated cases of elector independence (they are known as faithless electors) have occurred. For example, an elector in the District of Columbia refused to vote with the other electors for Gore and Lieberman in protest for the District of Columbia's "colonial status," and in 1988, an elector from West Virginia reversed her votes for the two Democratic candidates, Michael Dukakis and Lloyd Bentsen. In 2004, in an apparent mistake, an elector from Minnesota voted for John Edwards for both president and vice-president. Some states have laws that require electors to vote for their party's candidates and that penalize faithless electors. Although no such penalty has ever been enforced, the Supreme Court has affirmed the authority of the states to require their electors to take an oath to support the political party's candidates for president and vice-president.[3]

The electoral system under Article I, Section 1, proved to be problematic. It was possible, for example, for political opponents to be elected president and vice-president

Cyber Constitution
White House
The official website of the president of the United States is www.whitehouse.gov/. There are two sites for the vice-president. One located in the White House's webpages, www.whitehouse.gov/administration/vice-president-biden, and another in the Senate because of the vice-president's role as president of that body, www.senate.gov/pagelayout/senators/a_three_sections_with_teasers/leadership.htm

electoral college
The body empowered by the Constitution to elect the president and vice-president of the United States, composed of presidential electors chosen by the voters at each presidential election. In practice, however, the electoral college votes in accordance with the popular vote.

Cyber Constitution
Electoral College
The official website of the electoral college is www.archives.gov/federal-register/electoral-college/about.html

because all candidates ran for president and the candidate with the largest number of votes (had to be a majority of electors) was elected president and the candidate with the second largest number of votes, but not necessarily a majority, was elected vice-president. This happened in the election of 1796, where John Adams, a Federalist, was elected president and Thomas Jefferson, an anti-Federalist of the Democratic-Republican Party, was elected vice-president. The result was a contentious four years for the two men and the nation. The presidential election of 1800 exposed another flaw. Following a hotly contested and rancorous election between the Federalists, who supported Adam's re-election with Charles Pinckney as vice-president, and anti-Federalists, with Jefferson and Aaron Burr as their candidates for president and vice-president, respectively, the electoral college failed to select a president. The original constitution required the House of Representatives to resolve ties in the electoral college. Because Article I, Section 1, did not distinguish between president and vice-president when the electors voted, the two anti-Federalist candidates tied. Although Burr supported Jefferson for president, he campaigned for his election as president in the House of Representatives. His efforts were advanced by many Federalists who bitterly opposed Jefferson's election. One significant exception in the Federalist ranks was Alexander Hamilton, who lobbied Federalists to support Jefferson over Burr. This and several other political disagreements over many years between Burr and Hamilton led to their famous 1804 duel where Burr fatally shot Hamilton. Remarkably, it took 36 votes in the House of Representatives before Jefferson was selected. It was clear from these two elections that the electoral system had to be changed.

Change came quickly. The Twelfth Amendment was proposed by Congress in 1803 and ratified by the states in 1804. The amendment modified Article II, Section I, clause 3 to require electors to vote for president and vice-president separately, to require the same qualifications of the vice-president and president, and it delegates the resolution of ties for president to the House of Representatives and ties for vice-president to the Senate. Otherwise, the electoral college was left unchanged.

The Twelfth Amendment requires electors to "vote by ballot for President and Vice President, one of whom, shall not be an inhabitant of the same state with themselves." That is, if the presidential and vice-presidential candidates of the same party are from the same state as an elector, that elector may not vote for both. This is an obscure provision that narrowly missed its fifteen minutes of fame in the 2000 presidential election. Vice-presidential candidate Dick Cheney, long a resident of Wyoming, moved to Texas, the same domicile of presidential candidate Bush, then governor of Texas, several years before the election. He worked and lived in Texas until a few months before the election when he returned to Wyoming to register to vote. Three Texans filed a federal Twelfth Amendment claim, alleging that Cheney was an inhabitant of Texas. Therefore, Texas electors acted improperly by voting for both Bush and Cheney.[4] The district court that heard the case ruled in favor of Cheney, finding that the plaintiffs lacked standing, and also, because Cheney was born, raised, educated, and married in Wyoming; was a member of Congress representing; had a long history of voting in, and had recently relinquished his Texas voter's registration and driver's license in favor of Wyoming, he was an inhabitant of that state.

Undoubtedly, the Twelfth Amendment improved the electoral college system. But it remains imperfect in many ways. There is the possibility that electors will vote as they want in disregard to state laws or the will of the people. There is also the small state advantage problem. Because small states are guaranteed two electors plus additional electors equal to the number of votes they have in the House of Representatives, it is possible for the actual voter-to-elector ratio to be much higher than in larger states. The most serious weakness in the system is the possibility that a candidate can lose an election while garnishing the largest number of popular votes. This has happened four times in U.S. history: 1824 (John Quincy Adams prevailing over Andrew Jackson and others even though he had neither a majority of electoral votes

Protesters of the 2000 presidential election recount
© William Meyer/Alamy

nor popular votes), 1876 (Rutherford Hayes over Samuel Tilden), 1888 (Benjamin Harrison over Grover Cleveland), and most recently, 2000. In 2000, President George W. Bush, a Republican, defeated Vice-President Al Gore, a Democrat, by winning the majority of the electoral votes while Gore received greater than 500,000 more popular votes than Bush. A massive recount of the votes was undertaken following the election, and claims of isolated voter fraud and other irregularities were made by supporters and opponents of both candidates. Ultimately, the Supreme Court rendered the final decision in favor of Bush in a 5–4 decision.

Bush v. Gore
531 U.S. 98 (2000)

[The 2000 presidential election was the closest in U.S. history. The outcome centered on Florida, where the count was very close and because Florida had enough electoral votes to swing the election in favor of either candidate. Florida law is winner-takes-all; that is, all electoral votes are cast for the candidate with the greatest popular vote. Florida law required a recount because the initial tally identified Bush as the winner by less than one-half of 1 percent (2,909,135 vs. 2,907,351). The initial mechanical recount still showed Bush the victor, but by fewer votes. Vice-President Gore then demanded manual recounts in four counties. There was a dispute about the deadline for such recounts that ended up before the Florida Supreme Court twice and the U.S. Supreme Court once. On November 26, the Florida Elections Canvassing Commission certified Bush the victor. Pursuant to Florida law, Gore appealed this to a Florida trial court, where he lost. He appealed to a Florida court of appeals, which certified the case to the Florida Supreme Court. Specifically, Gore challenged the exclusion of thousands of votes that were not counted by the machines because they had hanging chads or other defects. On December 8, 2000, the Florida Supreme Court affirmed the lower court's decision to reject Gore's claims in regard to one County, but found that a recount was needed in Miami-Dade County, which had failed to manually tabulate 9,000 votes, enough possibly to change the outcome of the election. The Florida Supreme Court also ordered that the increases Gore had seen in the automatic recount should be included in the totals, reversing an earlier Florida court decision that they were to be excluded. The Court ordered the recounts to begin immediately. Governor Bush filed an action to stay the recount in the Supreme Court of the United States.]

The petition presents the following questions: whether the Florida Supreme Court established new standards for resolving Presidential election contests, thereby violating Art. II, §1, cl. 2, of the United States Constitution and failing to comply with 3 U.S.C. § 5 and whether the use of standardless manual recounts violates the Equal Protection and Due Process Clauses. With respect to the equal protection question, we find a violation of the Equal Protection Clause.

The closeness of this election, and the multitude of legal challenges which have followed in its wake, have brought into sharp focus a common, if heretofore unnoticed, phenomenon. Nationwide statistics reveal that an estimated 2% of ballots cast do not register a vote for President for whatever reason, including deliberately choosing no candidate at all or some voter error, such as voting for two candidates or insufficiently marking a ballot. . . . In certifying election results, the votes eligible for inclusion in the certification are the votes meeting the properly established legal requirements.

This case has shown that punch card balloting machines can produce an unfortunate number of ballots which are not punched in a clean, complete way by the voter. After the current counting, it is likely legislative bodies nationwide will examine ways to improve the mechanisms and machinery for voting.

The individual citizen has no federal constitutional right to vote for electors for the President of the United States unless and until the state legislature chooses a statewide election as the means to implement its power to appoint members of the Electoral College. U.S. Const., Art. II, §1. This is the source for the statement in *McPherson v. Blacker*, 146 U.S. 1, 35 (1892), that the State legislature's power to select the manner for appointing electors is plenary; it may, if it so chooses, select the electors itself, which indeed was the manner used by State legislatures in several States for many years after the Framing of our Constitution. *Id.*, at 28–33. History has now favored the voter, and in each of the several States the citizens themselves vote for Presidential electors. When the state legislature vests the right to vote for President in its people, the right to vote as the legislature has prescribed is fundamental; and one source of its fundamental nature lies in the equal weight accorded to each vote and the equal dignity owed to each voter. The State, of course, after granting the franchise in the special context of Article II, can take back the power to appoint electors.

The right to vote is protected in more than the initial allocation of the franchise. Equal protection applies as well to the manner of its exercise. Having once granted the right to vote on equal terms, the State may not, by later arbitrary and disparate treatment, value one person's vote over that of another. . . .

The Florida Supreme Court has ordered that the intent of the voter be discerned from such ballots. For purposes of resolving the equal protection challenge, it is not necessary to decide whether the Florida Supreme Court had the authority under the legislative scheme for resolving election disputes to define what a legal vote is and to mandate a manual recount implementing that definition. The recount mechanisms implemented in response to the decisions of the Florida Supreme Court do not satisfy the minimum requirement for non-arbitrary treatment of voters necessary to secure the fundamental right. Florida's basic command for the count of legally cast votes is to consider the "intent of the voter." *Gore v. Harris*, ___ So. 2d, at ___ (slip op., at 39). This is unobjectionable as an abstract proposition and a starting principle. The problem inheres in the absence of specific standards to ensure its equal application. The formulation of uniform rules to determine intent based on these recurring circumstances is practicable and, we conclude, necessary. . . .

The want of those rules here has led to unequal evaluation of ballots in various respects. See *Gore* v. *Harris,* ___ So. 2d, at ___ (slip op., at 51) (Wells, J., dissenting) ("Should a county canvassing board count or not count a 'dimpled chad' where the voter is able to successfully dislodge the chad in every other contest on that ballot? Here, the county canvassing boards disagree.") As seems to have been acknowledged at oral argument, the standards for accepting or rejecting contested ballots might vary not only from county to county but indeed within a single county from one recount team to another.

The record provides some examples. A monitor in Miami-Dade County testified at trial that he observed that three members of the county canvassing board applied different standards in defining a legal vote. 3 Tr. 497, 499 (Dec. 3, 2000). And testimony at trial also revealed that at least one county changed its evaluative standards during the counting process. Palm Beach County, for example, began the process with a 1990 guideline which precluded counting completely attached chads, switched to a rule that considered a vote to be legal if any light could be seen through a chad, changed back to the 1990 rule, and then abandoned any pretense of a *per se* rule, only to have a court order that the county consider dimpled chads legal. This is not a process with sufficient guarantees of equal treatment. . . .

The State Supreme Court ratified this uneven treatment. It mandated that the recount totals from two counties, Miami-Dade and Palm Beach, be included in the certified total. The court also appeared to hold *sub silentio* that the recount totals from Broward County, which were not completed until after the original November 14 certification by the Secretary of State, were to be considered part of the new certified vote totals even though the county certification was not contested by Vice President Gore. Yet each of the counties used varying standards to determine what was a legal vote. Broward County used a more forgiving standard than Palm Beach County, and uncovered almost three times as many new votes, a result markedly disproportionate to the difference in population between the counties.

In addition, the recounts in these three counties were not limited to so-called undervotes but extended to all of the ballots. The distinction has real consequences. A manual recount of all ballots identifies not only those ballots which show no vote but also those which contain more than one, the so-called overvotes. Neither category will be counted by the machine. This is not a trivial concern. At oral argument, respondents estimated there are as many as 110,000 overvotes statewide. As a result, the citizen whose ballot was not read by a machine because he failed to vote for a candidate in a way readable by a machine may still have his vote counted in a manual recount; on the other hand, the citizen who marks two candidates in a way discernable by the machine will not have the same opportunity to have his vote count, even if a manual examination of the ballot would reveal the requisite indicia of intent. Furthermore, the citizen who marks two candidates, only one of which is discernable by the machine, will have his vote counted even though it should have been read as an invalid ballot. The State Supreme Court's inclusion of vote counts based on these variant standards exemplifies concerns with the remedial processes that were under way.

That brings the analysis to yet a further equal protection problem. The votes certified by the court included a partial total from one county, Miami-Dade. The Florida Supreme Court's decision thus gives no assurance that the recounts included in a final certification must be complete. Indeed, it is respondent's submission that it would be consistent with the rules of the recount procedures to include whatever partial counts are done by the time of final certification, and we interpret the Florida Supreme Court's decision to permit this. This accommodation no doubt results from the truncated contest period established by the Florida Supreme Court in *Bush I*, at respondents' own urging. The press of time does not diminish the constitutional concern. A desire for speed is not a general excuse for ignoring equal protection guarantees.

In addition to these difficulties the actual process by which the votes were to be counted under the Florida Supreme Court's decision raises further concerns. That order did not specify who would recount the ballots. The county canvassing boards were forced to pull together ad hoc teams comprised of judges from various Circuits who had no previous training in handling and interpreting ballots. Furthermore, while others were permitted to observe, they were prohibited from objecting during the recount.

The recount process, in its features here described, is inconsistent with the minimum procedures necessary to protect the fundamental right of each voter in the special instance of a statewide recount under the authority of a single state judicial officer. Our consideration is limited to the present circumstances, for the problem of equal protection in election processes generally presents many complexities.

The question before the Court is not whether local entities, in the exercise of their expertise, may develop different systems for implementing elections. Instead, we are presented with a situation where a state court with the power to assure uniformity has ordered a statewide recount with minimal procedural safeguards. When a court orders a statewide remedy, there must be at least some assurance that the rudimentary requirements of equal treatment and fundamental fairness are satisfied. . . .

Upon due consideration of the difficulties identified to this point, it is obvious that the recount cannot be conducted in compliance with the requirements of equal protection and due process without substantial additional work. . . .

The Supreme Court of Florida has said that the legislature intended the State's electors to "participat[e] fully in the federal electoral process," as provided in 3 U.S.C. § 5. That statute, in turn, requires that any controversy or contest that is designed to lead to a conclusive selection of electors be completed by December 12. That date is upon us, and there is no recount procedure in place under the State Supreme Court's order that comports with minimal constitutional standards. Because it is evident that any recount seeking to meet the December 12 date will be unconstitutional for the reasons we have discussed, we reverse the judgment of the Supreme Court of Florida ordering a recount to proceed.

None are more conscious of the vital limits on judicial authority than are the members of this Court, and none stand more in admiration of the Constitution's design to leave the selection of the President to the people, through their legislatures, and to the political sphere. When contending parties invoke the process of the courts, however, it becomes our unsought responsibility to resolve the federal and constitutional issues the judicial system has been forced to confront.

The judgment of the Supreme Court of Florida is reversed, and the case is remanded for further proceedings not inconsistent with this opinion.

Had the plaintiffs prevailed, the electors would have had to choose whether to vote for Bush or Cheney. If they would have chosen Bush, Cheney would have lost to Democratic vice-presidential candidate Joe Lieberman, who would have earned a majority of the electoral votes. This would have left the president and vice-president divided by political party affiliation.

With the two-political-party system, it is unlikely that no candidate will receive a majority of electoral votes. But should dissatisfaction with the system lead to more third-party and independent candidates, the possibility of a plurality in the electoral college exists. The Twelfth Amendment provides that if no candidate wins a majority, the House of Representatives shall elect the president from the three candidates with the greatest number of electoral votes. Thomas Jefferson and John Quincy Adams were elected in this manner. However, each representative of the House is not entitled to vote. Each state is given one vote, equalizing the smaller and larger states. The Senate makes the decision for vice-president from the two highest candidates.

The original Constitution did not limit the number of terms a president may serve. The Twenty-Second Amendment, ratified in 1951 following President Franklin D. Roosevelt's four-term presidency, limits presidents to two terms. The Twenty-Fifth Amendment establishes rules of succession to the presidency. First, if the president dies, resigns, or is removed, the vice-president assumes the presidency. The new president is then empowered to nominate another vice-president, who must be confirmed by both houses of Congress.

If the president becomes unable to perform his or her responsibilities, the vice-president assumes the role of acting president. Presidential disability may be declared either by the president or by the vice-president and other officers in letters to the Speaker of the House and President Pro Tempore of the Senate. Congress is empowered to resolve any dispute between the president and vice-president (together with other executive officials) concerning the president's ability to perform the functions of the office.[5] Although this issue has never been presented, there can be little question that Congress's decision is a nonjusticiable political question.

Further succession is provided for by statute.[6] After the vice-president, the following officials would be appointed, in this order: speaker of the House, President Pro Tempore of the Senate, secretary of state, secretary of the treasury, secretary of defense, attorney general, secretary of the interior, secretary of agriculture, secretary of commerce, secretary of labor, secretary of health and human services, secretary of energy, secretary of education, and secretary of veterans affairs. Of course, replacements must satisfy the constitutional qualifications—that is, be thirty-five years of age, a natural-born citizen, and fourteen years a resident of the United States. Like federal judges, the president is shielded from financial coercion by Congress through Article II, Section 1, clause 7, which prohibits the president's salary from being decreased during his or her term.

5.3 SHARED POWERS

The framers included a thorough system of checks and balances between the executive and legislative branches, so most of the powers possessed by the president are shared with Congress. In most instances, the line between congressional authority and presidential authority is defined by practice.

Through the political question doctrine, the Court has managed to avoid many power conflicts between the president and Congress. When the Court has agreed to involve itself, it has taken two approaches. The first is a separation of functions approach. That is, in some cases the Court applies a strictly formal interpretation of the functions of the two branches. When looking at a case from this perspective, the Court asks the question, "To which branch is this function delegated?"

In most cases, however, the Court has taken a different approach to cases involving legislative–executive power conflicts. This second approach focuses more on check-and-balance principles than on strict separation principles. Functions are viewed as shared and cooperation is put at a premium. Look for these two views in the following discussions of domestic and foreign powers.

The result of practice and law has been favorable to the presidency. Most power conflicts between Congress and the president have concluded in favor of the president. In a few particular instances, Congress has attempted to control the growth of presidential authority. For example, through the War Powers Act, Congress attempted to limit the president's authority to commit the nation to war. However, in other instances, Congress has attempted to increase presidential authority over lawmaking. Delegations of legislative authority to the executive branch are discussed at length in Chapter 7. For the moment, bear in mind that through legislation, Congress controls, to some extent, executive power.

There is a reason the president often prevails in power struggles: the presidency is unified. Congress is collegial. Even more, it is fragmented. To resolve most matters, both houses must act. The president can act swiftly, often before Congress has had an opportunity to meet. As a result, even if a power is shared, the president tends to dominate. There is a positive correlation between the need for quick and efficient action and presidential dominance. That is, as the need for swift and efficient action increases, so does the likelihood that the president will be in the driver's seat.

5.4 DOMESTIC POWERS

The Constitution delegates to the president certain authorities. Other powers are inherent and have been defined through practice. Recall that few powers are possessed exclusively by one branch. Most presidential powers are closely shared with Congress, especially in the foreign affairs and military areas. This discussion begins with an examination of domestic presidential authority and then turns to foreign affairs.

5.4(a) Legislation

Congress is the primary governmental authority empowered to make law. But the president plays a role in lawmaking through three processes. First, the president participates in congressional lawmaking. Second, presidents comment on the constitutionality of laws and, in some cases, refuse to enforce them. Third, presidents have limited lawmaking authority. As to the former, the president affects congressional lawmaking both directly and indirectly. The president has a direct influence on congressional lawmaking through the veto power. Article I, Section 7, clause 2, requires all bills that have passed the House and Senate to be submitted to the president. The president may then sign the bill, making it law, or veto it. Any bills not returned to Congress within ten days become law automatically, unless Congress is not in session. In such a case, the bill dies as a consequence of the president's failure to return it. This is known as the **pocket veto.**

In the event of a veto, the Constitution requires the president to return the bill to the house where it originated. The president is required to attach "objections" to the bill for consideration by Congress. A two-thirds vote in both houses overrides a presidential veto.

pocket veto
The veto of a congressional bill by the president by retaining it until Congress is no longer in session, neither signing nor vetoing it. The effect of such inaction is to nullify the legislation without affirmatively vetoing it. The pocket veto is also available to governors under some state constitutions.

President Obama signs a bill into law in the Oval Office

Although not expressly stated in the Constitution, the president is de facto an initiator of legislation. By proposing a budget, returning bills with objections, and conferring with members of Congress concerning legislation, the president affects the development of legislation. In addition, the vice-president serves as the president of the Senate and is entitled to vote to break ties in that body.[7]

5.4(b) Signing Statements

Presidents can influence the enforcement of legislation through signing statements. A signing statement is just that, a written statement by a president about a piece of legislation, issued at the time of signing. Many signing statements are innocuous. A president may explain why he supports the law, emphasize the importance of the law to solve a problem, or recognize the individuals who initiated or shepherded the legislation through Congress.

Other statements, however, are deeper. Feeling handcuffed by the all-or-nothing approach, the Constitution offers a president (veto or not), presidents sometimes elect to sign bills but attach statements indicating that the president is of the opinion that one or more provisions of the law are unconstitutional. Quite commonly the constitutional complaint is interference with presidential authority under Article II. In some instances, presidents have used their signing statements to direct federal officers not to enforce the provisions believed to be unconstitutional. This is a controversial practice. Some scholars believe that the president's constitutional authority to question legislation ends when a bill is signed. Thereafter, the president has the duty to faithfully execute the entire law, as specifically required by Article II. Under this theory, the president must await a judicial pronouncement of unconstitutionality before refraining from enforcing the questioned provision. The counter-theory holds that the president may sign a bill into law and thereafter may choose to not enforce the questioned provision.

Although controversial at times, signing statements are not new. Although they were different in form, presidents dating back to Monroe have questioned the legitimacy of specific provisions of bills they signed into law. Even though presidents have long felt the freedom to voice their objections, there were only a few occasions where a president stated an intention to not follow the law before the twentieth century.[8] In 1909, President Theodore Roosevelt announced his intention to ignore a statutory restriction on the president's authority to appoint voluntary commissions, and President Woodrow Wilson indicated in a signing statement that a provision of the bill violated 32 treaties, and as such, he would not enforce it. In an interesting series of events, Congress passed and President Franklin D. Roosevelt signed a law that barred compensation to three federal employees found to be subversive by Congress. Although Roosevelt consented to enforcing it, he objected. In his objection he wrote that if the employees sued, he would direct the attorney general to join forces with the employees in opposing the law as unconstitutional, a deviation from the widely recognized obligation of the attorney general to defend statutes. The employees sued with the attorney general's support, Congress hired an attorney to defend the law, and the Supreme Court ruled in the employees' favor.[9]

The use of signing statements began to increase under President Jimmy Carter, but the greatest increases in their issuance have been in the George H. W. Bush, Clinton, George W. Bush, and Obama presidencies. President George H. W. Bush issued 232 during his presidency, most in the field of foreign affairs. His son, President George W. Bush, issued more signing statements questioning the constitutionality of bills than did all the presidents before him combined. Many of these resulted from President Bush's strong belief in the unitary executive. For example, he opposed congressional attempts to require executive officers to report to Congress without presidential consent or prior review, and he questioned Congress's authority to impose affirmative action requirements on federal hiring. Many others involved national security and military matters.[10]

The American Bar Association was so concerned about the potential threat to democracy that signing statements posed that it commissioned a task force to study the matter during the Bush presidency. The report, which was made public in 2006, recommended that signing statements not be used by presidents to indicate a refusal to enforce any provision of any law. The task force concluded that presidential authority to object to a bill is limited to the veto. Once signed, a president must await a judicial decision of unconstitutionality before refusing to enforce a law.

Although critical of President Bush's unprecedented use of signing statements prior to taking office, President Obama has not shied away from them. In 2009, for example, President Obama signed an appropriations bill that provided funding for the war in Afghanistan and post-war support for both Afghans and Iraqis. The bill also required the Secretary of the Treasury and other federal officials to take particular policy positions and vote in specific ways when representing the United States abroad. In a signing statement dated June 24, 2009, President Obama wrote:

> However, provisions of this bill . . . would interfere with my constitutional authority to conduct foreign relations by directing the Executive to take certain positions in negotiations or discussions with international organizations and foreign governments, or by requiring consultation with the Congress prior to such negotiations or discussions. I will not treat these provisions as limiting my ability to engage in foreign diplomacy or negotiations.[11]

5.4(c) Executive Orders, Proclamations, Memoranda

No provision in the Constitution gives the president the power to directly make law. Regardless, all American presidents have made law through **executive orders** and *presidential proclamations.* Orders and proclamations are tools used by the president to perform executive functions. As such, they are not an independent source of presidential authority. A president uses orders and proclamations only to enforce otherwise lawful presidential authority. If lawfully promulgated, orders and proclamations have the effect of statutes. To assure public notice, executive orders must be published in the **Federal Register.** It is estimated that there were as many as 20,000 executive orders (EOs) by 1907, when executive orders began to be numbered. By the time George W. Bush was elected in 2001, at least another 13,000 EOs had been issued. See Appendix D for examples of executive orders issued by several presidents.

All the executive powers discussed so far have derived from the Constitution or an act of Congress. Whether the president possesses additional power—inherent powers—has been the subject of intense debate since the formation of the Constitution. That question is at the heart of *Youngstown Sheet & Tube Co. v. Sawyer. Can we move Youngstown here?*

The *Youngstown* Court followed a strictly formal approach to separation of powers. It could find no authorization in the Constitution (or legislation) for President Truman to seize property; therefore, the action was invalidated. The dissent followed a more functional, shared-powers approach. The president as chief executive and commander-in-chief has the implied power to act in response to emergencies, assuming there is no prohibitory statute.

It appears that there is no inherent domestic presidential power. Clearly, Congress may extend emergency powers to a president. Whether the president may temporarily act while awaiting congressional action is unknown. History provides many example of the exercise of presidential authority without, or in anticipation of, congressional authorization. These usually involve national emergencies or national security. Truman's seizure is an example. Another notorious example is President Franklin D. Roosevelt's 1942 orders to relocate Japanese, German, and Italian residents of the West Coast, many of them citizens of the United States, into internment camps. Over 100,000 people were interned before the orders were rescinded in 1944. Although Congress followed the orders (E.O. 9066 and E.O. 9102) with enabling legislation, Roosevelt issued the orders

Cyber Constitution
Presidential Data
A site rich with presidential data, including signing statements, proclamations, speeches, and much more, belongs to the American Presidency Project, www.presidency.ucsb.edu/index.php

executive order
An order issued by the chief executive officer of government, whether national, state, or local.

Federal Register
An official publication, printed daily, containing regulations and proposed regulations issued by administrative agencies, as well as other rulemaking and other official business of the executive branch of government. All regulations are ultimately published in the *Code of Federal Regulations.*

under his Article II authority. The United States later apologized and paid reparations to the residents of the camps. Today the orders are generally regarded as exceeding presidential authority. It is also unlikely that Congress's authorization would make a difference today because such a law is likely to be found violative of the residents' Fifth Amendment due process and equal protection rights, contrary to the Supreme Court's 1944 decision in *Korematsu,* which is discussed later in this chapter. See Appendix D to read both of Roosevelt's relocation executive orders.

In *Youngstown,* the Court found that Congress had implicitly rejected the use of seizures before President Truman had acted. If it had not, it is possible that Congress's nonaction following the seizure could have been perceived by the Court as implicit approval, and the outcome might have been different.

Justice Jackson's outline of presidential authority is generally accepted and provides a good framework for reference. The president has the greatest authority when acting pursuant to the Constitution. Presidential power is at its next highest status when the president is acting pursuant to a statute, and weakest when acting against Congress. There is a "twilight" zone in the middle where the extent of presidential authority is not well defined. Justice Jackson was referring to situations in which presidential action is neither expressly permitted nor prohibited by the Constitution. Clearly, presidential authority is truly at its peak when expressly authorized by the Constitution. Conversely, presidential authority is at its lowest when adverse to the Constitution.

Youngstown Sheet & Tube Co. v. Sawyer
343 U.S. 579 (1952)

Mr. Justice Black delivered the opinion of the Court.

We are asked to decide whether President Truman was acting within his constitutional power when he issued an order directing the Secretary of Commerce to take possession of and operate most of the Nation's steel mills. The mill owners argue that the President's order amounts to lawmaking a legislative function which the Constitution has expressly confided to the Congress and not the President. The Government's position is that the order was made on findings of the President that his action was necessary to avert a national catastrophe which would inevitably result from a stoppage of steel production, and that in meeting this grave emergency the President was acting within the aggregate of his constitutional powers as the Nation's Chief Executive and Commander in Chief of the Armed Forces of the United States. The issue emerges here from the following series of events:

[Steel company management and steel workers' unions had a dispute over wages and other conditions. As a result, they could not reach a collective bargaining agreement. The Federal Mediation and Conciliation Service and federal Wage Stabilization Board attempted unsuccessfully to settle the dispute. The workers' union gave notice of intent to strike.] The indispensability of steel as a component of substantially all weapons and other war materials led the President to believe that the proposed work stoppage would immediately jeopardize our national defense and that governmental seizure of the steel mills was necessary in order to assure the continued availability of steel. Reciting these considerations for his action, the President, a few hours before the strike was to begin, issued Executive Order 10340. [The] order directed the Secretary of Commerce to take possession of most of the steel mills and keep them running. The Secretary immediately issued his own orders, calling upon the presidents of the various seized companies to serve as operating managers for the United States. . . . The next morning the President sent a message to Congress reporting his action. . . . [Congress never took action. The companies complied, but filed suit in federal court seeking an injunction prohibiting the order from being enforced. The companies prevailed in the district court.]

The President's power, if any, to issue the order must stem either from an act of Congress or from the Constitution itself. There is no statute that expressly authorizes the President to take possession of property as he did here. Nor is there any act of Congress to which our attention has been directed from which such a power can fairly be implied. . . .

Moreover, the use of the seizure technique to solve labor dispute in order to prevent work stoppages was not only unauthorized by any congressional enactment; prior to this controversy, Congress had refused to adopt that method of setting labor disputes. When the Taft-Hartley Act was under consideration in 1947. Congress rejected an amendment which would have authorized such governmental seizures in cases of emergency. . . .

It is clear that if the President had authority to issue the order he did, it must be found in some provision to the Constitution. . . . The contention is that presidential power should he implied from the aggregate of his powers under the Constitution. Particular reliance is placed on provisions in Article II which say that "The executive Power shall be vested in a President . . ."; that "he shall take Care that the Laws be faithfully executed"; and that he "shall be Commander in Chief of the Army and Navy of the United States."

The order cannot properly be sustained as an exercise of the President's military power as Commander in Chief of the Armed Forces. The Government attempts to do so by citing a number of cases upholding broad powers in military commanders engaged in day-to-day fighting in a theater of war. Such cases need not concern us here. Even though "theater of war" be an expanding concept, we cannot with faithfulness to our constitutional system hold that the Commander and Chief of the Armed Forces had the ultimate power as such to take possession of private property in order to keep labor disputes from stopping production. This is a job for the Nation's lawmakers, not for its military authorities.

Nor can the seizure order be sustained because of the several constitutional provisions that grant executive power to the President. In the framework of our Constitution, the President's power to see that the laws are faithfully executed refutes the idea that he is to be lawmaker. The Constitution limits his functions in the lawmaking process to the recommending of laws . . . and the vetoing of laws. . . .

The Founders of this Nation entrusted the lawmaking power to the Congress alone in both good and bad times. It would do no good to recall the historical events, the fears of power and the hopes for freedom that lay behind their choice. Such a review would but confirm our holding that this seizure order cannot stand.

The judgment of the District Court is affirmed.

Mr. Justice Jackson, concurring in the judgment and opinion of the Court.

. . . Presidential powers are not fixed but fluctuate, depending upon their disjunction or conjunction with those of Congress. . . .

1. When the President acts pursuant to an express or implied authorization of Congress, his authority is at its maximum, for it includes all that he possesses in his own right plus all that Congress can delegate. . . . If his act is held unconstitutional under these circumstances, it usually means that the Federal Government as an undivided whole lacks power. A seizure executed by the President pursuant to an Act of Congress would be supported by the strongest of presumptions and the widest latitude of judicial interpretation, and the burden of persuasion would rest heavily upon any who might attack it.

2. When the President acts in absence of either a congressional grant or denial of authority, he can only rely upon his own independent powers, but there is a zone of twilight in which he and Congress may have concurrent authority, or in which its distribution is uncertain. Therefore, congressional inertia, indifference or acquiescence

may sometimes, at least in practical matters, enable, if not invite, [presidential] measures. . . .

3. When the President takes measures incompatible with the expressed or implied will of Congress, his power is at its lowest ebb, for then he can rely only upon his own constitutional powers minus any constitutional powers of Congress over the matter. . . . [Justice Jackson analyzed the seizure under the third category and found that the president had acted unlawfully.]

Mr. Justice Burton, concurring.

. . . The present situation is not comparable to that of an imminent invasion or threatened attack. We do not face the issue of what might be the President's constitutional power to meet such catastrophic situations. Nor is it claimed that the current seizure is in the nature of a military command addressed by the President, as Commander-in-Chief, to a mobilized nation waging, or imminently threatened with, total war.

Mr. Justice Clark, concurring.

[The] Constitution does grant to the President extensive authority in times of grave and imperative national emergency. In fact, to my thinking, such a grant may well be necessary to the very existence of the Constitution itself. As Lincoln aptly said, "[is] it possible to lose the nation and yet preserve the Constitution?". . .

[Several] statutes furnish the guideposts for decision in this case. [N]either the Defense Production Act nor Taft-Hartley authorized the seizure challenged here, and the Government made no effort to comply with the procedures established by the Selective Service Act of 1948, a statute which expressly authorizes seizures when producers fail to supply necessary defense material. . . .

Mr. Chief Justice Vinson, with whom Mr. Justice Reed and Mr. Justice Minton join, dissenting.

The President of the United States directed the Secretary of Commerce to take temporary possession of the Nation's steel mills during the existing emergency because "a work stoppage would immediately jeopardize and imperil our national defense and the defense of those joined with us in resisting aggression, and would add to the continuing danger of our soldiers, sailors, and airmen engaged in combat in the field." . . .

Plaintiffs do not remotely suggest any basis for rejecting the President's finding that *any* stoppage of steel production would immediately place the Nation in peril. [According to the plaintiffs], the President is left powerless at the very moment when the need for action may be most pressing and when no one, other than he, is immediately capable of action. Under this view, he is left powerless [because the power belongs to Congress]. . . .

A review of executive action demonstrates that our Presidents have on many occasions exhibited the leadership contemplated by the Framers when they made the President Commander in Chief, and imposed upon him the trust to "take Care that the Laws be faithfully executed." With or without explicit statutory authorization,

Presidents have at such times dealt with national emergencies by acting promptly and resolutely to enforce legislative programs, at least to save those programs until Congress could act. Congress and the courts have responded to such executive initiative with consistent approval. . . .

Our first President displayed at once the leadership contemplated by the Framers. When the national revenue laws were openly flouted in some sections of Pennsylvania, President Washington, without waiting for a call from the state government, summoned the militia and took decisive steps to secure the faithful execution of the laws. [Hamilton,] whose defense of the Proclamation [of Neutrality concerning the French Revolution] has endured the test of time, invoked the argument that the Executive has the duty to do that which will preserve the peace until Congress acts. . . .

In an action furnishing a most apt precedent for this case, President Lincoln without statutory authority directed the seizure of rail and telegraph lines leading to Washington. . . .

The broad executive power granted by Article II to an officer on duty 365 days a year cannot, it is said, be invoked to avert disaster. Instead, the President must confine himself to sending a message to Congress recommending action. Under this messenger-boy concept of the Office, the President cannot even act to preserve legislative programs from destruction so that Congress will have something left to act upon. . . .

The President immediately informed Congress of his action and clearly stated his intention to abide by the legislative will. No basis for claims of arbitrary action, unlimited powers or dictatorial usurpation of congressional power appears from the facts of this case. On the contrary, judicial, legislative and executive precedents throughout our history demonstrate that in this case the President acted in full conformity with his duties under the Constitution. . . .

[The Court's decision was issued on June 2, and the union then struck for nearly two months. The war effort was not seriously affected by the strike.]

In addition to issuing orders, presidents also make proclamations and issue memoranda on a variety of topics. Some raise no legal issues and are more ceremonial in nature. Others are more substantive. For example, concerned about the large number of federal regulations that "preempt" or replace state laws, President Obama issued a memoranda in 2009 advising executive officials to be respectful of the prerogatives of the states when considering "preemption" of state laws. You can read this memorandum in Appendix D.

Unlike executive orders, however, memoranda are not law. A memorandum is an expression of a president's views and policy objectives that does not create substantive rights that may form the basis of legal action.

5.4(d) Impoundment and Nonenforcement of Laws

Does presidential authority include the power to not enforce laws? This issue arises in two contexts: refusal to spend congressionally appropriated funds and refusal to enforce law.

Impoundment *Impoundment* refers to a president's refusal to expend congressionally appropriated funds. Presidents have long claimed impoundment power, usually for economic reasons, such as to combat inflation. Opponents of the power assert that Article II imposes an affirmative obligation on the president to execute all of the laws and that the president lacks the power to refuse enforcement of particular laws. Further, because the Constitution expressly delegates fiscal powers to Congress, as well as the general power to make the nation's laws, a refusal to spend appropriated funds is a usurpation of legislative power.

The application of impoundment to specific sections of a law with many appropriations is much like the **line item veto.** The line item veto is not provided for by the Constitution or by statute. Lower courts have rejected the theory of implied impoundment power, at least in the domestic arena. In the foreign affairs context, presidential authority is likely greater. For example, Congress may not attempt to control diplomacy, which is an executive power, through appropriations. Thus, Congress could not appropriate funds to open an embassy in a nation where the executive has terminated relations.

line item veto
The right of a governor under most state constitutions to veto individual appropriations in an appropriation act rather than being compelled either to veto the act as a whole or to sign it into law. The president of the United States does not have a line item veto.

Executive/Prosecutorial Discretion   In terms of civil and criminal law, the authority of the executive to exercise prosecutorial discretion is well established. Prosecutorial discretion includes the power to decide whether and when to investigate, prosecute, settle, and appeal individual cases. With the exception of decisions that are malicious, arbitrary, or premised upon some improper motive (such as race), courts do not interfere.

However, the authority of the executive to refuse to enforce a law altogether, or to refuse to enforce the law against an entire class of people covered by the law, is questionable. Recall that Article II provides that the president "shall take Care that the Laws be faithfully executed." This language appears to compel the executive to enforce all statutes, at least all that are facially valid. If a law has been declared unconstitutional or otherwise invalid by a court, the executive has the contrary obligation not to enforce that law. Similarly, a law that is facially or obviously invalid should not be enforced. For example, the Supreme Court decided in *Texas v. Johnson*[12] that First Amendment freedom of expression includes burning the nation's flag. In that case, a Texas statute criminalizing this conduct was invalidated. The U.S. Congress responded by enacting a federal law criminalizing the same conduct, in obvious contravention of the First Amendment.[13] In such a case, the president could have issued an order to the U.S. attorneys, directing them not to enforce the law, without running afoul of his duty to enforce the laws.

One method presidents use to announce their opinions about the constitutionality of laws is presidential signing statements, as discussed earlier in this chapter.

5.4(e) Appointment and Removal of Officials

Article II, Section 2, clause 2, governs the appointment of the government's most senior officials. True to the framer's intention of separating powers subject to checks and balances, the appointments clause reads,

> [The president shall have the power to] nominate, and by and with the Advice and Consent of the Senate, shall appoint Ambassadors, other public Ministers and Consuls, Judges of the Supreme Court, and all other Officers of the United States, whose Appointments are not herein otherwise provided for, and which shall be established by Law: but the Congress may by Law vest the Appointment of such inferior Officers, as they think proper, in the President alone, in the Courts of Law, or in the Heads of Departments.

Naturally, as the chief executive, it is the president who is responsible for identifying the heads of departments. As a check on this power, the Senate must confirm presidential nominations of officers, or in the language of Article II, provide "advice and consent." The president may nominate any person, subject only to the qualifications

---

S I D E B A R

PRESIDENTIAL APPOINTMENTS OF SUPREME COURT JUSTICES

Although a president exercises no control over a justice after confirmation, presidents do attempt to select individuals with whom they share a political philosophy. Even though superficial and often unsuccessful, presidents tend to look to such factors as political party affiliation, prior political positions held, and opinions rendered, if the candidate has had judicial experience. For example, 82 percent of the nominees of Republican presidents have been Republican and 95 percent of the nominees of Democratic presidents have been from the Democratic Party.[14]

Another study indicates that a president's strength and popularity affect the likelihood of confirmation. For example, for presidents who would be re-elected, only 7.3 percent of their nominations were rejected. For presidents who were not re-elected, the rejection rate increased to 18.6 percent. Of presidents who could not be re-elected because they were in their second term, the rate was 26.3 percent. Finally, the rate of failure was the highest for those presidents who were not elected; it was 60 percent.[15]

established by Congress. Similarly, it appears that the Senate possesses the same authority. It may deny confirmation for any reason. In fact, the Constitution does not require the Senate to explain itself. The presidential nomination power of appointment is personal and may not be delegated, nor may the Senate delegate its advice and consent responsibility to another body.

Although the nation and its government were much smaller in 1787, the framers recognized that the responsibility to appoint all federal officers would be overwhelming to a president and to the Senate. Accordingly, they established an alternative appointment method for "inferior officers," which may be appointed, as Congress prescribes, by the president, courts of law, or heads of departments. If the appointment of an inferior officer is vested in the president, head of office, or court under Article II, Section 2, Congress can require Senate confirmation or not. It may also require confirmation by both the House of Representatives and the Senate. In most cases, however, congressional approval is not required, leaving the designated officials to make their appointments directly or under the oversight of the president or another executive officer.

The appointments clause does not further distinguish between, or better define, officers and inferior officers. Clearly, members of the president's cabinet, which is filled with the highest officers of the nation's most significant departments, are officers that must come to office through presidential nomination and Senate confirmation. The secretaries of state, treasury, defense, interior, agriculture, commerce, labor, education, health and human service, housing and urban development, energy, veterans affairs, transportation, and homeland security and the attorney general are members of the cabinet. There are hundreds, possibly more than a thousand, other positions that are considered officers under the appointments clause. Deputy-, assistant-, and under-secretaries of departments, the heads of non-cabinet offices, U.S. attorneys (responsible for representing the United States in civil and criminal matters), members of boards of collegially governed agencies, and all individuals who hold military commissions are officers. Additionally, the appointments clause is clear that ambassadors, public ministers and consuls, and judges of the Supreme Court must be nominated by the president and confirmed by Senate. Beyond justices of the Supreme Court, all federal judges that are appointed under Article III must undergo the nomination and confirmation process. This includes all federal trial (district) and appellate judges. As you will learn in a moment, there are non–Article III judges whose appointments have been delegated to Article III judges under the appointments clause.

Note that positions personal to the president do not require Senate approval. The president's administrative support personnel, spokesperson (White House Press Secretary), attorney (White House Counsel), chief of staff, and a variety of advisors are examples. There is sometimes a fine line between an advisor to the president and an officer of the United States. The Office of Legal Counsel to President Obama opined that any person who is delegated a sovereign power of the United States and who has continuing employment is an officer under the appointments clause.[16] A president must be careful when defining the duties of an advisor not to empower the individual with "sovereign powers," lest Senate confirmation, and quite possibly congressional creation of the position, will be required. In 2009, the Senate Judiciary Committee held hearings on this very issue because a number of senators were concerned that the so-called White House Czars or individuals who are appointed by the president as advisers over specific subject areas (e.g., drugs and green jobs) were wielding too much authority. The Senate investigation did not lead to immediate action, but in 2011, Congress decided to "defund" four Czar positions, including advisers for energy and climate, health reform, auto industry, and manufacturing. President Obama objected in a signing statement, claiming that the four positions were purely advisory, created under Article II, and that Congress had violated the separation of powers by its decision.[17]

The Office of Legal Counsel further defined sovereign authority as a delegation of authority to legally bind the United States; to interpret, implement, or execute law; and to command the military. By continuing, the Office of Legal Counsel excluded contractors and other transient employees, even if they exercise temporary sovereign authority. This definition of an officer has not been reviewed by the Supreme Court, and the Court has not provided its own precise definition.

So, what is an inferior officer? Naturally, it is an employee of the government that reports to a superior officer. In support of the idea that officers of the government must in some manner be connected to nation's elected officials, the Court has found that there needs to be accountability between inferior officers and the officers that undergo the presidential nomination and senatorial confirmation process.

Congress has three options when deciding where to vest an appointment: the president, the courts, or a head of department. Congress may not delegate the appointment of inferior officers to any other person or group, including itself. For example, a statute that delegated the appointment of the Commissioners of the Federal Election Commission to the President Pro Tempore of the Senate and speaker of the House was invalidated as to the executive and judicial functions the FEC performs (but not the legislative).[18] This case reflects the limitation on Congress's authority to delegate the appointment power of inferior officers. The authority of appointment must rest with an official from the correct branch of government in order to preserve the separation of powers. So, officials who are responsible for enforcing the law must be appointed by someone in the executive branch, and non–Article III judges must be appointed by Article III judges. Even though Congress may not appoint executive officials, it may establish qualifications for their appointment. These qualifications must be related to the position; arbitrary qualifications are invalid. For example, requiring a nominee for Surgeon General to be a physician is reasonable. In an effort to achieve ideological balance, Congress has also required that the composition of collegial bodies be balanced between Democrats and Republicans. The directors of the Federal Communications Commission, Federal Agricultural Mortgage Corporation, Federal Deposit Insurance Corporation, and Defense Nuclear Safety Board are examples. Congress may also establish reasonable conditions of office and commonly sets the length of appointment, particularly for so-called independent agencies (these are discussed in greater detail in the next chapter). The length of tenure varies from at-will to fifteen-year terms. Three- to five-year terms are common.

What constitutes an inferior officer can be a challenging question. An examination of an officer's duties and responsibilities, as well as whom the officer supervises and whom he or she is supervised by, is necessary. The nomination power may be delegated to courts of law, as well as to the president. Under this authority, Congress delegated the power to appoint special judges (inferior officers) to the chief judge of the Tax Court. That the Tax Court is not an Article III court is not dispositive. Legislatively established tribunals are "courts" under the appointments clause.[19]

Federal officials are mobile. Some officers change positions through promotion. Other officials change positions as requested by the president. In most circumstances, transferring officials must undergo the appointment process a second time. For example, a change from secretary of energy to secretary of state could not occur without Senate confirmation to the new position. However, when the change in position does not bring with it a substantial change in responsibility, a second confirmation may be unnecessary. For example, all commissioned military officers are nominated by the president and confirmed by the Senate. A change in rank does not require a new confirmation, nor does a change of an officer from a line position to military judge. However, promoting an officer to Chair of the Joint Chiefs of Staff requires confirmation.[20]

Article II, Section 2, provides that the president may make temporary appointments, or **recess appointments,** to fill vacancies while the Senate is not in session.

recess appointment
An appointment of an officer of the United States by the president while the Senate is in recess. The appointment expires at the end of the next session of the Senate if the appointee is not confirmed. Recess appointments are common. George Washington, for example, made a recess appointment of John Rutledge as chief justice of the Supreme Court in 1795 after John Jay, the nation's first chief justice, resigned to assume the role of governor of New York. Rutledge's nomination was rejected by the Senate during its next session, in part due to his unpopular and vocal political opinions and also because of concerns about his mental condition. Rather than remain chief justice until the end of the Senate's term, Rutledge resigned.

This applies to all positions for which the president holds the nomination power. The appointee must be confirmed by the Senate during its next session. If not, the appointment expires automatically at the end of the session.

Most of the work of the federal government is not performed by primary or inferior officers, but by federal employees. These persons may be appointed in whatever manner Congress wishes to impose, so long as the method comports with due process and equal protection. Most federal employees are hired through a civil service system.

The counterpart to appointment authority is removal authority. Once appointed, federal judges enjoy lifetime tenure. This is not true of executive officials. As part of the appointment power, as well as the power as chief executive, the president may remove executive branch "officers" who have undergone the nomination and confirmation process under Article II, Section 2. The president enjoys nearly unlimited discretion in the removal of cabinet members. The attorney general is an example. Because law enforcement and prosecution is an inherently executive function, presidential authority over federal law enforcement is significant. This has been recognized by Congress, which provides for presidential nomination and senatorial confirmation in the appointment of U.S. attorneys (federal prosecutors), yet the president may solely remove them. Many presidents have made significant changes to the staff of U.S. attorneys, who are appointed in every judicial district in the United States, at the time they take office. President George W. Bush found himself, as well as his Attorney General Alberto Gonzales, immersed in a controversy for the firing of several U.S. attorneys during Bush's second term in office. Many claimed the firings were politically motivated. Congress investigated and, ultimately, Gonzales and others resigned, at least in part, if not largely, due to the controversy. It was not questioned that President Bush possessed the authority to fire the prosecutors, and everyone acknowledged that past presidents had dismissed U.S. attorneys for partisan reasons. The controversy concerned whether they had been dismissed for decisions concerning specific cases involving prominent Republicans.

As to inferior officers, heads of independent agencies, and executive branch officials who serve quasi-legislative or quasi-judicial functions, Congress may limit the president's removal power in certain circumstances.

Other than impeachment (which is discussed in the chapter on Congress), the Constitution does not establish a method of removal of federal officers. Presidents have long held that they possess plenary removal authority over federal officers (see Figure 7-1). Removal, it has been contended, is part of the president's Article II executive power. In addition to this structural (unitary) theory, a democratic theory for direct presidential oversight is advanced; that is, agency officials, who are not elected, should be directly accountable to an individual who is elected. Additionally, some scholars also propose that direct accountability of all federal officers is necessary for a president to build a team and advance a vision.

Through the years, however, Congress has chosen to limit presidential power to terminate some inferior federal officials. The rationale for limiting the president's removal authority is that government agencies will be better focused on their missions if they are free from presidential politics. An agency whose head cannot be terminated by the president without cause is known as an **independent agency.** The Interstate Commerce Commission, established in 1887, was the nation's first independent agency. An agency whose head serves at the pleasure of the president is known as an **executive agency.** There are many executive and independent agencies. (See Figure 6-2.) Typically the president's authority to remove independent agency executives is limited to "cause." What agencies may Congress make independent is not exactly clear. Agencies that perform traditionally pure executive functions must remain as accountable to the president as possible, and a "for cause limitation" is likely violative of Article II.

independent agency
An agency whose head may be terminated by the president only for good cause.

executive agency
An agency whose head serves at the pleasure of the president.

Cabinet-levels officers, such as the secretary of the Department of Defense and attorney general of the United States, are examples.

In those cases where presidential authority is legitimately limited, disagreements over policy and politics do not constitute good cause, whereas corruption and incompetence do. In *Myers v. United States,* the constitutionality of limiting the president's authority to remove the postmaster of the United States was considered by the Supreme Court. *Myers* leaves the impression that Congress may not limit the presidential removal power whatsoever. Time would prove otherwise.

The Federal Trade Commission, which is the subject of the *Humphrey's Executor* case, was structured as an independent agency. Unlike the statute in *Myers,* however, Congress did not require Senate approval or removal; rather, it limited the reasons for which the president could remove an officer for cause. Compare the decision in *Humphrey's* to the *Myers* opinion.

Myers v. United States
272 U.S. 52 (1926)

[A federal statute (1863) provided that postmasters could be removed by the president only with Senate approval. Contrary to the law, a postmaster from Oregon, Myers, was removed by the postmaster general under orders from the president. Myers sued to recover his lost salary in the Court of Claims. He did not prevail. He died in the interim, but his estate brought an appeal to the Supreme Court alleging that the president was without the authority to terminate his employment.]

Mr. Chief Justice Taft delivered the opinion of the Court.

This case presents the question whether under the Constitution the President has the exclusive power of removing executive officers of the United States whom he has appointed by and with the advice and consent of the Senate. . . .

Made responsible under the Constitution for the effective enforcement of the law, the president needs as an indispensable aid to meet it the disciplinary influence upon those who act under him of a reserve power of removal. But it is contended that executive officers appointed by the President with the consent of the Senate are bound by the statutory law, and are not his servants to do his will, and that his obligation to care for the faithful execution of the law does not authorize him to treat them as such. The degree of guidance in the discharge of their duties that the president may exercise over executive officers varies with the character of their service as prescribed in the law under which they act. The highest and most important duties which his subordinates perform are those in which they act for him. In such cases they are exercising not their own but his discretion. This field is a very large one. It is sometimes described as political. . . . Each head of a department is and must be the President's alter ego in the matters of that department where the president is required by law to exercise authority. . . .

The imperative reasons requiring an unrestricted power to remove the most important of his subordinates in their most important duties must therefore control the interpretation of the Constitution as to all appointed by him.

. . . [T]he President should have a like power to remove his appointees charged with other duties than those above described. The ordinary duties of officers prescribed by statute come under the general administrative control of the President by virtue of the general grant to him of the executive power, and he may properly supervise and guide their construction of the statute under which they act in order to secure that unitary and uniform execution of the laws which article 2 of the Constitution evidently contemplated in vesting general executive power in the president alone. Laws are often passed with specific provision for the adoption of regulations by a department or bureau head to make the law workable and effective. The ability and judgment manifested by the official thus empowered, as well as his energy and stimulation of his subordinates, are subject which the president must consider and supervise in his administrative control. Finding such officers to be negligent and inefficient, the President should have the power to remove them. Of course there may be duties so peculiarly and specifically committed to the discretion of a particular officer as to raise a question whether the President may overrule or revise the officer's interpretation of his statutory duty in a particular instance. Then there may be duties of a quasi judicial character imposed on executive officers and members of executive tribunals whose decisions after hearing affect interests of individuals, the discharge of which the president cannot in a particular case properly influence or control. But even in such a case he may consider the decision after its rendition as a reason for removing the officer, on the ground that the discretion regularly entrusted to that officer by statute has not been on the whole intelligently or wisely exercised. Otherwise he does not discharge his own constitutional duty of seeing that the laws be faithfully executed. . . .

[The Court then noted that the First Congress created three executive departments—War, State, and Treasury—and that the secretaries of all three were removable by the president solely. The Court considered this evidence that the framers considered removal an executive power.]

Summing up . . . the facts as to acquiescence by all branches of the government in the legislative decision of 1789 as to executive officers, whether superior or inferior, we find that from 1789 to 1863 [when the statute at issue was adopted], a period of 74 years, there was no act of Congress, no executive act, and no decision of this court at variance with the declaration of the First Congress; but there was, as we have seen, clear affirmative recognition of it by each branch of government.

Our conclusion on the merits, sustained by the arguments before stated, is that article 2 grants to the president the executive power of the government—i.e., the general administrative control of those executing the laws, including the power of appointment and removal of executive officers—a conclusion confirmed by his obligation to take care that the laws be faithfully executed; that article 2 excludes the exercise of legislative power by Congress to provide for appointments and removals, except only as granted therein to Congress in the matter of inferior offices; that Congress is only given power to provide for appointments and removals of inferior officers after it has vested, and on condition that it does vest, their appointment in other authority than the President with the Senate's consent, that the provisions of the second section of article 2, which blend action by the legislative branch, or by part of it, in the work of the executive, are limitations to be strictly construed, and not to be extended by implication; that the president's power of removal is further established as an incident to his specifically enumerated function of appointment by and with the advice of the Senate, but that such incident does not by implication extend to removals the Senate's power of checking appointments; and, finally, that to hold otherwise would make it impossible for the President, in case of political or other difference with the Senate or Congress, to take care that the laws be faithfully executed. . . .

For the reasons given, we must therefore hold that the provision of the law of 1876 by which the unrestricted power of removal of first-class postmasters is denied the President is in violation of the Constitution and invalid. This leads to the affirmance of the judgment of the Court of Claims.

Humphrey's Executor v. United States
295 U.S. 602 (1935)

[Humphrey had been appointed to sit on the Federal Trade Commission (FTC). Statute established that FTC commissioners were to serve seven years and, further, that a commissioner could be removed by the president for inefficiency, neglect of duty, or malfeasance in office. President Roosevelt asked Humphrey to resign. He refused. Humphrey subsequently died, but his estate prosecuted an action against the United States in the Court of Claims for his lost pay. The Court of Claims certified two questions to the Supreme Court: (1) Does the Federal Trade Claims Act limit the removal of commissions by the president to the causes listed in the statute? (2) If so, is such a limitation constitutional?]

Mr. Justice Sutherland delivered the opinion of the Court.

First. The question first to be considered is whether, by the provisions of § 1 of the Federal Trade Act . . . the President's power is limited to removal for the specific causes enumerated therein. . . .

The commission is to be non-partisan; and it must, from the very nature of its duties, act with entire impartiality. It is charged with the enforcement of no policy except the policy of the law. Its duties are neither political nor executive, but predominately quasi-judicial and quasi-legislative. Like the Interstate Commerce Commission, its members are called upon to exercise the trained judgment of a body of experts "appointed by law and informed by experience."

The legislative reports in both houses of Congress clearly reflect the view that a fixed term was necessary to the effective and fair administration of the law. . . .

The debates in both houses demonstrate that the prevailing view was that the commission was not to be "subject to anybody in the government but . . . only the people of the United States"; free from "political domination or control" or the "probability or possibility of such a thing"; to be "separate and apart from any existing department of government—not subject to the orders of the President." . . .

Thus, the language of the act, the legislative reports, and the general purposes of the legislation as reflected by the debates, all combine to demonstrate the Congressional intent to create a body of experts who shall gain expertise by length of service—a body which shall be independent of executive authority *except in its selection*, and free to exercise its judgment without the leave or hindrance of any other official or any department of the government. To the accomplishment of these purposes, it is clear that Congress was of the opinion that length and certainty of tenure would vitally contribute. And to hold that, nevertheless, the members of the commission continue in office at the mere will of the President, might be to thwart, in large measure, the very ends which Congress sought to realize by definitely fixing the term of office.

We conclude that the intent of the act is to limit the executive power of removal to the causes enumerated, the existence of none of which is claimed here; and we pass to the second question.

Second. To support its contention that the removal provision of § 1, as we have just construed it, is an unconstitutional interference with the executive power of the President, the government's chief reliance [is] on *Myers v. United States*, 272 U.S. 52, 47 S. Ct 21. . . . [T]he narrow point actually decided [*in Myers*] was only that the President had power to remove a postmaster of the first class, without the advice and consent of the Senate as required by act of Congress. . . .

The office of postmaster is so essentially unlike the office now involved that the decision in the *Myers* case cannot be accepted as controlling our decision here. A postmaster is an executive officer restricted to the performance of executive functions. He is charged with no duty at all related to either the legislative or judicial power. The actual decision in the *Myers* case finds support in the theory that such an officer is merely one of the units in the executive department and, hence, inherently subject to the exclusive and illimitable power of removal by the Chief Executive, whose subordinate and aid he is. Putting aside *dicta*, which may be followed if sufficiently persuasive but which are not controlling, the necessary reach of the decision goes far enough to include all purely executive officers. It goes no farther;—much less does it include an officer who occupies no place in the executive department and who exercises no part of the executive power vested by the Constitution in the President.

The Federal Trade Commission is an administrative body created by Congress to carry into effect legislative policies embodied in the statute in accordance with the legislative standard therein prescribed, and to perform other specified duties as a legislative or as a judicial aid. Such a body cannot in any proper sense be characterized as an arm or an eye of the executive. Its duties are performed without executive leave and, in the contemplation of the statute, must be free from executive control. In administering the provisions of the statute in respect of "unfair methods of competition"—that is to say in filling in and administering the details embodied by that general standard—the commission acts in part quasi-legislatively and in part quasi-judicially. In making investigations and reports thereon for the information of Congress under § 6, in aid of the legislative power, it acts as a legislative agency. Under § 7, which authorizes the commission to act as a master in chancery under rules prescribed by the court, it acts as an agency of the judiciary. To the extent that it exercises any executive function—as distinguished from executive power in the constitutional sense—it does so in the discharge and effectuation of its quasi-legislative or quasi-judicial powers, or as an agency of the legislative or judicial departments of the government.

We think it plain under the Constitution that illimitable power of removal is not possessed by the President in respect of officers of the character of those just named. The authority of Congress, in creating quasi-legislative or quasi-judicial agencies, to require them to act in discharge of their duties independently of executive control cannot well be doubted; and that authority includes, as an appropriate incident, power to fix the period during which they shall continue in office, and to forbid their removal except for cause in the meantime. For this is quite evident that one who holds office only during the pleasure of another, cannot be depended upon to maintain an attitude of independence against the latter's will.

The fundamental necessity of maintaining each of the three general departments of government entirely free from the control or coercive influence, direct or indirect, of either of the others, has often been stressed and is hardly open to serious question. . . .

The result of what we now have said is this: Whether the power of the President to remove an officer shall prevail over the authority of Congress to condition the power by fixing a definite term and precluding a removal except for cause, will depend upon the character of the office; the *Myers* decision, affirming the power of the President alone to make the removal, is confined to purely executive officers; and as to officers of the kind here under consideration, we hold that no removal can be made during the prescribed term for which the officer is appointed, except for one or more of the causes named in the applicable statute.

To the extent that, between the decision in the *Myers* case, which sustains the unrestricted power of the President to remove purely executive officers, and our present decision that such power does not extend to an office such as that here involved, there shall remain a field of doubt, we leave such cases as may fall within it for future consideration and determination as they may arise.

In accordance with the foregoing, the questions submitted are answered.

Question No. 1, Yes.
Question No. 2, Yes.

Thus, it is clear that congressional ability to control the president's removal of federal officers hinges upon the character of the officer's responsibilities. If a position is purely executive, the person who fills it serves at the pleasure of the president, and Congress may not provide otherwise. Primary offices, such as cabinet offices, are purely executive. Others are as well—U.S. attorneys, for example. They are not temporary employees, they perform purely executive functions (e.g., prosecution of cases), they possess administrative authority, and they render policy decisions.

If an officer performs quasi-legislative or quasi-judicial functions, then Congress may control her tenure. Note that even when Congress may dictate the terms of an official's tenure, it may never control that tenure. For example, in a 1986 Supreme Court decision, *Bowsher v. Synar*,[21] a statute that empowered Congress to remove the comptroller general, an executive official, was invalidated because it violated the separation of powers principle. The Court found the statute to be a dangerous usurpation of executive power.

The issue concerning the power of Congress to limit presidential removal power surfaced again in 1978. To combat crime in government, Congress enacted the Ethics in Government Act in 1978. Pursuant to that statute, an independent counsel (also known as a *special prosecutor*) may be appointed to investigate and prosecute cases. The attorney general is required to request appointment under the statute after finding reasonable grounds to believe that a crime was committed, but the selection and appointment are made by a special panel of three federal judges. Once appointed, the independent counsel's judgment may not be interfered with by the attorney general or anyone else. An independent counsel may be removed by the attorney general only for good cause. The law was carefully tailored to provide the independent counsel with as much independence as possible without violating separations principles.

In *Morrison v. Olson*,[22] the constitutionality of the independent counsel law was considered. The issue was particularly challenging because the objective of the law is to shield the independent counsel from political pressures, although the prosecution function appears to be a "purely executive function" over which the president has plenary authority.

The Court upheld the independent counsel law in *Morrison* for the following reasons:

1. Unlike the situation in *Bowsher v. Synar,* the independent counsel law does not represent an attempt by Congress to control an executive function. The decision to have counsel appointed and removed is left to the attorney general.
2. An independent counsel is an inferior officer in terms of the appointments clause. The independent counsel's appointment is temporary; she does not exercise any policymaking authority, nor does she possess significant administrative authority. This being the case, it is proper for Congress to limit removal to good cause.
3. The use of federal judges to select the independent counsel is appropriate. They may not review the attorney general's decision to request appointment, and the statute does not empower them to supervise the investigation or prosecution of the case. Thus, there is no encroachment of the judiciary on executive turf. Nor does the role endanger the integrity of the judiciary. Further, the appointments clause specifically states that inferior officers may be appointed by courts.
4. The president's ability to perform his or her constitutionally assigned functions is not disturbed by this process, especially as the decision to appoint and the power to remove are vested in the executive (attorney general).

It can be reasonably argued that *Morrison* altered the test from "nature of function" to "is the president's ability to perform the constitutionally assigned functions impaired?" More likely, both standards continue to be viable and must be considered by a reviewing court.

Another twist challenging the unitary presidency is the so-called double-for-cause limitation. In such a structure, Congress creates an agency that reports to an independent agency. When this occurs, the lower agency's head can be removed only for cause and their supervisor's removal by the president is also limited to cause, further distancing the agency from the president. This happened in a law (commonly known as Sarbanes–Oxley) enacted in 2002 in response to a number of scandals that involved accounting firms and practices, including Enron. The purpose of the law is to improve accounting and accountability in public corporations. The issue that made its way to the Supreme Court in the 2010 case *Free Enterprise Fund v. Public Corporation Accounting Oversight Board (2010)* was whether the dual-for-cause limitation on presidential oversight was valid under Article II.

Cyber Constitution
Morrison v. Olson can be read at www.law.cornell. edu/supct/html/historics/ USSC_CR_0487_0654_ ZS.html

Free Enterprise Fund v. Public Corporation Accounting Oversight Board
561 U.S. __ (2010)

Our Constitution divided the "powers of the new Federal Government into three defined categories, Legislative, Executive, and Judicial." Article II vests "[t]he executive Power . . . in a President of the United States of America," who must "take Care that the Laws be faithfully executed." Art. II, §1, cl. 1. In light of "[t]he impossibility that one man should be able to perform all the great business of the State," the Constitution provides for executive officers to "assist the supreme Magistrate in discharging the duties of his trust."

Since 1789, the Constitution has been understood to empower the President to keep these officers accountable—by removing them from office, if necessary. See generally *Myers v. United States*, 272 U. S. 52 (1926). This Court has determined, however, that this authority is not without limit. In *Humphrey's Executor v. United States*, 295 U. S. 602(1935), we held that Congress can, under certain circumstances, create independent agencies run by principal officers appointed by the President, whom the President may not remove at will but only for good cause. Likewise, in *United States v. Perkins*, 116 U. S. 483 (1886), and *Morrison v. Olson*, 487 U. S. 654 (1988), the Court sustained similar restrictions on the power of principal executive officers—themselves responsible to the President—to remove their own inferiors. The parties do not ask us to reexamine any of these precedents, and we do not do so.

We are asked, however, to consider a new situation not yet encountered by the Court. The question is whether these separate layers of protection may be combined. May the President be restricted in his ability to remove a principal officer, who is in turn restricted in his ability to remove an inferior officer, even though that inferior officer determines the policy and enforces the laws of the United States?

We hold that such multilevel protection from removal is contrary to Article II's vesting of the executive power in the President. The President cannot "take Care that the Laws be faithfully executed" if he cannot oversee the faithfulness of the officers who execute them. Here the President cannot remove an officer who enjoys more than one level of good-cause protection, even if the President determines that the officer is neglecting his duties or discharging them improperly. That judgment is instead committed to another officer, who may or may not agree with the President's determination, and whom the President cannot remove simply because that officer disagrees with him. This contravenes the President's "constitutional obligation to ensure the faithful execution of the laws." . . .

Congress created the Board as a private "nonprofit corporation," and Board members and employees are not considered Government "officer[s] or employee[s]" for statutory purposes. The Board can thus recruit its members and employees from the private sector by paying salaries far above the standard Government pay scale. . . .

Unlike [private] organizations, however, the Board is a Government-created, Government-appointed entity, with expansive powers to govern an entire industry. Every accounting firm—both foreign and domestic—that participates in auditing public companies under the securities laws must register with the Board, pay it an annual fee, and comply with its rules and oversight. . . .

The Board promulgates auditing and ethics standards, performs routine inspections of all accounting firms, demands documents and testimony, and initiates formal investigations and disciplinary proceedings. The willful violation of any Board rule is treated as a willful violation of the Securities Exchange Act of 1934 —a federal crime punishable by up to 20 years' imprisonment or $25 million in fines ($5 million for a natural person). And the Board itself can issue severe sanctions in its disciplinary proceedings, up to and including the permanent revocation of a firm's registration, a permanent ban on a person's associating with any registered firm, and money penalties of $15 million ($750,000 for a natural person). Despite the provisions specifying that Board members are not Government officials for statutory purposes, the parties agree that the Board is "part of the Government" for constitutional purposes. . . .

The Act places the Board under the SEC's oversight, particularly with respect to the issuance of rules or the imposition of sanctions (both of which are subject to Commission approval and alteration). But the individual members of the Board—like the officers and directors of the self-regulatory organizations—are substantially insulated from the Commission's control. The Commission cannot remove Board members at will, but only "for good cause shown," "in accordance with" certain procedures. . . .

As explained, we have previously upheld limited restrictions on the President's removal power. In those cases, however, only one level of protected tenure separated the President from an officer exercising executive power. It was the President—or a subordinate he could remove at will—who decided whether the officer's conduct merited removal under the good-cause standard.

The Act before us does something quite different. It not only protects Board members from removal except for good cause, but withdraws from the President any decision on whether that good cause exists. That decision is vested instead in other tenured officers—the Commissioners—none of whom is subject to the President's direct control. The result is a Board that is not accountable to the President, and a President who is not responsible for the Board.

The added layer of tenure protection makes a difference. Without a layer of insulation between the

Commission and the Board, the Commission could remove a Board member at any time, and therefore would be fully responsible for what the Board does. The President could then hold the Commission to account for its supervision of the Board, to the same extent that he may hold the Commission to account for everything else it does.

A second level of tenure protection changes the nature of the President's review. Now the Commission cannot remove a Board member at will. The President therefore cannot hold the Commission fully accountable for the Board's conduct, to the same extent that he may hold the Commission accountable for everything else that it does. The Commissioners are not responsible for the Board's actions. They are only responsible for their own determination of whether the Act's rigorous good-cause standard is met. And even if the President disagrees with their determination, he is powerless to intervene—unless that determination is so unreasonable as to constitute "inefficiency, neglect of duty, or malfeasance in office."

This novel structure does not merely add to the Board's independence, but transforms it. Neither the President, nor anyone directly responsible to him, nor even an officer whose conduct he may review only for good cause, has full control over the Board. The President is stripped of the power our precedents have preserved, and his ability to execute the laws—by holding his subordinates accountable for their conduct—is impaired.

That arrangement is contrary to Article II's vesting of the executive power in the President. Without the ability to oversee the Board, or to attribute the Board's failings to those whom he *can* oversee, the President is no longer the judge of the Board's conduct. He is not the one who decides whether Board members are abusing their offices or neglecting their duties. He can neither ensure that the laws are faithfully executed, nor be held responsible for a Board member's breach of faith. This violates the basic principle that the President "cannot delegate ultimate responsibility or the active obligation to supervise that goes with it," because Article II "makes a single President responsible for the actions of the Executive Branch."

The diffusion of power carries with it a diffusion of accountability. . . .

The people do not vote for the "Officers of the United States." Art. II, §2, cl. 2. They instead look to the President to guide the "assistants or deputies . . . subject to his superintendence." Without a clear and effective chain of command, the public cannot "determine on whom the blame or the punishment of a pernicious measure, or series of pernicious measures ought really to fall." . . .

Free Enterprise Fund stands for the proposition that there this is a minimum level of accountability that officers must have to the president to be consistent with Article II, albeit with some congressionally imposed limitations. Congress, for example, may establish reasonable qualifications for appointment and may limit the president's authority to remove secondary, non-cabinet, officers to nonpolitical causes.

5.4(f) Reprieves and Pardons

Article II, Section 2, clause 1, states: "The President . . . shall have Power to grant Reprieves and Pardons for offenses against the United States, except in cases of impeachment." The framers borrowed this concept from England, where the Crown held an absolute power to pardon and otherwise alter sentences.

A full **pardon** has the effect of totally canceling both the conviction and the punishment. "[I]n the eyes of the law the offender is as innocent as if he had never committed the offense."[23] Therefore, a fully pardoned offender has all rights restored, and the pardoned offense may not be used to enhance sentences for later convictions. Accordingly, a lawyer-offender cannot be denied a license to practice law because of a pardoned offense.[24]

Pardons do not have to be complete. The president possesses the authority of **commutation of sentence.** By way of this authority, the president may lessen a sentence. A term of imprisonment may be reduced or a lesser punishment may be substituted for a greater one, such as life imprisonment for death.

For example, President George W. Bush commuted the sentence of Vice-President Cheney's past chief of staff, I. Lewis "Scooter" Libby, in 2007. Libby had been convicted of perjury and obstruction of justice in an investigation of an alleged disclosure of national security information. Specifically, it is alleged that Bush administration officials intentionally leaked the name of a Central Intelligence Agency operative for political reasons. Libby was not charged with disclosing the information, but with obstructing the investigation and committing perjury.

pardon
An act of grace by the chief executive of the government relieving a person of the legal consequences of a crime of which he or she has been convicted. A pardon erases the conviction.

commutation of sentence
A partial pardon that reduces the punishment for a crime. The president has the authority under Article II to issue reprieves and pardons. This includes the authority to commute a sentence.

Libby had been sentenced to pay a file of $250,000, to thirty months in prison, and probation. Through the commutation, the prison sentence was eliminated, but Libby was still required to serve probation and to pay the fine. President Bush, in his explanation of the commutation, explained that the damage to Libby's reputation and his extensive service to the United States justified the commutation.[25]

The president may also impose conditions upon pardons. Conditions must be reasonable and must not encroach upon constitutionally secured rights. Requiring restitution to victims or deportation of pardoned aliens is permissible. Prohibiting a pardoned offender from attending church or engaging in lawful political activities would not be valid. A condition may impose a disability that was not originally available, so long as the pardon on the whole truly reduces the sentenced punishment. Pardons may not be used to enhance sentences. For example, in *Schick v. Reed,* the Court upheld a commutation of a death sentence to life imprisonment without the possibility of parole, even though the law under which the offender was sentenced did not provide for life without the possibility of parole.[26] The president may revoke a pardon if an offender violates the conditions imposed.

S I D E B A R

FAMOUS PARDONS

Three of the best known pardons of recent times were the last-minute pardons of William Clinton, Ford's pardon of Richard Nixon, and Carter's pardons of the men who evaded the draft during the Vietnam Conflict.

On his last day in office, President Clinton pardoned 140 individuals, 31 percent of all the pardons he issued during his eight years in office. Many believe that several pardons were motivated by political and personal, not fairness, reasons—most notably, the pardons of Marc Rich, whose wife was a large financial contributor to Clinton, and Susan McDougal, who was convicted for contempt of court for refusing to testify about President Clinton's involvement in a financial scandal that became known as Whitewater. These and other pardons are sometimes referred to as Pardongate.

In June 1972, the Watergate Building in Washington, DC, which housed the Democratic National Headquarters, was burglarized. This event triggered two years of investigations by journalists, Congress, and prosecutors of the executive branch. President Nixon was implicated, a bill of impeachment was introduced in the House, and he resigned. On September 8, 1974, President Ford granted former President Nixon an unconditional pardon for any and all criminal acts committed while in office. A Michigan lawyer, Murphy, challenged the pardon. His primary allegation was that a pardon cannot be granted before an individual has been charged with a crime. The U.S. District Court for the Western District of Michigan rejected this claim.[27]

During the Vietnam Conflict, many men fled abroad, primarily to Canada, to avoid the draft. Many others failed to register for the draft or deserted after induction. President Ford established a clemency program on September 17, 1974, through which draft evaders and military deserters could perform up to two years of civilian service in exchange for a full pardon. This program was announced through Proclamation No. 4313. Approximately 22,000 persons took advantage of this pardon. This was a small percentage of the total evaders and deserters.

On January 21, 1977, President Carter issued Proclamation No. 4483, which extended Ford's pardon to all men who had evaded the draft from August 4, 1964, to March 28, 1973. The pardon covered approximately 13,000 men, including 7 who were in prison for draft evasion convictions and another 2,500 who were under indictment. The pardon did not include those who had used force or violence, the 4,500 deserters who were at large, or the 88,700 men who had received general or dishonorable discharges for deserting or being absent without leave.

Even though Presidents Ford's and Carter's pardons were controversial, they were not the first of a kind. There have been several presidential pardons of evaders, deserters, and enemies:

- President Thomas Jefferson granted full pardons to all deserters from the U.S. Army.
- President James Madison proclaimed a full pardon for deserters during the War of 1812.
- President Abraham Lincoln pardoned those who deserted during the Civil War.
- President Andrew Johnson pardoned ex-Confederates.
- President Theodore Roosevelt pardoned those individuals who had aided the insurrection in the Philippines.[28]

> **WILLIAM HOWARD TAFT: PRESIDENT, CHIEF JUSTICE, AND MORE**
>
> Most successful political figures hold several positions, elected and appointed, during their lives. Only one person, however, has served as both the nation's highest executive and its highest judicial officer.
>
> William Howard Taft was born on September 15, 1857, in Cincinnati, Ohio. He was married in June 1886, and he remained married to the same woman until his death at age 72. He was a Republican and held many positions before being elected president, including local prosecutor, state judge, federal judge, solicitor general of the United States, law school dean, governor-general of the Philippines, provisional governor of Cuba, acting secretary of state, and secretary of war. He was elected president and served from 1909 to 1913. Taft lost his re-election bid to Woodrow Wilson and accepted a position as professor of law at Yale, which he held until June 30, 1921, the date he began his term as chief justice of the Supreme Court. He was nominated by President Warren Harding. He served as chief justice until February 3, 1930.

SIDEBAR

Amnesty to entire classes of offenders are within the pardon power. Hence, President Carter's amnesty of all the men who evaded military service in Vietnam was lawful under the pardons clause. Presidents may also issue **reprieves** that have the effect of delaying the imposition of a punishment.

Any offense against the United States may be pardoned, with the exception of impeachments. The president has no authority to pardon or commute convictions and sentences for state or local offenses. In the case of a federal officer who is to be impeached and prosecuted for the same act, the underlying offenses that led to impeachment may be pardoned, but not the impeachment and removal from office by Congress.

Pardons do not make an offender whole. The government does not compensate the pardoned individual for any losses sustained as a consequence of arrest, trial, conviction, or sentence served. The pardoned offender is not entitled to compensation for property seized and sold before the pardon was granted. However, if seized property remains in the possession of the government, it is returned to the pardoned individual. Once pardoned, an individual loses the privilege against self-incrimination and may be compelled to testify about the crime.

The pardon power is vested in the president and may not be interfered with by Congress or the courts. Statutes limiting the pardon power are unconstitutional, and courts may not review the wisdom of granting or denying a pardon. The remedy for presidential indiscretion in the use of the pardon is at the polls, or, in the extreme, in removal from office through impeachment. Franklin D. Roosevelt issued 3,687 pardons, clemencies, and commutations, the largest number issued by any president. At zero, William Henry Harrison and James Garfield issued the least. Overall, the trend has been toward fewer pardons, clemencies, and commutations over the past thirty years.[29]

amnesty
An act of the government granting a pardon for a past crime. Amnesty is rarely exercised in favor of individuals, but is usually applied to a group or class of persons who are accountable for crimes for which they have not yet been convicted.

reprieve
The postponement of the carrying out of a sentence. A reprieve is not a commutation of sentence; it is merely a delay.

5.4(g) Chief Administrative Officer

The president sits at the apex of the federal bureaucracy. He or she is the chief administrative officer. This role includes the authority to develop and declare federal policy as it applies to executive functions, supervise lower executive officers, represent the nation in contract negotiations, manage federal properties, receive citizen complaints, recommend budgets for the government, issue executive orders, and promulgate administrative rules and regulations.

Many presidential functions may be delegated to lower federal officials. Some functions, however, may not be delegated. For example, the president must personally sign or veto bills, nominate officials, and sign pardons. Of course, the president may seek the advice of other officials when making these decisions.

5.4(h) Emergency Powers

The Constitution has several provisions that empower the federal government to respond to national, and sometimes local, emergencies:

1. Article IV, Section 4, requires the United States to guarantee every state a Republican form of government, to protect the states against invasion, and upon request by a state governor or legislature, to protect it against domestic violence.
2. Article I, Section 8, empowers Congress to provide for calling militias to execute federal law, to suppress insurrections, and to repel invasions.
3. Article I, Section 9, empowers Congress to suspend habeas corpus in cases of rebellion or invasion, or when the public safety requires it.

martial law
The state of martial law exists when civilian government has been replaced with military government. Civil liberties are typically greatly diminished during martial law. In the United States, martial law and the suspension of habeas corpus may be imposed by Congress only during times of invasion or insurrection and when civilian government is inoperable.

habeas corpus
Latin for "you have the body." A Writ whose purpose is to obtain immediate relief from illegal imprisonment by having the "body" (that is, the prisoner) delivered from custody and brought before the court. A writ of habeas corpus is a means for attacking the constitutionality of the statute under which, or the proceedings in which, the original conviction was obtained. There are numerous writs of habeas corpus, each applicable in different procedural circumstances. The full name of the ordinary writ of habeas corpus is *habeas corpus ad subjiciendum.*

Although the Constitution does not specifically refer to **martial law,** it has been imposed on several occasions by both presidents and governors. Andrew Jackson declared martial law in New Orleans during the War of 1812, Abraham Lincoln declared martial law in the rebellious states, and the governor of the Territory of Hawaii relinquished civilian governance in favor of martial law following the Japanese attack on Pearl Harbor in 1941. The territorial constitution was suspended, civilian courts closed, and severe restrictions on individual liberties were imposed. The islands government was placed in the hands of the U.S. military, where it remained until 1944.

Although "martial law" is not specifically mentioned in the Constitution, suspension of the right of **habeas corpus** is found. Indeed, martial law and the suspension of habeas corpus are often referred to as synonymous, although in reality martial law raises a great number of civil liberties issues that transcend habeas corpus.

Habeas corpus existed in the common law and was brought by the founders to this nation. Known as the Great Writ of Liberty, habeas corpus provides a mechanism for an individual to challenge her incarceration in court. The framers provided, in Article I, Section 9, clause 2, that "[t]he privilege of the Writ of Habeas Corpus shall not be suspended, unless when in Cases of Rebellion or Invasion the public Safety may require it." Contrary to the assertion of several presidents, this power does not belong to the president. The language of Article I is clear that the authority to suspend habeas corpus belongs to Congress. Lincoln's declaration of martial law (actually he delegated the authority to a military subordinate) and the suspension of habeas corpus was invalidated by Chief Justice Taney (pronounced Tawney), sitting a Circuit judge not as a justice of the Supreme Court, in *Ex Parte Merryman*, 17 F. Cas. 144 (1861). Note, however, that Lincoln ignored the Court's ruling and continued the suspension. After failing to obtain Congress's authorization in 1862, Lincoln was successful in obtaining congressional authorization to suspend habeas corpus in 1863.

But having a congressionally authorized suspension of habeas corpus does not end the inquiry. Habeas corpus may be suspended only in times of invasion or rebellion. In a unanimous decision, the Supreme Court stated in *Ex Parte Milligan*[30] that "[m]artial law cannot arise from a threatened invasion. The necessity must be actual and present; the invasion real, such as effectively closes the courts and deposes the civil administration." Whether martial law is constitutional is a justiciable question, meaning that it is subject to judicial review.[31]

Milligan stresses that the threat must be both present and genuine. Even more, civilian government must be disabled. The purpose of martial law is to establish order while civilian government is inoperable. The facts of *Milligan* are instructive. Milligan was a citizen of Indiana. He did not serve in the military during the Civil War, nor was he present in the rebel states during the war. He was charged with conspiracy to aid the Confederacy, tried in a military court, convicted, and sentenced to death. He sought habeas corpus, asserting that he had a right to be tried in a civilian court. The Court invalidated his conviction and held that he should have been tried in a common law court, not a military court, in spite of the 1863 congressional empowerment of the president to suspend the Writ. That Indiana was never the site of insurrection or fighting, that the civil courts in Indiana continued in operation, and that Milligan was a continuous twenty-year resident who did not serve in the military on either side during the war were proof that there was no threat justifying suspension of his right to habeas corpus and to be tried in a common law court by a jury of his peers.

SIDEBAR

CHIEF JUSTICE TANEY AND PRESIDENT LINCOLN

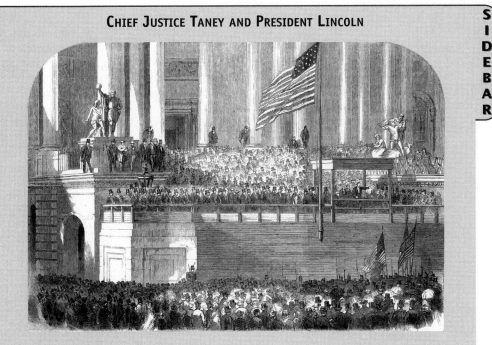

Lincoln inauguration
Photos.com/Thinkstock

Roger Taney had a distinguished career as a private attorney, attorney general of Maryland, secretary of war of the United States, and attorney general of the United States prior to joining the Supreme Court. Taney was first nominated to the Supreme Court as associate justice by President Andrew Jackson in 1835. Anti-Jacksonians in the Senate were successful in blocking Taney's confirmation to the Court, as they had done the year before to his nomination to become the secretary of the treasury. The 1834 elections brought a shift in power in the Senate, and Jackson nominated Taney again after the new Congress was in session, but this time to be the nation's fifth chief justice. The Senate confirmed him and he was sworn into office on March 28, 1836. Although highly regarded for his intellect and abilities, Taney is most commonly remembered for authoring the Court's decision in *Dred Scott v. Sandford*, 60 U.S. 393 (1857), where the Court ruled that slaves were not citizens as defined by the Constitution, that slaves were chattel that could not be taken from their owners without due process of law, and that the federal government lacked the authority to prohibit slavery in the territories (see Chapter 12 for a more thorough discussion of this case). Taney's hope that the decision would bring an end to the rising dispute between the north and the south proved to be 180 degrees wrong; the decision is regarded today as having deepened the conflict and hastened the Civil War. Lincoln, then an attorney involved in politics from Illinois, was vocal and public in the opposition to the decision. He was deferential to the Supreme Court's role in defining the Constitution while simultaneously critical of Taney's conclusions about slaves. The framers, he remarked, did not believe all people were equal in "color, size, intellect, moral developments, or social capacity," but they did believe all people equal in their pursuit of certain rights, including life, liberty, and pursuit of happiness, a reference to the language in the Declaration of Independence.

Taney administered the oath office to President Abraham Lincoln on March 4, 1861. The two were political opponents at this point, and the relationship only worsened during the Civil War. Taney's decision in *Merryman* was particularly troublesome to Lincoln. In 1861, Supreme Court justices also served as circuit appellate judges. As circuit judge Taney received a petition for a writ of habeas corpus from John Merryman, who was accused of burning bridges and other insurrection acts on behalf of the Confederacy. Taney issued the Writ, but federal officials refused to turn Merryman over to the court, citing President Lincoln's suspension of the Writ. Taney then issued the *Merryman* decision both *ex parte* (without the government presenting its case), which was not unusual in habeas corpus cases, and alone as a circuit judge. His language in *Merryman* was harsh but well reasoned, holding that the president did not have the authority to suspend the writ of habeas corpus. The decision no doubt embarrassed and frustrated the president. Lincoln and his subordinates chose to ignore the decision, and countless individuals were arrested and tried by the military, including entire state legislatures, city officials, and other southern sympathizers. Taney did not relent on the habeas issue. He encouraged other judges to issue writs of habeas corpus to review detentions resulting from Lincoln's martial law, causing more headaches for the Lincoln administration. There is evidence that military officials attempted to intimidate judges who followed Taney's lead.

A contemporary controversy in history concerns Lincoln's reaction to Taney's decision and efforts to thwart the suspension of habeas corpus. Ward Hill Lamon, Lincoln's law partner, friend, self-appointed body guard, and eventually U.S. marshal for the District of Columbia, wrote in his private papers in the late 1800s that Lincoln issued an arrest warrant for Taney. The reason it was not executed is not mentioned by Lamon, although Lincoln raised the question of who should serve the warrant with Lamon. Other records from the period show that Taney believed he might be arrested and a couple of secondary sources corroborate the existence of the warrant, or at least Lincoln's consideration of issuing it. But no official document has been found, nor has direct corroboration by a credible Lincoln contemporary, leaving historians unsure and divided. There are historians who believe the evidence, others do not, and yet others believe a different scenario. For example, it is possible that a key advisor to the president, for example, Secretary of State William H. Seward, suggested arresting Taney, and Lincoln refused. No doubt, Lincoln exceeded his authority in suspending habeas corpus, at least until Congress authorized the suspension in 1863. Lincoln's decision to ignore Taney's order (there was no appeal by the government) stretched his constitutional stance further. Of course, all of Lincoln's actions must be contextualized. The nation was in the greatest state of tumult it has ever experienced. The threat to the union came from within; enemies and espionage were ubiquitous. Regardless of context, the issuance of an arrest warrant for the nation's chief justice for the performance of his duties, if true, would have represented a deep threat to constitutionalism and rule of law. After both Taney's and Lincoln's deaths and the conclusion of the Civil War, the Supreme Court, in a unanimous decision, essentially affirmed Taney's *Merryman* decision in *Milligan*.

Posse Comitatus Act
Posse Comitatus is Latin for "power of the county." The Posse Comitatus Act forbids, without congressional authorization, the use of federal military as domestic law enforcement.

Insurrection Act
The Insurrection Act modifies the Posse Comitatus Act by granting the president limited authority to use federal military to quell insurrections and unrest.

Congress has addressed the use of federal military in times of crisis on several occasions. The most significant statutes are the **Posse Comitatus Act** of 1878 (18 U.S.C. sec. 1385) and the **Insurrection Act** of 1807 (10 U.S.C. sec. 331 et. seq.). The Posse Comitatus Act forbids the use of federal military to perform local police functions, except when authorized by Congress. The Insurrection Act details the use of the federal military by the president to quell domestic insurrections and unrest. Actions authorized under the Insurrection Act are an exception to the prohibition of the use of federal troops domestically found in the Posse Comitatus Act. In 2006, Congress greatly expanded presidential authority to declare a "national emergency"; take control of National Guard units, without state authorization; and deploy federal military into the states in response to the experience of Hurricane Katrina. The Insurrection Act limited presidential authority to act in this manner to insurrections, domestic violence, unlawful combination, and conspiracy. The 2006 changes added natural disasters, epidemics, serious public health emergencies, terrorist attacks, and other conditions. "Conditions" was not defined. This expansion of authority was repealed in 2008.[32]

Even a war that has not reached American soil increases both presidential and congressional domestic powers, beyond habeas corpus. The combination of executive and legislative war powers proved significant in the *Korematsu* case.

Japanese internment camp during World War II

© Everett Collection Inc / Alamy

Cyber Constitution
Civil War, Slavery,
Taney, and Lincoln Cases
Milligan may be read at
http://caselaw.lp.findlaw.
com/scripts/getcase.
pl?court=us&vol=
71&invol=2,
Merryman at http://
teachingamericanhistory.
org/library/index.asp?
document=442, and
Dred Scott at www.
law.cornell.edu/supct/
html/historics/USSC_
CR_0060_0393_ZS.html

In short, in *Korematsu* the Supreme Court decided that the exigencies of World War II (i.e., fear of a West Coast invasion, espionage, and sabotage) outweighed the civil liberties of the Japanese Americans living on the West Coast. Note that Justice Black's description of racial discrimination analysis became the precursor of contemporary equal protection law. Racial classifications are "suspect." He stated that the government must have a "pressing" governmental reason to racially classify and that courts must review such classifications with "rigid scrutiny." Today, *compelling* and *strict scrutiny* is the nomenclature. Pursuant to statute enacted in 1988, the United States tendered an apology and reparation of $20,000 to each surviving detainee.

Korematsu v. United States
323 U.S. 214 (1944)

[Congress enacted legislation in 1942 authorizing the president to restrict movement or residence within military areas and war zones. At the time, concern was building throughout the nation that the Japanese were going to invade the West Coast. This, matched with suspicions about the loyalty of citizens and aliens of Japanese ancestry, led President Roosevelt to issue an executive order authorizing military commanders to exclude persons from military areas and war zones. General DeWitt, commander of the Western Command, then issued several orders directed at Japanese persons. These included curfew, exclusion from certain areas, and internment in camps. When Korematsu failed to leave an area to be interned, he was prosecuted. The curfew order had been previously upheld in *Hirabayashi v. United States*, 320 U.S. 81 (1943).]

Mr. Justice Black delivered the opinion of the Court.

It should be noted, to begin with, that all legal restrictions which curtail the civil rights of a single racial group are immediately suspect. That is not to say that all such restrictions are unconstitutional. It is to say that courts must subject them to the most rigid scrutiny. Pressing public necessity may sometimes justify the existence of such restrictions; racial antagonism never can. . . .

The 1942 Act was attacked in the *Hirabayashi* case as an unconstitutional delegation of power; it was contended that the curfew order and other orders on which it rested were beyond the war powers of the Congress, the military authorities and of the President, as Commander in Chief of the Army; and finally that to apply the curfew order against none but citizens of Japanese ancestry amounted to a constitutionally prohibited discrimination solely on account of race. To these questions, we gave the serious consideration which their importance justified. We upheld the curfew order as an exercise of the power of the government to take steps necessary to prevent espionage and sabotage in an area threatened by Japanese attack. . . .

Here, as in the *Hirabayashi* case . . . "we cannot reject as unfounded the judgment of the military authorities and of Congress that there were disloyal members of that population, whose number and strength could not be precisely and quickly ascertained. We cannot say that the war-making branches of the Government did not have ground for believing that in a critical hour such persons could not readily be isolated and separately dealt with, and constituted a menace to the national defense and safety, which demanded that prompt and adequate measures be taken to guard against it."

Like curfew, exclusion of those of Japanese origin was deemed necessary because of the presence of an unascertained number of disloyal members of the group, most of whom we have no doubt were loyal to this country. It was because we could not reject the finding of the military authorities that it was impossible to bring about an immediate segregation of the disloyal from the loyal that we sustained the validity of the curfew order as applying to the whole group. In the instant case, temporary exclusion of the entire group was rested by the military on the same ground. The judgment that exclusion of the entire group was for the same reason a military imperative answers the contention that the exclusion was in the nature of group punishment based on antagonism to those of Japanese origin. That there were members of the group who retained loyalties to Japan has been confirmed by investigations made subsequent to the exclusion. Approximately five thousand American citizens of Japanese ancestry refused to swear unqualified allegiance to the United States and to renounce allegiance to the Japanese Emperor, and several thousand evacuees requested repatriation to Japan.

We uphold the exclusion order as of the time it was made and when the petitioner violated it. . . . In doing so, we are not unmindful of the hardships imposed by it upon a large group of American citizens. . . . But hardships are part of war, and war is an aggregation of hardships. All citizens alike, both in and out of uniform, feel the impact of war in greater or lesser measure. Citizenship has its responsibilities as well as its privileges, and in time of war the burden is always heavier. Compulsory exclusion of large groups of citizens from their homes, except under circumstances of direst emergency and peril, is inconsistent with our basic governmental institutions. But when under conditions of modern warfare our shores are threatened by hostile forces, the power to protect must be commensurate with the threatened danger. . . .

We are thus being asked to pass at this time upon the whole subsequent detention program in both assembly and relocation centers, although the only issues framed at the trial related to petitioner's remaining in the prohibited area in violation of the exclusion order. . . .

Some of the members of the Court are of the view that evacuation and detention in an Assembly Center were inseparable. After May 3, 1942, the date of Exclusion Order No. 34, Korematsu was under compulsion to leave the area not as he would choose but via an Assembly Center. The Assembly Center was conceived as a part of the machinery for group evacuation. The power to exclude includes the power to do it by force if necessary. And any forcible measure must necessarily entail some degree of detention or restraint whatever method of removal is selected. But whichever view is taken, it results in holding that the order under which petitioner was convicted was valid.

It is said that we are dealing here with the case of imprisonment of a citizen in a concentration camp solely because of his ancestry, without evidence or inquiry concerning his loyalty and good disposition towards the United States. Our task would be simple, our duty clear, were this a case involving the imprisonment of a loyal citizen in a concentration camp because of racial prejudice. Regardless of the true nature of the assembly and relocation centers—and we deem it unjustifiable to call them concentration camps with all the ugly connotations that term implies—we are dealing specifically with nothing but an exclusion order. To cast this case into outlines of racial prejudice, without reference to the real military dangers which were presented, merely confuses the issue. Korematsu was not excluded from the Military Area because of hostility to him or his race. He was excluded because we are at war with the Japanese Empire, because the properly constituted military authorities feared an invasion of our West Coast and felt constrained to take proper security measures, because they decided that the military urgency of the situation demanded that all citizens of Japanese ancestry be segregated from the West Coast temporarily, and finally, because Congress, reposing its confidence in this time of war in our military leaders—as inevitably it must—determined that they should have the power to do just this. There was evidence of disloyalty on the part of some, the military authorities considered that the need for action was great, and time was short. We cannot—by availing ourselves of the calm perspective of hindsight—now say that at that time these actions were unjustified.

Mr. Justice Roberts, dissenting.

This is not a case of keeping people off the streets at night . . . nor a case of temporary exclusion of a citizen from an area for his own safety or that of the community. . . . On the contrary, it is the case of convicting a citizen as a punishment for not submitting to imprisonment in a concentration camp, based on his ancestry, and solely because of his ancestry, without evidence or inquiry concerning his loyalty. . . .

Mr. Justice Murphy, dissenting.

This exclusion of "all persons of Japanese ancestry, both alien and nonalien," from the Pacific Coast area on the plea of military necessity in the absence of martial law ought not to be approved. Such exclusion goes over "the very brink of constitutional power" and falls into the ugly abyss of racism. . . .

[W]e must accord great respect and consideration to the judgments of the military authorities who are on the scene and who have full knowledge of the military facts. The scope of their discretion must, as a matter of necessity and common sense, be wide. And their judgments ought not to be overruled lightly by those whose training and duties ill-equip them to deal intelligently with matters so vital to the physical security of the nation.

At the same time, however, it is essential that there be definite limits to military discretion, especially where martial law has not been declared. Individuals must not be left impoverished of their constitutional rights on a plea of military necessity that has neither substance nor support. . . .

The judicial test of whether the Government, on a plea of military necessity, can validly deprive an individual of any of his constitutional rights is whether the deprivation is reasonably related to a public danger that is so "immediate, imminent, and impending" as not to admit of delay and not to permit of ordinary constitutional processes. . . .

But to infer that examples of individual disloyalty prove a group's disloyalty and justify discriminatory action against the entire group is to deny that under our system of law individual guilt is the sole basis for deprivation of rights. Moreover, this inference, which is at the very heart of the evacuation orders, has been used in support of the abhorrent and despicable treatment of minority groups by the dictatorial tyrannies which this nation is now pledged to destroy. To give constitutional sanction to that inference in this case, however well-intentioned may have been the military command on the Pacific Coast, is to adopt one of the cruelest of the rationales used by our enemies to destroy the dignity of the individual and to encourage and open the door to discriminatory actions against other minority groups in the passions of tomorrow.

Moreover, there was no adequate proof that the Federal Bureau of Investigation and the military and naval intelligence services did not have the espionage and sabotage situation well in hand. . . .

Mr. Justice Jackson, dissenting.

Korematsu was born on our soil, of parents born in Japan. The Constitution makes him a citizen of the United States by nativity and a citizen of California by residence. No claim is made that he is not loyal to this country. . . . Korematsu, however, has been convicted of an act not commonly a crime. It consists of merely being present in the state whereof he is a citizen, near the place where he was born, and where all his life he has lived. . . .

A citizen's presence in the locality, however, was made a crime only if his parents were of Japanese birth. Had Korematsu been one of four—the others being say, a German alien enemy, an Italian alien enemy, and a citizen of American born ancestors, convicted of treason but out on parole—only Korematsu's presence would have violated the order. The difference between their innocence and his crime would result, not from anything he did, said, or thought, different than they, but only in that he was born of different racial stock.

Now, if any fundamental assumption underlies our system, it is that guilt is personal and not inheritable. Even if all of one's antecedents had been convicted of treason, the Constitution forbids its penalties to be visited upon him, for it provides that "no Attainder of Treason shall work Corruption of Blood, or Forfeiture except during the Life of the Person attainted." Article 3, § 3, cl. 2. But here is an example to make an otherwise innocent act a crime merely because this prisoner is the son of parents as to whom he had no choice, and belongs to a race from which there is no way to resign. . . .

On the same day the Court issued *Korematsu,* it also issued *Ex Parte Endo.* While *Korematsu* addressed the authority of the president, with congressional authorization, to relocate people of Japanese ancestry during World War II, *Endo* examines the decision to intern U.S. citizens of Japanese ancestry in camps when no proof of disloyalty existed.

Ex Parte Endo
323 U. S. 283 (1944)

[Ms. Endo, a citizen of the Unites States of Japanese ancestry, was removed from Sacramento, California, to the Tule Lake War Relocation Center in California pursuant to the presidential (E.O. 9066) and military orders (issued by General De Witt, who was in charge of defending the West Coast), later affirmed by statute, discussed earlier in this chapter. She was removed and relocated in 1942. She was eventually transferred to a camp in Utah. Along with the orders requiring the evacuation and incarceration of people of Japanese ancestry from areas on the West Coast, General De Witt provided for the release, known as "leave" of individuals in the relocation centers. There were detailed rules concerning eligibility for leave. Loyalty to the United States was required, for example. Employment was one of the many factors as well. But if the War Relocation Authority decided that local community sentiment did not favor the presence of the individual, leave could be denied. She filed a petition of Writ of Habeas Corpus challenging her relocation and confinement, which was denied by the trial court, and she appealed.]

It is conceded by the Department of Justice and by the War Relocation Authority that appellant is a loyal and law-abiding citizen. They make no claim that she is detained on any charge, or that she is even suspected of disloyalty. Moreover, they do not contend that she may be held any longer in the Relocation Center. They concede that it is beyond the power of the War Relocation Authority to detain citizens against whom no charges of disloyalty or subversiveness have been made for a period longer than that necessary to separate the loyal from the disloyal and to provide the necessary guidance for relocation. But they maintain that detention for an additional period after leave clearance has been granted is an essential step in the evacuation program. Reliance for that conclusion is placed on the following circumstances.

It is argued that such a planned and orderly relocation was essential to the success of the evacuation program; that, but for such supervision, there might have been a dangerously disorderly migration of unwanted people to unprepared communities; that unsupervised evacuation might have resulted in hardship and disorder; that the success of the evacuation program was thought to require the knowledge that the federal government was maintaining control over the evacuated population except as the release of individuals could be effected consistently with their own peace and wellbeing and that of the nation; that, although community hostility towards the evacuees has diminished, it has not disappeared, and the continuing control of the Authority over the relocation process is essential to the success of the evacuation program. It is argued that supervised relocation, as the chosen method of terminating the evacuation, is the final step in the entire process, and is a consequence of the first step taken. It is conceded that appellant's detention pending compliance with the leave regulations is not directly connected with the prevention of espionage and sabotage at the present time. But it is argued that Executive Order No. 9102 confers power to make regulations necessary and proper for controlling situations created by the exercise of the powers expressly conferred for protection against espionage and sabotage. The leave regulations are said to fall within that category.

First. We are of the view that Mitsuye Endo should be given her liberty. In reaching that conclusion, we do not come to the underlying constitutional issues which have been argued. For we conclude that, whatever power the War Relocation Authority may have to detain other classes of citizens, it has no authority to subject citizens who are concededly loyal to its leave procedure.

It should be noted at the outset that we do not have here a question such as was presented in *Ex parte Milligan*, 4 Wall. 2, or in *Ex parte Quirin*, 317 U. S. 1, where the jurisdiction of military tribunals to try persons according to the law of war was challenged in habeas corpus proceedings.

Mitsuye Endo is detained by a civilian agency, the War Relocation Authority, not by the military. Moreover, the evacuation program was not left exclusively to the military; the Authority was given a large measure of responsibility for its execution, and Congress made its enforcement subject to civil penalties by the Act of March 21, 1942. Accordingly, no questions of military law are involved. . . .

A citizen who is concededly loyal presents no problem of espionage or sabotage. Loyalty is a matter of the heart and mind, not of race, creed, or color. He who is loyal is, by definition, not a spy or a saboteur. When the power to detain is derived from the power to protect the war effort against espionage and sabotage, detention which has no relationship to that objective is unauthorized.

Nor may the power to detain an admittedly loyal citizen or to grant him a conditional release be implied as a useful or convenient step in the evacuation program, whatever authority might be implied in case of those whose loyalty was not conceded or established. If we assume (as we do) that the original evacuation was justified, its lawful character was derived from the fact that it was an espionage and sabotage measure, not that there was community hostility to this group of American citizens. The evacuation program rested explicitly on the former ground, not on the latter, as the underlying legislation shows. The authority to detain a citizen or to grant him a conditional release as protection against espionage or sabotage is exhausted, at least when his loyalty is conceded. If we held that the authority to detain continued thereafter, we would transform an espionage or sabotage measure into something else. That was not done by Executive Order No. 9066 or by the Act of March 21, 1942, which ratified it. What they did not do, we cannot do. Detention which furthered the campaign against espionage and sabotage would be one thing. But detention which has no relationship to that campaign is of a distinct character. Community hostility even to loyal evacuees may have been (and perhaps still is) a serious problem. But if authority for their custody and supervision is to be sought on that ground, the Act of March 21, 1942, Executive Order No. 9066, and Executive Order No. 9102, offer no support. And none other is advanced. [Footnote 24] To read them that broadly would be to assume that the Congress and the President intended that this discriminatory action should be taken against these people wholly on account of their ancestry even though the government conceded their loyalty to this country. We cannot make such an assumption. As the President has said of these loyal citizens:

> Americans of Japanese ancestry, like those of many other ancestries, have shown that they can, and want to, accept our institutions and work loyally with the rest of us, making their own valuable contribution to the national wealth and wellbeing. In vindication of the very ideals for which we are fighting this war, it is important to us to maintain a high standard of fair, considerate, and equal treatment for the people of this minority, as of all other minorities.

We approach the construction of Executive Order No. 9066 as we would approach the construction of legislation in this field. That Executive Order must indeed be considered along with the Act of March 21, 1942, which ratified and confirmed it (*Hirabayashi v. United States, supra,* pp. 320 U. S. 87-91), as the Order and the statute together laid such basis as there is for participation by civil agencies of the federal government in the evacuation program. Broad powers frequently granted to the President or other executive officers by Congress so that they may deal with the exigencies of wartime problems have been sustained. And the Constitution, when it committed to the Executive and to Congress the exercise of the war power, necessarily gave them wide scope for the exercise of judgment and discretion so that war might be waged effectively and successfully. *Hirabayashi v. United States, supra,* p. 320 U. S. 93. At the same time, however, the Constitution is as specific in its enumeration of many of the civil rights of the individual as it is in its enumeration of the powers of his government. Thus, it has prescribed procedural safeguards surrounding the arrest, detention, and conviction of individuals. Some of these are contained in the Sixth Amendment, compliance with which is essential if convictions are to be sustained. And the Fifth Amendment provides that no person shall be deprived of liberty (as well as life or property) without due process of law. Moreover, as a further safeguard against invasion of the basic civil rights of the individual, it is provided in Art. I, Sec. 9 of the Constitution that "The Privilege of the Writ of Habeas Corpus shall not be suspended unless when in Cases of Rebellion or Invasion, the public Safety may require it." *See Ex Parte Milligan, supra.*

We mention these constitutional provisions not to stir the constitutional issues which have been argued at the bar, but to indicate the approach which we think should be made to an Act of Congress or an order of the Chief Executive that touches the sensitive area of rights specifically guaranteed by the Constitution. This Court has quite consistently given a narrower scope for the operation of the presumption of constitutionality when legislation appeared on its face to violate a specific prohibition of the Constitution. We have likewise favored that interpretation of legislation which gives it the greater chance of surviving the test of constitutionality. Those analogies are suggestive here. We must assume that the Chief Executive and members of Congress, as well as the courts, are sensitive to and respectful of the liberties of the citizen. In interpreting a war-time measure, we must assume that their purpose was to allow for the greatest possible accommodation between those liberties and the exigencies of war. We must assume, when asked to find implied powers in a grant of legislative or executive authority, that the lawmakers intended to place no greater restraint on the citizen than was clearly and unmistakably indicated by the language they used.

> The necessity for this legislation arose from the fact that the safe conduct of the war requires the fullest possible protection against either espionage or sabotage to national defense material, national defense premises, and national defense utilities.

That was the precise purpose of Executive Order No. 9066, for, as we have seen, it gave as the reason for the exclusion of persons from prescribed military areas the protection of such property "against espionage and against sabotage." And Executive Order No. 9102, which established the War Relocation Authority, did so, as we have noted, "in order to provide for the removal from designated areas of persons whose removal is necessary in the interests of national security." The purpose and objective of the Act and of these orders are plain. Their single aim was the protection of the war effort against espionage and sabotage. It is in light of that one objective that the powers conferred by the orders must be construed.

Mitsuye Endo is entitled to an unconditional release by the War Relocation Authority. . . .

The judgment is reversed, and the cause is remanded to the District Court for proceedings in conformity with this opinion.

Be aware that in another World War II case, *Duncan v. Kahanamoku,*[33] the Supreme Court reviewed the convictions of a civilian who was tried for embezzlement of stocks from another civilian, and in a companion case, a civilian was charged and convicted of resisting military officers who were attempting to arrest him. In both cases they were tried by military commission. Hawaii was operating under military command as a consequence of the attacks on Pearl Harbor in 1941. The Court invalidated the convictions, finding that martial law and military trials of civilians cannot be imposed when civilian courts were capable of operation.

5.5 FOREIGN AFFAIRS POWERS

Foreign affairs are exclusively a national concern. By uniting into one nation, the states agreed that jurisdiction over foreign affairs would be vested in the federal government. The foreign affairs power is shared between the president and Congress. The Constitution does not spell out the precise contours of these powers, and, because of the political question doctrine, the Court has issued few opinions in this area. The largest source of information in this area is practice, that is, the roles that the president and Congress

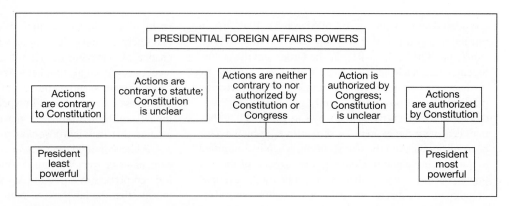

FIGURE 5-1

Presidential powers relating to foreign affairs

have historically accepted and performed. Through practice, the president has assumed most of the foreign affairs powers. Due to its unitary nature, the presidency has proven to operate more quickly and secretly than Congress, both important features in the foreign affairs arena (see Figure 5-1).

These principles were recognized by the Supreme Court in *United States v. Curtiss-Wright Export Corp.,* a 1936 Supreme Court decision that involved a presidential proclamation prohibiting the sale of arms to combatants in South America.[34] The proclamation had been approved by Congress. The defendants, who were convicted of selling arms to one of the prohibited parties, challenged the delegation to the president as an unlawful delegation of legislative authority. They prevailed in the lower court, but the Supreme Court reversed.

It found that federal power is different in foreign affairs than in the domestic sphere; specifically, the federal government possesses inherent foreign affairs powers. In reaching this conclusion, the Court reasoned that one purpose of the 1789 Constitution was to carve out some of the powers held by the states and place them into a federal government. For example, domestic powers that had previously belonged to the states were transferred to the federal government. However, only limited powers were vested in the federal government, with the states possessing the remainder. The *Curtiss-Wright* Court determined that the states had never held foreign affairs powers; rather, such powers passed directly from the British Crown to the United States (colonies) collectively. Therefore, foreign affairs powers had never belonged to the states. There is no evidence that the framers intended to change this arrangement in the new Constitution. Accordingly,

> [i]t results that the investment of the federal government with the powers of external sovereignty did not depend upon the affirmative grants of the Constitution. The powers to declare and wage war, to conclude peace, to make treaties, to maintain diplomatic relations with other sovereignties, if they never had been mentioned in the Constitution, would have vested in the federal government as necessary concomitants of nationality.

The Court then concluded that the "President alone has the power to speak or listen as a representative of the nation. . . . The President is the sole organ of the nation in its external relations, and its sole representative with foreign nations." The Court went further and concluded that the president could have issued the proclamation without congressional approval. Recall *Youngstown,* however. The president's power is at the lowest ebb when acting contrary to Congress's intent. Although the president could have acted in the absence of congressional approval in *Curtiss-Wright,* he could not have acted if Congress had explicitly disapproved.

Why did the Court trust the president with such broad authority? It said that foreign relations require "caution and unity of design," objectives that the president is more likely to realize than is Congress. The Court stated further:

[the President], not Congress, has the better opportunity of knowing the conditions which prevail in foreign countries, and especially is this true in time of war. He has his confidential sources of information. He has his agents in the form of diplomatic, consular and other officials. Secrecy in respect of information gathered by them may be highly necessary, and the premature disclosure of it productive of harmful results.

Some foreign affairs powers are exclusively, or at least nearly exclusively, held by the president. The president is the sole official of the United States responsible for communicating with foreign nations. Of course, the president may, and often does, delegate this power to subordinates. Through the Department of State and its secretary, the president engages in continuous contact with other nations. At times, members of Congress engage in dialogue with foreign powers, but this practice is of questionable constitutional and statutory validity.

The Supreme Court has recognized that it is the president who is responsible for recognizing foreign governments. This is a political question and nonreviewable by the courts.[35] The power to recognize governments includes the power to establish relations and develop foreign policy concerning recognized nations. Conversely, the president may order relations with a foreign power terminated and may withdraw the United States's diplomatic representatives from a nation.

So, through practice, federalism, congressional approval, and Supreme Court deference to the other two branches to determine the nature of their foreign affairs relationship, the president has dominated the foreign affairs arena. This has been largely true of the treaty and war powers as well.

5.6 TREATIES AND EXECUTIVE AGREEMENTS

5.6(a) Treaty Power

As previously mentioned, the Constitution empowers the president to "make Treaties, provided two thirds of the Senators present concur."[36] The treaty power is exclusively federal. Article I, Section 10, clause 1, prohibits states from entering into treaties, alliances, or confederations, and from granting letters of marque and reprisal. Clause 3 of that section further prohibits states from making agreements or compacts with other states or nations, without the consent of Congress, except in times of extreme emergency. A two-thirds majority in the Senate is required to confirm a treaty. Only two-thirds of the senators present are required, not two-thirds of the whole body.

Although treaty-making is a shared federal power, the president alone is responsible for negotiating with other nations. The president also decides which nations should be negotiated with, what the subject matter of negotiations should be, and who will represent the nation. Presidents may appoint any person to represent the country in negotiations, without congressional approval. In addition to the members of the professional diplomatic corps (foreign service personnel), presidents have used members of Congress, prominent businesspersons, and past presidents as negotiators. Former President Jimmy Carter, for example, has been actively involved in diplomatic efforts since leaving the Oval Office.

The Supremacy Clause declares that the "Constitution, and the Laws of the United States which shall be made in Pursuance thereof; and all Treaties made, or which shall be made, under the Authority of the United States, shall be the supreme Law of the Land."[37] The language of this article permits two constructions. The first construction focuses on the placement of the semicolon. The "laws of the United States," which refer primarily to statutes, are treated differently than treaties under this construction. The laws are subject to constitutional limitations, namely, "Constitution, and the Laws . . . which shall be made in Pursuance thereof," whereas treaties are not. Under this interpretation, treaties are made under the authority of the United States and are equal to the Constitution. The second construction reads the Constitution as limiting both laws and treaties. This interpretation has been adopted by the Court. For example, *Reid v. Covert*[38] involved two cases with nearly identical facts. Two women, both civilians, were charged with murdering their servicemen husbands. Both murders occurred while the men were serving abroad (one in Japan and the other in Great Britain). The United States had entered into executive agreements with both nations providing that military personnel and their families would be tried by U.S. military courts in the nation where the crime was alleged to have been committed. Accordingly, the women were tried in Great Britain and Japan—but military law denied the women rights they would have enjoyed in U.S. courts. The Supreme Court stated that the women were protected by the Bill of Rights because "[t]he United States is entirely a creature of the Constitution. Its power and authority have no other source."[39] The Court continued, "[no] agreement with a foreign nation can confer power on the Congress, or on any branch of Government, which is free from the restraints of the Constitution."[40] Accordingly, a president may not negotiate away the civil liberties of American citizens through the treaty power. The Court held that the women were entitled to the protections of the Constitution.

This defines the relationship between the Constitution and treaties, but what about the relationship between statutes and treaties? Which prevails if there is a conflict? Both are the supreme law of the land. Accordingly, they are of equal legal weight or authority. If a treaty and statute both deal with the same topic, courts attempt to interpret them as consistent with each other. If this is not possible, then the latest of the two prevails. Thus, Congress may amend or repeal a treaty by statute. Similarly, statutes may be amended or repealed by treaties. However, because of the international consequences of amending or repealing treaties, congressional intent is not inferred. Congress must clearly express an intent to alter an existing treaty.[41]

Federalism issues also arise in the treaty context. What if a treaty conflicts with state law? Even more, does the Tenth Amendment restrict the treaty power? The answer to the former question is that the state law is defeated, and to the second, the answer is no. The Supremacy Clause is the foundation for both answers. There is, of course, no problem with matters that fall squarely within the jurisdiction of the federal government. For example, a state law that affects commerce with other nations is voided by a treaty with contrary provisions. But the treaty power has proven much greater than that. The federal government may, through the treaty power, regulate matters that usually fall within the sphere of state authority. For example, in *Hauenstein v. Lynham*,[42] a state law that prohibited aliens from inheriting property was overridden by a treaty that provided otherwise.

SIDEBAR

EXECUTIVE AGREEMENT OR TREATY? CIRCULAR 175

When will the president rely on an executive agreement rather than on a treaty to memorialize an agreement with a foreign nation? The State Department has issued guidelines concerning when executive agreements are appropriate. The following factors are considered, as announced in the State Department's Circular 175:

1. The extent to which the agreement affects the nation as a whole
2. The extent to which state laws will be affected
3. Whether congressional action is necessary
4. Domestic and foreign practice
5. Congressional preference
6. The degree of formality desired
7. The expected duration of the agreement and the need for prompt conclusion
8. Whether the Constitution delegates the subject matter to the president[43]

These State Department guidelines are intended to assist its officials in the performance of their duties. Courts, however, may consider these factors, but need not rely on them. Rather, judicial review will center around federalism principles, particularly the nature of the executive agreement and whether Congress has approved or disapproved of it. If not, a reviewing court will determine whether the subject matter is inherently executive.

Missouri v. Holland (1920)[44] also stands for the principle that the Tenth Amendment does not limit the treaty power. In addition, the Court announced that federal power could be expanded through the treaty power. In 1913, Congress enacted a statute to protect migratory birds. That law was invalidated by lower federal courts as exceeding federal power. Later, the United States and Britain entered into a treaty that required protection of the same birds. Missouri claimed that the federal government had again exceeded its authority and encroached upon state powers. The Court rejected those claims. The Court reasoned that the Tenth Amendment does not create specific state powers; rather, it reserves to the states those powers not given to the federal government. The treaty power was delegated to the federal government, so the Tenth Amendment does not limit it. In further support of the decision, Justice Oliver Wendell Holmes, who wrote the majority opinion, noted that migratory birds are inherently a national concern and that the treaty did not encroach upon any constitutionally secured rights of citizens.

5.6(b) Executory and Self-Executing Treaties

Treaties are characterized as either **executory** or **self-executing.** An executory treaty is not immediately enforceable as domestic law. Congressional action is necessary to carry it into effect. An executory treaty is not, therefore, the supreme law of the land until Congress has enacted implementing legislation. A self-executing treaty, in contrast, requires no statute to implement its provisions. It is already in a form that courts can enforce.

5.6(c) Executive Agreements

In addition to treaties, the president may enter into an **executive agreement** with a foreign power. Treaties and executive agreements may be similar in substance, but in procedure they are very different. Treaties must be approved by the Senate, whereas executive agreements are entered into unilaterally by the president. Executive agreements are known by many names, including *executive agreement, memorandum of understanding, memorandum of arrangement,* and *technical agreement,* among others. In recent years, for example, the State Department reported the creation of 300 executive agreements a year through its office. The Defense Department reported a similar number, and there are many more from other agencies.[45]

There is no explicit language in the Constitution recognizing executive agreements, compacts, and accords. Regardless, they are an accepted presidential power. In fact, over 90 percent of all agreements with foreign nations are in the form of executive agreements, not treaties.

There are three types of executive agreements, each characterized by different sources of power.[46] The first is the *treaty-authorized executive agreement.* Of the three types of executive agreements, it most closely resembles a treaty, because the agreement is authorized by an existing treaty that has already been approved by the Senate. This is common, for example, for treaties that resolve large policy issues but not the details of implementation. The details are left to future negotiations, and the treaty contains a provision authorizing the president to enter into agreements with the treaty's signatories for this purpose. Because the requisite two-thirds Senate vote approves of such agreements, they are seldom found to be invalid. Of course, an agreement that exceeds the treaty authorization is not on the same footing. It is treated as one of the other two forms of executive agreements.

The second type of executive agreement is the *congressionally authorized* executive agreement. This is different from the treaty-authorized executive agreement in two respects. First, congressional approval usually occurs by majority vote in both houses, often through joint resolution. Second, approval usually comes after the agreement has been concluded and executed. Even though this form of agreement need not go through the two-thirds Senate approval procedure, it is checked by Congress and is generally accepted.

executory
Not yet fully performed, completed, fulfilled, or carried out; to be performed, either wholly or in part; not yet executed.

self-executing
Self-acting; going into effect without need of further action.

executive agreement
An agreement with a foreign government, made by the president acting within his or her executive powers.

The third form of executive agreement is the *solely executive agreement*. It is not approved by Congress in any fashion and is founded upon presidential power alone. Generally, this form of agreement is valid only if its subject matter is exclusively executive. Because of the absence of congressional involvement, this form is most questionable. An example is an agreement to recognize a foreign government. Because this is an executive, rather than congressional, power, the president may unilaterally enter into such an agreement. It has been estimated that only 7 percent of executive agreements are purely executive.[47]

All executive agreements that are premised entirely upon executive power may be altered by Congress. For purposes of analysis, Justice Jackson's three-part test of presidential power applies to executive agreements. If the president enters into a solely executive agreement concerning a subject that is exclusively executive, then Congress may not interfere. For example, Congress is without authority to amend an executive agreement recognizing a foreign power. The same would be true of armistice agreements, as the president possesses the power to end hostilities without congressional authorization. If the subject of an agreement is one over which the president and Congress share powers, however, then Congress may amend or abolish the agreement. Because congressionally approved agreements are not approved by the Senate, as are treaties, they differ in their effect on existing legislation. Recall that a treaty may amend an existing statute. This appears reasonable because both Congress (the Senate) and the president are acting. But only the president acts in executive agreements. For this reason, unless the president is acting within the sphere of exclusive executive powers, an executive agreement may not alter existing legislation. Even more, if an executive agreement is wholly inconsistent with statutory law, then it is void.[48]

Like treaties, executive agreements are limited by the Constitution. Executive agreements are law of the United States under the Supremacy Clause and prevail over conflicting state laws. The case *Dames & Moore v. Regan* illustrates the use of an executive agreement by President James Carter to free Americans who were held captive in Iran.

Dames & Moore v. Regan
453 U.S. 654 (1981)

Justice Rehnquist delivered the opinion of the Court.

On November 4, 1979, the American Embassy in Tehran was seized and our diplomatic personnel were captured and held hostage. In response to that crisis, President Carter, acting pursuant to the International Emergency Economic Powers Act, declared a national emergency on November 14, 1979, and blocked the removal or transfer of "all property and interests in property of the Government of Iran, its instrumentalities and controlled entities of the Central Bank of Iran which are or become subject to the jurisdiction of the United States. . . . "

[On] November 14, 1979, the Treasury Department's Office of Foreign Assets Control issued a regulation providing that "[u]nless licensed or authorized . . . any attachment, judgment, decree, lien, execution, garnishment, or other judicial process is null and void with respect to any property in which on or since [the date of the order] existed an interest of Iran." . . .

On December 19, 1979, petitioner Dames and Moore filed suit in the United States District Court [against] the Government of Iran, the Atomic Energy Organization of Iran, and a number of Iranian banks. [Dames and Moore] alleged that its wholly owned subsidiary, Dames

and Moore International, S.R.L., was a party to a written contract with the Atomic Energy Organization, and that the subsidiary's entire interest in the contract with the Atomic Energy Organization, and that the subsidiary's entire interest in the contract had been assigned to petitioner. [Dames and Moore] contended . . . it was owed $3,436,694.30 plus interest for services performed under the contract prior to the date of termination. The District Court issued orders of attachment directed against property of the defendants, and the property of certain Iranian banks was then attached to secure any judgment that might be entered against them.

On January 20, 1981, the Americans held hostage were released by Iran pursuant to an Agreement entered into the day [before]. [This] agreement stated "[i]t is the purpose . . . to terminate all litigation as between the Government of each party and the nationals of the other, and to bring about the settlement and termination of all such claims through binding arbitration." In furtherance of this goal, the Agreement called for the establishment of an Iran-United States Claims Tribunal which would arbitrate any claims not settled within six months. Awards of the Claims Tribunal are to be "final and binding" and "enforceable . . . in the courts of any nation in accordance with its laws." Under the Agreement, the United States is obligated

> to terminate all legal proceedings in United States courts involving claims of United States persons and institutions against Iran and its state enterprises, to nullify all attachments and judgments obtained therein, to prohibit all further litigation based on such claims, and to bring about the termination of such claims through binding arbitration.

In addition, the United States must "act to bring about the transfer" by July 19, 1981 of all Iranian assets held in this country by American banks. One billion dollars of these assets will be deposited in a security account in the Bank of England, to the account of the Algerian Central Bank, and used to satisfy awards rendered against Iran by the Claims Tribunal.

On January 19, 1981, President Carter issued a series of Executive Orders implementing the terms of the agreement. . . .

The parties and the lower court all agreed that much relevant analysis is contained in [*Youngstown*] Justice Black's opinion for the Court in that case [stated that the] "President's power, if any, to issue the order must stem either from an act of Congress or from the Constitution itself." Justice Jackson's concurring opinion elaborated in a general way the consequences of different types of interaction between the two democratic branches in assessing Presidential authority to act in any given case.

Although we have in the past found and do today find Justice Jackson's classification of executive actions into three categories analytically useful, Jackson himself recognized that his three categories represented "a somewhat oversimplified grouping," and it is doubtless the case that executive action in any particular instance falls, not neatly in one of three pigeonholes [recall the three: the President acting pursuant to statute, in the absence of any statute, and against statute]. . . . This is particularly true as respects cases such as the one before us, involving responses to international crises the nature of which Congress can hardly have been expected to anticipate in any detail.

[The] Government has principally relied on § 203 of the [International Emergency Economic Powers Act (IEEPA), which] provides in part:

> [The] President may [nullify], void, prevent or prohibit any acquisition, holding, withholding, use, transfer, withdrawal, transportation, importation or exportation of, or dealing in, or exercising any right, power, or privilege with respect to, or transactions involving, any property in which any foreign country or a national thereof has any interest; by any person, or with respect to any property, subject to the jurisdiction of the United States.

The Government contends that the acts of "nullifying" the attachments and ordering the "transfer" of the frozen assets are specifically authorized by the plain language of the above statute. . . .

Because the President's action in nullifying the attachments and ordering the transfer of assets was taken

pursuant to specific congressional authorization, it is "supported by the strongest of presumptions and the widest latitude of judicial interpretation, and the burden of persuasion would rest heavily upon any who might attack it." *Youngstown*, 343 U.S. at 637 (Jackson, J., concurring). Under the circumstances of this case, we cannot say that petitioner has sustained that heavy burden. A contrary ruling would mean that the Federal Government as a whole lacked the power exercised by the President, and that we are not prepared to say.

Although we have concluded that the IEEPA constitutes specific congressional authorization to the President to nullify the attachments and order the transfer of Iranian assets, there remains the question of the President's authority to suspend claims pending in American courts. Such claims have, of course, an existence apart from the attachments which accompany them. In terminating these claims [the] President purported to act under authority of both the IEEPA and so-called "Hostage Act." We conclude that neither the IEEPA nor the Hostage Act constitutes specific authorization of the President's action suspending claims. This is not to say that these statutory provisions are entirely irrelevant to the question of the validity of the President's action. We think both statutes highly relevant in the looser sense of indicating congressional acceptance of a broad scope for executive action in circumstances such as those presented in this case. [The] IEEPA delegates broad authority to the President to act in times of national emergency with respect to property of a foreign country. The Hostage Act similarly indicates congressional willingness that the President have broad discretion when responding to the hostile acts of foreign sovereigns. . . .

Although we have declined to conclude that the IEEPA or the Hostage Act directly authorizes the President's suspension of claims for the reasons noted, we cannot ignore the general tenor of Congress' legislation in this area in trying to determine whether the President is acting alone or at least with the acceptance of Congress. [Congress] cannot anticipate and legislate with regard to every possible action the President may find it necessary to take [for] every possible situation in which he might act. Such failure of Congress specifically to delegate authority does not, "especially . . . in the areas of foreign policy and national security," imply "congressional disapproval" of action taken by the Executive. On the contrary, the enactment of legislation closely related to the question of the President's authority in a particular case which evinces legislative intent to accord the President broad discretion may be considered to "invite" "measures on independent presidential responsibility." At least this is so where there is no contrary indication of legislative intent and when, as here, there is a history of congressional acquiescence in conduct of the sort engaged in by the President. . . .

In light of the foregoing—the inferences to be drawn from the character of the legislation Congress has enacted in the area such as the IEEPA and the Hostage Act, and from the history of acquiescence in executive claims

settlement—we conclude that the President was authorized to suspend pending claims. Justice Frankfurter pointed
out in *Youngstown*, "a systematic, unbroken, executive
practice, long pursued to the knowledge of the Congress
and never before questioned . . . may be treated as a gloss
on the 'Executive Power' vested in the President by § 1 of
Art. II." Past practice does not, by itself, create power, but
"long-continued practice, known to and acquiesced in by
Congress, would raise a presumption that the [act] had been
[committed] in pursuance of [Congress's] consent. . . . "

Our conclusion is buttressed by the fact that the means
chosen by the President to settle the claims of American
nationals provided an alternative forum, the Claims Tribunal, which is capable of providing meaningful relief. . . .

Just as importantly, Congress has not disapproved of
the action taken here. Though Congress has held hearings
on the Iranian Agreement itself, Congress has not enacted legislation, or even passed a resolution, indicating
its displeasure with the Agreement. Quite the contrary,
the relevant Senate Committee has stated that the establishment of the Tribunal is "of vital importance to the
United States." We are thus clearly not confronted with a
situation in which Congress has in some way resisted the
exercise of Presidential authority.

Although the executive agreement at issue in *Dames & Moore* was of the solely
executive type (i.e., it was never expressly approved by Congress), the Court found that
Congress had implicitly approved it. Because of inaction (failure to enact legislation disapproving of the agreement), a scheme of legislation that supported the power generally,
a history of presidential authority in the area, and provisions in the agreement intended
to protect the rights of interested individuals (claims tribunal), the agreement was upheld.

Congress has enacted several laws intended to control the presidential power to make
executive agreements. In some instances, Congress disapproves of executive agreements on
certain subjects in advance. In others, Congress disapproves of agreements after they have
been enacted. Also, federal legislation requires presidents to report all executive agreements
to Congress after execution. Figure 5-2 summarizes agreement creation and source.

TREATIES AND EXECUTIVE AGREEMENTS

Type of Agreement	Description/Method of Creation	Constitutional Source
Treaty —Executory —Self-executing	Presidential negotiation and drafting. Two-thirds favorable vote in Senate (of senators present).	—Art. II, § 2, cl. 2, establishes federal power and method. —Art. I, § 10, prohibits the states from making agreements with other nations, except in emergencies.
Treaty-authorized executive agreement	Existing treaty that has sena-torial approval authorizes the president to unilaterally make an agreement with a nation. Usually done to allow signatory nations to a treaty to resolve issues of implementation more easily.	—Art. II, § 2, cl. 2
Congressionally authorized executive agreement	Presidential negotiation and agreement authorized by both houses of Congress, usually by joint resolution.	—Inherent executive power —Congressional authorization —Practice
Solely executive agreement	President unilaterally negotiates and executes an agreement. Congress does not participate either before or after execution.	—Inherent executive power —Practice

FIGURE 5-2
Treaties and executive agreements

The final issue in this area is termination power. May a president terminate a treaty? An executive agreement? May Congress terminate either? The Constitution does not express a termination method.

It is argued that because treaties are approved by a two-thirds vote of the Senate, they must be terminated in the same manner. Conversely, it is argued that the president possesses the inherent power to terminate treaties. This area of law is not well defined, in part because the Supreme Court has treated the issue as a nonjusticiable political question.[49] Recall Justice Jackson's tripartite analysis in *Youngstown* when considering this issue.

Though there are no concrete answers, a few conclusions can be drawn. First, treaties most assuredly can be terminated when the president and Senate concur. Second, terminations with congressional approval (majority votes in both houses) are likely valid. Third, solely executive terminations are the most vulnerable. The extent to which the treaty regulates a subject within the president's domain is relevant. Also, congressional attitude, whether express or implied, will also be considered.

5.7 WAR POWERS

Article II, Section 2, clause 1, declares the president to be the commander-in-chief of the United States Army and Navy and of the state militias when called into national service. Only the army and navy are specifically mentioned because that was the whole of the military in 1789. It is not seriously questioned that the framers intended to include the entire military with the language. Therefore, the president is the commander-in-chief of all branches of the armed forces: U.S. Army, Navy, Marines, and Air Force. The framers specifically chose civilian command of the military to keep the military in check. As commander-in-chief, the president sits at the top of the hierarchy. He or she is the chief general and chief admiral of the armed forces. The extent to which the president becomes involved in the daily operations of the armed forces is left to his or her discretion. Although the Constitution delegates the power to regulate the armed forces to Congress,[50] the president may issue regulations covering the same subject. Congress is the final authority, and thus executive regulations, orders, and commands must be consistent with legislation to be valid. The power to promulgate regulations may be delegated to the secretaries of the armed forces.

The most controversial and discussed authority of the president concerns the initiation of hostilities and the commitment of American military forces to ventures abroad. The power to declare war clearly rests with Congress. Other methods were considered by the framers. Hamilton initially suggested that the Senate alone should possess the power. He argued that the Senate would be best suited to make the decision, because of its familiarity with foreign affairs through the treaty and related powers. (He later changed his opinion and advocated that it be a shared presidential and Senate power.) Randolph believed the power should lie with the House of Representatives, the true voice of the people. Butler argued that war-making is by its nature executive and should be delegated exclusively to the president. The delegates finally settled on excluding the president, but involving the entire Congress in the decision.[51] A simple majority vote in each house is required to declare war.

Even though the framers rejected presidential power to declare war, presidents have de facto exercised the power since the beginning. The first controversy actually involved a presidential decision not to use force. In 1798, George Washington issued a proclamation declaring the neutrality of the United States in a war between Great Britain and France. Alexander Hamilton defended President Washington's action, while James Madison argued that it was an invasion of Congress's authority to declare war. Madison reasoned that the power to declare war necessarily includes the power to declare peace. Since that time, presidents have on hundreds of occasions involved the United States in conflicts without congressional approval. Some presidents have openly resisted congressional involvement in the decision to commit troops. President Bush remarked, "I didn't have to get permission from some old goat in the United States Congress to kick Saddam Hussein out of Kuwait."[52] Of the hundreds of military ventures in which the United States has been involved, only five were accompanied by a declaration of war.

There have been more than two hundred instances of military action without declarations of war or other congressional authorization. The first occurred in 1798, when the United States and France had the first of several military conflicts over a two-year period. Such actions continue into the present day. Both Korean and Vietnam "wars" fall into this category. But Congress has authorized war on several occasions. It gave President Lyndon Johnson authority to use the military in southeast Asia through the Gulf of Tonkin resolution.[53] A precursor to the Vietnam War, it was repealed in 1971. Congress subsequently enacted the War Powers Resolution, discussed in the later paragraphs. Congress also authorized the nation's two most recent wars in Iraq and Afghanistan, as requested by President Bush.[54]

The source of presidential authority to make war is primarily the commander-in-chief power, but it is also custom. Clearly, presidents have often made "war" without congressional authorization. However, it is not likely that presidential authority can overcome adverse congressional resolution. If Congress prohibits, or requires a cessation of, military action, the president must comply. To do otherwise would not be the faithful execution of the laws.

Presidents have justified their unilateral decisions to use the military for several reasons: to defend national economic interests abroad, to defend U.S. citizens abroad, to assist foreign persons from abuse, and to honor treaty obligations. Clearly, presidential authority would be at its highest point if the United States were invaded. Unilateral presidential power to repel invasions cannot be seriously questioned.

Congress attempted to control presidential war-making authority through the War Powers Resolution of 1973.[55] Section 2 of the Resolution announces Congress's objective:

> It is the purpose of this joint resolution to fulfill the intent of the framers of the Constitution of the United States and to insure that the collective judgment of both the Congress and the President will apply to the introduction of United States Armed Forces into hostilities, or into situations where imminent involvement in hostilities is clearly indicated by the circumstances, and to the continued use of such forces in hostilities or in such situations.

The resolution provides that the president must notify Congress of any introduction of the U.S. military into hostilities, or situations where hostilities are imminent, within forty-eight hours. With few exceptions, Congress then has sixty days to act. If it cannot meet during this time, the president is authorized to continue the military action. If Congress does meet, it may declare war, authorize the action, require a termination of hostilities, or not act. If Congress does not act, the president is required to terminate the military action. The president has no veto power.[56] The constitutionality of the War Powers Resolution is questionable. One objection that has been voiced by several presidents is that it interferes with an inherent presidential power. Another objection concerns the absence of a presidential veto. The Supreme Court has invalidated the use of the **legislative veto** and the War Powers Resolution appears to be just that. See Chapter 7 for a further discussion of the legislative veto. Finally, the resolution may represent an unlawful delegation of Congress's war-making power to the president.

The precise relationship between Congress and the president in the war powers area is unknown. The federal judiciary has been reluctant to become involved in this area, usually ruling that these cases are nonjusticiable political questions. Instead, history, cooperation between the two branches, and public opinion shape this area of law. Once war has been initiated, the president is responsible for deciding military strategy and technique. These are command decisions with which Congress may not interfere.

legislative veto
An act of a legislature invalidating executive action in a particular instance. Generally, legislative vetos are unconstitutional. Once power is delegated by Congress to the president, it is generally prohibited from interfering with the president's enforcement.

The president supervises the war and its participants. His or her power is more limited in terms of military discipline, which Congress may regulate. The president alone executes congressional regulations of the military, and he or she may establish rules that do not conflict with congressional regulations. The president's largest limitation as to the conduct of wars is money. Congress alone may appropriate funds.

The powers of the federal government, at least of the political branches, are generally increased during times of war. The government's war power is most potent when Congress and the president join forces. The federal government may enact economic regulations (such as price and rental controls and rationing of food and supplies), draft servicepersons, and the like. Also, as previously discussed, the internment of Americans of the same ancestry as a war enemy was permitted during World War II, in spite of the absence of conflict on American soil, in the *Korematsu* case. Although presidential authority is enhanced during wartime, alone it is not as powerful as when accompanied by congressional support. This is evinced by the Court's invalidation of President Truman's seizure of steel mills (*Youngstown*) during the Korean Conflict.

Presidents may call state militias into active national service when necessary. By a statute, which was upheld by the Court, the president may now order state militias into service abroad without the consent of state officials. During domestic emergencies, such as invasion, the president may declare martial law. If Congress is unable to meet and has preapproved the action, the president may suspend habeas corpus. So long as Congress is unable to meet due to domestic hostility, the presidential authority to both legislate and execute laws will be increased.

5.7(a) War Against Terrorism

Presidential war authority has been the subject of considerable debate since the attacks on the United States on September 11, 2001. In response to the attacks, President Bush waged war against Afghanistan, Iraq, and, most controversially, terrorism. Congress reacted to the attacks by enacting the Uniting and Strengthening America by Providing Appropriate Tools Required to Intercept and Obstruct Terrorism (aka USA PATRIOT) Act in 2001. It was renewed in 2006. This law expanded the authority of law-enforcement officials in their prevention, detection, and punishment of terrorists. It also supplemented existing related laws, such as the Foreign Intelligence Surveillance Act, which regulates federal law-enforcement investigations of foreign intelligence targets.

Congress also passed a joint resolution, the Authorization for Use of Military Force (AUMF), authorizing the president to "use all necessary and appropriate force" against nations, organizations, and persons that planned or participated in the attacks.

Pursuant to the AUMF, other laws, and the president's inherent authority as commander-in-chief, President Bush issued Military Order 1. Through this order, Bush declared a national emergency, ordered the detention of al-Qaeda members who planned or participated in the attacks, and ordered the military trial of such individuals. The order provides defendants with the right to counsel, freedom of religious practice while in detention, humane treatment, and other protections.

In its battle with terrorism, the United States detained hundreds of individuals suspected of giving aid to al-Qaeda and the Taliban. Most of these individuals have been held at the U.S. Naval Base in Guantanamo Bay, Cuba. The United States has determined that the detainees are enemy combatants, and as such, the rules concerning their detention should follow standard wartime rules. For enemy combatants, this means detention until the war has ended. Indeed, many of the detainees at Guantanamo Bay have been held for years. Because the United States has characterized the detainees as prisoners of war and not criminal defendants, their detentions have not been reviewed by a court, they have not been tried, and they have not had the benefit of legal counsel. They are entitled, however, to certain protections under both international (e.g., Geneva Convention) and U.S. law. International law divides combatants (as opposed to noncombatant civilians) into two groups, lawful and unlawful.

The Supreme Court, in *Ex Parte Quirin*, 317 U.S. 1, 30–31 (1942), stated:

> By universal agreement and practice the law of war draws a distinction between the armed forces and the peaceful populations of belligerent nations and also between those who are lawful and unlawful combatants. Lawful combatants are subject to capture and detention as prisoners of war by opposing military forces. Unlawful combatants are likewise subject to capture and detention, but in addition they are subject to trial and punishment by military tribunals for acts which render their belligerency unlawful. The spy who secretly and without uniform passes the military lines of a belligerent in time of war, seeking to gather military information and communicate it to the enemy, or an enemy combatant who without uniform comes secretly through the lines for the purpose of waging war by destruction of life or property, are familiar examples of belligerents who are generally deemed not to be entitled to the status of prisoners of war, but to be offenders against the law of war subject to trial and punishment by military tribunals.

The War on Terror, however, is unlike traditional wars. Defining the enemy is more difficult than in past wars, and it is not likely to end with a surrender and peace agreement. The possibility that the War on Terror could continue for many years, possibly generations, exists. As such, many scholars question whether detainees should be treated in the same manner as enemy combatants of the past (e.g., Germans in World Wars I and II). A question that remains to be resolved is whether the government's efforts to detect and apprehend the terrorists are war or traditional law-enforcement actions. The Bush administration contends that the members of al-Qaeda are neither prisoners of war nor enemy combatants. Instead, the administration asserts that they are unlawful enemy combatants, subject to indeterminate detention and trial by military commission.

This was the position of the United States in *Ex Parte Quirin* more than sixty years earlier. In *Quirin*, a group of German-born U.S. citizens who returned to Germany before and at the outbreak of World War II were caught preparing for terrorist attacks on the United States. Traveling by submarine, the men reentered the United States and hid explosives on the shores of both New York and Florida. Although they wore German infantry uniforms when they came ashore, they shed the uniforms and dressed liked civilians as they proceeded to New York City to complete their sabotage mission. They were apprehended in Chicago, Illinois. Pursuant to an order of President Franklin D. Roosevelt concerning the detention and trial of unlawful combatants, the men were to be tried by military commission. The men challenged the president's authority to order trial by military commission, rather than by civil court. The Court upheld the presidential order both under Article II presidential authority and because Congress had empowered the president to issue such an order. The men were tried and convicted by military commission. Six were executed and two were sentenced to prison.

In 2004, the Supreme Court decided that the Guantanamo detainees possess a right to have their detention reviewed by federal courts through the habeas corpus procedure in *Rasul v. Bush* (2004). But what process is required? The U.S. Supreme Court heard a habeas corpus petition from a U.S. citizen detainee in *Hamdi v. Rumsfeld* (2004). In this case, the basic hearing rights of a detainee were outlined by the Supreme Court.

Hamdi v. Rumsfeld
542 U.S. 507 (2004)

Justice O'Connor delivered the opinion of the court.

At this difficult time in our Nation's history, we are called upon to consider the legality of the Government's detention of a United States citizen on United States soil as an "enemy combatant" and to address the process that is constitutionally owed to one who seeks to challenge his classification as such. The United States Court of Appeals for the Fourth Circuit held that petitioner's detention was legally authorized and that he was entitled to no further opportunity to challenge his enemy-combatant label. We now vacate and remand. We hold that although Congress authorized the detention of combatants in the narrow circumstances alleged here, due process demands that a citizen held in the United States as an enemy combatant be given a meaningful opportunity to contest the factual basis for that detention before a neutral decision-maker.

On September 11, 2001, the al Qaeda terrorist network used hijacked commercial airliners to attack prominent targets in the United States. Approximately 3,000 people were killed in those attacks. One week later, in response to these "acts of treacherous violence," Congress passed a resolution authorizing the President to "use all necessary and appropriate force against those nations, organizations, or persons he determines planned, authorized, committed, or aided the terrorist attacks" or "harbored such organizations or persons, in order to prevent any future acts of international terrorism against the United States by such nations, organizations or persons." Authorization for Use of Military Force ("the AUMF"), 115 Stat. 224. Soon thereafter, the President ordered United States Armed Forces to Afghanistan, with a mission to subdue al Qaeda and quell the Taliban regime that was known to support it.

This case arises out of the detention of a man whom the Government alleges took up arms with the Taliban during this conflict. His name is Yaser Esam Hamdi. Born an American citizen in Louisiana in 1980, Hamdi moved with his family to Saudi Arabia as a child. By 2001, the parties agree, he resided in Afghanistan. At some point that year, he was seized by members of the Northern Alliance, a coalition of military groups opposed to the Taliban government, and eventually was turned over to the United States military. The Government asserts that it initially detained and interrogated Hamdi in Afghanistan before transferring him to the United States Naval Base in Guantanamo Bay in January 2002. In April 2002, upon learning that Hamdi is an American citizen, authorities transferred him to a naval brig in Norfolk, Virginia, where he remained until a recent transfer to a brig in Charleston, South Carolina. The Government contends that Hamdi is an "enemy combatant," and that this status justifies holding him in the United States indefinitely—without formal charges or proceedings—unless and until it makes the determination that access to counsel or further process is warranted.

In June 2002, Hamdi's father, Esam Fouad Hamdi, filed the present petition for a writ of habeas corpus. . . . The elder Hamdi alleges in the petition that he has had no contact with his son since the Government took custody of him in 2001, and that the Government has held his son "without access to legal counsel or notice of any charges pending against him." The petition contends that Hamdi's detention was not legally authorized. It argues that, "[a]s an American citizen, . . . Hamdi enjoys the full protections of the Constitution," and that Hamdi's detention in the United States without charges, access to an impartial tribunal, or assistance of counsel "violated and continue[s] to violate the Fifth and Fourteenth Amendments to the United States Constitution." The habeas petition asks that the court, among other things, (1) appoint counsel for Hamdi; (2) order respondents to cease interrogating him; (3) declare that he is being held in violation of the Fifth and Fourteenth Amendments; (4) "[t]o the extent Respondents contest any material factual allegations in this Petition, schedule an evidentiary hearing, at which Petitioners may adduce proof in support of their allegations"; and (5) order that Hamdi be released from his "unlawful custody." Although his habeas petition provides no details with regard to the factual circumstances surrounding his son's capture and detention, Hamdi's father has asserted in documents found elsewhere in the record that his son went to Afghanistan to do "relief work," and that he had been in that country less than two months before September 11, 2001, and could not have received military training. The 20-year-old was traveling on his own for the first time, his father says, and "[b]ecause of his lack of experience, he was trapped in Afghanistan once that military campaign began."

The threshold question before us is whether the Executive has the authority to detain citizens who qualify as "enemy combatants." There is some debate as to the proper scope of this term, and the Government has never provided any court with the full criteria that it uses in classifying individuals as such. It has made clear, however, that, for purposes of this case, the "enemy combatant" that it is seeking to detain is an individual who, it alleges, was "part of or supporting forces hostile to the United States or coalition partners" in Afghanistan and who "engaged in an armed conflict against the United States" there. Brief for Respondents 3. We therefore answer only the narrow question before us: whether the detention of citizens falling within that definition is authorized.

The Government maintains that no explicit congressional authorization is required, because the Executive possesses plenary authority to detain pursuant to Article II of the Constitution. We do not reach the question whether Article II provides such authority, however, because we agree with the Government's alternative position, that Congress has in fact authorized Hamdi's detention, through the AUMF. . . .

The AUMF authorizes the President to use "all necessary and appropriate force" against "nations, organizations, or persons" associated with the September 11, 2001, terrorist attacks. 115 Stat. 224. There can be no doubt that individuals who fought against the United States in Afghanistan as part of the Taliban, an organization known to have supported the al Qaeda terrorist network responsible for those attacks, are individuals Congress sought to target in passing the AUMF. We conclude that detention of individuals falling into the limited category we are considering, for the duration of the particular conflict in which they were captured, is so fundamental and accepted an incident to war as to be an exercise of the "necessary and appropriate force" Congress has authorized the President to use.

The capture and detention of lawful combatants and the capture, detention, and trial of unlawful combatants, by "universal agreement and practice," are "important incident[s] of war." *Ex parte Quirin,* 317 U.S., at 28. The purpose of detention is to prevent captured individuals from returning to the field of battle and taking up arms once again. [C]aptivity in war is "neither revenge, nor punishment, but solely protective custody, the only purpose of which is to prevent the prisoners of war from further participation in the war" . . .

There is no bar to this Nation's holding one of its own citizens as an enemy combatant. [The Court then reviewed precedent on this point.] . . .

In light of these principles, it is of no moment that the AUMF does not use specific language of detention. Because detention to prevent a combatant's return to the battlefield is a fundamental incident of waging war, in permitting the use of "necessary and appropriate force," Congress has clearly and unmistakably authorized detention in the narrow circumstances considered here.

Hamdi objects, nevertheless, that Congress has not authorized the *indefinite* detention to which he is now subject. The Government responds that "the detention of enemy combatants during World War II was just as 'indefinite' while that war was being fought." We take Hamdi's objection to be not to the lack of certainty regarding the date on which the conflict will end, but to the substantial prospect of perpetual detention. We recognize that the national security underpinnings of the "war on terror," although crucially important, are broad and malleable. As the Government concedes, "given its unconventional nature, the current conflict is unlikely to end with a formal cease-fire agreement." The prospect Hamdi raises is therefore not far-fetched. If the Government does not consider this unconventional war won for two generations, and if it maintains during that time that Hamdi might, if released, rejoin forces fighting against the United States, then the position it has taken throughout the litigation of this case suggests that Hamdi's detention could last for the rest of his life.

It is a clearly established principle of the law of war that detention may last no longer than active hostilities. . . .

Hamdi contends that the AUMF does not authorize indefinite or perpetual detention. Certainly, we agree that indefinite detention for the purpose of interrogation is not authorized. Further, we understand Congress' grant of authority for the use of "necessary and appropriate force" to include the authority to detain for the duration of the relevant conflict, and our understanding is based on longstanding law-of-war principles. If the practical circumstances of a given conflict are entirely unlike those of the conflicts that informed the development of the law of war, that understanding may unravel. But that is not the situation we face as of this date. Active combat operations against Taliban fighters apparently are ongoing in Afghanistan. . . . The United States may detain, for the duration of these hostilities, individuals legitimately determined to be Taliban combatants who "engaged in an armed conflict against the United States." If the record establishes that United States troops are still involved in active combat in Afghanistan, those detentions are part of the exercise of "necessary and appropriate force," and therefore are authorized by the AUMF. . . .

Even in cases in which the detention of enemy combatants is legally authorized, there remains the question of what process is constitutionally due to a citizen who disputes his enemy-combatant status. Hamdi argues that he is owed a meaningful and timely hearing and that

"extra-judicial detention [that] begins and ends with the submission of an affidavit based on third-hand hearsay" does not comport with the Fifth and Fourteenth Amendments. The Government counters that any more process than was provided below would be both unworkable and "constitutionally intolerable." Brief for Respondents 46. Our resolution of this dispute requires a careful examination both of the writ of habeas corpus, which Hamdi now seeks to employ as a mechanism of judicial review, and of the Due Process Clause, which informs the procedural contours of that mechanism in this instance. . . .

Though they reach radically different conclusions on the process that ought to attend the present proceeding, the parties begin on common ground. All agree that, absent suspension, the writ of habeas corpus remains available to every individual detained within the United States. U.S. Const., Art. I, §9, cl. 2 ("The Privilege of the Writ of Habeas Corpus shall not be suspended, unless when in Cases of Rebellion or Invasion the public Safety may require it.") Only in the rarest of circumstances has Congress seen fit to suspend the writ. At all other times, it has remained a critical check on the Executive, ensuring that it does not detain individuals except in accordance with law. All agree suspension of the writ has not occurred here. . . .

[The Court then discussed the competing interests of the individual's interest in a fair process, especially when detention is involved, and the government's interest in preventing enemies from returning to the battlefield. The government also argued that its military officers need to be focused on waging war and they would be distracted from this duty by additional process for detainees.]

Striking the proper constitutional balance here is of great importance to the Nation during this period of ongoing combat. But it is equally vital that our calculus not give short shrift to the values that this country holds dear or to the privilege that is American citizenship. It is during our most challenging and uncertain moments that our Nation's commitment to due process is most severely tested; and it is in those times that we must preserve our commitment at home to the principles for which we fight abroad. . . .

We therefore hold that a citizen-detainee seeking to challenge his classification as an enemy combatant must receive notice of the factual basis for his classification, and a fair opportunity to rebut the Government's factual assertions before a neutral decisionmaker. . . .

At the same time, the exigencies of the circumstances may demand that, aside from these core elements, enemy combatant proceedings may be tailored to alleviate their uncommon potential to burden the Executive at a time of ongoing military conflict. Hearsay, for example, may need to be accepted as the most reliable available evidence from the Government in such a proceeding. Likewise, the Constitution would not be offended by a presumption in favor of the Government's evidence, so long as that presumption remained a rebuttable one and fair opportunity for rebuttal were provided. Thus, once the Government puts forth credible evidence that the habeas petitioner meets the enemy-combatant criteria, the onus could shift to the petitioner to rebut that evidence with more persuasive evidence that he falls outside the criteria. A burden-shifting scheme of this sort would meet the goal of ensuring that the errant tourist, embedded journalist, or local aid worker has a chance to prove military error while giving due regard to the Executive once it has put forth meaningful support for its conclusion that the detainee is in fact an enemy combatant. In the words of *Mathews*, process of this sort would sufficiently address the "risk of erroneous deprivation" of a detainee's liberty interest while eliminating certain procedures that have questionable additional value in light of the burden on the Government. 424 U.S., at 335.

We think it unlikely that this basic process will have the dire impact on the central functions of warmaking that the Government forecasts. The parties agree that initial captures on the battlefield need not receive the process we have discussed here; that process is due only when the determination is made to *continue* to hold those who have been seized. . . .

In sum, while the full protections that accompany challenges to detentions in other settings may prove unworkable and inappropriate in the enemy-combatant setting, the threats to military operations posed by a basic system of independent review are not so weighty as to trump a citizen's core rights to challenge meaningfully the Government's case and to be heard by an impartial adjudicator.

In so holding, we necessarily reject the Government's assertion that separation of powers principles mandate a heavily circumscribed role for the courts in such circumstances. Indeed, the position that the courts must forgo any examination of the individual case and focus exclusively on the legality of the broader detention scheme cannot be mandated by any reasonable view of separation of powers, as this approach serves only to *condense* power into a single branch of government. We have long since made clear that a state of war is not a blank check for the President when it comes to the rights of the Nation's citizens. *Youngstown Sheet & Tube*, 343 U.S., at 587. Whatever power the United States Constitution envisions for the Executive in its exchanges with other nations or with enemy organizations in times of conflict, it most assuredly envisions a role for all three branches when individual liberties are at stake. . . . Likewise, we have made clear that, unless Congress acts to suspend it, the Great Writ of habeas corpus allows the Judicial Branch to play a necessary role in maintaining this delicate balance of governance, serving as an important judicial check on the Executive's discretion in the realm of detentions. . . .

Because we conclude that due process demands some system for a citizen detainee to refute his classification, the proposed "some evidence" standard is inadequate. Any process in which the Executive's factual assertions go wholly unchallenged or are simply presumed correct without any opportunity for the alleged combatant to demonstrate otherwise falls constitutionally short. . . .

Today we are faced only with such a case. Aside from unspecified "screening" processes, Brief for Respondents 3–4, and military interrogations in which the Government suggests Hamdi could have contested his classification, Tr. of Oral Arg. 40, 42, Hamdi has received no process. An interrogation by one's captor, however effective an intelligence-gathering tool, hardly constitutes a constitutionally adequate factfinding before a neutral decisionmaker. . . .

There remains the possibility that the standards we have articulated could be met by an appropriately authorized and properly constituted military tribunal. Indeed, it is notable that military regulations already provide for such process in related instances, dictating that tribunals be made available to determine the status of enemy detainees who assert prisoner-of-war status under the Geneva Convention.

Note: The United States and Hamdi entered into an agreement following this decision. The agreement provided for his release in exchange for Hamdi's renunciation of his citizenship, his pledge not to travel to Afghanistan, Iraq, The United States, Israel, and other nations, and his release and waiver for any damages against the United States for his detention.

In response to *Hamdi,* the Department of Defense established Combatant Status Review Tribunals (CSRT) to determine if Guantanamo detainees are unlawful or lawful enemy combatants. The tribunals are staffed by military officers and are secret, and detainees enjoy few rights. For example, detainees are assigned personal representatives, but these individuals are not attorneys and are not charged with advocating for detainees they represent. Also, the government's evidence is presumed valid and detainees have little ability to refute the government's evidence because of his confinement, the inability to call witnesses and to prepare a defense, and the lack of legal representation.

In yet another case, Salim Ahmed Hamdan, who was alleged to have been a close aid to Osama bin Laden before his capture in Afghanistan, was charged with conspiracy to commit murder, conspiracy to attack civilians, and conspiracy to destroy property. Pursuant to Military Order 1, he was scheduled to be tried under military law by a military commission. He challenged this process through a petition for habeas corpus. He prevailed at the district court level but lost at the appellate court. The U.S. Supreme Court granted certiorari and heard oral arguments in late March 2006.

The Court issued its opinion in June 2006. The opinion, written by Justice Stevens, held that President Bush lacked the authority to create a military commission to try Hamdan that did not comply with statutory and treaty (Geneva Convention) provisions. Specifically, it held that the military commission did not comply with the U.S. Uniform Code of Military Justice (UCMJ), a congressionally authorized procedure, by allowing the accused and his attorney to be excluded from the trial, by allowing unsworn evidence to be received, and through other procedures that are inconsistent with the UCMJ. These procedures were also found to be in violation of the Geneva Conventions, treaties that the U.S. Congress has ratified. The Court also questioned whether a military commission, as opposed to a civilian court or military tribunal, was the right forum for Hamdan's trial. Accordingly, the Court concluded that Hamdan could not be tried by the appointed military commission. The majority indicated that the president could ask Congress to authorize the use of military commissions, but he did not have the sole authority to create them. The Court also noted that as an enemy combatant, Hamdan could be held until the war ends and that he could be tried by an ordinary military or civilian court, following the basic safeguards provided for in the UCMJ. In 2007, the charges against Hamdan were dismissed.

The Bush administration was successful in receiving congressional authorization for military commissions through the 2006 Military Commissions Act (MCA). The MCA authorized the president to establish military tribunals for the trial of alien unlawful enemy combatants. Soldiers of recognized enemy nations are "lawful" enemy combatants. Individuals and members of terrorist organizations are unlawful enemies. The MCA explicitly provides for fewer rights in military tribunals than in civilian courts. For example, habeas corpus was suspended altogether, enabling indefinite imprisonment of suspected terrorists. Judicial review of the detention of prisoners at Guantanamo had previously been limited by the Detainee Treatment Act of 2005 (DTA), which eliminated habeas corpus review but allowed CSRT decisions to be appealed to a federal court in Washington, DC. The court had not only exclusive jurisdiction over CSRT appeals but also non-mandatory jurisdiction. That is, it had the authority, with no appeal to the Supreme Court, to hear a case, or not. Further, the court's authority is to review the CSRT's review for compliance with the Department of Defense's procedures. It may not delve into the general legality of the procedures established by the Defense Department.

Cyber Constitution
Boumediene v. Bush
can be found at www. law.cornell.edu/supct/ html/06-1195.ZS.html

While *Hamdan* makes *it* is clear that Congress can create military tribunals, whether Congress can limit habeas corpus was the subject of a third Supreme Court on the subject, *Boumediene v. Bush, 553 U.S. 723* (2008). In Boumediene, the Court held that detainees at Guantanamo Bay, including enemy combatants, are entitled to habeas corpus. The Court rejected the government's theory that the constitution was not applicable at Guantanamo because the base lies outside the United States, finding that while Guantanamo is leased from Cuba, which is the *de jure* sovereign, the United States is a *de facto* sovereign over the base. Accordingly, the Court found the DTA's and MCA's suspension of the writ of habeas corpus unconstitutional.

President Obama opposed the MCA of 2006 as a senator and worked with Congress after his election as president to enact the MCA of 2009. The amendments provide for greater access to counsel by defendants, less use of hearsay evidence, greater access to witnesses by defendants, and other changes to bring military tribunals more in line with civilian courts.

5.8 PRESIDENTIAL PRIVILEGE

At common law, several confidentiality privileges developed to preserve the integrity of special relationships. Many of these continue today. For example, communications between attorneys and clients are confidential. Attorneys have an ethical obligation not to disclose the content of these communications, and courts may not compel their disclosure (with few exceptions). Physician–patient, clergy–parishioner, and therapist–patient are other examples. The privilege is intended to create an atmosphere of openness and freedom of communication.

The Constitution does not expressly provide for confidentiality between the president and his or her staff. However, presidents and their subordinates have long claimed that a privilege is inherent in the separation of powers. The privilege, it has been asserted, prohibits courts from ordering executive branch officials from disclosing internal communications or documents. The issue was first addressed by a federal court in the 1807 treason prosecution of Aaron Burr. At issue in *United States v. Burr*[57] was the production of a letter Aaron Burr had sent to President Thomas Jefferson. Chief Justice John Marshall, who sat as trial judge, ruled that President Jefferson was subject to the order of the court and could be ordered to produce the letter.[58] The issue remained dormant thereafter for many years. It surfaced again, with vigor, during and following the Nixon presidency. Consider *United States v. Nixon*.[59] Ultimately, President Nixon and many of his closest advisors were accused of conspiring to cover up the burglary. The Senate investigated the affair and eventually a special prosecutor, Archibald Cox, was appointed. Cox learned that President Nixon had been secretly taping Oval Office conversations, and he obtained subpoenas for those tapes and certain documents from President Nixon. Politically, Nixon responded by ordering his Attorney General Elliot Richardson to fire Cox. Richardson resigned rather than comply. Assistant Attorney General William Ruckelshaus then resigned for the same reason. Third in line of authority was Solicitor General Robert Bork (later an unsuccessful nominee to the Supreme Court). He relented and fired Cox. These events became known as the Saturday Night Massacre. Eventually, another special prosecutor, Leon Jaworski, was appointed, and he pressed the matter before the U.S. Supreme Court.

President Richard Nixon claimed that his tape recordings of Oval Office conversations and documents relating to the Watergate investigation were privileged from disclosure to a grand jury. The Court agreed that there should be an executive privilege if there were to be frank and open discussions in the White House, but it would not extend the privilege as far as President Nixon urged.

The Court held that presidential communications are presumed to be privileged. By asserting executive privilege, a president establishes a prima facie case of nondisclosure. However, the presumption may be overcome. In this particular case, the Court held that president Nixon's generalized privilege was defeated by "demonstrated, specific need for evidence in a pending criminal trial."[60] However, the Court also concluded that the trial court should first conduct an in-camera inspection of the records to determine if disclosure was appropriate. Records not material to the Watergate investigation were ordered to remain confidential. Ultimately, the Watergate scandal led to President Nixon's resignation, the only U.S. president to resign. Please refer back to Chapter 1 to read *United States v. Nixon,* 418 U.S. 683 (1974).

(a) President Nixon announcing his resignation
© Everett Collection Inc./Alamy

(b) Mark Felt (Deep Throat)
© Everett Collection Inc./Alamy

The Supreme Court has not had an opportunity to deal with the privilege in the context of national security, military, or diplomatic records. It is likely that the courts would find national security records to be privileged. Nor has the Court had to deal with the issue in the context of civil litigation. The need for information is more critical in criminal cases, in which both the public and the accused have more at stake than during civil litigation. For this reason, it will be more difficult to overcome the executive privilege in a civil case.[61]

Of course, the precise nature and facts of each case, civil or criminal, must be considered. After President Nixon resigned, he entered into an agreement with the General Services Administration (GSA) for the storage of over two million documents and 880 tape recordings relating to his presidency. In response, Congress passed a bill requiring the GSA to screen the materials and return private ones to President Nixon, preserve materials of historical value, make the materials available in judicial proceedings, and establish rules concerning public access to the materials. President Ford signed the bill into law, and Jimmy Carter, the newly elected president, supported the legislation. President Nixon challenged the law as violative of separation of powers principles and the executive privilege. The Court rejected those claims in *Nixon v. Administrator of General Services Administration* (1977).[62] In President Nixon's favor, the Court held that a former president may assert executive privilege. However, in this particular case, the fact that neither President Ford nor Carter supported Nixon's contentions made his position weaker. In further support of its rejection of the separations claim, the Court noted that the executive branch had been delegated the authority to maintain, screen, and determine public access to the materials.

As to his claim of privilege, the Court found that the standards set out in *United States v. Nixon* applied. However, instead of judicial in-camera inspection, Congress had delegated the review to the administrator of the GSA. The Court found this acceptable, as this person was an executive branch official and would be sensitive to executive concerns. The privilege was further overcome by the public need to preserve and reconstruct its history and the absence of support by Presidents Ford and Carter for Nixon's claim.

In summary, a president enjoys a limited privilege against being compelled to disclose records and other materials created in the course of executive duties. The Supreme Court has determined that issues relating to the presidential privilege are justiciable. (As announced in *Marbury v. Madison*,[63] it is the Court's duty to say what the law is.) A presidential assertion of privilege creates a presumption of nondisclosure that must be overcome by the party seeking the information. If the information sought concerns purely executive powers, such as diplomacy and national security, then the privilege may be absolute, or, at least, nearly impossible to overcome. If the matter is not as sensitive, then a generalized claim of privilege may be overcome by the need for information in a particular criminal case. To a lesser degree, this is also true in civil cases.

5.9 PRESIDENTIAL IMMUNITY

In addition to a privilege against disclosure of executive materials, presidents and their subordinates may also be immune from civil liability for actions committed in furtherance of their duties. Generally, the president is absolutely immune from suit and liability for official acts.[64] The scope of the immunity is broad—acts within the *outer perimeter* of official function are covered. This absolute immunity stems from the doctrine of separation of powers, the common law history, and the desire not to divert the attention of the president from his or her duties. Both sitting and past presidents enjoy this immunity. (See Figure 5-3.)

Lower executive officials are also entitled to immunity, but in most circumstances, it is not absolute. Rather, it is characterized as *qualified*. An executive official is entitled to absolute immunity only when performing a near-presidential function—that

Cyber Constitution
Nixon v. Fitzgerald
can be read at www.
law.cornell.edu/supct/
html/historics/USSC_
CR_0457_0731_ZS.html

PRESIDENTIAL PRIVILEGE AND IMMUNITY—IMPORTANT CASES

Privilege

United States v. Burr, 25 F. Cas. 30 (C.C.D.Va. 1807)	John Marshall, sitting as a trial judge, decided that President Thomas Jefferson could be ordered to produce a letter written by Aaron Burr as part of Burr's treason trial.
United States v. Nixon, 418 U.S. 904 (1974)	The Supreme Court ruled that although a presidential privilege exists, and is presumed to exist if asserted, it may be overcome by a specific need for evidence in a criminal case.
Nixon v. Administrator of General Services Administration, 433 U.S. 425 (1977)	Established that former presidents may assert the privilege. Also, a congressional delegation of authority to review a previous president's documents for privilege was approved.

Immunity

Nixon v. Fitzgerald, 457 U.S. 800 (1982)	Presidents are absolutely immune for official acts. Immunity extends to the outer perimeter of official function.
Harlow v. Fitzgerald, 457 U.S. 800 (1982)	Lower federal officials are shielded by absolute immunity when performing a purely executive function. Otherwise, lower officials are shielded by a qualified immunity.
Jones v. Clinton, 520 U.S. 681 (1997)	Presidents are not immune from civil litigation unrelated to the performance of official duties.

FIGURE 5-3
Important cases on presidential privilege and immunity

is, when the official is performing a function that is inherently executive and is closely tied to the presidency itself. It is likely that, to satisfy this test, an officer must have been acting under a direct delegation from the president. Military, national security, and diplomatic functions are most likely to fall into this category.

In most instances, an officer will be protected by a qualified immunity. Under the qualified immunity, an officer may be liable for acts that violate *clearly established law*. If the law is not clearly established, the officer is not liable for any injuries caused. The test is objective, not subjective. Thus, the question is whether a reasonably competent official would have known the law, not whether the officer-defendant knew the law.[65] To protect officials from pernicious litigation, courts are instructed to consider the state of the law in pretrial proceedings and to dismiss cases in which the law was not clearly established. Therefore, in the end, the official acting properly is immune from liability, but not from suit. Presidents are, in contrast, immune from both suit and liability.

As previously indicated, presidents and their subordinates are not immune from equitable relief (e.g., injunctions). Executive acts that are justiciable and unconstitutional may be enjoined by courts. Core executive functions, however, will not be reviewed under the nonjusticiability doctrine.

The president does not enjoy a privilege against civil actions unrelated to the performance of official duties. President William Clinton was sued by Paula Jones for sexual harassment, assault, and state tort claims in federal district court. President Clinton asserted that the action should be dismissed pending his departure from office. The district court accepted this position in part. The court ordered Clinton to respond to discovery, but further held that separations principles shielded President Clinton from trial until he had vacated the presidency. On appeal in 1996, the U.S. Court of Appeals for the Eighth Circuit reversed the trial court's decision. The court of appeals stated that the presidency is not a monarchy and that liability for unofficial acts does not threaten presidential performance. Accordingly, sitting presidents are subject to liability for "unofficial acts." The court did emphasize that trial courts must be sensitive to a president's schedule and time demands so as to avoid interfering with presidential functions.[66] The Supreme Court affirmed that decision in the following case.

Jones v. Clinton
520 U.S. 681 (1997)

This case raises a constitutional and a prudential question concerning the Office of the President of the United States. Respondent, a private citizen, seeks to recover damages from the current occupant of that office based on actions allegedly taken before his term began. The President submits that in all but the most exceptional cases the Constitution requires federal courts to defer such litigation until his term ends and that, in any event, respect for the office warrants such a stay. Despite the force of the arguments supporting the President's submissions, we conclude that they must be rejected.

Petitioner, William Jefferson Clinton, was elected to the Presidency in 1992, and re-elected in 1996. His term of office expires on January 20, 2001. In 1991 he was the Governor of the State of Arkansas. Respondent, Paula Corbin Jones, is a resident of California. In 1991 she lived in Arkansas, and was an employee of the Arkansas Industrial Development Commission.

On May 6, 1994, she commenced this action in the United States District Court for the Eastern District of Arkansas by filing a complaint naming petitioner and Danny Ferguson, a former Arkansas State Police officer, as defendants. The complaint alleges two federal claims, and two state law claims over which the federal court has jurisdiction because of the diverse citizenship of the parties. As the case comes to us, we are required to assume the truth of the detailed—but as yet untested—factual allegations in the complaint.

Those allegations principally describe events that are said to have occurred on the afternoon of May 8, 1991, during an official conference held at the Excelsior Hotel in Little Rock, Arkansas. The Governor delivered a speech at the conference; respondent—working as a state employee—staffed the registration desk. She alleges that Ferguson persuaded her to leave her desk and to visit the Governor in a business suite at the hotel, where he made "abhorrent" sexual advances that she vehemently rejected. She further claims that her superiors at work subsequently dealt with her in a hostile and rude manner, and changed her duties to punish her for rejecting those advances. Finally, she alleges that after petitioner was elected President, Ferguson defamed her by making a statement to a reporter that implied she had accepted petitioner's alleged overtures, and that various persons authorized to speak for the President publicly branded her a liar by denying that the incident had occurred.

Respondent seeks actual damages of $75,000, and punitive damages of $100,000. Her complaint contains four counts. The first charges that petitioner, acting under color of state law, deprived her of rights protected by the Constitution, in violation of Rev. Stat. §1979, 42 U.S.C. § 1983. The second charges that petitioner and Ferguson engaged in a conspiracy to violate her federal rights, also actionable under federal law. See Rev. Stat. §1980, 42 U.S.C. § 1985. The third is a state common law claim for intentional infliction of emotional distress, grounded primarily on the incident at the hotel. The fourth count, also based on state law, is for defamation, embracing both the comments allegedly made to the press by Ferguson and the statements of petitioner's agents. Inasmuch as the legal sufficiency of the claims has not yet been challenged, we assume, without deciding, that each of the four counts states a cause of action as a matter of law. With the exception of the last charge, which arguably may involve conduct within the outer perimeter of the President's official responsibilities, it is perfectly clear that the alleged misconduct of petitioner was unrelated to any of his official duties as President of the United States and, indeed, occurred before he was elected to that office.

In response to the complaint, petitioner promptly advised the District Court that he intended to file a motion to dismiss on grounds of Presidential immunity, and requested the court to defer all other pleadings and motions until after the immunity issue was resolved. Relying on our cases holding that immunity questions should be decided at the earliest possible stage of the litigation, 858 F. Supp. 902, 905 (ED Ark. 1994), our recognition of the "singular importance of the President's duties," id., at 904 (quoting Nixon v. Fitzgerald, 457 U.S. 731, 751 [1982]), and the fact that the question did not require any analysis of the allegations of the complaint . . . the court granted the request. Petitioner thereupon filed a motion "to dismiss . . . without prejudice and to toll any statutes of limitation [that may be applicable] until he is no longer President, at which time the plaintiff may refile the instant suit." Extensive submissions were made to the District Court by the parties and the Department of Justice.

The District Judge denied the motion to dismiss on immunity grounds and ruled that discovery in the case could go forward, but ordered any trial stayed until the end of petitioner's Presidency . . . [The appellate court reversed the decision to stay the trial.] . . .

The principal rationale for affording certain public servants immunity from suits for money damages arising out of their official acts is inapplicable to unofficial conduct. In cases involving prosecutors, legislators, and judges we have repeatedly explained that the immunity serves the public interest in enabling such officials to perform their designated functions effectively without fear that a particular decision may give rise to personal liability. We explained in *Ferri v. Ackerman,* 444 U.S. 193 (1979):

> As public servants, the prosecutor and the judge represent the interest of society as a whole. The conduct of their official duties may adversely affect a wide variety of different individuals, each of whom may be a potential source of future controversy. The societal interest in providing such public officials with the maximum ability to deal fearlessly and impartially with the public at large has long been recognized as an acceptable justification for official immunity. The point of immunity for such officials is to forestall an atmosphere of intimidation that would conflict with their resolve to perform their designated functions in a principled fashion. . . .

Moreover, when defining the scope of an immunity for acts clearly taken within an official capacity, we have applied a functional approach. "Frequently our decisions have held that an official's absolute immunity should extend only to acts in performance of particular functions of his office." Hence, for example, a judge's absolute immunity does not extend to actions performed in a purely administrative capacity. . . .

We are also unpersuaded by the evidence from the historical record to which petitioner has called our attention. He points to a comment by Thomas Jefferson protesting the subpoena *duces tecum* Chief Justice Marshall directed to him in the Burr trial, a statement in the diaries kept by Senator William Maclay of the first Senate debates, in which then Vice President John Adams and Senator Oliver Ellsworth are recorded as having said that "the President personally [is] not . . . subject to any process whatever," lest it be "put . . . in the power of a common Justice to exercise any Authority over him and Stop the Whole Machine of Government," and to a quotation from Justice Story's Commentaries on the Constitution. None of these sources sheds much light on the question at hand.

Respondent, in turn, has called our attention to conflicting historical evidence. Speaking in favor of the Constitution's adoption at the Pennsylvania Convention, James Wilson—who had participated in the Philadelphia Convention at which the document was drafted—explained

that, although the President "is placed [on] high," "not a single privilege is annexed to his character; far from being above the laws, he is amenable to them in his private character as a citizen, and in his public character by impeachment." This description is consistent with both the doctrine of presidential immunity as set forth in Fitzgerald, and rejection of the immunity claim in this case. With respect to acts taken in his "public character"—that is official acts—the President may be disciplined principally by impeachment, not by private lawsuits for damages. But he is otherwise subject to the laws for his purely private acts.

In the end, as applied to the particular question before us, we reach the same conclusion about these historical materials that Justice Jackson described when confronted with an issue concerning the dimensions of the President's power. "Just what our forefathers did envision, or would have envisioned had they foreseen modern conditions, must be divined from materials almost as enigmatic as the dreams Joseph was called upon to interpret for Pharoah. A century and a half of partisan debate and scholarly speculation yields no net result but only supplies more or less apt quotations from respected sources on each side. . . . They largely cancel each other. . . ."

Petitioner's strongest argument supporting his immunity claim is based on the text and structure of the Constitution. He does not contend that the occupant of the Office of the President is "above the law," in the sense that his conduct is entirely immune from judicial scrutiny. The President argues merely for a postponement of the judicial proceedings that will determine whether he violated any law. His argument is grounded in the character of the office that was created by Article II of the Constitution, and relies on separation of powers principles that have structured our constitutional arrangement since the founding.

As a starting premise, petitioner contends that he occupies a unique office with powers and responsibilities so vast and important that the public interest demands that he devote his undivided time and attention to his public duties. He submits that—given the nature of the office—the doctrine of separation of powers places limits on the authority of the Federal Judiciary to interfere with the Executive Branch that would be transgressed by allowing this action to proceed.

We have no dispute with the initial premise of the argument. Former presidents, from George Washington to George Bush, have consistently endorsed petitioner's characterization of the office. After serving his term, Lyndon Johnson observed: "Of all the 1,886 nights I was President, there were not many when I got to sleep before 1 or 2 a.m., and there were few mornings when I didn't wake up by 6 or 6:30." In 1967, the Twenty-fifth Amendment to the Constitution was adopted to ensure continuity in the performance of the powers and duties of the office; one of the sponsors of that Amendment stressed the importance of providing that "at all times" there be a President "who has complete control and will be able to perform" those duties. As Justice Jackson has pointed out, the Presidency concentrates executive authority "in a single head in whose choice the whole Nation has a part, making him the focus of public hopes and expectations. In drama, magnitude and finality his decisions so far overshadow any others that almost alone he fills the public eye and ear." . . .

It does not follow, however, that separation of powers principles would be violated by allowing this action to proceed . . .

Of greater significance, petitioner errs by presuming that interactions between the Judicial Branch and the Executive, even quite burdensome interactions, necessarily rise to the level of constitutionally forbidden impairment of the Executive's ability to perform its constitutionally mandated functions. "[O]ur . . . system imposes upon the Branches a degree of overlapping responsibility, a duty of interdependence as well as independence the absence of which 'would preclude the establishment of a Nation capable of governing itself effectively.'" Mistretta, 488 U.S., at 381 (quoting Buckley, 424 U.S., at 121). As Madison explained, separation of powers does not mean that the branches "ought to have no partial agency in, or no control over the acts of each other." The fact that a federal court's exercise of its traditional Article III jurisdiction may significantly burden the time and attention of the Chief Executive is not sufficient to establish a violation of the Constitution. Two long settled propositions, first announced by Chief Justice Marshall, support that conclusion.

First, we have long held that when the President takes official action, the Court has the authority to determine whether he has acted within the law. Perhaps the most dramatic example of such a case is our holding that President Truman exceeded his constitutional authority when he issued an order directing the Secretary of Commerce to take possession of and operate most of the Nation's steel mills in order to avert a national catastrophe. . . .

Second, it is also settled that the President is subject to judicial process in appropriate circumstances. [The Court then described several instances where presidents had participated in judicial proceedings] . . .

We add a final comment on two matters that are discussed at length in the briefs: the risk that our decision will generate a large volume of politically motivated harassing and frivolous litigation, and the danger that national security concerns might prevent the President from explaining a legitimate need for a continuance.

We are not persuaded that either of these risks is serious. Most frivolous and vexatious litigation is terminated at the pleading stage or on summary judgment, with little if any personal involvement by the defendant. See Fed. Rules Civ. Proc. 12, 56. Moreover, the availability of sanctions provides a significant deterrent to litigation directed at the President in his unofficial capacity for purposes of political gain or harassment. History indicates that the likelihood that a significant number of such cases will be filed is remote. Although scheduling problems may arise, there is no reason to assume that the District Courts will be either unable to accommodate the President's needs or unfaithful to the tradition—especially in matters involving national security—of giving "the utmost deference to Presidential responsibilities." Several Presidents, including petitioner, have given testimony without jeopardizing the Nation's security. In short, we have confidence in the ability of our federal judges to deal with both of these concerns . . .

If Congress deems it appropriate to afford the President stronger protection, it may respond with appropriate legislation. As petitioner notes in his brief, Congress has enacted more than one statute providing for the deferral of civil litigation to accommodate important public interests. . . .

The Federal District Court has jurisdiction to decide this case. Like every other citizen who properly invokes that jurisdiction, respondent has a right to an orderly disposition of her claims. Accordingly, the judgment of the Court of Appeals is affirmed.

5.10 MODERN CHALLENGES

The most significant contemporary constitution issue concerning the presidency is also a perennial one: executive power during war. The tension between the need for a strong executive and the nation's distrust of the aggregation of power during war is not new, but it is confounded by the war on terrorism. That the so-called war does not appear to be a war as historically defined is part of the problem. The long-term nature of the fight is one of the issues. During more traditional wars of the past, there was tolerance for increases in presidential power because the wars were not expected to be protracted. But the war on terrorism could last for decades, and any changes in the alignment of powers between the branches would be effectively permanent. Even more, challenges to civil liberties would also not be temporary. So as the nation moves forward, it will have to redefine what it means to be at war and reconstruct the basic interbranch relations in a manner that enables the executive to be not only responsive to threats but also proactive in deterring future terrorism. Simultaneously, the nation will have to preserve its long history of respecting privacy and civil liberties.

5.11 SUMMARY

The American presidency is unique. Instead of a monarch, we have an elected official as the head of our government. Unlike in many nations, executive power is not divided between two positions, a president and prime minister. Instead, Article II vests all executive authority in one person.

In terms of domestic power, the president is responsible for the enforcement of laws. This includes statutes and court orders. Presidential power in this context is largely defined by the other two branches. As to foreign affairs, Justice Jackson established a paradigm for understanding presidential authority. Presidential power is the greatest when authorized by the Constitution. After that, presidential power is greatest when authorized by Congress. The president, of course, acts without authority if the action is contrary to the Constitution. Presidential authority is weakest when contrary to an express statement of Congress. The cases in the middle—what Justice Jackson referred to as the twilight area—are the most complex to resolve.

To protect the integrity of the presidency, the law recognizes that a president must feel free to consult with advisors. Accordingly, presidential communications are privileged. The Supreme Court has held that a presidential assertion of privilege is prima facie proof of its applicability. This may be overcome, however, if a party can demonstrate a specific need for the evidence in a pending criminal trial.

Similarly, the president is immune from damages liability for the performance of presidential functions. The scope of presidential functions is drawn broadly in favor of the president. This rule prevents a disabling of the presidency by civil legislation and the fear of litigation. However, a sitting president may be subject to civil legislation that does not stem from the performance of official duties. In such cases, trial courts are to be sensitive to executive responsibilities when scheduling proceedings and other matters.

REVIEW QUESTIONS

1. What are the basic qualifications to be president, as established by Article II of the Constitution?

2. Identify the ways in which the president plays a role in lawmaking.

3. Justice Jackson's tripartite analysis of presidential power, announced in *Youngstown,* has been referred to by members of the Court on many occasions since that decision was rendered. Describe that analysis.

4. What is executive impoundment?

5. What is an executive order?

6. What is the presidential and congressional role in appointments (Supreme Court justices, etc.)?

7. Presidents may grant pardons and reprieves. Distinguish between the two.

8. Distinguish treaties from executive agreements.

9. Does the Constitution provide that the president may suspend habeas corpus?

10. Distinguish presidential privilege from presidential immunity.

ASSIGNMENTS: CONSTITUTIONAL LAW IN ACTION

The Constitution in Your Community

Assume that a local state judge has just retired, thereby creating a vacancy in the local felony court. Steve Smith, a local attorney, has retained the lobbying department of your law firm to advance his candidacy for appointment to the vacant judgeship.

Accordingly, your supervisor wants you to research your state's constitutional process for filing judicial vacancies in your state's courts. Prepare a memorandum wherein you outline your state's constitutional and/or statutory qualifications and procedures for appointing someone to a judicial position.

Going Federal

Assume that your law firm has been retained by the family of a man who has been incarcerated for a federal crime he insists he did not commit. The incarcerated man is 85 years old, and his family would like the president to pardon him or, at the very least, commute his sentence. Your supervising attorney would like you to research (1) the constitutional authority of, (2) the process to apply for, and (3) the process used by the president to review and issue pardons. Prepare a short memorandum (1–3 pages) answering these questions.

Moot Court

In response to the attacks on the United States on September 11, 2001, President Bush initiated wars against the Taliban in Afghanistan, Iraq, and "terror." Is the war against "terror" the same as the wars against Afghanistan and Iraq? Identify one constitutional issue that is raised by one of the possible differences between the war on terror and other more traditional wars. Break into two groups and debate both sides of the constitutional issue. Review the relevant sections of Articles I and II and the Authorization for Force in Iraq (2002) and the Authorization for the Use of Force Against Terrorists (2001), break into two groups and debate the constitutionality of all three wars.

NOTES

1. Article I, Section 1, clause 5.
2. Amendment XII.
3. *Ray v. Blair*, 343 U.S. 214 (1952).
4. See *Jones v. Bush*, 122 F. Supp. 2d 713 (N.D. Tex. 2000), relief den. 244 F.3d 144 (5th Cir. 2000.)
5. Amendment XXV, §§ 3 and 4.
6. 3 U.S.C. § 19.
7. Article I, Section 3, clause 4.
8. Report of American Bar Association Task Force on Presidential Signing Statements and the Separation of Powers Doctrine, August 2006 at www.abanet.org/media/docs/signstatereport.pdf.
9. *United States v. Lovett*, 328 U.S. 303 (1946)
10. *Id.* at page 7 onward.
11. Statement on Signing the Appropriations Act, 2009. President Barack Obama, June 24, 2009.
12. 491 U.S. 397 (1989).
13. The statute was declared unconstitutional in *United States v. Eichman*, 496 U.S. 310 (1990).
14. Thomas Halper, "Supreme Court Appointments: Criteria and Consequences," 21 *N.Y.L. Forum* 563 (1976).
15. Thomas Halper, "Senate Rejection of Supreme Court Nominees," 22 *Drake L. Rev.* 102 (1972).
16. Officers of the United States within the meaning of the appointments clause, U.S. Department of Justice, Office of Legal Counsel, Memo dated April 16, 2007, available at www.justice.gov/olc/2007/appointmentsclausev10.pdf.
17. See Emily Yehle, "Congress Can't Kill Advisory Posts, Obama Declares in Signing Statements," *The New York Times*, April 18, 2011, available at www.nytimes.com/gwire/2011/04/18/18 greenwire-congress-cant-kill-advisory-posts-obama-declar-22353.html, and Kate Phillips, "Senators Take on Czar Wars," *The New York Times*, October 7, 2009, available at http://thecaucus.blogs.nytimes.com/2009/10/07/senators-take-on-the-czar-wars/.
18. *Buckley v. Valeo*, 424 U.S. 1 (1976).
19. *Freytag v. Commissioner of Internal Revenue*, 501 U.S. 868 (1991).
20. *Weiss v. United States*, 114 S. Ct. 752 (1994).
21. 478 U.S. 714 (1986).
22. 487 U.S. 654 (1988).
23. *Ex Parte Garland*, 71 U.S. 333, 380 (1867).

24. *Id.*
25. See Amy Goldstein, "Bush Commutes Libby's Prison Sentence," WashingtonPost.com, July 3, 2007.
26. *Schick v. Reed,* 419 U.S. 256 (1974).
27. *Murphy v. Ford,* 390 F. Supp. 1372 (W.D. Mich. 1995).
28. See "Keeping His First Promise," *Time,* January 31, 1977; "Carter's First Act Touches Off a Storm," *U.S. News & World Report,* January 31, 1977; "Carter Pardons Draft Evaders, Orders a Study of Deserters," *New York Times,* January 22, 1977.
29. http://jurist.law.pitt.edu/pardonspres1.htm, citing P. S. Ruckman Jr., *Federal Executive Clemency in the United States,* 1995; *Los Angeles Times,* January 29, 2001.
30. 71 U.S. (4 Wall.) 2 (1866).
31. *Sterling v. Constantin,* 287 U.S. 378 (1932).
32. National Defense Authorization Act for Fiscal Year 2008, P.L. 110-181. Senator Patrick Leavy of Vermont was an opponent of the changes to the Insurrection Act and was the lead legislator in bringing about the repeal. See http://leahy.senate.gov/old_site/issues/InsurrectionAct/index.html.
33. 327 U.S. 324 (1946).
34. 299 U.S. 304 (1936).
35. *United States v. Pink,* 315 U.S. 203 (1942).
36. Article II, Section 2, clause 2.
37. Article VI, clause 2.
38. 354 U.S. 1 (1957).
39. *Id.* at 5–6.
40. *Id.* at 16.
41. *Cook v. United States,* 288 U.S. 102 (1933).
42. 100 U.S. 483 (1879).
43. 252 U.S. 416 (1920).
44. Richard Erikson, "The Making of Executive Agreements by the United States Department of Defense: An Agenda for Progress," 13 *B.U. Int'l L.J.* 45, 46 (1995).
45. See Kenneth Randall, "The Treaty Power," 51 *Ohio St. L.J.* 1089 (1990), and Jack Weiss, "The Approval of Arms Control Agreements as Congressional-Executive Agreements," 38 *U.C.L.A. L. Rev.* 1533 (1991) for further discussion of this topic.
46. Erikson, *supra* n. 30, at 46.
47. *United States v. Capps, Inc.,* 204 F.2d 655 (4th Cir. 1953).
48. Kenneth Randall, "The Treaty Power," 51 *Ohio St. L.J.* 1089 (1990).
49. *Goldwater v. Carter,* 444 U.S. 996 (1979).
50. Article I, Section 8, clause 14.
51. Thomas and Thomas, *The War-Making Powers of the President* 7 (SMU Press 1982).
52. Jane Stromseth, "Rethinking War Powers: Congress, the President, and the United Nations," 81 *Georgetown L.J.* 597, 597 (1993), citing 28 *Weekly Comp. Pres. Doc.* 1119–1121 (June 20, 1992).
53. Pub. L. 88-408, 78 Stat. 384 (1964).
54. Authorization for the Use of Force Against Iraq Resolution of 2002, Pub. L. No. 107–243, 116 Stat. 1498, et seq. and Authorization for Use of Force Against Terrorists of 2001, Pub. L. No. 107–140, 115 Stat. 224.
55. 50 U.S.C. § 1541 *et seq.*
56. *Id.*
57. 25 F. Cas. 30, 35 (C.C. D. Va. 1807).
58. Aaron Burr had previously killed his political nemesis Alexander Hamilton in a duel. Burr was charged with treason in this case because he allegedly stated in the letter to Jefferson that he intended to move to the southwest (Mexico) and establish a new government. Burr was acquitted, but the trial proved to be the last chapter of his political career.
59. 418 U.S. 904 (1974).
60. *Id.* at 713.
61. Since the *Nixon* case, several presidents have appeared in civil matters, either voluntarily or under subpoena. See Nowak and Rotunda, *Constitutional Law* § 7.1, n. 28 (West Hornbook 1991), for a list.
62. 433 U.S. 425 (1977).
63. 5 U.S. 137 (1803).
64. *Nixon v. Fitzgerald,* 457 U.S. 800 (1982).
65. *Harlow v. Fitzgerald,* 457 U.S. 800 (1982).
66. *Jones v. Clinton,* 72 F.3d 1354 (8th Cir. 1996), 1996 WL 5658.

6

Administrative Agencies in the Constitutional Scheme

A government big enough to give you everything you want is a government big enough to take away from you everything you have.

PRESIDENT GERALD FORD

LEARNING OBJECTIVES
At the end of this chapter you should be able to:

- Distinguish between executive and independent agencies.
- Explain the separations of powers problem that is created by modern agencies.
- Provide two examples of a separation of powers problem in the administrative agencies context, and explain how the problems have been addressed, including appropriate statutory and caselaw references.
- Define delegation and the limits on Congress to delegate legislative and judicial authorities, as defined by Supreme Court decision.
- Identify a contemporary issue concerning the authority of federal administrative agencies, and discuss the most likely future scenarios, referencing both historical analogs and caselaw.
- Brief a judicial opinion with no assistance. You should be successful in identifying the relevant facts. You should be successful in identifying the legal issue and analyzing the courts' rationale in at least 50 percent of your briefs.
- Apply what you have learned to a new set of facts that are given to you with no assistance.

6.1 INTRODUCTION

Since the beginning of this nation, administrative agencies have continuously increased in number, size, and power. The daily lives of all citizens are affected by administrative agencies. Consider these examples: The processing, manufacturing, packing, labeling, advertising, and sale of nearly all products in the United States is regulated by agencies such as the Food and Drug Administration and the Department of Agriculture; the Internal Revenue Service oversees the collection of taxes from all citizens; the Federal Aviation Administration regulates commercial air transportation; and the distribution of public welfare benefits (Aid to Dependent Children and food stamps) is regulated by the Department of Health and Human Services and the Department of Agriculture. These are only a few illustrations of the extent to which federal administrative agencies play a role in the daily lives of citizens. To get a complete picture, it is necessary to add state and local agencies. State departments of motor vehicles issue driver's licenses, register cars, and issue automobile tags; doctors, lawyers, barbers, plumbers, and electricians are among the many whose professions and trades are regulated by state agencies; state departments of revenue collect taxes; state and local governments regulate building and construction; and federal, state, and local agencies regulate the environment.

Cyber Constitution
Federal Agencies
You can read the stunning large list of federal agencies at www.usa.gov/ Agencies/Federal/All_ Agencies/index.shtml

Why do we need agencies at all? Why have they become so numerous and powerful? The answer to both questions is twofold. First, the job of governing has become too large for Congress, the courts, and the president to manage. There were four million citizens when the Constitution was adopted (1789). There are now over three hundred million people in the United States. People are more mobile, technology is changing at unprecedented speed, and other social changes have increased the demands on government. Congress does not have the time to make all the laws, the president to enforce all the laws, or the courts to adjudicate all the cases.

Second, agencies possess expertise. Every year Congress must deal with a large and diverse number of issues. Discrimination, environmental concerns, military and national security matters, and funding for science and art are but a few examples. Congress is too small to be expert in every subject. Agencies, however, specialize in and, as a result, possess technical knowledge and experience in their subject areas. They can hire specialists and benefit from continuous contact with the same subjects.

Where do administrative agencies fit into the U.S. constitutional scheme? What powers may they possess and who oversees them? These topics are explored in this chapter.[1]

6.2 AGENCIES AND SEPARATION OF POWERS PRINCIPLES

There is no constitutional provision establishing administrative agencies, nor is the role of agencies in the U.S. governmental structure defined. Regardless, agencies have been part of the federal government since the beginning. Agencies have been referred to as a "fourth branch" of government. This is not literally true, as the Constitution establishes only three branches. Even more, as you will learn, the Constitution demands that agencies remain accountable to the three constitutional branches. Unquestionably, agencies are vital components of government. Most of the work of government is conducted by administrative agencies. To satisfy their mandates, they are often empowered to perform the functions of all three branches of government. The Social Security Administration, for example, is delegated the authority to make rules (quasi-judicial authority), to enforce legislation and its own rules (executive authority), and to hear and decide claims. This arrangement creates separation of powers issues. In fact, many, if not most, contemporary separation of powers cases decided by the Supreme Court arise in the administrative context.

YOUR CONSTITUTIONAL VALUES

CAN YOUR CONDO ASSOCIATION ALSO BE YOUR COURT?

Most delegations of authority are to government officials, typically in the executive branch. However, privatization of government services raises interesting delegation questions. Similar questions are raised by state and local laws that empower private parties to regulate. May the government pass its authority to make rules or to hear and punish offenders to private parties? Privatization of prisons, for example, is becoming increasingly popular. The authority to discipline inmates is essential. Accordingly, delegations of prison operation must include the authority to accuse, adjudicate, and punish wrongdoers. The need to delegate rulemaking authority may also be needed. Are delegations to private parties different than delegations to government officials?

Outside the prison, examples of delegations to private parties much closer to home can be found. *Foley v. Osborne Court Condominium*, 1999 R.I. Super. Lexis 50 (1999), is just such a case. Foley owned two condominiums in the Osborne Court Condominiums (henceforth referred to as the Association). The Rhode Island statute regulating condominiums authorized condominium associations to make rules, levy fees, assess fines for rules violations, post liens for fees and fines owed by owners, and foreclose on owner's properties. Foreclosure required state court action, but the Association was delegated the authority, after a hearing, to fine owners.

Mr. Foley was accused of running afoul of the Association's bylaws and was fined on several occasions. After he failed to pay his fines, the Association placed a lien on Mr. Foley's two condominiums and began the process of auctioning them. The Association and Mr. Foley reached a settlement where he paid $10,000 in fines and his properties were removed from auction. However, he continued to violate the Association's rules, he was fined many times again, and his property was again set for foreclosure and auction. Mr. Foley petitioned to enjoin the sale, alleging that Rhode Island had unconstitutionally delegated judicial authority to condominium associations.

Mirroring the language of the U.S. Constitution, the Constitution of Rhode Island delegated the "judicial power of [the state] in one supreme court, and in such inferior courts as the general assembly may, from time to time, ordain and establish." While it was common in other Rhode Island statutes to permit debt collections without judicial intervention, none gave private parties the authority to impose fines. The Rhode Island Supreme Court found this authority to be judicial, and accordingly, it held the statute delegating the authority to be unconstitutional. What constitutional values were at play in this case? The rationale for the delegation was not discussed here. What reasons can you imagine for a legislator supporting such a bill? What values underlie these reasons? Are they similar to, or different from, the intent underlying the nondelegation doctrine?

6.3 APPOINTMENT AND CONTROL OF FEDERAL OFFICERS

Nearly every agency is created by Congress through its lawmaking power. Congress, the president, and constitutional courts are not "agencies" for purposes of this discussion. Legislation that creates an agency and defines its powers is known as **enabling legislation.** Once created, agencies fall into the executive branch.

Many agencies are overseen by one of the president's cabinet officers or another official that reports up to the president. Agencies may be headed by an individual or a group (collegial agencies). The relevant constitutional provision concerning the appointment of agency executives is Article II, Section 2, clause 2, which was discussed in the last chapter.

In addition to deciding who to nominate or appoint, presidents exert control of the bureaucracy in a variety of ways. For purely executive agencies, presidents can direct lower officials, within the bounds of the law. Regardless of whether an agency is independent or executive, the president can influence its authority, structure and organization, and budget through the lawmaking process. In extreme cases, presidents, from Washington to Obama, have claimed Article II authority to remove (fire) officers and inferior officers of executive agencies whom they have found unsatisfactory. For independent agencies, presidents (or officers who report to the president) often possess "for cause" removal authority, as defined by Congress. Malfeasance, misfeasance, and neglect of duty are commonly recognized by Congress as "cause" for removal. The authority of the president to remove officials was discussed more fully in the last chapter. Overall, most presidents have found it challenging to unite the administrative state behind a set of policy objectives. Even more, some presidents have been frustrated by their inability to get specific projects done. President Jimmy Carter, for example, experienced delay in getting a dead mouse removed from the White House when two agencies (General Services Administration and National Park Service) debated who had jurisdiction over the wall wherein the mouse laid dead.

enabling act
(enabling legislation)
(1) A statute that grants new powers or authority to persons or corporations. (2) A statute that gives the government the power to enforce other legislation or that carries out a provision of a constitution. The term also applies to a clause in a statute granting the government the power to enforce or carry out that statute. Such a provision is called an *enabling clause.*

6.4 DELEGATION

quasi-legislative
A term applied to the legislative functions of an administrative agency, such as rulemaking.

quasi-judicial
A term applied to the adjudicatory functions of an administrative agency, that is, taking evidence and making findings of fact and findings of law.

delegation of powers
The transfer of power from the president to an administrative agency.

As executive branch entities, administrative agencies perform executive functions. The preceding discussion of control of administrative officials mentioned that agencies may perform **quasi-legislative** and **quasi-judicial** functions. For example, administrative agencies are empowered to create rules (a quasi-legislative function) and to adjudicate cases (a quasi-judicial function). Agencies are given this power so that they may fulfill their mandate and free the constitutional branches from some of the ever-increasing burdens. From where do agencies receive these powers? From Congress. The act of granting quasi-judicial and quasi-legislative authority to an agency is referred to as **delegation.**

Separation of powers problems are created by delegations to agencies. How can Congress transfer its responsibility, or the responsibilities of the judiciary, to an agency? Does this not violate the separation of powers principle? The assertion that all delegations are unconstitutional has been rejected. There are, however, limits to the congressional delegation power. These limits are known as the *nondelegation doctrine.*

6.5 NONDELEGATION DOCTRINE

The Supreme Court has developed a nondelegation doctrine (also called the *delegation doctrine*) to preserve the integrity of the separation of powers. A delegation may be unlawful in two different ways, one quantitative and the other qualitative. A delegation may be unconstitutional if

1. It is excessive, *or*
2. It places control over an essential function of one branch in another branch.

A delegation may be "excessive" if Congress delegates too much of its or the judiciary's authority to an administrative agency or if an essential function of one of the two branches is transferred. For example, Congress may not abdicate its authority by establishing an agency responsible for lawmaking generally. Nor may it delegate certain essential functions, such as impeachment. This responsibility is to be performed by the House of Representatives and may not be delegated to anyone.

A delegation may also be violative of the Constitution if it places control over an essential function of one branch in another branch. For example, placing the authority to finally decide constitutional issues in an administrative agency would encroach upon an essential judicial function. See Figure 6-1 for a summary of cases that have shaped this area of law.

6.5(a) Quasi-Legislative Powers

Before 1934, delegations of legislative powers were routinely approved by the courts.[2] However, during Roosevelt's New Deal, the Supreme Court invalidated several laws either as exceeding federal power under the Commerce Clause (discussed in Chapter 5) or as excessive delegations of legislative powers.

Schechter Poultry Corp. v. United States, a 1935 Supreme Court decision,[3] was such a case. Congress had delegated to the president the authority to approve "codes of fair competition" for the poultry industry. The defendant corporation was convicted of violating the code established by an agency (acting through subdelegation from the president), over its objection that the delegation to the president was unlawful. The Supreme Court reversed the conviction because it found no solid policy statement to guide the agency when it created the code. In fact, the Court found that the policy statement issued by Congress had conflicting goals. For example, Congress wanted not only the code to discourage monopolies, but also to encourage cooperative actions among competitors.

DELEGATION: SUMMARY OF SELECTED CASES

Case	*Holding and Effect of Decision*
Whitman v. American Trucking Associations, 531 U.S. 457 (2001)	Delegation to EPA to set air quality standards upheld.
Touby v. United States, 500 U.S. 160 (1991)	Delegation to Attorney General to temporarily schedule drugs was approved. Question of whether more than an intelligible principle is required in penal cases raised but not decided.
Gomez v. United States, 490 U.S. 858 (1989); *Peretz v. United States,* 501 U.S. 923 (1991)	U.S. magistrate judges may preside over criminal pretrial proceedings. Consent of the parties is required to have a magistrate judge preside over a criminal trial.
Northern Pipeline Construction Co. v. Marathon Pipeline Co., 458 U.S. 50 (1932); *Granfinanciera, S.A. v. Nordberg,* 492 U.S. 33 (1989)	Under public rights doctrine, public issues may be decided by bankruptcy judges, but not private ones.
Mistretta v. United States, 488 U.S. 361 (1989)	Delegation of authority to administrative commission to establish sentencing guidelines was upheld.
Atlas Roofing Co. v. Occupational Safety & Health Review Commission, 430 U.S. 442 (1977)	Under public rights doctrine, OSHA may be delegated the authority to impose penalties on employers.
Arizona v. California, 373 U.S. 546 (1963)	Delegation to Secretary of Interior to decide water apportionment was upheld.
Lichter v. United States, 334 U.S. 546 (1948)	Delegation to recover excessive profits in governmental contracts was upheld.
NLRB v. Jones & Laughlin Steel Corp., 301 U.S. 1 (1937)	Under public rights doctrine, NLRB may be delegated the authority to hear unfair labor practice cases.
Schechter Poultry Corp. v. United States, 295 U.S. 495 (1935); *Panama Refining Co. v. Ryan,* 293 U.S. 388 (1935)	The only Supreme Court invalidations of delegations based upon nondelegation doctrine.
J.W. Hampton, Jr. & Co. v. United States, 276 U.S. 394 (1928)	Congress must provide an intelligible principle to guide agencies.

FIGURE 6-1

Selected cases on delegation

In *Panama Refining Co. v. Ryan,*[4] Congress authorized the president to prohibit the transportation of certain oil products in interstate commerce. The Supreme Court found the delegation unlawful because Congress granted too much legislative authority to the president, in particular the decision as to whether a product should be allowed into interstate commerce. The Court reasoned that the executive is charged with enforcing such prohibitions, not creating them.

By the late 1930s the Court had changed direction, and its scrutiny of legislation for delegation violations (and Commerce Clause excesses) lessened. Today, nearly all challenged delegations are validated. However, the Court requires that receiving agencies be provided with standards or an **intelligible principle** to guide them in the performance of the delegated responsibilities.[5] To satisfy the intelligible principle test, Congress must establish the overarching policy in an area and must provide basic guidelines concerning how the delegation is to be performed. The test is not rigorous. General policies and standards are adequate.

The intelligible principle test is designed to protect the integrity of the separation of powers and to keep agencies within the limits established by elected representatives. An intelligible principle facilitates congressional control and gives reviewing courts

intelligible principle test
The test used to determine if Congress has provided an agency with sufficient guidance in the performance of a delegated duty.

standards by which to judge the lawfulness of agency actions. The Supreme Court stated it this way: "A congressional delegation of power . . . must be accompanied by discernible standards, so that the delegatee's actions may be measured by its fidelity to the legislative will."[6]

There is no precise definition of "intelligible principle." To understand what is required by the test, it is best to examine specific cases.

Arizona v. California[7] represents a valid delegation. The Secretary of the Interior was delegated considerable authority over the apportionment of water from the Colorado River by the Boulder Canyon Project Act. The delegation was upheld because the statute ordered the secretary to consider various factors when deciding priority for water use. For example, he was ordered to consider river regulation, flood control, irrigation, domestic water consumption, and power production needs. The Court found that this provided the secretary with sufficient standards from which to work. If Congress had simply left the decision to the secretary's discretion, without listing the factors to be considered, the delegation would have failed.

In *Lichter v. United States,*[8] the Supreme Court upheld a delegation to administrative officers to recover "excessive profits" when renegotiating contracts involving war goods. Those who challenged the statute claimed that the phrase "excessive profits" was too vague and broad a delegation. The Court disagreed, holding that the phrase provided sufficient guidance and that the delegation was a proper exercise of congressional war powers.

An important case was handed down by the Supreme Court in 1989, *Mistretta v. United States.*[9] *Mistretta* involved a delegation to the U.S. Sentencing Commission. Congress established the commission to research sentencing in the federal courts and to draft a set of sentencing guidelines for use by federal judges. The enabling statute was challenged as an unlawful delegation of a legislative function, namely, determining what punishment should be imposed for criminal behavior.

The delegation was upheld for the following reasons: (1) the commission was mandated to use current sentencing averages as a "starting point," (2) the purposes and goals of sentencing (the policy issues) were established by Congress, and (3) the commission had to work within statutorily prescribed minimums and maximums when setting the guideline ranges (that is, the guidelines could not be used to sentence an individual to more or less time than Congress had set out by statute). The Court held that Congress had provided the commission with an intelligible principle by which it could perform its duties. In practice, the intelligible principle test has proven ineffective in controlling broad delegations. Justice Blackmun commented that when reviewing delegations, the Court "has been driven by a practical understanding that in our increasingly complex society, replete with ever changing and more technical problems, Congress simply cannot do its job absent an ability to delegate power under broad general directives."[10] Note, however, that the mandatory nature of the sentencing guidelines was later found to be violate of the right to trial by jury and today the guidelines are just that, advisory guidelines.[11] *There* is no indication, at this time, that the Court will revive the nondelegation doctrine in any meaningful way. The most recent case handed down by the Court again found a lawful delegation, contrary to the lower court's conclusion.[12]

The Court noted in that case that it had only found an intelligible principle lacking in two of its cases, *Schechter* and *Panama Refining,* affirming Congress's authority to delegate with minimal guidance. Many commentators have called for more meaningful review of statutes for excessive delegations of legislative authority, lest the nation will be increasingly governed by administrative officers. Examples of agencies stretching their authority too far can be found. Although well meaning, such extensions of authority are inconsistent with the U.S. architecture of government, which is designed to preserve liberty.

Cyber Constitution
Delegation Cases
You can read *Schecter* at www.law.cornell.edu/ supct/html/historics/ USSC_CR_0295_0495_ ZS.html, *Panama Refining* at http:// supreme.justia.com/ us/293/388/case.html, *Lichter* at http://supreme. justia.com/us/334/ 742/case.html, and *Arizona v. California* at http://supreme.justia.com/ us/373/546/case.html

Cyber Constitution
Federal Sentencing Commission
The U.S. Sentencing Commission continues its work in spite of the Supreme Court decision finding the mandatory nature of the guidelines violative of the Sixth Amendment. www. ussc.gov/

6.5(b) Quasi-Adjudicative Powers

In addition to delegating quasi-legislative powers to agencies, Congress may also empower agencies to perform quasi-adjudicative functions. For example, agency tribunals discipline license holders, fine violators, and resolve disputes between companies and consumers. In some instances, the agencies employ powers that have historically been exercised by courts of law. In fact, the transfer of cases from courts of law to administrative tribunals is increasing. The separation of powers issue is obvious when Congress transfers the authority to adjudicate a case from an Article III court to an administrative body. The purpose of Article III is twofold: to protect the integrity of the judiciary in the constitutional scheme and to assure that individuals will have their rights litigated before judges who are free from the domination of the political branches of government. Does this mean that all claims must be heard by Article III judges?

The Supreme Court addressed this issue as early as in 1932 in *Crowell v. Benson,*[13] in which it held that claims for damages resulting from work-related maritime injuries could be heard by an administrative official. The Court recognized in this case, however, that only certain cases can be transferred out of courts of law to Article I courts or officials.

The determination of whether a congressional delegation of judicial authority to an administrative agency is constitutional hinges upon the degree to which the delegation threatens the institutional integrity of the judicial branch. In 1986, the Court recognized four factors to be considered in this vein:

1. The extent to which the essential attributes of judicial power are reserved to Article III judges.
2. The extent to which the non–Article III tribunals exercise what are normally Article III powers.
3. The origins and importance of the right(s) to be adjudicated.
4. The reasons Congress chose to vest the adjudicatory power in an administrative officer or tribunal.[14]

All of these factors must be considered. The third factor has proven critical, however. Under what is known as the **public rights doctrine,** the Supreme Court treats the adjudication of public rights different from private rights. So-called public rights may be adjudicated by administrative officials, whereas private rights must be tried by Article III judges. Generally, when a case involves determining the liability between two private parties, it is a private-right case. But some apparent private rights may be adjudicated by administrative courts if they did not exist at the common law. A public rights case is one in which

1. The government is a party or
2. Congress has created a regulatory scheme, and a private right, which was not recognized to be common law, is integrated into that scheme.

The first category does not refer to criminal cases, even though the government is always a party in such cases.[15] A public right was found in *Atlas Roofing Co. v. Occupational Safety & Health Review Commission.*[16] The Occupational Safety and Health Act (OSHA) empowered the commission to impose civil penalties on employers for maintaining unsafe and unhealthy working conditions. The Court rejected the claims of punished employers that the nature of the claims covered by the act was private. On the contrary, no such remedy existed at the common law. The claim was a creation of Congress. Accordingly, it is public and may be adjudicated by an administrative agency.

Note that the right to have a claim heard by an Article III judge usually parallels the right to have a jury. The Seventh Amendment assures a jury trial in "[s]uits at common law, where the value in controversy shall exceed twenty dollars." As a

public rights doctrine
Rule providing that if a claim is public in nature and not private, Congress may delegate its adjudication to a non–Article III tribunal.

consequence, if a claim can be placed with an agency for adjudication, there is probably no right to a jury trial. Similar decisions have been reached in other cases. For example, an administrative tribunal may be charged with the responsibility of adjudicating unfair labor practice cases and awarding damages (back pay),[17] and the Commodity Futures Exchange Commission may entertain state-law counterclaims when customers of commodities brokers could seek money damages, even though these cases involve what appear to be private rights.[18] However, the availability of review by an Article III judge is important and may even be required for such a delegation to be valid.[19]

The use of U.S. bankruptcy judges has also been challenged. Bankruptcy judges are legislative, non–Article III judges. In *Northern Pipeline Construction Co. v. Marathon Pipe Line Co.*,[20] the Supreme Court invalidated a portion of the Bankruptcy Act that permitted bankruptcy judges to hear contract claims. Then, in 1989, the Supreme Court handed down *Granfinanciera, S.A. v. Nordberg*,[21] wherein it held that the act of a trustee in bankruptcy in recovering fraudulently conveyed property was private in nature, not public. Accordingly, the law that delegated the factual decision making in such cases to bankruptcy judges was invalidated. The Court did not answer the question of whether an Article I bankruptcy judge may preside over a jury trial that arises during a bankruptcy proceeding.

Interesting delegation issues have also arisen in the context of use of U.S. magistrate-judges. District judges (trial-level federal judges) are empowered under Article III of the Constitution. Article III judges undergo presidential nomination and Senate confirmation; magistrates do not. The positions of Article III judges are established under the Constitution; those of magistrates are not. Article II judges are insulated from political concerns by life tenure; magistrates are not. Article III judges may be removed only by Congress, through impeachment; magistrates may be removed by Article III judges.

Magistrate positions came into being through the Federal Magistrates Act, and are therefore creations not of the Constitution but of Congress. The Act delegates certain responsibilities to magistrates and allows Article III judges to delegate additional duties so long as the delegations are consistent with the Constitution and other laws of the United States.

Because magistrates are not Article III judges, only certain responsibilities may be delegated to them. For example, in *Gomez v. United States,* (1989)[22] it was determined that without the parties' consent, a magistrate may not be delegated the responsibility of conducting voir dire in a felony criminal case. The Court held that voir dire is a critical stage in the proceeding and so must be supervised by a constitutionally empowered judge. A later case, *Peretz v. United States,* (1991)[23] affirmed *Gomez,* but further explained that magistrate-judges may preside over criminal trials if the parties consent. If any party objects, then a district judge must preside over the critical stages of the case. The Court rejected the defendant's claim that conducting the voir dire is an inherently judicial function that cannot be delegated even with the consent of the parties (the defendant consented to have the magistrate-judge preside and then complained on appeal). The Court stated that the ultimate decision whether to invoke the magistrate's assistance is made by the district court, subject to veto by the parties. The decision whether to empanel the jury—the selection of which a magistrate has supervised—also remains entirely with the district court. Because the entire process takes place under the district court's total control and jurisdiction, there is no danger that use of the magistrate involves a congressional attempt to transfer jurisdiction to non–Article III tribunals for the purpose of emasculating constitutional courts. Because there was no separation of powers violation, the issue was whether a party may waive the right to have an Article III judge preside. The Court answered this affirmatively.

Gomez and *Peretz* stress the importance of agency accountability. When examining delegations of adjudicative power, courts look to whether the agency remains

Signing of the Constitution by Howard Chandler Christy
http://www.newscom.com

accountable to the judiciary. Whether the officer herself, such as with magistrate-judges, remains accountable to constitutional judges and whether the particular function is reviewed by constitutional judges are critical aspects.

Because the Act was drafted to keep magistrate-judges accountable to Article III judges, rather than to Congress or the president, most such delegations have been upheld. Under the Act, all decisions made by magistrates are reviewed de novo by district judges; magistrates may be removed by Article III judges; and magistrate-judges may not suffer a reduction in pay during their appointment. For these reasons, the Court has generally upheld the Act.

6.5(c) Criminal Law Powers

Special rules govern when agencies are delegated penal powers, that is, the power to establish what acts are criminal and what punishment should be meted out, and to try criminal charges. Because of the threat to civil liberties, agencies have limited authority in these areas.

In 1991 the Supreme Court issued a decision sustaining a delegation in the criminal law context. *Touby v. United States*[24] involved a statute that authorized the attorney general to temporarily declare a drug as Schedule I, controlled under the Controlled Substances Act. Possession, distribution, and use of controlled substances are criminal under that statute, and therefore the attorney general was delegated the responsibility of declaring penal law.

Congress delegated this power because it normally takes six months to a year to permanently schedule new drugs. Drug dealers took advantage of this gap in time by developing new "designer drugs" that were similar in effect to existing drugs but different in chemical composition. Until permanently scheduled, designer drugs could be possessed, distributed, and used lawfully. To resolve this problem, Congress delegated the authority to the attorney general to temporarily add, remove, or move drugs between schedules. The defendant raised two delegation issues: first, he claimed that the delegation to the attorney general was excessive; second, that more than an intelligible principle must be provided when Congress delegates penal rulemaking authority and that such was not done.

Accordingly, it is unknown whether Congress must provide more than an intelligible principle when delegating penal rulemaking authority. It is likely that a future

Cyber Constitution
Gomez v. United States
(1989) can be read at
http://supreme.justia.com/
us/490/858/case.html and
Peretz at http://supreme.
justia.com/us/501/923/
case.html

case may declare a higher standard. Whatever that standard proves to be, the Court stated that the statute at issue in *Touby* satisfies it.

Although Congress may delegate penal rulemaking to an agency, it may not delegate the power to establish penalties, with the possible exception of small fines. Congress may provide a range from which an agency establishes the penalty for a rule violation. Agencies may also act in a quasi-adjudicative role in criminal cases, although this power is very limited. Most administrative judges are not sufficiently connected to the judiciary to hear criminal cases. As discussed earlier, U.S. magistrates may hear criminal cases, although they may not preside over the voir dire (jury selection) in felony cases without the consent of both parties. U.S. magistrates may be delegated greater authority than administrative law judges because they are not officers of the executive branch, serve at the plea-sure of constitutionally selected judges, and are otherwise insulated from the political branches.

Touby v. United States
500 U.S. 160 (1991)

Justice O'Connor wrote the opinion of the Court.

Petitioners were convicted of manufacturing and conspiring to manufacture "Euphoria," a drug temporarily designated as a schedule I controlled substance pursuant to § 201(h) of the Controlled Substances Act. . . . We consider whether § 201(h) unconstitutionally delegates legislative power to the Attorney General and whether the Attorney General's subdelegation to the Drug Enforcement Administration (DEA) was authorized by statute.

I

In 1970, Congress enacted the Controlled Substances Act (Act). . . . The Act establishes five categories or "schedules" of controlled substances, the manufacture, possession, and distribution of which the Act regulates or prohibits violations involving schedule I substances carry the most severe penalties, as these substances are believed to pose the most serious threat to public safety. Relevant here, § 201(a) of the Act authorizes the Attorney General to add or remove substances, or to move a substance from one schedule to another. . . .

When adding a substance to a schedule, the Attorney General must follow specified procedures. First, the Attorney General must request a scientific and medical evaluation from the Secretary of Health and Human Services (HHS), together with a recommendation as to whether the substance should be controlled. A substance cannot be scheduled if the Secretary recommends against it. . . . Second, the Attorney General must consider eight factors with respect to the substance, including its potential for abuse, scientific evidence of its pharmacological effect, its psychic or physiological dependence liability, and whether the substance is an immediate precursor of a substance already controlled. . . . Third, the Attorney General must comply with the notice-and-hearing procedures of the Administrative Procedure Act . . . which permit comment by interested parties. . . . In addition,

the Act permits any aggrieved person to challenge the scheduling of a substance by the Attorney General in a court of appeals. . . .

It takes time to comply with these procedural requirements. From the time when law enforcement officials identify a dangerous new drug, it typically takes 6 to 12 months to add it to one of the schedules. . . . Drug traffickers were able to take advantage of this time gap by designing drugs that were similar in pharmacological effect to scheduled substances but differing slightly in chemical composition, so that existing schedules did not apply to them. These "designer drugs" were developed and widely marketed long before the Government was able to schedule them and initiate prosecutions. . . .

To combat the "designer drug" problem, Congress in 1984 amended the Act to create an expedited procedure by which the Attorney General can schedule a substance on a temporary basis when doing so is "necessary to avoid an imminent hazard to the public safety." § 201(h). . . . Temporary scheduling under § 201(h) allows the Attorney General to bypass, for a limited time, several of the requirements for permanent scheduling. The Attorney General need consider only three of the eight factors required for permanent scheduling. . . . Rather than comply with the APA notice-and-hearing provisions, the Attorney General need provide only a 30-day notice of the proposed scheduling in the *Federal Register*. . . . Notice also must be transmitted to the Secretary of the HHS, but the Secretary's prior approval of a proposed scheduling order is not required. . . . Finally, § 201(h) . . . provides that an order to schedule a substance temporarily "is not subject to judicial review." . . .

Because it has fewer procedural requirements, temporary scheduling enables the government to respond more quickly to the threat posed by dangerous new drugs. A temporary scheduling order can be issued 30 days after a new drug is identified, and the order remains valid for one year. During this 1-year period, the Attorney General presumably will initiate the permanent scheduling process, in which case the temporary scheduling order remains valid for an additional six months. . . .

The Attorney General promulgated regulations delegating to the DEA his powers under the Act, including the power to schedule controlled substances on a temporary basis. Pursuant to that delegation, the DEA Administrator issued an order scheduling temporarily 4-methylaminorex, known more commonly as "Euphoria," as a schedule I controlled substance. The Administrator subsequently initiated formal rulemaking procedures, following which Euphoria was added permanently to schedule I.

While the temporary scheduling order was in effect, DEA agents, executing a valid search warrant, discovered a fully operational drug laboratory in Daniel and Lyrissa Touby's home. The Toubys were indicted for manufacturing and conspiring to manufacture Euphoria. They moved to dismiss the indictment on the grounds that § 201(h) unconstitutionally delegates legislative power to the Attorney General, and that the Attorney General improperly delegated his temporary scheduling authority to the DEA. The United States District Court for the District of New Jersey denied the motion . . . and the Court of Appeals for the Third Circuit affirmed petitioner's subsequent convictions . . . and [we] now affirm.

II

The Constitution provides that "[a]ll legislative Powers herein granted shall be vested in a Congress of the United States. From this language the Court has derived the nondelegation doctrine: that Congress may not constitutionally delegate its legislative power to another Branch of government. "The nondelegation doctrine is rooted in the principle of separation of powers that underlies our tripartite system of government." . . .

We have long recognized that the nondelegation doctrine does not prevent Congress from seeking assistance, within proper limits, from its coordinate branches. . . .

Petitioners wisely concede that Congress has set forth in § 201(h) an "intelligible principle" to constrain the Attorney General's discretion to schedule controlled substances on a temporary basis. . . .

Petitioners suggest, however, that something more than an "intelligible principle" is required when Congress authorizes another Branch to promulgate regulations that contemplate criminal sanctions. They contend that regulations of this sort pose a heightened risk to individual liberty and that Congress must therefore provide more specific guidance. Our cases are not entirely clear as to whether or not more specific guidance is in fact required. . . . We need not resolve the issue today. We conclude that § 201(h) passes muster even if greater congressional specificity is required in the criminal context.

Although it features fewer procedural requirements than the permanent scheduling statute, § 201(h) meaningfully constrains the Attorney General's discretion to define criminal conduct. To schedule a drug temporarily, the Attorney General must find that doing so is "necessary to avoid an imminent hazard to the public safety."

. . . In making this determination, he is "required to consider" three factors: the drug's "history and current pattern of abuse"; "[t]he scope, duration, and significance of abuse"; and "[w]hat, if any, risk there is to the public health." . . . Included within these factors are three other factors on which the statute places a special emphasis; "actual abuse, diversion from legitimate channels, and clandestine importation, manufacture, or distribution." . . . The Attorney General also must publish 30-day notice of the proposed scheduling in the *Federal Register*, transmit notice to the Secretary of HHS, and "take into consideration any comments submitted by the Secretary in response."

In addition to satisfying the numerous requirements of § 201(h), the Attorney General must satisfy the requirements of § 202(b). . . . Thus, apart from the "imminent hazard" determination required by § 201(h), the Attorney General, if he wishes to add temporarily a drug to schedule I, must find it "has a high potential for abuse," that it "has no currently accepted medical use in treatment in the United States," and that "[t]here is a lack of accepted safety for use of the drug . . . under medical supervision."

It is clear that in §§ 201 (h) and 202(b) Congress has placed multiple specific restrictions on the Attorney General's discretion to define criminal conduct. These restrictions satisfy the constitutional requirements of the nondelegation doctrine.

Petitioners point to two other aspects of the temporary scheduling statute that allegedly render it unconstitutional. They argue first that it concentrates too much power in the Attorney General. Petitioners concede that Congress may legitimately authorize someone in the Executive Branch to schedule drugs temporarily, but argue that it must be someone other than the Attorney General because he wields the power to prosecute crimes. They insist that allowing the Attorney General both to schedule a particular drug and to prosecute those who manufacture that drug violates the principle of separation of powers. . . .

This argument has no basis in our separation of powers jurisprudence. The principle of separation of powers focuses on the distribution of power among the three coequal Branches . . . it does not speak to the manner in which authority is parceled out within a single Branch. The Constitution vests all executive power in the President . . . and it is the President to whom both the Secretary and the Attorney General report. Petitioners' argument that temporary scheduling authority should not be vested in one executive officer rather than another does not implicate separation-of-powers concerns; it merely challenges the wisdom of a legitimate policy judgment made by Congress.

[The Court also concluded that the attorney general's subdelegation was lawful.]

formal rulemaking
A process used by administrative agencies to create rules and regulations. The Administrative Procedure Act provides that formal rulemaking is required only when mandated by statute. Otherwise, informal rulemaking may be used by an agency. Formal rulemaking involves formal hearings and is more expensive and time consuming than informal rulemaking. This process is also known as *rulemaking on the record.*

informal rulemaking
A process used by administrative agencies to create rules and regulations. The Administrative Procedure Act provides that agencies may use this procedure unless formal rulemaking is required by statute. Informal rulemaking is less costly and less time consuming than its formal counterpart. This process is also known as *notice-and-comment rulemaking.*

Cyber Constitution
APA
The federal Administrative Procedure Act can be found at www.law.cornell.edu/uscode/5/usc_sup_01_5_10_I_30_5.html

legislative veto
An act of a legislature invalidating executive action in a particular instance. Generally, legislative vetos are unconstitutional. Once power is delegated by Congress to the president, it is generally prohibited from interfering with the president's enforcement.

6.5(d) Administrative Procedure Act

To govern the procedures used by administrative agencies, Congress enacted the Administrative Procedure Act (APA) in 1946.[25] The APA was intended to curb the growing power of agencies.

Among the many subjects the APA regulates are rulemaking and adjudication. Rulemaking is the administrative equivalent of lawmaking. The power to create substantive rules is not inherent; rather, it must be delegated to an agency by Congress. That delegation must be supported by an intelligible principle to confine the agency's authority.

The APA provides two rulemaking methods, formal and informal. In both, the public is given an opportunity to comment on proposed rulemaking. Public participation is greater in **formal rulemaking,** during which interested persons are allowed to participate orally in a hearing. Public participation in **informal rulemaking** is limited to written comment. A new rule must be published and an explanation of the agency's rationale in creating the rule must accompany the publication. An agency is required to explain its decision more thoroughly in formal rulemaking than in informal rulemaking. A properly promulgated rule has the effect of a statute.

The APA also governs agency adjudications, including agency notice to parties, participation requirements, and general procedures. Most agency hearings are presided over by administrative law judges (ALJs). ALJs are not Article III judges, but Congress has attempted to assure their independence by limiting their removal to good cause and placing their selection and compensation within the civil service system. Agency decisions are reviewable by courts.[26]

6.6 LEGISLATIVE VETO

One method that Congress used for many years to control agency behavior was the **legislative veto.** The term *legislative veto* refers to any process whereby Congress reviews, and possibly reverses, an agency decision. It is an attempt to control the implementation of delegated powers. Members of Congress are often more comfortable delegating broad powers to agencies if they know that they retain the power to review decisions of agencies and even more if Congress possesses the authority to reverse, alter, or veto decisions. The veto mechanism varied, but it was common for one house to be empowered to veto agency actions. The so-called legislative veto was the subject of the *Chadha* case.

Chadha specifically dealt with a one-house veto. But the Court's interpretation of the bicameralism and present clauses sees no way for Congress to bypass the bicameral and presentment of bills or resolutions to the president requirements. This was confirmed in another decision in which the Court invalidated the provision of a statute that permitted both houses to veto agency action without presentment to the president.[27] That same case extended the prohibition against legislative vetoes to independent agencies.

Immigration & Naturalization Service v. Chadha
426 U.S. 919 (1983)

[Chadha was an alien who had been residing in the United States under a student visa. His visa expired, and he applied to remain in the United States under a hardship provision of the Immigration Nationality Act (INA). The attorney general granted his request for suspension of deportation, but the House of Representatives, pursuant to a legislative veto provision of the INA, invalidated the attorney general's decision. That provision allowed either house of Congress to invalidate executive decisions concerning deportation. Chadha appealed the House's decision to the court of appeals, which invalidated the veto provision of the INA.]

Chief Justice Burger delivered the opinion of the Court.

We granted certiorari . . . [to review] a challenge to the constitutionality of a provision in § 244(c)(2) of the Immigration and Nationality Act . . . authorizing one House of Congress, by resolution, to invalidate the decision of the Executive Branch . . . to allow a particular deportable alien to remain in the United States. . . .

We turn now to the question whether action of one House of Congress under § 244(c)(2) violates strictures of the Constitution. We begin, of course, with the presumption that the challenged statute is valid. . . .

Our inquiry is sharpened rather than blunted by the fact that Congressional veto provisions are appearing with increasing frequency in statutes which delegate authority to executive and independent agencies:

> Since 1932, when the first veto provision was enacted into law, 295 congressional veto-type procedures have been inserted in 196 different statutes . . .

Justice White undertakes to make a case for the proposition that the one House veto is a useful "political invention," and we need not challenge that assertion. . . . But policy arguments supporting even useful "political inventions" are subject to the demands of the Constitution which defines powers and, with respect to this subject, sets out just how those powers are to be exercised. . . .

The Presentment Clauses

The records of the Constitutional Convention reveal that the requirement that all legislation be presented to the President before becoming law was uniformly accepted by the Framers. Presentment to the President and the Presidential veto were considered so imperative that the draftsmen took special pains to assure that these requirements could not be circumvented. During the final debate on Art. 1, § 7, cl. 2, James Madison expressed concern that it might easily be evaded by the simple expedient of calling a proposed law a "resolution" or "vote" rather than a "bill." As a consequence, Art I., § 7, cl. 3 [requiring bills, resolutions, and vote that require concurrence of both Houses to be presented to the President] . . . was added.

The decision to provide the President with a limited and qualified power to nullify proposed legislation by veto was based on the profound conviction of the Framers that the powers conferred on Congress were the powers to be most carefully circumscribed. It is beyond doubt that lawmaking was a power to be shared by both Houses and the President. . . .

Bicameralism

The bicameral requirement of Art. I, §§ 1, 7 was of scarcely less concern to the Framers than was the Presidential veto and indeed the two concepts are interdependent.

By providing that no law could take effect without the concurrence of the prescribed majority of the Members of both Houses, the Framers reemphasized their belief, already remarked upon in connection with the Presentment Clauses, that legislation should not be enacted unless it has been carefully and fully considered by the Nation's elected officials. In the Constitutional Convention debates on the need for a bicameral legislature, James Wilson, later to become a Justice of this Court, commented:

> Despotism comes on mankind in different shapes. Sometimes in an Executive, sometimes in a military, one. Is there danger of a Legislative despotism? Theory and practice both proclaim it. If the legislative authority be not restrained, there can be neither liberty nor stability; and it can only be restrained by dividing it within itself, into distinct and independent branches. In a single house there is no check, but the inadequate one, of the virtue and good sense of those who compose it. . . .

We see therefore that the Framers were acutely conscious that the bicameral requirement and the Presentment Clauses would serve essential constitutional functions. The President's participation in the legislative process was to protect the Executive Branch from Congress and to protect the whole people from improvident laws. . . . It emerges clearly that the prescription for legislative action in Art. I, §§ 1, 7 represents the Framers' decision that the legislative power of the Federal government be exercised in accord with a single, finely wrought and exhaustively considered, procedure.

The Constitution sought to divide the delegated powers of the new federal government into three defined categories, legislative, executive and judicial, to assure, as nearly as possible, that each Branch of government would confine itself to its assigned responsibility. . . .

Although not "hermetically" sealed from one another, the powers delegated to the three Branches are functionally identifiable. When any Branch acts, it is presumptively exercising the power the Constitution has delegated to it. When the Executive acts, it presumptively acts in an executive or administrative capacity as defined in Art. II. And when, as here, one House of Congress purports to act, it is presumptively acting within its assigned sphere.

Beginning with this presumption, we must nevertheless establish that the challenged action . . . is of the kind to which the procedural requirements of Art. 1, § 7 apply. Not every action taken by either House is subject to the bicameralism and presentment requirements of Art. I. Whether actions taken by either House are, in law and fact, an exercise of legislative power depends not on their form but upon "whether they contain matter which is properly to be regarded as legislative in its character and effect." . . .

Examination of the action taken here by one House pursuant to § 244(c)(2) reveals that it was essentially legislative in purpose and effect. In purporting to exercise power defined in Art. I, § 8, cl. 4, to "establish uniform Rule of Nationalization," the House took action that had the purpose and effect of altering the legal rights, duties and relations of persons, including the Attorney General, Executive Branch officials and Chadha, all outside the legislative branch. Section 244(c)(2) purports to authorize one House of Congress to require the Attorney General to deport an individual alien whose deportation otherwise would be cancelled under § 244. The one-House veto operated in this case to overrule the Attorney General and mandate Chadha's deportation; absent the House action, Chadha would remain in the United States. Congress had *acted* and its action has altered Chadha's status. . . .

Finally, we see that the Framers intended to authorize either House of Congress to act alone and outside of its prescribed bicameral legislative role; they narrowly and precisely defined the procedure for such action. There are but four provisions in the Constitution, explicit and unambiguous, by which one House may act alone with the unreviewable force of law, not subject to the President's veto:

(a) The House of Representatives alone was given the power to initiate impeachments. Art. I, § 2, cl. 6;

(b) The Senate alone was given the power to conduct trials following impeachment on charges initiated by the House and convict following trial. Art. I, § 3, cl. 5;

(c) The Senate alone was given final unreviewable power to approve or to disapprove presidential appointments. Art. II, § 2, cl. 2;

(d) The Senate alone was given final unreviewable power to ratify treaties negotiated by the President. Art. II, § 2, cl. 2.

Clearly, when the Draftsmen sought to confer special powers on one House independent of the other. House, or of the President, they did so in explicit, unambiguous terms. . . .

Since it is clear that the action by the House under § 244(c)(2) was not within any of the express constitutional exceptions authorizing one House to act alone, and equally clear that it was an exercise of legislative power, that action was subject to standards prescribed in Article I. . . .

V

We hold that the Congressional veto provision in § 244(c)(2) is severable from the Act and that it is unconstitutional. Accordingly, the judgment of the Court of Appeals is Affirmed.

[Justice Powell concurred with the judgment, but on different grounds. He concluded, "when Congress finds that a particular person does not satisfy the statutory criteria for permanent residence in this country it has assumed a judicial function in violation of the principle of separation of powers."

Justice White dissented. He concluded that the legislative veto is a good tool for keeping administrative agencies in check by elected representatives.]

Even though the Court could have decided *Chadha* on narrow grounds (e.g., that Congress had attempted to render a judicial decision in violation of the separation of powers), it chose to invalidate the legislative veto generally. Before this decision, Congress had placed veto provisions in many laws, including the War Powers Resolution, which empowered the president to commit U.S. armed forces to combat situations without congressional approval, subject to a requirement that the president report such actions to Congress and congressional authority to end the military action by joint resolution without presentment to the president. *Chadha* appears to render this provision of the War Powers Resolution unconstitutional, as well as similar provisions in other laws.

The invalidation of the legislative veto has not left Congress with recourse. Of course, Congress may veto agency decisions through resolutions that pass both houses and are signed by the president (or override presidential veto by two-thirds votes in both houses). Congress added a new program to its calendar in 1995 that is intended to increase its review of agency-created rules. **Corrections Day,** which occurs twice monthly, is an opportunity for members to introduce legislation to change or repeal agency rules. Congress also attempts to control agency decision making through oversight hearings. Informal methods, such as calls from individual members of Congress to agency officials, are also used to persuade agency officials to follow (or dissuade them from following) a particular course of action.

Corrections Day
Part of Congress's schedule; occurs twice a month. A time specially set aside for legislation intended to amend or repeal administrative rules.

6.7 MODERN CHALLENGES

The framers of the U.S. Constitution did not anticipate the enormous growth of the administrative state. Moreover, they did not foresee how the boundaries between the three branches would blur, particularly through the work of administrative agencies. The framers had a specific organizational vision for government: three branches with separately defined powers, limited by formal organizational and political checks that they exercise over one another. This framework operationalizes easily regardless of whether the balance of power swings in favor of the executive (unitary), Congress, or courts. It does not operationalize as easily in a model where a government entity performs the functions of all three branches. This is not a new challenge, but it is an enduring one. In the years to come, the federal government's health-care reform efforts are likely to give rise to many questions about governmental agencies and the exercise of governmental authority by private insurance and other companies.

6.8 SUMMARY

Although not specifically provided for in the Constitution, the administrative state is now an integral part of government in the United States. The number of agencies continually increases, as does the authority they possess. Although increasing, this power is checked. With the exception of independent agencies, the president acts as the chief of the administrative state. He controls the functioning of the agencies through control of agency heads, through the creation of rules governing their existence and functioning, and by collaboration with Congress in the creation of applicable statutes. Congress also wields a considerable amount of authority over agencies. It has the authority to create, reorganize, and disband them. In many instances, Congress must confirm presidential nominations of agency heads. Finally, Congress holds the purse strings.

The judiciary has not been silent on the rise of the administrative state. It has developed rules concerning delegations of authority, and the procedures agencies must follow when performing their functions. Although outside the scope of this book, the courts have also been active in defining the rights of citizens when dealing with agencies. This is not to say that all people are pleased with the state of administrative law. In spite of the checks previously discussed, Congress and the president appear unable to control the administrative machine at times. The Supreme Court's rejection of the legislative veto added another obstacle to Congress's desire to increase its oversight of agencies. Congress and the president are likely to seek new ways to control and oversee the nation's agencies in the years to come.

REVIEW QUESTIONS

1. Why are administrative agencies necessary in the contemporary United States?
2. What clause of the Constitution establishes administrative agencies?
3. What test is used to determine whether a delegation of power to an agency by Congress is lawful, that is, that Congress has not delegated too much power?
4. Distinguish independent agencies from executive agencies.
5. State the two ways a delegation may violate the Constitution.
6. Must Congress provide an agency with more than an intelligible principle when delegating criminal rulemaking authority?
7. What is a legislative veto? Is it constitutional?
8. What is the Administrative Procedure Act?

ASSIGNMENTS: CONSTITUTIONAL LAW IN ACTION

The Constitution in Your Community

As you learned in one of the "Your Constitutional Values," immigration is one of the most contentious and hotly debated issues in contemporary U.S. politics. The civil rights of immigrants, preservation of meaningful citizenship standards, national and personal identity, and federalism questions all converge to make "illegal" or "undocumented" immigrant status a third rail in politics. Ima, Cit, and Zen is a law firm that specializes in immigration and related issues. The decision has been made to open a new office in your state and you are one of the first employees hired. You have been directed to prepare a memorandum (1–3 pages) outlining your state's laws on immigration, if any. Does your state or local government have any law, policy, or practice that is specifically aimed at illegal immigrants? If so, what is that law, policy, or practice? Does it raise federal constitutional issues? If so, describe the law, policy, or practice as well as the constitutional issue(s). If you could not identify a law, policy, or practice in your locality, look to Arizona or another state to complete this exercise.

Going Federal

Assume that you work for a public interest group that has been asked to examine the constitutionality of the recent financial "bailout" program sponsored by the federal government. Recall that in 2008, Congress passed the Emergency Economic Stabilization Act of 2008, which authorized the President to make loans and provide other financial help to financial institutions in jeopardy of failing. One program known as "TARP," an acronym for "Troubled Assets Relief Program," also allowed the president to provide financial relief to financial institutions and other groups. The interest group that has retained your firm would like to know whether these congressional "bailout" measures constitute an unconstitutional delegation of authority by Congress to the president. See www.nytimes.com/2009/01/16/us/politics/16challenge.html. Prepare a memorandum (1–3 pages) discussing this question.

Moot Court

In 2010, the Dodd-Frank Wall Street Reform & Consumer Protection Act became law. Some analysts have argued that the new law constitutes a violation of the separation of powers doctrine. See www.fed-soc.org/doclib/20101209_BoydenShuDoddFrankWP.pdf. Divide into groups of two and prepare to argue the constitutionality, specifically whether the law violates the separation of powers.

NOTES

1. For a text on administrative law, see Daniel E. Hall, *Administrative Law: Bureaucracy in a Democracy*, 3rd ed. (Pearson/Prentice Hall 2006).
2. See, for example, *United States v. Gramaud,* 220 U.S. 506 (1911).
3. 295 U.S. 495 (1935).
4. 293 U.S. 388 (1935).
5. *J.W. Hampton, Jr. & Co. v. United States*, 276 U.S. 394 (1928).
6. *Eastlake v. Forest City Enterprises*, 426 U.S. 668 (1976).
7. 373 U.S. 546 (1963).
8. 334 U.S. 546 (1948).
9. 488 U.S. 361 (1989).
10. *Mistretta v. United States,* 488 U.S. 361, 372 (1989).
11. *United States v. Booker,* 220 (2005).
12. *Whitman v. American Trucking Assns, Inc.,* 531 U.S. 457 (2001).
13. 285 U.S. 22 (1932).
14. *Commodity Futures Trading Commission v. Schor,* 478 U.S. 833 (1986).
15. *Northern Pipeline Construction Co. v. Marathon Pipe Line Co.*, 458 U.S. 50, n. 24 (1982).
16. 430 U.S. 442 (1977).
17. *NLRB v. Jones & Laughlin Steel Corp.*, 301 U.S. 1 (1937).
18. *Commodity Futures Trading Commission v. Schor*, 478 U.S. 833 (1986).
19. *Atlas Roofing,* 430 U.S. 442 (1977).

20. 458 U.S. 50 (1982).
21. 492 U.S. 33 (1989).
22. 490 U.S. 858 (1989).
23. 501 U.S. 923 (1991).
24. 500 U.S. 160 (1991).
25. 5 U.S.C. § 551 *et seq.*
26. For a more thorough discussion of the APA and rulemaking and adjudication, see Daniel Hall, *Administrative Law*, chs. 3, 7 (Delmar/Lawyers Cooperative Publishing 1994).
27. *Process Gas Consumers Group v. Consumers Energy Council*, 463 U.S. 1216, reh'g denied, 463 U.S. 1250 (1983).

7

Contemporary Federalism: The State and Federal Relationship

Preoccupation by our people with the constitutionality, instead of with the wisdom of legislation or of executive action is preoccupation with false value. . . . Focusing attention on constitutionality tends to make constitutionality synonymous with wisdom.

JUSTICE FRANKFURTER[1]

In the compound republic of America, the power surrendered by the people is first divided between two distinct governments, and then the portion allotted to each subdivided among distinct and separate departments. Hence a double security arises to the rights of the people. The different governments will control each other, at the same time each will be controlled by itself.

JAMES MADISON[2]

LEARNING OBJECTIVES
At the end of this chapter you should be able to:

■ Define preemption and explain the most significant Supreme Court decisions defining the limits on congressional authority to preempt state laws.

■ Define the "Dormant Commerce Clause" and explain the most significant Supreme Court decisions defining it, including the state as market participant line of cases.

■ Define intergovernmental immunity and explain when it is applied.

■ Explain the contours of state constitutionalism, including the relationship between the federal and state constitutions. You should be able to cite examples of how state constitutions have been interpreted to protect individual rights to a greater extent than the U.S. Constitution.

■ Identify a contemporary issue concerning the relationship between the federal government and state government, and discuss the most likely future scenarios, referencing both historical analogs and caselaw.

■ Brief a judicial opinion with no assistance. You should be successful in identifying the relevant facts. You should be successful in identifying the legal issue and analyzing the court's rationale in at least 50 percent of your briefs.

■ Apply what you have learned to a new set of facts that are given to you with no assistance.

7.1 STATE AUTHORITIES

As you have previously learned, the framers intended to establish a stronger national government than existed under the Articles of Confederation. Indeed they did this, but some people feared that they had gone too far. The potential scope of the Supremacy and Necessary and Proper Clauses was of particular concern. Although the framers intended to strengthen the federal government, they did not intend to abolish the states. Rather, they created a limited federal government, carving out specific powers for it. The remaining power was intended to belong either to the states or to the people. These principles were enshrined in the Ninth and Tenth Amendments. See Figure 7-1, which illustrates the relationship between the rights held by the people and the respective authorities of the state and federal governments.

Amendment IX

The enumeration in the Constitution, of certain rights, shall not be construed to deny or disparage others retained by the people.

Amendment X

The powers not delegated to the United States by the Constitution, nor prohibited by it to the states, are reserved to the states, respectively, or to the people.

You may recall from Chapter 2 that the Supreme Court's perspective on the relationship of state and federal powers has vacillated between dual sovereignty and hierarchical federalism. You may want to review the discussion of these theories found in Chapter 2 before you read further.

The reserved powers of the states are commonly known as *police powers*. It is the police power that a state invokes when it performs the many functions people are accustomed to, such as declaring conduct criminal (most crimes, from theft to murder,

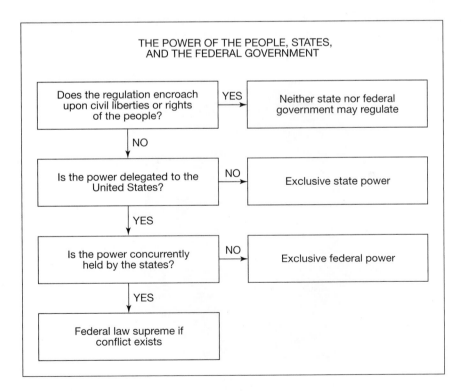

FIGURE 7-1

Respective powers of the people, the states, and the federal government

fall into state jurisdiction), providing education, issuing construction and building permits, licensing of professionals and trades people, the regulating of professionals and other occupations. Without a doubt, the federal government regulates for the general welfare today. Social security, occupational safety, welfare, and most recently, health care are examples of federal involvement in policy areas that historically belonged to the states.

An area of contention between the states and federal government in recent years has been physician-assisted suicide. The federal government has opposed the practice, while some states have authorized it. This issue came before the U.S. Supreme Court when the Attorney General issued an interpretive rule of the federal Controlled Substances Act, making it a federal crime for any physician to use a controlled substance to assist suicide in contradiction to Oregon's (voter-approved) Death with Dignity Act, which allowed physicians, with safeguards, to assist in the suicide of terminally ill patients. In its 2006 *Gonzales v. Oregon* decision (see Chapter 11), the Court penned:

> [T]he statute manifests no intent to regulate the practice of medicine generally. The silence is understandable given the structure and limitations of federalism, which allow the States "great latitude under their police powers to legislate as to the protection of lives, limbs, health, comfort, and quiet of all persons." . . . The structure and operation of the [Controlled Substances Act] presume and rely upon a functioning medical profession regulated under the States' police powers. . . .

Although the Court's decision in *Gonzales v. Oregon* was premised on more than federalism principles, its recognition of state authority against federal authority in this context is significant.

The states also have authority over physical boundaries; Article IV, Section 3, clause 1, prohibits Congress from establishing a state within the boundary of an existing state, joining states into one, or taking a portion of one state and making it a part of another without the consent of all the states involved.

As we have seen, the federal government has many powers as well. Some powers are exclusively federal—that is, a state may not simultaneously exercise them—such as

JAMES MADISON 1809-1817

James Madison, one of three authors of the *Federalist Papers* and the fourth president of the United States

akva / Shutterstock.com

coining money, conducting diplomacy with foreign nations, and declaring war. The converse is also true. Some subjects are purely local in nature, and Congress may not regulate them. This is true of regulating guns in and around schools, the subject of *United States v. Lopez* (see Chapter 5). Power over many policy areas, however, is concurrently held. Interstate commerce is such a subject. It is possible for both the state and the federal government to regulate interstate commerce. That legislation may be consistent, overlapping, conflicting, or complementary. Problems arise when state and federal regulations clash. This chapter examines the body of law governing these conflicts and other subject areas where federal and state powers intersect.

7.2 CONGRESSIONAL ACTION: PREEMPTION AND VALIDATION

If concurrent jurisdiction over a subject exists, and both state and federal governments have enacted legislation that is conflicting, then federal law prevails under the Supremacy Clause. Even more, in some circumstances, the federal government is deemed to have preempted state action. The **preemption** doctrine holds that in three instances, state regulation is precluded or invalidated by federal regulation:

preemption
The doctrine that once Congress has enacted legislation in a given field, a state may not enact a law inconsistent with the federal statute. A similar doctrine also governs the relationship between state governments and local governments.

1. When Congress expressly states that it intends to preempt state regulation;
2. When a state law is inconsistent with federal law, even though no express preemption statement has been made by Congress; and
3. When Congress has enacted a legislative scheme that comprehensively regulates a field.

The first of the three is self-explanatory; Congress preempts if it expressly states such through public law. As to the second and third types of preemption, several factors are considered by courts, including whether the subject has historically been state or federal, the need for uniformity, the likelihood of conflicts in administration of state and federal programs, and the pervasiveness of the federal regulatory scheme. As to the third type, Congress has sufficiently occupied a field whenever it is possible to reasonably infer that it left no room for the states to supplement federal law.

THE PHILOSOPHY OF STATES' RIGHTS

SIDEBAR

The framers were careful to preserve the sovereignty of the states. Three delegates to the Constitutional Convention (Gerry, Mason, and Randolph) refused to sign the Constitution because it extended too much power to the national government and, accordingly, took too much power from the states and the people. The states' rights controversy continues even today. But why did the framers believe so strongly in state, rather than federal, power? There are three answers.

First, they feared centralized power. These men had experienced the centralized power of the British monarchy and were of the belief that absolute power corrupts absolutely. They saw even lesser powers as having the same relative corruptive consequence.

Second, the framers believed that localized government is more responsive to local needs. Local leaders are members of the community; they live, work, and worship together. Accordingly, they are more sensitive to local concerns.

Third, it was a generally held belief at the time that republics had to be small to be successful. One of the anti-Federalist writers of the time, Brutus (a pseudonym), opposed the Constitution for this reason. In one of his essays, he quoted Montesquieu's *Spirit of Laws*:

It is natural to a republic to have only a small territory, otherwise it cannot long subsist. In a large republic there are men of large fortunes, and consequently of less moderation; these are trusts too great to be placed in any single subject; he has interest of his own; he soon begins to think that he may be happy, great and glorious, by oppressing his fellow citizens; and that he may raise himself to grandeur on the ruins of his country. In a large republic, the public good is sacrificed to a thousand views; it is subordinate to exceptions, and depends on accidents; In a small one, the interest of the public is easier perceived; better understood, and more within the reach of every citizen; abuses are of less extent, and of course are less protected.

Brutus stated:

[the] territory of the United States is of vast extent; it now contains near three million souls, and is capable of containing much more than ten times that number. Is it practicable for a country, so large and so numerous as they will soon become, to elect a representation, that will speak their sentiments, without their becoming so numerous as to be incapable of transacting public business? It certainly is not.[3]

If it is determined that Congress has preempted a policy area, all state laws, even if consistent with federal law, are void. The Court does not lightly infer preemption, and when a policy area is one that touches the states' police powers, preemption will not be found unless there is a "clear and manifest" intent by Congress.[4] Similarly, because preemption of an entire field totally divests the states of authority over a policy area, it is found only in extreme cases.[5]

Also, if Congress has expressed its attitude toward preemption, then courts are not to consider implicit preemption. This occurs in situations in which Congress has preempted some specific state regulations, but not all. That is, express preemption of one aspect of a subject precludes the possibility of a court finding implicit preemption of the entire subject. For example, the fact that Congress expressly preempts state licensing of interstate shipping indicates that it did not intend to preempt the entire field. Accordingly, state regulations that do not excessively burden interstate commerce are presumably valid.

Note that lawfully promulgated federal regulations may also preempt state law. Of course, Congress may specifically allow for concurrent state regulation, and often does. See Figure 7-2 for instances in which the Supreme Court found that federal law preempted state law.

John Jay, one of three authors of the *Federalist Papers* and the first chief justice of the United States

© Steven Wynn/Istockphoto.com

Congress may also announce the opposite of preemption: It may validate state legislation of interstate commerce. This is sometimes done before a state has regulated and sometimes after. In some instances, Congress requires federal approval of state laws and objectives before validation. For example, the federal Occupational Safety and Health Act regulated the training, testing, and licensing of hazardous waste site employees (among other things). Congress provided that federal law shall govern unless a state receives approval for its own plan from the U.S. Department of Labor.

PREEMPTION CASES

Chamber of Commerce v. Whiting	Arizona law that punished companies who hired unauthorized workers with lose of license to do business not preempted by federal law regulating the hiring, including fines, unauthorized workers.	*Form of Preemptions:* No Preemption.
American Ins. Ass'n v. Garamendi, 539 U.S. 396 (2003)	California law regulating insurance companies that may have defaulted on life insurance contracts with Jewish policy holders in Nazi Germany preempted by executive agreement with Germany.	*Form of Preepmtion:* Inconsistency and Implied.
Crosby v. National Trade Council, 530 U.S. 363 (2000)	Massachusetts law restricting state agencies in their commercial dealings with companies from Burma preempted by federal law regulating commercial activity with Burma.	*Form of Preemption:* Inconsistency.
Medtronic, Inc. v. Lohr, 518 U.S. 470 (1996)	Federal regulation and approval of medical devices did not preempt state remedies for negligence associated with use.	*Form of Preemption:* No Preemption.
Cipollone v. Liggett Group, Inc 505 U.S. 504 (1992)	Federal law requiring warnings on cigarettes preempted state law claims for failure to warn of dangers, but not state law claims on fraud.	*Form of Preemption:* No Preemption.
Gade v. National Solid Wastes Management Ass'n, 505 U.S. 88 (1992)	Illinois regulation of the training, testing, and licensing of hazardous waste site workers preempted by federal Occupational Safety and Health Act.	*Form of Preemption:* Express and inconsistency. Congress provided that federal law shall govern unless a state receives approval for its own plan from the Department of Labor.
Morales v. Trans World Airlines, Inc., 504 U.S. 374 (1992)	Language in the federal Airline Deregulation Act, stating that states shall not enforce laws "relating to rates, routes, or services," preempted state deceptive practices law against airlines for deceptive fares.	*Form of Preemption:* Express.
City of Burbank v. Lockhead Air Terminal, 411 U.S. 624 (1973)	City ordinance regulating aircraft noise by prohibiting flights during certain hours was preempted by Federal Aviation Act and the Noise Control Act.	*Form of Preemption:* Express.
Pennsylvania v. Nelson, 350 U.S. 497 (1956)	Pennsylvania criminal sedition act preempted by federal sedition laws.	*Form of Preemption:* Inconsistency and field occupation.
McDermott v. Wisconsin, 228 U.S. 115 (1913)	Wisconsin food labeling laws were invalidated because compliance with federal food labeling laws required violation of Wisconsin's laws.	*Form of Preemption:* Inconsistency.

FIGURE 7-2
Selected preemption cases

Illinois regulated the area without obtaining federal approval, leading the Court to conclude that the Illinois law was preempted by the federal government.[6]

Properly executed executive agreements, particularly those made with foreign nations, may also preempt state law. For example, a California law that regulated insurance companies that may have defaulted on life insurance contracts with Jewish policy holders in Nazi Germany was found to be preempted by a presidential agreement (not endorsed by Congress) that regulated the same subject in *Americans Ins. Ass'n v. Garamendi,* 539 U.S. 396 (2003).

In another case, *Crosby v. National Trade Council* (2000),[7] the Court took this analysis a step further and indicated that all extensive regulation of foreign affairs by a state is prohibited, either by implicit preemption or simply because the states lack the authority to delve too deeply into international matters.

In terms of federalism, the Rehnquist Court dealt most often with direct federal-state jurisdictional issues, carving out specific policy areas that belong to the states, exclusive of the federal government. Recall, for example, the decisions in *Lopez* (1995), *Printz* (1997), and *Morrison* (2000), discussed in Chapter 4. The Roberts Court has shown less of an interest in these issues and more in the thorny issue of preemption when concurrent jurisdiction exists.

The Court issued an abundance of cases, in Supreme Court terms, between 2008 and 2011. One of these is *Rowe v. New Hampshire Motor Transport Association.* In the late 1970s and early 1980s, the United States adopted a policy of deregulation of the airline and motor carrier industries. Congress's rationale for the deregulation was that better prices and improved service would result from a free market approach in both industries. To prevent the states from undermining the effort by regulating the industries themselves, the statutes that deregulated the industries provided that "no State . . . shall enact or enforce any law . . . relating to rates, routes, or services of any air carrier." In 2003, Maine enacted a statute intended to regulate the sales of, and to prevent teen use of, tobacco products. Although the intention of the law was not to regulate the trucking industry generally, its provisions that regulated the transport and delivery of tobacco products were held, by unanimous vote, to be preempted by the plain language of the federal statute. This is true, even if the state possesses the authority, as it claimed, to prohibit all shipments and sale of tobacco products within its border.

In *Riegel v. Medtronic, Inc.,* (2008), a federal law governing medical devices that preempted state tort law actions for injuries resulting from the medical devices was upheld. In two consumer safety cases, state attempts to bolster federal protections were upheld. In *Altria Group v. Good,* (2008), the Supreme Court held that the federal government's extensive regulation of tobacco including an express preemption of state labeling and warning requirements about smoking and health did not preempt a state law tort claim for fraudulent advertising by a tobacco company. Similarly, federal labeling requirements for prescription drugs were found to not preempt state laws that not only were consistent with but also furthered the protection of patients in *Wyeth v. Levine* (2009). In the same year the Court also determined that federal banking laws did not preempt state fair-lending laws in *Cuomo v. Clearing House.*[8]

The television personality Judge Alex was a party to another preemption case, *Preston v. Ferrer (see below).*

The Court reinforced the primacy of federal authority over arbitions in the 2011 decision AT&T v. Concepcion where the Court invalidated a lower court's application of California law which led to the invalidation of a provision of an arbitration agreement was invalid because it conflicted with the federal objective of encouraging speedy and efficient arbitration. Justice Breyer filed a dissent asserting that the decision is an afront to state authority.

In yet four additional 2011 decisions the Supreme Court decided that state tort law actions for defective design in vaccines are preempted by federal law, state tort actions against automobile manufacturers for installing lap belts but not shoulder belts are

Cyber Constitution
***Rowe v. New Hampshire Motor Transport Association* (2008)**
http://supreme.justia.com/us/552/06-457/

Cyber Constitution
***Riegel v. Medtronic, Inc.,* 552 U.S. 312 (2008)**
http://supreme.justia.com/us/552/06-179/

Cyber Constitution
***Altria Group v. Good* (2008)** http://supreme.justia.com/us/555/07-562/

Cyber Constitution
***Cuomo v. Clearing House* (2009)** http://supreme.justia.com/us/557/08-453/

not preempted by federal regulations empowering manufacturers to choose whether to install both, federal labeling law preempted state tort actions against a manufacturer of generic drugs for negligence from not providing adequate warnings about possible side effects, and that an Arizona law that punished corporations for hiring undocumented workers by loss of license to conduct business in Arizona. The Court held that the law was not preempted by a federal law that provides for fines in such circumstances. Even more, the federal law expressly preempted state laws that impose civil or criminal penalties on those who employ unauthorized workers. The Court found, however, that Congress intended to leave licensing, in all respects, to the states.[9]

Recent cases signal two interesting developments. The first was mentioned earlier. The Roberts Court is interested in preemption. The second is the increased strategic use of federalism theories, specifically preemption, by litigants in civil actions.

Preston v. Ferrer
552 U.S. 346 (2008)

[T]he Federal Arbitration Act (FAA or Act), 9 U. S. C. §1 *et seq.* (2000 ed. and Supp. V), establishes a national policy favoring arbitration when the parties contract for that mode of dispute resolution. The Act, which rests on Congress' authority under the Commerce Clause, supplies not simply a procedural framework applicable in federal courts; it also calls for the application, in state as well as federal courts, of federal substantive law regarding arbitration. More recently, in *Buckeye Check Cashing, Inc. v. Cardegna*, 546 U. S. 440 (2006) the Court clarified that, when parties agree to arbitrate all disputes arising under their contract, questions concerning the validity of the entire contract are to be resolved by the arbitrator in the first instance, not by a federal or state court.

The instant petition presents the following question: Does the FAA override not only state statutes that refer certain state-law controversies initially to a judicial forum, but also state statutes that refer certain disputes initially to an administrative agency? We hold today that, when parties agree to arbitrate all questions arising under a contract, state laws lodging primary jurisdiction in another forum, whether judicial or administrative, are superseded by the FAA.

This case concerns a contract between respondent Alex E. Ferrer, a former Florida trial court judge who currently appears as "Judge Alex" on a Fox television network program, and petitioner Arnold M. Preston, a California attorney who renders services to persons in the entertainment industry. Seeking fees allegedly due under the contract, Preston invoked the parties' agreement to arbitrate "any dispute . . . relating to the terms of [the contract] or the breach, validity, or legality thereof . . . in accordance with the rules [of the American Arbitration Association]."

Preston's demand for arbitration, made in June 2005, was countered a month later by Ferrer's petition to the California Labor Commissioner charging that the contract was invalid and unenforceable under the California Talent Agencies Act (TAA), Cal. Lab. Code Ann. §1700 *et seq.* (West 2003 and Supp. 2008). Ferrer asserted that Preston acted as a talent agent without the license required by the TAA, and that Preston's unlicensed status rendered the entire contract void. . . .

An easily stated question underlies this controversy. Ferrer claims that Preston was a talent agent who operated without a license in violation of the TAA. Accordingly, he urges, the contract between the parties, purportedly for "personal management," is void and Preston is entitled to no compensation for any services he rendered. Preston, on the other hand, maintains that he acted as a personal manager, not as a talent agent, hence his contract with Ferrer is not governed by the TAA and is both lawful and fully binding on the parties . . .

Section 2 [of FAA]"declare[s] a national policy favoring arbitration" of claims that parties contract to settle in that manner. *Southland Corp.*, 465 U. S., at 10. That national policy, we held in *Southland*, "appli[es] in state as well as federal courts" and "foreclose[s] state legislative attempts to undercut the enforceability of arbitration agreements." *Id.*, at 16. The FAA's displacement of conflicting state law is "now well-established," . . .

Ferrer attempts to distinguish *Buckeye* by arguing that the TAA merely requires exhaustion of administrative remedies before the parties proceed to arbitration. We reject that argument. . . .

Ferrer contends that the TAA is nevertheless compatible with the FAA because §1700.44(a) merely postpones arbitration until after the Labor Commissioner has exercised her primary jurisdiction. . . .

A prime objective of an agreement to arbitrate is to achieve "streamlined proceedings and expeditious results." That objective would be frustrated even if Preston could compel arbitration in lieu of *de novo* Superior Court review. Requiring initial reference of the parties' dispute to the Labor Commissioner would, at the least, hinder speedy resolution of the controversy. . . .

When parties agree to arbitrate all questions arising under a contract, the FAA supersedes state laws lodging primary jurisdiction in another forum, whether judicial or administrative. . . .

Dormant Commerce Clause
Judicial doctrine providing that even if federal power to regulate interstate and international commerce is not exercised, state power to regulate these areas is sometimes precluded.

***Cooley* doctrine**
Named for the case in which it was announced, *Cooley v. Board of Wardens*, 53 U.S. 299 (1851); provides that if a subject of interstate commerce is national in character, then regulation of that subject is exclusively federal.

7.3 CONGRESSIONAL INACTION: THE DORMANT COMMERCE CLAUSE

The discussion so far has been concerned with situations in which Congress has chosen to regulate. Difficult problems also arise when Congress does not act. Does the Commerce Clause preclude state action in some circumstances, even in the absence of federal legislation? The answer is yes—and when it does, it is referred to as the **Dormant Commerce Clause.**

Cooley v. Board of Wardens[10] is an early Dormant Commerce Clause case. Decided in 1851, its central holding has become known as the ***Cooley* doctrine.** If a subject in interstate commerce is by nature national in character or needs uniformity of law to be effective, then its regulation is exclusively federal. If not federal, then it falls within the state sphere. Largely premised upon dual federalism principles, *Cooley* has limited application in an era of cooperative federalism.

Today, the Dormant Commerce Clause prohibits a state from engaging in economic protectionism, using the law to favor local businesses over out-of-state

---

American Trucking Associations, Inc. v. Michigan Public Service Commission
545 U.S. 440 (2005)

[Pursuant to federal legislation, states were limited to charging a registration fee of $10 on trucks that travel in interstate commerce that are licensed in other states. Michigan had such a fee. In addition, Michigan established a fee—to support its road maintenance and enforcement—of $100 for all state-licensed intrastate carriers and another $100 for all carriers that make intrastate runs, regardless of whether the carrier is Michigan licensed. The fee had to be paid by all companies for all trucks, so long as they made an intrastate (Michigan location to Michigan location) haul. This is fee in question. It is a practice for some interstate carriers who have delivered a load or who are passing through a state with less than a full load to "top off" with another load and deliver it elsewhere, often within the same state, during the haul. This maximizes efficiency. The plaintiffs allege that because such intrastate deliveries comprise a smaller part of their business than for purely intrastate carriers, and because the fee is the same for both, the fee is disproportionately high to interstate trucking companies, and accordingly, it discriminates against interstate commerce.]

In this case, we consider whether a flat $100 fee that Michigan charges trucks engaging in intrastate commercial hauling violates the dormant Commerce Clause. We hold that it does not.

A subsection of Michigan's Motor Carrier Act imposes upon each motor carrier "for the administration of this act, an annual fee of $100.00 for each self-propelled motor vehicle operated by or on behalf of the motor carrier." The provision assesses the fee upon, and only upon, vehicles that engage in intrastate commercial operations—that is, on trucks that undertake point-to-point hauls between Michigan cities. Petitioners, USF Holland, Inc., a trucking company with trucks that engage in both interstate and intrastate hauling, and the American Trucking Associations, Inc. (ATA), asked the Michigan courts to invalidate the provision. Both petitioners told those courts that trucks that carry *both* interstate *and* intrastate loads engage in intrastate

business less than trucks that confine their operations to the Great Lakes State. Hence, because Michigan's fee is flat, it discriminates against interstate carriers and imposes an unconstitutional burden upon interstate trade. . . .

Our Constitution "was framed upon the theory that the peoples of the several states must sink or swim together." *Baldwin v. G. A. F. Seelig, Inc.,* 294 U.S. 511, 523 (1935). Thus, this Court has consistently held that the Constitution's express grant to Congress of the power to "regulate Commerce . . . among the several States," Art. I, §8, cl. 3, contains "a further, negative command, known as the dormant Commerce Clause," *Oklahoma Tax Comm'n v. Jefferson Lines, Inc.,* 514 U.S. 175, 179 (1995), that "create[s] an area of trade free from interference by the States," *Boston Stock Exchange v. State Tax Comm'n,* 429 U.S. 318, 328 (1977) (internal quotation marks omitted). This negative command prevents a State from "jeopardizing the welfare of the Nation as a whole" by "plac[ing] burdens on the flow of commerce across its borders that commerce wholly within those borders would not bear." *Jefferson Lines, supra,* at 180.

Thus, we have found unconstitutional state regulations that unjustifiably discriminate on their face against out-of-state entities, see *Philadelphia v. New Jersey,* 437 U.S. 617 (1978), or that impose burdens on interstate trade that are "clearly excessive in relation to the putative local benefits," *Pike v. Bruce Church, Inc.,* 397 U.S. 137, 142 (1970). We have held that States may not impose taxes that facially discriminate against interstate business and offer commercial advantage to local enterprises, see, *e.g., Oregon Waste Systems, Inc. v. Department of Environmental Quality of Ore.,* 511 U.S. 93, 99–100 (1994), that improperly apportion state assessments on transactions with out-of-state components, *Central Greyhound Lines, Inc. v. Mealey,* 334 U.S. 653 (1948), or that have the "inevitable effect [of] threaten[ing] the free movement of commerce by placing a financial barrier around the State," *American Trucking Assns., Inc. v. Scheiner,* 483 U.S. 266, 284 (1987).

Applying these principles and precedents, we find nothing in §478.2(1) that offends the Commerce Clause. To begin with, Michigan imposes the flat $100 fee only upon intrastate transactions—that is, upon activities taking place exclusively within the State's borders. Section 478.2(1) does not facially discriminate against interstate or out-of-state activities or enterprises. The statute applies evenhandedly to all carriers that make domestic journeys. It does not reflect an effort to tax activity that takes place, in whole or in part, outside the State. Nothing in our case law suggests that such a neutral, locally focused fee or tax is inconsistent with the dormant Commerce Clause. . . .

The record, moreover, shows no special circumstance suggesting that Michigan's fee operates in practice as anything other than an unobjectionable exercise of the State's police power. To the contrary, as the Michigan Court of Appeals pointed out, the record contains little, if any, evidence that the $100 fee imposes any significant practical burden upon interstate trade. . . .

They say that our earlier case, *American Trucking Assns., Inc. v. Scheiner*, 483 U.S. 266 (1987), requires invalidation of the $100 flat fee, even in the absence of such proof. We disagree.

In *Scheiner*, this Court invalidated a flat $25 "marker fee" and a flat "axle tax" that Pennsylvania levied upon all trucks (interstate and intrastate) that used its roads, including trucks that merely crossed Pennsylvania's borders to transport, say, Ohio goods to New Jersey customers. Data showed that the fees imposed a cost per mile on interstate trucks that was approximately "five times as heavy as the cost per mile borne by local trucks." at 286. The assessments largely helped to raise revenue "to improve and maintain [the State's] highways and bridges," at 270, thereby helping to cover costs likely to vary significantly with truck-miles traveled, sea. And the assessments did "not even purport to approximate fairly the cost or value of the use of Pennsylvania's roads." at 290. In light of these considerations, Pennsylvania's lump-sum taxes "threaten[ed] the free movement of commerce by placing a financial barrier around the State of Pennsylvania." at 284. We concluded that "[i]f each State imposed flat taxes for the privilege of making commercial entrances into its territory, there [was] no conceivable doubt that commerce among the States would be deterred."

The present fee, as we have said, taxes purely local activity; it does not tax an interstate truck's entry into the State nor does it tax transactions spanning multiple States. We lack convincing evidence showing that the tax deters, or for that matter discriminates against, interstate activities. 5. Nor is the tax one that, on its face, would seem to call for an assessment measured per mile rather than per truck. 6. Consequently, we lack any reason to infer that Michigan's lump-sum levy erects, as in *Scheiner,* an impermissible discriminatory road block.

Petitioners add that Michigan's fee fails the "internal consistency" test—a test that we have typically used where taxation of interstate transactions are at issue. Generally speaking, that test asks, "What would happen if all States did the same?" See, *e.g., Goldberg v. Sweet,* 488 U.S. 252, 261 (1989); *Jefferson Lines, supra,* at 185 (test looks to the structure of the tax to see whether its identical application by every State "would place interstate commerce at a disadvantage as compared with commerce intrastate"). We must concede that here, as petitioners argue, if all States did the same, an interstate truck would have to pay fees totaling several hundred dollars, or even several thousand dollars, were it to "top off" its business by carrying local loads in many (or even all) other States. But it would have to do so only because it engages in *local* business in all those States. An interstate firm with local outlets normally expects to pay local fees that are uniformly assessed upon all those who engage in local business, interstate and domestic firms alike. . . . A motor carrier is not special in this respect.

In sum, petitioners have failed to show that Michigan's fee, which does not seek to tax a share of interstate transactions, which focuses upon local activity, and which is assessed evenhandedly, either burdens or discriminates against interstate commerce, or violates the Commerce Clause in any other relevant way. See *Complete Auto Transit, Inc. v. Brady*, 430 U.S. 274, 279 (1977) (noting that a tax will be sustained where it is applied to an activity with a "substantial nexus" to the taxing State; where, if applied to interstate activity, it is "fairly apportioned"; where it does not discriminate; and where it is "fairly related to the services provided").

For these reasons, the judgment of the Michigan Court of Appeals is affirmed [and the fee is upheld].

It is so ordered.

---

businesses. This does not mean, however, that states may not impose reasonable state regulations on interstate and intrastate commerce. Michigan's fee on intrastate trucks to support road maintenance and enforcement was upheld by the Supreme Court in *American Trucking Associations, Inc. v. Michigan Public Service Commission.*

7.3(a) Discriminatory State Laws

Cooley does not address what is to be done with state laws that discriminate against interstate commerce. A state law is discriminatory and an invalid exercise of the police power when it favors local interests over out-of-state interests or intends to reduce the competitive advantage an out-of-state participant may have over locals. After all, one of the purposes of federal jurisdiction over interstate and international commerce was to bring an end to the local rivalries that existed under the Articles of Confederation. The

Cyber Constitution
Cooley v. Board of Wardens can be read at http://supreme.justia.com/us/53/299/case.html

Commerce Clause is premised upon a national market, and the states may not enact barriers to the interstate sale of products or services.

Discriminatory state laws are perceived as particularly pernicious by the Court and are scrutinized closely. State laws that are facially discriminatory are "virtually per se invalid."[11] Laws that place a state in economic isolation or favor its residents over out-of-state persons are per se unconstitutional. The Court will examine both the state's reason for regulating and the effect of the regulation on interstate commerce. If the state's objectives cannot be achieved in a less burdensome manner *and* outweigh the harm to interstate commerce, the law will be upheld. This is a rigorous standard for a state to meet. The Supreme Court summarized its Dormant Commerce Clause analysis in its decision *Department of Revenue v. Davis*.[12] First, the question whether the challenged action burdens interstate commerce must be answered. Second, the action is per se invalid, unless it can be shown to advance "a legitimate local purpose," and third, "that cannot be adequately served by reasonable nondiscriminatory alternatives." Finally, unless discriminatory for the forbidden purpose, the law is to be upheld unless its local benefits are greatly outweighted by the burden to interstate commerce. See Figure 7-3.

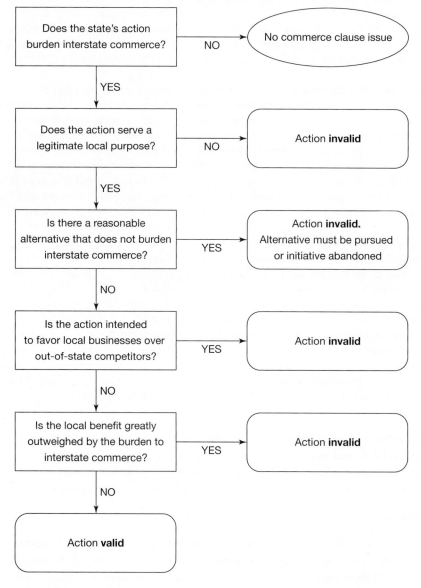

FIGURE 7-3

Framework for analyzing Dormant Commerce Clause cases

Accordingly, a New York statute that prohibited the sale of milk purchased out of state at a lower price than that obtainable in state was invalidated.[13] The Commerce Clause does not tolerate a state's attempt to discourage out-of-state products. A state statute that prohibited the sale of certain fish out of the state of Oklahoma, while allowing sale within the state, was void as violating the Dormant Commerce Clause.[14] In the 2005 case *Granholm v. Heald*,[15] the laws of two states that permitted in-state, but not out-of-state, wineries to make direct sales to consumers were stricken.

Attempts by a state to conserve its resources may also violate the Dormant Commerce Clause if the effect of these regulations is discrimination against out-of-state users or sellers. Although the Court has recognized that states have an interest in regulating water use, it has also determined that water is a commodity in interstate commerce subject to Dormant Commerce Clause jurisprudence. In *Sporhase v. Nebraska*,[16] the Court invalidated the reciprocity provision of a statute that prohibited the export of water to a state that does not permit water to be imported to Nebraska. The Court approved of other regulations that were intended to conserve water but found the reciprocity provision unlawfully discriminatory. As an aside, the Court noted that a state may create a limited preference for its own citizens when regulating vital natural resources. The reciprocity provision under review in the case, however, excessively obstructed interstate commerce.

Waste disposal laws have also been the subject of Dormant Commerce Clause jurisprudence. Increasingly, the disposal of human and hazardous wastes is becoming a problem for all cities and towns. In an effort to combat disposal problems, states and localities have enacted a multitude of laws concerning disposal areas, methods, access, and the like. Philadelphia, as well as other cities, attacked the problem of limited landfill space directly. It prohibited the importation of out-of-state solid and liquid wastes. The Court invalidated this law in the 1978 case of *City of Philadelphia v. New Jersey*.[17] Philadelphia could take action to curb its problem, such as prohibiting the disposal of wastes altogether or limiting disposal to certain types of wastes, but it could not discriminate against persons wanting to bring waste in from out of state.

A locality may not indirectly accomplish what it is prohibited from accomplishing directly. *Philadelphia* involved a direct discrimination, but *C&A Carbone v. Clarkstown*[18] involved a processing requirement that had the indirect effect of discriminating against out-of-state dumpers. Clarkstown had entered into a contract with a local solid waste processor, which agreed that the town would provide a certain amount of waste and the processor would process it (i.e., separate recyclable from nonrecyclable waste). A town ordinance then required all nonrecyclable wastes from all sources to be deposited with the private contractor to be processed and disposed. The ordinance was held unlawful because it prevented out-of-state processors from competing and because it increased the

YOUR CONSTITUTIONAL VALUES

FACING CONSEQUENCES FOR FACEBOOK

In 2004, Mark Zuckerberg, a student at Harvard University, created an online social network known as Facebook for Harvard University students. The popularity of Facebook spread quickly, and by 2006, several million high school students, college students, and other individuals had accounts throughout the United States and abroad. Facebook is designed to increase networking and communication among members. Users create personal profiles, post photos, exchange messages, and connect to other users in other ways. Facebook limits the access of each member to specific areas and data that is material to his or her life, for example, to other members from a specific college.

As is often true of new technology, the advent of Facebook, as well as blogs, online journals, and other Internet creations, has led to new legal questions.

Of course, journals, telephones, and other forms of communication preexisted Facebook. What is unique, however, is the ability to reach so many people, so quickly. In the short time Facebook has been in existence, college students have been disciplined for posting threatening messages, defamatory messages, and messages insulting to peers or instructors. Facebook has also been used to prove violations of law and university policy. For example, students at Northern Kentucky University were disciplined for violating the university's policy prohibiting alcohol on campus when photos of an on-campus party where alcohol was consumed appeared on Facebook.

Private institutions, where the First Amendment does not apply, have greater authority to discipline students for speech and association than do public institutions. However, disciplining and prosecuting students for posting threats or evidence of criminal behavior is relatively straightforward for both private and public institutions. However, other behaviors raise interesting First Amendment free speech and association questions in public institutions. For example, may a student be disciplined for posting messages with hate content? A Duquesne University student was disciplined for posting a message referring to gays as "subhuman." Would the result be the same if the student had been enrolled at a public university? One has a right to pen such ideas in a private journal. Does the public nature of Facebook change the outcome? What about posting sexual content about peers, faculty, or university administrators? May a student post the likeness of a peer or university employee? If so, may that photo be alerted? What about insulting statements? Students at Syracuse University, a private institution, were disciplined for penning statements such as "I'd rather watch my brother masturbate to midget porn with my mom than go to your class" and "I'd rather eat all the hair stuck in the drains of the showers than go to your class." On the one side, we have the values of free speech and association. On the other, the value of having harmonious institutions where students are free to exchange ideas without fear of national exposure is genuine, as is the desire to maintain privacy and dignity. For example, would you want the views you express in class broadcast to the world? How about the grades you earn on class assignments, which are seen by the student seated next to you in class? What about a description of your behavior at parties or with a lover?

The exact contours of the First Amendment's application to Facebook and other online communication tolls are likely to be the source of considerable attention by colleges, universities, and high schools, as well as by courts, in the years to come. What values are in competition in the Duquesne and Syracuse cases?

---

cost of depositing out-of-state waste in Clarkstown. Less restrictive alternatives existed for the town. If the town was genuinely concerned about the quality of processing, it could enact quality standards that would apply to all. Instead, it chose to discriminate against nonlocal processors and waste dumpers.

State laws requiring reciprocal action by other states have been closely scrutinized by the Court. In *Great Atlantic & Pacific Tea Co. v. Cottrell*,[19] a Mississippi law that permitted milk to enter the state from another state only if the other state had entered into a reciprocal inspection standards agreement, was invalidated. The Court rejected Mississippi's contention that the law was necessary to protect the health of its citizens. Further, the Court found that the health rationale was a pretext and that it was Mississippi's intention to favor local vendors. Also, in *Sporhase v. Nebraska*,[20] the Court struck down the reciprocity provision of a Nebraska law that restricted the exportation of water to states that permitted the importation of their water to Nebraska. Again, the Court found this to be unnecessarily discriminatory.

Not all discriminatory laws have failed. Maine's prohibition on the importation of certain baitfish, to prevent the introduction of certain parasites not common to Maine, was upheld. The Court held that Maine's interest in protecting local fisheries was significant and that there was no alternative method of achieving this objective that was less burdensome to interstate commerce.[21]

Alexander Hamilton, one of three authors of the *Federalist Papers*
© Steven Wynn/istockphoto.com

7.3(b) Burdensome State Laws

It is possible for state regulation to be nondiscriminatory, yet burdensome, to interstate commerce. Again, the Court weighs the state's interest against the burden on interstate commerce to determine whether the Dormant Commerce Clause has been violated. However, the test is not as rigorous as in the facially discriminatory cases discussed earlier. Accordingly, local regulation is more likely to be valid when challenged as burdensome than when challenged as facially discriminatory. In most of these cases, the state asserts that the regulation is necessary to protect the health and welfare of its citizens.

Many Dormant Commerce Clause cases have arisen in the context of state regulation of interstate transportation. Most state laws regulating transportation safety are validated by the Court. However, some overburden interstate commerce. For example, an Arizona law that prohibited trains with more than seventy freight cars or fourteen passenger cars was held unconstitutional. The Court noted that long trains were common throughout the United States and that company compliance with the law would be very burdensome to interstate commerce. A company would have to either change its practice nationwide or stop at the border of Arizona and reduce the length of its trains. If allowed, then every state could regulate train transportation and trains would be forced to stop at every border and make adjustments to comply with local law. Further, Arizona's evidence that shorter trains are safer was marginal. Thus, the burden on interstate commerce outweighed Arizona's interest in protecting its citizens.[22]

Similarly, an Illinois law requiring a certain mudflap on trucks was invalidated. The law would have prevented trucks from using a mudflap that was legal in nearly every other state. Again, the safety advantages were minimal, and the burden on interstate commerce high.[23] For nearly identical reasons, an Iowa law that forbade trucks longer than sixty-five feet from using its roads was held unconstitutional.[24] The

Court concluded that to comply, a truck would have to either avoid the state or stop at the border, detach the trailer that caused the vehicle to exceed the limit, and ship it separately. The burden on interstate commerce in both cases was significant. Further, the state's asserted safety concern was negated by the increased danger caused by the second alternative.

Some state laws that burden interstate commerce have been upheld. For example, state laws requiring railroads to have full crews on trains have been upheld. Also, a state law that prohibited the sale of milk in nonrecyclable plastic containers, but permitted the use of other nonrecyclable materials such as paperboard, was upheld because (1) its impact on interstate commerce was minimal, (2) it treated in-state and out-of-state retailers identically, and (3) the state had a legitimate conservation and waste disposal interest.[25]

7.3(c) Liquor Laws

State regulation of liquor requires special constitutional analysis due to the Twenty-First Amendment, Section 1. Section 2, which repealed prohibition, reads:

> The transportation or importation into any State, Territory, or possession of the United States for delivery or use therein of intoxicating liquors, in violation of the laws thereof, is hereby prohibited.

Cyber Constitution
The Dormant Commerce Clause
http://
nationalparalegal.edu/
conlawcrimproc_public/
CongressionalPowers/
DormantCommerceClause.
asp

Pursuant to this amendment, the states possess greater power over the interstate aspects of liquor than they do over other items. In particular, the Dormant Commerce Clause has limited application in the liquor arena. A state may tax, or otherwise discourage, the importation of liquor without violating the Dormant Commerce Clause.

Even so, broad state authority over liquor is not absolute. First, Congress regulates foreign trade and a state may not interfere with this authority, even when the trade subject is liquor. Second, extreme interferences with interstate commerce will be invalidated. For example, a New York law that required distillers to sell their products in New York at the lowest price in the United States violated the Commerce Clause.[26]

Earlier in this chapter, the decision of *Granholm v. Heald* was mentioned. The states in that case, Michigan and New York, raised the Twenty-First Amendment as a defense. The Supreme Court did not accept this argument, holding that the Twenty-First Amendment does not give the states the authority to favor in-state liquor businesses over out-of-state businesses.

Note that even though the federal government does not have the power to establish the drinking age, it may coerce the states into setting a minimum age. Hence, withholding of federal highway funds from states that did not enact and enforce a twenty-one-years-of-age drinking limit was deemed constitutional.[27]

7.3(d) State Taxation as Discriminatory and Burdensome

State taxes may also discriminate against or burden interstate commerce and, accordingly, violate the Dormant Commerce Clause. Yet tax revenues are needed by state and local governments to pay for the services they provide. It would be unfair to allow out-of-state market participants to avail themselves of local services but not to contribute revenues. For example, an out-of-state market participant may use the courts of a state to enforce a contract, the police to investigate fraud, and administrative agencies to file business claims of many varieties. In regard to discriminatory taxing, the Supreme Court applies the strict scrutiny test, as with other allegedly discriminatory laws. That is, the law is valid only if a government can show a compelling interest. The Court has held that laws intended to equalize the tax burdens between in-state and out-of-state participants are valid. Thus, if in-state market participants are shouldering most or all of a tax burden, the state may act. The Court established the following test:

1. If a state has identified an intrastate tax for which it is attempting to equalize the burden between in-state and out-of state participants, and
2. The taxing scheme leaves both sets of participants with approximately equal tax burdens, and
3. Approximately the same events are taxed.[28]

If all these criteria are met, the law will most probably pass the test.

The Supreme Court also developed a test concerning burdensome tax laws. It permits states and localities to extract a fair tax, yet prevents them from overburdening interstate commerce. The test was announced in *Complete Auto Transit, Inc. v. Brady,*[29] a 1977 case. Pursuant to this test, a state or local tax on a product or service in interstate commerce is valid if the tax:

1. Is applied to an activity with a substantial nexus to the taxing state, and
2. Is fairly apportioned, and
3. Does not discriminate against interstate commerce, and
4. Is fairly related to the services provided by the state.

Two interstate passenger bus transportation cases can be used to illustrate the application of this test. First, *Central Greyhound Line, Inc. v. Mealey*[30] involved an unapportioned tax on gross receipts from interstate bus tickets. The tax was based upon the total number of miles traveled. The law did not distinguish between intrastate and interstate miles. Applying the *Complete Auto Transit* test, it is clear that the activity was related to the taxing state. However, the second and third elements were not satisfied.

The second element has two aspects: internal and external consistency. To know whether internal consistency is satisfied, one must ask whether, if every state enacted an identical law, intrastate commerce would be favored. External consistency focuses on whether a state is taking more than its share of an interstate transaction. The tax in

---

STATE RIGHTS DON'T BELONG ONLY TO THE STATES

Any state may challenge federal law or action that it believes exceeds federal authority or that encroaches upon state authority. But the right to challenge federal law as encroaching upon state authority is not limited to the states; individuals who are affected by the federal law may assert the state rights defense as well. In *Bond v. United States* (S.Ct. 2011), the defendant wife discovered that a friend was pregnant by her husband. In revenge, she placed caustic substances on items her friend touched, including a mailbox, doorknob, and car door handle. The friend was burned, contacted federal authorities, and the defendant was charged and convicted of the federal offense of using chemicals to injure. The federal statute was enacted by Congress to comply with an international treaty the United States signed. The defendant challenged the law under the Tenth Amendment, claiming that such a prohibition amounts to an exercise of general police power a power that belongs to the states. She lost in both the trial and the appellate court. The appellate court found that she lacked standing to raise the federalism issue, and that it is the states that have an interest in protecting against federal incursions in their constitutional jurisdictional authorities.

The Supreme Court disagreed. It noted that federalism protects in a counterintuitive way, "freedom is enhanced by the creation of two governments, not one." Further, the division of authorities between the federal and state governments was intended to protect not only their respective roles but also individual freedoms. The Court found that "an individual has a direct interest in objecting to laws that upset the constitutional balance between the National Government and the States when the enforcement of those laws causes injury that is concrete, particular, and redressable." There is no doubt that criminal defendants have concrete interests and easily satisfy the case and controversy requirement since their liberties and reputations are in jeopardy. So Ms. Bond won her right to assert the federalism claim. The case was remanded to the trial court so that court could hear and decide whether the federal government exceeded its authority in enacting the law under which she was convicted. Note that the Court was clear in applying its analysis to both federalism and separation of powers claims.

S I D E B A R

Central Greyhound failed these elements because the possibility of duplicative taxes on interstate travel was presented. The state in which the ticket was purchased and the states through which a passenger traveled could all tax the trip. Because the tax on travel out of the state in which the ticket was purchased would be greater, the law unfairly discriminated against interstate commerce.

In a similar case decided in 1995, *Oklahoma Tax Commission v. Jefferson Lines,*[31] the Court examined a sales tax imposed on intrastate and interstate bus tickets. Jefferson paid the tax on the intrastate tickets it sold, but refused to pay the tax on interstate tickets. It relied on the *Central Greyhound* case in support of its position.

Again, the first element of the *Complete Auto Transit* test was satisfied. The tax was imposed by the state in which the ticket was sold. The Court rejected Jefferson's argument that *Central Greyhound* applied, finding that the sales tax in *Jefferson* was different from the gross receipts tax in *Central Greyhound.* The sales tax was identical for both in-state and out-of-state purchases (4.5 percent of the ticket price). Recall that the problem in *Central Greyhound* was the possibility of successive and duplicative taxes on interstate commerce. *Jefferson,* however, involved a transactional tax. The tax was imposed on the sale and delivery of the ticket. No other state could tax that activity. As to the fourth element, the Court found that the amount (first 4 percent, later 4.5 percent) was reasonably related to the services provided by the state. As to this element, a state does not have to prove that a taxpayer receives a direct benefit from a tax. Rather, it is enough that the tax reasonably relate to the types of services that benefit the taxpayer. The dissent in *Jefferson* argued that there is no meaningful difference between the two cases and that *Central Greyhound* should apply.

The Fourteenth Amendment's Due Process Clause also restricts a state's authority to tax out-of-state individuals. There must be a **minimum contact** between a state and the person taxed.[32] State citizenship may establish the requisite contact. Contact with a transaction may also satisfy due process. For example, the sale of goods in a state or the execution and performance of a contract in a state by out-of-state parties create minimum contacts. State taxation of the federal government may also be unconstitutional. This topic is discussed in Section 7.4.

7.3(e) State as Market Participant

States not only regulate commerce, but also participate in commerce, as buyers and, less often, as sellers. When a state is a participant in, as opposed to a regulator of, the market, the Dormant Commerce Clause does not apply. The Court has determined that although the Commerce Clause was intended to limit the states' power to regulate commerce, it was not intended to limit their ability to participate in the market. The Court has drawn a distinct line between states as regulators and states as market participants.

A state may purchase exclusively from local vendors and provide goods and services exclusively to local vendors, even though it may not require the same from local businesses. Accordingly, a state decision to sell cement produced at a state-owned plant to state residents only was validated by the Supreme Court.[33] A state may also charge higher prices to out-of-state purchasers when it is engaged in manufacturing or selling a product or service. States have taken advantage of this exception to the Dormant Commerce Clause and have solved problems that they could not remedy as regulators by becoming participants. For example, consider the nationwide waste disposal problem discussed earlier. Pursuant to the Dormant Commerce Clause, a state may not establish a regulatory scheme that discriminates against out-of-state disposers. This caused local and state governments to purchase landfills and disposal sites. By 1989, 81 percent of the nation's landfills were owned by a government.[34] As owners, local governments may limit disposal to residents. Kentucky's decision to tax bonds of other states but not its own was upheld by the Roberts Court in 2008 under the same rationale. Justice Souter, writing for the majority in *Department of Revenue v. Davis,* penned,

minimum contacts test
A doctrine under which a state court is permitted to acquire personal jurisdiction over a nonresident, although he or she is not personally served with process within the state, if he or she has had such a substantial connection with that state that due process is not offended by the court's exercise of jurisdiction over him or her.

[t]he Kentucky tax scheme falls outside the forbidden paradigm because the Commonwealth's direct participation favors, not local private entrepreneurs, but the Commonwealth and local governments. The Commonwealth enacted its tax code with an eye toward making some or all of its bonds more marketable. When it issues them for sale in the bond market, it relies on that tax code, and seller and purchaser treat the bonds and the tax rate as joined just as intimately, say, as the work force requirements and city construction contracts were in Boston. Issuing bonds must therefore have the same significance under the dormant Commerce Clause as government trash processing, junk car disposal, or construction.

In some instances, it is difficult to determine whether to treat a state as a market participant or as a regulator, because it may be both. If a state is a participant, but uses its regulatory power to interfere with the free market, then Dormant Commerce Clause analysis should be applied.[35] If state regulation is only incidental to its participation, then the state should not be limited by the Dormant Commerce Clause.

See Figure 7-3 for a summary of Commerce Clause cases.

7.3(f) Privileges and Immunities

There are two Privileges and Immunities Clauses in the Constitution. One is located in the Fourteenth Amendment. This provision is discussed further in the second part of this book. The other, which is the subject of this discussion, is found in Article IV, Section 2, clause 1, and states, "[t]he citizens of each State shall be entitled to all Privilege and Immunities of Citizens in the several States."

There is an intersection between some Commerce Clause cases and some privileges and immunities cases. When a state regulates to advance a local market over the interstate market, it simultaneously discriminates against interstate commerce and deprives the residents of other states of the privileges it extends to its own.

The clause is not absolute, however. A state may grant greater benefits to its own residents if *substantial cause* to do so exists. Further, the clause protects only fundamental rights. *Fundamental* in this context differs from other areas of constitutional law, such as in due process analysis. Here, *fundamental* refers to those rights that are important to the preservation of the Union—those that contribute to making this a federation as opposed to a confederation.

There is no bright line of demarcation between fundamental and nonfundamental rights. The right to practice law is fundamental, and a state law restricting that right to state residents is unconstitutional.[36] The right to earn a living as a commercial fisher is fundamental as well.[37] Sport hunting for elk is not fundamental, and, as such, is not protected by the Privileges and Immunities Clause.[38]

There is no way to know whether a court will analyze a case in terms of the Privileges and Immunities Clause or the Commerce Clause. However, the Commerce Clause has been the subject of more litigation and interpretation than has the Privileges and Immunities Clause, and appears to be a favored application. One important distinction between Commerce Clause and Privileges and Immunities Clause rulings can be made. Congress can legitimize state behavior under the Commerce Clause. Privileges and immunities jurisprudence, in contrast, transcends statutory law and cannot be altered by Congress.

7.4 INTERGOVERNMENTAL IMMUNITY

This section examines the authority of the federal government to regulate the states and vice versa. To begin with the latter, states are generally prohibited from regulating the federal government. Congress may consent to state regulation but rarely does. Thus, a state may not enact minimum wages that apply to federal employees or regulate the safety of federal employees while at work; since the 1819 decision in *McCulloch v. Maryland,*[39] it has been clear that states may not tax the federal government or its subunits.

Through time, the Supreme Court has cycled through hierarchical federalism and dual sovereignty periods. Justice Marshall's Court, for example, favored a strong

Cyber Constitution
Constitution and Citizenship Day
Federal law requires all civil authorities and schools, colleges, and universities that receive federal funds to observe Constitution and Citizenship Day and to provide "instruction of citizens in their responsibilities and opportunities as citizens of the United States and of the State and locality in which they reside." September 17 was selected for this celebration because that was the day in 1787 when thirty-nine delegates to the Constitutional Convention signed the new constitution. Another date is just as important and could easily have been chosen as Constitution Day. The Constitution required ratification by at least nine of the thirteen states for the new Constitution to be fully ratified. This occurred when New Hampshire approved on June 21, 1788. For more on Constitution Day, visit the Constitution Center at http://constitutioncenter. org/ncc_progs_ constitution_day.aspx. You can read the text of law at www.law. cornell.edu/uscode/36/ usc_sec_36_00000106— 000-.html. Ironically, some have questioned whether the law is constitutional. For a humorous discussion, see Nelson Lund, *Is Constitution Day Constitutional? The Green Bag*, Vol. 9 (3) (2006).

national government at the expense of state authority. Justice Taney, on the other hand, favored state authority. This philosophy underpinned the Court's 1857 decision in *Dred Scott v. Sandford*.[40] Some historians believe this decision was one of the causes of the Civil War. *Scott v. Sandford* held that Congress could not regulate slavery in the territories and affirmed that states, not the federal government, have the authority to define a person's status (citizen, slave, etc.). As a result of the northern victory in the Civil War and the enactment of the post–Civil War amendments, federal power increased significantly for several decades. The tide shifted again for a period and then, following Franklin D. Roosevelt's court-packing plan and the *switch in time that saved nine*, the Court again empowered the federal government. The tide has again shifted toward state rights in the past decade. However, an important state rights case dates back to 1976, *National League of Cities v. Usery*.[41]

Garcia v. San Antonio Metropolitan Transit Authority
469 U.S. 528 (1985)

Justice Blackmun delivered the opinion of the Court.

We revisit in these cases an issue raised in *National League of Cities v. Usery*. In that litigation, this Court, by a sharply divided vote, ruled that the Commerce Clause does not empower Congress to enforce the minimum-wage and overtime provisions of the Fair Labor Standards Act (FLSA) against the States "in areas of traditional governmental functions." Although *National League of Cities* supplies some examples of "traditional governmental functions," it did not offer a general explanation of how a "traditional" function is to be distinguished from a "nontraditional" one. Since then, federal and state courts have struggled with the task, thus imposed, of identifying a traditional function for purposes of state immunity under the Commerce Clause.

In the present cases, a Federal District Court concluded that municipal ownership and operation of a mass-transit system is a traditional governmental function and thus, under *National League of Cities*, is exempt from the obligation of the FLSA. Faced with the identical question, three Federal Courts of Appeals and one state appellate court have reached the opposite conclusion.

Our examination of this "function" standard applied in these and other cases over the last eight years now persuades us that the attempt to draw boundaries of state regulatory immunity in terms of "traditional governmental function" is not only unworkable but is also inconsistent with the established principles of federalism and, indeed, with those very federalism principles on which *National League of Cities*, purported to rest. That case, accordingly, is overruled. . . .

[The Court then discussed the difficulty in distinguishing traditional functions from nontraditional ones.]

We therefore now reject, as unsound in principle and unworkable in practice, a rule of state immunity from federal regulation that turns on a judicial appraisal of whether a particular governmental function is "integral" or "traditional." Any such rule leads to inconsistent results at the same time that it disserves principles of democratic self-governance, and it breeds inconsistency

precisely because it is divorced from those principles. If there are to be limits on the Federal Government's power to interfere with state functions—as undoubtably there are—we must look elsewhere to find them. We accordingly return to the underlying issue that confronted this Court in *National League of Cities*—the manner in which the Constitution insulates States from the reach of Congress' power under the Commerce Clause. . . .

The States unquestionably do "retai[n] a significant measure of sovereign authority." They do so, however, only to the extent that the Constitution has not divested them of their original powers and transferred those powers to the Federal Government. . . .

With rare exceptions, like the guarantee, in Article IV, § 3, of state territorial integrity, the Constitution does not carve out express elements of state sovereignty that Congress may not employ its delegated powers to displace. . . .

Apart from the limitation on federal authority inherent in the delegated nature of Congress' Article I powers, the principal means chosen by the Framers to ensure the role of the States in the federal system lies in the structure of the Federal Government itself. It is no novelty to observe that the composition of the Federal Government was designed in large part to protect the States from overreaching by Congress. The Framers thus gave the States a role in the selection both of the Executive and Legislative Branches of the Federal Government. The States were vested with indirect influence over the House of Representatives and the Presidency by their control of electoral qualifications and their role in presidential elections. . . . They were given more direct influence in the Senate, where each State received equal representation and each Senator was to be selected by the legislature of his State. . . . The significance attached to the States' equal representation in the Senate is underscored by the prohibition of any constitutional amendment divesting a State of equal representation without the State's consent. Art. V. . . .

We realize that changes in the structure of the Federal Government have taken place since 1789, not the least of which has been the substitution of popular election of Senators by the adoption of the Seventeenth Amendment in 1913, and that these changes may work to alter the influence of the States in the federal political process. Nonetheless, against this background, we are convinced that the fundamental limitation that the constitutional scheme imposes on the Commerce Clause to protect the "States as States" is one of process rather than one of result. . . .

Of course, we continue to recognize that the States occupy a special and specific position in our constitutional system and that the scope of Congress' authority under the Commerce Clause must reflect that position. . . .

These cases do not require us to identify or define what affirmative limits the constitutional structure might impose on federal action affecting the States under the Commerce Clause. We note and accept Justice Frankfurter's observation in *New York v. United States*, 326 U.S. 572 (1946):

> "The process of Constitutional adjudication does not thrive on conjuring up horrible possibilities that never happen in the real world and devising doctrines sufficiently comprehensive in detail to cover the remotest contingency. Nor need we go beyond what is required for a reasoned disposition of the kind of controversy now before the Court. . . ."

We do not lightly overrule recent precedent. We have not hesitated, however, when it has become apparent that a prior decision has departed from a proper understanding of congressional power under the Commerce Clause. Due respect for the reach of congressional power within the federal system mandates that we do so now. . . .

Justice Powell, with whom. The Chief Justice [Burger], Justice Rehnquist, and Justice O'Connor join, dissenting.

. . . Despite some genuflecting in the Court's opinion to the concept of federalism, today's decision effectively reduces the Tenth Amendment to meaningless rhetoric when Congress acts pursuant to the Commerce Clause. . . .

Today's opinion does not explain how the States' role in the electoral process guarantees that particular exercises of the Commerce Clause power will not infringe on residual State sovereignty. Members of Congress are elected from the various States, but once in office they are Members of the Federal Government. . . .

More troubling than the local infirmities in the Court's reasoning is the result of its holding, i.e., that federal political officials, invoking the Commerce Clause, are the sole judges of the limits of their own power. This result is inconsistent with the fundamental principles of our constitutional system. At least since *Marbury v. Madison* it has been the settled province of the federal judiciary "to say what the law is" with respect to the constitutionality of acts of Congress. . . .

In our federal system, the States have a major role that cannot be preempted by the National Government. As contemporaneous writings and the debates at the ratifying conventions make clear, the States' ratification of the Constitution was predicated on this understanding of federalism. Indeed, the Tenth Amendment was adopted specifically to ensure that the important role promised the States by the proponents of the Constitution was realized. . . .

By usurping functions traditionally performed by the State, federal overreaching under the Commerce Clause undermines the constitutionally mandated balance of power between the States and the Federal Government, a balance designed to protect our fundamental liberties. . . .

[The Tenth] Amendment states explicitly that "[t]he powers not delegated to the United States . . . are reserved to the States." The Court recasts this language to say that the States retain their sovereign powers "only to the extent that the Constitution has not divested them of their original powers and transferred those powers to the Federal Government." This rephrasing is not a distinction without a difference; rather, it reflects the Court's unprecedented view that Congress is free under the Commerce Clause to assume a State's traditional sovereign power, and to do so without judicial review of its action. . . .

Justice O'Connor, with whom Justice Powell and Justice Rehnquist join, dissenting.

[T]he Federal Government has, with this Court's blessing, undertaken to tell the States the age at which they can retire their law enforcement officers, and the regulatory standards, procedures, and even the agenda which their utilities commissions must consider and follow. . . . The political process has not protected against these encroachments on state activities, even though they directly impinge on a State's ability to make and enforce its laws. With the abandonment of essentials of state sovereignty and Congress is the latter's underdeveloped capacity for self-restraint . . .

National League was concerned with whether the federal Fair Labor Standards Act, which mandates the minimum wage and maximum work hours, could be applied to state employees. Initially, Congress exempted all public employees from the Act, but later amended the law to include employees of hospitals, institutions, and schools. The Supreme Court invalidated the law insofar as it reached state employees because "[o]ne undoubted attribute of state sovereignty is the States' power to determine the wages which shall be paid to those whom they employ in order to carry out their governmental functions." The Court stated further that application of the Act to the states "impermissibly interfere[s] with the integral governmental functions of these bodies" and threatens their "separate and independent existence." In short, "Congress may not exercise [its] power so as to force directly upon the States its choices as to how essential decisions regarding the conduct of integral governmental functions are to be made." (The essential functions the Court referred to are providing hospitals, schools, and fire and police protection.)

The *Usery* majority opinion was written by Justice Rehnquist and the vote count was 5–4. Justice Blackmun concurred, although he stated that he was "not untroubled by certain possible implications" of the decision. Nine years later, the Court reversed *Usery* in *Garcia v. San Antonio Metropolitan Transit Authority.* The legal issues in *Garcia* were nearly identical to those in *Usery*—whether the federal government's Fair Labor Standards Act provisions were binding on the states. The vote was again 5–4 but Justice Blackmun had crossed over to the other side.

Garcia inflicted a serious, but not fatal, wound to state sovereignty. The Court stated, "constitutional structure might impose" limits on the federal authority to regulate the states under the Commerce Clause. Through its quotation of Justice Frankfurter, it appeared to indicate that the limitation would prevent only "horrible" encroachments on state power.

Just such an encroachment was found in the 1992 case of *New York v. United States.*[42] Faced with a shortage of disposal sites for low-level radioactive waste throughout the United States, Congress enacted the Low-Level Radioactive Waste Policy Amendments Act. This statute imposed upon the states an obligation to provide for the disposal of waste generated within their borders. This could be done solely or in compact with other states. Congress established three incentives to bring the states into compliance:

1. *Financial:* States with disposal sites were authorized to impose a surcharge on waste received from states that did not establish their own disposal sites. One-fourth of the surcharge was to be collected by the federal government and then distributed to compliant states. The receiving state was authorized to keep the remaining three-quarters of the surcharge.
2. *Access:* Eventually, a state could refuse to receive waste from a state without its own disposal site.
3. *Take Title:* If a state had not provided for disposal of the waste by 1996, it would be required to take title to the waste from the private producer and be responsible for disposal and for all damages incurred by the waste's producer resulting from the state not timely taking possession of the waste.

The parties agreed that the federal government has the authority under the Commerce Clause to regulate the disposal of radioactive waste. The state of New York objected, however, to the manner of regulation. It asserted that Congress may regulate the private producers of the waste—individuals—but not the states. The Supreme Court agreed. The first two incentives were upheld as consonant with Congress's power under the Commerce and Spending Clauses. The Court reaffirmed the long-held rule that the federal government can attach conditions to the receipt of federal funds. Requiring a state to regulate in a particular manner is a permissible condition. Accordingly, it was lawful for the federal government to withhold federal highway funds from states that refused to adopt maximum-speed or minimum-drinking-age laws. It is also permissible, when Congress has the power to regulate a private activity directly, to give the states a choice to regulate the activity according to federal standards or have their laws preempted by federal laws. The Court decided, however, that these incentives possessed a characteristic not present in the third: state freedom of choice.

By either of these two methods, as by any other permissible method of encouraging a state to conform to federal policy choices, the residents of the state retain the ultimate decision as to whether or not the state will comply. If a state's citizens view federal policy as sufficiently contrary to local interests, they may elect to decline a federal grant. If state residents would prefer their government to devote its attention and resources to problems other than those deemed important by Congress, they may choose to have the federal government rather than the state bear the expense of a federally mandated regulatory program.

But the third provision, the take-title provision, is different. It directs that states either regulate as directed or take title to privately owned waste. There is no true choice, because Congress cannot compel either. It does not have the authority to order a state to enact laws, nor does it have the authority to require a state to subsidize a private business. Congress, therefore, "has crossed the line distinguishing encouragement from coercion," because the take-title provision amounts to a commandeering of state legislative power. "Whether one views the take title provision as lying outside Congress' enumerated powers, or as infringing upon the core of state sovereignty reserved by the Tenth Amendment, the provision is inconsistent with the federal structure of our Government established by the Constitution."

Accordingly, pursuant to *Garcia,* the federal government may regulate state activity, but *New York* prohibits Congress from directly compelling a state to regulate. Financial incentives are acceptable, and this is the method Congress uses to impose federal policy on the states. Hence, the federal government may withhold funds from states that do not regulate radioactive wastes, but it cannot require them to regulate the area. Some commentators have criticized this as a distinction without a difference.

Although it prohibited the federal government from mandating state regulation, the Court has softened the effect of *Garcia* by narrowly construing statutes that regulate states. In *Gregory v. Ashcroft,*[43] the Court refused to subject state judges to the federal Age Discrimination in Employment Act (ADEA), because they are "policymaking" officials. The Court concluded that Congress must clearly express an intent to include policymaking officials within the grasp of such a law. Because Congress had not, the officials were exempt. However, the impact of the decision is limited because the Court did not go so far as to say that Congress may not regulate state policymakers.

Then, in 1999, the Supreme Court reversed itself again, at least in part, in several decisions. First, in *Seminole Tribe of Florida v. Florida* (1996),[44] the Court held that states may not be involuntarily sued (by citizens) in federal court. Then, in *Alden v. Maine,*[45] the Court held that states must consent to be sued in their own courts. However, the Court's rationale did not center on the Tenth Amendment. Instead, the Court applied the Eleventh Amendment, which ends as follows:

> The Judicial power of the United States shall not be construed to extend to any suit in law or equity, commenced or prosecuted against one of the United States by Citizens of another State, or by Citizens or Subjects of any Foreign States.

This amendment was proposed and ratified in record time to counter the Supreme Court's decision in *Chisholm v. Georgia* (1793), which held that states may be held liable in federal courts. The language of the Eleventh Amendment applies the immunity only to citizens and subjects. Therefore, the federal government may sue a state and states may sue one another. Interestingly, the Eleventh Amendment's plain text does not bar citizens from suing their own states. Regardless, the Supreme Court rejected the possibility that a citizen may sue his or her own state in the 1890 case *Hans v. Louisiana.*

Also, the Court held in *Alden* that Eleventh Amendment immunity shields only states, not local forms of government. Further, the Court recognized that the Fourteenth Amendment carved civil rights cases out from immunity and that with appropriate implementation legislation, a state may be sued in federal court.

The Court extended state immunity from liability under the federal ADEA in *Kimel v. Florida Board of Regents*[46] (2000) and to the federal Americans with Disabilities Act in *Board of Trustees of University of Alabama v. Garrett* (2001).[47]

In 2003, however, the Court refused to extend state immunity to actions brought under the federal Family and Medical Leave Act in *Nevada Department of Human Resources v. Hibb*[48] because gender discrimination claims are subject to greater scrutiny than are either disabilities or age claims.

7.5 COMPACTS AND INTERSTATE COMITY

Article I, Section 10, clause 1, prohibits states from entering into treaties, alliances, or confederations with foreign nations. Clause 3 of this section further states, "[n]o State shall, without the Consent of Congress . . . enter into any Agreement or Compact with another State, or with a foreign Power."

Through these provisions, the framers granted exclusive federal jurisdiction in making treaties and a strong federal role in interstate compacts and agreements. There is no significant difference between a compact and an agreement, except that the former appears to refer to written agreements and the latter to oral agreements.

The purpose of requiring congressional approval of compacts is to protect the integrity of the nation. Congress, which will be mindful of concerns of national unity and cooperation, must consent to agreements between states that may change the character of the nation. Not all agreements or cooperative efforts between states need federal approval. Only those agreements that tend to change the power relationships of the states, threaten the integrity of the Union, or diminish the power of the federal government are subject to the consent clause. For example, an interstate cooperative effort to combat drug trafficking does not require congressional approval. However, an agreement between neighboring states to alter their borders or to combine into one state would.

full faith and credit
A reference to the requirement of Article IV of the Constitution that each state give "full faith and credit" to the "public acts, records, and judicial proceedings" of every other state. This means that a state's judicial acts must be given the same effect by the courts of all other states as they receive at home.

Cooperation, or *comity,* between the states is constitutionally mandated in some circumstances. Article IV, Section 1, demands that each state give its sister states' laws, records, and judicial proceedings **full faith and credit.** This means, with a few exceptions, that a judgment entered in one state can be enforced in another state. For example, suppose Nazarene obtains a judgment for $50,000 against Ronald in a Nebraska state court. Ronald moves to Montana immediately following the conclusion of the litigation. Nazarene is empowered under the Full Faith and Credit Clause to register her judgment in Montana and enforce it there, even though it was rendered in Nebraska. In some circumstances, the law of one state must be applied in the courts of another state. Assume that Nazarene and Ronald enter into a contract in Wyoming. That contract provides that all disputes arising under it shall be governed by the law of Wyoming, regardless of where litigated. So the law of Wyoming would apply, even if the case is filed in Nebraska. These are only a few examples of the application of the Full Faith and Credit Clause.

The interstate rendition clause, found in Article IV, Section 2, clause 2, provides that

> [a] Person charged in any State with Treason, Felony, or other Crime, who shall flee from Justice, and be found in another State, shall on demand of the executive Authority of the State from which he fled, be delivered up, to be removed to the State having Jurisdiction of the Crime.

In spite of the clause's plain language, until 1987 it was interpreted as not creating a binding obligation on state officials to extradite fugitives. However, the Supreme Court reexamined the clause in *Puerto Rico v. Branstad*[49] and held that the clause creates a mandatory duty to extradite fugitives properly demanded. A state may not examine the nature of the pending charges or make an independent determination of whether the fugitive will be treated fairly. The state may only satisfy itself that the extradition documents are proper, that the individual sought has been charged with a crime, and that the detainee is the person charged. If these are answered in the affirmative, then the state must extradite the fugitive to the demanding state. Failure or refusal to extradite is reviewable, and a federal court may order the extradition. A state may delay extradition if it is about to charge and try the sought individual with a crime and in other special circumstances.

Finally, the Privileges and Immunities Clause of Article IV also promotes interstate comity. See the discussion of this clause earlier in this chapter.

7.6 GUARANTEE AND MILITIA CLAUSES

The guarantee clause, Article IV, Section 4, states:

> The United States shall guarantee to every State in this Union a Republican Form of Government, and shall protect each of them against Invasion; and on Application of the Legislature, or of the Executive (when the Legislature cannot be convened) against domestic Violence.

This clause has not been invoked very often, and there are few cases defining its precise meaning. Congress relied on the guarantee clause to support its reconstruction efforts in the South following the Civil War. For example, Congress required the southern states to enact new constitutions respecting a Republican form of government. Similarly, Congress has reviewed the constitutions of territories that have applied for statehood to determine whether they should be admitted into the Union. Although it has never happened, Congress could nullify any state attempt to change to a non-Republican form of government.

A precise definition of "republican form of government" has not been rendered. Generally, it refers to a form of government that respects individual and property rights. Certainly, the electoral process is also an element of a Republican form of government. Therefore, it would not be Republican for a state to establish a government in which officials obtain their positions through inheritance.

The requirement of a Republican form of government does not mean that a state must establish a governmental structure identical to that of the United States. The states are generally free to design their governments in any manner they wish, so long as they remain Republican in nature. For example, a state may choose to have a unicameral legislature, as Nebraska has, even though the United States has chosen the bicameral model. Generally, Congress's decisions under the guarantee clause are nonjusticiable political questions. As such, federal courts will not interfere with Congress when it acts under the guarantee clause.

The guarantee clause also empowers the United States to protect the states from invasions and domestic violence. Even though the clause appears to limit federal intervention to quell domestic violence to occasions when state authorities have requested assistance, presidents have on many occasions, pursuant to congressional authorization, acted without such a request.[50]

Article I, Section 8, delegates to Congress the authority to provide for the national defense, establish a military, regulate the armed forces, and declare war. Congress also possesses power over the state militias. Article I, Section 8, clause 15, extends to Congress the power to call "forth the militia to execute the Laws of the Union, suppress Insurrections and repel Invasions." The Supreme Court upheld a statute that delegated the power to call state militias into national service without the consent of state officials.[51] The president may call on state militias to serve abroad, as well as domestically. Clause 16 of the same section gives Congress the power to organize, arm, and discipline the state militias (National Guard). However, the states retain the power to appoint officers and train the militias under the rules established by Congress. The power of the states to maintain militias under the original Constitution was questionable. Article I, Section 10, clause 3, states, "[n]o State shall, without the Consent of Congress . . . keep Troops, or Ships of War in time of Peace." However, the Second Amendment provides that the power of the states to maintain well-regulated militias shall not be infringed.

7.7 STATE CONSTITUTIONALISM AND THE NEW FEDERALISM

Every state has its own constitution. Like the federal Constitution, state constitutions contain declarations or bills of individual rights. In fact, many clauses in state bills of rights are worded identically, or nearly so, to the federal Constitution.

The state bills of rights were the foundation of civil rights, especially in criminal cases, for the first 150 years of the nation because the federal Bill of Rights was construed as limiting the power of the federal government only.* Thus, the Fourth Amendment's prohibition of unreasonable searches and seizures, the Eighth Amendment's prohibition of cruel and unusual punishments, and the Fifth Amendment's privilege against self-incrimination did not apply in state criminal proceedings.

This has changed. During the Warren Court era, almost the entire Bill of Rights was incorporated (See chapter 8). A right is incorporated, through the Fourteenth Amendment's Due Process Clause, if it is "fundamental and essential to an ordered liberty." As one of the post–Civil War amendments, the Fourteenth Amendment was written with the intention of limiting the states. Although it did not happen for many years after adoption, the Supreme Court eventually concluded that the Fourteenth Amendment incorporated all the rights that are fundamental to an ordered liberty. Today, only the Seventh Amendment's right to a jury trial in civil cases, the Fifth Amendment's right to grand jury indictment, and the Eighth Amendment's right to reasonable bail have not been incorporated. Therefore, federal constitutional law is now a significant factor in all criminal proceedings.

Note that there was a gap in time between the ratification of the Fourteenth Amendment (1868) and the Court's recognition of its incorporation of fundamental rights (1960s) through the **selective incorporation doctrine.** During that period, state constitutional law played a larger role in protecting civil liberties. For example, the Illinois Supreme Court ruled in 1882 that racial segregation was illegal.[52] The U.S. Supreme Court did not reach this conclusion until 1954.[53] Once it occurred, the effect of incorporation was the displacement of state constitutional law for many years. In recent years, however, there has been a rebirth in state constitutional law. This is often referred to as the *New Federalism.* One of the first and most dramatic statements of independent constitutionalism in recent decades was California Supreme Court's declaration that capital punishment is cruel and unusual under the California Constitution.[54] Then, in 1977, Justice William J. Brennan Jr. authored a law school journal article wherein he encouraged states to expand civil liberties through their own constitutions.[55]

State constitutional law may not decrease or limit federally secured rights, but a state may extend civil rights beyond what the federal Constitution secures. In some cases, this may occur expressly. For example, both Florida and Alaska constitutions expressly protect privacy, whereas the federal Constitution does not. Rather, a national right to privacy was only recently declared by the Supreme Court (as a *penumbra* or implied protection), and it is somewhat controversial because of the absence of express language in the Constitution establishing the right. The Washington state constitution protects "private affairs," which has been interpreted more broadly than *privacy* under the Fourth Amendment. Many states provide for education through their constitutions, although the federal Constitution does not contain a right to education. In addition to protecting freedom of religion, as does the First Amendment of the federal Constitution, Georgia's constitution protects freedom of "conscience."[56]

In some instances, a state constitution may expressly provide a protection that is implicit in the federal Constitution. For example, Florida's bill of rights protects "expression," whereas the national Constitution protects "speech." As you will learn later, however, the term *speech* has been interpreted as meaning "expression."

Cyber Constitution
State Constitutions
Links to the constitutions of each of the states can be found at www.findlaw.com/11stategov/indexconst.html

selective incorporation doctrine
Under the Due Process Clause of the Fourteenth Amendment, those rights in the federal Bill of Rights that are fundamental and necessary to an ordered liberty are applied against the states. Other incorporation theories exist.

---

*See the discussion of state and national powers compared in Chapter 2 for more on this subject.

STATE CONSTITUTIONALISM

What follows are a few examples of differences between state constitutions and the U.S Constitution. The list is not exhaustive; the particular states and rights chosen are intended only as illustrations.

Rights Expressed in State Constitutions but Not in the Federal Constitution

- EDUCATION—Texas (art. 7); Utah (art. X, § 1)
- VICTIM RIGHTS—Arizona (art. 2, § 2.1)
- RIGHT OF REVOLUTION—New Hampshire (art. I, § 10)
- WATER RIGHTS—Utah (art. XVII, § 1)
- CARE FOR THE NEEDY—New York (art. XVII, § 1)
- FREEDOM FROM PRIVATE DISCRIMINATION BASED UPON GENDER, RACE, ETHNICITY, CULTURE, POLITICAL BELIEFS, AND RELIGION—Montana (art. II, § 4)

Rights Implicitly Secured by the Federal Constitution and Expressly Protected by State Constitutions

- EXPRESSION (other than speech)—Implicitly protected by U.S. Constitution's First Amendment Free Speech Clause; expressly protected by Florida's constitution (art. I, § 4)
- PRIVACY—Implicitly protected by several amendments to the U.S. Constitution, including the Fourth, Fifth, Ninth, and Fourteenth; expressly protected by Florida (art. I, § 23) and Alaska (art. I, § 22).

Rights Expressed in Both State and Federal Constitutions but Interpreted More Broadly Under State Law,

- FREEDOM FROM UNREASONABLE SEARCHES AND SEIZURES—Pennsylvania rejected the U.S. Supreme Court's *Leon* (good faith exception to warrant requirement) decision. *Commonwealth v. Edmunds*, 586 A.2d 887 (Pa. 1991).
- FREEDOM FROM UNREASONABLE SEARCHES AND SEIZURES—Pennsylvania rejected the Supreme. Court's standing requirements for defendants in possession cases. *Commonwealth v. Sell*, 470 A.2d 457 (Pa. 1983).
- FREEDOM FROM SELF-INCRIMINATION—Hawaii's courts have interpreted Hawaii's counterpart clause as providing greater protection to the accused. *Hawaii v. Bowe*, 881 P.2d 538 (Haw. 1994).

FIGURE 7-4
Comparison of state constitutions with the federal Constitution

Also, many state constitutions protect individuals from one another. For example, the Illinois Free Speech Clause prohibits both public and private actors from encroaching upon an individual's freedom of expression; the federal Constitution restricts only government actors. Similarly, the Montana constitution's equal rights amendment prohibits gender-based discrimination by the state, persons, and corporations.

In other instances, the language of a state constitution may not expressly provide greater protection than the federal Constitution. Regardless, the courts of the state may interpret it as providing greater individual rights. This may happen even if the state constitutional provision uses language identical to its federal counterpart. Historically, this has not been so, however. Many state courts, if not most, interpreted their constitutional provisions as paralleling counterpart federal constitutional provisions. In rare cases, this is required by the state constitution.

Increasingly, however, this is not occurring. During the past three decades, commentators, judges, and attorneys have exhibited a renewed interest in state constitutional law. State constitutions are now viewed as an independent source of individual liberties. See Figure 7-4 for a comparison between selected state constitutions and the federal Constitution.

7.7(a) Approaches to Dual Constitutionalism

One scholar (John Shaw) has identified three approaches (models) to the relationship between federal and state constitutionalism (dual constitutionalism): **primacy, interstitial,** and **dual sovereignty.**[57]

The primacy approach treats state constitutions as the primary source of individuals' rights, with the federal Constitution acting as a backup or safety net. Under this

primacy
An approach to constitutional interpretation that requires state judges to apply their state's constitution before turning to the federal Constitution.

interstitial
An approach to constitutional interpretation that requires state judges to apply the federal Constitution before turning to their state's constitution.

dual sovereignty
An approach to constitutional interpretation that requires state judges to apply both federal and state constitutions simultaneously.

theory, courts have an obligation to examine claims under the state constitution before turning to the federal Constitution. At least three states (New Hampshire, Oregon, and Maine) have adopted this approach.

An interstitial approach, in contrast, views the federal Constitution as the fundamental source of individual rights, with the state constitutions as supplements. Using such an approach, courts look first to the federal Constitution and then to the appropriate state constitution. This is the most common approach.

The third approach, dual sovereignty, has been adopted by at least one state (Vermont). Under this approach, the federal and state constitutions are examined simultaneously. Then, rather than basing its decision on one or the other, a reviewing court will, if possible, decide the case using both, providing two independent sources to support its decision.

Bear in mind that most states have not identified which approach they follow. Nevertheless, through a reading of state constitutional decisions, one can often glean which of those models is most closely followed.

The primacy approach is growing in popularity, and there are now a number of instances in which state courts have determined that their constitutions protect criminal defendants to a greater extent than does the national constitution. Between 1977 and 1986, there were two hundred state constitutional decisions affording greater individual liberties than the federal Constitution. Only two years later, there were four hundred such decisions.[58] The Supreme Court of Pennsylvania has strongly asserted that its state's constitution has its own meaning, separate and independent from the federal Constitution. In a 1991 case, that Court stated:

> [T]he decisions of the [U.S. Supreme] Court are not, and should not be, dispositive of questions regarding rights guaranteed by counter-part provisions of State Law. Accordingly, such decisions are not mechanically applicable to state law issues, and state court judges and members of the bar seriously err if they so treat them. Rather, state court judges, and also practitioners, do well to scrutinize constitutional decisions by federal courts, for only if they are found to be logically persuasive and well-reasoned, paying due regard to precedent and the policies underlying specific constitutional guarantees, may they properly claim persuasive weight as guide posts when interpreting counter-part state guarantees.[59]

The California courts have taken a similar approach. Even if a provision's interpretation has paralleled that of national law, the courts favor citing state law over federal law. Whether a state court depends upon state or federal law when defining a right determines what court has the final word on the subject. If a right is founded upon federal law, the Supreme Court of the United States is the final arbiter. If a right is founded upon state law, the highest court of the state is the final arbiter—again assuming that no federal right is encroached upon by the state decision. For example, if a state court were to find that a fetus has a right to life in every instance, the decision would be void as violative of the federally secured right to privacy held by the mothers in some circumstances.

If a state court relies upon federal law when defining a right, the possibility of reversal by a federal court, usually the Supreme Court, exists. This is what occurred in California concerning the use of peyote, a drug made from cactus, by Native Americans. The Supreme Court of California decided in 1965 that the use of peyote by Native Americans during religious ceremonies was protected by the U.S. Constitution's First Amendment Free Exercise Clause.[60] That decision was not disturbed until 1990, when the Supreme Court of the United States decided that regulation of peyote as a drug was a reasonable burden upon the First Amendment[61] and, therefore, reversed the 1965 California decision. Although the defendant asserted both federal and state free exercise guarantees, the California Supreme Court relied entirely upon federal law in making its decision.

United States v. Leon
468 U.S. 897 (1984)

[Facially valid warrants were issued by a state judge. The searches conducted under the warrants produced narcotics and other evidence of narcotics violations.]

The respondents . . . filed motions to suppress the evidence seized pursuant to the warrant. The District Court held an evidentiary hearing and, while recognizing that the case was a close one, . . . granted the motions to suppress in part. It concluded that the affidavit was insufficient to establish probable cause. . . . In response to a request from the Government, the court made clear that Officer Rombach had acted in good faith. [This decision was affirmed on appeal before the Court of Appeals.]

The Government's petition for certiorari expressly declined to seek review of the lower courts' determinations that the search warrant was unsupported by probable cause and presented only the question "[w]hether the Fourth Amendment exclusionary rule should be modified so as not to bar the admission of evidence seized in reasonable, good-faith reliance on a search warrant that is subsequently held to be defective." . . .

[T]he exclusionary rule is designed to deter police misconduct rather than to punish the errors of judges and magistrates.

If exclusion of evidence obtained pursuant to a subsequently invalidated warrant is to have any deterrent effect, therefore, it must alter the behavior of the individual law enforcement officers or the policies of their departments. One could argue that applying the exclusionary rule in cases where the police failed to demonstrate probable cause in the warrant application deters future inadequate presentations or "magistrate shopping" and thus promotes the ends of the Fourth Amendment. Suppressing evidence obtained pursuant to a technically defective warrant supported by probable cause also might encourage officers to scrutinize more closely the form of the warrant and to point out suspected judicial errors. We find such arguments speculative and conclude that suppression of evidence obtained pursuant to a warrant should be ordered only on a case-by-case basis and only in those unusual cases in which exclusion will further the purposes of the exclusionary rule.

We conclude that the marginal or nonexistent benefits produced by suppressing evidence obtained in objectively reasonable reliance on a subsequently invalidated search warrant cannot justify the substantial costs of exclusion. We do not suggest, however, that exclusion is always inappropriate in cases where an officer has obtained a warrant and abided by its terms. . . . [A]n officer's reliance on the magistrate's probable-cause determination and on the technical sufficiency of the warrant he issues must be objectively reasonable . . . and it is clear that in some circumstances the officer will have no reasonable grounds for believing that the warrant was properly issued.

In many cases, courts must choose between competing rights. It is possible for a state to increase a right through its general police power, tipping the balance when weighing the competing rights. For example, the U.S. Supreme Court decided that individuals do not possess a First Amendment right to distribute handbills in privately owned shopping malls in *Lloyd Corp., Ltd. v. Tanner*, 407 U.S. 551 (1972). In that case, it recognized the Fourteenth Amendment property rights of mall owners to control their property. However, the Court reached the opposite conclusion when it reviewed the same facts, but within the context of a state constitution that extended free speech rights to the distribution of materials at privately owned malls that are open to the public in *Pruneyard Shopping Center v. Robins*, 447 U.S. 74 (1980). The extent to which a state constitutional provision extends a right to one against a federally secured right by another is important, as is the nature of the right that is diminished. The shopping center owner's rights in *Pruneyard* were not significantly affected; that is, they did not lose any value, nor was there reason to believe that other negative consequences, such as a loss of security, would result. If the deprivation had been greater, or if a more fundamental right was implicated, the outcome may have been different.

Some state courts have established tests to determine whether their state constitutions are parallel to, or more expansive than, the federal Constitution in securing individual liberties. The Supreme Court of Washington identified six factors to be taken into consideration:

1. Language of the state constitutional text,
2. Differences between the state and federal texts,

Cyber Constitution
New Federalism in Criminal Procedure
For an interesting empirical study of state constitutionalism in criminal procedure, including an appendix with examples of when states extend rights beyond what the U.S. Constitution protects, see David C. Brody, "Criminal Procedure Under State Law: An Empirical Examination of Selective New Federalism," *The Justice System Journal*, Vol. 23 (1), p. 75 (2002), available at www.ncsconline.org/WC/Publications/KIS_PreCriJSJV23No1.pdf.

3. Constitutional history,
4. Preexisting state law,
5. Structural differences between Washington state and the United States, and
6. Local concerns.[62]

Commonwealth v. Edmunds
526 Pa. 374 (1991)

[The defendant was convicted in the Court of Common Pleas, Criminal Division, of possession of marijuana and related offenses, and the defendant appealed. The Superior Court affirmed the conviction.]

The issue presented to this court is whether Pennsylvania should adopt the "good faith" exception to the exclusionary rule as articulated by the United States Supreme Court in the case of *United States v. Leon*, 468 U.S. 897, 104 S. Ct. 3405, 82 L. Ed. 2d 677 (1984). We conclude that a "good faith" exception to the exclusionary rule would frustrate the guarantees embodied in Article I, section 8, of the Pennsylvania Constitution. Accordingly, the decision of the Superior Court is reversed. . . .

The trial court held that the search warrant failed to establish probable cause that the marijuana would be at the location to be searched on the date it was issued. The trial court found that the warrant failed to set forth with specificity the date upon which the anonymous informants observed the marijuana. . . . However, the trial court went on to deny the defendant's motion to suppress the marijuana. Applying the rationale of *Leon*, the trial court looked beyond the four corners of the affidavit, in order to establish that the officers executing the warrant acted in "good faith" in relying upon the warrant to conduct the search. . . .

We must now determine whether the good-faith exception to the exclusionary rule is properly part of the jurisprudence of this Commonwealth, by virtue of Article 1, Section 8 of the Pennsylvania Constitution. In concluding that it is not, we set forth a methodology to be followed in analyzing future state constitutional issues which arise under our own Constitution. . . .

This Court has long emphasized that, in interpreting a provision of the Pennsylvania Constitution, we are not bound by the decisions of the United States Supreme Court which interpret similar (yet distinct) federal constitutional provisions. . . . [T]he federal constitution establishes certain minimum levels which are "equally applicable to the [analogous] state constitutional provision." . . . However, each state has the power to provide broader standards, and go beyond the minimum floor which is established by the federal Constitution. . . .

Here in Pennsylvania, we have stated with increasing frequency that it is both important and necessary that we undertake an independent analysis of the Pennsylvania Constitution, each time a provision of that fundamental document is implicated. . . .

The recent focus on the "New Federalism" has emphasized the importance of state constitutions with respect to individual rights and criminal procedure. As such, we find it important to set forth certain factors to be briefed and analyzed by litigants in each case hereafter implicating a provision of the Pennsylvania constitution. The decision of the United States Supreme Court in *Michigan v. Long*, 463 U.S. 1032, 103 S. Ct. 3469, 77 L. Ed. 2d 1201 (1983), now requires us to make a "plain statement" of the adequate and independent state grounds upon which we rely, in order to avoid any doubt that we have rested our decision squarely upon Pennsylvania jurisprudence. Accordingly, as a general rule it is important that litigants brief and analyze at least the following four factors:

1. text of the Pennsylvania constitutional provision;
2. history of the provision, including Pennsylvania case-law;
3. related case-law from other states;
4. policy considerations, including unique issues of state and local concern, and applicability within modern Pennsylvania jurisprudence.

Depending upon the particular issue presented, an examination of related federal precedent may be useful as part of the state constitutional analysis, not as binding authority, but as one form of guidance. . . . Utilizing the above four factors, and having reviewed *Leon*, we conclude that a "good-faith" exception to the exclusionary rule would frustrate the guarantees embodied in Article I, section 8 of our Commonwealth's Constitution. . . .

The United States Supreme Court in *Leon* made clear that, in its view, the sole purpose for the exclusionary rule under the 4th Amendment [to the Constitution of the United States] was to deter police misconduct. . . . The *Leon* majority also made clear that, under the Federal Constitution, the exclusionary rule operated as "a judicially created remedy designed to safeguard Fourth Amendment rights generally through its deterrent effect, rather than a personal constitutional right of the party aggrieved. . . ."

[T]he exclusionary rule in Pennsylvania has consistently served to bolster the twin aims of Article 1, section 8, to wit, the safeguarding of privacy and the fundamental requirement that warrants shall only be issued upon probable cause. . . .

The linch-pin that has been developed to determine whether it is appropriate to issue a search warrant is the test of probable cause. . . . It is designed to protect us from unwarranted and even vindictive incursions upon our privacy. It insulates from dictatorial and tyrannical rule by the state, and preserves the concept of democracy that assures the freedom of citizens. This concept is second to none in its importance in delineating the dignity of the individual living in a free society. . . .

Whether the United States Supreme Court has determined that the exclusionary rule does not advance the 4th Amendment purpose of deterring police conduct is irrelevant. Indeed, we disagree with the Court's suggestion in *Leon* that we in Pennsylvania have been employing the exclusionary rule all these years to deter police corruption. We flatly reject this notion. . . . What is significant, however, is that our Constitution has historically been interpreted to incorporate a strong right to privacy, and an equally strong adherence to the requirement of probable cause under Article 1, section 8. Citizens in this Commonwealth possess such rights, even where a police officer in "good faith" carrying out his or her duties inadvertently invades the privacy or circumvents the strictures of probable cause. To adopt a "good faith" exception to the exclusionary rule, we believe, would virtually emasculate those clear safeguards which have been carefully developed under the Pennsylvania Constitution over the past 200 years. . . .

The two case excerpts accompanying this section concern the *exclusionary rule,* a judicially created rule that requires the exclusion of evidence that was illegally obtained by the government from criminal trials. For example, if the police search a home without probable cause or a warrant, cocaine found in the home may not be used to convict the homeowner of possession of a controlled substance. The Constitution does not expressly provide for the exclusionary rule; rather, the Supreme Court has found it to be implicit in several amendments (e.g., the Fourth Amendment's protection from unreasonable searches and seizures). Several exceptions to the exclusionary rule have been made by the Court since it first announced the rule's existence. Some state courts have refused to adopt these exceptions into their own jurisprudence. This is the subject of the *Leon* and *Edmunds* cases, one issued by the Supreme Court of the United States, wherein it recognized a good-faith exception to the exclusionary rule, and the other by the Supreme Court of Pennsylvania, expressly rejecting the good-faith exception in state prosecutions. As another example, several states (including California, Hawaii, and Pennsylvania) have not followed the Supreme Court's lead in allowing statements made in violation of *Miranda* to be used by the prosecution in impeachment of a defendant.[63]

State constitutionalism has reached beyond criminal law. Several states guarantee a right to primary and secondary education through their constitutions. In New York, the state owes a duty to provide shelters to homeless families under a constitutional provision that requires the legislature to provide for the "[a]id, care, and support of the needy."[64] Even though the Supreme Court has held that indigent women have no right to have abortions funded by the federal government, the New Jersey Supreme Court has held otherwise concerning state funds.[65] These are but a few of the many instances in which a right has received greater protection under state law than under federal law.[66]

When a state court decides a case on **adequate and independent state grounds,** federal judicial review of any federal issues is unnecessary. Of course, the state law basis for the decision must be consistent with the U.S. Constitution for this rule to apply. State law is adequate in these cases if it logically resolves the issue without the support of federal constitutional law. The more troubling issue concerns the second prong, independence. Often, the issue is whether a state court decided a case upon state or federal constitutional principles. It is common for a state court to cite both state and federal constitutional provisions in support of a decision. In such cases, whether the state court relied upon federal or state caselaw, state or federal constitutional history, and the like must be considered. Generally, it must be plain that a decision is made upon state grounds to avoid review of federal legal issues.

adequate and independent state grounds doctrine Federal judicial review of a state decision in a case that includes both state and federal claims will not occur if the lower court's decision rested upon adequate and independent state law.

7.8 MODERN CHALLENGES

Federalism is evolutionary. As the United States changes, so do expectations for the United States and for the states. Today, many more activities, commercial and other, are directly interstate or international in character or indirectly affect interstate commerce, international commerce, and even international relations. This has contributed to the rise in federal authority over matters that were once the province of the states. On the other hand, notions of state sovereignty and the desire to have a more local, responsive, personal government bolster support for states' rights. There are many contemporary federalism issues. Immigration, waste disposal and storage, environment, law enforcement, and health care are examples of policy areas where thorny federalism issues will be debated in the future.

7.9 SUMMARY

Few disagree that the framers were successful in constructing a stronger national government through the Constitution. The contemporary issue is whether the federal government has become too large and powerful.

The states are empowered to regulate intrastate commerce, and the federal government is empowered to regulate interstate commerce. In 1789, intrastate and interstate commerce did not meet as often as they do in the contemporary highly mobile and technologically advanced world. The effect is that today, nearly all commerce has an interstate, if not international, dimension. Because state laws that burden, discriminate, or otherwise interfere with interstate commerce are invalid (via Dormant Commerce Clause theories), as well as those that conflict with federal law (via preemption), the authority of the state has greatly diminished. This remains controversial today.

Even more controversial, however, is the status of intergovernmental immunity. Today, the federal government has the authority to regulate the states. For example, state employees are entitled to the protections of federal minimum wage and maximum hours, occupational safety, and discrimination laws. A similar state law does not apply to federal employees working within the state.

A few policy areas remain within the jurisdiction of the states—the police powers, for example. In addition, the preservation of civil liberties by state constitutions, beyond that secured by the federal Constitution, has received considerable attention by state courts in recent years.

REVIEW QUESTIONS

1. Define preemption and identify its three forms.
2. Explain the Dormant Commerce Clause.
3. Discuss the significance of *Garcia v. San Antonio Metropolitan Transit Authority* to state–federal relations.
4. What role does Congress play in the creation of interstate compacts, if any?
5. What does the Full Faith and Credit Clause require of the states?
6. What does the interstate rendition clause require of the states?
7. Does Congress possess the authority to regulate state militias?
8. To what does the term *New Federalism* refer?

ASSIGNMENTS: CONSTITUTIONAL LAW IN ACTION

The Constitution in Your Community

You work for the local office of the public defender. You have a client, Ima Pothead, who has been charged with possession of illegal drugs. The police discovered the drugs in his home during the execution of a search warrant. The warrant was later invalidated by the presiding judge. The judge also held that the police executed the warrant in good faith. The judge scheduled a hearing for two weeks later on the question whether the drugs should be excluded from trial. Your charges against Ima Pothead will likely be dismissed if the seized drugs are excluded. You have been asked to prepare a memorandum (1–3 pages) on the issue. You will need to consider your state's approach to dual constitutionalism. Does your state constitution specifically address the issue? If so, how? If not, how has your state judiciary approached search and seizure questions? Does your state interpret its constitution identically to how the U.S. Constitution has been interpreted or independently? If independent, cite an example of a differing interpretation and an example where your state courts have interpreted the state constitution identically, even though not required to do so.

Going Federal

The U.S. Congress recently passed, and the president signed, the following law:

Practice of Law: USBA

> *Section One:* Admission, Regulation, Discipline The admission, regulation, and discipline of persons who render legal advice; appear on behalf of others in local, state, and federal courts; and otherwise act for another in legal contexts shall be regulated by the United States.
>
> *Section Two:* USBA; director There shall be created an executive agency known as the United States Bar Agency (USBA). The Secretary of Commerce of the United States shall appoint a director who shall be the executive officer of the USBA. The director shall serve for four years and may be removed for cause by the Secretary of Commerce. The director shall have the authority to make all needful rules for implementing these provisions in a manner prescribed by other federal law.
>
> *Preemption* All state laws inconsistent with these provisions are preempted and invalid.

You work for the attorney general of your state. The attorney general is concerned about the preemption and you have been directed to prepare a memorandum (1–3 pages) discussing the constitutionality (federalism question) of this statute.

Moot Court

Same-sex marriage is a hot button political and legal topic. Historically, marriage has been a policy area that belonged to the states. With the exception of indirect regulation (e.g., tax differences between individuals and married couples), the federal government left marriage to the states. That changed in 1996. The Full Faith and Credit Clause requires states to respect each other's laws and court judgments. Congress is delegated the authority to "prescribe the Manner in which such Acts, Records and Proceedings shall be proved, and the Effect thereof." Concerned that the Full Faith and Credit Clause would require all states to recognize same-sex marriages if one state permitted them, Congress enacted the Defense of Marriage Act in 1996. Commonly known as DOMA, the law expressly releases the states from having to recognize same-sex marriages of other states. DOMA was found by a federal trial court to violate both the Tenth Amendment and the Equal Protection Clause (see *Letourneau v. Office of Personnel Management*, Summary Judgment, July 8, 2010, U.S. District Court for the District of Massachusetts, Civil Action No. 09-10309-JLT). At the time of publication of this text, an appeal had been filed but had not been decided. Working in teams of two, prepare your own moot court. The first team should prepare a five-minute oral argument that DOMA violates the Tenth Amendment, and the second team will be responsible for preparing a five-minute oral argument defending DOMA. For purposes of this assignment, ignore the equal protection issue. You will learn more about individual rights later in this book!

NOTES

1. *Dennis v. United States,* 341 U.S. 494, 555 (1951) (concurring opinion).
2. Federalist No. 51.
3. Essay published in the *New York Journal* on October 18, 1787, taken from the creation of the constitution 109–111. Opposing viewpoints series (Green Haven Press 1995)
4. *Cipollone v. Liggett Group, Inc.,* 505 U.S. 504 (1992).
5. For an example when preemption was not complete, see *Mid-Con Freight Systems, Inc. v. Michigan Public Service Comm'n,* 545 U.S. 440 (2005).
6. *Gade v. National Solid Wastes Management Ass'n,* 505 U.S. 88 (1992).
7. 530 U.S. 363 (2000).
8. 557 U.S. __ (2009).
9. *Bruesewitz v. Wyeth, Williamson v. Mazda, Pliva v. Mensing,* and *Chamber of Commerce v. Whiting.*
10. 53 U.S. 299 (1851).
11. *United Food & Commercial Workers Union v. Brown Group,* 116 S. Ct. 1529 (1996); *Oregon Waste Systems, Inc. v. Department of Environmental Quality,* 114 S. Ct. 1345 (1995).
12. 553 U.S. 328 (2008).
13. *Baldwin v. G.A.F. Seelig, Inc.,* 294 U.S. 511 (1935).
14. *Hughes v. Oklahoma,* 441 U.S. 322 (1979).
15. 544 U.S. 460.
16. 458 U.S. 941 (1982).
17. 437 U.S. 617 (1978).
18. 114 S. Ct. 1677 (1994).
19. 424 U.S. 366 (1976).
20. 458 U.S. 941 (1982).
21. *Maine v. Taylor,* 477 U.S. 131 (1986).
22. *Southern Pacific Co. v. Arizona,* 325 U.S. 761 (1945).
23. *Bibb v. Navajo Freight Lines, Inc.,* 359 U.S. 520 (1959).
24. *Kassel v. Consolidated Freightways Corp.,* 450 U.S. 622 (1981).
25. *Minnesota v. Clover Leaf Creamery Co.,* 449 U.S. 456 (1981).
26. *Brown-Forman Distillers Corp. v. New York State Liquor Authority,* 476 U.S. 573 (1986).
27. *South Dakota v. Dole,* 483 U.S. 203 (1987).
28. *Oregon Waste Systems, Inc. v. Department of Environmental Quality,* 511 U.S. 93 (1995) *Fulton Corp. v. Faulkner,* 516 U.S. 325 (1996).
29. 430 U.S. 274 (1977).
30. 334 U.S. 653 (1948).
31. 115 S. Ct. 1331 (1995).
32. *International Shoe v. Washington,* 326 U.S. 310 (1945).
33. *Reeves, Inc. v. State,* 447 U.S. 429 (1980).
34. David Pomper, "Recycling *Philadelphia v. New Jersey*: The Dormant Commerce Clause, Postindustrial "Natural" Resources, and the Solid Waste Crisis," 137 *U. Pa. L. Rev.* 1309, 1311 (1989).
35. See *South-Central Timber Development, Inc. v. Wunnicke,* 467 U.S. 82 (1984).
36. *Supreme Court of Virginia v. Friedman,* 487 U.S. 59 (1988).
37. *Toomer v. Witsell,* 334 U.S. 385 (1948).
38. *Hicklin v. Orbeck,* 437 U.S. 518 (1978).
39. 17 U.S. 316 (1819).
40. 19 How. (60 U.S.) 393 (1857).
41. 426 U.S. 833 (1976).
42. 505 U.S. 144 (1992).
43. 501 U.S. 452 (1991).
44. 512 U.S. 44 (1996).
45. 527 U.S. 706 (1999).
46. 528 U.S. 62.
47. 531 U.S. 356.
48. 538 U.S. 721.
49. 483 U.S. 219 (1987).
50. See Chester Antieau, 2 *Modern Constitutional Law* § 14:6 (Lawyers Cooperative Publishing 1969).

51. *Perpich v. Department of Defense*, 110 S. Ct. 2418 (1990).
52. *Longress v. Board of Education*, 101 Ill. 308 (1882).
53. *Brown v. Board of Education*, 347 U.S. 483 (1954).
54. *People v. Anderson*, 493 P.2d 880 (Cal. 1972). This decision was reversed a few months later by constitutional amendment.
55. William J. Brennan Jr., "State Constitutions and the Protection of Individual Rights," 90 *Harv. L. Rev.* 489 (1977).
56. See Dorothy Beasley, "Federalism and the Protection of Individual Rights: The American State Constitutional Perspective," 11 *Ga. St. U. L. Rev.* 681 (1995).
57. This model was adopted from John Shaw, "Principled Interpretations of State Constitutional Law—Why Don't the 'Primacy' States Practice What They Preach?" 54 *U. Pitt. L. Rev.* 1019 (1993).
58. Helen Hershkoff, "State Constitutions: A National Perspective," 3 *Widener J. Pub. L.* 7 (1993).
59. *Commonwealth v. Ludwig,* 527 Pa. 472, 478 (1991).
60. *People v. Woody,* 61 Cal. 2d 716, 394 P.2d 813 (1965).
61. *Department of Human Resources v. Smith*, 494 U.S. 872 (1990).
62. *State v. Gunwall,* 106 Wash. 2d 54, 58 (1986).
63. See *People v. Disbrow,* 16 Cal. 3d 101, 545 P.2d 272 (1976) (California); *State v. Santiago,* 53 Haw. 254, 492 P.2d 657 (1971) (Hawaii); *Commonwealth v. Triplett,* 462 Pa. 244, 341 A.2d 62 (1975) (Pennsylvania).
64. *McCain v. Koch,* 502 N.Y.2d 720 (1987).
65. *Right to Choose v. Byrne,* 450 A.2d 925 (N.J. 1982).
66. See Joseph Cook, *Constitutional Rights of the Accused,* 2d ed. § 1:8, n. 16 (Lawyers Cooperative Publishing 1989) for a more thorough list.

8

The Bill of Rights

[A] bill of rights is what the people are entitled to against every government on earth, general or particular, and what no just government should refuse, or rest on inference.

THOMAS JEFFERSON, LETTER TO JAMES MADISON, DECEMBER 20, 1987[1]

LEARNING OBJECTIVES
At the end of this chapter you should be able to:

- Explain the historical purposes for adding a Bill of Rights to the Constitution.
- Discuss the practical and stylistic differences between the original Constitution and the Bill of Rights.
- Identify the basic liberties protected by the first ten amendments to the Constitution.
- Explain the difference between an enumerated right and an implicit right.
- Address how the Bill of Rights has been made applicable to the state and local governments.
- Identify a contemporary issue concerning the Bill of Rights, and discuss the most likely future scenarios, referencing both historical analogs and case law.
- Brief a judicial opinion with little outside assistance. You should be successful in identifying the relevant facts, identifying the legal issue(s), and analyzing the court's rationale in at least 60 percent of your briefs.
- Apply what you have learned to a new set of facts with little assistance.

8.1 WHY DO WE HAVE A BILL OF RIGHTS?

The first ten amendments to the Constitution are referred to as the **Bill of Rights.** These provisions, although considered a fundamental and inseparable part of the modern-day Constitution, were not included in the document when it was originally ratified in 1789.[2] In fact, some of the constitutional framers deemed such a supplemental list of rights to be unnecessary for, and perhaps even harmful to, protecting individual rights and liberties. Those who opposed a bill of rights asserted that if rights were specifically enumerated, they might be viewed as an exhaustive list of liberties, thereby leaving unprotected all other freedoms not specifically mentioned.[3] **James Madison,** the chief architect of the Bill of Rights, initially stated that the document was "unnecessary, because it was evident that the general government had no power but what was given it [by the Constitution]" and "dangerous, because an enumeration which is not complete is not safe." By omitting a bill of rights, some framers argued that citizens could always claim, in the face of governmental intrusion, that because citizens did not specifically limit the nature and extent of their freedoms, they reserved the right to do what they pleased.

But still other constitutional sponsors maintained that a bill of rights was necessary to preserve the blessings of liberty against governmental infringement. During the Constitutional Convention, George Mason, a delegate from Virginia, urged the delegates to adopt a bill of rights, claiming that such a document "would give great quiet to the people; and with the aid of the state declarations, a bill might be prepared in a few hours." Mason, along with delegates Charles Pinckney and Elbridge Gerry of Massachusetts and Edmund Randolph of Virginia, further believed that without a bill of rights, the powers vested in Congress under the proposed Articles eventually would lead to "monarchy or a tyrannical aristocracy." The efforts to include a bill of rights, however, were unsuccessful at the Constitutional Convention, and the Articles of the Constitution were adopted as an insulated document and sent to the states for ratification.

It was not until the ratification proceedings that the movement to include a bill of rights ultimately became successful. During the states' ratification debates, many delegates reintroduced objections to ratifying the proposed Constitution without the inclusion of a bill of rights. In Virginia, Patrick Henry questioned why the Constitution lacked specific protections for individual rights when the Declaration of Independence specifically recognized the "unalienable rights" of individuals and demanded protection for these rights against governmental interference. Henry asserted that without the inclusion of a bill of rights, the proposed Articles were inconsistent with the values and claims set forth in the nation's founding document.

Beyond the principled arguments surrounding the debate, the failure to include a bill of rights within the Constitution presented serious strategic problems for the framers seeking the document's ratification. Although many constitutional proponents believed that it was possible that the Constitution would be ratified by the requisite nine states even without including a bill of rights, some believed that Virginia, New York, and Massachusetts—three of the largest states at the time—were likely to vote against the new constitution without some guarantee that a bill of rights would be added. And given the size of these states, some framers believed that any constitution implemented without their approval stood little chance of succeeding in the long term. Accordingly, in an effort to secure the approval of these states and others, James Madison, who had opposed the inclusion of a bill of rights during the Constitutional Convention, along with other members of the Constitutional Convention, agreed to propose a bill of rights to the First Congress after the Constitution was ratified. This concession, along with other promotional efforts, ultimately secured unanimous ratification of the Constitution by the then thirteen states.

The First Congress was convened in March 1789. During this time, James Madison began to draft proposals for the new bill of rights, which were to be submitted for congressional consideration and approval and then to the states for ratification. In September 1789, after Madison had drafted a list of suggested amendments, Congress approved twelve amendments to the Constitution. The first of these amendments altered the manner by which seats in the House of Representatives were apportioned and, through a comparatively complex formula, sought to preserve the total number of House members as the nation grew. The second amendment barred congressional salaries from being effectuated prior to the following House election. However, during state ratification proceedings between November 1789 and December 1791, these two amendments were not approved by a sufficient number (eleven) of these states,[4] thereby leaving the remaining ten amendments as the adopted bill of rights. As a result, the amendment approved by Congress as the third amendment became the first amendment, the fourth amendment became the second amendment, and so forth. These ten provisions reflect the Bill of Rights as we know the document today. See Figure 8-1.

Be sure to note the Ninth Amendment, which provides that "[t]he enumeration in the Constitution, of certain rights, shall not be construed to deny or disparage others retained by the people." This provision was inserted to address the fears of some framers that the rights listed in the new Bill of Rights might be treated as the only individual liberties held by individuals. The Ninth Amendment's language suggests that there are other liberties beyond

Bill of Rights
The first ten amendments to the Constitution, which were written in 1789 and ratified in 1791, contain the primary civil liberties protected under the Constitution.

James Madison
A "founding father" of the Constitution and the chief architect of the Bill of Rights.

Cyber Constitution
History of the Bill of Rights http://www.billofrightsinstitute.org/

First Amendment

Bars government from passing laws respecting an establishment of religion

Bars government from prohibiting the free exercise of religion

Bars government from abridging the freedom of speech

Bars government from abridging the freedom of the press

Bars government from abridging the right to peacefully assemble

Bars government from abridging the right to petition government for redress of grievances

Second Amendment

Bars government from infringing on the right to bear arms

Third Amendment

In peacetime, bars government from quartering soldiers in homes without an owner's consent

During war, allows troops to be quartered in a manner prescribed by law

Fourth Amendment

Bars government from violating the right against unreasonable searches and seizures

Requires probable cause, oath or affirmation, and particularity for the issuance of warrants

Fifth Amendment

Requires grand jury indictment for charges of capital or infamous charges

Bars government from trying a person twice for the same offense (double jeopardy)

Bars government from compelling persons to testify against themselves in criminal cases

Bars government from depriving persons life, liberty, or property without due process of law

Bars government from taking private property for public use without just compensation

Sixth Amendment

Provides accused persons with the right to a speedy, public, and jury trial in criminal cases

Provides accused persons with the right to be notified of the criminal charges against them

Provides accused persons with the right to confront witnesses against them

Provides accused persons with the right to compel witnesses to appear on their behalf

Provides accused persons with the right to the assistance of legal counsel in criminal cases

Seventh Amendment

Provides the right to a jury trial in civil cases involving disputes valued over twenty dollars

Provides common law rules to be used when federal courts review common law suits

Eighth Amendment

Bars government from imposing excessive bail or fines

Bars government from inflicting cruel and unusual punishment

Ninth Amendment

Provides that the Constitution's enumeration of specific rights should not be interpreted to deny other rights retained by the people

Tenth Amendment

Provides that all powers not given to the United States or taken from the states by the Constitution are reserved to the States or to the people

FIGURE 8-1

Textual contents of the Bill of Rights

those written in the Bill of Rights that are to be protected against governmental intrusion. As discussed later, these implicit liberties include the rights to privacy, travel, and marriage.

Since the ratification of the Bill of Rights on December 15, 1791, seventeen additional amendments have been added to the Constitution. Some of these amendments address the manner in which governmental institutions fulfill their duties and exercise their powers. For example, the Seventeenth Amendment provides for the popular election of U.S. senators, the Twenty-Second Amendment places term limits on presidents, and the Twenty-Seventh Amendment imposes restrictions on congressional pay raises. Other amendments are designed to secure additional rights and liberties for individuals. For example, the Thirteenth Amendment bars slavery and involuntary servitude, the Fourteenth Amendment entitles individuals to equal protection and due process in state proceedings, and the Nineteenth Amendment gives women the right to vote. But even with these additional amendments, the Bill of Rights is still regarded as the primary document for protecting individual rights and liberties against governmental interference.

PRESIDENTS AND JUSTICES AS LAWYERS

Given the nature of the government service and its relationship to the law, lawyers have historically been attracted to elected office. As of 2008, twenty-five of the forty-three presidents of the United States had been attorneys. John Adams was the first. Barack Obama is the most recent. There were many accomplished attorneys between the two, including Abraham Lincoln and Martin van Buren.

Eight actually appeared before the Supreme Court of the United States. John Adams was the first. He appeared on several occasions, including his famous post-presidency appearance in the Amistad case, which was later popularized by a film of that name. James Polk, Abraham Lincoln, James Garfield, Benjamin Harrison, Grover Cleveland, William Howard Taft, and Richard Nixon were the other seven.

Interestingly, justices appointed to the Supreme Court do not have to be lawyers. But since 1957, the Court has been an all-lawyer bench. The last nonlawyer justice was Stanley Reed, who had received substantial legal training and education, but had never become a lawyer.

Source: See Norman Gross, "America's Lawyer-Presidents: From Law Office to Oval Office," 14 Sum Experience 4 (2004).

8.2 WHERE DO RIGHTS COME FROM?

One of the major questions debated by constitutional scholars is the source of individual rights. Some claim that these rights are created by the Constitution and that without the existence of this document, the enumerated rights therein would not exist. Others claim that people have individual rights by virtue of their birth and that these rights are not dependent upon any formal written document. In other words, some scholars view the Constitution as simply reaffirming and otherwise acknowledging rights that are vested in individuals independently from the document.

Upon reading the Constitution, one of the first things you may notice is the difference in the language between the Articles of the Constitution and the Bill of Rights. Generally, the powers held by the three branches of government under the Articles of the Constitution are treated as grants or investments of authority. For example, Article I provides that "All legislative Powers herein *granted* shall be *vested* in a Congress of the United States"; Article II states, "The executive Power shall be *vested* in a President"; Article III says, "The judicial Power of the United States, shall be *vested* in one Supreme Court, and in such inferior Courts as the Congress may from time to time ordain and establish." The use of the terms "granted" and "vested" in these provisions, along with the phrase "We the People . . . do ordain and establish this Constitution for the United States of America," found in the Preamble, suggests that the enumerated governmental powers found in the Constitution initially were not held by the government prior to the formation of the document, but instead were held by "the People" who ultimately chose to delegate these authorities to three governmental institutions.

The Preamble and Articles reflect a **social compact** or contract between two primary parties—the people and the government. Under this contract, the people have given their consent to political institutions to be their sovereign governing authority, granting to them certain powers of structure, process, and support. And in exchange, the government has agreed to provide the people with certain levels of protection and sustenance. This "agreement" provides that the parties' relationship may be changed under Article V's amendment procedure, depending upon the needs and desires of the parties. In other words, the duties and powers of the government are not inherent or unalienable; rather, they are dependent upon the continued consent of the governed and can be removed or altered at any time through constitutional amendment.[5]

Treating individuals' rights as the product of a negotiated contract is known as the **compact theory** of individual rights. Under this approach, rights are derived from an agreement or a compact between the individuals being protected and those individuals

social compact
A term used to describe the Constitution as a contract between two primary parties— the people and the government—wherein the people have given their consent to political institutions to be their sovereign governing authority, granting to them certain powers of structure, process, and support, and in exchange, the government has agreed to provide the people with certain levels of protection and sustenance.

compact theory
A theory of individual liberties that considers liberties to be the product of a negotiated contract. Under this approach, rights are derived from an agreement or compact between the individuals being protected and those individuals or institutions providing the protection. Through negotiation, individuals and institutions receive rights, powers, and protections by virtue of compact or constitution.

or institutions providing the protection. Through negotiation, individuals and institutions receive rights, powers, and protections by virtue of compact or constitution. Under this theory, people have rights to the freedom of speech, religion, and assembly because the Bill of Rights provides for these rights and secures them against governmental interference, and without these contractual (constitutional) provisions, these rights would not exist.[6]

Others assert that individuals have rights within the "laws of nature," and thus certain liberties regardless of whether any social compact is formed. This approach is called the **natural rights theory** of individual rights—a belief that some rights are vested in individuals by the "laws of nature" at the time of birth. This theory recognizes life itself as the source of certain individual rights, which exist independent of any constitution or contract. Natural rights theory insists that the rights enumerated in the Bill of Rights are natural, inherent, and unalienable to individuals.[7] Natural rights theory maintains there are certain fundamental privileges that are afforded to individuals simply as human beings and that are universal in application. As evidence of this theory, some point to the language of the Declaration of Independence, which cites to the "laws of nature" and provides that "all men . . . are endowed by their Creator with certain unalienable Rights." These provisions suggest that rights, while not always recognized or protected by governments, nevertheless are naturally vested in all persons at birth and held by virtue of their humanity until death.

Natural rights theorists also point to the language used in the Bill of Rights to support their theory. Unlike the words used in the Articles of the Constitution, the Bill of Rights does not speak in terms of *vesting, granting,* or *establishing* rights of speech, religion, press, and so on to the people. Instead, the document references the enumerated rights and freedoms as if they already existed, independent of the Constitution, and suggests that the Bill of Rights was drafted in order to ensure that these preexisting rights are protected by the government. For example, the First Amendment does not state that individuals are *vested* with the freedom of speech, freedom of the press, or right to peaceably assemble; rather, it provides that the government may not *abridge* these rights and freedoms. Similarly, the Fourth Amendment does not say that the people are *granted* the right to be secure in their persons, houses, papers, and effects, but instead, it provides protection of this right against unreasonable searches and seizures. Natural rights theorists maintain that this language suggests that the Bill of Rights protects all persons, regardless of their citizenship, against governmental interference.

The difference between compact theory and natural rights theory is much more than an academic debate. The nature and source of rights in the Bill of Rights have real and potentially enormous consequences, particularly during times of war, international conflict, and domestic disputes involving a person's nationality. Consider, for example, situations where the United States acts outside of its geographic jurisdiction against individuals who are not U.S. citizens. Under compact theory, foreign individuals likely would be considered to have few, if any, rights under the Bill of Rights to assert against the government's actions because they are not U.S. citizens, and thus they are not parties to the contract of the Constitution. But if rights are regarded as natural and universal, as natural rights theory suggests, then, in the face of action by the United States, foreign nationals would possess rights by virtue of their birth and regardless of their citizenship.

Consider the Supreme Court's opinion in *United States v. Verdugo-Urquidez,*[8] which addresses the issue of whether the Fourth Amendment's protections against unreasonable searches and seizures apply to foreign citizens who are arrested and whose homes are searched by American agents in other countries. Notice that one of the primary disagreements between the majority and dissenting opinions involves a debate between compact theory and natural rights theory. Notice as well the potential implications of this opinion for immigration laws, which seek to limit or eliminate the rights of undocumented residents in the United States, and for the United States's War on Terror, which includes establishing internment camps at places like Guantanamo Bay, Cuba, and holding foreign nationals as "enemy combatants" without charging them with any criminal offense.

natural rights theory
A theory of individual liberties that maintains that liberties are the result of the "laws of nature." This theory recognizes life itself as the source of certain individual rights, which exist independent of any constitution or contract. Natural rights theory insists that the rights enumerated in the Bill of Rights are natural, inherent, and unalienable to individuals.

Cyber Constitution
The Bill of Rights Project
http://www.vcsc.k12.in.us/
staff/mhutchison/rights/

United States v. Verdugo-Urquidez
494 U.S. 259 (1990)

Chief Justice Rehnquist delivered the opinion of the Court.

The question presented by this case is whether the Fourth Amendment applies to the search and seizure by United States agents of property that is owned by a nonresident alien and located in a foreign country. We hold that it does not.

Respondent Rene Martin Verdugo-Urquidez is a citizen and resident of Mexico. He is believed by the United States Drug Enforcement Agency (DEA) to be one of the leaders of a large and violent organization in Mexico that smuggles narcotics into the United States. Based on a complaint charging respondent with various narcotics-related offenses, the Government obtained a warrant for his arrest on August 3, 1985. In January 1986, Mexican police officers, after discussions with United States marshals, apprehended Verdugo-Urquidez in Mexico and transported him to the United States Border Patrol station in Calexico, California. There, United States marshals arrested respondent and eventually moved him to a correctional center in San Diego, California, where he remains incarcerated pending trial.

Following respondent's arrest, Terry Bowen, a DEA agent assigned to the Calexico DEA office, decided to arrange for searches of Verdugo-Urquidez's Mexican residences located in Mexicali and San Felipe . . . Thereafter, DEA agents working in concert with officers of the [Mexican Federal Judicial Police] searched respondent's properties in Mexicali and San Felipe and seized certain documents. In particular, the search of the Mexicali residence uncovered a tally sheet, which the Government believes reflects the quantities of marijuana smuggled by Verdugo-Urquidez into the United States. . . .

The Fourth Amendment provides:

> The right of the people to be secure in their persons, houses, papers, and effects, against unreasonable searches and seizures, shall not be violated, and no Warrants shall issue, but upon probable cause, supported by Oath or affirmation, and particularly describing the place to be searched, and the persons or things to be seized.

That text, by contrast with the Fifth and Sixth Amendments, extends its reach only to "the people." Contrary to the suggestion of amici curiae that the Framers used this phrase "simply to avoid [an] awkward rhetorical redundancy," "the people" seems to have been a term of art employed in select parts of the Constitution. The Preamble declares that the Constitution is ordained and established by "the people of the United States." The Second Amendment protects "the right of the people to keep and bear Arms," and the Ninth and Tenth Amendments provide that certain rights and powers are retained by and reserved to "the people." While this textual exegesis is by no means conclusive, it suggests that "the people" protected by the Fourth Amendment, and by the First and Second Amendments, and to whom rights and powers are reserved in the Ninth and Tenth Amendments, refers to a class of persons who are part of a national community or who have otherwise developed sufficient connection with this country to be considered part of that community. The language of these Amendments contrasts with the words "person" and "accused" used in the Fifth and Sixth Amendments regulating procedure in criminal cases.

What we know of the history of the drafting of the Fourth Amendment also suggests that its purpose was to restrict searches and seizures which might be conducted by the United States in domestic matters. The Framers originally decided not to include a provision like the Fourth Amendment, because they believed the National Government lacked power to conduct searches and seizures. Many disputed the original view that the Federal Government possessed only narrow delegated powers over domestic affairs, however, and ultimately felt an Amendment prohibiting unreasonable searches and seizures was necessary. Madison, for example, argued that "there is a clause granting to Congress the power to make all laws which shall be necessary and proper for carrying into execution all of the powers vested in the Government of the United States," and that general warrants might be considered "necessary" for the purpose of collecting revenue. The driving force behind the adoption of the Amendment, as suggested by Madison's advocacy, was widespread hostility among the former colonists to the issuance of writs of assistance empowering revenue officers to search suspected places for smuggled goods, and general search warrants permitting the search of private houses, often to uncover papers that might be used to convict persons of libel. The available historical data show, therefore, that the purpose of the Fourth Amendment was to protect the people of the United States against arbitrary action by their own Government; it was never suggested that the provision was intended to restrain the actions of the Federal Government against aliens outside of the United States territory. . . .

For better or for worse, we live in a world of nation-states in which our Government must be able to "functio[n] effectively in the company of sovereign nations." . . . Some who violate our laws may live outside our borders under a regime quite different from that which obtains in this country. Situations threatening to important American interests may arise halfway around the globe, situations which in the view of the political branches of our Government require an American response with armed force. If there are to be restrictions on searches and seizures which occur incident to such

American action, they must be imposed by the political branches through diplomatic understanding, treaty, or legislation.

The judgment of the Court of Appeals is accordingly Reversed.

. . .

Justice Brennan, with whom Justice Marshall joins, dissenting.

Today the Court holds that although foreign nationals must abide by our laws even when in their own countries, our Government need not abide by the Fourth Amendment when it investigates them for violations of our laws. I respectfully dissent. We investigate, prosecute, and punish them. We have recognized this fundamental principle of mutuality since the time of the Framers.

In drafting both the Constitution and the Bill of Rights, the Framers strove to create a form of Government decidedly different from their British heritage. Whereas the British Parliament was unconstrained, the Framers intended to create a Government of limited powers. The colonists considered the British Government dangerously omnipotent. After all, the British declaration of rights had been enacted not by the people, but by Parliament. Americans vehemently attacked the notion that rights were matters of "favor and grace," given to the people from the Government.

Thus, the Framers of the Bill of Rights did not purport to "create" rights. Rather, they designed the Bill of Rights to prohibit our Government from infringing rights and liberties presumed to be pre-existing. See e. g., U.S. Const., Amdt. 9 ("The enumeration in the Constitution of certain rights, shall not be construed to deny or disparage others retained by the people"). The Fourth Amendment, for example, does not create a new right of security against unreasonable searches and seizures. It states that "[t]he right of the people to be secure in their persons, houses, papers, and effects, against unreasonable searches and seizures, shall not be violated. . . ." The focus of the Fourth Amendment is on what the Government can and cannot do, and how it may act, not on against whom these actions may be taken. Bestowing rights and delineating protected groups would have been inconsistent with the Drafters' fundamental conception of a Bill of Rights as a limitation on the Government's conduct with respect to all whom it seeks to govern. It is thus extremely unlikely that the Framers intended the narrow construction of the term "the people" presented today by the majority.

Cyber Constitution
Arizona Anti-Immigration Law S.B. 1070 http://www.azleg.gov/legtext/49leg/2r/bills/sb1070s.pdf

Cyber Constitution
Temporary Injunction Against Arizona S.B. 1070 http://graphics8.nytimes.com/packages/pdf/national/20100729_ARIZONA_DOC.pdf

For example, in 2010, the State of Arizona passed the Support Our Law Enforcement and Safe Neighborhoods Act, which is also referred to as Arizona SB 1070. This is an anti-illegal immigration law that seeks to allow state law enforcement officials to regulate immigration. Under federal law, certain foreign nationals residing in the United States must register with federal authorities and possess official documentation. But Arizona SB 1070 goes beyond federal provisions by making it a state crime for a foreign national to be in Arizona without required documentation. The Arizona law also includes a provision that requires police officers, while enforcing other laws, to question a person about his or her immigration status, if there is "reasonable suspicion" that the person is in the United States illegally. Some have asserted that this provision violates the Fourth Amendment to the U.S. Constitution, which guards "the People" against unreasonable search and seizures. But others claim that undocumented aliens residing in the United States should not be protected by the Fourth Amendment and other constitutional provisions because they are in the country illegally. In light of the Court's ruling in *Verdugo-Urquidez*, assess whether undocumented residents stopped and questioned under the Arizona law would be able to assert protections under the Fourth Amendment.

8.3 TO WHOM DOES THE BILL OF RIGHTS APPLY?

One of the most frequently misunderstood areas of constitutional law involves the question of who must comply with the Bill of Rights. Specifically, students often ask why state and local governments have to comply with the Bill of Rights when the First Amendment begins by stating that "*Congress* shall make no law. . . ." The short answer to this question is that, even though the Bill of Rights mentions only Congress, state and local governments also must comply with most provisions of the Bill of Rights

Bullet holes in a sign warning of illegal activities near the border of Mexico and Arizona

Gila Photography/Shutterstock

because these provisions have been made applicable to these levels of government through the Fourteenth Amendment Due Process Clause. This, however, has not always been the case.

Initially, the Bill of Rights was interpreted and applied as placing limitations only on the federal government. For example, the Supreme Court held in *Barron v. The Mayor and City of Baltimore* (1833)[9] that the Fifth Amendment's provision regarding governmental takings of private property for public use and without just compensation was "a limitation on the exercise of power by the government of the United States, and is not applicable to the legislation of the States. . . ." In *Barron*, a wharf owner sued the mayor and city of Baltimore, claiming that the city deprived him of his property by completing harbor projects that reduced the access to and profitability of his wharf. Barron claimed that the Fifth Amendment should apply to limit state and local government conduct as well as that of the national government. The Supreme Court, however, disagreed, stating, "[h]ad the framers of [the] amendments intended them to be limitations on the powers of the State governments they would have imitated the framers of the original Constitution, and have expressed that intention." As a result, the Court made it clear that the Bill of Rights was "intended solely as a limitation on the exercise of power by the government of the United States, and [was] not applicable to legislation of the states."

The limited application and scope of the Bill of Rights eventually changed following the ratification of the **Fourteenth Amendment** to the Constitution. In the aftermath of the Civil War, Congress passed and the states ratified the Fourteenth Amendment, which includes a **Due Process Clause** that specifically applies to the states.[10] Section 1 of the Fourteenth Amendment provides, in relevant part, "nor shall any State deprive any person of life, liberty, or property, without due process of law. . . ." The 1868 ratification of the Due Process Clause, and other provisions within the Fourteenth Amendment, provided an explicit mandate to the states regarding civil liberties, a mandate that was not found in the original Bill of Rights. With the Fourteenth Amendment in place, the states are now required to protect liberty, as well as life and property, under mandate of the federal constitution.

It is important to note that the Constitution does not specifically mention local governments. But when the Constitution refers to "any state" or "the states," including

Fourteenth Amendment
An amendment ratified in 1868 that contains a Due Process Clause and Equal Protection Clause that applies to the states. The ratification of the Fourteenth Amendment provided explicit mandates to the states regarding civil liberties, mandates not found in the original Bill of Rights. Under this amendment, the states are required to protect liberty, as well as life and property, under mandate of the federal constitution.

Due Process Clause
A provision found in the Fifth and Fourteenth Amendments that government cannot deprive individuals of life, liberty, or property without due process of law.

such references in the Fourteenth Amendment, by implication, this reference includes local governments, such as counties, cities, townships, villages, and so on. The reason is that these smaller units of government are regarded essentially as agents or creatures of their respective state governments.[11] In other words, the reasoning is that because local governments are created by and largely regulated by the states, they should be subject to many of the constitutional duties imposed on the states. As a result, the Fourteenth Amendment's mandate that no state shall deprive a person of life, liberty, or property without due process of law also applies to local governments.

But even with the Due Process Clause in place in 1868, it was not clear that the Bill of Rights would apply to state and local governments. The Due Process Clause provided only that states must not deny life, liberty, or property without due process of law; it did not explicitly include any requirement that the states abide by the first ten amendments to the Constitution. And in the wake of the Fourteenth Amendment's ratification, courts began to grapple with two fundamental questions: What types of behavior does the term "liberty" include? And what "process" must be provided by states before liberty can be denied? Since these terms were not defined or further addressed by the Fourteenth Amendment, the scope and meaning of these provisions were uncertain.

In addressing the effect of the Due Process Clause in civil liberties cases, the Supreme Court was frequently urged to apply the constitutional standards established for protecting liberties under the Bill of Rights to resolve such disputes involving the states. Under this approach, if a state was accused of infringing upon an individual's liberty of speech, in violation of the Fourteenth Amendment Due Process Clause, the Court would simply apply the standards traditionally used for addressing similar cases under the First Amendment. This approach is known as the **incorporation doctrine** because it maintains, to varying degrees (see following discussion), that the provisions of the Bill of Rights ought to be applied to the states by "incorporating" them through the Due Process Clause. This doctrine maintains that when the Court considers whether a state is violating the Due Process Clause, there is essentially a footnote to the clause effectively stating, "please see the above-referenced provisions in the Bill of Rights." See Figure 8-2. In essence, the incorporation doctrine maintains that courts do not need to "reinvent the wheel" when it comes to interpreting the Due Process Clause of the Fourteenth Amendment. Under this doctrine, if a constitutional standard under the First Amendment is good enough to resolve free speech cases involving the federal government, it should be good enough for those disputes involving state governments as well.

incorporation doctrine
A legal theory that maintains that the Bill of Rights (or at least portions thereof) should be incorporated through the Fourteenth Amendment Due Process Clause and made applicable to the states.

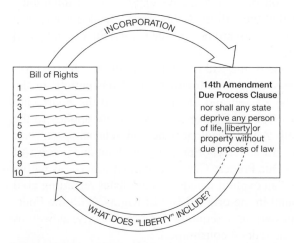

FIGURE 8-2

Incorporation Doctrine: Applying the Bill of Rights to the states

Hurtado v. California
110 U.S. 516 (1884)

On February 20, 1882, the state of California charged Joseph Hurtado with murdering Jose Antonio Stuardo. The state's charge against Hurtado did not come by way of grand jury indictment, but rather, through an information filed by the prosecutor. Following trial on the charge, a jury found Hurtado guilty of murder and he was later sentenced to death by the trial court. In his appeal, Hurtado asserts that his conviction should be reversed because his murder charge was not issued by a grand jury as required by the Fifth Amendment to the United States Constitution.

Matthews, J. delivers the opinion of the Court.

It is claimed on behalf of the prisoner that the conviction and sentence are void, on the ground that they are repugnant to that clause of the fourteenth article of amendment to the constitution of the United States, which is in these words: "Nor shall any state deprive any person of life, liberty, or property without due process of law." The proposition of law we are asked to affirm is that an indictment or presentment by a grand jury, as known to the common law of England, is essential to that "due process of law," when applied to prosecutions for felonies, which is secured and guaranteed by this provision of the constitution of the United States, and which accordingly it is forbidden to the states, respectively, to dispense with in the administration of criminal law . . .

We are to construe this phrase in the fourteenth amendment by the *usus loquendi* of the constitution itself. The same words are contained in the fifth amendment. That article makes specific and express provision for perpetuating the institution of the grand jury, so far as relates to prosecutions for the more aggravated crimes under the laws of the United States. It declares that "no person shall be held to answer for a capital or otherwise infamous crime, unless on a presentment or indictment of a grand jury, except in cases arising in the land or naval forces, or in the militia when in actual service in time of war or public danger; nor shall any person be subject for the same offense to be twice put in jeopardy of life or limb; nor shall he be compelled in any criminal case to be a witness against himself." It then immediately adds: "nor be deprived of life, liberty, or property without due process of law." According to a recognized canon of interpretation, especially applicable to formal and solemn instruments of constitutional law, we are forbidden to assume, without clear reason to the contrary, that any part of this most important amendment is superfluous. The natural and obvious inference is that, in the sense of the constitution, "due process of law" was not meant or intended to include, *ex vi termini*, the institution and procedure of a grand jury in any case. The conclusion is equally irresistible, that when the same phrase was employed in the fourteenth amendment to restrain the action of the states, it was used in the same sense and with no greater extent; and that if in the adoption of that amendment it had been part of its purpose to perpetuate the institution of the grand jury in all the states, it would have embodied, as did the fifth amendment, express declarations to that effect. Due process of law in the latter refers to that law of the land which derives its authority from the legislative powers conferred upon congress by the constitution of the United States, exercised within the limits therein prescribed, and interpreted according to the principles of the common law. In the fourteenth amendment, by parity of reason, it refers to that law of the land in each state which derives its authority from the inherent and reserved powers of the state, exerted within the limits of those fundamental principles of liberty and justice which lie at the base of all our civil and political institutions, and the greatest security for which resides in the right of the people to make their own laws, and alter them at their pleasure. "The fourteenth amendment," as was said by Mr. Justice BRADLEY in *Missouri v. Lewis*, 101 U.S. 22-31, "does not profess to secure to all persons in the United States the benefit of the same laws and the same remedies. Great diversities in these respects may exist in two states separated only by an imaginary line. On one side of this line there may be a right of trial by jury, and on the other side no such right. Each state prescribes its own modes of judicial proceeding." . . .

Tried by these principles, we are unable to say that the substitution for a presentment or indictment by a grand jury of the proceeding by information after examination and commitment by a magistrate, certifying to the probable guilt of the defendant, with the right on his part to the aid of counsel, and to the cross-examination of the witnesses produced for the prosecution, is not due process of law. It is, as we have seen, an ancient proceeding at common law, which might include every case of an offense of less grade than a felony, except misprision of treason; and in every circumstance of its administration, as authorized by the statute of California, it carefully considers and guards the substantial interest of the prisoner. It is merely a preliminary proceeding, and can result in no final judgment, except as the consequence of a regular judicial trial, conducted precisely as in cases of indictments. . . .

For these reasons, finding no error therein, the judgment of the supreme court of California is affirmed.

Harlan, J., dissenting.

"Due process of law," within the meaning of the national constitution, does not import one thing with reference to the powers of the states and another with reference to the powers of the general government. If particular proceedings, conducted under the authority of the general government, and involving life, are prohibited because not constituting that due process of law required by the fifth amendment of the constitution of the

United States, similar proceedings, conducted under the authority of a state, must be deemed illegal, as not being due process of law within the meaning of the fourteenth amendment. The words "due process of law," in the latter amendment, must receive the same interpretation they had at the common law from which they were derived, and which was given to them at the formation of the general government. . . .

It seems to me that too much stress is put upon the fact that the framers of the constitution made express provision for the security of those rights which at common law were protected by the requirement of due process of law, and, in addition, declared, generally, that no

person shall "be deprived of life, liberty, or property without due process of law." The rights, for the security of which these express provisions were made, were of a character so essential to the safety of the people that it was deemed wise to avoid the possibility that congress, in regulating the processes of law, would impair or destroy them. Hence, their specific enumeration in the earlier amendments of the constitution, in connection with the general requirement of due process of law, the latter itself being broad enough to cover every right of life, liberty, or property secured by the settled usages and modes of proceedings existing under the common and statute law of England at the time our government was founded. . . .

Palko v. State of Connecticut
302 U.S. 319 (1937)

The state of Connecticut charged Frank Jacob Palko with the murder of two police officers in 1935. Following a trial, Palko was convicted of second-degree murder and sentenced to life imprisonment. The state, however, sought to appeal Palko's conviction and sentence, seeking to retry Palko for first-degree murder and obtain a death sentence. Applying a Connecticut statute that allowed prosecutors to appeal criminal convictions in certain cases, Connecticut's supreme court of appeals agreed with the state, reversed Palko's conviction, and ordered a new trial. After a second trial, Palko was convicted of first-degree murder and sentenced to death. Palko appealed his conviction, asserting that the Fifth Amendment protection against double jeopardy applied to the states and barred his second trial.

Mr. Justice Cardozo delivered the opinion of the Court.

The argument for appellant is that whatever is forbidden by the Fifth Amendment is forbidden by the Fourteenth also. The Fifth Amendment, which is not directed to the States, but solely to the federal government, creates immunity from double jeopardy. No person shall be "subject for the same offense to be twice put in jeopardy of life or limb." The Fourteenth Amendment ordains, "nor shall any State deprive any person of life, liberty, or property, without due process of law." To retry a defendant, though under one indictment and only one, subjects him, it is said, to double jeopardy in violation of the Fifth Amendment, if the prosecution is one on behalf of the United States. From this the consequence is said to follow that there is a denial of life or liberty without due process of law, if the prosecution is one on behalf of the people of a state. . . .

We have said that in appellant's view the Fourteenth Amendment is to be taken as embodying the prohibitions of the Fifth. His thesis is even broader. Whatever would be a violation of the original bill of rights (Amendments 1 to 8) if done by the federal government is now equally

unlawful by force of the Fourteenth Amendment if done by a state. There is no such general rule.

The Fifth Amendment provides, among other things, that no person shall be held to answer for a capital or otherwise infamous crime unless on presentment or indictment of a grand jury. This court has held that, in prosecutions by a state, presentment or indictment by a grand jury may give way to informations at the instance of a public officer. *Hurtado v. California*, 110 U.S. 516, 4 S.Ct. 111, 292. The Fifth Amendment provides also that no person shall be compelled in any criminal case to be a witness against himself. This court has said that, in prosecutions by a state, the exemption will fail if the state elects to end it. The Sixth Amendment calls for a jury trial in criminal cases and the Seventh for a jury trial in civil cases at common law where the value in controversy shall exceed $20. This court has ruled that consistently with those amendments trial by jury may be modified by a state or abolished altogether. . . .

On the other hand, the Due Process Clause of the Fourteenth Amendment may make it unlawful for a state to abridge by its statutes the freedom of speech which the First Amendment safeguards against encroachment by the Congress, or the free exercise of religion, or the right of peaceable assembly, without which speech would be unduly trammeled, or the right of one accused of crime to the benefit of counsel. In these and other situations immunities that are valid as against the federal government by force of the specific pledges of particular amendments have been found to be implicit in the concept of ordered liberty, and thus, through the Fourteenth Amendment, become valid as against the states.

The line of division may seem to be wavering and broken if there is a hasty catalogue of the cases on the one side and the other. Reflection and analysis will induce a different view. There emerges the perception of a rationalizing principle which gives to discrete instances a proper order and coherence. The right to trial by jury and the immunity from prosecution except as the result of an indictment may have value and importance. Even so, they are not of the very essence of a scheme of ordered liberty. To abolish them is not to violate a "principle of justice so rooted in the traditions and conscience of our people as to be ranked as fundamental." Few would be so narrow or provincial as to maintain that a fair and enlightened system of justice would be impossible without them. What is true of jury trials and indictments is true also, as the cases show, of the immunity from compulsory self-incrimination. *Twining v. New Jersey* [211 U.S. 78 (1908)]. This too might be lost, and justice still be done. . . .

We reach a different plane of social and moral values when we pass to the privileges and immunities that have been taken over from the earlier articles of the Federal Bill of Rights and brought within the Fourteenth Amendment by a process of absorption. These in their origin were effective against the federal government alone. If the Fourteenth Amendment has absorbed them, the process of absorption has had its source in the belief that neither liberty nor justice would exist if they were sacrificed. This is true, for illustration, of freedom of thought and speech. Of that freedom one may say that it is the matrix, the indispensable condition, of nearly every other form of freedom. . . .

Our survey of the cases serves, we think, to justify the statement that the dividing line between them, if not unfaltering throughout its course, has been true for the most part to a unifying principle. On which side of the line the case made out by the appellant has appropriate location must be the next inquiry and the final one. Is that kind of double jeopardy to which the statute has subjected him a hardship so acute and shocking that our policy will not endure it? Does it violate those "fundamental principles of liberty and justice which lie at the base of all our civil and political institutions"? The answer surely must be "no." What the answer would have to be if the state were permitted after a trial free from error to try the accused over again or to bring another case against him, we have no occasion to consider. We deal with the statute before us and no other. The state is not attempting to wear the accused out by a multitude of cases with accumulated trials. It asks no more than this, that the case against him shall go on until there shall be a trial free from the corrosion of substantial legal error. This is not cruelty at all, nor even vexation in any immoderate degree. . . .

The judgment is affirmed.

Mr. Justice Butler dissents.

The incorporation doctrine, however, was not immediately accepted by the Court. Instead, throughout the rest of the nineteenth century and early part of the twentieth century, the Court generally relied upon its holding in *Barron v. The Mayor and City of Baltimore* to conclude that the Bill of Rights did not apply to the states.[12] For example, in *Hurtado v. California* (1884),[13] the Court refused to apply the Fifth Amendment's guarantee of a grand jury indictment in all capital cases to the states. The Court reasoned that the Fourteenth Amendment's Due Process Clause was not intended to include the Fifth Amendment's indictment provision. Similarly, in *Palko v. Connecticut* (1937),[14] the Court refused to apply the Fifth Amendment's guarantee against double jeopardy to the states, reasoning that such a right was not so "implicit in the concept of ordered liberty" to be included among the liberties protected by the Fourteenth Amendment's Due Process Clause. And in *Adamson v. California* (1947),[15] the Court used similar logic to reject the incorporation of the Fifth Amendment's protection against self-incrimination in a California case where the prosecutor criticized a criminal defendant for not testifying in his own defense.

Gradually, however, the Court changed its course and began to incorporate select provisions of the Bill of Rights through the Fourteenth Amendment's Due Process Clause, thereby making these provisions applicable to the states. For example, in *Benyton v. Maryland* (1969),[16] the Court reversed its decision in *Palko,* and found that the Fifth Amendment right against double jeopardy should be incorporated through the Due Process Clause. And in *Malloy v. Hogan* (1964),[17] the Court likewise rejected its holding in *Adamson,* finding that the states must abide by the Fifth Amendment's protection against self-incrimination. Note, however, that the Court has not reversed its holding in *Hurtado* to make the grand jury indictment provision of the Fifth Amendment applicable to the states.

Between 1896 and 1972, the Court used the Fourteenth Amendment's Due Process Clause to incrementally incorporate nearly all of the provisions of the Bill of Rights. And today, only four provisions remain unincorporated. See Figure 8-3.

Incorporated or Nonincorporated?	
1st Amendment:	Totally incorporated.
2nd Amendment:	Totally incorporated.
3rd Amendment:	Not incorporated.
4th Amendment:	Totally incorporated.
5th Amendment:	Incorporated except for provision guaranteeing criminal prosecution only on a grand jury indictment.
6th Amendment:	Totally incorporated.
7th Amendment:	Not officially incorporated.
8th Amendment:	Provision against "cruel and unusual punishments" has been incorporated, but provisions regarding "excessive fines" and "excessive bail" have not been officially incorporated.

FIGURE 8-3

Incorporated or Nonincorporated?

total incorporation doctrine
A theory held by some jurists and legal scholars maintaining that the Fourteenth Amendment requires all of the provisions of the Bill of Rights to be incorporated and applied to the states.

select incorporation doctrine
A theory held by some jurists and legal scholars that maintains that only select portions of the Bill of Rights, which are deemed to involve "preferred freedoms" or rights "implicit in the concept of ordered liberty," should be incorporated through the Due Process Clause and made applicable to the states.

Officially, the Court has not incorporated the Third Amendment right against quartering troops in a person's house, the Fifth Amendment right to indictment by grand jury, the Seventh Amendment right to jury trial in civil cases, and the Eighth Amendment right against excessive fines and bail. However, many states have their own constitutional protections for these and other liberties.[18]

The Court's rationale for incorporating provisions from the Bill of Rights through the Fourteenth Amendment has varied. Some members of the Court have maintained that the Fourteenth Amendment requires that all of the provisions of the Bill of Rights be incorporated because they are the same liberties referenced in the Due Process Clause. This approach is called the **total incorporation doctrine.** Others maintain that only select portions of the Bill of Rights, which are deemed to involve "preferred freedoms" or rights "implicit in the concept of ordered liberty," should be applied to the states. This approach is referred to as the **select incorporation doctrine.** Either way, the reality today is that most of the provisions found in the Bill of Rights apply to state and local governments through the Due Process Clause of the Fourteenth Amendment. And so when asked why the states are required to avoid the establishment of religion, even though the First Amendment explicitly says, "Congress shall make no law respecting an establishment of religion," the answer is that, despite its facially restrictive language, the First Amendment has been incorporated and made applicable to the states through the Fourteenth Amendment Due Process Clause.

In recent years, the proponents of the Second Amendment right to bear arms successfully urged the Supreme Court to incorporate this provision, thereby making it applicable to the state and local governments. For years, laws regulating the possession of weapons varied greatly from state to state. Moreover, many municipalities enacted local ordinances even more restrictive than the laws of the states in which they are located. During this time, many state gun-control statutes (1) outlawed concealed weapons; (2) limited access to, or ownership of, handguns; (3) severely restricted ownership of modified shotguns and rifles, such as those that have been "sawed off"; and (4) criminalized possession of high explosives and weapons of mass destruction. Most states also had laws controlling the possession of guns by underage youths and laws that make it a crime to carry guns on school property or to discharge a firearm under specified circumstances. Many state codes went to considerable lengths in describing those to whom handgun and weapons laws do not apply, such as law enforcement officers, correctional personnel, and military personnel.

Military items for sale. The Supreme Court recently held that Americans have the right to own a gun for self-defense anywhere they live, striking down Chicago's nearly thirty-year-old handgun ban but leaving the door open for other gun-control legislation.

Douglas Litchfield/Shutterstock

But recently, a number of individuals and organizations, like the National Rifle Association, argued that American citizens have a fundamental right to own firearms and that this right should apply to limit state and local regulations of firearms. Arguments in support of the right to own or carry weapons are often based on the Second Amendment to the U.S. Constitution, which reads, "[a] well regulated Militia, being necessary to the security of a free State, the right of the people to keep and bear Arms, shall not be infringed." Others, however, say that the individual ownership of handguns, rifles, shotguns, and other similar weapons has no place in a civilized society like ours. They argue that the Second Amendment is merely a restriction on the actions of the federal Congress—and that states are free to regulate or limit gun ownership as they see fit.

In response, the U.S. Supreme Court issued two important rulings regarding these challenges. In *District of Columbia v. Heller* (2008),[19] the Supreme Court considered whether a District of Columbia law barring the registration of handguns, prohibiting carrying a pistol without a license, and requiring all lawful firearms to be kept unloaded and either disassembled or trigger-locked violated the Second Amendment right of civilians seeking to possess firearms for private use. In a 5–4 ruling, the Court struck down the law, holding that the Second Amendment protects an individual's right to possess a firearm in non-militia settings, and allows persons to use firearms for lawful purposes, like self-defense within the home. The ruling essentially rejected the theory that the Second Amendment protected only a collective right to bear arms for the purposes of maintaining a well-regulated militia.

In *McDonald v. Chicago* (2010) (discussed later in the text), the Court held that the right to "keep and bear arms" is an individual right protected by the Second Amendment that applies to both federal and state governments. In a 5–4 decision, the Court found that the Second Amendment was incorporated through the Fourteenth Amendment and made applicable to state and local authorities. The Court, however, did not state exactly what limitations the Second Amendment placed on state and local governments when they seek to regulate firearm possession. The Court even cautioned that some firearm restrictions, such as those "prohibit[ing] . . . the possession of firearms by felons or mentally ill" and "laws forbidding the carrying of firearms in sensitive

Cyber Constitution
***District of Columbia v. Heller* (2008)** http://supreme.justia.com/us/554/07-290/opinion.html

places such as schools and government buildings, or laws imposing conditions and qualifications on the commercial sale of arms" would still likely be permissible. The Court's ruling in *McDonald* is likely to generate a substantial number of new legal challenges to current state and local firearm possession laws.

McDonald et al. v. City of Chicago, Illinois, et al.
561 U.S. ____ (2010)

Justice Alito announced the judgment of the Court . . .

Two years ago, in *District of Columbia v. Heller*, 554 U.S. ____ (2008), we held that the Second Amendment protects the right to keep and bear arms for the purpose of self-defense, and we struck down a District of Columbia law that banned the possession of handguns in the home. The city of Chicago (City) and the village of Oak Park, a Chicago suburb, have laws that are similar to the District of Columbia's, but Chicago and Oak Park argue that their laws are constitutional because the Second Amendment has no application to the States. We have previously held that most of the provisions of the Bill of Rights apply with full force to both the Federal Government and the States. Applying the standard that is well established in our case law, we hold that the Second Amendment right is fully applicable to the States. . . .

Chicago and Oak Park (municipal respondents) maintain that a right set out in the Bill of Rights applies to the States only if that right is an indispensable attribute of *any* "civilized" legal system. If it is possible to imagine a civilized country that does not recognize the right, the municipal respondents tell us, then that right is not protected by due process. And since there are civilized countries that ban or strictly regulate the private possession of handguns, the municipal respondents maintain that due process does not preclude such measures. In light of the parties' far-reaching arguments, we begin by recounting this Court's analysis over the years of the relationship between the provisions of the Bill of Rights and the States.

The Bill of Rights, including the Second Amendment, originally applied only to the Federal Government. In *Barron ex rel. Tiernan v. Mayor of Baltimore*, 7 Pet. 243 (1833), the Court, in an opinion by Chief Justice Marshall, explained that this question was "of great importance" but "not of much difficulty." In less than four pages, the Court firmly rejected the proposition that the first eight Amendments operate as limitations on the States, holding that they apply only to the Federal Government.

In the late 19th century, the Court began to consider whether the Due Process Clause prohibits the States from infringing rights set out in the Bill of Rights. . . .

[W]e now turn directly to the question whether the Second Amendment right to keep and bear arms is incorporated in the concept of due process. In answering that question, as just explained, we must decide whether the right to keep and bear arms is fundamental to *our* scheme of ordered liberty, or as we have said in a related context, whether this right is "deeply rooted in this Nation's history and tradition."

Our decision in *Heller* points unmistakably to the answer. Self-defense is a basic right, recognized by many legal systems from ancient times to the present day, and in *Heller*, we held that individual self-defense is "the *central component*" of the Second Amendment right. Explaining that "the need for defense of self, family, and property is most acute" in the home, *ibid.*, we found that this right applies to handguns because they are "the most preferred firearm in the nation to 'keep' and use for protection of one's home and family." Thus, we concluded, citizens must be permitted "to use [handguns] for the core lawful purpose of self-defense."

Heller makes it clear that this right is "deeply rooted in this Nation's history and tradition.". . . .

In sum, it is clear that the Framers and ratifiers of the Fourteenth Amendment counted the right to keep and bear arms among those fundamental rights necessary to our system of ordered liberty. . . .

Municipal respondents maintain that the Second Amendment differs from all of the other provisions of the Bill of Rights because it concerns the right to possess a deadly implement and thus has implications for public safety. And they note that there is intense disagreement on the question whether the private possession of guns in the home increases or decreases gun deaths and injuries.

The right to keep and bear arms, however, is not the only constitutional right that has controversial public safety implications. All of the constitutional provisions that impose restrictions on law enforcement and on the prosecution of crimes fall into the same category. . . .

In *Heller*, we held that the Second Amendment protects the right to possess a handgun in the home for the purpose of self-defense. Unless considerations of *stare decisis* counsel otherwise, a provision of the Bill of Rights that protects a right that is fundamental from an American perspective applies equally to the Federal Government and the States. We therefore hold that the Due Process Clause of the Fourteenth Amendment incorporates the Second Amendment right recognized in *Heller*. The judgment of the Court of Appeals is reversed, and the case is remanded for further proceedings.

It is so ordered.

SHOULD THE FIFTH AMENDMENT RIGHT TO A GRAND JURY INDICTMENT FOR FELONY PROSECUTIONS APPLY TO STATE AUTHORITIES?

Given the Supreme Court's 1884 ruling in *Hurtado v. California* (discussed earlier in the text), which ruled that states are not required to use the grand jury indictment system to charge persons with felonies, many have questioned whether this decision should be overruled. Particularly in light of the Supreme Court's ruling incorporating the Second Amendment right to bear arms (discussed earlier in the text), some questioned the wisdom of allowing states to avoid the grand jury process in felony cases.[20] Review the history and purpose of grand juries in the United States, including the materials found at the University of Dayton Law School's website: http://campus.udayton.edu/~grandjur/stategj/stateg. htm. Based on this information and your consideration of the Court's opinions in *Hurtado* and *McDonald v. Chicago* (2010) (discussed later in the text), discuss whether the Fifth Amendment right to a grand jury indictment in felony cases should be incorporated through the Fourteenth Amendment Due Process Clause and made applicable to the states.

Cyber Constitution
McDonald v. Chicago
(2010) http://supreme.
justia.com/us/561/08-1521/

8.4 WHAT RIGHTS ARE PROTECTED?

Some people may be tempted to read the Bill of Rights in much the same manner as they would read the Articles of the Constitution—as an exhaustive and restrictive list of provisions that are not to be added to or modified without formal amendment. But there are reasons to be cautious about equating the drafting strategies employed to write the Articles of the Constitution with those used to write the Bill of Rights.

The Articles were designed to be a document that limited government, with the powers and duties delegated to the newly formed government designed to be exhaustive and exclusive. Note, for example, Article I, Section 8, which provides an itemized (although, in some cases, vaguely worded) list of the powers vested in Congress—the power to regulate commerce, to coin money, to declare war, to establish post offices, and so on. The purpose of providing this detailed list was to ensure limited government, thereby making it known that if Congress was not constitutionally vested with a particular power, it was barred from exercising it. This drafting technique is captured in the Latin maxim ***"inclusio unis est exclusio alterius,"*** which means the inclusion of one item is the exclusion of all others. Under this theory, the framers maintained that they could limit the scope and power of government by enumerating or listing the government's specific powers in the constitution, and that such documentation, by implication, would curtail any subsequent argument that the government had powers beyond those listed in the Constitution. So essentially, the framers theorized that if they went to the trouble of delegating specific powers to the three branches of government, all other forms of power, not specifically mentioned, would be excluded. Indeed, the Tenth Amendment reinforces this principle by providing that those powers not given to the federal government are reserved to the states or to the people.

This drafting strategy of limiting items by omitting them from the Constitution, however, does not apply to the rights contained in the Bill of Rights. In contrast to their desire to limit the authority of the federal government, many of the framers wanted to ensure that the Bill of Rights was not viewed as an exhaustive list of rights held by individuals. In other words, the framers did not seek to apply the doctrine of *inclusio unis est exclusio alterius* to the Bill of Rights. Instead, the Ninth Amendment

Inclusio unis est exclusio alterius
A Latin maxim used as a principle in drafting some documents, meaning "the inclusion of one item is the exclusion of all others." Under this theory, the framers maintained that they could limit the scope and power of government by enumerating or listing the government's specific powers in the Constitution, and that such documentation, by implication, would curtail any subsequent argument that the government had powers beyond those listed in the Constitution.

Fundamental Rights Not Specifically Listed in the Bill of Rights but Deemed Protected by the Constitution
Right to privacy—*Griswold v. Connecticut* (1965)
Right to travel—*Shapiro v. Thompson* (1969)
Right to an abortion—*Roe v. Wade* (1973)
Freedom of association—*NAACP v. Alabama* (1958)
Right to marriage—*Zablocki v. Redhail* (1978)

FIGURE 8-4
Other fundamental liberties

penumbras
A penumbra is a lunar shadow. Justice Douglas used this term as a metaphor in *Griswold v. Connecticut* (1965) to describe an individual's right to privacy under the Constitution. According to Douglas, even though privacy is not specifically enumerated in the Bill of Rights, there are certain penumbras or shadows cast by the First, Third, Fourth, Fifth, and Ninth Amendments that reflect that a right to privacy is protected by the Constitution.

makes it clear that although certain rights are specifically enumerated in the first eight amendments, other rights, which are not explicitly listed, may be protected against governmental interference as well. This drafting technique later opened the door for the Supreme Court to conclude that the freedom to marry, the right to travel, the right to privacy, and other rights, which are not specifically mentioned in the Bill of Rights, are nonetheless fundamental rights protected by the Constitution. See Figure 8-4.

For example, notice how the Supreme Court used the Ninth Amendment, in conjunction with other amendments, in *Griswold v. Connecticut* (1965)[21] to conclude that the Constitution protects an individual's right to privacy even though such a right is not specifically enumerated in the document. Specifically, the opinion of Justice William Douglas found that there are certain **penumbras** or shadows cast by the First, Third, Fourth, and Fifth Amendments that reflect that a right to privacy,

Griswold v. Connecticut
381 U.S. 479 (1965)

Mr. Justice Douglas delivered the opinion of the Court.

Appellant Griswold is Executive Director of the Planned Parenthood League of Connecticut. Appellant Buxton is a licensed physician and a professor at the Yale Medical School who served as Medical Director for the League at its Center in New Haven—a center open and operating from November 1 to November 10, 1961, when appellants were arrested.

They gave information, instruction, and medical advice to married persons as to the means of preventing conception. They examined the wife and prescribed the best contraceptive device or material for her use. Fees were usually charged, although some couples were serviced free.

The statutes whose constitutionality is involved in this appeal are 53-32 and 54-196 of the General Statutes of Connecticut. The former provides:

> Any person who uses any drug, medicinal article or instrument for the purpose of preventing conception shall be fined not less than fifty dollars or imprisoned not less than sixty days nor more than one year or be both fined and imprisoned.

Section 54-196 provides:

> Any person who assists, abets, counsels, causes, hires or commands another to commit any offense may be prosecuted and punished as if he were the principal offender.

The appellants were found guilty as accessories and fined $100 each, against the claim that the accessory statute as so applied violated the Fourteenth Amendment. . . .

Coming to the merits, we are met with a wide range of questions that implicate the Due Process Clause of the Fourteenth Amendment. . . . We do not sit as a superlegislature to determine the wisdom, need, and propriety of laws that touch economic problems, business affairs, or social conditions. This law, however, operates directly on an intimate relation of husband and wife and their physician's role in one aspect of that relation.

The association of people is not mentioned in the Constitution nor in the Bill of Rights. The right to educate a child in a school of the parents' choice—whether public or private or parochial—is also not mentioned. Nor is the right to study any particular subject or any foreign language. Yet the First Amendment has been construed to include certain of those rights. . . .

[Our] cases suggest that specific guarantees in the Bill of Rights have penumbras, formed by emanations from those guarantees that help give them life and substance. Various guarantees create zones of privacy. The right of association contained in the penumbra of the First Amendment is one, as we have seen. The Third Amendment in its prohibition against the quartering of soldiers "in any house" in time of peace without the consent of the owner is another facet of that privacy. The Fourth Amendment explicitly affirms the "right of the people to be secure in their persons, houses, papers, and effects, against unreasonable searches and seizures." The Fifth Amendment in its self-incrimination clause enables the citizen to create a zone of privacy which government may not force him to surrender to his detriment. The Ninth Amendment provides: "The enumeration in the Constitution, of certain rights, shall not be construed to deny or disparage others retained by the people." . . .

The present case, then, concerns a relationship lying within the zone of privacy created by several fundamental constitutional guarantees. And it concerns a law which, in forbidding the use of contraceptives rather than regulating their manufacture or sale, seeks to achieve its goals by means having a maximum destructive impact upon that relationship. Such a law cannot stand in light of the familiar principle, so often applied by this Court, that a "governmental purpose to control or prevent activities constitutionally subject to state regulation may not be achieved by means which sweep unnecessarily broadly and thereby invade the area of protected freedoms." Would we allow the police to search the sacred precincts of marital bedrooms for telltale signs of the use of contraceptives? The very idea is repulsive to the notions of privacy surrounding the marriage relationship. . . .

Reversed.

Mr. Justice Goldberg, whom the Chief Justice and Mr. Justice Brennan join, concurring.

The Ninth Amendment reads, "The enumeration in the Constitution, of certain rights, shall not be construed to deny or disparage others retained by the people." The Amendment is almost entirely the work of James Madison. It was introduced in Congress by him and passed the House and Senate with little or no debate and virtually no change in language. It was proffered to quiet expressed fears that a bill of specifically enumerated rights could not be sufficiently broad to cover all essential rights and that the specific mention of certain rights would be interpreted as a denial that others were protected. . . .

In sum, I believe that the right of privacy in the marital relation is fundamental and basic—a personal right "retained by the people" within the meaning of the Ninth Amendment. Connecticut cannot constitutionally abridge this fundamental right, which is protected by the Fourteenth Amendment from infringement by the States. I agree with the Court that petitioners' convictions must therefore be reversed.

Mr. Justice Harlan, concurring in the judgment.

In my view, the proper constitutional inquiry in this case is whether this Connecticut statute infringes the Due Process Clause of the Fourteenth Amendment because the enactment violates basic values "implicit in the concept of ordered liberty," . . . The Due Process Clause of the Fourteenth Amendment stands, in my opinion, on its own bottom.

Mr. Justice White, concurring in the judgment.

In my view this Connecticut law as applied to married couples deprives them of "liberty" without due process of law, as that concept is used in the Fourteenth Amendment. I therefore concur in the judgment of the Court reversing these convictions under Connecticut's aiding and abetting statute.

Mr. Justice Black, with whom Mr. Justice Stewart joins, dissenting. . . .

The Court talks about a constitutional "right of privacy" as though there is some constitutional provision or provisions forbidding any law ever to be passed which might abridge the "privacy" of individuals. But there is not. . . .

although not explicitly enumerated, is nonetheless protected by the Constitution. Read the Court's opinion in Griswold and take note of the different approaches or tests the justices used to determine whether a particular right is protected by the Bill of Rights.

Given the Supreme Court's decision in *Griswold*, recognizing the implicit right to personal privacy, what other unenumerated rights might be implicitly protected by the Bill of Rights? Keep in mind that the Ninth Amendment cautions that "[t]he enumeration in the Constitution, of certain rights, shall not be construed to deny or disparage others retained by the people." This provision suggests that there are other rights held by persons, which although not listed in the Bill of Rights are still protected as individual liberties. What rights might these include? What about the right to the medicinal use of marijuana? Or the right to physician-assisted suicide? See Chapter 12. Or the right to view and possess obscene materials? See Chapter 9.

Does the Bill of Rights and/or the Due Process Clause contain an implicit right for individuals to obtain and use marijuana for medical purposes?

Juan Camilo Bernal/Shutterstock

8.5 WHAT DOES THE BILL OF RIGHTS REQUIRE OF THE GOVERNMENT?

Finally, it should be noted that the Bill of Rights and the Due Process Clause of the Fourteenth Amendment are generally written in negative language. For example, the First Amendment begins by stating "Congress shall make *no* law respecting an establishment of religion." The Fourth Amendment provides, in part, that "The right of the people to be secure . . . against unreasonable searches and seizures shall *not* be violated." And the Fourteenth Amendment provides "*nor* shall any state *deprive* any person life, liberty, or property without due process of law." Each of these provisions essentially tells the government what *not* to do—do not make a law respecting the establishment of religion, do not violate the right against unreasonable searches and seizures, and do not deny a person due process. But these provisions do not tell the government what it must affirmatively do, if anything, regarding civil liberties. In other words, generally speaking, the government's obligation with respect to individual rights is formed in the negative (do not interfere with certain rights) as opposed to the affirmative (government must promote and advance individual rights).

Consistent with the facial language of the Bill of Rights and Due Process Clause, the Supreme Court generally has refrained from imposing any affirmative obligations on the government when it comes to the Bill of Rights and Due Process Clause. As Chief Justice Rehnquist explained in *DeShaney v. Winnebago County Department of Social Services* (1989):[22]

> [N]othing in the language of the Due Process Clause itself requires the State to protect the life, liberty, and property of its citizens against invasion by private actors. The Clause is phrased as a limitation on the State's power to act, not as a guarantee of certain minimal levels of safety and security. It forbids the State itself to deprive individuals of life, liberty, or property without "due process of law," but its language cannot fairly be extended to impose an affirmative obligation on the State to ensure that those interests do not come to harm through other means. Nor does history support such an expansive reading of the constitutional text. Like its counterpart in the Fifth Amendment, the Due Process Clause of the Fourteenth Amendment was intended to prevent government "from abusing [its] power, or employing it as an instrument of oppression[.]" Its purpose was to protect the people from

---

Sections 25, 26, and 27 of the Republic of South Africa's Bill of Rights as adopted on 8 May 1996 and amended on 11 October 1996 by the Constitutional Assembly.

Property

25. (1) No one may be deprived of property except in terms of law of general application, and no law may permit arbitrary deprivation of property.

    (2) Property may be expropriated only in terms of law of general application
      a. for a public purpose or in the public interest; and
      b. subject to compensation, the amount of which and the time and manner of payment of which have either been agreed to by those affected or decided or approved by a court.

. . .

    (5) The state must take reasonable legislative and other measures, within its available resources, to foster conditions which enable citizens to gain access to land on an equitable basis. . . .

    (6) A person or community whose tenure of land is legally insecure as a result of past racially discriminatory laws or practices is entitled, to the extent provided by an Act of Parliament, either to tenure which is legally secure or to comparable redress.

    (9) Parliament must enact the legislation referred to in subsection (6).

. . .

Housing

26. (1) Everyone has the right to have access to adequate housing.

    (2) The state must take reasonable legislative and other measures, within its available resources, to achieve the progressive realisation of this right.

    (3) No one may be evicted from their home, or have their home demolished, without an order of court made after considering all the relevant circumstances. No legislation may permit arbitrary evictions.

Health care, food, water, and social security

27. (1) Everyone has the right to have access to
      a. health care services, including reproductive health care;
      b. sufficient food and water; and
      c. social security, including, if they are unable to support themselves and their dependants, appropriate social assistance.

    (2) The state must take reasonable legislative and other measures, within its available resources, to achieve the progressive realisation of each of these rights.

    (3) No one may be refused emergency medical treatment.

FIGURE 8-5

The Bill of Rights in context

the State, not to ensure that the State protected them from each other. The Framers were content to leave the extent of governmental obligation in the latter area to the democratic political processes.

    Consistent with these principles, our cases have recognized that the Due Process Clauses generally confer no affirmative right to governmental aid, even where such aid may be necessary to secure life, liberty, or property interests of which the government itself may not deprive the individual. . . .

Under this reasoning, the Bill of Rights is regarded as a document that protects several explicit and implied liberties held by individuals, but that does not impose any affirmative obligations upon government to promote or advance these liberties. The government fulfills its constitutional duty simply by refraining from interfering with these liberties.

Compare, however, the Bill of Rights adopted by the Republic of South Africa (see Figure 8-5), where, with respect to some enumerated liberties—property, housing, health care, and so on—the government has a constitutional duty to promote civil liberties through legislative and other means. Notice how the South African Bill of

Cyber Constitution
The Bill of Rights Game
http://www.texaslre.org/
BOR/billofrights.html

Rights includes affirmative language mandating that "[t]he state must take reasonable legislative and other measures" to support the rights identified in the Bill of Rights.

8.6 MODERN CHALLENGES

Seemingly, there will always be legal challenges related to the Bill of Rights. In the near future, there are likely to be several ongoing challenges involving the Second Amendment and the right to bear arms. Although the Supreme Court in *District of Columbia v. Heller* (discussed earlier in the text) interpreted this provision as protecting an individual right, not a collective right, and in *McDonald v. Chicago* (discussed earlier in the text) made the provision applicable to the states through the Fourteenth Amendment Due Process Clause, there are still many issues left unresolved. For example, like all other rights protected under the Bill of Rights, the right to bear arms is not, and cannot be, an absolute right that is protected under all circumstances. Even with Second Amendment freedoms, individuals still will not likely be able to carry guns into jails, planes, courtrooms, or government buildings. And many individuals, such as convicted felons, children, and the mentally disabled, may also be barred from recognizing their right to bear arms. In short, while the government may now have some constitutional obligation to honor Second Amendment freedoms, the question is to what extent will this right be counterbalanced and outweighed by strong governmental interests, such as national security, public safety, and the needs of law enforcement? Chances are there will be many constitutional cases in the next few years that seek to test the limits of the newly expanded rights under the Second Amendment.

In addition, with the incorporation of the Second Amendment, there likely will be new efforts to incorporate the remaining provisions of the Bill of Rights, which have yet to be incorporated. While there may be little, if any, pressing demand to incorporate the Third Amendment right against the quartering of troops, other yet-to-be-incorporated rights, such as the Fifth Amendment right to an indictment by a grand jury in felony cases and the Eighth Amendment rights against excessive bail and fines, may be the subjects of new litigation.

There also remain many questions left regarding who the Constitution protects. The Supreme Court has ruled that corporations have First Amendment rights to free speech (Chapter 9) and that foreign nationals held has enemy combatants may have different levels of constitutional protection in the courts (Chapter 5). In light of these rulings, the Court may be presented with additional questions about how the Bill of Rights should be applied to other groups of people and entities.

Finally, the ongoing debate over same-sex marriage may also test the substance of the Bill of Rights. For a number of years, the Supreme Court has found that the right to marry is a fundamental right protected by the Constitution, even though it is not specifically enumerated in the document. As the looming battles over same-sex marriage advance closer and closer to a Supreme Court showdown, constitutional scholars will continue to explore whether such marriage is one of those implicit freedoms suggested by the Ninth Amendment or a right that is simply not protected by the text or spirit of the Constitution.

8.7 SUMMARY

The Bill of Rights consists of the first ten amendments to the Constitution. They are regarded as safeguards to individual liberties, protecting such interests as the freedom of speech, freedom of religion, the right against unreasonable searches and seizures, and the right to be free from cruel and unusual punishment. The Bill of Rights was drafted in 1789, after the ratification of the Articles of the Constitution, fulfilling a promise made to those who were concerned that the Articles themselves did not do enough to guard against governmental encroachment of personal liberties.

For some, the freedoms contained in the Bill of Rights are natural rights, which are vested in all individuals as a matter of birthright. For others, these freedoms are not inherently given, but rather negotiated for under the terms of the Constitution. Either way, the Bill of Rights provides important limitations on governmental authority in the face of individual liberties.

Initially, the Bill of Rights was applied only to the federal government, not to state or local governments. But following the ratification of the Fourteenth Amendment, the Court began to slowly incorporate or apply most of the rights contained in the Bill of Rights to the states, using the Due Process Clause as the method for such incorporation. Today, all but four provisions of the Bill of Rights have been applied to the states.

Although the Bill of Rights contains several enumerated rights, the Court also has held that the document protects a number of additional rights as well. These rights include the right to privacy, marriage, travel, and association. Some members of the Court have justified the addition of these rights by referencing the Ninth Amendment, which makes it clear that the enumeration of certain rights within the Bill of Rights was not intended to exclude other rights of the people that still must be protected against governmental intrusion.

The Bill of Rights generally gives the government a number of negative instructions—do not interfere with the freedom of speech, do not engage in unreasonable searches and seizure, and so on. And while we hold these freedoms to be essential to the success and survival of our constitutional democracy, note that the government is under no obligation to promote or advance the freedom of speech or the right to privacy. The Bill of Rights simply tells the government not to interfere with these and other liberties.

REVIEW QUESTIONS

1. How does the Bill of Rights differ from the Articles of the Constitution?
2. Why was the Bill of Rights added to the Constitution?
3. Explain the difference between the compact theory and natural rights theory of civil liberties.
4. What was James Madison's role in drafting the Bill of Rights?
5. Why do state and local governments have to comply with most of the provisions in the Bill of Rights when the document begins with "Congress shall make no law"?
6. Explain how most of the liberties found in the Bill of Rights are incorporated through the Fourteenth Amendment Due Process Clause.
7. What rights are protected under the Bill of Rights even though they are not specifically listed in the document?
8. Where does the right to privacy come from?
9. What purpose does the Ninth Amendment serve?
10. What affirmative obligations are imposed on the government under the Bill of Rights?

ASSIGNMENTS: CONSTITUTIONAL LAW IN ACTION

The Constitution in Your Community

Assume that you are working as a paralegal for a newly formed law firm that wants to specialize in civil rights litigation. As a part of this new practice, the firm would like to represent individuals whose constitutional rights have allegedly been violated. A number of the attorneys with the new firm are not from your home state, and so they are not that familiar with your state's constitution. Certainly, all of the lawyers are well trained in U.S. constitutional law and the Bill of Rights. But they would like to know the extent to which your home state's constitution affords individuals greater legal protections in some areas. For example, does your home state constitution place greater restrictions on police search and seizures or custodial interrogations (see Chapter 13) than those imposed by the Fourth and Fifth Amendments to the U.S. Constitution? The attorneys need this information so that they can make strategic decisions as to what law to use in filing certain types of constitutional-based civil rights suits. Accordingly, you are asked to prepare a memorandum identifying whether and to what extent your home state's constitution either provides individuals with additional rights not protected under the Bill of Rights and/or affords greater legal protections for rights, such as speech, religion, etc., currently protected by the Bill of Rights.

Going Federal

In the wake of the Supreme Court's ruling in *District of Columbia v. Heller* (2008) and *McDonald v. Chicago* (2010) (discussed earlier in the text), a number of communities, including Chicago, have rewritten their gun-control laws in an effort to comply with the Court's ruling. For example, Westchester County, New York, Alan Kachalsky, and Christina Nikolov filed a federal complaint challenging the local handgun permit process. Using electronic resources, locate the complaint filed in *Kachalsky and Nikolov v. Westchester County*. Next, identify a handgun permit law in your jurisdiction or in a location that has recently revised its handgun laws in light of Heller and McDonald. Then, using the complaint filed in Kachalsky, prepare a federal complaint challenging your local handgun law under the Second Amendment.

Moot Court

In light of the Supreme Court's ruling in *McDonald v. Chicago* (2010), which incorporated the Second Amendment through the Fourteenth Amendment Due Process Clause, thereby making it applicable to the state and local governments, many people are left to wonder whether the Supreme Court should do the same with the yet-to-be-incorporated Fifth Amendment right to a grand jury indictment in felony cases. As discussed earlier, ever since the Court's ruling in *Hurtado v. California* (1884), states have been free under the Bill of Rights to use the grand jury process to indict persons for felonies or to use another system, such as the information process, whereby a prosecutor can directly charge person with a felony. Assume that you are working with a criminal defense attorney whose client was charged with a felony in a state jurisdiction that does not require a grand jury indictment. The attorney wishes to use the Supreme Court's reasoning in *McDonald* to challenge the constitutionality of the felony charge by arguing that the client's Fifth Amendment right has been violated. Working in teams of two, the first team should prepare a five-minute oral argument presentation wherein they use the Court's ruling in *McDonald* to support an argument that the Fifth Amendment right to a grand jury indictment ought to be incorporated through the Fourteenth Amendment and made applicable to the states. Conversely, the second team should prepare a five-minute oral argument asserting why the Court's ruling in *McDonald* should not be used to incorporate the Fifth Amendment right to a grand jury indictment.

NOTES

1. Thomas Jefferson, *The Papers of Thomas Jefferson*, Vol. 14, ed. Julian Boyd (Princeton, NJ: Princeton University Press 1950), p. 440.
2. Technically, the Articles of the Constitution were ratified on June 21, 1788, when New Hampshire became the ninth state to approve the document. Under Article VII of the new Constitution, only nine of the thirteen states were required to ratify the document to make it effective.

3. This theory is reflected in a Latin maxim that frequently governs legal disputes over contracts: "*inclusio unis est exclusio alterious*," which means "the inclusion of one is the exclusion of all others." Under this theory, if parties to a contract go to the trouble of enumerating a list of specific items to be covered by the agreement, by inference, the inclusion of these specific items bars any additional items from being covered after the contract is finalized.

4. The original Second Amendment affecting congressional pay raises was later adopted and ratified on May 7, 1992, as the Twenty-Seventh Amendment.

5. The Declaration of Independence provides that in order to secure unalienable rights, "governments are instituted among men, deriving their just powers from the consent of the governed."

6. Alan Dershowitz, *Rights from Wrongs: The Origins of Human Rights in the Experience of Injustice* (Basic Books 2004).

7. Louis Henkin, "Rights: Here and There," 81 *Columbia Law Review* 1582 (1981).

8. 494 U.S. 259 (1990).

9. 32 U.S. 23 (1833).

10. Note that the Fifth Amendment contains a Due Process Clause as well. But this clause has been interpreted to apply to the federal government. See *Bolling v. Sharpe*, 347 U.S. 497 (1954).

11. See Ted Gurr and Desmond King, *The State and the City* (Chicago: The University of Chicago Press 1987).

12. In 1896 and 1897, the Court did incorporate the Fifth Amendment's guarantee to just compensation for the government's taking of private property. See *Missouri Pacific Railway Co. v. Nebraska*, 164 U.S. 403 (1896); *Chicago, Burlington & Quincy Railway Co. v. Chicago*, 166 U.S. 226 (1897).

13. 110 U.S. 516 (1884).

14. 302 U.S. 319 (1937).

15. 332 U.S. 46 (1947).

16. 395 U.S. 784 (1969).

17. 378 U.S. 1 (1964).

18. See Robert Dowlut, "Federal and State Constitutional Guarantees to Arms," 15 *U. Dayton L. Rev.* 1–89 (1989).

19. 554 U.S. 570; 128 S. Ct. 2783 (2008).

20. "Prosecutor wants Philadelphia to revive grand jury system," *Pittsburg Tribune Review*, www.pittsburghlive.com/x/pittsburghtrib/news/regional/s_685904.html

21. 391 U.S. 145 (1965).

22. 489 U.S. 189 (1989).

9

First Amendment Freedoms of Expression, Association, and Press

The right to think is the beginning of freedom, and speech must be protected from the government because speech is the beginning of thought.

JUSTICE ANTHONY KENNEDY[1]

LEARNING OBJECTIVES
At the end of this chapter you should be able to:

■ Identify the differences between conduct, content, and viewpoint restrictions on speech.

■ Explain the vagueness and overbreadth doctrines, and apply them to legislative restrictions on expression.

■ Appreciate the differences between a ban and a regulation on speech and the distinction between public and nonpublic forums for speech.

■ Know the types of speech that are not protected by the First Amendment.

■ Identify the standards used to evaluate the right to the freedom of association.

■ Discuss the constitutional and legal issues that are related to the freedom of the press.

■ Identify a contemporary issue concerning freedom of expression under the First Amendment, and discuss the most likely future scenarios, referencing both historical analogs and caselaw.

■ Brief a judicial opinion with little outside assistance. You should be successful in identifying the relevant facts, identifying the legal issue(s), and analyzing the court's rationale in at least 70 percent of your briefs.

■ Apply what you have learned to a new set of facts with little assistance.

9.1 THE VALUES SERVED BY THE FREEDOM OF EXPRESSION

The First Amendment provides that "Congress shall make no law respecting an establishment of religion, or prohibiting the free exercise thereof; or abridging the freedom of speech, or of the press; or the right of the people peaceably to assemble, and to petition the Government for a redress of grievances." Within this provision, the Constitution offers protection for a number of different freedoms. The first two—the right to be free from the establishment of religion and the right to be free to exercise religion—will be covered in Chapter 10. The remaining freedoms of speech, press, assembly, and petition, while conceptually and fundamentally distinct from one another, all promote at least three common values: (1) the idea that governmental power can be limited by allowing individuals to critique and otherwise scrutinize their public officials and policies, (2) the notion that a democratic government functions best when conflicting interests are allowed to compete in an open marketplace, and (3) the belief that individual expression is a necessary condition for human health.

With regard to the first value, it is clear from the ratification proceedings surrounding the Articles of the Constitution that the First Amendment was designed to install additional checks and balances on governmental power. As discussed in Chapter 8, many of those debating the proposed constitution were concerned that it gave the new government too much authority and that additional measures were necessary to further guard against tyranny. To accommodate these concerns, the framers added a bill of rights following the ratification of the Constitution. And so just as the Articles of the Constitution sought to limit the power of the new government by separating its powers and by providing oversight authorities to each branch over the other branches, the First Amendment similarly provides legal mechanisms for scrutinizing and otherwise limiting governmental authority. Whether publicly protesting a piece of legislation, publishing a news article against a president's decision, gathering together for a common cause, or organizing a group demonstration to achieve greater legal protections, the First Amendment provides methods for individuals to interact with and to regulate governmental activity. As the Supreme Court has observed, "speech concerning public affairs . . . is the essence of self-government."[2]

And in reality, there are plenty of examples where these methods have been successful in limiting or directing governmental authority. In the 1950s, organized efforts by the National Association for the Advancement of Colored People led to the Supreme Court striking down school segregation. In the 1960s, public speeches and rallies led by Martin Luther King convinced Congress to pass legislation banning certain forms of discrimination. In the early 1970s, news stories written by Carl Bernstein and Bob Woodward of *The Washington Post* led to the resignation of President Richard Nixon and the criminal prosecution of several members of the president's staff. And in 2002, a voter initiative by California citizens resulted in Governor Gray Davis being removed from office and replaced by Arnold Schwarzenegger. In each instance, an individual or a group of individuals exercised their First Amendment freedoms to effectuate or change the power of government.

In addition to impacting public policy, the freedom of expression is also valued because it promotes peace and stability among diverse groups of people. In lobbying for the ratification of the Constitution, James Madison spoke in *Federalist No.10* of the impact of **factions** on government. Factions are individual or isolated interests that can destroy or substantially impair government if they are allowed to override the common good. According to Madison, there are two ways to deal with factions—eliminate them or manage them. For Madison, the first option was not realistic because it would result in a totalitarian government suppressing and otherwise quashing individual interests. As a result, Madison felt that the only way to address factions in a democratic society was to allow them to exist, but to manage them, so that one interest did not rise to dominate the rest. To that end, Madison believed that the Constitution would allow factions to be pitted against one another, thereby allowing them to be managed in a marketplace of competition.

Consistent with Madison's recommended treatment of factions, courts frequently have adopted the notion that the First Amendment fosters a **marketplace of ideas** for individuals to sell, purchase, and evaluate different concepts, thereby allowing individual factions to check one another. Through open exchange, based on speech, assembly, press, and petition, it is believed society will be in a better position to manage and balance the diversity of "products" (ideas) being offered.[3] In an often-quoted dissenting opinion, Justice Oliver Wendell Holmes supported this marketplace theory, stating,

> But when men have realized that time has upset many fighting faiths, they may come to believe even more than they believe the very foundations of their own conduct that the ultimate good desired is better reached by free trade in ideas—that the best test of truth is the power of the thought to get itself accepted in the competition of the market, and that truth is the only ground upon which their wishes safely can be carried out.[4]

Finally, the freedom of expression is also valued because it offers individuals an outlet for personal thoughts and creativity. Regardless of the practical benefits to government, it is believed that the First Amendment's protections provide individuals

factions
Individual or isolated interests that can destroy or substantially impair government if they are allowed to override the common good. According to James Madison in *Federalist No. 10*, the only way to address factions in a democratic society was to allow them to exist, but to manage them, so that one interest did not rise to dominate the rest. To that end, Madison believed that the Constitution would allow factions to be pitted against one another, thereby allowing them to be managed in a marketplace of competition.

marketplace of ideas
A phrase used in some free speech cases to describe the type of environment the First Amendment fosters for individuals to sell, purchase, and evaluate different ideas through speech. The idea is that if individual ideas are allowed to compete against one another through open exchange, using speech, assembly, press, and petition, society will be in a better position to manage and balance the diversity of "products" (ideas) being offered.

with a means for expressing themselves, thereby providing a healthy method of developing and releasing emotions and ideas. Rather than forcing individuals to bottle up their thoughts and beliefs, as is the case with more totalitarian governments, the First Amendment generally gives individuals the opportunity to release their innermost ideas and beliefs in public discourse. Of course, that often means that unpopular views and ideas will enter the public arena. For example, in some contexts, protesters will be allowed to burn a U.S. flag,[5] neo-Nazis will be permitted to march down Main Street,[6] and the KKK will be given a permit to erect a cross on the public square.[7] But such public expression of unpopular views is generally preferred to the suppression of ideas, which, if allowed to fester behind closed doors with no available outlet, may lead to far more destructive behavior. In other words, the expression of thought is generally viewed as being beneficial to human development. As Justice Anthony Kennedy stated, "[t]he right to think is the beginning of freedom, and speech must be protected from the government because speech is the beginning of thought."[8]

Cyber Constitution
Picketing Military Funerals with Offensive Speech http://www.nytimes.com/2011/03/03/us/03scotus.html?pagewanted=all

---

YOUR CONSTITUTIONAL VALUES

CAN A PERSON BE PROSECUTED FOR PRIVATELY EXPRESSING CRIMINAL THOUGHTS?

In 1998, Brian J. Dalton was charged with ten counts of pandering obscenity involving a minor and twenty counts of pandering sexually oriented material involving a minor in an Ohio state court. Dalton eventually pled guilty to five counts of pandering obscenity involving a minor and five counts of pandering sexually oriented material involving a minor. The trial court sentenced Dalton to eighteen months in prison.

After serving almost four months of his prison term, Dalton was granted judicial release and placed on probation for three years. However, shortly thereafter, Dalton was arrested for lack of participation in his sex-offender-treatment program, a violation of his probation. After his arrest, Dalton's mother contacted Scott Merrick, Dalton's probation officer. She told Merrick that she had visited Dalton's apartment and was concerned about some items she had discovered there. She asked Merrick to come to the apartment and remove those items.

That same day, Merrick and another probation officer met Dalton's mother at Dalton's apartment. When they arrived, she had already placed several items on Dalton's bed, including Dalton's personal, handwritten journal. Merrick took all of the items back to the probation department, where he began to read Dalton's journal. The journal depicted Dalton's personal fantasies of the violent torture and rape of a number of purely fictitious children. After reading Dalton's journal, Merrick contacted a detective from the Columbus Police Sexual Abuse Squad, who came to the probation department and took the journal.

Authorities later charged Dalton with two counts of pandering obscenity involving a minor. Both charges were based solely upon Dalton's personal journal discovered in his apartment. The trial court appointed an attorney to represent Dalton. In July 2001, Dalton entered a guilty plea to one count of pandering obscenity involving a minor in exchange for the dismissal of the other count of the indictment. The trial court accepted appellant's guilty plea and sentenced him to seven years in prison. In addition, the court found that Dalton violated the terms of his probation, and ordered him to serve the remainder of his original prison term consecutive to the seven-year prison term.

In August 2001, Dalton filed a motion to withdraw his guilty plea, asserting that, under the First Amendment, he should not have been charged with two

counts of pandering obscenity based on his personal thoughts in his journal. The trial court, however, denied Dalton's motion.

Based on your constitutional values, do you think Dalton's expression was protected by the First Amendment? What impact does the Court's decision in *Ashcroft v. Free Speech Coalition* (2002) (see later in this chapter) have on your decision?

To see how the court of appeals decided this case, go to *State v. Dalton*, 153 Ohio App.3d 286, 2003-Ohio-3813.

9.2 THE SCOPE AND SUBSTANCE OF THE FIRST AMENDMENT

First Amendment provisions protecting expression generally are not read or applied literally. The phrase "Congress shall make no law . . . abridging the freedom of speech, or of the press; or the right of the people peaceably to assemble, and to petition the Government for a redress of grievances" does not merely apply to Congress; nor does it simply apply to laws or legislation; nor does it provide absolute protection for all forms of speech, press, assembly, petition, and association. Instead, through judicial interpretation, the text of the First Amendment has been interpreted to apply to other bodies and layers of government, to extend to more governmental activity than just legislation, and to impose certain limits on individual expression.

As discussed in Chapter 8, the Supreme Court gradually has incorporated most of the provisions within the Bill of Rights, thereby making them applicable to the states. This is true for all rights of expression protected by the First Amendment. In 1927, the Supreme Court formally incorporated the freedom of speech through the Fourteenth Amendment and applied it to the states in *Fiske v. Kansas*,[9] although the Supreme Court had suggested in 1920 and 1925 that the states were obligated to protect this freedom.[10] In 1931, the Court incorporated the freedom of the press in *Near v. Minnesota*.[11] Six years later, in *DeJonge v. Oregon*,[12] the Court incorporated the freedom of assembly, an incorporation that has been interpreted to include the freedom to petition the government for redress of grievances. And in 1958, the Court decided *NAACP v. Alabama*,[13] concluding that the First Amendment implicitly included another freedom—the freedom of association—and made this right applicable to the states. Consequently, governments at all levels—federal, state, and local—are required to protect the freedom of expression, in its various forms, as required by the First Amendment.

Similarly, the First Amendment's protections extend to more than just laws passed by legislatures. In addition to legislation, the First Amendment also applies to executive, judicial, and administrative conduct that interferes with such freedoms. And so, for example, the First Amendment has been applied to presidential attempts to restrict the dissemination of information,[14] to judicial orders that restrict the press from public courtrooms,[15] and to administrative actions that try to curb "indecent" language on radio and television.[16]

Finally, it is important to appreciate that the First Amendment protections of expression are not absolute. Despite the seemingly unequivocal wording of the amendment, the rights of speech, press, assembly, petition, and association have been interpreted to have certain limitations. The most common statement offered to illustrate this point is the claim that individuals do not have the right to falsely shout "fire!" in a crowded theater.[17] The idea behind this is that, although this situation involves a person's speech, it also involves the safety of others, and there are times when a second value, such as human safety or national security, is going to trump or otherwise limit the value of speech. This trumping may also occur when a newspaper publishes false information, individuals threaten bodily harm to public officials, or people assemble or associate in a conspiracy to commit a crime. In each case, a competing value—a person's reputation, individual health, or public safety—likely will be deemed to outweigh the individual's interest in self-expression.

As discussed in the next section, the Supreme Court frequently adopts balancing tests or doctrines to resolve controversies over free expression. These balancing tests are designed not only to assist in resolving the immediate controversy before the Court, but also to provide other courts and litigants in future cases with some guidelines or standards for interpreting First Amendment protections. One may think of these balancing tests as scales used to weigh the value of expression against other competing values (national security, public safety, equality, etc.). In visualizing these tests as scales, there are two important considerations. First, has the Court "calibrated" the scale (balancing test) in advance of the "weigh-in" to favor one side over the other? In other words, has the Court presumed certain forms of expression to be constitutionally protected, thereby requiring the government to produce a very heavy (compelling) interest on the other side of the scale before the Court will find the right of expression to be unprotected? And second, how compelling (heavy) are the interests placed on each side of the scale? Appreciate the fact that the weighing of competing interests on each side of the scale involves certain value judgments to be made by those doing the weighing. As the Court has stated, "[i]t is pertinent to the decision before us to consider where on the scales of values we have in the past placed the type of speech now claiming constitutional immunity."[18]

9.3 BASIC APPROACHES TO FREEDOM OF SPEECH

One of the first questions that must be addressed when discussing the freedom of speech is the nature and scope of speech itself. Obviously, the First Amendment includes speech that involves verbal communication. But what about other types of human activity, such as electronic messaging, visual images, art, music, movies, signs, symbols, and dancing? These forms and activities, on the surface, are not pure forms of speech because they do not necessarily involve a person speaking verbally. At the same time, each has the potential for communicating ideas in a manner similar to that offered by verbal speech. Consistent with the latter observation, the Supreme Court often has treated nonverbal expression as "speech," as long as it communicates or expresses an idea that can readily be received and understood by others. Promoting the notion that the First Amendment should promote and protect a "marketplace of ideas," the Court has treated such things as books, movies, photographs, electronic texts and images, messages on clothing, flag burning, flag saluting, commercial advertising, and dancing as forms of speech.[19]

9.3(a) Conduct Verses Expression

There are times, however, when an individual's conduct will be viewed as just that—conduct—with very little or no communicative value. As a result, in examining the government's regulation of speech, the first issue that must be addressed is whether the government is regulating the expression of ideas (speech) or harmful behavior (conduct). In most cases, such an examination will involve contextual analysis and value judgments. If the case involves speech, the government likely will have to satisfy a more rigorous standard or balancing test. But if the case involves conduct, the government generally will be allowed more discretion in regulating the targeted activity, and in most cases, the government's actions will be permitted if they are reasonably related to a legitimate governmental interest. Read the Court's decision in *Texas v. Johnson* (1989) to see how the Court has considered this initial question regarding the difference between speech and conduct.

Texas v. Johnson
491 U.S. 397 (1989)

During the 1984 Republican National Convention in Dallas, Texas, Gregory Johnson participated in a political demonstration to protest the policies of the Reagan administration and some Dallas-based corporations. After a march through the city streets, Johnson burned an American flag while protesters chanted. No one was physically injured or threatened with injury, although several witnesses were seriously offended by the flag burning. Johnson was convicted of desecration of a venerated object in violation of a Texas statute, and a state court of appeals affirmed. However, the Texas Court of Criminal Appeals reversed, holding that the state, consistent with the First Amendment, could not punish Johnson for burning the flag in these circumstances. The state appealed that decision to the Supreme Court.

Justice Brennan delivered the opinion of the Court.

Johnson was convicted of flag desecration for burning the flag rather than for uttering insulting words. This fact somewhat complicates our consideration of his conviction under the First Amendment. We must first determine whether Johnson's burning of the flag constituted expressive conduct, permitting him to invoke the First Amendment in challenging his conviction. If his conduct was expressive, we next decide whether the State's regulation is related to the suppression of free expression. See, e.g., *United States v. O'Brien*, 391 U.S. 367, 377 (1968). If the State's regulation is not related to expression, then the less stringent standard we announced in *United States v. O'Brien* for regulations of noncommunicative conduct controls. If it is, then we are outside of O'Brien's test, and we must ask whether this interest justifies Johnson's conviction under a more demanding standard. A third possibility is that the State's asserted interest is simply not implicated on these facts, and in that event the interest drops out of the picture . . .

The First Amendment literally forbids the abridgment only of "speech," but we have long recognized that its protection does not end at the spoken or written word. While we have rejected "the view that an apparently limitless variety of conduct can be labeled 'speech' whenever the person engaging in the conduct intends thereby to express an idea," we have acknowledged that conduct may be "sufficiently imbued with elements of communication to fall within the scope of the First and Fourteenth Amendments[.]"

In deciding whether particular conduct possesses sufficient communicative elements to bring the First Amendment into play, we have asked whether "[a]n intent to convey a particularized message was present, and [whether] the likelihood was great that the message would be understood by those who viewed it." . . .

The State of Texas conceded for purposes of its oral argument in this case that Johnson's conduct was expressive conduct . . . Johnson burned an American flag as part—indeed, as the culmination—of a political demonstration that coincided with the convening of the Republican Party and its renomination of Ronald Reagan for President. The expressive, overtly political nature of this conduct was both intentional and overwhelmingly apparent. At his trial, Johnson explained his reasons for burning the flag as follows: "The American Flag was burned as Ronald Reagan was being renominated as President. And a more powerful statement of symbolic speech, whether you agree with it or not, couldn't have been made at that time. It's quite a just position [juxtaposition]. We had new patriotism and no patriotism." In these circumstances, Johnson's burning of the flag was conduct "sufficiently imbued with elements of communication," to implicate the First Amendment.

The government generally has a freer hand in restricting expressive conduct than it has in restricting the written or spoken word. It may not, however, proscribe particular conduct because it has expressive elements. . . . It is, in short, not simply the verbal or nonverbal nature of the expression, but the governmental interest at stake, that helps to determine whether a restriction on that expression is valid.

Thus, although we have recognized that where "'speech' and 'nonspeech' elements are combined in the same course of conduct, a sufficiently important governmental interest in regulating the nonspeech element can justify incidental limitations on First Amendment freedoms," we have limited the applicability of *O'Brien's* relatively lenient standard to those cases in which "the governmental interest is unrelated to the suppression of free expression." . . .

In order to decide whether *O'Brien's* test applies here, therefore, we must decide whether Texas has asserted an interest in support of Johnson's conviction that is unrelated to the suppression of expression. If we find that an interest asserted by the State is simply not implicated on the facts before us, we need not ask whether *O'Brien's* test applies. The State offers two separate interests to justify this conviction: preventing breaches of the peace and preserving the flag as a symbol of nationhood and national unity. We hold that the first interest is not implicated on this record and that the second is related to the suppression of expression.

Texas claims that its interest in preventing breaches of the peace justifies Johnson's conviction for flag desecration. However, no disturbance of the peace actually occurred or threatened to occur because of Johnson's burning of the flag. Although the State stresses the disruptive behavior of the protestors during their march toward City Hall, it admits that "no actual breach of the peace occurred at the time of the flagburning or in response to the flagburning." . . .

The State also asserts an interest in preserving the flag as a symbol of nationhood and national unity. . . . We are equally persuaded that this interest is related to expression in the case of Johnson's burning of the flag. The State, apparently, is concerned that such conduct will lead people to believe either that the flag does not stand for nationhood and national unity, but instead reflects other, less positive concepts, or that the concepts reflected in the flag do not in fact exist, that is, that we do not enjoy unity as a Nation. . . . We are thus outside of O'Brien's test altogether.

It remains to consider whether the State's interest in preserving the flag as a symbol of nationhood and national unity justifies Johnson's conviction. . . .

Whether Johnson's treatment of the flag violated Texas law thus depended on the likely communicative impact of his expressive conduct. Our decision in *Boos v. Barry*, [485 U.S. 312 (1988)], tells us that this restriction on Johnson's expression is content based. In *Boos*, we considered the constitutionality of a law prohibiting "the display of any sign within 500 feet of a foreign embassy if that sign tends to bring that foreign government into 'public odium' or 'public disrepute.'" Rejecting the argument that the law was content neutral because it was justified by "our international law obligation to shield diplomats from speech that offends their dignity," we held that "[t]he emotive impact of speech on its audience is not a 'secondary effect'" unrelated to the content of the expression itself.

According to the principles announced in *Boos*, Johnson's political expression was restricted because of the content of the message he conveyed. We must therefore subject the State's asserted interest in preserving the special symbolic character of the flag to "the most exacting scrutiny." . . .

The State's argument is not that it has an interest simply in maintaining the flag as a symbol of something, no matter what it symbolizes; indeed, if that were the State's position, it would be difficult to see how that interest is endangered by highly symbolic conduct such as Johnson's. Rather, the State's claim is that it has an interest in preserving the flag as a symbol of nationhood and national unity, a symbol with a determinate range of meanings. According to Texas, if one physically treats the flag in a way that would tend to cast doubt on either the idea that nationhood and national unity are the flag's referents or that national unity actually exists, the message conveyed thereby is a harmful one and therefore may be prohibited.

If there is a bedrock principle underlying the First Amendment, it is that the government may not prohibit the expression of an idea simply because society finds the idea itself offensive or disagreeable. . . .

In short, nothing in our precedents suggests that a State may foster its own view of the flag by prohibiting expressive conduct relating to it. . . .

It is not the State's ends, but its means, to which we object. It cannot be gainsaid that there is a special place reserved for the flag in this Nation, and thus we do not doubt that the government has a legitimate interest in making efforts to "preserv[e] the national flag as an unalloyed symbol of our country." . . .

The way to preserve the flag's special role is not to punish those who feel differently about these matters. It is to persuade them that they are wrong. . . .

The judgment of the Texas Court of Criminal Appeals is therefore

Affirmed.

Justice Kennedy, concurring.

With all respect to [the dissenters], I do not believe the Constitution gives us the right to rule as the dissenting Members of the Court urge, however painful this judgment is to announce. Though symbols often are what we ourselves make of them, the flag is constant in expressing beliefs Americans share, beliefs in law and peace and that freedom which sustains the human spirit. The case here today forces recognition of the costs to which those beliefs commit us. It is poignant but fundamental that the flag protects those who hold it in contempt. . . .

Chief Justice Rehnquist, with whom Justice White and Justice O'Connor join, dissenting.

The American flag, then, throughout more than 200 years of our history, has come to be the visible symbol embodying our Nation. It does not represent the views of any particular political party, and it does not represent any particular political philosophy. The flag is not simply another "idea" or "point of view" competing for recognition in the marketplace of ideas. Millions and millions of Americans regard it with an almost mystical reverence regardless of what sort of social, political, or philosophical beliefs they may have. I cannot agree that the First Amendment invalidates the Act of Congress, and the laws of 48 of the 50 States, which make criminal the public burning of the flag. . . .

Justice Stevens, dissenting.

The Court is . . . quite wrong in blandly asserting that respondent "was prosecuted for his expression of dissatisfaction with the policies of this country, expression situated at the core of our First Amendment values." Respondent was prosecuted because of the method he chose to express his dissatisfaction with those policies. Had he chosen to spray-paint—or perhaps convey with a motion picture projector—his message of dissatisfaction on the facade of the Lincoln Memorial, there would be no question about the power of the Government to prohibit his means of expression. The prohibition would be supported by the legitimate interest in preserving the quality of an important national asset. Though the asset at stake in this case is intangible, given its unique value, the same interest supports a prohibition on the desecration of the American flag.

9.3(b) Balancing Tests for Regulating Speech

The fact that a case involves a person's speech does not necessarily mean that it will be protected under the First Amendment. Assuming that the government is attempting to regulate speech, as opposed to conduct, the next question that must be addressed is to what extent government can regulate such speech. As we have discussed, the freedom of speech is not absolute. And in balancing the interests of speech against competing governmental interests, there has been an evolution of balancing tests created and modified by the Supreme Court.

In the early twentieth century, as the Court began to address matters under the Free Speech Clause, the Court initially adopted the **clear and present danger test.** This test was crafted in a unanimous opinion written by Justice Oliver Wendell Holmes in *Schenck v. United States* (1919).[20] See later in this chapter. In *Schenck*, the defendant was charged with attempts to cause insubordination in the military and obstruction of enlistment during World War I. Schenck was the secretary of the Socialist Party and had distributed pamphlets urging resistance to the draft, denouncing conscription, and challenging the motives of those supporting U.S. involvement in the war. Schenck asserted that his actions were protected under the First Amendment. But Justice Holmes rejected this claim, stating, "[t]he question in every case is whether the words used are used in such circumstances and are of such a nature as to create a clear and present danger that they will bring about the substantive evils that Congress has a right to prevent. It is a question of proximity and degree." This standard became known as the clear and present danger test and served as the initial prototype for balancing interests under the Free Speech Clause. Read the Court's opinion in *Schenck* to appreciate the contextual analysis used by the Court in adopting this initial test.

clear and present danger test
A theory adopted by the Supreme Court in the early twentieth century as a means to interpret and apply the Free Speech Clause of the First Amendment. Under this theory, Justice Holmes provided that "[t]he question in every case is whether the words used are used in such circumstances and are of such a nature as to create a clear and present danger that they will bring about the substantive evils that Congress has a right to prevent. It is a question of proximity and degree."

Schenck v. United States
249 U.S. 47 (1919)

Schenck held the position of Secretary within the Socialist Party, as organized in the United States. In this position, he was responsible for printing and distributing leaflets that urged men to oppose and resist the military draft during World War I. Based on these actions, federal authorities arrested and tried Schenck under the Espionage Act of 1917, which was enacted in the wake of the so-called "Red scare"—the fear of Communist invasion. After his conviction, Schenck challenged the constitutionality of the Espionage Act before the Supreme Court.

Mr. Justice Holmes delivered the opinion of the Court.

This is an indictment in three counts. The first charges a conspiracy to violate the Espionage Act of June 15, 1917, by causing and attempting to cause insubordination in the military and naval forces of the United States, and to obstruct the recruiting and enlistment service of the United States, when the United States was at war with the German Empire, to-wit, that the defendant willfully conspired to have printed and circulated to men who had been called and accepted for military service under the Act of May 18, 1917, a document set forth and alleged to be calculated to cause such insubordination and obstruction. The count

alleges overt acts in pursuance of the conspiracy, ending in the distribution of the document set forth. The second count alleges a conspiracy to commit an offense against the United States, to-wit, to use the mails for the transmission of matter declared to be non-mailable by title 12, 2, of the Act of June 15, 1917, to-wit, the above mentioned document, with an averment of the same overt acts. The third count charges an unlawful use of the mails for the transmission of the same matter and otherwise as above. The defendants were found guilty on all the counts. They set up the First Amendment to the Constitution forbidding Congress to make any law abridging the freedom of speech, or of the press, and bringing the case here on that ground have argued some other points also of which we must dispose.

The document in question upon its first printed side recited the first section of the Thirteenth Amendment, said that the idea embodied in it was violated by the conscription act and that a conscript is little better than a convict. In impassioned language it intimated that conscription was despotism in its worst form and a monstrous wrong against humanity in the interest of Wall Street's chosen few. It said, "Do not submit to intimidation," but in form at least confined itself to peaceful measures such as a petition for the repeal of the act. The other and later printed side of the sheet was headed "Assert Your Rights." It stated reasons for alleging that any one violated the Constitution when he refused to recognize "your right to assert your opposition to the draft," and went on, "If you do not assert and support your rights, you are helping to deny or disparage rights which it is the solemn duty of all citizens and residents of the United States to retain." It described the arguments on the other side as coming from cunning politicians and a mercenary capitalist press, and even silent consent to the conscription law as helping to support an infamous conspiracy. It denied the power to send our citizens away to foreign shores to shoot up the people of other lands, and added that words could not express the condemnation such cold-blooded ruthlessness deserves, &c., winding up, "You must do your share to maintain, support and uphold the rights of the people of this country." Of course the document would not have been sent unless it had been intended to have some effect, and we do not see what effect it could be expected to have upon persons subject to the draft except to influence them to obstruct the carrying of it out. The defendants do not deny that the jury might find against them on this point.

But it is said, suppose that that was the tendency of this circular, it is protected by the First Amendment to the Constitution. Two of the strongest expressions are said to be quoted respectively from well-known public men. It well may be that the prohibition of laws abridging the freedom of speech is not confined to previous restraints, although to prevent them may have been the main purpose. . . . We admit that in many places and in ordinary times the defendants in saying all that was said in the circular would have been within their constitutional rights. But the character of every act depends upon the circumstances in which it is done. The most stringent protection of free speech would not protect a man in falsely shouting fire in a theatre and causing a panic. It does not even protect a man from an injunction against uttering words that may have all the effect of force. The question in every case is whether the words used are used in such circumstances and are of such a nature as to create a clear and present danger that they will bring about the substantive evils that Congress has a right to prevent. It is a question of proximity and degree. When a nation is at war many things that might be said in time of peace are such a hindrance to its effort that their utterance will not be endured so long as men fight and that no Court could regard them as protected by any constitutional right. It seems to be admitted that if an actual obstruction of the recruiting service were proved, liability for words that produced that effect might be enforced. The statute of 1917 in section 4 punishes conspiracies to obstruct as well as actual obstruction. If the act, (speaking, or circulating a paper,) its tendency and the intent with which it is done are the same, we perceive no ground for saying that success alone warrants making the act a crime. . . .

Judgments affirmed.

Six years after *Schenck*, a majority of the Court rejected the clear and present test in *Gitlow v. New York* (1925).[21] In *Gitlow*, the defendant, who was a socialist, published a pamphlet called *Left Wing Manifesto*, which predicted the inevitability of a proletarian revolution in the United States. In a 7–2 opinion, the Court upheld the federal Advocacy of Criminal Anarchy statute, which barred advocating the overthrow of the government, as it was used against Gitlow. In upholding Gitlow's conviction, the Court declined to apply the clear and present danger test, and instead concluded that the government could restrict speech if the "natural tendency and probable effect [of the speech] was to bring about the substantive evil which the legislative body might prevent." This standard is known as the **bad tendency test** because it allowed the government to predetermine and ban types of speech that may have a *tendency* to bring about harm, regardless of whether the speech, in actuality, poses a clear and present danger. Essentially, under this standard, the Court concluded that the government did not have to wait until the dangers posed by speech were clear and present, but rather, it could identify harm potentially caused by certain forms of speech and take action against such speech.

Later, the Court resurrected and modified the clear and present danger test in *Dennis v. United States* (1951),[22] a case in which a member of the Communist Party was convicted under the federal Smith Act for knowingly conspiring to teach and advocate overthrow of government. In upholding Dennis's conviction, the Court found validity in a standard offered by Judge Learned Hand, a federal circuit court judge who earlier had ruled upon the case. Under Judge Hand's approach, the Court asked

bad tendency test
Another test used by the Court to interpret and apply the Free Speech Clause, which allows government to predetermine and ban types of speech that may have a *tendency* to bring about harm, regardless of whether the speech, in actuality, poses a clear and present danger.

"whether the gravity of the 'evil,' discounted by its improbability, justifies such invasion of free speech as is necessary to avoid the danger." Under this **probability test,** the likelihood that the speech will succeed in bringing about the identified harm is considered in addition to the traditional factors of whether the speech is advocating a clear and present danger.

The final standard in the Court's evolution of free speech doctrines is known as the ***Brandenburg* test.** In *Brandenburg v. Ohio* (1969)[23] (see later in this chapter), the Court reviewed the conviction of a Klu Klux Klan leader under an Ohio law barring a person from advocating violence or terrorism. Brandenburg was convicted based on a speech in which he claimed that if the government did not stop suppressing the white majority, "there might have to be revengenance [*sic*] taken." In reversing Brandenburg's conviction, the Court adopted what is regarded as the modern-day approach to free speech cases, concluding that before the government may suppress or punish speech, the speech must be "directed to inciting or producing imminent lawless action and . . . likely to incite or produce such action." Notice how the Court incorporated a value from the clear and present danger test (adopting an imminent or present requirement) with a value from the probability test (likelihood or probability of success). Read the opinion in *Brandenburg* to assess how the Court decided upon its current balancing test and how it applied this test to reverse Brandenburg's conviction.

probability test
A third approach to the Free Speech Clause adopted by some members of the Court in the mid-twentieth century. This test asks, "whether the gravity of the 'evil', discounted by its improbability, justifies such invasion of free speech as is necessary to avoid the danger."

***Brandenburg* test**
The current standard used by the Court in many free speech cases. Under this test adopted in *Brandenburg v. Ohio* (1969), the government may not suppress speech unless the speech is "directed to inciting or producing imminent lawless action and . . . likely to incite or produce such action."

Brandenburg v. Ohio
395 U.S. 444 (1969)

Per Curiam.

[Charles Brandenburg], a leader of a Ku Klux Klan group, was convicted under the Ohio Criminal Syndicalism statute for "advocat[ing] . . . the duty, necessity, or propriety of crime, sabotage, violence, or unlawful methods of terrorism as a means of accomplishing industrial or political reform" and for "voluntarily assembl[ing] with any society, group, or assemblage of persons formed to teach or advocate the doctrines of criminal syndicalism." Ohio Rev. Code Ann. 2923.13. He was fined $1,000 and sentenced to one to 10 years' imprisonment. The appellant challenged the constitutionality of the criminal syndicalism statute under the First and Fourteenth Amendments to the United States Constitution, but the intermediate appellate court of Ohio affirmed his conviction without opinion. The Supreme Court of Ohio dismissed his appeal. . . . We reverse.

The record shows that a man, identified at trial as the appellant, telephoned an announcer-reporter on the staff of a Cincinnati television station and invited him to come to a Ku Klux Klan "rally" to be held at a farm in Hamilton County. With the cooperation of the organizers, the reporter and a cameraman attended the meeting and filmed the events. Portions of the films were later broadcast on the local station and on a national network.

The prosecution's case rested on the films and on testimony identifying the appellant as the person who communicated with the reporter and who spoke at the rally. The State also introduced into evidence several articles appearing in the film, including a pistol, a rifle,

a shotgun, ammunition, a Bible, and a red hood worn by the speaker in the films.

One film showed 12 hooded figures, some of whom carried firearms. They were gathered around a large wooden cross, which they burned. No one was present other than the participants and the newsmen who made the film. Most of the words uttered during the scene were incomprehensible when the film was projected, but scattered phrases could be understood that were derogatory of Negroes and, in one instance, of Jews. Another scene on the same film showed the appellant, in Klan regalia, making a speech. The speech, in full, was as follows:

This is an organizers' meeting. We have had quite a few members here today which are—we have hundreds, hundreds of members throughout the State of Ohio. I can quote from a newspaper clipping from the Columbus, Ohio Dispatch, five weeks ago Sunday morning. The Klan has more members in the State of Ohio than does any other organization. We're not a revengent organization, but if our President, our Congress, our Supreme Court, continues to suppress the white, Caucasian race, it's possible that there might have to be some revengeance taken.

We are marching on Congress July the Fourth, four hundred thousand strong. From there we are dividing into two groups, one group to march on St. Augustine, Florida, the other group to march into Mississippi. Thank you.

The second film showed six hooded figures one of whom, later identified as the appellant, repeated a speech very similar to that recorded on the first film. The reference to the possibility of "revengeance" was omitted, and one sentence was added: "Personally, I believe the nigger should be returned to Africa, the Jew returned to Israel." Though some of the figures in the films carried weapons, the speaker did not. . . .

[The Court's] decisions have fashioned the principle that the constitutional guarantees of free speech and free press do not permit a State to forbid or proscribe advocacy of the use of force or of law violation except where such advocacy is directed to inciting or producing imminent lawless action and is likely to incite or produce such action. As we said in *Noto v. United States*, 367 U.S. 290, 297–298 (1961), "the mere abstract teaching . . . of the moral propriety or even moral necessity for a resort to force and violence, is not the same as preparing a group for violent action and steeling it to such action." A statute which fails to draw this distinction impermissibly intrudes upon the freedoms guaranteed by the First and Fourteenth Amendments. It sweeps within its condemnation speech which our Constitution has immunized from governmental control.

Measured by this test, Ohio's Criminal Syndicalism Act cannot be sustained. The Act punishes persons who "advocate or teach the duty, necessity, or propriety" of violence "as a means of accomplishing industrial or political reform"; or who publish or circulate or display any book or paper containing such advocacy; or who "justify" the commission of violent acts "with intent to exemplify, spread or advocate the propriety of the doctrines of criminal syndicalism"; or who "voluntarily assemble" with a group formed "to teach or advocate the doctrines of criminal syndicalism." Neither the indictment nor the trial judge's instructions to the jury in any way refined the statute's bald definition of the crime in terms of mere advocacy not distinguished from incitement to imminent lawless action.

Accordingly, we are here confronted with a statute which, by its own words and as applied, purports to punish mere advocacy and to forbid, on pain of criminal punishment, assembly with others merely to advocate the described type of action. Such a statute falls within the condemnation of the First and Fourteenth Amendments. . . .
Reversed.

9.4 FREEDOM OF SPEECH: THE REST OF THE STORY

While the *Brandenburg* standard is applied in many free speech cases, there are other situations where this test is insufficient. And in those cases, there may be other terms and tests that are important to evaluating the level of First Amendment protection. These items are outlined individually in the following sections. At the end of this discussion, a framework of questions is provided to help organize the individual terms and tests and to demonstrate how they can be used together to assess future free speech cases.

9.4(a) Content Versus Conduct

symbolic speech
Nonverbal communication that is akin to pure speech, including symbols (signs, flags, arm bands, or other tangible items) or conduct (hand gestures, burning objects, or other behavior). This nonverbal expression may receive First Amendment protection to the extent that it conveys a message capable of being received and understood by others.

As discussed earlier, one of the first considerations in free speech cases is whether the government is directly targeting the content of speech or whether it is trying to regulate conduct and, in so doing, is imposing a restriction on speech. For example, a law that bans signs critical of the government would be a policy directly aimed at curbing speech.[24] But a law that punishes disorderly conduct, if applied to a person screaming profanities at 2:00 a.m. in a neighborhood, would be an example of a conduct-focused law that affects speech. Typically, government will be given greater discretion to enforce laws that are focused on conduct, even if they slightly or indirectly impact speech, than to enforce laws that specifically target speech.

Pay particular attention to the concept of **symbolic speech,** which is nonverbal communication that is akin to pure speech. At first glance, a person's symbols (signs, flags, arm bands, or other tangible items) or conduct (hand gestures, burning objects, or other behavior) may appear not to be speech. But the Court has cautioned that such nonverbal expression will receive First Amendment protection to the extent that it conveys a message capable of being received and understood by others.[25]

9.4(b) Vagueness and Overbreadth

vagueness doctrine
A constitutional theory of due process that maintains that the government cannot impose legal standards that the average person cannot or is not likely to understand. Attempts to apply vague standards in regulating speech are generally deemed unconstitutional.

The vagueness and overbreadth doctrines are also critical to free speech analysis. The **vagueness doctrine** essentially maintains that the government cannot impose standards that the average person is not likely to understand. Consistent with the constitutional requirement that government provide due process of law (see Chapter 11), the Court requires governmental standards to be sufficiently clear and defined so that individuals can understand what is being prohibited. For example, a law that bans "indecent" communications on the Internet would be viewed as a vague standard for regulating speech because the term *indecent,* without a more precise definition, is not a readily and commonly understood term. Under these circumstances, it would be very difficult for individuals to conform their speech to meet this standard.[26] Such attempts to apply vague standards in regulating speech are generally deemed unconstitutional.

The **overbreadth doctrine** is also grounded in notions of due process, and generally provides that the government cannot regulate or prohibit more speech than is necessary to address the identified harm. For example, although the government may prohibit depictions of child pornography (see following discussion), it may not ban all forms of expression that "appear to be" child pornography because such a ban is likely to capture expression that does not include depictions of actual children.[27] Under the overbreadth doctrine, the Court essentially asks whether the government's restriction on speech is properly tailored to address the harm the government is seeking to prevent. But in cases where the government bans large amounts of protected speech in an effort to stop harmful speech, known as "burning the house down to roast the pig," such restrictions on speech will be deemed overly broad and therefore unconstitutional.

9.4(c) Ban Versus Regulation

Another consideration is the type of action taken by the government in restricting speech. Is it attempting to impose a complete **ban on speech** ("thou shall never criticize the government")? Or is it trying to impose a **time, place, and manner regulation** of speech (you must get a permit for a parade, and it can be held only between 9:00 a.m. and 7:00 p.m.)? A ban on speech prohibits expression at all times and in all places, whereas a regulation of speech allows expression in certain given contexts.[28] In most cases, governmental bans on speech will be scrutinized more rigorously under the First Amendment than reasonable time, place, and manner regulations of speech. In fact, in most cases where the government is seeking to impose a complete and direct ban on speech, the government will have to prove that its actions are necessary to promote a compelling governmental interest. This standard is known as the **strict scrutiny test** because it imposes the strictest burden upon government in its attempt to regulate speech.

Read the decision in *Republican Party of Minnesota v. White* (2002) to see how the Court determines whether to apply the strict scrutiny test and how the test actually works. Notice that even when members of the Court agree on the constitutional standard to be applied in a given case, they may not agree on the result it yields.

overbreadth doctrine
A constitutional theory of due process that generally provides that the government cannot regulate or prohibit more speech than is necessary to address the identified harm. Under this doctrine, the Court essentially asks whether the government's restriction on speech is properly tailored to address the harm the government is seeking to prevent.

ban on speech
A governmental policy barring a particular form of expression at any time or place or in any manner.

time, place, and manner regulation
A government restriction on speech that restricts speech but allows the expression in certain given contexts.

strict scrutiny test
A legal standard requiring the government to prove that its policy is necessary (or narrowly tailored) to promote a compelling governmental interest. This test imposes the strictest burden upon government in its attempt to regulate speech.

Republican Party of Minnesota v. White
536 U.S. 765 (2002)

Justice Scalia delivered the opinion of the Court.

The question presented in this case is whether the First Amendment permits the Minnesota Supreme Court to prohibit candidates for judicial election in that State from announcing their views on disputed legal and political issues.

Since Minnesota's admission to the Union in 1858, the State's Constitution has provided for the selection of all state judges by popular election. Since 1912, those elections have been non-partisan. Since 1974, they have

been subject to a legal restriction which states that a "candidate for a judicial office, including an incumbent judge," shall not "announce his or her views on disputed legal or political issues." This prohibition . . . is known as the "announce clause." Incumbent judges who violate it are subject to discipline, including removal, censure, civil penalties, and suspension without pay. Lawyers who run for judicial office also must comply with the announce clause. Those who violate it are subject to, *inter alia,* disbarment, suspension, and probation.

In 1996, one of the petitioners, Gregory Wersal, ran for associate justice of the Minnesota Supreme Court. In the course of the campaign, he distributed literature criticizing several Minnesota Supreme Court decisions on issues such as crime, welfare, and abortion. A complaint against Wersal challenging, among other things, the propriety of this literature was filed with the Office of Lawyers Professional Responsibility. . . . The Lawyers Board dismissed the complaint; with regard to the charges that his campaign materials violated the announce clause, it expressed doubt whether the clause could constitutionally be enforced. Nonetheless, fearing that further ethical complaints would jeopardize his ability to practice law, Wersal withdrew from the election. In 1998, Wersal ran again for the same office. Early in that race, he sought an advisory opinion from the Lawyers Board with regard to whether it planned to enforce the announce clause. The Lawyers Board responded equivocally, stating that, although it had significant doubts about the constitutionality of the provision, it was unable to answer his question because he had not submitted a list of the announcements he wished to make.

Shortly thereafter, Wersal filed this lawsuit in Federal District Court against respondents, seeking, *inter alia*, a declaration that the announce clause violates the First Amendment and an injunction against its enforcement. Wersal alleged that he was forced to refrain from announcing his views on disputed issues during the 1998 campaign, to the point where he declined response to questions put to him by the press and public, out of concern that he might run afoul of the announce clause. . . .

As the Court of Appeals recognized, the announce clause both prohibits speech on the basis of its content and burdens a category of speech that is "at the core of our First Amendment freedoms"—speech about the qualifications of candidates for public office. The Court of Appeals concluded that the proper test to be applied to determine the constitutionality of such a restriction is what our cases have called strict scrutiny, the parties do not dispute that this is correct. Under the strict-scrutiny test, respondents have the burden to prove that the announce clause is (1) narrowly tailored, to serve (2) a compelling state interest. In order for respondents to show that the announce clause is narrowly tailored, they must demonstrate that it does not "unnecessarily circumscrib[e] protected expression."

We think it plain that the announce clause is not narrowly tailored to serve impartiality (or the appearance of impartiality). . . . Indeed, the clause is barely tailored to serve that interest at all, inasmuch as it does not restrict speech for or against particular parties, but rather speech for or against particular issues. To be sure, when a case arises that turns on a legal issue on which the judge (as a candidate) had taken a particular stand, the party taking the opposite stand is likely to lose. But not because of any bias against that party, or favoritism toward the other party. Any party taking that position is just as likely to lose. The judge is applying the law (as he sees it) evenhandedly. . . .

The short of the matter is this: In Minnesota, a candidate for judicial office may not say "I think it is constitutional for the legislature to prohibit same-sex marriages." He may say the very same thing, however, up until the very day before he declares himself a candidate, and may say it repeatedly (until litigation is pending) after he is elected. As a means of pursuing the objective of open-mindedness that respondents now articulate, the announce clause is so woefully under inclusive as to render belief in that purpose a challenge to the credulous. . . .

Moreover, the notion that the special context of electioneering justifies an abridgment of the right to speak out on disputed issues sets our First Amendment jurisprudence on its head. "[D]ebate on the qualifications of candidates" is "at the core of our electoral process and of the First Amendment freedoms," not at the edges. "The role that elected officials play in our society makes it all the more imperative that they be allowed freely to express themselves on matters of current public importance." "It is simply not the function of government to select which issues are worth discussing or debating in the course of a political campaign." We have never allowed the government to prohibit candidates from communicating relevant information to voters during an election. . . .

The Minnesota Supreme Court's canon of judicial conduct prohibiting candidates for judicial election from announcing their views on disputed legal and political issues violates the First Amendment. Accordingly, we reverse the grant of summary judgment to respondents and remand the case for proceedings consistent with this opinion.

It is so ordered.

Justice O'Connor & Justice Kennedy concurring.

Justice Stevens, with whom Justice Souter, Justice Ginsburg, and Justice Breyer join, dissenting.

The disposition of this case on the flawed premise that the criteria for the election to judicial office should mirror the rules applicable to political elections is profoundly misguided. I therefore respectfully dissent.

Justice Ginsburg, with whom Justice Stevens, Justice Souter, and Justice Breyer join, dissenting.

Prohibiting a judicial candidate from pledging or promising certain results if elected directly promotes the State's interest in preserving public faith in the bench. When a candidate makes such a promise during a campaign, the public will no doubt perceive that she is doing so in the hope of garnering votes. And the public will in turn likely conclude that when the candidate decides an issue in accord with that promise, she does so at least in part to discharge her undertaking to the voters in the previous election and to prevent voter abandonment in the next. The perception of that unseemly quid pro quo—a judicial candidate's promises on issues in return for the electorate's votes at the polls—inevitably diminishes the public's faith in the ability of judges to administer the law without regard to personal or political self-interest. . . .

9.4(d) Public Versus Nonpublic Forum

A frequent distinction made in free speech cases is that between public forums and non-public forums. Generally, the Court has described **public forums** as properties historically associated with the exercise of First Amendment rights. This would include such places as public sidewalks, parks, and cartilages outside courthouses and statehouses.[29] Conversely, **nonpublic forums** are regarded as those places that are not historically associated with the exercise of First Amendment rights. Such locations may include military bases, jails, and certain interior portions of public buildings.[30] In most cases, the government will be given greater leeway to regulate speech in nonpublic forums than in public forums.[31]

In some cases, a clear distinction between public and nonpublic forums is hard to draw. For example, in *Morse v. Frederick* (2007), the Supreme Court upheld a public school's suspension of a student who held a vaguely written pro-drug message at a school-sponsored event. In *Morse*, during a school-sponsored event, a high school student unfurled a banner reading "BONG HiTS 4 JESUS." The principal of the school interpreted the banner's message as a promotion of illegal drug use and removed the banner. Later, the principal suspended one of the students involved in the banner's display. The student sued the school, arguing that he was being punished for his speech that was protected under the First Amendment. The Supreme Court, however, ruled 5-4 that a principal may restrict student speech at a school event, when that speech is reasonably viewed as promoting illegal drug use. The Court recognized that the school involved was a public institution. But the majority opinion also recognized that "schools may take steps to safeguard those entrusted to their care from speech that can reasonably be regarded as encouraging illegal drug use."

9.4(e) Content and Viewpoint Neutrality

The concepts of content neutrality and viewpoint neutrality are also important in many free speech controversies. **Content neutrality** (also known as subject-matter neutrality) means that the government, in attempting to regulate speech, is not discriminating against speech based on its content or subject matter. For example, a law that punishes "unruly behavior" takes no position on the content of speech that might result in a violation of this standard. However, a governmental action that prohibits public displays regarding war, either pro or con, would be an example of a content-based regulation of speech because it targets a specific subject matter for regulation.

Viewpoint neutrality means that the government does not favor one side or another within a given subject matter of speech. For example, a government ban on abortion-related demonstrations, while content based, would be viewpoint neutral. But if the government were to ban antiabortion protests, while allowing pro-choice demonstrations, such an approach would not be viewpoint neutral.

There are times when the Court will require the government to have content-neutral laws in place before it will be allowed to regulate speech. Such is often the case when the government attempts to regulate speech within a traditional public forum. In other instances, such as where the government attempts to regulate speech within a nonpublic forum, viewpoint neutrality will suffice.[32]

In *Christian Legal Society v. Martinez* (2010),[33] the Court relied upon the viewpoint neutrality doctrine in holding that a public law school can deny recognition to a religious student organization if the group refuses to comply with the school's anti-discrimination policy. At issue was a policy enforced by the University of California Hastings College of Law forbidding student organizations from engaging in discrimination based on "race, color, religion, national origin, ancestry, disability, age, sex or sexual orientation." One of the school's organizations, the Christian Legal Society (CLS), refused to admit gay or lesbian students, who CLS claimed did not maintain traditional Christian beliefs. In response, the law school informed CLS that it would no longer be recognized as an official student organization, thereby resulting in the loss of financial and other forms of support by the law school.

public forums
Properties historically associated with the exercise of First Amendment rights, including public sidewalks, parks, and cartilages outside courthouses and statehouses.

nonpublic forums
Places that are not historically associated with the exercise of First Amendment rights. Such locations may include military bases, jails, and certain interior portions of public buildings.

Cyber Constitution
Morse v. Frederick
(2007)
http://supreme.justia.com/us/551/06-278/

content neutrality
Also known as subject-matter neutrality, this term means that the government, in attempting to regulate speech, is not discriminating against speech based on its content or subject matter.

viewpoint neutrality
A term used to require the government not to favor one side or another within a given subject matter of speech.

Cyber Constitution
***CLS v. Martinez* (2010)**
http://supreme.justia.com/
us/561/08-1371/

obscenity
A form of unprotected sexual expression; material that, when viewed in its entirety (taken as a whole), appeals to a prurient (unhealthy) interest in sex; portrays sexual conduct in a patently offensive way; and lacks serious literary, artistic, political, or scientific value.

***Miller* Test**
A standard used to judge whether a material is obscene. In *Miller v. California* (1973), the Supreme Court defined obscenity as material that, when viewed in its entirety (taken as a whole) (1) appeals to a prurient (unhealthy) interest in sex; (2) portrays sexual conduct in a patently offensive way; and (3) lacks serious literary, artistic, political, or scientific value.

pornography
Materials that depict sexual expression, which may or may not meet the *Miller* standards of obscenity.

vulgarity
Expression, which is sometimes sexual in nature, that is regarded as highly crude and offensive.

profanity
Words, which often include slang references to sexual activity, that are viewed as highly offensive and impolite, but may still be afforded constitutional protection, as long as they do not fall into another category of unprotected speech, such as fighting words.

child pornography
Materials that depict actual children (persons under the age of eighteen) engaged in sexual conduct.

CLS sued the law school in federal court, claiming that the school violated the student members' rights to expressive association, free speech, free exercise of religion, and equal protection of the law. On appeal, the Supreme Court rejected CLS's claims, holding that a public university can restrict access to a student organization forum by policies that allow "all comers" to participate in the organization's activity. In a 5-4 decision, the Court found that the law school's policy was "a reasonable, viewpoint-neutral condition on access to the student-organization forum." For the majority opinion, the viewpoint neutrality of the school's policy was critical to its constitutionality. According to Justice Ginsburg's opinion, "[i]n requiring CLS—in common with all other student organizations—to choose between welcoming all students and forgoing the benefits of official recognition, we hold, Hastings did not transgress constitutional limitations."

9.4(f) Types of Speech

A final, although substantial, consideration is the nature and type of speech being regulated by the government. The Court has often noted that certain forms of speech are less protected or unprotected under the First Amendment. The Court has identified forms of expression, such as fighting words, defamation, obscenity, child pornography, and commercial speech, as types of speech that are somewhat removed from the pure political speech that, according to the Court, the First Amendment was designed to protect. Accordingly, the Court has drafted specialized balancing tests or doctrines to apply when these forms of expression are being regulated.

In the area of sexual expression, there is a fundamental constitutional distinction that is made between obscenity, pornography, vulgarity, and profanity. The Court has ruled that obscene materials generally are undeserving of any First Amendment protection. As the Court defined the term in *Miller v. California* (1973),[34] **obscenity** is a specific type of sexual expression, which is defined as material that when viewed in its entirety (taken as a whole) (1) appeals to a prurient (unhealthy) interest in sex; (2) portrays sexual conduct in a patently offensive way; and (3) taken as a whole, lacks serious literary, artistic, political, or scientific value. If a work meets each of these three standards, government may regulate, ban, or prosecute such materials. This is known as the ***Miller* test.** Interestingly, however, the Court has ruled that government may not punish the mere private possession of obscene materials by an individual.[35] As a result, obscenity prosecutions are mostly limited to the sale, distribution, or transmission of obscene materials.

While obscenity is categorized as a form of unprotected expression, **pornography** (materials that depict sexual expression but fall short of meeting the *Miller* standards), **vulgarity** (expression, which is sometimes sexual in nature, that is regarded as highly crude and offensive), and **profanity** (words, which often include slang references to sexual activity, that are viewed as highly offensive and impolite) are still afforded constitutional protection, as long as they do not fall into another category of unprotected speech, such as fighting words or child pornography (see following discussion).

Child pornography is another category of unprotected speech. Regardless of whether the expression meets *Miller's* obscenity standards, government may ban, regulate, or prosecute materials that depict actual children (persons under the age of eighteen) engaged in sexual conduct. And unlike obscene materials, government may also ban the mere possession of child pornography. The Court deemed this category of expression unprotected in *New York v. Ferber* (1982)[36] because this form of pornography has the potential to harm real children during the production of the materials and after they are distributed. Note, however, that in *Ashcroft v. Free Speech Coalition* (2002), the Court ruled that the unprotected category of child pornography is limited to those materials in which a real child, as opposed to a computer-generated or fictional child, is depicted.[37]

More recently, however, the Supreme Court ruled that Congress can prohibit the pandering of materials, which are advertised or represented as containing child pornography, even where, in reality, the materials do not contain actual child pornography. In *United States v. Williams* (2008),[38] the Court upheld a section of the federal PROTECT Act, which prohibits the pandering of "any material or purported material in a manner that reflects the belief, or that is intended to cause another to believe" that the material is illegal child pornography. The law punishes the advertising or presenting of material in ways that suggest it is child pornography. In a 7–2 ruling, the Court concluded that the law was constitutional because it targeted individuals who offer to engage in illegal transactions that are unprotected by the First Amendment.

Read the majority opinion by Justice Kennedy in *Ashcroft v. Free Speech Coalition* to understand the unprotected status of child pornography and the constitutional difficulties that the government often faces when it attempts to regulate sexual expression in cyberspace. Also, pay particular attention to the Court's treatment of the overbreadth doctrine as it is applied to the government's attempt to expand the definition of child pornography.

Cyber Constitution
United States v. Williams (2008) http://supreme.justia.com/us/553/06-694/

Cyber Constitution
The PROTECT Act
http://www.justice.gov/opa/pr/2003/April/03_ag_266.htm

"MOVIE DAY" AT THE SUPREME COURT

From the late 1950s through the early 1970s, the Supreme Court decided several cases involving the constitution and allegedly obscene materials. These cases included *Roth v. United States* and *Alberts v. California*, 354 U.S. 476 (1957); *Ginzburg v. United States*, 383 U.S. 463 (1966); *Miller v. California*, 413 U.S. 15 (1973); and *Paris Adult Theatre I v. Slaton*, 413 U.S. 49 (1973). In these and many other cases, the underlying materials at issue were pornographic films. Given this context, the members of the Court often saw it necessary to watch the films in order to determine whether they depicted obscenity or constitutionally protected sexual expression. Such viewings, it is reported, occurred in the basement of the Supreme Court building where the justices and their law clerks would gather to watch the movies.

One notable exception was Justice Hugo Black, who purportedly refused to attend the movie shows because he did not believe that watching such films would change his mind about the constitutional protection that should be afforded to the films. Regarded as an "absolutist" in the area of free speech, Black regularly found governmental regulations of adult films to be unconstitutional. For Black, when the First Amendment said, "Congress shall make no law . . . abridging the freedom of speech," the phrase "no law" should be interpreted and applied strictly and absolutely.

On a more humorous note, it is reported that, during "movie days," Justice Thurgood Marshall, who served on the bench from 1967 to 1991, would sit in the front row of the Court's "theater" and crack jokes about many of the scenes being depicted. It is also reported that Justice John Marshall Harlan, who was a justice from 1955 to 1971 and suffered from near-blindness due to extreme cataracts, had to rely upon Court colleagues to orally describe for him the visual events on the screen.

Sources: The Brethren, Bob Woodward and Scott Armstrong (Simon & Schuster 1979); Joyce Murdoch and Deb Price, *Courting Justice: Gay Men and Lesbians v. the Supreme Court* (Basic Books 2001).

Ashcroft v. Free Speech Coalition
535 U.S. 234 (2002)

Justice Kennedy delivered the opinion of the Court.

We consider in this case whether the Child Pornography Prevention Act of 1996 (CPPA) abridges the freedom of speech. The CPPA extends the federal prohibition against child pornography to sexually explicit images that appear to depict minors but were produced without using any real children. The statute prohibits, in specific circumstances, possessing or distributing these images, which may be created by using adults who look

like minors or by using computer imaging. The new technology, according to Congress, makes it possible to create realistic images of children who do not exist.

By prohibiting child pornography that does not depict an actual child, the statute goes beyond *New York v. Ferber*, 458 U.S. 747 (1982), which distinguished child pornography from other sexually explicit speech because of the State's interest in protecting the children exploited by the production process. As a general rule, pornography can be banned only if obscene, but under *Ferber*, pornography showing minors can be proscribed whether or not the images are obscene under the definition set forth in *Miller v. California*, 413 U.S. 15 (1973). *Ferber* recognized that "[t]he *Miller* standard, like all general definitions of what may be banned as obscene, does not reflect the State's particular and more compelling interest in prosecuting those who promote the sexual exploitation of children." . . .

The principal question to be resolved, then, is whether the CPPA is constitutional where it proscribes a significant universe of speech that is neither obscene under *Miller* nor child pornography under *Ferber*. . . .

As a general principle, the First Amendment bars the government from dictating what we see or read or speak or hear. The freedom of speech has its limits; it does not embrace certain categories of speech, including defamation, incitement, obscenity, and pornography produced with real children. While these categories may be prohibited without violating the First Amendment, none of them includes the speech prohibited by the CPPA. . . .

As we have noted, the CPPA is much more than a supplement to the existing federal prohibition on obscenity. Under *Miller v. California*, 413 U.S. 15 (1973), the Government must prove that the work, taken as a whole, appeals to the prurient interest, is patently offensive in light of community standards, and lacks serious literary, artistic, political, or scientific value. The CPPA, however, extends to images that appear to depict a minor engaging in sexually explicit activity without regard to the Miller requirements. The materials need not appeal to the prurient interest. Any depiction of sexually explicit activity, no matter how it is presented, is proscribed. The CPPA applies to a picture in a psychology manual, as well as a movie depicting the horrors of sexual abuse. It is not necessary, moreover, that the image be patently offensive. Pictures of what appear to be 17-year-olds engaging in sexually explicit activity do not in every case contravene community standards.

The CPPA prohibits speech despite its serious literary, artistic, political, or scientific value. The statute proscribes the visual depiction of an idea—that of teenagers engaging in sexual activity—that is a fact of modern society and has been a theme in art and literature throughout the ages. Under the CPPA, images are prohibited so long as the persons appear to be under 18 years of age. This is higher than the legal age for marriage in many States, as well as the age at which persons may consent to sexual relations. It is, of course, undeniable that some youths engage in sexual activity before the legal age, either on their own inclination or because they are victims of sexual abuse.

Both themes—teenage sexual activity and the sexual abuse of children—have inspired countless literary works. William Shakespeare created the most famous pair of teenage lovers, one of whom is just 13 years of age. *See* Romeo and Juliet, act I, sc. 2, l. 9 ("She hath not seen the change of fourteen years"). In the drama, Shakespeare portrays the relationship as something

splendid and innocent, but not juvenile. The work has inspired no less than 40 motion pictures, some of which suggest that the teenagers consummated their relationship. Shakespeare may not have written sexually explicit scenes for the Elizabethan audience, but were modern directors to adopt a less conventional approach, that fact alone would not compel the conclusion that the work was obscene.

Contemporary movies pursue similar themes. Last year's Academy Awards featured the movie, *Traffic*, which was nominated for Best Picture. The film portrays a teenager, identified as a 16-year-old, who becomes addicted to drugs. The viewer sees the degradation of her addiction, which in the end leads her to a filthy room to trade sex for drugs. The year before, *American Beauty* won the Academy Award for Best Picture. In the course of the movie, a teenage girl engages in sexual relations with her teenage boyfriend, and another yields herself to the gratification of a middle-aged man. The film also contains a scene where, although the movie audience understands the act is not taking place, one character believes he is watching a teenage boy performing a sexual act on an older man.

Ferber upheld a prohibition on the distribution and sale of child pornography, as well as its production, because these acts were "intrinsically related" to the sexual abuse of children in two ways. First, as a permanent record of a child's abuse, the continued circulation itself would harm the child who had participated. Like a defamatory statement, each new publication of the speech would cause new injury to the child's reputation and emotional well-being. Second, because the traffic in child pornography was an economic motive for its production, the State had an interest in closing the distribution network. "The most expeditious if not the only practical method of law enforcement may be to dry up the market for this material by imposing severe criminal penalties on persons selling, advertising, or otherwise promoting the product." Under either rationale, the speech had what the Court in effect held was a proximate link to the crime from which it came. . . .

In contrast to the speech in *Ferber*, speech that itself is the record of sexual abuse, the CPPA prohibits speech that records no crime and creates no victims by its production. Virtual child pornography is not "intrinsically related" to the sexual abuse of children, as were the materials in *Ferber*. While the Government asserts that the images can lead to actual instances of child abuse, the causal link is contingent and indirect. The harm does not necessarily follow from the speech, but depends upon some unquantified potential for subsequent criminal acts. . . .

The CPPA, for reasons we have explored, is inconsistent with *Miller* and finds no support in *Ferber*. The Government seeks to justify its prohibitions in other ways. It argues that the CPPA is necessary because pedophiles may use virtual child pornography to seduce children. There are many things innocent in themselves, however, such as cartoons, video games, and candy, that might be used for immoral purposes, yet we would not expect those to be prohibited because they can be misused. The Government, of course, may punish adults who provide unsuitable materials to children, and it may enforce criminal penalties for unlawful solicitation. The precedents establish, however, that speech within the rights of adults to hear may not be silenced completely in an attempt to shield children from it. In *Butler v. Michigan*, 352 U.S. 380, 381 (1957), the Court invalidated a statute prohibiting distribution of an indecent publication because of its tendency to "incite minors to violent or depraved or immoral acts." A unanimous Court agreed upon the important First Amendment principle that the State could not "reduce the adult population . . . to reading only what is fit for children." . . .

The Government submits further that virtual child pornography whets the appetites of pedophiles and encourages them to engage in illegal conduct. This rationale cannot sustain the provision in question. The mere tendency of speech to encourage unlawful acts is not a sufficient reason for banning it. The government "cannot constitutionally premise legislation on the desirability of controlling a person's private thoughts." . . . First Amendment freedoms are most in danger when the government seeks to control thought or to justify its laws for that impermissible end. The right to think is the beginning of freedom, and speech must be protected from the government because speech is the beginning of thought.

The Government next argues that its objective of eliminating the market for pornography produced using real children necessitates a prohibition on virtual images as well. Virtual images, the Government contends, are indistinguishable from real ones; they are part of the same market and are often exchanged. In this way, it is said, virtual images promote the trafficking in works produced through the exploitation of real children. The hypothesis is somewhat implausible. If virtual images were identical to illegal child pornography, the illegal images would be driven from the market by the indistinguishable substitutes. Few pornographers would risk prosecution by abusing real children if fictional, computerized images would suffice. . . .

Finally, the Government says that the possibility of producing images by using computer imaging makes it very difficult for it to prosecute those who produce pornography by using real children. Experts, we are told, may have difficulty in saying whether the pictures were made by using real children or by using computer imaging. The necessary solution, the argument runs, is to prohibit both kinds of images. The argument, in essence, is that protected speech may be banned as a means to ban unprotected speech. This analysis turns the First Amendment upside down.

The Government may not suppress lawful speech as the means to suppress unlawful speech. Protected speech does not become unprotected merely because

it resembles the latter. The Constitution requires the reverse. . . .

In sum, [the CPPA] covers materials beyond the categories recognized in *Ferber* and *Miller*, and the reasons the Government offers in support of limiting the freedom of speech have no justification in our precedents or in the law of the First Amendment. The provision abridges the freedom to engage in a substantial amount of lawful speech. For this reason, it is overbroad and unconstitutional. . . .

For the reasons we have set forth, the prohibitions of [the CPPA] are overbroad and unconstitutional. Having reached this conclusion, we need not address respondents' further contention that the provisions are unconstitutional because of vague statutory language.

The judgment of the Court of Appeals is affirmed.

It is so ordered.

Justice Thomas, concurring in the judgment.

Chief Justice Rehnquist, with whom Justice Scalia joins in part, dissenting.

I agree with Part II of Justice O'Connor's opinion concurring in the judgment in part and dissenting in part. Congress has a compelling interest in ensuring the ability to enforce prohibitions of actual child pornography, and we should defer to its findings that rapidly advancing technology soon will make it all but impossible to do so.

I also agree with Justice O'Connor that serious First Amendment concerns would arise were the Government ever to prosecute someone for simple distribution or possession of a film with literary or artistic value, such as "Traffic" or "American Beauty." I write separately, however, because the Child Pornography Prevention Act of 1996 (CPPA), 18 U.S.C. §2251 *et seq.,* need not be construed to reach such materials.

We normally do not strike down a statute on First Amendment grounds "when a limiting instruction has been or could be placed on the challenged statute." This case should be treated no differently.

Justice O'Connor, with whom The Chief Justice and Justice Scalia join as to Part II, concurring in the judgment in part and dissenting in part.

Although in my view the CPPA's ban on youthful-adult pornography appears to violate the First Amendment, the ban on virtual-child pornography does not. It is true that both bans are authorized by the same text: The statute's definition of child pornography to include depictions that "appea[r] to be" of children in sexually explicit poses. 18 U.S.C. §2256(8)(B). Invalidating a statute due to overbreadth, however, is an extreme remedy, one that should be employed "sparingly and only as a last resort." We have observed that "[i]t is not the usual judicial practice, . . . nor do we consider it generally desirable, to proceed to an overbreadth issue unnecessarily."

Heeding this caution, I would strike the "appears to be" provision only insofar as it is applied to the subset of cases involving youthful-adult pornography. . . .

fighting words
A category of unprotected speech that "by their very utterance inflict injury or tend to incite an immediate breach of the peace."

Another category of unprotected speech is **fighting words,** which are forms of expression that "by their very utterance inflict injury or tend to incite an immediate breach of the peace."[39] Essentially, fighting words are forms of expression that are likely to provoke a violent or otherwise harmful reaction by a reasonable person who sees, hears, or reads this expression. For example, a person who offers particularly cruel and hostile claims about another person's spouse or child might expect that his words would provoke a violent reaction by the other person. In many cases, fighting words are punished as a form of disorderly conduct—a criminal statute in many jurisdictions that bars outrageous and offensive conduct. Consistent with the balancing test established in *Brandenburg v. Ohio* (1969) (see earlier discussion), the Court has ruled that fighting words "are no essential part of any exposition of ideas, and are of such slight social value as a step to truth that any benefit that may be derived from them is clearly outweighed by the social interests in law and order."[40]

YOUR CONSTITUTIONAL VALUES

CAN A PERSON BE ARRESTED FOR USING PROFANITIES TOWARD A POLICE OFFICER?

On April 9, 1997, Officer Alan J. Oaks responded to an unknown problem at the residence of Richard Lowery in Chillicothe, Ohio. When Officer Oaks arrived at Lowery's home, Lowery approached the officer, pointing his finger at him and yelling, "You motherfuckers better do something." Officer Oaks told Lowery to lower his voice and to stop using profane language. Officer Oaks told Lowery to explain why the officer had been called to his residence. Lowery responded, "Fuck you, you motherfuckers never do anything." Officer Oaks noticed some children outside riding their bicycles and some neighbors outside of their homes. Officer Oaks again warned Lowery to stop using profane language. Lowery responded, "Fuck you."

Officer Oaks then arrested Lowery for violating Chillicothe Revised Ordinance 509.08(a), which provides that "No person, being in or upon any street, avenue, sidewalk, alley, bridge or public place, or being in a situation to be seen or observed from any street, avenue, alley, bridge or public place, shall commit or perpetrate or assist in the commission or perpetration of any lewd, indecent, obscene, filthy or lascivious act, gesture, movement or behavior, or shall utter or use any profane, indecent or obscene language."

On July 1, 1997, a trial court found Lowery guilty of using indecent or profane language in violation of Chillicothe Revised Ordinance 509.08. The trial court ordered Lowery to pay a $25.00 fine. Lowery appealed the verdict, claiming that the U.S. and Ohio Constitutions' freedom of speech provisions prohibit punishment for his statements because his language did not constitute "fighting words." The city, however, claimed that Lowery's language constituted "fighting words" and that the trial court correctly found the appellant guilty of using indecent or profane language.

Based on your Constitutional values, what do you think? Was Lowery's speech protected? Or did it constitute "fighting words"?

To see how an Ohio court of appeals decided this case, go to *City of Chillicothe v. Lowery*, Case No. 97 CA 2331, 1998 Ohio App. LEXIS 3336.

---

offensive speech
Expression that is likely to cause the sensibilities of others to be offended.

Two categories of speech that are often discussed along with fighting words are offensive speech and hate speech. **Offensive speech** is expression that is likely to cause the sensibilities of others to be offended. For example, calling a person unflattering names or revealing embarrassing information may result in the person being offended. In some cases, offensive speech can be a form of fighting words, where the speech is likely to provoke a violent response from a reasonable person. But in other cases, offensive speech can just transgress the sensibilities of others, without provoking a violent response. **Hate speech** may overlap many forms of offensive speech, but generally is regarded as expression that is directly aimed at insulting, derogating, or intimidating a particular class of individuals, often based on race, sex, religion, or ethnicity.

By itself, offensive speech or speech that expresses hateful attitudes is constitutionally protected.[41] Essentially, people are generally allowed to say offensive things to other people. For example, in *Snyder v. Phelps* (2011) (see photo earlier in this chapter), the Court held that a funeral protest by members of the Westboro Baptist Church was protected by the First Amendment and that a jury verdict siding with a family whose son had died on active duty in Iraq could not stand. In an 8–1 ruling, the Court upheld the right of protestors to express their views that the deaths of American service members in the Iraq War was the result of the nation's tolerant views toward homosexuality. The Court found that, although the protesters' expression may be viewed as outrageous and offense by many, it nonetheless was protected because it related to matters of public concern and was expressed in a public forum.

But if offensive expression (1) leads to a direct and immediate breach of the peace consistent with the *Brandenburg* or "fighting words" doctrine (discussed earlier in this chapter), (2) is defamatory (see following discussion), or (3) involves a significant amount of harmful conduct, which the government is permitted to regulate, it may become constitutionally unprotected. Appreciate how the dividing line between protected and unprotected offensive/hate speech often depends on the context in which the speech is being offered. For example, burning an American flag during political protest will likely be deemed protected expression, while offering the same message on the lawn of a VFW Hall may be found to be unprotected fighting words. Similarly, writing an opinion piece for a newspaper that contains racist ideas will likely be protected, while creating a hostile environment in your setting through the use of racist jokes or other messages will likely be treated as unprotected.

In 2010, the Supreme Court stuck down a federal statute that banned the commercial sale, creation, or possession of photos or other materials depicting animal cruelty. Under the law, Congress had made it a criminal offense to create, sell, or possess certain depictions of animal cruelty in interstate commerce. But in *United States v. Stevens* (2010),[42] the Court ruled 8-1 that the statute was substantially overbroad and unconstitutional under the First Amendment. The Court recognized the disturbing (offensive) nature of depictions of animal cruelty, but also recognized that the wholesale prohibition on such images went too far by not recognizing that such images might contribute to the marketplace of ideas on issues such as animal cruelty, hunting, and other topics, which can be discussed under the First Amendment.

Similarly, in 2011, the Court ruled that a California law prohibiting the sale of "violent video games" to minors violated the First Amendment. In *Brown v. Entertainment Merchants Ass'n* (2011), a 7–2 majority of the Court concluded that video games are a form of expression protected by the First Amendment and that minors have their own First Amendment rights just as adults. In his majority opinion, Justice Scalia applied the strict scrutiny test to what he described as a content-based regulation of speech. He then concluded that the state had failed to demonstrate a causal connection between violent video games and violent behavior by children. In a concurring opinion, Justice Alito suggested that a more carefully crafted statute might survive constitutional scrutiny.

Another category of unprotected speech is **defamation**, which is a false statement that causes injury to another. There are two primary forms of defamation—**slander** (verbal communications that are false and cause injury) and **libel** (written communications that are false and cause injury). In order for expression to be defamatory and, thus, unprotected, (1) it must be a statement of fact ("George sells drugs"), as opposed to a statement of opinion ("I think Suzie dresses provocatively"); (2) it must be false and capable of being proven as such; (3) it must cause injury to another (damage of reputation, loss of job, emotional distress, etc.); and (4) if the person harmed by the statement is a **public figure** (a person with particular notoriety in the community, which includes,

hate speech
Expression that is directly aimed at insulting, derogating, or intimidating a particular class of individuals, often based on race, sex, religion, or ethnicity.

Cyber Constitution
***Snyder v. Phelps* (2011)**
http://supreme.justia.com/us/562/09-751/

Cyber Constitution
***United States v. Stevens* (2010)** http://supreme.justia.com/us/559/08-769/

Cyber Constitution
***Brown v. Entertainment Merchants Ass'n*: Violent Video Games and the First Amendment** http://supreme.justia.com/us/564/08-1448/

defamation
A form of unprotected speech that involves a false statement that causes injury to another.

slander
A form of defamation that involves published verbal communications that are false and cause injury.

libel
A form of defamation that involves published written communications that are false and cause injury.

public figure
A person with particular notoriety in the community, including, but not limited to, public officials.

The Entertainment Consumers Association organizes a rally on the steps of the Supreme Court prior to the Court's hearing on California's appeal and debate whether the states can restrict the sale of violent games to children and teenagers, November 2, 2010, in Washington, DC

Olivier Douliery/Abaca Press/MCT/Newscom

malice
A legal standard in defamation cases involving public figures requiring the speech to be made with knowledge of the statement's falsity or reckless disregard as to its falsity.

commercial speech
Expression offered to promote the sale of a commodity or service.

***Central Hudson* test**
Constitutional standard for commercial speech adopted by the Court in *Central Hudson Gas & Electric Corp. v. Public Service Comm. of New York* (1980). This test considers whether (1) the speech concerns a lawful activity and is truthful and not misleading, (2) there is a substantial governmental interest in regulating the speech, (3) the government's regulation directly advances its substantial interest, and (4) there is a direct fit between the government's regulation and its claimed interest.

but is not limited to, public officials), the statement must be offered with **malice** (knowledge of the statement's falsity or reckless disregard as to its falsity).[43]

Commercial speech is also a category of underprotected speech for which the Court uses a specialized balancing test. Beginning with the proposition that commercial speech—expression offered to promote the sale of a commodity—should not receive less constitutional protection than political speech,[44] the Court has adopted a four-part approach to assess regulations of commercial speech. This approach is often referred to as the ***Central Hudson* test** because it was offered in *Central Hudson Gas & Electric Corp. v. Public Service Comm. of New York* (1980).[45] First, the Court considers whether the speech concerns a lawful activity and whether it is truthful and not misleading. Commercial speech that promotes unlawful activity (illegal narcotic sales) or that is false or misleading has the potential to harm the public, and therefore is regarded as unprotected speech. Second, the Court asks whether there is a substantial governmental interest in regulating the speech. Notice that this standard is less rigorous for the government than the "compelling" interest test, which must be met when attempting to regulate many forms of political speech.[46] Third, the Court evaluates whether the government's regulation directly advances its substantial interest. Essentially, the Court wants to know whether there is a direct fit between the government's regulation and its claimed interest. And finally, the Court considers whether the government's regulation is overbroad. Consistent with the overbreadth doctrine (discussed earlier), the Court requires that the government target no more expression than is necessary to satisfy its substantial interest.

9.4(g) Assessing Governmental Limitations on Speech

In the end, there are several concepts and doctrines that can be important to resolving free speech controversies. The challenge is knowing which terms and tests apply in a given dispute and understanding how they should be used. And while there is no mathematical formula or computer program for analyzing free speech controversies, there is a basic framework that can be applied. Within this framework, there are four basic considerations: (1) What is the government seeking to regulate—speech or conduct? (2) What standards are being used to regulate speech—are they clear, well defined, and sufficiently limited? (3) What is the scope of the government's action—a complete ban on speech or a more limited time, place, and manner restriction? (4) How much constitutional protection is traditionally afforded to the type of speech being targeted—fully protected (political speech), somewhat protected (commercial speech), or unprotected (obscenity, fighting words, child pornography, etc.)? Of course, within each of these four basic questions, there can be several additional questions and concepts that might need to be considered as well. And in the end, even after all of the relevant terms and tests are sufficiently identified and understood in a given case, the ultimate resolution of the case may come down to how a person interprets these standards and applies them to a particular set of facts.

Review the framework of analysis offered in Figure 9-1 to see how the various concepts and balancing tests outlined in Section 9.4 can be organized and applied in free speech disputes.

A Framework for Free Speech Analysis

I. What is being regulated, the content of speech or conduct?
  A. If purely conduct, proceed with rational basis test (Is regulation reasonably related to a legitimate governmental purpose?).
  B. If speech, go to the next step.

II. Do the government's standards for regulating/banning speech:
  A. Rely upon unduly vague terms or concepts (vagueness doctrine); or
  B. Impose overly broad restrictions on speech (overbreadth doctrine)?
  C. If so, the government's actions are unconstitutional.
  D. If not, proceed to next step.

III. Is the government seeking to regulate speech (impose reasonable time, place, and manner restrictions) or ban speech (remove it entirely)?

  A. If ban, is the speech at issue unprotected *per se*?
    1. Categories of unprotected speech (apply relevant test for each)
      (a) clear and present danger of imminent lawlessness (*Brandenburg* test)
      (b) obscene (*Miller* test)
      (c) fighting words (*Chaplinsky* and *Brandenburg*)
      (d) defamation (*New York Times Co. v. Sullivan*)
      (e) false or deceptive commercial speech (*Central Hudson* test)
      (f) child pornography (*New York v. Ferber* and *Ashcroft v. Free Speech Coalition*)
    2. If speech is unprotected, ban is valid as long as reasonable.
    3. If ban is of protected speech, apply strict scrutiny test (Is ban necessary to promote a compelling governmental interest?).

  B. If time, place, and manner regulation, does it involve a public forum (property historically associated with exercise of First Amendment rights—streets, sidewalks, parks) or a nonpublic forum (property not traditionally associated with exercise of First Amendment rights—military bases, schools, jails)?

    1. If regulation targets certain categories of speech (obscene, fighting words, defamation, commercial speech, child pornography), apply test appropriate for that category.
    2. If regulation involves a public forum, all of the following criteria must be met by the government:
      (a) regulation must be content neutral (not discriminate based on the subject of speech)
      (b) regulation must be narrowly tailored (not burden any more speech than necessary) to serve a significant governmental interest (traffic safety, orderly crowd, personal privacy)
      (c) regulation must leave open alternative channels of communication (allow other means of expressing oneself)
    3. If regulation involves a nonpublic forum, the following criteria must be met by the government
      (a) action must be viewpoint neutral (does not discriminate against sides of issue)
      (b) action must be reasonably related to a legitimate governmental purpose

---

FIGURE 9-1

Free speech: Putting it all together

9.5 SPEECH AND POLITICAL CAMPAIGNS

During the past several decades, there has been a general recognition that campaign fundraising and spending has gotten out of control and that the large amounts of money flowing in and out of campaigns is damaging the overall electoral process. According to the Federal Election Commission (FEC), candidates running for Congress during the 2004 general election raised $985.4 million and spent $911.8 million. This was a 20 percent increase in fundraising and an 18 percent increase in spending over the 2002 general election. And during the 2004 presidential campaign, the candidates and the national conventions generated more than $1 billion, which was a 56 percent increase over similar activity during the 2000 campaign. More critically, a large majority of campaign contributions came from a relatively few number of donors. For example, FEC records for the 2006 congressional election show that only 0.27 percent of eligible voters made financial contributions of $200 or more to a candidate, but that these donations represented 82 percent of individual contributions received by primary candidates.

Campaign finance reform laws
Legislation that seeks to change the way campaigns are run and funded. Often challenged as unconstitutional restrictions on political speech.

For years, Congress and other governmental authorities have tried to limit the harmful effects of money on elections by seeking to limit campaign contributions, expenditures, and other related facets of campaigns. These measures are called **campaign finance reform laws** because they seek to change the way campaigns are run and funded. The basic challenge to these efforts, however, has come by way of the first amendment, which the Supreme Court generally has interpreted as providing certain levels of constitutional protection to campaign contributions and expenditures as forms of political speech. By treating the transfer of money in and around political campaigns as a form of political speech, the Court has imposed certain parameters on the types of regulations government can impose on campaign finance.

Federal Election Campaign Act
Passed in 1971 and amended in 1974, this was the first major effort to control campaign finances at the federal level. The law included measures limiting the amount of money that could be donated and spent during federal campaigns. The Supreme Court reviewed this law in *Buckley v. Valeo* (1976) and upheld the contributions limitations, but struck down most of the limits on campaign spending.

The first major effort to control campaign finances at the federal level came in 1971, when Congress passed the **Federal Election Campaign Act.** This law, as amended in 1974, sought to control the flow of money in federal elections by imposing (1) a $1,000 contribution limit upon individuals and groups and a $5,000 limit on political action committees per candidate in an election, with an annual limitation of $25,000 imposed on individual donors; (2) a $1,000 expenditure limitation on individuals or groups seeking to spend money for a clearly identified candidate; (3) a personal contribution limitation for candidates and their relatives; (4) an overall expenditure limitation on candidates; and (5) record-keeping requirements for political committees in order to track and make public contributions and expenditures. Some elected officials objected to these regulations and challenged them in court, asserting among other things that the limitations imposed an unconstitutional restriction on political speech and the freedom of association. This effort quickly reached the Supreme Court.

In 1976, an incredibly divided Court issued its opinion in *Buckley v. Valeo* (1976),[47] wherein the Court upheld, among other things, the individual contribution limitations and the reporting provisions within the federal law. But the Court struck down the limitations on campaign expenditures, independent expenditures by individuals and groups, and expenditures by candidates from their personal funds. In a *per curiam* opinion, the Court rejected the notion that campaign contributions and expenditures were simply forms of conduct that could be broadly regulated by the government. Instead, the Court concluded that the contribution and expenditure limitations "implicate[d] fundamental First Amendment interests," including political speech and the freedom of association. The Court, however, also recognized Congress's interest in eliminating abuse and corruption in federal elections. In balancing the government's interest against the identified First Amendment concerns, the Court ruled that the contribution limitations did not unduly interfere with First Amendment rights of candidates, campaigns, and donors, but that the expenditure limitations were "significantly more severe" on the freedoms of expression and association.

The next major effort to enact campaign finance reform at the federal level occurred in 2002, when Congress passed the **Bipartisan Campaign Reform Act of 2002 (BCRA).** This law is also known as the McCain-Feingold Act, a term reflecting the names of the two primary senators, John McCain and Russ Feingold, who sponsored the law. BCRA was written in an effort to address some of the gaps that candidates, parties, and donors had exposed under the Federal Election Campaign Act (FECA). Two particular problems identified by BCRA were so-called soft money contributions and issue advocacy. **Soft money** refers to money that is not given directly by a donor to a campaign and that is not offered for the purpose of influencing a federal election. Soft money includes individual contributions to political parties for purposes of influencing state or local elections. Before BCRA, these contributions were largely unregulated under FECA, and national parties could solicit and receive these monies from state and local parties without restriction and use it to promote candidates for federal office. Proponents of BCRA viewed soft money as a way around the direct contribution (hard money) limitations imposed by FECA.

Issue advocacy is a form of electoral communication that mentions a candidate by name in association with a particular issue or cause, but stops short of actually urging the public to vote for or against the identified candidate. For example, an advertisement may address a proposed law regarding abortion and then urge viewers or listeners to "call Congressman Smith and tell him to vote against the law." This ad would not expressly state to vote for or against Congressman Smith, but the tenor and tone of the ad would offer strong overtones of support or opposition. BCRA proponents viewed issue ads as a way of getting around FECA, which limited the expenditure of funds for "communications that expressly advocate the election or defeat of a clearly identifiable candidate."

To address these and other issues, BCRA imposed several new limitations on campaign financing. Among these restrictions was a limitation on the spending of soft money by national political parties, officeholders, and candidates, and a ban on the use of general funds by corporations and unions for issue ads and other forms of "electioneering communications" within thirty days of a primary election and sixty days of a general election. The law also sought to stop individuals from making additional campaign contributions in the names of their children by barring persons under the age of seventeen from making political contributions.

In 2003, a divided Supreme Court upheld BCRA's restrictions on soft money and issue advocacy, but found the age restriction on donors to be unconstitutional. In *McConnell v. Federal Election Commission* (2003),[48] the Court essentially reaffirmed the basic tenets of *Buckley v. Valeo*, by recognizing the First Amendment value of campaign contributions but by also acknowledging the compelling interest of the government in ensuring uncorrupted elections at the federal level. But three more recent rulings by the Supreme Court have greatly undermined the *McConnell* ruling.

First, in 2006, the Court ruled in *Wisconsin Right to Life, Inc. v. Federal Election Commission* (2006)[49] that it did not intend to prohibit additional "as applied" challenges to the law that might be brought by parties asserting particular First Amendment interests not addressed in *McConnell*. In addition, a 5-4 majority of the Court found that BCRA unreasonably limited speech and violates the First Amendment rights of the plaintiffs. Writing for the majority, Chief Justice Roberts stated, "[d]iscussion of issues cannot be suppressed simply because the issues may also be pertinent in an election." But the majority stopped short of overruling the *McConnell* decision. In a strongly worded dissent, Justice Souter asserted, "[a]fter today, the ban on contributions by corporations and unions and the limitation on their corrosive spending when they enter the political arena are open to easy circumvention."

Then in *Davis v. Federal Election Commission* (2008),[50] the Court struck down the BCRA's so-called Millionaires' Amendment that had raised the limits on contributions to congressional candidates if their opponent spent above a threshold amount of

Bipartisan Campaign Reform Act of 2002 (BCRA)
Also known as the McCain-Feingold Act, this law sought to address some of the gaps that candidates, parties, and donors had exposed under the Federal Election Campaign Act of 1971. This law bans the use of soft money in federal elections and limits issue ads during periods immediately preceding elections. The Supreme Court upheld most of BCRA's provisions in *McConnell v. Federal Elections Commission* (2003).

soft money
Money that is not given directly by a donor to a campaign and that is not offered for the purpose of influencing a federal election. Soft money includes individual contributions to political parties for purposes of influencing state or local elections. The Bipartisan Campaign Reform Act of 2002 imposed substantial restrictions on the acceptance and use of this money in federal elections.

issue advocacy
A form of electoral communication that mentions a candidate by name in association with a particular issue or cause, but stops short of actually urging the public to vote for or against the identified candidate. The Bipartisan Campaign Reform Act of 2002 imposed substantial restrictions on the use of issue ads by unions and corporations during certain periods before federal elections.

$350,000 of personal funds on his or her campaign. This provision sought to address concerns that candidates with limited financial support could not effectively compete in federal elections. In a 5-4 ruling, the Supreme Court rejected both the contribution limits and the disclosure requirements associated with the Millionaires' Amendment, holding that "[w]hile BCRA does not impose a cap on a candidate's expenditure of personal funds, it imposes an unprecedented penalty on any candidate who robustly exercises that First Amendment right, requiring him to choose between the right to engage in unfettered political speech and subjection to discriminatory fundraising limitations." According to the majority opinion, "[this] burden is not justified by any governmental interest in eliminating corruption or the perception of corruption."

In 2010, the Court struck down several key provisions of the BCRA, including those prohibiting corporations and unions from using money from their general funds to pay for campaign ads. In *Citizens United v. Federal Elections Commission* (2010),[51] the Court considered whether the BCRA barred a conservative interest group from broadcasting a movie critical of then-Senator Hillary Clinton during the presidential primaries. The group asserted that the BCRA's "electioneering communications" ban, which prohibited corporations and nonprofits from airing broadcast ads referring a federal candidate thirty days before a primary election, was an unconstitutional restriction on free speech. In a 5-4 ruling, the Court struck down part of the BCRA that prohibited ads paid for by corporations and unions in the last days of election campaigns. Essentially, the Court removed the BCRA's limitations on independent expenditures that are not co-ordinated with candidates' campaigns. The Court, however, did not negate the BCRA's prohibitions on direct contributions to candidates from corporations and unions.

Most recently, in 2011, the Court struck down a provision of an Arizona campaign finance law that provided publicly financed candidates with matching funds in cases where a privately financed opponent exceeded funding levels beyond an initial public grant. In *Arizona Free Enterprise v. Bennett* (2011), a 5–4 majority ruled that matching funds substantially burden the free speech rights of the nonparticipating candidate, as well as outside groups making independent expenditures. The Court found that the state financing law could not be justified as a measure to level the playing field in campaigns or as an anti-corruption measure because it placed an excessive burden on other forms of protected speech, which are non-corrupting in nature.

Cyber Constitution
Arizona Free Enterprise v. Bennett (2011): **Campaign Finance Reform** http://supreme.justia.com/us/564/10-238/

Citizens United, Appellant v. Federal Election Commission
130 S.Ct. 876 (2010)

Justice Kennedy delivered the opinion of the Court.

Federal law prohibits corporations and unions from using their general treasury funds to make independent expenditures for speech defined as an "electioneering communication" or for speech expressly advocating the election or defeat of a candidate. Limits on electioneering communications were upheld in *McConnell v. Federal Election Comm'n*, 540 U. S. 93, 203–209 (2003). The holding of *McConnell* rested to a large extent on an earlier case, *Austin v. Michigan Chamber of Commerce*, 494 U. S. 652 (1990). *Austin* had held that political speech may be banned based on the speaker's corporate identity.

In this case we are asked to reconsider *Austin* and, in effect, *McConnell*. . . .

In January 2008, Citizens United released a film entitled *Hillary: The Movie*. We refer to the film as *Hillary*. It is a 90-minute documentary about then-Senator Hillary Clinton, who was a candidate in the Democratic Party's 2008 Presidential primary elections. *Hillary* mentions Senator Clinton by name and depicts interviews with political commentators and other persons, most of them quite critical of Senator Clinton. . . .

Before the Bipartisan Campaign Reform Act of 2002 (BCRA), federal law prohibited—and still does prohibit—corporations and unions from using general treasury funds to make direct contributions to candidates or independent expenditures that expressly advocate the election or defeat of a candidate, through any form of media, in connection with certain qualified federal elections. An electioneering communication is defined as "any broadcast, cable, or satellite communication" that "refers to a clearly identified candidate for Federal office" and is made within 30 days of a primary or 60 days of a general election. The Federal Election Commission's (FEC) regulations further define an electioneering communication as a communication that is "publicly distributed.". . .

The First Amendment provides that "Congress shall make no law . . . abridging the freedom of speech." Laws enacted to control or suppress speech may operate at different points in the speech process. . . .

The law before us is an outright ban, backed by criminal sanctions. Section 441b makes it a felony for all corporations—including nonprofit advocacy corporations—either to expressly advocate the election or defeat of candidates or to broadcast electioneering communications within 30 days of a primary election and 60 days of a general election. . . .

Speech is an essential mechanism of democracy, for it is the means to hold officials accountable to the people. The right of citizens to inquire, to hear, to speak, and to use information to reach consensus is a precondition to enlightened self-government and a necessary means to protect it. The First Amendment "'has its fullest and most urgent application' to speech uttered during a campaign for political office."

For these reasons, political speech must prevail against laws that would suppress it, whether by design or inadvertence. Laws that burden political speech are "subject to strict scrutiny," which requires the Government to prove that the restriction "furthers a compelling interest and is narrowly tailored to achieve that interest." . . . .

Premised on mistrust of governmental power, the First Amendment stands against attempts to disfavor certain subjects or viewpoints. Prohibited, too, are restrictions distinguishing among different speakers, allowing speech by some but not others. As instruments to censor, these categories are interrelated: Speech restrictions based on the identity of the speaker are all too often simply a means to control content. . . .

We find no basis for the proposition that, in the context of political speech, the Government may impose restrictions on certain disfavored speakers. Both history and logic lead us to this conclusion.

The Court has recognized that First Amendment protection extends to corporations.

This protection has been extended by explicit holdings to the context of political speech. Under the rationale of these precedents, political speech does not lose First Amendment protection "simply because its source is a corporation." The Court has thus rejected the argument that political speech of corporations or other associations should be treated differently under the First Amendment simply because such associations are not "natural persons.". . .

In *Buckley,* the Court addressed various challenges to the Federal Election Campaign Act of 1971 (FECA) as amended in 1974. These amendments created an independent expenditure ban separate from §610 that applied to individuals as well as corporations and labor unions.

Before addressing the constitutionality of §608(e)'s independent expenditure ban, *Buckley* first upheld §608(b), FECA's limits on direct contributions to candidates. The *Buckley* Court recognized a "sufficiently important" governmental interest in "the prevention of corruption and the appearance of corruption." . . . The Buckley Court explained that the potential for *quid pro quo* corruption distinguished direct contributions to candidates from independent expenditures. The Court emphasized that "the independent expenditure ceiling . . . fails to serve any substantial governmental interest in stemming the reality or appearance of corruption in the electoral process," because "[t]he absence of prearrangement and coordination . . . alleviates the danger that expenditures will be given as a *quid pro quo* for improper commitments from the candidate." *Buckley* invalidated §608(e)'s restrictions on independent expenditures, with only one Justice dissenting. . . .

Less than two years after *Buckley, Bellotti* reaffirmed the First Amendment principle that the Government cannot restrict political speech based on the speaker's corporate identity. . . .

Bellotti did not address the constitutionality of the State's ban on corporate independent expenditures to support candidates. In our view, however, that restriction would have been unconstitutional under *Bellotti*'s central principle: that the First Amendment does not allow political speech restrictions based on a speaker's corporate identity.

Thus the law stood until *Austin. Austin* "uph[eld] a direct restriction on the independent expenditure of funds for political speech for the first time in [this Court's] history.". . .

To bypass *Buckley* and *Bellotti*, the *Austin* Court identified a new governmental interest in limiting political speech: an antidistortion interest. *Austin* found a compelling governmental interest in preventing "the corrosive and distorting effects of immense aggregations of wealth that are accumulated with the help of the corporate form and that have little or no correlation to the public's support for the corporation's political ideas."

The Court is thus confronted with conflicting lines of precedent: a pre-*Austin* line that forbids restrictions on political speech based on the speaker's corporate identity and a post-*Austin* line that permits them. . . .

There is simply no support for the view that the First Amendment, as originally understood, would permit the suppression of political speech by media corporations. The Framers may not have anticipated modern business and media corporations. Yet television networks and major newspapers owned by media corporations have become the most important means of mass communication in modern times. The First Amendment was certainly not understood to condone the suppression of political speech in society's most salient media. It was understood as a response to the repression of speech and the press that had existed in England and the heavy taxes on the press that were imposed in the colonies. . . .

When Government seeks to use its full power, including the criminal law, to command where a person may get his or her information or what distrusted source he or she may not hear, it uses censorship to control thought. This is unlawful. The First Amendment confirms the freedom to think for ourselves. . . .

We need not reach the question whether the Government has a compelling interest in preventing foreign individuals or associations from influencing our Nation's political process. Section 441b is not limited to corporations or associations that were created in foreign countries or funded predominately by foreign shareholders. Section 441b therefore would be overbroad even if we assumed, *arguendo*, that the Government has a compelling interest in limiting foreign influence over our political process.

Due consideration leads to this conclusion: *Austin* should be and now is overruled. We return to the principle established in *Buckley* and *Bellotti* that the Government may not suppress political speech on the basis of the speaker's corporate identity. No sufficient governmental interest justifies limits on the political speech of nonprofit or for-profit corporations.

Given our conclusion we are further required to overrule the part of *McConnell* that upheld BCRA §203's extension of §441b's restrictions on corporate independent expenditures. The *McConnell* Court relied on the antidistortion interest recognized in *Austin* to uphold a greater restriction on speech than the restriction upheld in *Austin*, and we have found this interest unconvincing and insufficient. This part of *McConnell* is now overruled. . . .

Some members of the public might consider *Hillary* to be insightful and instructive; some might find it to be neither high art nor a fair discussion on how to set the Nation's course; still others simply might suspend judgment on these points but decide to think more about issues and candidates. Those choices and assessments, however, are not for the Government to make. "The First Amendment underwrites the freedom to experiment and to create in the realm of thought and speech. Citizens must be free to use new forms, and new forums, for the expression of ideas. The civic discourse belongs to the people, and the Government may not prescribe the means used to conduct it."

The judgment of the District Court is reversed with respect to the constitutionality of 2 U.S.C. §441b's restrictions on corporate independent expenditures. The judgment is affirmed with respect to BCRA's disclaimer and disclosure requirements. The case is remanded for further proceedings consistent with this opinion.

It is so ordered.

Robin and Laird Monahan are the brothers behind Amend the Constitution—Abolish Corporate Personhood. They are in the process of walking from San Francisco to Washington, DC, to publicize their cause—but took a short break to attend the "One Nation Working Together" rally at the Lincoln Memorial in Washington, DC, on October 2, 2010

Jeff Malet/Jeff Malet Photography/Newscom

9.6 FREEDOM OF ASSOCIATION

The First Amendment's textual reference to "the right of the people to peaceably assemble, and to petition the Government for a redress of grievances" offers a constitutional foundation for a right that is not explicitly mentioned in the Bill of Rights—the **freedom of association.** Essentially, this freedom includes the right of individuals to gather together and express themselves collectively. In many ways, this right is considered to be the plural version of the First Amendment's freedom of speech. Just as the freedom of speech generally is regarded as protecting an individual's right of expression (see previous discussion), the freedom of association is viewed as protecting the right of collective expression. And, despite any specific constitutional mention, this freedom nonetheless is deemed to be a fundamental right under the First Amendment. In fact, early in the nation's history, American observer and political philosopher Alexis de Tocqueville asserted, "The most natural privilege of a man next to the right of acting for himself, is that of combining his exertions with those of his fellow creatures and of acting in common with them. The right of association therefore appears to be as almost inalienable in its nature as the right of personal liberty. No legislator can attack it without impairing the foundations of society."[52]

The Supreme Court officially acknowledged the fundamental nature of the freedom of association in *NAACP v. Alabama* (1958),[53] a case in which Alabama's attorney general sought to acquire the membership lists of the NAACP. In response, the NAACP argued that providing the state's attorney general with the names of its members would likely lead to harassment, discrimination, and violence against its members. Moreover, because this case occurred during the age of segregation and legal discrimination, the group also believed that the disclosure of the list might lead to a chilling of speech and participation among its members. In a unanimous opinion, the Court sided with the NAACP, holding that the state's efforts violated the freedom of association that was held by the members of the NAACP. The Court connected this freedom to both the Due Process Clause and the right to the freedom of speech, stating, "[i]t is beyond debate that freedom to engage in association for the advancement of beliefs and ideas is an inseparable aspect of the 'liberty' assured by the Due Process Clause of the Fourteenth Amendment, which embraces the freedom of speech. . . ."[54] The fact that the Court tied the freedom of association to the freedom of expression has been a critical factor in deciding other cases involving this asserted right.

The freedom of association has been addressed in a number of different contexts. The right has been asserted in other cases where government sought the membership lists of organizations,[55] cases involving the firing or mistreatment of employees based on their political-party affiliations or political views,[56] and cases where private organizations have sought to exclude members based on race, sex, or sexual orientation.[57] Oftentimes, in balancing the private group's constitutional right to associate against the government's interest in law enforcement, the central question is, to what extent will the government's application of the law interfere with or undermine the expression of the private organization? In cases where the governmental action interferes with the primary message of the group, the right of association is more likely to be protected. But where the government's regulation does not substantially undermine the primary message of the group, the law will be upheld.

In 2000, the Supreme Court relied upon the freedom of association to uphold the right of the Boy Scouts of America to expel a scoutmaster because he was gay. In *Boy Scouts of America v. Dale* (see the following Court's opinion), the Court held that New Jersey could not enforce a state public accommodations law, which barred discrimination based on sexual orientation, against the Boy Scouts for their removal of James Dale, a troop leader. In a 5-4 ruling, the Court found that the state law infringed upon the organization's right to the freedom of association. Read the Court's opinion in *Boy Scouts of America v. Dale* (2000), and observe how the group's message (or lack thereof) lies at the heart of both the majority and dissenting opinions.

freedom of association
The First Amendment right of individuals to gather together and express themselves collectively.

Cyber Constitution
The Freedom Not to Associate
http://law2.umkc.edu/
faculty/projects/ftrials/
conlaw/association.htm

Boy Scouts of America v. Dale
530 U.S. 640 (2000)

Chief Justice Rehnquist delivered the opinion of the Court.

Petitioners are the Boy Scouts of America and the Monmouth Council, a division of the Boy Scouts of America (collectively, Boy Scouts). The Boy Scouts is a private, not-for-profit organization engaged in instilling its system of values in young people. The Boy Scouts asserts that homosexual conduct is inconsistent with the values it seeks to instill. Respondent is James Dale, a former Eagle Scout whose adult membership in the Boy Scouts was revoked when the Boy Scouts learned that he is an avowed homosexual and gay rights activist. The New Jersey Supreme Court held that New Jersey's public accommodations law requires that the Boy Scouts admit Dale. This case presents the question whether applying New Jersey's public accommodations law in this way violates the Boy Scouts' First Amendment right of expressive association. We hold that it does.

In *Roberts v. United States Jaycees*, 468 U. S. 609, 622 (1984), we observed that "implicit in the right to engage in activities protected by the First Amendment" is "a corresponding right to associate with others in pursuit of a wide variety of political, social, economic, educational, religious, and cultural ends." This right is crucial in preventing the majority from imposing its views on groups that would rather express other, perhaps unpopular, ideas. . . . Forcing a group to accept certain members may impair the ability of the group to express those views, and only those views, that it intends to express. Thus, "[f]reedom of association . . . plainly presupposes a freedom not to associate."

To determine whether a group is protected by the First Amendment's expressive associational right, we must determine whether the group engages in "expressive association." The First Amendment's protection of expressive association is not reserved for advocacy groups. But to come within its ambit, a group must engage in some form of expression, whether it be public or private.

Because this is a First Amendment case where the ultimate conclusions of law are virtually inseparable from findings of fact, we are obligated to independently review the factual record to ensure that the state court's judgment does not unlawfully intrude on free expression. The record reveals the following. The Boy Scouts is a private, nonprofit organization. According to its mission statement:

> It is the mission of the Boy Scouts of America to serve others by helping to instill values in young people and, in other ways, to prepare them to make ethical choices over their lifetime in achieving their full potential.

"The values we strive to instill are based on those found in the Scout Oath and Law." . . .

Thus, the general mission of the Boy Scouts is clear: "[T]o instill values in young people." The Boy Scouts seeks to instill these values by having its adult leaders spend time with the youth members, instructing and engaging them in activities like camping, archery, and fishing. During the time spent with the youth members, the scoutmasters and assistant scoutmasters inculcate them with the Boy Scouts' values—both expressly and by example. It seems indisputable that an association that seeks to transmit such a system of values engages in expressive activity.

Given that the Boy Scouts engages in expressive activity, we must determine whether the forced inclusion of Dale as an assistant scoutmaster would significantly affect the Boy Scouts' ability to advocate public or private viewpoints. This inquiry necessarily requires us first to explore, to a limited extent, the nature of the Boy Scouts' view of homosexuality.

The values the Boy Scouts seeks to instill are "based on" those listed in the Scout Oath and Law. The Boy Scouts explains that the Scout Oath and Law provide "a positive moral code for living; they are a list of 'do's' rather than 'don'ts.'" The Boy Scouts asserts that homosexual conduct is inconsistent with the values embodied in the Scout Oath and Law, particularly with the values represented by the terms "morally straight" and "clean."

The Boy Scouts asserts that it "teach[es] that homosexual conduct is not morally straight," and that it does "not want to promote homosexual conduct as a legitimate form of behavior." We accept the Boy Scouts' assertion. We need not inquire further to determine the nature of the Boy Scouts' expression with respect to homosexuality. . . .

We must then determine whether Dale's presence as an assistant scoutmaster would significantly burden the Boy Scouts' desire to not "promote homosexual conduct as a legitimate form of behavior." As we give deference to an association's assertions regarding the nature of its expression, we must also give deference to an association's view of what would impair its expression. That is not to say that an expressive association can erect a shield against antidiscrimination laws simply by asserting that mere acceptance of a member from a particular group would impair its message. But here Dale, by his own admission, is one of a group of gay Scouts who have "become leaders in their community and are open and honest about their sexual orientation." Dale was the copresident of a gay and lesbian organization at college and remains a gay rights activist. Dale's presence in the Boy Scouts would, at the very least, force the organization to send a message, both to the youth members and the world, that the Boy Scouts accepts homosexual conduct as a legitimate form of behavior.

Hurley [*v. Irish-American Gay, Lesbian, and Bisexual Group of Boston*, 515 U.S. 557 (1995)] is illustrative on this point. There we considered whether the application of Massachusetts' public accommodations law to require the organizers of a private St. Patrick's Day parade to include among the marchers an Irish-American gay, lesbian, and bisexual group, GLIB, violated the parade organizers' First Amendment rights. We noted that the parade organizers did not wish to exclude the GLIB members because of their sexual orientations, but because they wanted to march behind a GLIB banner. . . .

Here, we have found that the Boy Scouts believes that homosexual conduct is inconsistent with the values it seeks to instill in its youth members; it will not "promote homosexual conduct as a legitimate form of behavior." As the presence of GLIB in Boston's St. Patrick's Day parade would have interfered with the parade organizers' choice not to propound a particular point of view, the presence of Dale as an assistant scoutmaster would just as surely interfere with the Boy Scout's choice not to propound a point of view contrary to its beliefs. . . .

Having determined that the Boy Scouts is an expressive association and that the forced inclusion of Dale would significantly affect its expression, we inquire whether the application of New Jersey's public accommodations law to require that the Boy Scouts accept Dale as an assistant scoutmaster runs afoul of the Scouts' freedom of expressive association. We conclude that it does.

The judgment of the New Jersey Supreme Court is reversed, and the cause remanded for further proceedings not inconsistent with this opinion. . . .

Justice Stevens, with whom Justice Souter, Justice Ginsburg and Justice Breyer join, dissenting.

The majority holds that New Jersey's law violates BSA's right to associate and its right to free speech. But that law does not "impos[e] any serious burdens" on BSA's "collective effort on behalf of [its] shared goals," *Roberts v. United States Jaycees*, 468 U.S. 609, 622, 626-627 (1984), nor does it force BSA to communicate any message that it does not wish to endorse. New Jersey's law, therefore, abridges no constitutional right of the Boy Scouts. . . .

In light of BSA's self-proclaimed ecumenism, furthermore, it is even more difficult to discern any shared goals or common moral stance on homosexuality. Insofar as religious matters are concerned, BSA's bylaws state that it is "absolutely nonsectarian in its attitude toward . . . religious training." "The BSA does not define what

constitutes duty to God or the practice of religion. This is the responsibility of parents and religious leaders." In fact, many diverse religious organizations sponsor local Boy Scout troops. Because a number of religious groups do not view homosexuality as immoral or wrong and reject discrimination against homosexuals, it is exceedingly difficult to believe that BSA nonetheless adopts a single particular religious or moral philosophy when it comes to sexual orientation. This is especially so in light of the fact that Scouts are advised to seek guidance on sexual matters from their religious leaders (and Scoutmasters are told to refer Scouts to them); BSA surely is aware that some religions do not teach that homosexuality is wrong. . . .

The evidence before this Court makes it exceptionally clear that BSA has, at most, simply adopted an exclusionary membership policy and has no shared goal of disapproving of homosexuality. BSA's mission statement and federal charter say nothing on the matter; its official membership policy is silent; its Scout Oath and Law—and accompanying definitions—are devoid of any view on the topic; its guidance for Scouts and Scoutmasters on sexuality declare that such matters are "not construed to be Scouting's proper area," but are the province of a Scout's parents and pastor; and BSA's posture respecting religion tolerates a wide variety of views on the issue of homosexuality. Moreover, there is simply no evidence that BSA otherwise teaches anything in this area, or that it instructs Scouts on matters involving homosexuality in ways not conveyed in the Boy Scout or Scoutmaster Handbooks. In short, Boy Scouts of America is simply silent on homosexuality. There is no shared goal or collective effort to foster a belief about homosexuality at all—let alone one that is significantly burdened by admitting homosexuals. . . .

Furthermore, it is not likely that BSA would be understood to send any message, either to Scouts or to the world, simply by admitting someone as a member. Over the years, BSA has generously welcomed over 87 million young Americans into its ranks. In 1992 over one million adults were active BSA members. The notion that an organization of that size and enormous prestige implicitly endorses the views that each of those adults may express in a non-Scouting context is simply mind boggling. . . .

If we would guide by the light of reason, we must let our minds be bold. I respectfully dissent.

9.7 FREEDOM OF THE PRESS

Just like the freedoms of speech and association, the **freedom of the press** is grounded in the value of protecting and promoting expression. As the Supreme Court has observed, "[t]he freedom of speech and of the press guaranteed by the Constitution embraces at least the liberty to discuss publicly and truthfully all matters of public concern without previous restraint or fear of subsequent punishment."[58] But the First Amendment's textual inclusion of the freedom of the press leaves several practical questions about this freedom unanswered—questions that are inevitably addressed through the balancing of constitutional values.

freedom of the press
The First Amendment right guaranteeing some level of protection for press-based expression.

For example, what types of people and organizations are included in the category "the press"? Does it include just newspapers? What about radio, television, and Internet messages? Are Internet blogs considered part of the press? What about entertainment programs? Each of these questions presents, as Justice White put it, "practical and conceptual difficulties of a high order."[59] The Court has addressed press freedoms in terms of newspapers,[60] television stations,[61] and radio reporters.[62] But this treatment largely has left the constitutional status of numerous other informational outlets unresolved. In many cases, the Court simply has avoided labeling certain entities as "press" or "nonpress," by concentrating its rulings on the more general right to the freedom of speech. Essentially, the Court has approached many of these controversies from the standpoint that regardless of the press or nonpress status of the claimants, at the very least, they have First Amendment interests to speech.[63]

The Court's treatment of certain cases involving purported members of the press as simply free speech controversies raises another question regarding the freedom of the press, namely, given the First Amendment's specific reference to this right, should the press receive special constitutional status and protection beyond that afforded to other individuals under the freedom of speech provision? For some members of the Court, the press should be treated as a unique class deserving of special constitutional protection. For example, Justice Stewart referred to the press as the "fourth institution" of government and urged his colleagues to appreciate the fact that it was "the only organized private business that is given explicit constitutional protection."[64] But for other members of the Court, members of the press are to be afforded no greater constitutional status than that given to the ordinary citizen.

In many cases, the latter approach has ruled the day. For example, in 2005, *New York Times* reporter Judy Miller spent twelve weeks in jail for refusing to testify before a federal grand jury that was investigating purported leaks of confidential information by the Bush administration. Miller had argued, among other things, that the First Amendment protected her from revealing the confidential sources of her news information, but lower federal courts rejected this argument, finding that the First Amendment afforded Miller no special protection to withhold her testimony, and the Supreme Court declined to accept her appeal.[65] Still in other cases, the protection of the press is enhanced by state laws, many of which afford journalists with special privileges, including so-called **reporter shield laws,** which prevent reporters from being compelled to reveal their confidential news sources. In these jurisdictions, legislative and judicial efforts have attempted to fill the constitutional void by protecting and enhancing the status of the press.[66]

A final item that must be addressed with constitutional questions about press is how the Court should go about balancing competing interests against this constitutional freedom. There are three basic forms of constitutional controversy that can occur between the press and the government. First there are times when the government tries to prevent the press from disclosing information to third parties, such as the publication or transmission of sensitive or objectionable information. Second there are times when the government attempts to stop the press from accessing information, such as when the government refuses to provide public documents or attempts to close public meetings or trials. Finally there are times when the government seeks to acquire information from the press, such as when a prosecutor subpoenas a reporter for testimony during a criminal proceeding. In each of these instances, a balancing test is applied to determine whether the government's interest in blocking or obtaining information outweighs the values associated with a free press.

In cases where the government seeks to stop the press from disseminating information, the doctrine of **prior restraint** is highly important. Under this doctrine, there is a strong constitutional presumption against government restraining the press prior to its publication of information. As a result, the government generally will be required to demonstrate a compelling and immediate interest in restraining the press before it

---

reporter shield laws
State laws that prevent reporters from being compelled to reveal their confidential news sources.

Cyber Constitution
Reporter Shield Laws
http://iml.jou.ufl.edu/
projects/spring05/vaught/
state.html

prior restraint
An attempt by government to prevent or restrain expression, including press publication, before it is uttered.

will be allowed to override the First Amendment. In many cases, the government has failed in this attempt, such as in *New York Times v. United States* (1971).[67] In that case, the government sought to restrain *The New York Times* and *The Washington Post* from further publishing the so-called *Pentagon Papers*, which contained government studies related to the Vietnam War. The Court rejected the government's efforts, finding that any request for a prior restraint on press "bears a heavy presumption against its constitutional validity" and that the government had not met this heavy burden.

In cases where the government attempts to block access to information by the press, the First Amendment interests of the press are often balanced against other competing constitutional rights and powers. For example, where the press seeks to cover certain high-profile judicial proceedings, the courts must weigh the right of the defendant to receive a fair trial, as protected by the Sixth Amendment, against the right of a free press.[68] And where the press tries to compel the disclosure of government documents, the interests of national security and executive authority, which are often rooted, among other sources, in Article II of the Constitution, must be balanced against the public's right to know.[69]

YOUR CONSTITUTIONAL VALUES

SHOULD BOOK AUTHORS BE PROTECTED FROM DISCLOSING CONFIDENTIAL INFORMATION?

In 1997, Doris Angleton, the wife of Texas millionaire Robert Angleton, was found shot to death in Houston, Texas. Purportedly, she was killed just as she was about to file for divorce from her husband. The state of Texas charged her husband, Robert, with murder, asserting that he hired his brother, Roger Angleton, to kill Doris.

As news of Doris's death came to light, an aspiring writer, Vanessa Leggett, set out to investigate the case with the intention of writing a book. Leggett had worked as a private investigator and police instructor in Texas, but sought to begin a writing career. And so during the four years after Doris Angleton's death, Leggett investigated Doris's death by performing and taping interviews with several witnesses, including Roger Angleton, who was being held in a county jail pending trial. In February 1998, Roger committed suicide in his jail cell, but left a note indicating that his brother, Robert, was not responsible for Doris's death.

State investigators subpoenaed Leggett to testify before a grand jury, but she refused. Later, she agreed to provide prosecutors with some of the tapes she had made of her interviews, tapes that purportedly were incriminating to Robert Angleton. The state, however, did not use the tapes in its trial against Robert, nor did it call Leggett as a witness, and in 1998, Angleton was acquitted of murder by a state jury.

Shortly thereafter, a federal grand jury began to investigate Angleton's actions under federal law and sought Leggett's information through a subpoena. Leggett testified before the federal grand jury in December 2000 under the condition that she not be forced to reveal her confidential sources. But in June 2001, federal prosecutors subpoenaed Leggett again to the grand jury, only this time they wanted materials that would ostensibly reveal her sources.

This time, Leggett refused to comply with the subpoena and filed a motion to have it quashed based, in part, on the First Amendment claim that she was protected from testifying under the freedom of the press. But the federal district court rejected Leggett's motion and ordered her to testify. Ultimately, in July 2001, after again refusing to testify, Leggett was held in contempt of court and placed in jail. Leggett's appeal to the Fifth Circuit Court of Appeals was denied. The appeals court acknowledged that Leggett was "an aspiring freelance writer," but did not address her First Amendment objections. The Supreme Court declined to accept her case.

Leggett was eventually released in January 2002, after having spent 168 days in jail, which is believed to be the longest time served by an American journalist for a contempt citation.

Using your constitutional values, how would you address this matter? Should Leggett be included as a member of "the press" under the First Amendment? Should Leggett have been constitutionally protected from testifying before the federal grand jury?

For more information, go to Sue Ellison, "Vanessa Leggett: Defying Court Subpoenas in the Name of the First Amendment," *Montana Journalism Review*, Vol. 31 (Summer 2002).

Finally, where newspapers or reporters have sought special protection against governmental or third-party requests for information, typically the interest of the press in maintaining the confidentiality of news sources is pitted against the public's general interest in pursuing criminal investigations or the right to a fair trial.[70] In states with laws protecting press agents from encroachment from external seizure, the freedom of the press is relatively high. But in jurisdictions that lack legislative or judicial measures to shield news gatherers, protections for the press generally are at their lowest ebb.

9.8 MODERN CHALLENGES

As modern advances in communication evolve, so too will the doctrines and tests applied under the First Amendment. Today governments at all levels have sought to control the potentially-harmful effects of electronic communications. There are several legislative measures that have sought to curb expression through electronic means. For example, many contemporary laws ban soliciting a minor for sex in Internet chat rooms. But in some cases, the person being solicited is not really a minor, but rather, an adult law enforcement officer posing as a minor. The question in these cases is whether such communication between two adults is protected speech, or whether, because the solicitor believed the other person to be a minor, this is a form of illegal solicitation. The medium of cyberspace, where the reality of things being represented is not always as it appears, presents particular challenges for both legislators and courts when addressing the level of First Amendment protection to be afforded to cyber-based communications.

Another modern legislative trend is the passage of laws banning "sexting" by minors. For many years, criminal laws have prohibited the adult creation, use, possession, or distribution of materials depicting minors involved in sexual activity. And as discussed earlier in this chapter, child pornography is an unprotected category of expression, in part, because it can be used by adults to harm children. But what about cases where minors themselves create and transmit images of themselves, with no adult involvement whatsoever? Should minors who create sexually-explicit images of themselves be treated in the same manner as an adult who uses minors to create such images? Or should this autonomous act be given some level of protection under the First Amendment?

Finally, following the Supreme Court's ruling in *Citizens United v. FEC* (2010), there will be continuing debate as to whether and to what extent corporations should have First Amendment protections for their speech and advertising. On the one hand, corporate entities are associative groups that, like other organizations, may have a collective right to expression. On the other hand, corporations are essentially forms of legal fiction, with no tangible identity, and the framers of the Bill of Rights, no doubt, never envisioned such entities as having the freedom of speech. Many critics also are concerned about the mismatch of power that comes with allowing large corporate entities the freedom of speech and fear that such well-financed expression may drown out the voices of the less powerful and more modestly funded.

9.9 SUMMARY

The First Amendment contains a number of provisions that protect values associated with the freedom of expression. The explicitly referenced freedoms of speech, press, assembly, and the right to petition the government of redress of grievances, as well as the implicit freedom of association, are all based upon the belief that human expression is valuable to a democratic society. Such protections allow citizens to check and otherwise supervise their government; they allow competing individual interests or factions to check one another to prevent monopolies of interest, and they encourage human health by allowing individuals to release thoughts and feelings.

The freedoms of expression have all been incorporated through the Fourteenth Amendment Due Process Clause and made applicable to state and local governments. Moreover, these freedoms protect individuals against unconstitutional restrictions by any and all forms of government—legislative, executive, judicial, and administrative. These freedoms, however, are not absolute. Rather, the values of speech, press, assembly, redress of grievances, and association are balanced against other competing interests, such as national security, human safety, or other civil liberties. And through the use of various balancing tests, the Supreme Court weighs these competing interests against the values of expression to determine the appropriate constitutional standard for protecting First Amendment liberties.

The balancing test used to judge freedom of speech controversies has evolved over time. Beginning with the clear and present danger test adopted in 1919, the Court has gradually modified its approach to free speech cases, which has included brief periods where it used the bad tendency test and then the probability test. Currently, the Court uses the *Brandenburg* test, which provides that government may regulate or restrict speech when the speech is directed at inciting imminent lawless action and is likely to incite such action. This basic test, however, is only one consideration in free speech cases. Other questions must also be considered, including (1) whether the government is attempting to regulate speech or conduct, (2) whether the government's policy is vague or overly broad, (3) whether the government's action toward speech is a ban or a regulation, (4) whether the regulation applies to a public or nonpublic forum, and (5) whether the type of speech being regulated is regarded as constitutionally unprotected or underprotected, such as obscenity, fighting words, defamation, child pornography, or commercial speech.

The freedom of speech poses particular challenges when trying to regulate some of the abuses in political campaigns and elections. For years, policymakers have recognized the abuses of excessive money in campaigns and elections and have sought to regulate such abuses. But the Court has viewed financial campaign contributions to be a form of political speech. As a result, in recent years the Court has struck down a number of campaign finance reform measures that impose restrictions on campaign spending, including expenditures made by corporations and unions. Still in some cases the Court has regarded Congress's interest in preventing campaign abuse to be substantial and has upheld reasonable efforts to limit campaign contributions to candidates. However, the Court has refused to uphold limitations on the amount of money that can be spent by individual political campaigns.

The freedom of association includes the right of individuals to gather together and express themselves collectively. Despite any specific mention of this right in the First Amendment, the Court has found it to be implicitly protected and essential to protecting rights of expression. This right, however, often conflicts with other governmental interests, such as law enforcement and measures protecting equality, where the government is seeking to regulate the behavior of private groups. In these cases, the central question for the Court in balancing the two competing values is to what extent the government's actions would interfere with the primary message of the group.

The freedom of the press is also associated with the value of free expression consistent with the belief that the Constitution protects the liberty to discuss publicly and truthfully all matters of public concern. This provision, however, presents some practical problems. For example, what individuals should be included as members of "the press"? And should the press be given special protections for its expression above and beyond those given to individuals under the freedom of speech? Finally, in cases where the freedom of press is asserted, the Court often must balance competing governmental interests, such as national security, criminal investigation, and executive privilege, against this First Amendment liberty.

REVIEW QUESTIONS

1. Name the different types of expression protected by the First Amendment.
2. In what ways is the freedom of expression valuable to a constitutional democracy?
3. Discuss why the First Amendment has not been applied in a literal fashion to bar all forms of governmental interference with self-expression, regardless of the circumstances.
4. How has the balancing test used to resolve free speech cases evolved over time? What is the current standard for such cases?
5. Explain and discuss the relevance of the distinction between content and conduct when it comes to resolving free speech controversies.
6. How do the terms *vagueness, overbreadth, public forum, nonpublic forum, ban,* and *regulation* relate to free speech jurisprudence?
7. What is the constitutional difference between obscenity, pornography, profanity, and vulgarity?
8. Identify and discuss the constitutional standard for addressing governmental regulations of commercial speech.
9. What is the "fighting words" doctrine?
10. Describe the terms "soft money" and "advocacy advertisements." What has Congress done to regulate these items, and how has the Supreme Court viewed these legislative efforts?
11. Why is the freedom of association protected if it is not specifically mentioned in the First Amendment? What balancing test is used to weigh the freedom of association?
12. What practical problems are presented by the First Amendment's freedom of the press?

ASSIGNMENTS: CONSTITUTIONAL LAW IN ACTION

The Constitution in Your Community

Assume that you are working as a paralegal in a local prosecutor's office. You have been asked to work on a criminal case, where three defendants have been charged with disorderly conduct based on their behavior during a local football game. It seems that the three defendants got agitated after their team lost the game in double overtime.

Afterward, the defendants began shouting various barbs at passers-by. The first defendant yelled "You guys suck!" to members of the opposing team as they went into the locker room. The second defendant screamed "Your team is a bunch of inbred hicks who want to marry their sisters" to a group of opposing-team parents leaving the stadium. And the third defendant, shouted "Hey, you dumb cop, why don't you go back to the donut shop where you belong?" to an officer who was arresting the first two defendants. Each of the defendants maintains that his speech after the game was protected under the First Amendment.

Locate the disorderly conduct statute for your local jurisdiction or state. Then prepare a memorandum analyzing whether your prosecutor's office should proceed with criminal charges against each of the three defendants or whether some or all of the charges should be dropped based on constitutional protections under the First Amendment.

Going Federal

Assume that you are working for a criminal defense attorney, who has just been retained to represent Ima Reider, a librarian from a public university. It seems that federal authorities have charged Ms. Reider with violating provisions of the USA PATRIOT Act, which bars record keepers, including librarians, from discussing government searches of records within the custody of record keepers, including public libraries. Under the federal indictment, Ms. Reider is accused of telling a student at the university that FBI agents sought and obtained the student's library records during a search. Ms. Reider acknowledges her conversation with the student, but asserts that this form of speech is protected under the First Amendment.

Obtain a copy of the USA PATRIOT Act—the federal law passed shortly after September 11, 2001—and review the provisions that restrict certain record keepers from discussing governmental searches of private records, such as those from a library, academic records, or medical information. Prepare a three-page memorandum in which you address whether these restrictions are constitutional under the First Amendment.

Moot Court

Assume that you have been asked to assist a group of attorney in preparing for oral arguments in a First Amendment case challenging a law banning the sale of violent video games to minors. The case concerns a law that criminalizes the sale of violent video games to minors. Specifically, the law states, "[a] person may not sell or rent a video game that has been labeled as a violent video to a minor." Using the briefs filed in the U.S. Supreme Court case of *Schwarzenegger v. Entertainment Merchants Association*, Case No. 08-1448, prepare and present an oral argument that addresses the basic First Amendment issues involved in the dispute. The first team should prepare a five-minute oral argument presentation, wherein they assert that the law violated the expressive freedoms of minors under the First Amendment. Conversely, the second team should prepare a five-minute oral argument asserting why the law constitutes a reasonable and permissible regulation of speech under the First Amendment.

NOTES

1. *Ashcroft v. Free Speech Coalition*, 535 U.S. 234 (2002).
2. *Garrison v. Louisiana*, 379 U.S. 64 (1964).
3. Douglas M. Fraleigh and Joseph S. Tuman, *Freedom of Speech in the Marketplace of Ideas* (Bedford/St. Martin's 1996).
4. *Abrams v. United States*, 250 U.S. 616, 630 (1919), dissenting opinion.
5. *Texas v. Johnson*, 491 U.S. 397 (1989); *United States v. Eichmann*, 496 U.S. 310 (1990).
6. *Smith v. Collin*, 439 U.S. 916 (1978) (denying petition for writ of certiorari).

7. *Capitol Square Review Bd. v. Pinette*, 515 US 753 (1995).

8. *Ashcroft v. Free Speech Coalition*, 535 U.S. 234 (2002).

9. 274 U.S. 380 (1927).

10. See *Gitlow v. New York*, 268 U.S. 652 (1925) and *Gilbert v. Minnesota*, 254 U.S. 325 (1920) (both offering dicta suggesting that the First Amendment speech clause should be applied to the states).

11. 283 U.S. 697 (1931).

12. 299 U.S. 353 (1937).

13. 357 U.S. 449 (1958).

14. *New York Times Company v. United States*, 403 U.S. 670 (1971).

15. *Globe Newspaper Company v. Superior Court for the County of Norfolk*, 457 U.S. 596 (1982).

16. *Federal Communications Commission v. Pacifica Foundation*, 438 U.S. 726 (1978).

17. See *Schenck v. United States*, 249 U.S. 47 (1919), where Justice Holmes uses this example to justify certain governmental limitations on speech.

18. *Dennis v. United States*, 341 U.S. 494 (1951).

19. See *Kingsley International Corp. v. Regents of Univ. of New York*, 360 U.S. 684 (1959) (books and movies, including *Lady Chatterley's Lover*); *Reno v. ACLU*, 521 U.S. 844 (1997) (Internet communications); *A Book Named "John Cleland's Memoirs of a Woman of Pleasure" v. Massachusetts*, 383 U.S. 413 (1966) (book); *Schad v. Borough of Mt. Ephraim*, 452 U.S. 61 (1981) (nude dancing); *Cohen v. California*, 403 U.S. 15 (1971) (clothing messages); *West Virginia Bd. of Education v. Barnette*, 319 U.S. 624 (1943) (flag saluting); *Texas v. Johnson*, 491 US 397 (1989) (flag burning); *44 Liquormart, Inc. v. Rhode Island*, 517 U.S. 484 (1996) (commercial advertising).

20. 249 U.S. 47 (1919).

21. 268 U.S. 652 (1925).

22. 341 U.S. 494 (1951).

23. 395 U.S. 444 (1969).

24. See *Boos v. Barry*, 485 U.S. 312 (1988) (striking down a law prohibiting "the display of any sign within 500 feet of a foreign embassy if that sign tends to bring that foreign government into 'public odium' or 'public disrepute'").

25. See *Wooley v. Maynard*, 430 U.S. 705 (1977) (license plate messages); *Tinker v. Des Moines Independent Community School District*, 393 U.S. 503 (1969) (wearing arm bands to protest war).

26. *Reno v. American Civil Liberties Union*, 521 U.S. 844 (1997) (striking down Communications Decency Act of 1996, which, among other things, banned indecent Internet transmissions).

27. *Ashcroft v. Free Speech Coalition*, 535 U.S. 234 (2002) (striking down portions of the Child Pornography Prevention Act of 1996 because the phrases "appears to be" a minor and "conveys the impression" that a minor is depicted were unduly overbroad).

28. See *Renton v. Playtime Theatres, Inc.*, 475 U.S. 41 (1986) (upholding zoning ordinance keeping adult movie theaters out of residential neighborhoods, but allowing them to operate in other areas).

29. See *Hague v. CIO*, 307 U.S. 496 (1937) (public streets and meeting halls); *Edwards v. South Carolina*, 371 U.S. 229 (1963) (steps of state capitol building).

30. See *Greer v. Spock*, 424 U.S. 828 (1976) (military bases); *Adderly v. Florida*, 385 U.S. 39 (1966) (area surrounding jails).

31. See *Forsyth County v. The Nationalist Movement*, 505 U.S. 123 (1992) (striking down ordinance imposing a fee of up to $1,000 per day for parades).

32. See *Rosenberger v. The Rector and Visitors of the University of Virginia*, 515 U.S. 819 (1995) (5–4 ruling upholding the right for a student religious publication to receive funding from public university, wherein justice disagreed over the neutrality of the university's funding policy).

33. 561 U.S. __, 130 S.Ct. 2971 (2010)

34. 413 U.S. 15 (1973).

35. *Stanley v. Georgia*, 394 U.S. 561 (1969).

36. 458 U.S. 747 (1982).

37. 535 U.S. 234 (2002).

38. 553 U.S. 285 (2008).

39. *Chaplinsky v. New Hampshire*, 315 U.S. 568 (1942).

40. *Id.*

41. See *Cohen v. California*, 403 U.S. 15 (1971) (upholding the right of a man to wear a jacket bearing the phrase "Fuck the Draft," while in a courthouse, because there was no immediate

threat of breaching the peace); *R.A.V. v. City of St. Paul*, 505 U.S. 377 (1992) (striking down a sentencing law that allowed courts to enhance a defendant's punishment based on the message offered by his speech).

42. 561 U.S. __ (2010).

43. See *The New York Times Co. v. Sullivan*, 376 U.S. 254 (1964) (rejecting the defamation claim of an elected city official [a public figure] based on a lack of evidence that he was harmed and because the state's defamation statute did not address the requirement of malice).

44. See *Valentine v. Chrestensen*, 316 U.S. 52 (1942) (unanimously finding that there was no "restraint on the government as respects purely commercial advertising").

45. 447 U.S. 557 (1980).

46. Note that some members of the current Court, Justices Scalia and Thomas, have expressed the view that regulations of commercial speech should be made to satisfy the full rigors of the strict scrutiny analysis, not the less-strict standard of *Central Hudson*. See *Lorillard Tobacco Co. v. Reilly*, 533 U.S. 525 (2001).

47. 424 U.S. 1 (1976).

48. 540 U.S. 93 (2003).

49. 546 U.S. 410 (2006).

50. 554 U. S. 724 (2008).

51. 130 S.Ct. 876 (2010).

52. Alexis de Tocqueville, *Democracy in America*, Vol. 2, ed. Phillips Bradley (New York: Vintage Books 1954), p. 196.

53. 357 U.S. 449 (1958).

54. *Id.*

55. See *Communist Party v. Subversive Activities Control Board*, 367 U.S. 1 (1961) (requiring members of "subversive" organizations to register with control board); *Bryant v. Zimmerman*, 278 U.S. 63 (1928) (upholding New York law requiring KKK to submit membership lists); *Gibson v. Florida Legislative Investigation Committee*, 372 U.S. 539 (1963) (requiring government to show immediate and substantial interest for membership information).

56. *United States v. Harris*, 347 U.S. 612 (1954); *U.S. Civil Service Comm. v. National Assoc. of Letter Carriers*, 413 U.S. 548 (1973) (both upholding federal laws barring civil servants from participating in political campaigns); *Elrod v. Burns*, 427 U.S. 347 (1976); *Branti v. Finkel*, 445 U.S. 507 (1980); *Rutan v. Republican Party of Illinois*, 497 U.S. 62 (1990) (all striking down patronage-based or political-expression-based firings).

57. *Roberts v. United States Jaycees*, 468 U.S. 609 (1984) (upholding a Minnesota human rights law and requiring organization to admit women); *City of Dallas v. Stanglin*, 490 U.S. 1591 (1989) (upholding law barring sex-based discrimination and requiring club to admit women); *Hurley v. Irish-American Gay, Lesbian, and Bisexual Group of Boston*, 515 U.S. 557 (1995) (rejecting the application of Massachusetts public accommodation law to organizers of a St. Patrick's Day parade).

58. *Thornhill v. Alabama*, 310 U.S. 88 (1940).

59. *Branzburg v. Hayes*, 408 U.S. 665 (1972).

60. See *New York Times Co. v. United States*, 403 U.S. 670 (1971) (rejecting the Nixon administration's attempt to stop the *New York Times* from publishing "the Pentagon Papers").

61. *Branzburg v. Hayes, In re Pappas, and United States v. Caldwell*, 408 U.S. 665 (1972) (addressing the freedom of the press as it applies to television and newspaper reporters subpoenaed before a grand jury).

62. *Houchins v. KQED, Inc.*, 438 U.S. 1 (1978) (addressing press freedoms as applied to a radio reporter seeking access to interview state prisoners).

63. See *Simon & Schuster, Inc. v. Members of the New York State Crime Victims Bd.*, 502 U.S. 105 (1991) (the Court struck down New York's "Son-of-Sam" law barring criminals from profiting from stories about their crimes because it imposed "a financial burden on speakers because of the content of their speech."); *Denver Area Educational Telecommunications Consortium, Inc. v. F.C.C.*, 518 U.S. 727 (1996) (striking down portions of the federal Cable Television Consumer Protection and Competition Act because they violated principles of free speech).

64. Potter Stewart, "Or of the Press," 26 *Hastings Law Journal* 631 (1975); see also, *Branzburg v. Hayes, In re Pappas, and United States v. Caldwell*, 408 U.S. 665 (1972) (Stewart dissenting).

65. *In re Special Counsel Investigation*, Misc. No. 04-407, www.dcd.uscourts.gov/04ms407.pdf; files.findlaw.com/news.findlaw.com_/nytimes/docs/plame/_inregjmiller21505opn.

66. See, for example, Ohio Revised Code sections 2739.04 and 2739.12; Oklahoma Statute, Title 12, section 2506; Nevada Revised Statute, section 49.275.

67. 403 U.S. 670 (1971).

68. See *Sheppard v. Maxwell*, 385 U.S. 333 (1966) (overturning a conviction due to unfair publicity during trial); *Nebraska Press Association v. Stuart*, 427 U.S. 539 (1976) (rejecting a court-imposed gag order on the press).

69. *Cheney v. United States District Court for the District of Columbia*, 124 S. Ct. 2576 (2004) (rejecting efforts to obtain information about the vice-president's meetings with energy-related executives).

70. *Branzburg v. Hayes, In re Pappas, and United States v. Caldwell*, 408 U.S. 665 (1972) (rejecting request for constitutional-based reporter's privilege); *Cohen v. Cowles Media Co.*, 501 U.S. 663 (1991) (refusing constitutional protection for a newspaper against civil suits brought by a confidential news source).

10

Religion and the Constitution

Believing with you that religion is a matter which lies solely between man and his God, that he owes account to none other for his faith or his worship, that the legislative powers of government reach actions only, and not opinions, I contemplate with sovereign reverence that act of the whole American people which declared that their legislature should "make no law respecting an establishment of religion, or prohibiting the free exercise thereof," thus building a wall of separation between Church and State.

THOMAS JEFFERSON[1]

It may fairly be said that leaving accommodation [for religious practices] to the political process will place at a relative disadvantage those religious practices that are not widely engaged in; but that [is the] unavoidable consequence of democratic government. . . .

JUSTICE ANTONIN SCALIA[2]

LEARNING OBJECTIVES
At the end of this chapter you should be able to:

- Explain the historical background of the Establishment Clause and Free Exercise Clause.
- Understand the textual challenges and limitations of interpreting the plain language of the Establishment Clause and Free Exercise Clause.
- Identify, explain, and apply the three primary tests—the *Lemon* test, endorsement test, and coercion test—that are used to interpret the Establishment Clause.
- Identify and explain the evolving doctrines, including the strict scrutiny test and neutrality test, which are used to interpret the Free Exercise Clause.
- Discuss the significance of the Religious Freedom Restoration Act and the Religious Land Use and Institutionalized Persons Act, as they relate to religious freedom.
- Identify a contemporary issue concerning the freedom of religion under the First Amendment, and discuss the most likely future scenarios, referencing both historical analogs and caselaw.
- Brief a judicial opinion with no assistance. You should be successful in identifying the relevant facts, identifying the legal issue(s), and analyzing the court's rationale in at least 75 percent of your briefs.
- Apply what you have learned to a new set of facts with no assistance.

10.1 THE FOUNDING OF THE RELIGION CLAUSES

The first section of the First Amendment provides that "Congress shall make no law respecting an establishment of religion, or prohibiting the free exercise thereof." This provision contains two clauses relating to religious liberty: (1) the **Establishment Clause** (Congress shall make no law respecting an establishment of religion) and (2) the **Free Exercise Clause** (or prohibiting the free exercise thereof). These clauses are distinct in their scope and effect. The Establishment Clause generally regulates the extent to which government can participate in, assist, or otherwise further religious activity or organizations. The Free Exercise Clause addresses the extent to which government can interfere with an individual's religious practices.

It would be difficult to discuss the religion clauses without addressing the efforts of James Madison, the primary architect of these provisions. Prior to drafting the Bill of Rights, Madison worked to protect religious freedoms in Virginia.[3] One of Madison's most well known statements on religious freedom is his 1785 publication *Memorial and Remonstrance Against Religious Assessments*. This work, originally published anonymously, was written in opposition to the General Assessment Bill that was proposed in 1784 by the Virginia State Assembly. The bill was sought to enact a tax "for the support of Christian teachers [in order to] correct the morals of men, restrain their vices, and preserve the peace of society."[4] There was considerable opposition to the bill when it was made public in the spring of 1785, and upon the urging of George Mason and others, Madison agreed to write a memorial against the proposed legislation.

Madison, addressing his letter to the General Assembly of Virginia, called the proposed assessment bill "a dangerous abuse of power,"[5] and proceeded to list the reasons for remonstrating against it. Arguably, the most compelling reason offered by Madison against the bill was his first, wherein he stated:

> The Religion then of every man must be left to the conviction and conscience of every man; and it is the right of every man to exercise it as these may dictate. This right is in its nature an unalienable right. It is unalienable; because the opinions of men, depending only on the evidence contemplated by their own minds, cannot follow the dictates of other men: It is unalienable also; because what is here a right towards men, is a duty towards the Creator.[6]

Madison concluded his letter by calling religious freedom a "gift of nature," and asserted that the Virginia legislature had no authority to deteriorate such a right. Ultimately, Madison's letter, along with numerous other petitions, effectively discouraged the Assembly so much that in the fall of 1785, when the bill was to be voted upon, it did not even reach the Assembly floor.

The public outcry for religious freedom in Virginia was so overwhelming that in December 1785, Madison introduced a bill authored by Thomas Jefferson to the Virginia Assembly that included, among other things, a "Bill for Establishing Religious Freedom." The bill would have it "that all men shall be free to profess, and by argument to maintain, their opinions in matters of religion. . . ." The bill concluded by declaring that "the rights hereby asserted are of the natural rights of mankind, and that if any act shall be hereafter passed to repeal the present or to narrow its operation, such act will be an infringement of natural right." Although the bill was slightly altered by the Virginia Assembly, it was signed into law in January of 1786.[7]

Three years later, while serving in the First Congress under the new constitution, Madison was appointed to the Select Committee on Constitutional Amendments, whose primary responsibility was to develop a Bill of Rights for the Constitution. The first draft, proposed in the fall of 1789, included the clause: "No religion shall be established by Law, nor shall the equal rights of conscience be

Establishment Clause
The first provision of the First Amendment, which provides that "Congress shall make no law respecting an establishment of religion." This clause generally regulates the extent to which government can participate in, assist, or otherwise further religious activity or organizations.

Free Exercise Clause
The second provision of the First Amendment, which provides that "Congress shall make no law . . . prohibiting the free exercise [of religion] thereof." This clause addresses the extent to which government can interfere with an individual's religious practices.

infringed." However, after much debate, Congress adopted the phrase "Congress shall make no law respecting an establishment of religion, or prohibiting the free exercise thereof."

Cyber Constitution
**Pew Forum on Religion
and Public Life**
http://pewforum.org/

10.2 THE TEXTUAL MEANING OF THE RELIGION CLAUSES

The religion clauses can be viewed as two sides of the same coin. On the one side, the First Amendment provides that the government cannot go too far in advancing religion; on the other side, the amendment states that government cannot go too far in inhibiting religion. The problem, however, is determining just how far government can go in its relationship with religious activity.

Both clauses contain terms that are undefined, facially uncertain, and consequently, subject to different interpretations. The First Amendment does not specify what "respecting" means. Does it mean relating to or regarding? Does it mean giving honor or assistance to? The amendment also does not offer further explanation of what "an establishment of religion" constitutes. Does it mean the formal creation of a national church (the Church of the United States)? Does it mean providing assistance to already-established places of worship? And because the amendment does not elaborate on what types of activities are covered under the "free exercise [of religion]," does free exercise mean *doing* anything you want in the name of religion, or *believing* anything you want, or a combination of both? Without further constitutional definition or clarity, the meaning and scope of these provisions have largely been left to the courts, chiefly the Supreme Court.

Although the Establishment Clause and the Free Exercise Clause protect two different dimensions of religious liberty, the constitutional interpretation of both clauses largely has been conducted along the same ideological continuum. See Figure 10-1. On the one end of the spectrum, there is the **accommodationist approach,** which generally maintains that it is appropriate for government to accommodate or otherwise assist religious interests or organizations. This may come in the form of government funding for religious groups or allowing minority religious practices to be exempted from general legal requirements. On the other end of the spectrum, there is the **separationist approach,** which generally asserts that government should remain strictly separate or removed from religious activity. Under this approach, it is asserted that government should not aid, fund, or otherwise assist religious organizations or individual religious activity, but rather, there should be a high wall of separation between church and state.

For the most part, the Supreme Court generally has declined to accept either approach in its entirety when addressing cases under the Establishment Clause and Free Exercise Clause. Instead, the Court has adopted tests, doctrines, and general principles that function somewhere in between the accommodation and separation schools of thought. These standards have changed over time. As the membership of the Court has changed, its approaches to the religion clauses have moved along the ideological spectrum. At times the Court has been more accommodationist in nature, willing to allow

accommodationist approach
An interpretation of the religion clauses that maintains that it is appropriate for government to accommodate or otherwise assist religious interests or organizations.

separationist approach
A view of the religion clauses that generally asserts that government should remain strictly separate or removed from religious activity. Under this approach, it is asserted that government should not aid, fund, or otherwise assist religious organizations or individual religious activity.

| I─────────────────────────────────────I |
| **Accommodationist Theory**   **Separationist Theory** |
| (allow government to participate in,   (keep government and |
| accommodate, and support religion)   religion strictly separate) |

FIGURE 10-1
Theoretical continuum for the religion clauses

government to participate in religious exercises[8] and requiring government to accommodate certain minority religious practices.[9] At other times, the Court has been more separationist in its decisions, requiring government to divorce itself from religious activity[10] or not requiring government to accommodate minority religious practices that run afoul of general laws.[11] As a result, there is perhaps no other area of constitutional law that better illustrates the dynamic struggle over constitutional values than the First Amendment religion clauses.

There are two areas of constitutional interpretation, which are common to both the Establishment Clause and the Free Exercise Clause, that appear to be relatively resolved—the issue of incorporation and the meaning of the phrase "make no law." As addressed in Chapter 8, the Supreme Court gradually has incorporated most of the provisions with the Bill of Rights through the Fourteenth Amendment Due Process Clause, thereby making them applicable to all levels of government—federal, state, and local. The Establishment Clause and Free Exercise Clause are among these incorporated provisions. In 1940, the Court formally incorporated the Free Exercise Clause in *Cantwell v. Connecticut*.[12] And in 1947, the Court did the same with the Establishment Clause in *Everson v. Board of Education*.[13] As a result, all forms of government are bound by the conditions of the religion clauses.

In addition, the Court has broadly interpreted the phrase "Congress shall make no law" to apply to more governmental activity than just legislative acts or laws. The Court has held that the phrase "shall make no law" generally means that government "shall take no action"—legislative, executive, judicial, administrative, and so forth—respecting an establishment of religion or prohibiting the free exercise thereof. As a result, official actions taken by presidents, governors, mayors, public-school board officials, public administrators, and so on are subject to the religion clauses of the First Amendment.

A third term common to both clauses—*religion*—remains less definitive. Questions over the meaning of religion largely have been the subject of free exercise cases, where minority religions or belief systems with fewer established or majoritarian roots tend to be at issue. Within this context, religion has been interpreted to mean more than just an individual or organization who believes in a supreme being. Much of the Court's jurisprudence in this area came during the Vietnam War era, when some individuals sought "conscientious objector" exemptions from the draft based on the claim that the war violated their religious principles. In reviewing these claims, the Court found that the test for religion is "whether a given belief that is sincere and meaningful occupies a place in the life of its possessor parallel to that filled by the orthodox belief in God of one who clearly qualifies for [a religious exemption]."[14] The Court also granted conscientious objector status to an individual whose ethical and moral beliefs were of similar strength and importance to him as those based on religion.[15]

Consequently, the religion clauses cannot be read literally. One cannot say that the clauses apply only to Congress or only to legislative acts or that they only involve monotheistic or traditional religions. Instead, the Court has interpreted these three provisions—Congress, make no law, and religion—to mean much more than the facial language of the First Amendment might suggest. See Figure 10-2.

Cyber Constitution
Pillars of Church-State Law http://pewforum.org/Church-State-Law/Shifting-Boundaries-The-Establishment-Clause-and-Government-Funding-of-Religious-Schools-and-Other-Faith-Based-Organizations.aspx

---

Congress [to be interpreted as any level or branch of government] **shall make no law** [broadly understood to mean any form of governmental action] **respecting an establishment of religion** [which includes sincere and meaningful belief systems that are parallel to that filled by an orthodox belief in God] **or prohibiting the free exercise thereof.**

FIGURE 10-2
Annotated text of the religion clauses

CONSCIENTIOUS OBJECTORS

During the 1960s, the Supreme Court heard a number of cases involving "conscientious objectors" or "COs." Generally speaking, COs are regarded as individuals seeking to avoid war-time military service based on religious or other conscience-based objections. Since 1962, the U.S. Department of Defense has administered a formal policy for assessing conscientious objector status. Under these rules, those who feel that they cannot participate in war due to religious, ethical, or moral reasons (or a combination thereof) can seek an exemption from military training and/or service.

There are two basic conscientious objector categories: 1-O and 1-A-O. The 1-O exemption can be given to those who assert conscience-based inability to participate in military training and service as both a combatant and a noncombatant. In these cases, individuals may be required to perform civilian work in the place of military service. The 1-A-O exemption can be awarded to those who, based on conscience, cannot participate in military combat roles, but are not precluded from noncombatant military service.

Below are some excerpts from the "Instruction" provided by the U.S. Department of Defense to assist those seeking conscientious objector status and to aid those involved in reviewing applications for such status:

DEPARTMENT OF DEFENSE INSTRUCTION
NUMBER 1300.06, MAY 5, 2007

3. Definitions

3.1. <u>Conscientious Objection:</u> <u>General.</u> A firm, fixed, and sincere objection to participation in war in any form or the bearing of arms, by reason of religious training and/or belief. Unless otherwise specified, the term "Conscientious Objector" includes both Class 1-O and Class 1-A-O Conscientious Objectors.

3.1.1. <u>Class 1-O Conscientious Objector.</u> A member who, by reason of conscientious objection, sincerely objects to participation in military service of any kind in war in any form.

3.1.2. <u>Class 1-A-O Conscientious Objector.</u> A member who, by reason of conscientious objection, sincerely objects to participation as a combatant in war in any form, but whose convictions are such as to permit military service in a non-combatant status.

3.2. <u>Religious Training and/or belief:</u> Belief in an external power or "being" or deeply held moral or ethical belief, to which all else is subordinate or upon which all else is ultimately dependent, and which has the power or force to affect moral well-being. The external power or "being" need not be one that has found expression in either religious or societal traditions. However, it should sincerely occupy a place of equal or greater value in the life of its possessor. Deeply held moral or ethical beliefs should be valued with the strength and devotion of traditional religious conviction. The term "religious training and/or belief" may include solely moral or ethical beliefs even though the applicant may not characterize these beliefs as "religious" in the traditional sense, or may expressly characterize them as not religious. The term "religious training and/or belief" does not include a belief that rests solely upon considerations of policy, pragmatism, expediency, or political views. . . .

3.5. <u>War In Any Form.</u> The clause "war in any form" should be interpreted in the following manner:

3.5.1. An individual who desires to choose the war in which he or she will participate is not a Conscientious Objector under the law. The individual's objection must be to all wars rather than a specific war.

3.5 .2. A belief in a theocratic or spiritual war between the powers of good and evil does not constitute a willingness to participate in "war" within the meaning of this instruction.

4. Policy

It is DoD policy that:

4.1. Administrative discharge due to conscientious objection prior to the completion of an obligated term of service is discretionary with the Military Department concerned, based on a judgment of the facts and circumstances in the case. However, insofar as may be consistent with the effectiveness and efficiency of the Military Services, a request for classification as a conscientious objector and relief from or restriction of military duties in consequence thereof will be approved to the extent practicable and equitable. . . .

10.3 COMPETING INTERPRETATIONS OF THE ESTABLISHMENT CLAUSE

During most debates involving the Establishment Clause, there are two opposing arguments that encapsulate the various interpretations of the clause, each stressing a different word within the First Amendment. On one side of the debate, there is a tendency to focus on the term "establishment," using it to assert that as long as the government does not formally establish a national or statewide state church, synagogue, mosque, or similar institutions, the government does not violate the Establishment Clause. This is a frequent assertion of the accommodationist school of thought, which grounds much of its argument in the history of religion in the United States. This history suggests that many of those who came to America in the seventeenth and eighteenth centuries were fleeing countries, such as England, Italy, and Germany, that used state churches to persecute those outside the state-backed faith.[16] Accommodationists claim that the Establishment Clause was designed simply to ensure that the U.S. government did not become like its European counterparts and form a national religious organization. But short of that, accommodationists generally believe that the government can involve itself with religion in other ways, such as funding (money for religious-based schools), religious activities (prayer in public schools), and religious-oriented displays (nativity scenes on public property).

At the other side of the debate, there are those who focus on the textual language "respecting," arguing that this language means that, in addition to not forming a national religious institution, the government cannot do anything that respects or otherwise honors or furthers a religion that has been established by a nonstate entity in any form. These individuals, generally referred to as separationists, find support in the writings of James Madison, the chief architect of the Establishment Clause, who had argued that government support of religious organizations was harmful to the polity because such support would likely result in "pride and indolence in the clergy; ignorance and servility in the laity; in both, superstition, bigotry and persecution."[17] Separationists seek to reinforce the imagery of the "wall of separation between the garden of the church and the wilderness of the world," originally offered by Roger Williams in 1644[18] and reinforced by Thomas Jefferson and others discussing the proper relationship between government and religion. This approach asserts that both government and religion are best served when they remain distinct and separate from each other.

The reality is that the Supreme Court has not adopted completely either side of the debate as its approach to the Establishment Clause. The Court has not allowed government to advance religion in all forms, nor has it barred government from all interaction with religion. Rather, within the spectrum of the two polar-opposite interpretations, the Court has adopted a number of tests to resolve controversies under the clause. Within the realm of Establishment Clause cases, there are at least three primary tests that the Court currently employs. These tests vary in their approach. Some are more accommodationist in nature; others are more separationist.

10.4 TESTS USED TO INTERPRET AND APPLY THE ESTABLISHMENT CLAUSE

After a few decades of addressing Establishment Clause cases in the twentieth century, the Court in 1971 seemed to settle on a three-part standard known today as the *Lemon* **test.** This standard derives its name from the Court's decision in *Lemon v. Kurtzman* (excerpted here), a case involving state funding of religious schools. Under this test, the challenged government action must meet three guidelines: (1) it must have a secular (nonreligious) purpose, (2) its primary effect must neither advance nor inhibit religion, and (3) it must not foster an excessive entanglement with religion and government. Between 1971 and 1984, this was the primary test used by the Court to resolve Establishment Clause controversies.

In recent times, however, accommodationists have criticized the test for being too restrictive on government's efforts regarding religion. Some have even sought to

Lemon **test**
Legal standard developed by the Court in *Lemon v. Kurtzman* (1971) to evaluate Establishment Clause cases. Under this test, the challenged government action must meet three guidelines: (1) it must have a secular (nonreligious) purpose, (2) its primary effect must neither advance nor inhibit religion, and (3) it must not foster an excessive entanglement with religion and government.

Cyber Constitution
First Amendment Establishment Clause www. firstamendmentcenter. org/rel_liberty/ establishment/index.aspx

Lemon v. Kurtzman
403 U.S. 602 (1971)

Mr. Chief Justice Burger delivered the opinion of the Court.

These two appeals raise questions as to Pennsylvania and Rhode Island statutes providing state aid to church-related elementary and secondary schools. Both statutes are challenged as violative of the Establishment and Free Exercise Clauses of the First Amendment and the Due Process Clause of the Fourteenth Amendment.

Pennsylvania has adopted a statutory program that provides financial support to nonpublic elementary and secondary schools by way of reimbursement for the cost of teachers' salaries, textbooks, and instructional materials in specified secular subjects. Rhode Island has adopted a statute under which the State pays directly to teachers in nonpublic elementary schools a supplement of 15% of their annual salary. Under each statute state aid has been given to church-related educational institutions. We hold that both statutes are unconstitutional. . . .

The language of the religion clauses of the First Amendment is at best opaque, particularly when compared with other portions of the Amendment. Its authors did not simply prohibit the establishment of a state church or a state religion, an area history shows they regarded as very important and fraught with great dangers. Instead they commanded that there should be "no law respecting an establishment of religion." A law may be one "respecting" the forbidden objective while falling short of its total realization. A law "respecting" the proscribed result, that is, the establishment of religion, is not always easily identifiable as one violative of the Clause. A given law might not establish a state religion but nevertheless be one "respecting" that end in the sense of being a step that could lead to such establishment and hence offend the First Amendment. . . .

Every analysis in this area must begin with consideration of the cumulative criteria developed by the Court over many years. Three such tests may be gleaned from our cases. First, the statute must have a secular legislative purpose; second, its principal or primary effect must be one that neither advances nor inhibits religion, finally, the statute must not foster "an excessive government entanglement with religion."

Inquiry into the legislative purposes of the Pennsylvania and Rhode Island statutes affords no basis for a conclusion that the legislative intent was to advance religion. On the contrary, the statutes themselves clearly state that they are intended to enhance the quality of the secular education in all schools covered by the compulsory attendance laws. There is no reason to believe the legislatures meant anything else. . . .

The legislatures of Rhode Island and Pennsylvania have concluded that secular and religious education are identifiable and separable. In the abstract we have no quarrel with this conclusion.

The two legislatures, however, have also recognized that church-related elementary and secondary schools have a significant religious mission and that a substantial portion of their activities is religiously oriented. They have therefore sought to create statutory restrictions designed to guarantee the separation between secular and religious educational functions and to ensure that State financial aid supports only the former. All these provisions are precautions taken in candid recognition that these programs approached, even if they did not intrude upon, the forbidden areas under the religion clauses. We need not decide whether these legislative precautions restrict the principal or primary effect of the programs to the point where they do not offend the religion clauses, for we conclude that the cumulative impact of the entire relationship arising under the statutes in each State involves excessive entanglement between government and religion. . . .

Our prior holdings do not call for total separation between church and state; total separation is not possible in an absolute sense. Some relationship between government and religious organizations is inevitable. . . . Fire inspections, building and zoning regulations, and state requirements under compulsory school-attendance laws are examples of necessary and permissible contacts. . . . Judicial caveats against entanglement must recognize that the line of separation, far from being a "wall," is a blurred, indistinct, and variable barrier depending on all the circumstances of a particular relationship.

This is not to suggest, however, that we are to engage in a legalistic minuet in which precise rules and forms must govern. A true minuet is a matter of pure form and style, the observance of which is itself the substantive end. Here we examine the form of the relationship for the light that it casts on the substance.

In order to determine whether the government entanglement with religion is excessive, we must examine the character and purposes of the institutions that are benefited, the nature of the aid that the State provides, and the resulting relationship between the government and the religious authority. . . . Here we find that both statutes foster an impermissible degree of entanglement. . . .

Ordinarily political debate and division, however vigorous or even partisan, are normal and healthy manifestations of our democratic system of government, but political division along religious lines was one of the principal evils against which the First Amendment was intended to protect. The potential divisiveness of such conflict is a threat to the normal political process. . . . To have States or communities divide on the issues presented by state aid to parochial schools would tend to confuse and obscure other issues of great urgency. We have an expanding array of vexing issues, local and national, domestic and international, to debate and divide on. It conflicts with our whole history and tradition to permit questions of the religion clauses to assume such importance in our legislatures and in our elections that they could divert attention from the myriad issues and problems that confront every level of government. The highways of church and state relationships are not likely to be one-way streets, and the Constitution's authors sought to protect religious worship from the pervasive power of government. The history of many countries attests to the hazards of religion's intruding into the political arena or of political power intruding into the legitimate and free exercise of religious belief. . . .

The potential for political divisiveness related to religious belief and practice is aggravated in these two statutory programs by the need for continuing annual appropriations and the likelihood of larger and larger demands as costs and populations grow. The Rhode Island District Court found that the parochial school system's "monumental and deepening financial crisis" would "inescapably" require larger annual appropriations subsidizing greater percentages of the salaries of lay teachers. Although no facts have been developed in this respect in the Pennsylvania case, it appears that such pressures for expanding aid have already required the state legislature to include a portion of the state revenues from cigarette taxes in the program. . . .

We have no long history of state aid to church-related educational institutions comparable to 200 years of tax exemption for churches. Indeed, the state programs before us today represent something of an innovation. We have already noted that modern governmental programs have self-perpetuating and self-expanding propensities. These internal pressures are only enhanced when the schemes involve institutions whose legitimate needs are growing and whose interests have substantial political support. . . .

The merit and benefits of these schools, however, are not the issue before us in these cases. The sole question is whether state aid to these schools can be squared with the dictates of the religion clauses. Under our system the choice has been made that government is to be entirely excluded from the area of religious instruction and churches excluded from the affairs of government. The Constitution decrees that religion must be a private matter for the individual, the family, and the institutions of private choice, and that while some involvement and entanglement are inevitable, lines must be drawn.

Justice Douglas, whom Justice Black joins, concurring.

endorsement test
Another legal standard used to assess Establishment Clause issues. Under this standard, the Court essentially collapses the first two questions of the *Lemon* test (the secular purpose and primary effect requirements) by asking the more general question of whether the government's activity conveys a message of endorsement or disapproval of religion.

replace the *Lemon* test with more relaxed standards, which would make it easier for government to interact with religion. But thus far, the Court has resisted eliminating the *Lemon* test entirely. Instead, the Court has crafted more accommodation-friendly tests to supplement the *Lemon* test.

One of these other tests is the **endorsement test.** In 1984, the Court applied the *Lemon* test to rule in *Lynch v. Donnelly* that a crèche display in Pawtucket, Rhode Island, which included a Santa Claus, reindeer, carolers, and a "Seasons Greetings" sign, did not violate the Establishment Clause. However, in a concurring opinion, Justice O'Connor urged the Court to collapse the first two questions of the *Lemon* test (the secular purpose and primary effect requirements) by asking whether the government intends to convey a message of endorsement or disapproval of religion. This standard, commonly referred to as the endorsement test, replaces an inquiry into the government's purpose or the primary effect of its religion-friendly policy with a more general inquiry into whether the average person would view the government's action as either a public endorsement or a disapproval of religion.

Five years later, in *County of Allegany v. ACLU* (1989), Justice O'Connor's proposed new standard was supported by additional members of the Court. In that case, the Court was faced with two religious displays—a crèche prominently displayed inside the Allegany, Pennsylvania, courthouse on the grand staircase and an eighteen-foot-tall menorah displayed next to a forty-five-foot-tall Christmas tree located outside of the courthouse. Justice Blackmun, writing for a divided court, recognized the continued validity of the *Lemon* test, but also acknowledged that in recent years the Court focused on whether the challenged government policy has the effect of endorsing religion. The Court found such an unconstitutional endorsement with the crèche display because it was not surrounded by other secular symbols like the ones in *Lynch*. The Court, however, did not find such an endorsement with the menorah, because it appeared in the context of a Christmas tree, thereby making it appear less likely that the government intended to endorse a particular religion.

In 1992, the Court added a third approach to resolving Establishment Clause controversies by ruling that the coercive effect of the government's policy should be the primary consideration in such cases. In *Lee v. Weisman,* the Court ruled that a Judeo-Christian prayer offered during a public-school graduation ceremony violated the Establishment Clause. According to Justice Kennedy's opinion, the commence prayer created an environment wherein the government-sponsored prayer was likely to have a coercive effect on audience members and students who were attending the ceremony. This led to a new standard—the **coercion test**—which essentially asks whether the government is acting in a manner that may have a coercive effect on individuals to support or participate in a particular religion.

Notice that as the Court has added new "tools" to its Establishment Clause "toolbox," it has not removed (reversed) old ones. Rather, the three primary standards or tests have been allowed to coexist. This dynamic has given the members of the Court a certain amount of flexibility in resolving religion cases. But it has also made it particularly challenging when lower courts are seeking clarity in resolving new controversies. When do you apply the *Lemon* test? When do you apply the endorsement test? When do you apply the coercion test? Should all three be applied? Read the following opinion by the Ninth Circuit Court of Appeals in *Newdow v. United States Congress* (2002)—a case challenging the constitutionality of the "under God" provision found in the Pledge of Allegiance. Although this opinion was later reversed by the Supreme

coercion test
A third legal standard used to evaluate Establishment Clause cases. This test essentially asks whether the government is acting in a manner that may have a coercive effect on individuals to support or participate in a particular religion.

Newdow v. United States Congress
292 F.3d 597 (9th Cir. 2002)

Rev'd Sub Nom. Elk Grove Unified School District v. Newdow
542 U.S. 1 (2004)

Goodwin, Circuit Judge:

Newdow is an atheist whose daughter attends public elementary school in the Elk Grove Unified School District ("EGUSD") in California. In accordance with state law and a school district rule, EGUSD teachers begin each school day by leading their students in a recitation of the Pledge of Allegiance ("the Pledge"). The California Education Code requires that public schools begin each school day with "appropriate patriotic exercises" and that "[t]he giving of the Pledge of Allegiance to the Flag of the United States of America shall satisfy" this requirement. To implement the California statute, the school district that Newdow's daughter attends has promulgated a policy that states, in pertinent part: "Each elementary school class [shall] recite the pledge of allegiance to the flag once each day."

The classmates of Newdow's daughter in the EGUSD are led by their teacher in reciting the Pledge codified in federal law. On June 22, 1942, Congress first codified the Pledge as "I pledge allegiance to the flag of the United States of America and to the Republic for which it stands, one Nation indivisible, with liberty and justice for all." On June 14, 1954, Congress amended Section 1972 to add the words "under God" after the word "Nation." The Pledge is currently codified as "I pledge allegiance to the Flag of the United States of America, and to the Republic for which it stands, one nation under God, indivisible, with liberty and justice for all."

Newdow does not allege that his daughter's teacher or school district requires his, daughter to participate in reciting the Pledge. Rather, he claims that his daughter is injured when she is compelled to "watch and listen as her state-employed teacher in her state-run school leads her classmates in a ritual proclaiming that there is a God, and that our's [sic] is 'one nation under God.'"...

Over the last three decades, the Supreme Court has used three interrelated tests to analyze alleged violations of the Establishment Clause in the realm of public education: the three-prong test set forth in *Lemon v. Kurtzman,* 403 U.S. 602, 612–13 (1971); the "endorsement" test, first articulated by Justice O'Connor in her concurring opinion in *Lynch* [*v. Donnelly* 465 U.S. 668 (1984)], and later adopted by a majority of the Court in *County of Allegheny v. ACLU,* 492 U.S. 573 (1989); and the "coercion" test first used by the Court in *Lee* [*v. Weisman,* 505 U.S. 577, 580 (1992)]....

We are free to apply any or all of the three tests, and to invalidate any measure that fails any one of them....

We first consider whether the 1954 Act and the EGUSD's policy of teacher-led Pledge recitation survive the endorsement test....

In the context of the Pledge, the statement that the United States is a nation "under God" is an endorsement of religion. It is a profession of a religious belief, namely, a belief in monotheism. The recitation that ours is a nation "under God" is not a mere acknowledgment that many Americans believe in a deity. Nor is it merely descriptive of the undeniable historical significance of religion in the founding of the Republic. Rather, the phrase "one nation under God" in the context of the Pledge is normative. To recite the Pledge is not to describe the United States; instead, it is to swear allegiance to the values for which the flag stands: unity, indivisibility, liberty, justice, and—since 1954—monotheism . . . A profession that we are a nation "under God" is identical, for Establishment Clause purposes, to a profession that we are a nation "under Jesus," a nation "under Vishnu," a nation "under Zeus," or a nation "under no god," because none of these professions can be neutral with respect to religion. . . .

The Pledge, as currently codified, is an impermissible government endorsement of religion because it sends a message to unbelievers "that they are outsiders, not full members of the political community, and an accompanying message to adherents that they are insiders, favored members of the political community." . . .

Similarly, the policy and the Act fail the coercion test. Just as in *Lee,* the policy and the Act place students in the untenable position of choosing between participating in an exercise with religious content or protesting. As the Court observed with respect to the graduation prayer in that case: "What to most believers may seem nothing more than a reasonable request that the nonbeliever respect their religious practices, in a school context may appear to the nonbeliever or dissenter to be an attempt to employ the machinery of the State to enforce a religious orthodoxy." *Lee,* 505 U.S. at 592. Although the defendants argue that the religious content of "one nation under God" is minimal, to an atheist or a believer in certain non-Judeo-Christian religions or philosophies, it may reasonably appear to be an attempt to enforce a "religious orthodoxy" of monotheism, and is therefore impermissible. The coercive effect of this policy is particularly pronounced in the school setting given the age and impressionability of schoolchildren, and their understanding that they are required to adhere to the norms set by their school, their teacher and their fellow students. . . . Therefore, the policy and the Act fail the coercion test.

Finally we turn to the *Lemon* test, the first prong of which asks if the challenged policy has a secular purpose. Historically, the primary purpose of the 1954 Act was to advance religion, in conflict with the first prong of the *Lemon* test. The federal defendants "do not dispute that the words 'under God' were intended" "to recognize a Supreme Being," at a time when the government was publicly inveighing against atheistic communism. Nonetheless, the federal defendants argue that the Pledge must be considered as a whole when assessing whether it has a secular purpose. They claim that the Pledge has the secular purpose of "solemnizing public occasions, expressing confidence in the future, and encouraging the recognition of what is worthy of appreciation in society."

The flaw in defendants' argument is that it looks at the text of the Pledge "as a whole," and glosses over the 1954 Act. . . .

[T]he purpose prong of the *Lemon* test to the amendment that added the words "under God" to the Pledge, not to the Pledge in its final version. . . . the legislative history of the 1954 Act reveals that the Act's *sole* purpose was to advance religion, in order to differentiate the United States from nations under communist rule. . . .

This language reveals that the purpose of the 1954 Act was to take a position on the question of theism, namely, to support the existence and moral authority of God, while "deny[ing] . . . atheistic and materialistic concepts." Such a purpose runs counter to the Establishment Clause, which prohibits the government's endorsement or advancement not only of one particular religion at the expense of other religions, but also of religion at the expense of atheism.

Similarly, the school district policy also fails the *Lemon* test. Although it survives the first prong of *Lemon* because, as even Newdow concedes, the school district had the secular purpose of fostering patriotism in enacting the policy, the policy fails the second prong . . . "[T]he second *Lemon* prong asks whether the challenged government action is sufficiently likely to be perceived by adherents of the controlling denominations as an endorsement, and by the nonadherents as a disapproval, of their individual religious choices." Given the age and impressionability of schoolchildren, as discussed above, particularly within the confined environment of the classroom, the policy is highly likely to convey an impermissible message of endorsement to some and disapproval to others of their beliefs regarding the existence of a monotheistic God. Therefore the policy fails the effects prong of *Lemon,* and fails the *Lemon* test. In sum, both the policy and the Act fail the *Lemon* test as well as the endorsement and coercion tests. . . .

Reversed and Remanded.

Fernandez, Circuit Judge, concurring and dissenting.

Cyber Constitution
Newdow v. Rio Linda School District (2010)
http://undergod.procon.org/sourcefiles/9thcircuitrulingMar_2010.pdf

Court on procedural grounds,[19] and later rejected on the merits by the Ninth Circuit in 2010, it provides an excellent illustration of the current challenges facing courts in Establishment Clause cases, where at least three possible tests could be applied.

The three tests adopted by the Supreme Court in Establishment Clause cases have real implications for the debate between accommodationists and separationists. If each standard were plotted on the theoretical continuum offered at the outset of this chapter, most would agree that the *Lemon* test tends to be fairly separationist in its application, especially when compared to the other two standards. (See Figure 10-3.) While not forbidding all governmental support of religion, *Lemon*'s three-dimensional approach—reviewing the government's purpose, effect, and resulting relationship

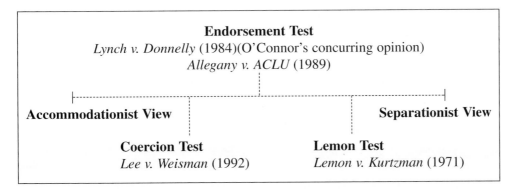

Endorsement Test
Lynch v. Donnelly (1984)(O'Connor's concurring opinion)
Allegany v. ACLU (1989)

Accommodationist View   **Separationist View**

Coercion Test   **Lemon Test**
Lee v. Weisman (1992)   *Lemon v. Kurtzman* (1971)

FIGURE 10-3
The ideological shift in Establishment Clause standards

with religion—is more likely to result in a finding of unconstitutionality than its one-dimensional endorsement and coercion counterparts.

Applying the endorsement test generally will result in greater latitude being afforded to government in its interaction with and support of religion. Imagine a situation where a government policy endorses government vouchers for schools, which on their face are not designed to assist religious schools. But in their application, the vast majority of parents who use these vouchers use them to fund their children's education at religious schools. Arguably, this results in the voucher programs having a primary effect of financially supporting religious-based education, which will likely be a fatal blow under the *Lemon* test. But when considered under the endorsement standard,

A rally on the steps of the U.S. Supreme Court in Washington, March 24, 2004, where the court was to hear arguments in a case dealing with the "Pledge of Allegiance." In contention before the Court was a passage from the pledge proclaiming "one nation under God," and whether it violated the First Amendment to the U.S. Constitution.

Paul J. Richards/Afp/Getty Images/Newscom

which asks whether it appears as though the government's program is endorsing one religion over another, it may not appear to the average person that such an endorsement is occurring because the government's program does not say anything about religion, nor does it take an active role in directing the use of the vouchers toward religious education. As a result, voucher programs stand a much better chance of constitutional survival under the endorsement test than under the *Lemon* test, thereby making the endorsement test more acccommodationist in nature.

YOUR CONSTITUTIONAL VALUES

CAN A JUDGE CONSULT THE BIBLE WHEN IMPOSING A CRIMINAL SENTENCE?

Between 1995 and 1997, James Arnett of Cincinnati, Ohio, sexually abused his girlfriend's daughter, Rachel, who was five years old when the abuse began. The state of Ohio ultimately indicted Arnett in November 1997 on ten counts of raping a minor under the age of thirteen. In January 1998, Arnett was indicted again on one count of pandering obscenity involving a minor. Arnett pled guilty to all of the charges and faced a sentencing hearing before Judge Melba Marsh of the Hamilton County Court of Common Pleas.

During the sentencing hearing, Judge Marsh told Arnett that, in trying to determine the proper sentence for him, she reviewed the nature of his offenses, the emotional and physical harm he had inflicted on his victim, and the medical and other evidence from the case. The judge also said that she considered the fact that recently she had given a convicted murderer a twenty-year sentence. But after discussing these factors, Judge Marsh told Arnett that she also consulted the Bible:

> And in looking at the final part of my [sentencing] struggle with you, I finally answered my question late at night when I turned to one additional source to help me. . . . And that [Bible] passage where I had the opportunity to look is Matthew 18:5, 6. "And whoso shall receive one such little child in my name, receiveth me. But, whoso shall offend one of these little ones which believe in me, it were better for him that a millstone were hanged about his neck, and he were drowned in the depth of the sea."

Following the discussion, the judge sentenced Arnett to fifty-one years in prison.

Arnett appealed his sentence to the Ohio Court of Appeals, asserting that Judge Marsh unconstitutionally applied her own religious beliefs during sentencing. The state appellate court agreed and vacated Arnett's sentence, concluding that Judge Marsh wrongly "factor[ed] in religion" when imposing Arnett's sentence. The Ohio Supreme Court, however, reversed this appellate court's decision, concluding that the judge's biblical reference did not violate Arnett's rights because it was not the sole basis of her sentencing decision, but rather "one of several reasons" or an "additional source" used by the judge.

In March 2001, Arnett filed a petition for writ of habeas corpus in federal district court. The district court subsequently found that the trial court's use of the Bible as a "final source of authority" constituted an impermissible factor for sentencing. On appeal, the Sixth Circuit, in a 2-1 ruling, reversed the district court's judgment and upheld the trial court's sentence, finding that "[t]here is nothing in the totality of the circumstances of Arnett's sentencing to indicate that the trial judge used the Bible as her 'final source of authority,' as found by the district court."

Given your constitutional values, how would you address this constitutional conflict?

Source: Arnett v. Jackson, 393 F.3d 681, 686 (6th Cir. 2005).

Finally, the coercion test appears to be even more accommodationist than the endorsement test because it only requires government not to force, physically, psychologically, or emotionally, individuals to participate in or support religious activity. Thus, a governmental program that supports religion is likely to be found constitutional as long as individuals do not feel compelled to go along with the program. Thus, a government program may be designed to support religion, have the effect of supporting religion, and result in excessive government entanglement (each a constitutional no-no under the *Lemon* test) or even appear to be endorsing religion in violation of the endorsement test, as long as it does not result in a coercive environment being created wherein individuals feel compelled to participate in the government-supported activity.

In the end, the outcome of Establishment Clause disputes largely may depend on the type of test employed. In essence, the means will likely determine the end. This dynamic is illustrated by the Court's companion decisions in *Perry v. Van Orden* and *McCreary v. ACLU* (2005) (see later in this chapter). These cases involved two public displays of the Ten Commandments, one on the lawn of the Capitol in Texas and another in a courthouse in Kentucky. Both cases yielded 5-4 rulings by the Court, with the Texas display being upheld and the Kentucky display being rejected. As you read these rulings, notice how the majority opinion in Perry emphasizes the Court's approach in *Lynch v. Donnelly,* while the majority opinion in *McCreary* relies on the "secular purpose" standard established under the *Lemon* test.

The slab displaying the Ten Commandments rests just north of the state Capitol in Austin, Texas

Shutterstock 1029337

Perry v. Van Orden
545 U.S. 677 (2005)

Chief Justice Rehnquist announced the judgment of the Court and delivered an opinion, in which Justice Scalia, Justice Kennedy, and Justice Thomas join.

The question here is whether the Establishment Clause of the First Amendment allows the display of a monument inscribed with the Ten Commandments on the Texas State Capitol grounds. We hold that it does.

The 22 acres surrounding the Texas State Capitol contain 17 monuments and 21 historical markers commemorating the "people, ideals, and events that compose Texan identity." The monolith challenged here stands 6-feet high and 3 1/2-feet wide. It is located to the north of the Capitol building, between the Capitol and the Supreme Court building. Its primary content is the text of the Ten Commandments. An eagle grasping the American flag, an eye inside of a pyramid, and two small tablets with what appears to be an ancient script are carved above the text of the Ten Commandments. Below the text are two Stars of David and the superimposed Greek letters Chi and Rho, which represent Christ. The bottom of the monument bears the inscription "PRESENTED TO THE PEOPLE AND YOUTH OF TEXAS BY THE FRATERNAL ORDER OF EAGLES OF TEXAS 1961."

The legislative record surrounding the State's acceptance of the monument from the Eagles—a national social, civic, and patriotic organization—is limited to legislative journal entries. After the monument was accepted, the State selected a site for the monument based on the recommendation of the state organization responsible for maintaining the Capitol grounds. The Eagles paid the cost of erecting the monument, the dedication of which was presided over by two state legislators.

Our cases, Januslike, point in two directions in applying the Establishment Clause. One face looks toward the strong role played by religion and religious traditions throughout our Nation's history. The other face looks toward the principle that governmental intervention in religious matters can itself endanger religious freedom.

This case, like all Establishment Clause challenges, presents us with the difficulty of respecting both faces. Our institutions presuppose a Supreme Being, yet these institutions must not press religious observances upon their citizens. One face looks to the past in acknowledgment of our Nation's heritage, while the other looks to the present in demanding a separation between church and state. Reconciling these two faces requires that we neither abdicate our responsibility to maintain a division between church and state nor evince a hostility to religion by disabling the government from in some ways recognizing our religious heritage. . . .

These two faces are evident in representative cases both upholding and invalidating laws under the Establishment Clause. Over the last 25 years, we have sometimes pointed to *Lemon v. Kurtzman,* as providing the governing test in Establishment Clause challenges. Yet, just two years after *Lemon* was decided, we noted that the factors identified in *Lemon* serve as "no more than helpful signposts." Many of our recent cases simply have not applied the *Lemon* test. Others have applied it only after concluding that the challenged practice was invalid under a different Establishment Clause test.

Whatever may be the fate of the *Lemon* test in the larger scheme of Establishment Clause jurisprudence, we think it not useful in dealing with the sort of passive monument that Texas has erected on its Capitol grounds. Instead, our analysis is driven both by the nature of the monument and by our Nation's history.

As we explained in *Lynch v. Donnelly*: "There is an unbroken history of official acknowledgment by all three branches of government of the role of religion in American life from at least 1789." For example, both Houses passed resolutions in 1789 asking President George Washington to issue a Thanksgiving Day Proclamation to "recommend to the people of the United States a day of public thanksgiving and prayer, to be observed by acknowledging, with grateful hearts, the many and signal favors of Almighty God." President Washington's proclamation directly attributed to the Supreme Being the foundations and successes of our young Nation.

In this case we are faced with a display of the Ten Commandments on government property outside the Texas State Capitol. Such acknowledgments of the role played by the Ten Commandments in our Nation's heritage are common throughout America. We need only look within our own Courtroom. Since 1935, Moses has stood, holding two tablets that reveal portions of the Ten Commandments written in Hebrew, among other lawgivers in the south frieze. Representations of the Ten Commandments adorn the metal gates lining the north and south sides of the Courtroom as well as the doors leading into the Courtroom. Moses also sits on the exterior east facade of the building holding the Ten Commandments tablets. . . .

Of course, the Ten Commandments are religious—they were so viewed at their inception and so remain. The monument, therefore, has religious significance. According to Judeo-Christian belief, the Ten Commandments were given to Moses by God on Mt. Sinai. But Moses was a lawgiver as well as a religious leader. And the Ten Commandments have an undeniable historical meaning, as the foregoing examples demonstrate. Simply having religious content or promoting a message consistent with a religious doctrine does not run afoul of the Establishment Clause. . . .

The placement of the Ten Commandments monument on the Texas State Capitol grounds is a far more passive use of those texts than was the case in *Stone,* where the text confronted elementary school students every day. Indeed, Van Orden, the petitioner here, apparently walked by the monument for a number of years before bringing this lawsuit. The monument is therefore also quite different from the prayers involved in *Schempp* and *Lee v. Weisman.* Texas has treated her Capitol grounds monuments as representing the several strands in the State's political and legal history. The inclusion of the Ten Commandments monument in this group has a dual significance, partaking of both religion and government. We cannot say that Texas' display of this monument violates the Establishment Clause of the First Amendment.

The judgment of the Court of Appeals is affirmed.

It is so ordered.

The concurring opinions of Justice Scalia, Justice Thomas, and Justice Breyer are omitted.

The dissenting opinions of Justice Stevens, with whom Justice Ginsburg joins, Justice O'Connor, and Justice Souter, with whom Justice Stevens and Justice Ginsburg join, are omitted.

McCreary County, Kentucky, v. ACLU
545 U.S. 844 (2005)

Justice Souter delivered the opinion of the Court.

In the summer of 1999, petitioners McCreary County and Pulaski County, Kentucky (hereinafter Counties), put up in their respective courthouses large, gold-framed copies of an abridged text of the King James version of the Ten Commandments, including a citation to the Book of Exodus. In McCreary County, the placement of the Commandments responded to an order of the county legislative body requiring "the display [to] be posted in 'a very high traffic area' of the courthouse." In Pulaski County, amidst reported controversy over the propriety of the display, the Commandments were hung in a ceremony presided over by the county Judge-Executive, who called them "good rules to live by" and who recounted the story of an astronaut who became convinced "there must be a divine God" after viewing the Earth from the moon. The Judge-Executive was accompanied by the pastor of his church, who called the Commandments "a creed of ethics" and told the press after the ceremony that displaying the Commandments was "one of the greatest things the judge could have done to close out the millennium." . . .

In November 1999, respondent American Civil Liberties Union of Kentucky sued the Counties in Federal District Court under 42 U.S.C. § 1983, and sought a preliminary injunction against maintaining the displays, which the ACLU charged were violations of the prohibition of religious establishment included in the First Amendment of the Constitution. Within a month, and before the District Court had responded to the request for injunction, the legislative body of each County authorized a second, expanded display, by nearly identical resolutions reciting that the Ten Commandments are "the precedent legal code upon which the civil and criminal codes of . . . Kentucky are founded" . . .

As directed by the resolutions, the Counties expanded the displays of the Ten Commandments in their locations, presumably along with copies of the resolution, which instructed that it, too, be posted. In addition to the first display's large framed copy of the edited King James version of the Commandments, the second included eight other documents in smaller frames, each either having a religious theme or excerpted to highlight a religious element. . . .

After argument, the District Court entered a preliminary injunction on May 5, 2000, ordering that the "display . . . be removed from [each] County Courthouse IMMEDIATELY" and that no county official "erect or cause to be erected similar displays." The court's analysis of the situation followed the three-part formulation first stated in *Lemon v. Kurtzman,* 403 U.S. 602 (1971). . . .

The Counties filed a notice of appeal from the preliminary injunction but voluntarily dismissed it after hiring new lawyers. They then installed another display in each courthouse, the third within a year. No new resolution authorized this one, nor did the Counties repeal the resolutions that preceded the second. The posting consists of nine framed documents of equal size, one of them setting out the Ten Commandments explicitly identified as the "King James Version" at Exodus 20:3–17, and quoted at greater length than before.

Assembled with the Commandments are framed copies of the Magna Carta, the Declaration of Independence, the Bill of Rights, the lyrics of the Star Spangled Banner, the Mayflower Compact, the National Motto, the Preamble to the Kentucky Constitution, and a picture of Lady Justice. The collection is entitled "The Foundations of American Law and Government Display". . . .

We granted certiorari, and now affirm. . . .

Ever since *Lemon v. Kurtzman* summarized the three familiar considerations for evaluating Establishment Clause claims, looking to whether government action has "a secular legislative purpose" has been a common, albeit seldom dispositive, element of our cases. Though we have found government action motivated by an illegitimate purpose only four times since *Lemon,* and "the secular purpose requirement alone may rarely be determinative . . . , it nevertheless serves an important function."

The touchstone for our analysis is the principle that the "First Amendment mandates governmental neutrality between religion and religion, and between religion and nonreligion." When the government acts with the ostensible and predominant purpose of advancing religion, it violates that central Establishment Clause value of official religious neutrality, there being no neutrality when the government's ostensible object is to take sides. . . .

Examination of purpose is a staple of statutory interpretation that makes up the daily fare of every appellate court in the country, and governmental purpose is a key element of a good deal of constitutional doctrine. With enquiries into purpose this common, if they were nothing but hunts for mares' nests deflecting attention from bare judicial will, the whole notion of purpose in law would have dropped into disrepute long ago.

But scrutinizing purpose does make practical sense, as in Establishment Clause analysis, where an understanding of official objective emerges from readily discoverable fact, without any judicial psychoanalysis of a drafter's heart of hearts. The eyes that look to purpose belong to an "objective observer," one who takes account of the traditional external signs that show up in the "text, legislative history, and implementation of the statute," or comparable official act. There is, then, nothing hinting at an unpredictable or disingenuous exercise when a court enquires into purpose after a claim is raised under the Establishment Clause. . . .

If someone in the government hides religious motive so well that the "objective observer, acquainted with the text, legislative history, and implementation of the statute," cannot see it, then without something more the government does not make a divisive announcement that in itself amounts to taking religious sides. A secret motive stirs up no strife and does nothing to make outsiders of nonadherents, and it suffices to wait and see whether such government action turns out to have (as it may even be likely to have) the illegitimate effect of advancing religion. . . .

[Here] once the Counties were sued, they modified the exhibits and invited additional insight into their purpose in a display that hung for about six months. This new one was the product of forthright and nearly identical Pulaski and McCreary County resolutions listing a series of American historical documents with theistic and Christian references, which were to be posted in order to furnish a setting for displaying the Ten Commandments and any "other Kentucky and American historical documen[t]" without raising concern about "any Christian or religious references" in them. As mentioned, the resolutions expressed support for an Alabama judge who posted the Commandments in his courtroom, and cited the fact the Kentucky Legislature once adjourned a session in honor of "Jesus Christ, Prince of Ethics."

In this second display, unlike the first, the Commandments were not hung in isolation, merely leaving the Counties' purpose to emerge from the pervasively religious text of the Commandments themselves. Instead, the second version was required to include the statement of the government's purpose expressly set out in the county resolutions, and underscored it by juxtaposing the Commandments to other documents with highlighted references to God as their sole common element. The display's unstinting focus was on religious passages, showing that the Counties were posting the Commandments precisely because of their sectarian content. That demonstration of the government's objective was enhanced by serial religious references and the accompanying resolution's claim about the embodiment of ethics in Christ. Together, the display and resolution presented an indisputable, and undisputed, showing of an impermissible purpose.

Today, the Counties make no attempt to defend their undeniable objective, but instead hopefully describe version two as "dead and buried." Their refusal to defend the second display is understandable, but the reasonable observer could not forget it. . . .

After the Counties changed lawyers, they mounted a third display, without a new resolution or repeal of the old one. The result was the "Foundations of American Law and Government" exhibit, which placed the Commandments in the company of other documents the Counties thought especially significant in the historical foundation of American government. In trying to persuade the District Court to lift the preliminary injunction, the Counties cited several new purposes for the third version, including a desire "to educate the citizens of the county regarding some of the documents that played a significant role in the foundation of our system of law and government." The Counties' claims did not, however, persuade the court, intimately familiar with the details of this litigation, or the Court of Appeals, neither of which found a legitimizing secular purpose in this third version of the display . . . . The conclusions of the two courts preceding us in this case are well warranted.

These new statements of purpose were presented only as a litigating position, there being no further authorizing action by the Counties' governing boards. And although repeal of the earlier county authorizations would not have erased them from the record of evidence bearing on current purpose, the extraordinary resolutions for the second display passed just months earlier were not repealed or otherwise repudiated. Indeed, the sectarian spirit of the common resolution found enhanced expression in the third display, which quoted more of the purely religious language of the Commandments than the first two displays had done. No reasonable observer could swallow the claim that the Counties had cast off the objective so unmistakable in the earlier displays. . . .

Given the ample support for the District Court's finding of a predominantly religious purpose behind the Counties' third display, we affirm the Sixth Circuit in upholding the preliminary injunction.

It is so ordered.

Justice O'Connor, concurring.

Justice Scalia, with whom The Chief Justice and Justice Thomas join, and with whom Justice Kennedy joins as to Parts II and III, dissenting.

For the foreseeable future, the Supreme Court likely will remain divided over its application of the Establishment Clause. This is particularly true when it comes to applying the clause to government-sponsored religious displays. Most recently, in *Salazar v. Buono* (2010), the Court could not even reach a majority opinion regarding the display of a cross within a federal national preserve. In *Buono*, the Court considered the constitutionality of a Latin cross placed by members of the Veterans of Foreign Wars (VFW) on federal land in the Mojave National Preserve in 1934 to honor American soldiers who died in World War I. Frank Buono, a retired Park Service employee who regularly visits the preserve, challenged the cross as a violation of the Establishment Clause. Initially, Buono prevailed in his challenge, obtaining an injunction against the cross from a federal district court. The Ninth Circuit Court of Appeals affirmed the lower court's ruling and upheld the injunction against the cross display.

But following this ruling, Congress passed the Department of Defense Appropriations Act (2004), which, in part, directed the secretary of the interior to transfer the cross and the land on which it stands to the VFW in exchange for privately owned land elsewhere in the preserve. Congress thought this land transfer would remedy the Establishment Clause problems with the cross, but Buono asserted that the new law did not correct the First Amendment violation because, even if technically the cross was now situated on private property, it was still in the middle of a large federal preserve. In 2010, a fractured Supreme Court ruled that the cross did not constitute an unconstitutional endorsement of religion. The Court, however, offered competing assessments of the case and remanded the case back to the district court. Some justices maintained that the district court needed to make additional findings of fact regarding the constitutionality of the cross in light of Congress's land transfer. Two justices asserted that Buono lacked standing to challenge Congress's land transfer in the case. At least one justice believed that the current record contained sufficient facts to rule in the government's favor. And four justices dissented from the Court's ruling, finding that Buono should prevail in the case. In short, the *Buono* decision illustrates just how deeply divisive the Establishment Clause remains in American jurisprudence—approximately 220 years after it was inserted in the First Amendment.

Cyber Constitution
***Salazar v. Buono* (2010)**
www.law.cornell.edu/
supct/html/08-472.
ZS.html

Mojave National Preserve, California, United States—the placement of the cross on public land was challenged in the case of *Salazar v. Buono*

r71/ZUMA Press/Newscom

10.5 THE FREE EXERCISE CLAUSE

As indicated earlier, the Free Exercise Clause can be interpreted along the same ideological continuum as that used with the Establishment Clause. One can apply an accommodationist perspective and conclude that government should afford religious practitioners with liberal exemptions and accommodations when public policy interferes with religious exercise. Or one can apply a separationist view by claiming that the Free Exercise Clause only requires government not to interfere with religious belief but allows government to compel individuals to comply with otherwise religiously neutral laws, which are of general applicability.

Initially, the Court adopted a separationist approach to the Free Exercise Clause. In 1879, the Court considered the constitutionality of a federal statute prohibiting polygamy as it applied to a Mormon who allegedly had married a second wife. In *Reynolds v. United States,*[20] the Court recognized that Congress had authority to implement such a statute, but also addressed the question of whether "those who make polygamy a part of their religion [should be] *excepted* from the operation of the statute."[21] The Court found no exception to be warranted, concluding, "[l]aws are made for the government of actions, and while they cannot interfere with mere religious belief and opinions, they may with practices."[22] The Court did not balance the religious interests of the Mormons with the government's interest, but instead relied on a distinction between "belief" and "action" as it interpreted the phrase "free exercise of religion."

Later, during the initial stages of the Court's "civil rights revolution," the Court shifted its approach to free exercise by adopting a more accommodationist-friendly balancing test to determine the religious liberties of individuals in the face of governmental interference. In *Cantwell v. Connecticut* (1940),[23] the Court interpreted the term "free exercise" as assessed in *Reynolds* to embrace two concepts—freedom to believe and freedom to act. According to the Court, "the first is absolute but, in the nature of things, the second cannot be."[24] But unlike *Reynolds,* the Court in *Cantwell* chose to employ a balancing test to determine the First Amendment rights of the religious petitioners. In determining whether three Jehovah's Witnesses should have been convicted under a breach of the peace statute for soliciting funds for religious purposes, the court maintained that the constitutionality of the conviction depended on the balancing of two conflicting interests—the religious and communicative rights of the petitioner versus the rights of the state, concluding:

> [I]n the absence of a statute narrowly drawn to define and punish specific conduct as constituting a clear and present danger to a substantial interest of the State, the petitioner's communication, considered in the light of the constitutional guarantees [free speech and religious expression], raised no such clear and present menace to public peace and order as to render him liable to conviction of the common law offense in question.[25]

compelling governmental interest test (also known as the strict scrutiny test) A constitutional litmus test that weighs the government's interest in advancing a particular policy against the free exercise interests of the individual. In order for the government's interest to outweigh the individual's, the government must prove that its interest is *necessary* to promote a *compelling* governmental interest. This standard is also used to assess other constitutional rights, including some free speech issues (see Chapter 9), fundamental freedoms (see Chapter 11), and some matters of equal protection (see Chapter 12).

With *Cantwell,* the Court essentially began to view religious freedom as a fundamental right with which the government could not interfere without a substantial or compelling governmental interest. This is known as the **compelling governmental interest test** or **strict scrutiny** standard. Under this approach, the government's interest in advancing a particular policy is essentially placed on a scale and weighed against the religious interests of the individual. And in order for the government's interest to outweigh the individual's, it must be substantial or compelling, not just of equal or slightly higher weight. The compelling interest or strict scrutiny test also places the burden on the government to prove that its interest is *necessary* to promote a *compelling* governmental interest. This test is contrasted with intermediate scrutiny (substantially related to an important governmental interest) and rational basis (rationally related to a legitimate governmental interest), both of which provide reduced levels of scrutiny or burden. See Chapter 11.

The Court solidified the balancing approach to free exercise cases in 1963, when it decided *Sherbert v. Verner*[26] (see later in this chapter). In *Sherbert,* the Court found that a South Carolina law, which denied unemployment benefits to a Seventh-Day Adventist whose religious practices precluded her from accepting jobs requiring work on Saturdays, violated the Free Exercise Clause. Justice Brennan, writing for the majority, acknowledged that the state's denial of benefits was an indirect infringement on the claimant's religious practices, but concluded that it was an infringement nonetheless. The Court then used the strict scrutiny test to evaluate the free exercise rights of the religious petitioner. In deciding the case, the Court asked, "whether some compelling state interest enforced in the eligibility provisions of the South Carolina statute justifies the substantial infringement of appellant's First Amendment right."[27] Elaborating on this standard, Justice Brennan stated, "[i]t is basic that no showing merely of a rational relationship to some colorable state interest would suffice; in this highly sensitive constitutional area, '[o]nly the gravest abuses, endangering paramount interests, give occasion for permissible limitation.'"[28] The significance of this decision is that the Court did not evaluate the state's law in a vacuum by limiting itself to reviewing the reasonableness of the statute. Instead, the court engaged in a balancing test, where the legitimacy of the state statute was weighed against competing First Amendment rights of the claimant.

The Court continued its strict scrutiny approach to free exercise cases in the landmark case of *Wisconsin v. Yoder.*[29] Much like *Sherbert,* the Court was faced with a neutral state law that indirectly discriminated against the religious practices of a minority religion. In *Yoder,* members of an Amish family sought an exemption from a state law that required children to attend school beyond the eighth grade because it conflicted with their religious practices. The Court decided in favor of the Amish, finding that the well-founded religious practices of the Amish outweighed the state's interest in compulsory school-attendance laws. Chief Justice Burger, in his opinion for the Court, reaffirmed the essence of the strict scrutiny test in free exercise cases, stating that "only those interests of the highest order and those not otherwise served can overbalance legitimate claims to the free exercise of religion."

Sherbert v. Verner
374 U.S. 398 (1963)

Appellant, a member of the Seventh-Day Adventist Church, was discharged by her South Carolina employer because she would not work on Saturday, the Sabbath Day of her faith. She was unable to obtain other employment because she would not work on Saturday, and she filed a claim for unemployment compensation benefits under the South Carolina Unemployment Compensation Act, which provides that a claimant is ineligible for benefits if he has failed, without good cause, to accept available suitable work when offered him. The State Commission denied appellant's application on the ground that she would not accept suitable work when offered, and its action was sustained by the State Supreme Court. . . .

Mr. Justice Brennan delivered the opinion of the Court. . . .

The door of the Free Exercise Clause stands tightly closed against any governmental regulation of religious beliefs as such. Government may neither compel affirmation of a repugnant belief, nor penalize or discriminate against individuals or groups because they hold religious views abhorrent to the authorities, nor employ the taxing power to inhibit the dissemination of particular religious views. On the other hand, the Court has rejected challenges under the Free Exercise Clause to governmental regulation of certain overt acts prompted by religious beliefs or principles. . . . The conduct or actions so regulated have invariably posed some substantial threat to public safety, peace or order.

Plainly enough, appellant's conscientious objection to Saturday work constitutes no conduct prompted by religious principles of a kind within the reach of state legislation. If, therefore, the decision of the South Carolina Supreme Court is to withstand appellant's constitutional challenge, it must be either because her disqualification as a beneficiary represents no infringement by the State of her constitutional rights of free exercise, or because any incidental burden on the free exercise of appellant's religion may be justified by a "compelling state interest in the regulation of a subject within the State's constitutional power to regulate. . . ."

We turn first to the question whether the disqualification for benefits imposes any burden on the free exercise of appellant's religion. We think it is clear that it does. In a sense the consequences of such a disqualification to religious principles and practices may be only an indirect result of welfare legislation within the State's general competence to enact; it is true that no criminal sanctions directly compel appellant to work a six-day week. But this is only the beginning, not the end, of our inquiry. For "[i]f the purpose or effect of a law is to impede the observance of one or all religions or is to discriminate invidiously between religions, that law is constitutionally invalid even though the burden may be characterized as being only indirect." Here not only is it apparent that appellant's declared ineligibility for benefits derives solely from the practice of her religion, but the pressure upon her to forego that practice is unmistakable. The ruling forces her to choose between following the precepts of her religion and forfeiting benefits, on the one hand, and abandoning one of the precepts of her religion in order to accept work, on the other hand. Governmental imposition of such a choice puts the same kind of burden upon the free exercise of religion as would a fine imposed against appellant for her Saturday worship. . . .

Significantly South Carolina expressly saves the Sunday worshipper from having to make the kind of choice which we here hold infringes the Sabbatarian's religious liberty. When in times of "national emergency" the textile plants are authorized by the State Commissioner of Labor to operate on Sunday, "no employee shall be required to work on Sunday . . . who is conscientiously opposed to Sunday work; and if any employee should refuse to work on Sunday on account of conscientious . . . objections he or she shall not jeopardize his or her seniority by such refusal or be discriminated against in any other manner." S. C. Code, 64-4. No question of the disqualification of a Sunday worshipper for benefits is likely to arise, since we cannot suppose that an employer will discharge him in violation of this statute. The unconstitutionality of the disqualification of the Sabbatarian is thus compounded by the religious discrimination which South Carolina's general statutory scheme necessarily effects.

We must next consider whether some compelling state interest enforced in the eligibility provisions of the South Carolina statute justifies the substantial infringement of appellant's First Amendment right. It is basic that no showing merely of a rational relationship to some colorable state interest would suffice. . . . No such abuse or danger has been advanced in the present case. The appellees suggest no more than a possibility that the filing of fraudulent claims by unscrupulous claimants feigning religious objections to Saturday work might not only dilute the unemployment compensation fund but also hinder the scheduling by employers of necessary Saturday work. But that possibility is not apposite here because no such objection appears to have been made before the South Carolina Supreme Court, and we are unwilling to assess the importance of an asserted state interest without the views of the state court. . . .

In holding as we do, plainly we are not fostering the "establishment" of the Seventh-Day Adventist religion in South Carolina, for the extension of unemployment benefits to Sabbatarians in common with Sunday worshippers reflects nothing more than the governmental obligation of neutrality in the face of religious differences, and does not represent that involvement of religious with secular institutions which it is the object of the Establishment Clause to forestall. Nor does the recognition of the appellant's right to unemployment benefits under the state statute serve to abridge any other person's religious liberties. Nor do we, by our decision today, declare the existence of a constitutional right to unemployment benefits on the part of all persons whose religious convictions are the cause of their unemployment. This is not a case in which an employee's religious convictions serve to make him a nonproductive member of society. Finally, nothing we say today constrains the States to adopt any particular form or scheme of unemployment compensation. Our holding today is only that South Carolina may not constitutionally apply the eligibility provisions so as to constrain a worker to abandon his religious convictions respecting the day of rest. . . .

The Court continued to employ the strict scrutiny standard in free exercise cases until 1990. Then, in what is widely viewed as a revolutionary development in free exercise jurisprudence, the Court switched to a far more separationist approach. In *Employment Division v. Smith* (1990)[30] (see later in this chapter), the Court addressed an Oregon unemployment compensation case wherein two Native Americans employed by a drug rehabilitation clinic were fired because they ingested peyote during a religious ceremony while off-duty. The Court, in a 5–4 decision, held that an individual's religious beliefs do not excuse him/her from complying with valid and neutral laws. The crux of the decision was that states can, but are not required to, provide exemptions to individuals whose religious practices are prohibited by a neutral state law. At the heart of the majority's decision was the statement "of the highest order and those not otherwise served can overbalance legitimate claims to the free exercise of religion."[31] While this test is not identical to the *Sherbert* test, it nevertheless reaffirms the general practice of balancing the two competing interests—religious liberty and governmental interest—and requires that the latter must be of great magnitude in order to override the former.[32]

> It may fairly be said that leaving accommodation to the political process will place at a relative disadvantage those religious practices that are not widely engaged in; but that unavoidable consequence of democratic government must be preferred to a system in which each conscience is a law unto itself or in which judges weigh the social importance of all laws against the centrality of all religious beliefs.[33]

In essence, the court preferred that the legislature be the source for creating exemptions to neutral laws, rather than individual conscience or judicial balancing tests. Justice Scalia, in his majority opinion, specifically rejected the use of the compelling interest test in free exercise cases, except in cases dealing with unemployment compensation. Scalia stated, "[i]f 'compelling interest' really means what it says . . . many laws will not meet the test. Any society adopting such a system would be courting anarchy. . . ."[34]

Notice the fundamental shift that occurs in *Smith*. Rather than constitutionally requiring government to balance the religious liberties of individuals with the competing governmental interests, *Smith* concludes that the First Amendment does not require such consideration. Instead, the Court concluded that laws that are neutral in form and generally applied will be deemed constitutional, regardless of their adverse impact on certain religious practices. This standard is called the **neutrality test** because it simply requires that government remain neutral in its application of policy by not intentionally targeting religious practices or by applying general laws in a disproportionate manner among all religions. Under *Smith*, as long as a policy is neutral in form and generally applied, it is constitutionally kosher.

10.6 CONTINUING THE DEBATE OVER THE FREE EXERCISE OF RELIGION

In 1993, Congress responded to the Court's decision in *Smith* by passing the **Religious Freedom Restoration Act (RFRA)**,[35] which, via statute, reinstated the compelling governmental interest test for free exercise cases. The RFRA bars government from substantially burdening an individual's exercise of religion, even if such burden stems from a neutral and generally applicable law, unless the government can demonstrate that the burden (1) furthers a compelling governmental interest and (2) is the least restrictive means of furthering such interest.

The Court, however, invalidated the RFRA as it applied to the states, finding that the Act went beyond the constitutional authority of Congress to regulate state policymaking in matters affecting religious exercise. In *City of Boerne v. Flores* (1997),[36] the Court observed that the text of the RFRA applied to all levels of government, but that Congress failed to justify the legislation as it applied to the states by asserting its powers under the Commerce or Spending Clauses. Instead, Congress tried to constitutionally justify the RFRA by its remedial powers under Section 5 of the Fourteenth Amendment. The Court concluded that the RFRA was not a form of remedial legislation, but rather an effort to create new legal obligations on the states. Accordingly, the Court ruled that the RFRA could not be applied to state action.

More recently, the Court unanimously affirmed the validity of the RFRA as it applies to the federal government. In *Gonzales v. O Centro Espirita Beneficiente Uniao Do Vegetal, et al.* (2006),[37] the Court held the federal government was required to comply with the statutory standards of the RFRA and that the government failed to meet those standards when it attempted to ban the importation of an hallucinogenic tea (hoasca) used by some Native Americans during tribal ceremonies. The Court concluded that the federal government did not support its ban on the substance with a narrowly tailored and compelling governmental interest, and therefore its ban could not be sustained in the face of competing religious interests. Thus, the Court has found that although the RFRA cannot be applied to the states, it is applicable to the federal government.

neutrality test
An approach to free exercise cases adopted in *Employment Division v. Smith* (1990) that maintains that governmental policies that are neutral in form and generally applied will be deemed constitutional, regardless of their adverse impact on certain religious practices.

Religious Freedom Restoration Act (RFRA)
A law passed by Congress in 1993 that sought to reinstate the strict scrutiny standard for free exercise cases. The RFRA bars the government from substantially burdening an individual's exercise of religion, even if such burden stems from a neutral and generally applicable law, unless the government can demonstrate that the burden (1) furthers a compelling governmental interest and (2) is the least restrictive means of furthering such interest.

Cyber Constitution
Religious Freedom Restoration Act http://uscode.house.gov/download/pls/42C21B.txt

Employment Division v. Smith
494 U.S. 872 (1990)

Justice Scalia delivered the opinion of the Court.

This case requires us to decide whether the Free Exercise Clause of the First Amendment permits the State of Oregon to include religiously inspired peyote use within the reach of its general criminal prohibition on use of that drug, and thus permits the State to deny unemployment benefits to persons dismissed from their jobs because of such religiously inspired use. . . .

Respondents Alfred Smith and Galen Black (hereinafter respondents) were fired from their jobs with a private drug rehabilitation organization because they ingested peyote for sacramental purposes at a ceremony of the Native American Church, of which both are members. When respondents applied to petitioner Employment Division (hereinafter petitioner) for unemployment compensation, they were determined to be ineligible for benefits because they had been discharged for work-related "misconduct." The Oregon Court of Appeals reversed that determination, holding that the denial of benefits violated respondents' free exercise rights under the First Amendment.

On appeal to the Oregon Supreme Court, petitioner argued that the denial of benefits was permissible because respondents' consumption of peyote was a crime under Oregon law. The Oregon Supreme Court reasoned, however, that the criminality of respondents' peyote use was irrelevant to resolution of their constitutional claim—since the purpose of the "misconduct" provision under which respondents had been disqualified was not to enforce the State's criminal laws but to preserve the financial integrity of the compensation fund, and since that purpose was inadequate to justify the burden that disqualification imposed on respondents' religious practice. . . . We granted certiorari.

Before this Court in 1987, petitioner continued to maintain that the illegality of respondents' peyote consumption was relevant to their constitutional claim. We agreed, concluding that "if a State has prohibited through its criminal laws certain kinds of religiously motivated conduct without violating the First Amendment, it certainly follows that it may impose the lesser burden of denying unemployment compensation benefits to persons who engage in that conduct." We noted, however, that the Oregon Supreme Court had not decided whether respondents' sacramental use of peyote was in fact proscribed by Oregon's controlled substance law, and that this issue was a matter of dispute between the parties. Being "uncertain about the legality of the religious use of peyote in Oregon," we determined that it would not be "appropriate for us to decide whether the practice is protected by the Federal Constitution." Accordingly, we vacated the judgment of the Oregon Supreme Court and remanded for further proceedings.

On remand, the Oregon Supreme Court held that respondents' religiously inspired use of peyote fell within the prohibition of the Oregon statute, which "makes no exception for the sacramental use" of the drug. It then considered whether that prohibition was valid under the Free Exercise Clause, and concluded that it was not. The court therefore reaffirmed its previous ruling that the State could not deny unemployment benefits to respondents for having engaged in that practice.

We again granted certiorari.

. . .

The Free Exercise Clause of the First Amendment, which has been made applicable to the States by incorporation into the Fourteenth Amendment, provides that "Congress shall make no law respecting an establishment of religion, or prohibiting the free exercise thereof. . . ." The free exercise of religion means, first and foremost, the right to believe and profess whatever religious doctrine one desires. Thus, the First Amendment obviously excludes all "governmental regulation of religious beliefs as such." . . .

But the "exercise of religion" often involves not only belief and profession but the performance of (or abstention from) physical acts: assembling with others for a worship service, participating in sacramental use of bread and wine, proselytizing, abstaining from certain foods or certain modes of transportation. It would be true, we think (though no case of ours has involved the point), that a State would be "prohibiting the free exercise [of religion]" if it sought to ban such acts or abstentions only when they are engaged in for religious reasons, or only because of the religious belief that they display. It would doubtless be unconstitutional, for example, to ban the casting of "statues that are to be used for worship purposes," or to prohibit bowing down before a golden calf.

Respondents in the present case, however, seek to carry the meaning of "prohibiting the free exercise [of religion]" one large step further. They contend that their religious motivation for using peyote places them beyond the reach of a criminal law that is not specifically directed at their religious practice, and that is concededly constitutional as applied to those who use the drug for other reasons. They assert, in other words, that "prohibiting the free exercise [of religion]" includes requiring any individual to observe a generally applicable law that requires (or forbids) the performance of an act that his religious belief forbids (or requires). As a textual matter, we do not think the words must be given that meaning. It is no more necessary to regard the collection of a general tax, for example, as "prohibiting the free exercise [of religion]" by those citizens who believe support of organized government to be sinful, than it is to regard the same tax as "abridging the freedom . . . of the press" of those publishing companies that must pay the tax as a condition of staying in business. It is a permissible reading of the text, in the one case as in the other, to say that if prohibiting the exercise of religion (or burdening the activity of printing) is not the object of the tax but merely the incidental effect of a generally applicable and otherwise valid provision, the First Amendment has not been offended.

Our decisions reveal that the latter reading is the correct one. We have never held that an individual's religious beliefs excuse him from compliance with an otherwise valid law prohibiting conduct that the State is free to regulate. On the contrary, the record of more than a century of our free exercise jurisprudence contradicts that proposition.

[Our] decisions have consistently held that the right of free exercise does not relieve an individual of the obligation to comply with a "valid and neutral law of general applicability on the ground that the law proscribes (or prescribes) conduct that his religion prescribes (or proscribes)." . . .

The only decisions in which we have held that the First Amendment bars application of a neutral, generally applicable law to religiously motivated action have involved not the Free Exercise Clause alone, but the Free Exercise Clause in conjunction with other constitutional protections, such as freedom of speech and of the press, or the right of parents, . . . to direct the education of their children. Some of our cases prohibiting compelled expression, decided exclusively upon free speech grounds, have also involved freedom of religion. And it is easy to envision a case in which a challenge on freedom of association grounds would likewise be reinforced by Free Exercise Clause concerns.

The present case does not present such a hybrid situation, but a free exercise claim unconnected with any communicative activity or parental right. Respondents urge us to hold, quite simply, that when otherwise prohibitable conduct is accompanied by religious convictions, not only the convictions but the conduct itself must be free from governmental regulation. We have never held that, and decline to do so now.

Respondents argue that even though exemption from generally applicable criminal laws need not automatically be extended to religiously motivated actors, at least the claim for a religious exemption must be evaluated under the balancing test set forth in *Sherbert v. Verner*, 374 U.S. 398 (1963). Under the *Sherbert* test, governmental actions that substantially burden a religious practice must be justified by a compelling governmental interest. Applying that test we have, on three occasions, invalidated state unemployment compensation rules that conditioned the availability of benefits upon an applicant's willingness to work under conditions forbidden by his religion. We have never invalidated any governmental action on the basis of the *Sherbert* test except the denial of unemployment compensation.

Even if we were inclined to breathe into *Sherbert* some life beyond the unemployment compensation field, we would not apply it to require exemptions from a generally applicable criminal law. The *Sherbert* test, it must be recalled, was developed in a context that lent itself to individualized governmental assessment of the reasons for the relevant conduct. . . .

The "compelling government interest" requirement seems benign, because it is familiar from other fields. But using it as the standard that must be met before the government may accord different treatment on the basis of race, or before the government may regulate the content of speech is not remotely comparable to using it for the purpose asserted here. What it produces in those other fields—equality of treatment and an unrestricted flow of contending speech—are constitutional norms; what it would produce here—a private right to ignore generally applicable laws—is a constitutional anomaly. . . .

Values that are protected against government interference through enshrinement in the Bill of Rights are not thereby banished from the political process. Just as a society that believes in the negative protection accorded to the press by the First Amendment is likely to enact laws that affirmatively foster the dissemination of the printed word, so also a society that believes in the negative protection accorded to religious belief can be expected to be solicitous of that value in its legislation as well. It is therefore not surprising that a number of States have made an exception to their drug laws for sacramental peyote use. But to say that a nondiscriminatory religious-practice exemption is permitted, or even that it is desirable, is not to say that it is constitutionally required, and that the appropriate occasions for its creation can be discerned by the courts. It may fairly be said that leaving accommodation to the political process will place at a relative disadvantage those religious practices that are not widely engaged in; but that unavoidable consequence of democratic government must be preferred to a system in which each conscience is a law unto itself or in which judges weigh the social importance of all laws against the centrality of all religious beliefs.

Because respondents' ingestion of peyote was prohibited under Oregon law, and because that prohibition is constitutional, Oregon may, consistent with the Free Exercise Clause, deny respondents unemployment compensation when their dismissal results from use of the drug. The decision of the Oregon Supreme Court is accordingly reversed.

It is so ordered.

Justice O'Connor, with whom Justice Brennan, Justice Marshall, and Justice Blackmun join as to Parts I and II, concurring in the judgment.

Although I agree with the result the Court reaches in this case, I cannot join its opinion. In my view, today's holding dramatically departs from well-settled First Amendment jurisprudence, appears unnecessary to resolve the question presented, and is incompatible with our Nation's fundamental commitment to individual religious liberty. . . .

I would therefore adhere to our established free exercise jurisprudence and hold that the State in this case has a compelling interest in regulating peyote use by its citizens and that accommodating respondents' religiously motivated conduct "will unduly interfere with fulfillment of the governmental interest." Accordingly, I concur in the judgment of the Court.

Justice Blackmun, with whom Justice Brennan and Justice Marshall join, dissenting.

This Court over the years painstakingly has developed a consistent and exacting standard to test the constitutionality of a state statute that burdens the free exercise of religion. Such a statute may stand only if the law in general, and the State's refusal to allow a religious exemption in particular, are justified by a compelling interest that cannot be served by less restrictive means. . . .

For these reasons, I conclude that Oregon's interest in enforcing its drug laws against religious use of peyote is not sufficiently compelling to outweigh respondents' right to the free exercise of their religion. Since the State could not constitutionally enforce its criminal prohibition against respondents, the interests underlying the State's drug laws cannot justify its denial of unemployment benefits. Absent such justification, the State's regulatory interest in denying benefits for religiously motivated "misconduct" is indistinguishable from the state interests this Court has rejected in [other cases]. The State of Oregon cannot, consistently with the Free Exercise Clause, deny respondents unemployment benefits.

I dissent.

Religious Land Use and Institutionalized Persons Act of 2000 (RLUIPA)
Another law passed by Congress that attempted to reinstate the strict scrutiny standard in Free Exercise Clause cases. RLUIPA reinstates strict scrutiny analysis in two types of cases: (1) those involving land-use regulation and (2) those involving religious exercise by institutionalized persons.

Cyber Constitution
Religious Land-Use and Institutionalized Persons Act of 2000
http://www.lc.org/resources/rluipa.htm

As for state governments, after the Court's decision in *Boerne* in 1997, Congress again sought to restore the strict scrutiny test by passing the **Religious Land Use and Institutionalized Persons Act of 2000 (RLUIPA)** in September 2000. More narrow in its coverage than the RFRA, and based on congressional power under the Spending and Commerce Clauses, the RLUIPA reinstates strict scrutiny analysis in two types of cases: (1) those involving land-use regulation and (2) those involving religious exercise by institutionalized persons. In *Cutter v. Wilkinson* (2005),[38] the Court unanimously affirmed the constitutional validity of the RLUIPA as it applied to an Ohio prison seeking to restrict the religious practices of its inmates. Thus, at least in some settings, states also must abide by the compelling governmental interest test. As for all other state settings not related to land use or institutionalized persons, it appears that the neutrality test established in *Smith* is the applicable standard. See Figure 10-4.

In light of Congress's legislative response to the *Smith* decision and the Court's ongoing review of this legislation, it is fair to say that the standards for cases involving the free exercise of religion are in a state of flux. It appears, at least for now, that the Court will not impose any affirmative *constitutional* obligations upon government to accommodate religious practices, as long as government's policies are neutral in form and uniformly applied. But Congress has imposed *legislative* requirements on

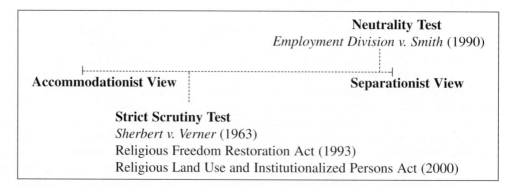

FIGURE 10-4
The ideological movement in free exercise jurisprudence

YOUR CONSTITUTIONAL VALUES

CAN GOVERNMENT ENFORCE FIRE CODE PROVISIONS AGAINST HAND-HELD CANDLES DURING RELIGIOUS CEREMONIES?

In 1991, David Dreyer, the fire marshal of Anderson Township, Ohio, sent letters to twenty churches in his district notifying them that they could not allow congregants to hold lighted candles during ceremonies. Dreyer maintained that such a practice was dangerous and violated the township's fire code. Later, Dreyer offered yet another warning to churches to avoid using hand-held candles in their Christmas services. "It's black and white in the fire code," Dreyer said, "[t]hey can't have candles in the pew area of the church." Violations of the fire code are punishable by a $25 fine, which could result in insurance problems for the churches.

In response to Dreyer's policy directive, Cincinnati Archbishop Daniel Pilarczyk filed a lawsuit against Anderson Township, claiming that its strict enforcement of the fire code violated religious freedom under the First Amendment. The archbishop sought a court order barring enforcement of the ordinance during Easter ceremonies. According to Pilarczyk, the candle flame symbolizes the resurrected Jesus Christ and is important to the Catholic tradition.

Eventually, the township and the Catholic Church avoided a constitutional showdown by working out a compromise allowing the candles to continue to be used but limiting the age of those permitted to hold them. Despite this compromise, the constitutional question remains, would the fire marshal have prevailed if this case had gone to court? Consider this matter in light of the Supreme Court's rulings in *Sherbert v. Verner* and *Employment Division v. Smith*, as well as the legislative provisions of the Religious Freedom Restoration Act of 1993 and the Religious Land Use and Institutionalized Persons Act of 2000. What are your constitutional values under the Free Exercise Clause? How would you decide the constitutional question raised by this case?

Using your constitutional values and the free exercise doctrines addressed in this chapter, how would you resolve the constitutional controversy?

Source: Rick Van Sant, "Archbishop Sues Over Candle Ban," *The Cincinnati Post* (April 7, 1993), p. A8.

---

governments in some settings that require interferences with religious practices to meet the strict scrutiny standard.

10.7 MODERN CHALLENGES

For several decades, constitutional challenges involving religion and government have remained a constant fixture in American jurisprudence. There is little reason to believe that such disputes will subside anytime soon.

There are a number of areas in which religion-related litigation is likely to continue. First, religious display cases will likely continue to dot court dockets. Despite the Supreme Court's rulings in *Perry v. Van Orden* and *McCreary v. ACLU*, governments, religious groups, and civil libertarian organizations continue to battle over what types of public displays violate the Establishment Clause. In what may appear like on ongoing cat-and-mouse game, some governments continue to try and find ways to present displays of manger scenes, the Ten Commandments, and other Christian-based symbols. The challenge for these governments is to develop religion-neutral or secular grounds for offering these displays. On the other side, civil libertarian groups remain ever vigilant in their practice of identifying and challenging government-sponsored symbols and displays that seek to make religion a part of the government's business.

Another area of contemporary concern involves the tax exempt status of some churches and other religious organizations. Generally speaking, the U.S. tax code has exempted religious organizations from paying most federal taxes, as long as the organization does not unduly engage in electoral and/or partisan affairs. In some cases, churches and other exempt religious institutions have been accused of using their pulpit and other institutional resources to lobby church members to take particular types of political action, including voting. It is likely that the Internal Revenue Service will continue to monitor religious institutions regarding these types of activities to assess whether they should remain exempt from paying federal taxes.

Finally, the so-called "War on Terror" and other similar campaigns likely will continue to result in allegations that governments are unnecessarily targeting and interfering with the free exercise of religion, particularly that of Muslims. Whether seeking to restrict the financial transactions and other contributions of individuals to Muslim-related organizations, regulate the location of Muslim-based structures (for example, the so-called ground zero mosque), or limit the types of clothing that can be worn during government-sponsored activities (schools, driver's license photos, airport security screenings), government at all levels likely will face constitutional scrutiny under the Free Exercise Clause and other legal protections of religious liberty.

10.8 SUMMARY

The First Amendment contains two religion clauses—the Establishment Clause and the Free Exercise Clause. The clauses can be viewed as two sides of the same coin. On the one side, the Establishment Clause limits the extent to which government aids or supports religious activity. On the other side, the Free Exercise Clause restricts government's ability to interfere with religious activity.

The religion clauses mean much more than would appear from the text of the First Amendment. The clauses limit more than just congressional action—they apply to the policies of state and local government as well. They also apply to more than just the laws or legislation passed by governments—they apply to all forms of governmental activity, including executive, judicial, and administrative action. And finally, the clauses also have been applied to more than just traditional or majoritarian religious organizations—they apply to other belief systems that individuals may substitute for a belief in a supreme being. As a result, one cannot read the religion clauses literally. To fully understand the scope of the religion clauses, one must appreciate how the Supreme Court has interpreted and enlarged the critical terms of these provisions.

Both religion clauses are subject to debate. Some claim that these provisions should be viewed as allowing the government to accommodate religious activity, either by allowing government to support religion, in one form or another, or by requiring government to accommodate certain individual religious practices. Others claim that the clauses ought to be viewed as creating a more separated relationship between government and religion, requiring government to avoid assisting religious activities or accommodating religious practices that run afoul of neutral and generally applicable laws.

The Supreme Court currently has three primary tests that it uses to interpret and apply the Establishment Clause. The *Lemon* test requires government actions that assist or support religion to (1) have a secular (nonreligious) purpose, (2) have a primary effect that neither advances nor inhibits religion, and (3) not foster an excessive entanglement with religion and government. The endorsement test asks whether, to the average viewer, the government action conveys a message of endorsement or disapproval of religion. And the coercion test asks whether the government is acting in a manner that may have a coercive effect on individuals to support or participate in a particular religion. Within recent case law, any or all of these tests may be applied to determine the constitutionality of the government's support of religion.

The Court has interpreted the Free Exercise Clause to mean that government is not required to accommodate religious practices as long as its policy is neutral in form and generally applied. Congress, however, has enacted the Religious Freedom Restoration Act and Religious Land Use and Institutionalized Persons Act, which, in some governmental settings, require the government to show that its interference with religious practice is necessary to promote a compelling governmental interest. As a result, to fully assess a person's religious liberty rights, one must examine the situation under both the Free Exercise Clause and the congressional legislation.

REVIEW QUESTIONS

1. Why are the religion clauses called "two sides of the same coin"?
2. What does the term *religion* mean under the First Amendment?
3. Why are the terms *respecting* and *establishment* important when interpreting the meaning of the Establishment Clause?
4. Compare and contrast the accommodationist view of the religion clauses with the separationist view.
5. What was James Madison's role in drafting the religion clauses?
6. Why might it be difficult to read the religion clauses literally?
7. Identify and explain the three tests or standards used by the Court to interpret and apply the Establishment Clause.
8. What is the neutrality test, and how does it differ from the *Sherbert* test in free exercise cases?
9. What has Congress done in response to the Court's decision in *Employment Division v. Smith*?

ASSIGNMENTS: CONSTITUTIONAL LAW IN ACTION

The Constitution in Your Community

Assume that you are working as a legal assistant for a civil rights firm. Your firm has been retained by a local woman, Ima A. Theest, who wants to challenge her local village council's practice of praying before council meetings. It seems that the village council in the town of Samsville has regularly said a prayer before starting its monthly meetings. The prayer is led by the mayor of the town and generally asks for "God's guidance" in making decisions regarding the public interest of the village. Typically, the mayor asks those in attendance at the meeting to bow their heads, before stating, "Dear God. We ask that you be present with us tonight as we deliberate and discuss matters that are important to your people. We ask that you guide us and strengthen us as we seek to act in the best interest of our community. Please give us wisdom and courage so that we may do good work and help those around us. We ask this in your name. Amen."

The mayor and council members defend the pre-meeting prayer by saying that it is part of a longstanding tradition within the community that merely offers the council and those in attendance at the meetings to have a moment of reflection before discussing matters of public importance. Ms. Theest, however, believes the council's prayer violates the First Amendment Establishment Clause, as well as the state's constitutional protections against religious compulsion. Accordingly, you are asked to prepare a memorandum identifying whether and to what extent the Establishment Clause and your home state's constitution prohibit the village council of Samsville from continuing with their pre-meeting prayer. Be sure to consider each of the Supreme Court's tests for interpreting the Establishment Clause, as well as any separate standards used under your state's constitution.

Going Federal

Assume that Jefferson School District, a local public school district, has adopted a policy for its students that bans the wearing of "any hat, cap, or other type of clothing on or around a student's head" during regular school hours. The school wants to reduce the number of distracting clothing items that may interfere with the educational process and to reduce potential artifacts that could be used for cheating on exams. Sheila Smith, a Jefferson high school student and a practicing Muslim, believes the school district's new policy interferes with her religious practice of wearing a burqa during the school day. She would like to file a federal lawsuit challenging the school's new policy as an unconstitutional infringement on her religious freedom. Consider Ms. Smith's challenge in light of the Supreme Court's ruling in *Employment Division v. Smith* (1990), the federal Religious Freedom Restoration Act, and any other legal protections for religious freedom afforded under your state's legal authorities. Then prepare a legal memorandum where you outline a federal complaint to be filed on behalf of Ms. Smith and assess the merits of her case.

Moot Court

Consider the history, wording, and context of the federal Pledge of Allegiance. Then read and outline the two Ninth Circuit Court of Appeals decisions regarding the constitutionality of the Pledge—*Newdow v. Carey* (2010) (upholding the constitutionality of the Pledge) (http://undergod.procon.org/sourcefiles/9thcircuitrulingMar_2010.pdf) and *Newdow v. Elk Grove School District*, 292 F.3d 597 (9th Cir. 2002) (finding the "under God" provision unconstitutional). Work in teams of two. The first team should prepare a five-minute oral argument presentation wherein they present arguments challenging the constitutionality of the "under God" provision within the Pledge. Conversely, the second team should prepare a five-minute oral argument asserting why the "under God" provision does not violate the Establishment Clause.

NOTES

1. Letter to a Committee of the Danbury (Connecticut) Baptist Association, January 1, 1802.
2. *Employment Division v. Smith,* 494 U.S. 872, 890 (1990).
3. Robert Alley, *The Supreme Court on Church and State* 9–10 (1988).
4. *Id.* at 10.
5. *Id.* at 18.
6. *Id.*
7. *Id.* at 26.
8. See *Marsh v. Chambers,* 463 U.S. 783 (1983) (allowing state legislative sessions to be opened with a chaplain); *Lynch v. Donnelly,* 465 U.S. 688 (1984) (allowing city-sponsored crèche display to stand as a part of a larger holiday season exhibit); *Agostini v. Felton,* 521 U.S. 203 (1997) (allowing public school teachers to be sent to parochial schools to provide remedial education).
9. See *Sherbert v. Verner,* 374 U.S. 398 (1963) (requiring state unemployment compensation system to accommodate a Seventh-Day Adventist who refused to work on the Sabbath); *Wisconsin v. Yoder,* 406 U.S. 205 (1972) (exempting Amish children from state law requiring school attendance beyond eighth grade); *Wooley v. Maryland,* 430 U.S. 705 (1977) (allowing exemption to Jehovah's Witnesses who did not want to display state license plate with the motto "Live Free or Die").

10. See *Engel v. Vitale,* 370 U.S. 421 (1962) (striking down nondenominational prayer reading in public school); *Abington School District v. Schempp,* 374 U.S. 203 (1963) (barring reading of Lord's Prayer and Bible verses in public school); *County of Allegheny v. ACLU,* 492 U.S. 573 (1989) (finding crèche display in city building to be unconstitutional).

11. See *Goldman v. Weinberger,* 475 U.S. 503 (1986) (upholding military dress code in face of request by Orthodox Jewish rabbi to wear a yarmulke); *Swaggart v. Bd. of Equalization,* 493 U.S. 378 (1990) (allowing state to impose sales tax on religious materials sold by ministerial organization); *Employment Division v. Smith,* 494 U.S. 872 (1990) (upholding state law banning peyote in face of challenge by Native Americans seeking to use the substance during ceremonies).

12. 310 U.S. 1 (1940).

13. 330 U.S. 1 (1947).

14. *United States v. Seeger,* 380 U.S. 163 (1965).

15. *Welsh v. United States,* 398 U.S. 333 (1970).

16. See Leonard Levy, *The Establishment Clause: Religion and the First Amendment* 61 (New York: Macmillan 1986).

17. James Madison, "Memorial and Remonstrance Against Religious Assessments" (1785).

18. Roger Williams, "The Bloudy Tenant of Persecution," for Cause of Conscience (1644).

19. *Elk Grove Unified School District v. Newdow,* 542 U.S. 1 (2004) (reversing the Ninth Circuit decision and dismissing the case based on a finding that Michael Newdow, as a noncustodial parent, lacked legal standing to assert the constitutional rights of his daughter).

20. 98 U.S. 145 (1879).

21. *Id.* at 166 (emphasis added).

22. *Id.*

23. 310 U.S. 296 (1940).

24. *Id.* at 303–304.

25. *Id.* at 311 (footnote omitted).

26. 374 U.S. 398 (1963).

27. *Id.* at 406.

28. *Id.* (citation omitted).

29. 406 U.S. 205 (1972).

30. 494 U.S. 872 (1990).

31. *Id.* at 215.

32. The tests articulated by *Sherbert* and *Yoder,* while not identical, require a two-step process: First, the government must show that the law serves an important interest of the state whether designated as "compelling" in *Sherbert* or "of the highest order" as in *Yoder*; second, the state must show that, by providing an exemption to the claimant, there will be a substantial harm to the government's interest.

33. *Id.*

34. *Id.*

35. 107 Stat. 1488, as amended, 42 U.S.C. §2000bb et seq.

36. 521 U.S. 507 (1997).

37. 546 U.S. 418 (2006).

38. 544 U.S. 709 (2005).

11

Substantive Due Process, Privacy, and Other Liberties

Liberty in the constitutional sense must mean more than freedom from unlawful government restraint; it must include privacy as well, if it is to be a repository of freedom. The right to be left alone is indeed the beginning of all freedom.

JUSTICE WILLIAM DOUGLAS (1952)[1]

LEARNING OBJECTIVES
At the end of this chapter you should be able to:

■ Explain the difference between the constitutional rights to substantive due process and procedural due process.

■ Identify the different approaches the Supreme Court has used to determine whether a particular activity constitutes a liberty interest protected by the Due Process Clause.

■ Understand the constitutional basis for recognizing and protecting a right of privacy under the Due Process Clause and Bill of Rights.

■ Identify and explain the history of the right to privacy as it relates to abortion and other reproductive freedoms.

■ Discuss the significance of the Court's ruling in *Lawrence v. Texas* and its implication for recognizing additional liberty interests under the Due Process Clause.

■ Explain the scope and protections afforded to economic liberties, including those protected under the Contract Clause, Takings Clause, and liberty and property provisions of the Due Process Clause.

■ Identify a contemporary issue concerning the right to privacy under the Due Process Clause of the Fourteenth Amendment, and discuss the most likely future scenarios, referencing both historical analogs and caselaw.

■ Brief a judicial opinion with no assistance. You should be successful in identifying the relevant facts, identifying the legal issue(s), and analyzing the court's rationale in at least 80 percent of your briefs.

■ Apply what you have learned to a new set of facts with no assistance.

11.1 SUBSTANTIVE DUE PROCESS

As briefly addressed in Chapter 8, the **Due Process Clause,** as contained in both the Fifth Amendment (applicable to the federal government) and the Fourteenth Amendment (applicable to the states), protects a person's right to liberty, in addition to the right to life and property. Specifically, the Due Process Clause provides that government cannot deprive any person of life, *liberty*, or property without due process of law. This clause provides an additional source for constitutional liberties that, while perhaps not specifically listed in the Bill of Rights, are nonetheless protected by the Constitution.

At the outset, it should be noted that the Due Process Cause in both Fifth and Fourteenth Amendments uses the term *person*, as opposed to *citizen* or *resident,* when identifying individuals who possess due process rights. As a result, even individuals who are not U.S. citizens may have a claim to due process protections under the Constitution. (See Chapter 8.)

There are two dimensions to the Due Process Clause as applied to liberties—procedural due process and substantive due process. **Procedural due process** is the requirement that government treat persons fairly while it attempts to interfere with their liberty interests. Put another way, procedural due process concerns *how* the government processes and safeguards individuals and their claims. Did the government give the person fair notice of its claim? Did the government give the person a chance to respond? Did the government give the person the right to appeal? All of these questions concern whether a person's claims were handled or processed in a fair manner.[2]

Substantive due process concerns the type or substance of behavior that is included as a "liberty" under the Due Process Clause. The primary question under this dimension of the Due Process Clause is *what* activities does "liberty" protect? Because "liberty" is nowhere defined in the Constitution, the Supreme Court has been left to assess its meaning. In recent years, the Court has interpreted the meaning and scope of the word "liberty" by considering whether a person's activity or conduct is either **"implicit in the concept of ordered liberty"** or "so rooted in the traditions and conscience of our people as to be ranked as fundamental."[3] For some justices, this legal inquiry involves a historical analysis to determine whether past governments or societies have provided protection for the identified activity. This essentially is a historical review. But for other justices, interpreting the meaning and scope of "liberty" under the Due Process Clause involves a more contemporary analysis. Under this approach, justices consider the nature and understanding of the asserted privacy right in light of modern-day culture.[4] For these justices, activities that were not protected in the past may nevertheless be deemed protected liberty interests today, because modern society has come to expect protection for these activities.

Over the years, the Supreme Court has identified several types of activities that are protected as liberty interests under the Due Process Clause. These include the right to privacy, parental choices regarding raising children, adult choices regarding consensual sexual activity, the right to travel, and women's decisions regarding reproduction and pregnancy. On the other hand, the Court has rejected other asserted rights, finding that they are not "implicit in the concept of ordered liberty," and therefore, not protected as liberty interests under the Due Process Clause. These include physician-assisted suicide, the right to die, and the private use of illegal narcotics.

11.2 THE RIGHT TO PRIVACY

11.2(a) Defining Privacy

The **right to privacy** has been defined in a number of different ways. Some define it as the "right to be left alone,"[5] while others refer to it as the "freedom of personal choice in matters of marriage and family life."[6] Still others see it as part of the "right to be secure in persons, houses, papers, and effects."[7] The reality is that personal privacy means different things to different people, and given the multitude of human activities to which it could be applied, it will continue to be asserted, though not necessarily constitutionally recognized, as protecting numerous dimensions of human behavior.

To various degrees, the individual right to privacy has been associated with a host of activities. These include matters relating to marriage, family education and

procedural due process
One dimension of the Due Process Clause as contained in the Fifth and Fourteenth Amendments. It requires government to treat persons fairly while it attempts to interfere with their liberty interests. Put another way, procedural due process concerns *how* the government processes and safeguards individuals and their claims.

substantive due process
A second dimension of the Due Process Clause that concerns the type or substance of behavior that is included as a "liberty" under the Due Process Clause. The primary question under this dimension of the Due Process Clause is *what* activities does "liberty" include.

implicit in the concept of ordered liberty
A phrase frequently offered by the Court as the standard for assessing whether a particular human activity will be included as a "liberty interest" under the Due Process Clause.

Cyber Constitution
The Due Process Clause
As contained in the Fourteenth Amendment, this clause prevents the states from denying persons life, liberty, or property without due process of law.
www.usconstitution.net/consttop_duep.html

right to privacy
Defined in a number of different ways, including the "right to be left alone"; the "freedom of personal choice in matters of marriage and family life"; and the "right to be secure in persons, houses, papers, and effects." The Court formally recognizes this right as a fundamental right of individuals, despite the fact that it is not specifically mentioned by the Constitution.

discipline, seeking medical information regarding birth control, obtaining reproductive-related procedures, including abortion, possessing (not selling or distributing) obscene materials in a home, cohabitating with persons of your choosing, and engaging in consensual, adult sexual conduct. In these settings, the right to privacy largely has been asserted as an independent form of liberty.

In other cases, the Court's treatment of privacy has been tethered to specific constitutional provisions affecting the rights of the criminally accused. For example, in cases where criminal defendants have alleged that the government breached their Fourth Amendment right against unreasonable searches and seizures, one of the initial questions the Court has asked is whether the defendant had a **reasonable expectation of privacy** in the area searched or the thing seized (see Chapter 13). In this context, the Court's consideration of privacy has gone to addressing the question of *reasonableness* of the government's search. The Fourth Amendment provides that "the right of the people to be secure in their persons, houses, papers, and effects, against *unreasonable* searches and seizures, shall not be violated . . ." (emphasis added). Notice that, textually, this provision guards against only unreasonable, as opposed to reasonable, searches and seizures. And one of the initial, though not always final, considerations that the Court has used to assess the reasonableness of a search is whether the defendant had a reasonable expectation of privacy in the location that was searched. If the location was a person's bedroom, it would likely be determined that the person had a reasonable expectation of privacy, and thus, at least initially, had some level of protection under the Fourth Amendment, although in some cases this protection is overridden by an otherwise reasonable government search. But if the police seized criminal contraband from a person's openly visible front lawn, it would likely be said that the person lacked a reasonable expectation of privacy and therefore was not protected under the Fourth Amendment.

reasonable expectation of privacy
A legal standard used by the Court to assess Fourth Amendment rights against unreasonable searches and seizures. Under this standard, the Court asks whether the individual had a reasonable expectation that a particular activity or location would be kept private.

11.2(b) Balancing Privacy Against Competing Interests

Like other civil liberties, the right to privacy is not absolute. Just because a person may have an expectation of privacy in his or her own home, relationships, or personal matters does not mean that the government will be unable to trump this right based on its own interests. As the Court has noted, "determining that a person has a 'liberty interest' under the Due Process Clause does not end the inquiry; 'whether [a person's] constitutional rights have been violated must be determined by balancing his liberty interests against the relevant state interests.'"[8] For example, in *Whalen v. Roe* (1976),[9] the Supreme Court upheld a governmental requirement that records be maintained on individuals who buy certain types of dangerous drugs. Similarly, in *Cruzan v. Missouri Department of Health* (1990),[10] the Court rejected the asserted privacy interests of parents who wanted to remove their daughter's feeding tube. And in *Kelly v. Johnson* (1976),[11] the Court allowed the government to regulate the length of a police officer's hair. In each of these cases, the Court weighed the interest of the state against the privacy interests of the individual and concluded that the government's interest outweighed that of the individual.

S I D E B A R

"HOME AWAY FROM HOME"

Unlike the early days of the Court when individual justices were expected to "ride circuit" by traveling across the country to hear appeals, the modern Court has occupied its current structure at One First Street N.E. (just across the street from the Capitol Building) since 1935. During this time, the Court has heard nearly all oral arguments in this building. A dramatic exception occurred in 2001, when on Friday, October 26, in the wake of the September 11 terrorist attacks, officials found traces of anthrax in the Supreme Court building. Due to this discovery, the Court was forced to hold the following week's oral arguments in the federal courthouse for the D.C. Circuit Court of Appeals, located just down the street from the Supreme Court building. This was the first and only time that the justices convened a session away from its "home" since the building was erected in 1935. The Court returned to its traditional courtroom a week later.

To the extent that privacy has been recognized, it has been treated as a **fundamental right** entitled to the utmost constitutional protection. Consequently, in recent years, the Court has evaluated privacy rights under the most rigorous of constitutional balancing tests—the **strict scrutiny test.** As addressed in Chapter 9, regarding the right to free speech; in Chapter 10, regarding the standard in some free exercise cases; and in Chapter 12, regarding racial discrimination, the strict scrutiny test requires the government to show that its infringement upon a fundamental right (privacy in this case) is necessary (or narrowly tailored) to serve a compelling governmental interest. Again, think of this standard as calibrating a scale before weighing the competing interests of the individual and the government. Under the strict scrutiny standard, the scale is adjusted before the "weigh-in" in favor of the individual's right to privacy and against the government's intrusion upon this right. In order for the government to outweigh the right to privacy, it will have to demonstrate that there is a compelling need for doing so and that its efforts are carefully crafted to fulfill this need.

11.2(c) Constitutional Sources of Privacy

As briefly addressed in Chapter 9, the right to privacy is not explicitly mentioned in the Bill of Rights—or anywhere else in the Constitution for that matter. There are, however, a number of constitutional provisions that have been interpreted as opening the door to recognizing and protecting this right. The first is the **Ninth Amendment,** which provides that "[t]he enumeration of certain rights in the bill of rights, shall not be construed to deny or disparage others retained by the people." This amendment suggests that, beyond those listed in the First through Eighth Amendments, there are other unenumerated rights that individuals retain that are to be protected against governmental intrusion. In other words, the Ninth Amendment states that the Bill of Rights should not be read as an exhaustive list of protected liberties and that other unspecified rights are still held by the people. And for some jurists, one of these other rights is privacy.

Another frequently cited source is the Due Process Clause, which, again, provides that government cannot deprive individuals of life, *liberty,* or property without due process of law. (See Section 11.1.) In recent years, the Court has frequently asked whether the asserted privacy right in a particular case is "implicit in the concept of ordered liberty" or "so rooted in the traditions and conscience of our people as to be ranked as fundamental."[12] And for some justices, under this analysis, the right to privacy is considered part of the "liberty" protected under the Due Process Clause.

The right to privacy has also been found to be implicitly located in the Bill of Rights. As addressed in Chapter 8, some justices view the First Amendment (right to speech, assembly, etc.), Third Amendment (protecting against the quartering of troops in a person's home), Fourth Amendment (guarding the right of the people to be secure in their persons, houses, papers, and effects against unreasonable searches), Fifth Amendment (barring forced self-incrimination), and Ninth Amendment (suggesting other unenumerated rights are to be protected) as casting penumbras (lunar shadows) of a privacy right. While these provisions do not specifically reference privacy, they are nonetheless deemed by some to imply such a right because they protect other activities (speech, home security, incrimination) that contain certain elements of privacy. This approach formed the basis for Justice Douglas's opinion in *Griswold v. Connecticut* (1965) (see following discussion), where the right to privacy was discussed as a penumbral or implicit right.

Some justices, however, have concluded that an individual right to privacy does not exist under the Constitution. Justices adopting this approach often justify their conclusion by observing that the right to privacy is not specifically stated in the Constitution or by finding that the asserted form of privacy (abortion, sodomy, right to die, etc.) is not "implicit in the concept of ordered liberty." The first justification is called the **strict constructionist** approach because it strictly construes the explicit words of the Constitution to determine whether a particular right is protected. And because there is no explicit reference to a right of privacy in the Constitution, this approach results

fundamental right
A constitutional right of the highest order and one to which utmost constitutional protection is applied, including strict scrutiny protection.

strict scrutiny test
Also addressed in Chapters 9 and 10, regarding the right to free speech and the free exercise of religion, this constitutional balancing test requires the government to show that its infringement upon a fundamental right is necessary (or narrowly tailored) to serve a compelling governmental interest.

Cyber Constitution
The Right to Privacy
www.law.umkc.edu/
faculty/projects/ftrials/
conlaw/rightofprivacy.
html

Ninth Amendment
A constitutional amendment providing that "[t]he enumeration of certain rights in the bill of rights, shall not be construed to deny or disparage others retained by the people." This amendment suggests that beyond those listed in the First through Eighth Amendments, there are other unenumerated rights that individuals retain that are to be protected against governmental intrusion.

strict constructionist
An approach to interpreting the Constitution that strictly construes the explicit words of the Constitution to determine whether a particular right is protected. This approach generally leads to the conclusion that there is no independent right of privacy.

original intent
An approach to interpreting the Constitution that uses historical analysis to assess what the authors of the Constitution meant or intended by a particular term or provision, including the term *liberty* within the Due Process Clause.

original understanding
An approach to interpreting the Constitution that is similar to original intent, except that it seeks to determine what the legal culture understood (as opposed to what the drafters intended) under the provision when it was originally written.

in the conclusion that there is no independent right of privacy. The second justification typically uses historical analysis to conclude that the asserted right of privacy is not protected because there is no long-standing tradition of protecting this form of privacy. This approach is known as **original intent** (assess what the authors of the Due Process Clause meant or intended by the term "liberty") or **original understanding** (assess what political and legal communities understood "liberty" to mean when the Due Process Clause was ratified). Either way, because this approach relies so much on the past, it is not likely to recognize more contemporary forms of privacy.

During the latter part of the nineteenth century and early part of the twentieth century, the Court referred to the notion of privacy in a number of cases. But the most common reference point for the Court's establishment of the right to privacy is its 1965 decision in *Griswold v. Connecticut*. In this case, the executive director of the Planned Parenthood League of Connecticut and its medical director were convicted as accessories to a crime for giving married persons information regarding birth control and for prescribing contraceptives. Under Connecticut law, it was a crime to use any drug or article to prevent conception. The Supreme Court overturned these convictions and invalidated the Connecticut law, but did so through a number of different opinions and rationales. Justice William Douglas delivered the opinion of the Court, wherein he concluded that the right to privacy, though not specifically referenced in the Bill of Rights, was nonetheless protected by the "penumbras" (shadows) of other explicit constitutional provisions, including personal freedoms found in the First, Third, Fourth, Fifth, and Ninth Amendments. Justice Arthur Goldberg concurred in the Court's opinion, but relied on the Ninth Amendment to justify his decision, stating, "[t]he language and history of the Ninth Amendment reveal that the Framers of the Constitution believed that there are additional fundamental rights, protected from governmental infringement, which exist alongside those fundamental rights specifically mentioned in the first eight constitutional amendments." Justice John Marshall Harlan II wrote a concurring opinion wherein he asserted that privacy is protected by the Due Process Clause of the Fourteenth Amendment because it is "implicit in the concept of ordered liberty." Justice Byron White also wrote a concurring opinion, finding that the Connecticut law unduly infringed upon the marital relationship, as protected by the Fourteenth Amendment. Justices Hugo Black and Potter Stewart dissented. Justice Black concluded that, because the right to privacy was not explicitly referenced in the Constitution, it should not be recognized as a liberty interest. Justice Stewart referred to the Connecticut statute as "an uncommonly silly law," but did not believe the judiciary was the appropriate venue to change it.

Since 1965, *Griswold* has served as the primary touchstone for privacy claims under the Constitution and has been instrumental in several Supreme Court rulings regarding abortion and reproductive freedoms, including the Court's landmark ruling in *Roe v. Wade* (1973).

11.3 REPRODUCTIVE LIBERTIES

Perhaps the most widely recognized case in all of modern constitutional law is *Roe v. Wade* (1973),[13] the case in which the Court struck down a Texas law outlawing abortion. Beginning with the premise that there is a particular zone of privacy that women have regarding their own bodies, the Court ruled that government could not interfere with this fundamental privacy interest absent a compelling governmental interest. In so doing, the Court effectively told government that it could not impose an outright ban on abortion during all stages of a woman's pregnancy. Moreover, the Court ruled that states may not criminalize abortions or make them too difficult to procure.[14]

More specifically, the Court held that the Due Process Clause of the Fourteenth Amendment protects the right to privacy, which includes a woman's qualified right to terminate her pregnancy. The Court concluded that, although government cannot override this privacy right, it does have legitimate interests in protecting both the pregnant woman's health and the potentiality of human life. In addressing the government's interest in regulating abortion procedures, the Court adopted a trimester approach, stating (1) for the stage prior to approximately the end of the first trimester, the abortion decision and its effectuation must be left to the medical judgment of the pregnant woman's attending physician; (2) for the stage subsequent to approximately the end of the first trimester, the state, in promoting its interest in the health of the mother, may, if it chooses, regulate the abortion procedure in ways that are reasonably related to maternal health; and (3) for the stage subsequent to viability, the state, in promoting its interest in the potentiality of human life, may, if it chooses, regulate, and even proscribe, abortion except where necessary, in appropriate medical judgment, for the preservation of the life or health of the mother.

Read the Court's decision in *Roe* and assess how the different groups of justices weighed the privacy interests of Jane Roe against the governmental interests asserted by Texas. Again, try to think of this constitutional controversy as two sets of values being weighed against each other on opposing sides of a scale. On the one side, there is the fundamental right to individual privacy held by a pregnant woman; on the other side, there is the asserted governmental interest in regulating medical procedures and protecting the fetus. As you read the opinion, notice how some justices regard the right to privacy as a fundamental right, thereby requiring the government to meet the strict scrutiny standard (the government must show that its policy is necessary to promote a compelling governmental interest). Notice too that for some justices, the sides of the scale begin to tip in the government's favor during the later stages of pregnancy. In other words, notice how some justices find that the government's interest becomes more compelling during the later stages of pregnancy.

Cyber Constitution
History of Abortion Laws
http://womenshistory.
about.com/od/
abortionuslegal/a/
abortion.htm

Roe v. Wade
410 U.S. 113 (1973)

Mr. Justice Blackmun delivered the opinion of the Court.

Jane Roe, a single woman who was residing in Dallas County, Texas, instituted this federal action in March 1970 against the District Attorney of the county. She sought a declaratory judgment that the Texas criminal abortion statutes were unconstitutional on their face, and an injunction restraining the defendant from enforcing the statutes.

Roe alleged that she was unmarried and pregnant; that she wished to terminate her pregnancy by an abortion "performed by a competent, licensed physician, under safe, clinical conditions"; that she was unable to get a "legal" abortion in Texas because her life did not appear to be threatened by the continuation of her pregnancy; and that she could not afford to travel to another jurisdiction in order to secure a legal abortion under safe conditions. . . .

The principal thrust of appellant's attack on the Texas statutes is that they improperly invade a right, said to be possessed by the pregnant woman, to choose to terminate her pregnancy. Appellant would discover this right in the concept of personal "liberty" embodied in the Fourteenth Amendment's Due Process Clause; or in personal, marital, familial, and sexual privacy said to be protected by the Bill of Rights or its penumbras, or among those rights reserved to the people by the Ninth

Amendment. Before addressing this claim, we feel it desirable briefly to survey, in several aspects, the history of abortion, for such insight as that history may afford us, and then to examine the state purposes and interests behind the criminal abortion laws.

It perhaps is not generally appreciated that the restrictive criminal abortion laws in effect in a majority of States today are of relatively recent vintage. Those laws, generally proscribing abortion or its attempt at any time during pregnancy except when necessary to preserve the pregnant woman's life, are not of ancient or even of common law origin. Instead, they derive from statutory changes effected, for the most part, in the latter half of the 19th century. . . .

Three reasons have been advanced to explain historically the enactment of criminal abortion laws in the 19th century and to justify their continued existence.

It has been argued occasionally that these laws were the product of a Victorian social concern to discourage illicit sexual conduct. Texas, however, does not advance this justification in the present case. . . .

A second reason is concerned with abortion as a medical procedure. When most criminal abortion laws were first enacted, the procedure was a hazardous one for the woman. This was particularly true prior to the *development of antisepsis. Antiseptic techniques, of* course, were based on discoveries by Lister, Pasteur, and others first announced in 1867, but were not generally accepted and employed until about the turn of the century. Abortion mortality was high. Even after 1900, and perhaps until as late as the development of antibiotics in the 1940's, standard modern techniques such as dilation and curettage were not nearly so safe as they are today. Thus, it has been argued that a State's real concern in enacting a criminal abortion law was to protect the pregnant woman, that is, to restrain her from submitting to a procedure that placed her life in serious jeopardy.

Modern medical techniques have altered this situation. Appellants and various *amici* refer to medical data indicating that abortion in early pregnancy, that is, prior to the end of the first trimester, although not without its risk, is now relatively safe. . . .

The third reason is the State's interest—some phrase it in terms of duty—in protecting prenatal life. Some of the argument for this justification rests on the theory that a new human life is present from the moment of conception. The State's interest and general obligation to protect life then extends, it is argued, to prenatal life. Only when the life of the pregnant mother herself is at stake, balanced against the life she carries within her, should the interest of the embryo or fetus not prevail. Logically, of course, a legitimate state interest in this area need not stand or fall on acceptance of the belief that life begins at conception or at some other point prior to live birth. In assessing the State's interest, recognition may be given to the less rigid claim that as long as at least potential life is involved, the State may assert interests beyond the protection of the pregnant woman alone. . . .

The Constitution does not explicitly mention any right of privacy. In a line of decisions, however . . . the Court has recognized that a right of personal privacy, or a guarantee of certain areas or zones of privacy, does exist under the Constitution. . . .

This right of privacy, whether it be founded in the Fourteenth Amendment's concept of personal liberty and restrictions upon state action, as we feel it is, or, as the District Court determined, in the Ninth Amendment's reservation of rights to the people, is broad enough to encompass a woman's decision whether or not to terminate her pregnancy. . . .

We, therefore, conclude that the right of personal privacy includes the abortion decision, but that this right is not unqualified, and must be considered against important state interests in regulation. . . .

Where certain "fundamental rights" are involved, the Court has held that regulation limiting these rights may be justified only by a "compelling state interest," and that legislative enactments must be narrowly drawn to express only the legitimate state interests at stake. . . .

Texas urges that, apart from the Fourteenth Amendment, life begins at conception and is present throughout pregnancy, and that, therefore, the State has a compelling interest in protecting that life from and after conception. We need not resolve the difficult question of when life begins. When those trained in the respective disciplines of medicine, philosophy, and theology are unable to arrive at any consensus, the judiciary, at this point in the development of man's knowledge, is not in a position to speculate as to the answer. . . .

In areas other than criminal abortion, the law has been reluctant to endorse any theory that life, as we recognize it, begins before live birth, or to accord legal rights to the unborn except in narrowly defined situations and except when the rights are contingent upon live birth. . . .

In view of all this, we do not agree that, by adopting one theory of life, Texas may override the rights of the pregnant woman that are at stake. We repeat, however, that the State does have an important and legitimate interest in preserving and protecting the health of the pregnant woman, whether she be a resident of the State or a nonresident who seeks medical consultation and treatment there, and that it has still another important and legitimate interest in protecting the potentiality of human life. These interests are separate and distinct. Each grows in substantiality as the woman approaches term and, at a point during pregnancy, each becomes "compelling."

With respect to the State's important and legitimate interest in the health of the mother, the "compelling" point, in the light of present medical knowledge, is at approximately the end of the first trimester. This is so because of the now-established medical fact that, until the end of the first trimester mortality in abortion may be less than mortality in normal childbirth. It follows that, from and after this point, a State may regulate the abortion procedure to the extent that the regulation reasonably relates to the preservation and protection of maternal health. Examples of permissible state regulation in this area are requirements as to the qualifications of the person who is to perform the abortion; as to the licensure of that person; as to the facility in which the procedure is to be performed, that is, whether it must be a hospital or may be a clinic or some other place of less-than-hospital status; as to the licensing of the facility; and the like.

This means, on the other hand, that, for the period of pregnancy prior to this "compelling" point, the attending physician, in consultation with his patient, is free to determine, without regulation by the State, that, in his medical judgment, the patient's pregnancy should be terminated. If that decision is reached, the judgment may be effectuated by an abortion free of interference by the State.

With respect to the State's important and legitimate interest in potential life, the "compelling" point is at viability. This is so because the fetus then presumably has the capability of meaningful life outside the mother's womb. State regulation protective of fetal life after viability thus has both logical and biological justifications. If the State is interested in protecting fetal life after viability, it may go so far as to proscribe abortion during that period, except when it is necessary to preserve the life or health of the mother.

Measured against these standards, Art. 1196 of the Texas Penal Code . . . sweeps too broadly. The statute makes no distinction between abortions performed early in pregnancy and those performed later, and it limits to a single reason, "saving" the mother's life, the legal justification for the procedure. The statute, therefore, cannot survive the constitutional attack made upon it here. . . .

To summarize and to repeat

1. A state criminal abortion statute of the current Texas type, that excepts from criminality only a lifesaving procedure on behalf of the mother, without regard to pregnancy stage and without recognition of the other interests involved, is violative of the Due Process Clause of the Fourteenth Amendment.

(a) For the stage prior to approximately the end of the first trimester, the abortion decision and its effectuation must be left to the medical judgment of the pregnant woman's attending physician.

(b) For the stage subsequent to approximately the end of the first trimester, the State, in promoting its interest in the health of the mother, may, if it chooses, regulate the abortion procedure in ways that are reasonably related to maternal health.

(c) For the stage subsequent to viability, the State in promoting its interest in the potentiality of human life may, if it chooses, regulate, and even proscribe, abortion except where it is necessary, in appropriate medical judgment, for the preservation of the life or health of the mother. . . .

This holding, we feel, is consistent with the relative weights of the respective interests involved, with the lessons and examples of medical and legal history, with the lenity of the common law, and with the demands of the profound problems of the present day. The decision leaves the State free to place increasing restrictions on abortion as the period of pregnancy lengthens, so long as those restrictions are tailored to the recognized state interests.

It is so ordered.

After the Court's 1973 decision in *Roe*, many federal and state governments sought to test the boundaries of the decision by passing laws regulating various aspects of abortion-related decisions and procedures. In many of these cases, the Court has been called upon to assess the constitutionality of these measures. In *Bigelow v. Virginia*,[15] the Court ruled that states could not bar newspapers from publishing abortion-related advertisements. In *Bellotti v. Baird* (1979),[16] the Court ruled that states could require minors to get parental permission before obtaining abortions as long as a judicial bypass procedure is available in cases where the minor does not want to seek or cannot obtain parental permission. In *Harris v. McRae* (1980),[17] the Court upheld the federal Hyde Amendment, which prevented Medicaid programs from funding certain types of abortions. In *Akron v. Akron Center for Reproductive Health* (1983),[18] the Court invalidated a number of city provisions that, among other things, required abortions sought after the first trimester to be performed in a hospital, imposed a twenty-four-hour delay between the patient's consent to an abortion and the actual procedure, and required fetal remains to be discarded in a "humane and dignified manner." In *Webster v. Reproductive Health Services* (1989),[19] the Court upheld a Missouri abortion law that, among other things, prohibited public employees or facilities from being used to perform abortions that were not necessary to protect the life of the woman and prohibited public monies from being spent to counsel women to have an abortion. And in *Rust v. Sullivan* (1991),[20] the Court upheld federal regulations barring organizations that receive federal monies under the Public Health Services Act from providing counseling regarding abortion. In each of these cases, to various degrees, the Court balanced the fundamental right to privacy, as it relates to abortion-related decisions and procedures, against the government's asserted interest in regulating medical procedures and protecting fetuses.

In 1992, the Court substantially altered its approach in abortion cases. In *Planned Parenthood of Southern Pennsylvania v. Casey* (1992)[21] (see later in this chapter), the court addressed five abortion-related regulations: (1) a requirement that physicians discuss the risks of an abortion with patients and obtain their written consent for the procedure; (2) a mandate that women wait twenty-four hours after giving their consent before they can obtain an abortion; (3) a requirement that unmarried minors get parental or judicial consent before an abortion; (4) a duty of physicians to notify public health authorities regarding abortions performed; and (5) a requirement that married women notify their spouses before obtaining an abortion. The court upheld all of these regulations except the spousal notification requirement.

In so doing, the Court made two fundamental changes to its abortion jurisprudence. First, the Court adopted an **"undue burden"** standard for abortion cases. Under this standard, the Court asks whether the challenged regulation imposes an undue burden on a woman's right to access or obtain an abortion. Second, the Court moved away from the trimester-based approach adopted in *Roe v. Wade* and began using framework that divided pregnancy into two stages—previability (the time when a fetus cannot survive outside the womb) and postviability (the time when external fetal survival is possible). The Court indicted that governments would have more substantial interests in regulating abortion procedures during the postviability stages.

undue burden
A legal standard used to review restrictions on abortion for their constitutionality. Under this standard, restrictions may not place an undue burden on a woman's right to choose an abortion.

Planned Parenthood v. Casey
505 U.S. 833 (1992)

Justice O'Connor, Justice Kennedy, and Justice Souter announced the judgment of the Court and delivered the opinion of the Court with respect to Parts I, II, III, V-A, V-C, and VI, an opinion with respect to Part V-E, in which Justice Stevens joins, and an opinion with respect to Parts IV, V-B, and V-D.

I.

Liberty finds no refuge in a jurisprudence of doubt. Yet, 19 years after our holding that the Constitution protects a woman's right to terminate her pregnancy in its early stages, *Roe v. Wade*, 410 U.S. 113 (1973), that definition of liberty is still questioned. Joining the respondents as *amicus curiae*, the United States, as it has done in five other cases in the last decade, again asks us to overrule *Roe*.

At issue in these cases are five provisions of the Pennsylvania Abortion Control Act of 1982, as amended in 1988 and 1989. . . . The Act requires that a woman seeking an abortion give her informed consent prior to the abortion procedure, and specifies that she be provided with certain information at least 24 hours before the abortion is performed. For a minor to obtain an abortion, the Act requires the informed consent of one of her parents, but provides for a judicial bypass option if the minor does not wish to or cannot obtain a parent's consent. Another provision of the Act requires that, unless certain exceptions apply, a married woman seeking an abortion must sign a statement indicating that she has notified her husband of her intended abortion. The Act exempts compliance with these three requirements in the event of a "medical emergency". . . .

After considering the fundamental constitutional questions resolved by *Roe*, principles of institutional integrity, and the rule of *stare decisis*, we are led to conclude this: the essential holding of *Roe v. Wade* should be retained and once again reaffirmed. . . .

II.

Constitutional protection of the woman's decision to terminate her pregnancy derives from the Due Process Clause of the Fourteenth Amendment. It declares that no State shall "deprive any person of life, liberty, or property, without due process of law." The controlling word in the cases before us is "liberty." . . .

The most familiar of the substantive liberties protected by the Fourteenth Amendment are those recognized by the Bill of Rights. We have held that the Due Process Clause of the Fourteenth Amendment incorporates most of the Bill of Rights against the States. . . .

Neither the Bill of Rights nor the specific practices of States at the time of the adoption of the Fourteenth Amendment marks the outer limits of the substantive sphere of liberty which the Fourteenth Amendment protects.

The inescapable fact is that adjudication of substantive due process claims may call upon the Court in interpreting the Constitution to exercise that same capacity which, by tradition, courts always have exercised: reasoned judgment. Its boundaries are not susceptible of expression as a simple rule. That does not mean we are free to invalidate state policy choices with which we disagree; yet neither does it permit us to shrink from the duties of our office. . . .

[T]he reservations any of us may have in reaffirming the central holding of *Roe* are outweighed by the explication of individual liberty we have given, combined with the force of *stare decisis*. We turn now to that doctrine.

III.

A.

[W]hen this Court reexamines a prior holding, its judgment is customarily informed by a series of prudential and pragmatic considerations designed to test the consistency of overruling a prior decision with the ideal of the rule of law, and to gauge the respective costs of reaffirming and overruling a prior case. . . .

Although *Roe* has engendered opposition, it has in no sense proven "unworkable," representing as it does a simple limitation beyond which a state law is unenforceable. While *Roe* has, of course, required judicial assessment of state laws affecting the exercise of the choice guaranteed against government infringement, and although the need for such review will remain as a consequence of today's decision, the required determinations fall within judicial competence. . . .

B.

In a less significant case, *stare decisis* analysis could, and would, stop at the point we have reached. But the sustained and widespread debate *Roe* has provoked calls for some comparison between that case and others of comparable dimension that have responded to national controversies and taken on the impress of the controversies addressed. Only two such decisional lines from the past century present themselves for examination, and in each instance the result reached by the Court accorded with the principles we apply today. . . .

Because neither the factual underpinnings of *Roe*'s central holding nor our understanding of it has changed (and because no other indication of weakened precedent has been shown), the Court could not pretend to be re-examining the prior law with any justification beyond a present doctrinal disposition to come out differently from the Court of 1973. To overrule prior law for no other reason than that would run counter to the view, repeated in our cases, that a decision to overrule should rest on some special reason over and above the belief that a prior case was wrongly decided.

C.

Our analysis would not be complete, however, without explaining why overruling *Roe*'s central holding would not only reach an unjustifiable result under principles of *stare decisis*, but would seriously weaken the Court's capacity to exercise the judicial power and to function as the Supreme Court of a Nation dedicated to the rule of law. . . .

A decision to overrule *Roe*'s essential holding under the existing circumstances would address error, if error there was, at the cost of both profound and unnecessary damage to the Court's legitimacy, and to the Nation's commitment to the rule of law. It is therefore imperative to adhere to the essence of *Roe*'s original decision, and we do so today.

IV.

We conclude that the basic decision in *Roe* was based on a constitutional analysis which we cannot now repudiate. The woman's liberty is not so unlimited, however, that,

from the outset, the State cannot show its concern for the life of the unborn and, at a later point in fetal development, the State's interest in life has sufficient force so that the right of the woman to terminate the pregnancy can be restricted.

That brings us, of course, to the point where much criticism has been directed at *Roe*, a criticism that always inheres when the Court draws a specific rule from what in the Constitution is but a general standard. We conclude, however, that the urgent claims of the woman to retain the ultimate control over her destiny and her body, claims implicit in the meaning of liberty, require us to perform that function. Liberty must not be extinguished for want of a line that is clear. And it falls to us to give some real substance to the woman's liberty to determine whether to carry her pregnancy to full term.

We conclude the line should be drawn at viability, so that, before that time, the woman has a right to choose to terminate her pregnancy. We adhere to this principle for two reasons. First, as we have said, is the doctrine of *stare decisis*. Any judicial act of line-drawing may seem somewhat arbitrary, but *Roe* was a reasoned statement, elaborated with great care. We have twice reaffirmed it in the face of great opposition. . . .

The second reason is that the concept of viability, as we noted in *Roe*, is the time at which there is a realistic possibility of maintaining and nourishing a life outside the womb, so that the independent existence of the second life can, in reason and all fairness, be the object of state protection that now overrides the rights of the woman. Consistent with other constitutional norms, legislatures may draw lines which appear arbitrary without the necessity of offering a justification. But courts may not. We must justify the lines we draw. And there is no line other than viability which is more workable. . . .

The woman's right to terminate her pregnancy before viability is the most central principle of *Roe v. Wade*. It is a rule of law and a component of liberty we cannot renounce. . . .

The trimester framework no doubt was erected to ensure that the woman's right to choose not become so subordinate to the State's interest in promoting fetal life that her choice exists in theory, but not in fact. We do not agree, however, that the trimester approach is necessary to accomplish this objective. A framework of this rigidity was unnecessary, and, in its later interpretation, sometimes contradicted the State's permissible exercise of its powers. . . .

We reject the trimester framework, which we do not consider to be part of the essential holding of *Roe* . . . A logical reading of the central holding in *Roe* itself, and a necessary reconciliation of the liberty of the woman and the interest of the State in promoting prenatal life, require, in our view, that we abandon the trimester framework as a rigid prohibition on all pre-viability regulation aimed at the protection of fetal life. . . .

The very notion that the State has a substantial interest in potential life leads to the conclusion that not all regulations must be deemed unwarranted. Not all burdens on the right to decide whether to terminate a pregnancy will be undue. In our view, the undue burden standard is the appropriate means of reconciling the State's interest with the woman's constitutionally protected liberty. . . .

Some guiding principles should emerge. What is at stake is the woman's right to make the ultimate decision, not a right to be insulated from all others in doing so. Regulations which do no more than create a structural mechanism by which the State, or the parent or guardian of a minor, may express profound respect for the life of the unborn are permitted, if they are not a substantial obstacle to the woman's exercise of the right to choose. Unless it has that effect on her right of choice, a state measure designed to persuade her to choose childbirth over abortion will be upheld if reasonably related to that goal. Regulations designed to foster the health of a woman seeking an abortion are valid if they do not constitute an undue burden. . . .

V.

A.

Because it is central to the operation of various other requirements, we begin with the statute's definition of medical emergency. Under the statute, a medical emergency is "[t]hat condition which, on the basis of the physician's good faith clinical judgment, so complicates the medical condition of a pregnant woman as to necessitate the immediate abortion of her pregnancy to avert her death or for which a delay will create serious risk of substantial and irreversible impairment of a major bodily function." . . .

[We] conclude that, as construed by the Court of Appeals, the medical emergency definition imposes no undue burden on a woman's abortion right. . . .

B.

Our prior decisions establish that, as with any medical procedure, the State may require a woman to give her written informed consent to an abortion. In this respect, the statute is unexceptional. Petitioners challenge the statute's definition of informed consent because it includes the provision of specific information by the doctor and the mandatory 24-hour waiting period. The conclusions reached by a majority of the Justices in the separate opinions filed today and the undue burden standard adopted in this opinion require us to overrule in part some of the Court's past decisions, decisions driven by the trimester framework's prohibition of all pre-viability regulations designed to further the State's interest in fetal life. . . .

C.

Section 3209 of Pennsylvania's abortion law provides, except in cases of medical emergency, that no physician shall perform an abortion on a married woman without receiving a signed statement from the woman that she has notified her spouse that she is about to undergo an abortion. . . .

[T]here are millions of women in this country who are the victims of regular physical and psychological abuse at the hands of their husbands. Should these women become pregnant, they may have very good reasons for not wishing to inform their husbands of their decision to obtain an abortion. . . .

The spousal notification requirement is thus likely to prevent a significant number of women from obtaining an abortion. It does not merely make abortions a little more difficult or expensive to obtain; for many women, it will impose a substantial obstacle. We must not blind ourselves to the fact that the significant number of women who fear for their safety and the safety of their children are likely to be deterred from procuring an abortion as surely as if the Commonwealth had outlawed abortion in all cases.

Section 3209 embodies a view of marriage consonant with the common law status of married women, but repugnant to our present understanding of marriage and of the nature of the rights secured by the Constitution. Women do not lose their constitutionally protected liberty when they marry. The Constitution protects all individuals, male or female, married or unmarried, from the abuse of governmental power, even where that power is employed for the supposed benefit of a member of the individual's family. These considerations confirm our conclusion that 3209 is invalid.

D.

We next consider the parental consent provision. Except in a medical emergency, an unemancipated young woman under 18 may not obtain an abortion unless she and one of her parents (or guardian) provides informed consent as defined above. If neither a parent nor a guardian provides consent, a court may authorize the performance of an abortion upon a determination that the young woman is mature and capable of giving informed consent and has, in fact, given her informed consent, or that an abortion would be in her best interests.

We have been over most of this ground before. Our cases establish, and we reaffirm today, that a State may require a minor seeking an abortion to obtain the consent of a parent or guardian, provided that there is an adequate judicial bypass procedure. Under these precedents, in our view, the one-parent consent requirement and judicial bypass procedure are constitutional. . . .

E.

Under the recordkeeping and reporting requirements of the statute, every facility which performs abortions is required to file a report stating its name and address as well as the name and address of any related entity, such as a controlling or subsidiary organization. In the case of state-funded institutions, the information becomes public.

[W]e [have] held that recordkeeping and reporting provisions that are reasonably directed to the preservation of maternal health and that properly respect a patient's confidentiality and privacy are permissible. We think that, under this standard, all the provisions at issue here except that relating to spousal notice are constitutional. Although they do not relate to the State's interest in informing the woman's choice, they do relate to health. The collection of information with respect to actual patients is a vital element of medical research, and so it cannot be said that the requirements serve no purpose other than to make abortions more difficult. Nor do we find that the requirements impose a substantial obstacle to a woman's choice. At most, they might increase the cost of some abortions by a slight amount. While at some point increased cost could become a substantial obstacle, there is no such showing on the record before us.

In recent years, much of the debate over abortion and the right to privacy has centered on a medical procedure sometimes referred to as partial-birth abortion. Some states and the federal government have sought to outlaw this particular medical procedure as a method for performing abortions. In so doing, some of these laws have failed to take into account the value this procedure might have in either saving the life of the pregnant woman or in preserving her health. Initially, such failure led the Court to conclude that these laws placed an "undue burden" on a woman's right to privacy.[22] However, in *Gonzales v. Carhart* (2007), the Court modified this policy by upholding the federal Partial-Birth Abortion Ban Act of 2003. Under this Act, Congress outlawed the so-called partial-birth abortions (properly known as intact dilation and evacuation procedures), but did not provide for an exception in cases where the health of the pregnant woman is in jeopardy. In a 5-4 ruling, the Court concluded the law's failure to include a health exception did not impose, at least based on the facial language of the statute, an undue burden on a woman's right to an abortion. The Court, however, noted that, if a case were presented where the medical science clearly demonstrated that the banned procedure was necessary to preserve a woman's health, the law's applied prohibition would be unconstitutional. But in *Carhart*, the Court found that such health risks were not clearly demonstrated.

Cyber Constitution
State Abortion Laws
http://www.guttmacher.
org/statecenter/spibs/
spib_OAL.pdf

Gonzales v. Carhart
550 U.S. 124 (2007)

Justice Kennedy delivered the opinion of the Court.

These cases require us to consider the validity of the Partial-Birth Abortion Ban Act of 2003 (Act), 18 U.S.C. §1531 (2000 ed., Supp. IV), a federal statute regulating abortion procedures. In recitations preceding its operative provisions the Act refers to the Court's opinion in *Stenberg v. Carhart*, 530 U.S. 914 (2000), which also addressed the subject of abortion procedures used in the later stages of pregnancy. Compared to the state statute at issue in *Stenberg*, the Act is more specific concerning the instances to which it applies and in this respect more precise in its coverage. We conclude the Act should be sustained against the objections lodged by the broad, facial attack brought against it. . . .

The Act proscribes a particular manner of ending fetal life, so it is necessary here, as it was in *Stenberg*, to discuss abortion procedures in some detail. . . .

Abortion methods vary depending to some extent on the preferences of the physician and, of course, on the term of the pregnancy and the resulting stage of the unborn child's development. Between 85 and 90 percent of the approximately 1.3 million abortions performed each year in the United States take place in the first three months of pregnancy, which is to say in the first trimester. The most common first-trimester abortion method is vacuum aspiration (otherwise known as suction curettage) in which the physician vacuums out the embryonic tissue. Early in this trimester an alternative is to use medication, such as mifepristone (commonly known as RU-486), to terminate the pregnancy. The Act does not regulate these procedures.

Of the remaining abortions that take place each year, most occur in the second trimester. The surgical procedure referred to as "dilation and evacuation" or "D&E" is the usual abortion method in this trimester. Although individual techniques for performing D&E differ, the general steps are the same. . . .

The abortion procedure that was the impetus for the numerous bans on "partial-birth abortion," including the

Act, is a variation of this standard D&E. The medical community has not reached unanimity on the appropriate name for this D&E variation. It has been referred to as "intact D&E," "dilation and extraction" (D&X), and "intact D&X." For discussion purposes this D&E variation will be referred to as intact D&E. The main difference between the two procedures is that in intact D&E a doctor extracts the fetus intact or largely intact with only a few passes. There are no comprehensive statistics indicating what percentage of all D&Es are performed in this manner. . . .

By the time of the *Stenberg* decision, about 30 States had enacted bans designed to prohibit the procedure. In 1996, Congress also acted to ban partial-birth abortion. President Clinton vetoed the congressional legislation, and the Senate failed to override the veto. Congress approved another bill banning the procedure in 1997, but President Clinton again vetoed it. In 2003, after this Court's decision in *Stenberg*, Congress passed the Act at issue here. On November 5, 2003, President Bush signed the Act into law. It was to take effect the following day.

The Act responded to *Stenberg* in two ways. First, Congress made factual findings. Congress determined that this Court in *Stenberg* "was required to accept the very questionable findings issued by the district court judge," but that Congress was "not bound to accept the same factual findings." Congress found, among other things, that "[a] moral, medical, and ethical consensus exists that the practice of performing a partial-birth abortion . . . is a gruesome and inhumane procedure that is never medically necessary and should be prohibited."

Second, and more relevant here, the Act's language differs from that of the Nebraska statute struck down in *Stenberg*. . . .

A defendant accused of an offense under this [law] may seek a "(d)(1) hearing before the State Medical Board on whether the physician's conduct was necessary to save the life of the mother whose life was endangered by a physical disorder, physical illness, or physical injury, including a life-endangering physical condition caused by or arising from the pregnancy itself." . . .

A woman upon whom a partial-birth abortion is performed may not be "(e) prosecuted under this section, for a conspiracy to violate this section, or for an offense under section 2, 3, or 4 of this title based on a violation of this section." . . .

We assume the following principles for the purposes of this opinion. Before viability, a State "may not prohibit any woman from making the ultimate decision to terminate her pregnancy." It also may not impose upon this right an undue burden, which exists if a regulation's "purpose or effect is to place a substantial obstacle in the path of a woman seeking an abortion before the fetus attains viability." On the other hand, "[r]egulations which do no more than create a structural mechanism by which the State, or the parent or guardian of a minor, may express profound respect for the life of the unborn are permitted, if they are not a substantial obstacle to the woman's exercise of the right to choose." . . .

We conclude that the Act is not void for vagueness, does not impose an undue burden from any overbreadth, and is not invalid on its face. . . .

Respondents contend the language described above is indeterminate, and they thus argue the Act is unconstitutionally vague on its face. "As generally stated, the void-for-vagueness doctrine requires that a penal statute define the criminal offense with sufficient definiteness that ordinary people can understand what conduct is prohibited and in a manner that does not encourage arbitrary and discriminatory enforcement." The Act satisfies both requirements. . . .

We next determine whether the Act imposes an undue burden, as a facial matter, because its restrictions on second-trimester abortions are too broad. A review of the statutory text discloses the limits of its reach. The Act prohibits intact D&E; and, notwithstanding respondents' arguments, it does not prohibit the D&E procedure in which the fetus is removed in parts.

The Act prohibits a doctor from intentionally performing an intact D&E. The dual prohibitions of the Act, both of which are necessary for criminal liability, correspond with the steps generally undertaken during this type of procedure. First, a doctor delivers the fetus until its head lodges in the cervix, which is usually past the anatomical landmark for a breech presentation. Second, the doctor proceeds to pierce the fetal skull with scissors or crush it with forceps. This step satisfies the overt-act requirement because it kills the fetus and is distinct from delivery. The Act's intent requirements, however, limit its reach to those physicians who carry out the intact D&E after intending to undertake both steps at the outset.

The Act excludes most D&Es in which the fetus is removed in pieces, not intact. If the doctor intends to remove the fetus in parts from the outset, the doctor will not have the requisite intent to incur criminal liability. . . .

Congress, it is apparent, responded to these concerns because the Act departs in material ways from the statute in *Stenberg*. It adopts the phrase "delivers a living fetus," instead of "delivering . . . a living unborn child, or a substantial portion thereof." The Act's language, unlike the statute in *Stenberg*, expresses the usual meaning of "deliver" when used in connection with "fetus," namely, extraction of an entire fetus rather than removal of fetal pieces. . . .

There can be no doubt the government "has an interest in protecting the integrity and ethics of the medical profession." Under our precedents it is clear the State has a significant role to play in regulating the medical profession. . . .

The Act's ban on abortions that involve partial delivery of a living fetus furthers the Government's objectives. No one would dispute that, for many, D&E is a procedure itself laden with the power to devalue human life. Congress could nonetheless conclude that the type of abortion proscribed by the Act requires specific regulation because it implicates additional ethical and moral concerns that justify a special prohibition. Congress determined that the abortion methods it proscribed had a "disturbing similarity to the killing of a newborn infant," and thus it was concerned with "draw[ing] a bright line that clearly distinguishes abortion and infanticide." The Court has in the past confirmed the validity of drawing boundaries to prevent certain practices that extinguish life and are close to actions that are condemned. . . .

Respect for human life finds an ultimate expression in the bond of love the mother has for her child. The Act recognizes this reality as well. Whether to have an abortion requires a difficult and painful moral decision. While we find no reliable data to measure the phenomenon, it seems unexceptionable to conclude some women come to regret their choice to abort the infant life they once created and sustained. Severe depression and loss of esteem can follow. . . .

In a decision so fraught with emotional consequence some doctors may prefer not to disclose precise details of the means that will be used, confining themselves to the required statement of risks the procedure entails. From one standpoint this ought not to be surprising. Any number of patients facing imminent surgical procedures would prefer not to hear all details, lest the usual anxiety preceding invasive medical procedures become the more intense. This is likely the case with the abortion procedures here in issue.

It is, however, precisely this lack of information concerning the way in which the fetus will be killed that is of legitimate concern to the State. The State has an interest in ensuring so grave a choice is well informed. It is self-evident that a mother who comes to regret her choice to abort must struggle with grief more anguished and sorrow more profound when she learns, only after the event, what she once did not know: that she allowed a doctor to pierce the skull and vacuum the fast-developing brain of her unborn child, a child assuming the human form. . . .

In sum, we reject the contention that the congressional purpose of the Act was "to place a substantial obstacle in the path of a woman seeking an abortion."

The Act's furtherance of legitimate government interests bears upon, but does not resolve, the next question: whether the Act has the effect of imposing an unconstitutional burden on the abortion right because it does not allow use of the barred procedure where "'necessary, in appropriate medical judgment, for [the] preservation of the . . . health of the mother.'" The prohibition in the Act would be unconstitutional, under precedents we here assume to be controlling, if it "subject[ed] [women] to significant health risks." . . .

There is documented medical disagreement whether the Act's prohibition would ever impose significant health risks on women. . . .

The question becomes whether the Act can stand when this medical uncertainty persists. The Court's precedents instruct that the Act can survive this facial attack. The Court has given state and federal legislatures wide discretion to pass legislation in areas where there is medical and scientific uncertainty. . . .

Medical uncertainty does not foreclose the exercise of legislative power in the abortion context any more than it does in other contexts. The medical uncertainty over whether the Act's prohibition creates significant health risks provides a sufficient basis to conclude in this facial attack that the Act does not impose an undue burden. . . .

A zero tolerance policy would strike down legitimate abortion regulations, like the present one, if some part of the medical community were disinclined to follow the proscription. This is too exacting a standard to impose on the legislative power, exercised in this instance under the Commerce Clause, to regulate the medical profession. Considerations of marginal safety, including the balance of risks, are within the legislative competence when the regulation is rational and in pursuit of legitimate ends. . . . The Act is not invalid on its face where there is uncertainty over whether the barred procedure is ever necessary to preserve a woman's health, given the availability of other abortion procedures that are considered to be safe alternatives. . . .

Respondents have not demonstrated that the Act, as a facial matter, is void for vagueness, or that it imposes an undue burden on a woman's right to abortion based on its overbreadth or lack of a health exception. . . .

It is so ordered.

Justice Thomas, with whom *Justice Scalia* joins, concurring.

I join the Court's opinion because it accurately applies current jurisprudence, including *Planned Parenthood of Southeastern Pa. v. Casey*, 505 U.S. 833 (1992). I write separately to reiterate my view that the Court's abortion jurisprudence, including *Casey* and *Roe v. Wade*, 410 U. S. 113 (1973), has no basis in the Constitution. . . .

Justice Ginsburg, with whom *Justice Stevens, Justice Souter,* and *Justice Breyer* join, dissenting.

Today's decision is alarming. It refuses to take *Casey* and *Stenberg* seriously. It tolerates, indeed applauds, federal intervention to ban nationwide a procedure found necessary and proper in certain cases by the American College of Obstetricians and Gynecologists (ACOG). It blurs the line, firmly drawn in *Casey*, between previability and postviability abortions. And, for the first time since *Roe*, the Court blesses a prohibition with no exception safeguarding a woman's health. . . .

Ultimately, the Court admits that "moral concerns" are at work, concerns that could yield prohibitions on any abortion. Notably, the concerns expressed are untethered to any ground genuinely serving the Government's interest in preserving life. By allowing such concerns to carry the day and case, overriding fundamental rights, the Court dishonors our precedent. . . .

11.4 THE RIGHT TO DIE

In the ongoing quest to determine what other activities are included in the right to privacy and what other forms of "liberty" are protected by the Constitution's Due Process Clauses, some have asserted that a "right to die" should be among them. To various degrees, individuals have asserted that one of the most private and personal decisions people can make is the manner and time of their death. Consistent with arguments made in other privacy and substantive due process cases, litigants have argued that, as the "owners" of their bodies, they should have a fundamental right to determine when and how they die.

living wills
A legal document in which a person provides instructions for medical treatment (or the lack thereof) in cases where the person becomes incapacitated.

The Court has acknowledged that constitutional privacy and other liberty interests allow individuals to refuse medical treatment. As Justice O'Connor observed, "the liberty guaranteed by the Due Process Clause must protect, if it protects anything, an individual's deeply personal decision to reject medical treatment, including the artificial delivery of food and water."[23] The Court has also recognized the value of **living wills,** which are legal documents in which a person provides instructions for medical treatment (or the lack thereof) in cases where the person becomes incapacitated. The Court has suggested that such instructions by the individual must be honored by government.[24] Thus, to the extent that the so-called right to die includes a right to refuse medical treatment or the right to direct the type of medical treatment a person receives, the Court has recognized a limited right for a person to die.

But the Supreme Court has not recognized the right to die as a fundamental right of privacy or liberty interest under the U.S. Constitution. In fact, Justice Scalia has asserted, "the Constitution has nothing to say about it."[25] To date, the Court has failed to recognize the right to die as a constitutional right. Instead, the Court has acknowledged that although the states on their own initiative may allow for such procedures as physician-assisted suicide, they are under no constitutional obligation to do so. In other words, the Court has stopped short of recognizing the right to privacy or the substantive right to due process as independent sources for an affirmative right to die under the Constitution.

Given the Court's general deference to the states in matters affecting death, much of the debate over the right to die has arisen out of state initiatives. For example, some states have banned physician-assisted suicide, while others have allowed for such a procedure. In *Washington v. Glucksberg* (1997) (see later in this chapter), the Court unanimously rejected an argument that the Fourteenth Amendment protected a liberty interest to commit physician-assisted suicide. In so doing, the Court upheld a state law expressly banning this form of suicide. But in *Gonzales v. Oregon* (2005) (see later in this chapter), the Court confronted an Oregon law that expressly allowed for physician-assisted suicide in some circumstances. While the underlying validity of the law itself was not challenged, the U.S. Attorney General declared that using controlled substances to assist suicide was not a legitimate medical practice and that dispensing or prescribing them for this purpose was unlawful under the federal Controlled Substances Act. The state of Oregon and others challenged the Attorney General's actions. And in a 6-3 ruling, the Court ruled against the Attorney General, concluding that he could not used the Controlled Substances Act to prohibit doctors from prescribing regulated drugs for use in physician-assisted suicide under state law permitting the procedure. As you read the *Glucksberg* and *Oregon* opinions, notice the deference given by the Court to the judgment of the state legislatures in each case.

Cyber Constitution
Right to Die Legal History www.euthanasia.cc/cases.html

Washington v. Glucksberg
521 U.S. 702 (1997)

Chief Justice Rehnquist delivered the opinion of the Court.

The question presented in this case is whether Washington's prohibition against "caus[ing]" or "aid[ing]" a suicide offends the Fourteenth Amendment to the United States Constitution. We hold that it does not. . . .

The plaintiffs asserted "the existence of a liberty interest protected by the Fourteenth Amendment which extends to a personal choice by a mentally competent, terminally ill adult to commit physician assisted suicide." Relying primarily on *Planned Parenthood v. Casey*, 505 U.S. 833 (1992), and *Cruzan v. Director, Missouri Dept. of Health*, 497 U.S. 261 (1990), the District Court agreed, and concluded that Washington's assisted suicide ban is unconstitutional because it "places an undue burden on the exercise of [that] constitutionally protected liberty interest." The District Court also decided that the Washington statute violated the Equal Protection Clause's requirement that "all persons similarly situated . . . be treated alike."

A panel of the Court of Appeals for the Ninth Circuit reversed, emphasizing that "[i]n the two hundred and five years of our existence no constitutional right to aid in killing oneself has ever been asserted and upheld by a court of final jurisdiction." The Ninth Circuit reheard the case en banc, reversed the panel's decision, and affirmed the District Court. . . .

We begin, as we do in all due process cases, by examining our Nation's history, legal traditions, and practices. In almost every State—indeed, in almost every western democracy—it is a crime to assist a suicide. The States' assisted suicide bans are not innovations. Rather, they are longstanding expressions of the States' commitment to the protection and preservation of all human life. Indeed, opposition to and condemnation of suicide—and, therefore, of assisting suicide—are consistent and enduring themes of our philosophical, legal, and cultural heritages. . . .

Against this backdrop of history, tradition, and practice, we now turn to respondents' constitutional claim.

The Due Process Clause guarantees more than fair process, and the "liberty" it protects includes more than the absence of physical restraint. The Clause also provides heightened protection against government interference with certain fundamental rights and liberty interests. . . .

But we "ha[ve] always been reluctant to expand the concept of substantive due process because guideposts for responsible decisionmaking in this unchartered area are scarce and open ended." By extending constitutional protection to an asserted right or liberty interest, we, to a great extent, place the matter outside the arena of public debate and legislative action. We must therefore "exercise the utmost care whenever we are asked to break new ground in this field," lest the liberty protected by the Due Process Clause be subtly transformed into the policy preferences of the members of this Court.

Our established method of substantive due process analysis has two primary features: First, we have regularly observed that the Due Process Clause specially protects those fundamental rights and liberties which are, objectively, "deeply rooted in this Nation's history and tradition," and "implicit in the concept of ordered liberty," such that "neither liberty nor justice would exist if they were sacrificed." Second, we have required in substantive due process cases a "careful description" of the asserted fundamental liberty interest. . . .

We now inquire whether this asserted right has any place in our Nation's traditions. Here, as discussed above, we are confronted with a consistent and almost universal tradition that has long rejected the asserted right, and continues explicitly to reject it today, even for terminally ill, mentally competent adults. To hold for respondents, we would have to reverse centuries of legal doctrine and practice, and strike down the considered policy choice of almost every State. . . .

The history of the law's treatment of assisted suicide in this country has been and continues to be one of the rejection of nearly all efforts to permit it. That being the case, our decisions lead us to conclude that the asserted "right" to assistance in committing suicide is not a fundamental liberty interest protected by the Due Process Clause. The Constitution also requires, however, that Washington's assisted suicide ban be rationally related to legitimate government interests. This requirement is unquestionably met here. As the court below recognized, Washington's assisted suicide ban implicates a number of state interests.

First, Washington has an "unqualified interest in the preservation of human life." The State's prohibition on assisted suicide, like all homicide laws, both reflects and advances its commitment to this interest. . . .

The State also has an interest in protecting the integrity and ethics of the medical profession. An contrast to the Court of Appeals' conclusion that "the integrity of the medical profession would [not] be threatened in any way by [physician assisted suicide]," the American Medical Association, like many other medical and physicians' groups, has concluded that "[p]hysician assisted suicide is fundamentally incompatible with the physician's role as healer." And physician assisted suicide could, it is argued, undermine the trust that is essential to the doctor patient relationship by blurring the time honored line between healing and harming.

Next, the State has an interest in protecting vulnerable groups—including the poor, the elderly, and disabled persons—from abuse, neglect, and mistakes. The Court of Appeals dismissed the State's concern that disadvantaged persons might be pressured into physician assisted suicide as "ludicrous on its face." We have recognized, however, the real risk of subtle coercion and undue influence in end of life situations. Similarly, the New York Task Force warned that "[l]egalizing physician assisted suicide would pose profound risks to many individuals who are ill and vulnerable. . . . The risk of harm is greatest for the many individuals in our society whose autonomy and well being are already compromised by poverty, lack of access to good medical care, advanced age, or membership in a stigmatized social group." If physician assisted suicide were permitted, many might resort to it to spare their families the substantial financial burden of end of life health care costs.

The State's interest here goes beyond protecting the vulnerable from coercion; it extends to protecting disabled and terminally ill people from prejudice, negative and inaccurate stereotypes, and "societal indifference." The State's assisted suicide ban reflects and reinforces its policy that the lives of terminally ill, disabled, and elderly people must be no less valued than the lives of the young and healthy, and that a seriously disabled person's suicidal impulses should be interpreted and treated the same way as anyone else's.

Finally, the State may fear that permitting assisted suicide will start it down the path to voluntary and perhaps even involuntary euthanasia. The Court of Appeals . . . noted, for example, that the "decision of a duly appointed surrogate decision maker is for all legal purposes the decision of the patient himself," that "in some instances, the patient may be unable to self administer the drugs and . . . administration by the physician . . . may be the only way the patient may be able to receive them," and that not only physicians, but also family members and loved ones, will inevitably participate in assisting suicide. Thus, it turns out that what is couched as a limited right to "physician assisted suicide" is likely, in effect, a much broader license, which could prove extremely difficult to police and contain. Washington's ban on assisting suicide prevents such erosion. . . .

We need not weigh exactly the relative strengths of these various interests. They are unquestionably important and legitimate, and Washington's ban on assisted suicide is at least reasonably related to their promotion and protection. We therefore hold that [the law] does not violate the Fourteenth Amendment, either on its face or "as applied to competent, terminally ill adults who wish to hasten their deaths by obtaining medication prescribed by their doctors." . . .

It is so ordered.

Justice O'Connor, concurring.

Death will be different for each of us. For many, the last days will be spent in physical pain and perhaps the despair that accompanies physical deterioration and a loss of control of basic bodily and mental functions. Some will seek medication to alleviate that pain and other symptoms.

The Court frames the issue in this case as whether the Due Process Clause of the Constitution protects a "right to commit suicide which itself includes a right to assistance in doing so," and concludes that our Nation's history, legal traditions, and practices do not support the existence of such a right. I join the Court's opinions because I agree that there is no generalized right to "commit suicide." But respondents urge us to address the narrower question whether a mentally competent person who is experiencing great suffering has a constitutionally cognizable interest in controlling the circumstances of his or her imminent death. I see no need to reach that question in the context of the facial challenges to the New York and Washington laws at issue here. . . .

Justice Stevens, concurring in the judgments.

The Court ends its opinion with the important observation that our holding today is fully consistent with a continuation of the vigorous debate about the "morality, legality, and practicality of physician assisted suicide" in a democratic society. I write separately to make it clear that there is also room for further debate about the limits that the Constitution places on the power of the States to punish the practice. . . .

Justice Souter, concurring in the judgment.

Protesters wave homemade signs to show their feelings over the Terri Schiavo affair—a legal battle in Florida between 1998–2005 regarding whether life-support treatments for Schiavo, who was in a medically vegetative state, could be stopped at the request of Shiavo's husband. Ultimately, the courts allowed Schiavo's husband to terminate the treatments, resulting in Schiavo's death in March 2005.

© PhotoStockFile/Alamy

Gonzales v. Oregon
546 U.S. 243 (2006)

Justice Kennedy delivered the opinion of the Court.

The question before us is whether the Controlled Substances Act allows the United States Attorney General to prohibit doctors from prescribing regulated drugs for use in physician-assisted suicide, notwithstanding a state law permitting the procedure. As the Court has observed, "Americans are engaged in an earnest and profound debate about the morality, legality, and practicality of physician-assisted suicide." The dispute before us is in part a product of this political and moral debate, but its resolution requires an inquiry familiar to the courts: interpreting a federal statute to determine whether Executive action is authorized by, or otherwise consistent with, the enactment.

In 1994, Oregon became the first State to legalize assisted suicide when voters approved a ballot measure enacting the Oregon Death With Dignity Act (ODWDA). ODWDA, which survived a 1997 ballot measure seeking its repeal, exempts from civil or criminal liability state-licensed physicians who, in compliance with the specific safeguards in ODWDA, dispense or prescribe a lethal dose of drugs upon the request of a terminally ill patient.

The drugs Oregon physicians prescribe under ODWDA are regulated under a federal statute, the Controlled Substances Act (CSA or Act). The CSA allows these particular drugs to be available only by a written prescription from a registered physician. In the ordinary course the same drugs are prescribed in smaller doses for pain alleviation.

A November 9, 2001 Interpretive Rule issued by the Attorney General addresses the implementation and enforcement of the CSA with respect to ODWDA. It determines that using controlled substances to assist suicide is not a legitimate medical practice and that dispensing or prescribing them for this purpose is unlawful under the CSA. The Interpretive Rule's validity under the CSA is the issue before us.

We turn first to the text and structure of the CSA. Enacted in 1970 with the main objectives of combating drug abuse and controlling the legitimate and illegitimate traffic in controlled substances, the CSA creates a comprehensive, closed regulatory regime criminalizing the unauthorized manufacture, distribution, dispensing, and possession of substances classified in any of the Act's five schedules. The Act places substances in one of five schedules based on their potential for abuse or dependence, their accepted medical use, and their accepted safety for use under medical supervision. Schedule I contains the most severe restrictions on access and use, and Schedule V the least. Congress classified a host of substances when it enacted the CSA, but the statute permits the Attorney General to add, remove, or reschedule substances. He may do so, however, only after making particular findings, and on scientific and medical mat-

ters he is required to accept the findings of the Secretary of Health and Human Services (Secretary). These proceedings must be on the record after an opportunity for comment.

The present dispute involves controlled substances listed in Schedule II, substances generally available only pursuant to a written, nonrefillable prescription by a physician. A 1971 regulation promulgated by the Attorney General requires that every prescription for a controlled substance "be issued for a legitimate medical purpose by an individual practitioner acting in the usual course of his professional practice."

To prevent diversion of controlled substances with medical uses, the CSA regulates the activity of physicians. To issue lawful prescriptions of Schedule II drugs, physicians must "obtain from the Attorney General a registration issued in accordance with the rules and regulations promulgated by him." The Attorney General may deny, suspend, or revoke this registration if, as relevant here, the physician's registration would be "inconsistent with the public interest." . . .

On November 9, 2001, without consulting Oregon or apparently anyone outside his Department, the [U.S.] Attorney General issued an Interpretive Rule announcing his intent to restrict the use of controlled substances for physician-assisted suicide. Incorporating the legal analysis of a memorandum he had solicited from his Office of Legal Counsel, the Attorney General ruled "assisting suicide is not a 'legitimate medical purpose' . . . and that prescribing, dispensing, or administering federally controlled substances to assist suicide violates the Controlled Substances Act. Such conduct by a physician registered to dispense controlled substances may 'render his registration . . . inconsistent with the public interest' and therefore subject to possible suspension or revocation. . . . The Attorney General's conclusion applies regardless of whether state law authorizes or permits such conduct by practitioners or others and regardless of the condition of the person whose suicide is assisted."

There is little dispute that the Interpretive Rule would substantially disrupt the ODWDA regime. Respondents contend, and petitioners do not dispute, that every prescription filled under ODWDA has specified drugs classified under Schedule II. A physician cannot prescribe the substances without DEA registration, and revocation or suspension of the registration would be a severe restriction on medical practice. Dispensing controlled substances without a valid prescription, furthermore, is a federal crime. . . .

In deciding whether the CSA can be read as prohibiting physician-assisted suicide, we look to the statute's text and design. The statute and our case law amply support the conclusion that Congress regulates medical practice insofar as it bars doctors from using their prescription-writing powers as a means to engage in illicit drug dealing and trafficking as conventionally understood. Beyond this, however, the statute manifests no intent to regulate the practice of medicine generally. The silence is understandable given the structure and limitations of federalism, which allow the States "great latitude under their police powers to legislate as to the protection of the lives, limbs, health, comfort, and quiet of all persons." . . .

Even though regulation of health and safety is "primarily, and historically, a matter of local concern," there is no question that the Federal Government can set uniform national standards in these areas. In connection to the CSA, however, we find only one area in which Congress set general, uniform standards of medical practice. Title I of the Comprehensive Drug Abuse Prevention and Control Act of 1970, of which the CSA was Title II, provides that "[The Secretary], after consultation with the Attorney General and with national organizations representative of persons with knowledge and experience in the treatment of narcotic addicts, shall determine the appropriate methods of professional practice in the medical treatment of the narcotic addiction of various classes of narcotic addicts, and shall report thereon from time to time to the Congress."

This provision strengthens the understanding of the CSA as a statute combating recreational drug abuse, and also indicates that when Congress wants to regulate medical practice in the given scheme, it does so by explicit language in the statute.

In the face of the CSA's silence on the practice of medicine generally and its recognition of state regulation of the medical profession it is difficult to defend the Attorney General's declaration that the statute impliedly criminalizes physician-assisted suicide. This difficulty is compounded by the CSA's consistent delegation of medical judgments to the Secretary and its otherwise careful allocation of powers for enforcing the limited objects of the CSA. The Government's attempt to meet this challenge rests, for the most part, on the CSA's

requirement that every Schedule II drug be dispensed pursuant to a "written prescription of a practitioner." A prescription, the Government argues, necessarily implies that the substance is being made available to a patient for a legitimate medical purpose. The statute, in this view, requires an anterior judgment about the term "medical" or "medicine." The Government contends ordinary usage of these words ineluctably refers to a healing or curative art, which by these terms cannot embrace the intentional hastening of a patient's death. It also points to the teachings of Hippocrates, the positions of prominent medical organizations, the Federal Government, and the judgment of the 49 States that have not legalized physician-assisted suicide as further support for the proposition that the practice is not legitimate medicine.

On its own, this understanding of medicine's boundaries is at least reasonable. The primary problem with the Government's argument, however, is its assumption that the CSA impliedly authorizes an Executive officer to bar a use simply because it may be inconsistent with one reasonable understanding of medical practice. Viewed alone, the prescription requirement may support such an understanding, but statutes "should not be read as a series of unrelated and isolated provisions." The CSA's substantive provisions and their arrangement undermine this assertion of an expansive federal authority to regulate medicine. . . .

The Government, in the end, maintains that the prescription requirement delegates to a single Executive officer the power to effect a radical shift of authority from the States to the Federal Government to define general standards of medical practice in every locality. The text and structure of the CSA show that Congress did not have this far-reaching intent to alter the federal-state balance and the congressional role in maintaining it.

The judgment of the Court of Appeals is Affirmed.

Justice Scalia, with whom Chief Justice Roberts and Justice Thomas join, dissenting.

Justice Thomas, dissenting.

11.5 LIBERTY AND HUMAN SEXUALITY

Cyber Constitution
The Terry Schiavo Case http://articles.cnn.com/2005-03-25/justice/schiavo.qa_1_michael-schiavo-robert-schindler-schiavo-case?_s=PM:LAW

For many individuals, one of the most private and intimate aspects of their lives is their sexuality. Decisions about whether to engage in sexual conduct, with whom to engage in such conduct, and the type of conduct in which to engage involve deeply personal considerations. On the other hand, government has often asserted an interest in regulating certain forms of sexual activity. At various times in history, governments have sought to ban the use of birth control,[26] criminalize adultery, stop mentally retarded persons from having sex,[27] force "habitual criminals" to be sterilized,[28] and preclude sexual activity between persons of the same sex.[29] In some cases, government has claimed that its laws are necessary to protect the health of the persons engaging in sexual activity, the safety of the public, or the well-being of the offspring that may be born out of such activity. In other cases, government has asserted less-tangible justifications, such as the promotion or maintenance of morality or ethics in the community.

Regardless of the asserted governmental interest, the analysis of constitutional controversies over the government's regulation of human sexuality is the same. The individual's interest in making personal decisions regarding sexuality is weighed against the government's interest in regulating such activity. For the most part, the Supreme Court has treated matters involving family relations and consensual sexual activity as fundamental liberty interests under the Due Process Clause. As a result, the Court, with some notable exceptions, has required government to demonstrate that its regulation of private and consensual sexual activity meets the strict scrutiny standard of constitutional review. That is, it must be shown to be necessary (or narrowly tailored) to promote a compelling governmental interest.

In recent years, much of the controversy over governmental interference with human sexuality has centered on the regulation of homosexuality. In 1986, the Supreme Court upheld a Georgia antisodomy law that was challenged as interfering with the liberty interest of homosexuals. In *Bowers v. Hardwick*, the Court in a 5-4 decision ruled that there was no constitutional right to engage in homosexual activity. Rather than approach the case from the traditional strict scrutiny framework, a majority of the Court first questioned whether there was even a protected liberty interest to be weighed against the government's interest. And for five justices, there simply was not.

Seventeen years later, however, the Court reversed its *Bowers* decision. In *Lawrence v. Texas* (2003) (see later in this chapter), the Court ruled in a 6-3 decision that a Texas law outlawing homosexual sodomy but permitting heterosexual sodomy deprived individuals of a liberty interest protected by the Fourteenth Amendment Due Process Clause. The Court further ruled that Texas had not demonstrated a sufficiently compelling interest to outweigh the liberty interest of individuals.

Read the Court's opinion in *Lawrence*. What accounts for the Court's reversal of *Bowers*? Is it the fact that six justices from the *Bowers* case had been replaced? Or do you find that more constitutional or evidence-based factors explain the Court's reversal?

Cyber Constitution
The Future of Sexual Liberties www. guttmacher.org/pubs/ tgr/06/4/gr060404.html

Lawrence v. Texas
539 U.S. 558 (2003)

Justice Kennedy delivered the opinion of the Court.

The question before the Court is the validity of a Texas statute making it a crime for two persons of the same sex to engage in certain intimate sexual conduct.

In Houston, Texas, officers of the Harris County Police Department were dispatched to a private residence in response to a reported weapons disturbance. They entered an apartment where one of the petitioners, John Geddes Lawrence, resided. The right of the police to enter does not seem to have been questioned. The officers observed Lawrence and another man, Tyron Garner, engaging in a sexual act. The two petitioners were arrested, held in custody over night, and charged and convicted before a Justice of the Peace.

The complaints described their crime as "deviate sexual intercourse, namely anal sex, with a member of the same sex (man)." The applicable state law is Tex. Penal Code Ann. §21.06(a) (2003). It provides: "A person commits an offense if he engages in deviate sexual intercourse with another individual of the same sex." . . .

The petitioners were adults at the time of the alleged offense. Their conduct was in private and consensual.

We conclude the case should be resolved by determining whether the petitioners were free as adults to engage in the private conduct in the exercise of their liberty under the Due Process Clause of the Fourteenth Amendment to the Constitution. For this inquiry we deem it necessary to reconsider the Court's holding in *Bowers* [*v. Hardwick*, 478 U.S. 186 (1986)]. . . .

The facts in *Bowers* had some similarities to the instant case. A police officer, whose right to enter seems not to have been in question, observed Hardwick, in his own bedroom, engaging in intimate sexual conduct with another adult male. The conduct was in violation of a Georgia statute making it a criminal offense to engage in sodomy . . . The Court, in an opinion by Justice White, sustained the Georgia law. . . .

The Court began its substantive discussion in *Bowers* as follows: "The issue presented is whether the Federal Constitution confers a fundamental right upon homosexuals to engage in sodomy and hence invalidates the laws of the many States that still make such conduct illegal and have done so for a very long time." That statement, we now conclude, discloses the Court's own failure to appreciate the extent of the liberty at stake. To say that the issue in *Bowers* was simply the right to engage in certain sexual conduct demeans the claim the individual put forward, just as it would demean a married couple were it to be said marriage is simply about the right to have sexual intercourse. The laws involved in *Bowers* and here are, to be sure, statutes that purport to do no more than prohibit a particular sexual act. Their penalties and purposes, though, have more far-reaching consequences, touching upon the most private human conduct, sexual behavior, and in the most private of places, the home. The statutes do seek to control a personal relationship that, whether or not entitled to formal recognition in the law, is within the liberty of persons to choose without being punished as criminals.

At the outset it should be noted that there is no longstanding history in this country of laws directed at homosexual conduct as a distinct matter. Beginning in colonial times there were prohibitions of sodomy derived from the English criminal laws passed in the first instance by the Reformation Parliament of 1533. The English prohibition was understood to include relations between men and women as well as relations between men and men. Nineteenth-century commentators similarly read American sodomy, buggery, and crime-against-nature statutes as criminalizing certain relations between men and women and between men and men. The absence of legal prohibitions focusing on homosexual conduct may be explained in part by noting that according to some scholars the concept of the homosexual as a distinct category of person did not emerge until the late 19th century. Thus early American sodomy laws were not directed at homosexuals as such but instead sought to prohibit nonprocreative sexual activity more generally. This does not suggest approval of homosexual conduct. It does tend to show that this particular form of conduct was not thought of as a separate category from like conduct between heterosexual persons.

Laws prohibiting sodomy do not seem to have been enforced against consenting adults acting in private. A substantial number of sodomy prosecutions and convictions for which there are surviving records were for predatory acts against those who could not or did not consent, as in the case of a minor or the victim of an assault. . . .

It was not until the 1970's that any State singled out same-sex relations for criminal prosecution, and only nine States have done so. Post-*Bowers* even some of these States did not adhere to the policy of suppressing homosexual conduct. Over the course of the last decades, States with same-sex prohibitions have moved toward abolishing them.

In summary, the historical grounds relied upon in *Bowers* are more complex than the majority opinion and the concurring opinion by Chief Justice Burger indicate. Their historical premises are not without doubt and, at the very least, are overstated. . . .

In all events we think that our laws and traditions in the past half century are of most relevance here. These references show an emerging awareness that liberty gives substantial protection to adult persons in deciding how to conduct their private lives in matters pertaining to sex. "[H]istory and tradition are the starting point but not in all cases the ending point of the substantive due process inquiry." . . .

In our own constitutional system the deficiencies in *Bowers* became even more apparent in the years following its announcement. The 25 States with laws prohibiting the relevant conduct referenced in the *Bowers* decision are reduced now to 13, of which 4 enforce their laws only against homosexual conduct. In those States where sodomy is still proscribed, whether for same-sex or heterosexual conduct, there is a pattern of nonenforcement with respect to consenting adults acting in private. The State of Texas admitted in 1994 that as of that date it had not prosecuted anyone under those circumstances.

Two principal cases decided after *Bowers* cast its holding into even more doubt. In *Planned Parenthood of Southeastern Pa. v. Casey*, 505 U.S. 833 (1992), the Court reaffirmed the substantive force of the liberty protected by the Due Process Clause. The Casey decision again confirmed that our laws and tradition afford constitutional protection to personal decisions relating to marriage, procreation, contraception, family relationships, child rearing, and education. . . .

Persons in a homosexual relationship may seek autonomy for these purposes, just as heterosexual persons do. The decision in *Bowers* would deny them this right.

The second post-*Bowers* case of principal relevance is *Romer v. Evans*, 517 U.S. 620 (1996). There the Court struck down class-based legislation directed at homosexuals as a violation of the Equal Protection Clause. *Romer* invalidated an amendment to Colorado's constitution which named as a solitary class persons who were homosexuals, lesbians, or bisexual either by "orientation, conduct, practices or relationships," *id.*, at 624 (internal quotation marks omitted), and deprived them of protection under state antidiscrimination laws. We concluded that the provision was "born of animosity toward the class of persons affected" and further that it had no rational relation to a legitimate governmental purpose. . . . The central holding of *Bowers* has been brought in question by this case, and it should be addressed. Its continuance as precedent demeans the lives of homosexual persons. . . .

The foundations of *Bowers* have sustained serious erosion from our recent decisions in *Casey* and *Romer*. When our precedent has been thus weakened, criticism from other sources is of greater significance. In the United States criticism of *Bowers* has been substantial and continuing, disapproving of its reasoning in all respects, not just as to its historical assumptions. The courts of five different States have declined to follow it in interpreting provisions in their own state constitutions parallel to the Due Process Clause of the Fourteenth Amendment.

To the extent *Bowers* relied on values we share with a wider civilization, it should be noted that the reasoning and holding in Bowers have been rejected elsewhere. The European Court of Human Rights has followed not *Bowers* but its own decision in *Dudgeon v. United Kingdom*. Other nations, too, have taken action consistent with an affirmation of the protected right of homosexual adults to engage in intimate, consensual conduct. The right the petitioners seek in this case has been accepted as an integral part of human freedom in many other countries. There has been no showing that in this country the governmental interest in circumscribing personal choice is somehow more legitimate or urgent.

The doctrine of *stare decisis* is essential to the respect accorded to the judgments of the Court and to the stability of the law. It is not, however, an inexorable command. *Payne v. Tennessee*, 501 U.S. 808, 828 (1991). In *Casey* we noted that when a Court is asked to overrule a precedent recognizing a constitutional liberty interest, individual or societal reliance on the existence of that liberty cautions with particular strength against reversing course. The holding in *Bowers*, however, has not induced detrimental reliance comparable to some instances where recognized individual rights are involved. Indeed, there has been no individual or societal reliance on *Bowers* of the sort that could counsel against overturning its holding once there are compelling reasons to do so. *Bowers* itself causes uncertainty, for the precedents before and after its issuance contradict its central holding.

The rationale of *Bowers* does not withstand careful analysis. In his dissenting opinion in *Bowers* Justice Stevens came to these conclusions:

> Our prior cases make two propositions abundantly clear. First, the fact that the governing majority in a State has traditionally viewed a particular practice as immoral is not a sufficient reason for upholding a law prohibiting the practice; neither history nor tradition could save a law prohibiting miscegenation from constitutional attack. Second, individual decisions by married persons, concerning the intimacies of their physical relationship, even when not intended to produce offspring, are a form of "liberty" protected by the Due Process Clause of the Fourteenth Amendment. Moreover, this protection extends to intimate choices by unmarried as well as married persons."

Justice Stevens' analysis, in our view, should have been controlling in *Bowers* and should control here.

Bowers was not correct when it was decided, and it is not correct today. It ought not to remain binding precedent. *Bowers v. Hardwick* should be and now is overruled. . . .

It is so ordered.

Justice O'Connor, concurring in the judgment.

The Court today overrules *Bowers v. Hardwick*, 478 U.S. 186 (1986). I joined *Bowers*, and do not join the Court in overruling it. Nevertheless, I agree with the Court that Texas' statute banning same-sex sodomy is unconstitutional. Rather than relying on the substantive component of the Fourteenth Amendment's Due Process Clause, as the Court does, I base my conclusion on the Fourteenth Amendment's Equal Protection Clause. . . .

Justice Scalia, with whom The Chief Justice and Justice Thomas join, dissenting.

Today's opinion is the product of a Court, which is the product of a law-profession culture, that has largely signed on to the so-called homosexual agenda, by which I mean the agenda promoted by some homosexual activists directed at eliminating the moral opprobrium that has traditionally attached to homosexual conduct. . . .

Let me be clear that I have nothing against homosexuals, or any other group, promoting their agenda through normal democratic means. Social perceptions of sexual and other morality change over time, and every group has the right to persuade its fellow citizens that its view of such matters is the best. That homosexuals have achieved some success in that enterprise is attested to by the fact that Texas is one of the few remaining States that criminalize private, consensual homosexual acts. But persuading one's fellow citizens is one thing, and imposing one's views in absence of democratic majority will is something else. I would no more require a State to criminalize homosexual acts—or, for that matter, display any moral disapprobation of them—than I would forbid it to do so. What Texas has chosen to do is well within the range of traditional democratic action, and its hand should not be stayed through the invention of a brand-new "constitutional right" by a Court that is impatient of democratic change. It is indeed true that "later generations can see that laws once thought necessary and proper in fact serve only to oppress"; and when that happens, later generations can repeal those laws. But it is the premise of our system that those judgments are to be made by the people, and not imposed by a governing caste that knows best. . . .

Justice Thomas, dissenting.

YOUR CONSTITUTIONAL VALUES

ARE ANTI-OBSCENITY LAWS UNCONSTITUTIONAL?

In August 2003, a federal grand jury in Pittsburgh, Pennsylvania, indicted Extreme Associates, Inc., a company that sells adult entertainment products, and its owners Robert Zicari and Janet Romano, on charges of commercial distribution of obscene materials in violation of federal obscenity laws. According to the indictment, Extreme Associates provided access to obscene videos on its website and also sold obscene materials through the U.S. mail.

In October 2003, the defendants responded to the charges by filing a motion to dismiss the indictment, asserting that the federal obscenity laws were unconstitutional. The defendants' motion relied chiefly on a 2003 ruling by the Supreme Court in *Lawrence v. Texas* (see excerpt in this chapter). In *Lawrence*, the Court struck down a Texas sodomy law that applied to same-sex couples, but not to opposite-sex couples. In part, a majority of the Court reasoned that the Texas ban violated due process rights of privacy. The Court also concluded that the state's moral disapproval of homosexuality did not provide a legitimate justification for criminalizing private, consensual gay sex. But in a strongly worded dissent, Justice Antonin Scalia argued that the majority opinion's reasoning ultimately would lead to the invalidation of obscenity laws.

Picking up where Justice Scalia left off, the Extreme Associates defendants moved to dismiss the indictment, asserting that *Lawrence* had essentially invalidated the frequently offered moral basis for federal obscenity laws.

Based on your constitutional values, what do you think? Should obscenity still be considered an unprotected form of expression under the First Amendment? If individuals have the constitutional right to possess obscene materials, per the Court's opinion in *Stanley v. Georgia*, should they also have the protected ability to acquire them? Is there a reason to ban obscenity other than the general claim that it is immoral?

To see how the federal courts approached this case, go to *United States v. Extreme Associates*, 352 F. Supp. 2d 578 (DCW Pa. 2005); rev'd by *United States v. Extreme Associates*, 431 F.3d 150 (3d Cir. 2005).

Cyber Constitution
Texas Law Against Sex Toys Overturned
www.msnbc.msn.
com/id/23155562/ns/
business-us_business/

11.6 MODERN CHALLENGES

Given the fact that "liberty" is not defined or otherwise restricted by the Due Process Clauses of the Fifth and Fourteenth Amendments, it is a practical certainty that parties will continue to seek the Supreme Court's recognition of their activities as a protected liberty interest under the Constitution. Many of the foreseeable debates in the next ten years are likely to involve old subjects with new twists. Some governments will continue to enact

Tyone Garner, left, and John Lawrence acknowledge applause at a rally at Houston City Hall celebrating the U.S. Supreme Court decision that overturned the Texas sodomy law on Thursday, June 26, 2003. Garner and Lawrence were arrested in 1998 under this law

ERICH SCHLEGEL KRT/Newscom

restrictive abortion regulations, which will result in an ongoing stream of litigation over whether these measures constitute an "undue burden" on a woman's right to privacy. Some more conservative states may even seek to ban abortion entirely, so as to generate a case that might revisit the core tenets of *Roe v. Wade* (1973). The so-called right to die is also likely to spark continued debate, as more state legislatures seek to pass laws that either allow for physician-assisted suicide or impose additional restrictions on such activity.

But in the post–*Lawrence v. Texas* (2003) world of due process, there likely will be many new and innovative arguments for protecting individual activity as a type of liberty interest. Proponents of same-sex marriage have argued that the right to choose a marital partner of the same sex should be a fundamental right protected by the Due Process Clause. Advocates for the freedom of sexual expression have asserted that obscenity laws and laws restricting the sale of sexual toys and devices violate basic notions of liberty and due process because they interfere with intimate choices involving sexual relations between consenting adults. The pursuit of these and other contemporary rights of privacy will not only provide a new body of case law under the Due Process Clause, but also further illustrate the belief held by some that the Constitution was designed to be a living document.

11.7 ECONOMIC LIBERTIES

For the most part, the previously-referenced liberties—privacy, abortion, death, and sexuality—all involve matters of individual autonomy, deeply personal choices, or the ability to control one's body. But another more public and open area of human activity, which has been addressed as a "liberty interest" under the Due Process Clause, is economic liberty or the freedom to interact with others concerning financial, commercial, or employment-related matters. Whether negotiating an employment contract, buying goods and services, or owning a home, economic liberties typically involve more social and public dynamics than some of the other, more private liberties (abortion, sexual activity, death) previously discussed. Nevertheless, the question remains as to what extent the Constitution protects personal choices regarding economic-related matters.

Three constitutional areas are most often recognized as being relevant to economic liberties: (1) the Due Process Clause, as cited in the Fifth and Fourteenth Amendments; (2) the **"Contract Clause,"** found in Article I, Section 10, which provides that states cannot impair the obligations of contracts; and (3) the Fifth Amendment right against governmental taking of private property for public use without just compensation, also known as the **Takings Clause** or **eminent domain** provision. Each of these provisions, to various degrees over time, has been used to address certain forms of economic liberty in the face of governmental interference.

11.7(a) Due Process and the Liberty of Contract

The ratification of the Fourteenth Amendment in 1868, which was viewed as a constitutional enhancement for racial equality, also coincided with the beginning of another social development—the Industrial Revolution. During the latter part of the nineteenth century and early part of the twentieth century, the U.S. economy was shifting from a primarily agrarian-based economy to one increasingly based on the industrial production and delivery of goods. These two developments—one legal and the other more social—quickly began to intersect with each other.

In *Santa Clara County v. Southern Pacific Railroad Co.* (1886),[30] the Supreme Court ruled that the term "person" as used in the Fourteenth Amendment Due Process Clause includes corporations, thereby affording these nonhuman organizations many of the same due process protections as those afforded to individuals. This ruling, which remains largely in effect today, has profoundly impacted constitutional law and industrial relations because it has given corporations legal standing under the Due Process Clause to challenge governmental regulations affecting businesses.

Contract Clause
A provision in Article I, Section 10, of the Constitution that provides that states cannot impair the obligations of contracts.

Takings Clause
A provision found in the Fifth Amendment that states that government cannot take private property for public use without just compensation. Also known as the *eminent domain provision.*

eminent domain
The process of government obtaining private property from individuals for public use under the Fifth Amendment. See also the *Takings Clause.*

liberty of contract
A liberty interest under the Fourteenth Amendment Due Process Clause as determined by the Court during the latter part of the nineteenth century and early part of the twentieth century (the laissez-faire era of the Court). The Court deemed this liberty interest to offer a constitutional right to engage in contractual relations without governmental interference.

laissez-faire era
A phrase used to describe the nature of the Supreme Court during the latter part of the nineteenth century and early part of the twentieth century. Also referred to as the *Lochner* era, this period is marked by the Court's frequent rejection of government regulation of business and the work setting.

Soon after its decision in *Santa Clara County*, the Court went a step further by interpreting the "liberty" provision of the Fourteenth Amendment to include an implicit **"liberty of contract"**—the constitutional right to engage in contractual relations without governmental interference. In *Allgeyer v. Louisiana* (1897), the Court struck down a Louisiana law that limited the sale of insurance policies, finding that it interfered with the liberty of contract. In his opinion, Justice Rufus Peckham announced the doctrine of liberty of contract, stating:

> The "liberty" mentioned in [the Fourteenth] Amendment means not only the right of the citizen to be free from the mere physical restraint of his person, as by incarceration, but the term is deemed to embrace the right of the citizens to be free in the enjoyment of all his faculties; to be free to use them in all lawful ways; to live and work where he will; to earn his livelihood by a lawful calling; to pursue any livelihood or avocation, and for that purpose to enter into all contracts which may be proper, necessary and essential to his carrying out to successful conclusion the purposes of the above mentioned.

During the next forty years following *Allgeyer*, the Court used the liberty of contract doctrine to strike down approximately two hundred federal and state laws. This period in the Court's history is known as the **laissez-faire era** or *Lochner* era of the Court (see Chapter 1, Section 1.7). The *Lochner* reference comes from *Lochner v. New York* (1905) (discussed later in this chapter), where the Court used the liberty of contract theory to invalidate a New York labor law that limited the number of hours bakers could work per week. This decision, perhaps more than any other, captures the Court's philosophy regarding the Due Process Clause and economic liberty during the Industrial Revolution.

Lochner v. New York
198 U.S. 45 (1905)

Mr. Justice Peckham, after making the foregoing statement of the facts, delivered the opinion of the court:

The indictment, it will be seen, charges that the plaintiff in error violated the 110th section of article 8, chapter 415, of the Laws of 1897, known as the labor law of the state of New York, in that he wrongfully and unlawfully required and permitted an employee working for him to work more than sixty hours in one week. . . .

The statute necessarily interferes with the right of contract between the employer and employees, concerning the number of hours in which the latter may labor in the bakery of the employer. The general right to make a contract in relation to his business is part of the liberty of the individual protected by the 14th Amendment of the Federal Constitution. *Allgeyer v. Louisiana*, 165 U.S. 578 (1897). Under that provision no state can deprive any person of life, liberty, or property without due process of law. The right to purchase or to sell labor is part of the liberty protected by this amendment, unless there are circumstances which exclude the right. There are, however, certain powers, existing in the sovereignty of each state in the Union, somewhat vaguely termed police powers, the exact description and limitation of which have not been attempted by the courts. Those powers, broadly stated, and without, at present, any attempt at a more specific limitation, relate to the safety, health, morals, and general welfare of the public. Both property and liberty are held

on such reasonable conditions as may be imposed by the governing power of the state in the exercise of those powers, and with such conditions the 14th Amendment was not designed to interfere. . . .

In every case that comes before this court, therefore, where legislation of this character is concerned, and where the protection of the Federal Constitution is sought, the question necessarily arises: Is this a fair, reasonable, and appropriate exercise of the police power of the state, or is it an unreasonable, unnecessary, and arbitrary interference with the right of the individual to his personal liberty, or to enter into those contracts in relation to labor which may seem to him appropriate or necessary for the support of himself and his family? Of course the liberty of contract relating to labor includes both parties to it. The one has as much right to purchase as the other to sell labor. . . .

We think the limit of the police power has been reached and passed in this case. There is, in our judgment, no reasonable foundation for holding this to be necessary or appropriate as a health law to safeguard the public health, or the health of the individuals who are following the trade of a baker. If this statute be valid, and if, therefore, a proper case is made out in which to deny the right of an individual, *sui juris*, as employer or employee, to make contracts for the labor of the latter under the protection of the provisions of the Federal Constitution, there would seem to be no length to which legislation of this nature might not go . . . We think that there can be no fair doubt that the trade of a baker, in and of itself, is not an unhealthy one to that degree which would authorize the legislature to interfere with the right to labor, and with the right of free contract on the part of the individual, either as employer or employee. In looking through statistics regarding all trades and occupations, it may be true that the trade of a baker does not appear to be as healthy as some other trades, and is also vastly more healthy than still others. To the common understanding the trade of a baker has never been regarded as an unhealthy one. . . .

It seems to us that the real object and purpose were simply to regulate the hours of labor between the master and his employees (all being men, *sui juris*), in a private business, not dangerous in any degree to morals, or in any real and substantial degree to the health of the employees. Under such circumstances the freedom of master and employee to contract with each other in relation to their employment, and in defining the same, cannot be prohibited or interfered with, without violating the Federal Constitution.

The judgment of the Court of Appeals of New York, as well as that of the Supreme Court and of the County Court of Oneida County, must be reversed and the case remanded to the County Court for further proceedings not inconsistent with this opinion.

Reversed.

Mr. Justice Harlan (with whom Mr. Justice White and Mr. Justice Day concurred) dissenting:

Mr. Justice Holmes dissenting:

This case is decided upon an economic theory which a large part of the country does not entertain. If it were a question whether I agreed with that theory, I should desire to study it further and long before making up my mind. But I do not conceive that to be my duty, because I strongly believe that my agreement or disagreement has nothing to do with the right of a majority to embody their opinions in law. It is settled by various decisions of this court that state constitutions and state laws may regulate life in many ways which we as legislators might think as injudicious, or if you like as tyrannical, as this, and which, equally with this, interfere with the liberty to contract. . . .

I think that the word "liberty," in the 14th Amendment, is perverted when it is held to prevent the natural outcome of a dominant opinion, unless it can be said that a rational and fair man necessarily would admit that the statute proposed would infringe fundamental principles as they have been understood by the traditions of our people and our law. It does not need research to show that no such sweeping condemnation can be passed upon the statute before us. A reasonable man might think it a proper measure on the score of health. Men whom I certainly could not pronounce unreasonable would uphold it as a first installment of a general regulation of the hours of work. Whether in the latter aspect it would be open to the charge of inequality I think it unnecessary to discuss.

Between 1897 and 1937, with some exceptions,[31] the Court generally viewed governmental regulations of business and contractual relations with utmost suspicion, and absent an extraordinary governmental interest, deemed these measures unconstitutional under the Due Process Clause. Even after the stock market crash in 1929, the ensuing Great Depression, and several laws passed under President Franklin Roosevelt's New Deal plan, the Court still looked with disfavor upon governmental interferences with business. Similar to the scrutiny afforded to fundamental rights in modern constitutional jurisprudence, the Court applied a heightened form of review to governmental regulation of business affairs.

However, in 1937, the Court dramatically altered its approach to economic liberties under the Due Process Clause. Earlier in the year, President Roosevelt had proposed to Congress that the size of the Supreme Court be enlarged to fifteen members. This is known as the **court-packing plan.** Publicly, President Roosevelt claimed that such an enlargement was necessary because six justices on the Court were over seventy years of age and the Court needed assistance with its workload. Historians, however, generally regard this plan as a strategy to change the membership of the Court so that the New Deal legislation previously rejected by the Court would subsequently be found constitutional. Many of the Court's decisions rejecting New Deal legislation were the result of 5–4 or 6–3 decisions. The general belief is that Roosevelt wanted to add additional members to the Court to tip the scales of justice in his favor.

Regardless of Roosevelt's motive, just a few months after President Roosevelt offered this proposal, the Court changed its doctrine regarding the liberty of contract. The change came in *West Coast Hotel v. Parrish* (1937),[32] where the Court upheld a Washington state minimum-wage law. The difference in the case was the vote of Justice Owen Roberts, who previously had voted to strike down New Deal policies under

court-packing plan
A phrase used to describe President Franklin Roosevelt's proposal in early 1937 to enlarge the Supreme Court by six members in order to ensure that his New Deal plan would be found constitutional. This proposal never became reality because the Court ultimately began approving social and economic legislation passed by Congress and state governments, thereby eliminating the perceived need to enlarge the Court.

the switch in time that saved nine
A phrase used to describe the change in the Court's approach to economic and social legislation, chiefly marked by the Court's opinion in *West Coast Hotel v. Parrish* (1937), where the Court upheld a Washington state minimum-wage law. The difference or "switch" in the case was the vote of Justice Owen Roberts, who previously had voted to strike down New Deal policies under the doctrine of liberty of contract. In *West Coast Hotel,* however, Roberts switched sides and voted to uphold the Washington law. This change not only negated any New Deal–related motive for Roosevelt's court-packing plan (which Congress never adopted), but also ushered in a new era of jurisprudence regarding economic liberty under the Due Process Clause.

Cyber Constitution
Liberty of Contract
http://caselaw.lp.findlaw.com/data/constitution/amendment14/03.html

the doctrine of liberty of contract. In *West Coast Hotel,* however, Roberts switched sides and voted to uphold the Washington law. This change, known as **"the switch in time that saved nine,"** not only negated any New Deal–related motive for Roosevelt's court-packing plan (which Congress never adopted), but also ushered in a new era of jurisprudence regarding economic liberty under the Due Process Clause.[33] In his opinion for the newly formed 5–4 majority, Chief Justice Hughes rejected the heightened constitutional scrutiny afforded to economic liberties, and in its place offered a more limited standard:

> The Constitution does not speak of freedom of contract. It speaks of liberty and prohibits the deprivation of liberty without due process of law. In prohibiting that deprivation, the Constitution does not recognize an absolute and uncontrollable liberty. Liberty in each of its phases has its history and connotation. But the liberty safe-guarded is liberty in a social organization which requires the protection of law against the evils which menace the health, safety, morals, and welfare of the people. Liberty under the Constitution is thus necessarily subject to restraints of due process, and regulation which is reasonable in relation to its subject and is adopted in the interests of the community is due process.

The Court's opinion in *West Coast Hotel* suggested that legislation regulating economic affairs would upheld under the Due Process Clause as long as it met the rational basis test (was rationally related to a legitimate governmental interest). With few exceptions, this has been the relevant constitutional standard in economic liberty cases under the Due Process Clause since 1937. Thus, absent the presence of another, more fundamental liberty interest, governmental restrictions on economic liberties will be reviewed under the Due Process Clause using the rational basis test.

11.7(b) The Contract Clause

One constitutional provision outside of the Bill of Rights and Fourteenth Amendment that has impacted economic liberties is the so-called Contract Clause found in Article I, Section 10. This provision prohibits states from "impairing the Obligation of Contracts." At first blush, this clause would appear to prohibit the states from passing any legislation that interferes with or otherwise impairs a contractual obligation previously formed under the law. And so, for example, if a tenant signs a lease with a landlord for an apartment and the lease allows the landlord to increase the rent after one year, the Contract Clause would seem to prohibit the state government from enacting a rent control law (a law that regulates the amount landlords can charge for rental units) that would apply to the previously formed contract. However, while this seemingly straightforward application of the Contract Clause reflects the Supreme Court's early interpretation of this provision, it does not comport with the Court's contemporary application, which typically allows government greater discretion to pass legislation that promotes societal interests, even if it interferes with previously established contracts.

The first major case addressing the Contract Clause was *Fletcher v. Peck* (1810),[34] where a party to a private land contract challenged a Georgia law that effectively invalidated the private land transfer. In an opinion written by Chief Justice John Marshall, the Court ruled that Georgia's law could not be applied to interfere with the private land contract. The Court concluded, "the state of Georgia was restrained, either by general principles, which are common to our free institutions, or by the particular provisions of the constitution of the United States, from passing a law whereby the estate of the plaintiff . . . could be constitutionally and legally impaired and rendered null and void."

Nine years after *Fletcher,* the Court reinforced its interpretation of the Contract Clause in *Trustees of Dartmouth College v. Woodward* (1819),[35] ruling that the New Hampshire legislature could not change the charter of Dartmouth College to allow for an expanded and modified board of trustees because the nature and size of the board had previously been established under a charter between the college and the English Crown in 1769. This ruling, along with others during the Marshall era, established restrictions on state government under the Contract Clause and formalized constitutional respect for private contracts. Moreover, during this period, the Marshall Court also interpreted the Contract Clause to apply to public contracts as well, thereby limiting the ability of legislatures to modify the terms of agreements involving governmental parties.

With time, the Court's interpretation of the Contract Clause began to change in a way that allowed for greater legislative discretion and less deference to contractual agreements. This change is illustrated by the Court's ruling in *Home Building & Loan Association v. Blaisdell* (1934), wherein the Court upheld a Minnesota law enacted during the Depression that restricted certain mortgaged property from being repossessed. In what amounted to a fundamental change in the Court's Contract Clause jurisprudence, the Court elevated societal interests, as represented by public policy, over private interests in contracts, stating, "not only is the [contract clause] qualified by the measure of control which the state retains over remedial processes, but the state also continues to possess authority to safeguard the vital interests of its people. It does not matter that legislation appropriate to that end 'has the result of modifying or abrogating contracts already in effect.'"

Consequently, since 1934, the Court generally has interpreted the Contract Clause in a manner that allows government to enact legislation that benefits the general welfare even if it interferes with private contracts. It should be noted, however, that in cases involving public contracts, the Court has expressed a willingness to provide greater scrutiny under the Contract Clause to laws that interfere with these agreements. For example, in *United States Trust Co. of New York v. State of New Jersey* (1977),[36] the Court invalidated a New Jersey law that interfered with a contractual covenant with a trustee and bondholder of the Port Authority, which previously had been established under an agreement between the states of New York and New Jersey. In a 4-3 ruling, the Court concluded that the New Jersey legislation was not reasonable under the circumstances, and therefore, could not impair the contractual rights of the Port Authority.

As a result, while the contemporary Contract Clause may offer little protection to economic liberties, especially in the face of societal needs, it may provide some restrictions on governmental interference when the government itself is involved in the making of the contract.

11.7(c) The Takings Clause

There is perhaps no other constitutional provision impacting economic liberties that has generated more debate and discussion in recent times than the "Takings Clause" of the Fifth Amendment. This provision states, "private property [shall not] be taken for public use, without just compensation," and generally allows government to assert the power of eminent domain—the ability of government to take private property for public use. Over the years, the Takings Clause jurisprudence has involved three major questions: (1) What is a taking? (2) What is public use? (3) What is just compensation?

For the most part, the last question involving compensation has not resulted in any major Supreme Court rulings. Parties involved in eminent domain cases typically used property adjusters or appraisers to establish a fair market value for the property being taken by the government. And while these matters often result in disagreements between the property owner and the government, courts usually resolve these disputes using market-based factors to establish the amount of compensation owed to the property owner for the government's taking.

Questions involving whether the government has done enough to have "taken" a person's property have resulted in a number of Supreme Court rulings. Obviously, in cases where the government officially says to a property owner, "we want to your property" there is really no dispute over whether a taking has occurred. But in other cases where government has sought to regulate (as opposed to take) property, some property owners have asserted that the regulation substantially impairs the value of the property as to amount to a virtual taking of the property. In these cases, the Court has had to determine how far government can go in regulating property before it will be deemed a taking under the Fifth Amendment.

Cyber Constitution
History of the Takings Clause http://law.wustl.edu/landuselaw/Articles/Brief_Hx_Taking.htm

In *Pennsylvania Coal Co. v. Mahon* (1922),[37] the Court established its initial standard in takings cases, holding that "property may be regulated to a certain extent, [but] if regulation goes too far it will be recognized as a taking." Although the Court failed to establish a "brightline rule," it made it clear that the property owner had the evidentiary burden to demonstrate that the government's action resulted in a virtually complete loss of use of the property. The Court later applied this standard to the facts in *United States v. Causby* (1946),[38] finding that a farmer's land had been virtually taken by the government installation of a military airport adjacent to the land. Later, in *Agins v. Tiburon* (1980),[39] the Court clarified its standard, cautioning that a land-use regulation will not result in a taking if it "substantially advance[s] legitimate state interests" and does not "den[y] an owner economically viable use of his land."

The Court has applied various forms of this standard in more recent rulings. In *Nollan v. California Coastal Commission* (1987),[40] the Court in a 5-4 ruling found a California regulation requiring property owners seeking building permits to grant the state an easement across their property to be a taking. In *Lucas v. South Carolina Coastal Commission* (1992), the Court in a 6-3 ruling concluded that government had to defend its promulgation of land-use regulations by something more than just "public interest," but that the Takings Clause applied only when owners are totally deprived of the economic value of their property. And in *Tahoe-Sierra Preservation Council, Inc. v. Tahoe Regional Planning Agency* (2002),[41] the Court ruled 6-3 that a local government could impose, without effectuating a taking, a three-year moratorium on new building around Lake Tahoe in order to allow regional development of natural resource and development plans.

The last question, involving whether a governmental taking is for public use, has also generated substantial controversy. In some cases, governments have openly seized private property under the power of eminent domain only to turn the property over to private entities for development. Governments typically argue that such transfers are for public use because the private redevelopment will result in more tax revenue being generated from the land and in some cases a more aesthetically pleasing environment for the public. Property owners, on the other hand, see such takings as seizure for private profit, not public use, and assert they are unconstitutional under the Fifth Amendment.

Buildings and demolition in the 17-acre area in Manhattan Valley in New York where Columbia University is expanding their campus
Alamy Images BTC3HN

In recent years, the Court generally has allowed these types of takings, finding that they are ultimately, although indirectly, for public use. In *Hawaii Housing Authority v. Midkiff* (1984),[42] the Court upheld legislation allowing the state to seize residential private property and to sell it to tenants who occupied the land. The Court supported the state's conclusion that too much of its land was concentrated in the hands of a few property owners and that such concentration resulted in adverse market conditions for housing in Hawaii. Accordingly, the Court found that although the seized land was sold to private owners, the ultimate objective of the state was to benefit the public as a whole. Similarly, in *Kelo v. City of New London* (2005) (see excerpt), the Court upheld a local government's taking of private homes for private land redevelopment, finding that the government sought to correct the blighted condition of the area and increase economic opportunities for the community, both of which are public purposes.

Kelo v. City of New London
125 S. Ct. 2655 (2005)

Justice Stevens delivered the opinion of the Court.

In 2000, the city of New London approved a development plan that, in the words of the Supreme Court of Connecticut, was "projected to create in excess of 1,000 jobs, to increase tax and other revenues, and to revitalize an economically distressed city, including its downtown and waterfront areas." In assembling the land needed for this project, the city's development agent has purchased property from willing sellers and proposes to use the power of eminent domain to acquire the remainder of the property from unwilling owners in exchange for just compensation. The question presented is whether the city's proposed disposition of this property qualifies as a "public use" within the meaning of the Takings Clause of the Fifth Amendment to the Constitution. . . .

The disposition of this case therefore turns on the question whether the City's development plan serves a "public purpose." Without exception, our cases have defined that concept broadly, reflecting our longstanding policy of deference to legislative judgments in this field. . . .

Viewed as a whole, our jurisprudence has recognized that the needs of society have varied between different parts of the Nation, just as they have evolved over time in response to changed circumstances. Our earliest cases in particular embodied a strong theme of federalism, emphasizing the "great respect" that we owe to state legislatures and state courts in discerning local public needs. For more than a century, our public use jurisprudence has wisely eschewed rigid formulas and intrusive scrutiny in favor of affording legislatures broad latitude in determining what public needs justify the use of the takings power. . . .

Just as we decline to second-guess the City's considered judgments about the efficacy of its development plan, we also decline to second-guess the City's determinations as to what lands it needs to acquire in order to effectuate the project. "It is not for the courts to oversee the choice of the boundary line nor to sit in review on the size of a particular project area. Once the question of the public purpose has been decided, the amount and character of land to be taken for the project and the need for a particular tract to complete the integrated plan rests in the discretion of the legislative branch."

In affirming the City's authority to take petitioners' properties, we do not minimize the hardship that condemnations may entail, notwithstanding the payment of just compensation. We emphasize that nothing in our opinion precludes any State from placing further restrictions on its exercise of the takings power. Indeed, many States already impose "public use" requirements that are stricter than the federal baseline. Some of these requirements have been established as a matter of state constitutional law, while others are expressed in state eminent domain statutes that carefully limit the grounds upon which takings may be exercised. As the submissions of the parties and their *amici* make clear, the necessity and wisdom of using eminent domain to promote economic development are certainly matters of legitimate public debate. This Court's authority, however, extends only to determining whether the City's proposed condemnations are for a "public use" within the meaning of the Fifth Amendment to the Federal Constitution. Because over a century of our case law interpreting that provision dictates an affirmative answer to that question, we may not grant petitioners the relief that they seek.

The judgment of the Supreme Court of Connecticut is affirmed.

It is so ordered.

Justice Kennedy, concurring.

I join the opinion for the Court and add these further observations.

This Court has declared that a taking should be upheld as consistent with the Public Use Clause, U.S. Const., Amdt. 5., as long as it is "rationally related to a conceivable public purpose." This deferential standard of review echoes the rational-basis test used to review economic regulation under the Due Process and Equal Protection Clauses. The determination that a rational-basis standard of review is appropriate does not, however, alter the fact that transfers intended to confer benefits on particular, favored private entities, and with only incidental or pretextual public benefits, are forbidden by the Public Use Clause.

This taking occurred in the context of a comprehensive development plan meant to address a serious city-wide depression, and the projected economic benefits of the project cannot be characterized as *de minimus*. The identity of most of the private beneficiaries were unknown at the time the city formulated its plans. The city complied with elaborate procedural requirements that facilitate review of the record and inquiry into the city's purposes. In sum, while there may be categories of cases in which the transfers are so suspicious, or the procedures employed so prone to abuse, or the purported benefits are so trivial or implausible, that courts should presume an impermissible private purpose, no such circumstances are present in this case.

For the foregoing reasons, I join in the Court's opinion.

Justice O'Connor, with whom *The Chief Justice*, *Justice Scalia*, and *Justice Thomas* join, dissenting.

Over two centuries ago, just after the Bill of Rights was ratified, Justice Chase wrote:

> "An *act* of the Legislature (for I cannot call it a law) contrary to the great first principles of the social compact, cannot be considered a rightful exercise of legislative authority. . . . A few instances will suffice to explain what I mean . . . [A] law that takes property from A and gives it to B: It is against all reason and justice, for a people to entrust a Legislature with *such* powers; and, therefore, it cannot be presumed that they have done it." Calder v. Bull, 3 Dall. 386, 388 (1798) (emphasis deleted).

Today the Court abandons this long-held, basic limitation on government power. Under the banner of economic development, all private property is now vulnerable to being taken and transferred to another private owner, so long as it might be upgraded—*i.e.*, given to an owner who will use it in a way that the legislature deems more beneficial to the public—in the process. To reason, as the Court does, that the incidental public benefits resulting from the subsequent ordinary use of private property render economic development takings "for public use" is to wash out any distinction between private and public use of property—and thereby effectively to delete the words "for public use" from the Takings Clause of the Fifth Amendment. Accordingly I respectfully dissent.

Justice Thomas, dissenting.

Cyber Constitution
The States' Response to *Kelo* www.ncsl.org/default.aspx?tabid=13252

Notice that the Court in *Kelo* advised that state and local governments are free to impose further restrictions on themselves, beyond the Fifth Amendment, when it comes to limiting the power of eminent domain. And, in fact, many state and local entities have done just that in the wake of *Kelo*.[43] Consequently, while the term "public use" appears to have an expansive and malleable meaning under the Fifth Amendment, state and local standards may provide greater protections for private property owners in the face of governmental takings.

11.8 MODERN CHALLENGES

For more than seventy years, the protection of economic liberties has largely taken a constitutional backseat to the greater public interests protected by the Commerce Clause, Tax and Spending Clause, and Necessary and Proper Clause. Since 1937, Congress generally has been able to regulate economic activities without much fear of constitutional limitation by the Due Process Clause. During the next several years, however, there likely will be many challenges made to this contemporary constitutional paradigm. The Supreme Court's ruling in *United States v. Lopez* (1995) (see Chapter 4) already has spawned more constitutional challenges to government regulations under the Commerce Clause. Though not regularly successful, these new challenges present persistent calls to change the old way of thinking about government regulations of commercial activity.

The Court's ruling in *Kelo v. City of New London* (2005) has also invited new approaches to governmental regulations of property. To protest the *Kelo* ruling, many state legislatures have enacted greater legal protections for private property, which seek to provide property owners with legal rights beyond those afforded by the Takings Clause of the Fifth Amendment. In the near future, governments are likely to face more difficult hurdles in taking private property, particularly where the purported governmental use of such property is not overtly in the public interest.

Finally, the so-called Tea Party movement, largely organized in 2010 by individuals seeking to ostensibly foster a more limited form of government, could also generate additional challenges to economic regulations, including those affecting health care, food safety, and education. By some measures, the Tea (Taxed Enough Already) Party movement is promoting many of the same arguments as those who advanced pre-New Deal era of laissez-faire economics. And for some, the theory of "liberty of contract" should, once again, be used to preclude government from interfering with many types of business affairs. It is way too early to know whether this contemporary movement will have any jurisprudential effect. But such theories and arguments are likely to be advanced in new forms of litigation.

11.9 SUMMARY

The Fourteenth Amendment provides that the states shall not deprive any person of life, liberty, or property without due process of law. The Fifth Amendment imposes the same obligation upon the federal government. There are two dimensions to due process—procedural due process and substantive due process. Procedural due process governs *how* the government processes the claims and grievances of individuals. Substantive due process asks what types of activities are included under the term "liberty." Over time, the Court has addressed a number of rights that are not specifically enumerated in the Bill of Rights, but that are nonetheless protected as civil liberties under the Due Process Clause.

One of these rights is privacy. The right to privacy has been called, among other things, the "right to be left alone." The term *privacy* is not explicitly found in the Bill of Rights or anywhere else in the Constitution. Rather, privacy is deemed to be the right implicitly found in either (1) the Ninth Amendment's reference to other rights "retained by the people," (2) the "liberty" interest protected by the Due Process Clauses of the Fifth and Fourteenth Amendments, or (3) the shadows cast by the privacy-related rights explicitly stated in the First, Third, Fourth, Fifth, and Ninth Amendments. To the extent that privacy has been recognized as a constitutional right, it is treated as a fundamental right, which is to be afforded the utmost constitutional protection. This means that governmental interferences with privacy will have to meet the strict scrutiny standard of constitutional review—government will have to show that its intrusion is necessary (or narrowly tailored) to meet a compelling governmental interest.

One of the first considerations in cases where an individual's right to privacy is asserted is whether the activity at issue is actually included under the right to privacy. Matters relating to marriage and family education and discipline; seeking information from physicians about birth control and reproductive procedures, including abortion; cohabitating with persons of your choosing; and engaging in consensual, adult sexual conduct have been treated as items included in privacy interests. But not all privacy interests will withstand the strict scrutiny standard. In some cases, the government will be able to demonstrate that its compelling and narrowly tailored interest outweighs the individual's interest in privacy. As a result, the right to privacy, like all other constitutional liberties, is not absolute.

There are three major areas in which the right to privacy has been addressed—abortion, death-related matters, and individual sexuality. Since 1973, the Supreme Court has recognized that the right to privacy protects a woman's right to select an abortion as a medical procedure. However, the Court also has recognized that the government can still regulate this procedure under the strict scrutiny standard. Currently, the primary question in abortion cases is whether the government's regulation of abortion imposes an undue burden on the woman's choice regarding abortion. If it does, the regulation is unconstitutional. If it does not, the government will be permitted to impose its regulation.

In the so-called right to die cases, the Court has not recognized an absolute right to die as part of the right to privacy. The Court generally has required government to honor the wishes of dying persons regarding the course of their medical care. This allows individuals to refuse medical treatment or dictate their wishes through a living will. But the Court has refused to hold that individuals have a constitutional right to assisted suicide. Instead, the Court has found that the states may provide for such a right, but are not required to do so under the Constitution.

Finally, some members of the Court have treated individual choices regarding consensual sex between adults as matters of privacy. For these justices, the ability to choose who, how, and whether to be with someone sexually is a matter of personal choice not to be interfered with by government absent a compelling and narrowly tailored interest.

Another area of civil liberties addressed under the Due Process Clause and other constitutional provisions is economic liberties. Initially, the Court concluded that a liberty of contract was protected under the Due Process Clause. However, in the modern era, the Court has moved away from recognizing and protecting such a right. Similarly, while the Court used the Contract Clause, found in Article I, Section 10, to limit the government's interference in private agreements during much of the nineteenth century, the Court generally has allowed governments to enact laws in the public interest, even when such laws interfere with previously established contracts.

The Fifth Amendment's Takings Clause also provides limits on the government's interference with private property, requiring the government to demonstrate public use for the taking and to provide just compensation. In some cases, governmental regulations have been so onerous as to constitute a taking under the Fifth Amendment, but in other cases, the government has been permitted to substantially regulate private property without it being deemed a taking. In certain cases, the government has been permitted to take private property and turn it over to private developers if such a transfer will benefit the public as a whole.

REVIEW QUESTIONS

1. What is the difference between substantive and procedural due process?
2. How does the Court determine what activities are protected under the "liberty" provision of the Due Process Clause?
3. How has the right to privacy been defined, and what activities does this right protect?
4. Where is the right to privacy found in the Constitution?
5. What is a *penumbra,* and how does it relate to the right to privacy?
6. Why do some justices refuse to recognize a constitutional right to privacy?
7. Explain how the right to abortion relates to the right to privacy.
8. What standards or tests has the Supreme Court used to evaluate governmental attempts to regulate abortion?
9. What is *partial-birth abortion,* and how is it affected by the right to privacy?
10. What privacy-related controversies have arisen over the "right to die"?
11. What is a living will, and how is it impacted by the right to privacy?
12. To what extent can government regulate individual choices regarding sexuality?
13. What is the "liberty of contract," and to what extent has the Court protected this right over time?
14. To what extent does the Contract Clause protect economic liberties?
15. What constitutional questions arise when the government exercises its power of eminent domain, and how has the Court addressed these questions?

ASSIGNMENTS: CONSTITUTIONAL LAW IN ACTION

The Constitution in Your Community

Assume that you are working as a legal assistant in a law firm. Your firm has just been retained by Bob Stanton, a local man whose wife, Freda, is suffering from a terminal illness. It seems that Freda has been suffering from severe pain due to her illness and is asking her husband to help end her life. Despite medical assistance and pain medication, Freda says that her pain is unbearable. Bob has retained your firm to advise him on the legal parameters for assisting his wife. Specifically, Bob wants to know if Freda has the freedom to end her life, and if so, how it can be done.

Using the laws from your home state, along with the basic standards of due process discussed in *Washington v. Glucksberg* (1997) and *Gonzales v. Oregon* (2005), prepare a legal memorandum outlining the legal standards for assisted suicide in your state. Be sure to address (1) whether your state allows for physician-assisted suicide; (2) any criminal laws that exist regarding suicide; (3) whether these laws interfere with the right to privacy, liberty, and/or due process; (4) how your state handles living wills, including the extent to which your state recognizes them, and what is necessary for these individual declarations to be honored in court.

Going Federal

Assume you are working as a legal professional for the Village of Takings, a local government in your home state. Within the village, there is a row of five houses on a street that a local developer would like to obtain for the purposes of demolishing them and building newer and more expensive homes on the lots. The developer has tried to negotiate directly with the home owners, but they have refused to sell their properties. As a result, the developer has sought the assistance of the village, requesting that the government seize the properties by eminent domain and convey them to the developer for redevelopment. The developer maintains that the village and the public would benefit from this transaction because the new homes built on the lots would generate four times the amount of property tax revenue for the village than is generated by the current homes.

The village has agreed to acquire the properties via eminent domain. But the homeowners have filed suit in federal court, asserting that the village's actions violate the Takings Clause of the Fifth Amendment because the acquisition of their properties is not for "public use." The village needs to respond to the homeowners' complaint. Using the Supreme Court's decision in *Kelo v. City of New London*, as well as any other applicable legal or constitutional standard in your jurisdiction, prepare a legal memorandum where you respond to the homeowners' primary argument that the taking is not for public use.

Moot Court

Locate and review your state's criminal laws regarding the sale and distribution of obscene materials (your state's anti-obscenity statutes). Then read and outline the Supreme Court's decision in *Lawrence v. Texas* (2003), along with the court rulings in *United States v. Extreme Associates*, 352 F. Supp. 2d 578 (DCW Pa. 2005); rev'd by *United States v. Extreme Associates*, 431 F.3d 150 (3d Cir. 2005). Work in teams of two; the first team should prepare a five-minute oral argument presentation wherein they present arguments challenging the constitutionality of the state's obscenity statute, asserting that it violates the liberty interest protected under the Fourteenth Amendment Due Process Clause. Conversely, the second team should prepare a five-minute oral argument asserting why the state's laws against obscenity do not infringe upon any constitutionally protected liberty interest.

NOTES

1. *Public Utilities Commission v. Pollack*, 343 U.S. 451 (1952) (Douglas dissenting).
2. See *Young v. Harper*, 520 U.S. 193 (1997) (addressing procedural protections for parole hearings and substantive protections against unfair imprisonment).
3. See *Washington v. Glucksberg*, 521 U.S. 702 (1997) (Chief Justice Rehnquist's opinion).
4. See Edward Keynes, *Liberty, Property, and Privacy: Toward a Jurisprudence of Substantive Due Process* (Pennsylvania State University Press 1996).
5. *Id.*
6. *Moore v. City of East Cleveland*, 431 U.S. 494 (1977) (Justice Powell's opinion).
7. U.S. Constitution, Fourth Amendment.
8. *Cruzan v. Director, Missouri Department of Health*, 497 U.S. 261 (1990), quoting *Youngberg v. Romeo*, 457 U.S. 307 (1982).
9. 429 U.S. 589 (1976).
10. 497 U.S. 261 (1990).
11. 425 U.S. 238 (1976).
12. See *Washington v. Glucksberg*, 521 U.S. 702 (1997) (Chief Justice Rehnquist's opinion).
13. 410 U.S. 113 (1973).
14. *Doe v. Bolton*, 410 U.S. 179 (1973) (a companion case to *Roe* striking down a state law requiring that abortions be performed in licensed hospitals and be approved by a hospital committee).
15. 421 U.S. 809 (1975).
16. 443 U.S. 622 (1979).
17. 448 U.S. 297 (1980).
18. 462 U.S. 416 (1983).
19. 492 U.S. 490 (1989).
20. 500 U.S. 377 (1991).
21. 500 U.S. 833 (1992).
22. *Stenberg v. Carhart*, 530 U.S. 914 (2000).
23. *Cruzan v. Director, Missouri Department of Health*, 497 U.S. 261 (1990) (O'Connor concurring).
24. *Id.*
25. *Id.*
26. See *Griswold v. Connecticut*, 391 U.S. 145 (1965).
27. *Buck v. Bell*, 274 U.S. 200 (1927).
28. *Skinner v. Oklahoma*, 316 U.S. 535 (1942).
29. *Lawrence v. Texas*, 539 U.S. 558 (2003).
30. 118 U.S. 398 (1886).
31. See *Muller v. Oregon*, 208 U.S. 412 (1980) (upholding an Oregon law limiting the number of hours women could work per day); *Jacobson v. Massachusetts*, 197 U.S. 11 (1905) (upholding state law requiring small pox vaccinations); *Holden v. Hardy*, 169 U.S. 366 (1898) (upholding a state regulation limiting the number of hours miners could work in a day).
32. 300 U.S. 379 (1937).
33. See Daniel E. Hall, *Administrative Law: Bureaucracy in a Democracy*, 3rd ed., (Pearson Prentice Hall, 2006).
34. 10 U.S. 87 (1810).
35. 17 U.S. 518 (1819).
36. 431 U.S. 1 (1977).
37. 260 U.S. 393 (1922).
38. 328 U.S. 258 (1946).
39. 447 U.S. 255 (1980).
40. 483 U.S. 825 (1987).
41. 535 U.S. 302 (2002).
42. 467 U.S. 229 (1984).
43. See *City of Norwood v. Horney*, et al., 110 Ohio St.3d 353, 2006-Ohio-3799 (using state constitutional standards to reject a local government's attempt to take private homes for the purpose of expanding private shopping mall).

12

Equal Protection

Our constitution is color-blind, and neither knows nor tolerates classes among citizens. In respect of civil rights, all citizens are equal before the law.

JUSTICE JOHN HARLAN, DISSENTING IN *PLESSY V. FERGUSON* (1896)[1]

In order to get beyond racism, we must first take account of race. There is no other way.

JUSTICE HARRY BLACKMUN, CONCURRING IN *REGENTS OF THE UNIVERSITY OF CALIFORNIA V. BAKKE* (1978)[2]

LEARNING OBJECTIVES
At the end of this chapter you should be able to:

- Identify the constitutional and statutory sources for equal protection at the federal and state levels of government.
- Explain the state action requirement for equal protection cases.
- Discuss the methods used to address nongovernmental forms of discrimination, including private-based employment discrimination and disparate treatment in places of public accommodation.
- Identify the three levels of constitutional scrutiny employed by courts under the Equal Protection Clause.
- Discuss the evolution of the Supreme Court's approach to addressing racial discrimination under the Equal Protection Clause.
- Discuss the doctrines for reviewing sex-based and sexual-orientation-based discrimination, including equal protection analysis for state bans on same-sex marriage.
- Identify the constitutional scrutiny used to assess government distinctions based on alienage, marital status of birth parents, age, and wealth.
- Identify a contemporary issue concerning equal protection under the Fourteenth Amendment, and discuss the most likely future scenarios, referencing both historical analogs and caselaw.
- Brief a judicial opinion with no assistance. You should be successful in identifying the relevant facts, identifying the legal issue(s), and analyzing the court's rationale in at least 85 percent of your briefs.
- Apply what you have learned to a new set of facts with no assistance.

12.1 EQUALITY AS A CONSTITUTIONAL VALUE

One may wonder how a constitutional democracy that essentially began with a Declaration of Independence stating that it was a "self-evident" truth that "all men are created equal"[3] could draft and adopt a constitution that largely failed to recognize and protect the value of equality

security
A primary value promoted by the Constitution that seeks stability, safety, and reliable institutions.

liberty
One of the three primary values promoted by the Constitution, particularly the Bill of Rights, which involves the ability to act and think without government interference.

equality
The third primary value promoted by the Constitution, chiefly by the Due Process Clause and Equal Protection Clause. The standard that similarly situated persons ought to be treated similarly.

Cyber Constitution
Dred Scott v. Sandford
Reargued in Second Life www.youtube.com/watch?v=LL-A6fOh6Nk

among certain individuals, including women and racial minorities. But the reality is that the two primary values promoted by the early Constitution were **security** (national security and economic viability), which was primarily advanced within the Articles of the Constitution, and **liberty** (individual freedom to act without government interference), which was protected primarily by the Bill of Rights. The third basic constitutional value that we know today—**equality** (the notion that similarly situated persons ought to be treated similarly)—was given little attention, at least as it related to mass participation, and in fact, a number of constitutional provisions actually served to undermine this value.[4]

Originally, Article I, Section 2, which established how the population of states would be counted for congressional representation and tax purposes, excluded untaxed Indians and treated a slave as three-fifths of a whole person. Article I, Section 9, barred Congress from passing laws prohibiting slavery until 1808. And Article IV, Section 2, ensured that slaves who escaped to free states would be returned to their state of servitude if they were caught. In addition, the Constitution afforded no explicit protections to women, blacks, other racial or ethnic minorities, the poor, or the disabled.[5] Instead, the Constitution largely allowed the states to determine for themselves which persons would be free, be legally able to vote, attend schools, serve on juries, have access to public accommodations, and otherwise participate in the full benefits of citizenship. The result was that the states, to various degrees, regularly precluded certain groups of individuals from fully participating in political, economic, and social activities.

There is perhaps no more infamous a case in American constitutional law than *Dred Scott v. Sandford* (1857), wherein the Supreme Court ruled, among other things, that Dred Scott, a slave, was not considered a person under the Constitution, and therefore could not bring a lawsuit for his freedom in federal court. Read the Court's opinion in *Dred Scott* to understand the tenure and tone of racial inequality under the antebellum Constitution.

Dred Scott v. Sandford
60 U.S. 396 (1857)

The plaintiff [Dred Scott] was a negro slave, belonging to Dr. Emerson, who was a surgeon in the army of the United States. In the year 1834, he took the plaintiff from the State of Missouri to the military post at Rock Island, in the State of Illinois, and held him there as a slave until the month of April or May, 1836 . . . Dr. Emerson removed the plaintiff from said military post at Rock Island to the military post at Fort Snelling . . . in the Territory known as Upper Louisiana . . . until the year 1838. . . .

Before the commencement of this suit, said Dr. Emerson sold and conveyed the plaintiff [and his family] to the defendant, as slaves, and the defendant has ever since claimed to hold them, and each of them, as slaves.

[Scott and his family sued in federal court seeking their freedom. Scott based his claim on the fact that he had traveled with Emerson to Illinois, a free state, and to other free northern territories. As was the legal practice at the time, courts allowed slaves who were temporarily domiciled in free states to become permanently free. Scott sought the help of the federal courts in getting this legal practice applied to him and his family.]

Mr. Chief Justice Taney delivered the opinion of the court.

The question is simply this: Can a negro, whose ancestors were imported into this country, and sold as slaves, become a member of the political community formed and brought into existence by the Constitution of the United States, and as such become entitled to all the rights, and privileges, and immunities, guarantied by that instrument to the citizen? One of which rights is the privilege of suing in a court of the United States in the cases specified in the Constitution. . . .

The words "people of the United States" and "citizens" are synonymous terms, and mean the same thing. They both describe the political body who, according to our republican institutions, form the sovereignty, and who hold the power and conduct the Government through their representatives. They are what we familiarly call the "sovereign people," and every citizen is one of these people, and a constituent member of this sovereignty. The question before us is, whether the class of persons described in the plea in abatement compose a portion of this people, and are constituent members of this sovereignty? We think they are not, and that they are not included, and were not intended to be included, under the word "citizens" in the Constitution, and can therefore claim none of the rights and privileges which that instrument provides for and secures to citizens of the United States. On the contrary, they were at that time considered as a subordinate and inferior class of beings, who had been subjugated by the dominant race, and, whether emancipated or not, yet remained subject to their authority, and had no rights or privileges but such as those who held the power and the Government might choose to grant them. . . .

In the opinion of the court, the legislation and histories of the times, and the language used in the Declaration of Independence, show, that neither the class of persons who had been imported as slaves, nor their descendants, whether they had become free or not, were then acknowledged as a part of the people, nor intended to be included in the general words used in that memorable instrument.

It is difficult at this day to realize the state of public opinion in relation to that unfortunate race, which prevailed in the civilized and enlightened portions of the world at the time of the Declaration of Independence, and when the Constitution of the United States was framed and adopted. But the public history of every European nation displays it in a manner too plain to be mistaken.

They had for more than a century before been regarded as beings of an inferior order, and altogether unfit to associate with the white race, either in social or political relations; and so far inferior, that they had no rights which the white man was bound to respect; and that the negro might justly and lawfully be reduced to slavery for his benefit. He was bought and sold, and treated as an ordinary article of merchandise and traffic, whenever a profit could be made by it. This opinion was at that time fixed and universal in the civilized portion of the white race. It was regarded as an axiom in morals as well as in politics, which no one thought of disputing, or supposed to be open to dispute; and men in every grade and position in society daily and habitually acted upon it in their private pursuits, as well as in matters of public concern, without doubting for a moment the correctness of this opinion. . . .

We refer to these historical facts for the purpose of showing the fixed opinions concerning that race, upon which the statesmen of that day spoke and acted. It is necessary to do this, in order to determine whether the general terms used in the Constitution of the United States, as to the rights of man and the rights of the people, was intended to include them, or to give to them or their posterity the benefit of any of its provisions.

The language of the Declaration of Independence is equally conclusive:

It begins by declaring that, "when in the course of human events it becomes necessary for one people to dissolve the political bands which have connected them with another, and to assume among the powers of the earth the separate and equal station to which the laws of nature and nature's God entitle them, a decent respect for the opinions of mankind requires that they should declare the causes which impel them to the separation."

It then proceeds to say: "We hold these truths to be self-evident: that all men are created equal; that they are endowed by their Creator with certain unalienable rights; that among them is life, liberty, and the pursuit of happiness; that to secure these rights, Governments are instituted, deriving their just powers from the consent of the governed." . . .

But there are two clauses in the Constitution which point directly and specifically to the negro race as a separate class of persons, and show clearly that they were not regarded as a portion of the people or citizens of the Government then formed.

One of these clauses reserves to each of the thirteen States the right to import slaves until the year 1808, if it thinks proper. And the importation which it thus sanctions was unquestionably of persons of the race of which we are speaking, as the traffic in slaves in the United States had always been confined to them. And by the other provision the States pledge themselves to each other to maintain the right of property of the master, by delivering up to him any slave who may have escaped from his service, and be found within their respective territories. By the first above-mentioned clause, therefore, the right to purchase and hold this property is directly sanctioned and authorized for twenty years by the people who framed the Constitution. And by the second, they pledge themselves to maintain and uphold the right of the master in the manner specified, as long as the Government they then formed should endure. And these two provisions show, conclusively, that neither the description of persons therein referred to, nor their descendants, were embraced in any of the other provisions of the Constitution; for certainly these two clauses were not intended to confer on them or their posterity the blessings of liberty, or any of the personal rights so carefully provided for the citizen. . . .

[U]pon a full and careful consideration of the subject, the court is of opinion that . . . Dred Scott was not a citizen of Missouri within the meaning of the Constitution of the United States, and not entitled as such to sue in its courts; and, consequently, that the Circuit Court had no jurisdiction of the case, and that the judgment on the plea in abatement is erroneous . . .

[Taney's opinion continues by addressing the constitutionality of the Missouri Compromise of 1820 (a congressional act that outlawed slavery in all northern federal territories), and concludes that the Act was unconstitutional because it undermined the sovereign rights of states to determine for themselves whether to be free or slave states.]

Justice McLean and Justice Curtis dissented from the opinion of the Court.

sameness
A theory of equality based on the notion that each person should be given the same amount and type of resources and opportunities, regardless of the individual's circumstances.

proportionality
A theory of equality based on the notion that resources and opportunities ought to be allocated based upon individual circumstances.

Thirteenth Amendment
Ratified in 1865, this amendment bans "involuntary servitude" (slavery) within the United States.

Fourteenth Amendment
An amendment ratified in 1868 that contains a Due Process Clause and Equal Protection Clause that apply to the states. The ratification of the Fourteenth Amendment provided explicit mandates to the states regarding civil liberties, mandates not found in the original Bill of Rights. Under this amendment, the states are required to protect liberty, as well as life and property, under mandate of the federal constitution.

Privileges or Immunities Clause
Prohibits states from denying persons the privileges or immunities of American citizenship.

Due Process Clause
Fifth and Fourteenth Amendment provision that provides that the federal government may not deprive a person of life, liberty, or property without due process of law. This clause requires, among other things, that government treat individuals fairly during the criminal process, which may include such protections as the right to a fair trial, the right to be free from outrageous conduct by prosecutors or judges, the right to a full and fair appeal of a conviction, and the right to humane conditions of confinement. The Sixth Amendment provides several standards for the criminal process.

The notion of equality was found in the early Constitution in other forms. In Article I, some attention was given to equality of representation in Congress. Each state was given the same number of senators—two—thereby recognizing a notion of equality based on **"sameness"** (give everyone the same amount regardless of their circumstances), and each state was allocated delegates to the House of Representatives based on their respective populations, thereby establishing a notion of equality based on **proportionality** (allocate resources based on circumstances). But these two values did little to ensure other dimensions of equality among individuals. Likewise, Article IV, Section 2, provides that "[t]he Citizens of each State shall be entitled to all Privileges and Immunities of Citizens in the several States." At first glance this clause would appear to promote an element of equality among people. But in reality, this provision gave protections only to "citizens"—a group that, under most state and national laws, often did not include, at least completely, women, blacks, or other minorities during the early years of the democracy. Thus, despite initial reference to the value of equality in the Declaration of Independence, one would be hard pressed to claim that the early Constitution recognized equality among individuals as a significant value.

Beyond the text of the Constitution, the claim that there should be equality among persons was repeatedly stressed by the abolitionists, members of the women's rights movement, and other groups during the first half of the nineteenth century.[6] The concept of equality was further emphasized in President Lincoln's Emancipation Proclamation, an executive order issued in January 1, 1863, asserting that former slaves within "rebellious areas" were to be treated as free persons.[7] This value was also implicitly recognized in Abraham Lincoln's Gettysburg Address, a speech delivered in November 1863, during the Civil War. In this speech, Lincoln asserted that "our fathers brought forth on this continent, a new nation, conceived in Liberty, and dedicated to the proposition that all men are created equal."[8]

But equality among the masses largely did not begin to be recognized as a constitutional value until after the Civil War, when the Thirteenth, Fourteenth, and Fifteenth Amendments were enacted. The **Thirteenth Amendment,** ratified in 1865, bans "involuntary servitude" (slavery) within the United States. The **Fourteenth Amendment,** added in 1868, does a number of things, but chiefly, it provides the following: (1) the **Privileges or Immunities Clause,** which prohibits states from denying persons the privileges or immunities of American citizenship; (2) the **Due Process Clause,** which prevents the states from denying persons life, liberty, or property without due process of law; and (3) the **Equal Protection Clause,** which precludes the states from denying persons equal protection of the law. The Fourteenth Amendment also provides an **enforcement clause** in Section 5 that allows Congress to pass legislation to enforce the aforementioned provisions. And the **Fifteenth Amendment,** ratified in 1870, provides that government cannot deny persons the right to vote based on race, color, or previous servitude. Combined, these three amendments introduced, at least textually, the notion that equality was a constitutional value.

Later, other amendments were added to further promote sex-based, racial, and age-based equality in voting. In 1920, the **Nineteenth Amendment** was ratified, thereby guaranteeing voting rights regardless of a person's sex. The **Twenty-Fourth Amendment,** ratified in 1964, prohibits poll taxes or other taxes, which had been employed in some jurisdictions as a means of preventing blacks from voting. And the **Twenty-Sixth Amendment,** added in 1971, ensures that persons eighteen years and older are entitled to vote. Within each of these amendments is the implicit notion that equality matters under the Constitution.

The result is that, today, three primary values are represented in the Constitution—security, liberty, and equality. And, arguably, all modern-day constitutional controversies, when distilled down to their basic arguments, involve a tension between at least two, and often all three, of these values (see Figure 12-1).

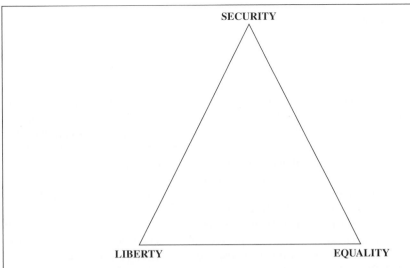

EXAMPLES OF TENSION BETWEEN AND AMONG CONSTITUTIONAL VALUES:

Roe v. Wade (1973) (abortion)—the government's interest in protecting the unborn (security) v. the right of pregnant women to govern their own bodies (liberty)

Texas v. Johnson (1989) (flag burning)—the government's interest in promoting the flag as a national symbol (security/order) v. the individual interest of political protest (liberty).

Boy Scouts of America v. Dale (2000) (sexual-orientation discrimination)—the Boy Scout's interest in freedom of association (liberty) v. the individual and state interest in negating discrimination (equality and security).

Lawrence v. Texas (2003) (same-sex sodomy)—the state interest in advancing the majoritarian will (morality) of the people v. the individual interest in sexual freedom (liberty) and being treated similarly to opposite-sex couples (equality).

FIGURE 12-1
Competing constitutional values

12.2 SETTING THE STAGE FOR EQUAL PROTECTION

The Fourteenth Amendment's Equal Protection Clause has been one of the primary vehicles for protecting constitutional equality. But the text of this provision applies only to state governments ("No *state* shall . . . deny any person within its jurisdiction the equal protection of the laws." (emphasis added). This narrow textual scope raises three initial questions: (1) How is the *federal* government held accountable for equal protection when the Fourteenth Amendment applies only to state action? (2) How involved does government have to be in denying equality before it will be considered subject to the Equal Protection Clause? (3) How are nongovernmental entities, such as private employers and owners of public accommodations (hotels, restaurants, etc.), held accountable when they deny equality?

12.2(a) State and Federal Sources for Equal Protection

The short answer to the first question is that the federal government is also constitutionally required to afford equal protection of the law. But the source for this requirement is the Fifth Amendment Due Process Clause ("No person . . . shall be deprived of life, liberty, or property, without due process of law"), not the Fourteenth Amendment Equal Protection Clause. The Supreme Court has ruled that, while the Fourteenth Amendment Equal Protection Clause is limited to state governmental action, the Fifth Amendment's Due Process Clause should be interpreted as including an implicit protection of equal protection. Essentially, the Court has found that one element of "due process" under the Fifth Amendment is that individuals should be treated equally under

Equal Protection Clause
Precludes the states from denying persons equal protection of the law.

enforcement clause
Found in Section 5 of the Fourteenth Amendment, this provision allows Congress to pass legislation to enforce the other clauses contained within the amendment, including Equal Protection Clause and Due Process Clause. This provision serves as the constitutional basis for many forms of federal civil rights legislation.

Fifteenth Amendment
Ratified in 1870, this amendment states that government cannot deny persons the right to vote based on race, color, or previous servitude.

Nineteenth Amendment
Ratified in 1920, this amendment guarantees voting rights regardless of a person's sex, thereby essentially affording women the right to vote.

Twenty-Fourth Amendment
Ratified in 1964, this amendment prohibits poll taxes or other taxes, which had been employed in some jurisdictions as a means of preventing blacks from voting.

Twenty-Sixth Amendment
Ratified in 1971, this amendment ensures that persons eighteen years and older are entitled to vote.

Bolling v. Sharpe
347 U.S. 497 (1954)

Mr. Chief Justice Warren delivered the opinion of the Court.

This case challenges the validity of segregation in the public schools of the District of Columbia. The petitioners, minors of the Negro race, allege that such segregation deprives them of due process of law under the Fifth Amendment. They were refused admission to a public school attended by white children solely because of their race. They sought the aid of the District Court for the District of Columbia in obtaining admission. That court dismissed their complaint. The Court granted a writ of certiorari before judgment in the Court of Appeals because of the importance of the constitutional question presented.

We have this day held that the Equal Protection Clause of the Fourteenth Amendment prohibits the states from maintaining racially segregated public schools. The legal problem in the District of Columbia is somewhat different, however. The Fifth Amendment, which is applicable in the District of Columbia, does not contain an Equal Protection Clause as does the Fourteenth Amendment which applies only to the states. But the concepts of equal protection and due process, both stemming from our American ideal of fairness, are not mutually exclusive. The "equal protection of the laws" is a more explicit safeguard of prohibited unfairness than "due process of law," and, therefore, we do not imply that the two are always interchangeable phrases. But, as this Court has recognized, discrimination may be so unjustifiable as to be violative of due process.

Classifications based solely upon race must be scrutinized with particular care, since they are contrary to our traditions and hence constitutionally suspect. As long ago as 1896, this Court declared the principle "that the Constitution of the United States, in its present form, forbids, so far as civil and political rights are concerned, discrimination by the General Government, or by the States, against any citizen because of his race." . . .

Although the Court has not assumed to define "liberty" with any great precision, that term is not confined to mere freedom from bodily restraint. Liberty under law extends to the full range of conduct which the individual is free to pursue, and it cannot be restricted except for a proper governmental objective. Segregation in public education is not reasonably related to any proper governmental objective, and thus it imposes on Negro children of the District of Columbia a burden that constitutes an arbitrary deprivation of their liberty in violation of the Due Process Clause.

In view of our decision that the Constitution prohibits the states from maintaining racially segregated public schools, it would be unthinkable that the same Constitution would impose a lesser duty on the Federal Government. We hold that racial segregation in the public schools of the District of Columbia is a denial of the due process of law guaranteed by the Fifth Amendment to the Constitution. . . .

It is so ordered.

the law. As a result, through the Fifth Amendment, the right to equal protection has been found to apply as much to federal action as it does to state action.

Read the Court's opinion in *Bolling v. Sharpe* (1954), a companion case to the famous school-desegregation case of *Brown v. Board of Education* (1954) (see §12.4 "Race-Based Classifications"), to fully appreciate how federal action is subject to the constitutional standards of equal protection.

12.2(b) The Need for "State" Action

The next basic question is how much governmental action must be involved for the case to be governed under the Fifth or Fourteenth Amendment? This is known as the **"State action" requirement,** referring not as much to "state" as a specific unit of government, but rather, to "state" as public or official conduct by government. Thus, when the phrase "state action" is used in equal protection cases, it is essentially referring to any form of governmental conduct—state, local, or federal.

"State action" requirement
An essential element to any due process or equal protection claim that requires sufficient government action—federal, state, or local—to be involved.

The need for state action in equal protection cases is consistent with other areas of constitutional law. Before a constitutional provision will be found to apply, there must first be some form of governmental conduct. In most cases, the role of the government will be readily apparent—Congress will pass a law, a local school board will enact a resolution, a police officer will take official action, and so on. As a result, in these cases, the initial issue of state action will have an easy answer. But in other equal protection cases, the answer is not so clear.

Take, for example, the Court's ruling in *Shelley v. Kraemer* (1948),[9] a case involving judicial enforcement of racially exclusive restrictive covenants in private land sales. In *Shelley*, Louis Kraemer, a white landowner in Missouri, sought to stop the sale of a neighboring house to J. D. Shelley, a black homebuyer. Kraemer asserted that there was a restrictive covenant (a legal provision in the deed to the home) that prevented the house from being sold to members of "the Negro or Mongolian race." At first glance, this case did not appear to involve any state action sufficient to make it constitutional matter of equal protection. Instead, it appeared to be a controversy between two owners of private land. And in fact, the Missouri Supreme Court found as much, ruling that the land covenant did not violate Shelley's right to equal protection. But the U.S. Supreme Court disagreed, holding that the judicial enforcement of the land covenant by Missouri courts did, in fact, involve state action—the courts themselves are state actors. As a result, the Court concluded that Missouri's judicial enforcement of the private land covenant deprived Shelley of equal protection.

In other cases, the presence of state action has not been found. For example, in *Moose Lodge v. Irvis* (1972),[10] the Court ruled that a private club's exclusion of blacks as members did not involve sufficient state action for equal protection purposes simply because the lodge used a state-provided liquor license during its hours of operation. This case and others illustrate the difficulty in answering the "state action" question in equal protection cases.[11] But before proceeding with any equal protection analysis, it first must be addressed.

Cyber Constitution
**Equal Protection
Over the Years**
www.youtube.com/
watch?v=tpWMPGRjtkE

12.2(c) Nongovernmental Discrimination

In many cases, discrimination comes at the hands of nongovernmental agents, businesses, private landowners, etc. Thus, the last basic question is, how can nongovernmental agents and entities be required to protect equality when the Equal Protection Clause applies only to state action?

The simple answer is that legislatures at all layers of government—federal, state, and local—have, at times, passed legislation prohibiting, to various degrees, nongovernmental agents from discriminating. This is called **civil rights legislation.** At the federal level, these laws are found in many different forms, ranging from the 1964 Civil Rights Act, which bars racial discrimination in places of public accommodation and prevents discrimination based on race, sex, and national origin in private employment decisions, to the Americans with Disabilities Act (ADA), which precludes discrimination based on disability (see Figure 12-2). State and local governments have also passed measures designed to promote equality and preclude discrimination. And in many cases, these laws are more encompassing than federal legislation. For example, many state and local jurisdictions prohibit discrimination against gay, lesbian, bisexual, and transgender individuals—a form of discrimination not explicitly covered by federal civil rights legislation.[12]

civil rights legislation
Laws designed to prohibit government and nongovernment agents from discriminating.

The fact that nongovernmental discrimination is largely regulated by legislative statutes, not constitutional mandates, does not eliminate constitutional controversies. For years, the ability of legislature to enact civil rights legislation targeting private or nongovernmental behavior was challenged as an unconstitutional exercise of legislative power. In the immediate aftermath of the Civil War, Congress attempted to ban racial discrimination in many nongovernmental settings. The Civil Rights Act of 1875 outlawed operators of places of public accommodations (hotels, restaurants, schools, churches, etc.) from denying people the "full enjoyment" of these places based on race or religion. Congress passed this law based on the enforcement provisions of the Thirteenth Amendment, which allows Congress to pass legislation enforcing the ban on involuntary servitude, and the Fourteenth Amendment, which allows Congress to enforce the Equal Protection Clause. But in *The Civil Rights Cases* (1883)[13]—a group of cases challenging the 1875 law—the Supreme Court struck down the law, holding that the enforcement clauses did not allow Congress to target the behavior of private individuals. In an 8–1 ruling, the Court ruled that discrimination in places of public

Civil Rights Act of 1871 (commonly known as "Section 1983)"—provides that anyone who, under color of state or local law, causes a person to be deprived of rights guaranteed by the U.S. Constitution, or federal law, can be ordered to pay for damages caused to that person.

Title II of the Civil Rights Act of 1964—provides that all persons are entitled to the full and equal enjoyment of the "goods, services, facilities, privileges, advantages and accommodations of any place of public accommodation . . . without discrimination or segregation on the ground of race, color, religion, or national origin."

Title VI of the Civil Rights Acts of 1964—provides that no person shall, on the basis of race, color, or national origin, be excluded from participation in, be denied the benefits of, or be subjected to discrimination under any program or activity receiving federal financial assistance.

Title VII of the Civil Rights Act of 1964—prohibits employers with fifteen or more employees from discriminating based on race, color, religion, sex, and national original.

Title VIII of the Civil Rights Act of 1964 (passed as the Civil Rights Act of 1968)—prohibits discrimination in the sale or rental of housing on the basis of race, color, religion, sex, familial status, or national origin. It also prohibits such discrimination in any residential real-estate transaction, including the making or purchasing of loans.

Title IX of the Civil Rights Act of 1964 (passed as the Federal Education Act of 1972)—provides that no person shall, on the basis of sex, be excluded from participation in, be denied the benefits of, or be subjected to discrimination under any program or activity receiving federal financial assistance.

Voting Rights Act of 1965—prohibits racial discrimination in elections.

Pregnancy Discrimination Act (1978)—amends the 1964 Civil Rights Act to clarify that sex-based discrimination includes discrimination based on pregnancy.

Age Discrimination in Employment Act (1967)—protects individuals who are 40 years of age or older from employment discrimination based on age.

Americans with Disabilities Act (1990)—bars discrimination against anyone who has a mental or physical disability in the area of employment, public services, transportation, public accommodations, and telecommunications.

FIGURE 12-2

Examples of federal civil rights legislation

accommodation did not involve slavery or state action, and therefore was not properly regulated under the Thirteenth and Fourteenth Amendments.

For decades, Congress struggled to pass civil rights legislation that would both effectively and constitutionally address discrimination inflicted by nongovernmental agents. Ultimately, Congress found success in passing the Civil Rights Act of 1964, legislation that banned racial discrimination in places of public accommodation and prohibited employment discrimination based on race, sex, religion, color, or national origin. Congress based this legislation, in part, on the interstate Commerce Clause of Article I, Section 8 (see Chapter 5, Section 4.5). And in *Heart of Atlanta Motel, Inc. v. United States* (1964) and *Katzenbach v. McClung* (1964),[14] the Supreme Court upheld this law, finding that, because discrimination in employment and places of public accommodation *affects* interstate commerce, Congress has the power to regulate it under Article I of the Constitution. Later, the Court also found that other antidiscrimination laws were constitutional under the enforcement clauses of the Thirteenth, Fourteenth, and Fifteenth Amendments, a decision that effectively reversed the Court's 1883 decision in *The Civil Rights Cases*.[15]

As a result, Congress has targeted nongovernmental discrimination by passing legislation under the Commerce Clause and/or the enforcement clauses of the Thirteenth, Fourteenth, and Fifteenth Amendments. To this extent, equality within nongovernmental settings is largely governed by statutory mandates, not constitutional provisions. It is important to note that some civil rights legislation applies to governmental entities as well. For example, Title VII of the 1964 Civil Rights Act, which prohibits employment discrimination based on race, sex, religion, and other characteristics, has been used to assess some government-based employment decisions. In *Ricci v. Destfano* (2009),[16] a group of New Haven, Connecticut firefighters sued their city's fire department after it threw out civil service examination test results. The city discarded the test result based on its belief that the results were racially disparate and, if maintained, would lead to lawsuits alleging racial discrimination. White and Hispanic firefighters who passed the exams sued the city, asserting that discarding the test results discriminated against them based on their race in violation of Title VII of the Civil Rights Act of 1964. In a 5–4 ruling, the Supreme Court agreed with the firefighters, finding that, under Title VII, the city did not demonstrate a "strong basis in evidence" for discarding the test results as a remedy for past discrimination.

It should also be noted that civil rights legislation is still being challenged as an unconstitutional exercise of congressional authority under the enforcement clauses— primarily that power found in Section 5 of the Fourteenth Amendment. Litigants have argued, with some success, that some legislation, such as the Family Medical Leave Act and the Americans with Disabilities Act (ADA), is not really *enforcing* the equal protection provision of the Fourteenth Amendment, but rather *creating* new rights not governed by the clause.[17] Consequently, in many contemporary cases, there is a dispute over whether Congress is properly exercising its enforcement powers under the Fourteenth Amendment, with the central issue being whether Congress is enforcing equal protection standards or creating new standards (see *Tennessee v. Lane* (2004), excerpted in this chapter).

It is important to note that some civil rights legislation applies to governmental agents as well. For example, the ADA requires governmental entities to ensure reasonable accommodations for certain disabilities. Thus, even if government is not responsible for protecting equality under the Constitution, it may be held accountable under legislative standards. Read the Court's opinion in *Tennessee v. Lane* (2004), a case involving state courts' liability under the ADA. Observe how a majority of the Court finds justification for the ADA in Section 5 of the Fourteenth Amendment, which allows Congress to enact legislation to further enforce the Equal Protection Clause and other provisions of the amendment.

Cyber Constitution
Equal Opportunity Employment Commission
www.eeoc.gov/

Tennessee v. Lane
541 US 509 (2004)

Justice Stevens delivered the opinion of the Court.

Title II of the Americans with Disabilities Act of 1990 (ADA or Act), provides that "no qualified individual with a disability shall, by reason of such disability, be excluded from participation in or be denied the benefits of the services, programs or activities of a public entity, or be subjected to discrimination by any such entity." The question presented in this case is whether Title II exceeds Congress' power under §5 of the Fourteenth Amendment.

In August 1998, respondents George Lane and Beverly Jones filed this action against the State of Tennessee and a number of Tennessee counties, alleging past and ongoing violations of Title II. Respondents, both of whom are paraplegics who use wheelchairs for mobility, claimed that they were denied access to, and the services of, the state court system by reason of their disabilities. Lane alleged that he was compelled to appear to answer a set of criminal charges on the second floor of a county court-

house that had no elevator. At his first appearance, Lane crawled up two flights of stairs to get to the courtroom. When Lane returned to the courthouse for a hearing, he refused to crawl again or to be carried by officers to the courtroom; he consequently was arrested and jailed for failure to appear. Jones, a certified court reporter, alleged that she has not been able to gain access to a number of county courthouses, and, as a result, has lost both work and an opportunity to participate in the judicial process. Respondents sought damages and equitable relief.

The State moved to dismiss the suit on the ground that it was barred by the Eleventh Amendment. The District Court denied the motion without opinion, and the State appealed. The United States intervened to defend Title II's abrogation of the States' Eleventh Amendment immunity. On April 28, 2000, after the appeal had been briefed and argued, the Court of Appeals for the Sixth Circuit entered an order holding the case in abeyance pending our decision in *Board of Trustees of Univ. of Ala. v. Garrett*, 531 U.S. 356 (2001).

In *Garrett*, we concluded that the Eleventh Amendment bars private suits seeking money damages for state violations of Title I of the ADA. We left open, however, the question whether the Eleventh Amendment permits suits for money damages under Title II. . . .

The ADA was passed by large majorities in both Houses of Congress after decades of deliberation and investigation into the need for comprehensive legislation to address discrimination against persons with disabilities. In the years immediately preceding the ADA's enactment, Congress held 13 hearings and created a special task force that gathered evidence from every State in the Union. The conclusions Congress drew from this evidence are set forth in the task force and Committee Reports, described in lengthy legislative hearings, and summarized in the preamble to the statute. Central among these conclusions was Congress' finding that "individuals with disabilities are a discrete and insular minority who have been faced with restrictions and limitations, subjected to a history of purposeful unequal treatment, and relegated to a position of political powerlessness in our society, based on characteristics that are beyond the control of such individuals and resulting from stereotypic assumptions not truly indicative of the individual ability of such individuals to participate in, and contribute to, society." . . .

Invoking "the sweep of congressional authority, including the power to enforce the fourteenth amendment and to regulate commerce," the ADA is designed "to provide a clear and comprehensive national mandate for the elimination of discrimination against individuals with disabilities." It forbids discrimination against persons with disabilities in three major areas of public life: employment, which is covered by Title I of the statute; public services, programs, and activities, which are the subject of Title II; and public accommodations, which are covered by Title III.

Title II prohibits any public entity from discriminating against "qualified" persons with disabilities in the provision or operation of public services, programs, or activities. The Act defines the term "public entity" to include state and local governments, as well as their agencies and instrumentalities . . . Title II's enforcement provision incorporates by reference §505 of the Rehabilitation Act of 1973, which authorizes private citizens to bring suits for money damages.

The Eleventh Amendment renders the States immune from "any suit in law or equity, commenced or prosecuted . . . by Citizens of another State, or by Citizens or Subjects of any Foreign State." Even though the Amendment "by its terms . . . applies only to suits against a State by citizens of another State," our cases have repeatedly held that this immunity also applies to unconsented suits brought by a State's own citizens. Our cases have also held that Congress may abrogate the State's Eleventh Amendment immunity. To determine whether it has done so in any given case, we "must resolve two predicate questions: first, whether Congress unequivo-cally expressed its intent to abrogate that immunity; and second, if it did, whether Congress acted pursuant to a valid grant of constitutional authority."

The first question is easily answered in this case. The Act specifically provides: "A State shall not be immune under the eleventh amendment to the Constitution of the United States from an action in Federal or State court of competent jurisdiction for a violation of this chapter." . . . The question, then, is whether Congress had the power to give effect to its intent. . . .

We have . . . repeatedly affirmed that "Congress may enact so-called prophylactic legislation that proscribes facially constitutional conduct, in order to prevent and deter unconstitutional conduct." *Nevada Dept. of Human Resources v. Hibbs*, 538 U.S. 721, 727–728 (2003). *See also City of Boerne v. Flores*, 521 U. S. 507, 518 (1997). . . .

Congress' §5 power is not, however, unlimited. While Congress must have a wide berth in devising appropriate remedial and preventative measures for unconstitutional actions, those measures may not work a "substantive change in the governing law." . . . In *Boerne*, we recognized that the line between remedial legislation and substantive redefinition is "not easy to discern," and that "Congress must have wide latitude in determining where it lies." But we also confirmed that "the distinction exists and must be observed," and set forth a test for so observing it: Section 5 legislation is valid if it exhibits "a congruence and proportionality between the injury to be prevented or remedied and the means adopted to that end." . . .

Congress' chosen remedy for the pattern of exclusion and discrimination described above, Title II's requirement of program accessibility, is congruent and proportional to its object of enforcing the right of access to the courts. The unequal treatment of disabled persons in the administration of judicial services has a long history, and has persisted despite several legislative efforts to remedy the problem of disability discrimination. Faced with considerable evidence of the shortcomings of previous legislative responses, Congress was justified in concluding that this "difficult and intractable proble[m]" warranted "added prophylactic measures in response."

The remedy Congress chose is nevertheless a limited one. Recognizing that failure to accommodate persons with disabilities will often have the same practical effect as outright exclusion, Congress required the States to take reasonable measures to remove architectural and other barriers to accessibility. But Title II does not require States to employ any and all means to make judicial services accessible to persons with disabilities, and it does not require States to compromise their essential eligibility criteria for public programs. It requires only "reasonable modifications" that would not fundamentally alter the nature of the service provided, and only when the individual seeking modification is otherwise eligible for the service. . . .

Judged against this backdrop, Title II's affirmative obligation to accommodate persons with disabilities in the administration of justice cannot be said to be "so out of proportion to a supposed remedial or preventive object that it cannot be understood as responsive to, or designed to prevent, unconstitutional behavior." It is, rather, a reasonable prophylactic measure, reasonably targeted to a legitimate end.

For these reasons, we conclude that Title II, as it applies to the class of cases implicating the fundamental right of access to the courts, constitutes a valid exercise of Congress' §5 authority to enforce the guarantees of the Fourteenth Amendment. The judgment of the Court of Appeals is therefore affirmed.

It is so ordered.

Justice Souter, Justice Ginsburg, Justice Breyer join, concurring.

Chief Justice Rehnquist, Justice Kennedy, Justice Scalia and Justice Thomas join, dissenting.

In the end, appreciate that even if a discrimination case is not governed under the Equal Protection Clause—either because it involves a nongovernmental entity or because it involves a form of governmental discrimination not fully protected against by the Fourteenth Amendment (age, disability, family medical problems, etc.)—the provisions of federal, state, or local civil rights legislation may apply to preclude the identified form of discrimination.

12.3 THE EQUAL PROTECTION CLAUSE

The Equal Protection Clause, whether explicitly found in the Fourteenth Amendment or implicitly found in the Fifth Amendment, guards against governmental discrimination by telling governments not to deny any person "the equal protection of the laws." But when you think about it, governments at all levels discriminate (make distinctions) on a daily basis. Police officers give tickets to some speeding drivers, but not to others. The government forces some taxpayers to pay higher taxes than other taxpayers. And public school teachers assign some students "A" grades, while others are given lower marks. Each of these examples involves a form of governmental discrimination or distinction.

On at least one level, the government in each case is denying individual's equal protection of the law. But if the government made these distinctions (tickets, taxes, and grades) based on factors that are deemed non-suspicious (driving above the speed limit, making a lot of income, or performing poorly on academic tests), most of us probably would find these forms of discrimination acceptable under the Constitution. If, however, the government made these distinctions based on other more suspicious factors (the driver's race, the taxpayer's religion, or the student's sex), most would likely question the constitutionality of such conduct. Thus, a central question in all equal protection cases is, how suspicious or suspect is the government's basis for discriminating? (See Figure 12-3.)

12.3(a) How Suspicious is the Discrimination?

In the past, the Court has suggested that there are three core considerations for assessing whether a form of discrimination is suspicious or suspect.[18] The first is whether there has been a **history of discrimination** based on the identified characteristic (race, sex,

history of discrimination
One of the three criteria used to determine whether a form of discrimination will be deemed suspect under the Due Process Clause. This involves a retrospective examination of whether and to what extent the characteristic has been unjustifiably mistreated in the United States.

Three questions to consider when evaluating the level of suspicion associated with a form of discrimination.

1. Is there a documented history of discrimination based on the identified characteristic?

2. Is the characteristic immutable?

3. Without sufficient constitutional protection, is it likely that the majoritarian process will continue to discriminate based on this characteristic?

FIGURE 12-3
Determining the suspiciousness of discrimination

religion, wealth, rate of speed, academic performance). This involves a retrospective examination of whether and to what extent the characteristic has been unjustifiably mistreated in the United States. If the characteristic is race or sex, there is an unfortunate history of harmful discrimination based on these factors. But if the characteristic is speeding or academic performance, the history of unjustifiable discrimination is less pronounced. Ultimately, if there is a well-documented accounting of discrimination based on the characteristic, there is a greater likelihood it will be deemed suspicious or suspect.

immutable characteristic
Another factor used to determine whether a form of discrimination will be deemed suspect under the Equal Protection Clause. An immutable characteristic is an attribute of a person that is not readily changeable. A person's race, sex, and eye color are considered immutable characteristics because they cannot be easily changed.

The second consideration is whether the basis of discrimination involves an **immutable characteristic** (an unchangeable attribute of a person). A person's race, sex, and eye color are considered immutable characteristics because they cannot be easily changed. However, a person's wealth, driving ability, or academic proficiency would not be considered immutable because they could be changed with time. The more immutable is the characteristic, the more suspicious or suspect it will be considered.

The third consideration involves a prediction about the future; namely, whether, without sufficient constitutional protection, it is likely that **majoritarian procedures** (democratic processes such as legislative action, electoral results, influence of public opinion, etc.) will continue to allow the identified characteristic to be used as a basis for discrimination. This is a more difficult assessment. But note that the operative phrase is "majoritarian procedure," which involves more than asking whether a majority or minority of people have this characteristic. Even if a majority of people have the identified feature, it is still possible that the majoritarian process could discriminate against them. For example, although women comprise a numeric majority of American residents, the majority of officials within Congress, the presidency, and the Supreme Court are men, which makes it possible for women to be treated unfavorably by the processes these institutions follow.[19] Again, this last consideration is likely to be much more subjective than the first two, but the Court, at times, has treated it as a relevant factor.

majoritarian process
A third consideration in determining whether a form of discrimination is suspect in nature. This essentially involves a prediction about the future, namely, whether, without sufficient constitutional protection, it is likely that democratic processes (such as legislative action, electoral results, influence of public opinion, etc.) will continue to allow the identified characteristic to be used as a basis for discrimination.

In the end, these three considerations can be used to classify the level of suspiciousness assigned to the form of discrimination present in a given case. There is no scientific precision to this process. If a characteristic meets two out of three considerations, it does not automatically make it suspect or semi-suspect. Rather, these considerations are just that—considerations—to be discussed before assigning a level of suspiciousness to a given category of characteristics.

12.3(b) What Constitutional Standard Applies?

suspect classification
A type of distinction or discrimination that is highly questionable and deserves the highest form of judicial scrutiny. Governmental distinctions based on race and alienage (in some cases) have been deemed "suspect" forms of discrimination.

To date, the Supreme Court has identified three categories or classifications of suspiciousness—suspect, semi-suspect, and non-suspect. Think of these categories as "smell tests." Some forms of discrimination immediately smell very bad (racial discrimination), while other forms do not initially offend the senses (grades on tests). Characteristics that are assigned to the **suspect classification** are considered highly suspicious or malodorous—at least initially, they smell very bad. The Court has assigned governmental distinctions based on race, alienage (in some cases), and discrimination that interferes with fundamental rights (voting, interstate travel, marriage, etc.) (see Section 12.8) as "suspect" forms of discrimination. Characteristics assigned to the **semi-suspect classification** are somewhat suspicious; they do not smell perfectly clean, but they are not entirely suspicious or malodorous. The Court has included sex-based (male v. female) discrimination and distinctions based on whether a person's parents were married when the person was born (known as legitimacy/illegitimacy in some circles) as forms of semi-suspect discrimination. And finally, all other forms of discrimination are assigned to the **non-suspect classification**—forms that are deemed "clean smelling," at least at the outset. Essentially, if a characteristic does not fall into one of the first two classifications, by default, it will be placed into this last classification. The Court has treated a person's wealth, age, alienage (in some cases), sexual

semi-suspect classification
A type of distinction or discrimination that is partially or somewhat suspicious under the Constitution and that deserves heightened, though not the highest, form of judicial scrutiny. This includes sex-based (male v. female) discrimination and distinctions based on whether a person's parents were married when the person was born.

THE FOURTEENTH AMENDMENT LEGITIMACY DEBATE

As was mentioned in Chapter 1, a minor, but perennial debate concerning the legitimacy of the Fourteenth Amendment exists. Amendments 13, 14, and 15, commonly known as Reconstruction or Post–Civil War Amendments, were enacted immediately following the Civil War. There are two theories about the illegitimacy of the amendment. The first concerns its initiation, and the second, its ratification.

Amendments to the Constitution must be proposed using one of two methods, vote by two-thirds of the states or two-thirds of both the U.S. House and the Senate. The Fourteenth Amendment was initiated using the latter. However, the senators of eleven southern states and one senator from New Jersey were excluded from the Senate for the vote. For this reason, some contend that the amendment was not constitutionally initiated.

In terms of ratification, the Constitution requires ratification by three-fourths of state legislatures or by conventions in three-fourths of the states. There were thirty-seven states in the union when the amendment was proposed. Accordingly, twenty-eight states were required for ratification. The amendment failed when thirteen states refused to ratify. In reaction, Congress enacted several Reconstruction Acts targeting the states that refused to ratify the amendment. These states' governments were disbanded and new governments were constructed in their place. In addition, the same states were placed under martial law, and their representation in Congress was revoked until the amendment was ratified.

orientation, and discrimination depriving individuals of education, welfare, or housing as non-suspect forms of discrimination for equal protection purposes.

The classification process is important because it determines the type of constitutional standard or test that will be applied to the government's discrimination. Like other standards used in constitutional law, equal protection cases involve weighing individual and governmental interests against each other. And each classification of discrimination has a corresponding standard or calibration for the scale. In cases where a suspect classification is involved, the government must meet the **strict scrutiny test**—it must show that its suspect form of discrimination is necessary (narrowly tailored) to meet a compelling governmental interest. In cases involving a semi-suspect form of discrimination, the government must satisfy the **intermediate scrutiny test**—it must show that its semi-suspect form of discrimination is substantially related to an important governmental interest. And in cases where the discrimination is non-suspect, the government must satisfy the **rational basis test**—it must show that its non-suspect distinction is rationally related to a legitimate governmental interest (see Figure 12-4).

Obviously, it is much more difficult for the government to meet the strict scrutiny test than the rational basis test. This has given rise to the adage "strict in theory,

non-suspect classification
Forms of discrimination that are not suspicious under the Constitution and thus require only minimal judicial scrutiny. This includes discrimination based on a person's wealth, age, alienage (in some cases), sexual orientation, and discrimination depriving individuals of education, welfare, or housing.

strict scrutiny test
A constitutional standard requiring the government to show that its suspect form of discrimination is necessary (narrowly tailored) to meet a compelling governmental interest (see also Chapters 9, 10, and 11).

intermediate scrutiny test
A constitutional standard used in cases involving a semi-suspect form of discrimination that requires the government to show that its semi-suspect form of discrimination is substantially related to an important governmental interest.

rational basis test
A constitutional standard used to review cases involving a non-suspect form of discrimination that requires the government to show that its non-suspect distinction is rationally related to a legitimate governmental interest.

Level of Discrimination	Legal Standard Applied	Forms of Discrimination Where Applied
Suspect	**Strict Scrutiny**—Is the government action necessary to promote a compelling governmental interest?	Race Fundamental rights (right to travel, vote, marry, etc.)
Semi-suspect	**Intermediate Scrutiny**—Is the government action substantially related to an important governmental interest?	Sex Marital status of person's parents at time of birth (legitimacy/illegitimacy)
Rational basis	**Rational Basis Test**—Is the government action rationally related to a legitimate governmental interest?	Age Income/wealth Sexual orientation

FIGURE 12-4

Scrutinizing discrimination—how closely does the court look?

fatal in fact"[20]—a belief that if the government is held to the strict scrutiny standard, its policy will likely be declared unconstitutional. But in reality, some governmental distinctions have passed the strict scrutiny test,[21] while others have failed the rational basis test.[22] The point is, regardless of which constitutional standard of scrutiny is applied, the competing interests of the individual and government must be weighed and judged based against each other.

In addition, it is important to note that some state and local governments through their own constitutions or charters have elevated certain types of discrimination to higher levels of scrutiny. For example, Hawaii and some other states have identified sex-based discrimination as a suspect form of discrimination.[23] Consequently, if this form of discrimination were addressed under the state, as opposed to federal, Constitution, the government would have to satisfy the strict scrutiny standard. Just

Equal Protection: A Framework for Analysis

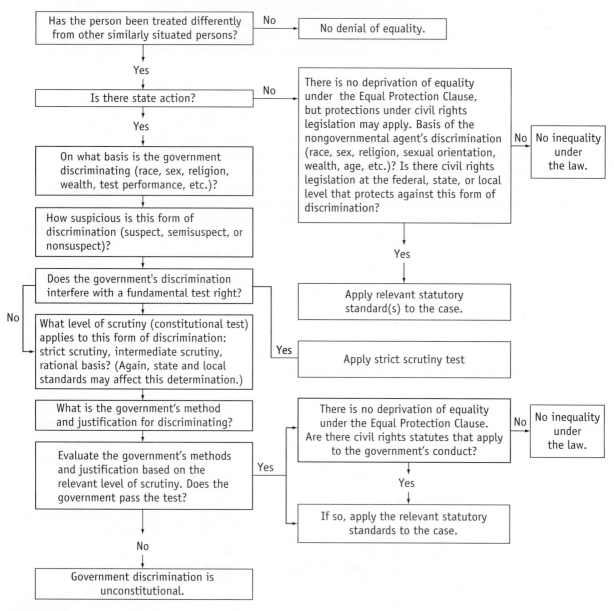

FIGURE 12-5

Putting it all together—assessing legal protections for equality

keep in mind that there are state and local constitutional standards that may enhance the level of protection afforded to a particular classification.

12.3(c) Putting It All Together: State Action, Civil Rights Laws, and Equal Protection

In the end, there will always be forms of discrimination in law and policy. The challenge is sorting out permissible forms of discrimination from those forms that are either unconstitutional or in violation of civil rights laws. Like other areas of constitutional law, there is no precise formula or program to determine the difference between the two. But a general framework can be used to help organize such a review. This framework involves asking several questions, including the following: (1) Is the government treating someone differently from another similarly-situated person? (2) If so, on what basis is the government discriminating (race, sex, religion, wealth, test performance, etc.)? (3) Is the government interfering with a fundamental right? (4) How suspicious is this form of discrimination (suspicious, semi-suspicious, or non-suspicious)? (5) What test (constitutional standard) applies to this form of discrimination (strict scrutiny, intermediate scrutiny, or rational basis)? (6) What is the government's justification (excuse) for discriminating? (7) Does the government's justification for making such a distinction outweigh the individual's interest in equal protection based on the applicable test (scale)? When combined with the other basic considerations relevant to matters of legal equality (see Sections 12.1 and 12.2), these questions provide a basic outline for reviewing equal protection under the Constitution and civil rights legislation. See Figure 12-5.

12.4 RACE-BASED CLASSIFICATIONS

12.4(a) The Separate but Equal Doctrine

As the Court's opinion in *Dred Scott v. Sandford* (1857) (see Section 12.1) illustrates, racial minorities in the United States had little, if any, constitutional protection against inequality under the pre–Civil War Constitution. And the practical reality is that, even with the postwar passage of the Thirteenth, Fourteenth, and Fifteenth Amendments, blacks and other racial minorities fared little better during the several decades that followed the war. Although the Thirteenth Amendment banned involuntary servitude, the Fourteenth Amendment guaranteed equal protection, and the Fifteenth Amendment banned race-based voting discrimination, governments still used race to treat individuals differently and unfairly. One of the primary tools for such discrimination came in the form of **segregation**—policies that separated individuals based on race. In many areas, these policies used race as a basis to separate drinking fountains, seating (as in the case of theaters, restaurants, courtrooms, transportation, etc.), and schools.

segregation
A policy used to discriminate whereby individuals are separated based on a particular attribute, such as race, sex, and so on.

The Supreme Court initially sanctioned some segregation policies under the Equal Protection Clause based on the **separate but equal doctrine**—a legal theory holding that as long as government provides individuals with relatively the same amount of resources or services, it may segregate individuals based on race without denying them equal protection. This theory was promulgated in *Plessy v. Ferguson* (1896) (excerpted in this chapter), a case wherein the Court upheld Louisiana's race-based segregation of public transportation. In an 8–1 ruling, the Court reasoned that even with segregated seating, blacks were still afforded the same public transportation. In a now-famous dissenting opinion, Justice John Harlan voted to strike down Louisiana's segregation policy, asserting that it bestowed a "badge of slavery or servitude" upon blacks in society. This dissent later became the rationale for many contemporary antidiscrimination laws.

separate but equal doctrine
A legal theory promulgated in *Plessy v. Ferguson* (1896) holding that as long as government provides individuals with relatively the same amount of resources or services, it may segregate individuals based on race without denying them equal protection. This theory was rejected by the Court in *Brown v. Board of Education* (1954).

Booking photo of Rosa Parks at the time of her arrest for refusing to give up her seat on a Montgomery, Alabama, bus to a white passenger on December 1, 1955.
© Everett Collection Inc/Alamy

Plessy v. Ferguson
163 U.S. 537 (1896)

Mr. Justice Brown, after stating the facts in the foregoing language, delivered the opinion of the court.

This case turns upon the constitutionality of an act of the general assembly of the state of Louisiana, passed in 1890, providing for separate railway carriages for the white and colored races.

The first section of the statute enacts "that all railway companies carrying passengers in their coaches in this state, shall provide equal but separate accommodations for the white, and colored races, by providing two or more passenger coaches for each passenger train, or by dividing the passenger coaches by a partition so as to secure separate accommodations: provided, that this section shall not be construed to apply to street railroads. No person or persons shall be permitted to occupy seats in coaches, other than the ones assigned to them, on account of the race they belong to." . . .

The constitutionality of this act is attacked upon the ground that it conflicts both with the thirteenth amendment of the constitution, abolishing slavery, and the fourteenth amendment, which prohibits certain restrictive legislation on the part of the states. . . .

The object of the [fourteenth] amendment was undoubtedly to enforce the absolute equality of the two races before the law, but, in the nature of things, it could not have been intended to abolish distinctions based upon color, or to enforce social, as distinguished from political,

equality, or a commingling of the two races upon terms unsatisfactory to either. Laws permitting, and even requiring, their separation, in places where they are liable to be brought into contact, do not necessarily imply the inferiority of either race to the other, and have been generally, if not universally, recognized as within the competency of the state legislatures in the exercise of their police power. The most common instance of this is connected with the establishment of separate schools for white and colored children, which have been held to be a valid exercise of the legislative power even by courts of states where the political rights of the colored race have been longest and most earnestly enforced. . . .

So far, then, as a conflict with the fourteenth amendment is concerned, the case reduces itself to the question whether the statute of Louisiana is a reasonable regulation, and with respect to this there must necessarily be a large discretion on the part of the legislature. In determining the question of reasonableness, it is at liberty to act with reference to the established usages, customs, and traditions of the people, and with a view to the promotion of their comfort, and the preservation of the public peace and good order. Gauged by this standard, we cannot say that a law which authorizes or even requires the separation of the two races in public conveyances is unreasonable, or more obnoxious to the fourteenth amendment than the acts of congress requiring separate schools for colored children in the District of Columbia, the constitutionality of which does not seem to have been questioned, or the corresponding acts of state legislatures. . . .

If the two races are to meet upon terms of social equality, it must be the result of natural affinities, a mutual appreciation of each other's merits, and a voluntary consent of individuals. . . . Legislation is powerless to eradicate racial instincts, or to abolish distinctions based upon physical differences, and the attempt to do so can only result in accentuating the difficulties of the present situation. If the civil and political rights of both races be equal, one cannot be inferior to the other civilly or politically. If one race be inferior to the other socially, the constitution of the United States cannot put them upon the same plane. . . .

The judgment of the court below is therefore affirmed.

Mr. Justice Harlan dissenting.

In respect of civil rights, common to all citizens, the constitution of the United States does not, I think, permit any public authority to know the race of those entitled to be protected in the enjoyment of such rights. Every true man has pride of race, and under appropriate circumstances, when the rights of others, his equals before the law, are not to be affected, it is his privilege to express such pride and to take such action based upon it as to

him seems proper. But I deny that any legislative body or judicial tribunal may have regard to the race of citizens when the civil rights of those citizens are involved. Indeed, such legislation as that here in question is inconsistent not only with that equality of rights which pertains to citizenship, national and state, but with the personal liberty enjoyed by every one within the United States. . . .

The white race deems itself to be the dominant race in this country. And so it is, in prestige, in achievements, in education, in wealth, and in power. So, I doubt not, it will continue to be for all time, if it remains true to its great heritage, and holds fast to the principles of constitutional liberty. But in view of the constitution, in the eye of the law, there is in this country no superior, dominant, ruling class of citizens. There is no caste here. Our constitution is color-blind, and neither knows nor tolerates classes among citizens. In respect of civil rights, all citizens are equal before the law. . . .

In my opinion, the judgment this day rendered will, in time, prove to be quite as pernicious as the decision made by this tribunal in the *Dred Scott* Case. . . .

The arbitrary separation of citizens, on the basis of race, while they are on a public highway, is a badge of servitude wholly inconsistent with the civil freedom and the equality before the law established by the constitution. It cannot be justified upon any legal grounds.

12.4(b) Ignoring *Plessy: Brown v. Board of Education*

The separate but equal doctrine established in *Plessy* served as the equal protection standard in race-based cases for more than fifty years. Under this doctrine, governmental distinctions based on race were upheld as long as they provided somewhat equal resources or services and met the rational basis test (were rationally related to a legitimate governmental interest).

But in 1954 the Court refused to follow this policy in one of its most famous rulings—*Brown v. Board of Education* (1954) (often called "*Brown I,*" excerpted in this chapter). *Brown I* was one of five cases the Court accepted for review in 1951 involving racial segregation in public schools. In addition to *Brown I,* which involved a Kansas school district, the other cases involved challenges to school segregation policies in Delaware, South Carolina, Virginia, and the District of Columbia (see *Bolling v. Sharpe* in Section 12.2). The Court's decision in *Brown I* was unanimous in refusing to enforce the separate but equal doctrine established in *Plessy.* As you read *Brown I,* note the significance the Court placed on the value of education in American society and how the Court used the psychological impact of racial segregation to justify its ruling.

In *Brown I,* the Court did not issue an order to enforce its ruling. Instead, the Court, concerned about how schools and states might react to the ruling, scheduled a separate hearing to determine an appropriate remedy. In 1955, following this additional round of oral arguments, the Court announced its second decision in *Brown* (often referred to as "*Brown II,*" also excerpted in this chapter), wherein it instructed lower courts to issue orders that were "necessary and proper" to integrate black students into public school "on a racially nondiscriminatory basis with all deliberate speed." This process is known as **desegregation.**

desegregation
The process by which the policies and effects of exclusion and separation are reversed and corrected.

Brown v. Board of Education I
347 U.S. 483 (1954)

Mr. Chief Justice Warren delivered the opinion of the Court.

These cases come to us from the States of Kansas, South Carolina, Virginia, and Delaware. They are premised on different facts and different local conditions, but a common legal question justifies their consideration together in this consolidated opinion.

In each of the cases, minors of the Negro race, through their legal representatives, seek the aid of the courts in obtaining admission to the public schools of their community on a nonsegregated basis. In each instance, they had been denied admission to schools attended by white children under laws requiring or permitting segregation according to race. This segregation was alleged to deprive the plaintiffs of the equal protection of the laws under the Fourteenth Amendment. . . .

The plaintiffs contend that segregated public schools are not "equal" and cannot be made "equal," and that hence they are deprived of the equal protection of the laws. Because of the obvious importance of the question presented, the Court took jurisdiction. Argument was heard in the 1952 Term, and reargument was heard this Term on certain questions propounded by the Court. . . .

In the first cases in this Court construing the Fourteenth Amendment, decided shortly after its adoption, the Court interpreted it as proscribing all state-imposed discriminations against the Negro race. The doctrine of "separate but equal" did not make its appearance in this Court until 1896 in the case of *Plessy v. Ferguson*, [163 U.S. 537 (1896)], involving not education but transportation. American courts have since labored with the doctrine for over half a century. . . .

In approaching this problem, we cannot turn the clock back to 1868 when the [Fourteenth] Amendment was adopted, or even to 1896 when *Plessy v. Ferguson* was written. We must consider public education in the light of its full development and its present place in American life throughout the Nation. Only in this way can it be determined if segregation in public schools deprives these plaintiffs of the equal protection of the laws.

Today, education is perhaps the most important function of state and local governments. Compulsory school attendance laws and the great expenditures for education both demonstrate our recognition of the importance of education to our democratic society. It is required in the performance of our most basic public responsibilities, even service in the armed forces. It is the very foundation of good citizenship. Today it is a principal instrument in awakening the child to cultural values, in preparing him for later professional training, and in helping him to adjust normally to his environment. In these days, it is doubtful that any child may reasonably be expected to succeed in life if he is denied the opportunity of an education. Such an opportunity, where the state has undertaken to provide it, is a right which must be made available to all on equal terms.

We come then to the question presented: Does segregation of children in public schools solely on the basis of race, even though the physical facilities and other "tangible" factors may be equal, deprive the children of the minority group of equal educational opportunities? We believe that it does. . . .

To separate [black school children] from others of similar age and qualifications solely because of their race generates a feeling of inferiority as to their status in the community that may affect their hearts and minds in a way unlikely ever to be undone. . . .

Whatever may have been the extent of psychological knowledge at the time of *Plessy v. Ferguson*, this finding is amply supported by modern authority. Any language in *Plessy v. Ferguson* contrary to this finding is rejected.

We conclude that in the field of public education the doctrine of "separate but equal" has no place. Separate educational facilities are inherently unequal. Therefore, we hold that the plaintiffs and others similarly situated for whom the actions have been brought are, by reason of the segregation complained of, deprived of the equal protection of the laws guaranteed by the Fourteenth Amendment. This disposition makes unnecessary any discussion whether such segregation also violates the Due Process Clause of the Fourteenth Amendment.

Because these are class actions, because of the wide applicability of this decision, and because of the great variety of local conditions, the formulation of decrees in these cases presents problems of considerable complexity. On reargument, the consideration of appropriate relief was necessarily subordinated to the primary question— the constitutionality of segregation in public education. We have now announced that such segregation is a denial of the equal protection of the laws. In order that we may have the full assistance of the parties in formulating decrees, the cases will be restored to the docket, and the parties are requested to present further argument . . . [on the appropriate remedy].

It is so ordered.

12.4(c) Implementing *Brown*'s Mandate: School Desegregation Cases

The "all deliberate speed" instruction from the Court in *Brown II* offered no firm guideline to school districts or courts regarding how desegregation was to be implemented and, perhaps more critically, gave no firm deadline for such implementation.

The result is that, even though more than fifty years have passed since the Court's *Brown* decisions, many assert that these rulings have not been fully implemented.

In the immediate aftermath of *Brown*, many school districts simply refused to integrate their educational facilities, choosing to spend more time on "deliberating" desegregation and less time on "speeding" it up.[24] Many members of Congress openly chastised the Court for its decision, asserting that it was unconstitutional. And the Court received little initial backing from then-president Dwight Eisenhower, although Eisenhower eventually did send federal authorities into Little Rock, Arkansas, to enforce a federal desegregation order. The Court nonetheless stood behind its decision.[25]

Brown v. Board of Education II
349 U.S. 294 (1955)

Mr. Chief Justice Warren delivered the opinion of the Court.

These cases were decided on May 17, 1954. The opinions of that date, declaring the fundamental principle that racial discrimination in public education is unconstitutional, are incorporated herein by reference. All provisions of federal, state, or local law requiring or permitting such discrimination must yield to this principle. There remains for consideration the manner in which relief is to be accorded.

Because these cases arose under different local conditions and their disposition will involve a variety of local problems, we requested further argument on the question of relief. In view of the nationwide importance of the decision, we invited the Attorney General of the United States and the Attorneys General of all states requiring or permitting racial discrimination in public education to present their views on that question. The parties, the United States, and the States of Florida, North Carolina, Arkansas, Oklahoma, Maryland, and Texas filed briefs and participated in the oral argument. . . .

Full implementation of these constitutional principles may require solution of varied local school problems. School authorities have the primary responsibility for elucidating, assessing, and solving these problems; courts will have to consider whether the action of school authorities constitutes good faith implementation of the governing constitutional principles. Because of their proximity to local conditions and the possible need for further hearings, the courts which originally heard these cases can best perform this judicial appraisal. Accordingly, we believe it appropriate to remand the cases to those courts.

In fashioning and effectuating the decrees, the courts will be guided by equitable principles. Traditionally, equity has been characterized by a practical flexibility in shaping its remedies and by a facility for adjusting and reconciling public and private needs. These cases call for the exercise of these traditional attributes of equity power. At stake is the personal interest of the plaintiffs in admission to public schools as soon as practicable on a nondiscriminatory basis. To effectuate this interest may call for elimination of a variety of obstacles in making the transition to school systems operated in accordance with the constitutional principles set forth in our May 17, 1954, decision. Courts of equity may properly take into account the public interest in the elimination of such obstacles in a systematic and effective manner. But it should go without saying that the vitality of these constitutional principles cannot be allowed to yield simply because of disagreement with them.

While giving weight to these public and private considerations, the courts will require that the defendants make a prompt and reasonable start toward full compliance with our May 17, 1954, ruling. Once such a start has been made, the courts may find that additional time is necessary to carry out the ruling in an effective manner. The burden rests upon the defendants to establish that such time is necessary in the public interest and is consistent with good faith compliance at the earliest practicable date. . . . During this period of transition, the courts will retain jurisdiction of these cases.

The judgments below, except that in the Delaware case, are accordingly reversed and the cases are remanded to the District Courts to take such proceedings and enter such orders and decrees consistent with this opinion as are necessary and proper to admit to public schools on a racially nondiscriminatory basis with all deliberate speed the parties to these cases. . . .

It is so ordered.

During the 1960s and 1970s, much of the Court's time was spent on reviewing the orders of federal district courts, who were the chief supervisors of school desegregation plans, and trying to provide them with guidance in their rulings. In *Alexander v. Holmes County Board of Education* (1969),[26] the Court refused to allow additional time for southern school districts to implement *Brown*. In *Carter v. West Feliciana Parish School Board* (1970),[27] the Court again ordered southern school districts to speed up the process of desegregation. And in *Swann v. Charlotte-Mecklenberg Board of Education* (1974),[28] the Court upheld court-ordered busing as a method of achieving school desegregation. But overall, little aggregate progress was made in achieving full implementation of *Brown*, and the Court's membership began to change.

With the addition of new justices appointed by Presidents Nixon, Reagan, and Bush between 1969 and 1992, the Court began to limit district courts' authority to fashion desegregation orders and to allow school districts to reduce their desegregation efforts. In *Milliken v. Bradley* (1974),[29] the Court, in a 5–4 decision, reversed a lower-court ruling that had allowed Detroit, Michigan, to impose an *inter*district busing plan (busing children among different school districts) as a means for solving *intra*district segregation problems (problems within a single district). In *Board of Education of Oklahoma City Public Schools v. Dowell* (1991),[30] the Court, in a 5–3 ruling, held that school districts under federal desegregation orders could end forced busing of students and begin implementing neighborhood schools, even though this plan would likely result in a racial imbalance among the schools. In his majority opinion, Chief Justice Rehnquist held that desegregation orders could be ended if "the vestiges of past discrimination" were eliminated. In *Freeman v. Pitts* (1992),[31] the Court unanimously ruled that federal courts could withdraw from supervising school districts incrementally, even when full compliance with Brown in all areas of school operations has not been achieved. And in *Missouri v. Jenkins* (1995),[32] the Court, in a 5–4 ruling, found that a federal district court erred by ordering Missouri to increase teacher salaries and fund remedial "quality education" programs as a means to achieve desegregation within its public schools.

Today, to be sure, policies imposed by school districts and states that require racial segregation in schools are constitutionally prohibited. These overt forms of separation are referred to as *de jure* **segregation,** meaning segregation established or formally reinforced by law. The Equal Protection Clause, per *Brown*, clearly guards against this form of discrimination.

But the fact of the matter remains that within and among many public school systems, children are still segregated by race due to factual circumstances. This is known as *de facto* **segregation.** With regard to this form of segregation, the Court has ruled that the Equal Protection Clause does not apply to racially segregated schools that are not the result of state-mandated (*de jure*) discrimination. According to Chief Justice Rehnquist, "[School desegregation orders] are not intended to operate in perpetuity. . . . Dissolving a desegregation decree after the local authorities have operated in compliance with it for a reasonable period of time properly recognizes . . . that a federal court's regulatory control of [public school] systems not extend beyond the time required to remedy the effects of past intentional discrimination."[33]

12.4(d) Race as a Suspect Form of Discrimination

Since *Brown*, the Court generally has treated race-based classifications as highly suspect forms of discrimination. Certainly, at least when applied to black Americans, race meets all three criteria for a suspect classification (see Section 12.3)—there is a well-documented history of discrimination against blacks, race is an immutable characteristic, and there are sound arguments that the majoritarian process continues to discriminate based on race, at least to some degree.

But, interestingly, the Court has not limited its classification of race as a suspect category to cases involving alleged discrimination against black Americans or other racial minorities. Instead, the Court has treated all racial distinctions—even those that discriminate against Caucasians—as a suspect form of discrimination. Despite the fact that Caucasian Americans would not likely meet either the first or the third consideration for being a suspect class (no history of discrimination and no current threat from the majoritarian process), the Court essentially has grouped all forms of racial distinctions into the suspect category.[34] As a result, in most cases, the government is required to justify all forms of race-based discrimination, regardless of the racial classification, under the strict scrutiny standard.

---

de jure segregation
Segregation established or formally reinforced by law or policy.

de facto segregation
Segregation created based on factors (social, economic, etc.) not directly linked to contemporary law or public policy.

In *Parents Involved in Community Schools v. Seattle School Dist. No. 1* and *Meredith v. Jefferson County Board of Education* (2007) (excerpted in this chapter), the Court decided two companion cases involving school districts in Louisville and Seattle that had used students' race as a factor in an effort to integrate their schools. These policies were defended as an effort to ensure diversity within and among the schools. The Court, however, in a sharply divided 5–4 ruling, struck down the policies under the Equal Protection Clause, finding that they fell short of meeting the strict scrutiny standard. Much of the discussion between and among the plurality, concurring, and dissenting opinions centered on whether the decision was consistent with the legacy of the Court's decision in *Brown v. Board of Education*. As you read the decision, assess which opinion within the decision comes closest to meeting the letter and spirit of the Court's landmark ruling in *Brown*.

Cyber Constitution
Gratz and *Grutter*: **Split Decision on Affirmative Action** www.npr.org/news/specials/michigan/

Parents Involved in Community Schools v. Seattle School Dist. No. 1 and Meredith v. Jefferson County Board of Education
551 U.S. 701 (2007)

Chief Justice Roberts announced the judgment of the Court, and delivered the opinion of the Court with respect to Parts I, II, III-A, and III-C, and an opinion with respect to Parts III-B and IV, in which Justices Scalia, Thomas, and Alito join.

The school districts in these cases voluntarily adopted student assignment plans that rely upon race to determine which public schools certain children may attend. The Seattle school district classifies children as white or non-white; the Jefferson County school district as black or "other." In Seattle, this racial classification is used to allocate slots in oversubscribed high schools. In Jefferson County, it is used to make certain elementary school assignments and to rule on transfer requests. In each case, the school district relies upon an individual student's race in assigning that student to a particular school, so that the racial balance at the school falls within a predetermined range based on the racial composition of the school district as a whole. Parents of students denied assignment to particular schools under these plans solely because of their race brought suit, contending that allocating children to different public schools on the basis of race violated the Fourteenth Amendment guarantee of equal protection. The Courts of Appeals below upheld the plans. We granted certiorari, and now reverse.

Both cases present the same underlying legal question—whether a public school that had not operated legally segregated schools or has been found to be unitary may choose to classify students by race and rely upon that classification in making school assignments. . . .

It is well established that when the government distributes burdens or benefits on the basis of individual racial classifications, that action is reviewed under strict scrutiny. *Johnson v. California*, 543 U.S. 499, 505-506 (2005); *Grutter v. Bollinger*, 539 U.S. 306, 326 (2003). As the Court recently reaffirmed, "racial classifications are simply too pernicious to permit any but the most exact connection between justification and classification."

Gratz v. Bollinger, 539 U.S. 244, 270 (2003). In order to satisfy this searching standard of review, the school districts must demonstrate that the use of individual racial classifications in the assignment plans here under review is "narrowly tailored" to achieve a "compelling" government interest.

Without attempting in these cases to set forth all the interests a school district might assert, it suffices to note that our prior cases, in evaluating the use of racial classifications in the school context, have recognized two interests that qualify as compelling. The first is the compelling interest of remedying the effects of past intentional discrimination. *See Freeman v. Pitts*, 503 U.S. 467, 494 (1992). Yet the Seattle public schools have not shown that they were ever segregated by law, and were not subject to court-ordered desegregation decrees. The Jefferson County public schools were previously segregated by law and were subject to a desegregation decree entered in 1975. In 2000, the District Court that entered that decree dissolved it, finding that Jefferson County had "eliminated the vestiges associated with the former policy of segregation and its pernicious effects," and thus had achieved "unitary" status. Jefferson County accordingly does not rely upon an interest in remedying the effects of past intentional discrimination in defending its present use of race in assigning students. . . .

The second government interest we have recognized as compelling for purposes of strict scrutiny is the interest in diversity in higher education upheld in *Grutter*, 539 U.S., at 328. The specific interest found compelling in *Grutter* was student body diversity "in the context of higher education." The diversity interest was not focused on race alone but encompassed "all factors that may contribute to student body diversity." . . .

In the present cases, by contrast, race is not considered as part of a broader effort to achieve "exposure to widely diverse people, cultures, ideas, and viewpoints"; race, for some students, is determinative standing alone.

The districts argue that other factors, such as student preferences, affect assignment decisions under their plans, but under each plan when race comes into play, it is decisive by itself. It is not simply one factor weighed with others in reaching a decision, as in *Grutter*; it is the factor. Like the University of Michigan undergraduate plan struck down in *Gratz*, 539 U.S., at 275, the plans here "do not provide for a meaningful individualized review of applicants" but instead rely on racial classifications in a "nonindividualized, mechanical" way . . .

Perhaps recognizing that reliance on *Grutter* cannot sustain their plans, both school districts assert additional interests, distinct from the interest upheld in *Grutter*, to justify their race-based assignments. In briefing and argument before this Court, Seattle contends that its use of race helps to reduce racial concentration in schools and to ensure that racially concentrated housing patterns do not prevent nonwhite students from having access to the most desirable schools. Jefferson County has articulated a similar goal, phrasing its interest in terms of educating its students "in a racially integrated environment." Each school district argues that educational and broader socialization benefits flow from a racially diverse learning environment, and each contends that because the diversity they seek is racial diversity—not the broader diversity at issue in *Grutter*—it makes sense to promote that interest directly by relying on race alone. . . .

The plans are tied to each district's specific racial demographics, rather than to any pedagogic concept of the level of diversity needed to obtain the asserted educational benefits. In Seattle, the district seeks white enrollment of between 31 and 51 percent (within 10 percent of "the district white average" of 41 percent), and nonwhite enrollment of between 49 and 69 percent (within 10 percent of "the district minority average" of 59 percent). In Jefferson County, by contrast, the district seeks black enrollment of no less than 15 or more than 50 percent, a range designed to be "equally above and below Black student enrollment systemwide," based on the objective of achieving at "all schools . . . an African-American enrollment equivalent to the average district-wide African-American enrollment" of 34 percent. In Seattle, then, the benefits of racial diversity require enrollment of at least 31 percent white students; in Jefferson County, at least 50 percent. There must be at least 15 percent nonwhite students under Jefferson County's plan; in Seattle, more than three times that figure. This comparison makes clear that the racial demographics in each district—whatever they happen to be—drive the required "diversity" numbers. The plans here are not tailored to achieving a degree of diversity necessary to realize the asserted educational benefits; instead the plans are tailored, in the words of Seattle's Manager of Enrollment Planning, Technical Support, and Demographics, to "the goal established by the school board of attaining a level of diversity within the schools that approximates the district's overall demographics." . . .

This working backward to achieve a particular type of racial balance, rather than working forward from some demonstration of the level of diversity that provides the purported benefits, is a fatal flaw under our existing precedent. We have many times over reaffirmed that "[r]acial balance is not to be achieved for its own sake." . . . *Grutter* itself reiterated that "outright racial balancing" is "patently unconstitutional."

Accepting racial balancing as a compelling state interest would justify the imposition of racial proportionality throughout American society, contrary to our repeated recognition that "[a]t the heart of the Constitution's guarantee of equal protection lies the simple command that the Government must treat citizens as individuals, not as simply components of a racial, religious, sexual or national class." Allowing racial balancing as a compelling end in itself would "effectively assur[e] that race will always be relevant in American life, and that the 'ultimate goal' of 'eliminating entirely from governmental decisionmaking such irrelevant factors as a human being's race' will never be achieved." . . .

While we do not suggest that greater use of race would be preferable, the minimal impact of the districts' racial classifications on school enrollment casts doubt on the necessity of using racial classifications. In *Grutter*, the consideration of race was viewed as indispensable in more than tripling minority representation at the law school—from 4 to 14.5 percent. Here the most Jefferson County itself claims is that "because the guidelines provide a firm definition of the Board's goal of racially integrated schools, they 'provide administrators with the authority to facilitate, negotiate and collaborate with principals and staff to maintain schools within the 15–50% range.'" Classifying and assigning schoolchildren according to a binary conception of race is an extreme approach in light of our precedents and our Nation's history of using race in public schools, and requires more than such an amorphous end to justify it. . . .

If the need for the racial classifications embraced by the school districts is unclear, even on the districts' own terms, the costs are undeniable . . . Government action dividing us by race is inherently suspect because such classifications promote "notions of racial inferiority and lead to a politics of racial hostility," "reinforce the belief, held by too many for too much of our history, that individuals should be judged by the color of their skin," and "endorse race-based reasoning and the conception of a Nation divided into racial blocs, thus contributing to an escalation of racial hostility and conflict." . . .

In *Brown v. Board of Education*, 347 U.S. 483 (1954) (*Brown I*), we held that segregation deprived black children of equal educational opportunities regardless of whether school facilities and other tangible factors were equal, because government classification and separation on grounds of race themselves denoted inferiority. It was not the inequality of the facilities but the fact of legally separating children on the basis of race on which the Court relied to find a constitutional violation in 1954. The next Term, we accordingly stated that "full compliance" with *Brown* I required school districts "to achieve a system of determining admission to the public schools on a nonracial basis."

The parties and their *amici* debate which side is more faithful to the heritage of Brown, but the position of the plaintiffs in Brown was spelled out in their brief and could not have been clearer: "[T]he Fourteenth Amendment prevents states from according differential treatment to American children on the basis of their color or race." What do the racial classifications at issue here do, if not accord differential treatment on the basis of race? As counsel who appeared before this Court for the plaintiffs in *Brown* put it: "We have one fundamental contention which we will seek to develop in the course of this argument, and that contention is that no State has any authority under the Equal-Protection Clause of the Fourteenth Amendment to use race as a factor in affording educational opportunities among its citizens." There is no ambiguity in that statement. And it was that position that prevailed in this Court, which emphasized in its remedial opinion that what was "[a]t stake is the personal interest of the plaintiffs in admission to public schools as soon as practicable on a nondiscriminatory basis," and what was required was "determining admission to the public schools on a nonracial basis." What do the racial classifications do in these cases, if not determine admission to a public school on a racial basis? . . .

The judgments of the Courts of Appeals for the Sixth and Ninth Circuits are reversed, and the cases are remanded for further proceedings.

It is so ordered.

Justice Thomas, concurring.

Today, the Court holds that state entities may not experiment with race-based means to achieve ends they deem socially desirable. I wholly concur in The Chief Justice's opinion. I write separately to address several of the contentions in Justice Breyer's dissent . . . Contrary to the dissent's arguments, resegregation is not occurring in Seattle or Louisville; these school boards have no present interest in remedying past segregation; and these race-based student-assignment programs do not serve any compelling state interest. Accordingly, the plans are unconstitutional. Disfavoring a color-blind interpretation of the Constitution, the dissent would give school boards a free hand to make decisions on the basis of race—an approach reminiscent of that advocated by the segregationists in *Brown v. Board of Education*, 347 U.S 483 (1954). This approach is just as wrong today as it was a half-century ago. The Constitution and our cases require us to be much more demanding before permitting local school boards to make decisions based on race.

Justice Kennedy, concurring in part and concurring in the judgment.

Our Nation from the inception has sought to preserve and expand the promise of liberty and equality on which it was founded. Today we enjoy a society that is remarkable in its openness and opportunity. Yet our tradition is to go beyond present achievements, however significant, and to recognize and confront the flaws and injustices that remain. This is especially true when we seek assurance that opportunity is not denied on account of race. The enduring hope is that race should not matter; the reality is that too often it does.

This is by way of preface to my respectful submission that parts of the opinion by The Chief Justice imply an all-too-unyielding insistence that race cannot be a factor in instances when, in my view, it may be taken into account. The plurality opinion is too dismissive of the legitimate interest government has in ensuring all people have equal opportunity regardless of their race. The plurality's postulate that "[t]he way to stop discrimination on the basis of race is to stop discriminating on the basis of race," is not sufficient to decide these cases. Fifty years of experience since *Brown v. Board of Education*, 347 U.S. 483 (1954), should teach us that the problem before us defies so easy a solution. School districts can seek to reach *Brown*'s objective of equal educational opportunity. The plurality opinion is at least open to the interpretation that the Constitution requires school districts to ignore the problem of de facto resegregation in schooling. I cannot endorse that conclusion. To the extent the plurality opinion suggests the Constitution mandates that state and local school authorities must accept the status quo of racial isolation in schools, it is, in my view, profoundly mistaken.

The statement by Justice Harlan that "[o]ur Constitution is color-blind" was most certainly justified in the context of his dissent in *Plessy v. Ferguson*, 163 U.S. 537, 559 (1896). The Court's decision in that case was a grievous error it took far too long to overrule. *Plessy*, of course, concerned official classification by race applicable to all persons who sought to use railway carriages. And, as an aspiration, Justice Harlan's axiom must command our assent. In the real world, it is regrettable to say, it cannot be a universal constitutional principle. . . .

The decision today should not prevent school districts from continuing the important work of bringing together students of different racial, ethnic, and economic backgrounds. Due to a variety of factors—some influenced by government, some not—neighborhoods in our communities do not reflect the diversity of our Nation as a whole. Those entrusted with directing our public schools can bring to bear the creativity of experts, parents, administrators, and other concerned citizens to find a way to achieve the compelling interests they face without resorting to widespread governmental allocation of benefits and burdens on the basis of racial classifications.

With this explanation I concur in the judgment of the Court.

Justice Stevens, dissenting.

While I join Justice Breyer's eloquent and unanswerable dissent in its entirety, it is appropriate to add these words.

There is a cruel irony in The Chief Justice's reliance on our decision in *Brown v. Board of Education*, 349 U.S. 294 (1955). The first sentence in the concluding paragraph of his opinion states: "Before *Brown*, schoolchildren were told where they could and could not go to school based on the color of their skin." This sentence reminds me of Anatole France's observation: "[T]he majestic equality of the la[w], forbid[s] rich and poor alike to sleep under bridges, to beg in the streets, and to steal their bread." The Chief Justice fails to note that it was only black schoolchildren who were so ordered; indeed, the history books do not tell stories of white children struggling to attend black schools. In this and other ways, The Chief Justice rewrites the history of one of this Court's most important decisions. . . .

It is my firm conviction that no Member of the Court that I joined in 1975 would have agreed with today's decision.

Justice Breyer, with whom Justice Stevens, Justice Souter, and Justice Ginsburg join, dissenting.

The historical and factual context in which these cases arise is critical. In *Brown*, this Court held that the government's segregation of schoolchildren by race violates the Constitution's promise of equal protection. The Court emphasized that "education is perhaps the most important function of state and local governments." And it thereby set the Nation on a path toward public school integration. . . .

In dozens of subsequent cases, this Court told school districts previously segregated by law what they must do at a minimum to comply with Brown's constitutional holding. The measures required by those cases often included race-conscious practices, such as mandatory busing and race-based restrictions on voluntary transfers. . . .

The upshot is that myriad school districts operating in myriad circumstances have devised myriad plans, often with race-conscious elements, all for the sake of eradicating earlier school segregation, bringing about integration, or preventing retrogression. Seattle and Louisville are two such districts, and the histories of their present plans set forth typical school integration stories.

I describe those histories at length in order to highlight three important features of these cases. First, the school districts' plans serve "compelling interests" and are "narrowly tailored" on any reasonable definition of those terms. Second, the distinction between *de jure* segregation (caused by school systems) and *de facto* segregation (caused, e.g., by housing patterns or generalized societal discrimination) is meaningless in the present context, thereby dooming the plurality's endeavor to find support for its views in that distinction. Third, real-world efforts to substitute racially diverse for racially segregated schools (however caused) are complex, to the point where the Constitution cannot plausibly be interpreted to rule out categorically all local efforts to use means that are "conscious" of the race of individuals. . . .

The Founders meant the Constitution as a practical document that would transmit its basic values to future generations through principles that remained workable over time. Hence it is important to consider the potential consequences of the plurality's approach, as measured against the Constitution's objectives. To do so provides further reason to believe that the plurality's approach is legally unsound. . . .

[This] opinion's reasoning is long. But its conclusion is short: The plans before us satisfy the requirements of the Equal Protection Clause. And it is the plurality's opinion, not this dissent that "fails to ground the result it would reach in law." . . .

The last half-century has witnessed great strides toward racial equality, but we have not yet realized the promise of *Brown*. To invalidate the plans under review is to threaten the promise of *Brown*. The plurality's position, I fear, would break that promise. This is a decision that the Court and the Nation will come to regret.

I must dissent.

12.4(e) Affirmative Action

affirmative action
Any policy that seeks to promote greater opportunities for individuals of an identifiable group whose members have been previously excluded from or who are currently underrepresented in particular educational, employment, or social settings, using *proactive* (affirmative) measures, as opposed to more punitive methods (criminal laws, civil rights legislation, etc.).

The constitutionally suspect status of race becomes a more controversial subject when applied to affirmative action programs. As a concept, an **affirmative action** is any policy that seeks to promote greater opportunities for individuals of an identifiable group, whose members have been previously excluded from or who are currently underrepresented in particular educational, employment, or social settings, using *proactive* (affirmative) measures, as opposed to more punitive methods (criminal laws, civil rights legislation, etc.). Affirmative action comes in many different forms. It could involve an employer advertising job vacancies in minority-read publications in an effort to attract more minority applicants; it could involve colleges considering race, sex, or other group status as a factor during their admission process; or it could involve a requirement that employers interview at least one person from an underrepresented group before making a job offer. In each case, a proactive or affirmative step is taken to promote the value of equality in a given setting.

When governments consider race (or the related characteristics of color, ethnicity, or national origin) in affirmative action programs, one of the initial constitutional questions has been whether race should still be deemed a suspect classification subject to strict scrutiny analysis. On the one hand, it is still race, and as identified earlier, this is regarded as a suspicious classification. But on the other hand, when race is used in an attempt to *promote* equality (as with affirmative action policies), as opposed to being used as an intentional effort to *deny* equality (as with segregation laws), one may find it less suspicious and therefore deserving of a less rigid constitutional scrutiny.

Initially, a number of Supreme Court members agreed with the latter argument, finding that when race is used in affirmative action programs, heightened scrutiny is not appropriate, and that a less-strict intermediate scrutiny standard is warranted, which allows governments to show that the programs are substantially related to an important governmental interest. In *Regents of the University of California v. Bakke* (1978),[35] the Court considered the affirmative action policy enacted by the medical school at the University of California at Davis, which had reserved (set aside) sixteen of its one hundred openings for minority applicants. Five justices (Powell, Burger, Stevens, Stewart, and Rehnquist) found the school's policy to be a quota-based program that denied white applicants equal protection. As such, the Court struck down this form of affirmative action. But within the opinion, five justices (Powell, Brennan, White, Marshall, and Blackmun) concluded that race could be considered as a part of a college's admissions program.

For a period of time after *Bakke*, some members of the Court treated race-based affirmative action programs as semi-suspect forms of discrimination, subject to the intermediate scrutiny analysis. In *Fullilove v. Klutznick* (1980),[36] the Court, in a 6–3 decision, applied the intermediate scrutiny test to uphold a congressional program that set aside 10 percent of funds for a public works project for minority-controlled businesses. And in *Metro Broadcasting, Inc. v. Federal Communications Commission* (1990),[37] five members of the Court applied the intermediate standard to uphold another affirmative action plan adopted by Congress.

But as the Court's membership changed during the 1980s and 1990s, so too did its approach to affirmative action programs. In *City of Richmond v. J.A. Croson* (1989),[38] six justices voted to strike down Richmond, Virginia's, set-aside program for public contracts. More important, a majority of the Court concluded that race-based affirmative action policies, at least at the state and local levels, should be subject to strict scrutiny analysis and that such programs must be narrowly tailored to address identifiable forms of past discrimination. Six years later, the Court applied this approach to federal affirmative action programs as well. In *Adarand Constructors, Inc. v. Pena* (1995),[39] the Court overruled its decision in *Metro Broadcasting*, holding that even congressional affirmative action plans must survive the most exacting form of constitutional scrutiny. As a result, the Court currently applies the strict scrutiny standard of review to all forms of government-sponsored, race-based, affirmative action programs.

Applying strict scrutiny to affirmative action programs certainly makes it more difficult for these programs to pass constitutional muster, but in some cases, the programs have passed the test. Critical to assessing the constitutionality of affirmative action programs is the government's justification for the program (its purported compelling interest for adopting the program) and the means by which the government is furthering this interest (how tailored the program is to the government's interest). Read the Court's opinions in *Grutter v. Bollinger et al.* (2003) and *Gratz et al. v. Bollinger et al.* (2003) (both excerpted in this chapter), which involve two different affirmative action programs at the University of Michigan. Notice the Court's emphasis on the asserted interest of the university as well as the attempted means of accomplishing this interest. In the end, the Court applied strict scrutiny to both programs, upholding one of them (*Grutter*) and striking down the other (*Gratz*).

Grutter v. Bollinger et al.
539 U.S. 306 (2003)

Justice O'Connor delivered the opinion of the Court.

This case requires us to decide whether the use of race as a factor in student admissions by the University of Michigan Law School (Law School) is unlawful.

The Law School ranks among the Nation's top law schools. It receives more than 3,500 applications each year for a class of around 350 students. Seeking to "admit a group of students who individually and collectively are among the most capable," the Law School looks for individuals with "substantial promise for success in law school" and "a strong likelihood of succeeding in the practice of law and contributing in diverse ways to the well-being of others."

More broadly, the Law School seeks a "mix of students with varying backgrounds and experiences who will respect and learn from each other." . . .

The hallmark of that policy is its focus on academic ability coupled with a flexible assessment of applicants' talents, experiences, and potential "to contribute to the learning of those around them." The policy requires admissions officials to evaluate each applicant based on all the information available in the file, including a personal statement, letters of recommendation, and an essay describing the ways in which the applicant will contribute to the life and diversity of the Law School. In reviewing an applicant's file, admissions officials must consider the applicant's undergraduate grade point average (GPA) and Law School Admissions Test (LSAT) score because they are important (if imperfect) predictors of academic success in law school. The policy stresses that "no applicant should be admitted unless we expect that applicant to do well enough to graduate with no serious academic problems." . . .

The policy aspires to "achieve that diversity which has the potential to enrich everyone's education and thus make a law school class stronger than the sum of its parts." The policy does not restrict the types of diversity contributions eligible for "substantial weight" in the admissions process, but instead recognizes "many possible bases for diversity admissions." The policy does, however, reaffirm the Law School's longstanding commitment to "one particular type of diversity," that is, "racial and ethnic diversity with special reference to the inclusion of students from groups which have been historically discriminated against, like African-Americans, Hispanics and Native Americans, who without this commitment might not be represented in our student body in meaningful numbers." By enrolling a "'critical mass' of [under-represented] minority students," the Law School seeks to "ensur[e] their ability to make unique contributions to the character of the Law School." . . .

The Equal Protection Clause provides that no State shall "deny to any person within its jurisdiction the equal protection of the laws." Because the Fourteenth Amendment "protect[s] persons, not groups," all "governmental action based on race—a group classification long recognized as in most circumstances irrelevant and therefore prohibited—should be subjected to detailed judicial inquiry to ensure that the personal right to equal protection of the laws has not been infringed." We are a "free people whose institutions are founded upon the doctrine of equality." It follows from that principle that "government may treat people differently because of their race only for the most compelling reasons."

We have held that all racial classifications imposed by government "must be analyzed by a reviewing court under strict scrutiny." This means that such classifications are constitutional only if they are narrowly tailored to further compelling governmental interests. . . .

With these principles in mind, we turn to the question whether the Law School's use of race is justified by a compelling state interest. Before this Court, as they have throughout this litigation, respondents assert only one justification for their use of race in the admissions process: obtaining "the educational benefits that flow from a diverse student body." In other words, the Law School asks us to recognize, in the context of higher education, a compelling state interest in student body diversity. . . .

Today, we hold that the Law School has a compelling interest in attaining a diverse student body.

The Law School's educational judgment that such diversity is essential to its educational mission is one to which we defer. The Law School's assessment that diversity will, in fact, yield educational benefits is substantiated by respondents and their amici. Our scrutiny of the interest asserted by the Law School is no less strict for taking into account complex educational judgments in an area that lies primarily within the expertise of the university. Our holding today is in keeping with our tradition of giving a degree of deference to a university's academic decisions, within constitutionally prescribed limits.

We have long recognized that, given the important purpose of public education and the expansive freedoms of speech and thought associated with the university environment, universities occupy a special niche in our constitutional tradition. . . .

As part of its goal of "assembling a class that is both exceptionally academically qualified and broadly diverse," the Law School seeks to "enroll a 'critical mass' of minority students." The Law School's interest is not simply "to assure within its student body some specified percentage of a particular group merely because of its race or ethnic origin." That would amount to outright racial balancing, which is patently unconstitutional. Rather, the Law School's concept of critical mass is defined by reference to the educational benefits that diversity is designed to produce. . . .

These benefits are not theoretical but real, as major American businesses have made clear that the skills needed in today's increasingly global marketplace can only be developed through exposure to widely diverse people, cultures, ideas, and viewpoints. What is more, high-ranking retired officers and civilian leaders of the United States military assert that, "[b]ased on [their] decades of experience," a "highly qualified, racially diverse officer corps . . . is essential to the military's ability to fulfill its principle mission to provide national security." . . .

We [also] find that the Law School's admissions program bears the hallmarks of a narrowly tailored plan. . . .

We are satisfied that the Law School's admissions program . . . does not operate as a quota. Properly understood, a "quota" is a program in which a certain fixed number or proportion of opportunities are "reserved exclusively for certain minority groups." Quotas "impose a fixed number or percentage which must be attained, or which cannot be exceeded," and "insulate the individual from comparison with all other candidates for the available seats." In contrast, "a permissible goal . . . require[s] only a good-faith effort . . . to come within a range demarcated by the goal itself," and permits consideration of race as a "plus" factor in any given case while still ensuring that each candidate "compete[s] with all other qualified applicants" . . .

Here, the Law School engages in a highly individualized, holistic review of each applicant's file, giving serious consideration to all the ways an applicant might contribute to a diverse educational environment. The Law School affords this individualized consideration to applicants of all races. There is no policy, either *de jure* or *de facto*, of automatic acceptance or rejection based on any single "soft" variable. Unlike the program at issue in *Gratz v. Bollinger*, the Law School awards no mechanical, predetermined diversity "bonuses" based on race or ethnicity. . . .

We are mindful, however, that "[a] core purpose of the Fourteenth Amendment was to do away with all governmentally imposed discrimination based on race." Accordingly, race-conscious admissions policies must be limited in time. This requirement reflects that racial classifications, however compelling their goals, are potentially so dangerous that they may be employed no more broadly than the interest demands. Enshrining a permanent justification for racial preferences would offend this fundamental equal protection principle. We see no reason to exempt race-conscious admissions programs from the requirement that all governmental use of race must have a logical end point. The Law School, too, concedes that all "race-conscious programs must have reasonable durational limits."

In the context of higher education, the durational requirement can be met by sunset provisions in race-conscious admissions policies and periodic reviews to determine whether racial preferences are still necessary to achieve student body diversity. Universities in California, Florida, and Washington State, where racial preferences in admissions are prohibited by state law, are currently engaged in experimenting with a wide variety of alternative approaches. Universities in other States can and should draw on the most promising aspects of these race-neutral alternatives as they develop. . . .

We take the Law School at its word that it would "like nothing better than to find a race-neutral admissions formula" and will terminate its race-conscious admissions program as soon as practicable. It has been 25 years since Justice Powell first approved the use of race to further an interest in student body diversity in the context of public higher education. Since that time, the number of minority applicants with high grades and test scores has indeed increased. We expect that 25 years from now, the use of racial preferences will no longer be necessary to further the interest approved today.

In summary, the Equal Protection Clause does not prohibit the Law School's narrowly tailored use of race in admissions decisions to further a compelling interest in obtaining the educational benefits that flow from a diverse student body. . . .

It is so ordered.

Justice Ginsburg, with whom Justice Breyer joins, concurring.

Chief Justice Rehnquist, Justice Scalia, Justice Kennedy, and Justice Thomas dissent.

Gratz et al. v. Bollinger et al.
539 U.S. 244 (2003)

Chief Justice Rehnquist delivered the opinion of the Court.

We granted *certiorari* in this case to decide whether "the University of Michigan's use of racial preferences in undergraduate admissions violate[s] the Equal Protection Clause of the Fourteenth Amendment." Because we find that the manner in which the University considers the race of applicants in its undergraduate admissions guidelines violates these constitutional and statutory provisions, we reverse that portion of the District Court's decision upholding the guidelines. . . .

The University has changed its admissions guidelines a number of times during the period relevant to this litigation, and we summarize the most significant of these changes briefly. The University's Office of Undergraduate Admissions (OUA) oversees the [College of Literature,

Science and the Arts (CSA)] admissions process. In order to promote consistency in the review of the large number of applications received, the OUA uses written guidelines for each academic year. Admissions counselors make admissions decisions in accordance with these guidelines. . . .

Beginning with the 1998 academic year, the OUA [adopted] . . . a "selection index," on which an applicant could score a maximum of 150 points. This index was divided linearly into ranges generally calling for admissions dispositions as follows: 100–150 (admit); 95–99 (admit or postpone); 90–94 (postpone or admit); 75–89 (delay or postpone); 74 and below (delay or reject).

Each application received points based on high school grade point average, standardized test scores, academic quality of an applicant's high school, strength or weakness of high school curriculum, in-state residency, alumni relationship, personal essay, and personal achievement or leadership. Of particular significance here, under a "miscellaneous" category, an applicant was entitled to 20 points based upon his or her membership in an underrepresented racial or ethnic minority group. The University explained that the "development of the selection index for admissions in 1998 changed only the mechanics, not the substance of how race and ethnicity were considered in admissions." . . .

During 1999 and 2000, the OUA used the selection index, under which every applicant from an underrepresented racial or ethnic minority group was awarded 20 points. Starting in 1999, however, the University established an Admissions Review Committee (ARC), to provide an additional level of consideration for some applications. Under the new system, counselors may, in their discretion, "flag" an application for the ARC to review after determining that the applicant (1) is academically prepared to succeed at the University, (2) has achieved a minimum selection index score, and (3) possesses a quality or characteristic important to the University's composition of its freshman class, such as high class rank, unique life experiences, challenges, circumstances, interests or talents, socioeconomic disadvantage, and underrepresented race, ethnicity, or geography. After reviewing "flagged" applications, the ARC determines whether to admit, defer, or deny each applicant.

Petitioners argue, first and foremost, that the University's use of race in undergraduate admissions violates the Fourteenth Amendment. Specifically, they contend that this Court has only sanctioned the use of racial classifications to remedy identified discrimination, a justification on which respondents have never relied. Petitioners further argue that "diversity as a basis for employing racial preferences is simply too open-ended, ill-defined, and indefinite to constitute a compelling interest capable of supporting narrowly-tailored means." But for the reasons set forth today in *Grutter v. Bollinger*, the Court has rejected these arguments of petitioners. . . .

It is by now well established that "all racial classifications reviewable under the Equal Protection Clause must be strictly scrutinized." This "standard of review . . . is not dependent on the race of those burdened or benefited by a particular classification." Thus, "any person, of whatever race, has the right to demand that any governmental actor subject to the Constitution justify any racial classification subjecting that person to unequal treatment under the strictest of judicial scrutiny."

To withstand our strict scrutiny analysis, respondents must demonstrate that the University's use of race in its current admission program employs "narrowly tailored measures that further compelling governmental interests." Because "[r]acial classifications are simply too pernicious to permit any but the most exact connection between justification and classification," our review of whether such requirements have been met must entail "a most searching examination." We find that the University's policy, which automatically distributes 20 points, or one-fifth of the points needed to guarantee admission, to every single "underrepresented minority" applicant solely because of race, is not narrowly tailored to achieve the interest in educational diversity that respondents claim justifies their program. . . .

The LSA's policy automatically distributes 20 points to every single applicant from an "underrepresented minority" group, as defined by the University. The only consideration that accompanies this distribution of points is a factual review of an application to determine whether an individual is a member of one of these minority groups. Moreover . . . the LSA's automatic distribution of 20 points has the effect of making "the factor of race . . . decisive" for virtually every minimally qualified underrepresented minority applicant. . . .

Respondents contend that "[t]he volume of applications and the presentation of applicant information make it impractical for [LSA] to use the . . . admissions system" upheld by the Court today in *Grutter*. But the fact that the implementation of a program capable of providing individualized consideration might present administrative challenges does not render constitutional an otherwise problematic system. Nothing in Justice Powell's opinion in *Bakke* signaled that a university may employ whatever means it desires to achieve the stated goal of diversity without regard to the limits imposed by our strict scrutiny analysis.

We conclude, therefore, that because the University's use of race in its current freshman admissions policy is not narrowly tailored to achieve respondents' asserted compelling interest in diversity, the admissions policy violates the Equal Protection Clause of the Fourteenth Amendment. . . . Accordingly, we reverse that portion of the District Court's decision granting respondents summary judgment with respect to liability and remand the case for proceedings consistent with this opinion.

It is so ordered.

Justices O'Connor, Thomas, and Breyer concurring. Justices Stevens, Souter and Ginsburg dissenting.

12.5 MODERN CHALLENGES

For the foreseeable future, race-based cases, involving both equal protection claims and civil rights legislation, are likely to remain a part of the American legal landscape. Under the Equal Protection Clause, the Supreme Court appears to be settled on using the strict scrutiny test to review all forms of government-sponsored distinctions based on race. But even with this constitutional standard in place, there are two primary areas in which legal professionals will find ongoing challenges.

The first area involves evidentiary questions about whether government officials are using race or ethnicity when making official decisions affecting individuals. In many cases, the use of race or ethnicity as a component of official action is not overt or readily admitted to by government. Instead, identifying race-based decisions is often a matter of circumstantial evidence that is gained through probing questions and intense investigative pursuits. For legal professionals working in civil rights and discrimination cases, this evidentiary challenge will always be a regular part of the job.

The second area in which many legal professionals find themselves is responding to the Supreme Court's rulings in the affirmative action cases of *Parents Involved in Community Schools v. Seattle School Dist. No. 1* (2007), *Meredith v. Jefferson County Board of Education* (2007), *Grutter v. Bollinger et al.* (2003), and *Gratz et al. v. Bollinger et al.* (2003). Despite the constitutional challenges presented by these cases, many public employers and schools still wish to promote diverse and inclusive work and education settings. But these policies must be justified, written, and applied in ways that meets the Court's redeveloped approach to equal protection and strict scrutiny analysis. Thus, in the near future, many legal professionals may be involved in reexamining and rewriting affirmative action policies in light of the Court's recent precedent.

12.6 SEX-BASED CLASSIFICATIONS

As briefly identified in Section 12.1, equality for women was not valued substantially, if at all, in the early Constitution. The right of women to vote or otherwise participate in the political process was simply not addressed by the text of the original document. Even after the addition of the Fourteenth Amendment in 1868, there was little, if any, recognition, at least among the courts, that the Equal Protection Clause might afford women greater legal protection against government discrimination. And even after the passage of the Nineteenth Amendment in 1920, courts generally held that this amendment was limited to preventing sex-based voting discrimination, not other forms of governmental distinction. As a result, until the 1970s, courts largely viewed sex-based discrimination as non-suspect, to be upheld as long as the government's policy was rationally related to a legitimate governmental interest.

The non-suspect approach to sex discrimination was illustrated in a variety of cases. In *Bradwell v. Illinois* (1873),[40] decided just a few years after the Fourteenth Amendment was ratified, the Supreme Court upheld an Illinois law excluding women from practicing law in the state. In *Muller v. Oregon* (1908),[41] the Court upheld a state law limiting the number of hours women could work in certain industries. And in *Hoyt v. Florida* (1961),[42] the Court ruled that women could be excluded from mandatory jury duty. In each of these cases, the implicit reasoning of the Court was that, as long as the government's sex-based distinctions were rational and related to a legitimate governmental objective, they did not violate the Equal Protection Clause or any other constitutional provision.

During the 1970s, the Court began to change its approach to sex-based equal protection cases. Beginning in *Reed v. Reed* (1971), where the court struck down an Idaho law preferring male heirs over female heirs in intestate probate proceedings, the Court started to take a closer look at sex discrimination. Although the *Reed* Court "officially" applied the rational basis test to the Idaho law, the substance of its scrutiny appeared to be far more exacting than earlier forms of the Court's deferential standard. Two years later, the Court was more overt about changing the scrutiny standard in sexual equality cases. In *Frontiero v. Richardson* (1973) (see later in this chapter), four justices concluded that, contrary to earlier rulings, sex should be deemed a suspect category for equal protection purposes, and therefore the strict scrutiny standard ought to apply. The remaining justices, however, did not go along with this conclusion.

Frontiero v. Richardson
411 U.S. 677 (1973)

Mr. Justice Brennan announced the judgment of the Court and an opinion in which Mr. Justice Douglas, Mr. Justice White, and Mr. Justice Marshall join.

The question before us concerns the right of a female member of the uniformed services to claim her spouse as a "dependent" for the purposes of obtaining increased quarters allowances and medical and dental benefits [under federal law] on an equal footing with male members. Under these statutes, a serviceman may claim his wife as a "dependent" without regard to whether she is in fact dependent upon him for any part of her support. A servicewoman, on the other hand, may not claim her husband as a "dependent" under these programs unless he is in fact dependent upon her for over one-half of his support. Thus, the question for decision is whether this difference in treatment constitutes an unconstitutional discrimination against servicewomen in violation of the Due Process Clause of the Fifth Amendment. . . .

Although the legislative history of these statutes sheds virtually no light on the purposes underlying the differential treatment accorded male and female members, a majority of the three-judge District Court surmised that Congress might reasonably have concluded that, since the husband in our society is generally the "bread-winner" in the family—and the wife typically the "dependent" partner—"it would be more economical to require married female members claiming husbands to prove actual dependency than to extend the presumption of dependency to such members." Indeed, given the fact that approximately 99% of all members of the uniformed services are male, the District Court speculated that such differential treatment might conceivably lead to a "considerable saving of administrative expense and manpower."

At the outset, appellants contend that classifications based upon sex, like classifications based upon race, alienage, and national origin, are inherently suspect and must therefore be subjected to close judicial scrutiny. We agree and, indeed, find at least implicit support for such an approach in our unanimous decision only last Term in *Reed v. Reed*, 404 U.S. 71 (1971). . . .

There can be no doubt that our Nation has had a long and unfortunate history of sex discrimination. Traditionally, such discrimination was rationalized by an attitude of "romantic paternalism" which, in practical effect, put women, not on a pedestal, but in a cage. Indeed, this paternalistic attitude became so firmly rooted in our national consciousness that, 100 years ago, a distinguished Member of this Court was able to proclaim:

> Man is, or should be, woman's protector and defender. The natural and proper timidity and delicacy which belongs to the female sex evidently unfits it for many of the occupations of civil life. The constitution of the family organization, which is founded in the divine ordinance, as well as in the nature of things, indicates the domestic sphere as that which properly belongs to the domain and functions of womanhood. The harmony, not to say identity, of interests and views which belong, or should belong, to the family institution is repugnant to the idea of a woman adopting a distinct and independent career from that of her husband. . . .

As a result of notions such as these, our statute books gradually became laden with gross, stereotyped distinctions between the sexes and, indeed, throughout much of the 19th century the position of women in our society was, in many respects, comparable to that of blacks under the pre–Civil War slave codes. . . .

Moreover, since sex, like race and national origin, is an immutable characteristic determined solely by the accident of birth, the imposition of special disabilities upon the members of a particular sex because of their sex would seem to violate "the basic concept of our system that legal burdens should bear some relationship to individual responsibility. . . ." And what differentiates sex from such nonsuspect statuses as intelligence or physical disability, and aligns it with the recognized suspect criteria, is that the sex characteristic frequently bears no relation to ability to perform or contribute to society. As a result, statutory distinctions between the sexes often have the effect of invidiously relegating the entire class of females to inferior legal status without regard to the actual capabilities of its individual members. . . .

With these considerations in mind, we can only conclude that classifications based upon sex, like classifications based upon race, alienage, or national origin, are inherently suspect, and must therefore be subjected to strict judicial scrutiny. Applying the analysis mandated by that stricter standard of review, it is clear that the statutory scheme now before us is constitutionally invalid.

The sole basis of the classification established in the challenged statutes is the sex of the individuals involved. Thus, under [the federal law], a female member of the uniformed services seeking to obtain housing and medical benefits for her spouse must prove his dependency in fact, whereas no such burden is imposed upon male members. In addition, the statutes operate so as to deny benefits to a female member, such as appellant Sharron Frontiero, who provides less than one-half of her spouse's support, while at the same time granting such benefits to a male member who likewise provides less than one-half of his spouse's support. Thus, to this extent at least, it may fairly be said that these statutes command "dissimilar treatment for men and women who are . . . similarly situated."

Moreover, the Government concedes that the differential treatment accorded men and women under these statutes serves no purpose other than mere "administrative convenience." . . .

In any case, our prior decisions make clear that, although efficacious administration of governmental programs is not without some importance, "the Constitution recognizes higher values than speed and efficiency." And when we enter the realm of "strict judicial scrutiny," there can be no doubt that "administrative convenience" is not a shibboleth, the mere recitation of which dictates constitutionality. On the contrary, any statutory scheme which draws a sharp line between the sexes, solely for the purpose of achieving administrative convenience, necessarily commands "dissimilar treatment for men and women who are . . . similarly situated," and therefore involves the "very kind of arbitrary legislative choice forbidden by the [Constitution]." . . . We therefore conclude that, by according differential treatment to male and female members of the uniformed services for the sole purpose of achieving administrative convenience, the challenged statutes violate the Due Process Clause of the Fifth Amendment insofar as they require a female member to prove the dependency of her husband.

Reversed.

Mr. Justice Stewart concurs in the judgment, agreeing that the statutes before us work an invidious discrimination in violation of the Constitution. . . .

Mr. Justice Powell, with whom The Chief Justice and Mr. Justice Blackmun join, concurring in the judgment.

Mr. Justice Rehnquist dissents for the reasons stated by Judge Rives in his opinion for the District Court, *Frontiero v. Laird*, 341 F. Supp. 201 (1972).

I agree that the challenged statutes constitute an unconstitutional discrimination against servicewomen in violation of the Due Process Clause of the Fifth Amendment, but I cannot join the opinion of Mr. Justice Brennan, which would hold that all classifications based upon sex, "like classifications based upon race, alienage, and national origin," are "inherently suspect and must therefore be subjected to close judicial scrutiny." It is unnecessary for the Court in this case to characterize sex as a suspect classification, with all of the far-reaching implications of such a holding. *Reed v. Reed*, 404 U.S. 71 (1971), which abundantly supports our decision today, did not add sex to the narrowly limited group of classifications which are inherently suspect. In my view, we can and should decide this case on the authority of *Reed* and reserve for the future any expansion of its rationale.

As the Court's decision in *Frontiero* reveals, the level of suspiciousness properly assigned to sex-based governmental distinctions is a challenging question. It would appear that such distinctions—at least when applied to women—satisfy the first two concerns for suspect classifications: (1) there is a substantial history of sex-based discrimination in the United States, and (2) a person's sex is an immutable characteristic. But because women constitute a majority of the population in the United States, thereby making it at least numerically possible for them to control the majoritarian process, some find that sex-based distinctions, at least when applied to women, fall short of meeting all three benchmarks for a suspect class. And yet, even assuming that some people may not find this final factor to be completely satisfied, there is little debate about the first two factors.

Two years after the Court's near-identification of sex as a suspect class, the Court agreed to treat sex as a quasi- or semi-suspect form of discrimination, deserving of a heightened, though not entirely strict, form of scrutiny. In *Craig v. Boren* (1976),[43] the Court struck down an Oklahoma liquor law that prohibited men, but not women, from buying 3.2 percent beer. After reviewing its earlier rulings in *Reed* and *Frontiero*, the Court announced, "[t]o withstand constitutional challenge, previous cases establish that classifications by gender must serve important governmental objectives and must be substantially related to achievement of those interests." And as applied to Oklahoma's law, the Court found that the state did not meet this standard.

Since its ruling in *Craig*, the Court generally has accepted that the intermediate scrutiny test applies to its sex-based equal protection cases. In some cases, this has resulted in sex-based distinctions being declared unconstitutional,[44] while in other cases, the government distinctions have been upheld.[45] But in recent years, new voice has been given to the idea of enhancing the constitutional scrutiny for sex-based classifications by making sex a fully suspect classification. Justice Ruth Bader Ginsburg, who as a lawyer argued a number of sex discrimination cases before the Court, has suggested that governments must offer an "exceedingly persuasive" justification before they will be allowed to make sex-based distinctions in public policy. Writing for a six-member majority in *United States v. Virginia* (1996) ("VMI case," excerpted in this chapter), Justice Ginsburg introduced the "exceedingly persuasive" phrase to describe the prevailing standard in sex-based equal protection cases. Read the Court's opinion in the VMI case to assess whether Justice Ginsburg is actually calling for an elevated form of scrutiny for sexual equality cases or whether her terminology is just another term reflective of the intermediate scrutiny standard. Note too the opinions by Chief Justice Rehnquist and Justice Scalia, both of whom challenge the use of the phrase "exceedingly persuasive."

United States v. Virginia
518 U.S. 515 (1996)

Justice Ginsburg delivered the opinion of the Court.

Virginia's public institutions of higher learning include an incomparable military college, Virginia Military Institute (VMI). The United States maintains that the Constitution's equal protection guarantee precludes Virginia from reserving exclusively to men the unique educational opportunities VMI affords. We agree.

Founded in 1839, VMI is today the sole single-sex school among Virginia's 15 public institutions of higher learning. VMI's distinctive mission is to produce "citizen-soldiers," men prepared for leadership in civilian life and in military service. VMI pursues this mission through pervasive training of a kind not available anywhere else in Virginia. Assigning prime place to character development, VMI uses an "adversative method" modeled on English public schools and once characteristic of military instruction. VMI constantly endeavors to instill physical and mental discipline in its cadets and impart to them a strong moral code. The school's graduates leave VMI with heightened comprehension of their capacity to deal with duress and stress, and a large sense of accomplishment for completing the hazardous course. . . .

Neither the goal of producing citizen-soldiers nor VMI's implementing methodology is inherently unsuitable to women. And the school's impressive record in producing leaders has made admission desirable to some women. Nevertheless, Virginia has elected to preserve exclusively for men the advantages and opportunities a VMI education affords. . . .

In 1990, prompted by a complaint filed with the Attorney General by a female high-school student seeking admission to VMI, the United States sued the Commonwealth of Virginia and VMI, alleging that VMI's exclusively male admission policy violated the Equal Protection Clause of the Fourteenth Amendment. . . .

Today's skeptical scrutiny of official action denying rights or opportunities based on sex responds to volumes of history. As a plurality of this Court acknowledged a generation ago, "our Nation has had a long and unfortunate history of sex discrimination." *Frontiero v. Richardson*, 411 U.S. 677, 684 (1973). . . .

In 1971, for the first time in our Nation's history, this Court ruled in favor of a woman who complained that her State had denied her the equal protection of its laws. *Reed v. Reed*, 404 U.S. 71, 73 (holding unconstitutional Idaho Code prescription that, among "several persons claiming and equally entitled to administer [a decedent's estate], males must be preferred to females"). Since *Reed*, the Court has repeatedly recognized that neither federal nor state government acts compatibly with the equal protection principle when a law or official policy denies to women, simply because they are women, full citizenship stature-equal opportunity to aspire, achieve, participate in and contribute to society based on their individual talents and capacities.

Without equating gender classifications, for all purposes, to classifications based on race or national origin, the Court, in post-*Reed* decisions, has carefully inspected official action that closes a door or denies opportunity to women (or to men). To summarize the Court's current directions for cases of official classification based on gender: Focusing on the differential treatment or denial of opportunity for which relief is sought, the reviewing court must determine whether the proffered justification is "exceedingly persuasive." The burden of justification is demanding and it rests entirely on the State. The State must show "at least that the [challenged] classification serves important governmental objectives and that the discriminatory means employed' are 'substantially related to the achievement of those objectives.'" The justification must be genuine, not hypothesized or invented post hoc in response to litigation. And it must not rely on overbroad generalizations about the different talents, capacities, or preferences of males and females. . . .

Measuring the record in this case against the review standard just described, we conclude that Virginia has shown no "exceedingly persuasive justification" for excluding all women from the citizen-soldier training afforded by VMI. We therefore affirm the Fourth Circuit's initial judgment, which held that Virginia had violated the Fourteenth Amendment's Equal Protection Clause. Because the remedy proffered by Virginia—the Mary Baldwin [Virginia Women's Institute for Leadership (VWIL)] program—does not cure the constitutional violation, i.e., it does not provide equal opportunity, we reverse the Fourth Circuit's final judgment in this case. . . .

The Fourth Circuit initially held that Virginia had advanced no state policy by which it could justify, under equal protection principles, its determination "to afford VMI's unique type of program to men and not to women." Virginia challenges that "liability" ruling and asserts two justifications in defense of VMI's exclusion of women. First, the Commonwealth contends, "single-sex education provides important educational benefits," and the option of single-sex education contributes to "diversity in educational approaches." Second, the Commonwealth argues, "the unique VMI method of character development and leadership training," the school's adversative approach, would have to be modified were VMI to admit women. We consider these two justifications in turn.

[I]t is not disputed that diversity among public educational institutions can serve the public good. But Virginia has not shown that VMI was established, or has been maintained, with a view to diversifying, by its categorical exclusion of women, educational opportunities within the State. . . .

In sum, we find no persuasive evidence in this record that VMI's male-only admission policy "is in furtherance of a state policy of 'diversity.'" . . . A purpose genuinely to advance an array of educational options, as the Court of Appeals recognized, is not served by VMI's historic and constant plan—a plan to "affor[d] a unique educational benefit only to males." However "liberally" this plan serves the State's sons, it makes no provision whatever for her daughters. That is not equal protection.

Virginia next argues that VMI's adversative method of training provides educational benefits that cannot be made available, unmodified, to women. Alterations to accommodate women would necessarily be "radical," so "drastic," Virginia asserts, as to transform, indeed "destroy," VMI's program. . . .

The notion that admission of women would downgrade VMI's stature, destroy the adversative system and, with it, even the school, is a judgment hardly proved, a prediction hardly different from other "self-fulfilling prophec[ies]," once routinely used to deny rights or opportunities. . . .

Women's successful entry into the federal military academies, and their participation in the Nation's military forces, indicate that Virginia's fears for the future of VMI may not be solidly grounded. The State's justification for excluding all women from "citizen-soldier" training for which some are qualified, in any event, cannot rank as "exceedingly persuasive," as we have explained and applied that standard. . . .

VMI . . . offers an educational opportunity no other Virginia institution provides, and the school's "prestige"—associated with its success in developing "citizen-soldiers"—is unequaled. Virginia has closed this facility to its daughters and, instead, has devised for them a "parallel program," with a faculty less impressively credentialed and less well paid, more limited course offerings, fewer opportunities for military training and for scientific specialization. VMI, beyond question, "possesses to a far greater degree" than the VWIL program "those qualities which are incapable of objective measurement but which make for greatness in a . . . school," including "position and influence of the alumni, standing in the community, traditions and prestige." Women seeking and fit for a VMI-quality education cannot be offered anything less, under the State's obligation to afford them genuinely equal protection. . . .

For the reasons stated, the initial judgment of the Court of Appeals is affirmed, the final judgment of the Court of Appeals is reversed, and the case is remanded for further proceedings consistent with this opinion.

It is so ordered.

Justice Thomas took no part in the consideration or decision of this case.

Chief Justice Rehnquist, concurring in judgment.

Justice Scalia, dissenting.

Today the Court shuts down an institution that has served the people of the Commonwealth of Virginia with pride and distinction for over a century and a half. To achieve that desired result, it rejects (contrary to our established practice) the factual findings of two courts below, sweeps aside the precedents of this Court, and ignores the history of our people. As to facts: it explicitly rejects the finding that there exist "gender-based developmental differences" supporting Virginia's restriction of the "adversative" method to only a men's institution, and the finding that the all-male composition of the Virginia Military Institute (VMI) is essential to that institution's character. As to precedent: it drastically revises our established standards for reviewing sex-based classifications. And as to history: it counts for nothing the long tradition, enduring down to the present, of men's military colleges supported by both States and the Federal Government. . . .

12.7 SEXUAL ORIENTATION

One of the most dynamic questions in contemporary jurisprudence is how equal protection standards should be applied to lesbians, gays, bisexuals, and transgendered individuals. Topics ranging from homosexuals serving in the military to same-sex marriage to legal benefits for domestic partners all involve questions of equality and sexual orientation. The bottom-line issue in most of these controversies is whether government may discriminate against individuals based on the fact that they are gay, lesbian, bisexual, or transgendered. Perhaps more specifically, the question is whether sexual orientation is a suspect, semi-suspect, or non-suspect classification.

Cyber Constitution
***Lawrence v. Texas
(2002)*** http://supreme.
justia.com/us/539/558/
case.html

In recent years, the Supreme Court has had a number of opportunities to squarely address this issue. But generally, the Court has avoided this central question. In *Bowers v. Hardwick* (1986), the Court upheld a Georgia sodomy statute as challenged by a homosexual man, finding that there was no constitutional right to engage in homosexual sodomy. But the Court avoided placing homosexuality in a particular classification for equal protection purposes. Clearly though, the implication was that homosexuality was a non-suspect classification. Even in *Lawrence v. Texas* (2003)[46] (see excerpt in Chapter 11), where the Court reversed *Bowers* in the process of striking down a Texas law barring same-sex sodomy, the Court generally avoided the direct question of whether sexual orientation was a suspect classification. Instead, the Court decided the case on due process grounds, concluding that the Texas law interfered with the liberty of making personal decisions about sexual relations. In a concurring opinion, Justice O'Connor asserted that the case should be decided on equal protection grounds, stating that the clause "is essentially a direction that all persons similarly situated should be treated alike."[47] She further concluded that rational basis review (non-suspect scrutiny) applied because the Texas law inhibited "personal relationships." Despite this finding, O'Connor, like the rest of the Court, failed to address homosexuality in light of the three indicators of suspiciousness.

Likewise, the Court avoided the central question in two cases involving state-enacted civil rights legislation protecting against sexual-orientation discrimination. In *Hurley v. Irish-American Gay, Lesbian, and Bisexual Group of Boston* (1995),[48] the Court refused to enforce a Massachusetts public accommodations law to require the organizers of a private St. Patrick's Day parade to include an Irish-American gay, lesbian, and bisexual group because the Court found that such compelled inclusion would violate the parade organizers' First Amendment rights. Similarly, in *Boy Scouts of America v. Dale* (2000)[49] (excerpt in Chapter 9), the Court refused to apply a New Jersey civil rights law to require the Boy Scouts to retain a homosexual troop leader because the Court concluded that it would violate the organization's right to the freedom of association. In both cases, the Court easily avoided the equal protection status of homosexuals.

Perhaps the closest the Court has come to directly addressing the level of scrutiny to be applied to government distinctions based on sexual orientation was in *Romer v. Evans* (1996) (excerpted in this chapter). In *Romer*, the Court struck down a Colorado constitutional amendment (Amendment 2) barring state and local entities from enacting legal protections against sexual-orientation discrimination. In writing for the Court, Justice Kennedy observed:

> The Fourteenth Amendment's promise that no person shall be denied the equal protection of the laws must co-exist with the practical necessity that most legislation classifies for one purpose or another, with resulting disadvantage to various groups or persons. We have attempted to reconcile the principle with the reality by stating that, if a law neither burdens a fundamental right nor targets a suspect class, we will uphold the legislative classification so long as it bears a rational relation to some legitimate end. Amendment 2 fails, indeed defies, even this conventional inquiry.

Notice that Kennedy's opinion avoids any direct evaluation of homosexuality as a suspect classification. Instead, it suggests that, because the Colorado amendment fails even the most minimal level of scrutiny—the rational basis test—there is no reason to evaluate it under a more rigorous standard. Read the Court's opinion in *Romer* to assess the possible reasons for the Court avoiding a complete scrutiny assessment for sexual orientation.

One issue that has yet to reach the Supreme Court but that has received plenty of attention elsewhere is same-sex marriage. During the past decade, a large majority of states

Romer v. Evans
517 U.S. 620 (1996)

Justice Kennedy delivered the opinion of the Court.

One century ago, the first Justice Harlan admonished this Court that the Constitution "neither knows nor tolerates classes among citizens." Unheeded then, those words now are understood to state a commitment to the law's neutrality where the rights of persons are at stake. The Equal Protection Clause enforces this principle and today requires us to hold invalid a provision of Colorado's Constitution.

The enactment challenged in this case is an amendment to the Constitution of the State of Colorado, adopted in a 1992 statewide referendum. The parties and the state courts refer to it as "Amendment 2," its designation when submitted to the voters. The impetus for the amendment and the contentious campaign that preceded its adoption came in large part from ordinances that had been passed in various Colorado municipalities. . . . Amendment 2 repeals these ordinances to the extent they prohibit discrimination on the basis of "homosexual, lesbian or bisexual orientation, conduct, practices or relationships."

Yet Amendment 2, in explicit terms, does more than repeal or rescind these provisions. It prohibits all legislative, executive or judicial action at any level of state or local government designed to protect the named class, a class we shall refer to as homosexual persons or gays and lesbians. The amendment reads: "No Protected Status Based on Homosexual, Lesbian, or Bisexual Orientation. Neither the State of Colorado, through any of its branches or departments, nor any of its agencies, political subdivisions, municipalities or school districts, shall enact, adopt or enforce any statute, regulation, ordinance or policy whereby homosexual, lesbian or bisexual orientation, conduct, practices or relationships shall constitute or otherwise be the basis of or entitle any person or class of persons to have or claim any minority status, quota preferences, protected status or claim of discrimination. This Section of the Constitution shall be in all respects self-executing." . . .

The State's principal argument in defense of Amendment 2 is that it puts gays and lesbians in the same position as all other persons. So, the State says, the measure does no more than deny homosexuals special rights. This reading of the amendment's language is implausible. . . .

The Fourteenth Amendment's promise that no person shall be denied the equal protection of the laws must co-exist with the practical necessity that most legislation classifies for one purpose or another, with resulting disadvantage to various groups or persons. We have attempted to reconcile the principle with the reality by stating that, if

a law neither burdens a fundamental right nor targets a suspect class, we will uphold the legislative classification so long as it bears a rational relation to some legitimate end.

Amendment 2 fails, indeed defies, even this conventional inquiry. First, the amendment has the peculiar property of imposing a broad and undifferentiated disability on a single named group, an exceptional and, as we shall explain, invalid form of legislation. Second, its sheer breadth is so discontinuous with the reasons offered for it that the amendment seems inexplicable by anything but animus toward the class that it affects; it lacks a rational relationship to legitimate state interests.

Taking the first point, even in the ordinary equal protection case calling for the most deferential of standards, we insist on knowing the relation between the classification adopted and the object to be attained. The search for the link between classification and objective gives substance to the Equal Protection Clause; it provides guidance and discipline for the legislature, which is entitled to know what sorts of laws it can pass; and it marks the limits of our own authority. In the ordinary case, a law will be sustained if it can be said to advance a legitimate government interest, even if the law seems unwise or works to the disadvantage of a particular group, or if the rationale for it seems tenuous. . . . By requiring that the classification bear a rational relationship to an independent and legitimate legislative end, we ensure that classifications are not drawn for the purpose of disadvantaging the group burdened by the law.

Amendment 2 confounds this normal process of judicial review. It is at once too narrow and too broad. It identifies persons by a single trait and then denies them protection across the board. The resulting disqualification of a class of persons from the right to seek specific protection from the law is unprecedented in our jurisprudence. The absence of precedent for Amendment 2 is itself instructive; "[d]iscriminations of an unusual character especially suggest careful consideration to determine whether they are obnoxious to the constitutional provision." . . .

The primary rationale the State offers for Amendment 2 is respect for other citizens' freedom of association, and in particular the liberties of landlords or employers who have personal or religious objections to homosexuality. Colorado also cites its interest in conserving resources to fight discrimination against other groups. The breadth of the Amendment is so far removed from these particular justifications that we find it impossible to credit them. We cannot say that Amendment 2 is directed to any identifiable legitimate purpose or discrete objective. It is a status-based enactment divorced from any factual context from which we could discern a relationship to legitimate state interests; it is a classification of persons undertaken for its own sake, something the Equal Protection Clause does not permit. "[C]lass legislation . . . [is] obnoxious to the prohibitions of the Fourteenth Amendment. . . ."

We must conclude that Amendment 2 classifies homosexuals not to further a proper legislative end but to make them unequal to everyone else. This Colorado cannot do. A State cannot so deem a class of persons a stranger to its laws. Amendment 2 violates the Equal Protection Clause, and the judgment of the Supreme Court of Colorado is affirmed.

It is so ordered.

Justice Scalia, with whom the Chief Justice and Justice Thomas join, dissenting.

Today's opinion has no foundation in American constitutional law, and barely pretends to. The people of Colorado have adopted an entirely reasonable provision which does not even disfavor homosexuals in any substantive sense, but merely denies them preferential treatment. Amendment 2 is designed to prevent piecemeal deterioration of the sexual morality favored by a majority of Coloradans, and is not only an appropriate means to that legitimate end, but a means that Americans have employed before. Striking it down is an act, not of judicial judgment, but of political will. I dissent.

Cyber Constitution
Court Rules on Federal Defense of Marriage Act
www.youtube.com/
watch?v=bX9mH6QBcRI

passed constitutional and legislative measures banning same-sex marriages. A number of state supreme courts have upheld these bans in the face of equal protection challenges. And in 1996, Congress passed the Defense of Marriage Act (DOMA), which provides a federal definition of marriage that excludes same-sex marriage and allows states to refuse recognition to same-sex marriages as well, even if such marriages are legally established in other jurisdictions. Despite these legislative and voter-initiated rejections of same-sex marriage, a number of states have recognized these marriages as legally valid.

Currently, there are seven jurisdictions in the United States that recognize same-sex marriage—Massachusetts, Connecticut, Iowa, Vermont, New Hampshire, New York and the District of Columbia. (See Table 12-1.) In addition, a federal district court has rejected California's ban on same-sex marriage, but this decision has been stayed pending appellate

TABLE 12-1 Legal Recognition of Same-Sex Marriage in the United States

Jurisdiction	Date	Method	Source
Massachusetts	Nov. 18, 2003	State Supreme Court Decision	*Goodridge v. Dept. of Public Health*, 798 N.E.2d 941 (Mass. 2003)
Vermont	Sep. 1, 2009	State Legislature Enactment	H.0275—Permitting Same-Sex Marriage and the Clergy's Right to Refuse to Solemize a Marriage
Connecticut	Oct. 10, 2008	State Supreme Court decision	*Kerrigan v. Commissioner of Public Health*, 289 Conn. 135, 957 A.2d 407 (2008)
Iowa	Apr. 3, 2009	State Supreme Court decision	*Varnum v. Brien*, 763 N.W.2d 862 (Iowa 2009)
District of Columbia	Dec. 18, 2009	Act of Legislative Council	Religious Freedom and Civil Marriage Equality Amendment Act 2009
New Hampshire	June 3, 2009	State Legislature Enactment	House Bill 73
California*	Aug. 4, 2010	U.S. District Court Decision	*Perry v. Schwarzenegger*, 704 F. Supp. 2d 921 (N.D. Cal. 2010)
New York	June 24, 2011	State Legislature Enactment	Assembly Bill 08354

*A ruling by the U.S. District Court for the Northern District of California struck down California's Proposition 8, which bans same-sex marriage in the state. This ruling has been stayed pending appellate review of the District Court's judgment.

review. Some state and local governments provide marriage-like benefits to same-sex couples, including New Jersey (recognizing civil unions), California, Oregon, Nevada, and Washington.

Massachusetts was the first state in the United States to recognize same-sex marriages. This was the result of the Massachusetts Supreme Court decision in *Goodridge v. Massachusetts Department of Public Health* (2003) (excerpted in this chapter), where the court ruled that the state could no longer bar same-sex couples from receiving marriage licenses. But in so doing, the court, like Justice Kennedy's opinion in *Romer,* avoided a full consideration of whether homosexuality was a suspect classification. Instead, using a *Romer*-like approach, the court stated, "we conclude that the marriage ban does not meet the rational basis test for either due process or equal protection. Because the statute does not survive rational basis review, we do not consider the plaintiffs' arguments that this case merits strict judicial scrutiny."[50] However, in a concurring opinion, Justice Greaney regarded the ban on same-sex marriage to be a form of highly suspicious discrimination warranting strict scrutiny analysis. For Greaney, the ban interfered with the fundamental right of marriage and constituted sex-based (as opposed to sexual orientation) discrimination, both of which require strict scrutiny analysis under Massachusetts law.

Cyber Constitution
Varnum v. Brien **(2009)**
http://graphics8.nytimes.
com/packages/pdf/
us/20090403iowa-text.
pdfhttp://graphics8.
nytimes.com/packages/
pdf/us/20090403iowa-
text.pdf

Goodridge v. Massachusetts Department of Public Health
440 Mass. 309, 334, 798 NE2d 941, 963 (2003)

Marshall, C. J.

Marriage is a vital social institution. The exclusive commitment of two individuals to each other nurtures love and mutual support; it brings stability to our society. For those who choose to marry, and for their children, marriage provides an abundance of legal, financial, and social benefits. In return it imposes weighty legal, financial, and social obligations. The question before us is whether, consistent with the Massachusetts Constitution, the Commonwealth may deny the protections, benefits, and obligations conferred by civil marriage to two individuals of the same sex who wish to marry. We conclude that it may not. The Massachusetts Constitution affirms the dignity and equality of all individuals. It forbids the creation of second-class citizens. In reaching our conclusion we have given full deference to the arguments made by the Commonwealth. But it has failed to identify any constitutionally adequate reason for denying civil marriage to same-sex couples.

We are mindful that our decision marks a change in the history of our marriage law. Many people hold deep-seated religious, moral, and ethical convictions that marriage should be limited to the union of one man and one woman, and that homosexual conduct is immoral. Many hold equally strong religious, moral, and ethical convictions that same-sex couples are entitled to be married, and that homosexual persons should be treated no differently than their heterosexual neighbors. Neither view answers the question before us. Our concern is with the Massachusetts Constitution as a charter of governance for every person properly within its reach. "Our obligation is to define the liberty of all, not to mandate our own moral code." . . .

We begin by considering the nature of civil marriage itself. Simply put, the government creates civil marriage.

In Massachusetts, civil marriage is, and since pre-Colonial days has been, precisely what its name implies: a wholly secular institution. No religious ceremony has ever been required to validate a Massachusetts marriage. . . .

Tangible as well as intangible benefits flow from marriage. The marriage license grants valuable property rights to those who meet the entry requirements, and who agree to what might otherwise be a burdensome degree of government regulation of their activities. The Legislature has conferred on "each party [in a civil marriage] substantial rights concerning the assets of the other which unmarried cohabitants do not have."

The benefits accessible only by way of a marriage license are enormous, touching nearly every aspect of life and death. The department states that "hundreds of statutes" are related to marriage and to marital benefits. . . .

Without the right to marry—or more properly, the right to choose to marry—one is excluded from the full range of human experience and denied full protection of the laws for one's "avowed commitment to an intimate and lasting human relationship." Because civil marriage is central to the lives of individuals and the welfare of the community, our laws assiduously protect the individual's right to marry against undue government incursion. Laws may not "interfere directly and substantially with the right to marry." . . .

The Massachusetts Constitution protects matters of personal liberty against government incursion as zealously, and often more so, than does the Federal Constitution, even where both Constitutions employ essentially the same language. That the Massachusetts Constitution is in some instances more protective of individual liberty interests than is the Federal Constitution is not surprising. Fundamental to the vigor of our Federal system of government is that "state courts are absolutely free to interpret state constitutional provisions to accord greater protection to individual rights than do similar provisions of the United States Constitution."

The Massachusetts Constitution requires, at a minimum, that the exercise of the State's regulatory authority not be "arbitrary or capricious." Under both the equality and liberty guarantees, regulatory authority must, at very least, serve "a legitimate purpose in a rational way"; a statute must "bear a reasonable relation to a permissible legislative objective." Any law failing to satisfy the basic standards of rationality is void. . . .

The department argues that no fundamental right or "suspect" class is at issue here, and rational basis is the appropriate standard of review. For the reasons we explain below, we conclude that the marriage ban does not meet the rational basis test for either due process or equal protection. Because the statute does not survive rational basis review, we do not consider the plaintiffs' arguments that this case merits strict judicial scrutiny. . . .

The department has had more than ample opportunity to articulate a constitutionally adequate justification for limiting civil marriage to opposite-sex unions. It has failed to do so. The department has offered purported justifications for the civil marriage restriction that are starkly at odds with the comprehensive network of vigorous, gender-neutral laws promoting stable families and the best interests of children. It has failed to identify any relevant characteristic that would justify shutting the door to civil marriage to a person who wishes to marry someone of the same sex.

The marriage ban works a deep and scarring hardship on a very real segment of the community for no rational reason. The absence of any reasonable relationship between, on the one hand, an absolute disqualification of same-sex couples who wish to enter into civil marriage and, on the other, protection of public health, safety, or general welfare, suggests that the marriage restriction is rooted in persistent prejudices against persons who are (or who are believed to be) homosexual. "The Constitution cannot control such prejudices but neither can it tolerate them. Private biases may be outside the reach of the law, but the law cannot, directly or indirectly, give them effect." Limiting the protections, benefits, and obligations of civil marriage to opposite-sex couples violates the basic premises of individual liberty and equality under law protected by the Massachusetts Constitution. . . .

So ordered.

Greaney, J. (concurring).

I agree with the result reached by the court, the remedy ordered, and much of the reasoning in the court's opinion. In my view, however, the case is more directly resolved using traditional equal protection analysis. . . .

The equal protection infirmity at work here is strikingly similar to (although, perhaps, more subtle than) the invidious discrimination perpetuated by Virginia's anti-miscegenation laws and unveiled in the decision of *Loving v. Virginia*, [388 US. 1 (1967)]. In its landmark decision striking down Virginia's ban on marriages between Caucasians and members of any other race on both equal protection and substantive due process grounds, the United States Supreme Court soundly rejected the proposition that the equal application of the ban (*i.e.*, that it applied equally to whites and blacks) made unnecessary the strict scrutiny analysis traditionally required of statutes drawing classifications according to race, and concluded that "restricting the freedom to marry solely because of racial classifications violates the central meaning of the Equal Protection Clause." That our marriage laws, unlike antimiscegenation laws, were not enacted purposely to discriminate in no way neutralizes their present discriminatory character.

With these two propositions established (the infringement on a fundamental right and a sex-based classification), the enforcement of the marriage statutes as they are currently understood is forbidden by our Constitution unless the State can present a compelling purpose further by the statutes that can be accomplished in no other reasonable manner. . . .

Spina, J. (dissenting, with whom Sosman and Cordy, JJ., join).

Sosman, J. (dissenting, with whom Spina and Cordy, JJ., join).

Cordy, J. (dissenting, with whom Spina and Sosman, JJ., join).

The Massachusetts marriage statute does not impair the exercise of a recognized fundamental right, or discriminate on the basis of sex in violation of the equal rights amendment to the Massachusetts Constitution. Consequently, it is subject to review only to determine whether it satisfies the rational basis test. Because a conceivable rational basis exists upon which the Legislature could conclude that the marriage statute furthers the legitimate State purpose of ensuring, promoting, and supporting an optimal social structure for the bearing and raising of children, it is a valid exercise of the State's police power. . . .

Cyber Constitution
Perry v. Schwarzenegger
(2010) http://documents.
nytimes.com/us-district-
court-decision-perry-v-
schwarzenegger

12.8 MODERN CHALLENGES

Equal protection cases involving sex and sexual-orientation-based distinctions are likely to remain constant fixtures among modern civil rights cases. Certainly, cases involving discrimination against gays, lesbians, and bisexuals are on the cutting edge of contemporary civil rights law. For many, it is the primary civil rights movement of the current era. And while many state and local governments have employed heightened legal scrutiny for these claims, resulting in the strict scrutiny test being used as a product of state or local law,

Former Solicitor General Ted Olson shakes hands with other gay rights advocates celebrating a few hours after a federal judge struck down a California voter-approved ban on same-sex marriage. In the landmark *Perry vs. Schwarzenegger*, U.S. District Chief Judge Vaughn R. Walker said Proposition 8, passed by voters in 2008, violated the federal constitutional rights of gays and lesbians to marry their partners of choice. The ruling is expected to be appealed to the U.S. Ninth Circuit Court of Appeals and then up to the U.S. Supreme Court

mg4/mg4/ZUMA Press/Newscom

the more universal question still remains as to what level of constitutional scrutiny is most appropriate under the federal standards for equal protection. Perhaps the federal same-sex marriage case of *Perry v. Schwarzenegger* currently percolating through the Ninth Circuit will lead to a formal and complete review by the Supreme Court. But for now, the appropriate constitutional scrutiny for these cases remains open to dispute in many jurisdictions.

In cases involving sex-based forms of discrimination, constitutional scholars and legal advocates continue to see what, if any, impact Justice Ginsburg's opinion in *United States v. Virginia* (1996) will have on the level of constitutional scrutiny applied to these cases. Certainly, Justice Ginsburg and others would like to apply an increased form of scrutiny to sex-based classifications beyond the currently used intermediate form of scrutiny. Whether this involves employing the full-blown strict scrutiny standard or the "exceedingly persuasive" standard suggested in *United States v. Virginia* remains an open debate. For now, legal professionals working on behalf of plaintiffs will continue to advance the higher levels of scrutiny as the appropriate standard for review, while those defending against sex-based claims will continue to cite the intermediate level of scrutiny as the established standard of review.

12.9 OTHER CHARACTERISTIC-DRIVEN CLASSIFICATIONS

As is evident from the Supreme Court's decisions regarding the equal protection rights of homosexuals, the Court has been somewhat reluctant to identify additional characteristics or classifications as being suspect or semi-suspect. As a result, for many equal protection claims that do not involve race, sex, or interference with a fundamental right (see following discussion), the rational basis standard will be the framework for constitutional analysis. Keep in mind, though, that in many cases the discrimination at issue may also be governed by civil rights legislation or state and local constitutional standards, which may provide greater legal protection than that afforded under the Equal Protection Clause.

12.9(a) Alienage

One classification that, at times, the Court has found to be suspect is **alienage**—a person's status as a non–U.S. citizen. In *Graham v. Richardson* (1971),[51] the court declared that alienage was a suspect category deserving of strict scrutiny analysis. Consistent with this finding, the Court has struck down a Texas law barring a non–U.S. citizen from becoming a notary public, a New York law prohibiting resident aliens from receiving state financial aid and scholarships, and a Connecticut law prohibiting aliens from practicing law.[52] But the Court has carved out three large exceptions to this approach— exceptions that allow the rational basis standard to be applied in many alienage cases.

The first exception involves non–U.S. citizens who are in the United States illegally. The Court has stated that these individuals "cannot be treated as a suspect class because their presence in this country in violation of federal law is not a constitutional irrelevancy."[53] The second exception involves congressional legislation affecting aliens. Because Article I of the Constitution gives Congress specific authority to regulate immigration and naturalization, the Court generally has not held alienage-based distinctions made by Congress to be suspect. The last exception applies to governmental employment (at all levels). The Court has ruled that where public positions involve **"important governmental functions,"** the government may deny such jobs to non–U.S. citizens. Under the important governmental functions test, noncitizens have been denied jobs as police officers, public school teachers, and probation officers.[54]

Given the nature and scope of the three exceptions to the strict scrutiny standard in alienage cases, it is fair to say that the exceptions have often overridden the rule. And in cases where an exception is applicable, governmental discrimination against non–U.S. citizens will be upheld if it is rationally related to a legitimate governmental interest.

12.9(b) Parents' Marital Status at Birth ("Illegitimacy")

At times, some governments have treated children whose biological parents are married when the child is born differently from those children whose parents are not married at the time of the child's birth. Within many facets of the law, this has given rise to the pejorative labeling of children as "legitimate" (born to married parents) and "illegitimate" (born to unmarried parents). And in some cases, governments have afforded lesser legal benefits and rights to those parents and children involved in births out-of-wedlock than to those involved in "wedlock" births.

The Supreme Court has offered mixed signals with regard to the proper equal protection analysis for these cases. In *Matthews v. Lucas* (1976),[55] the Court treated the federal Social Security Act's distinct and adverse treatment of "illegitimate" children as semi-suspect, thereby warranting intermediate scrutiny. This approach was followed in *Trimble v. Gordon* (1977),[56] where the Court struck down an Illinois law that permitted "illegitimate" children to inherit from their mothers, but not their fathers, ruling that the law was not "substantially related to a permissible state interest." But the Court has also applied the non-suspect approach to these cases. In *Levy v. Louisiana* (1968),[57] the Court used the rational basis standard to invalidate a state law allowing only "legitimate" children to bring an action for the wrongful death of a parent. And in recent cases, the Court has given less attention to the intermediate scrutiny standard. In fact, in *Michael H. v. Gerald D.* (1989),[58] Justice Scalia's plurality opinion referred to "illegitimacy" as a "legal construct, not a natural trait," and concluded that the rational basis standard was applicable. As a result, it appears that equal protection for individuals affected by out-of-wedlock births lies either at the non-suspect or at the semi-suspect level.

12.9(c) Age

The Court has made it clear that, under the Equal Protection Clause, age is a non-suspect classification entitled only to rational basis review. In *Massachusetts Board of Retirement v. Murgia* (1976),[59] the Court upheld a state law that required certain police officers to retire at fifty years of age, finding that it was rationally related to the state's legitimate interest in maintaining an effective means of law enforcement. Three years later, in *Vance v. Bradley* (1979),[60] the Court upheld a similar mandatory-retirement law at the federal level, concluding that it was rationally related to a legitimate governmental interest. More recently, in *Kimel v. Florida Board of Regents* (2000),[61] the Court reiterated the non-suspect nature of age-based classifications under the Equal Protection Clause. In an opinion by Justice O'Connor, the Court explained the non-suspect nature of age by stating, "[o]ld age . . . does not define a discrete and insular minority because all persons, if they live out normal life spans, will experience it."

While age is not a suspect form of discrimination for equal protection purposes, in some instances, it is afforded heightened protection under federal civil rights legislation. In 1967, Congress passed the **Age Discrimination in Employment Act (ADEA),** barring employers from using age to disadvantage employees between the age of forty and seventy. The Supreme Court has limited the scope of the ADEA by ruling that it (1) does not bar states from enacting mandatory-retirement laws, (2) does not allow state employees to bring suits against states in federal courts to enforce its mandates, and (3) does not stop an employer from favoring an older employee over a younger one.[62] But generally speaking, within the employment context, the ADEA affords much greater legal protection than the Equal Protection Clause for age-based deprivations of equality.

Age Discrimination in Employment Act (ADEA) A federal statute barring employers from discriminating based on advanced age.

12.9(d) Wealth

Like its treatment of age, the Court, during the modern era, generally has regarded wealth or *indigency* (the lack of wealth) as a non-suspect classification for equal protection purposes. The Court's deferential treatment of wealth-based government distinctions has resulted in many forms of economic policy, including tax code provisions, public program funding, and economic development decisions, surviving equal protection scrutiny, as long as they are rationally related to a legitimate governmental interest. For example, in *Fitzgerald v. Racing Association of Iowa et al.* (2003),[63] the Court applied the rational basis test to uphold an Iowa law that taxed the proceeds from racetrack slot machines at a higher level than proceeds generated from riverboat slot machines. Deferring to the economic objectives of state legislators, the Court concluded that a rational legislator could conclude that the tax policy would further the state's economic interests, and therefore the policy met the basic standard for equal protection.

In some cases, however, the financial values exercised by legislators have had a profound impact on other dimensions of individual liberty. This is particularly true with the public financing decisions that some state legislatures have made regarding public education.

During the past several years, there have been a number of cases in which individuals have challenged their state's method for financing public schools.[64] In most of these cases, the plaintiffs have asserted that the state's reliance on real estate taxes to fund much of public education has resulted in disparate educational resources and opportunities for children. Essentially, the assertion is that school districts located in areas with higher land values receive more funding as compared to districts with much lower land values. In many of these cases, the plaintiffs have prevailed. But largely these decisions have been based on state constitutional provisions, not protections under the Fourteenth Amendment's Equal Protection Clause.[65]

On the one hand, state policies governing the funding of public schools involve wealth-based distinctions, which, as identified earlier, are subject to non-suspect scrutiny. On the other hand, funding decisions impact the quality of education, which, as the Court addressed in *Brown v. Board of Education I* (1954) (see excerpt earlier in this chapter), is a critical state-provided service that is necessary for many to have in order to become informed, effective, and productive citizens. This suggests that government distinctions that impact the quality of education, including those that involve financial matters, may warrant a higher degree of equal protection review.

In 1973, the Supreme Court reviewed this question under the Equal Protection Clause and concluded that school funding decisions were non-suspect forms of discrimination to be afforded nothing greater than rational basis review. Read the Court's opinion in *San Antonio Independent School District v. Rodriguez* (1973). Note that, in addition to treating public funding decisions regarding education as a non-suspect form of discrimination, the Court also refused to identify the ability to receive an education as a fundamental right.

San Antonio School District v. Rodriguez
411 U.S. 1 (1973)

Mr. Justice Powell delivered the opinion of the Court.

This suit attacking the Texas system of financing public education was initiated by Mexican-American parents whose children attend the elementary and secondary schools in the Edgewood Independent School District, an urban school district in San Antonio, Texas. They brought a class action on behalf of schoolchildren throughout the State who are members of minority groups or who are poor and reside in school districts having a low property tax base. . . . The complaint was filed in the summer of 1968 and a three-judge court was impaneled in January 1969. In December 1971, the panel rendered its judgment in a *per curiam* opinion holding the Texas school finance system unconstitutional under the Equal Protection Clause of the Fourteenth Amendment. The State appealed, and we noted probable jurisdiction to consider the far-reaching constitutional questions presented. For the reasons stated in this opinion, we reverse the decision of the District Court. . . .

Until recent times, Texas was a predominantly rural State and its population and property wealth were spread relatively evenly across the State. Sizable differences in the value of assessable property between local school districts became increasingly evident as the State became more industrialized and as rural-to-urban population shifts became more pronounced. The location of commercial and industrial property began to play a significant role in determining the amount of tax resources available to each school district. These growing disparities in population and taxable property between districts were responsible in part for increasingly notable differences in levels of local expenditure for education. . . .

The school district in which appellees reside, the Edgewood Independent School District, has been compared throughout this litigation with the Alamo Heights Independent School District. This comparison between the least and most affluent districts in the San Antonio area serves to illustrate the manner in which the dual system of finance operates and to indicate the extent to which substantial disparities exist despite the State's impressive progress in recent years. Edgewood is one of seven public school districts in the metropolitan area. Approximately 22,000 students are enrolled in its 25 elementary and secondary schools. The district is situated in the core-city sector of San Antonio in a residential neighborhood that has little commercial or industrial property. The residents are predominantly of Mexican-American descent: approximately 90% of the student population is Mexican-American and over 6% is Negro. The average assessed property value per pupil is $5,960—the lowest in the metropolitan area—and the median family income ($4,686) is also the lowest. At an equalized tax rate of $1.05 per $100 of assessed property—the highest in the metropolitan area—the district contributed $26 to the education of each child for the 1967—1968 school year above its Local Fund Assignment for the Minimum Foundation Program. The Foundation Program contributed $222 per pupil for a state-local total of $248. Federal funds added another $108 for a total of $356 per pupil.

Alamo Heights is the most affluent school district in San Antonio. Its six schools, housing approximately 5,000 students, are situated in a residential community quite unlike the Edgewood District. The school population is predominantly "Anglo," having only 18% Mexican-Americans and less than 1% Negroes. The assessed property value per pupil exceeds $49,000, and the median family income is $8,001. In 1967–1968 the local tax rate of $.85 per $100 of valuation yielded $333 per pupil over and above its contribution to the Foundation Program. Coupled with the $225 provided from that Program, the district was able to supply $558 per student. Supplemented by a $36 per-pupil grant from federal sources, Alamo Heights spent $594 per pupil. . . .

Texas virtually concedes that its historically rooted dual system of financing education could not withstand the strict judicial scrutiny that this Court has found appropriate in reviewing legislative judgments that interfere with fundamental constitutional rights or that involve suspect classifications. . . .

We must decide, first, whether the Texas system of financing public education operates to the disadvantage of some suspect class or impinges upon a fundamental right explicitly or implicitly protected by the Constitution, thereby requiring strict judicial scrutiny. If so, the judgment of the District Court should be affirmed. If not, the Texas scheme must still be examined to determine whether it rationally furthers some legitimate, articulated state purpose and therefore does not constitute an invidious discrimination in violation of the Equal Protection Clause of the Fourteenth Amendment. . . .

We are unable to agree that this case, which in significant aspects is *sui generis*, may be so neatly fitted into the conventional mosaic of constitutional analysis under the Equal Protection Clause. Indeed, for the several reasons that follow, we find neither the suspect-classification nor the fundamental-interest analysis persuasive. . . .

The case comes to us with no definitive description of the classifying facts or delineation of the disfavored class. Examination of the District Court's opinion and of appellees' complaint, briefs, and contentions at oral argument suggests, however, at least three ways in which the discrimination claimed here might be described. The Texas system of school financing might be regarded as discriminating (1) against "poor" persons whose incomes fall below some identifiable level of poverty or who might be characterized as functionally "indigent," (2) against those who are relatively poorer than others, or (3) against all those who, irrespective of their personal incomes, happen to reside in relatively poorer school districts. . . .

However described, it is clear that appellees' suit asks this Court to extend its most exacting scrutiny to review a system that allegedly discriminates against a large, diverse, and amorphous class, unified only by the common factor of residence in districts that happen to have less taxable wealth than other districts. The system of alleged discrimination and the class it defines have none of the traditional indicia of suspectness: the class is not saddled with such disabilities, or subjected to such a history of purposeful unequal treatment, or relegated to such a position of political powerlessness as to command extraordinary protection from the majoritarian political process.

We thus conclude that the Texas system does not operate to the peculiar disadvantage of any suspect class. But in recognition of the fact that this Court has never heretofore held that wealth discrimination alone provides an adequate basis for invoking strict scrutiny, appellees have not relied solely on this contention. They also assert that the State's system impermissibly interferes with the exercise of a "fundamental" right and that accordingly the prior decisions of this Court require the application of the strict standard of judicial review. It is this question—whether education is a fundamental right, in the sense that it is among the rights and liberties protected by the Constitution—which has so consumed the attention of courts and commentators in recent years.

Education, of course, is not among the rights afforded explicit protection under our Federal Constitution. Nor do we find any basis for saying it is implicitly so protected. As we have said, the undisputed importance of education will not alone cause this Court to depart from the usual standard for reviewing a State's social and economic legislation. . . .

In sum, to the extent that the Texas system of school financing results in unequal expenditures between children who happen to reside in different districts, we cannot say that such disparities are the product of a system that is so irrational as to be invidiously discriminatory. . . .

Reversed.

Mr. Justice Stewart, concurring.

Mr. Justice Brennan, dissenting.

Although I agree with my Brother White that the Texas statutory scheme is devoid of any rational basis, and for that reason is violative of the Equal Protection Clause, I also record my disagreement with the Court's rather distressing assertion that a right may be deemed "fundamental" for the purposes of equal protection analysis only if it is "explicitly or implicitly guaranteed by the Constitution." . . .

Here, there can be no doubt that education is inextricably linked to the right to participate in the electoral process and to the rights of free speech and association guaranteed by the First Amendment. This being so, any classification affecting education must be subjected to strict judicial scrutiny, and since even the State concedes that the statutory scheme now before us cannot pass constitutional muster under this stricter standard of review, I can only conclude that the Texas school-financing scheme is constitutionally invalid.

Mr. Justice White, with whom Mr. Justice Douglas and Mr. Justice Brennan join, dissenting. . . .

Mr. Justice Marshall, with whom Mr. Justice Douglas concurs, dissenting. . . .

In my judgment, the right of every American to an equal start in life, so far as the provision of a state service as important as education is concerned, is far too vital to permit state discrimination on grounds as tenuous as those presented by this record. Nor can I accept the notion that it is sufficient to remit these appellees to the vagaries of the political process which, contrary to the majority's suggestion, has proved singularly unsuited to the task of providing a remedy for this discrimination. I, for one, am unsatisfied with the hope of an ultimate "political" solution sometime in the indefinite future while, in the meantime, countless children unjustifiably receive inferior educations that "may affect their hearts and minds in a way unlikely ever to be undone." *Brown v. Board of Education*, 347 U.S. 483, 494 (1954). I must therefore respectfully dissent. . . .

12.10 CLASSIFICATIONS THAT INTERFERE WITH FUNDAMENTAL RIGHTS

As illustrated in *San Antonio Independent School District v. Rodriguez,* there are some equal protection cases where the Court asks whether governmental distinctions, regardless of their level of suspiciousness, impact on the exercise of fundamental constitutional rights. If so, the Court has expressed a willingness to apply strict scrutiny analysis. Of course, the Court in *Rodriguez* concluded that education was not a fundamental right under the Constitution, and therefore only rational basis review applied, but this has not been the result in other equal protection contests.

In a number of cases, the Court has concluded that a governmental distinction, which, in and of itself, is non-suspect, may nonetheless warrant strict scrutiny analysis if it interferes with a fundamental liberty interest. For example, in *Zablocki v. Redhail* (1978),[66] the Court applied the Equal Protection Clause to invalidate a Wisconsin law that prohibited individuals who were under child-support obligations from getting married without a judicial determination that the individual's child-support obligations were being met and would continue to be met. The Court noted that the right to marry is "of fundamental importance for all individuals" and that "the decision to marry has been placed on the same level of importance as decisions relating to procreation, childbirth, child rearing, and family relationships." The Court further found that because the Wisconsin law interfered with the fundamental right to marry, it could be justified only if it met the strict scrutiny standard, which the Court concluded it did not.

The Court has adopted this approach to other cases as well. In *Skinner v. Oklahoma* (1942),[67] the Court invalidated a state law requiring "habitual criminals" to be sterilized, holding that the law created a distinction among persons that interfered with the fundamental right to procreate. In *Griffin v. Illinois* (1956),[68] the Court applied the Equal Protection Clause to reject a state policy that prevented indigent criminal defendants from obtaining trial transcripts, finding that it interfered with defendants' fundamental right to access the courts. Similarly, in *Douglas v. California* (1963),[69] the Court found

YOUR CONSTITUTIONAL VALUES

SHOULD EDUCATION BE A FUNDAMENTAL RIGHT?

In *San Antonio v. Rodriguez* (1973), the Supreme Court rejected the claim that education is a fundamental right under the United States. Consequently, litigants increasingly have turned to state courts and state constitutions in an effort to address inequities in public education. These cases have taken two primary approaches. The first is the equal protection approach, which, like the argument in *Rodriguez*, asserts that disparities in funding public education infringe upon a fundamental right to education. These are known as "equity" cases. The second category of cases are referred to as "adequacy" suits. These claims generally rely on state constitutional provisions requiring the government to provide an "adequate" public education and use statistical analysis of the state's funding programs to argue that the state's funding is inadequate.

The results of these state challenges have been mixed. In equity-based cases, challengers have been successful at times in getting greater constitutional protection for education under state constitutional provisions. For example, in *Pauley v. Kelly*, 255 S.E.2d 859 (1979), the Supreme Court of Appeals of West Virginia ruled that education was a fundamental right under the state's constitution. But in other cases, state courts have refused to acknowledge education as a more valued liberty. The Nebraska Supreme Court, for example, in *Gould v. Orr*, 506 N.W.2d 349 (1993), held that equal funding in public education was not protected under the then-state constitution. The addition of adequacy-based claims to lawsuits beginning in the 1980s has led to greater success for many challengers to public education financing programs. In fact, since 1989, challengers have prevailed in nearly two-thirds of their court cases. See http://schoolfunding.info/.

How has your state approached education under its constitution, court decisions, and legislative enactments? Based on your constitutional values, do you find that your state has sufficiently and properly protected "the right to an education"?

For more information, see www.educationjustice.org/resources.html.

a state's denial of appellate counsel to criminal defendants to be invidious discrimination under the Equal Protection Clause. And in *Harper v. Virginia State Board of Elections* (1966), the Court struck down a $1.50 poll tax (a wealth-based distinction) because it interfered with the fundamental right to vote.[70]

Read the Court's opinion in *Shapiro v. Thompson* (1969), where the Court addressed the right to interstate travel as being a fundamental right under the Equal Protection Clause. Consider how the Court reached its conclusion that such a right exists and is fundamental, despite not being explicitly referenced in the Constitution. Also consider whether other unenumerated rights (education, marriage, etc.) should also be treated as fundamental under the Equal Protection Clause.

One may wonder why the Court has addressed "fundamental rights" under the Equal Protection Clause when this is also the central focus under the Due Process Clause (see Chapter 11). Recall that under due process analysis, some matters, such as privacy, birth control, and consensual adult relations, have been treated as fundamental rights, deserving of strict scrutiny protection. Why, then, would the Court bring fundamental rights into the picture under equal protection analysis when such rights could be (and have been) assessed under the Due Process Clause?

There is no clear answer to this question. In fact, there appears to be little rhyme or reason to the Court's application of its due process approach, as compared to its equal protection approach. For example, in *Lawrence v. Texas* (2003) (see Chapter 11), although the Court rejected Texas's same-sex sodomy statute on due process grounds, arguably, it could have just as easily addressed and invalidated the law on equal protection grounds. In fact, Justice O'Connor, in her concurring opinion in *Lawrence*, concluded that the equal protection route was the better way to go. Ultimately, as the

Shapiro v. Thompson
394 U.S. 618 (1969)

Mr. Justice Brennan delivered the opinion of the Court.

[This] is an appeal from a decision of a three-judge District Court holding unconstitutional a State or District of Columbia statutory provision which denies welfare assistance to residents of the State or District who have not resided within their jurisdictions for at least one year immediately preceding their applications for such assistance. We affirm. . . .

There is no dispute that the effect of the waiting-period requirement in each case is to create two classes of needy resident families indistinguishable from each other except that one is composed of residents who have resided a year or more, and the second of residents who have resided less than a year, in the jurisdiction. On the basis of this sole difference the first class is granted and the second class is denied welfare aid upon which may depend the ability of the families to obtain the very means to subsist—food, shelter, and other necessities of life. . . . The interests which appellants assert are promoted by the classification either may not constitutionally be promoted by government or are not compelling governmental interests.

Primarily, appellants justify the waiting-period requirement as a protective device to preserve the fiscal integrity of state public assistance programs. It is asserted that people who require welfare assistance during their first year of residence in a State are likely to become continuing burdens on state welfare programs. Therefore, the argument runs, if such people can be deterred from entering the jurisdiction by denying them welfare benefits during the first year, state programs to assist long-time residents will not be impaired by a substantial influx of indigent newcomers. . . .

We do not doubt that the one-year waiting-period device is well suited to discourage the influx of poor families in need of assistance. An indigent who desires to migrate, resettle, find a new job, and start a new life will doubtless hesitate if he knows that he must risk making the move without the possibility of falling back on state welfare assistance during his first year of residence, when his need may be most acute. But the purpose of inhibiting migration by needy persons into the State is constitutionally impermissible.

This Court long ago recognized that the nature of our Federal Union and our constitutional concepts of personal liberty unite to require that all citizens be free to travel throughout the length and breadth of our land uninhibited by statutes, rules, or regulations which unreasonably burden or restrict this movement. . . .

We have no occasion to ascribe the source of this right to travel interstate to a particular constitutional provision. . . .

We recognize that a State has a valid interest in preserving the fiscal integrity of its programs. It may legitimately attempt to limit its expenditures, whether for public assistance, public education, or any other program. But a State may not accomplish such a purpose by invidious distinctions between classes of its citizens. It could not, for example, reduce expenditures for education by barring indigent children from its schools. Similarly, in the cases before us, appellants must do more than show that denying welfare benefits to new residents saves money. The saving of welfare costs cannot justify an otherwise invidious classification.

In sum, neither deterrence of indigents from migrating to the State nor limitation of welfare benefits to those regarded as contributing to the State is a constitutionally permissible state objective. . . .

The argument that the waiting-period requirement facilitates budget predictability is wholly unfounded. The records in all three cases are utterly devoid of evidence that either State or the District of Columbia in fact uses the one-year requirement as a means to predict the number of people who will require assistance in the budget year. . . .

The argument that the waiting period serves as an administratively efficient rule of thumb for determining residency similarly will not withstand scrutiny. The residence requirement and the one-year waiting-period requirement are distinct and independent prerequisites for assistance under these three statutes, and the facts relevant to the determination of each are directly examined by the welfare authorities. Before granting an application, the welfare authorities investigate the applicant's employment, housing, and family situation and in the course of the inquiry necessarily learn the facts upon which to determine whether the applicant is a resident.

Similarly, there is no need for a State to use the one-year waiting period as a safeguard against fraudulent receipt of benefits; for less drastic means are available, and are employed, to minimize that hazard. . . .

We conclude therefore that appellants in these cases do not use and have no need to use the one-year requirement for the governmental purposes suggested. Thus, even under traditional equal protection tests a classification of welfare applicants according to whether they have lived in the State for one year would seem irrational and unconstitutional. But, of course, the traditional criteria do not apply in these cases. Since the classification here touches on the fundamental right of interstate movement, its constitutionality must be judged by the stricter standard of whether it promotes a compelling state interest. Under this standard, the waiting-period requirement clearly violates the Equal Protection Clause. . . .

Affirmed.

Mr. Justice Stewart, concurring.

"The constitutional right to travel from one State to another . . . has been firmly established and repeatedly recognized." This constitutional right, which, of course, includes the right of "entering and abiding in any State in the Union" is not a mere conditional liberty subject to regulation and control under conventional due process or equal protection standards. "[T]he right to travel freely from State to State finds constitutional protection that is quite independent of the Fourteenth Amendment." As we made clear in *Guest*, it is a right broadly assertable against private interference as well as governmental action. Like the right of association, it is a virtually unconditional personal right, guaranteed by the Constitution to us all. . . .

The Court today, therefore, is not "contriving new constitutional principles." It is deciding these cases under the aegis of established constitutional law.

Mr. Chief Justice Warren, with whom Mr. Justice Black joins, dissenting.

Mr. Justice Harlan, dissenting.

Cyber Constitution
Equal Protection Standards in Song www.youtube.com/watch?v=M_Xymr1YVzQ

Massachusetts Supreme Court acknowledged in *Goodridge v. Massachusetts Department of Public Health* (2003) (excerpted earlier in text), regardless of whether a case is reviewed under the Equal Protection Clause or the Due Process Clause, a court may end up applying the same level of scrutiny.

In the end, the important thing to note is that in some equal protection cases, courts will apply strict scrutiny analysis to governmental distinctions—regardless of whether they involve semi-suspect or non-suspect classifications—if they interfere with fundamental rights.

12.11 VOTING RIGHTS

Unlike many cases involving campaign finance reform or post-election employment, which often center on First Amendment issues of political speech and the right of association (see Chapter 9), the right to vote has traditionally been debated based on notions of equal protection.

At the outset it must be observed that there is no general or affirmative right to vote mentioned in the original Constitution. Under the Articles of the Constitution, qualifications and other issues involving voting were largely left to the states to decide. For example, in Article I, Section 2, the Constitution provides that members of the House of Representatives will be chosen by voters in each state who have "[q]ualifications requisite for Electors of the most numerous Branch of the State Legislature." In other words, in order to vote for a member of the U.S. House of Representatives, a person had to meet the qualifications for voting in a state election for the state's largest legislative chamber. Given this constitutional deference to the states under the original Constitution, the right to vote was generally determined on a state-by-state basis, resulting in widespread and substantial forms of voter discrimination.

Early in the nation's history, some states excluded non-landowners from voting. Drawing upon a practice used in the British colonies, some states limited the right to vote to white male landowners. Still other states restricted voting based on religion. Most of these barriers were removed during the early to middle nineteenth century, but many other obstacles were left in place during a substantial portion of the nation's history. Most notably, racial minorities (enfranchised in 1870) and women (enfranchised in 1920) were excluded from voting for many years. Gradually, however, the Constitution was amended to provide more uniform (national) and inclusive voting qualifications. The Fifteenth Amendment states that the right to vote cannot be denied based on race. The Nineteenth Amendment ensures that a person's sex cannot be used to disqualify individuals from voting. The Twenty-Fourth Amendment bars the use of poll taxes from being applied in federal elections. And the Twenty-Sixth Amendment guarantees that persons over eighteen years of age cannot be prohibited from voting based on age.

These voting rights amendments to the Constitution dramatically expanded the right to vote, but these amendments did not resolve all issues regarding voting and equality. Many other matters have been left to the Supreme Court to resolve. Chief among these disputes is the battle over where and how legislative districts are drawn by state legislatures. A term often used to describe this process is called **gerrymandering,** which is a form of drawing or redrawing geographic boundaries for electoral districts based on a particular motive, such as reelecting the incumbent, including or excluding minority voters, or increasing political party control. Even today, states are afforded considerable discretion when drawing and dividing geographic boundaries for legislative districts, but constitutional challenges can be asserted when race-based reasons are used in the process. For years, black voters argued that many states were drawing their legislative districts in a manner that diluted the collective voting strength of black voters. In some cases, it was argued that states were trying to consolidate black voters by creating districts that were malapportioned, assigning large numbers of black residents to a single district, thereby limiting the number of black representatives likely to be elected. In other states, it was asserted that the legislatures were seeking to draw district lines in such a way as to distribute black residents among so-called white districts in order to dilute their voting strength.

Initially, the Supreme Court refused to consider the argument that these redistricting efforts amounted to racial discrimination under the Fourteenth and Fifteenth Amendments. Instead, the Court deemed these issues to be "political questions," which were best resolved by the other branches of government. For example, the Court refused to consider the merits of *Colegrove v. Green* (1946),[71] wherein black voters tried to challenge the electoral districts in Illinois, which maintained gross disparities among the voting power of black and white voters. Instead, the Court deemed the case to involve a nonjusticiable political question.

The Court's approach to malapportioned districts dramatically changed in 1962, when in *Baker v. Carr*,[72] the Court ruled that such disputes were justiciable and that lower courts could examine whether state efforts in drawing or maintaining legislative districts involved racial discrimination. While the Court did not address the underlying

gerrymandering
The process of drawing or redrawing geographic boundaries for electoral districts based on a particular motive, such as reelecting the incumbent, including or excluding minority voters, or increasing political party control.

question of whether the challenged district in *Baker* was unconstitutional, the Court's ruling nonetheless had an enormous impact on voting rights cases because it essentially opened the courthouse doors to future cases regarding voter discrimination and voting rights. As a result, this opinion is widely regarded as one of the most important Supreme Court rulings of all time.

One year after *Baker v. Carr*, in *Gray v. Sanders*,[73] the Court struck down Georgia's use of a county-based system of primary elections in state elections because it diluted the voting power of those living in urban areas. In this opinion, Justice William Douglas asserted that "[t]he conception of political equality from the Declaration of Independence to Lincoln's Gettysburg address, to the Fifteenth, Seventeenth, and Nineteenth Amendments can mean only one thing—one person, one vote." This is known as the **one person, one vote principle,** which generally holds that, in order to be constitutional, states must draw electoral districts in a manner that evenly (though not necessarily with mathematical perfection) distributes the population so that individual voting power can be relatively equal among the districts.

One year later, the Court issued seven opinions addressing malapportionment issues. These cases included *Wesberry v. Sanders* (1964),[74] which struck down malapportioned congressional districts in Georgia, and *Reynolds v. Sims* (1964),[75] which invalidated state legislative districts in Alabama. In each of these cases, the Court emphasized that the doctrine of one person one vote was "the essence of self-government."

Following these landmark rulings, Congress passed the **Voting Rights Act of 1965,** which prohibits any "voting qualification or prerequisite to voting" that denies the right to vote based on race or color. This law was designed to supplement the Fifteenth Amendment by specifically banning such practices as literacy, educational, and "good moral character" tests, which were being used by some authorities as a means of racial discrimination. In *South Carolina v. Katzenbach* (1966),[76] the Supreme Court upheld the constitutionality of the Voting Rights Act, finding it to be a proper exercise of congressional authority under Section 2 of the Fifteenth Amendment, which authorizes Congress to enforce the amendment through "appropriate legislation." Originally, the Voting Rights Act was set to expire in 1970, but since its passage in 1965, Congress has renewed the law on several occasions. Congress also has amended the statute to include protections for citizens with limited English proficiency and to make it clear that voting discrimination does not need to be intentional in order to violate the act (the law uses a "results test").

Despite the constitutional amendments and civil rights legislation protecting the right to vote, the battle over voting rights and equality continues today. Many cases continue to address the issue of legislative redistricting, where the district lines drawn by state legislatures are challenged under the Fifteenth Amendment and the Voting Rights Act of 1965. In many cases, there is a twist on the debate from the 1960s. Instead of claiming that the state legislature drew district boundaries in an effort to exclude minority voters, the claim is often that such redistricting is designed to afford greater minority representation by creating so-called minority districts. The Supreme Court, however, has concluded that the motive—inclusion or exclusion—generally does not matter and that the central question in any case involving race and redistricting is whether the state can satisfy the demands of strict scrutiny analysis. As a divided Court held in *Shaw v. Reno* (1993),[77] race-based redistricting is unconstitutional under the Fourteenth Amendment unless the government can demonstrate a compelling interest for creating black or Hispanic districts.

12.12 MODERN CHALLENGES

As long as state legislatures are involved in the process of redrawing legislative and other voting districts, there will likely be equal protection challenges asserted by voters who feel disenfranchised based on race or other prohibited classifications. For

---

one person, one vote principle
A doctrine adopted by the Supreme Court in the 1960s, which generally holds that, in order to be constitutional, states must draw electoral districts in a manner that evenly (though not necessarily with mathematical perfection) distributes the population so that individual voting power can be relatively equal among the districts.

Voting Rights Act of 1965
Major piece of civil rights legislation that prohibits any "voting qualification or prerequisite to voting" that denies the right to vote based on race or color. This law was designed to supplement the Fifteenth Amendment by specifically banning such practices as literacy, educational, and "good moral character" tests, which were being used by some authorities as a means of racial discrimination.

Cyber Constitution
History of Voting Rights
www.aclu.org/voting-rights

Cyber Constitution
Voting Rights Act
www.justice.gov/crt/voting/intro/intro_b.php

legislators seeking to defend their redistricting efforts, the challenge will be either to offer and prove that there are race-neutral reasons for redrawing the district's boundaries or, if based on race, to show that the redrawn lines are necessary to promote a compelling governmental interest. For voters or interest groups fighting against policies that impact voting rights, the challenge will be to prove that such policies are based on race or another prohibited criterion and that they do not meet the rigors of the strict scrutiny standard of review. For legal professionals assigned to these cases, the work can be tedious and fact intensive, involving substantial amounts of demographic and census data, geographic evidence, and legislative history.

12.13 SUMMARY

The value of equality was not substantially present in or protected by the early pension of the Constitution. But with the passage of the Thirteenth, Fourteenth, and Fifteenth Amendments following the Civil War, notions that similarly situated people ought to be treated similarly began to enter the formal constitutional dialogue of the Court. The chief provision that protects equality is the Fourteenth Amendment's Equal Protection Clause, which tells the states not to deny persons the equal protection of the law. The Court has read the same requirement into the Fifth Amendment's Due Process Clause by requiring the federal government to provide equal protection to persons as well.

To be governed by the constitutional principles of equal protection, there must first be state action. In other words, the government must be sufficiently involved in the practice of denying equality for there to be a constitutional remedy. If nongovernmental action is involved, the situation may be governed by civil rights legislation, which has been enacted to various degrees by federal, state, and local governments, requiring employers, owners of public accommodations, and other entities to comply with certain legislative standards for equality. Civil rights legislation is applicable to governmental action as well in some cases.

Governments can discriminate in a number of ways—some are more suspicious than others. Generally, the Court has gauged the level of suspicion applied to government distinctions by considering (1) whether there has been a substantial history of the relevant type of discrimination, (2) whether the classification used to discriminate involves an immutable (not easily changeable) characteristic, and (3) whether it is likely that this characteristic will continue to be used by the majoritarian process to discriminate in the future. If the government engages in a form of highly suspicious discrimination (as with race, color, or, in some cases, alienage), its policy will be reviewed under the strict scrutiny standard and will be upheld only if it is necessary (narrowly tailored) to promote a compelling governmental interest. Government distinctions that are not in and of themselves suspect but that interfere with fundamental liberties of individuals (the right to vote, travel, get married, raise children, etc.) are also reviewed under the strict scrutiny test. If the government's discrimination is somewhat suspicious or semi-suspect (as in the case of sex-based discrimination), it will be reviewed under the intermediate scrutiny standard, which requires the government to prove that its policy is substantially related to an important governmental interest. And finally, if the government's discrimination is non-suspect (as is the case with most forms of government action, including distinctions based on age and wealth), it will be reviewed under the rational basis test, requiring the government to show that its policy is rationally related to an important governmental interest.

Voting rights have presented unique challenges under the Equal Protection Clause. Initially, voter qualifications were left to the states to decide, which resulted in substantial discrimination against women and minorities at the ballot box. Gradually, however, through constitutional amendments and federal legislation, greater legal protections have been implemented to guard against racial and sex-based discrimination during the voting process.

REVIEW QUESTIONS

1. How does the value of equality compare to the values of security and liberty?

2. Where is the value of equality evidenced in the Constitution?

3. Why does the federal government have to provide equal protection of the law when the Fourteenth Amendment applies to the states?

4. What is state action, and why is it relevant to equal protection analysis?

5. What criteria are used to determine whether a government is engaging in a suspicious form of discrimination?

6. What is civil rights legislation? Provide five different examples of this legislation. How does it work with or supplement the Equal Protection Clause?

7. What constitutional standard is used to evaluate suspect forms of governmental discrimination? Semi-suspect? Non-suspect?

8. What characteristics or classifications have been deemed to involve suspect forms of discrimination? Semi-suspect? Non-suspect?

9. What is a fundamental liberty, and how does it relate to equal protection analysis?

10. What is a badge of servitude, and how has it been used in the development of equal protection under the Constitution?

11. Explain the doctrine of "one person one vote." How has this doctrine enhanced voting rights under the Constitution?

ASSIGNMENTS: CONSTITUTIONAL LAW IN ACTION

The Constitution in Your Community

Assume that you are working as a legal assistant in a law firm. Your firm has just been retained by Sheila Smith, a city employee in your local town, who has just been turned down for a promotion by her city supervisor. Ms. Smith strongly believes that she did not receive the promotion because she is an African American female who is a lesbian. Without judging the factual merits of Ms. Smith's claim, your supervising attorney would like to know the constitutional and legal standards for assessing Ms. Smith's case.

To that end, you are asked to research the relevant legal standards for discrimination that might apply to Ms. Smith's case. Specifically, you are asked to research the types of federal, state, and local protections that might apply to Ms. Smith's case and prepare a five-page legal memorandum outlining your findings. Be sure to consider whether your state or local government has any constitutional or charter provisions that afford greater protection against race, sex, or sexual-orientation discrimination. Also check whether your state or local government has enacted civil rights legislation to protect certain groups against discrimination? Also address how these protections compare to those afforded under the Fourteenth Amendment Equal Protection Clause.

Going Federal

Between 1993 and September 2011, the U.S. military maintained a "don't ask, don't tell" policy with respect to gay, lesbian, and bisexual service members. The policy allowed the military to discharge any openly homosexual member of the military. This policy was later repealed by Congress in 2011.

Despite the recent political judgment of Congress to repeal the "don't ask, don't tell" policy, you are asked to assess the constitutionality of the former law. Accordingly, you are asked to review a federal judge's order in *The Log Cabin Republicans v. United States* (found at http://graphics8.nytimes.com/packages/pdf/PhillipsDecision. pdf). Based on this review and using core Equal Protection Clause standards, prepare a five-page written argument, either in favor of or against the judge's ruling. Assess whether the don't ask, don't tell" policy was consistent with the Equal Protection standards of the U.S. Constitution.

Moot Court

Locate and review the appellate briefs filed in *Perry v. Schwarzenegger*, the same-sex marriage case challenging California's Proposition 8 before the Ninth Circuit Court of Appeals. The briefs can be found at www.ca9.uscourts.gov/content/view.php?pk_id=0000000472. Working in teams of two, the first team should prepare a five-minute oral argument wherein members present arguments, based on equal protection standards, challenging the constitutionality of California's ban on same-sex marriage. Conversely, the second team should prepare a five-minute oral argument asserting why California's ban on same-sex marriage complies with the requirements of the Fourteenth Amendment's Equal Protection Clause.

NOTES

1. *Plessy v. Ferguson*, 163 U.S. 537 (1896).
2. 438 U.S. 265 (1978).
3. Declaration of Independence, July 4, 1776.
4. See Paul Finkelman, "The Proslavery Origins of the Electoral College," 23 *Cardozo L. Rev.* 1145–1157 (2002); "The Founders and Slavery: Little Ventured, Little Gained," 13 *Yale J. L. & Humanities* 413–449 (2001).
5. *See Letter from Abigail Adams to John Adams*, March 31, 1776, L. H. Butterfield, Marc Friedlaender, and Mary-Jo Kline, eds., *The Book of Abigail and John: Selected Letters of the Adams Family, 1762–1784* (Cambridge: Harvard University Press 1975) (where years before the Constitution was written, Abigail Adams cautioned her husband, John Adams, to "remember the ladies" when establishing government authority: "I long to hear that you have declared an independency. . . . In the new Code of Laws which I suppose it will be necessary for you to make I desire you would Remember the Ladies, and be more generous and favourable to them than your ancestors. Do not put such unlimited power into the hands of the Husbands. Remember all Men would be tyrants if they could. If particular care and attention is not paid to the Ladies we are determined to foment a Rebellion, and will not hold ourselves bounds by any Laws in which we have no voice, or Representation.").
6. See James M. McPherson, *The Struggle for Equality: Abolitionists and the Negro in the Civil War and Reconstruction* (Princeton University Press 1964); Jean V. Matthews, *Women's Struggle for Equality: The First Phase, 1828–1876,* American Ways Series (Chicago: Ivan R. Dee 1997).
7. *The Gettysburg Address*, Gettysburg, Pennsylvania, November 19, 1863.
8. See Allen C. Guelzo, *Lincoln's Emancipation Proclamation: The End of Slavery in America* (Simon and Schuster 2004).
9. 334 U.S. 1 (1948).
10. 407 U.S. 163 (1972).
11. See also *San Francisco Arts & Athletics, Inc. v. United States Olympic Committee (USOC)*, 483 U.S. 522 (1987) (holding that the USOC was not engaging in state action); *Brentwood Academy v. Tennessee Secondary School Athletic Assoc.*, 531 U.S. 288 (2001) (finding an athletic association to be participating in state action by working with state school officials).
12. See Lambda Legal Defense Fund, "Summary of States Which Prohibit Discrimination Based on Sexual Orientation," www.lambdalegal.org/cgi-bin/iowa/news/resources.html?record=185.
13. 109 U.S. 3 (1883).
14. 379 U.S. 241 (1964); 379 U.S. 294 (1964).
15. See *Jones v. Alfred H. Mayer, Co.*, 392 U.S. 409 (1968) (adopting Justice Harlan's dissenting opinion in *The Civil Rights Cases* that private discrimination imposes a badge and incident of slavery barred by the Thirteenth Amendment).
16. *Ricci v. DeStefano*, 129 S. Ct. 2658, 2671 (2009).
17. See *Nevada Department of Human Resources v. Hibbs*, 538 U.S. 721 (2003); *Board of Trustees of the University of Alabama v. Garrett*, 531 U.S. 356 (2001); *Kimel v. Florida Board of Regents*, 528 U.S. 62 (2000); *City of Boerne v. Flores*, 521 U.S. 507 (1997).

18. See *Frontiero v. Richardson*, 411 U.S. 677 (1973); *Regents of the University of California v. Bakke*, 428 U.S. 265 (1978) (concurring opinion) for a discussion of these considerations.

19. See *id.* for a discussion of women (sex as a characteristic for discrimination) and the majoritarian process.

20. See *Regents of the University of California v. Bakke*, 428 U.S. 265 (1978) (concurring opinion) ("[it] should be strict—not 'strict' in theory and fatal in fact. . . ."); *Fullilove v. Klutznick*, 448 U.S. 448, 519 (1980) (Marshall, J., concurring in judgment) ("we wish to dispel the notion that strict scrutiny is 'strict in theory, but fatal in fact.'").

21. *Grutter v. Bollinger et al.*, 539 U.S. 306 (2003) (finding a race-based affirmative action policy constitutional).

22. *Romer v. Evans*, 517 U.S. 620 (1996) (striking down an amendment to Colorado's Constitution that discriminated based on sexual orientation).

23. The Constitution of the State of Hawaii, Article I, Section 3, provides, "Equality of rights under the law shall not be denied or abridged by the State on account of sex. The legislature shall have the power to enforce, by appropriate legislation, the provisions of this section."

24. See *Griffin v. Prince Edward County School Board*, 377 U.S. 218 (1964) (wherein Justice Hugo Black asserted, "There has been entirely too much deliberation and not enough speed" in enforcing *Brown*.).

25. See *id.* (applying the Fourteenth Amendment to stop school boards from closing all schools instead of desegregating them); *Cooper v. Aaron*, 358 U.S. 1 (1958) (refusing to allow the Little Rock, Arkansas, school board an extension to delay its desegregation order).

26. 396 U.S. 19 (1969).

27. 396 U.S. 290 (1970).

28. 402 U.S. 1 (1971).

29. 418 U.S. 717 (1974).

30. 498 U.S. 237 (1991).

31. 503 U.S. 467 (1992).

32. 515 U.S. 70 (1995).

33. *Board of Education of Oklahoma City Public Schools v. Dowell*, 498 U.S. 237 (1991).

34. See *Regents of the University of California v. Bakke*, 428 U.S. 265 (1978) (wherein Justice Powell rejects the argument that discrimination against "the white majority" is "benign," while the four concurring justices [Brennan, White, Marshall, and Blackmun] found that "whites as a class [do not] have the 'traditional indicia of suspectness'").

35. 428 U.S. 265 (1978).

36. 448 U.S. 448 (1980).

37. 497 U.S. 547 (1990).

38. 488 U.S. 469 (1989).

39. 515 U.S. 200 (1995).

40. 83 U.S. 130 (1873).

41. 208 U.S. 412 (1908). (This ruling came during the pre–New Deal era—a time when the Court was regularly striking down social legislation designed to regulate working conditions [see Chapter 1, Section 1.7]).

42. 368 U.S. 57 (1961).

43. 429 U.S. 190 (1976).

44. See *Califano v. Goldfarb*, 430 U.S. 199 (1977) (striking down section of Social Security Act giving different benefits to widows and widowers); *J.E.B. v. Alabama ex rel. T.B.*, 511 U.S. 127 (1994) (prohibiting sex-based discrimination during jury selection).

45. See *Rostker v. Goldberg*, 453 U.S. 57 (1981) (allowing Selective Service Act to require males to register for the draft, but not females); *Michael M. v. Superior Court of Sonoma County*, 450 U.S. 464 (1981) (allowing California statutory rape law to treat men more severely than women).

46. 539 U.S. 558 (2003).

47. *Id.*

48. 515 U.S. 557 (1995).

49. 530 U.S. 640 (2000).

50. *Goodridge v. Massachusetts Department of Public Health*, 440 Mass. 309, 334, 798 NE2d 941, 963 (2003).

51. 403 U.S. 365 (1971).

52. See *In re Griffiths*, 413 U.S. 717 (1973) (practice of law); *Nyquist v. Mauclet*, 432 U.S. 1 (1977) (financial aid); and *Bernal v. Fainter*, 467 U.S. 216 (1984) (notary public).

53. *Plyler v. Doe*, 457 U.S. 202 (1982) (although the Court has distinguished those who actually enter the country illegally from the children who are born into these circumstances and who were not responsible for an illegal entry).

54. See *Foley v. Connelie*, 435 U.S. 291 (1978) (police officers); *Ambach v. Norwick*, 441 U.S. 68 (1979) (public school teachers); and *Cabell v. Chavez-Salido*, 454 U.S. 432 (1982) (probation officers).

55. 427 U.S. 495 (1976).

56. 430 U.S. 762 (1977).

57. 391 U.S. 68 (1968).

58. 491 U.S. 110 (1989).

59. 427 U.S. 307 (1976).

60. 440 U.S. 93 (1979).

61. 528 U.S. 62 (2000).

62. *Gregory v. Ashcroft*, 501 U.S. 452 (1991); *Kimel v. Florida Board of Regents*, 528 U.S. 62 (2000); *General Dynamics Land Systems v. Cline*, 540 U.S. 581 (2004).

63. 539 U.S. 103 (2003).

64. See Michele Moser and Ross Rubenstein, "The Equality of Public School District Funding in the United States: A National Status Report," *Public Administration Review*, Vol. 62, 2002.

65. See *DeRolph v. State of Ohio*, 78 Ohio St.3d 193, 677 N.E.2d 733 (1997) (a case declaring Ohio's system of funding public schools unconstitutional, but also a case that has not been implemented by the courts or the legislature).

66. 434 U.S. 374 (1978).

67. 316 U.S. 535 (1942).

68. 351 U.S. 12 (1956).

69. 372 U.S. 353 (1963).

70. 383 U.S. 663 (1966). There are other cases where the Court struck down state voting measures under the Equal Protection Clause. See, for example, *Kramer v. Union Free School District*, 395 U.S. 621 (1969) (property requirement to vote in school district elections); *Reynolds v. Sims*, 377 U.S. 533 (1964) (state reapportionment schemes that denied voters equal voting power [one person/one voting theory]).

71. 328 U.S. 549 (1946).

72. 369 U.S. 186 (1962).

73. 372 U.S. 368 (1963).

74. 376 U.S. 1 (1964).

75. 377 U.S. 533 (1964).

76. 383 U.S. 301 (1966).

77. 509 U.S. 630 (1993). See also *Hunt v. Cromartie*, 532 U.S. 234 (2001); *Georgia v. Ashcroft*, 539 U.S. 461 (2003); *Vieth v. Jubelirer*, 541 U.S. 267 (2004); *League of United Latin American Citizens v. Perry*, 548 U.S. 399 (2006).

13

Civil Liberties in the Criminal Justice System

The criminal is to go free because the constable has blundered.

JUDGE (LATER JUSTICE) BENJAMIN CARDOZO (1926)[1]

Our cases have consistently recognized that unbending application of the exclusionary sanction to enforce ideals of governmental rectitude would impede unacceptably the truth-finding functions of judge and jury.

JUSTICE BYRON WHITE (1984)[2]

LEARNING OBJECTIVES
At the end of this chapter you should be able to:

- Discuss the use of the exclusionary rule and the fruit of the poisonous tree doctrine in criminal cases.

- Identify the differences between a seizure of a person, an arrest, and an investigatory detention.

- Explain the process for evaluating the constitutionality of search and seizure issues within criminal cases.

- Understand the legal standard of probable cause as it applies to search and arrest warrants.

- Identify the exceptions to the warrant requirement under the Fourth Amendment.

- Appreciate the importance of Miranda warnings in processing criminal defendants.

- Identify the stages of a criminal case during which a defendant or suspect has the right to an attorney under either the Fifth or the Sixth Amendment.

- Recognize the many different rights that are associated with affording defendants "the right to a fair trial."

- Identify the limitations of the right against double jeopardy, including the many exceptions to the double jeopardy rule.

- Appreciate the constitutional parameters for criminal sentencing.

- Identify a contemporary issue concerning the constitutional limitations on government in processing criminal cases, and discuss the most likely future scenarios, referencing both historical analogs and caselaw.

- Brief a judicial opinion with no assistance. You should be successful in identifying the relevant facts, identifying the legal issue(s), and analyzing the court's rationale in at least 90 percent of your briefs.

- Apply what you have learned to a new set of facts with no assistance.

13.1 CONSTITUTIONAL VALUES IN THE CRIMINAL CONTEXT

Several provisions within the Bill of Rights address the rights of individuals whose contact with government involves suspicion or accusation of criminal activity. These provisions are found primarily in the Fourth, Fifth, Sixth, and Eighth Amendments. Of course, more general constitutional protections involving due process, equal protection, free speech, and other liberties may also be relevant in addressing individual liberties in the criminal context.

Within the Fourth Amendment, there are two primary provisions. The **search and seizure provision** bars government from engaging in unreasonable searches and seizures of persons, houses, papers, and effects. And the **warrant provision** provides that the government must demonstrate probable cause before a warrant will be issued by a judge. These two provisions, which are often interrelated, provide the basic constitutional context for addressing government searches of persons and places, seizures of evidence, and arrests of individuals.[3]

The Fifth Amendment contains four clauses relevant to the criminal justice system. The **grand jury provision** requires government to obtain a **grand jury indictment** (a formal charge by a group of citizens sitting as a jury who have reviewed the evidence and decided that there is sufficient cause to charge a person with a criminal offense) in order to charge a person with a **capital offense** (an offense punishable by death) or an "otherwise infamous crime," which is usually read to mean a **felony** (generally defined to mean a crime for which the punishment may include a year or more of incarceration).[4] The **Double Jeopardy Clause** provides that government may not punish a person twice for the same offense.[5] The **self-incrimination provision** states that, within a criminal case, individuals cannot be forced to provide testimony against themselves.[6] And lastly, the **Due Process Clause** provides that the federal government may not deprive a person of life, liberty, or property without due process of law. This clause, which is repeated in the Fourteenth Amendment and thereby made applicable to the states, requires, among other things, that government treat individuals fairly during the criminal process. This may include such protections as the right to a fair trial, the right to be free from outrageous conduct by prosecutors or judges, the right to a full and fair appeal of a conviction, and the right to humane conditions of confinement.[7]

The Sixth Amendment provides several standards for the criminal process. The **speedy trial provision** provides individuals with a right to a speedy trial.[8] Similarly, the **public trial provision** states that individuals are also entitled to a public trial.[9] The **jury trial provision** provides that individuals have a right to have their criminal cases decided by an impartial jury (as opposed to a judge) within the jurisdiction where the crime was allegedly committed.[10] The **information provision** requires government to notify defendants of the nature and cause of the criminal charges. The **confrontation clause** provides the accused with the right to confront (generally interpreted as to view and cross-examine) any witnesses providing testimony against them.[11] The **compulsory process clause** allows defendants to compel witnesses to appear on their behalf.[12] And the **assistance of counsel provision** provides that the accused has the right to have counsel (an attorney) assist in defending against the criminal charges.[13]

Finally, the Eighth Amendment contains three primary provisions. The **excessive bail provision** states that the amount of bail (the collateral imposed by a court as a condition for pretrial release of the defendant) cannot be excessive. The **excessive fines provision** provides that a fine (a postconviction punishment in the form of monetary payment) cannot be excessive. And the **Cruel and Unusual Punishment Clause** provides that government may not inflict cruel and unusual punishment upon individuals.[14]

In addition to applying to federal prosecutions, the Supreme Court has made most of the aforementioned rights applicable to state and local prosecutions via the Fourteenth Amendment Due Process Clause. See Chapter 8. The two exceptions are the Fifth Amendment right to a grand jury indictment in capital and felony cases and the Eighth Amendment right against excessive bail and fines. These two provisions have not been formally incorporated and applied to the states.[15] However, many states, through their own constitutions or statutes, require capital and felony indictments to be issued by grand juries and provide defendants, to various degrees, with the right to reasonable bail pending trial.

Search and Seizure Clause
Fourth Amendment provision that precludes government from engaging in unreasonable searches and seizures of persons, houses, papers, and effects.

warrant provision
Fourth Amendment provision that requires government to demonstrate probable cause before a warrant will be issued by a judge.

grand jury provision
Fifth Amendment clause that requires government to obtain a grand jury indictment in order to charge someone with a capital offense or felony.

grand jury indictment
A formal charge by a group of citizens sitting as a jury who have reviewed the evidence and decided that there is sufficient cause to charge a person with a criminal offense.

capital offense
An offense punishable by death.

felony
Generally defined to mean a crime for which the punishment may include a year or more of incarceration.

Double Jeopardy Clause
Fifth Amendment provision that government may not punish a person twice for the same offense.

self-incrimination provision
Fifth Amendment clause stating that within a criminal case, persons cannot be forced to provide testimony against themselves.

Due Process Clause
A provision found in the Fifth and Fourteenth Amendments, which states that government cannot deprive individuals of life, liberty, or property without due process of law.

speedy trial provision
Sixth Amendment clause that provides individuals with a right to a speedy trial.

public trial provision
Sixth Amendment clause stating that individuals are entitled to a public trial.

jury trial provision
Sixth Amendment provision that individuals have a right to have their criminal cases decided by an impartial jury (as opposed to a judge) within the jurisdiction where the crime was allegedly committed.

Information provision
Sixth Amendment provision that requires government to notify defendants of the nature and cause of the criminal charges.

confrontation clause
Sixth Amendment clause that provides the accused with the right to confront (generally interpreted as to view and cross-examine) any witnesses providing testimony against them.

compulsory process clause
Sixth Amendment clause that allows defendants to compel witnesses to appear on their behalf.

assistance of counsel provision
Sixth Amendment clause that provides that the accused has the right to have counsel (an attorney) assist in defending against the criminal charges.

excessive bail provision
Eighth Amendment clause stating that the amount of bail, which is the collateral imposed by a court as a condition for pretrial release of the defendant, cannot be excessive.

excessive fines provision
Eighth Amendment clause that provides that a fine, which is a postconviction punishment in the form of monetary payment, cannot be excessive.

Cruel and Unusual Punishment Clause
Eighth Amendment provision that government may not inflict cruel and unusual punishment upon individuals.

Savana Redding (L), age 19, is seen in front of the Supreme Court on April 21, 2009. The Supreme Court ruled that a strip search performed on Redding at her Arizona school violated the Fourth Amendment ban on unreasonable searches. Another student accused Redding of giving out prescription-strength ibuprofen, the equivalent of two over-the-counter Advils, when she was in eighth grade. No pills were found.
www.newscom.com I.D. upiphotos945602

The role of constitutional values is readily apparent when applying the Bill of Rights to the criminal justice system. Because many of the phrases, such as "unreasonable search and seizure," "speedy trial," "assistance of counsel," "excessive bail," and "cruel and unusual punishment," are not defined or further addressed in the Constitution, it is ultimately up to jurists to determine the meaning and scope of these terms based on some source of constitutional values. What must a law enforcement officer do to make a search unreasonable? How long must a criminal defendant wait for trial before such trial is no longer speedy? How painful or strange must punishment be before it is considered cruel and unusual? These questions, left unanswered by the explicit text of the Bill of Rights, ultimately require the application of values from beyond the text. What is evident is that as the membership of the Supreme Court has changed, the values brought by new justices to the Court and used to address these questions have also changed. Within many areas, this has resulted in the creation of new doctrines, tests, rules, and exceptions that make criminal procedure one of the most dynamic and fluctuating facets of constitutional law.

13.2 UNREASONABLE SEARCHES AND SEIZURES

The Fourth Amendment prohibits the government from conducting unreasonable searches and seizures of persons, houses, papers, and effects. It also requires that warrants be based on probable cause. There are three primary categories of search and

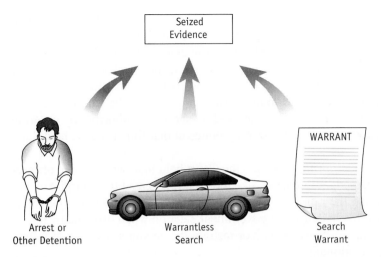

FIGURE 13-1
Primary categories of search and seizure under the Fourth Amendment

seizure under the Fourth Amendment: (1) the seizure, detention, or arrest of persons; (2) searches and seizures of evidentiary materials conducted pursuant to a valid warrant; and (3) warrantless searches and seizures. See Figure 13-1. Each category has its own set of constitutional standards and doctrines.

13.2(a) The Arrest, Seizure, and Detention of Persons

The most serious form of search and seizure under the Fourth Amendment is the seizure, arrest, or other detention of persons. In many cases, governmental seizures of individuals will be obvious, particularly in cases where the person is arrested by police and taken into custody. In other cases, law enforcement may stop short of formally arresting someone, but the officers' actions may still constitute a type of seizure or detention under the Fourth Amendment.

Seizure of Persons   The Fourth Amendment may apply to police detentions that fall short of full-blown arrests. In other words, in some cases, police may seize a person without formally arresting them. **Seizure of a person** occurs when law enforcement officer uses force or the threat of force to detain a person, thereby causing the person to reasonably believe that he or she cannot freely leave the presence of the official.[16] In these situations, a seizure will be determined based on the **totality of the circumstances**—the overall context of the detention, including what actions and words the officer used, the location of the detention, and the length of the stop—and an assessment of **reasonableness**—what a reasonable person would believe under the circumstances.

   In *Michigan v. Chesternut* (1988), the Supreme Court unanimously ruled that police pursuits do not *per se* constitute a seizure under the Fourth Amendment. In *Chesternut*, the defendant saw a police car approaching and began to run. As police started to follow him "to see where he was going," the defendant discarded a number of packets containing illegal drugs. After his arrest, the defendant tried to suppress the drug evidence, asserting that it was obtained by police during an unconstitutional seizure of his person. The Court, however, held that the officers' pursuit of the defendant did not constitute a "seizure" under the Fourth Amendment. The Court reasoned that the appropriate test is whether a reasonable person, viewing the particular police conduct as a whole and within the setting of all of the surrounding circumstances, would have concluded that the police had in some way restrained his liberty so that he was not free to leave.

seizure of a person
Occurs when a law enforcement officer uses force or the threat of force to detain a person, thereby causing the person to reasonably believe that he or she cannot freely leave the presence of the official.

totality of the circumstances
A legal standard used to review arrests and seizures of persons and property to determine whether probable cause or reasonable suspicion exists. Under this standard, the overall context of the detention or seizure is reviewed, including what actions and words the officer used, the location of the detention, and the length of the stop.

reasonableness
A legal standard that attempts to assess what a reasonable person would believe or do under the circumstances.

Similarly, in *California v. Hodari D.* (1991),[17] where a defendant fled and began discarding drug evidence after the police told him to stop, the Court likewise concluded the defendant was not seized as he discarded the drug evidence. The Court ruled that, to constitute a seizure of the person, just as to constitute an arrest, there must be either the application of physical force, however slight, or, where that is absent, submission to an officer's "show of authority" to restrain the subject's liberty. The Court concluded that, even though the police may have displayed a "show of authority" by ordering Hodari to halt, the defendant was not seized by police at that time because he did not comply with the police order.

But in *Brendlin v. California* (2007),[18] the Court held that, when police officers make a traffic stop, a passenger in the car, like the driver, is seized for Fourth Amendment purposes. Applying the rationale from *Bostick*, the Court ruled that a person is seized and thus entitled to challenge the government's action when officers, by physical force or a show of authority, terminate or restrain the person's freedom of movement through means intentionally applied.

Arrests In many criminal cases, a law enforcement officer physically takes a person into custody against their will for purposes of initiating criminal prosecution or investigation. This is called an **arrest.** There are two basic types of arrests—arrests made pursuant to an arrest warrant and warrantless arrests.

An **arrest warrant** is a judicial order authorizing law enforcement officers to arrest a person. In some cases, arrest warrants are procured immediately after a grand jury issues an indictment. But in other cases, an arrest warrant can be issued without any grand jury action. An arrest warrant must be based on probable cause (see Section 13.2(a)(2)(A)).

At common law, an arrest warrant was a more critical factor in determining the validity of an arrest. Under common law principles, officers could make warrantless arrests only in cases where they reasonably believed the suspect committed a felony or where they actually witnessed the suspect committing a misdemeanor in their presence. Today, however, although the Fourth Amendment states that warrants must be supported by probable cause, it does not specifically require all arrests or arrest-like detentions be made pursuant to a warrant.

Under normal circumstances, the Court still requires police to obtain a warrant before arresting individuals within their homes.[19] These are known as **home arrests.** And generally, unless police are operating under exigent circumstances (see the following paragraph), a warrant is necessary to make a nonconsensual entry into a private residence to arrest someone inside. With a court-issued arrest warrant, police are authorized to enter a person's home and effectuate an arrest, although normally they must knock and announce their identity and purpose before making a forcible entry into the home.

In some cases, police may effectuate a **warrantless arrest** inside a person's home, if the officers are operating under **exigent circumstances.** These might include situations where officers have received the consent of the home owner, or someone who has apparent authority over the home, to enter the home; cases where police are in hot pursuit of a suspect who runs into a home; and situations where an immediate danger exists, such as the possible escape of the suspect or the possible destruction of criminal evidence.

The vast majority of arrests are made without a warrant. These are known as warrantless arrests. In these cases, particularly where an arrest is made in a public place, officers can make an arrest if they have probable cause to believe that a crime has occurred. Thus, to be constitutional, both arrest warrants and warrantless arrests must be based on probable cause. The Court generally allows police to make other forms of warrantless arrests as long as they have probable cause to believe the suspect has committed a crime. For example, in *Atwater v. Lago Vista* (2001),[20] the Court held that the Fourth Amendment does not require police to have an arrest warrant to effectuate

Cyber Constitution
Brendlin v. California
(2007) http://supreme.justia.com/us/551/06-8120/

arrest
A governmental seizure of an individual, whereby a person is apprehended by a public official and taken into custody for purposes of criminal process.

arrest warrant
A judicial order supported by probable cause authorizing a law enforcement agent to arrest an individual.

home arrests
An arrest that occurs with an individual's home; usually requires a warrant.

exigent circumstances
An exception to the warrant requirement that allows home arrests where pressing needs of the public outweigh the individual's right to privacy.

Cyber Constitution
Atwater v. Lago Vista
(2001) http://supreme.justia.com/us/532/318/case.html

an arrest for a minor criminal offense, such as a misdemeanor seat belt violation punishable only by a fine. In *Atwater*, police arrested Gail Atwater for violating a Texas seat belt law. The law made it a misdemeanor, punishable only by a fine, for failing to secure any small child riding in the front of a vehicle. Police pulled Atwater over, verbally berated her, handcuffed her, placed her in his squad car, and drove her to the local police station, where she was made to remove her shoes, jewelry, and eyeglasses, and empty her pockets. Officers also took her "mug shot" and placed her, alone, in a jail cell for about an hour, after which she was taken before a magistrate and released on bond. Atwater challenged her arrest, arguing that it was an unreasonable seizure of her person under the Fourth Amendment. But the Supreme Court disagreed, concluding that because the officer had probable cause to believe Atwater was committing a criminal offense, even though a minor offense, the arrest was not unreasonable under the Fourth Amendment.

13.2(a)(2)(A) The Need for Probable Cause **Probable cause** is a legal standard requiring the warrant-issuing judge or warrantless-arrest-making law enforcement officer to have sufficient, articulable, and trustworthy information to reasonably believe that a person has committed a crime.[21] The Supreme Court has approached the probable cause standard as a degree of probability that cannot be easily defined out of context. Specifically, the Court has stated, "[t]he probable-cause standard is incapable of precise definition or quantification into percentages because it deals with probabilities and depends on the totality of the circumstances. We have stated, however, that the substance of all the definitions of probable cause is a reasonable ground for belief of guilt, and that the belief of guilt must be particularized with respect to the person to be searched or seized."[22] As a result, like many other constitutional concepts in criminal cases, determining whether an officer had probable cause to arrest is based on the totality of the circumstances and a reflection on what is reasonable under those circumstances.

13.2(a)(2)(B) Use of Deadly Force In some cases, police use **deadly force,** which is perhaps the most severe form of governmental seizure, to apprehend criminal suspects. Under the Supreme Court's analysis, the use of deadly force to seize or stop individuals is unreasonable under the Fourth Amendment, unless the officer has probable cause to believe that the person presents a substantial threat of death or serious physical harm to the officer or other persons.[23] In other words, the use of deadly force by police officers can be constitutional when the person or persons in question are believed to present an immediate life-threatening danger to people around them. For example, an armed man in a shopping mall shooting at random without regard to the safety of the people around him, and refusing or being unwilling to negotiate, would likely warrant the usage of deadly force as a means to prevent further danger to the community.

The leading case in this area is *Tennessee v. Garner* (1985), where the Supreme Court ruled that "deadly force . . . may not be used unless necessary to prevent the escape and the officer has probable cause to believe that the suspect poses a significant threat of death or serious physical injury to the officer or others." This is generally known as the **reasonableness test.**

More recently, in *Scott v. Harris* (2007),[24] the Court held that a police officer's attempt to terminate a dangerous high-speed car chase that threatens the lives of innocent bystanders does not violate the Fourth Amendment, even when it places the fleeing motorist at risk of serious injury or death. In *Harris*, a police officer in a high-speed chase of a suspect applied his cruiser's bumper to the rear of a suspect's car, which caused the suspect to wreck his car and sustain serious injuries. Applying the reasonableness test established in *Garner*, the Court found that because the car chase suspect posed a substantial and immediate risk of serious physical injury to others, the police officer's attempt to terminate the chase by forcing the suspect off the road was reasonable under the Fourth Amendment.

probable cause
A legal standard requiring the officer to have sufficient and trustworthy information to reasonably believe that a person has committed a crime.

deadly force
The application of potentially deadly techniques by police in an effort to apprehend or stop individuals. The use of deadly force to seize or stop individuals is unreasonable under the Fourth Amendment unless the officer has probable cause to believe that the person presents a substantial threat of death or serious physical harm to the officer or other persons.

Cyber Constituiton
Tennessee v. Garner
(1985) http://supreme.justia.com/us/471/1/case.html

reasonableness test
Legal standard used to judge whether use of deadly force by police was constitutional; force must be necessary to prevent the escape of the suspect, and the officer must have probable cause to believe that the suspect poses a significant threat of death or serious physical injury to the officer or others.

Terry **Stop**
Also known as a "stop
and frisk," this can be
conducted during an
investigatory stop where
the officer has reasonable
suspicion that the
person is armed, thereby
allowing the police to
frisk an individual.

Cyber Constitution
Scott v. Harris **(2007)**
http://supreme.justia.com/
us/550/05-1631/

investigatory detention
An officer's relatively
brief stop of an
individual for purposes of
conducting a reasonable
investigation of possible
criminal activity. In these
situations, an officer must
have reasonable suspicion
that the person being
stopped is involved in
criminal activity.

reasonable suspicion
A less rigorous legal
standard than probable
cause, which generally
requires an officer to
have articulable facts that
would lead a reasonable
person to suspect that
criminal activity is afoot.

Cyber Constitution
Illinois v. Wardlow
(2000) http://supreme.
justia.com/us/528/119/
case.html

Cyber Constitution
Florida v. J.L. **(2000)**
http://supreme.justia.com/
us/529/266/case.html

Investigatory Detentions (Terry Stops) Separate from situations involving an arrest, the Supreme Court also has interpreted the Fourth Amendment to allow officers to briefly detain persons for legitimate investigative purposes, even where the officer does not have probable cause to believe that a crime has occurred. This is known as an **investigatory detention** or a *Terry* **stop.** The term derives from the Supreme Court's landmark ruling in *Terry v. Ohio* (1968),[25] where the Court ruled that, during investigatory stops, if a reasonably prudent officer believes that his safety or that of others is endangered, he may make a reasonable search for weapons of the person believed by him to be armed and dangerous regardless of whether he has probable cause to arrest that individual for crime. In *Terry*, the Court upheld the patdown search conducted by Cleveland police officers of three men who were stopped on suspicion of robbery. During the investigatory stop, an officer patted down a suspect's outside clothing and found a pistol in the suspect's overcoat pocket. The suspect was then charged with carrying a concealed weapon. The Court concluded that the officer's protective seizure and limited search were reasonable under the Fourth Amendment, both at their inception and as conducted.

Specifically, an investigatory detention or stop is a police officer's relatively brief stop of a person for purposes of conducting a reasonable investigation of possible criminal activity. An investigatory stop is different from an arrest. With a stop, police ostensibly are not making an arrest or arrest-like seizure of a person—at least initially. Rather they wish to briefly detain a person to investigate what might be criminal activity.

13.2(a)(3)(A) Need for Reasonable Suspicion In order for investigatory detentions to be constitutional under the Fourth Amendment, an officer must have reasonable suspicion that the person being stopped is involved in criminal activity. **Reasonable suspicion** is less stringent standard than probable cause. And although the Court has not specifically defined the concept, reasonable suspicion generally requires an officer to have articulable facts that would lead a reasonable person to suspect that criminal activity is afoot.[26] Reasonable suspicion is not as rigorous a standard as probable cause (see earlier in this chapter), but it does require the officer to have more than just a vague hunch or gut feeling about possible criminal activity. And like probable cause, determining whether an officer has reasonable suspicion to stop someone is based on the totality of the circumstances and the degree of reasonableness underlying the officer's judgment.

In *Illinois v. Wardlow* (2000), William Wardlow was walking in a Chicago neighborhood known for high levels of illegal drug trafficking. After seeing a group of police cars, Wardlow began running. Police caught up with Wardlow and stopped him. An officer then conducted a protective patdown search for weapons (see discussion later in this chapter) because, in his experience, there were usually weapons in the vicinity of narcotics transactions. The officer found a handgun during the patdown and arrested Wardlow for unlawful possession of a firearm.

The Supreme Court was asked to determine whether officers had reasonable suspicion to stop Wardlow for an investigatory detention. The Court found that Wardlow's presence in a high-crime area, by itself, did not provide a reasonable, particularized suspicion of criminal activity, but that the neighborhood's characteristics were relevant to the officer's judgment to make the stop. The Court further found that Wardlow's unprovoked flight, when coupled with the neighborhood characteristics, provided the officers with the reasonable suspicion necessary to conduct an investigatory detention. According to the Court, the reasonable suspicion determination must be based on commonsense judgments and inferences about human behavior.

But in *Florida v. J.L.* (2000),[27] the Court ruled that an anonymous tip to police that a person is carrying a gun is not, by itself, sufficient to justify a police officer's stop and frisk of that person. In *J.L.*, the Court observed that the officers' suspicion that the defendant was carrying a gun came not from their own observations, but from a call made by an unknown caller from an unknown location. According to the Court, this anonymous tip lacked sufficient indicia of reliability to provide reasonable suspicion to make a *Terry* stop because it did not provide predictive information. As a result, it left the police without means to test the informant's knowledge or credibility.

13.2(a)(3)(B) Detention Must Be Relatively Brief   Assuming that an officer's initial detention of a person is based on reasonable suspicion of criminal activity, there are a number of other conditions that affect whether the stop will remain constitutional while it is executive. For one, investigatory detentions must be relatively brief in time. This means that the officer cannot detain a person any longer than is necessary to confirm or reject the officer's initial suspicion.

For example, if an officer stops a person believing him to be a parole violator, the officer can detain him only long enough to confirm or deny the person parole status, unless the officer develops more suspicion or probable cause of additional criminal activity during the brief stop (see below). If an officer unreasonably prolongs the investigatory detention to the point where the initially brief stop actually develops into a seizure or arrest-like situation (see arrest earlier in text), the officer must have probable cause for such a detention.

13.2(a)(3)(C) Police Patdowns or Frisks   One of the most critical events that occur during an investigatory stop is the frisking or patting down of the detained individual. This is sometimes called a **stop and frisk** or *Terry* **frisk.** The Supreme Court has ruled that officers are permitted to **frisk** (to pat the outer clothing of an individual) a person during an investigatory stop if the officer has reasonable suspicion that the person is armed and dangerous. The purpose of this limited search is to ensure the officer's safety by certifying the stopped person does not have any weapons on or about his person. As discussed below, the evidence seized by police during this frisking process often serves as the basis of criminal charges.

stop and frisk or *Terry* **frisk**
Police technique employed during investigatory detentions, whereby the person detained is patted down for weapons.

frisk
To pat the outer clothing of an individual.

13.2(a)(3)(D) Stop and Identify Laws   A number of states have adopted **stop and identify laws,** which require individuals properly detained by police to provide their identity to the investigating officer during the stop.[28] The wording of these laws varies from state to state, but generally, they allow an officer to ask or require suspects to disclose their identity during an investigatory stop.

In some cases, the Supreme Court has found these laws to be unconstitutionally vague. For example, in *Kolender v. Lawson* (1983),[29] the Court invalidated a California law because its wording was too broad and imprecise. The law required persons who loiter or wander on the streets to identify themselves and to account for their presence when requested by a peace officer. The Court invalidated the statute, finding that it failed to clarify what is contemplated by the requirement that a suspect provide a "credible and reliable" identification.

stop and identify laws
Laws in some jurisdictions that require individuals to provide their identity to the investigating officer during the stop.

But in *Hiibel v. Sixth Judicial District of Nevada* (2004),[30] the Court upheld a Nevada law requiring properly detained persons to provide their identity to law enforcement officers. The Nevada law read in relevant part:

> Any peace officer may detain any person whom the officer encounters under circumstances which reasonably indicate that the person has committed, is committing or is about to commit a crime. . . . The officer may detain the person pursuant to this section only to ascertain his identity and the suspicious circumstances surrounding his presence abroad. Any person so detained shall identify himself, but may not be compelled to answer any other inquiry of any peace officer.

Cyber Constitution
***Hiibel v. Sixth Judicial District of Nevada* (2004)**
http://supreme.justia.com/us/542/177/case.html

The Court found that, in contrast to the "credible and reliable" identification requirement in *Kolender,* the Nevada Supreme Court has interpreted the Nevada law to require only that a suspect disclose his name. It apparently does not require him to produce a driver's license or any other document. As a result, the Court ruled that *Terry*-search principles (discussed earlier in this chapter) permit a state to require a suspect to disclose his name in the course of a *Terry* stop. According to the Court, the Nevada statute was consistent with Fourth Amendment prohibitions against unreasonable searches and seizures because it properly balanced the intrusion on the individual's interests against the promotion of legitimate government interests.

13.2(a)(3)(E) Motor Vehicle Stops   One area of personal seizure that has presented unique constitutional challenges under the Fourth Amendment is the detention of persons operating motorized vehicles. Generally speaking, the Court has required that governmental stops of persons operating motorized vehicles be based on either probable cause (to make a full seizure or arrest of the person) or reasonable suspicion (to briefly investigate possible illegal activity, including the violation of traffic laws). Consistent with these standards, the Court has held that officers cannot randomly stop persons in automobiles without sufficient cause or suspicion just to check their driver's information.[31]

The Court, however, has ruled that police may engage in pretextual stops of motorists, if the officers have probable cause to believe that the driver has committed a traffic violation or some other crime. In *Whren v. Brown* (1996),[32] police stopped a driver in a high-drug-crime neighborhood, after the driver failed to use his turn signal before making a turn. Although the underlying motive of police in making the stop may have been to investigate possible drug activity, for which they lacked reasonable suspicion or probable cause, the Court ruled that the officers were nonetheless justified in making the stop because they had probable cause to believe that a traffic violation occurred. According to the Court, since an actual traffic violation occurred, the ensuing search and seizure of the offending vehicle was reasonable, regardless of what other personal motivations the officers might have had for stopping the vehicle.

In some cases, officers engaging in traffic stops detain more than just the driver of the vehicle. Read the Court's opinion in *Brendlin v. California* (2007), where the Court considered whether passengers involved in a traffic stop are detained under the Fourth Amendment, thereby allowing them to challenge the legality of the traffic stop.

Brendlin v. California
551 U.S. 249 (2007)

Justice Souter delivered the opinion of the Court.

Early in the morning of November 27, 2001, Deputy Sheriff Robert Brokenbrough and his partner saw a parked Buick with expired registration tags. In his ensuing conversation with the police dispatcher, Brokenbrough learned that an application for renewal of registration was being processed. The officers saw the car again on the road, and this time Brokenbrough noticed its display of a temporary operating permit with the number "11," indicating it was legal to drive the car through November. The officers decided to pull the Buick over to verify that the permit matched the vehicle, even though, as Brokenbrough admitted later, there was nothing unusual about the permit or the way it was affixed. Brokenbrough asked the driver, Karen Simeroth, for her license and saw a passenger in the front seat, petitioner Bruce Brendlin, whom he recognized as "one of the Brendlin brothers." He recalled that either Scott or Bruce Brendlin had dropped out of parole supervision and asked Brendlin to identify himself. Brokenbrough returned to his cruiser, called for backup, and verified that Brendlin was a parole violator

with an outstanding no-bail warrant for his arrest. While he was in the patrol car, Brokenbrough saw Brendlin briefly open and then close the passenger door of the Buick. Once reinforcements arrived, Brokenbrough went to the passenger side of the Buick, ordered him out of the car at gunpoint, and declared him under arrest. When the police searched Brendlin incident to arrest, they found an orange syringe cap on his person. A patdown search of Simeroth revealed syringes and a plastic bag of a green leafy substance, and she was also formally arrested. Officers then searched the car and found tubing, a scale, and other things used to produce methamphetamine.

Brendlin was charged with possession and manufacture of methamphetamine, and he moved to suppress the evidence obtained in the searches of his person and the car as fruits of an unconstitutional seizure, arguing that the officers lacked probable cause or reasonable suspicion to make the traffic stop. He did not assert that his Fourth Amendment rights were violated by the search of Simeroth's vehicle, but claimed only that the traffic stop was an unlawful seizure of his person. The trial court denied the suppression motion after finding that the stop was lawful and Brendlin was not seized until Brokenbrough ordered him out of the car and formally arrested him. Brendlin pleaded guilty, subject to appeal on the suppression issue, and was sentenced to four years in prison. . . .

A person is seized by the police and thus entitled to challenge the government's action under the Fourth Amendment when the officer, "by means of physical force or show of authority," terminates or restrains his freedom of movement, *Florida v. Bostick*, 501 U. S. 429, 434 (1991), "*through means intentionally applied.*" Thus, an "unintended person . . . [may be] the object of the detention," so long as the detention is "willful" and not merely the consequence of "an unknowing act." A police officer may make a seizure by a show of authority and without the use of physical force, but there is no seizure without actual submission; otherwise, there is at most an attempted seizure, so far as the Fourth Amendment is concerned.

When the actions of the police do not show an unambiguous intent to restrain or when an individual's submission to a show of governmental authority takes the form of passive acquiescence, there needs to be some test for telling when a seizure occurs in response to authority, and when it does not. The test was devised by Justice Stewart in *United States v. Mendenhall*, 446 U. S. 544 (1980), who wrote that a seizure occurs if "in view of all of the circumstances surrounding the incident, a reasonable person would have believed that he was not free to leave." Later on, the Court adopted Justice Stewart's touchstone, but added that when a person "has no desire to leave" for reasons unrelated to the police presence, the "coercive effect of the encounter" can be measured better by asking whether "a reasonable person would feel free to decline the officers' requests or otherwise terminate the encounter." . . .

The State concedes that the police had no adequate justification to pull the car over, but argues that the passenger was not seized and thus cannot claim that the evidence was tainted by an unconstitutional stop. We resolve this question by asking whether a reasonable person in Brendlin's position when the car stopped would have believed himself free to "terminate the encounter" between the police and himself. We think that in these circumstances any reasonable passenger would have understood the police officers to be exercising control to the point that no one in the car was free to depart without police permission.

A traffic stop necessarily curtails the travel a passenger has chosen just as much as it halts the driver, diverting both from the stream of traffic to the side of the road, and the police activity that normally amounts to intrusion on "privacy and personal security" does not normally (and did not here) distinguish between passenger and driver. An officer who orders one particular car to pull over acts with an implicit claim of right based on fault of some sort, and a sensible person would not expect a police officer to allow people to come and go freely from the physical focal point of an investigation into faulty behavior or wrongdoing. . . .

It is also reasonable for passengers to expect that a police officer at the scene of a crime, arrest, or investigation will not let people move around in ways that could jeopardize his safety. . . .

Brendlin was seized from the moment Simeroth's car came to a halt on the side of the road, and it was error to deny his suppression motion on the ground that seizure occurred only at the formal arrest. It will be for the state courts to consider in the first instance whether suppression turns on any other issue. The judgment of the Supreme Court of California is vacated, and the case is remanded for further proceedings not inconsistent with this opinion.

It is so ordered.

13.2(a)(3)(F) Traffic Checkpoints In some circumstances, however, the Court has permitted suspicionless stops to occur. For example, the Court has authorized the use of **sobriety checkpoints,** which typically involve the stopping of vehicles at a fixed checkpoint without any particularized suspicion in order to detect drunk driving. The Court has ruled that these checkpoints are permissible as long as officers stop cars based on some neutral and articulable standard (for example, every fifth car).

In *Michigan Department of State Police v. Sitz* (1988),[33] the Court upheld a Michigan program that established a sobriety checkpoint pilot program in early 1986. Under the program, police-operated checkpoints were to be set up at selected sites along state roads. All vehicles passing through a checkpoint would be stopped and their drivers briefly examined for signs of intoxication. In cases where a checkpoint officer detected signs of intoxication, the motorist would be directed to a location out of the traffic flow where an officer would check the motorist's driver's license and car registration and, if warranted, conduct further sobriety tests. All other drivers would be permitted to resume their journey immediately. The Court concluded that the public's

sobriety checkpoints
A police procedure that involves the stopping of vehicles at a fixed checkpoint without any particularized suspicion in order to detect drunk driving.

Cyber Constitution
***Michigan Department of State Police v. Sitz* (1988)**
http://supreme.justia.com/
us/496/444/case.html

interest in preventing drunk driving and maintaining safe roadways outweighs the limited burden on a driver being stopped.

13.2(a)(3)(G) Other Motor Vehicle Stops   The Supreme Court also has given law enforcement greater constitutional leeway to conduct international border stops, where usually every car is stopped to determine the occupants' citizenship. The Court has concluded that national security interests and the constitutional authority given to Congress under Article I to regulate immigration justify greater governmental intrusions during border stops.[34]

And in cases involving boats, the Court generally has not required government to demonstrate probable cause or reasonable suspicion before stopping operators given the difficulty in conducting fixed checkpoints in the sea and the compelling need to maintain safe waterways.[35]

13.2(b) Evidentiary Searches and Seizures

Beyond the seizure of persons, the Fourth Amendment also applies to searches and seizures of places and things. But this provision does not apply to searches and seizures of all places and things. Rather, the Supreme Court has held that the Fourth Amendment search and seizure provision applies only to governmental conduct that interferes with an individual's reasonable expectation of privacy.[36] Thus, at the outset of all evidentiary searches and seizures, legal professionals must assess whether two primary conditions are met: (1) a search or seizure must involve some type of substantial governmental action and (2) the search or seizure must interfere with a person's reasonable expectation of privacy.

governmental conduct
Action that is performed by police officers and their agents performing work that is funded or facilitated by public resources.

Governmental Conduct   **Governmental conduct** involves law enforcement officers and their agents performing work that is funded or facilitated by public resources. Certainly, this includes state highway patrol officers, state detectives, local police officers, FBI agents, DEA agents, and other publicly paid authorities performing a law enforcement function. For example, in *Ferguson v. City of Charleston* (2001),[37] staff members at a state hospital conducted a diagnostic test on a non-consenting pregnant patient to see if she was using cocaine. The Supreme Court invalidated this search, finding that, because the hospital was a state-run facility, its staff members were government actors subject to the Fourth Amendment's requirements.

In some cases, governmental conduct might include private citizens acting as informants at the behest and direction of law enforcement. For example, if public authorities instruct a jail inmate to elicit a confession from another inmate, this might involve sufficient government conduct to invoke the Fourth Amendment. But such conduct would not likely include conduct by mall security guards, bouncers, or other private security employees.[38]

reasonable expectation of privacy
A legal standard used by the Court to assess Fourth Amendment rights against unreasonable searches and seizures. Under this standard, the Court asks whether the individual had a reasonable expectation that a particular activity or location would be kept private.

Reasonable Expectation of Privacy   In addition, in order for the Fourth Amendment to be applicable, individuals asserting this right must show that they had a reasonable expectation of privacy in the place or property that was searched. A **reasonable expectation of privacy** is a reasonable person's legitimate expectation that certain property or places will not be involuntarily viewed or inspected by third parties. Such an expectation is determined based on the totality of the circumstances.

The leading case in this area is *Katz v. United States* (1967).[39] *Katz* involved a defendant whose phone conversation was seized by government authorities by means of an electronic listening device placed on the outside of a telephone booth. The Supreme Court ruled that the Fourth Amendment protected the defendant from the warrantless eavesdropping because he "justifiably relied" upon the privacy of the telephone booth. In a concurring opinion, Justice John Harlan observed that a Fourth Amendment search occurs when the government violates a subjective expectation of privacy that society recognizes as reasonable. Over the years, the Court has relied on this observation in holding that a Fourth Amendment search does *not* occur—even when the explicitly protected location of a *house* is concerned—unless "the individual manifested a subjective expectation of privacy in the object of the challenged search" and "society [is] willing to recognize that expectation as reasonable."[40] This is generally known as the ***Katz* test.** Under the *Katz* test, the Supreme Court has found that a person generally has a reasonable expectation of privacy in their own home and body.

For example, in *Kyllo v. United States* (2001),[41] the Court ruled that the warrantless governmental use of thermal imaging equipment to explore details of a private home was presumptively unreasonable. In *Kyllo*, authorities suspected the defendant was growing marijuana in his home and used a thermal imaging device to scan the house to determine if the amount of heat emanating from it was consistent with the high-intensity lamps typically used for indoor marijuana growth. The scan showed that the defendant's garage roof and a side wall were relatively hot compared to the rest of his home and substantially warmer than the neighboring units. Based in part on the thermal imaging, a federal magistrate judge issued a warrant to search Kyllo's home, where the agents found marijuana growing.

The Supreme Court, however, rejected this use of thermal imaging, stating, "[w]e have said that the Fourth Amendment draws 'a firm line at the entrance to the house.' That line, we think, must be not only firm but also bright–which requires clear specification of those methods of surveillance that require a warrant . . . Where, as here, the Government uses a device that is not in general public use, to explore details of the home that would previously have been unknowable without physical intrusion, the surveillance is a 'search' and is presumptively unreasonable without a warrant."

But in other cases, the Court has found no such reasonable expectation of privacy. The Court has approved governmental intrusions into areas held out to the public, such as a person's handwriting and the scent coming from their luggage at an airport.[42] The Court has reasoned that, because reasonable persons have little or no expectation of privacy in places or property that are readily available to the public or held out to the public, these items and locations are not entitled to Fourth Amendment protection. In particular, the Court has developed the **open fields doctrine,** which holds that places outside the curtilage (the immediate, enclosed area surrounding a house or dwelling) of a home are generally held out to the public. The Court has used the doctrine to approve searches involving a person's barn, airplane and helicopter flyovers, and discarded garbage left at a home's curbside.[43]

The Process for Evaluating Evidentiary Searches and Seizures   There are four basic steps in assessing the constitutionality of searches and seizures. At the outset, courts must determine whether the defendant had a Fourth Amendment right that was violated by governmental authorities during the search. This involves two questions: (1) Was there sufficient governmental conduct involved in the search? (2) Did the defendant have a reasonable expectation of privacy in the place or thing that was searched? Each of these questions must be answered in the affirmative in order for the defendant to assert the Fourth Amendment against a search or seizure. If both of these questions are positively answered, the court must determine whether the search was conducted pursuant to a valid warrant. If not, the court must determine whether there was a constitutionally recognized exception that allowed the authorities to conduct the search without a court-approved search warrant. See Figure 13-2.

13.2(c) Warrant-Based Searches and Seizures

The plain text of the Fourth Amendment includes the statement that "no warrants shall issue, but upon probable cause, supported by oath or affirmation, and particularly describing the place to be searched, and the persons or things to be seized." A **search warrant** is essentially written authorization from a court to perform a search. The language

---

***Katz* test**
Legal standard used to assess reasonable expectation of privacy; supports notion that persons must manifest a subjective expectation of privacy in the object of the challenged search.

Cyber Constitution
Katz v. United States
(1967) http://supreme.justia.com/us/389/347/

Cyber Constitution
Kyllo v. United States
(2001) http://supreme.justia.com/us/533/27/

open fields doctrine
An exception to the warrant requirement for searches and seizures that allows law enforcement officers to search and seize areas or items located in open and public view.

search warrant
Written authorization from a court to perform a search that is supported by probable cause.

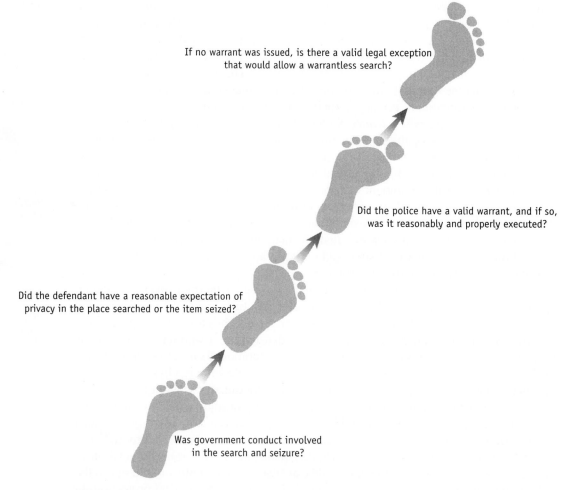

If no warrant was issued, is there a valid legal exception that would allow a warrantless search?

Did the police have a valid warrant, and if so, was it reasonably and properly executed?

Did the defendant have a reasonable expectation of privacy in the place searched or the item seized?

Was government conduct involved in the search and seizure?

FIGURE 13-2
Four basic steps for evaluating searches and seizures

of the Fourth Amendment suggests that the Constitution places great value on the use of warrants when police search places or seize property or persons. It also suggests that the underlying constitutional value to the Fourth Amendment is *reasonableness*, and that one measure of reasonableness is the presence of a search warrant. Because the Fourth Amendment stresses the importance of a warrant, and warrants are considered a strong measurement of the reasonableness of a search, searches and seizures performed without warrants are presumed unconstitutional.[44] Of course, this does not mean that all warrantless searches are unconstitutional. As will be discussed later in this chapter, the Supreme Court has identified several situations where a warrantless search can be deemed reasonable, and therefore, valid under the Fourth Amendment.

Overall, if law enforcement properly executes a valid search warrant, generally the search will be deemed reasonable, and therefore, constitutional under the Fourth Amendment. But if the search warrant is invalid, or if it is executed in an unreasonable manner, the search may be declared unconstitutional.

Validity of a Search Warrant As briefly discussed in the previous section, the Supreme Court generally has deemed searches performed with a valid warrant to be reasonable and, therefore, constitutional under the Fourth Amendment. The validity of a search warrant is assessed based on four primary factors: (1) whether the warrant was issued by a neutral and detached judicial authority, (2) whether the warrant was based on a finding of probable cause, (3) whether the warrant provides sufficiently detailed or particular instructions to the police officer about the person or places to be searched and the items to be seized, and (4) whether the warrant was properly executed.

With respect to **judicial neutrality and detachment,** generally, the judicial authority (typically, a judge or magistrate) issuing the warrant must not have a conflict of interest in evaluating the request for the warrant or its execution. This requires the judicial authority to be sufficiently objective (neutral) regarding the persons or matters involved in the search warrant and to not have a personal stake in issuing the warrant. Individuals who are working in law enforcement, conducting the search, or receiving compensation based on the issuance of a warrant would not be regarded as neutral and detached.[45]

The warrant must also be supported by probable cause, which as discussed earlier in text is a legal standard requiring sufficient, articulable, and trustworthy information to reasonably believe that a person has committed a crime. In most cases, an officer appears before a judicial authority with an application for a search warrant and an attached **affidavit** asserting the basis for the requested warrant. Within the application and affidavit, the officer must supply the judicial authority with the requisite amount of facts to support a finding of probable cause.

Like many other evidentiary standards in criminal justice, the judge or magistrate reviews the totality of the circumstances within the application and affidavit to determine whether probable cause exists for the warrant. Under most circumstances, probable cause must be found within the four corners (within the page of paper) of the application and affidavit. This is known as the **four corners rule.** Under this standard, magistrates/judges cannot rely on verbal exchanges or other undocumented information provided by the applying officer to find probable cause for the warrant.

If there are insufficient facts within the application and affidavit to support probable cause, or if the officer seeking the warrant intentionally or recklessly provided materially false statements to the magistrate/judge, the warrant could be deemed invalid, thereby causing any subsequent search to be ruled unconstitutional. This is determined by the trial court during a **Franks hearing.** In *Franks v. Delaware* (1978),[46] the Supreme Court held that "where the defendant makes a substantial preliminary showing that a false statement knowingly and intentionally, or with reckless disregard for the truth, was included by the affiant in the warrant affidavit, and if the allegedly false statement is necessary to the finding of probable cause, the Fourth Amendment requires that a hearing be held at the defendant's request."

In addition to demonstrating probable cause, a warrant must also particularly describe the place to be searched and the items to be seized. In other words, the judge or magistrate must be sufficiently precise in the warrant so as to avoid a general or overreaching search by the executing officer. This is known as the **particularity requirement.** For example, a warrant authorizing officers to search "any property owned by John Smith for any criminal contraband" likely would be too broad to satisfy the particularity requirement of the Fourth Amendment. But if a warrant authorized police to search "the residence at 704 Houser Street for illegal narcotics," this likely would be sufficiently particular.

Execution of Warrant
Once a warrant has been issued by a judicial authority, it must be properly and fairly executed by law enforcement. This includes the requirement that a public police officer, as opposed to a private figure, execute the warrant within a reasonable time period after it has been issued and that the search be conducted within the scope outlined in the warrant.

In some cases, police officers may request a **no-knock warrant,** which, if granted, allows them to enter the place to be searched without knocking on the door or otherwise notifying the property occupants of the police presence. The purpose of no-knock warrants is to protect the safety of the officers in situations where occupants of dwelling may respond violently upon hearing police officers at the door. According to the U.S. Department of Justice:

---

judicial neutrality and detachment
Fourth Amendment standard required for the person issuing a search warrant that generally requires the judicial authority to be free of conflicts of interest in evaluating the request for the warrant or its execution and sufficiently objective (neutral) regarding the persons or matters involved in the search warrant.

affidavit
A written statement made under oath typically completed by a police officer when seeking a search warrant.

four corners rule
To be valid, a search warrant application must demonstrate probable cause within the four corners (within the page of paper) of the application and affidavit.

Franks hearing
A type of hearing to determine whether a search warrant was supported by probable cause or based on falsities or misrepresentations of the truth.

particularity requirement
Fourth Amendment standard for warrants that requires the judicial authority issuing a warrant to be sufficiently precise in writing the warrant so as to avoid a general or overreaching search by the executing officer.

no-knock warrant
A warrant that allows officers to execute a warrant without knocking on the door of the search premises.

Federal judges and magistrates may lawfully and constitutionally issue "no-knock" warrants where circumstances justify a no-knock entry, and federal law enforcement officers may lawfully apply for such warrants under such circumstances. Although officers need not take affirmative steps to make an independent re-verification of the circumstances already recognized by a magistrate in issuing a no-knock warrant, such a warrant does not entitle officers to disregard reliable information clearly negating the existence of exigent circumstances when they actually receive such information before execution of the warrant.

For years, the Supreme Court had held that police were required to knock and announce their presence before executing a warrant on a dwelling, unless they reasonably believed their safety would be jeopardized. This is known as the **knock and announce rule.** But this requirement was relaxed in *Hudson v. Michigan* (2006).[47] In *Hudson*, police obtained a warrant authorizing a search for drugs and firearms at the home of Booker Hudson. When police executed the warrant, they announced their presence, but waited only a short time before entering Hudson's home. In a 5-4 ruling, the Court upheld the search, observing that "the social costs of applying the exclusionary rule to knock-and-announce violations are considerable." As a result, the Court concluded that "[r]esort to the massive remedy of suppressing evidence of guilt is unjustified." In short, the Court ruled that the failure of police officers to knock and announce their presence before executing a warrant will not result in evidence being suppressed under the exclusionary rule.

Despite this ruling, there still may be situations where the unreasonable execution of a perfectly valid warrant may result in an unconstitutional search under the Fourth Amendment. Many states have their own constitutional or statutory standards for executing search warrants. And some specifically require police to engage in certain procedural actions, including in some cases knocking and announcing their presence, before making a warranted entry into a dwelling.

Good Faith Exception   Even in cases where a search warrant is deemed invalid, the fruits of a resulting search may not result in the suppression of evidence, if the executing officer relied in good faith on the apparent validity of the warrant. This rather substantial exception to the valid warrant requirement is known as the **good faith exception** or *Leon* **rule.** This exception is also viewed as a general exception to the exclusionary rule.

In *United States v. Leon* (1984),[48] the Court ruled that an invalid warrant, which appears on its face to be valid, will not automatically result in an unconstitutional search if the officer executing the warrant reasonably relied on the facial validity of the warrant. In *Leon*, a police officer obtained a search warrant from a judge, which he believed was valid. The officer then used the warrant to a property where large quantities of drugs and other evidence were found. The district court, however, ruled that the affidavit used to procure the warrant did not establish probable cause for the warrant. The Supreme Court ruled that, despite the probable cause deficiency with the warrant, the Fourth Amendment exclusionary rule does not bar the use of the obtained evidence because the officer acted in reasonable reliance on the search warrant. As a result, even if a warrant is ultimately proven to be deficient because it is not supported by probable cause, a search executed based on the warrant nevertheless can be upheld, if the executing officer had no reason to believe the warrant was deficient.

The Court's reasoning behind this rule is that the Fourth Amendment was designed to punish police overreaching and misconduct, and therefore, should not apply to officers who, in good faith, rely on a seemingly valid warrant. This exception would not apply if (1) the officer executing the warrant made misrepresentations to the judge or magistrate in order to obtain the warrant, (2) the warrant is so deficient on its face that any reasonable officer should know that it is unsupported by probable cause, or (3) the application and/or affidavit is so deficient in probable cause that no reasonable officer would have relied on it. It is important to note that some state jurisdictions have rejected the good faith exception, and instead, rely on state constitutional principles to exclude evidence procured through defective search warrants in state cases.

knock and announce rule
A requirement in some state jurisdictions that police knock and announce their presence before executing a warrant on a dwelling.

Cyber Constitution
Hudson v. Michigan (2006) http://supreme.justia.com/us/new-cases/04-1360.pdf

good faith exception or *Leon* rule
An exception to the valid warrant requirement that holds that an invalid warrant, which appears on its face to be valid, will not automatically result in an unconstitutional search if the officer executing the warrant reasonably relied on the facial validity of the warrant.

Cyber Constitution
United States v. Leon (1984) http://supreme.justia.com/us/468/897/

13.2(d) Warrantless Evidentiary Searches and Seizures

Perhaps the largest percentage of criminal searches and seizures involve warrantless searches of places or things. Again, because the Fourth Amendment stresses the importance of a warrant, searches and seizures performed without warrants are presumed unconstitutional.[49] There are exceptions to this presumption that allow law enforcement to engage in warrantless searches and still use the fruit from these searches during a criminal trial. But because of the constitutional presumption against warrantless searches, the government bears the burden of demonstrating that a valid exception excuses the lack of a warrant in a particular case.

Exceptions to the Warrant Requirement   Over the years, the Court has recognized a number of exceptions to the Fourth Amendment warrant requirement that allow law enforcement officers to perform warrantless searches and still comply with the Constitution. Arguably, these exceptions have become so numerous as to greatly overshadow the general presumption against warrantless searches.

13.2(d)(1)(A) Search Incident to a Lawful Arrest   The first exception is a **search incident to a lawful arrest.** Under this exception, if police are conducting a valid arrest of a person, they may conduct a warrantless search of the arrestee. This search may include inspections of the area within the "wingspan" of the suspect, a protective sweep of the larger area around the suspect if other criminal suspects are believed to be in the vicinity, and search of the passenger seat of the suspect's automobile.[50] Similarly, police may take a full inventory (the administrative equivalent of a search) of a suspect's possessions, including items within the suspect's automobile, when the suspect and these items are held pursuant to an incarceration of the suspect.[51] The basic theory behind this exception is that arrests and incarcerations are often such dynamic and hostile situations that may involve dangerous items or the threat of harm, as to make it impractical for police to obtain a search warrant prior to performing these procedures.

The leading case for this exception is *Chimel v. California* (1969),[52] where the Supreme Court held that when an arrest is made, it is reasonable for the officer to search the arrestee for weapons and evidence. According to the Court, such a search includes the area within the arrestee's immediate control—areas where defendants may gain access to a weapon or an evidence. This is sometimes referred to as the **wingspan rule.** As a result, generally speaking, police can search the room in which the arrest is made. In addition, the Supreme Court generally has recognized that police officers can conduct a **protective sweep** of the location where the defendant is arrested, if authorities reasonably believe that accomplices may be present in the area and threaten the safety of the officers. Essentially, a protective sweep is a larger search of a location whereby the officers assess other rooms or areas of a property to see if other persons or harmful devices are present.

But more recently, the Court held that police cannot search inside an arrested person's vehicle after the person is taken away from the car, unless police have reason to believe that there is criminal evidence inside the vehicle. In *Arizona v. Gant* (2009) (see later in this chapter), the Court refused to apply the incident to a lawful arrest exception to car searches where the driver/arrested person no longer has access to the vehicle. Read the Court's opinion in *Gant* to appreciate the limitations on this exception to warrantless searches.

13.2(d)(1)(B) Consent Searches   Another exception to the warrant requirement is **consent searches.** These are searches performed with the permission or consent of a person who has actual or apparent authority over the property being searched. The Court has held that a person's consent to a search must be made voluntarily and intelligently, meaning that police cannot unreasonably coerce a person to consent or take advantage of a person who does not have sufficient mental ability to consent.[53] For example, police cannot falsely announce that they have a warrant to search a home in order to obtain

search incident to a lawful arrest
An exception to the Fourth Amendment warrant requirement that allows police to search an arrestee during a valid arrest of a person.

wingspan rule
A rule under the search incident to a lawful arrest exception; allows police to search the immediate area around an arrested person.

protective sweep
During warrantless searches conducted pursuant to a lawful arrest, police are permitted to search the surrounding premises, if authorities reasonably believe that accomplices may be present in the area and threaten the safety of the officers.

consent searches
An exception to the Fourth Amendment warrant requirement that allows police to perform searches with the permission or consent of a person who has actual or apparent authority over the property being searched.

Arizona v. Gant
556 U.S. 332 (2009)

Justice Stevens delivered the opinion of the Court.

After Rodney Gant was arrested for driving with a suspended license, handcuffed, and locked in the back of a patrol car, police officers searched his car and discovered cocaine in the pocket of a jacket on the backseat. Because Gant could not have accessed his car to retrieve weapons or evidence at the time of the search, the Arizona Supreme Court held that the search-incident-to-arrest exception to the Fourth Amendment's warrant requirement, as defined in *Chimel v. California*, 395 U. S. 752 (1969), and applied to vehicle searches in *New York v. Belton*, 453 U. S. 454 (1981), did not justify the search in this case. We agree with that conclusion.

Under *Chimel*, police may search incident to arrest only the space within an arrestee's "immediate control," meaning "the area from within which he might gain possession of a weapon or destructible evidence." The safety and evidentiary justifications underlying *Chimel*'s reaching-distance rule determine *Belton*'s scope. Accordingly, we hold that *Belton* does not authorize a vehicle search incident to a recent occupant's arrest after the arrestee has been secured and cannot access the interior of the vehicle . . . [W]e also conclude that circumstances unique to the automobile context justify a search incident to arrest when it is reasonable to believe that evidence of the offense of arrest might be found in the vehicle.

. . .

Consistent with our precedent, our analysis begins, as it should in every case addressing the reasonableness of a warrantless search, with the basic rule that "searches conducted outside the judicial process, without prior approval by judge or magistrate, are *per se* unreasonable under the Fourth Amendment—subject only to a few specifically established and well-delineated exceptions." Among the exceptions to the warrant requirement is a search incident to a lawful arrest. The exception derives from interests in officer safety and evidence preservation that are typically implicated in arrest situations. . . .

The State does not seriously disagree with the Arizona Supreme Court's conclusion that Gant could not have accessed his vehicle at the time of the search, but it nevertheless asks us to uphold the search of his vehicle under the broad reading of *Belton* discussed above. The State argues that *Belton* searches are reasonable regardless of the possibility of access in a given case because that expansive rule correctly balances law enforcement interests, including the interest in a bright-line rule, with an arrestee's limited privacy interest in his vehicle.

For several reasons, we reject the State's argument. First, the State seriously undervalues the privacy interests at stake. Although we have recognized that a motorist's privacy interest in his vehicle is less substantial than in his home, the former interest is nevertheless important and deserving of constitutional protection . . . A rule that gives police the power to conduct such a search whenever an individual is caught committing a traffic offense, when there is no basis for believing evidence of the offense might be found in the vehicle, creates a serious and recurring threat to the privacy of countless individuals. Indeed, the character of that threat implicates the central concern underlying the Fourth Amendment—the concern about giving police officers unbridled discretion to rummage at will among a person's private effects . . .

Contrary to the State's suggestion, a broad reading of *Belton* is also unnecessary to protect law enforcement safety and evidentiary interests. Under our view, *Belton* and *Thornton* permit an officer to conduct a vehicle search when an arrestee is within reaching distance of the vehicle or it is reasonable to believe the vehicle contains evidence of the offense of arrest. Other established exceptions to the warrant requirement authorize a vehicle search under additional circumstances when safety or evidentiary concerns demand. . . .

These exceptions together ensure that officers may search a vehicle when genuine safety or evidentiary concerns encountered during the arrest of a vehicle's recent occupant justify a search. Construing *Belton* broadly to allow vehicle searches incident to any arrest would serve no purpose except to provide a police entitlement, and it is anathema to the Fourth Amendment to permit a warrantless search on that basis. . . .

Police may search a vehicle incident to a recent occupant's arrest only if the arrestee is within reaching distance of the passenger compartment at the time of the search or it is reasonable to believe the vehicle contains evidence of the offense of arrest. When these justifications are absent, a search of an arrestee's vehicle will be unreasonable unless police obtain a warrant or show that another exception to the warrant requirement applies. The Arizona Supreme Court correctly held that this case involved an unreasonable search. Accordingly, the judgment of the State Supreme Court is affirmed.

It is so ordered.

consent from the homeowner. Like many other standards in criminal procedure, the validity of a person's consent will be judged based on the totality of the circumstances. Factors such as the person's age, mental capacity, state of intoxication, and language barriers can be considered to assess whether a person voluntarily and intelligently consented to a search.

The Court has ruled that a consent search will be valid even if the consenting person did not really have authority to consent to the search, as long as the police had a reasonable belief that the person was authorized to give consent for the search.[54] This is known as the **apparent authority rule,** and it generally recognizes that other people may have authority to give consent to search a home and the focus should be on what the officers reasonably believed regarding the consenting person's authority over the home.

Sometimes consent-based searches can be complicated. For example, in *Georgia v. Randolph* (2006),[55] the defendant's estranged wife gave police permission to search the marital residence for items of drug use, after the defendant, who was also present, had clearly refused to give consent. Essentially, when the police asked for consent to search the home, the wife said yes, but the husband/defendant said no. Based on the subsequent search, the defendant was indicted for possession of cocaine. The Supreme Court, however, invalidated this search, finding that the physically present co-occupant's clear refusal to permit entry rendered the warrantless entry and search unreasonable and invalid as to him.

In addition, the scope of a person's consent can also be limited, thereby limiting the scope of the search performed. For example, if a person authorizes police to search the bathroom of her home, but police also search two bedrooms and a hall closet, the additional searches generally would be deemed beyond the scope of consent. As a result, any criminal contraband obtained in these additional searches would not qualify for the consent exception for warrantless searches.

13.2(d)(1)(C) Plain View Searches

Searches and seizures of property within plain view also provide an exception to the warrant requirement. Under the **plain view doctrine,** if police are lawfully in location where they plainly see evidence of criminal activity, they may search and seize the evidence without a warrant.[56] There are three basic requirements for this exception: (1) police must have legal authority to be in a location, (2) they must find an item in plain view, and (3) they must have probable cause to believe the item is evidence of a crime. As a result, if police are searching a home for illegal aliens pursuant to a valid warrant and they discover illegal narcotics in plain sight, they do not need an additional warrant to seize the narcotics. The Court has reasoned that, even without a warrant, the search and seize of criminal contraband within plain view is not unreasonable.

In *Arizona v. Hicks* (1987),[57] police lawfully entered the defendant's apartment to search for a shooting suspect. Inside the apartment, an officer noticed two sets of expensive stereo components, which he suspected were stolen. The officer read and recorded the serial numbers from the components, moving some of them to do so. Based on these serial numbers, officers learned the components were stolen and charged the defendant with robbery. Upon review, however, the Supreme Court invalidated the search. The Court concluded that, while the mere recording of the serial numbers did not constitute a "seizure," the moving of the equipment was a "search" separate and apart from the search that was the lawful objective (the shooting) of entering the apartment. The Court refused to apply the plain view doctrine to the search because the serial numbers were not in the officer's plain view.

13.2(d)(1)(D) Terry Searches (Stop and Frisk)

The Court also has interpreted stop-and-frisk situations (*Terry* stops) (see earlier in text) as an exception to the warrant requirement. Recall from the earlier discussion that officers are permitted to briefly detain and question individuals when they have reasonable suspicion that the individuals are engaged or about to engage in criminal activity. Police are also permitted to perform a frisk or patdown of the person to assess whether the person is armed and/or dangerous. The Supreme Court has identified this frisking or patting down during a *Terry* stop as another type of permissible warrantless search. This is known as the **stop-and-frisk exception.** It maintains that officers conducting a brief investigation of a person based on reasonable suspicion may conduct a warrantless

apparent authority rule
Used to judge some types of consent searches; allows police to rely on consent given by persons that police reasonably believed are authorized to give consent.

Cyber Constitution
Georgia v. Randolph
(2006) http://supreme. justia.com/us/547/04- 1067/

plain view doctrine
Another exception to the Fourth Amendment warrant requirement that allows police to search and seize items if they are lawfully in a location where they plainly see evidence of criminal activity.

Cyber Constitution
***Arizona v. Hicks* (1987)**
http://supreme.justia.com/ us/480/321/

stop-and-frisk exception
An exception to the Fourth Amendment warrant requirement that allows officers, who are conducting a brief investigation of a person based on reasonable suspicion, to conduct a warrantless "patdown" of the person's outer clothing in order to ensure that the person is not armed or dangerous.

plain-feel exception
Allows officers performing stop and frisks to seize nonweapon forms of contraband (drugs, drug paraphernalia, etc.) that the officer reasonably detects as a part of a properly executed patdown.

Cyber Constitution
Minnesota v. Dickerson
(1993) http://supreme.justia.com/us/508/366/

exigent circumstances exception
An exception to the Fourth Amendment warrant requirement that allows officers to conduct warrantless searches where there is a need to apprehend a dangerous person or prevent an imminent and serious threat to the police or public.

hot-pursuit rule
A form of the exigent circumstances exception to the warrant requirement that allows police to enter places without a warrant where they are pursuing a fleeing felon, where evidence may be destroyed or evaporated, where contaminated food or narcotics present immediate danger, and where an ongoing crisis poses a threat to public safety.

evanescent evidence exception
A type of exigent circumstances situation that allows police to perform warrantless seizures of evidence that may be destroyed or evaporated.

public safety exception
An exception to the *Miranda* requirement that has allowed police, in at least one instance, to question a suspect in custody without supplying the requisite warnings when the questions were designed to address an imminent matter of public safety.

"patdown" of the person's outer clothing in order to ensure that the person is not armed or dangerous.[58]

While conducting a *Terry* stop and frisk, police officers may discover criminal contraband, including illegal drugs and firearms. Such discoveries gathered during *Terry* searches can lead to an arrest or to a more invasive search based on probable cause. It is important to note, however, that the scope of the officer's initial frisking or patdown must be for weapons, not other criminal contraband. But in the course of conducting a patdown for weapons, officers may either see or feel items that they reasonably believe to be elements of criminality. This may include non-weapon forms of contraband (drugs, drug paraphernalia, etc.) that the officer reasonably detects as a part of a properly executed patdown.

As discussed earlier, under the plain view doctrine, officers may seize items that they can patently observe during the course of an investigation. But in addition, the Supreme Court has also ruled that police may seize items that they reasonably discover through plain touch or feel during a properly-conducted investigatory stop. This is known as the **plain-feel exception** to the warrant requirement. In *Minnesota v. Dickerson* (1993),[59] the Court held that police may seize nonthreatening contraband detected through the sense of touch during a protective patdown search of the sort permitted by *Terry,* so long as the search stays within the bounds marked by *Terry.*

For example, while conducting a protective patdown for weapons, officers may feel something that they reasonably believe may be a crack pipe, bag of illegal narcotics, a weapon, or other criminal contraband. Assuming the officer's suspicion is reasonable—which again is based on the totality of the circumstances, including the officer's experience and knowledge of articulable facts—the officer may conduct a more invasive search of the suspect item, including reaching into the suspect's pockets or pants, and this search generally will be deemed reasonable under the Fourth Amendment.

13.2(d)(1)(E) Exigent Circumstances Another exception to the warrant requirement developed by the Court is the **exigent circumstances exception,** which generally allows law enforcement officers to conduct warrantless searches where there is a need to apprehend a dangerous person or prevent an imminent and serious threat to the police or public.[60] Although the Court has made it clear that this is not a general or catch-all exception, it has approved some warrantless searches conducted under particular circumstances of exigency.

These include cases where the police are pursuing fleeing felons, who may run into a home or other place that is traditionally associated with a reasonable expectation of privacy. In such instances, police are permitted to continue the pursuit without the search becoming unreasonable under the Fourth Amendment. This is known as the **hot-pursuit rule.**

The Court has also authorized police to perform warrantless seizures of evidence that may be destroyed or evaporated. This is called the **evanescent evidence exception,** and it generally recognizes situations where police cannot obtain a warrant before evidence may dissipate or otherwise disappear. For example, in *Cupp v. Murphy* (1973),[61] during a police station detention, police took samples from a murder suspect's fingernails over his protests and without a warrant. The Court ruled that this intrusion, which was undertaken to preserve highly evanescent evidence, did not violate the Fourth Amendment.

The Court also has sanctioned warrantless searches performed during circumstances that pose an imminent threat to public safety.[62] This is known as the **public safety exception.** For example, if authorities view a home on fire or see children in trouble on private property, they can access and search the property within the scope of the emergency. The Court, however, has held that the exigent circumstances exception should not be applied to cases where the police would have a reasonable opportunity to obtain a warrant in time to address the perceived threat.[63]

13.2(d)(1)(F) Vehicle Searches   The Court also has applied a warrant exception to many automobile searches. Under the **automobile exception,** police generally may search a vehicle without a warrant as long as they have probable cause that the vehicle or a part thereof contains evidence of criminality.[64] The Court has theorized that this exception is appropriate because vehicles can be readily moved, thereby making the acquisition of a warrant impractical. The Court also has suggested that people have a lesser expectation of privacy in their automobiles because they are used among the public and on public roads.

As a result, in addition to warrantless automobile searches conducted under the *Terry* stop or stop-and-frisk exception (see earlier in text), police may also search areas within vehicles and any containers therein if they have probable cause to believe that these areas or containers hold criminal contraband or the instruments of crime. Of course, if police believe the vehicle itself is evidence of a crime, they may seize the entire vehicle.

automobile exception
Another exception to the warrant requirement that allows police to search a vehicle without a warrant if they have probable cause to believe that the vehicle or part thereof contains evidence of criminality.

13.2(d)(1)(G) Administrative and Border Searches   There are several other specialized settings for which the Court has approved warrantless searches. These include, but are not limited to, international-border stops, where officials may stop vehicles at fixed checkpoints, even without reasonable suspicion, and search them for criminal contraband or persons unauthorized to enter the country. The Court has also authorized warrantless and suspicion-less searches of airline passengers boarding planes and businesses that are substantially regulated by the government, including gun and liquor stores.[65] And for similar reasons, the Court has upheld warrantless drug

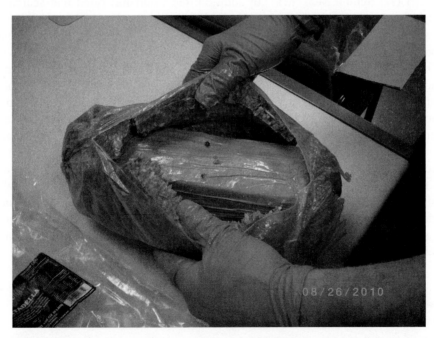

Police in the United States found a kilo of cocaine hidden inside this slab of sausage meat. A police dog sniffed out the drugs, which had been stashed inside the hollowed-out piece of bologna. Officials were tipped off by postal inspectors in Puerto Rico who had been investigating similar shipments. After the dog confirmed there were drugs inside, the package was put back together and delivered to a house in Holyoke, Massachusetts, by an undercover agent. When a woman sitting outside the property signed for it, police executed a search warrant and arrested Juan Rodriguez, 30, on cocaine-trafficking charges. Police said the coke had a street value of around 100,000 USD.

testing of employees involved in public safety occupations, such as railroad workers and customs officials. When conducted in a neutral and fair manner, the seizures of bodily fluids from some public safety professionals may be conducted, even without reasonable suspicion.[66]

In addition, the Court has ruled that prison officials can conduct warrantless searches of a prisoner's cell and personal property.[67] The Court reasoned that, given the circumstances surrounding incarceration, prisoners have no reasonable expectation of privacy within their prison cells or within the property found therein. As a result, the Court found that generally prisoners have no Fourth Amendment rights when officials search their prison cell or personal property.

And even after prisoners are released, they may have limited Fourth Amendment safeguards against warrantless searches. The Court has also approved warrantless stops and searches of persons on parole. In *Samson v. California* (2006), the Supreme Court upheld a police officer's warrantless and suspicionless search of a parolee, which was conducted pursuant to a California statute that required persons on parole to "agree in writing to be subject to search or seizure by a parole officer or other peace officer . . . with or without a search warrant and with or without cause." The Court upheld the search and the statute, finding that parolees have fewer expectations of privacy and that California's law was a reasonable measure designed to ensure public safety.

In each of these settings, the Court generally has found that the heightened interest in maintaining public safety outweighs the need for a warrant or probable cause in government searches.

13.2(d)(1)(H) School Searches   In addition, the Court has ruled that searches of public school property, including student lockers, may be performed based on reasonable suspicion. In *New Jersey v. T. L. O.* (1985),[68] the Court recognized that public school children have legitimate expectations of privacy, but that these interests must be weighed against the school's need to maintain an effective learning environment. In balancing these two interests, the Court held that school officials need not obtain a warrant before searching students who are under their authority and that searches do not need to be based on probable cause. Instead, the legality of a student search depends simply on the reasonableness of the search, based on all the circumstances.

In *Safford Unified School District #1 v. Redding* (2009), the Court ruled that a school search will be permissible in its scope when the measures adopted are reasonably related to the objectives of the search, and not excessively intrusive in light of the student's age and sex and the nature of the infraction. Read the following Court's opinion in *Redding*, which involves a school administrator's strip search of a junior high school student. Notice how the Court applies the reasonable suspicion standard to searches performed in public school settings.

Safford Unified School District #1 v. Redding
129 S.Ct. 2633 (2009)

Justice Souter delivered the opinion of the Court.

The events immediately prior to the search in question began in 13-year-old Savana Redding's math class at Safford Middle School one October day in 2003. The assistant principal of the school, Kerry Wilson, came into the room and asked Savana to go to his office . . .

Wilson then showed Savana four white prescription-strength ibuprofen 400-mg pills, and one over-the-counter blue naproxen 200-mg pill, all used for pain and inflammation but banned under school rules without advance permission. He asked Savana if she knew anything about the pills. Savana answered that she did not . . . Helen Romero, an administrative assistant, came into the office, and together with Wilson they searched Savana's backpack, finding nothing.

At that point, Wilson instructed Romero to take Savana to the school nurse's office to search her clothes for pills. Romero and the nurse, Peggy Schwallier, asked

Savana to remove her jacket, socks, and shoes, leaving her in stretch pants and a T-shirt (both without pockets), which she was then asked to remove. Finally, Savana was told to pull her bra out and to the side and shake it, and to pull out the elastic on her underpants, thus exposing her breasts and pelvic area to some degree. No pills were found. . . .

. . .

The Fourth Amendment "right of the people to be secure in their persons . . . against unreasonable searches and seizures" generally requires a law enforcement officer to have probable cause for conducting a search. . . .

In [*New Jersey v. T. L. O.*, 469 U. S. 325 (1985)], we recognized that the school setting "requires some modification of the level of suspicion of illicit activity needed to justify a search," and held that for searches by school officials "a careful balancing of governmental and private interests suggests that the public interest is best served by a Fourth Amendment standard of reasonableness that stops short of probable cause." We have thus applied a standard of reasonable suspicion to determine the legality of a school administrator's search of a student, and have held that a school search "will be permissible in its scope when the measures adopted are reasonably related to the objectives of the search and not excessively intrusive in light of the age and sex of the student and the nature of the infraction."

. . .

Perhaps the best that can be said generally about the required knowledge component of probable cause for a law enforcement officer's evidence search is that it raise a "fair probability," or a "substantial chance," of discovering evidence of criminal activity. The lesser standard for school searches could as readily be described as a moderate chance of finding evidence of wrongdoing.

This suspicion of Wilson's was enough to justify a search of Savana's backpack and outer clothing . . . And the look into Savana's bag, in her presence and in the relative privacy of Wilson's office, was not excessively intrusive, any more than Romero's subsequent search of her outer clothing.

Here it is that the parties part company, with Savana's claim that extending the search at Wilson's behest to the point of making her pull out her underwear was constitutionally unreasonable. The exact label for this final step in the intrusion is not important, though strip search is a fair way to speak of it. . . .

Savana's subjective expectation of privacy against such a search is inherent in her account of it as embarrassing, frightening, and humiliating. The reasonableness of her expectation (required by the Fourth Amendment standard) is indicated by the consistent experiences of other young people similarly searched, whose adolescent vulnerability intensifies the patent intrusiveness of the exposure. . . .

The indignity of the search does not, of course, outlaw it, but it does implicate the rule of reasonableness as stated in *T. L. O.*, that "the search as actually conducted [be] reasonably related in scope to the circumstances which justified the interference in the first place." The scope will be permissible, that is, when it is "not excessively intrusive in light of the age and sex of the student and the nature of the infraction."

Here, the content of the suspicion failed to match the degree of intrusion. Wilson knew beforehand that the pills were prescription-strength ibuprofen and over-the-counter naproxen, common pain relievers equivalent to two Advil, or one Aleve. He must have been aware of the nature and limited threat of the specific drugs he was searching for, and while just about anything can be taken in quantities that will do real harm, Wilson had no reason to suspect that large amounts of the drugs were being passed around, or that individual students were receiving great numbers of pills. . . .

In sum, what was missing from the suspected facts that pointed to Savana was any indication of danger to the students from the power of the drugs or their quantity, and any reason to suppose that Savana was carrying pills in her underwear. We think that the combination of these deficiencies was fatal to finding the search reasonable. . . .

The strip search of Savana Redding was unreasonable and a violation of the Fourth Amendment. . . .

It is so ordered.

YOUR CONSTITUTIONAL VALUES

CAN THE PRESIDENT CONDUCT WARRANTLESS WIRETAPS TO FIGHT TERRORISM?

After the September 11, 2001, terrorist attacks, President Bush authorized the National Security Agency (NSA) to conduct wiretaps of international telephone and other electronic communications between individuals in the United States and others abroad without obtaining a warrant or other judicial approval (TSP policy). Administration officials contended that such warrantless interceptions were necessary to fight the War on Terror and to prevent another 9/11-style attack. Prior to this policy, investigators were required to obtain a warrant from a court authorized under the Foreign Intelligence Surveillance Act (FISA) either before or shortly after conducting these types of wiretaps. Supporters of the TSP claimed that it was constitutional and pointed primarily to the president's commander-in-chief power under Article II of the Constitution and the Authorization for Use of Military Force, which Congress had passed, allowing the president to use "all necessary and appropriate" force to respond to the 9/11 attacks, as legal justification for the policy.

In response to the policy, several groups joined with the American Civil Liberties Union (ACLU) and filed an action in federal district court in Michigan seeking to stop the program. Opponents of TSP asserted that it violated several basic constitutional principles, including the Fourth Amendment right against unreasonable searches and seizures, the First Amendment right to free speech, basic notions of privacy, and the separation of powers.

On August 17, 2006, District Court Judge Anna Diggs Taylor agreed with the challengers, finding, among other things, that the TSP violated the Fourth Amendment right against unreasonable and warrantless searches and seizures. Judge Diggs Taylor wrote:

> [T]he Fourth Amendment, about which much has been written, in its few words requires reasonableness in all searches. It also requires prior warrants for any reasonable search, based upon prior-existing probable cause, as well as particularity as to persons, places, and things, and the interposition of a neutral magistrate between Executive branch enforcement officers and citizens. In enacting FISA, Congress made numerous concessions to stated executive needs. They include delaying the applications for warrants until after surveillance has begun for several types of exigencies, reducing the probable cause requirement to a less stringent standard, provision of a single court of judicial experts, and extension of the duration of approved wiretaps from thirty days (under Title III) to a ninety day term.
>
> All of the above Congressional concessions to Executive need and to the exigencies of our present situation as a people, however, have been futile. The wiretapping program here in litigation has undisputedly been continued for at least five years, it has undisputedly been implemented without regard to FISA and of course the more stringent standards of Title III, and obviously in violation of the Fourth Amendment. . . .
>
> The President of the United States is himself created by that same Constitution.

Following Judge Diggs Taylor's ruling, the Bush administration appealed the order to the Sixth Circuit Court of Appeals. Then, on January 17, 2007—just days before the Sixth Circuit was to hear oral arguments in the case—the Bush administration, through Attorney General Alberto Gonzales, announced that federal investigators would be conducting future surveillance through the FISA court. The administration then argued to the Sixth Circuit that this recent change in policy made the pending case moot and urged the court to dismiss the ACLU action. On July 6, 2007, the Sixth Circuit issued a 2–1 opinion, vacating the lower court's ruling based on the conclusion that the ACLU lacked standing to bring its claims. Based on your constitutional values, what do you think? Should the president be permitted to conduct warrantless wiretaps of international communications in the name of fighting terrorism? Or do the Fourth Amendment and companion legislative measures bar such activity?

In October 2007, the ACLU asked the Supreme Court to review the case but the Court denied this petition without comment.

For more information, see Judge Diggs Taylor's opinion in *ACLU, et al. v. National Security Agency, et al.*, Case No. 06-CV-10204, U.S. District Court for Eastern District of Michigan (2006); and Sixth Circuit Opinion in Case Nos. 06-2095; 06-2140.

A Framework for Search and Seizure Analysis

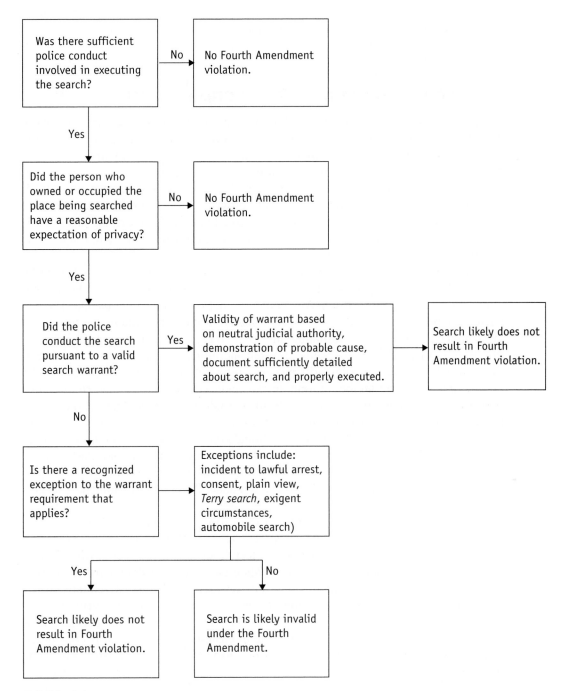

FIGURE 13-3
Framework for evidentiary searches and seizures

13.3 MODERN CHALLENGES

Fourth Amendment search and seizure cases are likely to remain a constant presence on American court dockets. For most cases, the basic approach or legal framework for evaluating these cases is the same. But the practical reality is that, like snowflakes, no two criminal cases are ever the same. There is always some difference of fact present in new cases. And given the legal standards that typically applied in search and seizure cases, which involve questions of reasonableness and totality of circumstance, a slight difference of fact can make a difference in the outcome of the case. As a result, for legal professionals working on Fourth Amendment issues, the important thing to remember is to pay attention to the details of fact that distinguish your current case from the precedent of cases that might apply.

13.4 THE RIGHT AGAINST SELF-INCRIMINATION

The Fifth Amendment provides that individuals have a right against self-incrimination. This basically means that government cannot coerce or force individuals to provide incriminating statements against themselves, including confessions, within a criminal context. Of course, the Fifth Amendment does not preclude individuals from knowingly, intelligently, and voluntarily providing statements to government, nor does it prevent individuals from being compelled to provide nonincriminating statements or testify in situations where they do not face criminal liability. In short, the provision is designed to bar the government from employing unreasonable tactics against suspects during custodial criminal investigations.

The right against self-incrimination under the Fifth Amendment is bolstered by additional protections under the Due Process Clause, within the Fifth and Fourteenth Amendments, as well as the Sixth Amendment right to counsel. Under the Due Process Clause (no person shall be deprived of life, liberty, or property without due process of law), police are barred from inflicting unduly coercive techniques to extract information from individuals.[69] Thus, within any self-incrimination case, the first consideration is whether the person voluntarily provided information to the police or whether the circumstances reflect that the information was induced more heavy-handed measures by government. In addition, while the Fifth Amendment provides protection against self-incrimination even before a person is formally charged with a crime, the Sixth Amendment right to counsel provides additional protections against compulsory statements once adversarial proceedings (usually the filing of a criminal charge) have started. As a result, in cases where a person provides police with information *after* being charged with a crime, the right to counsel under the Sixth Amendment must also be assessed. See Section 13.5.

At the outset, it must be noted that the Fifth Amendment right against self-incrimination applies to testimony or statements, not to physical evidence. Thus, while police cannot compel a person to testify during his or her own criminal trial, the Supreme Court has ruled that police can require a defendant or suspect to provide other forms of evidence that may be used against the defendant during trial. This may include the production of a blood, saliva, DNA, handwritings samples, and/or tangible evidence (documents, weapons, etc.) within the person's possession. However, a person's silence while in custody or during trial is considered testimonial in nature and generally cannot be used by the government against the defendant.[70]

13.4(a) Custodial Interrogation Requirement

custodial interrogations
Police-led questioning of a suspect while in police custody.

The right against self-incrimination is activated when police engage in **custodial interrogations** of suspects. There are three basic elements to a custodial interrogation. First, an authorized law enforcement officer must be involved in extracting information from the person. This is called the government conduct requirement. Private security guards or other nongovernmental persons, who are not working in conjunction with police, are not bound by the Fifth Amendment, and thus they are not constitutionally restricted in obtaining confessions from individuals. But if police direct or cause a nongovernmental person to interrogate another person who is in custody, this delegation of task may constitute government conduct.

Tareq and Michaele Salahi, who were subpoenaed to testify, attend a hearing on "The United States Secret Service and Presidential Protection: An Examination of a System Failure" on Capitol Hill, January 20, 2010, in Washington, DC. The Salahis snuck into a presidential event and met President Obama without authorization. At the hearing, the Salahis invoked their Fifth Amendment right against self-incrimination rather than testify.
Olivier Douliery/MCT/Newscom

Second, a person must be within governmental custody before Fifth Amendment protections will apply. In many cases, **custodial requirement** means that the police have physically apprehended someone and restrained the person's ability to leave. In this setting, custody is determined based on whether a person's ability to move is restricted in a substantial manner. In other contexts, however, the government may stop short of arresting or substantially detaining a person, but nonetheless create a situation where the person reasonably believes he or she is in custody. In this situation, the Supreme Court has held that custody is assessed based on whether a reasonable person (not the actual suspect) placed in similar circumstances would feel free to leave the presence of police.[71]

Finally, the Fifth Amendment protection against self-incrimination applies where government is actually interrogating an individual. **Interrogation** includes questions asked by police in an effort to obtain incriminating information, as well as other forms of police conduct that are designed or likely to elicit an incriminating response from the person in custody. If a person held in police custody voluntarily offers information without being asked or provoked by police, the Fifth Amendment would not prevent such information from being used against the individual. In some cases, police can engage in conversation directly with suspects or within the presence of suspects without such talk being labeled an interrogation.[72] Likewise, basic questions asked by police during the "booking" process—name, address, age, and so on—likely will not be deemed questions of an interrogating nature.[73]

13.4(b) Miranda Warnings

Once it is determined that police are engaging in a custodial interrogation, the question is what do the police need to do in order to comply with the Fifth Amendment in performing this task? The Supreme Court has ruled that, prior to engaging in custodial interrogation, police must inform suspects of their constitutional rights if it wishes to

custodial requirement
A standard requirement before a person will have a constitutional right against self-incrimination. In some cases, custody is determined based on whether a person's ability to move is restricted in a substantial manner. In other cases, custody is based on whether a reasonable person (not the actual suspect) placed in similar circumstances would feel free to leave the presence of police.

interrogation
Efforts, including questions, by police designed to obtain incriminating information.

use evidence gathered during such interrogations. As the Court held in the now-famous case of *Miranda v. Arizona* (1966),[74] police must inform suspects that (1) they have the right to remain silent, (2) anything they say can and will be used against them in court, (3) they have the right to the presence of an attorney, and (4) if they cannot afford an attorney, one will be provided for them.

Miranda warnings
Information the police must provide to suspects before a custodial interrogation, which includes notice that (1) they have the right to remain silent; (2) anything they say can and will be used against them in court; (3) they have the right to the presence of an attorney; and (4) if they cannot afford an attorney, one will be provided for them.

The *Miranda* **warnings** are designed to ensure that prior to police questioning, individuals are informed of two basic rights under the Constitution—the right to be silent and the right to an attorney. Note that the right to an attorney under the Fifth Amendment and *Miranda* is fundamentally distinct from the right to counsel under the Sixth Amendment. See Section 13.5. And as the Court reaffirmed in *Missouri v. Seibert* (2004), if police fail to provide *Miranda* warnings prior to eliciting incriminating statements from a suspect, such statements likely will be deemed to be involuntary, and therefore inadmissible. But if these warnings are provided, suspects may waive either or both of their basic rights and agree to talk to police. If this occurs, the government has the burden of proving that any waiver made by a suspect was made knowingly, intelligently, and voluntarily.[75]

In cases where a suspect has asserted a right to remain silent, prior to or during an interrogation, the police must immediately stop questioning the defendant regarding the particular offense for which he is being interrogated. The Court has ruled that police can restart questioning if: (1) the defendant initiates such questioning on his own, (2) the police seek to ask questions about another offense, or (3) the police "scrupulously honor" the suspect's request not to talk, wait a sufficient amount of time before trying to continue the questioning, and do not coerce the suspect into resuming the questioning. In cases where a suspect has invoked his right to the presence of an attorney, the rule is more clear and strict: police must cease all questioning—even that related to other offenses—until an attorney is provided or until the suspect initiates, own his own accord, additional conversation.[76]

As with many other doctrines of criminal procedure, the Supreme Court has limited the scope of the *Miranda* rule in recent years. Most notably, the Court has carved out a public safety exception to the *Miranda* requirement that has allowed police, in at least one instance, to question a suspect in custody without supplying the requisite warnings when the questions were designed to address an imminent matter of public safety.[77] In addition, the Court has held that *Miranda* warnings are not required prior to a person's grand jury testimony; voluntary (as opposed to involuntary) statements made in violation of *Miranda* can still be used to impeach the defendant's testimony during trial, should the defendant decide to testify, and the use of evidence acquired in violation of *Miranda* may be deemed to be **harmless error** (an error made during trial that ostensibly would not change the outcome of the case), meaning that a court believes that the person would have been convicted even if the incriminating statement evidence had been excluded.[78]

harmless error
An error made during trial that ostensibly does not change the outcome of the case.

Cyber Constitution
Florida v. Powell (2010)
http://supreme.justia.com/
us/559/08-1175/

More recently, the Supreme Court ruled in *Florida v. Powell* (2010) that law enforcement officers do not have to provide suspects with the precise language of the *Miranda* warnings. According to the Court, different words that communicate the same essential message of the *Miranda* language are sufficient to comply with the Fifth Amendment.

13.4(c) Basic Framework for Self-Incrimination Issues

In most self-incrimination cases, the basic outline for reviewing the constitutionality of a defendant's statements, confessions, and other incriminating information is the same. As illustrated in Figure 13-4, legal professionals must ask a series of questions to determine whether a defendant's statements were voluntarily offered, whether the statements were given during a custodial interrogation, whether *Miranda* warnings were given and waived, and, if not, whether there is some recognized exception to the Fifth Amendment that applies.

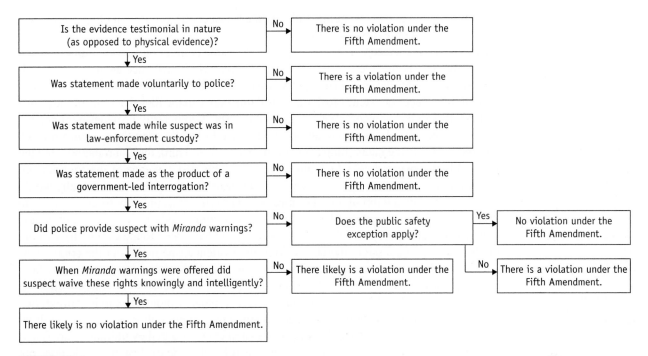

FIGURE 13-4
Framework for evaluating defendant's statements

13.5 THE EXCLUSIONARY RULE

Upon finding that the government has engaged in an unreasonable search and seizure under the Fourth Amendment or infringed upon the right against self-incrimination under the Fifth Amendment, the big question is what can the Court do about it? The Supreme Court's response to this question has gradually, although not consistently or thoroughly, been to exclude from the evidence items that are unconstitutionally obtained by the government. This is called the **exclusionary rule.**

The Court first adopted the exclusionary rule in *Weeks v. United States* (1914),[79] when it declared the rule to apply to evidence unconstitutionally seized by federal authorities. The Court, however, did not apply this rule to state agents until its ruling in *Mapp v. Ohio* (1962). As applied today, the rule is designed to deter police misconduct by essentially imposing a type of "death penalty" to evidence that is obtained outside of constitutional parameters. If imposed, the rule bars unconstitutionally or illegally obtained evidence from being used by the government against the accused.

In some cases, the Court has applied the exclusionary rule to more than just the initial item of evidence obtained by police in violation of the Constitution excluding any other evidence derived from the initial piece of evidence. This is known as the **"fruit of the poisonous tree doctrine."** This metaphoric doctrine likens "the poisonous tree" to the evidence initially obtained by police in violation of the Constitution and "the fruit" to all other evidence that "grew" out of the ill-gotten evidence or "poisonous tree."[80] So, for example, if police seize a person's diary during an illegal search of a home and then use the diary entries to seize additional evidence outside of the home, the fruit of the poisonous tree doctrine would exclude the additional items from evidence at trial because those items are fruit from an original and poisonous search.

While in theory the fruit of the poisonous tree doctrine could lead to a substantial expansion of the exclusionary rule, the Supreme Court has imposed a number of restrictions on its application. First, the Court has ruled that if police can show that the derived evidence was obtained by a source that is separate or independent from the originally tainted method, they can still use the evidence. This is called the **independent source rule.** As

exclusionary rule
A judically created remedy for violations of the Fourth, Fifth, or Sixth Amendment, which is used to exclude unconstitutionally obtained evidence from a criminal trial.

fruit of the poisonous tree doctrine
A doctrine that extends the exclusionary rule to all evidence obtained as a result of the initial piece of unconstitutionally obtained evidence.

independent source rule
An exception to the exclusionary rule that will not exclude evidence if police can show that it was obtained by a source that is separate or independent from the originally tainted method.

an example, if police unconstitutionally coerce a suspect into confessing to a crime, they cannot use this confession.[81] But if the police use a valid warrant based on information unrelated to the coerced confession to obtain the same confession from a journal located in the suspect's home, the confession will be admissible as evidence against the defendant. Second, under the **intervening circumstances rule,** evidence will be admissible if new circumstances or events break the causal link between the illegal actions of the police and the ill-gotten evidence.[82] For example, if a suspect voluntarily provides to police the same evidence that the officers had originally seized illegally, then the evidence may be admissible due to the intervening event of the confession. Third, the Court has adopted the **inevitable discovery rule,** which allows illegally obtained evidence or the fruit derived therefrom to be admitted if the government can show that the evidence eventually would have been discovered through proper means.[83] Thus, if police illegally force a suspect to disclose the location of a murder victim, but the victim's body is found in a public and open location, the police could claim the body would have been found eventually without the defendant's confession, thereby making the evidence (the body, not the confession) admissible. Fourth, as discussed previously, the Court also has adopted the good faith exception or Leon rule, which allows illegally obtained evidence to be introduced if the police can show that they relied in good faith on a judicial order or search warrant. See earlier in text. This exception also includes situations where police act in good faith on laws or rules that they reasonably believe are valid even though they ultimately are found to be invalid.[84] Finally, the Supreme Court has ruled that the exclusionary rule does not apply to grand jury hearings and civil proceedings and, in some cases, where the prosecution seeks to use illegally obtained evidence to impeach a criminal defendant's testimony during trial.[85] All told, these doctrines and limitations have served to substantially limit the scope of the exclusionary rule and fruit of the poisonous tree doctrine.

It should be noted that a number of states relying on their own constitutional protections have not enforced some of the exceptions to these exclusionary rules under their own constitutions. For example, in Georgia, the State Supreme Court has refused to recognize a good faith exception to the Fourth Amendment. Thus, under some state constitutions, a search performed by state police, such as that conducted in *United States v. Leon* (1984) (see section 13.5), would result in the evidence being excluded. In addition, the exclusionary rule may not be the only remedy available to those whose rights are violated under the Fourth, Fifth, and Sixth Amendments. Individuals may also pursue civil action, under federal or state law, for money damages against officials who breach their rights of privacy during arrests and searches and seizures.[86]

13.6 THE RIGHT TO COUNSEL

The Sixth Amendment provides, "[i]n all criminal prosecutions, the accused shall . . . have the assistance of counsel for his defence." As addressed in Section 13.4, the right to counsel is also protected under the Fifth Amendment as a part of the right against self-incrimination. The primary difference is that the Supreme Court has interpreted the Sixth Amendment to apply after formal charges have been filed against a defendant, while the Fifth Amendment right to counsel during custodial interrogation can be present even before charges have been filed. But the Court also has ruled that even after charges have been filed against a defendant, the Sixth Amendment right to counsel applies only to "critical stages" of the prosecution "where substantial rights of a criminal accused may be affected."[87] This "critical stage" demarcation by the Court has resulted in a long and detailed case analysis to determine which of the many criminal proceedings are considered "critical," thereby resulting in the Sixth Amendment right to counsel, and which are deemed noncritical, resulting in no right to counsel.

Most discussions of the "critical stage" requirement under the Sixth Amendment begin with the Court's ruling in *Gideon v. Wainwright* (1963),[88] the landmark case in which the Court ruled that a defendant had a constitutional right to an attorney during state criminal proceedings and that if he could not afford an attorney, the state was

intervening circumstances rule
Another exception to the exclusionary rule that allows evidence to be admitted if new circumstances or events break the causal link between the illegal actions of the police and the ill-gotten evidence.

inevitable discovery rule
Another exception to the exclusionary rule that allows illegally obtained evidence or the fruit derived therefrom to be admitted if the government can show that the evidence eventually would have been discovered through proper means.

required to appoint one. Prior to *Gideon*, the Court had held that the right to counsel and court-appointed counsel for indigent counsel was a right within federal trials and state trials involving the possibility of the death penalty. But *Gideon* was the first case to make the Sixth Amendment right to counsel widely applicable to the vast majority of state criminal proceedings. This includes, but is not limited to, the right to counsel during all felony trials; misdemeanor cases where imprisonment is actually imposed, as opposed to cases where jail time is a possibility (see *Scott v. Illinois* (1979)); arraignments; postcharge lineups; postcharge interrogations (regardless of whether they are custodial); and appeals as a matter of right.[89] The Court, however, has ruled that the Sixth Amendment right to counsel does not apply to misdemeanor trials when actual imprisonment is not imposed, the taking of handwriting and voice exemplars, photo identifications, discretionary appellate proceedings (appeals over which courts have discretion to accept or deny), parole hearings, and habeas corpus proceedings.[90]

Cyber Constitution
Scott v. Illinois **(1979)**
http://supreme.justia.com/us/440/367/

In cases where counsel is denied to an individual during a critical *pretrial* stage, any evidence gathered by the government as a result of such denial can be excluded. In other cases where the government wrongly denies a defendant during a qualified court proceeding or the defendant receives the ineffective assistance of counsel (see following discussion) during trial, the verdict of the trial or other proceeding can be reversed.

The more dynamic question under the Sixth Amendment right to counsel is whether a person who had counsel during criminal proceedings actually received sufficient and competent service from the lawyer to comply with constitutional standards. In other words, under the Sixth Amendment, persons are not just entitled to an attorney; they are entitled to the **effective assistance of counsel.** As a result, if a person has an attorney during criminal proceedings, but the attorney's services are deficient, it may be a violation of the right to counsel. In *Strickland v. Washington* (1984),[91] the Supreme Court held that defendants seeking to prove a violation of the right to counsel based on deficient representation must show two things: (1) the attorney's representation fell below objective standards of reasonableness (it was deficient), and (2) there is a reasonable probability that the outcome of the criminal proceedings would have been different but for counsel's deficient performance. Later in *Lockhart v. Fretwell* (1993),[92] the Court suggested that a defendant, in some cases, may also be required to prove that the counsel's deficiency caused the result to be fundamentally unfair or unreliable. Under these standards, in cases where counsel is proved to be ineffective during trial or appellate proceedings, a defendant's conviction can be reversed.

Of course, the right to counsel, like other constitutional rights, can be waived. This is known as *pro se* (for yourself) counsel or representation. In order to do this, defendants do not need to show that they are competent in the law or even capable of representing themselves. They only need to show that they are sufficiently competent to make a valid waiver of their rights. This course of action, however, generally is not recommended and has led to the expression "the person who represents himself has a fool for a client."

To better understand how the *Strickland* test is applied to IAC claims, read the following Supreme Court's ruling in *Padilla v. Kentucky* (2010). In *Padilla*, the Court ruled 7–2 that Sixth Amendment guarantee of effective assistance of counsel requires a criminal defense lawyer to advise a noncitizen client that pleading guilty to an aggravated felony will trigger mandatory, automatic deportation.

effective assistance of counsel
The more specific standard used to assess the right to counsel under the Sixth Amendment. To prove a violation of the right to counsel, a defendant must show two fundamental things: (1) the attorney's representation fell below objective standards of reasonableness (it was deficient) and (2) there is a reasonable probability that the outcome of the criminal proceedings would have been different but for counsel's deficient performance.

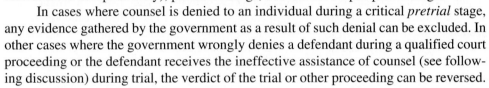

Padilla v. Kentucky
559 U.S. __ (2010)

Justice Stevens delivered the opinion of the Court.

Petitioner Jose Padilla, a native of Honduras, has been a lawful permanent resident of the United States for more than 40 years. Padilla served this Nation with honor as a member of the U. S. Armed Forces during the Vietnam War. He now faces deportation after pleading

guilty to the transportation of a large amount of marijuana in his tractor-trailer in the Commonwealth of Kentucky.

In this postconviction proceeding, Padilla claims that his counsel not only failed to advise him of this consequence prior to his entering the plea, but also told him that he "did not have to worry about immigration status since he had been in the country so long." Padilla relied on his counsel's erroneous advice when he pleaded guilty to the drug charges that made his deportation virtually mandatory. He alleges that he would have insisted on going to trial if he had not received incorrect advice from his attorney . . . . . .

Under *Strickland* [*v. Washington*], we first determine whether counsel's representation "fell below an objective standard of reasonableness." Then we ask whether "there is a reasonable probability that, but for counsel's unprofessional errors, the result of the proceeding would have been different." . . .

The weight of prevailing professional norms supports the view that counsel must advise her client regarding the risk of deportation. "[A]uthorities of every stripe—including the American Bar Association, criminal defense and public defender organizations, authoritative treatises, and state and city bar publications—universally require defense attorneys to advise as to the risk of deportation consequences for non-citizen clients. . . ." . . .

In the instant case, the terms of the relevant immigration statute are succinct, clear, and explicit in defining the removal consequence for Padilla's conviction. Padilla's counsel could have easily determined that his plea would make him eligible for deportation simply from reading the text of the statute, which addresses not some broad classification of crimes but specifically commands removal for all controlled substances convictions except for the most trivial of marijuana possession offenses. Instead, Padilla's counsel provided him false assurance that his conviction would not result in his removal from this country. This is not a hard case in which to find deficiency: The consequences of Padilla's plea could easily be determined from reading the removal statute, his deportation was presumptively mandatory, and his counsel's advice was incorrect. . . .

Accepting his allegations as true, Padilla has sufficiently alleged constitutional deficiency to satisfy the first prong of *Strickland*. Whether Padilla is entitled to relief on his claim will depend on whether he can satisfy *Strickland*'s second prong, prejudice, a matter we leave to the Kentucky courts to consider in the first instance. . . .

It is our responsibility under the Constitution to ensure that no criminal defendant—whether a citizen or not—is left to the "mercies of incompetent counsel." To satisfy this responsibility, we now hold that counsel must inform her client whether his plea carries a risk of deportation. Our longstanding Sixth Amendment precedents, the seriousness of deportation as a consequence of a criminal plea, and the concomitant impact of deportation on families living lawfully in this country demand no less. . . .

The judgment of the Supreme Court of Kentucky is reversed, and the case is remanded for further proceedings not inconsistent with this opinion.

It is so ordered.

13.7 THE RIGHT AGAINST DOUBLE JEOPARDY

One of the most misunderstood rights in criminal procedure is the right against double jeopardy. The Fifth Amendment provides in relevant part that "[no person shall] be subject for the same offence to be twice put in jeopardy of life or limb." The basic concept of double jeopardy is that after the government has tried (placed in jeopardy) a person once, it cannot do it again for the same offense. And while this provision is seemingly self-explanatory, the Supreme Court has interpreted the terms "same offence" and "jeopardy" in ways that preclude a strict application of the words within this provision.

The text of the clause makes it clear that it applies only to criminal proceedings, not to civil cases. Thus, a person may be tried in a criminal case and then later tried in civil proceedings or vice versa. The classic example of this principle is O. J. Simpson, who was initially acquitted of homicide charges in a state criminal case, but then was later found liable for the same homicide in a civil case. The logic behind allowing these double trials is that a person is not truly jeopardized of life or limb (usually only monetary loss) in a civil case. But at times, the distinction between civil and criminal proceedings is not always clear. For example, in *United States v. Ursery* (1996),[93] the defendant argued that the government could not prosecute him for drug offenses *and*, based on the same offenses, force him to forfeit his property that was involved in committing his drug offenses through civil forfeiture proceedings (actions where government seeks to acquire private property used in the commission of criminal acts—typically drug offenses). The Supreme Court, however, rejected this argument, finding that civil forfeiture proceedings were not considered punishment under the Fifth Amendment.

The Court has ruled that a defendant is placed in jeopardy (jeopardy attaches) at different times depending on the nature of the proceeding. In a jury trial, jeopardy attaches when the jury is sworn to duty. In a bench trial, where a judge is the trier of fact, jeopardy is initiated when the first witness is sworn for testimony. And even though juvenile proceedings normally are not regarded as criminal in nature, jeopardy nonetheless still attaches in these proceedings when they commence.[94] It is also important to note that once jeopardy attaches for a particular offense, it also attaches for all lesser included offenses and most higher-level offenses that could be charged for the same act.[95] For example, if a person is charged with a single count of robbery, and jeopardy attaches to this case, the government normally could not charge the defendant with theft (a lesser included offense) or aggravated robbery (a higher-level offense) based on the same act. The principle underlying this rule is that the prosecution should not be able to get a second or third attempt to convict a person by merely adjusting the level of charge in order to gain another trial. The one primary exception to this limitation is homicide charges, where a defendant charged with assaulting another person may be charged with homicide (a higher-level offense) if the victim later dies as a result and within a specified time period after the assault.

The Court has carved out a number of exceptions to the Double Jeopardy Clause. First, the clause does not bar multiple prosecutions by different sovereign governments. Under the **dual sovereignty doctrine,** federal and state governments may try a person for the same act, and two or more states may try a person for the same act because they are separate sovereigns. However, two municipalities within the same state may not impose multiple punishments because they are technically of the same sovereign (agents of the same state). Second, a person may be tried multiple times if the prior trial ended due to **manifest necessity** (a compelling need to stop the trial prior to a verdict being reached), which may include a **hung jury** (a jury that cannot reach a decision after sufficient deliberations) or the declaration of a **mistrial** (the termination of a trial prior to a verdict) where the prosecution did not intentionally seek to cause the mistrial. The logic behind this exception is that double jeopardy should bar a second trial only if the first trial was resolved based on the merits of the case. Third, individuals may be tried again in cases where their initial conviction was reversed on appeal. The theory behind this exception is that "[i]t would be a high price indeed for society to pay were every accused granted immunity from punishment because of any defect sufficient to constitute reversible error in the proceedings leading to conviction." If, however, a person's conviction is reversed due to insufficient evidence being offered during the first trial, the prosecution will be barred from initiating a second trial. Finally, it is also possible to place persons in jeopardy a second time if they breach the terms of their plea agreement with the government.[96] Under the scenario, if a defendant enters a plea agreement to avoid a trial, but then fails to live up to the agreement's terms, the government could seek to invalidate the agreement and try the defendant on the initial charges.

Perhaps the most challenging aspect of the Double Jeopardy Clause is determining when two offenses are actually the same. For example, if a person is convicted of speeding, reckless driving, and driving under influence, all based on the same act of driving, it may seem as though the driver is being punished in multiple ways for the same offense. But the Supreme Court has ruled that two or more criminal charges are not the same offense, for double jeopardy purposes, if each charge requires proof of an additional criminal element (another form of intent or an additional act). This is known as the **Blockburger test.**[97] Under this analysis, the government probably would be able to proceed against the driver with the three charges because each of the offenses is likely to contain a unique or additional element from the other charges. For example, in *Yeager v. United States* (2009), the Supreme Court ruled 6–3 that the Double Jeopardy Clause bars the government from retrying a defendant who was acquitted of some charges on factually related counts on which the jury failed to reach a verdict.

13.8 THE RIGHT TO A FAIR TRIAL

There are a number of other constitutional protections that impact an individual's rights during trial proceedings. Chief among them are the right to a fair, public, and speedy trial; the right to due process; and the right to equal protection.

dual sovereignty doctrine
A legal theory associated with the Double Jeopardy Clause that provides that federal and state governments may try a person for the same act just as two or more states may try a person for the same act because they are separate sovereigns.

manifest necessity
A compelling need to stop the trial prior to a verdict being reached.

hung jury
A jury that cannot reach a decision after sufficient deliberations.

mistrial
The termination of a trial prior to a verdict.

Blockburger test
A legal standard created by the Supreme Court under the Double Jeopardy Clause that provides that two or more criminal charges are not the same offense if each charge requires proof of an additional criminal element (another form of intent or an additional act).

Cyber Constitution
Yeager v. United States
(2009) http://supreme.
justia.com/us/557/08-67/

right to a fair trial
A general term used to describe a variety of fairness-based rights during a criminal trial, including the right to a speedy and public trial by an impartial jury and the right to due process.

The Sixth Amendment provides the accused with an explicit right to a speedy and public trial, by an impartial jury. When combined with more general protections of due process under the Fifth and Fourteenth Amendments, this provision is the foundation for what most people refer to as the **right to a fair trial.** Under the Sixth Amendment, the basic right to a public trial ensures that most trial proceedings will be open to the public. However, in rare occasions, trials or pretrial proceedings may be closed to the public if such closure is necessary to ensure the defendant receives a fair trial. Even in cases where defendants may want to close their criminal proceedings from the public, the freedom of the press—a competing constitutional value in some cases—likely will prohibit a judge from closing the proceedings.[98]

The right to a speedy trial under the Sixth Amendment is designed to ensure that defendants are not held in custody for unreasonable periods of time before their trial. The Supreme Court, however, has not provided a clear definition of speedy trial. Instead, the Court has ruled that pretrial delays should be evaluated based on the totality of the circumstances, which includes an assessment of the time of and reason for the delay, whether the defendant asserted his rights, and the nature of prejudice to the defendant. For example, in *Doggett v. United States* (1992),[99] the Court held that the speedy trial provision was violated when the federal government failed to make reasonable efforts to apprehend the defendant after he was indicted, resulting in an eight-and-one-half-year delay between the defendant's indictment and his trial. It is important to note that the right to a speedy trial begins when the defendant has been arrested or charged with a criminal offense.[100] In addition, defendants may also have statutory rights that provide even greater speedy trial rights. For example, the federal government and many state governments have passed more specific measures that set a clear timetable for bringing a person to trial. Of course, like most other rights, a person's right to a speedy trial—under both the Constitution and any relevant statute—can be waived, and in many cases, defendants agree to waive their speedy trial rights in order to afford their attorneys more time to prepare for trial.

The right to a jury trial is protected at both state and federal levels. But there are a number of important caveats. First, the Supreme Court has ruled that the right to a jury trial exists only with regard to **serious offenses**—defined as an offense for which a defendant could receive more than six months of imprisonment. If a person faces six months or less of incarceration, the offense is presumed to be petty and no absolute right to a jury trial exists.[101] Under many state constitutional standards, however, defendants are eligible for jury trials if they face the possibility of any jail time whatsoever. Second, the Court has ruled that the Sixth Amendment does not entitle a person to a twelve-person jury. Instead, the Court has ruled that there must be at least six jurors to decide a case. But again, many state constitutions and laws have supplemented the Court's standards by requiring larger jury memberships (typically twelve jurors in felony cases). Third, the Court has not required jury verdicts to be unanimous under the Sixth Amendment, except in cases where there are only six members of the jury. Many states, on the other hand, require unanimity. Finally, in many jurisdictions, a defendant can unilaterally waive the right to a jury trial and have the case decided by a judge, but in the federal system, both the defendant and the prosecutor must agree to waive a jury trial.

serious offenses
Offenses for which a defendant could receive more than six months of imprisonment.

In recent years, the Supreme Court has used the Sixth Amendment right to a jury trial to strike down some sentencing laws at the state and federal levels. During the 1980s and 1990s, many states and the federal government passed sentencing regulations that allowed judges to enhance a defendant's sentence beyond the statutory maximum penalty if aggravating factors, such as the use of a gun or the infliction of extreme cruelty, were present in the case. Under a typical scenario, a defendant would be convicted of an offense during trial and then, during sentencing, a judge would make a number of other factual findings not made by the jury and use them to increase the defendant's sentence. The Supreme Court, however, ruled that allowing judges to enhance a defendant's sentence based on facts that are not decided by a jury or admitted by the defendant (typically within a plea agreement) violates the Sixth Amendment guarantee to a jury trial.

In *Apprendi v. New Jersey* (2000),[102] the Supreme Court questioned the fact-finding authority of judges in making sentencing decisions, ruling that other than the fact of a prior conviction, any fact that increases the penalty for a crime beyond the pre-scribed statutory maximum is, in effect, an element of the crime that must be submitted to a jury and proved beyond a reasonable doubt. The Court held that "under the Due Process Clause of the Fifth Amendment and the notice and jury trial guarantees of the Sixth Amendment, any fact (other than prior conviction) that increases the maximum penalty for a crime must be charged in an indictment, submitted to a jury, and proven beyond a reasonable doubt." The *Apprendi* case raised the question of whether judges can deviate from established sentencing guidelines or apply sentence enhancements based on judicial determinations—as opposed to jury findings or defendant admissions—of aggravating factors that deviate from those guidelines.

Similarly, in *Ring v. Arizona* (2002),[103] the Supreme Court held that Arizona's capital sentencing law, which allowed judge-determined facts to serve as the basis of a death sentence, violated the Sixth Amendment right to a trial by jury. The *Ring* decision effectively overturned death penalty sentencing practices in as many as nine states. Essentially, *Ring* established that juries, not judges, must decide the facts that lead to a death sentence.

In *Blakely v. Washington* (2004),[104] the U.S. Supreme Court extended *Apprendi* and *Ring* by effectively invalidating sentencing schemes that allow judges rather than juries to determine any factor that imposes a mandatory increase in a defendant's crimi-nal sentence, except for prior convictions. The Court found that because the facts sup-porting Blakely's increased sentence (a determination that he had acted with deliberate cruelty in kidnapping his estranged wife) were neither admitted by Blakely nor found by a jury, the sentence violated Blakely's Sixth Amendment right to trial by jury. The *Blakely* decision required the sentencing laws of several jurisdictions to be rewritten.

Finally, in two 2005 cases, the U.S. Supreme Court further expanded the influ-ence of *Apprendi*, *Ring,* and *Blakely* by applying their rationale to the federal sentencing guidelines. In *United States v. Booker*,[105] a Wisconsin federal jury convicted Freddie Booker of possessing and distributing crack cocaine and also determined that Booker had 92.5 grams of crack in his possession. Under federal sentencing guidelines, that amount of the drug would have limited Booker's maximum prison sentence to 21 years and 10 months. During sentencing, however, the trial judge determined that Booker had distributed an additional 566 grams of crack cocaine, had perjured himself at trial, and had twenty-three prior convictions. As a result, the judge sentenced Booker to 30 years in prison. In other words, the judge-determined facts were used to enhance Booker's sentence beyond what the federal sentencing guidelines called for based on the jury-determined facts. Accordingly, Booker argued that the use of judge-determined facts to enhance his sentence violated his Sixth Amendment right to a trial by jury.

In *Booker*, and its companion case, *United States v. Fanfan* (2005),[106] the Supreme Court held that, to the extent that the federal sentencing guidelines required the judge to enhance a defendant's sentence based on facts not found by juries or admitted to by defendants, they violated the Sixth Amendment right to trial by jury. In other words, the Court found that federal sentencing guidelines unconstitutionally forced judges to increase sentences based on their own factual findings rather than on those of a jury. The Court further declared that the federal guidelines are "effectively advisory" in nature and do not impose mandatory requirements upon federal judges. In effect, the Court's ruling now allows federal judges to consider federal guideline ranges for sentencing but does not require them to tailor the sentence to the confines of the guideline factors. For some, the Court's decision essentially restored judicial discretion in federal sentencing.[107] Read the Court's opinion in *United States v. Booker* and *United States v. Fanfan* (2008) (later in text) to assess its potential impact on judicial decisions in sentencing hearings.

United States v. Booker and United States v. Fanfan
543 U.S. 220 (2005)

Justice Stevens delivered the opinion of the Court in part.

The question presented in each of these cases is whether an application of the Federal Sentencing Guidelines violated the Sixth Amendment. In each case, the courts below held that binding rules set forth in the Guidelines limited the severity of the sentence that the judge could lawfully impose on the defendant based on the facts found by the jury at his trial . . . We hold that both courts correctly concluded that the Sixth Amendment as construed in *Blakely* does apply to the Sentencing Guidelines. In a separate opinion authored by Justice Breyer, the Court concludes that in light of this holding, two provisions of the Sentencing Reform Act of 1984 (SRA) that have the effect of making the Guidelines mandatory must be invalidated in order to allow the statute to operate in a manner consistent with congressional intent.

Respondent Booker was charged with possession with intent to distribute at least 50 grams of cocaine base (crack). Having heard evidence that he had 92.5 grams in his duffel bag, the jury found him guilty of violating 21 U.S.C. § 841(a)(1). That statute prescribes a minimum sentence of 10 years in prison and a maximum sentence of life for that offense. §841(b)(1)(A)(iii).

Based upon Booker's criminal history and the quantity of drugs found by the jury, the Sentencing Guidelines required the District Court Judge to select a "base" sentence of not less than 210 nor more than 262 months in prison. The judge, however, held a post-trial sentencing proceeding and concluded by a preponderance of the evidence that Booker had possessed an additional 566 grams of crack and that he was guilty of obstructing justice. Those findings mandated that the judge select a sentence between 360 months and life imprisonment; the judge imposed a sentence at the low end of the range. Thus, instead of the sentence of 21 years and 10 months that the judge could have imposed on the basis of the facts proved to the jury beyond a reasonable doubt, Booker received a 30-year sentence. . . .

It has been settled throughout our history that the Constitution protects every criminal defendant "against conviction except upon proof beyond a reasonable doubt of every fact necessary to constitute the crime with which he is charged." It is equally clear that the "Constitution gives a criminal defendant the right to demand that a jury find him guilty of all the elements of the crime with which he is charged." These basic precepts, firmly rooted in the common law, have provided the basis for recent decisions interpreting modern criminal statutes and sentencing procedures. . . .

In *Jones v. United States* (1999) . . . we noted . . . a "rule requiring jury determination of facts that raise a sentencing ceiling" in state and federal sentencing guidelines systems.

In *Apprendi v. New Jersey* (2000), the defendant pleaded guilty to second-degree possession of a firearm for an unlawful purpose, which carried a prison term of 5-to-10 years. Thereafter, the trial court found that his conduct had violated New Jersey's "hate crime" law because it was racially motivated, and imposed a 12-year sentence. This Court set aside the enhanced sentence. We held: "Other than the fact of a prior conviction, any fact that increases the penalty for a crime beyond the prescribed statutory maximum must be submitted to a jury, and proved beyond a reasonable doubt."

. . .

In *Ring v. Arizona* (2002), we reaffirmed our conclusion that the characterization of critical facts is constitutionally irrelevant. There, we held that it was impermissible for "the trial judge, sitting alone" to determine the presence or absence of the aggravating factors required by Arizona law for imposition of the death penalty. "If a State makes an increase in a defendant's authorized punishment contingent on the finding of a fact, that fact—no matter how the State labels it—must be found by a jury beyond a reasonable doubt." . . .

In *Blakely v. Washington* (2004), we dealt with a determinate sentencing scheme similar to the Federal Sentencing Guidelines. There the defendant pleaded guilty to kidnaping, a class B felony punishable by a term of not more than 10 years. Other provisions of Washington law, comparable to the Federal Sentencing Guidelines, mandated a "standard" sentence of 49-to-53 months, unless the judge found aggravating facts justifying an exceptional sentence. Although the prosecutor recommended a sentence in the standard range, the judge found that the defendant had acted with "deliberate cruelty" and sentenced him to 90 months.

For reasons explained in *Jones*, *Apprendi*, and *Ring*, the requirements of the Sixth Amendment were clear. The application of Washington's sentencing scheme violated the defendant's right to have the jury find the existence of "any particular fact" that the law makes essential to his punishment. That right is implicated whenever a judge seeks to impose a sentence that is not solely based on "facts reflected in the jury verdict or admitted by the defendant." . . . The determination that the defendant acted with deliberate cruelty, like the determination in *Apprendi* that the defendant acted with racial malice, increased the sentence that the defendant could have otherwise received. Since this fact was found by a judge using a preponderance of the evidence standard, the sentence violated Blakely's Sixth Amendment rights. . . .

If the Guidelines as currently written could be read as merely advisory provisions that recommended, rather than required, the selection of particular sentences in response to differing sets of facts, their use would not implicate the Sixth Amendment. We have never doubted the authority of a judge to exercise broad discretion in imposing a sentence within a statutory range. . . .

All of the foregoing support our conclusion that our holding in *Blakely* applies to the Sentencing Guidelines. We recognize, as we did in *Jones, Apprendi,* and *Blakely,* that in some cases jury factfinding may impair the most expedient and efficient sentencing of defendants. But the interest in fairness and reliability protected by the

right to a jury trial—a common-law right that defendants enjoyed for centuries and that is now enshrined in the Sixth Amendment—has always outweighed the interest in concluding trials swiftly. . . .

Accordingly, we reaffirm our holding in *Apprendi:* Any fact (other than a prior conviction) which is necessary to support a sentence exceeding the maximum authorized by the facts established by a plea of guilty or a jury verdict must be admitted by the defendant or proved to a jury beyond a reasonable doubt.

The constitutional right to due process guarantees a criminal defendant's right to receive certain materials from the government for trial purposes. In *Brady v. Maryland* (1963),[108] the Supreme Court ruled that, upon request, defendants are entitled to any **exculpatory evidence** (items that might lead to the defendant's exoneration) within the prosecutor's control or possession. The Court held that "the suppression by the prosecution of evidence favorable to an accused upon request violates due process where the evidence is material either to guilt or punishment, irrespective of the good faith or bad faith of the prosecution." Under the so-called ***Brady* rule,** "[t]he question is not whether the defendant would more likely than not have received a different verdict with the evidence, but whether in its absence he received a fair trial, understood as a trial resulting in a verdict worthy of confidence."[109] In addition, in *Giglio v. United States* (1972),[110] the Court ruled that, upon request, a defendant is also entitled to materials within the prosecutor's possession that may be used to impeach government witnesses. These materials might include the witness's criminal record or plea agreements or other deals between the witness and the prosecution.

exculpatory evidence
Materials or information that might lead to a defendant's exoneration.

***Brady* rule**
A legal standard adopted by the Court that requires the prosecution to provide exculpatory evidence within the possession of the government to the defendant.

The constitutional right to equal protection also provides certain safeguards to defendants. For example, this right prohibits **selective prosecution**—the process of selecting a person for criminal charge based on a prohibited criterion. While proving selective prosecution is a difficult task, requiring the defendant to meet a "heavy burden," such a burden is met where it is shown that the government initiated criminal proceedings "deliberately based upon an unjustifiable standard such as race, religion, or other arbitrary classification."[111]

selective prosecution
The process of selecting a person for criminal charge based on a prohibited criterion, such as race, sex, or ethnicity.

Equal protection guarantees have also been employed to ensure fair and impartial juries in criminal cases. In *Batson v. Kentucky* (1986),[112] the Supreme Court ruled that, under the Equal Protection Clause, prosecutors cannot exclude potential jurors from serving on a jury solely based on their race or based on "the assumption that black jurors as a group will be unable impartially to consider the State's case against a black defendant." Later, in *J.E.B. v. Alabama ex rel. T.B.* (1994),[113] the Court imposed the same restriction with regard to the exclusion of jurors based on sex. More recently, in *Snyder v. Louisiana* (2008), the Court conducted a *Batson* analysis of the prosecutor's exclusion of African American jurors in a death penalty case and found evidence that the prosecutor's exclusion of jurors was based on race.

Cyber Constitution
Batson v. Kentucky
(1986) http://supreme.justia.com/us/476/79/

13.9 CRUEL AND UNUSUAL PUNISHMENT

Perhaps no other provision within criminal procedure invites more debate over constitutional values than the Eighth Amendment ban on cruel and unusual punishment. The Cruel and Unusual Punishment Clause provides that government may not inflict cruel and unusual punishment upon individuals. But the undefined and rather subjective terms "cruel" and "unusual" have sparked controversy and led to fluxuation within the Court as to the practical meaning and effect of this provision.

Cyber Constitution
Snyder v. Louisiana
(2008) http://supreme.justia.com/us/552/06-10119/index.html

Genarlow Wilson holds his sister Jaiya as his mother Juanness Bennett looks after Wilson walked out of the Burruss Correctional Training Facility in Forsyth, Georgia, on Friday, October 26, 2007. The Georgia Supreme Court ordered Wilson's release after it ruled his ten-year sentence for consensual oral sex with his fifteen-year-old girlfriend constituted cruel and unusual punishment.
117/117/ZUMA Press/Newscom

The Supreme Court first incorporated the cruel and unusual punishment ban, thereby making it applicable to the states, in *Robinson v. California* (1962).[114] This is significant because the vast majority of punishments (criminal sentences)—including those in the form of the death penalty—occur at the state, not federal, level. As a result, the Court's incorporation of the cruel and unusual punishment provision in 1962 made it possible for a substantial amount of issues to be presented to the Court under the Eighth Amendment.

As interpreted by the Court, there are four primary dimensions to the cruel and unusual punishment provision. First, courts cannot impose punishments that are grossly disproportionate to the committed offense. This is regarded as the **proportionality doctrine.** As an example, in *Coker v. Georgia* (1977),[115] the Court ruled that a state cannot impose the death penalty for a rape conviction, if the crime does not involve the death of another. The Court has indicated that the proportionality of a punishment should be evaluated by looking at (1) the seriousness of the offense and the severity of the imposed punishment, (2) the types of sentences given to other defendants for the

proportionality doctrine
A legal doctrine under the Cruel and Unusual Punishment Clause that requires criminal punishment to be proportional to the crime committed.

same offense in the same jurisdiction, and (3) the types of sentences given in similar cases in other jurisdictions. Currently, some so-called **three-strikes-and-you're-out laws**—statutes that impose life sentences for repeat (usually third) offenses, regardless of the seriousness of the offense—which have been passed in some jurisdictions, are being challenged under this dimension of the Eighth Amendment.

Second, the Eighth Amendment bars government from imposing punishment for **status crimes** or personal characteristic offenses—attempts to punish individuals based on their reputation or propensity for certain behavior. For example, in *Powell v. Texas* (1968),[116] the Court struck down a state law making it a crime to be a "common drunkard." Under the Court's ruling, government can punish a person for being under the influence of alcohol in public or while driving, but it cannot punish someone based solely on their reputation for such activity.

The third dimension involves the **death penalty** or **capital punishment.** Since 1976, the Court has ruled that the death penalty does not inherently violate the Eighth Amendment. The Court initially struck down the death penalty in *Furman v. Georgia* (1972)[117] because some states allowed triers of fact (usually juries) to impose death as a punishment without giving them sufficient standards or guidance when making their decisions. But after the Court's 1972 ruling, many states revised their death penalty laws consistent with the *Furman* ruling and the Court upheld these new forms in *Gregg v. Georgia* (1976).[118] In *Gregg*, the Court ruled that the death penalty is constitutionally permitted if implemented under a statutory scheme that provides the trier of fact with reasonable discretion, sufficient information about the defendant, and legal standards for rendering the decision.

Since *Gregg*, the Court has ruled that the death penalty can be applied to adults who are convicted of directly committing murder. In recent years, however, the Court has begun to limit the application of capital punishment in some cases. In *Atkins v. Virginia* (2002),[119] the Court held that the death penalty could not be imposed on individuals with mental retardation. This ruling reversed a 1989 decision that had allowed such executions to occur. And in *Roper v. Simmons* (2005),[120] the Court ruled that the Eighth Amendment bars the execution of juveniles (persons who were under eighteen years of age at the time of their offense). This ruling reversed another 1989 opinion, which had allowed persons sixteen years of age and older to be executed. Both of these recent rulings acknowledged that the constitutional standards of what is "cruel and unusual" are not fixed or finite but can change over time. In *Atkins*, the Court asserted, "[a] claim that punishment is excessive is judged not by the standards that prevailed in 1685 when Lord Jeffreys presided over the 'Bloody Assizes' or when the Bill of Rights was adopted, but rather by those that currently prevail." And in both *Atkins* and *Roper*, a majority of the Court recognized that public and legislative values regarding the execution of mentally retarded and underage persons had changed since 1989, thereby warranting a change in the constitutional standard of what is cruel and unusual. Note too that in both cases, some justices also considered international or "world community" standards regarding the death penalty as a part of their opinion.

More recently, in *Kennedy v. Louisiana* (2008), the Court, in a 5-4 ruling, held that states cannot impose capital punishment for the crime of child rape, when the sexual offense does not involve homicide. Read the excerpt from the majority opinion (later in this chapter), and assess whether there are any non-homicide criminal offenses that should be eligible for the death penalty.

And finally, the Court, at times, has applied the Eighth Amendment to redress unreasonable prison and other confinement conditions that inmates have faced after being sentenced. The Court, however, appears divided on whether the Eighth Amendment should apply to treatment imposed outside of criminal sentencing. In *Wilson v. Seiter* (1991),[121] the Court denied the claim of a prison inmate subjected to rat-infested and overcrowded conditions in an Ohio prison. The Court ruled that, in cases where prison inmates are using the general conditions of their surroundings to assert their

three-strikes-and-you're-out laws
Statutes in some states that impose life sentences for repeat (usually third) offenses, regardless of the seriousness of the offense.

status crimes
Also known as personal characteristic offenses, these are attempts to punish individuals based on their reputation or propensity for certain behavior and are generally prohibited as cruel and unusual punishment.

death penalty or capital punishment
The imposition of death as criminal punishment. Since 1976, the Court has ruled that the death penalty does not inherently violate the Eighth Amendment.

Eighth Amendment claim, they must demonstrate that prison officials engaged in "deliberate indifference" in responding to unreasonably harsh conditions. But in *Hudson v. McMillian* (1992),[122] the Court found that a prison inmate's Eighth Amendment right was violated when a prison guard used excessive force against him. The Court indicated that in "excessive force" cases, the Eighth Amendment will apply if prison officials "maliciously and sadistically used force to cause harm." Interestingly, in both of these cases, Justice Thomas asserted that the Eighth Amendment should be limited to punishment imposed as a part of a court's sentencing and should not be applied to conditions that arise in prisons after sentencing.

bail
The collateral imposed by a court as a condition for pretrial release of the defendant.

The Eighth Amendment contains two other provisions—the excessive bail provision, which provides that the amount of **bail** cannot be excessive, and the excessive fines provision, which provides that **fines** cannot be excessive. But the Supreme Court has yet to formally apply these provisions to the states through the Fourteenth Amendment Due Process Clause. However, the imposition of unreasonable punishments through fines, particularly when the defendant is indigent, may run afoul of other constitutional standards, including equal protection.[123]

fines
A postconviction punishment in the form of monetary payment.

Kennedy v. Louisiana
554 U.S. 407 (2008)

Justice Kennedy delivered the opinion of the Court.

The National Government and, beyond it, the separate States are bound by the proscriptive mandates of the Eighth Amendment to the Constitution of the United States, and all persons within those respective jurisdictions may invoke its protection. Patrick Kennedy, the petitioner here, seeks to set aside his death sentence under the Eighth Amendment. He was charged by the respondent, the State of Louisiana, with the aggravated rape of his then-8-year-old stepdaughter. After a jury trial petitioner was convicted and sentenced to death under a state statute authorizing capital punishment for the rape of a child under 12 years of age. This case presents the question whether the Constitution bars respondent from imposing the death penalty for the rape of a child where the crime did not result, and was not intended to result, in death of the victim. We hold the Eighth Amendment prohibits the death penalty for this offense. The Louisiana statute is unconstitutional. . . .

The Eighth Amendment, applicable to the States through the Fourteenth Amendment, provides that "[e]xcessive bail shall not be required, nor excessive fines imposed, nor cruel and unusual punishments inflicted." The Amendment proscribes "all excessive punishments, as well as cruel and unusual punishments that may or may not be excessive." The Court explained . . . that the Eighth Amendment's protection against excessive or cruel and unusual punishments flows from the basic "precept of justice that punishment for [a] crime should be graduated and proportioned to [the] offense." Whether this requirement has been fulfilled is determined not by the standards that prevailed when the Eighth Amendment was adopted in 1791 but by the norms that "currently prevail." The Amendment "draw[s] its meaning from the evolving standards of decency that mark the progress of a maturing society." This is because "[t]he standard of extreme cruelty is not merely descriptive, but necessarily embodies a moral judgment. The standard itself remains the same, but its applicability must change as the basic mores of society change."

Evolving standards of decency must embrace and express respect for the dignity of the person, and the punishment of criminals must conform to that rule. As we shall discuss, punishment is justified under one or more of three principal rationales: rehabilitation, deterrence, and retribution. It is the last of these, retribution, that most often can contradict the law's own ends. This is of particular concern when the Court interprets the meaning of the Eighth Amendment in capital cases. When the law punishes by death, it risks its own sudden descent into brutality, transgressing the constitutional commitment to decency and restraint.

For these reasons we have explained that capital punishment must "be limited to those offenders who commit 'a narrow category of the most serious crimes' and whose extreme culpability makes them 'the most deserving of execution.'" Though the death penalty is not invariably unconstitutional, the Court insists upon confining the instances in which the punishment can be imposed.

Applying this principle, we held . . . that the execution of juveniles and mentally retarded persons are punishments violative of the Eighth Amendment because the offender had a diminished personal responsibility for the crime. The Court further has held that the death penalty can be disproportionate to the crime itself where the crime did not result, or was not intended to result, in death of the victim. . . .

In these cases the Court has been guided by "objective indicia of society's standards, as expressed in legislative enactments and state practice with respect to executions." The inquiry does not end there, however. Consensus is not dispositive. Whether the death penalty is disproportionate to the crime committed depends as well upon the standards elaborated by controlling precedents and by the Court's own understanding and interpretation of the Eighth Amendment's text, history, meaning, and purpose.

Based both on consensus and our own independent judgment, our holding is that a death sentence for one who raped but did not kill a child, and who did not intend to assist another in killing the child, is unconstitutional under the Eighth and Fourteenth Amendments. . . .

Louisiana is the only State since 1964 that has sentenced an individual to death for the crime of child rape; and petitioner and Richard Davis, who was convicted and sentenced to death for the aggravated rape of a 5-year-old child by a Louisiana jury in December 2007, are the only two individuals now on death row in the United States for a nonhomicide offense.

After reviewing the authorities informed by contemporary norms, including the history of the death penalty for this and other nonhomicide crimes, current state statutes and new enactments, and the number of executions since 1964, we conclude there is a national consensus against capital punishment for the crime of child rape. . . .

The judgment of the Supreme Court of Louisiana upholding the capital sentence is reversed. This case is remanded for further proceedings not inconsistent with this opinion.

It is so ordered.

13.10 MODERN CHALLENGES

Applying civil liberties in the criminal setting is one of the most challenging aspects of constitutional law. Criminal arrests, searches and seizures, trials, and other procedures all occur in highly dynamic settings of human interaction, often with enormous consequences for individuals at stake. As a result, criminal cases can invite a substantial level of emotions and values to the interpretation of constitutional provisions.

In the past few decades, legislators at all levels have sought to regulate human behavior through criminal sanctions—either by writing new criminal laws to punish previously lawful behavior or by enhancing the punishment for existing criminal acts. Either way, the reality is that a large portion of human behavior in American society is controlled by criminal law. The question for future legislators, law enforcement officers, and judges is how much longer this type of governmental monitoring can continue without the nation (or portions thereof) becoming a type of police state. In many cases, this question will be answered by determining the extent to which our constitutional liberties limit the scope and substance of governmental action in the criminal setting.

13.11 SUMMARY

The rights of the criminally accused are primarily contained in the Fourth, Fifth, Sixth, and Eighth Amendments, with more general protections afforded in the Due Process and Equal Protection Clauses of the Fourteenth Amendment. The Supreme Court generally has refused to apply these provisions literally, but instead has developed a series of tests, doctrines, and exceptions to effectuate these constitutional protections. Many of these standards have changed over time based on the makeup of the Court and its members' constitutional values.

The Fourth Amendment protects individuals from unreasonable searches and seizures. This includes the right not to be arrested without probable cause, which is an evidentiary standard that requires police to possess trustworthy facts that would cause a reasonable person to believe that the arrestee has committed a crime. The government can perform other investigative detentions that fall short of full-blown arrests if they are brief in duration and based on reasonable suspicion, a lower evidentiary standard than probable cause. During these brief stops, police can frisk an individual to ensure the officer's safety.

The Fourth Amendment also prohibits government from conducting unreasonable searches and seizures of those places and things in which individuals have a reasonable expectation of privacy. The Court has stated that generally a search warrant is necessary for a search. A valid warrant must be issued by a neutral and detached judicial authority and be based on probable cause. A warrant must also be executed in a proper manner, without unreasonable delay, and within the scope of the permission granted in the warrant. If the police obtain a warrant, which is later determined to be invalid, the search conducted pursuant to the warrant may still be constitutional if the police can demonstrate that they relied in good faith on the warrant when conducting the search.

In cases where the police fail to obtain a warrant prior to an evidentiary search, the Court has carved out several exceptions that may authorize the search. These include searches incident to a lawful arrest, searches of items in plain view, consent searches, stop-and-frisk searches, searches conducted in some exigent circumstances—such as hot pursuit—and some automobile searches.

The Fifth Amendment precludes police from forcing people to incriminate themselves. The right against self-incrimination occurs when police engage in custodial interrogation. Before police begin custodial interrogations, they must provide *Miranda* warnings to the suspects, informing them of the right to remain silent and the right to an attorney, unless there is an imminent need to protect public safety. At a minimum, a suspect's statements must be voluntary in order to be admissible at trial. In addition, if a suspect asks for an attorney, all questioning must stop unless and until an attorney is provided. If the suspect asserts the right to remain silent, police must scrupulously honor the request for a significant period of time before trying to question the suspect again.

To guard against governmental violations of the Fourth and Fifth Amendments, the Supreme Court created the exclusionary rule, which generally prohibits evidence illegally obtained by the police from being used against the defendant at trial. Under the fruit of the poisonous tree doctrine, all other evidence obtained as a result of the initial illegality must be excluded from evidence as well. Exceptions to the exclusionary rule include the independence source, intervening circumstances, inevitable discovery, and good faith doctrines.

The Sixth Amendment protects the right to counsel after criminal charges are filed. This right exists at all critical stages of the prosecution, including arraignment, guilty pleas, trials, and sentencing. A person can assert the right to counsel only in cases where incarceration is actually imposed. The right to counsel includes the right to the effective assistance of counsel. To prove a case of ineffective assistance, defendants must show that their attorney was deficient and that, but for the deficiency, the result of the proceeding would have been different.

The right against double jeopardy generally precludes the government from placing a person in criminal jeopardy more than once. This right applies to cases where the same sovereign seeks to prosecute a person for a second time after a final judgment on the merits of the case is issued.

The right to a fair trial encompasses the Sixth Amendment right to a public, speedy, and jury trial, as well as more general rights of due process and equal protection. In most cases, the right to a public trial is absolute except where trial publicity may infringe upon the right to a fair trial. The right to a speedy trial is determined based on the totality of the circumstances, requiring the court to consider the length of and reason for the delay and the resulting prejudice to the defendant. The right to a jury trial exists in trials involving all serious offenses, which typically means offenses for which a person faces more than six months of incarceration. In most states, each of these rights is supplemented with state constitutional or statutory protections. Due process protections ensure that prosecutors treat defendants fairly during trial by giving them sufficient notice and providing them with exculpatory evidence and materials, where available, to impeach the government's witnesses. The right to equal protection guards against selective prosecution and prohibits the prosecutor's use of race or sex to exclude potential members from the jury.

Finally, under the Eighth Amendment, the government is barred from engaging in cruel and unusual punishment. This includes a prohibition on imposing punishment that is disproportionate to the offense and punishing a person based on his or her status or reputation in society. The Court has not barred the death penalty or capital punishment under the Eighth Amendment in all cases. But in recent years, the Court has prohibited the death penalty in cases involving juvenile and mentally retarded defendants. In addition, the Eighth Amendment may also apply to prohibit harsh prison conditions that are malicious in nature or to which prison officials are "deliberately indifferent."

REVIEW QUESTIONS

1. What basic protections of criminal procedure do the Fourth, Fifth, Sixth, and Eighth Amendments provide?
2. What must the police do to conduct a constitutionally valid arrest?
3. What is the difference between probable cause and reasonable suspicion, and under what circumstances do these standards apply?
4. What are the requirements for a valid warrant?
5. Under what circumstances may police conduct a search and seizure without a valid warrant?
6. What is a stop and frisk, or *Terry*, search?
7. When are police required to provide suspects with *Miranda* warnings? What is the purpose of these warnings and what do they include?
8. Under what circumstances may police obtain confessions without providing *Miranda* warnings?
9. During what stages of the criminal process does a person have a Sixth Amendment right to counsel?
10. What factors are used to assess whether a person received the effective assistance of counsel?
11. What is the exclusionary rule, and how does it relate to the fruit of the poisonous tree doctrine?
12. Describe the exceptions to the exclusionary rule as developed by the Supreme Court.
13. Under what circumstances does the Fifth Amendment right against double jeopardy bar the government from trying or punishing a person a second time?
14. What constitutional protections are designed to ensure a person a fair trial?
15. What governmental practices have been prohibited or limited under the Eighth Amendment ban on cruel and unusual punishment?

ASSIGNMENTS: CONSTITUTIONAL LAW IN ACTION

The Constitution in Your Community

Assume that you are working for a public defender's officer and that one of the attorneys in the office has been assigned to represent Tiffany Jones in *State v. Jones*, Case No. 2011-0655. The prosecutor in your local jurisdiction has charged Ms. Jones with two criminal offenses—contributing to the delinquency of a minor and supplying a minor with alcohol.

Tiffany, who is twenty-five years old, was staying at her parents' house, while they were away on vacation. She was watching the home along with her sister, Sheila Jones, who is seventeen and still in high school. After working an eight-hour shift at her job, Tiffany arrived at her parents' home, entered the front door, and went upstairs to change out of her work clothes. When she arrived at the house, Tiffany heard loud music coming from the backyard and assumed that her sister might have some friends over. While Tiffany was upstairs changing, a police officer walked into the bedroom and began questioning her about the people in the backyard and the presence of beer. Although, Tiffany explained that she just got home, the officer arrested her and initiated the two criminal charges outlined above.

According to the officer's report, police received a phone call from one of the neighbors complaining about loud music coming from the Jones home. When police arrived at the house, they heard the loud music and noticed several young-looking individuals in the backyard. One officer went immediately to the backyard and began asking for identification from the individuals. The other officer went to the front door, opened it, and went upstairs, where he found Tiffany, who was the only adult on the premises.

Tiffany's attorney would like to file a motion to suppress the police findings within the home, particularly the discovery of Tiffany in the bedroom. The attorney's position is that the officer's entrance into the home was unconstitutional under the Fourth Amendment, and but for this illegal entry, the officer would not have found Tiffany.

Based on the materials in this chapter, particularly those addressing the exclusionary rule, prepare a legal memorandum for the attorney wherein you outline the legal issues for a motion to suppress. Specifically, address whether the officer's search of the Jones home was constitutional and whether the officer's observations made within the home should be excluded from evidence during trial.

Going Federal

Assume you are working in a U.S. Attorney's office in the criminal division. You are working with an Assistant United States Attorney (AUSA) who is assigned to the grand jury room. As a part of your job, you help to coordinate witnesses and exhibits to be presented before grand juries. In one case, the grand jury has subpoenaed Luke Atmee to testify. Mr. Atmee is a witness to a purported federal bank robbery offense, but he fears that he may also be a suspect in the case. As a result, he does not wish to offer any incriminating statements to the grand jury in violation of his Fifth Amendment rights.

During Mr. Atmee's testimony before the grand jury, he has asserted a Fifth Amendment right not to respond to several questions posed by the prosecutor. Specifically, Mr. Atmee has refused to answer the following questions, based on his claim that his responses might tend to incriminate him:

> *What is your name?*
>
> *Do your friends call you by any other name?*
>
> *How tall are you?*
>
> *How much do you weigh?*
>
> *How old are you?*
>
> *Please state the following in a normal tone of voice: "Give me cash; I have a gun."*
>
> *Print the following in your normal handwriting: "Put the money in this bag; I have a gun."*
>
> *Do you know the person in this photo?*
>
> *Where were you on October 22, 2011?*

After refusing to answer these questions, the AUSA working with the grand jury wants to seek an order from the magistrate judge assigned to the grand jury compelling Mr. Atmee to answer the questions listed above. But before doing this, the AUSA wants to make sure that he is entitled to gain answers to each of these questions. Accordingly, you are asked to review each question to determine whether Mr. Atmee has a

Fifth Amendment right not to answer the individual questions. Prepare a memorandum for the AUSA wherein you outline whether Mr. Atmee has a testimonial privilege to remain silent in the face of these questions or whether the district court can compel him to respond.

Moot Court

Locate your state's constitutional and statutory provisions regarding the death penalty. Identify the efforts that have been made to implement, reinstate, or remove capital punishment in your state. Work in teams of two. The first team should prepare and present a five-minute oral argument, based on constitutional standards regarding cruel and unusual punishment, challenging your state's approach to the death penalty. Conversely, the second team should prepare a five-minute oral argument asserting why your state's approach to the death penalty complies with constitutional standards.

NOTES

1. *People v. Defore*, 242 N.Y. 13, 21, 150 N.E. 585, 587 (1926).
2. *United States v. Leon*, 468 U.S. 902 (1984).
3. See *Wolf v. Colorado*, 338 U.S. 25 (1949), and *Carroll v. United States*, 267 U.S. 132 (1925).
4. See *Hurtado v. California*, 110 U.S. 516 (1884) (discussing the grand jury provision but refusing to apply it to state prosecutions).
5. See *Benton v. Maryland*, 395 U.S. 784 (1969).
6. See *Malloy v. Hogan*, 378 U.S. 1 (1964).
7. See *Ward v. City of Monroeville*, 409 U.S. 57 (1972) (barring mayor from presiding over trial because of city's financial interest in imposing fines); *Batson v. Kentucky*, 476 U.S. 79 (1989) (precluding prosecutor's use of race to exclude jurors during voir dire).
8. See *Klopfer v. North Carolina*, 386 U.S. 213 (1967).
9. See *In re Oliver*, 333 U.S. 257 (1948).
10. See *Duncan v. Louisiana*, 391 U.S. 145 (1968).
11. See *Pointer v. Texas*, 380 U.S. 400 (1965).
12. See *Washington v. Texas*, 388 U.S. 14 (1967).
13. See *Gideon v. Wainwright*, 372 U.S. 335 (1963) (applicable to felony cases); *Argersinger v. Hamlin*, 407 U.S. 25 (1972) (applicable to misdemeanor cases if sentence includes imprisonment).
14. See *Robinson v. California*, 370 U.S. 660 (1962).
15. See *Hurtado v. California*, 110 U.S. 516 (1884).
16. See *Florida v. Bostick*, 501 U.S. 429 (1991) (finding that officials boarding a transport bus and asking passengers for identification and request to search luggage did not result in a seizure under the Fourth Amendment).
17. 499 U.S. 621 (1991).
18. 551 U.S. 249 (2007).
19. See *Payton v. New York*, 445 U.S. 573 (1980).
20. 532 U.S. 318 (2001).
21. See *Beck v. Ohio*, 379 U.S. 89 (1964).
22. *Maryland v. Pringle*, 540 U.S. 366, 371 (2003) (citations omitted).
23. See *Tennessee v. Garner*, 471 U.S. 1 (1985).
24. *Scott v. Harris*, 550 U.S. 372 (2007).
25. 392 U.S. 1 (1968).
26. See *United States v. Sokolow*, 490 U.S. 1 (1989) (finding that defendant's activity at an airport, which included traveling under a different name than that which matched his phone number, paying for a ticket with small bills, and appearing nervous, gave rise to reasonable suspicion of illegal activity).
27. 529 U.S. 266 (2000).
28. See Ala. Code §15—5—30 (West 2003); Ark. Code Ann. §5—71—213(a)(1) (2004); Colo. Rev. Stat. §16—3—103(1) (2003); Del. Code Ann., Tit. 11, §§1902(a), 1321(6) (2003); Fla. Stat. §856.021(2) (2003); Ga. Code Ann. §16—11—36(b) (2003); Ill. Comp. Stat., ch. 725, §5/107—14 (2004); Kan. Stat. Ann. §22—2402(1) (2003); La. Code Crim. Proc. Ann., Art. 215.1(A) (West 2004); Mo. Rev. Stat. §84.710(2) (2003); Mont. Code Ann. §46—5—401(2)

(a) (2003); Neb. Rev. Stat. §29—829 (2003); N. H. Rev. Stat. Ann. §§594:2 and 644:6 (Lexis 2003); N. M. Stat. Ann. §30—22—3 (2004); N. Y. Crim. Proc. Law §140.50(1) (West 2004); N. D. Cent. Code §29—29—21 (2003); R. I. Gen. Laws §12—7—1 (2003); Utah Code Ann. §77—7—15 (2003); Vt. Stat. Ann., Tit. 24, §1983 (Supp. 2003); Wis. Stat. §968.24 (2003).

29. 461 U.S. 352 (1983).
30. 542 U.S. 177 (2004).
31. See *Delaware v. Prouse*, 440 U.S. 468 (1979).
32. 517 U.S. 806 (1996).
33. 496 U.S. 444 (1990).
34. See *Martinez v. Fuerte*, 428 U.S. 543 (1976).
35. See *United States v. Villamonte-Marquez*, 462 U.S. 579 (1983).
36. See *Rakas v. Illinois*, 439 U.S. 128 (1978).
37. 532 U.S. 67 (2001).
38. See *United States v. Jacobsen*, 466 U.S. 109 (1984) (finding insufficient governmental conduct in search of package opened by a private freight operator).
39. 389 U.S. 347 (1967).
40. *California v. Ciraolo*, 476 U.S. 207 (1986).
41. 533 U.S. 27 (2001).
42. See *United States v. Mara*, 410 U.S. 19 (1973) (handwriting); *United States v. Place*, 462 U.S. 696 (1983) (luggage sniffed by drug dogs); *California v. Greenwood*, 486 U.S. 35 (1988) (curbside garbage); *California v. Ciraolo*, 476 U.S. 207 (1986) (police flying over a person's home).
43. See *Florida v. Riley*, 488 U.S. 445 (1989) (flyover); *United States v. Dunn*, 480 U.S. 294 (1987) (search of barn); *California v. Greenwood*, 486 U.S. 35 (1988).
44. See *Dow Chemical Co. v. United States*, 476 U.S. 227 (1986).
45. See *Coolidge v. New Hampshire*, 403 U.S. 443 (1971) (state attorney general not neutral); *Lo-Ji Sales, Inc. v. New York*, 442 U.S. 319 (1979) (magistrate participating in execution of warrant); *Connally v. Georgia*, 429 U.S. 245 (1977) (magistrate got paid for issuing warrant).
46. 438 U.S. 154 (1978).
47. 126 S.Ct. 1836 (2006).
48. 468 U.S. 897 (1984).
49. See *Dow Chemical Co. v. United States*, 476 U.S. 227 (1986).
50. See *Chimel v. California*, 395 U.S. 752 (1969) (wingspan rule allowing police to inspect areas where suspect might obtain weapons or other items); *Maryland v. Buie*, 494 U.S. 325 (1990) (allowing protective sweeps of premises); *New York v. Belton*, 453 U.S. 454 (1981) (permitting search of passenger seat area upon arresting driver).
51. See *Illinois v. Lafayette*, 459 U.S. 986 (1983) (search pursuant to incarceration); *Colorado v. Bertine*, 479 U.S. 367 (1987) (allowing inspection of contents of impounded vehicle).
52. 395 U.S. 752 (1969).
53. See *Bumper v. North Carolina*, 391 U.S. 543 (1968) (officers cannot induce consent by falsely claiming they have a search warrant).
54. See *Illinois v. Rodriguez*, 497 U.S. 177 (1990) (apparent authority is sufficient), but see *Georgia v. Randolph*, 547 U.S. 103, 126 S.Ct. 1515 (2006).
55. 547 U.S. 103 (2006).
56. See *Arizona v. Hicks*, 480 U.S. 321 (1987).
57. 480 U.S. 321 (1987).
58. See *Terry v. Ohio*, 392 U.S. 1 (1968).
59. See *Minnesota v. Dickerson*, 508 U.S. 366 (1993).
60. See *Minnesota v. Olson*, 495 U.S. 91 (1990).
61. 414 U.S. 291 (1973).
62. See *United States v. Santana*, 427 U.S. 38 (1976) (pursuit of suspect into private home); *Schmerber v. California*, 384 U.S. 757 (1966) (warrantless seizure of blood sample suspect to contain alcohol); *North American Cold Storage v. City of Chicago*, 211 U.S. 306 (1908) (emergency search of contaminated food); *Michigan v. Tyler*, 436 U.S. 499 (1978) (search conducted during burning fire).
63. See *Mincey v. Arizona*, 437 U.S. 385 (1978) (search of a murder scene).
64. See *Carroll v. United States*, 267 U.S. 132 (1925) (addressing theory behind exception); *California v. Acevedo*, 500 U.S. 565 (1991) (searches of containers within vehicles).
65. See *United States v. Martinez-Fuerte*, 428 U.S. 543 (1976) (border checkpoints); *Colonnade Catering Corp. v. United States*, 397 U.S. 72 (1970) (liquor-related business); *United States v. Biswell*, 406 U.S. 311 (1972) (gun-related business).

66. See *Skinner v. Railway Labor Executive's Assoc.*, 489 U.S. 602 (1989); *National Treasury Employees Union v. Von Raab*, 489 U.S. 656 (1989) (both involving employee drug testing).
67. See *Hudson v. Palmer*, 468 U.S. 517 (1984).
68. 469 U.S. 325 (1985).
69. See *Brown v. Mississippi*, 297 U.S. 278 (1936) (police beat defendant to get confession).
70. See *Gilbert v. California*, 388 U.S. 263 (1967) (handwriting and voice samples); *Schmerber v. California*, 384 U.S. 757 (1966) (blood samples); *Greer v. Miller*, 483 U.S. 756 (1987) (cannot comment on suspect's silence after arrest and *Miranda* warnings); *Griffin v. California*, 380 U.S. 609 (1965) (cannot comment on silence during trial).
71. See *Orozco v. Texas*, 394 U.S. 324 (1969) (suspect questioned in his bedroom).
72. *Nix v. Williams*, 467 U.S. 431 (1984).
73. See *Rhode Island v. Innis*, 446 U.S. 291 (1980) (police comments about threat posed by missing gun not an interrogation).
74. 384 U.S. 436 (1966).
75. See *Colorado v. Spring*, 479 U.S. 564 (1987) (discussing waiver requirements).
76. See *Michigan v. Mosely*, 423 U.S. 96 (1975) (addressing assertion of right to remain silent); *Edwards v. Arizona*, 451 U.S. 477 (1981) (right to counsel).
77. See *New York v. Quarles* 467 U.S. 649 (1984).
78. See *United States v. Wong*, 431 U.S. 174 (1977) (grand jury); *Mincey v. Arizona*, 437 U.S. 385 (1978) (impeachment); *Greer v. Miller*, 483 U.S. 756 (1987) (harmless error).
79. 232 U.S. 383 (1914).
80. See *Wong Sun v. United States*, 371 U.S. 471 (1963).
81. See *Segura v. United States*, 468 U.S. 796 (1984).
82. See *Brown v. Illinois*, 422 U.S. 590 (1975).
83. See *Nix v. Williams*, 467 U.S. 431 (1984).
84. See *United States v. Leon*, 468 U.S. 897 (1984) (invalid search warrant); *Michigan v. DeFillippo*, 443 U.S. 41 (1979) (facially valid statute).
85. See *United States v. Calandra*, 414 U.S. 338 (1974) (grand jury); *United States v. Janis*, 428 U.S. 433 (1976) (civil proceedings); *Harris v. New York*, 401 U.S. 222 (1971) (impeachment).
86. See Federal Civil Rights Law, 42 U.S.C. § 1983; *Bivens v. Six Unknown Named Agents of the Federal Bureau of Narcotics*, 403 U.S. 388 (1971) (providing monetary relief for a Fourth Amendment violation).
87. *Mempa v. Rhay*, 389 U.S. 128, 134 (1967).
88. 372 U.S. 335 (1963).
89. See *Gideon v. Wainwright*, 372 U.S. 335 (1963) (felonies); *Hamilton v. Alabama*, 368 U.S. 52 (1961) (arraignments); *Moore v. Illinois*, 434 U.S. 220 (1977) (postcharge lineups); *Massiah v. United States*, 377 U.S. 201 (1964) (postcharge interrogations); *Douglas v. California*, 372 U.S. 353 (1963) (appeals as a matter of right).
90. See *Gilbert v. California*, 388 U.S. 263 (1967) (handwriting and voice exemplars); *United States v. Ash*, 413 U.S. 300 (1973) (photo identifications); *Ross v. Moffitt*, 417 U.S. 600 (1974) (discretionary appeals); *Gagnon v. Scarpelli*, 411 U.S. 778 (1973) (parole hearings); *Pennsylvania v. Finely*, 481 U.S. 55 (1987) (habeas proceedings).
91. 466 U.S. 668 (1984).
92. 506 U.S. 364 (1993).
93. 518 U.S. 267 (1996).
94. See *Crist v. Bretz*, 437 U.S. 28 (1978) (jury trials); *Breed v. Jones*, 421 U.S. 519 (1975) (juvenile proceedings).
95. See *Harris v. Oklahoma*, 433 U.S. 682 (1977) (less included offenses); *Brown v. Ohio*, 432 U.S. 161 (1977) (high-level offenses); *Diaz v. United States*, 223 U.S. 442 (1912) (exception to rule in homicide cases).
96. See *Heath v. Alabama*, 474 U.S. 82 (1986) (separate sovereigns); *Illinois v. Somerville*, 410 U.S. 458 (1973) (manifest necessity); *Burks v. United States*, 437 U.S. 1 (1978) (retrial after appeal).
97. The name of this test comes from the Court's opinion in *Blockburger v. United States*, 284 U.S. 299 (1932); see also *Missouri v. Hunter*, 459 U.S. 359 (1983) (successive punishments for the same crime).
98. See *Press-Enterprise Co. v. Superior Court*, 478 U.S. 1 (1986) (competing interest of the press in public trials).
99. 505 U.S. 647 (1992).
100. See *Barker v. Wingo*, 407 U.S. 514 (1972); *Doggett v. United States*, 505 U.S. 647 (1992).
101. See *Blanton v. City of North Las Vegas*, 489 U.S. 538 (1989).

102. *Apprendi v. New Jersey*, 530 U.S. 466 (2000).
103. *Ring v. Arizona*, 536 U.S. 584 (2002).
104. *Blakely v. Washington*, 542 U.S. 296 (2004).
105. *United States v. Booker*, 543 U.S. 220 (2005).
106. *United States v. Fanfan*, 543 U.S. 220 (2005).
107. Tony Mauro, "Supreme Court: Sentencing Guidelines Advisory, Not Mandatory," Law.com, January 1, 2005 (accessed July 4, 2009).
108. 373 U.S. 83 (1963).
109. *Kyles v. Whitley*, 514 U.S. 419, 434 (1995).
110. 405 U.S. 150 (1972).
111. *Bordenkircher v. Hayes*, 434 U.S. 357, 364 (1978).
112. 476 U.S. 79 (1986).
113. 511 U.S. 127 (1994).
114. 370 U.S. 660 (1962).
115. 433 U.S. 584 (1977).
116. 392 U.S. 514 (1968).
117. 408 U.S. 238 (1972).
118. 428 U.S. 153 (1976).
119. 536 U.S. 304 (2002).
120. 543 U.S. 551 (2005).
121. 501 U.S. 294 (1992).
122. 503 U.S. 1 (1992).
123. See *Williams v. Illinois*, 399 U.S. 235 (1970) (nonpayment of fine); *Tate v. Short*, 401 U.S. 395 (1971) (restrictive fines).

APPENDIX A

Constitution of the United States of America

We the People of the United States, in Order to form a more perfect Union, establish Justice, insure domestic Tranquility, provide for the common defense, promote the general Welfare, and secure the Blessings of Liberty to ourselves and our Posterity, do ordain and establish this Constitution of for the United States of America.

ARTICLE I

Section 1

All legislative Powers herein granted shall be vested in a Congress of the Unites States, which shall consist of a Senate and House of Representatives.

Section 2

The House of Representatives shall be composed of Members chosen every second Year by the People of the several States, and the Electors in each State shall have the Qualifications requisite for Electors of the most numerous Branch of the State Legislature.

No Person shall be a Representative who shall not have attained to the Age of twenty five Years, and been seven Years a Citizen of the United States, and who shall not, when elected, be an Inhabitant of that State in which he shall be chosen.

Representatives and direct Taxes shall be apportioned among the several States which may be included within this Union, according to their respective Numbers, which shall be determined by adding to the whole number of free Persons, including those bound to Service for a Term of Years, and excluding Indians not taxed, three fifths of all other Persons. The actual Enumeration shall be made within three Years after the first Meeting of the Congress of the United States, and within every subsequent Term of ten Years, in such Manner as they shall by Law direct. The Number of Representatives shall not exceed one for every thirty Thousand, but each State shall have at Least one Representative; and until such enumeration shall be made, the State of New Hampshire shall be entitled to chuse three, Massachusetts eight, Rhode-Island and Providence Plantations one, Connecticut five, New-York six, New Jersey four, Pennsylvania eight, Delaware one, Maryland six, Virginia ten, North Carolina five, South Carolina five, and Georgia three.

When vacancies happen in the Representation from any State, the Executive Authority thereof shall issue Writs of Election to fill such Vacancies.

The House of Representative shall chuse their Speaker and other Officers: and shall have the sole Power of Impeachment.

Section 3

The Senate of the United States shall be composed of two Senators from each State, *chosen by the Legislature thereof* for six Years; and each Senator shall have one Vote.

Immediately after they shall be assembled in Consequence of the first Election, they shall be divided as equally as may be into three Classes. The Seats of the Senators of the first Class shall be vacated at the Expiration of the second Year, of the second Class at the Expiration of the Fourth Year, and of the third Class at the Expiration of the sixth Year, so that one third may be chosen every second Year: *and if Vacancies happen by Resignation, or otherwise, during the Recess of the Legislature of any State, the Executive thereof may make temporary Appointments until the next Meeting of the Legislature, which shall then fill such Vacancies.*

No Person shall be a Senator who shall not have attained to the Age of thirty Years, and been nine Years a Citizen of the United States, and who shall not, when elected, be an Inhabitant of that State for which he shall be chosen.

The Vice President of the United Sates shall be President of the Senate, but shall have no Vote, unless they be equally divided.

The Senate shall chuse their other Officers, and also a President pro-tempore, in the Absence of the Vice President, or when he shall exercise the Office of President of the United States.

The Senate shall have the sole Power to try all Impeachments. When sitting for that Purpose, they shall be on Oath or Affirmation. When the President of the United States is tried, the Chief Justice shall preside: And no Person shall be convicted without the Concurrence of two thirds of the Members present.

Judgment in cases of Impeachment shall not extend further than to removal from Office, and disqualification to hold and enjoy any Office of honor, Trust or Profit under the United States: but the Party convicted shall nevertheless be liable and subject to Indictment, Trail, Judgment and Punishment, according to law.

Section 4

The Times, Places and Manner of holding Elections for Senators and Representatives, shall be prescribed in each State by the Legislature thereof; but the Congress may at any time by Law make or alter such Regulations, except as to the Places of chusing Senators.

The Congress shall assemble at least once in every Year, and such Meeting shall be on the *first Monday in December*, unless they shall by Law appoint a different Day.

Section 5

Each House shall be the Judge of the Elections, Returns and Qualifications of its own Members, and a Majority of each shall constitute a Quorum to do Business; but a smaller Number may adjourn from day to day, and may be authorized to compel the Attendance of absent Members, in such Manner, and under such Penalties as each House may provide.

Each House may determine the Rules of its Proceedings, punish its Members for disorderly Behaviour, and, with the Concurrence of two thirds, expel a Member.

Each House shall keep a Journal of its Proceedings, and from time to time publish the same, excepting such Parts as may in their Judgment require Secrecy; and the Yeas and Nays of the Members of either House on any question shall, at the Desire of one fifth of those Present, be entered on the Journal.

Neither House, during the Session of Congress, shall, without the Consent of the other, adjourn for more than three days, nor to any other Place than that in which the two Houses shall be sitting.

Section 6

The Senators and Representatives shall receive a Compensation for their Services, to be ascertained by Law, and paid out of the Treasury of the United States. They shall in all Cases, except Treason, Felony and Breach of the Peace, be privileged from Arrest during their Attendance at the Session of their respective Houses, and in going to and returning from the same; and for any Speech or Debate in either House, they shall not be questioned in any other Place.

No Senator or Representative shall, during the Time for which he was elected, be appointed to any civil Office under the Authority of the United States, which shall have been created, or the Emoluments whereof shall have been encreased during such time; and no Person holding any Office under the United States, shall be a Member of either House during his Continuance in Office.

Section 7

All Bills for raising Revenue shall originate in the House of Representatives; but the Senate may propose or concur with Amendments as on other Bills.

Every Bill which shall have passed the House of Representatives and the Senate, shall, before it becomes a Law, be presented to the President of the United States. If he approve he shall sign it, but if not he shall return it, with his Objections to that House in which it shall have originated, who shall enter the Objections at large in their Journal, and proceed to reconsider it. If after such Reconsideration two thirds of that House shall agree to pass the Bill, it shall be sent, together with the Objections, to the other House, by which it shall likewise be reconsidered, and if approved by two thirds of that House, it shall become a Law. But in all such Cases the Votes of both Houses shall be determined by Yeas and Nays, and the Names of the Persons voting for and against the Bill shall be entered on the Journal of each House respectively. If any Bill shall not be returned by the President within ten Days (Sundays excepted) after it shall have been presented to him, the Same shall be a Law, in like Manner as if he had signed it, unless the Congress by their Adjournment prevent its Return, in which Case it shall not be a Law.

Every Order, Resolution, or Vote to which the Concurrence of the Senate and House of Representatives may be necessary (except on a question of Adjournment) shall be presented to the President of the United States; and before the Same shall take Effect, shall be approved by him, or being disapproved by him, shall be repassed by two thirds of the Senate and House of Representatives, according to the Rules and Limitations prescribed in the Case of a Bill.

Section 8

The Congress shall have Power to lay and collect Taxes, Duties, Imposts and Excises, to pay the Debts and provide for the common Defense and general Welfare of the United States; but all Duties, Imposts and Excises shall be uniform throughout the United States;

To borrow Money on the credit of the United States;

To regulate Commerce with foreign Nations, and among the several States, and with the Indian Tribes;

To establish an uniform Rule of Naturalization, and uniform Laws on the subject of Bankruptcies throughout the United States;

To coin Money, regulate the Value thereof, and of foreign Coin, and fix the Standard of Weights and Measures;

To provide for the Punishment of counterfeiting the Securities and current Coin of the United States;

To establish Post Offices and post Roads;

To promote the Progress of Science and useful Arts, by securing for limited Times to Authors and Inventors the exclusive Rights to their respective Writings and Discoveries;

To constitute Tribunals inferior to the supreme Court;

To define and punish Piracies and Felonies committed on the high Seas, and Offences against the Law of Nations;

To declare War, grant Letters of Marque and Reprisal, and make Rules concerning Captures on Land and Water;

To raise and support Armies, but no Appropriation of Money to that Use shall be for a longer Term than two Years;

To provide and maintain a Navy;

To make Rules for the Government and Regulation of the land and naval Forces;

To provide for calling forth the militia to execute the laws of the union, suppress Insurrections and repel Invasions;

To provide for organizing, arming, and disciplining the Militia, and for governing such Part of them as may be employed in the Service of the United States, reserving to the States respectively, the Appointment of the Officers, and the Authority of training the Militia according to the discipline prescribed by Congress;

To exercise exclusive Legislation in all Cases whatsoever, over such District (not exceeding ten Miles square) as may, by Cession of particular States, and the Acceptance of Congress, become the Seat of the Government of the United States, and to exercise like Authority over all Places purchased by the Consent of the Legislature of the State in which the Same shall be, for the Erection of Forts, Magazines, Arsenals, dock-Yards, and other needful Buildings; —And

To make all Laws which shall be necessary and proper for carrying into Execution the foregoing Powers, and all other Powers vested by this Constitution in the Government of the United States, or in any Department of Officer thereof.

Section 9

The Migration of Importation of such Persons as any of the States now existing shall think proper to admit, shall not be prohibited by the Congress prior to the Year one thousand eight hundred and eight, but a Tax or duty may be imposed on such Importation, not exceeding ten dollars for each Person.

The Privilege of the Writ of Habeas Corpus shall not be suspended, unless when in Cases of Rebellion or Invasion the public Safety may require it.

No Bill of Attainder or ex post facto Law shall be passed.

No Capitation or other direct, Tax shall be laid, *unless in Proportion to the Census or enumeration herein before directed to be taken.*

No Tax or Duty shall be laid on Articles exported from any State.

No Preference shall be given by any Regulation of Commerce or Revenue to the Ports of one State over those of another; nor shall Vessels bound to, or from, one State be obliged to enter, clear, or pay Duties in another.

No Money shall be drawn from the Treasury, but in Consequence of Appropriations made by Law; and a regular Statement and Account of the Receipts and Expenditures of all publish Money shall be published from time to time.

No Title of Nobility shall be granted by the United States: And no Person holding any Office of Profit or Trust under them, shall, without the Consent of the Congress, accept of any present, Emolument, Office, or Title, of any kind whatever, from any King, Prince, or foreign State.

Section 10

No State shall enter into any Treaty, Alliance, or Confederation; grant Letters of Marque and Reprisal; coin Money; emit Bills of Credit; make any Thing but gold and silver Coin a Tender in Payment of Debts; pass any Bill of Attainder, ex post facto Law, or Law impairing the Obligation of Contracts, or grant any Title of Nobility.

No State shall, without the Consent of the Congress, lay any Imposts or Duties on Imports or Exports, except what may be absolutely necessary for executing its inspection Laws: and the net Produce of all Duties and Imposts, laid by any State on Imports or Exports, shall be for the Use of the Treasury of the United States; and all such Laws shall be subject to the Revision and Controul of the Congress.

No State shall, without the Consent of Congress, lay any Duty of Tonnage, keep Troops, or Ships of War in time of Peace, enter into any Agreement or Compact with another State, or with a foreign Power, or engage in War, unless actually invaded, or in such imminent Danger as will not admit of delay.

ARTICLE II

Section 1

The executive Power shall be vested in a President of the United States of America. He shall hold his Office during the Term of four Years, and, together with the Vice President, chosen for the same Term, be elected, as follows:

Each State shall appoint, in such Manner as the Legislature thereof may direct, a Number of Electors, equal to the whole number of Senators and Representatives to which the State may be entitled in the Congress: but no Senator or Representative, or Person holding an Office of Trust of Profit under the United States, shall be appointed an Elector.

The Electors shall meet in their respective States, and vote by Ballot for two Persons, of whom one at least shall not be an Inhabitant of the same State with themselves. And they shall make a List of all the Persons voted for, and of the Number of Votes for each; which List they shall sign and certify, and transmit sealed to the Seat of the Government of the United States, directed to the President of the Senate. The President of the Senate shall, in the Presence of the Senate and House of Representatives, open all the Certificates, and the Votes shall then be counted. The Person having the greatest Number of Votes shall be the President, if such Number be a Majority of the whole Number of Electors appointed; and if there be more than one who have such Majority, and have an equal Number of Votes, then the House of Representatives shall immediately chuse by Ballot one of them for President; and if no Person have a Majority, then from the five highest on the List the said House shall in like Manner chuse the President. But in chusing the President, the Votes shall be taken by States, the Representation from each State having one Vote; A quorum for this purpose shall consist of a Member or Members from two thirds of the States, and a Majority of all the States shall be necessary to a Choice. In every Case, after the Choice of the President, the Person having the greatest Number of Votes of the Electors shall be the Vice President. But if there should remain two or more who have equal Votes, the Senate shall chuse from them by Ballot the Vice President.

The Congress may determine the Time of chusing the Electors, and the Day on which they shall give their Votes; which Day shall be the same throughout the United States.

No Person except a natural born Citizen, or a Citizen of the United States, at the time of the Adoption of this Constitution, shall be eligible to the Office of President; neither shall any Person be eligible to that Office who shall not have attained to the Age of thirty five Years, and been fourteen Years a Resident within the United States.

In Case of the Removal of the President from office, or of his Death, Resignation, or Inability to discharge the Powers and Duties of the said Office, the Same shall devolve on the Vice President, and the Congress may by Law provide for the Case of Removal, Death, Resignation or Inability, both of the President and Vice President, declaring what Officer shall then act as President, and such Officer shall act accordingly, until the Disability be removed, or a President shall be elected.

The President shall, at stated Times, receive for his Services, a Compensation, which shall neither be increased nor diminished during the Period for which he shall have been elected, and he shall not receive within that Period any other Emolument from the United States, or any of them.

Before he enter on the Execution of his Office, he shall take the following Oath or Affirmation:— "I do solemnly swear (or affirm) that I will faithfully execute the Office of President of the United States, and will to the best of my Ability, preserve, protect and defend the Constitution of the United States."

Section 2

The President shall be Commander in Chief of the Army and Navy of the United States, and of the Militia of the several States, when called into the actual Service of the United States; he may require the Opinion, in writing, of the principal Officer in each of the executive Departments, upon any Subject relating to the Duties of their respective Offices, and he shall have Power to grant Reprieves and Pardons for Offences against the United States, except in Cases of Impeachment.

He shall have Power, by and with the Advice and Consent of the Senate, to make Treaties, provided two thirds of the Senators present concur; and he shall nominate, and by and with the Advice and Consent of the Senate, shall appoint Ambassadors, other public Ministers and Consuls, Judges of the supreme Court, and all other Officers of the United States, whose Appointments are not herein otherwise provided for, and which shall be established by Law: but the Congress may by Law vest the Appointment of such inferior Officers, as they think proper, in the President alone, in the Courts of Law, or in the Heads of Departments.

The President shall have Power to fill up all Vacancies that may happen during the Recess of the Senate, by granting Commissions which shall expire at the End of their next Session.

Section 3

He shall from time to time give to the Congress Information of the State of the Union, and recommend to their Consideration such Measures as he shall judge necessary and expedient; he may, on extraordinary Occasions, convene both Houses, or either of them, and in Case of Disagreement between them, with Respect to the Time of Adjournment, he may adjourn them to such Time as he shall think proper; he shall receive Ambassadors and other public Ministers; he shall take Care that the Laws be faithfully executed, and shall Commission all the Officers of the United States.

Section 4

The President, Vice President and all civil Officers of the United States, shall be removed from Office on Impeachment for, and Conviction of, Treason, Bribery, or other high Crimes and Misdemeanors.

ARTICLE III

Section 1

The judicial Power of the United States shall be vested in one supreme Court, and in such inferior Courts as the Congress may from time to time ordain and establish. The Judges, both of the supreme and inferior Courts, shall hold their Offices during good Behaviour, and shall, at stated Times, receive for their Services a Compensation, which shall not be diminished during their Continuance in Office.

Section 2

The judicial Power shall extend to all Cases, in Law and Equity, arising under this Constitution; the Laws of the United States, and Treaties made, or which shall be made, under their Authority; —to all Cases affecting Ambassadors, other public Ministers and Consuls; —to all Cases of admiralty and maritime Jurisdiction; —to Controversies to which the United States shall be a Party; —to Controversies between two or more States; —*between a State and Citizens of another State*; —between Citizens of different States; —between Citizens of the same State claiming Lands under Grants of different States, and between a State, or the Citizens thereof, and foreign States, Citizens or Subjects.

In all Cases affecting Ambassadors, other public Ministers and Consuls, and those in which a State shall be Party, the supreme Court shall have original Jurisdiction. In all the other Cases before mentioned, the supreme Court shall have appellate Jurisdiction, both as to Law and Fact, with such Exceptions, and under such Regulations as the Congress shall make.

The Trial of all Crimes, except in Cases of Impeachment, shall be by Jury; and such Trial shall be held in the State where the said Crimes shall have been committed; but when not committed within any Sate, the Trial shall be at such Place or Places as the Congress may by Law have directed.

Section 3

Treason against the United States, shall consist only in levying War against them, or in adhering to their Enemies, giving them Aid and Comfort. No Person shall be convicted of Treason unless on the Testimony of two Witnesses to the same overt Act, or on Confession in open Court.

The Congress shall have Power to declare the Punishment of Treason, but no Attainder of Treason shall work Corruption of Blood, or Forfeiture except during the Life of the Person attainted.

ARTICLE IV

Section 1

Full Faith and Credit shall be given in each State to the public Acts, Records, and judicial proceedings of every other State. And the Congress may by general Laws prescribe the Manner in which such Acts, Records and Proceedings shall be proved, and the Effect thereof.

Section 2

The Citizens of each State shall be entitled to all Privileges and Immunities of Citizens in the several States.

A Person charged in any State with Treason, Felony, or other Crime, who shall flee from Justice, and be found in another State, shall on Demand of the executive Authority of the State from which he fled, be delivered up, to be removed to the State having Jurisdiction of the Crime.

No Person held to Service or Labour in one State, under the Laws thereof, escaping into another, shall, in Consequence of any Law or Regulation therein, be discharged from such Service or Labour, but shall be delivered up on Claim of the Party to whom such Service or Labour may be due.

Section 3

New States may be admitted by the Congress into this Union; but no new State shall be formed or erected within the Jurisdiction of any other State; nor any State be formed by the Junction of two or more States, or Parts of States, without the consent of the Legislatures of the States concerned as well as of the Congress.

The Congress shall have Power to dispose of and make all needful Rules and Regulations respecting the Territory or other property belonging to the United States; and nothing in this Constitution shall be so construed as to Prejudice any Claims of the United States, or of any particular State.

Section 4

The United States shall guarantee to every State in this Union a Republican Form of Government, and shall protect each of them against Invasion; and on Application of the Legislature, or of the Executive (when Legislature cannot be convened), against domestic Violence.

ARTICLE V

The Congress, whenever two thirds of both Houses shall deem it necessary, shall propose Amendments to this Constitution, or, on the Application of the Legislatures of two thirds of the several States, shall call a Convention for proposing Amendments, which, in either Case, shall be valid to all Intents and Purposes, as

Part of this Constitution, when ratified by the Legislatures of three fourths of the several States, or by Conventions in three fourths thereof, as the one or the other Mode of Ratification may be proposed by the Congress; Provided that no Amendment which may be made prior to the Year One thousand eight hundred and eight shall in any Manner affect the first and fourth Clauses in the Ninth Section of the first Article; and that no State, without its Consent, shall be deprived of its equal Suffrage in the Senate.

ARTICLE VI

All Debts contracted and Engagements entered into, before the Adoption of this Constitution, shall be as valid against the United States under this Constitution, as under the Confederation.

This Constitution, and the Laws of the United States which shall be made in Pursuance thereof; and all Treaties made, or which shall be made, under the Authority of the United States, shall be the supreme Law of the Land; and the Judges in every State shall be bound thereby, any Thing in the Constitution or Laws of any State to the Contrary notwithstanding.

The Senators and Representative before mentioned, and the Members of the several State Legislatures, and all executive and judicial Officers, both of the United States and of the several States, shall be bound by Oath or Affirmation, to support this Constitution; but no religious Test shall ever be required as a Qualification to any Office or public Trust under the United States.

ARTICLE VII

The Ratification of the Conventions of nine States, shall be sufficient for the Establishment of this Constitution between the States so ratifying the Same.

The Word, "the," being interlined between the seventh and eighth Lines of the first Page, the Word "Thirty" being partly written on an Erazure in the fifteenth Line of the first Page, the Words "is tried" being interlined between the thirty second and thirty third Lines of the first Page and the Word "the" being interlined between the forty third and forty fourth Lines of the second Page.

Attest William Jackson Secretary

Done in Convention by the Unanimous Consent of the States present the Seventeenth Day of September in the Year of our Lord one thousand seven hundred and Eighty seven and of the Independence of the United States of America the Twelfth In witness whereof We have hereunto subscribed our Names,

G. Washington

Presidt and deputy from Virginia

Delaware

Geo: Read

Gunning Bedford jun

John Dickinson

Richard Bassett

Jaco: Broom

Maryland

James McHenry

Dan of St Thos. Jenifer

Danl. Carroll

Virginia

John Blair

James Madison Jr.

North Carolina

Wm. Blount

Richd. Dobbs Spaight

Hu Williamson

South Carolina

J. Rutledge

Charles Cotesworth Pinckney

Charles Pinckney

Pierce Butler

Georgia

William Few

Abr Baldwin

New Hampshire

John Langdon

Nicholas Gilman

Massachusetts

Nathaniel Gorham

Rufus King

Connecticut

Wm. Saml. Johnson

Roger Sherman

New York

Alexander Hamilton

New Jersey

Wil: Livingston

David Brearley

Wm. Paterson

Jona: Dayton

Pennsylvania

B Franklin

Thomas Mifflin

Robt. Morris

Geo. Clymer

Thos. FitsSimons

Jared Ingersoll

James Wilson

Gouv Morris

AMENDMENT I (1791)

Congress shall make no law respecting an establishment of religion, or prohibiting the free exercise thereof; or abridging the freedom of speech, or of the press; or the right of the people peaceably to assemble, and to petition the Government for a redress of grievances.

AMENDMENT II (1791)

A well regulated Militia being necessary to the security of a free state, the right of the people to keep and bear Arms, shall not be infringed.

AMENDMENT III (1791)

No Soldier shall, in time of peace be quartered in any house, without the consent of the Owner, nor in time of war, but in a manner to be prescribed by law.

AMENDMENT IV (1791)

The right of the people to be secure in their persons, houses, papers, and effects, against unreasonable searches and seizures, shall not be violated, and no Warrants shall issue, but upon probable cause, supported by Oath or affirmation, and particularly describing the place to be searched, and the persons or things to be seized.

AMENDMENT V (1791)

No person shall be held to answer for a capital, or otherwise infamous crime, unless on a presentment or indictment of a Grand Jury, except in cases arising in the land or naval forces, or in the Militia, when in actual service in time of War or public danger; nor shall any person be subject for the same offence to be twice put in jeopardy of life or limb; nor shall be compelled in any criminal case to be a witness against himself, nor be deprived of life, liberty, or property, without due process of law; nor shall private property be taken for public use, without just compensation.

AMENDMENT VI (1791)

In all criminal prosecutions, the accused shall enjoy the right to a speedy and public trail, by an impartial jury of the State and district wherein the crime shall have been committed, which district shall have been previously ascertained by law, and to be informed of the nature and cause of the accusation; to be confronted with the witnesses against him; to have compulsory process for obtaining witness in his favor; and to have the Assistance of Counsel for his defense.

AMENDMENT VII (1791)

In Suits at common law, where the value in controversy shall exceed twenty dollars, the right of trial by jury shall be preserved, and no fact tried by a jury, shall be otherwise reexamined in any Court of the United States, than according to the rules of the common law.

AMENDMENT VIII (1791)

Excessive bail shall not be required, nor excessive fines imposed, nor cruel and unusual punishments inflicted.

AMENDMENT IX (1791)

The enumeration in the Constitution, of certain rights, shall not be construed to deny or disparage others retained by the people.

AMENDMENT X (1791)

The powers not delegated to the United States by the Constitution, nor prohibited by it to the States, are reserved to the States respectively, or to the people.

AMENDMENT XI (1798)

The Judicial power of the United States shall not be construed to extend to any suit in law or equity, commenced or prosecuted against one of the United States by Citizens of another State, or by Citizens or Subjects of any Foreign State.

AMENDMENT XII (1804)

The Electors shall meet in their respective states and vote by ballot for President and Vice-President, one of whom, at least, shall not be an inhabitant of the same state with themselves; they shall name in their ballots the person voted for as President, and in distinct ballots the person voted for as Vice-President, and they shall make distinct lists of all persons voted for as President, and of all persons voted for as Vice-President, and of the number of votes for each, which lists they shall sign and certify, and transmit sealed to the seat of the government of the United States, directed to the President of the Senate; —The President of the Senate shall, in the presence of the Senate and House of Representatives, open all the certificates and the votes shall then be counted; —The person having the greatest number of votes for President, shall be the President, if such number be a majority of the whole number of Electors appointed; and if no person have such majority, then from the persons having the highest numbers not exceeding three on the list of those voted for as President, the House of Representative shall choose immediately, by ballot, the President. But in choosing the President, the votes shall be taken by states, the representation from each state having one vote; a quorum for this purpose shall consist of a member or members from two-thirds of the states, and a majority of all the states shall be necessary to a choice. And if the House or Representatives shall not choose a President whenever the right of choice shall devolve upon them, before the fourth day of March next following, then the Vice-President shall act as President, as in the case of the death or other constitutional disability of the President—The person having the greatest number of votes as Vice-President, shall be the Vice-President, if such number be a majority of the whole number of Electors appointed, and if no person have a majority, then from the two highest numbers on the list, the Senate shall choose the Vice-President; A quorum for the purpose shall consist of two-thirds of the whole number of Senators, and a majority of the whole number shall be necessary to a choice. But no person constitutionally ineligible to the office of President shall be eligible to that of Vice-President of the United States.

AMENDMENT XIII (1865)

Section 1

Neither slavery nor involuntary servitude, except as a punishment for crime whereof the party shall have been duly convicted, shall exist within the United States, or any place subject to their jurisdiction.

Section 2

Congress shall have power to enforce this article by appropriate legislation.

AMENDMENT XIV (1868)

Section 1

All persons born or naturalized in the United States and subject to the jurisdiction thereof, are citizens of the United States and of the State wherein they reside. No State shall make or enforce any law which shall abridge the privileges or immunities of citizens of the United States; nor shall any State deprive any person of life, liberty, or property, without due process of law; nor deny to any person within its jurisdiction the equal protection of the laws.

Section 2

Representatives shall be apportioned among the several States according to their respective numbers, counting the whole number of persons in each State, excluding Indians not taxed. But when the right to vote at any election for the choice of electors for President and Vice-President of the United States, Representatives in Congress, the Executive and Judicial officers of a State, or the members of the Legislature thereof, is denied to any of the male inhabitants of such State, being twenty-one years of age, and citizens of the United States, or in any way abridged, except for participation in rebellion, or other crime, the basis of representation therein shall be reduced in the proportion which the number of such male citizens shall bear to the whole number of male citizens twenty-one years of age in such State.

Section 3

No person shall be a Senator or Representative in Congress, or elector of President and Vice-President, or hold any office, civil or military under the United States, or under any State, who, having previously taken an oath, as a member of Congress, or as an officer of the United States, or as a member of any State legislature, or as an executive or judicial officer of any State, to support the Constitution of the United States, shall have engaged in insurrection or rebellion against the same, or given aid or comfort to the enemies thereof. But Congress may by a vote of two-thirds of each House, remove such disability.

Section 4

The validity of the public debt of the United States, authorized by law, including debts incurred for payment of pensions and bounties for services in suppressing insurrection or rebellion, shall not be questioned. But neither the United States nor any State shall assume or pay any debt or obligation incurred in aid of insurrection or rebellion against the United States, or any claim for the loss or emancipation of any slave; but all such depts, obligations and claims shall be held illegal and void.

Section 5

The Congress shall have power to enforce, by appropriate legislation, the provisions of the article.

AMENDMENT XV (1870)

Section 1

The right of citizens of the Unites States to vote shall not be denied or abridged by the United States or by any State on account of race, color, or previous condition of servitude.

Section 2

The Congress shall have power to enforce this article by appropriate legislation.

AMENDMENT XVI (1913)

The Congress shall have power to lay and collect taxes on incomes, from whatever source derived, without apportionment among the several States, and without regard to any census or enumeration.

AMENDMENT XVII (1913)

The Senate of the United States shall be composed of two Senators from each State, elected by the people thereof, for six years; and each Senator shall have one vote. The electors in each State shall have the qualifications requisite for electors of the most numerous branch of the State legislatures.

When vacancies happen in the representation of any State in the Senate, the executive authority of such State shall issue writs of election to fill such vacancies: *Provided*, That the legislature of any State may empower the executive thereof to make temporary appointments until the people fill the vacancies by election as the legislature may direct.

This amendment shall not be so construed as to affect the election or term of any Senator chosen before it becomes valid as part of the Constitution.

AMENDMENT XVIII (1919)

Section 1

After one year from the ratification of this article the manufacture, sale, or transportation of intoxicating liquors within, the importation thereof into, or the exportation thereof from the United States and all territory subject to the jurisdiction thereof for beverage purposes is hereby prohibited.

Section 2

The Congress and the several States shall have concurrent power to enforce this article by appropriate legislation.

Section 3

This article shall be inoperative unless it shall have been ratified as an amendment to the Constitution by the legislatures of the several States, as provided by the Constitution, within seven years from the date of the submission hereof to the States by the Congress.

AMENDMENT XIX (1920)

The right of citizens of the United States to vote shall not be denied or abridged by the United States or by any State on account of sex

Congress shall have power to enforce this article by appropriate legislation.

AMENDMENT XX (1933)

Section 1

The terms of the President and Vice-President shall end at noon on the 20th day of January, and the terms of Senators and Representatives at noon on the 3rd day of

January, of the years in which such terms would have ended if this article had not been ratified; and the terms of their successors shall then begin.

Section 2

The Congress shall assemble at least once in every year, and such meeting shall begin at noon on the 3rd day of January, unless they shall by law appoint a different day.

Section 3

If, at the time fixed for the beginning of the term of the President, the president elect shall have died, the Vice President elect shall become President. If a President shall not have been chosen before the time fixed for the beginning of his term, or if the President elect shall have failed to qualify, then the Vice President elect shall act as President until a President shall have qualified; and the Congress may by law provide for the case wherein neither a President elect nor a Vice President elect shall have qualified, declaring who shall then act as President, or the manner in which one who is to act shall be selected, and such person shall act accordingly until a President or Vice President shall have qualified.

Section 4

The Congress may by law provide for the case of the death of any of the persons from whom the House of Representatives may choose a President whenever the right of choice shall have devolved upon them, and for the case of the death of any of the persons from whom the Senate may choose a Vice President whenever the right of choice shall have devolved upon them.

Section 5

Sections 1 and 2 shall take effect on the 15th day of October following the ratification of this article.

Section 6

This article shall be inoperative unless it shall have been ratified as an amendment to the Constitution by the legislatures of three-fourths of the several States within seven years from the date of its submission.

AMENDMENT XXI (1933)

Section 1

The eighteenth article of amendment to the Constitution of the United States is hereby repealed.

Section 2

The transportation or importation into any State, Territory or possession of the United States for delivery or use therein of intoxicating liquors, in violation of the laws thereof, is herby prohibited.

Section 3

This article shall be inoperative unless it shall have been ratified as an amendment to the Constitution by convention in the several States, as provided in the Constitution, within seven years from the date of the submission hereof to the State by the Congress.

AMENDMENT XXII (1951)

Section 1

No person shall be elected to the office of the President more than twice, and no person who has held the office of President, or acted as President, for more than two years of a term to which some other person was elected President shall be elected to the office of the President more than once. But this Article shall not apply to any person holding the office of President when this Article was proposed by the Congress, and shall not prevent any person who may be holding the office of President, or acting as President, during the term within which this Article becomes operative from holding the office of President or acting as President during the remainder of such term.

Section 2

This Article shall be inoperative unless it shall have been ratified as an amendment to the Constitution by the legislatures of three-fourths of the several States within seven years from the date of its submission to the States by the Congress.

AMENDMENT XXIII (1961)

Section 1

The District constituting the seat of Government of the United States shall appoint in such manner as the Congress may direct.

A number of electors of President and Vice President equal to the whole number of Senators and Representatives in Congress to which the District would be entitled if it were a State, but in no event more than the least populous State; they shall be in addition to those appointed by the States, but they shall be considered, for the purposes of the election of President and Vice President, to be electors appointed by a State; and they shall meet in the District and perform such duties as provide by the twelfth article of amendment.

Section 2

The Congress shall have power to enforce this article by appropriate legislation

AMENDMENT XXIV (1964)

Section 1

The right of citizens of the United States to vote in any primary or other election for President or Vice President, for electors for President or Vice President, or for Senator or Representative in Congress, shall not be denied or abridged by the United States or any State by reason of failure to pay any poll tax or other tax.

Section 2

The Congress shall have power to enforce this article by appropriate legislation.

AMENDMENT XXV (1967)

Section 1

In case of the removal of the President from office or of his death or resignation, the Vice President shall become President.

Section 2

Whenever there is a vacancy in the office of the Vice President, the President shall nominate a Vice President who shall take office upon confirmation by a majority vote of both Houses of Congress.

Section 3

Whenever the President transmits to the President pro tempore of the Senate and the Speaker of the House of Representatives his written declaration that he is unable to discharge the powers and duties of his office, and until he transmits to them a written declaration to the contrary, such powers and duties shall be discharged by the Vice President as Acting President.

Section 4

Whenever the Vice President and a majority of either the principal officers of the executive departments or of such other body as Congress may by law provide, transmit to the President pro tempore of the Senate and the Speaker of the House of Representatives their written declaration that the President is unable to discharge the powers and duties of his office, the Vice President shall immediately assume the powers and duties of the office as Acting President.

Thereafter, when the president transmits to the President pro tempore of the Senate and the Speaker of the House of Representative his written declaration that no inability exists, he shall resume the powers and duties of his office unless the Vice President and a majority of either the principal officers of the executive department or of such other body as Congress may by law provide, transmit within four days to the President pro tempore of the Senate and the Speaker of the House of Representatives their written declaration that the President is unable to discharge the powers and duties of his office. Thereupon Congress shall decide the issue, assembling within forty-eight hours for that purpose if not in session. If the Congress, within twenty-one days after receipt of the latter written declaration, or, if Congress is not in session, within twenty-one days after Congress is required to assemble, determines by two-thirds vote of both the Houses that the President is unable to discharge the powers and duties of his office, the Vice President shall continue to discharge the same as Acting President; otherwise, the President shall resume the powers and duties of his office.

AMENDMENT XXVI (1971)

Section 1

The right of citizens of the United States, who are eighteen years of age or older, to vote shall not be denied or abridged by the United States or by any State on account of age.

Section 2

The Congress shall have power to enforce this article by appropriate legislation.

AMENDMENT XXVII (1992)

No law varying the compensation for the services of the senators and representatives shall take effect, until an election of representatives shall have intervened.

APPENDIX B

Briefing and Analyzing Cases

Decisions of courts are often written and are commonly referred to as *judicial opinions* or cases. These cases are published in law reporters so they may be used as precedent. Many cases appear in this text for your education. Your instructor may also require that you read other cases, often from your jurisdiction. The cases included in your book have been edited, citations have been omitted, and legal issues not relevant to the subject discussed have been excised. There is a common method that students of the law use to read and analyze, also known as briefing, cases.

Most judicial opinions are written using a similar format. First, the name of the case appears with the name of the court, the cite (location where the case has been published), and the year. When the body of the case begins, the name of the judge, or judges, responsible for writing the opinion appears directly before the first paragraph. The opinion contains an introduction to the case, which normally includes the procedural history of the case. This is followed by a summary of the facts that led to the dispute, the court's analysis of the law that applies to the case, and the court's conclusions and orders, if any.

Most opinions used here are from appellate courts, where many judges sit at one time. After the case is over, the judges vote on an outcome. The majority vote wins, and the opinion of the majority is written by one of those judges. If other judges in the majority wish to add to the majority opinion, they may write one or more *concurring opinions*. Concurring opinions appear after majority opinions in the law reporters. When a judge who was not in the majority feels strongly about his or her position, he or she may file a dissenting opinion, which appears after the concurring opinions, if any. Only the majority opinion is law, although concurring and dissenting opinions are often informative.

During your legal education, you may be instructed to "brief" a case. Even if your instructor does not require you to brief cases, you may want to, as many learners understand a case better after they have completed a brief. Here are suggestions for reading and understanding cases.

First, read the case. Do not take notes during your first reading. Get a "feel" for the case—the facts, the Court's tone, and the outcomes.

Second, brief the case. What follows is a suggested briefing format.

A very common format for briefing judicial decisions is IRAC. The acronym represents Issue, Rules, Analysis, and Conclusion. It is recommended that you employ a modified form of IRAC that adds the facts of the case, hence FIRAC. See Figure B-1.

Begin your brief by identifying the most important and material **FACTS** of the case. Not all facts mentioned by the court are material to the issue you are studying. It is possible for a court to reference an immaterial fact, or more likely, it had to address more legal issues than you have read about, and accordingly, it has included facts that could be material to a separate legal issue. Remember, you are reading cases that have been edited and pared down to the topic you are studying.

Identify the legal **ISSUE** in the case. Issue spotting is a very important legal skill. The issue is the legal question the court is answering. The facts of the case give rise to and frame the legal issue(s) of the case.

What **RULE**(s) applies to the issue you have identified? The rules are the laws, from whatever source, that guide the analysis. The rules come in many forms. The law that directly applies to the issues and facts is known as doctrinal law. But other process rules may apply as well, such as the rules of statutory or constitutional interpretation, stare decisis, etc. Often, some knowledge of the law, or at least a good intuition, is needed to identify an issue. This is one of the challenges of being a legal neophyte.

ANALYZE the case, applying the law to the facts of the case. Remember, the law is "blind." The politics and social dimensions of cases are immaterial. Like Mr. Spock in *Star Trek*, engage in objective, logical (legal) analysis and leave your personal opinions

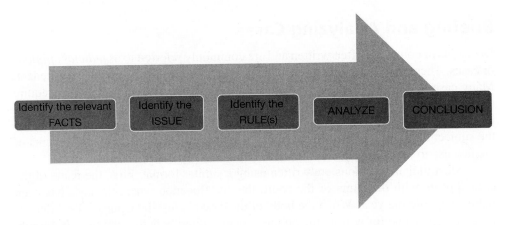

FIGURE B-1
Framework for briefing cases

out of the mix. Often during analysis, new legal issues will emerge. Be prepared to add them to your analysis. See the example below to understand how this happens.

Draw a **CONCLUSION.** Students often want to jump to the "final answer." What is important is that you can identify and frame an issue and analyze the problem. Your final conclusion is less important (unless you are a judge!). In most cases, your conclusion will not be about guilt or innocence. It will be about the application of a law to a set of facts.

Finally, depending on your objective, you may also want to discuss any concurring and/or dissenting opinions.

Here is a simple example of the application of the FIRAC model.

EXAMPLE: Gun Possession in the Home

Facts

In response to rising homicides and robberies involving guns, MegaTown enacts an ordinance making it a class A misdemeanor punished by as much as one year in jail and a fine of $10,000 for the possession of a handgun anywhere in the city, including in the home. One evening, A. Sih, a resident of MegaTown, phoned the police to report that she heard a noise in her home. She invited the two officers who were dispatched to her residence to come into her home to search for possible intruders. While they did not find an intruder, they discovered a handgun sitting on a table in the living room. The officers inquired about the gun and she replied, "I keep it for safety. I don't think the neighborhood is safe. I work with a local group that identifies and reports trouble in the neighborhood. Gang members have threatened me." They issued Ms. Sih a citation for possession of the firearm in violation of city ordinance. She filed a motion to dismiss the citation on the grounds that the ordinance violates the Second Amendment to the U.S. Constitution. She did not challenge the ordinance's prohibition of guns in public places. She challenged its provision making it unlawful to possess a gun in the home. The motion was denied by the trial judge. Subsequently, she pled guilty and was sentenced to sixty days in jail and a $1,000 fine. She has appealed the judge's denial of her motion to dismiss. The judge agreed to stay her punishment pending appeal.

Issue

May MegaTown forbid the possession of handguns in the home? More specifically, is MegaTown's ordinance forbidding handgun possession in one's home consistent with the Second Amendment to the U.S. Constitution?

Rules

The Second Amendment to the U.S. Constitution provides that "A well regulated Militia, being necessary to the security of a free state, the right of the people to keep and bear Arms, shall not be infringed."

> *This is an example of where some knowledge of the law is necessary in order to identify the issue. One would have to know, at some level, that there is a protection of gun ownership to know to turn to the Constitution.*
>
> *Additionally, as an issue is researched, new legal issues often emerge. In this case, for example, you would learn as you read the Supreme Court's cases that an issue that must be addressed is whether the Second Amendment applies against the states or just against the federal government, as was the framers' intention at the time of the adoption of the Bill of Rights. This analysis requires the application of a new rule, the Fourteenth Amendment's due process clause (which is used to "incorporate" or apply the Bill of Rights to the states).*

Analysis

1. The Second Amendment reads, "A well regulated Militia, being necessary to the security of a free state, the right of the people to keep and bear Arms, shall not be infringed."
2. Initially, the rights found in the first ten amendments (Bill of Rights) limited only the federal government, as intended by the framers. The Civil War dramatically changed the federal system. The adoption of the Thirteenth, Fourteenth, and Fifteenth Amendments is the most significant legal change resulting from the Civil War. Although it took some time after the ratification of the Fourteenth Amendment (see *Barron ex rel. Tiernan v. Mayor of Baltimore*, 7 Pet. 243 (1833)), the Supreme Court eventually held that rights that are fundamental and necessary to an ordered liberty are incorporated and apply against the states under the Fourteenth Amendment's due process guarantee, see *Hurtado v. California* (1884) and *Chicago, B. & Q. R. Co. v. Chicago* (1897). Because only those rights that are fundamental and necessary to an ordered liberty are incorporated, the process has become known as selective incorporation, as opposed to Justice Black's theory that the Fourteenth Amendment totally incorporated the first eight amendments.
3. Evidence from the Constitutional Convention makes it clear that the Second Amendment's Right to Bear Arms Clause is independent of its Militia Clause. Accordingly, there is an individual right to bear arms.
4. There is considerable evidence that possession of a handgun in the home for personal security is "deeply rooted" in U.S. and English history. The framers of the Constitution, both Federalists and anti-Federalists, considered gun ownership and self-defense important to freedom. Attempts to disarm the colonists by the King of England were met with hostility. At the time of the adoption of the Second Amendment, the states commonly protected the right through their constitutions and the framers purposely replicated those protections in the U.S. Constitution. Congress has on more than one occasion recognized the importance of gun ownership to personal safety and to the protection of civil rights. For example, Congress acted on several occasions to protect gun ownership by African-Americans in southern states following the Civil War, where whites were permitted to own guns and African-Americans, who were not permitted to possess weapons, were the target of violence by unrelenting rebels.
5. The right to self-defense and defense of family is most acute in the home.
6. Accordingly, possession of a handgun in the home is a fundamental right intended to be protected from federal governmental intervention under the Second Amendment.

7. Because it is fundamental and necessary to an ordered liberty, the right to bear arms is incorporated under the Fourteenth Amendment and applies against the states (which includes localities).

8. MegaTown's desire to address the rising number of homicides and robberies is genuine. However, it does not justify a full prohibition of gun possession for all residents, in all homes. MegaTown's law forbidding gun possession in the home directly conflicts with the Second Amendment.

You will want to cite the cases, statutes, and constitutional provisions that stand for the principles you are advancing.

Conclusion

MegaTown's ordinance violates the Second Amendment's right to bear arms in the home, and Ms. Sih's conviction must be overturned. The Court made no judgment about MegaTown's regulation of guns in public places.

Note: This example draws from two Supreme Court decisions: *McDonald v. Chicago* (2010) and *Washington, D.C. v. Heller* (2008).

History of United States Justices By Seat

Chief Justice		Associate Justice (Seat 1)		Associate Justice (Seat 2)		Associate Justice (Seat 3)	
The seat of Chief Justice was established by the Constitution and organized on September 24, 1789 by the Judiciary Act of 1789 [see 1 *Stat.* 73].		This seat was established on September 24, 1789 by the Judiciary Act of 1789 [see 1 *Stat.* 73].		This seat was established on September 24, 1789 by the Judiciary Act of 1789 [see 1 *Stat.* 73].		This seat was established on September 24, 1789 by the Judiciary Act of 1789 [see 1 *Stat.* 73].	
Jay	October 19, 1789 – June 29, 1795	Wilson	October 5, 1789 – August 21, 1798	Cushing	February 2, 1790 – September 13, 1810	Blair	February 2, 1790 – October 25, 1795
J. Rutledge	August 12, 1795 – December 15, 1795	Washington	February 4, 1799 – November 26, 1829	Story	February 3, 1812 – September 10, 1845	S. Chase	February 4, 1796 – June 19, 1811
Ellsworth	March 8, 1796 – December 15, 1800	Baldwin	January 18, 1830 – April 21, 1844	Woodbury	September 23, 1845 – September 4, 1851	Duvall	November 23, 1811 – January 14, 1835
J. Marshall	February 4, 1801 – July 6, 1835	Grier	August 10, 1846 – January 31, 1870	Curtis	October 10, 1851 – September 30, 1857	Barbour	May 12, 1836 – February 25, 1841
Taney	March 28, 1836 – October 12, 1864	Strong	March 14, 1870 – December 14, 1880	Clifford	January 21, 1858 – July 25, 1881	Daniel	January 10, 1842 – May 31, 1860
S.P. Chase	December 15, 1864 – May 7, 1873	Woods	January 5, 1881 – May 14, 1887	Gray	January 9, 1882 – September 15, 1902	Miller	July 21, 1862 – October 13, 1890
Waite	March 4, 1874 – March 23, 1888	L. Lamar	January 18, 1888 – January 23, 1893	Holmes	December 8, 1902 – January 12, 1932	Brown	January 5, 1891 – May 28, 1906
Fuller	October 8, 1888 – July 4, 1910	H. Jackson	March 4, 1893 – August 8, 1895	Cardozo	March 14, 1932 – July 9, 1938	Moody	December 17, 1906 – November 20, 1910
E. White	December 19, 1910 – May 19, 1921	Peckham	January 6, 1896 – October 24, 1909	Frankfurter	January 30, 1939 – August 28, 1962	J. Lamar	January 3, 1911 – January 2, 1916

Taft	July 11, 1921 – February 3, 1930	Lurton	January 3, 1910 – July 12, 1914	Goldberg	October 1, 1962 – July 25, 1965	Brandeis	June 5, 1916 – February 13, 1939
Hughes	February 24, 1930 – June 30, 1941	McReynolds	October 12, 1914 – January 31, 1941	Fortas	October 4, 1965 – May 14, 1969	Douglas	April 17, 1939 – November 12, 1975
Stone	July 3, 1941 – April 22, 1946	Byrnes	July 8, 1941 – October 3, 1942	Blackmun	June 9, 1970 – August 3, 1994	**Stevens**	December 19, 1975 – present
Vinson	June 24, 1946 – September 8, 1953	W. Rutledge	February 15, 1943 – September 10, 1949	**Breyer**	August 3, 1994 – present	**Kagan**	August 7, 2010 – present
Warren	October 5, 1953 – June 23, 1969	Minton	October 12, 1949 – October 15, 1956				
Burger	June 23, 1969 – September 26, 1986	Brennan	October 16, 1956 – July 20, 1990				
Rehnquist	September 26, 1986 – September 3, 2005	**Souter**	October 9, 1990 – present				
J. Roberts	September 29, 2005 – present	**Sotomayor**	August 8, 2009 – present				

Associate Justice (Seat 4)		Associate Justice (Seat 5)		Associate Justice (Seat 6)		Associate Justice (Seat 7)	
This seat was established on September 24, 1789 by the Judiciary Act of 1789 [see 1 *Stat.* 73].		This seat was established on September 24, 1789 by the Judiciary Act of 1789 [see 1 *Stat.* 73].		This seat was established on February 24, 1807 by the Seventh Circuit Act [see 2 *Stat.* 420].		This seat was established on March 3, 1837 by the Eighth and Ninth Circuits Act [see 5 *Stat.* 176].	
J. Rutledge	February 15, 1790 – March 5, 1791	Iredell	May 12, 1790 – October 20, 1799	Todd	May 4, 1807 – February 7, 1826	Catron	May 1, 1837 – May 30, 1865
T. Johnson	August 6, 1792 – January 16, 1793	Moore	April 21, 1800 – January 26, 1804	Trimble	June 16, 1826 – August 25, 1828	This seat was abolished on July 23, 1866 by the Judicial Circuits Act [see 14 *Stat.* 209].	
Paterson	March 11, 1793 – September 9, 1806	W. Johnson	May 7, 1804 – August 4, 1834	McLean	January 11, 1830 – April 4, 1861		
Livingston	January 20, 1807 – March 18, 1823	Wayne	January 14, 1835 – July 5, 1867	Swayne	January 27, 1862 – January 24, 1881		
Thompson	September 1, 1823 – December 18, 1843	This seat was abolished upon the death of James Moor Wayne per the *Judicial Circuits Act* [see 14 *Stat.* 209].		Matthews	May 17, 1881 – March 22, 1889		
Nelson	February 27, 1845 – November 28, 1872			Brewer	January 6, 1890 – March 28, 1910		

Hunt	January 9, 1873 – January 27, 1882				Hughes	October 10, 1910 – June 10, 1916		
Blatchford	April 3, 1882 – July 7, 1893				Clarke	October 9, 1916 – September 18, 1922		
White	March 12, 1894 – December 18, 1910				Sutherland	October 2, 1922 – January 17, 1938		
Van Devanter	January 3, 1911 – June 2, 1937				Reed	January 31, 1938 – February 25, 1957		
Black	August 19, 1937 – September 17, 1971				Whittaker	March 25, 1957 – March 31, 1962		
Powell	January 7, 1972 – June 26, 1987				White	April 16, 1962 – June 28, 1993		
Kennedy	February 18, 1988 – present				**Ginsburg**	August 10, 1993 – present		

Associate Justice (Seat 8)	
This seat was established on March 3, 1837 by the Eighth and Ninth Circuits Act [see 5 *Stat.* 176].	
McKinley	January 9, 1838 – July 19, 1852
Campbell	April 11, 1853 – April 30, 1861
Davis	December 10, 1862 – March 4, 1877
Harlan (I)	December 10, 1877 – October 14, 1911
Pitney	March 18, 1912 – December 31, 1922
Sanford	February 19, 1923 – March 8, 1930
O. Roberts	June 2, 1930 – July 31, 1945
Burton	October 1, 1945 – October 13, 1958
Stewart	October 14, 1958 – July 3, 1981
O'Connor	September 25, 1981 – January 31, 2006
Alito	January 31, 2006 – present

Associate Justice (Seat 9)	
This seat was established on March 3, 1863 by the Tenth Circuit Act [see 12 *Stat.* 794].	
Field	May 20, 1863 – December 1, 1897
McKenna	January 26, 1898 – January 5, 1925
Stone	March 2, 1925 – July 2, 1941
R. Jackson	July 11, 1941 – October 9, 1954
Harlan (II)	March 28, 1955 – September 23, 1971
Rehnquist	January 7, 1972 – September 26, 1986
Scalia	September 26, 1986 – present

Associate Justice (Seat 10)	
This seat was established on April 10, 1869 by the Circuit Judges Act of 1869 [see 16 *Stat.* 44].	
Bradley	March 23, 1870 – January 22, 1892
Shiras	October 10, 1892 – February 23, 1903
Day	March 2, 1903 – November 13, 1922
Butler	January 2, 1923 – November 16, 1939
Murphy	February 5, 1940 – July 19, 1949
Clark	August 24, 1949 – June 12, 1967
T. Marshall	October 2, 1967 – October 1, 1991
Thomas	October 23, 1991 – present

APPENDIX D

Selected Executive Orders and Memoranda

EXECUTIVE ORDER 9066 (PRESIDENT ROOSEVELT 1942)

Authorizing the Secretary of War to Prescribe Military Areas

Whereas the successful prosecution of the war requires every possible protection against espionage and against sabotage to national-defense material, national-defense premises, and national-defense utilities as defined in Section 4, Act of April 20, 1918, 40 Stat. 533, as amended by the Act of November 30, 1940, 54 Stat. 1220, and the Act of August 21, 1941, 55 Stat. 655 (U.S.C., Title 50, Sec. 104);

Now, therefore, by virtue of the authority vested in me as President of the United States, and Commander in Chief of the Army and Navy, I hereby authorize and direct the Secretary of War, and the Military Commanders whom he may from time to time designate, whenever he or any designated Commander deems such action necessary or desirable, to prescribe military areas in such places and of such extent as he or the appropriate Military Commander may determine, from which any or all persons may be excluded, and with respect to which, the right of any person to enter, remain in, or leave shall be subject to whatever restrictions the Secretary of War or the appropriate Military Commander may impose in his discretion. The Secretary of War is hereby authorized to provide for residents of any such area who are excluded therefrom, such transportation, food, shelter, and other accommodations as may be necessary, in the judgment of the Secretary of War or the said Military Commander, and until other arrangements are made, to accomplish the purpose of this order. The designation of military areas in any region or locality shall supersede designations of prohibited and restricted areas by the Attorney General under the Proclamations of December 7 and 8, 1941, and shall supersede the responsibility and authority of the Attorney General under the said Proclamations in respect of such prohibited and restricted areas.

I hereby further authorize and direct the Secretary of War and the said Military Commanders to take such other steps as he or the appropriate Military Commander may deem advisable to enforce compliance with the restrictions applicable to each Military area hereinabove authorized to be designated, including the use of Federal troops and other Federal Agencies, with authority to accept assistance of state and local agencies.

I hereby further authorize and direct all Executive Departments, independent establishments and other Federal Agencies, to assist the Secretary of War or the said Military Commanders in carrying out this Executive Order, including the furnishing of medical aid, hospitalization, food, clothing, transportation, use of land, shelter, and other supplies, equipment, utilities, facilities, and services.

This order shall not be construed as modifying or limiting in any way the authority heretofore granted under Executive Order No. 8972, dated December 12, 1941, nor shall it be construed as limiting or modifying the duty and responsibility of the Federal Bureau of Investigation, with respect to the investigation of alleged acts of sabotage or the duty and responsibility of the Attorney General and the Department of Justice under the Proclamations of December 7 and 8, 1941, prescribing regulations for the conduct and control of alien enemies, except as such duty and responsibility is superseded by the designation of military areas hereunder.

Executive Order 9066 was followed by this executive order:

EXECUTIVE ORDER 9102 (PRESIDENT ROOSEVELT 1942)

War Relocation Authority

By virtue of the authority vested in me by the Constitution and statutes of the United States, as President of the United States and Commander in Chief of the Army and

Navy, and in order to provide for the removal from designated areas of persons whose removal is necessary in the interests of national security, it is ordered as follows:

1. There is established in the Office for Emergency Management of the Executive Office of the President the War Relocation Authority, at the head of which shall be a Director appointed by and responsible to the President.

2. The Director of the War Relocation Authority is authorized and directed to formulate and effectuate a program for the removal, from the areas designated from time to time by the Secretary of War or appropriate military commander under the authority of Executive Order No. 9066 of February 19, 1942, of the persons or classes of persons designated under such Executive Order, and for their relocation, maintenance, and supervision.

3. In effectuating such program the Director shall have authority to
   (a) Accomplish all necessary evacuation not undertaken by the Secretary of War or appropriate military commander, provide for the relocation of such persons in appropriate places, provide for their needs in such manner as may be appropriate, and supervise their activities.
   (b) Provide, insofar as feasible and desirable, for the employment of such persons at useful work in industry, commerce, agriculture, or public projects, prescribe the terms and conditions of such public employment, and safeguard the public interest in the private employment of such persons.
   (c) Secure the cooperation, assistance, or services of any governmental agency.
   (d) Prescribe regulations necessary or desirable to promote effective execution of such program, and, as a means of coordinating evacuation and relocation activities, consult with the Secretary of War with respect to regulations issued and measures taken by him.
   (e) Make such delegations of authority as he may deem necessary.
   (f) Employ necessary personnel, and make such expenditures, including the making of loans and grants and the purchase of real property, as may be necessary, within the limits of such funds as may be made available to the Authority.

4. The Director shall consult with the United States Employment Service and other agencies on employment and other problems incident to activities under this Order.

5. The Director shall cooperate with the Alien Property Custodian appointed pursuant to Executive Order No. 9095 of March 11, 1942, in formulating policies to govern the custody, management, and disposal by the Alien Property Custodian of property belonging to foreign nationals removed under this Order or under Executive Order No. 9066 of February 19, 1942; and may assist all other persons removed under either of such Executive Orders in the management and disposal of their property.

6. Departments and agencies of the United States are directed to cooperate with and assist the Director in his activities hereunder. The Departments of War and Justice, under the direction of the Secretary of War and the Attorney General, respectively, shall insofar as consistent with the national interest provide such protective, police, and investigational services as the Director shall find necessary in connection with activities under this Order.

7. There is established within the War Relocation Authority the War Relocation Work Corps. The Director shall provide, by general regulations, for the enlistment in such Corps, for the duration of the present war, of persons removed under this Order or under Executive Order No. 9066 of February 19, 1942, and shall prescribe the terms and conditions of the work to be performed by such Corps, and the compensation to be paid.

8. There is established within the War Relocation Authority a Liaison Committee on War Relocation, which shall consist of the Secretary of War, the Secretary of

the Treasury, the Attorney General, the Secretary of Agriculture, the Secretary of Labor, the Federal Security Administrator, the Director of Civilian Defense, and the Alien Property Custodian, or their deputies, and such' other persons or agencies as the Director may designate. The Liaison Committee shall meet at the call of the Director and shall assist him in his duties.

9. The Director shall keep the President informed with regard to the progress made in carrying out this Order, and perform such related duties as the President may from time to time assign to him.

10. In order to avoid duplication of evacuation activities under this Order and Executive Order No. 9066 of February 19, 1942, the Director shall not undertake any evacuation activities within military areas designated under said Executive Order No. 9066, without the prior approval of the Secretary of War or the appropriate military commander.

11. This Order does not limit the authority granted in Executive Order No. 8972 of December 12, 1941; Executive Order No. 9066 of February 19, 1942; Executive Order No. 9095 of March 11, 1942; Executive Proclamation No. 2525 of December 7, 1941; Executive Proclamation No. 2526 of December 8, 1941; Executive Proclamation No. 2527 of December 8, 1941; Executive Proclamation No. 2533 of December 19, 1941; or Executive Proclamation No. 2537 of January 14, 1942; nor does it limit the functions of the Federal Bureau of Investigation.

> [Although E.O. 9066 appears somewhat innocuous, if not cryptic, it was understood to be used to relocate residents of the west coast of Japanese descent and to a lesser extent, German and Italian descent. The order was a consequence of the fear of espionage following Japan's attack on Pearl Harbor and the belief that the west coast was vulnerable to attack. It is also believed that the historical context of racism towards Japanese on the west coast contributed to the relocation decision. Congress quickly enacted 18 U.S.C. sec. 97a (1942) which made it a crime to disobey the military commander in charge or the Secretary of War in their relocation efforts. Over 100,000 people, many citizens of the United States, were relocated and interned. President Roosevelt rescinded E.O. 9066 in 1944 and the interned individuals (most people of Japanese ethnicity but also individuals of German and Italian ancestry) were released. Unfortunately, many lost their homes and land, in addition to their liberty, as a consequence of relocation. In 1988 Congress, with the support of President Reagan, formally apologized to the internees. Subsequently all internees were paid $20,000 in reparations by the United States.]

EXECUTIVE ORDER 12291 (PRESIDENT REAGAN 1981)

Federal regulation

By the authority vested in me as President by the Constitution and laws of the United States of America, and in order to reduce the burdens of existing and future regulations, increase agency accountability for regulatory actions, provide for presidential oversight of the regulatory process, minimize duplication and conflict of regulations, and insure well-reasoned regulations, it is hereby ordered as follows:

Sec. 1. Definitions.   For the purposes of this Order:

(a) "Regulation" or "rule" means an agency statement of general applicability and future effect designed to implement, interpret, or prescribe law or policy or describing the procedure or practice requirements of an agency, but does not include:

   (1) Administrative actions governed by the provisions of Sections 556 and 557 of Title 5 of the United States Code;

   (2) Regulations issued with respect to a military or foreign affairs function of the United States; or

   (3) Regulations related to agency organization, management, or personnel.

(b) "Major rule" means any regulation that is likely to result in:
  (1) An annual effect on the economy of $100 million or more;
  (2) A major increase in costs or prices for consumers, individual industries, Federal, State, or local government agencies, or geographic regions; or
  (3) Significant adverse effects on competition, employment, investment, productivity, innovation, or on the ability of United States-based enterprises to compete with foreign-based enterprises in domestic or export markets.
(c) "Director" means the Director of the Office of Management and Budget.
(d) "Agency" means any authority of the United States that is an "agency" under 44 U.S.C. 3502 (1), excluding those agencies specified in 44 U.S.C. 3502(10).
(e) "Task Force" means the Presidential Task Force on Regulatory Relief.

Sec. 2. General Requirements.

In promulgating new regulations, reviewing existing regulations, and developing legislative proposals concerning regulation, all agencies, to the extent permitted by law, shall adhere to the following requirements:

(a) Administrative decisions shall be based on adequate information concerning the need for and consequences of proposed government action;
(b) Regulatory action shall not be undertaken unless the potential benefits to society for the regulation outweigh the potential costs to society;
(c) Regulatory objectives shall be chosen to maximize the net benefits to society;
(d) Among alternative approaches to any given regulatory objective, the alternative involving the least net cost to society shall be chosen; and
(e) Agencies shall set regulatory priorities with the aim of maximizing the aggregate net benefits to society, taking into account the condition of the particular industries affected by regulations, the condition of the national economy, and other regulatory actions contemplated for the future.

Sec. 3. Regulatory Impact Analysis and Review.

(a) In order to implement Section 2 of this Order, each agency shall, in connection with every major rule, prepare, and to the extent permitted by law consider, a Regulatory Impact Analysis. Such Analysis may be combined with any Regulatory Flexibility Analyses performed under 5 U.S.C. 603 and 604.
(b) Each agency shall initially determine whether a rule it intends to propose or to issue is a major rule, provided that, the Director, subject to the direction of the Task Force, shall have authority, in accordance with Sections 1(b) and 2 of this Order, to prescribe criteria for making such determinations, to order a rule to be treated as a major rule, and to require any set of related rules to be considered together as a major rule.
(c) Except as provided in Section 8 of this Order, agencies shall prepare Regulatory Impact Analyses of major rules and transmit them, along with all notices of proposed rule-making and all final rules, to the Director as follows:
  (1) If no notice of proposed rulemaking is to be published for a proposed major rule that is not an emergency rule, the agency shall prepare only a final Regulatory Impact Analysis, which shall be transmitted, along with the proposed rule, to the Director at least 60 days prior to the publication of the major rule as a final rule;
  (2) With respect to all other major rules, the agency shall prepare a preliminary Regulatory Impact Analysis, which shall be transmitted, along with a notice of proposed rulemaking, to the Director at least 60 days prior to the publication of a notice of proposed rulemaking, and a final Regulatory Impact Analysis, which shall be transmitted along with the final rule at least 30 days prior to the publication of the major rule as a final rule;

(3) For all rules other than major rules, agencies shall submit to the Director, at least 10 days prior to publication, every notice of proposed rulemaking and final rule.

(d) To permit each proposed major rule to be analyzed in light of the requirements stated in Section 2 of this Order, each preliminary and final Regulatory Impact Analysis shall contain the following information:

(1) A description of the potential benefits of the rule, including any beneficial effects that cannot be quantified in monetary terms, and the identification of those likely to receive the benefits;

(2) A description of the potential costs of the rule, including any adverse effects that cannot be quantified in monetary terms, and the identification of those likely to bear the costs;

(3) A determination of the potential net benefits of the rule, including an evaluation of effects that cannot be quantified in monetary terms;

(4) A description of alternative approaches that could substantially achieve the same regulatory goal at lower cost, together with an analysis of this potential benefit and costs and a brief explanation of the legal reasons why such alternatives, if proposed, could not be adopted; and

(5) Unless covered by the description required under paragraph (4) of this subsection, an explanation of any legal reasons why the rule cannot be based on the requirements set forth in Section 2 of this Order.

(e) (1) The Director, subject to the direction of the Task Force, which shall resolve any issues raised under this Order or ensure that they are presented to the President, is authorized to review any preliminary or final Regulatory Impact Analysis, notice of proposed rulemaking, or final rule based on the requirements of this Order.

(2) The Director shall be deemed to have concluded review unless the Director advises an agency to the contrary under subsection (f) of this Section:

(A) Within 60 days of a submission under subsection (c)(1) or a submission of a preliminary Regulatory Impact Analysis or notice of proposed rule making under subsection (c)(2);

(B) Within 30 days of the submission of a final Regulatory Impact Analysis and a final rule under subsection (c)(2); and

(C) Within 10 days of the submission of a notice of proposed rulemaking or final rule under subsection (c)(3).

(f) (1) Upon the request of the Director, an agency shall consult with the Director concerning the review of a preliminary Regulatory Impact Analysis or notice of proposed rulemaking under this Order, and shall, subject to Section 8(a)(2) of this Order, refrain from publishing its preliminary Regulatory Impact Analysis or notice of proposed rulemaking until such review is concluded.

(2) Upon receiving notice that the Director intends to submit views with respect to any final Regulatory Impact Analysis or final rule, the agency shall, subject to Section 8(a)(2) of this Order, refrain from publishing its final Regulatory Impact Analysis or final rule until the agency has responded to the Director's views, and incorporated those views and the agency's response in the rulemaking file.

(3) Nothing in this subsection shall be construed as displacing the agencies' responsibilities delegated by law.

(g) For every rule for which an agency publishes a notice of proposed rulemaking, the agency shall include in its notice:

(1) A brief statement setting forth the agency's initial determination whether the proposed rule is a major rule, together with the reasons underlying that determination; and

(2) For each proposed major rule, a brief summary of the agency's preliminary Regulatory Impact Analysis.

(h) Agencies shall make their preliminary and final Regulatory Impact Analyses available to the public.

(i) Agencies shall initiate reviews of currently effective rules in accordance with the purposes of this Order, and perform Regulatory Impact Analyses of currently effective major rules. The Director, subject to the direction of the Task Force, may designate currently effective rules for review in accordance with this Order, and establish schedules for reviews and Analyses under this Order.

Sec. 4. Regulatory Review.   *Before approving any final major rule, such agency shall:*

(a) Make a determination that the regulation is clearly within the authority delegated by law and consistent with congressional intent, and include in the Federal Register at the time of promulgation a memorandum of law supporting that determination.

(b) Make a determination that the factual conclusions upon which the rule is based have substantial support in the agency record, viewed as a whole, with full attention to public comments in general and the comments of persons directly affected by the rule in particular.

Sec. 5. Regulatory Agendas.

(a) Each agency shall publish, in October and April of each year, an agenda of proposed regulations that the agency has issued or expects to issue, and currently effective rules that are under agency review pursuant to this Order. These agendas may be incorporated with the agendas published under 5 U.S.C. 602, and must contain at the minimum:

    (1) A summary of the nature of each major rule being considered, the objectives and legal basis for the issuance of the rule, and an approximate § *13196* schedule for completing action on any major rule for which the agency has issued a notice of proposed rulemaking;

    (2) The name and telephone number of a knowledgeable agency official for each item on the agenda; and

    (3) A list of existing regulations to be reviewed under the terms of this Order, and a brief discussion of each such regulation.

(b) The Director, subject to the direction of the Task Force, may, to the extent permitted by law:

    (1) Require agencies to provide additional information in an agenda; and

    (2) Require publication of the agenda in any form.

Sec. 6. The Task Force and Office of Management and Budget.

(a) To the extent permitted by law, the Director shall have authority, subject to the direction of the Task Force, to:

    (1) Designate any proposed or existing rule as a major rule in accordance with Section 1(b) of this Order;

    (2) Prepare and promulgate uniform standards for the identification of major rules and the development of Regulatory Impact Analyses;

    (3) Require an agency to obtain and evaluate, in connection with a regulation, any additional relevant data from any appropriate source;

    (4) Waive the requirements of Sections 3, 4, or 7 of this Order with respect to any proposed or existing major rule;

    (5) Identify duplicative, overlapping and conflicting rules, existing or proposed, and existing or proposed rules that are inconsistent with the policies underlying

statutes governing agencies other than the issuing agency or with the purposes of this Order, and, in each such case, require appropriate interagency consultation to minimize or eliminate such duplication, overlap, or conflict;

(6) Develop procedures for estimating the annual benefits and costs of agency regulations, on both an aggregate and economic or industrial sector basis, for purposes of compiling a regulatory budget;

(7) In consultation with interested agencies, prepare for consideration by the President recommendations for changes in the agencies' statutes; and

(8) Monitor agency compliance with the requirements of this Order and advise the President with respect to such compliance.

(b) The Director, subject to the direction of the Task Force, is authorized to establish procedures for the performance of all functions vested in the Director by this Order. The Director shall take appropriate steps to coordinate the implementation of the analysis, transmittal, review, and clearance provisions of this Order with the authorities and requirements provided for or imposed upon the Director and agencies under the Regulatory Flexibility Act, 5 U.S.C. 601 *et seq.*, and the Paperwork Reduction Plan Act of 1980, 44 U.S.C. 3501 *et seq.*

Sec. 7. Pending Regulations.

(a) To the extent necessary to permit reconsideration in accordance with this Order, agencies shall, except as provided in Section 8 of this Order, suspend or postpone the effective dates of all major rules that they have promulgated in final form as of the date of this Order, but that have not yet become effective, excluding:

(1) Major rules that cannot legally be postponed or suspended;

(2) Major rules that, for good cause, ought to become effective as final rules without reconsideration. Agencies shall prepare, in accordance with Section 3 of this Order, a final Regulatory Impact Analysis for each major rule that they suspend or postpone.

(b) Agencies shall report to the Director no later than 15 days prior to the effective date of any rule that the agency has promulgated in final form as of the date of this Order, and that has not yet become effective, and that will not be reconsidered under subsection (a) of this Section:

(1) That the rule is excepted from reconsideration under subsection (a), including a brief statement of the legal or other reasons for that determination; or

(2) That the rule is not a major rule.

(c) The Director, subject to the direction of the Task Force, is authorized, to the extent permitted by law, to:

(1) Require reconsideration, in accordance with this Order, of any major rule that an agency has issued in final form as of the date of this Order and that has not become effective; and

(2) Designate a rule that an agency has issued in final form as of the date of this Order and that has not yet become effective as a major rule in accordance with Section 1(b) of this Order.

(d) Agencies may, in accordance with the Administrative Procedure Act and other applicable statutes, permit major rules that they have issued in final form as of the date of this Order, and that have not yet become effective, to take effect as interim rules while they are being reconsidered in accordance with this Order, provided that, agencies shall report to the Director, no later than 15 days before any such rule is proposed to take effect as an interim rule, that the rule should appropriately take effect as an interim rule while the rule is under reconsideration.

(e) Except as provided in Section 8 of this Order, agencies shall, to the extent permitted by law, refrain from promulgating as a final rule any proposed major rule that has been published or issued as of the date of this Order until a final

Regulatory Impact Analysis, in accordance with Section 3 of this Order, has been prepared for the proposed major rule.

(f)   Agencies shall report to the Director, no later than 30 days prior to promulgating as a final rule any proposed rule that the agency has published or issued as of the date of this Order and that has not been considered under the terms of this Order:

    (1)   That the rule cannot legally be considered in accordance with the Order, together with a brief explanation of the legal reasons barring such consideration; or

    (2)   That the rule is not a major rule, in which case the agency shall submit to the Director a copy of the proposed rule.

(g)   The Director, subject to the direction of the Task Force, is authorized, to the extent permitted by law, to:

    (1)   Require consideration, in accordance with this Order, of any proposed major rule that the agency has published or issued as of the date of this Order; and

    (2)   Designate a proposed rule that an agency has published or issued as of the date of this Order, as a major rule in accordance with Section 1(b) of this Order.

(h)   The Director shall be deemed to have determined that an agency's report to the Director under subsections (b), (d), or (f) of this Section is consistent with the purposes of this Order, unless the Director advises the agency to the contrary:

    (1)   Within 15 days of its report, in the case of any report under subsections (b) or (d); or

    (2)   Within 30 days of its report, in the case of any report under subsection (f).

(i)   This Section does not supersede the President's Memorandum of January 29, 1981, entitled "Postponement of Pending Regulations," which shall remain in effect until March 30, 1981.

(j)   In complying with this Section, agencies shall comply with all applicable provisions of the Administrative Procedure Act, and with any other procedural requirements made applicable to the agencies by other statutes.

Sec. 8. Exemptions.

(a)   The procedures prescribed by this Order shall not apply to:

    (1)   Any regulation that responds to an emergency situation, provided that, any such regulation shall be reported to the Director as soon as is practicable, the agency shall publish in the Federal Register a statement of the reasons why it is impracticable for the agency to follow the procedures of this Order with respect to such a rule, and the agency shall prepare and transmit as soon as is practicable a Regulatory Impact Analysis of any such major rule; and

    (2)   Any regulation for which consideration or reconsideration under the terms of this Order would conflict with deadlines imposed by statute or by judicial order, provided that, any such regulation shall be reported to the Director together with a brief explanation of the conflict, the agency shall publish in the Federal Register a statement of the reasons why it is impracticable for the agency to follow the procedures of this Order with respect to such a rule, and the agency, in consultation with the Director, shall adhere to the requirements of this Order to the extent permitted by statutory or judicial deadlines.

(b)   The Director, subject to the direction of the Task Force, may, in accordance with the purposes of this Order, exempt any class or category of regulations from any or all requirements of this Order.

Sec. 9. Judicial Review.

(a)   This Order is intended only to improve the internal management of the Federal government, and is not intended to create any right or benefit, substantive or procedural, enforceable at law by a party against the United States, its agencies, its officers or any person. The determinations made by agencies under Section 4 of this Order, and any Regulatory Impact Analyses for any rule, shall be made part of the whole record of agency action in connection with the rule.

Sec. 10. Revocations. *Executive Orders No. 12044, as amended, and No. 12174 are revoked.*

EXECUTIVE ORDER 12866 (PRESIDENT CLINTON 1993)

Regulatory Planning and Review

The American people deserve a regulatory system that works for them, not against them: a regulatory system that protects and improves their health, safety, environment, and well-being and improves the performance of the economy without imposing unacceptable or unreasonable costs on society; regulatory policies that recognize that the private sector and private markets are the best engine for economic growth; regulatory approaches that respect the role of State, local, and tribal governments; and regulations that are effective, consistent, sensible, and understandable. We do not have such a regulatory system today.

With this Executive order, the Federal Government begins a program to reform and make more efficient the regulatory process. The objectives of this Executive order are to enhance planning and coordination with respect to both new and existing regulations; to reaffirm the primacy of Federal agencies in the regulatory decision-making process; to restore the integrity and legitimacy of regulatory review and oversight; and to make the process more accessible and open to the public. In pursuing these objectives, the regulatory process shall be conducted so as to meet applicable statutory requirements and with due regard to the discretion that has been entrusted to the Federal agencies.

Accordingly, by the authority vested in me as President by the Constitution and the laws of the United States of America, it is hereby ordered as follows:

Section 1. Statement of Regulatory Philosophy and Principles.

(a) *The Regulatory Philosophy.* Federal agencies should promulgate only such regulations as are required by law, are necessary to interpret the law, or are made necessary by compelling public need, such as material failures of private markets to protect or improve the health and safety of the public, the environment, or the well-being of the American people. In deciding whether and how to regulate, agencies should assess all costs and benefits of available regulatory alternatives, including the alternative of not regulating. Costs and benefits shall be understood to include both quantifiable measures (to the fullest extent that these can be usefully estimated) and qualitative measures of costs and benefits that are difficult to quantify, but nevertheless essential to consider. Further, in choosing among alternative regulatory approaches, agencies should select those approaches that maximize net benefits (including potential economic, environmental, public health and safety, and other advantages; distributive impacts; and equity), unless a statute requires another regulatory approach.

(b) *The Principles of Regulation.* To ensure that the agencies' regulatory programs are consistent with the philosophy set forth above, agencies should adhere to the following principles, to the extent permitted by law and where applicable:

(1) Each agency shall identify the problem that it intends to address (including, where applicable, the failures of private markets or public institutions that warrant new agency action) as well as assess the significance of that problem.

(2) Each agency shall examine whether existing regulations (or other law) have created, or contributed to, the problem that a new regulation is intended to

correct and whether those regulations (or other law) should be modified to achieve the intended goal of regulation more effectively.

(3) Each agency shall identify and assess available alternatives to direct regulation, including providing economic incentives to encourage the desired behavior, such as user fees or marketable permits, or providing information upon which choices can be made by the public.

(4) In setting regulatory priorities, each agency shall consider, to the extent reasonable, the degree and nature of the risks posed by various substances or activities within its jurisdiction.

(5) When an agency determines that a regulation is the best available method of achieving the regulatory objective, it shall design its regulations in the most cost-effective manner to achieve the regulatory objective. In doing so, each agency shall consider incentives for innovation, consistency, predictability, the costs of enforcement and compliance (to the government, regulated entities, and the public), flexibility, distributive impacts, and equity.

(6) Each agency shall assess both the costs and the benefits of the intended regulation and, recognizing that some costs and benefits are difficult to quantify, propose or adopt a regulation only upon a reasoned determination that the benefits of the intended regulation justify its costs.

(7) Each agency shall base its decisions on the best reasonably obtainable scientific, technical, economic, and other information concerning the need for, and consequences of, the intended regulation.

(8) Each agency shall identify and assess alternative forms of regulation and shall, to the extent feasible, specify performance objectives, rather than specifying the behavior or manner of compliance that regulated entities must adopt.

(9) Wherever feasible, agencies shall seek views of appropriate State, local, and tribal officials before imposing regulatory requirements that might significantly or uniquely affect those governmental entities. Each agency shall assess the effects of Federal regulations on State, local, and tribal governments, including specifically the availability of resources to carry out those mandates, and seek to minimize those burdens that uniquely or significantly affect such governmental entities, consistent with achieving regulatory objectives. In addition, as appropriate, agencies shall seek to harmonize Federal regulatory actions with related State, local, and tribal regulatory and other governmental functions.

(10) Each agency shall avoid regulations that are inconsistent, incompatible, or duplicative with its other regulations or those of other Federal agencies.

(11) Each agency shall tailor its regulations to impose the least burden on society, including individuals, businesses of differing sizes, and other entities (including small communities and governmental entities), consistent with obtaining the regulatory objectives, taking into account, among other things, and to the extent practicable, the costs of cumulative regulations.

(12) Each agency shall draft its regulations to be simple and easy to understand, with the goal of minimizing the potential for uncertainty and litigation arising from such uncertainty.

Sec. 2. Organization.   An efficient regulatory planning and review process is vital to ensure that the Federal Government's regulatory system best serves the American people.

(a) *The Agencies.* Because Federal agencies are the repositories of significant substantive expertise and experience, they are responsible for developing regulations and assuring that the regulations are consistent with applicable law, the President's priorities, and the principles set forth in this Executive order.

(b) *The Office of Management and Budget.* Coordinated review of agency rulemaking is necessary to ensure that regulations are consistent with applicable law, the President's priorities, and the principles set forth in this Executive order, and that decisions made by one agency do not conflict with the policies or actions taken or planned by another agency. The Office of Management and Budget (OMB) shall carry out that review function. Within OMB, the Office of Information and Regulatory Affairs (OIRA) is the repository of expertise concerning regulatory issues, including methodologies and procedures that affect more than one agency, this Executive order, and the President's regulatory policies. To the extent permitted by law, OMB shall provide guidance to agencies and assist the President, the Vice President, and other regulatory policy advisors to the President in regulatory planning and shall be the entity that reviews individual regulations, as provided by this Executive order.

(c) *The Vice President.* The Vice President is the principal advisor to the President on, and shall coordinate the development and presentation of recommendations concerning, regulatory policy, planning, and review, as set forth in this Executive order. In fulfilling their responsibilities under this Executive order, the President and the Vice President shall be assisted by the regulatory policy advisors within the Executive Office of the President and by such agency officials and personnel as the President and the Vice President may, from time to time, consult.

Sec. 3. Definitions.   For purposes of this Executive order:

(a) "Advisors" refers to such regulatory policy advisors to the President as the President and Vice President may from time to time consult, including, among others:

    (1) the Director of OMB;

    (2) the Chair (or another member) of the Council of Economic Advisers;

    (3) the Assistant to the President for Economic Policy;

    (4) the Assistant to the President for Domestic Policy;

    (5) the Assistant to the President for National Security Affairs;

    (6) the Assistant to the President for Science and Technology;

    (7) the Assistant to the President for Intergovernmental Affairs;

    (8) the Assistant to the President and Staff Secretary;

    (9) the Assistant to the President and Chief of Staff to the Vice President;

    (10) the Assistant to the President and Counsel to the President;

    (11) the Deputy Assistant to the President and Director of the White House Office on Environmental Policy; and

    (12) the Administrator of OIRA, who also shall coordinate communications relating to this Executive order among the agencies, OMB, the other Advisors, and the Office of the Vice President.

(b) "Agency," unless otherwise indicated, means any authority of the United States that is an "agency" under 44 U.S.C. 3502(1), other than those considered to be independent regulatory agencies, as defined in 44 U.S.C. 3502(10).

(c) "Director" means the Director of OMB.

(d) "Regulation" or "rule" means an agency statement of general applicability and future effect, which the agency intends to have the force and effect of law, that is designed to implement, interpret, or prescribe law or policy or to describe the procedure or practice requirements of an agency. It does not, however, include:

    (1) Regulations or rules issued in accordance with the formal rulemaking provisions of 5 U.S.C. 556, 557;

    (2) Regulations or rules that pertain to a military or foreign affairs function of the United States, other than procurement regulations and regulations involving the import or export of non-defense articles and services;

(3) Regulations or rules that are limited to agency organization, management, or personnel matters; or

(4) Any other category of regulations exempted by the Administrator of OIRA.

(e) "Regulatory action" means any substantive action by an agency (normally published in the **Federal Register**) that promulgates or is expected to lead to the promulgation of a final rule or regulation, including notices of inquiry, advance notices of proposed rulemaking, and notices of proposed rulemaking.

(f) "Significant regulatory action" means any regulatory action that is likely to result in a rule that may:

(1) Have an annual effect on the economy of $100 million or more or adversely affect in a material way the economy, a sector of the economy, productivity, competition, jobs, the environment, public health or safety, or State, local, or tribal governments or communities;

(2) Create a serious inconsistency or otherwise interfere with an action taken or planned by another agency;

(3) Materially alter the budgetary impact of entitlements, grants, user fees, or loan programs or the rights and obligations of recipients thereof; or

(4) Raise novel legal or policy issues arising out of legal mandates, the President's priorities, or the principles set forth in this Executive order.

Sec. 4. *Planning Mechanism.*

In order to have an effective regulatory program, to provide for coordination of regulations, to maximize consultation and the resolution of potential conflicts at an early stage, to involve the public and its State, local, and tribal officials in regulatory planning, and to ensure that new or revised regulations promote the President's priorities and the principles set forth in this Executive order, these procedures shall be followed, to the extent permitted by law:

(a) *Agencies' Policy Meeting.* Early in each year's planning cycle, the Vice President shall convene a meeting of the Advisors and the heads of agencies to seek a common understanding of priorities and to coordinate regulatory efforts to be accomplished in the upcoming year.

(b) *Unified Regulatory Agenda.* For purposes of this subsection, the term "agency" or "agencies" shall also include those considered to be independent regulatory agencies, as defined in 44 U.S.C. 3502(10). Each agency shall prepare an agenda of all regulations under development or review, at a time and in a manner specified by the Administrator of OIRA. The description of each regulatory action shall contain, at a minimum, a regulation identifier number, a brief summary of the action, the legal authority for the action, any legal deadline for the action, and the name and telephone number of a knowledgeable agency official. Agencies may incorporate the information required under 5 U.S.C. 602 and 41 U.S.C. 402 into these agendas.

(c) *The Regulatory Plan.* For purposes of this subsection, the term "agency" or "agencies" shall also include those considered to be independent regulatory agencies, as defined in 44 U.S.C. 3502(10).

(1) As part of the Unified Regulatory Agenda, beginning in 1994, each agency shall prepare a Regulatory Plan (Plan) of the most important significant regulatory actions that the agency reasonably expects to issue in proposed or final form in that fiscal year or thereafter. The Plan shall be approved personally by the agency head and shall contain at a minimum:

(A) A statement of the agency's regulatory objectives and priorities and how they relate to the President's priorities;

(B) A summary of each planned significant regulatory action including, to the extent possible, alternatives to be considered and preliminary estimates of the anticipated costs and benefits;

(C) A summary of the legal basis for each such action, including whether any aspect of the action is required by statute or court order;

(D) A statement of the need for each such action and, if applicable, how the action will reduce risks to public health, safety, or the environment, as well as how the magnitude of the risk addressed by the action relates to other risks within the jurisdiction of the agency;

(E) The agency's schedule for action, including a statement of any applicable statutory or judicial deadlines; and

(F) The name, address, and telephone number of a person the public may contact for additional information about the planned regulatory action.

(2) Each agency shall forward its Plan to OIRA by June 1st of each year.

(3) Within 10 calendar days after OIRA has received an agency's Plan, OIRA shall circulate it to other affected agencies, the Advisors, and the Vice President.

(4) An agency head who believes that a planned regulatory action of another agency may conflict with its own policy or action taken or planned shall promptly notify, in writing, the Administrator of OIRA, who shall forward that communication to the issuing agency, the Advisors, and the Vice President.

(5) If the Administrator of OIRA believes that a planned regulatory action of an agency may be inconsistent with the President's priorities or the principles set forth in this Executive order or may be in conflict with any policy or action taken or planned by another agency, the Administrator of OIRA shall promptly notify, in writing, the affected agencies, the Advisors, and the Vice President.

(6) The Vice President, with the Advisors' assistance, may consult with the heads of agencies with respect to their Plans and, in appropriate instances, request further consideration or inter-agency coordination.

(7) The Plans developed by the issuing agency shall be published annually in the October publication of the Unified Regulatory Agenda. This publication shall be made available to the Congress; State, local, and tribal governments; and the public. Any views on any aspect of any agency Plan, including whether any planned regulatory action might conflict with any other planned or existing regulation, impose any unintended consequences on the public, or confer any unclaimed benefits on the public, should be directed to the issuing agency, with a copy to OIRA.

(d) *Regulatory Working Group.* Within 30 days of the date of this Executive order, the Administrator of OIRA shall convene a Regulatory Working Group ("Working Group"), which shall consist of representatives of the heads of each agency that the Administrator determines to have significant domestic regulatory responsibility, the Advisors, and the Vice President. The Administrator of OIRA shall chair the Working Group and shall periodically advise the Vice President on the activities of the Working Group. The Working Group shall serve as a forum to assist agencies in identifying and analyzing important regulatory issues (including, among others (1) the development of innovative regulatory techniques, (2) the methods, efficacy, and utility of comparative risk assessment in regulatory decision-making, and (3) the development of short forms and other streamlined regulatory approaches for small businesses and other entities). The Working Group shall meet at least quarterly and may meet as a whole or in subgroups of agencies with an interest in particular issues or subject areas. To inform its discussions, the Working Group may commission analytical studies and reports by OIRA, the Administrative Conference of the United States, or any other agency.

(e) *Conferences.* The Administrator of OIRA shall meet quarterly with representatives of State, local, and tribal governments to identify both existing and proposed regulations that may uniquely or significantly affect those governmental entities. The Administrator of OIRA shall also convene, from time to time, conferences with representatives of businesses, nongovernmental organizations, and the public to discuss regulatory issues of common concern.

Sec. 5. Existing Regulations.   In order to reduce the regulatory burden on the American people, their families, their communities, their State, local, and tribal governments, and their industries; to determine whether regulations promulgated by the executive branch of the Federal Government have become unjustified or unnecessary as a result of changed circumstances; to confirm that regulations are both compatible with each other and not duplicative or inappropriately burdensome in the aggregate; to ensure that all regulations are consistent with the President's priorities and the principles set forth in this Executive order, within applicable law; and to otherwise improve the effectiveness of existing regulations:

(a) Within 90 days of the date of this Executive order, each agency shall submit to OIRA a program, consistent with its resources and regulatory priorities, under which the agency will periodically review its existing significant regulations to determine whether any such regulations should be modified or eliminated so as to make the agency's regulatory program more effective in achieving the regulatory objectives, less burdensome, or in greater alignment with the President's priorities and the principles set forth in this Executive order. Any significant regulations selected for review shall be included in the agency's annual Plan. The agency shall also identify any legislative mandates that require the agency to promulgate or continue to impose regulations that the agency believes are unnecessary or outdated by reason of changed circumstances.

(b) The Administrator of OIRA shall work with the Regulatory Working Group and other interested entities to pursue the objectives of this section. State, local, and tribal governments are specifically encouraged to assist in the identification of regulations that impose significant or unique burdens on those governmental entities and that appear to have outlived their justification or be otherwise inconsistent with the public interest.

(c) The Vice President, in consultation with the Advisors, may identify for review by the appropriate agency or agencies other existing regulations of an agency or groups of regulations of more than one agency that affect a particular group, industry, or sector of the economy, or may identify legislative mandates that may be appropriate for reconsideration by the Congress.

Sec. 6. Centralized Review of Regulations.   The guidelines set forth below shall apply to all regulatory actions, for both new and existing regulations, by agencies other than those agencies specifically exempted by the Administrator of OIRA:

(a) *Agency Responsibilities.*
  (1) Each agency shall (consistent with its own rules, regulations, or procedures) provide the public with meaningful participation in the regulatory process. In particular, before issuing a notice of proposed rulemaking, each agency should, where appropriate, seek the involvement of those who are intended to benefit from and those expected to be burdened by any regulation (including, specifically, State, local, and tribal officials). In addition, each agency should afford the public a meaningful opportunity to comment on any proposed regulation, which in most cases should include a comment period of not less than 60 days. Each agency also is directed to explore and, where appropriate, use consensual mechanisms for developing regulations, including negotiated rulemaking.

(2) Within 60 days of the date of this Executive order, each agency head shall designate a Regulatory Policy Officer who shall report to the agency head. The Regulatory Policy Officer shall be involved at each stage of the regulatory process to foster the development of effective, innovative, and least burdensome regulations and to further the principles set forth in this Executive order.

(3) In addition to adhering to its own rules and procedures and to the requirements of the Administrative Procedure Act, the Regulatory Flexibility Act, the Paperwork Reduction Act, and other applicable law, each agency shall develop its regulatory actions in a timely fashion and adhere to the following procedures with respect to a regulatory action:

(A) Each agency shall provide OIRA, at such times and in the manner specified by the Administrator of OIRA, with a list of its planned regulatory actions, indicating those which the agency believes are significant regulatory actions within the meaning of this Executive order. Absent a material change in the development of the planned regulatory action, those not designated as significant will not be subject to review under this section unless, within 10 working days of receipt of the list, the Administrator of OIRA notifies the agency that OIRA has determined that a planned regulation is a significant regulatory action within the meaning of this Executive order. The Administrator of OIRA may waive review of any planned regulatory action designated by the agency as significant, in which case the agency need not further comply with subsection (a)(3)(B) or subsection (a)(3)(C) of this section.

(B) For each matter identified as, or determined by the Administrator of OIRA to be, a significant regulatory action, the issuing agency shall provide to OIRA:

(i) The text of the draft regulatory action, together with a reasonably detailed description of the need for the regulatory action and an explanation of how the regulatory action will meet that need; and

(ii) An assessment of the potential costs and benefits of the regulatory action, including an explanation of the manner in which the regulatory action is consistent with a statutory mandate and, to the extent permitted by law, promotes the President's priorities and avoids undue interference with State, local, and tribal governments in the exercise of their governmental functions.

(C) For those matters identified as, or determined by the Administrator of OIRA to be, a significant regulatory action within the scope of section 3(f)(1), the agency shall also provide to OIRA the following additional information developed as part of the agency's decision-making process (unless prohibited by law):

(i) An assessment, including the underlying analysis, of benefits anticipated from the regulatory action (such as, but not limited to, the promotion of the efficient functioning of the economy and private markets, the enhancement of health and safety, the protection of the natural environment, and the elimination or reduction of discrimination or bias) together with, to the extent feasible, a quantification of those benefits;

(ii) An assessment, including the underlying analysis, of costs anticipated from the regulatory action (such as, but not limited to, the direct cost both to the government in administering the regulation and to businesses and others in complying with the regulation, and any adverse effects on the efficient functioning of the economy, private markets (including productivity, employment, and competitiveness), health, safety, and the natural environment), together with, to the extent feasible, a quantification of those costs; and

(iii) An assessment, including the underlying analysis, of costs and benefits of potentially effective and reasonably feasible alternatives to the planned regulation, identified by the agencies or the public (including improving the current regulation and reasonably viable nonregulatory actions), and an explanation why the planned regulatory action is preferable to the identified potential alternatives.

(D) In emergency situations or when an agency is obligated by law to act more quickly than normal review procedures allow, the agency shall notify OIRA as soon as possible and, to the extent practicable, comply with subsections (a)(3)(B) and (C) of this section. For those regulatory actions that are governed by a statutory or court-imposed deadline, the agency shall, to the extent practicable, schedule rulemaking proceedings so as to permit sufficient time for OIRA to conduct its review, as set forth below in subsection (b)(2) through (4) of this section.

(E) After the regulatory action has been published in the **Federal Register** or otherwise issued to the public, the agency shall:

(i) Make available to the public the information set forth in subsections (a)(3)(B) and (C);

(ii) Identify for the public, in a complete, clear, and simple manner, the substantive changes between the draft submitted to OIRA for review and the action subsequently announced; and

(iii) Identify for the public those changes in the regulatory action that were made at the suggestion or recommendation of OIRA.

(F) All information provided to the public by the agency shall be in plain, understandable language.

(b) *OIRA Responsibilities.* The Administrator of OIRA shall provide meaningful guidance and oversight so that each agency's regulatory actions are consistent with applicable law, the President's priorities, and the principles set forth in this Executive order and do not conflict with the policies or actions of another agency. OIRA shall, to the extent permitted by law, adhere to the following guidelines:

(1) OIRA may review only actions identified by the agency or by OIRA as significant regulatory actions under subsection (a)(3)(A) of this section.

(2) OIRA shall waive review or notify the agency in writing of the results of its review within the following time periods:

(A) For any notices of inquiry, advance notices of proposed rulemaking, or other preliminary regulatory actions prior to a Notice of Proposed Rulemaking, within 10 working days after the date of submission of the draft action to OIRA;

(B) For all other regulatory actions, within 90 calendar days after the date of submission of the information set forth in subsections (a)(3)(B) and (C) of this section, unless OIRA has previously reviewed this information and, since that review, there has been no material change in the facts and circumstances upon which the regulatory action is based, in which case, OIRA shall complete its review within 45 days; and

(C) The review process may be extended (1) once by no more than 30 calendar days upon the written approval of the Director and (2) at the request of the agency head.

(3) For each regulatory action that the Administrator of OIRA returns to an agency for further consideration of some or all of its provisions, the Administrator of OIRA shall provide the issuing agency a written

explanation for such return, setting forth the pertinent provision of this Executive order on which OIRA is relying. If the agency head disagrees with some or all of the bases for the return, the agency head shall so inform the Administrator of OIRA in writing.

(4) Except as otherwise provided by law or required by a Court, in order to ensure greater openness, accessibility, and accountability in the regulatory review process, OIRA shall be governed by the following disclosure requirements:

(A) Only the Administrator of OIRA (or a particular designee) shall receive oral communications initiated by persons not employed by the executive branch of the Federal Government regarding the substance of a regulatory action under OIRA review;

(B) All substantive communications between OIRA personnel and persons not employed by the executive branch of the Federal Government regarding a regulatory action under review shall be governed by the following guidelines:

(i) A representative from the issuing agency shall be invited to any meeting between OIRA personnel and such person(s);

(ii) OIRA shall forward to the issuing agency, within 10 working days of receipt of the communication(s), all written communications, regardless of format, between OIRA personnel and any person who is not employed by the executive branch of the Federal Government, and the dates and names of individuals involved in all substantive oral communications (including meetings to which an agency representative was invited, but did not attend, and telephone conversations between OIRA personnel and any such persons); and

(iii) OIRA shall publicly disclose relevant information about such communication(s), as set forth below in subsection (b)(4)(C) of this section.

(C) OIRA shall maintain a publicly available log that shall contain, at a minimum, the following information pertinent to regulatory actions under review:

(i) The status of all regulatory actions, including if (and if so, when and by whom) Vice Presidential and Presidential consideration was requested;

(ii) A notation of all written communications forwarded to an issuing agency under subsection (b)(4)(B)(ii) of this section; and

(iii) The dates and names of individuals involved in all substantive oral communications, including meetings and telephone conversations, between OIRA personnel and any person not employed by the executive branch of the Federal Government, and the subject matter discussed during such communications.

(D) After the regulatory action has been published in the **Federal Register** or otherwise issued to the public, or after the agency has announced its decision not to publish or issue the regulatory action, OIRA shall make available to the public all documents exchanged between OIRA and the agency during the review by OIRA under this section.

(5) All information provided to the public by OIRA shall be in plain, understandable language.

Sec. 7. Resolution of Conflicts. To the extent permitted by law, disagreements or conflicts between or among agency heads or between OMB and any agency that cannot be resolved by the Administrator of OIRA shall be resolved by the President, or by the Vice President acting at the request of the President, with the relevant agency head (and, as appropriate, other interested government officials). Vice Presidential and Presidential consideration of such disagreements may be initiated only by the Director, by the head of the issuing agency, or by the head of an agency that has a significant interest in the regulatory action at issue. Such review will not be undertaken at the request of other persons, entities, or their agents.

Resolution of such conflicts shall be informed by recommendations developed by the Vice President, after consultation with the Advisors (and other executive branch officials or personnel whose responsibilities to the President include the subject matter at issue). The development of these recommendations shall be concluded within 60 days after review has been requested.

During the Vice Presidential and Presidential review period, communications with any person not employed by the Federal Government relating to the substance of the regulatory action under review and directed to the Advisors or their staffs or to the staff of the Vice President shall be in writing and shall be forwarded by the recipient to the affected agency(ies) for inclusion in the public docket(s). When the communication is not in writing, such Advisors or staff members shall inform the outside party that the matter is under review and that any comments should be submitted in writing.

At the end of this review process, the President, or the Vice President acting at the request of the President, shall notify the affected agency and the Administrator of OIRA of the President's decision with respect to the matter.

Sec. 8. Publication.   Except to the extent required by law, an agency shall not publish in the **Federal Register** or otherwise issue to the public any regulatory action that is subject to review under section 6 of this Executive order until

1. the Administrator of OIRA notifies the agency that OIRA has waived its review of the action or has completed its review without any requests for further consideration, or
2. the applicable time period in section 6(b)(2) expires without OIRA having notified the agency that it is returning the regulatory action for further consideration under section 6(b)(3), whichever occurs first. If the terms of the preceding sentence have not been satisfied and an agency wants to publish or otherwise issue a regulatory action, the head of that agency may request Presidential consideration through the Vice President, as provided under section 7 of this order. Upon receipt of this request, the Vice President shall notify OIRA and the Advisors. The guidelines and time period set forth in section 7 shall apply to the publication of regulatory actions for which Presidential consideration has been sought.

Sec. 9. Agency Authority.   Nothing in this order shall be construed as displacing the agencies' authority or responsibilities, as authorized by law.

Sec. 10. Judicial Review.   Nothing in this Executive order shall affect any otherwise available judicial review of agency action. This Executive order is intended only to improve the internal management of the Federal Government and does not create any right or benefit, substantive or procedural, enforceable at law or equity by a party against the United States, its agencies or instrumentalities, its officers or employees, or any other person.

Sec. 11. Revocations.   Executive Orders Nos. 12291 and 12498; all amendments to those Executive orders; all guidelines issued under those orders; and any exemptions from those orders heretofore granted for any category of rule are revoked.

EXECUTIVE ORDER 13132 (PRESIDENT CLINTON 1999)

Federalism

By the authority vested in me as President by the Constitution and the laws of the United States of America, and in order to guarantee the division of governmental responsibilities between the national government and the States that was intended by the Framers of the Constitution, to ensure that the principles of federalism established by the Framers guide the executive departments and agencies in the formulation and implementation of policies, and to further the policies of the Unfunded Mandates Reform Act, it is hereby ordered as follows:

Section 1. Definitions. *For purposes of this order:*

(a) "Policies that have federalism implications" refers to regulations, legislative comments or proposed legislation, and other policy statements or actions that have substantial direct effects on the States, on the relationship between the national government and the States, or on the distribution of power and responsibilities among the various levels of government.

(b) "State" or "States" refer to the States of the United States of America, individually or collectively, and, where relevant, to State governments, including units of local government and other political subdivisions established by the States.

(c) "Agency" means any authority of the United States that is an "agency" under 44 U.S.C. 3502(1), other than those considered to be independent regulatory agencies, as defined in 44 U.S.C. 3502(5).

(d) "State and local officials" means elected officials of State and local governments or their representative national organizations.

Sec. 2. Fundamental Federalism Principles. *In formulating and implementing policies that have federalism implications, agencies shall be guided by the following fundamental federalism principles:*

(a) Federalism is rooted in the belief that issues that are not national in scope or significance are most appropriately addressed by the level of government closest to the people.

(b) The people of the States created the national government and delegated to it enumerated governmental powers. All other sovereign powers, save those expressly prohibited the States by the Constitution, are reserved to the States or to the people.

(c) The constitutional relationship among sovereign governments, State and national, is inherent in the very structure of the Constitution and is formalized in and protected by the Tenth Amendment to the Constitution.

(d) The people of the States are free, subject only to restrictions in the Constitution itself or in constitutionally authorized Acts of Congress, to define the moral, political, and legal character of their lives.

(e) The Framers recognized that the States possess unique authorities, qualities, and abilities to meet the needs of the people and should function as laboratories of democracy.

(f) The nature of our constitutional system encourages a healthy diversity in the public policies adopted by the people of the several States according to their own conditions, needs, and desires. In the search for enlightened public policy, individual States and communities are free to experiment with a variety of approaches to public issues. One-size-fits-all approaches to public policy problems can inhibit the creation of effective solutions to those problems.

(g) Acts of the national government—whether legislative, executive, or judicial in nature—that exceed the enumerated powers of that government under the Constitution violate the principle of federalism established by the Framers.

(h) Policies of the national government should recognize the responsibility of—and should encourage opportunities for—individuals, families, neighborhoods, local governments, and private associations to achieve their personal, social, and economic objectives through cooperative effort.

(i) The national government should be deferential to the States when taking action that affects the policymaking discretion of the States and should act only with the greatest caution where State or local governments have identified uncertainties regarding the constitutional or statutory authority of the national government.

Sec. 3. Federalism Policymaking Criteria.   *In addition to adhering to the fundamental federalism principles set forth in section 2, agencies shall adhere, to the extent permitted by law, to the following criteria when formulating and implementing policies that have federalism implications:*

(a) There shall be strict adherence to constitutional principles. Agencies shall closely examine the constitutional and statutory authority supporting any action that would limit the policymaking discretion of the States and shall carefully assess the necessity for such action. To the extent practicable, State and local officials shall be consulted before any such action is implemented. Executive Order 12372 of July 14, 1982 ("Intergovernmental Review of Federal Programs") remains in effect for the programs and activities to which it is applicable.

(b) National action limiting the policymaking discretion of the States shall be taken only where there is constitutional and statutory authority for the action and the national activity is appropriate in light of the presence of a problem of national significance. Where there are significant uncertainties as to whether national action is authorized or appropriate, agencies shall consult with appropriate State and local officials to determine whether Federal objectives can be attained by other means.

(c) With respect to Federal statutes and regulations administered by the States, the national government shall grant the States the maximum administrative discretion possible. Intrusive Federal oversight of State administration is neither necessary nor desirable.

(d) When undertaking to formulate and implement policies that have federalism implications, agencies shall:
  (1) encourage States to develop their own policies to achieve program objectives and to work with appropriate officials in other States;
  (2) where possible, defer to the States to establish standards;
  (3) in determining whether to establish uniform national standards, consult with appropriate State and local officials as to the need for national standards and any alternatives that would limit the scope of national standards or otherwise preserve State prerogatives and authority; and
  (4) where national standards are required by Federal statutes, consult with appropriate State and local officials in developing those standards.

Sec. 4. Special Requirements for Preemption.   *Agencies, in taking action that preempts State law, shall act in strict accordance with governing law.*

(a) Agencies shall construe, in regulations and otherwise, a Federal statute to preempt State law only where the statute contains an express preemption provision or there is some other clear evidence that the Congress intended preemption of State law, or where the exercise of State authority conflicts with the exercise of Federal authority under the Federal statute.

(b) Where a Federal statute does not preempt State law (as addressed in subsection (a) of this section), agencies shall construe any authorization in the statute for the issuance of regulations as authorizing preemption of State law by rulemaking only when the exercise of State authority directly conflicts with the exercise of Federal authority under the Federal statute or there is clear evidence to conclude that the Congress intended the agency to have the authority to preempt State law.

(c) Any regulatory preemption of State law shall be restricted to the minimum level necessary to achieve the objectives of the statute pursuant to which the regulations are promulgated.

(d) When an agency foresees the possibility of a conflict between State law and Federally protected interests within its area of regulatory responsibility, the agency shall consult, to the extent practicable, with appropriate State and local officials in an effort to avoid such a conflict.

(e) When an agency proposes to act through adjudication or rulemaking to preempt State law, the agency shall provide all affected State and local officials notice and an opportunity for appropriate participation in the proceedings.

Sec. 5. Special Requirements for Legislative Proposals. *Agencies shall not submit to the Congress legislation that would:*

(a) directly regulate the States in ways that would either interfere with functions essential to the States' separate and independent existence or be inconsistent with the fundamental federalism principles in section 2;

(b) attach to Federal grants conditions that are not reasonably related to the purpose of the grant; or

(c) preempt State law, unless preemption is consistent with the fundamental federalism principles set forth in section 2, and unless a clearly legitimate national purpose, consistent with the federalism policymaking criteria set forth in section 3, cannot otherwise be met.

Sec. 6. Consultation.

(a) Each agency shall have an accountable process to ensure meaningful and timely input by State and local officials in the development of regulatory policies that have federalism implications. Within 90 days after the effective date of this order, the head of each agency shall designate an official with principal responsibility for the agency's implementation of this order and that designated official shall submit to the Office of Management and Budget a description of the agency's consultation process.

(b) To the extent practicable and permitted by law, no agency shall promulgate any regulation that has federalism implications, that imposes substantial direct compliance costs on State and local governments, and that is not required by statute, unless:

    (1) funds necessary to pay the direct costs incurred by the State and local governments in complying with the regulation are provided by the Federal Government; or

    (2) the agency, prior to the formal promulgation of the regulation,

        (A) consulted with State and local officials early in the process of developing the proposed regulation;

        (B) in a separately identified portion of the preamble to the regulation as it is to be issued in the Federal Register, provides to the Director of the Office of Management and Budget a federalism summary impact statement, which consists of a description of the extent of the agency's prior consultation with State and local officials, a summary of the nature of their concerns and the agency's position supporting the need to issue the regulation, and a statement of the extent to which the concerns of State and local officials have been met; and

(C) makes available to the Director of the Office of Management and Budget any written communications submitted to the agency by State and local officials.

(c) To the extent practicable and permitted by law, no agency shall promulgate any regulation that has federalism implications and that preempts State law, unless the agency, prior to the formal promulgation of the regulation,

(1) consulted with State and local officials early in the process of developing the proposed regulation;

(2) in a separately identified portion of the preamble to the regulation as it is to be issued in the Federal Register, provides to the Director of the Office of Management and Budget a federalism summary impact statement, which consists of a description of the extent of the agency's prior consultation with State and local officials, a summary of the nature of their concerns and the agency's position supporting the need to issue the regulation, and a statement of the extent to which the concerns of State and local officials have been met; and

(3) makes available to the Director of the Office of Management and Budget any written communications submitted to the agency by State and local officials.

Sec. 7. Increasing Flexibility for State and Local Waivers.

(a) Agencies shall review the processes under which State and local governments apply for waivers of statutory and regulatory requirements and take appropriate steps to streamline those processes.

(b) Each agency shall, to the extent practicable and permitted by law, consider any application by a State for a waiver of statutory or regulatory requirements in connection with any program administered by that agency with a general view toward increasing opportunities for utilizing flexible policy approaches at the State or local level in cases in which the proposed waiver is consistent with applicable Federal policy objectives and is otherwise appropriate.

(c) Each agency shall, to the extent practicable and permitted by law, render a decision upon a complete application for a waiver within 120 days of receipt of such application by the agency. If the application for a waiver is not granted, the agency shall provide the applicant with timely written notice of the decision and the reasons therefore.

(d) This section applies only to statutory or regulatory requirements that are discretionary and subject to waiver by the agency.

Sec. 8. Accountability.

(a) In transmitting any draft final regulation that has federalism implications to the Office of Management and Budget pursuant to Executive Order 12866 of September 30, 1993, each agency shall include a certification from the official designated to ensure compliance with this order stating that the requirements of this order have been met in a meaningful and timely manner.

(b) In transmitting proposed legislation that has federalism implications to the Office of Management and Budget, each agency shall include a certification from the official designated to ensure compliance with this order that all relevant requirements of this order have been met.

(c)   Within 180 days after the effective date of this order, the Director of the Office of Management and Budget and the Assistant to the President for Intergovernmental Affairs shall confer with State and local officials to ensure that this order is being properly and effectively implemented.

Sec. 9. Independent Agencies.   *Independent regulatory agencies are encouraged to comply with the provisions of this order.*

Sec. 10. General Provisions.

(a)   This order shall supplement but not supersede the requirements contained in Executive Order 12372 ("Intergovernmental Review of Federal Programs"), Executive Order 12866 ("Regulatory Planning and Review"), Executive Order 12988 ("Civil Justice Reform"), and OMB Circular A-19.

(b)   Executive Order 12612 ("Federalism"), Executive Order 12875 ("Enhancing the Intergovernmental Partnership"), Executive Order 13083 ("Federalism"), and Executive Order 13095 ("Suspension of Executive Order 13083") are revoked.

(c)   This order shall be effective 90 days after the date of this order.

Sec. 11. Judicial Review.   *This order is intended only to improve the internal management of the executive branch, and is not intended to create any right or benefit, substantive or procedural, enforceable at law by a party against the United States, its agencies, its officers, or any person.*

EXECUTIVE ORDER 13228 (PRESIDENT GEORGE W. BUSH 2001)

Establishing the office of homeland security and the homeland security council

(a)   By the authority vested in me as President by the Constitution and the laws of the United States of America, it is hereby ordered as follows:

Section 1. Establishment.   *I hereby establish within the Executive Office of the President an Office of Homeland Security (the "Office") to be headed by the Assistant to the President for Homeland Security.*

Sec. 2. Mission.   The mission of the Office shall be to develop and coordinate the implementation of a comprehensive national strategy to secure the United States from terrorist threats or attacks. The Office shall perform the functions necessary to carry out this mission, including the functions specified in Section 3 of this order.

Sec. 3. Functions.   The functions of the Office shall be to coordinate the executive branch's efforts to detect, prepare for, prevent, protect against, respond to, and recover from terrorist attacks within the United States.

(a)   *National Strategy.* The Office shall work with executive departments and agencies, State and local governments, and private entities to ensure the adequacy of the national strategy for detecting, preparing for, preventing, protecting against, responding to, and recovering from terrorist threats or attacks within the United States and shall periodically review and coordinate revisions to that strategy as necessary.

(b)   *Detection.* The Office shall identify priorities and coordinate efforts for collection and analysis of information within the United States regarding threats of terrorism against the United States and activities of terrorists or terrorist groups within the United States. The Office also shall identify, in coordination with the Assistant to the President for National Security Affairs, priorities for collection of intelligence outside the United States regarding threats of terrorism within the United States.

   (i) In performing these functions, the Office shall work with Federal, State, and local agencies, as appropriate, to:

      (A) facilitate collection from State and local governments and private entities of information pertaining to terrorist threats or activities within the United States;

      (B) coordinate and prioritize the requirements for foreign intelligence relating to terrorism within the United States of executive departments and agencies responsible for homeland security and provide these requirements and priorities to the Director of Central Intelligence and other agencies responsible for collection of foreign intelligence;

      (C) coordinate efforts to ensure that all executive departments and agencies that have intelligence collection responsibilities have sufficient technological capabilities and resources to collect intelligence and data relating to terrorist activities or possible terrorist acts within the United States, working with the Assistant to the President for National Security Affairs, as appropriate;

      (D) coordinate development of monitoring protocols and equipment for use in detecting the release of biological, chemical, and radiological hazards; and

      (E) ensure that, to the extent permitted by law, all appropriate and necessary intelligence and law enforcement information relating to homeland security is disseminated to and exchanged among appropriate executive departments and agencies responsible for homeland security and, where appropriate for reasons of homeland security, promote exchange of such information with and among State and local governments and private entities.

   (ii) Executive departments and agencies shall, to the extent permitted by law, make available to the Office all information relating to terrorist threats and activities within the United States.

(c) *Preparedness.* The Office of Homeland Security shall coordinate national efforts to prepare for and mitigate the consequences of terrorist threats or attacks within the United States. In performing this function, the Office shall work with Federal, State, and local agencies, and private entities, as appropriate, to:

   (i) review and assess the adequacy of the portions of all Federal emergency response plans that pertain to terrorist threats or attacks within the United States;

   (ii) coordinate domestic exercises and simulations designed to assess and practice systems that would be called upon to respond to a terrorist threat or attack within the United States and coordinate programs and activities for training Federal, State, and local employees who would be called upon to respond to such a threat or attack;

   (iii) coordinate national efforts to ensure public health preparedness for a terrorist attack, including reviewing vaccination policies and reviewing the adequacy of and, if necessary, increasing vaccine and pharmaceutical stockpiles and hospital capacity;

   (iv) coordinate Federal assistance to State and local authorities and nongovernmental organizations to prepare for and respond to terrorist threats or attacks within the United States;

   (v) ensure that national preparedness programs and activities for terrorist threats or attacks are developed and are regularly evaluated under appropriate standards and that resources are allocated to improving and sustaining preparedness based on such evaluations; and

(vi) ensure the readiness and coordinated deployment of Federal response teams to respond to terrorist threats or attacks, working with the Assistant to the President for National Security Affairs, when appropriate.

(d) *Prevention.* The Office shall coordinate efforts to prevent terrorist attacks within the United States. In performing this function, the Office shall work with Federal, State, and local agencies, and private entities, as appropriate, to:

(i) facilitate the exchange of information among such agencies relating to immigration and visa matters and shipments of cargo; and, working with the Assistant to the President for National Security Affairs, ensure coordination among such agencies to prevent the entry of terrorists and terrorist materials and supplies into the United States and facilitate removal of such terrorists from the United States, when appropriate;

(ii) coordinate efforts to investigate terrorist threats and attacks within the United States; and

(iii) coordinate efforts to improve the security of United States borders, territorial waters, and airspace in order to prevent acts of terrorism within the United States, working with the Assistant to the President for National Security Affairs, when appropriate.

(e) *Protection.* The Office shall coordinate efforts to protect the United States and its critical infrastructure from the consequences of terrorist attacks. In performing this function, the Office shall work with Federal, State, and local agencies, and private entities, as appropriate, to:

(i) strengthen measures for protecting energy production, transmission, and distribution services and critical facilities; other utilities; telecommunications; facilities that produce, use, store, or dispose of nuclear material; and other critical infrastructure services and critical facilities within the United States from terrorist attack;

(ii) coordinate efforts to protect critical public and privately owned information systems within the United States from terrorist attack;

(iii) develop criteria for reviewing whether appropriate security measures are in place at major public and privately owned facilities within the United States;

(iv) coordinate domestic efforts to ensure that special events determined by appropriate senior officials to have national significance are protected from terrorist attack;

(v) coordinate efforts to protect transportation systems within the United States, including railways, highways, shipping, ports and waterways, and airports and civilian aircraft, from terrorist attack;

(vi) coordinate efforts to protect United States livestock, agriculture, and systems for the provision of water and food for human use and consumption from terrorist attack; and

(vii) coordinate efforts to prevent unauthorized access to, development of, and unlawful importation into the United States of, chemical, biological, radiological, nuclear, explosive, or other related materials that have the potential to be used in terrorist attacks.

(f) *Response and Recovery.* The Office shall coordinate efforts to respond to and promote recovery from terrorist threats or attacks within the United States. In performing this function, the Office shall work with Federal, State, and local agencies, and private entities, as appropriate, to:

(i) coordinate efforts to ensure rapid restoration of transportation systems, energy production, transmission, and distribution systems; telecommunications; other utilities; and other critical infrastructure facilities after disruption by a terrorist threat or attack;

      (ii) coordinate efforts to ensure rapid restoration of public and private critical information systems after disruption by a terrorist threat or attack;

     (iii) work with the National Economic Council to coordinate efforts to stabilize United States financial markets after a terrorist threat or attack and manage the immediate economic and financial consequences of the incident;

    (iv) coordinate Federal plans and programs to provide medical, financial, and other assistance to victims of terrorist attacks and their families; and

     (v) coordinate containment and removal of biological, chemical, radiological, explosive, or other hazardous materials in the event of a terrorist threat or attack involving such hazards and coordinate efforts to mitigate the effects of such an attack.

(g) *Incident Management.* The Assistant to the President for Homeland Security shall be the individual primarily responsible for coordinating the domestic response efforts of all departments and agencies in the event of an imminent terrorist threat and during and in the immediate aftermath of a terrorist attack within the United States and shall be the principal point of contact for and to the President with respect to coordination of such efforts. The Assistant to the President for Homeland Security shall coordinate with the Assistant to the President for National Security Affairs, as appropriate.

(h) *Continuity of Government.* The Assistant to the President for Homeland Security, in coordination with the Assistant to the President for National Security Affairs, shall review plans and preparations for ensuring the continuity of the Federal Government in the event of a terrorist attack that threatens the safety and security of the United States Government or its leadership.

(i) *Public Affairs.* The Office, subject to the direction of the White House Office of Communications, shall coordinate the strategy of the executive branch for communicating with the public in the event of a terrorist threat or attack within the United States. The Office also shall coordinate the development of programs for educating the public about the nature of terrorist threats and appropriate precautions and responses.

(j) *Cooperation with State and Local Governments and Private Entities.* The Office shall encourage and invite the participation of State and local governments and private entities, as appropriate, in carrying out the Office's functions.

(k) *Review of Legal Authorities and Development of Legislative Proposals.* The Office shall coordinate a periodic review and assessment of the legal authorities available to executive departments and agencies to permit them to perform the functions described in this order. When the Office determines that such legal authorities are inadequate, the Office shall develop, in consultation with executive departments and agencies, proposals for presidential action and legislative proposals for submission to the Office of Management and Budget to enhance the ability of executive departments and agencies to perform those functions. The Office shall work with State and local governments in assessing the adequacy of their legal authorities to permit them to detect, prepare for, prevent, protect against, and recover from terrorist threats and attacks.

(l) *Budget Review.* The Assistant to the President for Homeland Security, in consultation with the Director of the Office of Management and Budget (the "Director") and the heads of executive departments and agencies, shall identify programs that contribute to the Administration's strategy for homeland security and, in the development of the President's annual budget submission, shall review and provide advice to the heads of departments and agencies for such programs. The Assistant to the President for Homeland Security shall provide advice to the Director on the level and use of funding in departments and agencies for homeland security-related activities and, prior to the Director's forwarding of the proposed annual budget submission to the President for transmittal to the Congress, shall certify to the Director the funding levels that the Assistant to the President for Homeland Security believes are necessary and appropriate for the homeland security-related activities of the executive branch.

Sec. 4. Administration.

(a) The Office of Homeland Security shall be directed by the Assistant to the President for Homeland Security.

(b) The Office of Administration within the Executive Office of the President shall provide the Office of Homeland Security with such personnel, funding, and administrative support, to the extent permitted by law and subject to the availability of appropriations, as directed by the Chief of Staff to carry out the provisions of this order.

(c) Heads of executive departments and agencies are authorized, to the extent permitted by law, to detail or assign personnel of such departments and agencies to the Office of Homeland Security upon request of the Assistant to the President for Homeland Security, subject to the approval of the Chief of Staff.

Sec. 5. Establishment of Homeland Security Council.

(a) I hereby establish a Homeland Security Council (the "Council"), which shall be responsible for advising and assisting the President with respect to all aspects of homeland security. The Council shall serve as the mechanism for ensuring coordination of homeland security-related activities of executive departments and agencies and effective development and implementation of homeland security policies.

(b) The Council shall have as its members the President, the Vice President, the Secretary of the Treasury, the Secretary of Defense, the Attorney General, the Secretary of Health and Human Services, the Secretary of Transportation, the Director of the Federal Emergency Management Agency, the Director of the Federal Bureau of Investigation, the Director of Central Intelligence, the Assistant to the President for Homeland Security, and such other officers of the executive branch as the President may from time to time designate. The Chief of Staff, the Chief of Staff to the Vice President, the Assistant to the President for National Security Affairs, the Counsel to the President, and the Director of the Office of Management and Budget also are invited to attend any Council meeting. The Secretary of State, the Secretary of Agriculture, the Secretary of the Interior, the Secretary of Energy, the Secretary of Labor, the Secretary of Commerce, the Secretary of Veterans Affairs, the Administrator of the Environmental Protection Agency, the Assistant to the President for Economic Policy, and the Assistant to the President for Domestic Policy shall be invited to attend meetings pertaining to their responsibilities. The heads of other executive departments and agencies and other senior officials shall be invited to attend Council meetings when appropriate.

(c) The Council shall meet at the President's direction. When the President is absent from a meeting of the Council, at the President's direction the Vice President may preside. The Assistant to the President for Homeland Security shall be responsible, at the President's direction, for determining the agenda, ensuring that necessary papers are prepared, and recording Council actions and Presidential decisions.

Sec. 6. Original Classification Authority.   *I hereby delegate the authority to classify information originally as Top Secret, in accordance with Executive Order 12958 or any successor Executive Order, to the Assistant to the President for Homeland Security.*

Sec. 7. Continuing Authorities.   *This order does not alter the existing authorities of United States Government departments and agencies. All executive departments and agencies are directed to assist the Council and the Assistant to the President for Homeland Security in carrying out the purposes of this order.*

Sec. 8. General Provisions.

(a) This order does not create any right or benefit, substantive or procedural, enforceable at law or equity by a party against the United States, its departments, agencies or instrumentalities, its officers or employees, or any other person.

(b) References in this order to State and local governments shall be construed to include tribal governments and United States territories and other possessions.

(c) References to the "United States" shall be construed to include United States territories and possessions.

Sec. 9. Amendments to Executive Order 12656.   *Executive Order 12656 of November 18, 1988, as amended, is hereby further amended as follows:*

(a) Section 101(a) is amended by adding at the end of the fourth sentence: ", except that the Homeland Security Council shall be responsible for administering such policy with respect to terrorist threats and attacks within the United States."

(b) Section 104(a) is amended by adding at the end: ", except that the Homeland Security Council is the principal forum for consideration of policy relating to terrorist threats and attacks within the United States."

(c) Section 104(b) is amended by inserting the words "and the Homeland Security Council" after the words "National Security Council."

(d) The first sentence of section 104(c) is amended by inserting the words "and the Homeland Security Council" after the words "National Security Council."

(e) The second sentence of section 104(c) is replaced with the following two sentences: "Pursuant to such procedures for the organization and management of the National Security Council and Homeland Security Council processes as the President may establish, the Director of the Federal Emergency Management Agency also shall assist in the implementation of and management of those processes as the President may establish. The Director of the Federal Emergency Management Agency also shall assist in the implementation of national security emergency preparedness policy by coordinating with the other Federal departments and agencies and with State and local governments, and by providing periodic reports to the National Security Council and the Homeland Security Council on implementation of national security emergency preparedness policy."

(f) Section 201(7) is amended by inserting the words "and the Homeland Security Council" after the words "National Security Council."

(g) Section 206 is amended by inserting the words "and the Homeland Security Council" after the words "National Security Council."

(h) Section 208 is amended by inserting the words "or the Homeland Security Council" after the words "National Security Council."

MILITARY ORDER 1 (PRESIDENT GEORGE W. BUSH 2001)

Detention, treatment, and trial of certain non-citizens in the war against terrorism

By the authority vested in me as President and as Commander in Chief of the Armed Forces of the United States by the Constitution and the laws of the United States of America, including the Authorization for Use of Military Force Joint Resolution

(Public Law 107-40, 115 Stat. 224) and sections 821 and 836 of title 10, United States Code, it is hereby ordered as follows:

Section 1. Findings.

(a) International terrorists, including members of al Qaida, have carried out attacks on United States diplomatic and military personnel and facilities abroad and on citizens and property within the United States on a scale that has created a state of armed conflict that requires the use of the United States Armed Forces.

(b) In light of grave acts of terrorism and threats of terrorism, including the terrorist attacks on September 11, 2001, on the headquarters of the United States Department of Defense in the national capital region, on the World Trade Center in New York, and on civilian aircraft such as in Pennsylvania, I proclaimed a national emergency on September 14, 2001 (Proc. 7463, Declaration of National Emergency by Reason of Certain Terrorist Attacks).

(c) Individuals acting alone and in concert involved in international terrorism possess both the capability and the intention to undertake further terrorist attacks against the United States that, if not detected and prevented, will cause mass deaths, mass injuries, and massive destruction of property, and may place at risk the continuity of the operations of the United States Government.

(d) The ability of the United States to protect the United States and its citizens, and to help its allies and other cooperating nations protect their nations and their citizens, from such further terrorist attacks depends in significant part upon using the United States Armed Forces to identify terrorists and those who support them, to disrupt their activities, and to eliminate their ability to conduct or support such attacks.

(e) To protect the United States and its citizens, and for the effective conduct of military operations and prevention of terrorist attacks, it is necessary for individuals subject to this order pursuant to Section 2 hereof to be detained, and, when tried, to be tried for violations of the laws of war and other applicable laws by military tribunals.

(f) Given the danger to the safety of the United States and the nature of international terrorism, and to the extent provided by and under this order, I find consistent with Section 836 of title 10, United States Code, that it is not practicable to apply in military commissions under this order the principles of law and the rules of evidence generally recognized in the trial of criminal cases in the United States district courts.

(g) Having fully considered the magnitude of the potential deaths, injuries, and property destruction that would result from potential acts of terrorism against the United States, and the probability that such acts will occur, I have determined that an extraordinary emergency exists for national defense purposes, that this emergency constitutes an urgent and compelling government interest, and that issuance of this order is necessary to meet the emergency.

Sec. 2. Definition and Policy.

(a) The term "individual subject to this order" shall mean any individual who is not a United States citizen with respect to whom I determine from time to time in writing that:

    (1) there is reason to believe that such individual, at the relevant times,

        (i) is or was a member of the organization known as al Qaida;

        (ii) has engaged in, aided or abetted, or conspired to commit, acts of international terrorism, or acts in preparation therefor, that have caused, threaten to cause, or have as their aim to cause, injury to or adverse effects on the United States, its citizens, national security, foreign policy, or economy; or

> (iii) has knowingly harbored one or more individuals described in subparagraphs (i) or (ii) of subsection 2(a)(1) of this order; and

(2) it is in the interest of the United States that such individual be subject to this order.

(b) It is the policy of the United States that the Secretary of Defense shall take all necessary measures to ensure that any individual subject to this order is detained in accordance with Section 3, and, if the individual is to be tried, that such individual is tried only in accordance with Section 4.

(c) It is further the policy of the United States that any individual subject to this order who is not already under the control of the Secretary of Defense but who is under the control of any other officer or agent of the United States or any State shall, upon delivery of a copy of such written determination to such officer or agent, forthwith be placed under the control of the Secretary of Defense.

Sec. 3. Detention Authority of the Secretary of Defense. *Any individual subject to this order shall be—*

(a) detained at an appropriate location designated by the Secretary of Defense outside or within the United States;

(b) treated humanely, without any adverse distinction based on race, color, religion, gender, birth, wealth, or any similar criteria;

(c) afforded adequate food, drinking water, shelter, clothing, and medical treatment;

(d) allowed the free exercise of religion consistent with the requirements of such detention; and

(e) detained in accordance with such other conditions as the Secretary of Defense may prescribe.

Sec. 4. Authority of the Secretary of Defense Regarding Trials of Individuals Subject to this Order.

(a) Any individual subject to this order shall, when tried, be tried by military commission for any and all offenses triable by military commission that such individual is alleged to have committed, and may be punished in accordance with the penalties provided under applicable law, including life imprisonment or death.

(b) As a military function and in light of the findings in Section 1, including subsection (f) thereof, the Secretary of Defense shall issue such orders and regulations, including orders for the appointment of one or more military commissions, as may be necessary to carry out subsection (a) of this section.

(c) Orders and regulations issued under subsection (b) of this section shall include, but not be limited to, rules for the conduct of the proceedings of military commissions, including pretrial, trial, and post-trial procedures, modes of proof, issuance of process, and qualifications of attorneys, which shall at a minimum provide for—

(1) military commissions to sit at any time and any place, consistent with such guidance regarding time and place as the Secretary of Defense may provide;

(2) a full and fair trial, with the military commission sitting as the triers of both fact and law;

(3) admission of such evidence as would, in the opinion of the presiding officer of the military commission (or instead, if any other member of the commission so requests at the time the presiding officer renders that opinion, the opinion of the commission rendered at that time by a majority of the commission), have probative value to a reasonable person;

(4) in a manner consistent with the protection of information classified or classifiable under Executive Order 12958 of April 17, 1995, as amended, or any

successor Executive Order, protected by statute or rule from unauthorized disclosure, or otherwise protected by law, (A) the handling of, admission into evidence of, and access to materials and information, and (B) the conduct, closure of, and access to proceedings;

(5) conduct of the prosecution by one or more attorneys designated by the Secretary of Defense and conduct of the defense by attorneys for the individual subject to this order;

(6) conviction only upon the concurrence of two-thirds of the members of the commission present at the time of the vote, a majority being present;

(7) sentencing only upon the concurrence of two-thirds of the members of the commission present at the time of the vote, a majority being present; and

(8) submission of the record of the trial, including any conviction or sentence, for review and final decision by me or by the Secretary of Defense if so designated by me for that purpose.

Sec. 5. Obligation of Other Agencies to Assist the Secretary of Defense.

(a) Departments, agencies, entities, and officers of the United States shall, to the maximum extent permitted by law, provide to the Secretary of Defense such assistance as he may request to implement this order.

Sec. 6. Additional Authorities of the Secretary of Defense.

(a) As a military function and in light of the findings in section 1, the Secretary of Defense shall issue such orders and regulations as may be necessary to carry out any of the provisions of this order.

(b) The Secretary of Defense may perform any of his functions or duties, and may exercise any of the powers provided to him under this order (other than under section 4(c)(8) hereof) in accordance with section 113(d) of title 10, United States Code.

Sec. 7. Relationship to Other Law and Forums.

(a) Nothing in this order shall be construed to—
  (1) authorize the disclosure of state secrets to any person not otherwise authorized to have access to them;
  (2) limit the authority of the President as Commander in Chief of the Armed Forces or the power of the President to grant reprieves and pardons; or
  (3) limit the lawful authority of the Secretary of Defense, any military commander, or any other officer or agent of the United States or of any State to detain or try any person who is not an individual subject to this order.

(b) With respect to any individual subject to this order—
  (1) military tribunals shall have exclusive jurisdiction with respect to offenses by the individual; and
  (2) the individual shall not be privileged to seek any remedy or maintain any proceeding, directly or indirectly, or to have any such remedy or proceeding sought on the individual's behalf, in (i) any court of the United States, or any State thereof, (ii) any court of any foreign nation, or (iii) any international tribunal.

(c) This order is not intended to and does not create any right, benefit, or privilege, substantive or procedural, enforceable at law or equity by any party, against the United States, its departments, agencies, or other entities, its officers or employees, or any other person.

(d) For purposes of this order, the term "State" includes any State, district, territory, or possession of the United States.

(e) I reserve the authority to direct the Secretary of Defense, at any time hereafter, to transfer to a governmental authority control of any individual subject to this order. Nothing in this order shall be construed to limit the authority of any such governmental authority to prosecute any individual for whom control is transferred.

Sec. 8. Publication.

(a) This order shall be published in the Federal Register.

PRESIDENTIAL DOCUMENTS

Executive Order 13422 (President George W. Bush 2007)

Further Amendment to Executive Order 12866 on Regulatory Planning and Review By the authority vested in me as President by the Constitution and laws of the United States of America, it is hereby ordered that Executive Order 12866 of September 30, 1993, as amended, is further amended as follows:

Sec. 1. Section 1 is amended as follows:

(a) Section 1(b)(1) is amended to read as follows:

> (1) Each agency shall identify in writing the specific market failure (such as externalities, market power, lack of information) or other specific problem that it intends to address (including, where applicable, the failures of public institutions) that warrant new agency action, as well as assess the significance of that problem, to enable assessment of whether any new regulation is warranted.

(b) by inserting in section 1(b)(7) after "regulation" the words "or guidance document".

(c) by inserting in section 1(b)(10) in both places after "regulations" the words "and guidance documents".

(d) by inserting in section 1(b)(11) after "its regulations" the words "and guidance documents".

(e) by inserting in section 1(b)(12) after "regulations" the words "and guidance documents".

Sec. 2. Section 2 is amended as follows:

(a) by inserting in section 2(a) in both places after "regulations" the words "and guidance documents".

(b) by inserting in section 2(b) in both places after "regulations" the words "and guidance documents".

Sec. 3. Section 3 is amended as follows:

(a) by striking in section 3(d) "or rule" after "Regulation";

(b) by striking in section 3(d)(1) "or rules" after "Regulations";

(c) by striking in section 3(d)(2) "or rules" after "Regulations";

(d) by striking in section 3(d)(3) "or rules" after "Regulations";

(e) by striking in section 3(e) "rule or" from "final rule or regulation";

(f) by striking in section 3(f) "rule or" from "rule or regulation";

(g) by inserting after section 3(f) the following:

> (g) "Guidance document" means an agency statement of general applicability and future effect, other than a regulatory action, that sets forth a policy on a statutory, regulatory, or technical issue or an interpretation of a statutory or regulatory issue.

(h)   "Significant guidance document"—
  (1)   Means a guidance document disseminated to regulated entities or the general public that, for purposes of this order, may reasonably be anticipated to:
    (A)   Lead to an annual effect of $100 million or more or adversely affect in a material way the economy, a sector of the economy, productivity, competition, jobs, the environment, public health or safety, or State, local, or tribal governments or communities;
    (B)   Create a serious inconsistency or otherwise interfere with an action taken or planned by another agency;
    (C)   Materially alter the budgetary impact of entitlements, grants, user fees, or loan programs or the rights or obligations of recipients thereof; or
    (D)   Raise novel legal or policy issues arising out of legal mandates, the President's priorities, or the principles set forth in this Executive order; and
  (2)   Does not include:
    (A)   Guidance documents on regulations issued in accordance with the formal rulemaking provisions of 5 U.S.C. 556, 557;
    (B)   Guidance documents that pertain to a military or foreign affairs function of the United States, other than procurement regulations and regulations involving the import or export of non-defense articles and services;
    (C)   Guidance documents on regulations that are limited to agency organization, management, or personnel matters; or
    (D)   Any other category of guidance documents exempted by the Administrator of OIRA."

Sec. 4. Section 4 is amended as follows:

(a)   Section 4(a) is amended to read as follows: "The Director may convene a meeting of agency heads and other government personnel as appropriate to seek a common understanding of priorities and to coordinate regulatory efforts to be accomplished in the upcoming year."

(b)   The last sentence of section 4(c)(1) is amended to read as follows: "Unless specifically authorized by the head of the agency, no rulemaking shall commence nor be included on the Plan without the approval of the agency's Regulatory Policy Office, and the Plan shall contain at a minimum:".

(c)   Section 4(c)(1)(B) is amended by inserting "of each rule as well as the agency's best estimate of the combined aggregate costs and benefits of all its regulations planned for that calendar year to assist with the identification of priorities" after "of the anticipated costs and benefits".

(d)   Section 4(c)(1)(C) is amended by inserting ", and specific citation to such statute, order, or other legal authority" after "court order".

Sec. 5. Section 6 is amended as follows:

(a)   by inserting in section 6(a)(1) "In consultation with OIRA, each agency may also consider whether to utilize formal rulemaking procedures under 5 U.S.C. 556 and 557 for the resolution of complex determinations" after "comment period of not less than 60 days."

(b)   by amending the first sentence of section 6(a)(2) to read as follows: "Within 60 days of the date of this Executive order, each agency head shall designate one of the agency's Presidential Appointees to be its Regulatory Policy Officer, advise OMB of such designation, and annually update OMB on the status of this designation."

Sec. 6. Sections 9–11 are redesignated respectively as sections 10–12.

Sec. 7. After section 8, a new section 9 is inserted as follows:

"Sec. 9. Significant Guidance Documents.   Each agency shall provide OIRA, at such times and in the manner specified by the Administrator of OIRA, with advance notification of any significant guidance documents. Each agency shall take such steps as are necessary for its Regulatory Policy Officer to ensure the agency's compliance with the requirements of this section. Upon the request of the Administrator, for each matter identified as, or determined by the Administrator to be, a significant guidance document, the issuing agency shall provide to OIRA the content of the draft guidance document, together with a brief explanation of the need for the guidance document and how it will meet that need. The OIRA Administrator shall notify the agency when additional consultation will be required before the issuance of the significant guidance document."

Sec. 8. Newly designated section 10 is amended to read as follows:

"Sec. 10. Preservation of Agency Authority.   Nothing in this order shall be construed to impair or otherwise affect the authority vested by law in an agency or the head thereof, including the authority of the Attorney General relating to litigation."

MEMORANDUM FOR THE HEADS OF EXECUTIVE DEPARTMENTS AND AGENCIES (PRESIDENT BARACK OBAMA, MAY 20, 2009)

Subject: Preemption

From our Nation's founding, the American constitutional order has been a Federal system, ensuring a strong role for both the national Government and the States. The Federal Government's role in promoting the general welfare and guarding individual liberties is critical, but State law and national law often operate concurrently to provide independent safeguards for the public. Throughout our history, State and local governments have frequently protected health, safety, and the environment more aggressively than has the national Government.

An understanding of the important role of State governments in our Federal system is reflected in longstanding practices by executive departments and agencies, which have shown respect for the traditional prerogatives of the States. In recent years, however, notwithstanding Executive Order 13132 of August 4, 1999 (Federalism), executive departments and agencies have sometimes announced that their regulations preempt State law, including State common law, without explicit preemption by the Congress or an otherwise sufficient basis under applicable legal principles.

The purpose of this memorandum is to state the general policy of my Administration that preemption of State law by executive departments and agencies should be undertaken only with full consideration of the legitimate prerogatives of the States and with a sufficient legal basis for preemption. Executive departments and agencies should be mindful that in our Federal system, the citizens of the several States have distinctive circumstances and values, and that in many instances it is appropriate for them to apply to themselves rules and principles that reflect these circumstances and values. As Justice Brandeis explained more than 70 years ago, "[i]t is one of the happy incidents of the federal system that a single courageous state may, if its citizens choose, serve as a laboratory; and try novel social and economic experiments without risk to the rest of the country."

To ensure that executive departments and agencies include statements of preemption in regulations only when such statements have a sufficient legal basis:

1. Heads of departments and agencies should not include in regulatory preambles statements that the department or agency intends to preempt State law through the regulation except where preemption provisions are also included in the codified regulation.

2. Heads of departments and agencies should not include preemption provisions in codified regulations except where such provisions would be justified under legal principles governing preemption, including the principles outlined in Executive Order 13132.

3. Heads of departments and agencies should review regulations issued within the past 10 years that contain statements in regulatory preambles or codified provisions intended by the department or agency to preempt State law, in order to decide whether such statements or provisions are justified under applicable legal principles governing preemption. Where the head of a department or agency determines that a regulatory statement of preemption or codified regulatory provision cannot be so justified, the head of that department or agency should initiate appropriate action, which may include amendment of the relevant regulation.

Executive departments and agencies shall carry out the provisions of this memorandum to the extent permitted by law and consistent with their statutory authorities. Heads of departments and agencies should consult as necessary with the Attorney General and the Office of Management and Budget's Office of Information and Regulatory Affairs to determine how the requirements of this memorandum apply to particular situations.

This memorandum is not intended to, and does not, create any right or benefit, substantive or procedural, enforceable at law or in equity by any party against the United States, its departments, agencies, or entities, its officers, employees, or agents, or any other person.

The Director of the Office of Management and Budget is authorized and directed to publish this memorandum in the Federal Register.

Barack Obama

accommodationist approach An interpretation of the religion clauses that maintains that it is appropriate for government to accommodate or otherwise assist religious interests or organizations.

adequate and independent state grounds doctrine Federal judicial review of a state decision in a case that includes both state and federal claims will not occur if the lower court's decision rested upon adequate and independent state law.

advisory opinion A judicial interpretation of a legal question requested by the legislative or executive branch of government. Typically, courts prefer not to give advisory opinions and federal courts are generally prohibited from rendering advisory opinions.

affectation doctrine Rule that provides Congress with authority to regulate intrastate activities that affect interstate commerce. Even though individual activity may not affect interstate commerce, the total effect of all individuals who engage in the activity may affect interstate commerce and provide Congress with the jurisdiction to regulate the activity.

affidavit A written statement made under oath typically completed by a police officer when seeking a search warrant.

affirmative action Any policy that seeks to promote greater opportunities for individuals of an identifiable group, whose members have been previously excluded from or who are currently underrepresented in particular educational, employment, or social settings, using *proactive* (affirmative) measures, as opposed to more punitive methods (criminal laws, civil rights legislation, etc.).

Age Discrimination in Employment Act (ADEA) Passed in 1967, this form of civil rights legislation bars employers from using age to disadvantage employees between the ages of forty and seventy.

alienage A person's status as a non-U.S. citizen. Viewed as a suspect classification in some cases, but in others, where an important governmental function is being performed, is treated as a non-suspect form of discrimination.

amnesty An act of the government granting a pardon for a past crime. Amnesty is rarely exercised in favor of individuals, but is usually applied to a group or class of persons who are accountable for crimes for which they have not yet been convicted.

anti-Federalist (1) A person who opposes establishment of a strong, centralized government in favor of local control. (2) A party that opposes establishment of a strong, centralized government in favor of local control.

apparent authority rule Used to judge some types of consent searches; allows police to rely on consent given by persons that police reasonably believed are authorized to give consent.

appellate jurisdiction The authority of one court to review the proceedings of another court or of an administrative agency.

arrest A governmental seizure of an individual, whereby a person is apprehended by a public official and taken into custody for purposes of criminal process.

arrest warrant A judicial order supported by probable cause authorizing a law enforcement agent to arrest an individual.

assistance of counsel provision Sixth Amendment clause providing that the accused has the right to have counsel (an attorney) assist in defending against the criminal charges.

automobile exception Another exception to the warrant requirement that allows police to search a vehicle without a warrant if they have probable cause to believe that the vehicle or part thereof contains evidence of criminality.

avoidance The Supreme Court's practice of avoiding constitutional issues by deciding cases upon nonconstitutional grounds.

bad tendency test Another test used by the Court to interpret and apply the First Amendment free speech provision, which allows government to predetermine and ban types of speech that may have a *tendency* to bring about harm, regardless of whether the speech, in actuality, poses a clear and present danger.

bail The collateral imposed by a court as a condition for pretrial release of the defendant.

ban on speech A governmental policy barring a particular form of expression at any time or place or in any manner.

bicameral Two-chambered, referring to the customary division of a legislature into two houses (a Senate and a House of Representatives).

bill A proposed law, presented to the legislature for enactment, that is, a legislative bill.

bill of attainder A legislative act that inflicts capital punishment upon named persons without a judicial trial. Congress and the state legislatures are prohibited from issuing bills of attainder by the Constitution.

Bill of Rights The first ten amendments to the Constitution, which were written in 1789 and ratified in 1791, contain the primary civil liberties protected under the Constitution.

Bipartisan Campaign Reform Act of 2002 (BCRA) Also known as the McCain-Feingold Act, this law sought to address some of the gaps that candidates, parties, and donors had exposed under the Federal Election Campaign Act of 1971. This law bans the use of soft money in federal elections and limits issue ads during periods immediately preceding elections. The Supreme Court upheld most of BCRA's provisions in *McConnell v. Federal Elections Commission* (2003) but struck down portions of the law in *Citizens United v. FEC* (2010).

Blockburger test A legal standard created by the Supreme Court under the Double Jeopardy Clause that provides that two or more criminal charges are not the same offense if each charge requires proof of an additional criminal element (another form of intent or an additional act).

***Brady* Rule** A legal standard adopted by the Court that requires the prosecution to provide exculpatory evidence within the possession of the government to the defendant.

***Brandenburg* test** The current standard used by the Court in many free speech cases. Under this test adopted in *Brandenburg v. Ohio* (1969), the government may not suppress speech unless the speech is "directed to inciting or producing imminent lawless action and . . . likely to incite or produce such action."

Campaign finance reform laws Legislation that seeks to change the way campaigns are run and funded. Often challenged as unconstitutional restrictions on political speech.

canons of construction and interpretation A set of judicially created rules that govern the interpretation of written law, such as statutes, regulations, and constitutions.

capable of repetition yet evading review An exception to the mootness doctrine, which provides that if an alleged harm may be repeated, but by its nature cannot be judicially determined in the normal legal process, that harm may become the basis of jurisdiction.

capital offense An offense punishable by death.

***Central Hudson* test** Constitutional standard for commercial speech adopted by the Court in *Central Hudson Gas & Electric Corp. v. Public Service Comm. of New York* (1980). This test considers whether (1) the speech concerns a lawful activity and is truthful and not misleading, (2) there is a substantial governmental interest in regulating the speech, (3) the government's regulation directly advances its substantial interest, and (4) there is a direct fit between the government's regulation and its claimed interest.

child pornography Materials that depict actual children (persons under the age of eighteen) engaged in sexual conduct.

civil rights legislation Laws designed to prohibit government and nongovernment agents from discriminating.

class action An action brought by one or several plaintiffs on behalf of a class of persons. A class action may be appropriate when there has been injury to so many people that their voluntarily and unanimously joining in a lawsuit is improbable and impracticable. In such a situation, injured parties who wish to do so may, with the court's permission, sue on behalf of all. A class action is sometimes referred to as a *representative action*.

clear and present danger test A theory adopted by the Supreme Court in the early twentieth century as a means to interpret and apply the Free Speech Clause of the First Amendment. Under this theory, Justice Holmes provided that "[t]he question in every case is whether the words used are used in such circumstances and are of such a nature as to create a clear and present danger that they will bring about the substantive evils that Congress has a right to prevent. It is a question of proximity and degree."

code (1) The published statutes of a jurisdiction, arranged in systematic form. (2) A portion of the statutes of a jurisdiction, especially the statutes relating to a particular subject.

codification (1) The process of arranging laws in a systematic form covering the entire law of a jurisdiction or a particular area of the law; the process of creating a code. (2) The process of turning a common law rule into a statute.

coercion test A third legal standard used to evaluate Establishment Clause cases. This test essentially asks whether the government is acting in a manner that may have a coercive effect on individuals to support or participate in a particular religion.

collateral consequences An exception to the mootness doctrine providing for jurisdiction in cases in which the primary issue is moot, but secondary—*collateral*—issues remain.

Commerce Clause The clause in Article I, Section 8, of the Constitution that gives Congress the power to regulate commerce between the states and between the United States and foreign countries. Federal statutes that regulate business and labor are based upon this power.

commercial speech Expression offered to promote the sale of a commodity or service.

commutation of sentence The substitution of a less severe punishment for a more severe punishment.

compact theory A theory of individual liberties that considers liberties to be the product of a negotiated contract. Under this approach, rights are derived from an agreement or compact between the individuals being protected and those individuals or institutions providing the protection. Through negotiation, individuals and institutions receive rights, powers, and protections by virtue of compact or constitution.

compelling governmental interest test or strict scrutiny test A constitutional litmus test that weighs the government's interest in advancing a particular policy against the free exercise interests of the individual. In order for the government's interest to outweigh the individual's, the government must prove that its interest is *necessary* to promote a *compelling* governmental interest. This standard is also used to assess other constitutional rights, including some free speech issues (see Chapter 9), fundamental freedoms (see Chapter 11), and some matters of equal protection (see Chapter 12).

compulsory process clause Sixth Amendment clause that allows defendants to compel witnesses to appear on their behalf.

confrontation clause Sixth Amendment clause that provides the accused with the right to confront (generally interpreted as to view and cross-examine) any witnesses providing testimony against them.

consent searches An exception to the Fourth Amendment warrant requirement that allows police to perform searches with the permission or consent of a person who has actual or apparent authority over the property being searched.

content neutrality Also known as subject-matter neutrality, this term means that the government, in attempting to regulate speech, is not discriminating against speech based on its content or subject matter.

Contract Clause A provision in Article I, Section 10 of the Constitution that provides that states cannot impair the obligations of contracts.

Cooley doctrine Named for the case in which it was announced, *Cooley v. Board of Wardens*, 53 U.S. 299 (1851); provides that if a subject of interstate commerce is national in character, then regulation of that subject is exclusively federal.

cooperative federalism The theory that the national government is supreme to the state governments. The powers of the national government are read broadly and the Tenth Amendment is read as not granting any specific powers to the states.

Corrections Day Part of Congress's schedule; occurs twice a month. A time specially set aside for legislation intended to amend or repeal administrative rules.

countermajoritarian institution Because its members are not elected by the people, are not accountable to the people, and are not required to consider public opinion in their decision making, the Supreme Court is considered by most to be a countermajoritarian institution. This does not mean, however, that the Court has historically been countermajoritarian in its decision making.

court of general jurisdiction Generally, another term for trial court, that is, a court having jurisdiction to try all classes of civil and criminal cases except those that can be heard only by a court of limited jurisdiction.

court of limited jurisdiction A court whose jurisdiction is limited to civil cases of a certain type or that involve a limited amount of money, or whose jurisdiction in criminal cases is confined to petty offenses and preliminary hearings. A court of limited jurisdiction is sometimes called a *court of special jurisdiction*.

court-packing plan A phrase used to describe President Franklin Roosevelt's proposal in early 1937 to enlarge the Supreme Court by six members in order to ensure that his New Deal plan would be found constitutional. This proposal never became reality because the Court ultimately began approving social and economic legislation passed by Congress and state governments, thereby eliminating the perceived need to enlarge the Court.

Cruel and Unusual Punishment Clause Eighth Amendment provision that provides that government may not inflict cruel and unusual punishment upon individuals.

custodial interrogations Police-led questioning of a suspect while in police custody.

custodial requirement A standard requirement before a person will have a constitutional right against self-incrimination. In some cases, custody is determined based on whether a person's ability to move is restricted in a substantial manner. In other cases, custody is based on whether a reasonable person (not the actual suspect) placed in similar circumstances would feel free to leave the presence of police.

de facto segregation Segregation created based on factors (social, economic, etc.) not directly linked to law or public policy.

de jure segregation Segregation established or formally reinforced by law or policy.

de novo Anew; over again; a second time.

deadly force The application of potentially deadly techniques by police in an effort to apprehend or stop individuals. The use of deadly force to seize or stop individuals is unreasonable under the Fourth Amendment unless the officer has probable cause to believe that the person presents a substantial threat of death or serious physical harm to the officer or other persons.

death penalty or capital punishment The imposition of death as criminal punishment. Since 1976, the Court has ruled that the death penalty does not inherently violate the Eighth Amendment.

declaratory judgment (declaratory relief) A judgment that specifies the rights of the parties but orders no relief. Nonetheless, it is a binding judgment and the appropriate remedy for the determination of an actionable dispute when the plaintiff is in doubt as to his or her legal rights.

defamation A form of unprotected speech that involves a false statement that causes injury to another.

delegation of powers The transfer of power from the president to an administrative agency.

desegregation The process by which the policies and effects of exclusion and separation are reversed and corrected.

dictum (obiter dictum) Expressions or comments in a court opinion that are not necessary to support the decision made by the court; they are not binding authority and have no value as precedent. If nothing else can be found on point, an advocate may wish to attempt to persuade by citing cases that contain dicta.

distinguishing on the facts Choosing not to apply a rule from a previous case because its facts differ from the case sub judice.

diversity jurisdiction The jurisdiction of a federal court arising from diversity of citizenship, when the jurisdictional amount has been met.

diversity of citizenship A ground for invoking the original jurisdiction of a federal district court, the basis of jurisdiction being the existence of a controversy between citizens of different states.

Dormant Commerce Clause Judicial doctrine providing that even if federal power to regulate interstate and international commerce is not exercised, state power to regulate these areas is sometimes precluded.

Dormant Commerce Clause Doctrine The idea that state laws that unduly burden interstate commerce, even if the subject is unregulated by the national government, are invalid under federalism principles, because the regulation of interstate and foreign commerce belongs exclusively to the federal government.

Double Jeopardy Clause Fifth Amendment provision that provides that government may not punish a person twice for the same offense.

dual federalism The theory that the national government and the state governments are coequal sovereigns. The national government is supreme only when its jurisdiction is explicitly granted by the Constitution.

dual sovereignty An approach to constitutional interpretation that requires state judges to apply both the federal and state constitutions simultaneously.

dual sovereignty doctrine A legal theory associated with the Double Jeopardy Clause that provides that federal and state governments may try a person for the same act just as two or more states may try a person for the same act because they are separate sovereigns.

Due Process Clause A provision found in the Fifth and Fourteenth Amendments, which states that government cannot deprive individuals of life, liberty, or property without due process of law. This clause requires, among other things, that government treat individuals fairly during the criminal process, which may include such protections as the right to a fair trial, the right to be free from outrageous conduct by prosecutors or judges, the right to a full and fair appeal of a conviction, and the right to humane conditions of confinement. The Sixth Amendment provides several standards for the criminal process. As contained in the Fourteenth Amendment, this clause prevents the states from denying persons life, liberty, or property without due process of law. Found in section 1 of the Fourteenth Amendment, this clause provides, "nor shall any State deprive any person of life, liberty, or property, without due process of law." The Supreme Court has interpreted this clause as making most of the provisions within the Bill of Rights applicable to the states.

effective assistance of counsel The more specific standard used to assess the right to counsel under the Sixth Amendment. To prove a violation of the right to counsel, a defendant must show two fundamental things: (1) the attorney's representation fell below objective standards of reasonableness (it was deficient), and (2) there is a reasonable probability that the outcome of the criminal proceedings would have been different but for counsel's deficient performance.

electoral college The body empowered by the Constitution to elect the president and vice-president of the United States, composed of presidential electors chosen by the voters at each presidential election. In practice, however, the electoral college votes in accordance with the popular vote.

eminent domain The process of government obtaining private property from individuals for public use under the Fifth Amendment. See also the *Takings Clause*.

en banc French term for "on the bench." A court, particularly an appellate court, with all the judges sitting together (sitting en banc) in a case.

enabling act (enabling legislation) (1) A statute that grants new powers or authority to persons or corporations. (2) A statute that gives the government the power to enforce other legislation or that carries out a provision of a constitution. The term also applies to a clause in a statute granting the government the power to enforce or carry out that statute. Such a provision is called an *enabling clause*.

endorsement test Another legal standard used to assess Establishment Clause issues. Under this standard, the Court essentially collapses the first two questions of the *Lemon* test (the secular purpose and primary effect requirements) by asking the more general question of whether the government's activity conveys a message of endorsement or disapproval of religion.

enforcement clause Found in Section 5 of the Fourteenth Amendment, this provision allows Congress to pass legislation to enforce the other clauses contained within the amendment, including Equal Protection Clause and Due Process Clause. This provision serves as the constitutional basis for many forms of federal civil rights legislation.

Equal Protection Clause Precludes the states from denying persons equal protection of the law.

equality The third primary value promoted by the Constitution, chiefly by the Due Process Clause and Equal Protection Clause. The standard that similarly situated persons ought to be treated similarly.

Establishment Clause The first provision of the First Amendment, which provides that "Congress shall make no law respecting an establishment of religion." This clause generally regulates the extent to which government can participate in, assist, or otherwise further religious activity or organizations.

evanescent evidence exception A type of exigent circumstances situation that allows police to perform warrantless seizures of evidence that may be destroyed or evaporated.

ex post facto law A law making a person criminally liable for an act that was not criminal at the time it was committed. The Constitution prohibits both Congress and the states from enacting such laws.

excessive bail provision Eighth Amendment clause stating that the amount of bail, which is the collateral imposed by a court as a condition for pretrial release of the defendant, cannot be excessive.

excessive fines provision Eighth Amendment clause that provides that a fine, which is a postconviction punishment in the form of monetary payment, cannot be excessive.

exclusionary rule A judicially created remedy for violations of the Fourth, Fifth, or Sixth Amendments, which is used to exclude unconstitutionally obtained evidence from a criminal trial.

exculpatory evidence Materials or information that might lead to a defendant's exoneration.

executive agency An agency whose head serves at the pleasure of the president.

executive agreement An agreement with a foreign government, made by the president acting within his or her executive powers.

executive order An order issued by the chief executive officer of government, whether national, state, or local.

executory Not yet fully performed, completed, fulfilled, or carried out; to be performed, either wholly or in part; not yet executed.

exigent circumstances exception An exception to the Fourth Amendment warrant requirement that allows officers to conduct warrantless searches where there is a need to apprehend a dangerous person or prevent an imminent and serious threat to the police or public.

exigent circumstances An exception to the warrant requirement that allows home arrests where pressing needs of the public outweigh the individual's right to privacy.

factions Individual or isolated interests that can destroy or substantially impair government if they are allowed to override the common good. According to James Madison in *Federalist No. 10*, the only way to address factions in a democratic society was to allow them to exist, but to manage them, so that one interest did not rise to dominate the rest. To that end, Madison believed that the Constitution would allow factions to be pitted against one another, thereby allowing them to be managed in a marketplace of competition.

Federal Election Campaign Act Passed in 1971 and amended in 1974, this was the first major effort to control campaign finances at the federal level. The law included measures limiting the amount of money that could be donated and spent during federal campaigns. The Supreme Court reviewed this law in *Buckley v. Valeo* (1976) and upheld the contributions limitations, but struck down most of the limits on campaign spending.

federal jurisdiction The jurisdiction of the federal courts. Such jurisdiction is based upon the judicial powers granted by Article III of the Constitution and by federal statutes.

Federal Register An official publication, printed daily, containing regulations and proposed regulations issued by administrative agencies, as well as other rulemaking and other official business of the executive branch of government. All regulations are ultimately published in the *Code of Federal Regulations.*

Federalism A governmental structure in which two or more levels of government operate concurrently with jurisdiction over the same citizens, and in which each governmental entity has some autonomy over specific policy areas. This is opposed to a *unitary system,* where there is one centralized government; and a *confederation,* where two or more governments combine to create a confederation government that has no direct authority over the citizens of each of its members.

Federalist (1) A person who supports a strong, centralized government. (2) A political party that advocates a strong, centralized government.

felony Generally defined to mean a crime for which the punishment may include a year or more of incarceration.

Fifteenth Amendment Ratified in 1870, this amendment states that government cannot deny persons the right to vote based on race, color, or previous servitude.

fighting words A category of unprotected speech that "by their very utterance inflict injury or tend to incite an immediate breach of the peace."

fines A postconviction punishment in the form of monetary payment.

formal rulemaking A process used by administrative agencies to create rules and regulations. The Administrative Procedure Act provides that formal rulemaking is required only when mandated by statute. Otherwise, informal rulemaking may be used by an agency. Formal rulemaking involves formal hearings and is more expensive and time consuming than informal rulemaking. This process is also known as *rulemaking on the record.*

Fourteenth Amendment The ratification of the Fourteenth Amendment provided explicit mandates to the states regarding civil liberties, mandates not found in the original Bill of Rights. Under this amendment, the states are required to protect liberty, as well as life and property, under mandate of the federal constitution. Ratified in 1868, this amendment provides for several things, but primarily it provides the privileges or immunities clause, the Due Process Clause for states, and the Equal Protection Clause for states. This amendment was designed to promote equality and fairness in the aftermath of the Civil War and abolition of slavery.

Free Exercise Clause The second provision of the First Amendment, which provides that "Congress shall make no law . . . prohibiting the free exercise [of religion] thereof." This clause addresses the extent to which government can interfere with an individual's religious practices.

freedom of association The First Amendment right of individuals to gather together and express themselves collectively.

freedom of the press The First Amendment right guaranteeing some level of protection for press-based expression.

frisk To pat the outer clothing of an individual.

fruit of the poisonous tree doctrine A doctrine that extends the exclusionary rule to all evidence obtained as the result of the initial piece of unconstitutionally obtained evidence.

full faith and credit A reference to the requirement of Article IV of the Constitution that each state give "full faith and credit" to the "public acts, records, and judicial proceedings" of every other state. This means that a state's judicial acts must be given the same effect by the courts of all other states as they receive at home.

fundamental right A constitutional right of the highest order and one to which utmost constitutional protection is applied, including strict scrutiny protection.

gerrymandering Manipulating the boundary lines of a political district to give an unfair advantage to one political party or to dilute the political strength of voters of a particular race, color, or national origin.

good faith exception or *Leon* rule An exception to the valid warrant requirement that holds that an invalid warrant, which appears on its face to be valid, will not automatically result in an unconstitutional search if the officer executing the warrant reasonably relied on the facial validity of the warrant.

governmental conduct Action that is performed by police officers and their agents performing work that is funded or facilitated by public resources.

grand jury indictment A formal charge by a group of citizens sitting as a jury who have reviewed the evidence and decided that there is sufficient cause to charge a person with a criminal offense.

grand jury provision Fifth Amendment clause that requires government to obtain a grand jury indictment in order to charge someone with a capital offense or felony.

habeas corpus Latin for "you have the body." A writ whose purpose is to obtain immediate relief from illegal imprisonment by having the "body" (that is, the prisoner) delivered from custody and brought before the court. A writ of habeas corpus is a means for attacking the constitutionality of the statute under which, or the proceedings in which, the original conviction was obtained. There are numerous writs of habeas corpus, each applicable in different procedural circumstances. The full name of the ordinary writ of habeas corpus is *habeas corpus ad subjiciendum.*

harmless error An error made during trial that ostensibly does not change the outcome of the case.

hate speech Expression that is directly aimed at insulting, derogating, or intimidating a particular class of individuals, often based on race, sex, religion, or ethnicity.

hierarchical federalism The theory that the national government is supreme to the state governments. The powers of the national government are read broadly, and the Tenth Amendment is read as not granting any specific powers to the states.

history of discrimination One of the three criteria used to determine whether a form of discrimination will be deemed suspect under the Due Process Clause. This involves a retrospective examination of whether and to what extent the characteristic has been unjustifiably mistreated in the United States.

home arrests An arrest that occurs with an individual's home; usually requires a warrant.

hot-pursuit rule A form of the exigent circumstances exception to the warrant requirement that allows police to enter places without a warrant where they are pursuing a fleeing felon, where evidence may be destroyed or evaporated, where contaminated food or narcotics present immediate danger, and where an ongoing crisis poses a threat to public safety.

hung jury A jury that cannot reach a decision after sufficient deliberations.

immutable characteristic Another factor used to determine whether a form of discrimination will be deemed suspect under the Equal Protection Clause. An immutable characteristic is an attribute of a person that is not readily changeable. A person's race, sex, and eye color are considered immutable characteristics because they cannot be easily changed.

impeachment The constitutional process by which high elected officers of the United States, including the president, may be removed from office. The accusation (articles of impeachment) is made by the House of Representatives and tried by the Senate, which sits as an impeachment court. Under the Constitution, the grounds for impeachment are "treason, bribery, or other high crimes and misdemeanors."

implicit in the concept of ordered liberty A phrase frequently offered by the Court as the standard for assessing whether a particular human activity will be included as a "liberty interest" under the Due Process Clauses.

important governmental functions A legal standard development by the Court that allows government to discriminate against aliens when the position or function for which the alien seeks an opportunity involves an important government function, including jobs as police officers, public school teachers, and probation officers.

inclusio unis est exclusio alterius A Latin maxim used as a principle in drafting some documents, meaning "the inclusion of one item is the exclusion of all others." Under this theory, the framers maintained that they could limit the scope and power of government by enumerating or listing the government's specific powers in the Constitution, and that such documentation, by implication, would curtail any subsequent argument that the government had powers beyond those listed in the Constitution.

incorporation The Bill of Rights was intended to be applied only against the national government. However, the Supreme Court determined that most of the rights contained therein were "incorporated" by the Due Process Clause of the Fourteenth Amendment. A right is *incorporated* if it is fundamental and necessary to an ordered liberty. Once incorporated, the right applies against the states.

incorporation doctrine A legal theory that maintains that the Bill of Rights (or at least portions thereof) should be incorporated through the Fourteenth Amendment Due Process Clause and made applicable to the states.

independent agency An agency whose head may be terminated by the president only for good cause.

independent counsel Under federal statute, counsel who may be specially appointed to investigate and prosecute high government officials for crimes committed in office.

independent source rule An exception to the exclusionary rule that will not exclude evidence if police can show that it was obtained by a source that is separate or independent from the originally tainted method.

indigency A person's status as lacking wealth, which the Court has treated as a nonsuspect classification for equal protection purposes.

inevitable discovery rule Another exception to the exclusionary rule that allows illegally obtained evidence or the fruit derived therefrom to be admitted if the government can show that the evidence eventually would have been discovered through proper means.

informal rulemaking A process used by administrative agencies to create rules and regulations. The Administrative Procedure Act provides that agencies may use this procedure unless formal rulemaking is required by statute. Informal rulemaking is less costly and less time consuming than its formal counterpart. This process is also known as *notice-and-comment rulemaking.*

information provision Sixth Amendment provision that requires government to notify defendants of the nature and cause of the criminal charges.

Insurrection Act The Insurrection Act modifies the Posse Comitatus Act by granting the president limited authority to use federal military to quell insurrections and unrest.

intelligible principle test The test used to determine if Congress has provided an agency with sufficient guidance in the performance of a delegated duty.

intergovernmental immunity doctrine The doctrine that both the states and the national government possess some immunity from the regulation of the other under federalism principles. Generally, the federal government enjoys greater immunity than do the states.

intermediate scrutiny test A constitutional standard used in cases involving a semisuspect form of discrimination that requires the government to show that its semisuspect form of discrimination is substantially related to an important governmental interest.

interrogation Efforts, including questions, by police designed to obtain incriminating information.

interstitial An approach to constitutional interpretation that requires state judges to apply the federal Constitution before turning to their state's constitution.

intervening circumstances rule Another exception to the exclusionary rule that allows evidence to be admitted if new circumstances or events break the causal link between the illegal actions of the police and the ill-gotten evidence.

investigatory detention An officer's relatively brief stop of an individual for purposes of conducting a reasonable investigation of possible criminal activity. In these situations, an officer must have reasonable suspicion that the person being stopped is involved in criminal activity.

issue advocacy A form of electoral communication that mentions a candidate by name in association with a particular issue or cause, but stops short of actually urging the public to vote for or against the identified candidate. The Bipartisan Campaign Reform Act of 2002 imposed substantial restrictions on the use of issue ads by unions and corporations during certain periods before federal elections.

James Madison A "founding father" of the Constitution and the chief architect of the Bill of Rights.

joint resolution A resolution passed by both houses of a bicameral legislature and eligible to become a law if signed by the chief executive or passed over the chief executive's veto.

judicial activism (1) Use of judicial decisions to engage in social engineering. (2) A judicial philosophy that gives little deference to precedent, and therefore commonly results in the abrogation of prior decisions.

judicial neutrality and detachment Fourth Amendment standard required for the person issuing a search warrant that generally requires the judicial authority to be free of conflicts of interest in evaluating the request for the warrant or its execution and sufficiently objective (neutral) regarding the persons or matters involved in the search warrant.

judicial review The power of the judiciary, as the final interpreter of the law, to declare an act of a coordinate governmental branch or state unconstitutional. The power is not expressly stated in the Constitution, but the Supreme Court announced that the judiciary possesses this power in *Marbury v. Madison,* 5 U.S. (1 Cranch) 137 (1803).

jurisdiction A term used in several senses: (1) In a general sense, the right of a court to adjudicate lawsuits of a certain kind. (2) In a specific sense, the right of a court to determine a particular case; in other words, the power of the court over the subject matter of, or the property involved in, the case at bar. (3) In a geographical sense, the power of a court to hear cases only within a specific territorial area.

jury trial provision Sixth Amendment provision that individuals have a right to have their criminal cases decided by an impartial jury (as opposed to a judge) within the jurisdiction where the crime was allegedly committed.

justiciability doctrine Rules that limit the authority of federal courts to hear cases, such as ripeness, mootness, political question, and standing.

***Katz* test** Legal standard used to assess reasonable expectation of privacy; supports notion that persons must manifest a subjective expectation of privacy in the object of the challenged search.

knock and announce rule A requirement in some state jurisdictions that police knock and announce their presence before executing a warrant on a dwelling.

laissez-faire era A phrase used to describe the nature of the Supreme Court during the latter part of the nineteenth century and early part of the twentieth century. Also referred to as the *Lochner* era, this period is marked by the Court's frequent rejection of government regulations of business and the work setting.

legislative veto An act of a legislature invalidating executive action in a particular instance. Generally, legislative vetos are unconstitutional. Once power is delegated by Congress to the president, it is generally prohibited from interfering with the president's enforcement.

***Lemon* test** Legal standard developed by the Court in *Lemon v. Kurtzman* (1971) to evaluate Establishment Clause cases. Under this test, the challenged government action must meet three guidelines: (1) it must have a secular (nonreligious) purpose, (2) its primary effect must neither advance nor inhibit religion, and (3) it must not foster an excessive entanglement with religion and government.

libel A form of defamation that involves published written communications that are false and cause injury.

liberty One of the three primary values promoted by the Constitution, particularly the Bill of Rights, which involves the ability to act and think without government interference.

liberty of contract A liberty interest under the Fourteenth Amendment Due Process Clause as determined by the Court during the latter part of the nineteenth and early part of the twentieth centuries (the laissez-faire era of the Court). The Court deemed this liberty interest to offer a constitutional right to engage in contractual relations without governmental interference.

line item veto The right of a governor under most state constitutions to veto individual appropriations in an appropriation act rather than being compelled either to veto the act as a whole or to sign it into law. The president of the United States does not have a line item veto.

literalism An approach to interpreting the Constitution that focuses on the literal meanings of its words, rather than on other factors, such as the original intent of the framers. There are two forms of literalism, historical and contemporary. *Historical literalism* defines terms in the context of when the particular provision being considered was ratified. *Contemporary literalism* uses contemporary definitions.

living wills A legal document in which a person provides instructions for medical treatment (or the lack thereof) in cases where the person becomes incapacitated.

majoritarian process A third consideration in determining whether a form of discrimination is suspect in nature. This essentially involves a prediction about the future, namely, whether, without sufficient constitutional protection, it is likely that democratic processes (such as legislative action, electoral results, influence of public opinion, etc.) will continue to allow the identified characteristic to be used as a basis for discrimination.

malice A legal standard in defamation cases involving public figures requiring the speech to be made with knowledge of the statement's falsity or reckless disregard as to its falsity.

manifest necessity A compelling need to stop the trial prior to a verdict being reached.

marketplace of ideas A phrase used in some free speech cases to describe the type of environment the First Amendment fosters for individuals to sell, purchase, and evaluate different ideas through speech. The idea is that, if individual ideas are allowed to compete against one another through open exchange, using speech, assembly, press, and petition, society will be in a better position to manage and balance the diversity of "products" (ideas) being offered.

marking up The detailed revision of a bill by a legislative committee.

minimum contacts test A doctrine under which a state court is permitted to acquire personal jurisdiction over a nonresident, although he or she is not personally served with process within the state, if he or she has had such a substantial connection with that state that due process is not offended by the court's exercise of jurisdiction over him or her.

***Miller* Test** A standard used to judge whether a material is obscene. In *Miller v. California* (1973), the Supreme Court defined obscenity as material that, when viewed in its entirety (taken as a whole) (1) appeals to a prurient (unhealthy) interest in sex; (2) portrays sexual conduct in a patently offensive way; and (3) lacks serious literary, artistic, political, or scientific value.

***Miranda* warnings** Information the police must provide to suspects before a custodial interrogation, which includes notice that (1) they have the right to remain silent; (2) anything they say can and will be used against them in court; (3) they have the right to the presence of an attorney; and (4) if they cannot afford an attorney, one will be provided for them.

mistrial The termination of a trial prior to a verdict.

modernism An approach to interpreting the Constitution that allows courts to consider changes in social, economic, and political forces.

natural law A term referring to the concept that there exists, independent of manmade law, a law laid down (depending upon one's beliefs) by God or by nature, which human society must observe in order to be happy and at peace.

natural right A right existing under natural law, independent of manmade law.

natural rights theory A theory of individual liberties that maintains that liberties are the result of the "laws of nature." This theory recognizes life itself as the source of certain individual rights, which exist independent of any constitution or contract. Natural rights theory insists that the rights enumerated in the Bill of Rights are natural, inherent, and unalienable to individuals.

Necessary and Proper Clause Article I of the Constitution grants to Congress the power to make all laws "necessary and proper" for carrying out its constitutional responsibilities. The Supreme Court has long interpreted this provision to mean that Congress has the right to enact not only those laws that are absolutely indispensable, but any laws that are reasonably related to effectuating the powers expressly granted to it by the Constitution.

neutrality test An approach to free exercise cases adopted in *Employment Division v. Smith* (1990) that maintains that governmental policies that are neutral in form and generally applied will be deemed constitutional, regardless of their adverse impact on certain religious practices.

Nineteenth Amendment Ratified in 1920, this amendment guarantees voting rights regardless of a person's sex, thereby essentially affording women the right to vote.

no-knock warrant A warrant that allows officers to execute a warrant without knocking on the door of the search premises.

Ninth Amendment A constitutional amendment providing that "[t]he enumeration of certain rights in the bill of rights, shall not be construed to deny or disparage others retained by the people." This amendment suggests that beyond those listed in the First through Eighth Amendments, there are other unenumerated rights that individuals retain that are to be protected against governmental intrusion.

nonpublic forums Places that are not historically associated with the exercise of First Amendment rights. Such locations may include military bases, jails, and certain interior portions of public buildings.

nonsuspect classification Forms of discrimination that are not suspicious under the Constitution and thus require only minimal judicial scrutiny. This includes discrimination based on a person's wealth, age, alienage (in some cases), sexual orientation, and discrimination depriving individuals of education, welfare, or housing.

obscenity A form of unprotected sexual expression. As the Court defined the term in *Miller v. California* (1973), obscenity is a specific type of sexual expression that: (1) taken as a whole, appeals to a prurient (unhealthy) interest in sex; (2) portrays sexual conduct in a patently offensive way; and (3) taken as a whole, lacks serious literary, artistic, political, or scientific value.

offensive speech Expression that is likely to cause the sensibilities of others to be offended.

one person, one vote principle A doctrine adopted by the Supreme Court in the 1960s, which generally holds that, in order to be constitutional, states must draw electoral districts in a manner that evenly (though not necessarily with mathematical perfection) distributes the population so that individual voting power can be relatively equal among the districts.

open fields doctrine An exception to the warrant requirement for searches and seizures that allows law enforcement officers to search and seize areas or items located in open and public view.

original intent An approach to interpreting the Constitution that uses historical analysis to assess what the authors of the Constitution meant or intended by a particular term or provision, including the term "liberty" within the Due Process Clauses. This view maintains that judicial interpretation of the Constitution should be based on the words of the Constitution itself and the framers' "original intent," not on a contemporary understanding of the Constitution in the context of current realities. Adherents of this doctrine are sometimes referred to as *strict constructionists*.

original jurisdiction The jurisdiction of a trial court, as distinguished from the jurisdiction of an appellate court.

original understanding An approach to interpreting the Constitution that is similar to original intent, except that it seeks to determine what the legal culture understood (as opposed to intended) under the provision when it was originally written.

origination clause Article I, Section 7, clause 1, of the U.S. Constitution, which requires all revenue-raising bills to originate in the House of Representatives.

overbreadth doctrine A constitutional theory of due process that generally provides that the government cannot regulate or prohibit more speech than is necessary to address the identified harm. Under this doctrine, the Court essentially asks whether the government's restriction on speech is properly tailored to address the harm the government is seeking to prevent.

pardon An act of grace by the chief executive of the government, relieving a person of the legal consequences of a crime of which he or she has been convicted. A pardon erases the conviction.

parens patriae Latin for "the parent of the country."

particularity requirement Fourth Amendment standard for warrants that requires the judicial authority issuing a warrant to be sufficiently precise in writing the warrant so as to avoid a general or overreaching search by the executing officer.

pendent jurisdiction The rule that even though there is no diversity of citizenship, a federal court has the right to exercise jurisdiction over a state matter if it arises out of the same transaction as a matter already before the federal court.

penumbras A penumbra is a lunar shadow. Justice Douglas used this term as a metaphor in *Griswold v. Connecticut* (1965) to describe an individual's right to privacy under the Constitution. According to Douglas, even though privacy is not specifically enumerated in the Bill of Rights, there are certain penumbras or shadows cast by the First, Third, Fourth, Fifth, and Ninth Amendments that reflect that a right to privacy is protected by the Constitution.

plain-feel exception Allows officers performing stop and frisks to seize nonweapon forms of contraband (drugs, drug paraphernalia, etc.) that the officer reasonably detects as a part of a properly executed patdown.

plain-meaning rule The rule that in interpreting a statute whose meaning is unclear, the courts will look to the "plain meaning" of its language to determine legislative intent. The plain-meaning rule is in opposition to the majority view of statutory interpretation, which takes legislative history into account.

plain view doctrine Another exception to the Fourth Amendment warrant requirement that allows police to search and seize items if they are lawfully in a location where they plainly see evidence of criminal activity.

plenary Full; complete.

pocket veto The veto of a congressional bill by the president by retaining it until Congress is no longer in session, neither signing nor vetoing it. The effect of such inaction is to nullify the legislation without affirmatively vetoing it. The pocket veto is also available to governors under some state constitutions.

police power (1) The power of government to make and enforce laws and regulations necessary to maintain and enhance the public welfare and to prevent individuals from violating the rights of others. (2) The sovereignty of each of the states of the United States that is not surrendered to the federal government under the Constitution.

political question A nonjudicial issue. The political question doctrine states that, under the Constitution, certain questions belong to the nonjudicial branches of the federal government to resolve.

pornography Materials that depict sexual expression, which may or may not meet the *Miller* standards of obscenity.

Posse Comitatus Act Posse Comitatus is Latin for "power of the county." The Posse Comitatus Act forbids, without congressional authorization, the use of federal military as domestic law enforcement.

prayer Portion of a bill in equity or a petition that asks for equitable relief and specifies the relief sought.

preemption The doctrine that once Congress has enacted legislation in a given field, a state may not enact a law inconsistent with the federal statute. A similar doctrine also governs the relationship between the state government and local governments.

preemption doctrine Doctrine that state laws that interfere with federal laws are invalid pursuant to the Supremacy Clause.

pretext principle A law that is enacted by Congress supposedly under one of its enumerated powers, when the law's true purpose is to regulate a subject belonging to the states, is invalid. Today, the affectation doctrine has made the pretext principle of little significance.

primacy An approach to constitutional interpretation that requires state judges to apply their state's constitution before turning to the federal Constitution.

prior restraint An attempt by government to prevent or restrain expression, including press publication, before it is uttered.

Privileges or Immunities Clause Prohibits states from denying persons the privileges or immunities of American citizenship.

probability test A third approach to the Free Speech Clause adopted by some members of the Court in the mid-twentieth century. This test asks "whether the gravity of the 'evil,' discounted by its improbability, justifies such invasion of free speech as is necessary to avoid the danger."

probable cause A legal standard requiring the officer to have sufficient and trustworthy information to reasonably believe that a person has committed a crime.

procedural due process One dimension of the Due Process Clause as contained in the Fifth and Fourteenth Amendments. It requires government to treat persons fairly while it attempts to interfere with their liberty interests. Put another way, procedural due process concerns *how* the government processes and safeguards individuals and their claims.

profanity Words, which often include slang references to sexual activity, that are viewed as highly offensive and impolite, but may still be afforded constitutional protection, as long as they do not fall into another category of unprotected speech, such as fighting words.

proportionality A theory of equality based on the notion that resources and opportunities ought to be allocated based upon individual circumstances.

proportionality doctrine A legal doctrine under the Cruel and Unusual Punishment Clause that requires criminal punishment to be proportional to the crime committed.

pseudonym A fictitious name. A plaintiff may sometimes be permitted to file a case using a fictitious name, if the plaintiff has a legitimate interest in protecting his or her privacy, such as when the facts of the case are embarrassing or the plaintiff's life may be threatened.

public figure A person with particular notoriety in the community, including, but not limited to, public officials.

public forums Properties historically associated with the exercise of First Amendment rights, including public sidewalks, parks, and cartilages outside courthouses and statehouses.

public rights doctrine Rule providing that if a claim is public in nature and not private, Congress may delegate its adjudication to a non-Article III tribunal.

public safety exception An exception to the *Miranda* requirement that has allowed police, in at least one instance, to question a suspect in custody without supplying the requisite warnings when the questions were designed to address an imminent matter of public safety.

public trial provision Sixth Amendment clause stating that individuals are entitled to a public trial.

quasi-judicial A term applied to the adjudicatory functions of an administrative agency, that is, taking evidence and making findings of fact and findings of law.

quasi-legislative A term applied to the legislative functions of an administrative agency, such as rulemaking.

rational basis test A constitutional standard used to review cases involving a non-suspect form of discrimination that requires the government to show that its non-suspect distinction is rationally related to a legitimate governmental interest.

reasonable expectation of privacy A legal standard used by the Court to assess Fourth Amendment rights against unreasonable searches and seizures. Under this standard, the Court asks whether the individual had a reasonable expectation that a particular activity or location would be kept private.

reasonable suspicion A less rigorous legal standard than probable cause, which generally requires an officer to have articulable facts that would lead a reasonable person to suspect that criminal activity is afoot.

reasonableness A legal standard that attempts to assess what a reasonable person would believe or do under the circumstances.

reasonableness test Legal standard used to judge whether use of deadly force by police was constitutional; force must be necessary to prevent the escape of the suspect, and the officer must have probable cause to believe that the suspect poses a significant threat of death or serious physical injury to the officer or others.

recess appointment An appointment of an officer of the United States by the president while the Senate is in recess. The appointment expires at the end of the next session of the Senate if the appointee is not confirmed. Recess appointments are common. George Washington, for example, made a recess appointment of John Rutledge as chief justice of the Supreme Court in 1795 after John Jay, the nation's first chief justice, resigned to assume the role of governor of New York. Rutledge's nomination was rejected by the Senate during its next session, in part due to his unpopular and vocal political opinions and also because of concerns about his mental condition. Rather than remain chief justice until the end of the Senate's term, Rutledge resigned.

Religious Freedom Restoration Act (RFRA) A law passed by Congress in 1993 that sought to reinstate the strict scrutiny standard for free exercise cases. The RFRA bars government from substantially burdening an individual's exercise of religion, even if such burden stems from a neutral and generally applicable law, unless the government can demonstrate that the burden (1) furthers a compelling governmental interest, and (2) is the least restrictive means of furthering such interest.

Religious Land Use and Institutionalized Persons Act of 2000 (RLUIPA) Another law passed by Congress that attempted to reinstate the strict scrutiny standard in Free Exercise Clause cases. RLUIPA reinstates strict scrutiny analysis in two types of cases: (1) those involving land-use regulation, and (2) those involving religious exercise by institutionalized persons.

remand The return of a case by an appellate court to the trial court for further proceedings, for a new trial, or for entry of judgment in accordance with an order of the appellate court.

removal of case The transfer of a case from a state court to a federal court.

reporter shield laws State laws that prevent reporters from being compelled to reveal their confidential news sources.

reprieve The postponement of the carrying out of a sentence. A reprieve is not a commutation of sentence; it is merely a delay.

right to a fair trial A general term used to describe a variety of fairness-based rights during a criminal trial, including the right to a speedy and public trial by an impartial jury and the right to due process.

right to privacy Defined in a number of different ways, including the "right to be left alone"; the "freedom of personal choice in matters of marriage and family life"; and the "right to be secure in persons, houses, papers, and effects."

The Court formally recognizes this right as a fundamental right of individuals, despite the fact that it is not specifically mentioned by the Constitution.

rule of four An internal rule of the Supreme Court, which provides that a case will be reviewed by the Court if four justices wish it to be reviewed.

sameness A theory of equality based on the notion that each person should be given the same amount and type of resources and opportunities regardless of individual circumstances.

Search and Seizure Clause Fourth Amendment provision that precludes government from engaging in unreasonable searches and seizures of persons, houses, papers, and effects.

search incident to a lawful arrest An exception to the Fourth Amendment warrant requirement that allows police to search an arrestee during a valid arrest of a person.

search warrant Written authorization from a court to perform a search that is supported by probable cause.

security A primary value promoted by the Constitution that seeks stability, safety, and reliable structures.

segregation A policy used to discriminate whereby individuals are separated based on a particular attribute, such as race, sex, and so on.

seizure of a person Occurs when a law enforcement officer uses force or the threat of force to detain a person, thereby causing the person to reasonably believe that he or she cannot freely leave the presence of the official.

selective incorporation A theory held by some jurists and legal scholars that maintains that only select portions of the Bill of Rights, which are deemed to involve "preferred freedoms" or rights "implicit in the concept of ordered liberty," should be incorporated through the Due Process Clause and made applicable to the states.

selective prosecution The process of selecting a person for criminal charge based on a prohibited criterion, such as race, sex, or ethnicity.

self-incrimination provision Fifth Amendment clause stating that within a criminal case, persons cannot be forced to provide testimony against themselves.

self-executing Self-acting; going into effect without need of further action.

semi-suspect classification A type of distinction or discrimination that is partially or somewhat suspicious under the Constitution and that deserves heightened, though not the highest, form of judicial scrutiny. This includes sex-based (male v. female) discrimination and distinctions based on whether a person's parents were married when the person was born.

separate but equal doctrine A legal theory promulgated in *Plessy v. Ferguson* (1896) holding that as long as government provides individuals with relatively the same amount of resources or services, it may segregate individuals based on race without denying them equal protection. This theory was rejected by the Court in *Brown v. Board of Education* (1954).

separationist approach A view of the religion clauses that generally asserts that government should remain strictly separate or removed from religious activity. Under this approach, it is asserted that government should not aid, fund, or otherwise assist religious organizations or individual religious activity.

serious offenses Offenses for which a defendant could receive more than six months of imprisonment.

severability rule A rule of interpretation that allows a court to remove unconstitutional portions from a law and leave the remainder intact.

Shays' Rebellion Daniel Shays, a veteran of the American Revolutionary War, and a group of fellow farmers rebelled in protest of economic conditions. This incident was cited by many as justification for abandoning the Articles of Confederation, the theory being that a stronger national government could provide better economic conditions and that a national military would be most effective in defeating rebellions.

slander A form of defamation that involves published verbal communications that are false and cause injury.

sobriety checkpoints A police procedure that involves the stopping of vehicles at a fixed checkpoint without any particularized suspicion in order to detect drunk driving.

social compact A term used to describe the Constitution as a contract between two primary parties—the people and the government wherein the people have given their consent to political institutions to be their sovereign governing authority, granting to them certain powers of structure, process, and support, and in exchange, the government has agreed to provide the people with certain levels of protection and sustenance.

soft money Money that is not given directly by a donor to a campaign and that is not offered for the purpose of influencing a federal election. Soft money includes individual contributions to political parties for purposes of influencing state or local elections. The Bipartisan Campaign Reform Act of 2002 imposed substantial restrictions on the acceptance and use of this money in federal elections.

sovereign immunity The principle that the government specifically, the United States or any state of the United States—is immune from suit except when it consents to be sued.

special master A person appointed by the court to assist with certain judicial functions in a specific case.

speedy trial provision Sixth Amendment clause that provides individuals with a right to a speedy trial.

standing The legal capacity to bring and to maintain a lawsuit. A person is without standing to sue unless some interest of his or hers has been adversely affected or unless he or she has been injured by the defendant. The term "standing to sue" is often shortened simply to "standing."

stare decisis Latin for "standing by the decision." Stare decisis is the doctrine that judicial decisions stand as precedents for cases arising in the future. It is a fundamental policy of our law that, except in unusual circumstances, a court's determination on a point of law will be followed by courts of the same or lower rank in later cases presenting the same legal issue, even though different parties are involved and many years have elapsed.

"state action" requirement An essential element to any due process or equal protection claim that requires sufficient government action—federal, state, or local—to be involved.

status crimes Also known as personal characteristic offenses, these are attempts to punish individuals based on their reputation or propensity for certain behavior and are generally prohibited as cruel and unusual punishment.

statute A law enacted by a legislature; an act.

stop-and-frisk exception An exception to the Fourth Amendment warrant requirement that allows officers, who are conducting a brief investigation of a person based on reasonable suspicion, to conduct a warrantless "patdown" of the person's outer clothing in order to ensure that the person is not armed or dangerous.

stop and frisk or *Terry* **frisk** Police technique employed during investigatory detentions, whereby the person detained is patted down for weapons.

stop and identify laws Laws in some jurisdictions that require individuals to provide their identity to the investigating officer during the stop.

strict constructionist An approach to interpreting the Constitution that strictly construes the explicit words of the Constitution to determine whether a particular right is protected. This approach generally leads to the conclusion that there is no independent right of privacy.

strict scrutiny test A legal standard requiring the government to prove that its policy is necessary (or narrowly tailored) to promote a compelling governmental interest. This test imposes the strictest burden upon government in its attempt to justify regulate speech.

sub judice Before the court for consideration and determination.

substantive due process A second dimension of the Due Process Clause that concerns the type or substance of behavior that is included as a "liberty" under the Due Process Clause. The primary question under this dimension of the Due Process Clause is *what* activities does "liberty" include.

Supremacy Clause The provision in Article VI of the Constitution that "this Constitution and the laws of the United States . . . shall be the supreme law of the land, and the judges in every state shall be bound thereby."

suspect classification A type of distinction or discrimination that is highly questionable and that deserves the highest form of judicial scrutiny. Governmental distinctions based on race and alienage (in some cases) have been deemed "suspect" forms of discrimination.

symbolic speech Nonverbal communication that is akin to pure speech, including symbols (signs, flags, arm bands, or other tangible items) or conduct (hand gestures, burning objects, or other behavior). This nonverbal expression may receive First Amendment protection to the extent that it conveys a message capable of being received and understood by others.

Takings Clause A provision found in the Fifth Amendment that states that government cannot take private property for public use without just compensation. Also known as the *eminent domain provision*.

***Terry* stop** Also known as a "stop and frisk," this can be conducted during an investigatory stop where the officer has reasonable suspicion that the person is armed, thereby allowing the police to frisk an individual.

the switch in time that saved nine A phrase used to describe the change in the Court's approach to economic and social legislation, chiefly marked by the Court's opinion in *West Coast Hotel v. Parrish* (1937), where the Court upheld a Washington State minimum-wage law. The difference or "switch" in the case was the vote of Justice Owen Roberts, who previously had voted to strike down New Deal policies under the doctrine of liberty of contract. In *West Coast Hotel*, however, Roberts switched sides and voted to uphold the Washington law. This change not only negated any New Deal-related motive for Roosevelt's court-packing plan (which Congress never adopted), it also ushered in a new era of jurisprudence regarding economic liberty under the Due Process Clause.

Thirteenth Amendment Ratified in 1865, this amendment bans "involuntary servitude" (slavery) within the United States.

three-strikes-and-you're-out laws Statutes in some states that impose life sentences for repeat (usually third) offenses, regardless of the seriousness of the offense.

time, place, and manner regulation A government restriction on speech that allows the expression in certain given contexts.

total incorporation doctrine A theory held by some jurists and legal scholars maintaining that the Fourteenth Amendment requires that all of the provisions of the Bill of Rights be incorporated and applied to the states.

totality of the circumstances A legal standard used to review arrests and seizures of persons and property to determine whether probable cause or reasonable suspicion exists. Under this standard, the overall context of the detention or seizure is reviewed, including what actions and words the officer used, the location of the detention, and the length of the stop.

Twenty-Fourth Amendment Ratified in 1964, this amendment prohibits poll taxes or other taxes, which had been employed in some jurisdictions as a means of preventing blacks from voting.

Twenty-Sixth Amendment Ratified in 1971, this amendment ensures that persons eighteen years and older are entitled to vote.

undue burden A legal standard used to review restrictions on abortion for their constitutionality. Under this standard, restrictions may not place an undue burden on a woman's right to choose an abortion.

unitary executive A theory that the Constitution vests all executive authority in the president of the United States. In a strong unitary executive system, Congress is without the authority to delegate executive authority, independent of the president, to any officer or agency or to limit presidential authority to remove or direct executive subordinates.

use immunity A guarantee given to a person that if he or she testifies against others, his or her testimony will not be used against him or her if he or she is prosecuted for involvement in the crime.

vagueness doctrine A constitutional theory of due process that maintains that the government cannot impose legal standards that the average person cannot or is not likely to understand. Attempts to apply vague standards in regulating speech are generally deemed unconstitutional.

viewpoint neutrality A term used to require the government not to favor one side or another within a given subject matter of speech.

voluntary cessation of illegal acts An exception to the mootness doctrine, providing that if an alleged harm has been ceased in order to avoid review, and there is a reasonable likelihood that the harm will reoccur or be recommenced, then the case may be heard.

vulgarity Expression, which is sometimes sexual in nature, that is regarded as highly crude and offensive.

Voting Rights Act of 1965 Major piece of civil rights legislation that prohibits any "voting qualification or prerequisite to voting" that denies the right to vote based on race or color. This law was designed to supplement the Fifteenth Amendment by specifically banning such practices as literacy, educational, and "good moral character" tests, which were being used by some authorities as a means of racial discrimination.

warrant provision Fourth Amendment provision that requires government to demonstrate probable cause before a warrant will be issued by a judge.

wingspan rule A rule under the search incident to a lawful arrest exception; allows police to search the immediate area around an arrested person.

***Younger* doctrine** The doctrine, drawn from *Younger v. Harris*, that federal courts will abstain in most cases from interfering with state court proceedings, even if federal constitutional issues are present. Except in extreme cases, federal review of federal constitutional issues must wait until appeal or habeas corpus review.

INDEX